THE RISE AND DEVELOPMENT OF

# WESTERN CIVILIZATION

# THE RISE AND
# DEVELOPMENT OF

**JOHN L. STIPP**
*Knox College*

**ALLEN W. DIRRIM**
*San Fernando Valley State College*

**C. WARREN HOLLISTER**
*University of California, Santa Barbara*

# VOLUME II

*John Wiley & Sons, Inc.*

NEW YORK   LONDON   SYDNEY

# WESTERN
# CIVILIZATION

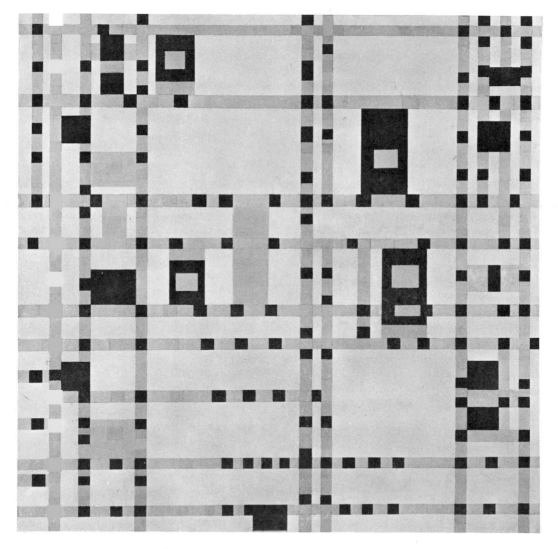

Frontispiece: Louis XIV

*Historical Pictures Service—Chicago*

Title-page illustration: Broadway Boogie Woogie

By Piet Mondrian. Reproduced by permission of The Museum of Modern Art, New York, N. Y.

*To our parents*

# Preface

Several assumptions underlie this account of the rise and development of Western civilization. One is that the modern college student possesses a quickened intellectual curiosity. Given a reasonably comprehensive body of data, he may be trusted to reach responsible judgments on his own. Another —only seemingly contradictory to the first— is that he needs some guidelines to keep him on the main paths; otherwise he may easily become lost in a forest of facts. This book deliberately focuses attention on pivotal decisions and developments. Where they are encountered, the tempo slows to allow treatment in depth. Where they are not present, the narrative passes over details that are mainly of interest only to the specialist. For the most part, the problems that invite this kind of study are problems whose nature or "solution" bears upon our own times.

A third premise, closely related to the second, rests in the belief that historical trends or movements deserve emphasis over separate, particular events. Of course this does not mean neglect of the latter; the pages of this book actually contain almost a distressing amplitude of them. The point is that a sustained effort is made to present them so that they reveal the larger concerns of man and the spirit of the times that envelops them.

A fourth assumption is that no meaningful understanding of the various facets of human experience—religion, politics, literature, economics, art, philosophy—can come from studying them in isolation. In the section on Nazi Germany, for example, close attention is called to the interpenetrating influences of certain philosophic outlooks—in this case, those of Schopenhauer and Nietzsche—and of Wagnerian music, as they bore upon the Führer's grand designs to create a thousand-year Reich.

Finally, encompassing these beliefs is a fundamental faith that the collective memory of man that we call history is not an academic—and sometimes dispensable— discipline in essence, but a requisite for the enlargement of man. The eminent historian, Carl Becker, phrased this faith in compelling words:

> The value of history is, indeed, not scientific but moral: by liberalizing the mind, by deepening the sympathies, by fortifying the will, it enables us to control, not society, but ourselves —a much more important thing; it prepares us to live more humanely in the present and to meet rather than to foretell the future.

The results of recent research, published in articles and monographic and general works, have been used throughout. Naturally, they have modified a number of opinions and conclusions that were once firmly held. But a critical, and at times stubborn, insistence that new findings prove to be more than merely new has saved, it is hoped, both writers and readers from misunderstanding in the name of new understanding. At all times we have stood ready, where it seemed necessary, to report that from the available evidence no conclusions could be reached, however important the event or object under study. On a few occasions we have had to confess that from the evidence it seemed that no conclusions were ever likely to be reached. On the whole, however, we are left with the feeling that the material in the pages that follow offers opportunities enough, for those who want to know, to learn where Western man has been and how he got where he is. Any lesser purpose seems hardly worthwhile.

*March 1967*

JOHN L. STIPP
ALLEN W. DIRRIM
C. WARREN HOLLISTER

# Acknowledgments

We express appreciation to a number of our colleagues who have carefully read portions of the manuscript and have made many helpful suggestions. They are not, of course, to be held accountable for any errors of fact or interpretation, for which we must bear sole responsibility.

Loren Baritz, University of Rochester

Gene A. Brucker, University of California (Berkeley)

Sidney A. Burrell, Boston University

Gerald D. Feldman, University of California (Berkeley)

John G. Gagliardo, University of Illinois (Chicago)

Boyd H. Hill, University of California (Los Angeles)

Jeffry Kaplow, Columbia University

Walter LeFeber, Cornell University

Orest Ranum, Columbia University

Carl E. Schorske, University of California (Berkeley)

William B. Slottman, University of California (Berkeley)

George H. Stein, State University of New York (Binghamton)

Edward R. Tannenbaum, New York University

George V. Taylor, University of North Carolina

Richard S. Westfall, Indiana University

We also express our collective debt to Jere Donovan of *Time* magazine for maps that have made portions of this history instructively graphic beyond the power of words. We are equally obligated to Nancy Unger, Associate Editor of John Wiley & Sons, not only for her work with the illustrations, but also for her assistance in deciding what was editorially fit and proper. Above all, we owe thanks to our editor, William L. Gum, for his steady encouragement and his thorough, sensitively informed supervision of a very long, very complicated task. Each of us is under special obligation to particular individuals. We should like to express this obligation in separate statements.

Although this book is a joint effort, particular responsibilities are involved: Allen W. Dirrim for Chapters I through VIII, John L. Stipp for Chapters IX through XVII, Perry Viles of the University of Pennsylvania for a complete reworking of Chapter IV, and C. Warren Hollister for general editorial concern and advice.

I express my appreciation to colleagues, notably Professor Darrall Morse, for testing ideas and providing suggestions. I am also indebted to Mrs. Earl Field for assistance on some of the illustrations. Especial acknowledgment is due Perry Viles, University of Pennsylvania, who provided most of Chapter IV.

A. W. D.

Grateful acknowledgments are made to: my wife Cleo, not only for patient understanding throughout, but for careful reading of galley proof of many sections of my portion of the book; Mrs. Jo Ann Robinson, Jr., for typing some of the early versions of various chapters and for sustained interest in the work from beginning to end; Mr. Mark Lawrence and other members of the Seymour Library Staff for their inestimable assistance; and Miss Mary Mangieri, who bore prime responsibility for transmuting my portion of Volume II from baffling script to type manuscript, and for reading galley proof.

J. L. S.

# List of Maps

Maps by J. Donovan

# Contents

*Chapter* *XVII*

THE RISE AND DEVELOPMENT OF
# WESTERN CIVILIZATION

# I

# Governments and Societies in the Age of Absolutism

Custom, "the legislation of the Middle Ages," had been for centuries the principal regulator of people's lives and institutions in Western Europe. In rural villages each generation followed the procedures of its forebears in ploughing, planting, harvesting, pasturing, worshiping, and celebrating. Each locality had accumulated its own precedents for making and implementing communal decisions that were binding on the whole. With central governments, each town stood in a special relationship defined by charters and recorded compromises. Other corporate institutions such as guilds, religious foundations, courts, and diets had their own privileges, rights, legal jurisdictions, and exemptions. These arrangements were reinforced by vested interests as well as custom. Most people, when they thought about them at all, believed them to be part of a divine order of the universe. Hence, even the idea of premeditated change seemed to be a kind of sacrilege.

Within the framework of supposedly time-less and changeless custom, innovations were rationalized either as the restatement of long-recognized principles or as the restitution of an older authority or model. Under the guise of the restitution of an older authority, Italian jurists revived Roman law beginning in the eleventh century. Renaissance humanists modified the medieval heritage with other classical precedents. Although the Protestant reformers of the sixteenth century broke the religious uniformity of Western Europe, they, too, used a norm of the past for the determination of creed and church polity. Indeed in early modern times most major innovations were cloaked and limited by precedents of the past.

Out of the crises of both the Renaissance and Reformation emerged authoritarian governments that claimed to be arbiters of society and thought. By 1660 divine-right kings were trying to obtain absolute control over military, political, legal, economic, and cultural affairs—hence, the label "absolut-

1

ism" has often been used to describe this type of regime. These kings—with their standing armies, their bureaucracies, and their control over established churches—attempted to impose domestic order and to extend their hereditary domains. In theory, divine-right kings acknowledged no earthly limitation; they were accountable to God alone. But the societies that they ruled were still basically medieval hierarchies. In part, royal absolutism came into being to defend the "liberties" that the privileged orders, by themselves, could no longer maintain against rival groups at home and foreign invaders. When the nobles, clergy, and urban oligarchies turned to their kings for the protection of their traditional prerogatives, they often had to give up their former political autonomy. Some absolute monarchs, however, were not content to protect privileges. Strengthened by the new powers surrendered to them, they attempted to reshape their society, making it dependent upon their personal will. But, in doing this, they jeopardized their alliance with the old aristocracy by elevating commoners to the highest offices. After 1660 the most effective monarchs—Louis XIV of France, Frederick William I of Prussia, Leopold I of Austria, and Peter the Great of Russia—had to deal with an alienated nobility. Their successes and failures are our main concern in this chapter.

Other monarchs claimed but did not attempt to wield this kind of unlimited authority. They cooperated with the privileged orders whose political and social claims they respected. We shall refer to their kingdoms, which remained firmly in the grip of custom, as "aristocratic monarchies."

Only a few seventeenth-century states were outside the political mold of monarchical authoritarianism. These included oligarchic Venice, the Imperial Free Cities of Germany, and the Swiss Confederacy; the two most important ones were the Dutch Republic and England. The Dutch fought off absolutism in the "Eighty Years' War"

against Spain (1576–1648). England escaped it in 1688 by revolution. These two states went furthest in developing new constitutions, but their revolutions were still far from complete at the beginning of the eighteenth century. In both instances, commercial expansion and the growth of large commercial and professional middle classes attended the overthrow of absolutism. But in the Dutch Republic the impetus of commercial expansion subsided by 1660. In decline, the Dutch Republic adopted a tightly closed oligarchy, as had other once-thriving commercial cities such as Venice and Nuremberg. In England the commercial classes continued to expand with the nation's commercial growth, but they shared power without ruling. Almost everywhere else in Europe this commercial motor of sociopolitical change was not running.* Banking, trading, and manufacture were either stagnant or in decline.

* One small exception was the German city of Hamburg, the banking and transshipping point for English, Dutch and French trade entering Germany. Revolting against an exclusive patriciate, Hamburg's townsmen established a more broadly based constitution in 1712.

# A. The Nature of Absolutism

## THE ALL-POWERFUL MONARCHY IN THEORY AND PRACTICE

In the late Middle Ages civil lawyers, clergymen, and royal publicists began to claim autocratic powers for kings who traced their descent from feudal times. They interpreted feudal monarchy as a lord-subject relationship without the reciprocal rights and obligations of the lord-vassal concept. Following the precedent of canon lawyers who put the popes above the Church's law, civil lawyers used imperial Roman law from the time of Justinian to exalt kings above custom. They especially emphasized the precept "What the king wills is law." Kings instituted extraordinary courts that followed their personal command rather than the procedures and substance of traditional law. They also attempted to override local custom by appointing officials possessing their delegated sovereign authority. Thus buttressed by Roman law, they could exclude all except themselves and their favorites from the "mysteries of state." But the most prevalent doctrine of autocracy after the Reformation was divine right. Roman Catholic and Protestant clergy appointed by kings cited scripture, especially the Old Testament and Romans XIII, to prove that kings were direct agents of God, that their power was subject to no limitation except Him and His revelation, and that resistance to a divinely ordained ruler was a cardinal sin. If these kings ruled tyrannically, they were only punishing human wickedness for God. A few monarchist propagandists, such as Bishop Bossuet in France, added still another—a secular and modern—argument for authoritarian rule. They accepted the premises of Jean Bodin and Thomas Hobbes that complete centralization of state authority was rational, necessary, and natural. But this theory was frowned upon as being too secular until the "enlightened despots" of the eighteenth century made it their own. Seventeenth-century advocates of royal absolutism depicted their kings as ruling in the image of God, simultaneously manifesting traits of feudal and classical heroes.

Absolute monarchs built royal supremacy into the machinery of their governments. Their new standing armies provided security from invasion and put in royal hands the only armed forces permitted within their states. Frequently kings substituted chains of military command for civil administration. The bellicose traditions of the aristocracy could be channeled away from feudal or civil conflicts into wars that used these armies against rival dynasts. To equip, supply, and pay their soldiers, monarchs sought the power to tax without interference from traditional representative assemblies. When these assemblies resisted, they and their members were excluded from affairs of state as thoroughly as other subjects. The Cortes, Estates General, and many German diets, for example, were no longer summoned. With the powers to tax and to maintain standing armies, autocratic kings conducted foreign affairs subject only to the limits of their own ambitions and available resources; the age of absolutism was marked by nearly continuous warfare. Royal diplomats served as the agents of aggrandizement. Imitating a Venetian custom, kings sent permanent resident agents equipped with pensions and gifts to buy their way into favorable agreements and information. For workaday espionage and fraud they employed secret agents who could be disavowed when caught. Royal control over

*An officer and musketeer of the French Guards.*

military and foreign affairs set precedents for executive discretion that long survived the demise of monarchical forms of government.

In domestic affairs, however, absolutism was more often a superficial façade than a reality. No absolute monarch had as much control over his subjects as did the king and Parliament of England, both of which exacted only semivoluntary obedience. Absolutism was effective in dealing with nonprivileged subjects, but—on the broad front of domestic affairs—it was hemmed in by numerous practical restraints. A backward technology was a major curb on royal absolutism; slow transport and communications limited its range to the vicinity of capitals and provincial administrative centers. Agrarian economies could not support armed forces or bureaucracies proportionate to those of either England or the Dutch Republic. Moreover, the officers who served the throne were often more devoted to personal gain than to royal authority. Rather than public trusts, offices were generally considered pri-

vate property. In France, for example, the king could remove by judicial process officials who acted independently of his direct supervision, but he was obliged to compensate most of them for their loss. Still more important in limiting royal authority were the vested interests of the privileged classes and the strong hold of custom among the masses; no monarch could completely eliminate these restraints.

## THE BRAKES OF CUSTOM, PRIVILEGE, AND POVERTY

Strikingly absent from the configuration of absolutist society were the large commercial middle classes—bankers, merchants, and entrepreneurs—comparable to those in England and the Dutch Republic. The rest of Europe remained primarily agrarian. Only France had an extensive professional and commercial middle class, and even its ambitions were set by the aristocracy. In Brandenburg-Prussia, Poland, Russia, and the Habsburg Danubian monarchy, no such class existed except for officials.

Throughout Europe peasants made up the great bulk of the population. They differed widely in status. In Western Europe they were for the most part legally free, but, unlike the leaseholders of England and the Dutch Republic, they were still subject to manorial services, monopolies, and restrictions, and they had only a limited access to royal justice. In most instances taxes, tithes, and various services took more than two thirds of their gross incomes and energies. Western European peasants, particularly in France, were obtaining *de facto* ownership of their holdings, but east of the Elbe River serfdom during the seventeenth century was taking a firmer hold and expanding. Eastern European lords worked their estates with forced labor and had legal powers of life and limb over their serfs, who were bound to the soil as personal property. Power to exact peasant services, dues, and rents belonged primarily to the nobility, the state, and the

*A procession of French clergy.*

*An English nonconformist minister.*

Greek Orthodox and Roman Catholic churches. Even though the clergy and aristocracy (the two principal privileged orders) no longer dominated government, they continued to dominate absolutist society in both Eastern and Western Europe.

Royal absolutism was the political antithesis of decentralized feudalism because it subordinated the nobles to the king. But even when absolute monarchs facilitated the rise of commoners into the aristocracy, they still used their political powers to preserve the hierarchic social order. Formal division of society into the estates of the late Middle Ages—nobles, clergy, and commoners— lasted until the French Revolution. Besides maintaining their traditional social ties with the monarchy, the nobles became officers of the royal army and held the most prestigious offices in the state and the church, thus sharing power with titled and privileged officials, themselves on the way to becoming nobles. In these ways absolute monarchy remained basically, although not entirely, a conservative social force. At the apex of the social pyramid stood the king. He alone had the power to promote limited numbers of men of ability or wealth. But he lacked the power, and usually the will, to dilute endlessly the old aristocracy or to invade and destroy existing privileges and vested interests.

In the simplest kind of hierarchy, as for example in France, the established clergy retained its preeminent position among the estates. In Roman Catholic kingdoms the clergy retained its prestige as the first estate and continued to educate the nobility's offspring, but its ranks were staffed at the top by noblemen or commoners elevated by the king. Protestant churchmen were more likely to come from professional ranks, especially the sons of clergy. The Reformation had produced religious minorities too large to eradicate without civil war, but the still prevalent belief that religious uniformity was necessary for domestic peace was reflected in the universal acceptance of established churches. Formal adherence to their tenets was a *sine qua non* for entrance into honorable professions. By teaching the common people obedience to divine-right rulers, the established churches supported royal absolutism as long as it was consistent with clerical privileges. "No king, no bishop; no

*A French lawyer with robe.*

bishop, no king" was a commonplace formula. In Roman Catholic countries such as France and Spain, where the Church retained great wealth, the established hierarchy also made considerable contributions to the royal treasury.

Among the privileged laymen, highest honors and preferment went to the nobility, itself a hierarchy of ranks. Law and custom recognized two different types of noble patents—titles inherited from knightly or military ancestors and titles acquired by service and made hereditary by purchase or gratuitous royal grant. Despite rivalries between them, hereditary and service nobles shared common traits: they held landed estates, rights to local milling and baking monopolies, tolls, and legal jurisdictions over peasants; they were exempt from common taxes and believed that acts of manual labor or trade in goods not produced on their own estates were

demeaning. In France the minority of nobles that engaged in commerce failed to overcome this tradition. Fighting wars was the occupation with the most prestige, but military undertakings often proved too costly for noble resources and forced noble families to negotiate despised marriage compacts with wealthy commoners.

Privilege was territorial as well as social. Local estates and courts maintained their "liberties" against incursions by royal officials. These liberties consisted of the privileges and political or legal autonomy of the local clergy, nobles, and bourgeoisie. They were incorporated in law codes and customs and were preserved and bolstered by local diets and courts. Usually they thrived on the periphery of the monarchy, outside the range of effective centralized control. The absolute monarchies never supplanted this maze of economic and legal localisms and always retained a strongly federal, provincial aspect.

On the fringe of privileged ranks in Western Europe lived the upper bourgeoisie. Aspiring to attain nobility, these professionals, bankers, and great merchants acquired offices and land with manorial rights. They received tax exemptions and other privileges from royal and municipal offices and sometimes patents of nobility from the king. Like nobles, they disdained and avoided manual labor. They, along with the clergy and nobility, were the only representatives to those provincial and central diets that survived, and their representation in Poland and other parts of Eastern Europe was scant indeed. From their ranks kings, overriding resistance from the older nobility, recruited the most aggressive centralizers among the royal bureaucrats. Adventurers from the West often entered the service of monarchs in Eastern Europe and received privileges and titles there. The leading absolute rulers of the late seventeenth and early eighteenth centuries ennobled more commoners than the older nobility would tolerate, but after the kings' deaths the nobles recovered much lost ground.

A hierarchy also existed within the bourgeoisie. It ranged from scholars and councillors at the top down through officials, notaries, and merchants (wholesale and retail) and masters of corporate guilds. These master craftsmen inherited their status but were considered less respectable if they actually worked with their hands.

Journeymen, apprentices, domestic workers, day workers, and agriculturists who lived within town walls constituted an unprivileged majority subject to excise and other taxes. They were forbidden to band together for mutual political or economic advantage, even if they had desired to do so. For them, rapid social ascent was difficult if not impossible.

In the hierarchies of all classes the hereditary family, not the individual, was the unit of society. Hereditary rights were most conspicuous among, but not limited to, families of political rulers, whose right to rule was inherited as an indefeasible, inalienable right. Among them marriages sealed treaties, and conflicting claims arose when male lines died out. The principle of heredity also prevailed among the nobility and bourgeoisie. Families sought marriage alliances to increase their fortunes or status. Since private and public rights were not sharply separated, dowries and legacies included offices of church and state, profitable legal jurisdictions, and manorial dues, as well as lands and securities. Money enough to give a daughter a large dowry or a son an education was the principal means of social ascent. At the middle level of the townspeople, guild masterships passed almost exclusively by inheritance and marriage. By voluntary or compulsory systems similar to the nobility's entails, even landholding peasants prevented the division of estates among heirs. Normally, the individual's status was determined for life by the position of the family into which he was born, and the social order strengthened family control over him.

Seldom could kings break through the bulwarks of family loyalties and class privileges,

*A merchant and his accounts.*

*A master silversmith's shop, about 1700.*

*Concluding an arranged marriage.*

but they were no less constrained by the inertia of custom that prevailed in the countryside. Upward of 80 per cent of Europe's population was rural; usually it was over 90 per cent. Even where personal movement was not legally prohibited, most village people lived, worked, and died without leaving the same villages that their ancestors had inhabited since time immemorial. Tradition ordered their daily lives much the same as it had the lives of their forebears, and it made novelty an object of fear.

The villages of the countryside also had their hierarchy based on access to land. Western European leaseholders held full, half, quarter, or lesser hides or estates. The system of entails left all but the eldest sons to become squatters on the commons, work in domestic industries or as day laborers, wander, plunder, or enter the army. Similar differentiations existed among the serf populations of Eastern Europe. But even the larger leaseholders of Western Europe often lacked the means of supporting their families, especially following droughts. The peasantry lived on the brink of famine not only because its obligations to state, church, and lord took the greater part of its productivity, but also because agriculture was bound by tradition to backward methods.

The peasants' only method for replenishing the soil was to let one third to one half of the land lie fallow each year. This alone could not prevent the soil's eventual exhaustion, and more and more tracts became wasteland. Cereals, the basic foodstuff for man and beast and the best sources of calories per acre of cultivated land, seldom returned more than five times their seed in good weather on good soil. Twofold or threefold harvests were most common. Until seed grasses were introduced to provide cold-weather forage, large numbers of cattle could not be kept over winter. Manure for fertilizer was therefore short. Thus agriculture was tied to a cycle of diminishing returns, and periodically subsistence fell catastrophically short.

Good harvests one after another supported

*Peasants harvesting.*

a growth of population, but short harvests brought local and regional famines. France was one of the most productive and prosperous continental states of the seventeenth century, but there were large regional famines there in 1629–1630, 1648–1651, 1660–1661, 1693–1694, and 1709–1710. No year of Louis XIV's seventy-two-year reign was without famine in some province. Starvation or malnutrition brought death first to the weaker members of the lower classes: children, women, old persons, and beggars. (Half the children died before the age of one.) Average longevity was probably not more than twenty-five, certainly not over thirty. Peasant women were weathered and old at that age. At forty, village men were often graybeards. Upper-class persons who reached adulthood lived longer, averaging perhaps fifty. Paradoxically country folk suffered more than townspeople from food shortages. Town governments stocked grain in warehouses, but even so famine caused deprivation and unemployment within their jurisdictions. High grain prices consumed greater proportions of spendable income and shrank markets for industrial goods. Craftsmen as well as peasants were obliged to sell tools and equipment—their capital goods—to subsist during protracted shortages, and they were perennially in debt.

Using force to prevent the redistribution of wealth, authoritarian rulers maintained stability at the top of the social order. But at the lower levels of town society, food shortages were the most common cause of riot and disorder. Peasants, on the other hand, seem to have accepted famine with greater resignation, although they frequently revolted against new or heavier taxes. In France and other absolutist kingdoms, especially Russia, such revolts spread across entire regions. Despite the relatively small population there was much unemployment. Officials tried to compel the unemployed to work but in vain; the capital to provide them with jobs was either lacking or being put to other purposes.

Basic poverty thus curtailed the absolute ruler's credit and revenues. It also set limits upon his militarism. Louis XIV could muster the largest army in Western Europe since the Roman Empire, but its range was limited by a lack of fodder and oats for its horses. And this was true even though the French monarch geared his policy for power rather than his subjects' welfare.

## ECONOMIC POLICIES OF ABSOLUTIST STATES

The continental monarchies were preoccupied with raising money for war. The policies followed by royal officials to increase revenues were later described as "mercantilism." But mercantilism has become an ambiguous word. On the Continent it departed significantly from the mercantilism practiced by England and the Dutch Republic, which relied upon commercial economies.

Many continental rulers tried to achieve the mercantilist goal of a favorable balance of trade, and they waged economic warfare to secure it. But they had to work within the framework and limitations of their feudal traditions. Some of their officials, like Louis XIV's principal finance minister Colbert, had long-range visions of economic expansion. Colbert tried to facilitate commerce by standardizing production methods, tariffs, and commercial law for the whole kingdom. Such efforts have been depicted as a phase of

*A peasant family (by Louis Le Nain, 1642).*

"state-building," as a response to the need created by international power politics for more economic centralization. Usually such policies, and Colbert's were no exception, amounted to intensified collection of traditional taxes rather than basic reform. State-building might make the regime militarily stronger, but its emphasis upon centralization, industry, and commerce trod on the toes of privileged interests and offended traditional sensibilities. And kings persisted in waging wars that their mercantilist officials considered economically ruinous. Even under the strongest autocrats, mercantilism became at most a compromise between aggressive foreign policies and the inertia of tradition.

Nevertheless governments did intervene extensively in the domestic economy. On larger estates in Western Europe, peasants—important as taxpayers, billeters of troops, and suppliers of military transportation—were protected against the nobility. Wage rates were fixed at low levels to make domestic products more competitive in foreign markets. Demanding more work, rulers reduced the number of religious holidays, enacted repressive measures against idleness, suppressed some monasteries and boarding schools, and encouraged the growth of population. Industrial production codes prescribed universal standards of quality. Initially justified as a means of insuring quality, these codes soon became mere devices to collect inspection fees and to curb innovations harmful to craftsmen's monopolies. In the interests of local, provincial, and national self-sufficiency, governments also regulated the grain trade. Some mercantilists favored the removal of restrictions on grain shipments, but the persistence of famines reinforced demands for local control.

Self-sufficiency was a major objective of mercantilist policy. To create military independence and to check the outward flow of hard money, governments established enterprises to produce luxury goods and founded royal arsenals. Tariffs checked the importation of all goods competing with domestic products. To secure colonial products unavailable at home, governments with access to the ocean chartered monopolistic trading and colonizing companies. In England and the Dutch republic such companies' resources buoyed up state credit at low rates of interest, but elsewhere they required the spur of state initiative and capital.

Rather than concentrating power in the hands of the state, these chartered companies gave public power to private groups of merchants. The same was true of the practice of farming tax collection out to private contractors and establishing monopolies to raise revenues from the sale of such necessities as salt. Thus absolute monarchies often extended the range of economic privilege to private individuals and families. But because mercantilist policies were secular and because they accorded greater prominence to merchants, they tended to undermine the religious and social foundations of the regimes that practiced them.

# B. The Effective Absolutist Regimes

If every European monarch aspired to unlimited authority, few came close to realizing it. Those that did were engaged in almost continuous warfare. The pace-setter for authoritarianism in all of Europe was Louis XIV. The Austrian Habsburgs, the Hohenzollerns, and some smaller German princes charted courses similar to his. Eastern Europe also boasted its great autocrat, Peter the Great, who thrust Russia into European affairs and built up his power at home by borrowing technology and institutions from the West.

## THE FRANCE OF LOUIS XIV

After the Peace of the Pyrenees in 1659, France replaced Spain as the most powerful and resplendent absolute state of Western Europe. In population and resources, except commercial wealth, it exceeded all other states of Europe. France's army and diplomacy dominated European politics, and her language became the *lingua franca* of upper-class Europe. French manners, fashions, music, art, and court life were aped as far east as Russia. Behind this great expansion of influence lay not only the work of Louis XIV and his ministers but the organization built by his Bourbon predecessors and the Cardinal-Ministers Richelieu and Mazarin.*

By ending the struggle for the French crown and then issuing the Edict of Nantes (1598) to pacify the Huguenots (whose faith he had once espoused), Henry IV had

* For a more extensive discussion of their work, see Volume I, Chapter 15.

brought peace to France. His chief minister, Sully, had begun to build a royal bureaucracy that subordinated the provinces to the King. But this incipient absolutism flagged with Henry's assassination in 1610 and the resurgence of the aristocracy under the regency that ruled during Louis XIII's childhood. Thereafter Louis' principal minister, Cardinal Richelieu, and Cardinal Mazarin, who presided over affairs during the wars that came to a conclusion in 1659, proceeded to suppress opposition and to build a royal autocracy.

Following a revolt by the Huguenots and nobility, Richelieu revoked those parts of the Edict of Nantes that granted the Huguenots autonomous political and military rights. He also displaced the rebellious nobility from critical decision-making and command posts in the central government. The office of *intendant,* staffed by appointees of common birth (who could be removed by the crown), represented royal authority in the provinces. Among other things, the *intendants* brought royal governors, who were local nobles, under surveillance and reported on their conduct of affairs. Nobles and holders of hereditary offices resented Mazarin as an Italian adventurer who enriched himself in office during Louis XIV's minority. But in 1648 a prolonged revolt, the *Fronde,* failed to unseat him. Likewise it failed to check royal taxation or dislodge the system of *intendants.* When Mazarin died after concluding the long war with Spain by the Peace of the Pyrenees (1659), he bequeathed intact to Louis XIV's personal control the machinery of absolutism developed during the previous half century.

## The King's Personal Monarchy

In attempting to fulfill and improve on Mazarin's paternalism, Louis XIV resolved to have no prime minister. Reacting against the civil wars of the 1640s, he was determined to exclude the nobility from making high-level decisions. When queried by a Church official as to whom he should address himself on questions of public affairs after Mazarin's death, Louis replied, "To myself." Like his Bourbon predecessors, he considered the state his private inheritance.

> Kings [he wrote] are absolute *seigneurs* [lords], and from their nature have full and free disposal of all property both secular and ecclesiastical, to use it as wise dispensers, that is to say, in accordance with the requirements of their State.[1]

The statement traditionally attributed to him, "I am the state," is apocryphal, but it illustrates his attitude. A Venetian ambassador once reported:

> The King maintains the most impenetrable secrecy about affairs of State. The ministers attend council meetings, but he confides his plans to them only when he has reflected at length upon them and has come to a definite decision. I wish you might see the King. His expression is inscrutable; his eyes like those of a fox. He never discusses State affairs except with his ministers in council. When he speaks to courtiers he refers only to their respective prerogatives and duties. Even the most frivolous of his utterances has the air of being the pronouncement of an oracle.[2]

In administering the state Louis proved to be diligent and industrious. After formal court rituals in the morning, he met in the afternoons with his high councillors. Unfortunately for France and Europe, he pursued glory and power for their own sake. The "Sun King" basked in the admiration of his own subjects and the amazement it aroused in neighboring countries. With this advantage, he wrote, there was nothing he could not obtain eventually. His wars of aggression were financed, however, by the tax administration that he inherited, and it placed tremendous burdens on the French peasantry. Moreover his aggressiveness re-

1. Quoted by Jean Longnon, ed., *A King's Lessons in Statecraft: Louis XIV: Letters to his Heirs,* translated by Herbert Wilson, A. & C. Boni, New York, 1925, p. 149.
2. Quoted by Louis Bertrand, *Louis XIV,* translated by Cleveland B. Chase, Longmans, Green & Co., London and New York, 1928, pp. 292–293.

*Louis XIV as a chivalric, classical hero.*

former hunting lodge just outside Paris, Louis constructed a huge palace built at tremendous expense and staffed by nearly fifteen thousand servants. Apart from the palace's role in setting the court and art fashions of Europe, it served Louis' purpose of gathering the greater nobility around the court. In return for personal services exalting the monarchy, he gave them pensions and made them financially dependent upon his favor.

Although this strategy succeeded in making politically impotent parasites out of the higher nobility, the court of Versailles had its drawbacks. It removed the King and his court from the realities of everyday life, and it permeated the court with an air of sycophancy. These results were sources of fundamental weaknesses in the regime.

Louis also threatened the privileged orders by depriving the old provincial assemblies of their functions and by overawing the *parlements* (high law courts). Only once near the end of his reign did the Parlement of Paris assert its claim to nullify a royal law by refusing to register it. Insofar as possible, the *intendants* and royal councils carried on the direction of state affairs.

### The Machinery of State

Louis' administration of France became a model for absolutism in other parts of Europe. In deciding matters of high policy the King attended three councils in person— War, Finance, and Foreign Affairs. They were made up of ministers of state. Lesser councils dealt with justice and internal administration. Officials did the work, but the King personally made decisions, which were then communicated to his diplomats and military commanders. For domestic affairs they were directed to the provinces through the *intendants* whose authority was absolute, at least in theory. ("The *intendant*," Louis wrote, "is the king present in the provinces.") In practice, however, they were often thwarted by provincial institutions, especially the *parlements*. Although France's central-

peatedly led other states to form coalitions against him and to frustrate his conquests. His failures and the pressures of his wars on the French people so transformed his image that the appellation "the Great," which his contemporaries used, failed to carry into the future.

Louis continued the Bourbon policy of subordinating the political and economic life of France to the direction of the monarchy. He built a bureaucracy of elevated commoners who owed their positions to the monarch alone. It excluded the nobility and high clergy. He set up special courts to discipline nobles, but his greatest thrust at their political power was indirect. At Versailles, a

*Colbert.*

ized government wielded unprecedented authority, there were limits to its functions. Louis XIV was never able to unify the kingdom completely. He had direct command of the army and foreign affairs, but even in the army corruption and traditional privileges tempered his control.

Early in Louis' reign Mazarin appointed and put at the sovereign's disposal a number of outstanding officials: de Louvois over the army, de Lionne over foreign affairs, and particularly Jean Baptiste Colbert (1619–1683). An ennobled draper's son who had been manager of Mazarin's personal fortune, Colbert became Controller of France in 1665. His efforts to strengthen France's economic capacity for war became so familiar that one form of mercantilism is usually designated by his name. His successes and failures graphically illustrate the gulf between the aims and accomplishments of the royal government.

## "Colbertism"

As finance minister Colbert worked assiduously to increase tax revenues, expand commerce, and reduce debts and corruption. He hit hard at speculation in government securities, many of them bogus, which passed from hand to hand. He instituted a drastic investigation of the tax farmers, the richest class in France, to force the return of ill-gotten gain.* By administering financial affairs efficiently, he nearly doubled revenues within six years and temporarily decreased the basic land tax. By stimulating economic activity, he sought further income without raising tax levels. The government took the initiative in encouraging industry—notably silk, lace, drapery, luxury goods, forestry, sugar refining, iron, and glassware. It sponsored colonial trading companies to build an empire in North America and India. To make the quality of French exports uniform and acceptable, Colbert promulgated minutely detailed industrial production codes drawn up by guildmasters. These codes, which specified minimum standards for manufacture, were enforced over the whole of France by the *intendants*. To stimulate trade and commerce Colbert built roads and canals. He proposed abolition of the provincial tariffs and grain trade regulations that hindered the flow of goods. Foreign goods, especially Dutch merchandise, he sought to exclude by heavy protective tariffs in 1664 and 1667. He strove to make France self-sufficient in grain by prohibiting the export of wheat. Finally he tried to standardize the legal procedures of the royal courts.

Although Colbert supplied money for Louis' war machine, most of his ventures failed. War costs mounted faster than revenues. Few basic reforms were implemented. The system of farming taxes to private contractors continued to plague the kingdom until the Revolution of 1789. Private French capital failed to support Colbert's industries

* Tax farmers were men who paid a lump sum to the treasury periodically in return for authority to collect taxes from the King's subjects.

and trading companies, going instead to state bonds (*rentes*). His industrial production codes stifled technological innovations and encouraged craftsmen to maintain the *status quo*. Only luxury goods and necessities found a ready market, for there was no broad purchasing power necessary to the success of new consumer industries. Colbert's prohibitive tariffs helped precipitate war with the Dutch, who forced their downward revision in the treaty of Nimwegen in 1678. Grain famines and revolts against exorbitant taxes did not cease. Nor did Colbert's attempted revision of the legal system give real unity to France, for approximately 400 different "systems" still existed in 1789. Even his supreme effort to incorporate the "Five Great Farms" in northern France into the largest tariff-free zone in Europe was not a complete success. The rest of France kept its traditional tolls, and extreme confusion over conflicting weights, measures, and tolls left the country an economic hodgepodge until the Revolution swept them away at the end of the eighteenth century.

Although Colbert is often depicted as an opponent of Louis' aggressive wars, he advocated economic warfare: exclusionist tariffs, colonial struggles waged by private companies, and the seizure of Dutch wealth. Moreover he was dedicated to the splendor of Louis—"For the king's glory, no sacrifice was too great," he wrote—and his fiscal measures financed his monarch's campaigns. Most of the revenue came from the *taille,* a headtax on the peasantry. In the recently acquired border provinces that retained their estates it was moderate, but in the older provinces it was particularly burdensome. The *gabelle* or government salt monopoly likewise varied according to province. As the pressure of war intensified after Colbert's death, taxes extended to include marriages, births, and deaths. Even in some of the richer areas the peasantry was in a state of semi-starvation during Louis' wars.

Royal military expenditures thus exceeded the kingdom's taxable wealth, especially during famines. But without Colbert's management the consequences would have been graver. From the *intendants* he solicited detailed and precise tax lists and information on business activity, population, and the temper of the people. Collated in government archives, the *intendants'* reports constituted a large store of information necessary to policy-making.

## The State and the Arts

In charge of royal buildings, Colbert was in a position to regiment architecture and plastic arts as well as the economy of Europe's most influential state. At the Gobelins royal factory he assembled an army of painters, sculptors, engravers, weavers, cabinet makers, and other artists under the leadership of the painter Charles Lebrun. But Versailles was Colbert's principal artistic concern. As an effort of major construction, it is matched only by the architect Christopher Wren's rebuilding of London after the Great Fire of 1666.

Colbert wielded his influence to tame baroque elaborateness with classical simplicity. The Catholic Reformation that had inspired baroque emotionalism was over. Classical baroque was dedicated not to an otherworldly religion but to a secular hero, Louis XIV. The Royal Academy of Sculpture and Painting set the tone of official taste, returning to the principles of Aristotle and of the Italian High Renaissance. Versailles' exterior was classical; its gardens were rigidly symmetrical and geometrical. Its interior, however, was classical baroque, done in themes drawn from the ancient world but laden with allegorical rather than literal meaning. Lebrun instructed his painters to avoid Venetian models as too colorful, the Flemish and Dutch as too literal and bourgeois. Versailles was designed not for comfort or utility but for magnificence. It was the culmination in grandeur of the courts of the late Renaissance. It set the norm for courtly architecture and furnishings to such a degree that other monarchs felt obliged to imitate it. Likewise

*Versailles and its classical gardens.*

its operas, ballets, and plays set Europe's standards of entertainment.

Besides artists, Louis XIV patronized men of letters. The leading classical writers—Corneille, Racine, and Molière—were brought to court as willing or reluctant courtiers. During the first years of the personal monarchy there was a great outpouring of their dramas and satires. Nicolas Boileau-Despréaux (1636–1711), royal historiographer, more or less set official canons of writing and became the arbiter of literary taste. Attacking the affectations or "preciousness" of the overrefined and highly personal authors in the salons of Paris, he appealed for good sense, reason, and rigidly disciplined imagination. He led in formulating the rules of neoclassicism that spread over Europe.

Under royal patronage, writers, like artists, gained status and lost independence. They appealed to a limited audience and scorned the romances, imitative poems and plays, letters, and polemical religious works that most literate Frenchmen read. Courtiers looked down upon popular culture as much

as upon provincial nobles. In the quarrel that broke out over the relative merits of ancient and modern authors, they sided squarely with the ancients. Literary advances are often singled out as the most enduring accomplishments of Louis' reign, but they occurred in the years prior to 1685. As the classical "greats" died or retired they were not replaced. Louis became less generous as he grew older and came under the influence of the pious Madame de Maintenon. As the atmosphere of Versailles, influenced by piety and family misfortunes, turned to cold formality, artistic creativity froze.

## One King, One Church

The Church as well as the arts felt the steely grip of royal absolutism. For a time it appeared that Louis, like the Protestant rulers of Germany, would try to create a national (Gallican) Church. The Concordat of Bologna (1516), which the Council of Trent had not nullified, empowered French kings to make most high Church appointments. Louis' appointees supported him against the papacy, but he still lacked the power to name prelates in parts of southern France. During the 1670s he determined to bring these posts under royal sway. This extension of government power precipitated a sharp quarrel with the pope who refused to confirm the King's appointments. During the deadlock that ensued, many Church offices fell vacant, and the monarchy collected their revenues. In 1682 a national Church council led by Bishop Bossuet supported the King. It reiterated the position of the Gallican Church that the pope's spiritual powers were limited to those confirmed by a council. After protracted conflict that cost Louis the diplomatic support of the papacy, he and the pope reached a compromise. Then monarch, pope, and Jesuits joined in common effort against the French Jansenists, a mystical Catholic cult professing Calvinist morals and St. Augustine's theology of predestination. The Jansenists also advocated a state church, which ought to have pleased Louis, had they not been allied with the *parlements* and nobility resisting his authority. He destroyed the major centers of their activity but failed to extirpate their spiritual influence. It survived until the late eighteenth century.

Fast abandoning the Bourbon policy of toleration, Louis also attacked the Huguenots. Here, too, he yielded to the pressure of the clergy and his advisors, who after 1655 demanded the complete elimination of Protestantism. Noble families of "political Huguenots" went back to the Roman Church. Financial inducements were offered to apostates, while church closures canceled their privileges and narrowed the range of toleration. Then dragoons were stationed in Huguenots' homes to harass them. Royal troops forced nominal conversions in the public squares of southern towns. Finally on the specious argument that there were few dissenters left in France, the King revoked the Edict of Nantes in 1685.

Louis forbade the Huguenots to emigrate, but over 200,000 of them escaped the kingdom. Their numbers included skilled artisans, scholars, merchants, soldiers, and professional men. Their talents enriched Prussia, the English colonies, and other new Protestant homelands. After their emigration, Protestant states were solidified against Louis' foreign policy. This episode momentarily reinjected religion into Europe's dynastic power struggles. By abandoning toleration, Louis convinced non-Catholic peoples that Roman Catholics could not be trusted.

## Louis XIV and Europe

The France of Louis XIV epitomized aggressive diplomacy during a century in which warfare decisively influenced institutions. During the Thirty Years' War, France's standing army had borrowed tactics from the Dutch and Swedes in order to defeat Spanish formations that had been invincible for a century and a half. As personal ruler, Louis lavished resources and attention upon the army. Under de Louvois the army adopted improved artillery, bayonets, and a quicker-firing muzzle-loading handgun. Soldiers donned uniforms and were given a serious military education. Their administrators centralized command and devoted great attention to supply. Marshal de Vauban, an engineering genius, devised scientific ways to reduce fortresses that were precise enough to predict the time of capitulation. Upon occasion the King, following such predictions, assembled the court, complete with orchestra, to witness the fall of an enemy. The nature of military discipline is indicated by the name of Louis' inspector-general, Jean Martinet. Nobles filled the officer corps, whereas commissioned recruiting captains, often corrupt, hired or impressed the common soldiery. By 1678 the standing army reached 279,000 men, a formidable and expensive force, and it continued to grow.

Louis sought first to conquer those territories in the Spanish Netherlands that had escaped Mazarin's grasp during the Thirty Years' War. When the queen's father, the king of Spain, died in 1665, Louis claimed

*A Prussian military parade in Berlin.*

the Spanish Netherlands as her inheritance. Catching Spain diplomatically isolated, French armies under de Condé and de Turenne swept through a series of Flemish forts and Franche-Comté in 1667 and 1668. French diplomats forestalled interference by the Austrian Habsburgs by promising them generous slices of Spanish territory upon the death of the sickly Spanish king, Charles II. The task of organizing resistance to French expansion fell to Jan De Witt, Grand Pensionary of Holland, who brought England and Sweden into a triple alliance with the Dutch Republic. Louis opted for peace, retained his conquests in the Low Countries, and then set his diplomatic corps the task of dissolving De Witt's defenses. In 1670 he detached Charles II of England, who was at loggerheads with Parliament, from the alliance. Charles accepted a French subsidy, joined France against the Dutch Republic, and promised to announce his adherence to Roman Catholicism as soon as possible. In 1672 Sweden also switched sides. In Germany a horde of diplomatic agents well laden with gifts neutralized all of the princes except the elector of Brandenburg. Thus did Louis prepare for the next onslaught.

Without a declaration of war, French armies invaded Lorraine and Holland in 1672. The overwhelmed Dutch met all of Louis' demands, but the King raised his terms for peace. Desperation and fear of defeat brought William of Orange to power in the Dutch Republic. The Dutch opened dikes and flooded fields to stop the invasion. Wil-

liam enlisted foreign assistance. He allied with Brandenburg, Austria, Spain, Denmark, several German states, and eventually England. In 1675 Brandenburg defeated Louis' only remaining ally, Sweden. Although French forces had meanwhile reconquered Franche-Comté, the war had become a stalemate. The French secured peace by making a separate settlement with the Dutch. At Nimwegen in 1678 the Dutch received favorable trade arrangements and the restoration of their territory. Spain ceded to France Franche-Comté and a chain of forts extending from Dunkirk to the Meuse River. France, which had been militarily strengthened but had lost an irreplaceable general (de Turenne), was faced with revolts against war taxation in several provinces and would have to live with the marriage alliance between English and Dutch royal houses.

Having acquired Franche-Comté, France was mistress of her eastern frontier. Now Louis XIV's ambition, heightened by success, extended to the Rhine itself. He paved the way with clever diplomacy and inflated legal claims. The Peace of Westphalia had ceded ambiguous rights to France in Alsace in 1648. Now French jurists laid claim to full sovereignty before specially constituted "Chambers of Reunion," courts set up in frontier cities. As the courts consistently rendered decisions favorable to France, the French army occupied their territorial awards. Theoretically, by taking advantage of outdated feudal relationships, the Chambers of Reunion could have pushed French claims progressively across most of Germany.

Meanwhile French diplomacy—which was setting the language and procedures, open and secret, for all of Europe—was disarming German resistance to this creeping expansion. The French King posed as the protector of the "liberties" of German princes against the emperor; by 1683 Louis himself had hopes of being elected emperor. By the same date he had reconstructed an alliance system consisting of Sweden, Poland, Turkey, Brandenburg, Saxony, Bavaria, and Hungarian

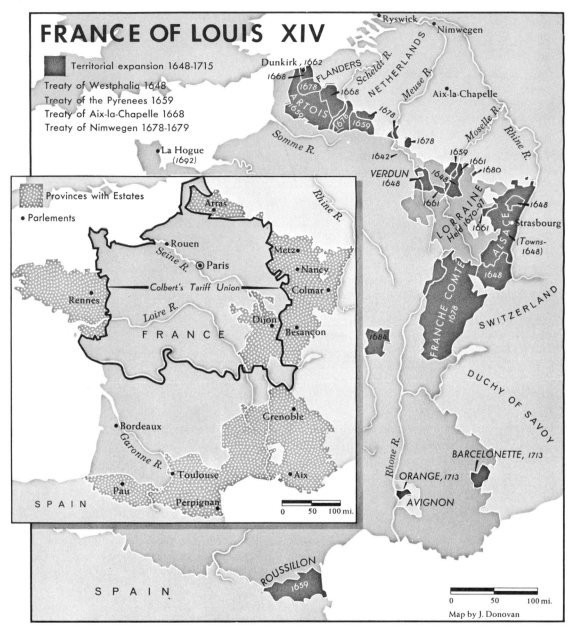

FRANCE OF LOUIS XIV

Territorial expansion 1648-1715

Treaty of Westphalia 1648
Treaty of the Pyrenees 1659
Treaty of Aix-la-Chapelle 1668
Treaty of Nimwegen 1678-1679

Provinces with Estates
• Parlements

Colbert's Tariff Union

Map by J. Donovan

leaders in revolt against the Habsburgs. When the Turks laid seige to Vienna in 1683, Louis played a waiting game hoping to save Europe from the Turks at Austrian expense. But he miscalculated; the Habsburgs drove the Turks from Vienna. Then they purchased temporary peace in the West by recognizing the work of the Chambers of Reunion. They

used the time thus gained to turn the Turkish retreat into a rout. Belgrade fell in 1688. Louis, fearing the loss of his Turkish ally, invaded and devastated the Palatinate.

As Louis came to the peak of his power in Europe after Nimwegen, his personal life and the tone of his court were changing. His shapely, vivacious mistress, Madame de

Montespan, "as wicked as the devil himself," gave way in royal favor to Madame de Maintenon, governess of the royal bastards. With the advent of de Maintenon, whom the King married secretly in 1684, puritanical winds blew through the royal corridors. Comedy was banned at court, and the atmosphere at Versailles became sober and stiff. During the same years the King turned to persecuting the Huguenots. Thus the complement of aggressiveness abroad was suppression at home.

By 1685 Louis, expanding along the Rhine, revoking the Edict of Nantes, and reviving French colonial and commercial power, had again lost his allies. William of Orange began organizing the League of Augsburg. In 1688 Louis again miscalculated when he did not oppose William's ascension to the throne of England as co-ruler with James II's daughter Mary.* Louis assumed that civil war would neutralize Great Britain, but instead of starting a civil war, William assumed rule over a united country in a bloodless revolution. France was now opposed by a coalition of the Empire, the major German states including Brandenburg, the Dutch Republic, Spain, Savoy, and England. The exhausting War of the League of Augsburg (1689–1697) was the first major European struggle to extend to the rest of the world; in the English colonies of North America it was known as King William's War. The League turned back French expansion. At Ryswick in 1697 peace terms substantially restored prewar boundaries. It gave Emperor Leopold peace in the West again, thus allowing him to drive the Turks eastward until, suspicious once again of France, he called a halt in 1699.

## The War of Spanish Succession

Louis made peace in 1697 because he could not risk being at war with Spain when

*Charles II, the end of a line.*

the feeble, childless Charles II died. Otherwise he might forfeit his claims to Charles' empire. By accidents of birth and death, there were three dynastic claimants to this, the largest European empire—the French Dauphin, the duke of Bavaria, and Emperor Leopold I.† And the struggle among them came to pose the chief threat to peace in Europe. Louis negotiated first with England and the Dutch republic. Together these three states drew up a partition treaty in 1698 that substituted a balance of power for the strict system of legitimate succession. By its terms the weakest contender, the duke of Bavaria, would have received Spain, her colonies, and the Spanish Netherlands. Thus

---

* James II was forced into exile, and when he died his son became the new Stuart pretender under the name of James III.

† Dauphin was the designation for the French king's eldest son or heir apparent. The Spanish mothers of both the French and Bavarian claimants had renounced their rights of succession.

no one dynasty would have monopolized power in Europe. But the treaty was never carried out. The Austrian Habsburgs refused to recognize it, and the Bavarian duke died before Charles II.

Again Europe faced the threat of general war over the Spanish throne. In 1699 a second partition treaty among the same parties allotted those lands previously promised to Bavaria to a branch of the Austrian Habsburgs. France was to receive Naples, Sicily, and Milan, the last to be exchanged for Lorraine. But Leopold of Austria was not content with part of the loaf. He preferred to claim the whole. Likewise the Spanish court opposed partition. Just before his death in 1700, Charles II drew up a will, a "crop of dragon's teeth," which bequeathed the entire empire to Louis' grandson Philip. If he and his younger brother refused the inheritance, all of Charles' domains would then go to an Austrian archduke. A more devastating threat to peace could scarcely have been contrived. Louis was now faced with the most difficult choice of his reign. To accept the will was to violate the second partition treaty and to secure Spain as an ally in a war against Austria, Great Britain, and the Dutch Republic. To reject the will meant war with both Austria and Spain with the dubious assistance of the commercial powers. Since he had to fight in either case, the temptation of defiantly taking the whole proved too strong to resist. Needlessly provoking the English and the Dutch, Louis announced the eventual union of the Spanish and French thrones, recognized James Stuart (III) as the legitimate king of England, issued a series of strong decrees regulating Spanish colonial trade—at the expense of both the English and the Dutch—and seized Dutch-controlled forts in the Spanish Netherlands. Again a grand coalition formed against France. As allies Louis had only Spain, Portugal, Cologne, and Bavaria.

The war for Charles II's inheritance, called Queen Anne's War in England's American colonies, spread overseas between 1701 and

1713. It remained isolated, however, from a contemporary Great Northern War for Baltic supremacy. France had now lost the military leadership of de Turenne and de Condé, whereas England and Austria had the outstanding services of the Duke of Malborough and Prince Eugene of Savoy. In the battle of Blenheim (1704) Marlborough drove French forces back across the Rhine. Following the battle at Ramillies (1706), he forced them out of the Spanish Netherlands. Meanwhile Prince Eugene expelled them from Italy. As France suffered defeats unmatched in the past two centuries, Austria overran Bavaria; Gibraltar fell to the English; Portugal was detached from Louis' camp. French morale fell very low during the extremely cold winter months of 1708 and 1709. As early as 1706 Louis had decided upon peace, but his foes, as their fortunes improved, raised their demands. Finally in 1710 he offered to surrender Alsace and Lorraine and to supply money to drive his grandson from the throne of Spain. But the allies demanded that Louis himself drive Philip from Spain during a two-month truce. He rejected this demand, and France and Spain began to rally.

At the same time, the anti-French alliance disintegrated. In 1711 the Austrian claimant to Spain died, and his rights reverted to the Habsburg emperor. England found herself fighting to unite the Spanish and Austrian thrones. This union would upset the balance of power as much as if Louis would seize the whole domain. Weary of war, concerned about commerce, and fearful of Austrian Habsburg dominance, a peace party—the Tories—took charge in England and negotiated a separate peace with France. Two treaties—Utrecht (1713) and Rastatt (1714), known together as the Peace of Utrecht—halted the devastating war. Louis' grandson Philip retained possession of Spain and her colonies on the condition that the French and Spanish thrones would never be joined. The Austrian Habsburgs received Naples, Sardinia, Milan, and the Spanish Netherlands, where the Dutch were granted

WESTERN EUROPE AFTER UTRECHT, 1721

*Map by J. Donovan*

the right to garrison forts in order to forestall any new French invasion. The house of Savoy received Sicily and the status of kingdom. The Hohenzollern rulers of Prussia were also allowed to call themselves "king," and they received a small territory (Guelderland) along the lower Rhine. The lion's share of the spoils of war went to England. She retained Gibraltar, Minorca, Newfoundland, Acadia, St. Kitts, and Hudson Bay. In Spain's American colonies British merchants gained a limited right to trade, which served as an entrée for large-scale smuggling. The South Sea Company also obtained a monopoly of the Spanish colonial slave trade (*Asiento*). In subsequent decades Spain was to upset the peace arrangements in Italy, and France was to obtain Lorraine (1739). Despite these changes, however, the Peace of Utrecht stands as one of the most important territorial settlements in modern European history.

## Epilogue to Glory

Louis XIV's death in 1715 brought to a close the longest reign in European history. He had raised France to a peak of glory, but his reputation for greatness did not survive even the latter part of his reign. Deeply tired of Louis' wars, clergymen, intellectuals, disaffected nobles, merchants, and even military leaders like de Vauban criticized him severely. Louis outlived many critics or silenced them by censorship. But after his death the aristocracy was able to reassert its influence. Despising his "reign of the vile bourgeoisie," the resurgent aristocrats played upon popular desires for peace and stability and took advantage of the minority of Louis XV to assume more control over public policy. In exalting the monarchy, Louis had provided its opponents with explosive ammunition. And they had at their disposal the lines of cultural communications that he had laid across Europe. Subsequent generations of critics could spread their assault on absolutism far beyond the borders of France.

## HABSBURG AND HOHENZOLLERN

In the Old Regime, dynastic state boundaries were set by births, deaths, and marriages within ruling families as well as by conquest. Ruling families inherited diverse territories with a variety of laws, customs, and constitutions. Provincial diets usually put provincial interests first and tried to prevent outsiders from holding local positions of power and privilege. This particularism was especially notable in the provinces of Central Europe held by the Habsburgs and Hohenzollerns. Compared to them, Louis XIV's territories were contiguous and relatively homogeneous. Hohenzollern lands were scattered from the Rhine to the Niemen rivers, whereas the Habsburgs ruled peoples of diverse languages along the Danube. Despite the disunity of their holdings, these two families tried to administer them as coherent

states. Thus they laid the basis for future rivalry over the control of German affairs.

## Absolutism in the Habsburg Danubian Monarchy

The Peace of Westphalia (1648) left the Habsburg emperors of the Holy Roman Empire with an empty title. It admitted their rivals, France and Sweden, to direct participation in German affairs. Their authority was further diluted by the growing independence of the larger German principalities—Bavaria, Brandenburg-Prussia, Saxony, and Hanover —which had their own armies and foreign dynastic ties. Against the strength of his competitors, Leopold I (1658–1705) had no chance of recovering imperial authority. To counter French and Swedish designs on Germany, he was obliged to make Hanover an electorate and to concede royalty to the Hohenzollerns as kings "in Prussia."

Leopold was Louis XIV's most consistent opponent, but until 1697 his opposition was sporadic and feeble. In 1668 he agreed to divide the Spanish empire with France. In the Dutch War he gave the beleaguered Dutch no assistance until 1673. Then he appeased the French king by allowing France to annex German territory through the "Chambers of Reunion."* And during the War of the League of Augsburg, William III was more conspicuous than Leopold in organizing Europe against French aggression. Irked by Leopold's ineffectiveness in Western Europe, the papal nuncio at Vienna even opined that Leopold, who had been trained for the clergy in Spain, should act more decisively and trust less in Providence.

But Austria's relative ineffectiveness against Louis XIV stemmed more from conscious policy than from weakness. Unable to prosecute a long two-front war, Leopold gave first priority to the extension of his domains eastward. While Louis XIV nibbled at Alsace and the Empire, the Austrian ruler was en-

---

* For their activities, see p. 17.

gaged in conquering Hungary, driving the Turks from positions they had held for more than a century. Thus the Habsburgs laid the basis for a strong Danubian monarchy that continued to order the political affairs of Central Europe for more than two centuries.

When the Tyrol escheated to Leopold in 1665, he became the first Habsburg monarch to rule personally the whole Habsburg patrimony. Besides the Tyrol there were Upper Austria, Lower Austria, Carniola, Carinthia, Styria, the German provinces, Bohemia, and Hungary. But Leopold controlled only the western fourth of Hungary, a band 40 to 80 miles wide, and the Magyar nobility made his hold on that portion tenuous. Since 1222 it had claimed the right to elect its own king and to resist any monarch who infringed upon its privileges. Actually the nobles refused to submit to any authority. Their restiveness under foreign rule, Habsburg or Turkish, gave each power ample opportunity to intervene in Hungarian affairs at the other's expense.

In 1663 a revived Ottoman military machine conquered Transylvania, selling 80,000 captives as slaves. This event caused the Magyar nobility to join Austria in defeating the Turks at St. Gotthard. But Leopold struck an immediate truce with the invaders. Interpreting this truce as a device to reduce them to submission as Bohemia had been subjected to Vienna after 1620, Magyar nobles conspired to establish an independent state. They were fully justified in suspecting Austrian motives, but in 1683 the Ottomans launched a major invasion aimed at the conquest of Vienna. Stopped at the gates of that city by King Jan Sobieski of Poland in the defenders' eleventh hour of endurance, the Turks were finally driven out of Hungary. Leopold, who had found a capable general in Prince Eugene of Savoy, terminated the eastern drive in 1699. The Treaty of Karlowitz in that year recognized Habsburg authority over Transylvania and almost all

of Hungary. Despite her heavy contributions to the victory, Poland received only one small territory. Leopold now turned his attention westward to deal with the impending crisis over the Spanish succession.

Using the stability gained in the East to strengthen his position in the West, Leopold now made a bid for his sons to inherit the whole Spanish empire. In this he failed, but the Peace of Utrecht awarded to his successor the old Spanish Netherlands, Milan, Tuscany, Naples, and Sicily. Historians have joined the papal nuncio in deriding Leopold for indecisiveness, but he enlarged Habsburg domains far more than Louis XIV expanded those of France. After Utrecht, Prince Eugene of Savoy returned to the eastern front to turn back a renewed Turkish counterattack. The Treaty of Passarowitz (1718) confirmed Turkish losses of 1699* and marked the demise of the Ottomans as an offensive threat to the newly established Habsburg empire on the Danube.

Leopold I admired the power and prerogatives of Louis XIV and tried to imitate them by being his own first minister. Like his opposite number in France, he made the higher nobility dependent on the court for its honors and privileges. His central government was compartmentalized into a privy council, a war council, an imperial treasury, and an imperial chancery. But these were considerably weaker than the institutions of France. The German provinces retained their privileged estates. In order to raise money and troops, Leopold had to negotiate with each diet, which then supervised its own levies. The privy council remained an advisory rather than an executive body, and the imperial treasury's revenue was limited to mineral rights and indirect taxes.

In the chancery a group called the "cameralists" stood ready to assert the authority

---

* In addition, the Ottomans ceded the remainder of Hungary, western Walachia, and parts of Bosnia and Serbia.

Map by J. Donovan

— Holy Roman Empire

0    100    200    300 mi.

of the crown more rigorously than Leopold himself. But at the outset of his reign their authority was effective only in Bohemia, which had been reduced after 1620 to a hereditary monarchy directly under the Viennese court. Leopold summoned the Magyar estates to Pressburg in 1687 to ratify an absolutist constitution which abolished their rights to elect and resist the king. It equated Protestantism, long associated with political dissent, with treason and was meant to stamp it out.

24

Unlike the Bohemian nobles, the turbulent, ungovernable Magyars were not displaced. For one thing the monarchy lacked a middle class from which to draw loyal bureaucrats. In the eastern part of the Habsburg realm only Transylvania was ruled directly from Vienna. Hungary's administration remained in the hands of the nobility, although its finances were subject to central control. The nobles were confirmed in their privileged rule over an enserfed peasantry, and in order to enforce this settlement, Austria was obliged to garrison the kingdom with 30,000 troops during the War of Spanish Succession. After the war Leopold's successors Joseph I (1705–1711) and Charles VI (1711–1740) won over individual rebel leaders. Charles VI's Pragmatic Sanction of 1713 proclaimed as an established fact that his German, Bohemian, and Hungarian possessions were administratively unified. In the German provinces a centralized state with officials comparable to *intendants* did not take form until the reign of Maria Theresa after 1740. But in the eastern, non-German parts of the monarchy, absolutism was firmly entrenched during the reign of Leopold I.

## *The Rise of Brandenburg-Prussia*

Hohenzollern lands were even more scattered than those of the Habsburg patrimony, but within a few decades the rulers of Brandenburg, who had the title "Elector of the Holy Roman Empire," instituted a more effective absolutism. After the Thirty Years' War the Hohenzollerns ruled Cleves, Mark, Ravensburg, Halberstadt, Cammin, Minden, Magdeburg, Brandenburg, Eastern Pomerania, and Prussia—all as separate principalities. Each had its own diet or assembly and its own customary law. In the first half of the seventeenth century the elector's power over these diets had reached its nadir. A long series of economic crises had enabled the nobility to humble city, peasant, and ruler alike. The electors had been forced to side with the nobles (Junkers), who dominated

*The Great Elector (by Andreas Schlüter).*

state and society, thus reducing formerly free peasants to serfdom and towns to decadence. But the Junkers were undone by military weakness and depression during the Thirty Years' War.

During that war the Junkers resisted taxation and failed to provide for defense. Fiscal weakness and poverty (Brandenburg was known as "the sandbox of the Empire") left Hohenzollern domains to the mercies of foreign invaders. The war precipitated a conflict between the electors and their noble-dominated diets over the electors' desire to administer, defend, and expand their dynastic territories as a single state. The war forced some efforts along these lines: a central privy council for all Hohenzollern lands was established, and during the 1630s a centralized war commissariat began to develop independently of the local assemblies. But these diets were still wed to parochial interests and privilege, and Frederick William, the Great Elector who acceded to power in 1640, was forced to cooperate with them temporarily.

In 1653 Brandenburg witnessed the first

RISE OF BRANDENBURG-PRUSSIA

Map by J. Donovan

test of strength between an elector and a provincial diet. Frederick William confirmed the old privileges of the nobles and granted them full power over the peasantry. He also acknowledged their tax exemptions and their privilege of importing and exporting their products duty free, prerogatives that weighed heavily on townsmen and peasants. In return, the Junkers pledged Frederick William a long-term grant of money. Actually the diet had unwittingly voted its own extinction when it abdicated financial control because the outbreak of the Baltic War (1655–1660) enabled the elector to secure further taxes without its consent. After 1653 no full diet met again in Brandenburg. In 1667, on his own authority, Frederick William imposed excise taxes on production and trade. His tax collectors were soon administering the cities, but urban crafts were prohibited in the countryside, and control remained in the Junkers' hands.

The elector used his new powers in Brandenburg to wrest concessions from other provincial diets. Taxes supported his standing army, and, in turn, the army collected the taxes he needed. When peace was signed in 1660 Frederick William did not disband his army as had been the custom. He maintained

it and used it to centralize further the Hohenzollern state. Like Brandenburg, Prussia also lost its diet. The Great Elector broke its power during a war with Louis XIV from 1672 to 1678 when the War Commissariat collected military and excise taxes, pushing aside the diet and local officials. Still, as in Brandenburg, the Junkers in Prussia preserved their power over the peasantry, their administrative offices, and exclusive rights to trade in grain.

As in the eastern Hohenzollern lands, autocratic military rule superseded civilian control in the smaller territories of north-central Germany such as Magdeburg. But along the Rhine in Cleves and Mark, stronger towns, diets, and a less downtrodden peasantry blunted the thrust of electoral absolutism. Here the War Commissariat obtained large taxes but little administrative power. The Great Elector exempted the nobility from taxation and gave it extensive legal jurisdictions, but the Rhenish provinces retained their assemblies and never conformed to the eastern pattern of autocracy, serfdom, and suppression of town life.

Between 1653 and 1688 the Great Elector became one of Europe's most powerful rulers; his standing army and its administration made this development possible. At the end of the Thirty Years' War the Privy Council had been the highest legal and administrative body for both military and civil matters, but in 1660 it lost control of military affairs to the War Commissariat. This organization had originally been responsible for assembling, equipping, provisioning, and financing the army. Steadily it encroached upon civilian affairs. It stripped local diets of fiscal power, and its agents extended their authority over guilds, town government, and courts. It also came to control taxes, trade, settlement of the Huguenots, and numerous other matters.

Hohenzollern absolutism paralleled many developments in France. Agents of the War Commissariat had powers resembling Louis XIV's *intendants*. Its bureaucracy operated under military regimentation. Corruption was less widespread, although family influence and nepotism were common. The Hohenzollern government also gained greater cooperation from the nobility than the French rulers ever enjoyed. It is true that both the Great Elector and Frederick William I placed commoners in positions of high authority. But noblemen filled most of the offices at all times, and they kept control of the countryside and the army. Their political loyalties shifted away from the local diets to the monarch. Still that loyalty was conditioned by their own interests, to which the Great Elector had made important concessions. Absolutism stopped at the gates of the landed estates; the Junkers were exempted from all its controls except military conscription. In return for their service in the military bureaucracy, most of the population was abandoned to their rule.

The Hohenzollerns guaranteed to the Junker class control over both rural and urban affairs, a guarantee that proved very costly. Taxes per capita were probably double those of France. These heavy taxes drained potential capital from the economy, thus undercutting the Great Elector's mercantilist policies, which were designed to

*Frederick William I reviewing his "giant guards."*

stimulate economic growth. They actually crippled the growth of towns, commerce, and industry.

Under the Great Elector's successors, Frederick (1688–1713) and Frederick William I (1713–1740), Prussian absolutism became increasingly centralized. The military bureaucracy grew as the Hohenzollerns struggled to contain Louis XIV along the Rhine and to assume supremacy in the Baltic area. In 1723 the General Directory was formed, uniting civil and military chains of command into a single body. Created to save the state from near bankruptcy, it became the nucleus around which the power of the eighteenth-century Prussian state was built.

Frederick William I devoted special attention to the army. Indeed Prussia was sometimes referred to as "an army with a state." At great expense he recruited giants from all over Europe for his palace guard at Potsdam. To Frederick II, who succeeded him in 1740, he bequeathed a large army (80,000 men) and a centralized bureaucracy. The one great chink in the absolutist armor was the power and degree of independence that aristocratic officials enjoyed. Furthermore, the nobles resented the tax that Frederick William I imposed on them in order to help support his army. As the nobility had risen up in France after the death of Louis XIV, so the nobility of

Prussia renewed its bid for power when Frederick William died.

## THE EMERGENCE OF RUSSIA AS A EUROPEAN POWER STATE

By the eighteenth century Russia came to resemble Brandenburg-Prussia as a society composed of serfs and lords and governed by a military bureaucracy. Since English and Dutch traders had made contact with Russia in the sixteenth century, Russian rulers had borrowed technology from the West to undergird their military power. Peter the Great (1682–1725) accelerated this Westernization and by territorial expansion brought Russian power to bear upon Western and Central Europe. Absolutism in Russia, however, rested upon political, social, religious, and intellectual traditions quite different from those of any Western or Central European state.

### The Muscovite Tradition

Forged by the grand dukes of Moscow, the Russian state never experienced that feudal decentralization which vested nobles, churchmen, and town councils in the West with legal and political autonomy. No diets defended the vested interests of privileged Russians. Ivan III (1462–1505) stripped the autonomous city-state Novgorod of its republican institutions and dispersed its commercial families. Ivan IV (1533–1584) dealt similarly with the city of Pskov. When the government later fostered industry and trade it was under paternal state direction.

The grand dukes could suppress urban autonomy more easily than aristocratic power. Ruling an agrarian state and short of money, they were obliged to reward their servants with land and privileges that became hereditary. To undermine the growing influence of the hereditary nobles (the *boyars*), Ivan IV (the first tsar) called a representative advisory assembly, the *zemski sobor,* but this body never achieved the status of a Western diet. He also attempted to replace the *boyars* with a new nobility of service wholly dependent upon his own person. When these measures failed, Ivan broke the *boyars'* power by using a secret police and a system of extraordinary courts, both of which engaged in assassination and torture. But eventually the service nobility, too, acquired hereditary privileges that threatened his power. Although the struggle between tsar and nobility went on, the Russian aristocracy remained considerably weaker than its Western counterpart.

The Russian Orthodox Church was another potential rival to the tsar. Russian Christianity stemmed from Constantinople (Byzantium) where caesaropapism—the subordination of the Church to secular rulers or caesars (hence czars or tsars)—was well established. During Moscow's wars of expansion, Russian churchmen nationalized Orthodoxy into the doctrine that the tsar was the only Christian king and Moscow, the "Third Rome," the only capital of pure Christianity on the face of the earth. This messianic doctrine made holy crusades of Moscow's wars. And the hold that religious leaders assumed over the Russian masses threatened the secular ruler who aimed to concentrate all power in himself.

Russian Orthodoxy and the heritage of Tartar rule* set thought and customs in Russia apart from Western traditions. Orthodox theology remained impervious to scholastic efforts toward reconciling faith with reason. Russian thought was untouched by the Renaissance revival of classical languages and literatures. Prior to Peter the Great the country had but one printing press and no universities or intellectuals to foster Western culture. Russian clothing and customs, such as the seclusion of women, struck the inhabitants of Western Europe as Oriental and alien.

---

* The dukes of Muscovy overturned Tartar suzerainty in 1480.

## The Early Romanovs

Ivan IV did not establish internal security or a stable succession of rule by his reign of terror against the nobility; when his son died in 1598, the male line of the Muscovite house became extinct, and Russia plunged into chaos. The last tsar's father-in-law, Boris Godunov, tried to restore order and found a dynasty, but after he died in 1604, the army unseated and killed his heir. From 1605 to 1613 Russia was beset by a "Time of Troubles"—bitter faction, fighting, foreign invasion, internal brigandage, and famine. Swedish and Polish troops entered Moscow and vied to make their candidates tsar. Finally in 1613 the *zemski sobor* selected Michael Romanov, who secured order and drove out the Poles and Swedes. His dynasty lasted until another time of troubles and social disintegration in 1917.

Michael's son Alexis waged wars of expansion and followed policies that foreshadowed the social regimentation completed by his son, Peter the Great. Tax associations of townsmen were organized to support the army. The royal treasury imposed an excessive salt tax and debased the coinage. These measures provoked riots and disorder and were undercut by the large-scale peculation of tax farmers. But popular resistance failed to check Alexis' progressive oppression of the peasantry and the Church.

Before the advent of the Romanovs the Russian peasantry had been divided among free farmers, bondsmen, and slaves, but the freer peasants had been losing status since the thirteenth century. By 1500 they were on their way toward chattel serfdom. As their condition deteriorated, many of them sought freedom and land by escaping to the borderlands in the Don, Dnieper, and Ural river valleys, where they formed egalitarian "Cossack" republics that bore the brunt of frontier fighting. Russian authorities then severely restricted peasant freedom of movement. A new law code in 1649 declared them to be a homogeneous mass of serfs bound to the soil. By this time the Cossack areas were losing their attractiveness, as Cossack leaders began to emulate Russian nobles. Soon the tsars were ruling the Cossack territories and enforcing serfdom. Discontented Cossacks revolted repeatedly. During the seventeenth and eighteenth centuries their uprisings spread to old Russia. Between 1667 and 1671 the Cossack, Stenka Razin, led the whole lower Volga in rebellion before he was captured and executed.

In reasserting tsarist control over the Church, Alexis had to deal with Nikon, Patriarch of Moscow. Nikon urged liturgical reforms that would have facilitated Russian annexation of Greek Orthodox Slavs living under Polish and Turkish rule. But because the Patriarch challenged the Tsar's supreme authority, he was banished. Alexis continued the reforms, however, against the determined opposition of the "Old Believers," Russians who insisted upon keeping the faith of their fathers as it was. Thousands of dissenters were executed or exiled; others burned themselves to death rather than submit. Many Old Believers, sure that the end of the world was at hand, found convincing proof that Alexis' successor, Peter the Great, was the Anti-Christ. This schism weakened the Church, and Peter ultimately reduced it to a department of state under lay control.

## Peter the Great (1682–1725)

Peter transformed Russia from an isolated, landlocked state into a major European power. Petrine Russia adopted Western technology, built a navy, and entered into diplomatic relations with Western chanceries. At Peter's death it extended from the Baltic Sea to the Kurile Islands north of Japan. These rapid changes were mainly the work of the eccentric giant who became tsar in 1682.

The young Tsar was unconventional by any standards. Nearly seven feet tall, he

*Peter the Great.*

further attracted attention by a jerky walk and nervous facial contortions. A drunken tutor from the bureaucracy gave him a meager formal education, but he learned mainly from experiences that left him disrespectful of the conventions of Russian society and gave him the tastes of an artisan proud of his calluses. At the outset of his reign his elder half-sister and half-brother intrigued with the palace guard, the *streltsy,* to purge his relatives and many old *boyars.* His half-sister, Sophia, became regent over both boys as co-tsars, but when she made a second bid for power in 1689, Sophia was confined to a convent. Little impressed with the *streltsys'* contribution to order, Peter set out to consolidate all power in his own hands. He devoted himself to military exercises by commanding a play regiment of grooms and servants (later soldiers supplied from the arsenals of Moscow). From the foreign or "German" quarter of Moscow he acquired a mistress, a fascination for Western technical skills and languages, and rowdy companions. At the age of sixteen he married a nobleman's daughter, but he preferred shipbuilding, sailing, military exercises, and

life in the German suburb to life with her.* In all of these unconventional exploits, Peter was accompanied by Menshikov, a courtier of low birth who remained his principal advisor. Fired by exuberant energy, the Tsar always kept moving. And he drove his people as hard as himself.

In 1695 Peter began to apply his acquired skills by launching an attack on Turkey, then engaged in war with the Habsburgs. Aided by Russia's first fleet, which Peter assembled on the Don, his army took Azov. The courts of Europe took note of this victory, and their curiosity increased when the Tsar made his "Grand Embassy" to the West. Ostensibly it was to arrange a coalition against the Turks, but its primary purpose was to acquire the technical knowledge that Russia lacked.

## The Tsar Westernizer

The events of Peter's itinerary were most extraordinary. Traveling incognito as "Mein Herr Peter Mikhailov," an uncommissioned officer in the party, he insisted upon being received with the honors of state. At one German court he mistook his dancing partner's corset stays for protruding ribs; in London he and his companions left the house of their host a shambles. In the Netherlands he discussed the Quaker religion with William Penn. But his mission was to acquire technical knowledge, to sate his catholic curiosity. In England he visited factories, arsenals, and shipyards, taking copious notes; in the Netherlands he even served as a shipwright carpenter. In Vienna, where he stopped to negotiate an alliance against the Turks, news reached him that the *streltsy* had revolted again. Stopping only

---

* Eventually she retired to a convent to care for their son, Alexis, who was nurtured on her grievances. Peter then married Catherine, a gifted former Lithuanian servant girl whose charms had attracted the court. Later Catherine succeeded Peter to the throne. His son, Alexis, became involved with Peter's traditionalist opposition and, accused of treasonable plotting, was tortured to death.

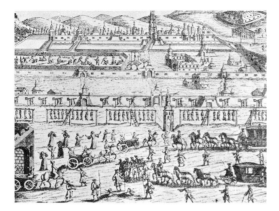

*Mass execution of the* Streltsy.

*Satirical cartoon of Peter's order to clip beards.*

to negotiate with Augustus, Elector of Saxony and King of Poland, Peter hastened home.

Peter's ferocity in putting down the *streltsy* and the radicalness of his new reform edicts expressed his determination to imitate Western European absolutism. In quelling the revolt, he and Menshikov punished the innocent with the guilty in order to break the guards' power permanently. The Tsar then ordered courtiers to shave their beards and adopt Western dress; peasants and priests could escape the order only by paying a special tax. But to Orthodox Russian Christians beards were a sacrosanct part of the human body, created in the image of God. Politically the assault on beards and Oriental dress was a thrust at the Old Believers who had sympathized with the *streltsy*. To gain revenue Peter also affronted the traditionalists by promoting the use of (taxed) tobacco. Most of his subjects considered smoking no less a defilement of the human body than the shaving of beards. These two official acts augured a more comprehensive effort by the Tsar to introduce foreign, Western culture into Russia during the remainder of his reign.

## Peter's Foreign Policy

Constant warfare filled the rest of Peter's reign, and military demands became the primary motive for the subsequent reforms

that are so closely linked to his name. He fought on all frontiers, making Russia an empire. But his overriding goal was to gain unimpeded access to the Baltic and Black seas.

Peter first thrust a new fleet against the Turks while they were at war with Austria. But at Karlowitz in 1699 Austria made peace, leaving Russia to fight the Turks alone. Peter finally secured a truce in 1700, after having allied his country with Denmark, Poland, and Saxony for the purpose of partitioning Sweden's Baltic empire. On the same day that he learned of the Turkish truce, he declared war on Sweden. But also on the same day King Charles XII of Sweden knocked Denmark out of the war. At Narva, on the Estonian border, Peter massed 60,000 raw recruits under the command of foreign officers. With only 8000 men Charles XII handed the Russians a terrifying setback. Luckily for Peter, Charles opted not to follow up his victory, turning instead to pursue Augustus into Poland.

The Tsar spent the years between 1700 and 1709 feverishly training a new peasant

EXPANSION OF PETRINE RUSSIA

army with which he conquered Ingria and Livonia, the two Swedish possessions nearest Russia. These territories gave him access to the Baltic and provided the site for the city of St. Petersburg, the Tsar's window on the West, founded on a barren moor in 1703. Built by forced labor at a tremendous sacrifice of life, St. Petersburg became the capital of Russia, a monument to Peter's Western orientation.

By 1708 Charles XII moved into the Ukraine on an ill-fated expedition. In vain he sought alliances with dissident Cossacks and Turks. The winter of 1708 depleted his forces, and the local population, maltreated at his hands, launched guerrilla warfare against him. Peter cut off Charles' supply and reinforcement columns. At Poltava in 1709 the Tsar's larger army decisively defeated the Swedes. Charles fled to Turkey where he intrigued for a new Turkish attack on Russia. Meanwhile Peter reconstructed his northern alliance against Sweden, conquering Karelia and more of Livonia. He also laid claim to Courland on the Baltic, but in 1711 the Turks forced him to surrender all the territory he had gained in 1700; he thereby lost his access to the Black Sea.

Russia fared better in the Great Northern War for Baltic supremacy. Using his refurbished navy Peter took Finland and threatened Sweden itself. He hoped to gain the Swedish crown by marriage and to widen his grip on northern Germany by diplomacy. His diplomacy, however, began to falter as his occupying armies turned the German princes against him. And after Charles XII's death in 1718, England prevented Russia from overrunning Sweden. But the Treaty of Nystad in 1721 forced the Swedes to cede most of their Baltic empire to Russia. Although this treaty restored Finland to Sweden, it recognized Russian possession of the Baltic coast from Riga to Viborg. Peter had acquired not one but nine ports and bases on the Baltic. Russia seemed about to become a major naval and maritime power, but after Peter's death the fleets deteriorated rapidly.

## Russian Administrative Absolutism

Keeping the war machine going on all frontiers took immense manpower and money and necessitated administrative reorganization. In order to maintain his huge standing army the Tsar conscripted the enserfed subjects of his nobles. (His recruiting system,

with its twenty-five-year term of enlistment, lasted until 1874.) His campaigns also required conscript labor, whose losses often equaled those of the army. Peter relied upon nobles and foreign adventurers to lead the army and bureaucracy, forcing the nobility to share preferment with newcomers. In 1722 the Tsar instituted a Table of Ranks to determine the status of his servants. It organized the army, civil service, and the court into fourteen parallel grades. Children of nobles were obliged to start at the bottom grade, but all became nobles upon appointment to the lowest officer rank in the army or upon promotion to the eighth rank in the court or civil service. Those attaining noble status were granted lands, the exclusive right to own serfs, and other privileges that later became hereditary. In order to equip themselves for service, the children of the nobility were required to attend state schools, another petrine innovation. But the schools were few, and resistance to them debilitatingly strong. Like his predecessors, Peter could not regiment all classes for state service without great opposition.

In a country lacking commercial capital and banking institutions the raising of money to finance administration and wars was a major undertaking. Because the treasury had no credit, all expenses had to be met currently. Tax revenues trebled during Peter's reign, and the Great Northern War brought a financial crisis that led to a host of new military and indirect taxes. He employed "revenue-finder" boards to discover new taxable items.* His government established monopolies to raise revenue on such items as salt, tobacco, cod liver oil, potash, and coffins. It also commandeered monastic revenues and debased the coinage again. These measures were in addition to the traditional direct tax on households and implements.

---

* The list grew to include lands, rents, sales, horse collars, hats, boots, horse hides, beehives, hot baths, chimney stacks, beards, moustaches, nuts, watermelons, and cucumbers.

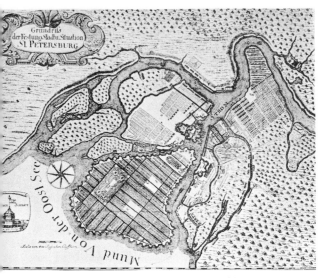

*Layout of St. Petersburg in 1738.*

The levy on households, which had been the principal source of revenue, began to dry up as householders evaded it, fled, or were conscripted. The government replaced it with a head or "soul" tax, applicable to all male peasants. The backbone of the revenue structure until 1886, this tax was collected by the lords of the village communes. Since anyone enrolled on their tax registers was automatically a serf, this tax system helped spread serfdom. Nevertheless, the treasury did not reap the principal benefit from the new taxes, for officials, embezzling this and other public money, apparently took as much as 70 per cent of all collections.

Peter's effort to introduce Western mercantilist policies fared no better than his tax reforms. In order to encourage industry, mining, and commerce under paternal direction of the state, he enacted high protective tariffs and leased state-built factories to private individuals on favorable terms. Entrepreneurs who copied Western technology were given tax exemptions, interest-free loans, and the coveted privilege of owning serfs. Peter also sent technicians abroad for training and wooed skilled immigrants. Overall, Peter's program of economic de-velopment failed, even though the country became self-sufficient in some industrial lines and exported iron and sailcloth. Capitalists, distrustful of officials and regulations, failed to meet his expectations. Rather than increasing revenues, his mercantilism added to state expenditures.

Repeated attempts to reorganize the central administration also failed. In practice the central government was more often represented by military commanders than by civil authorities. In most of Russia the local nobles constituted the only government. Neither military rule, savage punishments, decentralization, nor secret informers eliminated the bribery and corruption that riddled the bureaucracy from top to bottom. The most notorious offender was Prince Menshikov, Peter's closest associate, who accumulated a legendary fortune without losing favor. Against the bureaucracy and military authorities, the public resorted to fraud and violence on a local, sometimes on a general, scale.

However, Peter did succeed in bringing the Orthodox Church, the largest organization in Russia, under secular control. When the current patriarch died in 1700 he named no successor. Several years later the Holy Synod, a collegiate board headed by a lay procurator, assumed control of the Church. The state thus silenced, to some extent, clerics who opposed such reforms as secular education, limited toleration, and the Julian calendar. The Holy Synod itself was charged with dispelling ignorance and superstition by improving education. But the regulation establishing it revealed still another, more important, purpose—namely, the elimination of the patriarch as a competitor of the tsar for the spiritual allegiance of the masses. The subordination of the Church to the state served Russian autocracy until 1917.

Peter's impact upon Russian society and government was decisive and long-lived. Despite its failings, in practice the structure he built held firm until the nineteenth century, much of it until 1917. He brought absolutism to its highest point with the undoing of the old nobility, the elimination of the *zemski sobor* (Russia's only representative institution) and the assertion of the tsar's right to name his own successor. He did not, however, implement a system of succession, failing even to name a ruler to follow himself. Violence and intrigue continued to determine who would hold the reins of power. The strongest force in the state was an immense standing army, and the palace guard decided the fates of the tsars and tsarinas who followed.

Peter gained a reputation as a Westernizer. Conservative nativists accused him of despoiling the Russian soul with heresy, rationalism, and foreign values. Certainly he borrowed institutions, techniques, and outlooks from France, Sweden, England, and the Dutch Republic. St. Petersburg remained the capital and the center of intercourse with the West. By dynastic marriage and intrigue, the Romanov dynasty became basically German. The petrine state assumed a lasting place in the European state system. Nevertheless Peter's Westernization was selective. Mainly it modified and strengthened existing institutions that resisted deep penetration by Western culture. The army was modernized, but it remained the basic tool for administration. Serfdom was extended and riveted into law and practice by the state. Some of the higher nobles eventually accepted Westernization, but over the larger society of enserfed peasants and boorish lords it lay as a shallow veneer. A question remains whether Peter really wanted to Westernize or whether he borrowed European technology to defend Russia against Western encroachment. In either case his experience indicated the limitations of absolutism even in a state where organized opposition was not possible.

# C. Aristocratic Monarchies

Alongside the divine-right kingdoms that we have discussed stood other monarchies whose rulers laid equal claim to unlimited authority but whose effective power was too weak to be considered absolute at all. Some of them—Spain and Sweden, for example—had been Europe's leading states but were now in decline. None of them had the strength to hold its own in the dynastic power struggles of the second half of the seventeenth century. In all of them the trend of political development was toward decentralization, away from absolutism.

## SPAIN AND ITALY

There was a close relationship between the rising star of France in Western Europe and the falling star of the Spanish Habsburg empire. Spain emerged from the Thirty Years' War and the Bourbon-Habsburg conflict with an immense empire, still Europe's largest, and great imperial pride. But her men and materials had been overcommitted and overexpended during a previous century of warfare. The efforts of Philip IV's war minister, de Olivares, to revitalize Spain and shunt some of the burdens of empire onto kingdoms other than Castile had come to naught. To put down revolts against de Olivares' "Castilianization" the King was forced to confirm the territorial privileges of the Catalans. The Portuguese, whose revolt in 1640 opened a second front in the Iberian Peninsula until peace was signed with France in 1659, slipped away completely. Thereafter Louis XIV denied the exhausted Habsburgs any respite from his encroachment upon the Spanish Netherlands and along France's eastern frontier.

During the final phases of the Thirty Years' War, Spain suffered an acute depression, and evidence of recovery was hardly perceptible for the rest of the century. Inflation reached dizzy heights prior to 1680, when a particularly severe deflation occurred. Imports of bullion from the New World came to a halt, and foreign smugglers, abetted by monopolistic colonial trade laws, paid no duties in Castile's inadequately defended empire. Although the ruined middle classes recovered somewhat in Catalonia, they were displaced in the rest of the empire by French, Dutch, and English merchants. These merchants dominated Spain's economic life and monopolized her trade with the Americas.

Meanwhile, depression deepened the great gulf between the poor and the wealthy privileged minority. By 1700 nobility, Church, and crown held an estimated 95 per cent of the land. The shepherds' guild (*Mesta*) maintained its privileges at the expense of Spanish agriculture, but its flocks were mere shadows of what they had once been. Seignorial oppression of the peasants went unchecked, and vagabondage and banditry became alternate ways of life. Increasing numbers found a living within the Church. The aristocracy failed conspicuously as a ruling minority. Both courtiers and impoverished *hidalgos* abhorred the manual labor, commerce, and economic investment, which the crown tried to make respectable in 1680. Educated churchmen likewise failed in leadership. They cherished contemplative passivity and disdained reason.

The postwar government of Philip V momentarily arrested Spain's decline. To some degree he imitated Louis XIV in subordinating the Church and the nobility to central control. He restored authority and commerce in the empire. Yet he could not fundamentally cure the hardening of Spain's social and political arteries. Schemes of reform failed without exception. By and large the empire remained impervious to contemporary commercial change, rationalized government, secular science, and speculative thought. And failure to cope with these developments hastened its relative decline.

Like Spain, whose decaying and corrupt authority still dominated the peninsula, Italy was caught in a midcentury depression. Her cities, population, and trade continued to decline, until, by 1700, most Italian principalities were completely agrarian. Venice, still a maritime state independent of Spain, was beset by a long series of wars with the Turks, and her capital resources flowed steadily from commerce to land. Commercial life still flickered in Lombardy, Tuscany, and Piedmont, but their societies were dominated by the routine of petty courts. Intellectual life and even the arts, save for music and baroque architecture, were in a state of decay. Italy was a major stopping point on the "grand tour" of every young European aristocrat, but it had become a museum for the greatness of the past rather than a showplace of vitality for the present.

## THE HOLY ROMAN EMPIRE

The Peace of Westphalia fragmented the Holy Roman Empire permanently into hundreds of petty states. Kings of France, Sweden, and Castile, princes of the Empire, worked against coordinated action. No imperial bureaucracy existed. In 1663 the Reichstag (Imperial Diet) went into permanent session as an assembly of delegates instructed by their states. Effective business practically ceased. The Imperial High Court was notorious for the jurisdictions exempted from its authority and for delays of a half century or more in deciding cases, long after the original litigants had died. Political theorists began to dispute both the holy and the Roman origins of this empire, considering it instead a contractual republic of princes. In any case, politics were determined by the particularism of innumerable states.

Individual German princes were inspired by Louis XIV, and a number of them built smaller versions of Versailles near their capitals. But not all German principalities became little "absolute monarchies." In some of them the diets remained active and standing armies small. Some German diets became the sole preserve of the landed nobility; others, privileged oligarchies that they were, preserved traditions that later joined with parliamentary government.

Economic decline accompanied particularistic politics. Seeking fat revenues and self-sufficiency, German princes crisscrossed the Empire with a maze of rigid barriers to commerce and production. These barriers delayed the recovery of the economy from the disasters of the Thirty Years' War. As late as 1668 one official said: "There is hardly any trade and enterprise, all commerce is ruined, no money is to be found either among the great or among the small people." [3] It was more than a century before the Empire regained its 1618 level of prosperity. During its prolonged weakness, German towns fell more completely than before into princely hands. Even closed urban oligarchies in the Imperial Free Cities accepted the aristocratic dictum that trade was ignoble. Many governments pursued mercantilistic policies as a means of spurring economic activity, but since their taxes sapped the capital and initiative of their productive subjects, it is debatable whether they should be praised for sponsoring production or condemned for making consumption impossible. The same question, of course, applies to the policies of the effective states such as Brandenburg-Prussia and Russia.

## NORTHERN AND EASTERN EUROPE

### Denmark, Sweden, and Poland

In Scandinavia the political pattern was more uniform than in the Empire. Sweden was a major power in control of most of the Baltic coast between 1660 and 1710. Her warrior-king, Charles XII, tried also to ac-

quire Poland but lacked the population and resources for such a large-scale enterprise. After Charles was killed and Sweden was defeated in the Great Northern War, noble factions dominated political life there. Similar factions controlled the Kingdom of Denmark, which was exhausted by generations of dynastic warfare with Sweden.

Poland, however, furnished the classic case of aristocratic decentralization. Extending from the Baltic almost to the Black Sea in the fifteenth and sixteenth centuries, she was now surrounded by aggressive neighbors who took advantage of her internal weakness to invade her repeatedly. An exceedingly numerous nobility, the only class represented in the local and central diets, crushed town interests, the peasantry, and the authority of the elective monarchy. Political life centered around the conflicts of a few great noble families, behind which the lesser nobles arrayed themselves in factions. By the middle of the seventeenth century decisive action by the central government was hardly possible. The diet kept the army ridiculously small. Foreign-sponsored candidates (Augustus the Strong of Saxony was one "successful" example) contested for the empty honor. By the infamous *liberum veto* any delegate to the central diet could, and on critical occasions did, rise to end further deliberations. Only the inability of her foes to cooperate preserved Poland from dismemberment until the late eighteenth century.

### The Ottoman Decline

By virtue of its hold on the Balkan Peninsula and the southern Ukraine, the Ottoman Empire was a major European power with its base in Asia Minor and the Near East. Nominally the sultans also ruled North Africa from Egypt to Algeria. Formidable as this imperial giant seemed, internal decay and failure to keep pace with its opponents were sapping its relative strength, as its retreat before the Habsburgs showed. A long succession of capable sultans had come to an end in 1566. Thereafter strong leaders rose in

---

3. Quoted by the *New Cambridge Modern History*, V, *The Ascendancy of France 1648–88*, University Press, Cambridge, 1961, p. 434.

times of crisis, but the roots of deterioration were beyond their power to extirpate. Ottoman power had rested on a feudal cavalry and the famed Janissary corps of infantry, recruited as tribute from Balkan Christian communities. No longer terror-inspiring, the Janissaries were becoming a self-perpetuating and privileged Moslem force that made and unmade sultans and officials as harem intrigues and bribery dictated. They neglected the navy and spurned new military inventions such as the bayonet.

Devoid of commercial safeguards and improvements, the Ottoman economy got along no better than the government. Western merchants, backed by their governments, preyed on Turkish commerce. Unsupported by protective tariffs, native production remained at the handicraft level. Formerly the rural population had enjoyed a better life than most European peasants; but now it fell into the bondage of the privileged orders. In-

tellectually the Turks remained pre-Renaissance, and the dead weight of tradition stifled innovations. Even by using terror, reformers were unable to check the decline.

Ottoman power was temporarily revived by the Kiuprili dynasty of Grand Viziers, the sultans' chief administrators. Believing that territorial conquest and the seizure of slaves could generate vitality, they resumed military pressure upon the Danube. Venice, Poland, and Russia joined Austria in a holy league to drive them from Europe.* The results we have seen in the Treaty of Karlowitz.† Freed from fear of Ottoman oppression, Europe now took up the "eastern question." To what state or states would the territories of the weakened Empire fall? Because Europeans could not answer this question, the Turkish Empire lived on for nearly two more centuries. Nevertheless its losses of territory and internal trade indicated Europe's continued expansion to the east.

# D. The Maritime States: England and the Dutch Republic

Declining monarchies and former commercial centers remained most heavily caked with custom. They were governed by the aristocratic and clerical traditions of medieval times. Competitive power struggles forced some innovations upon absolutist states, but even so these states continued to preserve social privileges and a hierarchic society. Neither type of monarchy made fundamental changes in its socioeconomic structure or introduced new concepts of government. Such changes were peculiar to the maritime states, England and the Dutch Republic. Even they retained much that was traditional or even medieval, especially the notion that government should be limited or contractual in nature. But they instituted a broader governing

class and set constitutional limits to the powers of the state. As a result, these governments commanded more obedience from their subjects voluntarily than the absolutisms that arrogated all initiative to the crown or to aristocracies of birth.

In both England and the Dutch Republic, authoritarian Roman law yielded to the political demands of aristocratic and commercial groups whose strength lay in trade, finance, industry, and rationalized agriculture. By their wealth and credit they created more

---

* One casualty of this war was the Parthenon, which the Turks used as a powder magazine in defending the Peloponnesus from Venetian invasion.

† See page 23.

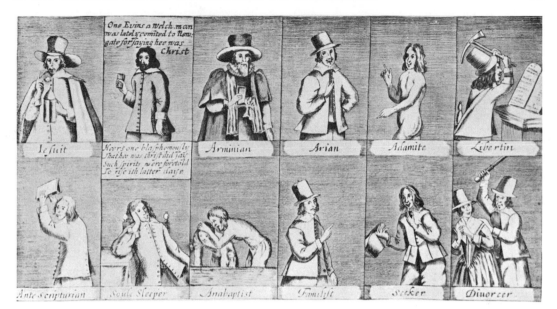

*Religious diversity: a derogatory view of sectarianism.*

military resources than any impoverished absolutism ever enjoyed. Significantly geography partially guaranteed both countries against foreign invasion. England was protected by the sea, the Dutch Republic by its system of rivers, canals, and floodable fields. Thus they could escape from the two primary instruments of absolutism: a permanent standing army and extraparliamentary taxation to finance it. From their relative abundance these maritime states probably spent more per capita on arms than any absolute monarchy, but their money went largely for navies, which were difficult to deploy against domestic foes, and mercenary armies raised for specific occasions.

These states diverged from authoritarianism not only politically but also in their religious and intellectual activity. The prevailing formula of the Reformation (the religion of the prince determines the religion of the people) gave way to compromise with limited toleration. Religious pluralism undercut rigorous censorship and divine-right kingship. It challenged the established authorities, which barred nonconformists from secular

trades. Though often precariously, radical sectarians maintained their existence. And secular humanists could resume the Renaissance's speculation about politics and society that had been interrupted by the Reformation and religious wars. As refuges for exiles and as establishers of freer societies for their own subjects, England and the Dutch republic, along with the English colonies of North America, became the seedbeds of those liberal and humanitarian heresies that flowered during the eighteenth-century Enlightenment.

## THE DUTCH REPUBLIC

Constitutionally the Dutch republic was a confederation of disparate provinces whose diets sent instructed delegates to the common States General. In Guelderland feudal nobles ruled over subsistent tenant farmers. In Utrecht authority was vested in Protestant canons who had replaced electors of the former Roman Catholic bishop. The richest and most powerful provinces were the commercial states of Zeeland and Holland, ruled by tight republican oligarchies of regents. Led by the Grand Pensionary of Holland, Jan De Witt, the regents coordinated the Republic's affairs from 1650 to 1672, defending its aristocratic, decentralized constitution. Humanistic Calvinists or Arminians, the regents had the tacit support of both Roman Catholics and the sectarians whom they protected from Calvinist persecution.

Jan De Witt was locked in a political tug of war with the House of Orange, which traditionally had filled the chief executive, judicial, and military office of stadtholder in each province. Behind the Orange faction stood the orthodox Calvinist clergy, the discontented urban poor, and most of the local authorities in the rural provinces. To check Orangist monarchical ambitions, De Witt in 1670 secured acceptance in all seven provinces of an eternal edict barring the young William of Orange from the stadtholderates. But failures in foreign policy brought down De Witt and the regents' government. When the French invaded in 1672 he was murdered during an Orangist revolution. Though he did not become a monarch and establish a court, William of Orange, dealing through favorites, directed Dutch affairs as King of England until his death in 1702. During the peace after the War of Spanish Succession the regents' oligarchy again took power, but by then the Dutch Republic's economy and politics had stagnated.

Experimenting with a compromise between liberty and order, the Dutch Republic of the seventeenth century became a haven of personal freedom in absolutist Europe, a laboratory of liberalism. But as its commerce declined, its political evolution followed the earlier course of Venice. Dutch greatness had filled the interim between Spanish and French hegemony on the Continent. After 1650 its economy ceased to expand. In the latter half of the century it consolidated and defended its previous gains against its greatest rivals, the merchants and navy of England. Between 1652 and 1678 the republic fought a series of commercial wars

*Jan De Witt and the mob that lynched him.*

with England on even terms, but at the end of the War of Spanish Succession it failed to share in the commercial spoils, which fell instead to England.

In great part the Dutch Republic declined because its resources and population were insufficient to compete with stronger rivals. Internal decay was also responsible. At its peak the Dutch economy pioneered in commercial agriculture and adopted technical skills and techniques for sustaining a dense population. The republic's level of education was probably the highest in Europe. But even when commerce was expanding, the lower classes could barely subsist and were burdened by heavy excise taxes. Despite extensive organized charity, hunger was widespread and prompted many youths to enlist in the navy and the merchant marine. By the end of the seventeenth century the Dutch had lost their technological leadership. Investment flowed into banking, insurance, life annuities, state debts, and foreign plantations; such investments did not provide domestic employment. Amsterdam remained the financial capital of Europe, but the domestic economy had lost its dynamism.

## THE TRIUMPH OF THE ENGLISH PARLIAMENT

England, Europe's other major maritime power, had also experimented with republican government after the execution of Charles I in 1648. Three years later Oliver Cromwell proposed a union of the two kingless states, but instead of uniting, they fell to fighting for control of sea lanes. Becoming less and less popular at home, Cromwell's government deteriorated into a military dictatorship, which his son and political heir was unable to maintain. Fed up with the rule of Puritan saints, the people of England restored the Stuart court in 1660. An able monarch coming to the throne on a wave of religious and political reaction against the Puritan revolution, Charles II posed a serious challenge to parliamentary authority. But the Restoration proved to be only an interlude before Parliament took control of the royal succession and ultimately of most of the powers of the crown itself.

*Charles II, the Stuart Restoration.*

### The Stuart Restoration

Like his Stuart predecessors, Charles II was an absolutist in outlook. But England differed sharply from the conditions that fostered autocracy in many continental kingdoms. Economically the English lower classes may have been no better off than the French peasantry, but they enjoyed at least a modicum of civil rights and had left behind them for good the servile conditions of much of the continental peasantry east of the Rhine. Not popular rights but the organized power of the upper classes, however, had been and continued to be the great barrier to Stuart absolutism: Parliament, the common law courts, and the unpaid justices of the peace who came from the gentry. Moreover the social distance between the enlarged merchant classes and the lower aristocracy was smaller than in the continental kingdoms.*

* English landlords who improved and managed their own estates enjoyed respect that only the court nobility, for example, held in France.

The two groups were tied by intermarriage and were represented in the same house of Parliament, where their participation in affairs of state had given them a national outlook.

Still Charles II had great political abilities; had he lived longer, he might have been able to put Stuart concepts of government into effect. The Restoration Settlement was moderate enough not to create large numbers of foes for him. Crown and church lands were restored, but confiscated Cavalier estates that had been resold often remained in Cromwellian hands. Only about twenty persons, who had not been quick enough to declare for the Stuarts, were executed for their part in the civil wars. The least moderate part of the Settlement was a series of laws designed to break Puritan power forever, the Clarendon Code. These laws removed Puritan clergymen from their benefices, barred Puritans from political activity, and prohibited nonconformist teaching and worship assemblies. But the Clarendon Code was the work of the "Cavalier Parliament," not the King.

Benefiting from popular reactions against Puritan rule, Charles' partisans in Parliament protected royal authority. Broader treason and censorship laws enhanced his powers. He was able to select those acts of the interregnum that he wished to retain as binding laws. The legislators granted him revenues for life, which, fed by commercial prosperity, yielded greater incomes than anyone anticipated. Bombay and New Amsterdam (present-day New York City) were added to England's commercial empire. Charles' diplomatic alignment with Louis XIV was unpopular, but French subsidies made him more independent of Parliament. He balanced suspension of penalties against Catholics with similar exemptions to Protestant dissenters. Though his court was an affront to Puritans, it catered to science, art, and literature. Many a powerful pen supported him. His radical opposition led by the Earl of Shaftesbury discredited itself by republican tendencies, involvement in plots that revived the specter of civil war, and the use of unsubstantiated evidence to secure the execution of Catholics accused of conspiracy.

The most irreconcilable issue between King and Parliament was religion. Charles had pro-Catholic proclivities and a French Catholic queen. His brother and heir apparent, James, Duke of York, was an open Catholic. Suspicion that the King had bound himself to Louis XIV in order to restore Catholicism in England was founded in fact; the secret Treaty of Dover (1670) had just such stipulations. By exempting Catholics and Protestant dissenters from the penalties of law, Charles aroused religious ire and the constitutional objection that he was setting himself above the law. Parliament rebuffed him with the Test Act of 1673. It required officeholders to denounce the Roman Catholic form of communion and to take the Anglican sacrament annually. Anglicanism became the necessary badge for political privilege and advancement. Even the Duke of York was forced out of the Admiralty by its terms. But did its provisions extend to the crown itself? James' heir apparency inevitably raised that question in English politics.

Bills to exclude the Duke of York from succeeding to the throne failed in Parliament, but they became the issue around which political factions formed. The Whig party—composed of progressive landlords, merchants, and Protestant dissenters—originated these bills. The Whigs' opponents were the Tories, a court party whose religious views were High Anglican and whose viewpoints represented the more conservative landed gentlemen. Committed as a matter of religious conscience to the passive obedience of subjects to legitimate kings, the Tories supported Charles II and received offices and favors from him. Radical republican and Whig plotters pushed conservative Whigs into the King's camp also. With their support Charles was empowered by a corporation act to revoke municipal charters and to replace Whig with Tory councils. Meanwhile trade expanded and with it royal revenues. At his death in 1685 Charles was at the peak of his power. For the moment parliamentary government had ceased to function.

## James II and the "Glorious Revolution"

James II inherited the throne, Charles' revenues, and his brother's conflicts. His accession was contested by the Duke of Monmouth, Charles II's illegitimate son. Counting upon Whig support, Monmouth led an insurrection against James. Bloodily suppressed by James, the revolt put a standing army at his disposal. In violation of the Test Act he appointed Roman Catholic officials and revived the Court of High Commission to deal with religious offenders. He acted rapidly to remove recalcitrant judges, maintain his standing army, and force suspension of legal penalties against Catholics and Protestant dissenters. These actions opened old

*James II, an unwelcome king.*

and tender sores, but Englishmen would probably have put up with him if he had had no male heir. In 1688, however, the queen bore a son.

Threatened with an eventual Roman Catholic succession, prominent Whigs and Tories cooperated in inviting William of Orange and his wife, Mary, James' Protestant daughter by an earlier marriage, to the throne. Others organized conspiracies in the army and navy in order to disarm the King. Committed to divine-right monarchy, the Anglican Tories were caught in a serious dilemma. Their qualms with respect to overturning James II were eased when he elected to flee rather than to fight. Officially he was held to have abdicated. But there still remained his legitimate son and heir. On this issue the Tories salved their consciences by believing the myth that a commoner child had been smuggled into the queen's chamber in a warming pan. The royal heir did not exist! Later Anglicans who participated in the revolution of 1688 refused to take oaths to the new monarchs as legitimate sovereigns, and many Anglicans became Jacobites, that is, Stuart counterrevolutionaries.

## The Revolutionary Settlement and After

The "Glorious Revolution" of 1688 established the constitutional supremacy of Parliament. The Bill of Rights in 1689 confirmed Parliament's past demands against Stuart kings. It limited royal authority over a peacetime standing army to a specific number of years. It defined treason more narrowly, thus making this crime more difficult to prove in court. James II's bid for support from religious dissenters had forced Anglicans to promise them toleration, though not political and civic rights. An act of 1689 exempted all except Roman Catholics and Unitarians from punitive penalties. Formal censorship, but not stringent libel laws, lapsed in 1695.* The crown, whose succession Parliament now determined, retained considerable powers. After the judiciary's independence was confirmed by an act of 1701, the English constitution had a balance and division of executive, legislative, and judicial powers. But royal prerogatives gradually dwindled. Queen Anne (1702–1714) was the last English monarch to wield a royal veto. During the eighteenth century executive and legislative functions began to merge in the cabinet, a committee standing between king and Parliament.

Clearly Parliament was replacing the court as the source of both favor and corruption, an unmistakable indication that power had shifted. But Parliament was an oligarchy, part of the same oligarchy from which local justices and jurists were drawn. To a degree, individual rights were protected by the division of the oligarchy into factions of Whig and Tory. But when they were in solid agreement, as upon economic and social

* The press became freer in England's American colonies because libel was much more narrowly construed.

policy, their sympathies were distinctly aristocratic. Parliament, not the people, was sovereign, and its two houses were substantially under the control of the same coterie of agrarian and commercial interests.

Having men of means involved in politics marshaled unexpected power behind the English government. As distrust dissolved between king and Parliament, the latter's purse strings loosened. Royal debts became state debts and after 1694 were handled by the Bank of England. The accession of William and Mary marked a revolution in English foreign policy. England became the fore-most opponent of Louis XIV, both in Europe and overseas. For her increased power, she was amply rewarded at the end of the War of Spanish Succession with colonial territory and commercial concessions.

Thus in cooperation with the central government, men experienced in trade, finance, and administration were laying the basis for England's colonial and commercial supremacy during the eighteenth century. Unlike trade and production in the Dutch Republic, British commerce continued to expand until the end of the eighteenth century, when it became the basis for urban industrialization.

---

# E. Interpreting Absolutism: A Paradox

German historians of the nineteenth century made conventional the interpretation that divine-right monarchy was an evolutionary stepping stone to the "modern nation state." Thereafter absolutism was generally treated as an episode in the centralization of authority which delivered *coups de grâce* to the local power of nobles and churchmen. Historians have also considered absolutism as a part of the "rise of the middle class" who served as officials to kings and as beneficiaries of mercantilist economics. Some have also tied mercantilism and the absolute state's large-scale purchases of military supplies to the growth of capitalism. Taken together these interpretations conceive of absolutism as a force working for modernization.

Individual parts of these interpretations have merit, but as a whole they tend to confuse the *ideology* of absolutism with a *reality* that was quite different. Some absolute regimes did develop trained central bureaucracies, which modern states have imitated. But more generally they established standing professional armies that were authorized monopolies of violence within the state. Both these armies and bureaucracies took autonomy away from the old nobility. But no monarch stripped the aristocracy of its economic and social privileges. Instead, most absolute rulers multiplied the number of privileged offices and granted hereditary rights to new officeholders. Under these officials, not uniformity but endless diversity prevailed in domestic affairs. Jurisdictions were traditional, many, and confused. Villages and towns ignored or defied orders and edicts. Even taxes, the principal point of contact between state and subject, varied drastically according to social status and locality. Uniformity was more characteristic of religion, for the established churches were the most centralized institutions. In the aristocratic monarchies executive authority had little centralizing effect and commanded even less obedience.

Absolutism has often been cited by historians as a major factor in the rise of the middle classes and capitalism. But this alleged connection is tenuous if not misleading. It is a blunt fact that the two capitalist commercial states, the Dutch Republic and England, rejected royal absolutism and that divine-right kings flourished in agrarian societies. If absolute monarchs promoted commerce and industry, it was for the purpose of revenues under the aegis of paternal bureaucracies and within the framework of privilege. Merchants becoming officials ceased being merchants and adopted aristocratic social codes that made commerce demeaning. Old aristocratic values permeated even the declining mercantile city-states. When absolute monarchs decreed that commerce and industrial investment were respectable, their edicts had no effect. They were nullified by the nobility whose privileges the same monarchs preserved. Crown and court reached accommodations with bankers and merchants, but prevailing attitudes repudiated commercial society. Royal tax policies favored the aristocracy further. Outside of England and the Dutch Republic, nobles, clergy, officials, and privileged wealthy commoners were not taxed except as a last resort and then seldom successfully. Burdens of state fell primarily on the working classes, those engaged in production. Taxes thus cut deeply into the spendable income of the common people and reduced markets for consumer goods other than luxuries and bare necessities. Rather than being challenged by a new class of capitalist entrepreneurs, absolute monarchs were threatened by the privileged officeholders they had created.

Power presumably was the preoccupation of absolute kings. But the paradox of absolutism is partly that the maritime states, with no centralized bureaucracies, were more efficient in creating and marshaling power. French hegemony on the Continent was as attributable to numerical superiority as to Louis XIV's organization. Louis was great as long as his potential foes were weak and divided. But he was checked on land and defeated at sea when the maritime states with smaller populations combined against him after 1689. Absolutism may have been stronger than the kingdoms dominated by the aristocracy, but it was proportionately weaker than the sociopolitical order of England and the Dutch Republic.

Finally we are led by events to question the permanence of absolute monarchy as an effective type of government, apart from dominating personalities. After the major power struggles of East and West closed at the beginning of the eighteenth century, the leading absolutisms reverted back to governments by aristocracy. The "enlightened despots" attempted to revive centralized authority in the second half of the century. But the aristocratic monarchies and republican oligarchies, rather than Louis XIV or Peter the Great, prefigured the dominant political trend after 1715.

Where rapid economic growth and revolution did not occur, the cake of custom held firm and absorbed the innovations of the most powerful authoritarians who had lived in the "age of absolutism."

## SELECTED READINGS

Ashley, Maurice, *Louis XIV and the Greatness of France,* English Universities Press, London, 1957.

   A very readable, short account of the "Sun King's" reign in the Teach Yourself History series.

* Beloff, Max, *The Age of Absolutism 1660–1815,* Hutchinson University Library, London, 1954, and Harper Torchbook.

   Interpretation that considers societies rather than governments decisive in the age of absolutism.

Boxer, Charles R., *The Dutch Seaborne Empire 1600–1800,* Alfred A. Knopf, New York, 1965.

   A social history of both the Dutch Republic and the Dutch Empire in the series, The History of Human Society, edited by J. H. Plumb.

* The asterisk (*) denotes paperback.

Carsten, Francis L., ed., *The Ascendancy of France 1648–88,* Volume V, *The New Cambridge Modern History,* University Press, Cambridge, 1961.

    Exhaustively thorough for Europe in the age of Louis XIV, useful for reference.

Clark, G. N., *The Later Stuarts, 1660–1714,* Clarendon Press, Oxford, 1949.

    A dispassionate scholarly account in the Oxford History of England.

Cole, Charles W., *French Mercantilism 1683–1700,* Columbia University Press, New York, 1943.

    One of the author's several detailed works on French mercantilism, especially informative on the industrial production codes after Colbert.

Davies, R. Trevor, *Spain in Decline, 1621–1700,* Macmillan, London; St. Martin's Press, New York, 1957.

    A rambling posthumous work useful in assessing the causes of decay in the aristocratic monarchy of Spain.

Fay, Sidney B., *The Rise of Brandenburg-Prussia to 1786,* H. Holt, New York, 1937.

    A short, classic description of the consolidation of Prussian military absolutism which needs to be supplemented by the works of Francis L. Carsten (see Selected Readings, Volume I, Chapter XIII).

Figgis, John N., *The Divine Right of Kings,* University Press, Cambridge, 1922 (2nd ed.).

    An analysis of the major ideology of royal absolutism.

Holborn, Hajo, *A History of Modern Germany 1648–1840,* Alfred A. Knopf, New York, 1966.

    A lucid treatment based on recent scholarship which is part of the author's projected three-volume History of Modern Germany.

King, James E., *Science and Rationalism in the Government of Louis XIV, 1661–1683,* Johns Hopkins Press, Baltimore, 1949.

    A detailed interpretation of the reign of Louis XIV which links efficient government with the rational viewpoint of contemporary science.

*Lewis, W. H., *The Splendid Century, Life in the France of Louis XIV,* Doubleday Anchor Books, Garden City, N. Y., 1957.

    Aspects of French society, omitting institutions that the author considers tedious to write.

Lough, John, *Introduction to Seventeenth Century France,* Longmans, Green & Co., London, 1960.

    A literary approach to the period that is well illustrated but carries key points, unfortunately, in French.

Maland, David, *Europe in the Seventeenth Century,* St. Martin's Press, New York, 1966.

    New, exceptionally well-balanced textbook of the period by a British scholar.

*Nussbaum, Frederick L., *The Triumph of Science and Reason 1660–1685,* Harper & Brothers, New York, 1953, and Harper Torchbook.

    A general account emphasizing intellectual developments and recognizing absolutism as a façade of aristocratic society.

Petrie, Charles, *Earlier Diplomatic History 1492–1713,* Hollis & Carter, London, 1949.

    Short manual of exceedingly complex diplomatic relationships; the second half is applicable to this chapter.

Rosenberg, Hans, *Bureaucracy, Aristocracy and Autocracy, The Prussian Experience 1660–1815,* Harvard University Press, Cambridge, 1958.

    A sociological investigation of the Prussian bureaucracy and its rivalry with the monarchy and the aristocracy.

Schevill, Ferdinand, *The Great Elector,* Chicago University Press, Chicago, 1947.

    A political and institutional biography of Frederick William, the founder of Prussian absolutism.

Sumner, B. H., *Peter the Great and the Emergence of Russia,* English Universities Press, London, 1956.

    Another short, moving account in the Teach Yourself History Series; it emphasizes the military basis of Peter's administration.

Trevelyan, G. M., *The English Revolution, 1688–1689,* Butterworth, London, 1938.

A well-written study in the Home University Library by the author of several well-known works on the Stuarts.

*Wolf, John B., *The Emergence of the Great Powers 1685–1715,* Harper and Brothers, New York, 1951, and Harper Torchbook.
An account of the power struggles in which seventeenth-century absolutism culminated; a volume in the Rise of Modern Europe series.

See also the works by J. H. Elliott, Eli Heckscher, David Ogg, and George N. Clark in Selected Readings, Volume I, Chapter XV.

# II

# *The Secularization of Thought—the Seventeenth and Eighteenth Centuries*

We saw in the preceding chapter that power struggles between divine-right monarchs whittled away otherworldly concepts of society and politics. Strained to mobilize force, heads of state had to take stock of their resources and to press first and foremost for revenues. At the end of his wars, Louis XIV, the epitome of divine-right absolutism, had to reconcile himself to the secular principle of the balance of power in international relations. At home, absolute rulers and their courts became secular in outlook long before the bulk of their subjects, who were mainly peasants bound by tradition to established churches. But during the seventeenth and eighteenth centuries a large section of the intellectual elite also lost its attachment to otherworldly concerns.

The new tone of politics was only one indication of a growing interest in worldly matters; the other great secularizing forces were the accumulation of wealth through commerce and technology, the continued vitality of humanism, the impact of scientific advances, and the stimulus of travel literature.

Secularization first penetrated deeply those areas of northwestern Europe where the pursuit of wealth and comfort were primary social goals. Although England and the Dutch Republic retained established churches, they did not forcibly impose religious uniformity the way most absolutist states did. The fact that different religious groups could live together peacefully bred tolerance. At the same time, trading profits enlarged the mercantile classes, which began to set their own goals independently of the aristocracy and the established churches. English and Dutch farmers became more market oriented, and many villages began to produce goods for commercial entrepreneurs. As the English and Dutch governments catered increasingly to commercial

49

interests, their effective power became stronger than that of any absolutist regime. Their strength, however, derived from the voluntary action and private initiative of their subjects rather than from royal paternalism and doctrines of resignation to divine will. Finally, in the more open commercial societies, science and technology imparted a sense of control over nature.

Overseas commerce combined with missionary activity added another dimension to this secularization, and travel literature reporting the customs of non-Europeans became common, especially in northwestern Europe. How far this literature in itself helped to break down European parochialism is difficult to assess. Nevertheless, because this literature seemed to demonstrate that "noble savages" could live naturally and happily without Europe's Christian institutions, critics of European conditions used it to bolster their assault on the otherworldly foundations of authoritarianism.

The seventeenth century produced a more secular humanism than that of the Renaissance. The "new" humanism was more involved in the problems raised by scientific developments than in the ideas of classical literature. Hence it, too, contributed to the secularization of thought.

More than any other single factor, the demonstrable success of seventeenth-century science brought past authority into doubt and provided the intellectual foundation for new world views. Science did not openly undermine tradition until philosophical conclusions were drawn from its discoveries and methodology. When this happened, however, by the second half of the eighteenth century, popularized science and secular humanism merged into the qualified optimism of the Enlightenment. Popular writers of the Enlightenment competed with the clergy in defining morality, religious doctrine, and the goals of society. Theirs was a new secular gospel, which they hoped to spread through national systems of education oriented toward natural sciences, modern languages, economics, and modern history. This goal was not to be realized for over a century, and then only where industrialization and urbanization were firmly rooted.

The writers of the Enlightenment were not without effective foes in their own day. In traditional agrarian societies, social and religious safeguards functioned without fanfare. More vocal opposition came from Protestant revivalists who sought to salvage the primacy of spirit and revelation from the secular onslaught. Seen in historical perspective, these revivalists were the progenitors of nineteenth-century romantics, who taught that feelings are the fundamental guide to life and truth. But in some respects even this outlook indicated that the salvation of souls was no longer the predominant goal of religion and society.

## THE "SCIENTIFIC REVOLUTION"

By breaking with the prevalent Western intellectual tradition, science became a revolutionary force. But this break did not come about suddenly, nor was it always overt. Indeed no clear distinction existed between natural science and natural philosophy before the end of the seventeenth century. Until the seventeenth century, when it became universally important to intellectuals (still a small minority of the population), the study of nature had been cultivated for centuries by isolated scholars. Fourteenth-century schoolmen in England and France had already questioned Aristotle's explanation of motion. During the Italian Renaissance the University of Padua had become a center for Aristotelian scientists seeking natural causes for natural phenomena. Meanwhile literary humanists were rediscovering Greek and Hellenistic scientific works, including parts of the writings of Euclid and Archimedes; in 1543 the publication of

Archimedes' theories contributed significantly to the revival of science.*

These ancient works increased both Europe's store of knowledge and its supply of misinformation; these works also undermined faith in the version of Aristotle that philosophers and theologians had propagated, because they revealed that the ancients had disagreed on fundamental conclusions. In trying to decide among conflicting authorities, some early natural philosophers were driven to make their own analyses and observations. On the basis of their own experience artists and engineers, such as Leonardo da Vinci, also questioned prevailing authorities. Although the influence of their work was restricted, the impetus toward new investigations was growing. Navigators needing more and better instruments slowly demonstrated anomalies in prevailing Ptolemaic astronomy, as did an increasing number of persons who, dissatisfied with the Julian calendar, wanted a reliable system for dating Easter and other significant events.

## Copernicus' Challenge to Ptolemaic Astronomy

The discoveries in astronomy illustrate how slowly early modern science progressed. Prevailing traditions in 1500 stemmed from Aristotle and Ptolemy, who asserted that a stationary earth occupied the center of the universe. According to them, stars, sun, planets, and the moon were held in circular orbits around the earth by crystalline spheres. The source of motion was an alleged "prime mover" identified with the Christian God. In the heavens, where Dante and lesser men had located Paradise, perfection was expressed in circular motion and immutability, and it reigned as the supreme law.

* Not all Hellenistic science was recovered in time to make such a contribution. Aristarchus and Eratosthenes, for example, were not known until after Copernicus had been accepted in astronomy.

On earth, at whose center Hell was popularly pictured, imperfection was expressed in irregular vertical and horizontal motion and degeneration. But the low prestige of earth was redeemed by theology. According to the Christian epic, earth was the stage for the unique drama of Creation, Incarnation, and Redemption, which gave cosmic significance to human life. Thus physics, astronomy, and theology were integrated into a consistent cosmology or description of the universe. As Copernicus and other early astronomers learned, any effort to reformulate this cosmology was not only difficult but also dangerous.

Nicholas Copernicus, a Polish-German churchman, had probably come to doubt Ptolemaic astronomy as a student in Italy. He made few observations, and these were without the aid of a telescope. Instead he assembled older observations and arguments in favor of a simplified and more symmetrical scheme in which the planets, including the earth, revolved around the sun within an envelope of fixed stars. His model or theory of the universe explained why planets at times appeared to be moving backward, a problem that had troubled the Greeks. He published his description of the universe, *On the Revolutions of the Heavenly Orbs,* in 1543, the year of his death. The preface, written anonymously by a Lutheran clergyman, described Copernicus' conclusions as merely mathematical hypotheses, which they were. But they were sufficiently in conflict with specific passages in the Scripture to lead both Calvin and Luther to condemn their author as "the fool who would overturn the whole science of astronomy." In the Roman Catholic world, Copernicus' thesis was brought into disrepute by the case of the philosopher Giordano Bruno. In addition to asserting the plurality of worlds and the infinity of the universe, Bruno adopted the concept of a sun-centered cosmos. For advocating these "heresies" he was burned at the stake in 1600. In 1616 Church authorities

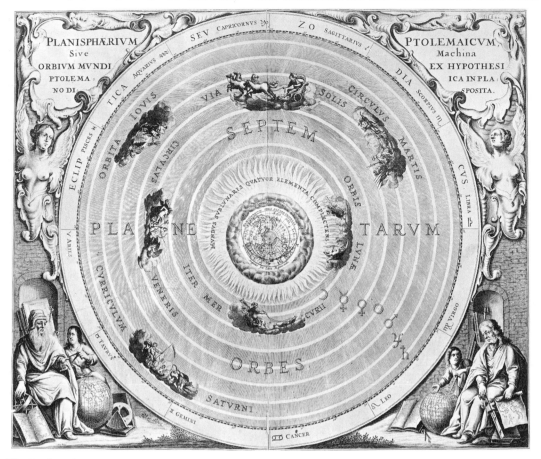

*The Ptolemaic system.*

placed Copernicus' book on the *Index of Prohibited Works,* where it remained for more than two centuries. Copernicus, whose strongest argument was the greater simplicity of his explanation, also failed to win contemporary academicians. They raised pertinent objections, some of which were not explained satisfactorily until the nineteenth century.

Still, practicing astronomers could not long avoid the issues that Copernicus had raised. The heavens themselves enlivened the cosmological debate in 1572 when a new star appeared and again in 1618 when a new comet came into view. In the past, comets had been interpreted as divine signs of impending doom. So was this one. But

it also caused astronomers to question the existence of crystalline spheres supporting the planets and to doubt the sharp distinction held to exist between the immutable heavens and the mutable earth.

Vindication for Copernicus' sun-centered hypothesis, but not other parts of his system that proved untenable, awaited the accumulation of observations by Tycho Brahe (1546–1601), the improvement of his theory by Johannes Kepler (1571–1630), the invention of the telescope, and the later achievements of Isaac Newton (1642–1727) and his generation.

In the thirty-year course of accumulating a mass of exceedingly accurate observations with the naked eye, the Danish astronomer

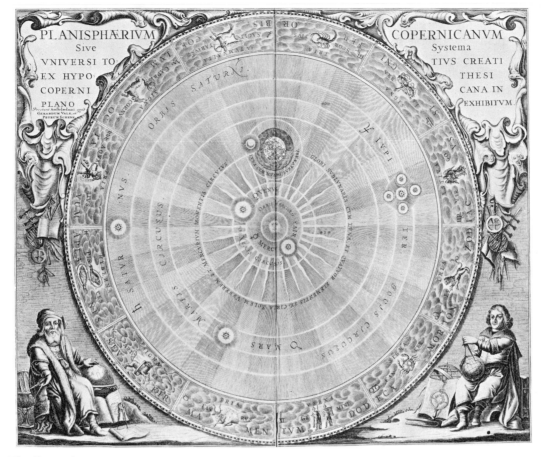

*The Copernican system.*

*Kepler's computations.*

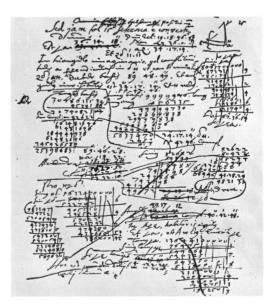

Tycho Brahe proposed a mathematical theory of the solar system that still put the earth at its center. Brahe worked at Prague, where his successor Johannes Kepler was another client of the emperor. Kepler obtained Brahe's great store of recorded observations. But he found that they gave more support to a sun-centered explanation of the solar system than to Brahe's own conclusions. Inspired by scientific zeal, astrology, and fantasies of the aesthetic orderliness of the universe (which he related to the harmonies of the musical scale), Kepler energetically worked out a series of laws describing planetary motion. Kepler discovered that the planets' paths were elliptical. He related their paths to their irregular velocities in orbit, and he formulated a law relating the time required by the planets to complete a full revolution in orbit to their distance from the sun. He also set forth plans for an astronomic telescope. Brahe's observations and Kepler's mathematical analyses destroyed Ptolemaic concepts of the universe, but they failed to answer fully the question of what held it together or governed its motion. Ptolemy had fallen into disrepute, but there was as yet no complete alternative.

## Galileo's Contributions to Modern Science

While Kepler worked in Prague, Galileo Galilei (1546–1642) and his successors pursued another line of scientific development in Italy. Here knowledge of Hellenistic scientists, notably Archimedes, had been revived, and Italian science seemed destined to succeed to the glory of Italian art. An industrious student and mathematical genius, Galileo started his career in physics and mechanics in opposition to Aristotelian teachings. By mathematical description and analysis he worked out laws of ballistic trajectories, pendulum movements, and uniform acceleration. He worked at a highly abstract level, considering neither causal theories nor observable effects of resistance. His conclusion that the velocity of a body falling freely in a vacuum was proportional to the elapsed time of fall laid the foundations for mechanics, the field of natural phenomena that was most productive of seventeenth-century scientific methodology. His studies of motion and falling bodies were directly related to controversies over Copernican astronomy. Anti-Copernicans argued that if the earth were in motion and turning on its axis, terrestrial motion would be distorted. In meeting their objections, Galileo partially formulated the concept of inertia. He carried his astronomy much fur-

*To view other worlds: Galileo's telescopes.*

ther, however, with a new instrument, the telescope. Learning of its invention in the Netherlands, he built such an instrument for his own use. With it he detected sunspots, saw the four satellites of Jupiter, followed the phases of Venus, studied the mountains and valleys on the surface of the moon, and noted that the Milky Way was a dense cluster of stars. All these observations were new. In 1610 he published the *Message of the Stars*. This work demonstrated that the same laws applied both to the earth and the heavens and that Aristotelian natural philosophy was as unreliable in astronomy as in mechanics.

Galileo's fame spread, but he aroused intense opposition in the universities and churches. Scholars who had devoted their lives to examining nature within an Aristotelian framework rejected his conclusions and even refused to look through his telescope. By 1616 a board of inquiry appointed by the Roman Inquisition had enjoined him to make only hypothetical statements concerning cosmology. Even so, in 1632 he published in Italian for a lay audience the *Dialogue on the Two Principal Systems of the Universe, the Ptolemaic and the Copernican.* Technically the Aristotelian, Simplicio, won the debate with the Copernican, but his victory was undeserved from the evidence used by his opponent. The *Dialogue* revealed that Galileo possessed remarkable literary talents as a propagandist for the new science. He had support within the Church (Pope Urban VIII himself likely supplied the tract's title) but its publication set off a controversy similar to that stirred up in the nineteenth century by popularizers of biological evolution. Clearly Galileo's criterion for scientific truth was not the authority of the Church. For defying its authority he was summoned before the Inquisition in 1632, forced to retract his conclusions, and put under house arrest for the remainder of his life. Protestant authorities were no less hostile toward Galileo; individual clergymen denounced him, and Protestant schools used anti-Copernican textbooks throughout the century. Spectacular as Galileo's accomplishments were, he merely initiated, and not entirely accurately, the broad lines of inquiry that were left to a new generation to follow up.* And follow them up it did. Isaac Newton, the great synthesizer of the new cosmology, was born the same year that Galileo died.

## The Organization of Science: Scientific Societies

Spurned by the universities and official scholarship, Galileo and his successors could

*Louis XIV at the Paris Observatory, 1662.*

tie themselves to no existing institution to coordinate or disseminate their work. Men of disparate interests who shared a common enthusiasm for the "new philosophy" banded together in informal groups that evolved into formal scientific societies. Galileo himself belonged to the new Roman *Accademia dei Lincei,* which sponsored his reports on sunspots in 1613. When that society disappeared in 1657, it was temporarily replaced by the *Accademia del Cimento* (Academy of Experiments), which flourished in Florence under Medici patronage only from 1657 to 1667.

More permanent and important were the societies given official sponsorship in France and England. The French *Académie des Sciences* founded in 1666 received financial support from the French crown. And in 1662 Charles II of England chartered, but did not subsidize, the Royal Society of London for the Promotion of Natural Knowledge. Other scientific societies were founded later in Russia and in a few German states.

---

* In fact, Galileo's *Dialogue* failed to clinch his argument that the earth rotated about the sun. He "proved" its rotation by referring to the ebb and flow of the tides. This argument was erroneous and retrograde. Oblivious to Kepler's contemporary work, which was ensconced in an impossible literary style, he continued to follow Copernicus' theory that the planets followed circular orbits.

These societies varied somewhat in their organization, but they performed similar functions. Their members experimented individually and in groups with new instruments. Duplicating experiments of others, they verified or corrected previous findings. Through corresponding secretaries and by publishing monographs and journals they disseminated detailed reports of their work to foreign scholars, irrespective of political or sectarian boundaries. The *Accademia del Cimento,* for example, working with the first physical laboratory in Europe, repeated and extended Galileo's experiments, employed the barometer invented by Torricelli, studied vacuums, computed the velocity of sound, and engaged in unproductive studies of the digestive processes of animals. The French society succeeded in computing the approximate speed of light, measuring the length of a degree of latitude, and applying the telescope to angular measurement in surveying. The Royal Society of London reached a high level of prestige as Isaac Newton and his contemporaries completed the mathematical synthesis of seventeenth-century astronomy and physics. Although the scope of the societies' interests extended to natural history and medicine, their greatest achievements during the early years lay in the field of physics; here their advances eventually carried them beyond the point where amateurs could make contributions.

Seeking to formulate universal natural laws, the scientific societies set secular, often utilitarian goals. Their membership was open to men of accomplishment without regard to birth. They encouraged clarity and precise objective description, choosing to avoid philosophical speculation beyond what was observable and definable in the world of nature. Robert Hooke, curator of experiments for the Royal Society of London, has left us with a succinct statement of the leading society's objectives:

To improve the knowledge of naturall things, and all useful Arts, Manufactures, Mechanik

practices, Engynes and Inventions by Experiments—(not meddling with Divinity, Metaphysics, Moralls, Politiks, Grammar, Rhetorick, or Logick).

To attempt the recovering of such allowable arts and inventions as are lost.

To examine all systems, theories, principles, hypotheses, elements, histories, and experiments of all things naturall, mathematicall, and mechanicall, invented, recorded or practiced, by any considerable author ancient or modern. . . .

In the mean time this Society will not own any hypothesis, system, or doctrine of the principles of naturall philosophy, proposed or mentioned by any philosopher ancient or modern, nor the explication of any phenomena whose recourse must be had to originall causes (as not being explicable by heat, cold, weight, figure, and the like, as effects produced thereby): nor dogmatically define, nor fix axioms of scientificall things, but will question and canvass all opinions, adopting nor adhering to none, till by mature debate and clear arguments, chiefly such as are deduced from legitimate experiments, the truth of such experiments be demonstrated invincibly.[1]

Not all of these societies, however, were as aloof from nonscientific influence as Hooke's statement would indicate. Governments urged that more attention be given to "useful discoveries" in navigation or war machinery, and the French society was apparently influenced by politics, as were the Berlin Academy (founded in 1700) and the St. Petersburg Academy (which began in 1724). Nevertheless, by consciously standing apart from politics and traditional religious metaphysics, the scientific societies caused eyebrows to be raised. The *Accademia del Cimento*—and Italian leadership in science—lapsed in 1667, when its Medici benefactor became a cardinal in the Church and when one of its members was indicted by the Inquisition. Traditionalists also attacked the

1. Quoted by Martha Ornstein, *The Rôle of Scientific Societies in the Seventeenth Century,* Chicago University Press, Chicago, 1928, pp. 108–109.

Royal Society of London for trying to subvert religion, but Thomas Sprat, who became an Anglican bishop, answered the charges in his celebrated history of the society in 1667. Unlike the Italian societies, the Royal Society survived unscathed.

## Scientific Instruments

The rapid expansion of scientific knowledge depended in part on the invention and elaboration of instruments that extended the senses. For aid in building such instruments, scientists turned to skilled craftsmen. In the seventeenth century these craftsmen and scientists developed the telescope, the microscope, the thermometer, the barometer, the air pump, and the clock; in the eighteenth century they built electrometers and delicate scales, which helped to open new fields of physical and chemical research.

In studying Galileo, we have already noted the effects of the discovery of the simple telescope. Kepler laid down plans for an improved refracting instrument, and Isaac Newton developed a reflecting model. The development of both types drew upon the same optical and glass-grinding skills as the microscope that was first produced in the Netherlands. But the usefulness of both the telescope and the microscope was limited at first by color distortions of lens images, incomplete optical theory, and imperfect lens-grinding techniques. When Newton's telescope was improved in the eighteenth century, it extended the astronomers' range beyond the solar system. But the lenses of the compound microscope were not corrected until the nineteenth century, when biological studies could finally flourish. Meanwhile Otto von Guericke's air pump was employed in experiments to defy Aristotle's dictum that "nature abhors a vacuum." Primitive thermometers and barometers both originated in Italy.

Another critical instrument, the pendulum clock, which was essential to quantitative measurement, was not developed until 1657

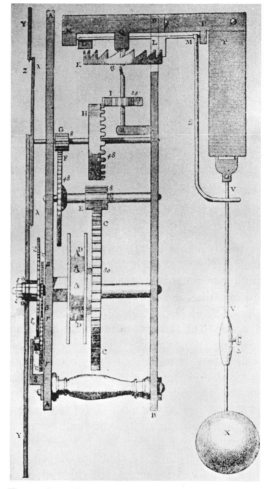

*Exact time: Huygens' clock.*

by the Dutchman, Christian Huygens. His invention partially solved the difficulties Galileo had experienced using a primitive and inaccurate water clock, but for navigation at sea accurate spring-driven clocks were still needed. Several governments offered substantial prizes, and a number of men devoted much attention to the problem. After a period of sixty years of work, practical chronometers were developed in the eighteenth century. Thus making possible for the first time accurate determination of longitude, they were a great boon to navigation and commerce.

In many ways the clock became the most

expressive symbol of new mechanistic concepts of the universe and society. Popularizers of the new science described the universe as a gigantic clockwork whose operations were regular, repetitive, and predictable. They reduced God to the position of the master clockmaker who had designed and set it in motion. Later the clock would assume a central role in the organization of complex industrial societies.

## Mathematics and the Completion of the Copernican Revolution in Astronomy

Much of the data that physical scientists collected was neither useful nor intelligible until mathematics (which developed rapidly during the seventeenth century) made it possible to incorporate these data into theories. The symbols of multiplication, division, addition, and decimals as we use them today were standardized after 1600. In the same period the Scotsman John Napier invented logarithms (1614). Henry Briggs provided one of the most useful innovations for rapid calculation, the slide rule based on logarithms. In France in the 1650s Pierre de Fermat and Blaise Pascal opened another new line of mathematics, the study of probabilities. To solve problems of motion, European mathematicians learned to apply the algebra they had borrowed from the Arabs to geometry; René Descartes* led the way in this field. Equally indispensable for the study of motion, and hence for the Newtonian theories in celestial mechanics, was the invention of the calculus, done concurrently by Newton and by Gottfried Wilhelm von Leibniz (1646–1716). Leibniz' system of notation was adapted for general use outside of England.

Mathematics and the experimental work of astronomers and physicists after Galileo and Kepler laid the basis for a more systematic explanation of the solar system. Both

*See pp. 67–68.

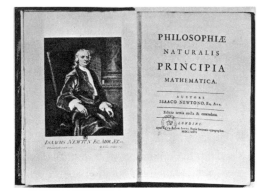

*Newton and his classic third edition.*

men had given impetus to the notion of an orderly, mechanistic universe, but neither one had provided answers to fundamental questions. What kept the planets in motion? What held them in their orbits? Or, assuming some gravitational force as Kepler did, what kept them from plummeting to its center? Many men furnished partial answers to these questions. Among them, René Descartes formulated a law of inertia that explained the planets' continued motion. Christian Huygens described the mathematical principles of centrifugal force. From these principles, Robert Hooke of the Royal Society developed a working theory of gravitational attraction. However, credit for mathematically demonstrating the operation of gravity in the solar system belonged not to Hooke, but to his colleague, Isaac Newton, a genius among the giants of the Royal Society.

Newton was born and trained at the very time when mathematics and physics were ready for a synthesizer of his ability. In the lesser developed fields of optics and chemistry, to which he devoted more time, his contributions were less. After graduating from Cambridge, Newton spent a momentous year in the country (1664–1665). During this time he formulated the calculus, discovered the compound nature of white light, and arrived at the essentials of the law of gravitation. In 1687 he finally published his magnum opus, *Philosophiæ Naturalis Princi-*

*pia Mathematica* (*The Mathematical Principles of Natural Philosophy*).

This complex treatise explained natural mathematical principles of matter in motion but cautiously refrained from speculation on ultimate causes. The best known part of it described the celestial mechanism in terms of mass, attraction, and the laws of motion. It incorporated Kepler's laws of planetary motion into a general mathematical model. Newton's model for matter in motion was to remain "valid" until challenged in the late nineteenth and early twentieth centuries by the theory of relativity. So sweeping was his concept of the constitution of the "World Machine" that intellectuals soon found themselves in a universe from which animistic spirits seemed to have been banished. Although Newton believed that his investigation supported religion, it seemed to be at war with traditional theology.

After publishing the *Principia,* Newton's enthusiasm for science, which had never been zealous, flagged. On two occasions he served in Parliament. Later he became master of the mint when the Whig government was replacing the coinage during the early phases of the War of Spanish Succession. He spent part of his energies in a personal conflict with Leibniz over who had precedence in the invention of the calculus. Each charged the other with plagiarism. From 1703 to 1709 he served as president of the Royal Society. During these years he published the *Opticks,* an influential summary of his work on the physical properties of light. His last scientific publication suggested hypotheses to explain the phenomena of light, gravitation, and the composition of matter. Upon his death he received honors previously reserved to royalty.

## Electricity

After Newton, scientists devoted themselves largely to the elaboration of his principles in physics, astronomy, and mathematics. The Royal Society lost its practical interests and became an aloof club of pure

*An early experiment with static electricity, 1774.*

scientists, leaving technical undertakings for industry to new associations. And the somnolent universities of the eighteenth century made almost no scientific contributions. Nevertheless, science progressed. The study of heat, conceived of primarily as a fluid rather than energy, became important, and Fahrenheit formulated tables of specific heat for various substances. But the most striking development of eighteenth-century physics lay in the field of electricity.

Certain aspects of electricity had been studied by William Gilbert (1540–1603), a physician at the court of Queen Elizabeth. The extent to which electricity was conceived of as static can be seen from the fact that he derived the term from the Greek word for amber after observing that amber rubbed on fur attracted hair, straw, and other small objects. Gilbert also worked with magnetism, particularly the dip or inclination of a magnetic compass needle, which he sought to make serviceable to mariners. But in order to study electricity further, investigators had to learn how to generate and store a charge. Otto von Guericke, who had already invented an air pump and demonstrated the force of atmospheric pressure, made some advance in this direction with a machine that generated static electricity by friction. The first major breakthrough came in 1745, when a Leyden jar was invented for storing static electrical charges. Although electrical attraction and repulsion had been noted earlier, Benjamin Franklin first set forth the theory of negative and positive electrical charges. This was a far more basic contribution than his famous kite experiment of 1752, which demonstrated that lightning was electricity.

A further breakthrough in the study of electricity came in 1800 when a northern Italian, Count Alessandro Volta (1745–1827) invented a primitive "wet cell" battery that produced a steady supply of current. Joseph Priestley (1733–1804) and other English experimenters soon learned of Volta's achievement and used it for the electrolysis of water into hydrogen and oxygen. Shortly thereafter Sir Humphry Davy began to develop a theory that explained the chemical origins of Volta's electrical current. Not only was the development of electricity thus highly international in character, but it also formed a bridge to modern chemistry.

## The Birth of Modern Chemistry

Traditional natural philosophy did not recognize physics and chemistry as separate studies. All earthly things were considered imperfect compounds of four elements—earth, air, fire, and water—each of which had inherent propensities for movement. Alchemy, the esoteric art of changing one substance into another, thus seemed a reasonable pursuit to most men of learning. In their trial-and-error pursuit of new remedies, doctors sometimes worked with a different set of assumptions. So did metallurgists. Gradually there developed the basis for a pure science of chemistry. But until the generation of Robert Boyle and Robert Hooke, all chemists lacked the apparatus and ideas needed to overturn sterile traditional notions.

Robert Boyle (1627–1691), son of an English earl, was one of the first and most influential members of the Royal Society. He set out to apply the basic concepts of Galileo and Descartes to chemistry. Although his chemical experiments failed to explain the composition of matter, he did destroy the notion that there were only four elements. Boyle also demonstrated that all substances could not be compounded from them as the

*An experiment with breath by Lavoisier.*

alchemists taught. He concluded that something in the air was necessary for combustion, but, again, he could not think of a way to isolate and identify oxygen. His success was greater in formulating laws describing the behavior of gases, and his works, notably *The Sceptical Chymist* (1661), did provide a basis for subsequent research.

For several generations after Boyle, chemists stumbled over the problem of relating gases to solids and fluids. Many of them were misled by the "phlogiston theory," which emanated from Germany. This theory was designed to explain the heat and light given off by combustion and the weight gained by certain substances when they were burned. "Phlogiston" was an imaginary "fluid" of negative weight given off by a burning object. This theory, although it offered explanations for some phenomena, reflected the lack of knowledge about the active chemical role of gases. This subject was pursued with success in England and Scotland by Henry Cavendish (1731–1810), Joseph Black (1728–1799), and Joseph Priestley. They succeeded in producing and differentiating gases such as oxygen and hydrogen, and their discoveries concerning the active chemical role of gases seriously undermined the old theory.

The French chemist Antoine Laurent Lavoisier (1743–1794) finally overthrew the phlogiston theory. In contact with Priestley and others, by 1778 Lavoisier developed the new theory of oxidation. He explained that weight gained by the residue of an "oxidized" object was due not to an elusive fluid but to the fixation of oxygen during the process. Meanwhile Cavendish analyzed the ratio of hydrogen and oxygen in water (1782), thus adding to the emphasis placed upon quantitative measurement by Lavoisier. In 1787 Lavoisier gave his theory a new and lasting terminology for the known elements. His work indicated great progress, but in certain aspects of metallurgy and applied technology procedures that as yet had no scientific explanation were still being used.

## Biology

Biology was even slower than chemistry in responding to new scientific concepts. At the beginning of the modern era it too was enmeshed in methods and concepts that explained little and resisted change. Its inheritance included the fixity of species, animistic concepts of the "soul" of plants, and the belief that certain animals represented moral virtues and vices, concepts as firmly rooted as the stability of the earth in the center of the universe. Early modern biologists were primarily catalogers of types of plants and animals, but they lacked an overall system of classification that would give order to their catalogs.

With the microscope, investigators extended their range of knowledge concerning the complexity of living things. Marcello Malpighi, an Italian anatomist, used this new instrument to examine body tissues. Anton van Leeuwenhoek's unexcelled microscopic work revealed the existence of protozoa, bacteria, and red corpuscles of the blood. The Englishmen Nehemiah Grew, a contemporary of Malpighi and Leeuwenhoek, observed the sexual reproduction of plants.

This sexual aspect of plant life was further developed until Carolus Linnaeus (1707–1778) of Sweden finally used it as the basis for classifying the plant kingdom into genera and species. In early editions of his *System of Nature* (1735 *et seq.*)—which included animal, vegetable, and mineral categories because minerals were thought to "grow" in the ground—Linnaeus supported the concept of the fixity of species. (In the nineteenth century his work was to be used by religious fundamentalists as an authoritative argument against Charles Darwin.) Ironically by 1760 he himself had conceded that new species can rise from stable hybridization. By the end of the century other biologists also disputed the fixity of species, notably the Frenchman Georges Buffon (1707–1788). Buffon seemed to be a harbinger of Darwin, but he did not make evolutionary change into a synthesizing principle as Darwin did. Thus the added element of evolutionary change in biology did not appear to upset the concept of the Newtonian world machine until the nineteenth century.

## Medicine and Public Health

Medicine was retarded until microbiology had progressed beyond the primitive concepts that had characterized it in the seventeenth and eighteenth centuries. Meanwhile the Hellenistic medicine of Galen, and, to a lesser extent, of Hippocrates, dominated medical thought and practice. According to traditional Greek medicine, the health of the body was dependent upon the balance of the four humors: blood, phlegm, yellow bile (choler), and black bile. As long as this theory prevailed through the nineteenth century so did the general practice of bleeding. In the nineteenth century this theory also gave rise to the name cholera, on the presumption that that disease was caused by a surfeit of one of these humors, choler. Early modern remedies were prescribed according to "signatures": a liver-shaped plant was used for diseases of the liver; an Indian wood was given to cure an "Indian" disease such as syphilis. The list of popular remedies included the exorcism of spirits and the "royal touch" of kings for the cure of scrofula. Alchemy and astrological cures (hence influenza from the purported *influence* of the stars) also figured in medicine.

*Bleeding a gentleman in the sixteenth century.*

difficult to overturn than Aristotle's physics. For one thing, doctors of medicine lectured from texts, leaving actual contact with cadavers, dissection knife, and most patients to barber-surgeons who lacked the prestige of having had a philosophical education. Renaissance artists sometimes practiced dissection illicitly and achieved far greater detail than anatomists. Their realism was reflected in Andreas Vesalius' *On the Fabric of the Human Body,* which was published in 1543, the same year that Copernicus' major work appeared. Vesalius, a Fleming who had worked at Paris, Padua, Bologna, and Pisa threw his work together hastily without any intention of assaulting Galen's authority. But his attempt to describe human anatomy part by part, layer by layer, inadvertently piled up evidence against Galen. Facing a hostile reception, Vesalius suspended his work to become court physician to Charles V. Nevertheless anatomy was the earliest medical science to be emancipated from speculative philosophy and the authority of the ancients.

Other advances were made by men who tackled new problems. Immediately after the discovery of America, virulent strains of syphilis swept across Europe. In addition, the mortality rate from scurvy among sailors on long voyages was astoundingly high. Doctors had to deal with these problems as well as gunshot wounds, the by-product of new military weaponry. Especially noteworthy was the uneducated military surgeon, Ambroise Paré (1510–1590), who discovered by chance that cauterization of wounds with boiling oil was less effective than ligatures and dressings.

The generation of doctors following Paré produced a significant synthesis in the field of physiology. After an education at Padua, William Harvey (1578–1657) demonstrated —insofar as he could without a microscope —the circulation of the blood. Inspired by analogies between mechanics and the operation of valves in the veins, he described the heart as a mechanical pump forcing blood

Neither physician nor patient understood cause and effect relationships; practitioners who proceeded by trial and error were the first to approach such an understanding.

One early rebel against the authority of traditional medicine was Paracelsus (1493–1541), a German physician and alchemist. With a stream of invective he attacked contemporary doctors for using logic rather than experience. This iconoclast introduced a medical chemistry steeped in alchemy but nevertheless empirical to a degree. Driven from his teaching post in the medical school at Basel and condemned by Catholic and Protestant clergymen, the wandering Paracelsus left behind him a succession of medical practitioners who relied on chemical cures.

A more cautious revolt grew out of the Italian medical schools, where dissection was practiced in order to illustrate the texts of Galen. Unfortunately Galen had used animals rather than human cadavers for his descriptions, but his authority was more

*Empirical anatomy: Vesalius.*

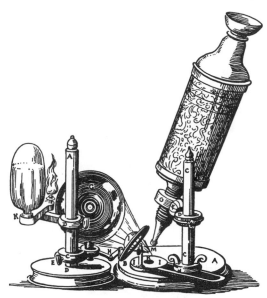

*Compound microscope, 1665.*

through the arteries whence it returned through the veins. Thus he replaced Galen's postulate that the two types of blood—one emanating from the liver, the other from the heart—ebbed and flowed within the veins and arteries. Harvey worked on this hypothesis for ten years prior to publishing his conclusions in 1628. Another generation or two passed before medical scientists accepted it. Not until Malpighi used a microscope to discover capillaries connecting arteries and veins in the tissues of a frog's lungs was Harvey's thesis of circulation empirically confirmed.

Despite Harvey's achievements, most attempts to proceed solely on mechanical principles failed. Members of the Royal Society showed that part of the air inhaled into the lungs was essential to life and that combustion and breathing were similar processes. As blood was viewed as a vehicle for carrying air (oxygen was not identified and

named until later) and nourishment, scientific societies attempted inconsequential experiments with blood transfusions, usually from animals to humans. For further success the life sciences depended on the advance of chemistry, microscopy, and clinical medical observations. But they also lacked organizing ideas with which to establish meaningful relationships between known facts. No theory of the origin of disease was forthcoming until the nineteenth century.

Public health remained primarily a local and humanitarian concern. Isolated doctors produced descriptions of epidemics and treatises on occupational diseases. Local governments ordered the cleaning of streets and the provision of water (usually by under-supervised private companies), but in neither case were the standards used nor the level of enforcement sufficient to eliminate the continued threat of epidemics. Control of rats by 1720 brought the end of bubonic plague epidemics except in the jails, but other urban epidemics, including diseases totally new in Western Europe, still took heavy tolls. Humanitarian reformers, especially the Quakers in England, concerned themselves

*Sick ward in an eighteenth-century prison.*

with "jail fever," the treatment of the mentally ill, and high infant mortality; they built hospitals, some of them specialized. With all its shortcomings improved public health probably accounted in part for Europe's rapid increase of population after 1750.

Once bubonic plague was curbed, progress in the control of smallpox began. After 1722 upper-class Englishmen began to use innoculation—a practice of long standing in the Near and Far East—to give the patient a mild case as a means of achieving immunity. Using this dangerous procedure was preferable to contracting a virulent case, but innoculation was impracticable for most people because it required isolation. Nevertheless, it became popular when Voltaire and others proclaimed its utility on the Continent. At the very end of the eighteenth century, Edward Jenner, an English country doctor, discovered a vaccine of cowpox serum for the disease. Jenner had become interested in

milkmaids' immunity to smallpox after they had contracted cowpox. After long study and discussion, he first vaccinated a small boy in 1796. The experiment worked to give him immunity. After Jenner published his findings in 1798, vaccination for smallpox spread through the Western world and substantially reduced the death rate.

## The Methodology of Science

Because age-old authorities were overturned in so many fields, it is usually assumed that a revolution in scientific methodology had taken place—a "scientific revolution." Both scientists and their propagandists consciously rejected philosophers' concerns with things beyond (meta) nature (physics) as speculation. "We are to admit," Newton wrote, "no more causes of natural things than such as are both true and sufficient to explain their appearances." This conscious shaking loose from theological authority appears to have been part of that revolution. So was the scientists' spurning of the allegories that theologians used to reconcile science with sacred texts.

But scientific spokesmen did not speak with one voice in defining scientific methodology. The English philosopher Francis Bacon saw it primarily as empiricism, the use of inductive logic to give meaning to direct observations. But René Descartes, author of a classic essay on method, emphasized the necessity of first having a set of hypotheses, even a completely new metaphysics, before empirical testing could take place. Both Bacon and Descartes, who were intimately connected with scientific developments, were immensely impressed with contemporary discoveries. Subsequently, however, Western men have gone through further such revolutions within the same branches of science. These additional "revolutions" have inspired both philosophers and historians to inquire more deeply into the nature of scientific changes. As a result of these inquiries, historians of science have come to view the new syntheses of this period less as absolute changes than as recurrent aspects of scientific methodology itself.

Purged of magical and animistic beliefs held by primitive peoples, modern science was a continuation of man's efforts to predict natural phenomena, to make them useful to human comfort and survival, or to satisfy curiosity. Since ancient times "natural philosophers" have developed theories or models for that purpose. Whether or not they conform to ultimate reality is a problem for philosophical speculation. Historically, routine scientific research has gone on within the framework of such theories and models until one of them failed to make new or previously neglected data meaningful. Then a crisis occurred, which lasted until someone conceived a new model. Though the new model gained credence by eliminating anomalies in the old one, it would retain the "valid" parts.

The coincidence of several such crises during the seventeenth and eighteenth centuries gave rise to the somewhat exaggerated idea that a "scientific revolution" had occurred. Scientists and popularizers of science were certain they had found a new criterion of *ultimate truth*. Yet experience was to demonstrate that in contrast to the timeless absolutes of traditional theology and philosophy, "natural laws" were authoritative rather than authoritarian. Authoritarians assumed that the premises from which they derived all knowledge, natural or supranatural, were unquestionable. For many of them the existence of awesome, unresolved mysteries was proof of the gulf separating puny man from his omniscient, sovereign, and inscrutable God. In propagating their doctrines, authoritarians relied on indoctrination protected by censorship and coercion. Popularizers of science also usually quenched the human thirst for absolutes with a similar authoritarianism. And even early modern scientists often assumed that their ideas described ultimate reality unconditioned by the human mind and the position of the observer relative to the thing observed.

But the operation of scientific methodology has depended upon quite different conditions. Scientific laws or rules have constantly had to stand the test of new evidence and new concepts for interpreting old and new facts. In order for such an interchange to operate fully, freedom of inquiry and of communications has been indispensable. Ultimately scientific authority rests upon intellectual assent of peers in the field. Thus scientific "truth" is secular and open-minded.

Although natural philosophers disavowed metaphysics, certain implicit or explicit metaphysical assumptions were eventually drawn from their ideas and general approach. And these assumptions, which belong to the philosophy of science, were at variance with both Catholic and Protestant concepts of divine immanence in the world. Behind the superficial chaos of observable natural phenomena, science presupposed regularity rather than supranatural intervention. Mathematically regular "natural laws" came to be set in opposition to arbitrary miracles. Although scientists like Newton specifically disavowed this conclusion, it was inherent in their mechanistic approach to nature. They justified their probing into this world as the unveiling of a "second scripture" or laying bare the handiwork of God. But their deity was a "constitutional" sovereign, since his power was circumscribed by immutable natural laws that the human mind could make progressively more intelligible.

## SCIENTIFIC PHILOSOPHY AND THE NEW HUMANISM

Quietly at first, the application of new scientific concepts overturned one old authority after the other. Only exceptional persons like the English poet John Donne perceived that even man's self image—as the special creation dwelling at the center of a cosmically purposeful universe—was crumbling before the onslaught of the Copernican revolution during the seventeenth century.

From Donne's time to the present, critics of science and technology have shared his lament that

> . . . [the] new Philosophy calls all in doubt,
> The Element of fire is quite put out;
> The Sun is lost, and th'earth, and no man's wit
> Can well direct him where to looke for it.[2]

The new humanists were optimists who foretold progress in the future if reason were applied to nature and the fetters of the past were thrown off. Their humanism was grafted onto the older humanism of the Renaissance. In the sixteenth century humanists like Jean Bodin* had learned to study institutions—and even deities—of the past in relation to their historical environment. Some Renaissance humanists had also anticipated progress through the use of reason and the study of nature. Science more than classical letters would confirm this attitude henceforth. In the new humanism science became an idol, a myth. Bernard de Fontenelle, secretary of the French Academy and popularizer of its members' achievements, sensed this when he wrote, "Pure physics is being elevated into a new kind of theology."

Thinkers who drew their premises from mechanical science were preoccupied with questions raised by the "scientific revolution." They gave Aristotelian philosophy short shrift, arguing that past thought was no aid but rather a prejudice to be overcome, a burdensome ballast to be jettisoned. Still there remained the inexorable question of the relationship of science to religion: what role could divine miracles play within a mechanistic universe governed by mathematical natural laws? When traditionally accepted truths were replaced by scientific

---

* For Bodin, see Volume I, page 539.

2. From *An Anatomie of the World,* 1611, in the *Complete Poetry and Selected Prose of John Donne and the Complete Poetry of William Blake,* New York, The Modern Library, 1941, p. 171.

and mathematical axioms, questions about the origin and validity of human knowledge became inescapable. What role could man's mind play? Was it the repository of innate self-evident laws or merely an associative device responding to its environment? To what fields was scientific methodology applicable? Could quantitative measurement be applied meaningfully to social phenomena as well as to matter in motion? Most thinkers who thought that it could went no further than to postulate certain axioms of social relationships and to cloak them in words of mechanistic science, such as the balance of power or the balance of property. A few ventured into the collection of primitive statistics. According to some observers, European thought began to take on a quantitative quality greater than in any other civilization of the past.

Scientific philosophers who followed the new models of natural philosophy were unanimous in repudiating, even scoffing at, Aristotelianism. They used concepts, terms, and problems produced by contemporary science. But they failed to agree on conclusions drawn from these common roots. They began by denying the authority and categories of scholasticism, which had survived both the Renaissance and the Reformation only slightly scathed. The catchwords of scientific philosophy in the seventeenth and eighteenth centuries were "reason" and "nature." These two terms became as integral a part of new mechanistic world views as divine law and deductive logic had been to scholasticism, or as solitary, irrational faith had been to Protestantism. But "reason" and "nature" became volatile words employed by sharply differing schools of thought. Not only did various philosophers define them in varying ways in the seventeenth century, but men of the Enlightenment were to redefine them in the eighteenth century. And in the nineteenth century, romantics and evolutionists were to revise their meaning drastically again.

Most seventeenth-century scientific philosophers held that with reason men could set all past and present prejudices aside. Mathematics seemed to have demonstrated that fundamental truths could be found within the mind itself. For *rationalists* the "nature of things" could be deduced from innate ideas in the mind. Although they sometimes lauded empirical investigation, they relied upon *innate* ideas (called "Platonic" after their first champion, Plato), usually conceived in mathematical terms, as the key to understanding and explaining the world of nature. *Empiricists,* on the other hand, though no less committed to reason and nature, considered knowledge to be the mind's response to *external* stimuli. At most the mind was an associative device that would sort out clear and distinct ideas from the more reliable types of sensation. Like scientists, which they themselves often were, scientific philosophers usually pursued a middle course between pure rationalism and pure empiricism. In practice, however, these categories were more theoretical than actual.

## Platonic Rationalism

Seventeenth-century rationalists self-consciously proclaimed a revolution. But their zeal for innovation obscured their close ties to the Platonic philosophy of the past.

The thought of the Italian pantheist, Giordano Bruno (1548–1600) illustrates the link between Platonism and the newer rationalism. To Bruno physical nature was a visible manifestation of divinity. It was expressed in laws of nature which man could understand without the aid of revelation. Nature was the creation of God, and by the very nature of His unlimited powers He would have created every conceivable level or degree of being, perfect and imperfect. Creation must therefore consist of an infinite universe, an infinite number of worlds, and a physical order representing a great unbroken chain of being descending from the Creator to the lowest inanimate thing. Even if it were evil, each finite being in this chain reflected the full power of God. Thus nature reveals

God by its harmony, beauty, fullness, and orderliness.

As we have seen, Bruno adopted Copernicus' concept of a sun-centered universe. But he died at the stake before Galileo published his major works and before Newton was born. Instead he drew upon the Platonism of the Italian Renaissance,* the same philosophy that inspired Copernicus and played a major role in Kepler's aesthetic and geometrical view of the universe. Later it was to merge with the rationalism of Spinoza† and Leibniz.‡ Intellectually radical, because in pantheism men found a religious sanction for revolutionary science, this Platonic rationalism did not offend the existing social order. Rather it shored up that hierarchic order, as it had in the Middle Ages, with a cosmic rationale.

## The Cartesian Revolution

René Descartes (or des Cartes, hence Cartesian), not Bruno, was the first person since Aristotle to start afresh in building a philosophical system. A budding mathematical genius disgusted with the authorities taught in the universities, Descartes in 1619 developed the notion of applying mathematics to all nature. In the following decade he worked to found a complete metaphysics based on the premise that ultimate reality would have to be explained theoretically before meaningful experimentation could take place. The starting point for his new system was the one reality he could not refute by systematic doubt: "I think, hence I am." Although he advocated experimentation, he preferred the ultimate certainty of such "clear and distinct" ideas arrived at by introspection and deduction to the chaotic complexities of experience. From his central single axiom he proceeded to deduce the existence of God and of a material world in motion. Beside this material world and

---

* See Volume I, p. 492.
† See this volume, pp. 68–69.
‡See this volume, pp. 71–72.

sharply separated from it was the realm of the mind. The human mind obtained real knowledge of the external world by innate ideas such as the concept of God, the axioms of mathematics, and common notions of space, time, and motion. Mind and matter did not interact in Descartes' universe save in the human brain. Accepting Galen's erroneous statement that only man had a pineal gland, Descartes concluded that it was the cosmic meeting point of mind and matter. The supernatural intervention of God was required to hold this dualistic universe together. Descartes' dogmatic system thus saved the prestige of man and insulated religion, politics, and moral affairs from empirical study.

Nevertheless, Cartesianism offended traditionalists, and Descartes' works were placed on the Roman Catholic *Index of Prohibited Books*.* Once the shock of his iconoclasm passed, however, many clergymen of Europe's established churches invoked Descartes' principles as a means of preventing scientific philosophy—especially empiricism—from making further inroads into the politics and morals over which theologians claimed authority.

Despite the conservative uses to which his ideas were put, Descartes did much to popularize scientific discoveries and methodology on the Continent, especially through his *Discourse on Method* (1637). As a mathematician, Descartes was at the very center of the "scientific revolution." He set forth logical steps of analysis—that is, the breaking of complex questions down into simpler parts and the progressive solution of simpler to more complex questions. Des-

cartes also gave general currency to certain scientific discoveries, but on some points he was scientifically behind the times. He continued to deny the possibility of a vacuum, for example. His metaphysical speculations concerning the mechanics of the universe contained fertile concepts, but its actual details were of no use to Newton. Descartes' emphasis upon rational hypothesis may have been healthy for science, but his methodology was invoked generally in the seventeenth and eighteenth centuries to obstruct empiricism.

## Dutch Rationalism and Baruch Spinoza

For most of his mature life (from 1629 to 1649) Descartes took refuge in the Dutch Republic, the outpost of personal freedom and cross-roads of heterodoxy in seventeenth-century Europe. Besides Descartes other prominent antitraditional thinkers sojourned or at least visited there: Pierre Bayle of France, John Locke of England, and Leibniz of Germany. Native Dutchmen such as Christian Huygens were in the forefront of the scientific revolution. In addition, prominent Dutch statesmen speculated on statistical approaches to taxation and insurance. Classical humanism flourished, and radical religious movements with antimetaphysical bents were tolerated: Quakers, Mennonites, and Unitarians. Among educated and secure townsmen, the ethical and tolerant spirit of Erasmus and Sebastianus Castellio had lived on through the Reformation. In other words, major solvents of tradition were at work in the Netherlands. At some point Baruch Spinoza (1632–1677) drew upon them all.

Born in Amsterdam of well-to-do Jewish-Portuguese immigrant parents, Spinoza became involved with a Mennonite group, Cartesian philosophy, prominent scientists such as Huygens, and friends with radical economic and political views. Excommunicated by the Jewish community, he renounced

---

* That is, being contrary to faith and morals, they could not be read without permission of a bishop or other administrative official. (In 1966 the Curia, the papal administration, gave notice that ecclesiastical penalties for reading such books were no longer being enforced. The hierarchy now depends on moral suasion, and it is more a matter of individual conscience whether one reads such works.)

business to become a lens grinder near The Hague, where he lived in a garret and produced political and philosophic writings until his death. In his youth Spinoza was deeply involved with utilitarian statistical approaches to social and political problems. But he was disillusioned by the French invasion of 1672, when his republican party lost power. Thereafter he turned more exclusively to a contemplative rationalism that culminated in his posthumously published *Ethics.*

In the *Ethics* Spinoza sought to establish absolute certainty by rigid mathematical reasoning. The work laid down theorems and axioms and demonstrated ethical principles like a Euclidean textbook in geometry. It was probably the most rigorous application of what the French philosophers called *l'esprit géométrique,* the geometric spirit. Everything would be better done, they argued, at the hands of a geometer. But Spinoza was an original thinker who went beyond French Cartesianism. Mind and matter he held to be two coordinate aspects of a God who existed in a mystical pantheistic union with nature. Led by the intellectual love of God, morally free man could rise above capricious passions by understanding them and acting upon his reasoned though hedonistic will. "An emotion which is a passion," he wrote "ceases to be a passion as soon as we form a clear and distinct idea of it." Spinoza's highest level of knowledge permits the intellectual to transcend time and to view life dispassionately "under the aspect of eternity." But Spinoza's geometrical proof broke down on the question of immortality, thus forcing this, "the God-intoxicated man," to shift to mysticism and ethical behavior founded upon psychological insight. With Bruno, Spinoza saw no cosmic viciousness in a nature replete with both good and evil, and he postulated an infinite universe and a plurality of worlds. These heresies plus his point-by-point rejection of Calvinist asceticism endeared him neither to Calvinists nor to Jewish authorities.

## The Empiricists: Bacon, Hobbes, and Locke

Rationalists drew inspiration from the successful use of mathematics in science. For them mathematical truths in the mind seemed to correspond to the structure of the universe. Banish passion, prejudice, and traditional error, they said, and reason could provide keys to understanding the universe. Empiricists also condemned prejudices, passion, and tradition, but they disputed the existence of innate ideas in the mind. For them the mind was not a storehouse of such master ideas but, in John Locke's phrase, it was a *blank tablet* on which experience wrote. The mind was a device that sorted and associated the data of experience derived from the senses. In fact, however, seventeenth-century empiricists did not maintain this view consistently. Instead they started with nonempirical assumptions and made room for the compelling authority of what was "clear and distinct" or "self-evident," even while consciously rejecting innate ideas. Boundaries separating rationalists from empiricists were geographical as well as methodological. On the Continent, Cartesianism swept the field as Spinoza's career illustrates. But an empirical tradition maintained itself in revolutionary seventeenth-century England.

An early spokesman of English empiricism was James I's Lord Chancellor, Francis Bacon (1561–1626). Bacon called for a new science that would establish man's dominion over nature. Isolated writers since the Renaissance had hailed and lauded new inventions, but Bacon optimistically predicted that if the universities were overhauled and scientific societies for cooperative research were founded, the mysteries of the universe could be unveiled in a single generation. As a first step he set out to dispel the "idols" or harmful mental habits that had perverted reason and led to the repetition of error in the past. He spoke against the Idol of the Tribe, the desire of men to see only what

*A voyage to new logic: Bacon's* Novum Organum.

they wanted to believe. Another snare was the Idol of the Cave, the transformation of personal prejudices and limited personal experience into universal principles. In labeling the Idol of the Market Place, Bacon referred to confusion resulting from different meanings of words. Lastly he denounced the Idol of the Theater, stubborn commitment to particular schools of thought that had become untenable.

In order to become free of these idols Bacon said that men had to disentangle science from theology for the mutual benefit of both. He denied that nature was Satan's bailiwick; the created world was, he affirmed, a second Scripture whose study would reinforce religion. "It is . . . most wise to render unto faith the things that are faith's," he wrote in the *New Logic,* but it was apparent

that he left it to the scientist, not the theologian, to define the boundary between science and religion.

Bacon was a popularizer of science rather than a scientist, and his influence was limited. In his lifetime he remained a lonely clarion. He sought but failed to reform the universities' curriculum. A proud place-seeker and a political absolutist, he was impeached and deposed by Parliament on charges of bribery. During the English civil wars, science tended to be identified with Puritan revolutionaries, his opponents, but the restored Charles II put part of Bacon's cherished plans for a scientific society into operation thirty-four years after his death. Committed to the utilitarian application of science, the society's early members touted Bacon as its intellectual father.

Bacon lived and wrote without knowing the works of Galileo. Such was not the case with Thomas Hobbes (1588–1679), who made mechanistic science the basis for a materialist philosophy. To him only matter and motion were real, and sense perceptions, conveying the motion of matter to the mind (itself a special kind of matter), were the source of all knowledge. Believing that he had destroyed the basis for transcendent knowledge, Hobbes argued that man was distinguished from beast by his ability to use symbols and language. Hobbes' political philosophy made use of still another device borrowed from science—the concept of a "state of nature" abstracted from experience. In a state of nature life was "nasty, brutish, and short." But man escaped the natural "war of all against all" by creating a state and establishing a political contract. Under this contract the state, by imposing a uniform ideology, was empowered to secure order.

Hobbes' empirical "psychology" was modified by John Locke (1632–1704), the Whig theorist of the English Revolution of 1688. A member of the Royal Society, Locke was a physician and the secretary of the Earl of Shaftesbury, a radical Whig who led the fight against James II's accession.

*Title page of Hobbes'* Leviathan, *1651.*

From discussions within these radical intellectual circles, Locke concluded that conflicts over terminology and contradictory assertions arose because men carried their inquiries beyond the mind's possible experience.

After considering the origins and validity of human knowledge for twenty years, Locke published *An Essay Concerning Human Understanding* in 1690. In it he states that the mind derives its ideas from sensory data. They are recorded as on a blank sheet of paper, and their range is limited to areas of human sensation and experience. No room was left for Platonic universal ideas. Moreover, valid sensations were not sensible qualities such as color but the mathematical, physical primary qualities of solidity, extension, form, and motion. Yet Locke did not maintain that the mind was wholly passive.

He accorded it the ability to originate ideas through active reflection, repeating, comparing, and uniting sensations in a practically infinite variety of ways. It could not formulate metaphysical realities. Knowledge of these might be obtained from Christian revelation, subject always to the test of reason.

In *An Essay Concerning Human Understanding* Locke accepts the compelling validity of "clear and distinct" or self-evident ideas. Among these were the natural rights that justified revolution in his political philosophy. He also anticipated the development of a system of mathematically demonstrable ethics. In contrast to Hobbes, who wanted the state to enforce uniformity of opinion, Locke wanted an exchange of ideas, which required limited religious toleration.

Locke's dedication to empiricism and his denunciation of innate ideas endeared him to many thinkers of the eighteenth-century Enlightenment. More immediately, however, he was refuted by continental rationalists, especially by the mathematician Gottfried Wilhelm von Leibniz.

Leibniz was the brilliant German mathematician who had discovered infinitesimal calculus at the same time as Newton. He upheld innate ideas and based a comprehensive metaphysical explanation of the universe upon them. Like Bruno he postulated a created universe composed of an infinite number of substances ("monads") arranged in a cosmic hierarchy or chain of being. Each monad was self-contained and totally isolated from all others, but all were directed by innate mind or spirit in harmony with the order pre-established by God (the "Monad of Monads"). Believing that harmony was the essence of the universe, Leibniz labored to negotiate a religious reunion, proposed a confederation of European states, and worked on a universal language. All of these dreams failed, but Leibniz' confidence in the power of reason to heal human schisms was reflected in the eighteenth-century Enlightenment. Reformers, however, had difficulty accepting his dictum "that this is the best of all possible worlds," which was commonly given a conservative interpretation.

## The Politics of Reason

Whether rationalist, empiricist, or a combination of both, scientific philosophers of the seventeenth century broke from the otherworldly religious creeds of the sixteenth century. So did political theorists who reacted against the general violence during the religious wars. They discredited warring creeds as a basis for political life and bequeathed a doctrine of natural law to subsequent generations. Humanists like Jean Bodin in the sixteenth and Hugo Grotius in the seventeenth century replaced theology with secular concepts of sovereignty and the common weal. They based their theories not on divine revelation but on rational natural laws. Borrowing terms from the physical sciences, English empiricists went further in putting politics on a secular utilitarian footing. Their analyses substituted the "state of nature" for the Garden of Eden and contractual relationships between the ruler and the ruled for authority by divine right. This new political philosophy was a compound of humanism and contemporary science. By the eighteenth century, terms taken from mechanics such as "balanced government" and "the balance of power" became general in Western Europe.

Political philosophers of the seventeenth century demonstrated that their new premises could be used to support revolution, confederation, or absolute states. But even those who advanced absolutism were at variance with traditional concepts.

To prevent further civil warfare of the kind he had witnessed in England and France, Thomas Hobbes prescribed a thoroughgoing absolutism. Convinced that men would never cease warring against one another in a state of nature, he proposed in his *Leviathan* of 1651 to make the state a "mortal god" with the unlimited power to. set all moral and religious values. It would be contractual, rational, and utilitarian in

origin. Once entered into, the contract between state and people was irrevocable. In international relations, however, Hobbes foresaw no contract that might curtail wars. Rather he believed that the nations were trapped in a state of nature and would carry out an insatiable struggle for power that would cease only in death.

Most advocates of divine-right monarchy received Hobbes' rationale for absolutism coldly. It was too bluntly this-worldly, materialistic, and utilitarian, leaving no grounds for asserting the divine origins of political authority. Some enlightened despots of the eighteenth century, however, aimed at Hobbes' model.

No less secular was another theorist of the English civil wars, James Harrington. A contemporary and admirer of Hobbes, Harrington was preoccupied with the distribution of property. Whereas Hobbes found the basis of the state in absolute legal power, Harrington advocated republican government under written constitutional law. He did so because he believed that an imbalance between economic and political power perverted the constitution and could cause revolution as in seventeenth-century England. His ideal commonwealth, detailed plans for which he set forth in *The Commonwealth of Oceana* of 1656, should be a government of laws, not men. Among the devices to secure this end were secret ballots, a separation of policy-making and consultative powers, and rotation in office (which he compared to the circulation of the blood). Harrington's legacy fell primarily to radical Whigs in England and to the American revolution.

Still a different concept of government based on natural law emerged in the Dutch Republic and the Empire. In rebelling against Spain in the sixteenth century, the Dutch had appealed to both natural law and chartered rights. Government in the Dutch Republic became a confederation recognizing individual and corporate rights. Johannes Althusius, a German theorist, formulated a concept of divided sovereignty in which families, communes, associations, and provinces were granted enough strength to set limits upon the power of the central government. The Dutch humanist Hugo Grotius (1583–1645) concurred that associations might limit central governments. He conceived of the state as an agreement among individual holders of rights, whose autonomous associations could coexist within it. But his concept of revolution did not go beyond the *fait accompli* represented by the Dutch Republic. Grotius' main concern, however, was with international relations, a field in which he exerted considerable influence. Reacting against the religious wars, he tried to detach politics from theology. His major work, *On the Law of War and Peace,* set down the principle that relations between sovereigns should be governed by reason and natural law; their own self-interest and preservation dictated restraint. Grotius considered natural law to be as self-evident and as self-enforcing as the axioms of geometry.

In England John Locke made natural law a revolutionary doctrine. Prior to his writing, English colonists in North America had demonstrated their ability to institute government by voluntary compact, an accomplishment that contradicted the premises of contemporary authoritarianism. In England itself Locke's radical circle worked against the Catholic Stuart absolutism of James II, and Locke wrote a justification for the Revolution of 1688. Like Hobbes, the English philosopher assumes an initial "state of nature." But to him natural man was neither fallen, as theological politics assumed, nor brutish, as Hobbes had said. Instead Locke agreed with Harrington that man possessed a certain sociability. To guarantee certain natural rights—life, liberty, and property—men in a state of nature entered a social contract. Locke could not demonstrate empirically either the existence of these rights or the formation of a contract. Nevertheless, they furnished the basis for asserting that natural rights were anterior to government.

Title page of Grotius' On the Law of War and Peace, *his book that explained the law of nature and of nations.*

Government was instituted, Locke argued, by a second contract with a ruler. Should the ruler flagrantly transgress upon individual rights, the ruled might revoke the contract, that is, revolt. In this way Locke provided a justification for overturning James II. In so doing, he shifted the emphasis of political theory from the indefeasible right of rulers to the inalienable rights of subjects.

Locke appropriated from Hobbes the ideas of a state of nature and a contractual government, but he used them to refute Hobbes' absolutism. Rather than a monolithic state, Locke advocated a balance of social and political powers. From the revolutionary thinkers of the Puritan Commonwealth he borrowed the notion of a separation and balance of executive and legislative powers, which was as prominent a part of his political theory as the right of revolution.

This idea of a "balanced government" whose primary function was the protection of property, the only natural right that Locke discussed at length, was far more congenial to the thought of the eighteenth century than his rationale for revolution. It was forgotten that he defined property as life, liberty, and the fruit of labor. His precepts of balanced government were invoked on behalf of the English constitution as a perfect balance of aristocracy, monarchy, and democracy. But his doctrines could also serve the cause of revolution, as American colonists demonstrated in 1776. In any case, whether given a conservative or revolutionary interpretation, Locke's legacy was secular rather than religious.

Natural law theorists were primarily concerned with domestic rather than international politics. They left foreign affairs in a state of nature regulated only by the doctrine of rational self-interest. Increasingly that doctrine was supplemented by the notion of a balance of power, a phrase borrowed from physics. The Peace of Utrecht (1713) deepened Western Europe's commitment to a balance of power and weakened the tradition of inheritance by divine right. Subsequent to that treaty the Western powers intervened diplomatically in other wars in order to prevent any one state from gaining hegemony.

## Rational Religion

World views based on revelation and supernatural intervention could not be reconciled with the premises of scientific philosophy and natural law politics. A collision was inevitable; whether its outcome would be endless hostility or a satisfactory compromise remained to be seen. When the contest began, traditional theology had a strong hold on intellectuals. But it could scarcely remain firm during civil and military conflicts in which religious truths were decided by the strongest battalions. Rulers and theorists reacted to this situation by making internal peace more important than confessional partisanship. Classical humanists responded by deepening their thought and expanding their influence. Men who had studied the genealogy of the ancient gods were, in effect, acquainted with comparative religion, and from the Renaissance on, some of them had formed a "deistic" point of view. Behind varying and perhaps inconsequential rituals and creeds they discovered general moral precepts. For humanists such as Jean Bodin and Hugo Grotius, these precepts, themselves imperfect manifestations of natural law, constituted real or natural religion.

Commerce and colonization also worked to undermine traditional religious creeds. Christian merchants traded with heretics wherever a profit was to be made, often even in wartime. Their societies seemed to benefit as a result. Entrepreneurs likewise defied prohibitions on "usury", the taking of exorbitant interest. Missionaries coming into contact with other religions had to broaden their points of view. The Jesuit order, formerly the shock troops of aggressive Catholic reform, publicized native customs and mores. A few of them even proposed merging Buddhism with the Roman Catholic Church. Such a suggestion obviously fell upon deaf ears in Europe, but it was indicative of one important result of European expansion. For the mercantile people who profited from increased trade, salvation was no longer a solitary goal. Now they sought secular happiness also.

Thus in many parts of Europe conditions were ripe for a redefinition of doctrines that would include humanism, a secular ethic, and the new world view of science and scientific philosophy. But this redefinition was less radical in the older commercial states, where secularization was already far advanced in practice and where a certain stability had been achieved. It was stated most uncompromisingly by intellectuals who admired these societies but whose environment was still the Old Regime. In elaborating ideas and ideals—often borrowed from the more secular, commercial societies—

these intellectuals broke more decisively with past religious traditions than the intellectuals of the Renaissance or the Reformation.

Early scientists such as Copernicus, Kepler, Galileo, Boyle, Pascal, and Newton saw no conflict between their work and their religion. Kepler, for example, was certain that proving the existence of an orderly mechanistic universe would increase the glory of God. Boyle and Newton conceived of God as the giver of laws and the imparter of motion within the divine plan of creation. Newton left this "clockwinder God" with the function of making occasional repairs. On the basis of Old Testament genealogy, he assumed with contemporary clergymen that creation had occurred about 4004 B.C. Their calculation did not differ appreciably from those of Francis Bacon or Blaise Pascal, who accepted scientific methodology in the physical realm but relied upon revelation for religious truth. Nevertheless these scientists no longer relied on theology to explain natural phenomena. And henceforth the boundaries between religion and science would not prove easy to maintain.

As new generations sought to interpret the scope of modern science they raised more and more questions about the nature of religion. Were scientific methodology and conclusions relevant to religion? Did traditional religion uphold Newton's principle that natural law is simple? Was the record of miracles that supported revelation genuine? Or could miracles occur at all in a mechanistic universe? How could the many competing claims of absolute truth, both in Europe and overseas, be reconciled? Given the limitations of human knowledge, could absolute truth be known and enforced? Would it not be discovered by reason from nature rather than from authoritarian institutions and records? Could all the ethical standards in the Holy Scriptures be considered just or even moral? Particularly in England and the Netherlands, where religious unity was lacking, attempts to answer

such questions led to the emergence of a rational religion that gradually transformed faith in revelation into faith in reason or piety.

Humanists sparked this transformation. In 1627 Hugo Grotius proposed an Erasmian Christianity based on piety rather than doctrine alone. His *Concerning the Truth of the Christian Religion* adhered to Scripture but interpreted it according to its environment at the time of its composition. An Englishman, Edward Herbert of Cherbury (1583–1648), went further in the direction of universality. Through the study of comparative religion and through introspection he set out to find the universal religious principles on which all rational men could agree. He eliminated the sacraments and the concept of God-chosenness whether of nation or the predestined "elect." His emphasis fell instead upon the worship of a Supreme Being, conscience, and piety. In the Netherlands Spinoza arrived at similar conclusions. Later in the century Pierre Bayle (1647–1706) began publishing from the Netherlands the *Historical and Critical Dictionary* in the same year that Louis XIV revoked the Edict of Nantes (1685). The *Dictionary* lashed out against superstition, intolerance, and dogmatic assertions. It appealed to the primacy of moral conscience over all Scripture that seemed to command violent behavior. At the same time Locke was reconciling faith and reason in his *Reasonableness of Christianity*. Locke defined reason as "natural revelation," which served as a check upon recorded miracles. According to him, those who had not been exposed to Christianity could learn moral law by the light of nature. In Germany Johann Semler (1725–1791) followed a similar course in biblical criticism, treating the Scriptures as historical evidence rather than literal, inspired injunctions.

All proponents of rational religion pressed in the direction of universality, minimized dogma, and emphasized morality. Few followed Hobbes and Spinoza in making faith a function of politics and the social order. Nevertheless, all rationalists had replaced revelation with reason in determining ethics. Their outlook, which led to a more explicit scientific Deism in the eighteenth century, appealed primarily to the educated upper classes, and it made a deep impression on the more open-minded clergy of several established churches. But it elicited little enthusiasm from the uneducated masses, who often joined emotional fundamentalist revolts against it.

As the new science and philosophy spread, the premises of religious rationalism became increasingly those of scientific natural law. Locke and others had set the main lines of Deistic thought, but it came more into vogue and became more secular as Newton's concepts of a mechanistic universe were popularized. By 1789 Newton's *Principia* had run through eighteen English editions, and no less than forty books describing his accomplishment had appeared in English alone. Many of these popularizations carried the conviction that Newton had banished mystery from the universe, making it entirely explainable by mathematical laws. Alexander Pope quipped,

> Nature and Nature's laws lay hid in night:
> God said, Let Newton be! and all was light.

Newtonian science provided the two principal Deistic arguments for the existence of a Supreme Being: (1) that He was necessary as the first cause of the universe, and (2) that the flawless order of that universe presupposed an intelligent creator. Since the laws of the universe were uniform and universal, the Deists rejected miracles and relegated prophecy and rites to superstition. They professed a faith in immortality primarily as a sanction for ethics, since the focus of their interest was on this world. They examined traditional Christianity for ethical utility and humanitarianism and found it seriously lacking in both. Their faith was set upon the existence of a Su-

preme Being who seldom intervened in the affairs of men but also upon man's capacity to reform.

The new humanism of the seventeenth century bequeathed to the Enlightenment of the eighteenth century a belief in the possibility of human progress. Through reason man could discover and use the laws of nature that applied to him and his society. The Supreme Being was a constitutional sovereign subject also to the laws of nature. As He assumed less responsibility for daily affairs, man assumed more. Resignation gave way to reform. Orthodoxy gave way to benevolence. Heaven gave way to posterity. Thus the progressive secularization of thought remade religion, and this has continued until the present time.

## THE ENLIGHTENMENT

In the eighteenth century the effort to popularize science and the new humanism and to use these new outlooks as a basis for improving the political and social order was known as the Enlightenment. French publicists who called themselves *philosophes* led this effort. Rapidly expanding its commerce and caught up in new sociopolitical tensions, France produced intellectuals who were receptive to the radical thought of the previous century. Disillusioned with existing institutions and outlooks, the *philosophes* were attracted to views based on Newton's science and Locke's psychology. Together with travel literature, some of which they edited, their writings helped break down European parochialism. And their works made France, whose cultural and social standards had begun to dominate the Continent under Louis XIV, the radiant center of the Enlightenment. England and the Netherlands provided few new stimuli to radical eighteenth-century thought. But Scots, Italians, Germans, and other European intellectuals, who constituted a cosmopolitan rather than a national sort of elite, joined the *philosophes* in their mission of enlightening their contemporaries and posterity with new knowledge. They even found some followers in benighted Spain.

## The Prominence of the French Philosophes

Among the publicists of the Enlightenment the most prolific were the *philosophes* of France. Writers elsewhere wrestled with the same problems, often making basic contributions, but it was such men as Montesquieu, Voltaire, Condillac, Diderot, and Condorcet who set the Enlightenment's basic tone. Unlike previous continental intellectuals, they depended for their livelihood not on patronage of church and state but on a reading public of middle classes, clergy, and aristocrats. The tastes of their public were those of the salons, where the influence of women, the requirements of urbanity and wit, and the atmosphere of pleasure-seeking and graceful behavior prevailed. Intermittently the authorities censored the works of the French *philosophes,* but the inconsistency of this censorship only sharpened demands for the forbidden books, advertised the *philosophes'* plea for intellectual freedom, and encouraged them to disguise their criticisms by means of satire and ridicule.

Many *philosophes* had both a humanist education and scientific interests. They became simplifiers and popularizers of scientific discoveries and the views based upon them. Their interests being primarily social, they proclaimed a challenging and relatively new objective, a *science of society*. They assumed that societies operated in accordance with natural laws as axiomatic and binding as the mathematical laws that governed the physical universe. They championed empiricism, but they more often used reason than research as a tool. Without becoming slavish imitators, they advocated borrowing foreign, especially English, institutions that seemed to conform to the laws of nature.

The *philosophes* assumed that these laws could help rational men improve their lot

*Voltaire expounding to friends.*

and accepted or rejected existing institutions solely on the basis of their social utility. They rejected theological sanction, vested interests, or mere historical survival as justifications for the continued existence of these institutions. Without adopting Locke's ideas of natural rights, they brought many of the institutions of their time into question when their usefulness to society could not be demonstrated. For the most part, however, they sought not their destruction but their redirection to propagate the Enlightenment's faith in human betterment.

Without being consciously revolutionary, the *philosophes* took positions squarely at odds with inherited institutions. According to them, the reform of society required that freedom of thought replace authoritarian censorship and indoctrination by the Church. They condemned the priesthood for using coercion and manipulating popular hopes and fears. They attacked clerical obscurantism as the most serious threat to social progress. They provided no blueprint, but it was clear that the French Church, made vulnerable by doctrinal warfare between Jesuits and Jansenists, would have to be remodeled. Some *philosophes* wanted its conflicting doctrines replaced by a universal natural Deism without sacraments and rites. All of this "reformism" meant that they rejected the doctrine of the depravity of man. By education, at least the upper echelons of society could be transformed. Education, a

*"Noble savages" negotiating with William Penn (Benjamin West).*

key part of the *philosophes'* program, should pass from the Church to the state and be oriented toward citizenship, science, practical arts, and modern languages.

Discredited by foreign defeats, financial crises, and internal conflicts, the French state was especially vulnerable to criticism. All of the *philosophes* denounced arbitrary government and the violation of rights of property and person. They also opposed economic regulations, clerical influences, and systems of forced labor. Their ideal enlightened ruler would legislate according to the dictates of natural law or social utility to advance the arts, the sciences, and the general welfare. Against the divine prerogatives of the monarchy and the Church, they appealed to nature and the natural goodness of man.

Along with "reason," the word "natural" became their touchstone for testing institutions. Unfortunately that word was (and still

is) used in a variety of confusing and contradictory ways. Among other things it meant (1) the ideal determined by reason, what ought to be, (2) the customary or usual, what was or was done, (3) the worldly as opposed to the supernatural, thus making miracles unnatural, and often (4) the primitive or untarnished original state of nature inhabited by the "noble savage" and reported by travel literature. Thus the repeated proposition that man should discover the laws of nature and conform to them was ambiguous. The *philosophes* believed that "nature," unmolested by arbitrary authority, would operate harmoniously as a unifying force.

Most of the *philosophes* considered "social science" an instrument of progress. Past history made some of them pessimistic; Voltaire, for example, believed that progress would always be limited. Condorcet, however, postulated perfectibility as an inexorable law of nature replacing divine Providence. In either case the golden age for man was to be found in the future rather than in revelation or in a past era of excellence. (As Fontenelle had explained earlier, moderns were really the ancients, for they had at their disposal the experience of those who had gone before them.)

The *philosophes* assumed that knowledge of nature would make men virtuous, but as another part of their program for progress, they called for sweeping humanitarian reforms. Following in the footsteps of the Quakers, they attacked slavery, torture, secret accusations, arbitrary imprisonment, cruel and unusual punishments, treatment of the insane as criminals, and the inferior status of women. Many also attacked war and militarism. Although they advocated a state in which the individual had a stake in property and civic rights, their patriotism was cultural and not based upon emotional hatred or disparagement of foreigners. As a means of curtailing warfare they relied upon enlightened self-interest working through a balance of power. Rarely did a *philosophe* think that reason should be supplemented by institutions to resolve international conflicts. They were cosmopolitans rather than internationalists.

## Montesquieu and Historical Empiricism

Rational criticism of the existing regime in France had begun during the reign of Louis XIV, but it first obtained wide currency and general significance with Montesquieu. During the aristocratic resurgence following the death of Louis XIV, Baron de Montesquieu (1689–1755) opened an era with *The Persian Letters* (1721). This satire placed caustic remarks on French government, religion, and manners in the mouth of a visiting oriental. Then, after many years of research and travel, Montesquieu published in 1748 *The Spirit of the Laws.* Here, by inductive methods, he tried to go behind the apparent diversity of governmental systems

*Montesquieu's chateau near Bordeaux.*

and find a natural law of constitutional and social structure. His sources were both ancient and contemporary. In the England of his own time he found a political freedom that contrasted with the "tyranny" of Louis XIV. That freedom, he concluded, was guaranteed by a separation of the executive, legislative, and judicial powers and by the maintenance of the hereditary nobility with a veto over legislation. Everywhere he found constitutions conditioned by climate and environment to which wise legislators were obliged to adjust specific enactments.

*The Spirit of the Laws,* although blemished with naïve associations of cause and effect and with rambling formlessness, remained a fountainhead of constitutions that embodied the principle of a separation of powers and systems of checks and balances among those powers. At the same time it served as a sharp criticism of the tyranny of monarchs ruling without the nobility and other intermediate orders of society.

In Italy Giovanni Battista Vico (1668–1744) manifested independently of Montesquieu a similar sense of history and a similar attempt to get at the "spirit" behind differing external forms of government and society. Vico traced an evolutionary cycle of intellectual and institutional development, which he considered to be universally characteristic of all societies. He saw them passing through an initial stage of savage emotion characterized by a theocratic state, an imaginative stage with aristocratic government, and a third

*Voltaire (Houdon).*

1778), the undisputed prince of *philosophe* letters—expressed the anti-aristocratic viewpoint of the middle class. A political realist who praised English constitutionalism and considered absolutism appropriate for Russia, Voltaire differed sharply from Montesquieu about what was best for France. There he championed an enlightened despotism that would curb the nobility. A promising poet who was twice imprisoned in the Bastille at a nobleman's instigation, Voltaire crossed the Channel and imbibed English philosophy, literature, science, and Deism. Returning for fifteen years to the Duchy of Lorraine on the French frontier, he popularized Newton, Locke, and the whole English social system as sharp contrasts to contemporary French thought and institutions. A star of the salons and a confidante of princes, notably Frederick the Great of Prussia, Voltaire finally settled in 1758 at Ferney, an estate on the French-Swiss frontier, where he spent most of the remainder of his life writing, supervising his estates and factories, and entertaining guests who made their pilgrimage to him. He produced a flood of plays, histories, essays, satires, letters, and deistic sermons, today filling nearly ninety volumes of collected works. His work conveyed the Enlightenment's message of free thought, common sense, and hatred of fanaticism, ignorance, persecution, and war. He took up individual cases of injustice under the aegis of his sharp and witty pen. Hostile to revolution and aloof from democratic sentiments, at least until his old age, he urged rulers to enact the *philosophes'* program of civil rights and freedoms for their citizens.

Voltaire displayed a humanitarian rage toward intolerance and inhumanity. In this vein his name is most closely linked with criticism of organized Christianity. *Écrasez l'infâme*—"crush the infamous thing" (namely intolerance)—he wrote. He held the organized church largely responsible for the ignorance, superstition, servility, and fanaticism of the masses. He deplored its role in

phase of knowledge and civilization within monarchical or republican government. Vico's evolutionary approach and his treatment of institutions as projections of a group mind made little impact on his contemporaries, but his works belie the charge of nineteenth-century romantics that the Enlightenment lacked a historical sense and that it preached purely rational abstractions. In addition to Montesquieu (who also wrote on the fall of Rome) and Vico, the Englishman Edward Gibbon and the Scotsman David Hume were avid historians; Voltaire also produced major historical works.

## Voltaire and Humanitarian Rage

Whereas Montesquieu represented the enlightened nobility, Jean François Marie Arouet—better known as Voltaire (1694–

perverting justice and supporting cruelties. Purged of its evils, however, the church could serve a useful social purpose.

As a moralist-historian Voltaire flayed the past for its follies; he also introduced Far Eastern subjects into universal history. His amateurish effort served mainly to compare Frenchmen unfavorably with the rational Chinese, but it indicated a universal point of view. Although much of Voltaire's work was clever, witty, superficial, and borrowed, his literary power carried the Enlightenment to its widest audience.

Many indignant voices carried the Enlightenment's gospel of humanitarianism, but an Italian, the Marchese Cesare di Beccaria produced one of its most cogent treatises on a common theme. His *Crimes and Punishments* of 1764, a systematic indictment of contemporary court procedures and penal codes, became a classic in enlightened criminology. He denied the efficacy of increasingly severe penal codes, torture, and unusual punishments as deterrents to crime. Criminals would be more effectively curbed, he argued, simply by punishment that was certain and limited to the offense.

## The Enlightenment's Problem of Knowledge

By denying divinely implanted innate ideas as the source of truth, the leaders of the Enlightenment proceeded to secularize thought drastically. Distrusting rationalist systems of all kinds, they followed Locke's empiricism in setting limits on human knowledge by excluding innate ideas. According to Voltaire, "Locke has set forth human reason just as an excellent anatomist explains the parts of the human body." Denis Diderot, another outstanding *philosophe*, said: "Nothing is in the intellect that was not first in the senses." But by the middle of the eighteenth century fundamental dilemmas appeared in the *philosophes'* empirical doctrine of knowledge. Locke had acknowledged the disparity between sensory data, which could be mis-

leading, and what he took to be the external reality of extension, motion, weight, and so forth. But did these Lockean categories actually conform to reality in the external world? Or were they entirely subjective forms imposed by the mind or human passions?

During the first half of the century, Locke's authority was little questioned by enlightened writers, but as early as 1709 the Anglo-Irish bishop, George Berkeley, had pushed empiricism to its logical extreme, thereby exposing the dilemmas it created. If only specific triangles were real, then there could be no true "abstract genuine idea" of triangle. On the other hand, things not perceived had no meaningful reality. "To be is to be perceived," he concluded. Berkeley opted for a complete subjective idealism. But he accepted only other minds as being real without being perceived.

David Hume, a Scottish philosopher in revolt against all rationalist systems, adhered to a thoroughgoing empiricism; he questioned all knowledge except individual sensory experience. He assigned supernatural knowledge insufficiently attested by miracles to the realm of subjective hopes and fears. At the same time he doubted the reality of cause-and-effect relationships as mental habits. Likewise he attacked self-evident propositions, rational religion based on the assumption of a universal human nature, and rational morality. No man, Hume said in effect, had ever observed a "state of nature." Hence, assumptions drawn from such an idea were unverifiable. In order to discover human nature, he urged the study of psychology, history, and anthropology. Since reason was a slave to the passions, sound human relations could not be based on it. They could rest only on an ethic of moral sentiment or on the ability to put oneself into the "shoes" of another. Hume thus divorced "reason" from "nature" and substituted an alliance between "nature" and "feeling."

French *philosophes* also had to take up the problem of knowledge in order to support their empirical position. Among them

Étienne de Condillac wrestled with it most systematically beginning in 1746 with *The Essay of the Origin of Human Knowledge* (or *Sense Perceptions*). Condillac was primarily concerned with the "natural history of the soul," the progressive development of the mind. In a famous illustration he compared this development to a statue acquiring human mental capabilities. According to Condillac, knowledge came from the senses, but it was the passions that determined their primacy and their impact on the mind. In short, with Condillac and Diderot, who also wrote on the same problem, the Enlightenment began to abandon the rationalist faith in reason's ability to command emotions and to seek to direct the passions in the direction of human happiness and social usefulness. Voltaire's "humanitarian rage" was an illustration of such use of passionate feeling.

## Diderot and the Encyclopedists

Not all the *philosophes'* work was individual; their crowning collective achievement was the seventeen-volume *Encyclopédie* published from 1751 to 1780 under the principal editorship of Denis Diderot (1713–1784). It had no less a purpose than to "bring together all the knowledge scattered over the face of the earth, to lay its general system before the men with whom we live . . . so that our children will know more, and so that they may at the same time be greater in virtue and in happiness . . . ." Its contributors included such men as Montesquieu, Turgot, Rousseau, d'Alembert, Holbach, Voltaire, and especially Diderot. In order to pass the scrutiny of the censors, the political and religious articles were orthodox, but its columns carried the Enlightenment's assault on existing institutions and values in unsuspected places. The *Encyclopédie* was much more than a philosophic compilation; it became the outstanding work popularizing the Newtonian revolution and Bacon's ideas of inductive science on the Continent. Its technical articles and plates, drawn to reproducible specifications, provided a storehouse

of skills, for technology's future social significance was not lost on Diderot and his collaborators. The *Encyclopédie* was too large, too unwieldly a work to be as effective as Voltaire's tracts. Nevertheless, as a vehicle for spreading the Enlightenment, it reinforced the activities of the salons, the Masonic lodges, an increasing number of scientific societies, newspapers, and public libraries and museums which appeared both in Europe and America.

The Encyclopedists carried faith in empiricism and in the overwhelming influence of environment to its limits. Diderot explained human conduct entirely in natural terms, and occasionally he concluded that environment determined it. On a similar basis Claude Helvétius built up a morality based upon people's aversion to pain and attraction to pleasure. His political doctrine was utilitarianism—the greatest good for the greatest number. These ideas were later expanded in England by philosophic radicals led by Jeremy Bentham. French materialism reached its culmination in the works of Baron d'Holbach (1723–1789) whose *System of Nature,* published anonymously in 1770, explained everything in terms of matter and motion and denied the existence of free will, soul, and God. In stressing the emotions as wellsprings of human behavior, these *philosophes* sought to redirect antisocial feelings into useful paths. In so doing they put natural forces above an abstract deity as a basis for morality.

## Condorcet and Progress

Although the outbreak of the French Revolution has sometimes been blamed on subversion by the *philosophes,* only the Marquis de Condorcet (1743–1794) lived through its early phases and had the opportunity to translate their thoughts into action once the monarchy had given way. Mathematician turned popular philosopher, Encyclopedist, anticlerical advocate of economic freedom, and activist for antislavery and feminism, Condorcet turned his home into a salon. His visitors included Thomas Paine, Thomas Jefferson, and Adam Smith. A constitutional monarchist at the outbreak of the Revolution, he helped pen the French constitution of 1791. As the Revolution progressed, his thought became more and more democratic. But he was eventually put in jail; he died, perhaps a suicide, during the Terror of 1794. During his last few weeks, which he spent hiding from the revolutionary authorities, he penned a celebrated work on progress, *Sketch of the Intellectual Progress of Mankind.* This selective account of the human past predicted the spread of the Enlightenment and the perfectibility of man in a world of equal states and equality of individuals. The vehicles of such progress were to be democratic revolution, technology, and accumulation of knowledge.

Condorcet's main counterpart as an advocate of progress as an inexorable law of nature was Joseph Priestley, the English chemist. Priestley, a founder of modern Unitarianism, seconded and elaborated upon Condorcet's concept of progress as a law of nature.

The idea of progress as expressed by Condorcet and Priestley has sometimes been taken as typical of the Enlightenment as a whole. Most *philosophes,* however, thought only of limited or conditional progress. Pessimistic with respect to the lower classes becoming enlightened, not a few thought that savagery was a natural state from which men could escape only temporarily. For still others, progress was a temporary, cyclical phenomena. Yet it is fair to say that a conditional faith in progress based upon the accumulation of knowledge typified the Enlightenment.

## Rousseau and the Emancipation of Passions

The idea of harnessing the emotions or passions to useful ends was shared by many writers of the Enlightenment and was brought to a climax by Jean Jacques Rousseau (1712–1778), Genevan born and self-

*Business, politics, and coffee: Lloyd's in the eighteenth century.*

educated wanderer. A plebeian misfit in the exaggerated refinement of Parisian salons. Rousseau became the prophet of revolt against the *philosophes'* rationalism and materialsm. In 1749 he bounded into fame by winning an essay contest on the question, "Has the Restoration of Sciences and Arts Tended to Corrupt or Purify Morals?" By charging that luxury and cities had corrupted man, he attacked the cherished assumption of many *philosophes* that increased knowledge automatically brought progress. In the *Discourse on Inequality* (1755) he broadened his criticism to indict the morally corrupting influence of society and rule by and for the rich, thereby questioning the existence of a natural harmony between self-interest and society. According to Rousseau, a moral revolution was the first prerequisite for progress.

Rousseau sketched the path this moral revolution should take in his *Social Contract* (1762). If existing society corrupted natural man, then government ought to be transformed into an expression of popular will. For Rousseau, only the "general will" could legitimately bind men to law and government. Therefore the *Social Contract* could be construed as a call for popular revolution against monarchical and aristocratic governments. Perfect democracy, however, could only exist in small states such as his native

Geneva. For large states such as France, he proposed a sovereign restrained from tyranny through forced submission to periodic local assemblies in each province. Rosseau's chief concern was to maintain civic spirit and curb materialistic self-interest. To this end he wanted citizens to be indoctrinated with group pride and civic religion. This proposal seemed to contradict his commitment to the individual's moral autonomy. It also conflicted with his contemporary tract on education, *Émile,* which advocated a natural spontaneous education of youth apart from artificial social contacts.

The life and writings of Rousseau abound in paradoxes, different sides of which have been adopted by the most diverse schools of politics. An unfettered individualist, he would surrender all individual rights to the state— once its authority had been made legitimate. Although contributing to a revolutionary climate that considered the *status quo* immoral, he considered revolutionary cures worse than the disease.

Rousseau's *Confessions* provides a possible key to his thought and personality. In this autobiographical sketch he portrayed at length his moods, reveries, and feelings. His ideal norm for human societies is the better but unrealized nature of Jean Jacques himself, tortured by his own shortcomings to preach social virtues. His idea that a moral revolution must precede progress gave unity to his thought. His intuitive approach, his denial of natural harmony, his refusal to equate virtue with knowledge, and his uncompromising conclusion that contemporary society and its spokesmen were corrupt made a break between him and the *philosophes* inevitable. In his declining years his belief that he was being persecuted became a mania. Nevertheless Rousseau's approach admirably suited the tastes of those who wanted governments responsive to their peoples and who sought immediate solutions to practical problems that the Enlightenment's intellectualism failed to provide. As a diverse and fertile writer, he stands as the

fountainhead of such nineteenth-century movements as the religious revival, democracy, romanticism, socialism, and especially nationalism. For the divine right of kings, he substituted the natural right of peoples. This principle called the legitimacy of all existing governments into question, but it contributed less to effective representative government than Montesquieu's constitutionalism.

Meanwhile some of Rousseau's younger contemporaries perverted his emphasis on the emancipation of the passions. The Italian adventurer and gambler, Casanova, who at one point associated with the *philosophes* in Paris, made a profession of libertinism and bragged about it in his memoirs. The Marquis de Sade, whose works became popular at the end of the century, gave a peculiar rationalization to perversion and the pursuit of personal pleasure alone; he defined virtue as inaction and argued that the strong man must be wholeheartedly evil. Yet even extremists like Casanova and Sade were not wholly out of accord with the Enlightenment's resurrection of naturalness in opposition to the doctrine of the depravity of man.

## Kant and Moral Consciousness

An admirer of Rousseau far removed from the libertinism just described was Immanuel Kant, the greatest thinker of the German Enlightenment. Kant took up the problem of knowledge by subordinating both reason and empiricism to moral consciousness. He reversed Locke's doctrine that the mind was a blank tablet on which experience writes. He posited instead an active and synthesizing mind. It was the mind, not reality itself, that provided experience with the categories of time, space, and causation. Having thus refuted rationalism, he vitiated empiricism with the argument that the senses do not penetrate beyond a shadow world of unreal phenomena. Only the moral and aesthetic self—the inner experience of moral freedom, responsibility, and beauty—could give man access to "things in themselves." Kant thus made pietistic faith and the guidance of moral sentiment drawn from Rousseau and Hume intellectually respectable. Kant's reliance upon faith reflected the "religion of the heart" of his pietistic background.* But on politics he differed from most German Pietists, who became ardent nationalists. Kant was a universalist who proposed international institutions to provide eternal peace. As a whole his thought deeply affected Protestant theology, romanticism, English democratic theory, and, by the end of the nineteenth century, German democratic socialism. His emphasis upon duty as an imperative of the moral self was also propagated as a political doctrine by the German absolute states.

## Economic Thought of the Enlightenment

In so far as it was not mercantilist or traditionalist, eighteenth-century economic thought reflected the economic and social changes taking place in the more prosperous Western countries. Like the more specialized economic theorists, the *philosophes* wanted to replace medieval property rights with concepts of private ownership. When "enlightened" economic writers spoke of property, most of them meant landed rather than commercial wealth. The *philosophes* idealized the English colonies of North America and England, where restrictions on the exchange of land had partially broken down in the sixteenth century. They assumed that if property could be exchanged freely it would naturally be dispersed among greater numbers of owners. This distribution would be facilitated by abolishing laws restricting full rights of ownership and by requiring the division of estates in inheritance. Tax reform and state guarantees of property rights were essential also. Property was central to the *philosophes'* social theory; they considered it the social counterpart to the physical law of gravitation. Property held

society together by giving men a stake in it and by involving them in its political affairs. A few successors of Rousseau devised socialist plans for distributing wealth, but most economists of the Enlightenment left its distribution to the unhindered operation of natural laws.

Eighteenth-century economic thought was directed against mercantilism no less than against older forms of property rights. Encouraged by their own economic strength and harassed by complicated regulations, entrepreneurs and landlords in England and France became critical of government paternalism. Using analogies from the physical sciences, they argued that natural economic forces, given free play, would establish their own beneficial harmony. Whereas mercantilists depended upon government supervision and national antagonisms, economists of the Enlightenment emphasized the natural harmony that would prevail when individuals and states pursued their enlightened self-interest. Governments should abandon intervention and let the self-regulating mechanism of the market, which operated according to natural laws, work for the common good.

The first "scientific" school of political economy, the Physiocrats, arose in France among the followers of François Quesnay (1694–1774), who claimed to have discovered the self-evident laws regulating the flow of money. Apart from government regulation of interest rates, the Physiocrats advocated leaving the economy to the natural laws of supply and demand and to man's enlightened self-interest (*laissez faire*). Government, which they would vest in an absolute monarchy, should guarantee the natural and limitless rights of property, security, and (economic) liberty. The Physiocrats agreed with many mercantilists that internal trade barriers were intolerable, but the bulk of their outlook was a reaction against the policies of Colbert. They denounced restrictive industrial production codes, guild regulations, protective tariffs, commercial wars,

* For Pietism, see page 87.

and the mercantilist emphasis upon industry and foreign commerce. Sympathetic to estate holders, they publicized their new agricultural techniques and accorded full rights over communal property to them. Only agriculture and extractive industries, they asserted, produced wealth; manufacturing and the professions were "sterile." As a substitute for forced peasant labor and the cumbersome tax structure of the times, they advocated a single tax on the net product of the land. This reform would have swept away many administrative cobwebs and inequalities.

Prior to the French Revolution the Physiocrats' influence was small. In 1776 Turgot, Louis XVI's reforming minister of finance, was dismissed for championing their views. In that same year, Adam Smith, who had praise as well as criticism for them, published a more comprehensive explanation of economic phenomena, *An Inquiry Concerning the Wealth of Nations.*

In this classic treatise Smith (1723–1790) shared the Physiocrats' optimistic faith in the natural harmony of the economic mechanism, provided that men recognized their true self-interests. But in contrast to the Physiocrats, Smith emphasized trade and labor, especially the division of labor, as principal sources of wealth. To government he assigned three tasks: (1) national defense, (2) the administration of justice with the purpose of protecting each member of society against oppression by any other member, and (3) the construction and maintenance of essential public utilities. Traditionally Smith's name has become more closely identified with *laissez-faire* economics than that of any other man. Yet his criticism of certain business practices on moral grounds sets him apart from many later adherents and practitioners of *laissez faire* who used this principle to justify such practices. Smith's edifice rested upon the premise that the greatest social benefits would result when each individual was allowed to pursue his own rational self-interest. Despite his moral strictures he insisted that natural economic processes need be guided only by the "invisible hand" of natural law. Although he did not break completely with the mercantilists on navigation acts and tariffs, he warned against the political dangers of high protective tariffs, and he roundly criticized monopolistic corporations, such as the East India Company, that exercised governmental powers.

Smith's advocacy of *laissez faire* was seconded by Jeremy Bentham, in whose utilitarian morality egoism (the securing of pleasure and the avoidance of pain) was the motive force behind individuals and societies. But Bentham also advocated inheritance laws and other reforms to lessen the inequality of economic relationships, as long as property was not disturbed. Other advocates of *laissez faire* such as Edmund Burke believed that traditional property rights and economic relationships were regulated by evolutionary laws of nature and God. Whatever form they took, *laissez-faire* economic theories made inroads only in Western Europe, where a prosperous middle class had risen or where landlords became restive about communal agriculture. These theories were an outstanding example of the secularization of thought.

## POPULAR RELIGIOUS REACTIONS TO SCIENCE AND REASON

As "world views"—explanations of the universe and man's place in it—rationalism, Deism, and sceptical empiricism satisfied only part of the educated classes. The conservative rationalism that upheld the social hierarchy and taught resignation to the *status quo* as "the best of all possible worlds" did penetrate the established Protestant churches. But rationalists chastened by the religious wars to decry "enthusiasm" in all forms could not hold the loyalty of those who craved a "religion of the heart," an emotional experience of conversion, and a humanitarian morality. Already in revolt against the narrow creeds of the Reformation, several emotional religious movements also spurned the new secular world views. But even though these emotional religious groups could not accommodate themselves to new natural philosophies, their doctrines, too, were less otherworldly than past creeds of salvation, and they put more emphasis upon moral precepts of human conduct They were creeds of secular "works" as well as faith.

The English civil wars of the seventeenth century spawned several new religious sects that sponsored secular reforms, but the Society of Friends—or Quakers—was at the same time the most spiritualistic and worldly among them. Rejecting a professional clergy —whom they identified as "hirelings of princes"—tithes, sacraments, and the external paraphernalia of worship, the Quakers emphasized a private faith for living that transcended the boundaries of creed, nationality, race, and social class in the same way that natural law did for scientists and secular philosophers. Although a small sect, the Quakers included an inordinate number of wealthy businessmen who devoted much time and money to the relief of poverty, unemployment, alcoholism, slavery, scandalous prison conditions, and inadequate medical facilities. In Pennsylvania the Quakers established a government that invoked the death penalty for only two offenses (treason and murder), in contrast to hundreds of capital offenses on the statute books of European states. Pennsylvania's fame as the most prosperous English colony in North America made many *philosophes* use it as an example of the benefits of humanitarianism. Only in their insistence upon nonviolence and international political organization did the Quakers deviate from the humanitarian ideal that Western men still profess to see in themselves.

In the aftermath of the Thirty Years' War another new religious sect, the German Pietists, had also begun to reject the rationalism and scholasticism of the "stone churches." Although the Pietists repudiated both science and reason, they were not wholly outside the secular currents about them. They found a moral sense within the heart that enabled men to achieve salvation. Theirs was an emotional faith of personal experience, contrition, and conversion. Conversion was expected to transform the individual's private life. Since separatist churches were illegal in the German states, the Pietists founded lay associations for worship and workhouses to serve the unemployed and impoverished. Others migrated to Pennsylvania.

Pietism formed the basis for an emotional religious revival that spread over the Protestant world during the eighteenth century. Against the mechanistic world view of Deism the Protestant revival asserted "fundamentalism,"—that is, absolute faith in the literal meaning of the Bible. The number of dogmas inherited from the Reformation was pared down to a few basic ones, but those that were retained reasserted the active intervention of divine spirit in human affairs. Unlike traditional orthodoxies that checked emotion and denied all conscience except that sworn to their own doctrines, the eighteenth-century revivalists emphasized piety and taught that salvation depended not upon predestination or sacraments but upon the individual's religious and moral rebirth. In the eighteenth century the German Pietists turned more directly against science, cosmopolitan French culture, and aristocratic social norms. Their lower-class sympathies stimulated the foundation of philanthropic institutions and schools that were designed to train the heart more than the intellect. German Pietism shared with the *philosophes* an emphasis upon individualism, but its individualism was more compatible with and merged into romanticism.*

In England and British North America, Methodism challenged the drift toward rationalism. This new revivalist sect was organized by George Whitefield and the Wesley brothers, John (1703–1791) and

* See page 185.

*Evangelism in a home: John Wesley.*

*A witchcraft trial in Massachusetts, 1692.*

Charles. Calling passionately for personal conversion, these early Methodists revived fundamental doctrines of man's utter depravity, of the Atonement, and of divine intervention. They revived Puritanism in England, particularly among the industrial workers and miners. Neglected by the established church, these urban laborers were innoculated by their religion against revolutionary doctrines of natural rights. Like the German Pietists they, too, identified themselves thoroughly with nationalism during the wars of the French Revolution. In North America the revival initiated by Whitefield and the Wesleys was redefined by Jonathan Edwards (1703–1758), a prophet of the "Great Awakening." With descriptions of hellfire and the writhing of the damned, Edwards preached an austere, anti-intellectual brand of Calvinism. Temporarily he had great success, and the revival movement followed the frontier westward.

Protestant revivalism in Europe recruited principally from those members of the middle and lower classes who were at odds with their theologically liberal but socially conservative establishments. To some extent it was, like the Enlightenment, subversive of the *status quo.* It pressed for humanitarian reforms, the extension of literacy among the lower classes, and a combination of self-help and mutual assistance. These ascetic fundamentalist movements promoted dedication to hard work and disciplined labor; they were also vehicles of religious nationalism, which was ultimately to threaten the legitimacy of princely continental states. In England their revival tactics were later to be copied by agitators who denounced agricultural tariffs (corn laws) and the unreformed House of Commons before urban audiences.

One form of protest against the secularization of thought in religious circles was a renewed belief in witchcraft, especially during the seventeenth century. In a sense this response was a desperate reassertion of the continued intervention of supernatural spirits in human affairs. Seventeenth-century Roman Catholic prelates in the Rhineland conducted extensive investigations and trials of witches. So did Calvinists in Switzerland, Scotland, and Massachusetts. In the eighteenth century, John Wesley, among others, would assert that he who disbelieves in witchcraft disbelieves in God. But the days of *religious* witchcraft proceedings in the Western world were dying out; to later, more secular Europeans educated in science, they seemed hopelessly benighted. They were an integral part of the older spiritual view of the universe which even Protestant fundamentalism could not maintain on the basis of biblical authority alone.

Within two centuries, European thought had gone far toward a secular outlook especially in assuming natural causes for natural phenomena. This was true not only for explanations of the heavens' movements but also of the human body and the organization of society. Humanists had charted this secular course, but it was the scientific revolution that gave it its major impetus. As the frontiers of the unknown were pressed back, mysterious and spiritualistic explanations receded. In this sense the scientific revolution gave birth to those outlooks that today are usually reckoned "modern." Its impact was sufficient to force even religious diehards against science and secularization to abandon some of their tenets.

The new thought of the seventeenth and eighteenth centuries deserves emphasis because of its overwhelming importance for the future. Yet it left a varied and confused legacy, no more providing a unifying ideology than the religious authoritarianism that had preceded it. Some empiricists, like Hobbes, were authoritarian, whereas others, like Locke, advocated constitutional government. There was no common standard of values. Many scientific philosophers were certain that a self-evident standard of ethics was not only possible but immediately forthcoming. But no such standard appeared, and voices like Hume's soon raised to question the validity of the quest. Moreover, as Hume foresaw, scientific "natural laws" were subject to constant revision. Metaphysical assumptions deduced from the natural sciences and applied to society could be as shifty as traditional concepts. Nevertheless, humanitarianism gained wider currency than in any

*Scene from a slave ship.*

previous period of Western history. Indifferent toward heaven and convinced that life on earth could be improved, the publicists of the Enlightenment popularized reform as a social goal. As the *philosophes* knew, this trail had been blazed before them by religious sectarians, especially the Quakers and Anabaptists; it also attracted those contemporary religious movements that rejected rational and mechanistic world views.

Although humanitarianism was professed more widely than before, secularized thought had not yet deeply penetrated European society. It remained the property of a narrow, albeit powerful, elite. Even in France the *philosophes* converted only a minority of the clergy, nobles, and literate middle classes. Literate Frenchmen apparently read more in works that reconciled traditional religious doctrines with popularized science than in the *Encyclopédie*. Dissatisfied peasants knew nothing of the *philosophes*. In Eastern and Southern Europe, the Enlightenment was hardly felt at all. In fact, most Europeans had little reason to take an optimistic view toward this world. Optimism was generally the prerogative of those who benefited from commerce or royal patronage. And even among them deep pessimism was common.

Many major social and political trends of the eighteenth century ran counter to the hopes of the Enlightenment. Although progress in commerce and technology increased the total wealth of France and England, rapid population growth aggravated poverty, vagabondage, and infanticide even in prosperous areas. The *philosophes* condemned slavery, but the slave trade had never been brisker. In order to implement their reforms, most enlightened thinkers counted upon converting monarchs who, they assumed, would have the power to carry them out. But monarchical power in eighteenth-century Europe was contested by a resurgent nobility whose interests conflicted with "enlightened despotism." Kings themselves were unreliable converts, and renewed power struggles consumed their principal energies. In short, law and persuasion—the favored means for implementing the *philosophes'* "new design for living"—gave way to revolution by the end of the eighteenth century. The fate of the *philosophes'* "search for humanity" was to be determined by foreign and domestic struggles in their own and subsequent centuries; again and again reactionaries were to attack their goals and values. In the twentieth century these conflicts were to be fought with unheard of violence as fascists mobilized traditionalists to banish the Enlightenment's influence from Western society.

## SELECTED READINGS

*Becker, Carl L., *The Heavenly City of the Eighteenth-Century Philosophers,* Yale University Press, New Haven, 1932.
   A popular series of essays propounding the dubious thesis that the *philosophes* were reconstructing medieval philosophy with more up-to-date materials.

Beer, Max, *An Inquiry into Physiocracy,* G. Allen and Unwin, London, 1939.
   An analysis of the doctrines of early *laissez-faire* economists that links them to practices of the medieval towns and exposes weaknesses in their method.

Brinton, Howard, *Friends for 300 Years, the History and Beliefs of the Society of Friends since George Fox Started the Quaker Movement,* Harper, New York, 1952.
   A brief sketch of the Quaker organization, doctrines, and social action. Chapter 8, "The Meeting and the World," is especially pertinent.

*Bronowski, J., and Mazlish, B., *The Western Intellectual Tradition from Leonardo to Hegel,* Harper, New York and Evanston, 1962.
   Brilliant intellectual history of Europe from the Renaissance to the early nineteenth century particularly sensitive to the impact of science.

*Bury, J. B. *The Idea of Progress, An Inquiry into Its Growth and Origin,* Dover Publications, New York, 1955.
   An older discussion, with some omissions, of early advocates of the idea of progress.

*Butterfield, Herbert, *The Origins of Modern Science 1300–1800,* The Free Press, New York.
   A history of the "scientific revolution" by an author who considers science the most influential force making the modern world.

*Cassirer, Ernst, *The Philosophy of the Enlightenment,* Beacon Press, Boston, 1955.
   A classic account that rehabilitates the *philosophes* as serious thinkers.

———, *The Question of Jean-Jacques Rousseau,* Columbia University Press, New York, 1954.
   A probe of Rousseau's fundamental ideas which confirms his claim that all of his works had a consistent theme; indispensable for distinguishing Rousseau from the French *philosophes.*

Cobban, Alfred, *In Search of Humanity, the Role of the Enlightenment in Modern History,* George Braziller, New York, 1960.
   A sympathetic account and an appeal for a return to the Enlightenment's humanitarian principles.

Feuer, Lewis S., *Spinoza and the Rise of Liberalism,* Beacon Press, Boston, 1958.
   One of the few detailed works in English relating seventeenth-century Dutch thought to its environment.

Gay, Peter, *The Party of Humanity, Essays in

* Asterisk (*) denotes paperback.

*the French Enlightenment,* Alfred A. Knopf, New York, 1964.

Interpretative essays rescuing the *philosophes,* especially Voltaire, from charges of frivolity and utopianism and dissociating them from the rhetoric of the revolution.

*Gierke, Otto, *Natural Law and the Theory of Society, 1500 to 1800,* Beacon Press, Boston, 1957.

A detailed exposition of early modern social and political theory by a German critic of rational natural law.

*Hall, A. R., *The Scientific Revolution 1500– 1800, The Formation of the Modern Scientific Attitude,* Beacon Press, Boston, 1954.

A narrative manual of scientific developments organized according to subject.

*Koyré, Alexandre, *From the Closed World to the Infinite Universe,* Harper, New York, 1958.

Traces the destruction of the conception of the cosmos as an earth or man centered, finite, hierarchically ordered whole by the new philosophy and science of the seventeenth century.

*Kuhn, Thomas S., *The Structure of Scientific Revolutions,* University of Chicago Press, Chicago and London, 1962.

An attempt to acquaint nonscientists with scientific methodology, particularly helpful in emphasizing the role of conceptual models in scientific advances.

*Lovejoy, Arthur O., *The Great Chain of Being, A Study of the History of an Idea,* Harper, New York, 1960.

Traces a basic assumption of classical and medieval thought through the rationalism of the seventeenth and eighteenth centuries.

Manuel, Frank E., *The Eighteenth Century Confronts the Gods,* Harvard University Press, Cambridge, 1959.

Explores explanations by the men of the Enlightenment of popular religious beliefs, especially deification of gods in the past.

More, Louis T., *Isaac Newton, a Biography,* Charles Scribner's Sons, New York and London, 1934.

Factual biography of the leading scientist of the period.

Morley, John, *Diderot and the Encyclopedists,* Macmillan Company, London, 1923.

Old account of the Encyclopedists by a Victorian Liberal who also wrote on Voltaire and Rousseau.

Pinson, Koppel S., *Pietism as a Factor in the Rise of German Nationalism,* Columbia University Press, New York, 1934.

A study of the political implications of emotional fundamentalism in the German states.

Robbins, Caroline, *The Eighteenth-Century Commonwealthman,* Harvard University Press, Cambridge, 1959.

An in-depth examination of the transmission of English radical thought from the civil wars through the eighteenth century.

*Santillana, Giorgio de, *The Crime of Galileo,* University of Chicago, 1955.

An investigation of the quarrel between the Church and Galileo, with an eye to political measures taken in the United States after World War II against outspoken scientists.

Schapiro, J. Selwyn, *Condorcet and the Rise of Liberalism,* Harcourt, Brace, New York, 1934.

Sympathetic biography of the only *philosophe* who lived to participate in the French Revolution; a study in activism.

Smith, Preserved, *The History of Modern Culture,* Volume II, *The Enlightenment,* Holt, New York, 1934.

Detailed comprehensive account that neglects the continued force of tradition.

Vyverberg, Henry, *Historical Pessimism in the French Enlightenment,* Harvard University Press, Cambridge, 1958.

A necessary corrective to the notion that unqualified optimism dominated the thought of the Enlightenment.

* Willey, Basil, *The Seventeenth-Century Background; Studies in the Thought of the Age in Relation to Poetry and Religion,* Columbia

University Press, New York, 1952, and an Anchor paperback; and

*———, *The Eighteenth-Century Background; Studies on the Idea of Nature in the Thought of the Period,* Columbia University Press, New York, 1953, and a Beacon paperback.

Lucid works based on England that show drastic changes in the meanings of the slogans "reason" and "nature" and that emphasize conservative uses of rationalism.

Wolf, A., *A History of Science, Technology and Philosophy in the Sixteenth and Seventeenth Centuries,* G. Allen and Unwin, London, 1950.

Standard detailed account useful for reference.

See also the relevant sections of the volumes by Friedrich, Nussbaum, Wolf, Roberts, and Gershoy in the Rise of Modern Europe series edited by W. L. Langer.

# III

# The Decline of Absolutism, 1720 to 1787

Monarchical absolutism came to a provisional climax in the great wars that engulfed Europe at the beginning of the eighteenth century. In their wake, these wars left financial exhaustion, disillusionment with the personal rule of warrior-kings, and a weariness with conflict that temporarily curbed the expansion of royal absolutism. Other factors helped to lengthen this momentary pause in the growth of absolute royal power in many European states. A series of succession crises weakened many of the major dynasties, and local aristocracies exploited this weakness to make renewed bids for power and to consolidate their positions. The resurgence of aristocratic opposition to central executive authority was general during this century. In themselves, war-weariness, financial exhaustion, and aristocratic aggrandizement may have been sufficient to account for a general decline of absolutism. But in Western Europe, especially, two other significant factors were operative. One of these, the erosion of the otherworldly religious ideol-

ogy of the divine right of kings, we have traced in the preceding chapter. The other was the rapid growth of commerce, which gradually created a social basis for a democratic response to the revival of the aristocracy late in the century.

Succession crises were a perennial source of weakness in the institution of hereditary monarchy, but the early eighteenth century produced so many of them that they had a cumulative and general impact. The Hanoverians of Britain, represented in the person of George I, were a new dynasty whose succession was tenuous even after the failure of a Stuart counterrevolution in 1715. Until he begat an heir, undisputed succession in France hinged on the precarious health of young Louis XV. Charles VI of Austria had only a daughter to succeed him to thrones that law customarily reserved for males. And in Russia after the death of Peter I in 1725, rather than strict succession, intrigues at court and among the palace guards made and unmade rulers. Their domestic insecurity made these weak dynasts reluctant to go to war; they much preferred the tedium of diplomacy to armed conflict, which could produce unlooked-for and unwanted results at home. In domestic affairs, continental rulers still claimed absolute authority, and they retained a formidable arsenal of arbitrary powers, but they were unable to check a slow aggrandizement by the aristocracy.

The aristocratic character of society gave this segment of the eighteenth century a distinctive stability and an aura of fine living. Mediating between sovereigns or central governments and commoners, the aristocracy served to give society a certain balance; but in its claims to autonomous privileges and in its virtual monopoly of social power, it was as absolute as any king. In France immediately after 1715, titled peers tried and failed to replace Louis XIV's central government with a series of aristocratic executive councils, called collectively the Polysynodie; but ennobled officials and magistrates succeeded where they failed. Local affairs in Central, Eastern, and Southern Europe were firmly in the hands of nobles and gentry. In the Dutch Republic, the German Imperial Cities, and Italian city-states, "Venetian oligarchies" consisting of urban patricians even more exclusive than the aristocracies of monarchical states, filled offices and judicial benches. Even in commercialized England, Parliament was filled almost exclusively by landed gentry. These local privileged oligarchies were not easily dislodged. Following the outbreak of general war again after 1740, "enlightened despots" of the continental monarchies attempted with some success to re-assert absolute executive powers. But their aristocracies were so firmly entrenched that they were able to block or dilute much enlightened reform and, while their despots were preoccupied with making war, sometimes exacted further concessions from them.

For Western Europe this period of declining absolutism was an age of empire and trade as well as of aristocratic dominance.

Trade expanded more rapidly than during any previous commercial revolution. Among the colonial products that formed the major sources of new wealth were sugar, slaves, tobacco, dyestuffs, tea, coffee, and precious metals. In both Britain and France great commercial companies gained such wealth and influence after the War of Spanish Succession that they attempted to take over and manage the inflated debts of their respective states. Both experiments ended in "bubbles," or financial panics, but solid commerical gains continued unabated. England united with Scotland in 1707 to become Britain and emerged as the greatest colonial and imperial power, but she was not the only beneficiary of the expanding commercial sector of the European economy. France, whose foreign trade expanded nearly fivefold during this period, entered more positively into the ranks of the maritime states. Others—notably the Austrian Habsburgs, the Prussian Hohenzollerns, and the Bourbons of Spain —also sought to harness commercial profits to their power. Spain still held a large empire, but the dynamic rivals for an overseas empire were Britain and France. After 1740 their imperial conflicts again merged with the dynastic struggles of the Continent.

The vast colonial and commercial expansion of this century had profound consequences for the European world. It enlarged the boundaries of an Atlantic civilization whose distinctive features set it increasingly apart from older European societies; in many cases its water routes of communication brought its parts closer together than adjacent continental points that were dependent upon expensive and difficult overland transportation; commercialization created new problems and strains on the domestic institutions of the mother countries and on the mercantilist ties between them and their colonies. Britain's commercial and industrial cities became centers of agitation for radical reform. In France conflicts between aristocrats and the monarch were complicated by the growing ranks of the economically influential commercial bourgeoisie. Those whose profits and livelihood were tied up with commerce became restive with old institutions and policies that were no longer appropriate to their needs. This was even more true among the British colonists of North America. On the outer fringes of Western civilization, they took advantage of imperial rivalries to forge a revolutionary challenge to both oligarchy and absolutism. Their example proved contagious. Still it was France—where renewed power struggles caused deepening financial difficulties—and not the American Colonies, which became the wellspring of European revolutions in the generations after 1789.

## THE COMPETITIVE STATE SYSTEM, AROUND 1720 TO 1740

After Louis XIV failed to create a personal European empire, negotiators at Utrecht restored the balance of power. Ignoring a plan for a federation of states, the major powers agreed instead to consult regularly in diplomatic congresses. This machinery for the peaceful settlement of international disputes was stillborn, however. It failed to replace the competitive system in which each state pursued its own interests individually or collectively. On the other hand, in the years following Utrecht, several major powers did work in a concert based on alliances to preserve the general peace.

That peace and concert, which successfully prevented general war until 1740, rested on a minor diplomatic revolution, an alliance between recent foes, Britain and France. An understanding between these two powers, each of which had been of pivotal importance in their earlier hostile alliances, was considered a sure guarantee of general peace. The architect of the alliance was Lord Stanhope, a belligerent Whig soldier who involved Britain everywhere in continental affairs. The agreement secured both dynasties which were momentarily weak, and Stanhope extended the alliance to include

other major powers. In combination with the Dutch, who joined the alliance in 1717, Britain and France cooperated to frustrate an invasion of Habsburg Italy by Spain in violation of the terms of Utrecht. The aim of the Spanish court was to secure a throne for Don Carlos, the infant son of Philip V. Reacting against this invasion and desperate to secure the consent of other powers to the eventual succession of his daughter to the throne, Charles VI took Austria into the alliance in 1718. In 1720 the allies thrust Spain out of Italy, except that Don Carlos did receive rights to succeed in Parma, Piacenza, and Florence. Spain was then more or less forced to join the allied powers. Meanwhile they intervened to bring an end in 1721 to a potentially dangerous war between Sweden and Russia in the Baltic, which at one point had threatened to involve many other states.

The concert now had five members. But by 1725 it had virtually collapsed. Spain, still harboring designs on Italy, withdrew in that year and now sought to accomplish her goals by a diplomatic alliance with Austria herself. In addition to her annoyance with the maritime powers because of their opposition to her Italian plans, Spain was resentful of the British occupation of Gibraltar and bitter over both British and French smuggling in Spanish America. Charles VI of Austria, for his part, was increasingly unhappy with his dependence on the Maritime Powers for subsidies, and was eager to share in the immense profits of overseas commerce. He irritated France, which had a virtual monopoly on the Mediterranean trade with the Levant, by developing Trieste for trade with the Levant and alarmed both England and the Dutch Republic by chartering a new commercial company, the Ostend Company, to trade with the Far East from the Austrian Netherlands. Spain protected the company's ships, but the Dutch preyed on them at every opportunity. The Austro-Spanish alliance, combined with an Austro-Russian accord of 1726, led to the formation

*British press gang at work.*

of a rival league, including Britain, France, Sweden, and Denmark, and by 1727 war clouds once again spread over Europe. War was desired by no one, however, and lengthy negotiations finally led to a peaceful solution in 1731. Charles abandoned the Ostend Company and his alliance with Spain, and the Maritime Powers in return recognized Maria Theresa as his heir. Reluctantly and temporarily Spain recognized Britain's treaty rights to trade in Spanish America and gave up hopes of recovering Gibraltar. Thus the Mediterranean problem, one of the great threats to peace of the post-Utrecht period, appeared to have been resolved.

Events in Poland, however, soon disrupted this fragile settlement. In 1733 Augustus the Strong, the ambitious dynast who ruled both Saxony and Poland, died. The Polish throne was an elective one, and the death of a king invariably invited the interference of foreign powers—Austria, Sweden, Russia, and, lately, also France—who sought to bribe the Polish electors to choose for the throne a man favorable to their own interests. In this case, reacting against Austrian and Russian intervention, the Polish nobles selected not the Austro-Russian candidate, Augustus' son, but the French candidate, Stanislas Leszczynski, father-in-law of Louis XV. The French had only a navy to assist the installation of their man; the Russians

used troops to put their candidate, Augustus III, on the throne, and this they did without great difficulty. Nominally, this row caused the so-called War of Polish Succession (1733–1736), but it was not fought over Poland or by Poles. Rather, it was a dreary war of maneuver, involving old grievances as well as new, in which France and Spain fought Austria, which had some Russian support, in northern Italy and along the Rhine. France conquered Lorraine from Austria, and Stanislas, forced to abdicate from the Polish throne, was made Duke of Lorraine. In a comic opera of diplomacy the previous Duke of Lorraine was transferred to Tuscany, whose own graud duke had conveniently just died without heirs. Lorraine was to revert to French control upon the death of Stanislas. Don Carlos of Spain surrendered his northern Italian duchies to become ruler of the new Bourbon Kingdom of the Two Sicilies. After this settlement the period of relative stability in European international affairs was succeeded by an era of general wars. But this stability had undergirded a generation of reconstruction, which laid the foundations of aristocratic dominance until the eighteenth century.

## THE POLITICS OF OLIGARCHY AND STABILITY, 1720 TO 1740

Against efficient absolute monarchs, aristocrats reacted by reasserting claims to positions of enhanced honor and power. Many of the aristocrats involved in this movement were not of the old feudal nobility, who could trace their titles to past centuries. Rather, the bulk of them were office holders, magistrates, and councillors whose aristocratic lineage was recent and, in many cases, purchased. In (kingless) republics, self-perpetuating "constituted bodies" staffed by the same families from one generation to the next were no less common than in the monarchies. Since titles and offices were not subject to purchase, republican oligarchies were often more closed to new blood and the influence of new riches than were the monarchies that practiced venality (the sale of offices). In both republics and monarchies, however, these aristocratic bureaucracies claimed considerable power over their subjects; theirs was an inherited right to rule. Usually they traced their authority back to medieval origins. Drawing incomes from manorial revenues, loans to the state, and the emoluments of public office, these oligarchies were the backbone of a "cult of stability" in domestic affairs.

This cult predominated in a world half modern, half medieval, and the interests of both central governments and commoners were sacrificed to it. Entrenched bureaucratic power led such men as Voltaire in France and John Adams in America to conclude that a strong executive was necessary to defend the interests of the many against the few. Later in the century such power was the target of both enlightened despots and democratic revolutionaries.

## France

In calling no Estates General, in curbing the provincial estates, and in restricting the *parlements,* Louis XIV had trampled upon the institutions and prerogatives of the older aristocracy. Titled peers led the first counter-revolt against his government after his death in 1715. Louis XV's regent, the Duke of Orleans, fearful of his own shaky position, permitted them to dominate the government from 1715 to 1718 through their ascendancy in a series of central councils called the Polysynodie. Lacking technical competence, however, they became bogged down in ceremonial trivia and jurisdictional disputes, which finally put an end to this experiment. Leadership of the aristocracy then passed to educated nobles of the robe, especially the jurists of the *parlements,* most of whose old powers were now restored. So alarmed was the regent by their power that he contemplated abolishing all hereditary privileges. Instead, however, he turned to the expedi-

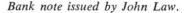

*Bank note issued by John Law.*

ency of centralizing financial power in accordance with a plan submitted to him by John Law, a Scottish gambler, adventurer, and financier of unusual talents. Law's scheme had the double merit of promising to cope with both war debts and problems of power.

On no matter had the aristocracy floundered worse than in handling the king's debts. Accounts were chaotic, and there was no budget. Speculators had bought government annuities on terms exceedingly disadvantageous to the crown. Repudiation of debts was the only solution that most of the nobility could suggest, and that, of course, would ruin credit in the future. France had no centralized financial institution comparable to the Bank of England, which had been eminently successful during the past war. After memorializing several European governments without success, Law gained the Regent's favor and established a central, note-issuing bank in France in 1716. Then he founded the Company of the West (Mississippi Company) to trade with Louisiana. Soon it absorbed all other French chartered companies, gaining a monopoly of French colonial trade. Law had promised the Regent that he would extinguish the royal debt. The company now exchanged its shares for certificates of debt, which it planned to pay off through trading profits and by acquiring a monopoly on the collection of internal indirect taxes.

The scheme was not a total failure. Law's

*Contemporary satire of the Mississippi Bubble in which Folly and Chance run down True Commerce.*

bank notes stimulated trade as promised. But the purchase of shares in the Company became a speculative mania, in which the price of shares skyrocketed to many times their real worth. In 1720 the "Mississippi Bubble" broke, taking many investors from paper riches to rags. In the disillusionment which followed, the Parlement of Paris canceled Law's charters. Only his original trading company survived and continued to prosper. The Regent was convinced that Law's downfall was the work of rival financiers, but the unfortunate Scot was driven from the country nonetheless. Not until after the Revolution of 1789 did the French people overcome prejudices, which the Mississippi Bubble had ingrained more deeply, against central banking, bank notes, and even joint stock ventures. Nor were the government accounts in any better order as a result of Law's scheme.

Unlike Louis XIV, the new French monarch had no taste for affairs of state. After he came of age in 1726, Louis XV turned them over to the seventy-two-year-old Cardinal Fleury. A cautious administrator who avoided offending vested interests, Fleury worked for retrenchment and recovery. He stabilized the coinage, provided security for highways, and built better roads than England's. Tax farming was not abolished, but the Cardinal kept taxes down by avoiding the expenses of war. Fleury worked for stability at home and abroad, but his policies

did not check the growing power of the nobility of the robe, whose obstructionism eventually crippled the central government and made "French absolutism" a misnomer.

Nobles of the robe, who now filled numerous judicial and other official positions in the monarchy, had been considered a part of the bourgeoisie a century before. After 1715 their ascent was indicated by their social merger with the older nobility. Better educated and organized, they proved to be better defenders of aristocratic interests than the older nobles, whose tastes, views, and interests they gradually acquired. They bought up legal jurisdictions, manors, state loans, and profitable survivals of the manorial system. Rigorous collectors of these obligations, they became an integral part of the "feudal reaction" that began to exacerbate relations between landlords and peasants around midcentury. In their religion, they supported Jansenism, a puritanical Catholicism which opposed papal centralism, the Jesuits, and a state-directed church. Supported by the *parlements* against the central government, the Jansenists engaged in doctrinal brawls with the Jesuits that discredited the French Church and made it vulnerable to attacks by the *philosophes* of the Enlightenment. By portraying themselves as defenders of liberty against arbitrary government, these nobles, who constituted the membership of the *parlements,* also discredited the monarchy. But at the same time, they blocked reforms. More than any other group, the nobles of the robe protected the provincial and social privileges that made France's nominal absolutism a contradiction in terms. But prior to 1789 their refurbished feudalism could offer no substitute for it.

In a distinctly separate compartment of French life, but coincident with the aristocratic resurgence, was the development of an overseas empire and colonial trade. In Martinique, Guadeloupe, and Santo Domingo, French planters had the most productive sugar islands of the West Indies. French traders vied with English companies

*Cardinal Fleury.*

for illicit trade with the Spanish empire. They encroached upon the decrepit Portuguese empire in India and increasingly came into hostile contact with the English East India Company. Marseilles was a prosperous port for trade with the Levant, which French merchants made virtually their own. As a result of the War of Spanish Succession, France had lost part of North America to Britain. French efforts to build a self-sustaining society in Canada and Louisiana failed, but merchants traded with the Indians and returned a profitable supply of furs. French commerce thrived during the first half of the century, but it affected a lesser proportion of the population than was the case in England.

## Britain

It has been said that eighteenth-century England was a federation of country houses, the ancestral seats of the gentry who, as in the past, filled most of the offices and the benches of the House of Commons. Titled nobles were few in number and lacked privileges that continental nobles enjoyed, such as tax exemption.* Among the governing classes, social class lines were not tightly drawn, but coteries of families, knit together by intermarriage and personal acquaintanceship, formed the basic units of political life. Within the aristocracy, Whigs and Tories—and factional subdivisions of each—contended for positions of power and prestige.

In addition to being a constitutional kingdom dominated by the gentry, England was fast displacing the Dutch Republic as Europe's principal entrepôt of colonial trade. Merchants as well as "improving landlords" had social respectability and influence. Younger sons of the aristocracy entered trade and married heiresses of mercantile fortunes. Thus the aristocracy was attentive to trade and harkened to publicists such as Daniel Defoe, who attributed England's manifest wealth to commerce.

. . . Trade is the Wealth of the World [Defoe wrote]; Trade makes the Difference as to Rich and Poor, between one Nation and another; Trade nourishes Industry, Industry begets Trade; Trade dispenses the natural Wealth of the World, and Trade raises new Species of Wealth, which Nature knew nothing of; Trade has two Daughters, whose fruitful Progeny in Arts may be said to employ Mankind; namely

MANUFACTURE
and
NAVIGATION.[1]

With respect to both commerce and industry, Defoe was not wide of the mark. Better balanced and protected than French commerce, British overseas trade increased rapidly during the century. The growth of western ports such as Liverpool, Bristol, and Glasgow reflected this expansion and Britain's strategic advantage over both the Dutch Republic and France. In North America, Britain had a unique series of moderately

---

* The nearest parallel to the continental nobility were the English lords who exploited Ireland.

1. Quoted by J. H. Plumb, *England in the Eighteenth Century* (Penguin Books, Baltimore, 1950), p. 21.

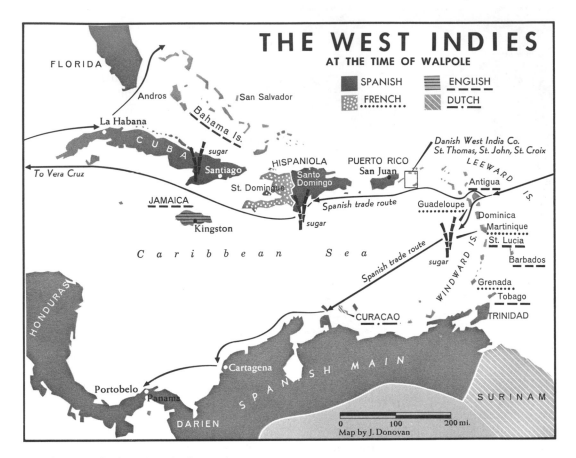

THE WEST INDIES
AT THE TIME OF WALPOLE

SPANISH    ENGLISH
FRENCH    DUTCH

Map by J. Donovan

populous agricultural colonies. They supplied raw materials and markets, but they did not fit well into the mercantilists' mold. Their lines of commerce gravitated more naturally toward the French and Spanish West Indies and to other parts of Europe than to Britain. More congenial to British strategic interests, as mercantilists saw them, were Jamaica and the Barbados, producers of sugar, tobacco, and dyestuffs. The half century following the Peace of Utrecht was also prosperous for the English East India Company. It vied with the French for primacy in the former Portuguese mercantile empire in India and southeast Asia. A similar rivalry was taking place in the Mediterranean and in the Levant, where Dutch and Italian markets and influence were giving way to French and English merchants. Naval bases such as Gibraltar secured this trade against Spaniards and Barbary pirates. Technological advances helped British traders undersell their competitors in all areas. Cheap coal, which early steam pumping engines helped to obtain, was one such factor. Also, by 1750 British craftsmen had overtaken the Dutch in the art of finishing cloth and could produce calicos that equaled the native Indian cotton product. In other words, the technological advances that would later blossom into the "industrial revolution" were already working to enhance Britain's strategic advantages by the middle of the eighteenth century.*

By 1720 Britain had accumulated large reserves of capital from commerce. This relative abundance of investment funds

* Industrialization is discussed in greater detail in Chapter VI.

brought interest rates down* and provided money for the improvement of other sectors of the economy, notably agriculture and industry. To channel and direct the flow of that capital, Britain also had a major financial institution, the Bank of England. It handled exchange, issued notes, and floated the public debt. In the last role it funneled private savings to public use and tied the moneyed classes to the existing system of government. Their representation in Parliament gave assurance that the debt would not be repudiated, that it would be considered a national, not just a royal, obligation. Even though the interest rate declined from 5 per cent to 3 per cent from 1717 to 1749, the debt rose from about £1 million when the bank was chartered to about £80 million by the middle of the eighteenth century. Its certificates were readily taken up as gilt-edged securities. But despite the Bank's effective mobilization of capital for the War of Spanish Succession, its facilities were partially bypassed in 1720 by political leaders confronted with the difficulties of paying for the war.

It was these scandal-ridden difficulties that brought the fall of the radical Whig, Stanhope, and the rise of Robert Walpole, who stood for stability and peace. Stanhope's aggressive foreign policy alienated Walpole and other Whigs. He was defeated in Parliament when he tried to liberalize government policy by removing civic disabilities from Dissenters and to strip the crown of its power to create new peers.† Then came the discrediting events of the "South Sea Bubble," an episode that paralleled the Mississippi Bubble in France and led to a reshuffling of the Whig ministry.

Walpole had established a sinking fund to retire part of the debt at reduced rates of interest. Its bonds became prized securities among investors. But in 1720 directors of the South Sea Company obtained authority to take over other parts of the debt, exchanging its stock for bonds. Walpole opposed the scheme, but the directors liberally plied leading politicians and the king's mistresses with stock. The company got its way, and a mania of speculation in its shares followed. In 1720 the "Bubble" broke into a financial panic. No general depression of commerce occurred, but Parliament reacted by restricting the incorporation of banks, a measure that eventually became a serious obstacle to Britain's industrial expansion. Uncompromised by the scandal, Walpole served as a "screen" to save the dynasty and drove the implicated Whigs from office.

A landed gentleman who had married into a family trading in Baltic timber, Walpole was a representative of the cult of stability, not of Stanhope's radical Whiggery. "I am no Saint," he wrote, "no Spartan, no Reformer." He considered the nobility an indispensable element of any free government. Preferring to "let sleeping dogs lie," he cautiously avoided offending any great interest except those who pressed for war. To merchant entrepreneurs he gave a free hand by forbidding labor to organize. Toward the North American Colonists his policy was "salutary neglect." Parliament regulated trade, but the "prime minister" (as Walpole was called by his opponents, much to his own discomfort) neglected to enforce a tariff on foreign molasses imposed on the Colonies by Parliament in 1733. His reluctance to offend great interests became even clearer the same year when he abandoned a bill to extend excise duties to colonial products sold in England. Intended to relieve tax rates on land, the Excise Bill evoked a storm of protest in London. Led by Lord Bolingbroke's popular press, opponents of the tax depicted it as a step toward tyranny, a monster that would enable officials to ride roughshod over common people. Threatened with insurrec-

---

* Large supplies of capital had had a similar effect in the Dutch Republic, it will be recalled, in the seventeenth century.

† That power had been used to push through Parliament ratification of the Peace of Utrecht, which Stanhope considered a betrayal of British victory.

*Cabinet session at the time of Walpole.*

*Master of patronage: the Duke of Newcastle.*

tion in London, Walpole retreated and withdrew the proposed taxes.

But Walpole's reluctance to confront great opposition must not be misunderstood: he dominated British politics more thoroughly than any previous minister. He is often considered Britain's first prime minister working with a cabinet. Following the scandal of the Bubble, he joined the inner circle of the Privy Council, the precursor of England's modern cabinet. This early committee of ministers was responsible to both Parliament and the king. Meetings were informal, often at dinner, and no records were kept. One man, Walpole, acted to secure the king's assent to measures they agreed upon collectively. For this purpose he found George I's favorite mistress and George II's queen, Caroline, most useful. His power over England's political machine, however, was not along the lines of cabinet government that developed during the nineteenth century. Instead, it rested upon the Duke of Newcastle's control over patronage, that is, the power to make appointments, influence the letting of contracts, and so on.

The powerful but colorless Newcastle made loyalty to Walpole an unconditional qualification for appointments to offices of church and state. Through his patronage, he controlled Parliament. Bishops in the House of Lords and Scottish M.P.s were absolutely under his command. Indirectly, so was a majority of other members, for, apart from dispersal of offices, Newcastle controlled nominations for Parliament from the counties. After 1733 Walpole became increasingly unpopular, but as long as Newcastle and George II supported him, he continued to hold power.

In tying his policies to powerful vested interests, Walpole failed to respond to new problems brought by social changes. At the top, British society was remarkably stable and uniform. At the bottom of the social pyramid riots, looting, vagabondage, unpaid debts, drunkenness, and ever-present death and crime were festering. Officials responded

*"Polling at an Election" by William Hogarth.*

*The state of the urban poor: "Beer Street and Gin Lane" by William Hogarth.*

with penalties more and more severe. They filled prisons and constantly employed the gallows, but they failed to get at the roots of poverty and unrest. Politically, however, the lower segments of society were inarticulate and impotent. Walpole's downfall came from quarters quite different and more powerful.

His foremost critic had been Lord Bolingbroke, a Tory who had joined the Stuart pretender abroad for a time after 1715. Bolingbroke's London press had raked the "prime minister" for corruption and a lack of patriotism. During the War of Polish Succession, his line of attack gained other powerful supporters. British merchants engaged in wholesale smuggling in Spanish America condemned enforcement of the Spanish customs regulations as aggression against British honor. Walpole took the accurate but unpopular view that boarding English vessels for customs inspection was within Spain's treaty rights. Much of the public debate focused on an atrocity, the story of Captain Jenkins who had lost an ear during a boarding, an ear whose desiccated remains he carried about in a box. Agitators for war with Spain seized upon his plight, and the

war which followed was popularly known as the War of Jenkins' Ear. As France supported Spain in trying to limit British trade in her colonies, other powerful English leaders turned against Walpole's pacific stance. William Pitt the elder joined the chorus for war. He portrayed French prosperity and prestige as the cause of British poverty. When Newcastle and George II also came out for war, Walpole was forced to change his policy. War was officially declared in 1739 and soon became general. Forced to fight against his will, Walpole resigned in 1742.

## The Prevalence of Aristocratic Stabilization

France and Britain furnish only two examples, albeit major ones, of stabilization under aristocratic oligarchies between 1720 and 1740. Nearly everywhere else in eighteenth-century Europe, a similar aristocratic consolidation was also taking place.

The most dramatic shift from absolutism to aristocracy occurred in Sweden. Exhausted by Charles XII's catastrophic aggressiveness, Swedes looked back upon his reign as a national disaster that had lost an empire, and they imposed a restrictive constitution on the monarchy in 1720. Nobles used the occasion of royal disrepute to lay claims to all offices and to oppress the peasantry. Their "era of liberty" (during which they divided into factions that catered to foreign bribes) lasted until a royal counter-revolution in 1772. When that royal *coup d'état* occurred, it had the support of burghers, peasantry, and clergy.

Poland set the pace of aristocratic resurgence among the nobles of Eastern and Central Europe. There the nobility assembled in provincial diets and a national diet (*Sjem*) representing them. The government was essentially a republic of serf-owning lords, where a single vote in the *Sjem* was sufficient to veto any piece of legislation (the *liberum veto*). Too jealous of executive authority to entrust taxes, an army, or even a bureaucracy to their elected king, in practice the lords were ungovernable. Although Poland was in anarchy and little respected as a state, her nobles were the idols of aristocrats of other states.

On the heels of Peter the Great's autocracy, Russian nobles secured the succession of women rulers whom they hoped to control. Reaction to autocracy went so far that in 1726 Prince Golitsyn, who had read John Locke, led a movement aimed at restricting the Tsarina, in the same way that the English Whigs had limited the authority of William and Mary after 1688. But in his country this attempt was not much understood or supported, and a counterrevolt by Empress Anne (1730–1740) took advantage of the nobles' divisions to assure her own succession. Nevertheless, she was obliged to exempt the privileged nobility from compulsory service to the state.

In Habsburg lands, the Polish example attracted the dissident nobility. Hungarian officials drawn from the gentry and titled families refused to bow to Habsburg officials from Vienna. Great serf-owning landholders of Hungary, Bohemia, and the German Habsburg duchies monopolized power in local diets. Charles VI brought many of them to court to serve as imperial officials. But by winning over a part of the great nobles he secured neither cooperation from the provincial aristocracy nor harmony among the great noble officials. Because it signified that the dynasty's prerogatives took precedence over provincial constitutions, his greatest domestic achievement was to obtain the diets' acceptance of Maria Theresa as his heir. In this he succeeded, but while factions wrangled at court, the power of the Austrian state waned.

To a degree, Bourbon Spain under Philip V was an exception to the general decentralization of authority seen elsewhere in Europe. Slowly and patiently the new king revamped the administration, setting up provincial administrative organs, the intendancies, on the model of France. But for the most part, the condition for maintaining his theoretical absolutism was to refrain from exercising it. Philip greatly enlarged the number of grandees and titled noblemen. They lived from revenues collected by bailiffs who exploited one of the most impoverished peasant populations in Europe. In Spain, an oligarchical balance between clerical and noble lords was not so much a novelty as it was the conservation of the immediate past.

## Prussia: An Exception

While one continental autocracy after another lurched in the direction of inefficient oligarchy or in some cases even aristocratic anarchy, Prussian absolutism under Frederick William I reached its prime.* Like previous great absolutists, the Elector-King continued to compensate the aristocracy with economic and social favors while using talented commoners as his highest advisors and administrators. Frederick William was never able to alleviate all rivalry between

---

* For his consolidation of power immediately after the Great Northern War, see pages 27–28.

these administrators and the local Junker dominated governments, but he mobilized Prussia's meager human and material resources to build a "Sparta of the North." His state served as the headquarters and magazine for Central Europe's largest army, but after the Great Northern War that ended in 1721, it fought no battles under his rule.

Although the Elector-King held his growing military power in reserve, its very existence tipped the balance of power in Prussia's favor. Realizing this, his successor, Frederick II, determined to exploit the advantage for the immediate seizure of Silesia, because as he assessed Europe's power relationships, he thought he could carry it off with impunity.

## THE RENEWED STRUGGLE FOR POWER, 1740 TO 1763

### The War of Austrian Succession

In 1740 occurred the event toward which Charles VI had aimed his reign—his death. As Maria Theresa ascended the thrones of the Habsburg inheritance, a peaceful succession seemed assured. All the major European powers and the Habsburg diets themselves had given advance approval of Charles' Pragmatic Sanction that enabled a woman to rule all except the Holy Roman Empire. But this assurance and Europe's short respite from armed power politics was destroyed by Frederick II. Laying specious dynastic claim to Silesia, he suddenly set the Continent ablaze by wresting that province from the young Habsburg princess. By 1741 France, Bavaria, Spain, Prussia, and Saxony had agreed to partition the Habsburg empire, leaving Maria Theresa only her eastern Austrian and Hungarian provinces. Meanwhile the war for overseas trade and empire, which Britain initiated in 1739 with the War of Jenkins' Ear, merged with the continental dynastic struggle. There followed a series of wars lasting until 1748, collectively known as the War of Austrian Succession.

Led by Louis XV and tradition-minded noblemen, France undertook to lead the coalition against Austria. It appeared to be irresistible, but Maria Theresa proved to be resourceful in defending her patrimony, and the allies were racked by mutual jealousies. To avert French hegemony and to avoid sharing the spoils of war, Frederick II repeatedly deserted his allies. Though tied by a Bourbon family compact, France and Spain could not agree on a common policy for the conquest of Italy. France's preoccupation with war on the Continent diverted her resources from fighting her real enemy, Britain. The French court sought to win overall victory on land, making gains on the Continent that could be exchanged for imperial territories at the peace table. This strategy worked as French armies conquered most of the Austrian Netherlands, which Britain tried vainly to defend in 1745. But Britain gained victories in the Colonies and on the seas that canceled French gains in Europe. American Colonists and the British fleet took Louisburg, the fortress that commanded the mouth of the St. Lawrence River, the indispensable gateway to French Canada. Thus both sides waged an exhausting war without gaining a clear-cut victory.

In 1748 financial exhaustion, or fear of it, brought both the dynastic and imperial conflicts to an end in the Peace of Aix-la-Chapelle. This peace restored boundaries as they were before the war except that Frederick II retained Silesia. It did nothing to assuage the imperial antagonisms between Britain and France, nor did it reduce Maria Theresa's resolve to retake Silesia at the first favorable moment. For these reasons, Aix-la-Chapelle endured only as a truce, not as a lasting pacification.

### The Seven Years' War, 1756 to 1763

Hostilities first began again in the race for overseas empire. In both Britain and France, publicists ascribed prosperity to the rapid increase in colonial trade. The port cities and planters of both kingdoms displayed the

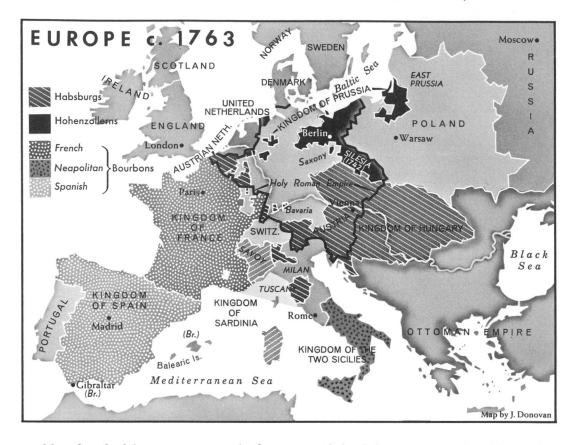

EUROPE c. 1763

Map by J. Donovan

wealth of colonial commerce; and they echoed the conviction that greater wealth and security were to be had by eliminating the competition represented by the other. The Anglo-French conflict now encircled the globe; it focused on West Indian plantations, slave-shipping stations in Africa, trading "factories" in India, and control of the North American continent. The plantations produced a cash crop of great economic importance—sugar. They imported foodstuffs, clothing, and, because the life-expectancy of slaves was short, an ever-increasing amount of "black gold." In India conflict grew out of expansionist policies by rival East India companies. When the French company's profits lagged, Dupleix, its director, subdued the native states of the Deccan and subjected them to taxes and tributes. Officials of the English company backed rival native rulers, thus precipitating warfare between native protégés of the two companies. Abandoning strictly commercial objectives for the assumption of political authority, the two companies were locked in a war for the domination of India. This occurred while their European governments were officially at peace; but in 1756 their colonial war merged with the Seven Years' War.

Hostilities broke out in North America two years before the main war began in Europe, and, unlike India, they involved government troops of both countries. In North America the issue was not so much markets or prized colonies as it was a struggle for strategic locations for an empire.

After the War of Spanish Succession, France developed Louisiana and began linking it to Canada by forts and settlements along the north-south river systems. With the erection of Fort Duquesne (present-day Pittsburgh) in 1754, they completed a chain of forts north and south. Manned by royal troops, the French positions initially had superior military strength. But lacking on-the-spot resources and population, they were too weak, even with the aid of the Indians, for a long war of attrition. To no avail the French government cared for its colonies with expensive paternalism. Private investment was slight, for French investors preferred state annuities or offices to hazardous North American ventures, especially after the Mississippi Bubble. Frenchmen did not emigrate to North America in great numbers. Religious dissenters were excluded, and the lower classes were discouraged by efforts to reconstitute the manorial system of France in America. Most French settlers were trappers, traders, churchmen, and soldiers. Cut off from the mother country by British naval power, New France could not support large military forces.

Although militarily disorganized, the populous agricultural and commercial mainland colonies of Britain had greater endurance and easier access to Europe. Their interests clashed most sharply with the French in the Ohio River valley over trade, Indian loyalties, and especially land. In the first clashes of 1754 and 1755, the French and Indians drove off the British and their Indian allies. Then both home governments committed themselves to a greater collision by reinforcing their respective colonial claims. When pro-war forces in Britain were able to promote raids against French shipping in 1755, maritime hostilities became inevitable. In part, then, the world war which followed was a struggle for control over the American mainland east of the Mississippi River and north of Florida.

Despite their bellicosity overseas, neither the French nor the British government wanted war on the Continent. But this was not true of Maria Theresa, who would not be reconciled to the loss of Silesia and to the possibility of Prussian hegemony in the Empire and in Central Europe. Her foreign minister, Count von Kaunitz, operating on the assumption that the traditional Austro-French antagonism had lost much of its importance in the face of the new threat from Prussia, had worked diligently at Versailles since about 1749 to align France with Austria against Prussia but without success. During a few months of 1756, however, Kaunitz' aims materialized into a diplomatic revolution to which Britain, by negotiating a subsidiary treaty with Russia, inadvertently and indirectly contributed. Caught between British-ruled Hanover and Russia, Frederick became alarmed. Discounting France as a serious ally and contemptuous of her performance as a partner in the last war, he hastened to tie himself to Britain as protector of George II's principality of Hanover. Motivated by pique with Prussia and Britain, French and Russian diplomats now bound their countries to Austria against Prussia. Immediately plans for the reduction of Prussia were drawn up, with Russia and Austria taking the lead. When Frederick became aware of these plans, by surprise attack he seized Saxony, a passive partner in the negotiations against him, and held it during the remainder of the Seven Years' War as a tribute-producing vassal state. Again, Frederick's precipitous action started a general continental war, which merged with the Anglo-French struggle for empire overseas.

As in the War of Austrian Succession, continental warfare diverted French energies from an all-out effort in the Colonies. In the previous war, France had salvaged her colonial losses by seizing parts of the Austrian Netherlands as hostage territories, to be bargained with at the conference table. But this time Austria was an ally. The same strategy could now work only by taking enemy territory in Hanover, but it was too far away and too well defended. Unless Prussia were destroyed, France was committed to a war she could not win.

The destruction of Prussia was less an aim of France, however, than of Austria and Russia; and only narrowly did they miss achieving it. Together they put Frederick's military prowess to its supreme test. The allied sovereigns' failure to cooperate, however, allowed him for a time simply to defeat each in turn. But his position became so precarious, due to the massive demands on manpower, money, and supplies, that he actually contemplated suicide early in 1762. Russia's sudden withdrawal from the war saved him. Peter III, who succeeded the Prussophobe Empress Elizabeth in January 1762, admired Frederick very much and switched from foe to ally. Catherine II, Peter's wife and successor (she had her imbecilic husband done away with after only a few months of his reign) did not resume the war against Prussia, thus enabling Frederick to survive.

While Prussian and other British-subsidized German troops pinned France down on the Continent, Britain reaped great gains overseas. Rallied by William Pitt the Elder, British forces swept away most of the French colonial empire. A commoner, Pitt came to power after the older Whig ministry had suffered reverses. With national pride as a basis for popularity and with the support of aggressive merchants, Pitt became virtual dictator of wartime Britain. By popular consent, he became the absolute manager of a war for imperial expansion.

In contrast to Britain's unity of command and power, France was racked by internal conflicts and inability to raise adequate taxes. Ultimately, French hopes of victory came to hinge on plans for an invasion of Britain, but the naval power to reach English shores was lacking. By 1760 Canada fell to Britain and her Colonists; parts of the French West Indies were lost; and French forces in India yielded to British sea power and the resourcefulness of the East India Company's agent, Robert Clive. Though saddled with heavy war debts, Britain prospered while French shipping, commerce, and credit suffered disastrously.

Attrition and Russian withdrawal from the war made peace necessary. In Europe

*Lord Clive (after a Gainsborough portrait).*

the Peace of Paris of 1763 restored prewar boundaries and therefore did not resolve the rivalry between Austria and Prussia. Colonial peace came as a result of domestic British politics. In an attempt to unseat the Whig oligarchy that had ruled since 1715, George III replaced Pitt with Lord Bute. Bute, fearful of Britain's immense successes and not quite able to believe them in any case, granted lenient peace terms, but Britain retained the preeminent power she had gained during the war. France was driven from the North American continent, retaining only two offshore islands and fishing rights. To placate Spain for the loss of Florida to Britain, France ceded Louisiana to her. The French West Indies were restored, but in India France retained only unfortified trading stations. Her political power there was definitely broken.

France's humiliation and the discrediting of her Bourbon monarchy were not the only legacies of the Seven Years' War. Its scope and intensity challenged the *philosophes'* optimistic antimilitarism, because it demonstrated that within the competitive state system enlightened self-interest was insufficient to stop wars. Rather, reason had become an adjunct of *raison d'état*, a tool of predatory states. The war also demonstrated that Britain's parliamentary regime, antimilitaristic at home but the largest spender on arms, had proved more than a match for declining absolutism in France. The price of victory for Britain, however, was the loss of all her allies on the Continent. Previously it was the Austrian court which had become disillusioned with "perfidious Albion"; now it was Frederick II who deserted England for an alliance with Russia. Against British predominance, the balance of power now worked to isolate Britain completely, generating general suspicion, hostility, and jealousy, which helped to make the American Revolution successful. The war also gave impetus to a new form of absolutism cast in the secular language of the Enlightenment— enlightened despotism. In a sense, both of the two major radical political programs of the late eighteenth century, enlightened despotism and democratic revolution, were offsprings of the midcentury wars.

## Imperial Rivalry and the War of the American Revolution

As we shall soon see in greater detail, the American Revolution was simultaneously a civil war and a national revolt against Britain. But its success was also the result of renewed imperial rivalry that aligned France and the other major powers against Britain. Whetting the long knife of revenge, the French court stood ready to give the rebellious Colonists immediate covert aid. As soon as the Colonists' victory over Burgoyne at Saratoga demonstrated their resolve to pursue independence seriously with force, France concluded a permanent alliance and a commercial convention with the new republic in 1778.

*Shipbuilding at Toulon.*

French aid was the foreign mainstay of the American Revolution,* but it was not the only assistance the Colonies received. When Spain joined France against Britain in 1779, but not as an ally of the Colonists, Britain lost control over the seas. At great loss to its trade, the Dutch Republic made loans to the Continental Congress and became an active, but ineffective, belligerent in 1780. Russia and several other continental states in 1780 formed the League of Armed Neutrality, designed to stop British search and seizure on the high seas. Only the general hostility toward Britain within the context of continental rivalries can fully explain the paradox of the aid given by Europe's absolute and aristocratic states to this republican revolution. Even France had no intention of creating a powerful new state in North America. When American negotiators became aware of this, they violated their alliance with France to accept Lord Shelburne's offer for a separate peace.

The international war of the American Revolution did not come to an end with the

---

* The battle of Yorktown in 1781 illustrated the impact of this aid. While French troops aided the Americans on land, a French fleet offshore prevented British relief of their beleaguered and encircled troops.

*Europe's great carve: the Polish Cheese.*

preliminary peace between Britain and the United States. After that, Britain won the naval war with France and Spain in West Indian waters. Undiverted by the continental war, France had lost its last bid for empire under the Old Regime. Her defeat paved the way for the Peace of Paris of 1783. This peace recognized American independence, but it also transferred Florida from Britain to Spain, an unmistakable indication that more than a colonial revolt was involved in the war.

## Eastern Power Struggles and the First Partition of Poland

While France and Britain fought for empire overseas, Austria, Prussia, and Russia annexed territories shorn from Poland and the Ottoman Empire. Poland's misfortune was to be the buffer between the three great Eastern powers. Because of internal weakness, Poland, territorially the third largest

state in Europe, incited the appetites and mutual distrust of her stronger neighbors. Prior to their actual partition of the kingdom, they worked to preserve the nobles' "freedoms," that is, they maintained the constitutional anarchy that virtually disarmed the kingdom and made it subject to their manipulation. Russia was particularly successful in this. In 1763 Catherine II installed as king her former lover, Stanislas Poniatowski, who succeeded Augustus III, another Russian nominee. Content with this virtual control over Poland, Catherine in 1768 launched an invasion of the Ottoman Empire to secure the northern shores of the Black Sea, territories which Peter the Great had first won, then lost.

With an uncanny political eye, Frederick II perceived that the Russian invasion of the Ottoman Empire provided him an opportunity to take part of Poland. Russian gains along the Black Sea would rouse Habsburg fears of Russian power. If the two powers began hostilities, he might even be dragged unwillingly into war with Austria. By a power play, however, he might avoid such a war and force Catherine II to partition Poland, giving him West Prussia, a territory that would form a land bridge between Pomerania and East Prussia. Hoping thus to consolidate his eastern territories into a single block, Frederick proposed the partition of Poland to Catherine in 1772. To pacify Maria Theresa, she, too, would share the spoils. Catherine reluctantly agreed. The plan shocked Maria Theresa, but as Frederick noted cynically, "The more she wept for Poland, the more she took of it." Frederick got his land bridge, Catherine took White Russia, and Maria Theresa annexed Galicia. A revolutionary act, the first partition of Poland had only *raison d'état* to justify it. In no way could monarchical legitimacy, which in theory underlay absolutism itself, be invoked in its defense.

This rape of Polish territory neither checked Russia's war on Turkey nor reconciled Austria with Prussia. Catherine's peace with the Turks in 1774 resulted in Russian acquisition of Azov, permitted Russian ships to operate on the Black Sea, and placed Christians within the Ottoman Empire under a vague Russian protection. Far from satisfying Catherine, this limited success whetted her desire for more. She turned to Maria Theresa's son and successor, Joseph II, with plans for a joint partition of all Ottoman territory in Europe. The acquiescence of Frederick II, who had just frustrated Joseph's plans to round out his domains by exchanging the Austrian Netherlands for part of Bavaria, was to be purchased by suggestions of a further partition of Poland. Russia started the war by invading the Crimea and territories between the Black and Caspian seas. Weakened by internal resistance to his enlightened despotism, Joseph II did not field an army until 1788. Meanwhile Catherine parried a futile bid by Sweden's enlightened despot, Gustavus III, to regain the Baltic empire lost in 1721. This series of power plays in Eastern Europe did not cease until Poland was entirely absorbed by two further partitions in 1793 and 1795. But it was halted temporarily by the aggressive expansion of revolutionary France after 1793, which directed the Eastern powers' attention westward.

ENLIGHTENED DESPOTISM

The great wars of the midcentury decisively affected the domestic policies of several monarchs as they tried to reconstitute and streamline their authority and central institutions. This new impetus to centralization came at the same time that the French Physiocrats and many other *philosophes* were calling for "enlightened despots" to reform their states in accordance with the enlightened standards of Reason and Nature. In practice the autocratic implementation of the Enlightenment's "laws of nature" bade fair to strengthen the central power of the state. Therefore, eighteenth-century rulers and officials pursued both enlightened despotism and power politics with little sense of contradiction. Some centralizers—Maria Theresa, for example—abhorred the Enlightenment and its secularism. On the other hand, Catherine II, a devotee to enlightened principles, pursued traditionalist policies. Thus the boundaries between the older form of absolutism and enlightened despotism were often blurred and confused. But with a few exceptions, it was true that most eighteenth-century absolutists viewed their states as secular rather than otherworldly entities. They agreed with Frederick II that "the king is the first servant of the state," a phrase which implied that the state was a secular bureaucratic machine rather than an instrument of divine will.

The idea that society should be managed by philosopher-kings was as old as Plato, but eighteenth-century rulers had a rather specific program of enlightened policies in mind. First and foremost was the centralization of administration and justice in separate, parallel institutions. Thereby, all sub-

*Empress Maria Theresa.*

jects would be under the same laws, taxes, and officials. Among other things, local uniformity entailed adjusting the serfs' status to make them to a greater extent legal personalities subject more directly to the state than to their lords and, incidentally, subject also to conscription. Made uniform within, the state would also use its power to simplify its boundaries, making its territory compact and thereby rationally manageable. Clerical orders such as the Jesuits, who spurned natural reason and transcended the state's boundaries, had to be abolished or subordinated to secular authority. Enlightened domestic policy also required that the established churches relinquish control over censorship, education, welfare, and family affairs. Under secular officials there would be intellectual freedom except in politics, and freer exchange of goods. Compared to absolutism of the past, enlightened rulers placed more emphasis on humanitarianism and economic well-being. All initiative, however, lay with hereditary monarchs. En-

lightened despots would do everything *for* the people; nothing would be done *by* the people except under royal supervision.

### Maria Theresa and Joseph II

Charles VI's Pragmatic Sanction securing Maria Theresa's succession bound all Habsburg territories permanently under a single ruler for the first time. Nevertheless, it was still more appropriate to speak of a Habsburg dynasty than a Habsburg state. A congeries of duchies and kingdoms gathered together by dynastic marriage and the fortunes of war, the Habsburg empire was inhabited by Germans, Hungarians, Czechs, Slovenes, Slovaks, Croats, Flemings, Walloons, Italians, and, by the end of the century, Poles and Ruthenians also. Unlike their Hohenzollern rivals in Prussia, the Habsburgs had retained provincial diets that shared executive powers with the cosmopolitan court in Vienna.

As a result of her conflict with Prussia, after 1740 Maria Theresa sharply modified this policy of collaboration with local nobles and churchmen in the diets. For the sake of efficiency, she set out to build a military state. Around her she established an advisory council of experts headed by Count von Kaunitz and Count von Haugwitz. Under their guidance, she introduced new royal officials comparable to the French *intendants,* who gave her domains more unity. So did a tariff union between Bohemia and the German provinces. To strengthen her power, the first female Habsburg ruler taxed the nobility, limited nobles' jurisdictions over and dues from the peasantry, laid plans for a system of state education, and had the laws codified in a more humane, orderly, and secular direction. Above all, she reorganized the army in order to cope with Prussia.

Total consolidation of the Habsburg empire, however, posed too many problems for her to accomplish. Preoccupied with waging war and retaining her patrimony, Maria Theresa made no determined effort to impose her centralization on Hungary, the Austrian Netherlands, and northern Italy. To the Hungarians in particular, she made concessions of local autonomy in order to secure their military assistance and acceptance of her authority.

Maria Theresa was too pious to sympathize with the secular *philosophes.* Never could her attitude be described as "enlightened." But Joseph II, her son and co-ruler from 1765 to 1780, took over the reins of government and was determined to make "philosophy" the legislator of the empire. Undaunted by the power of his opposition, Joseph undertook to reduce the power of the clergy, nobles, and chartered towns throughout the empire. This assault on privilege was the reflection both of his personal enlightenment and of his desire to increase the state's vitality and power. Deliberately bypassing the provincial diets, the defenders of privileged interests, he divided the realm into administrative districts supervised directly from Vienna. He had the civil and penal laws codified for application to all subjects alike. In conformity with the Enlightenment's humanitarianism, these codes substantially reduced the number of capital offenses. More than his mother, he threatened the nobility with a land tax and the abolition or reduction of peasant dues.

Since the Catholic Reformation, the Habsburg dynasty had identified itself with an intolerant Roman Catholicism. Impatient with clerical resistance, Joseph turned this traditional policy upside down. He embarked upon anticlerical religious policies derogatorily dubbed "Josephism," that aimed at a thorough-going secularization of the monarchy. In general he sought to bring the Church under state control. The Jesuits, who operated directly under papal authority, were expelled. Papal bulls now required the approval of the emperor, and the clergy had to take an oath of allegiance to him. Joseph further curtailed the Church's autonomy by stripping it of control over education; he personally appointed prelates, taxed the

Church's lands, abolished many contemplative monastic orders, and reduced the number of bishoprics. In some instances "Josephism" also entailed state regulation of ritual and clerical education. Except in political matters, which remained under stringent censorship, he decreed intellectual freedom. To Protestants and Jews, Joseph extended toleration of private worship, but his enlightenment was not sufficient to tolerate Deists and atheists. Revenues taken from the Church were assigned to a system of free compulsory state education, to charity, and to newly founded medical facilities at Vienna. Catholic reaction to "Josephism" was severe; in the Austrian Netherlands it was the core of a revolution designed to frustrate the Emperor's policies.

In order to protect her source of taxes from the peasantry, Maria Theresa had curbed the nobility's power to increase their receipts from the peasants. Joseph went much further. Initially he proposed free peasant schools, the freedom to buy and sell land, and the opportunity to commute forced labor into payments of money. Eventually he tried to emancipate all peasants from the remnants of serfdom—to give them freedom of marriage, to enable them to move, improve their land tenure, and reduce their total obligations and dues. Surveys by his officials indicated that peasants had been paying about 73 per cent of their gross incomes to Church, landlord, and state. Joseph proposed reducing it to 30 per cent. But when he attempted to implement these reforms, the privileged orders resisted with force. He utterly failed to free the peasants under noble and clerical lords. Only those living on the royal domains, which in Hungary were practically non-existent, were freed during his reign.

The Emperor's policy toward the peasantry was part of a more comprehensive general economic reform, which entailed restriction of the guilds, reduction of industrial controls, and the removal of internal trade barriers. He revived Charles VI's project of

*The "revolutionary emperor," Joseph II.*

founding a commercial company in the Austrian Netherlands, but foreign opposition and war expenses negated his efforts.

As a theory of government, enlightened despotism was predicated on the prince's absolute sovereignty, his ability to alter society by edict. To execute his reforms, Joseph needed an immensely larger bureaucracy than he possessed, and one more committed to his goals than were the aristocrats who filled most of the important official posts of his government. No supply of such men existed. Even had they been available, it is unlikely that they would have succeeded, for the Emperor simply lacked the power and public support to decree and implement the overturn of existing privileges and property relationships. Hungarian nobles revolted

successfully against all of his reforms. Belgian towns took to arms also. His reforms for the peasantry stirred up revolts but little effective support for his policies. Joseph could enlist no powerful segment of society behind him. Moreover, pressures of taxes and conscripts to prosecute the Turkish war after 1788 forced him to reverse his own stance. In 1790 he died a disillusioned man. "Here lies a prince whose intentions were pure," he ordered inscribed upon his tombstone, "but who had the misfortune to see all his plans miscarry." Joseph painted the picture too darkly. His administrative reorganization, legal codification, emancipation of the peasants on the royal domains, and his stimulus to medical research in Vienna survived the aristocratic counterattack that followed. But his brother-successor, Leopold II, former enlightened despot of Tuscany, was forced to cancel most of Joseph's other changes. Ironically the reaction had at its disposal the same central institutions, including secret police, that Joseph had created to implement his reforms.

### Frederick II, 1740 to 1786

Frederick II of Prussia was more the heir than the builder of an efficient bureaucratic absolutism. Most of his "enlightened" reforms were simply continuations of his predecessors' policies. This is not to say, however, that he was not a child of the Enlightenment. Far from it. As a youth he defied the traditions of his dynasty. A devotee of French culture and educated by a French tutor, Frederick dabbled in arts and letters, played the flute well, wrote histories and bad verse in French, and even penned an essay attacking Machiavelli and his conception of statecraft. His relationship with his father, Frederick William I, was particularly stormy. On one occasion, the elder Hohenzollern ordered him shot as a deserter but settled for temporary confinement. Nevertheless, after 1732 Frederick served as a commander of a regiment of grenadiers, and for the rest of his life he made the code of the barracks his own guide to life. From his personal experience and education, he effected a peculiarly Prussian fusion of tradition, reason, custom, and enlightenment, which he enforced on his subjects as the head of the Prussian state.

From the French Enlightenment Frederick appropriated a completely secular attitude toward life. Neither religious nor political passions had a legitimate place. Revealed religion he held to be an "absurd system of fables," but his Protestant state was tolerant rather than anticlerical. Describing himself "to a certain measure pope of the Lutherans," he abandoned the label "Christian magistrate," which his predecessors had proudly displayed since the Reformation. Moreover, he also denied that the state was the personal property of the dynasty; rather, it was something above and beyond both king and people, something to which they owed their lives and fortunes.

Reason was to order state, church, society, economics, and high policy. But for Frederick the rule of reason was severe, a deterministic providence that made statesmen and soldiers stoic marionettes. Their duty was not to humanity in general but to the concrete historical state. Self-interest, not international agreements, determined the relationships between these states. "The fundamental principle of great states at any time," he wrote, "is to subordinate all in order to expand their own power without ceasing." In 1740, therefore, he felt secure in invading Silesia without diplomatic preparations or alliances, because he calculated that the self-interests of the other states would force them either to join him or to accept the outcome. It was his harsh duty to exploit Prussia's opportunity; equally harsh necessity would force others to recognize it. Frederick's foreign and domestic policies were based on clever, detached analyses of human motivations, but he distrusted and despised all men as hopelessly depraved. Only the nobility was partially redeemed by virtue of its military valor and relative de-

*Frederick II reviewing his troops at Potsdam.*

tachment from selfish worldly concerns. The nobles best conformed to his military doctrine that the object of battle was not to win by maneuver but to attack and destroy the enemy, preferably at the center of his power. Frederick was as much a military commander as a civilian administrator. State power, not individual well-being, was his overriding concern, though he tended to see the latter as realizable only through the former. In a real sense, his enlightened ideas were secularizations of the religious doctrines of church, state, and society that had prevailed during the religious wars. The one great exception was his hostility to enthusiasm and emotional passion. His regime was founded on a rational royalism; violence was to be constrained by reason, the reason of state.

Frederick's redefinition of enlightened values did not prevent him from collecting leading European intellectuals at Sans Souci, his palace at Potsdam, in an attempt to make his court the literary and scientific center of Europe. His closest intellectual ties were with the continental rationalists, but for forty years he maintained contact with Voltaire. Although punctuated with quarrels, his patronage of the great *philosophe* enhanced his reputation, for Voltaire gave him favorable publicity as a beacon of light in the midst of clerical obscurantists. Rousseau, to be sure, denounced him as a fraud, but Frederick's sponsorship of the Enlightenment put him in good stead with influential makers of public opinion throughout his reign.

Hohenzollern strength had grown through an unbroken succession of able administrators on the throne. Frederick's reign was no exception. The king displayed phenomenal energy as he conducted journeys of inspection (often incognito) and issued reports and instructions that flowed down to every level of his bureaucratic machine. With the possible exception of establishing more direct contact with serfs on private estates, he needed no innovations to introduce the legal absolutism demanded of conventional enlightened despots.

In economic policy, Frederick made no breach in the mercantilistic tradition of his predecessors. His main concern, like theirs, was to raise revenues for the army. Frederick made no change in the tax and toll structure that sharply separated town from country and gave privileged exemptions to the Junkers, the noble landlords. He retained the tightly administered system of exploiting revenues from the royal domains, which in Prussia were very extensive. But his wars consumed far more revenues than the Hohenzollern lands produced. Subsidies from England and levies on conquered territories gave only partial relief. To expand economic activity and to enable war-devastated areas to recover, the king enlarged the role of the bureaucracy in economic affairs. To secure a favorable balance of trade and tariff revenues, heavy duties were placed on foreign goods, especially luxury products and Saxon textiles. In addition to military industries, the state threw its weight behind the production of luxuries such as silk and porcelain. In 1765 the government founded a bank to finance new industries. Monopolies were established for colonial products that were

particularly in demand, such as coffee and tobacco. The acquisition of Silesia added a territory rich in textiles, iron, lead, and coal. Some of these industries, especially luxuries, continued to grow. By 1783 Prussia was exporting about one third of its manufactures.

Agriculture was still Prussia's basic occupation, and devastation during the Seven Years' War dealt the rural economy a serious blow. Frederick's government provided seed and stock for its recovery. Travelers were sent to England to observe and report on new procedures. Skilled foreign peasants ("colonists") were brought in to occupy wastelands and new areas recovered from swamp and forest, and the government advertised the cultivation of new crops such as potatoes. But Prussian agriculture did not undergo an "agricultural revolution" comparable to that of England in the eighteenth century. Customary methods of farming and land tenure were little touched.

Because revenues continued to flow into the treasury and because Prussia became an exporting state, Frederick's mercantilism has generally been considered a marked success. The growth of population from about 2 million to 6 million, partly as a result of conquest, is often cited to demonstrate the point. There is, however, another side to the coin, one which indicates that Prussia was headed toward a major social-economic crisis.

State capitalism and bureaucratic paternalism crowded out individual enterprise at every level. There was, for example, a state bank, but no large private banks survived. Because state taxes were heavy and the landed aristocracy was largely exempt, peasant and urban incomes were sharply reduced by taxes, which left little capital for productive investment. Frederick proposed the emancipation of the peasants, whom he sympathetically described as "the beasts of burden of human society," but like Joseph II he could free only those on the royal domains. Their emancipation did not result in any reduction of army and billeting services, taxes, and cartage (the obligation to put teams, wagons, and drivers at the service of the state).

In the cities, wage rates were fixed by law at a low level, and most craftsmen were forbidden to practice outside the towns. Commoners lacked the purchasing power to buy heavy industrial or luxury goods. While these industries produced more than their markets could absorb, general consumer industries failed. Probably sustained by high-priced colonial commodities such as sugar and the cultivation of potatoes, the population, however, increased rapidly. Between 1757 and 1805 births are estimated to have exceeded deaths by 30 per cent. Silesia grew especially fast in spite of major famines during the 1770s. Pressure of youth upon "places" in society hit all classes. Even the Junkers became heavily indebted in trying to provide for their more numerous surviving offspring. Unemployment, vagabondage, and crime increased, and authorities tried in vain to repress them with more severe laws. Frederick's economic policies certainly had areas of success; but they could not cope with this rapid increase in population. Those in positions of power within the bureaucracy responded to this population pressure by forcefully maintaining the traditional social order. But Prussia's disinherited "surplus population," which plagued other states of the Old Regime also, provided one of the dynamic social forces behind the revolutionary and romantic assault on reason in the following generation.

Unlike Joseph II, Frederick did not attempt to alter the distribution of wealth, power, and privilege. On the contrary, he gave the nobility more authority in the bureaucracy than it possessed under his predecessors. The law code he ordered compiled preserved intact the social order of three estates. The nobles' accrual of power within the bureaucracy enabled them to resist basic reforms. When Frederick died childless and with no one trained to succeed

*Catherine II: despot, enlightened or otherwise.*

him, decay set in. The reign of Frederick William II (1786–1797) was one of reaction against the Enlightenment. Fundamental reform awaited the shock of Napoleonic invasions.

## Catherine II

Catherine the Great was one of the trio of best-known enlightened despots who ruled major states of Europe in the eighteenth century. But practical application of the Enlightenment's principles in Russia had even less chance than in Prussia. After Peter the Great's death, Western influences had continued to affect the narrow intellectual circles at the court, the nobility, and the bureaucracy. Through foreign travel, tutors, and literature they became attached to French culture, rococo art, and the writings of the *philosophes*. On no one did the Enlightenment seem to make a deeper impression than on the obscure German princess who became the slighted wife of Peter III. Upon his removal and murder in 1762, she became Catherine II, Empress of Russia.

Herself widely read, Catherine sponsored French culture, wrote Russian histories, and maintained a lively correspondence with such *philosophes* as Voltaire, d'Alembert, Baron d'Holbach, and Diderot, whom she enticed to come to St. Petersburg. The climax of her enlightened idealism came in setting forth an Instruction for a convention called in 1767 to prepare the way for a new codification of Russian law. Justifying autocracy but adopting the principle that "people do not exist for the ruler, but the ruler for the people," the Instruction borrowed most of its contents from Montesquieu and Beccaria. Among other things, it advocated equality before and freedom under the law. It denounced torture and serfdom and criticized the concentration of ownership of large estates in a few hands.

This convention, the first real Russian deliberative assembly, represented all social classes except serfs under private landlords, which were about half the population. But as a vehicle for translating Catherine's intentions into concrete proposals, it was a dismal failure. Long sessions repeatedly failed to achieve agreement on particulars. Noble delegates construed "freedom" to authorize their extension of power over the peasantry and denounced critics of serfdom as "traitors to their class." Townsmen interpreted "equality" to mean their equality with nobles in sharing privileges such as the holding of serfs. Although Catherine denounced these perversions of enlightened principles and instigated discussions of serfdom, she failed to define clearly the convention's function. In 1768, long after she herself had ceased to take it seriously, its sessions were suspended. By 1774 its committees ceased to meet. Apart from stirring up discussion of controversial subjects, the convention had no practical significance.

Catherine's enlightened principles can also be seen at work in a variety of specific measures. In 1764 the state secularized most of the land belonging to the Church. She was instrumental in establishing foundling hospitals, medical facilities, a public library, and the practice of inoculation against smallpox. Her most lasting reform was probably the reorganization of local government along lines that remained essentially unchanged until 1917. In 1775 she ordered the erection of fifty identical provincial governments, each with a noble governor. At both the provincial and district level an attempt was made to separate justice from administration and, within justice, civil from criminal jurisdiction. Local authorities had power over all classes, but the administrators were drawn from the nobility alone. Thus the nobles, now free from compulsory service to the state, became the legal masters of the provinces. The towns, allowed to hold land in 1766 and chartered for their own self-government in 1785, seemed to have been an exception to noble dominance. But in fact the privileged urban classes, who controlled the town governments, lacked financial and police powers and found themselves subordinated to the nobility.

To portray Catherine as a faithful executrix of the Enlightenment would be to distort the major weight of her reign's significance for Russian development. She was more concerned with an aggressive foreign policy than with the worsening condition of most of her subjects' lives. As avidly enthusiastic for Machiavelli as for the *philosophes,* she adopted the traditional Russian political system of intrigue among favorites. (Diderot once characterized her as a combination of the soul of Brutus and the charms of Cleopatra.) From the time she, a non-Russian, seized the throne, she played that system as a master. Had she been sincerely and primarily devoted to enlightened principles, it is difficult to see how she could have carried out reforms and kept power. As a matter of practical politics, she was dependent upon an ascendant nobility for provincial and local government. Since the death of Peter the Great, this nobility had secured almost total exemption from obligations. The state, lacking a trained and obedient bureaucracy, had assisted the nobles' reduction of the mass of the Russian population to their will.

Instead of ameliorating the deep social ills of Russian society, Catherine legitimized and extended them. The nobles secured confirmation of their gains during the previous half century in a Letter of Grace of 1785. It constituted them henceforth as "an estate . . . separated by its rights and privileges from the rest of the people." Exempted from military service, personal taxation, and corporal punishment, they were confirmed in their rights to buy and sell land freely, to trade, and to operate mines and factories. To the hereditary nobility was given the exclusive privilege of owning serfs, a privilege which was becoming the foundation of Russian society and its chief curse.

Despite the state's interest in the serf as the principal source of taxes, the serf became almost a chattel slave. Not only was the lord his overseer, tax collector, and landlord, to whom he owed undefined amounts of labor and fees, but the lord (or his bailiff) also served as policeman, judge, jury, and sometimes (as a result of beatings) executioner. With this boundless power, lords eroded peasants' rights to the use of the land. While exactions in labor and fees were increased, peasant's appeals to the government were forbidden by law. Individual lords were forbidden to emancipate their serfs, who on occasion were detached from their land and sold at increasing prices at public auction. Although administrators of the central bureaucracy occasionally protested against the nobles' usurpations, laws defining noble-serf relationships were not passed. Instead, administrative practice acquiesced in the serfs' declining status. Even though Catherine herself could denounce serfdom and its advocates, she did nothing to mitigate the condition of peasants on Church lands that the government confiscated and turned over to private lords. Moreover, for the convenience

*Flogging of a Russian peasant.*

of tax collection through noble lords, the government granted to magnates in newly acquired districts similar powers over their peasants. Thus serfdom reached its apogee in the late eighteenth century.

With all the avenues of political expression blocked off to the peasantry, an estate sunk in ignorance, superstition, and tradition, the only reaction to its worsening condition could be resignation or rebellion. Numerous peasant conspiracies and revolts threatened Catherine's rule, but all channels of discontent merged in the massive Pugachev Rebellion of 1773 to 1775, during which peasant restiveness loosed itself in a furious counterattack. Pugachev, a Don Cossack veteran encouraged by Old Believer priests,* organized nomads, adventurers, and disgruntled peasants into a great army. Sweeping along the Volga River and the Ural Mountains, they terrorized the nobility and clergy. Defeated at first, government forces finally caught Pugachev and executed him after the strength of his forces had been sapped by famine. Pugachev's suppression firmly reestablished noble superiority and snuffed out all further thought of reform.

The riveting of servitude on the peasantry

* See Chapter 1, page 29.

*Russian peasant family at the time of Catherine the Great.*

became the most salient feature of Russian tsarist society. Squeezed by exactions of both state and nobility, the serfs could neither improve their lot on present lands nor migrate to others. Yet neither the state nor the nobility appears to have profited from the system. Despite increased taxes and dues, Catherine's government went deeper into debt. The greater part of the nobility became unproductive administrators, dwelling often in towns as absentees from their estates. As the social distance between peasant and noble increased, the nobility lost its sense of reality. It repudiated its Russian environment in favor of French ideas, clothes, fashions, manners, and language. So cut off from actual conditions were Russian recipients of the Enlightenment that they would have been impotent to change the system even had they desired to. Moreover, commercial urbanization bringing social, economic, and intellectual changes in Western Europe, was arrested in Russia by the lords' absolute rights over the peasants and by their pronounced economic and trading privileges, which tended to hinder the growth of the tiny indigenous middle class. At Catherine's death, the urban population constituted not more than 4 per cent of the total population. The path of gradual change was thus virtually closed on the eve of the gigantic population increase that was to come during the nineteenth century.

## Enlightened Despotism in the Lesser States

The major states had no monopoly of enlightened despots. Indeed, the chances for their success seemed to have been greater in smaller states that had neither the resources nor the desire to become embroiled in major wars.

Latin Europe produced several cases of secular anticlerical reform similar to the program attempted by Joseph II. In Savoy the Old Regime was overhauled by uniform laws, curtailment of the Church, emancipation of the serfs, and reorganization of taxes and administration. In Tuscany Joseph's brother Leopold successfully carried out a similar set of policies. Don Carlos, who became Charles III of Spain in 1759, reorganized the administration of the Kingdom of the Two Sicilies along the lines of Bourbon France. From 1759 to 1788 he made Spain the seat of a reform movement designed to revive Spanish power. Hindering both centralization of secular authority and reform were the Inquisition and the Roman Catholic clergy. Charles curbed both, centralized his administration in a council of state, proclaimed economic reforms, and attempted, with only small success, to break the landholding monopoly of nobles and clergy. But Charles did revitalize Spanish power in Europe and the New World. Meanwhile, Portugal had a brief period of reforming absolutism under the police-state measures of the able Marquis de Pombal, who served as the king's chief minister. In expelling the Jesuits, Pombal initiated what soon became a universal aspect of enlightened despotism in Catholic states.

Among the many smaller German states there were instances of enlightened rule. The dukes of Baden and Saxe-Weimar followed such formulas, giving some slight roots to German liberalism and the basis for a cultural renaissance, involving such important literary figures as Johann Gottfried von Herder and Johann Wolfgang von Goethe.

Other German despots followed quite unenlightened courses. The landgrave of Hesse-Cassel, for example, made a fortune by selling his subjects as soldiers ("Hessians"), a practice that others followed on a smaller scale. Within the Holy Roman Empire there was no general pattern of enlightened despotism.

Earlier in the century Sweden had provided the most spectacular shift from absolutism to aristocratic oligarchy. In 1772, with the *coup d'état* of Gustavus III, Swedish politics shifted as decisively back to absolutism. But Gustavus coupled reform with an ill-fated attack on Russia to recover the Swedish Baltic empire. Denmark, too, had its absolutist reformer in the person of Johann Friedrich von Struensee, a royal doctor who cared for the debilitated king. Taking control of the administration and of the queen, whose lover he was, he issued a flood of decrees in his brief tenure in office. Both he and Gustavus III were killed at the instigation of nobles who resisted the drastic curtailment of their powers that absolutist reform entailed. Struensee was executed by judicial decree in 1772; Gustavus was assassinated in 1792.

## THE COLLAPSE OF ABSOLUTISM AND THE RISE OF DEMOCRATIC MOVEMENTS IN THE MARITIME STATES

Enlightened despotism was one of two major responses to the resurgent aristocracy during the eighteenth century. With varying degrees of success, enlightened despots contended with aristocrats in agrarian kingdoms whose commerce and industry were relatively backward. Such "revolutions" as occurred in these states were either counter-revolutions of the privileged classes against enlightened reforms or hopeless uprisings of the peasantry. In the more commercially developed societies, especially in the Atlantic maritime states, a different evolution led to the second response: demands for the democratization of political institutions and the social structure. In Britain's older North American Colonies, where semidemocratic institutions were indigenous, this movement became overtly revolutionary after the Seven Years' War. In Britain itself, democratic elements sought means short of revolution to reverse the growing oligarchical trend of British institutions, especially the English and Irish parliaments. There were also democratic movements that led to open revolution in Geneva and the Low Countries. Except for the American Revolution, whose success was due partly to the diplomatic alignment of Europe, all of these movements failed. But by 1787 French absolutism was on the point of collapse because of rapidly deepening financial crises and the obstructionism of the aristocracy. France had not fully become a maritime state, and before 1787 the democratic movement was more latent than actual and had not yet become distinct from the rebelliousness of the aristocracy. As events proved, however, France had developed the potential for the most significant of the revolutionary democratic movements.

### The Failure of the Democratic Movement in Great Britain

Walpole's fall in 1742 brought no change in the methods he had used to manage Parliament. Backed by the Duke of Newcastle, his successors disposed of proposed reforms as easily as he had done. Charges of corruption were widespread, but no reform in the parliamentary system occurred until after the Seven Years' War.

This delay came in part because discontented elements pinned their faith on William Pitt, a prophet of empire, and on war with France, all of which detracted from interest in reform. As early as 1746 Pitt considered proposals to conquer Canada and to ruin French commerce. Immensely popular in London, he was not acceptable to George II as head of the government until the Seven Years' War. Under his direction in that war,

*William Pitt the Elder (Earl of Chatham).*

Britain carried the day in one theater of war after another: North America, India, North Africa, and on the seas in general. The trade and the industry that supplied Britain flourished as the victories mounted. While British debts, taxes, and nationalistic fervor grew, Pitt would not make peace. After his resignation in 1761 over the question of the conduct of the war, that task was undertaken by Newcastle on terms that Pitt denounced as too lenient. Although the peace was unpopular in London, it gave the small but vocal movement for parliamentary reform a new impetus.

Revived agitation for reform coincided with a long period of government weakness and embarrassment in foreign affairs. George III, who ascended the throne in 1760, replaced Newcastle, who had been the real power behind the scenes since Walpole's emergence, with Lord Bute. Bute was not a member of Parliament, and his appointment stirred its opposition. Parliament began to assert its independence of the crown on the

one hand and its abhorrence of popular reform movements on the other. Newcastle's dismissal disrupted the patronage system that ministers had used to control Parliament, and when the lever of patronage ceased to be an effective means to secure unity between crown and Parliament, the controlling Whigs broke into rival factions. George III searched in vain for a stable coalition until he found it temporarily under Lord North, appointed in 1770. George meanwhile attempted personally to appropriate the temporarily disorganized system of patronage and influence in order to build up in Parliament a body of supporters loyal to himself and thus to reestablish the integrity of the executive powers of the crown within the constitution as he interpreted it. The unpopularity of this royal bid for increased influence, together with Britain's entry into the American Revolution with no allies and with the British people themselves sharply divided on the justice of the war, resulted in the temporary coincidence of two separate reform movements which produced a near revolution in Britain in 1780. One, largely within Parliament, sought to strip the crown of its control over "placemen" (that is, those who enjoyed the benefits of government patronage) in the House of Commons, while making no concessions to democratic control over the House. The other, mainly outside of Parliament, aimed to make the House of Commons more representative of the population.

The extraparliamentary movement was led by radicals from the new industrial bourgeoisie. Many of them were religious dissenters who were being discriminated against under the present system. While the decadent universities were firmly wed to things as they were, dissenting academies taught science, economics, and history, as well as rational religion and more modern approaches to new social problems. Joseph Priestley, chemist and founder of modern Unitarianism, and Richard Price, later to be a target of Edmund Burke's polemics for teaching the doctrine of

*Portraiture of the English oligarchy: "Mrs. Grace Dalrymple Elliott" by Gainsborough.*

natural rights, were among their teachers and leaders. Literate men, whose practical and political interests were not served by parliamentary representation as then constituted, also formed technical societies, clubs, and workingmen's associations, which joined in the campaign to democratize Parliament.

Early popular discontent with Parliament's oligarchy centered around the personality of John Wilkes, a townsman of recent wealth who founded a newspaper, the *North Briton,* in 1762. When it attacked Bute's "ministerial despotism" with a more than merely implied slap at the king himself, the crown tried to suppress it by arresting Wilkes, a member of Parliament, and the paper's staff. The courts declared the general warrants on which Wilkes and his associates were arrested illegal, but Parliament expelled him. His

leadership among dissenters was weakened by discovery of a lascivious essay on women among his personal papers, but after a short stay in France, Wilkes was elected and re-elected to Parliament. When that body consistently refused to seat him, his case became the cause of public meetings and agitation against Parliament. Elected mayor of London, he secured the city's support in publishing debates of Parliament for the first time. This was a major step in the subjection of Parliament to public scrutiny. Finally admitted to Parliament, Wilkes introduced an abortive bill for universal manhood suffrage, but he gradually disappeared from prominence during the American Revolution.

British democrats perceived in that revolution many of the same elements of the fight they were waging at home. One Major Cartwright, for example, refused to serve in America and proposed home rule for the Colonies and thorough democratization of Parliament. When the popular reform movement organized local "associations" and called for a national General Association, a representative body that might rival and perhaps even displace Parliament, it alarmed parliamentary Whigs and country gentlemen alike. In 1780 the Association Movement, which had its counterpart among Protestants in Ireland, was badly compromised by the Gordon riots in London.* Ignited by mild but extremely unpopular parliamentary concessions to Roman Catholics and by lower class frustrations, these riots destroyed sections of unpoliced London. More destructive of property than any single episode during the French Revolution in Paris, the Gordon riots revealed the latent violence at the bottom of Britain's social order. It also demonstrated the gulf between the lower classes themselves and the would-be reformers of Parliament, for Priestley's house

* Named after an eccentric Scotsman, Lord George Gordon, the riots followed his presentation of a petition to the House of Commons protesting reduction of penalties against Roman Catholics.

*Mob firing Newgate Prison during the Gordon Riots.*

was destroyed and Wilkes tried to quiet the disturbance.

After the Association Movement petered out, bills to reform Parliament also failed. Between 1782 and 1785 the younger Pitt introduced a series of bills to redistribute parliamentary seats and to broaden the suffrage. They failed without exception.

The only successful reform was the parliamentary one for which Edmund Burke was spokesman. And its success weakened the executive still further. He introduced bills that reduced some corruption by barring certain placemen and contractors from sitting in Commons. These measures weakened the executive but did not democratize the legislature. Threatened by a new and radical urban society, Whig and Tory lords drew together to preserve their own power. But they relied upon their own control of Parliament, not on the authority of an absolute monarch, to secure that goal. Burke himself, although sympathetic to the American Revolution,

now turned to defending the existing British constitution as perfection itself.

## The American Revolution

Meanwhile the thirteen mainland colonies of Great Britain in North America succeeded in breaking free from the Empire. Only those colonies which had been most successful in transplanting European populations and civilization overseas were involved. In 1700 they had a population of 200,000. By mid-century there were nearly two million in these thirteen colonies. Over two thirds of them were native-born, and their birth rate was prodigious. In Philadelphia, New York, and Boston they possessed commercial cities of significance. In the middle and northern Colonies shipbuilding, distilling, and commerce, including the slave trade, flourished. Pennsylvania, the most prosperous and populous Colony, was a world leader in the production of raw iron. Unlike their nearest counterparts within the British Empire, the West Indies, the mainlanders had apparently unlimited opportunities for expansion. Land speculation was rampant among the wealthy, whereas less fortunate elements could find new opportunities on the frontiers. They had at hand well-rooted, if not oligarchical, institutions. Each Colony possessed a legislature with a popularly elected house paralleling the British House of Commons. And these legislatures used their power to blunt the authority of royal officials. In short, the mainland Colonies had developed to a point at which they were able to articulate local interests with considerable success. Once the French barrier was removed by the Seven Years' (French and Indian) War, their dependence upon the British for military protection, already weak, diminished still more.

The growing Colonial self-confidence assured that if the Empire were to remain a harmonious body, constitutional means of resolving divergent interests within it would have to be found. Before 1775 Americans had based their resistance to unpopular

British enactments on their rights as Englishmen guaranteed by local charters and grants. Thus they defended themselves as part of the corporate structure of the British constitution. Despite non-English immigration and geographical isolation from Europe and from each other, their culture, governmental systems, and principal trading relationships were English. The common British connection was useful in mediating local conflicts resulting from each Colony's pursuit of its own particularistic course. Overlapping territorial claims, differing religious institutions, divergent economic and trade patterns, and local loyalties discouraged cooperation in common enterprise. This was most exasperating to the British government in wartime. Nor were relationships within each Colony without conflicts, such as those between debtors and creditors, orthodox and non-conformists, and frontier and tidewater interests. For reasons that varied in different colonies, discontented elements challenged the commercial, family, and religious oligarchies whose control over government and its spoils mitigated the democratizing effect of broad suffrage. During the decade of discontent that preceded the American Revolution, part of the Colonial leadership (the radicals or patriots) came to espouse separation from Britain as a necessary step in the realization of their own goals.

## The Colonial Rift with Britain, 1763 to 1775

Parliament claimed full sovereignty over the Colonies as "dependent corporations," but until the midcentury wars, the implications of this claim were muted by Britain's failure to enforce its authority fully. Americans paid less taxes than any people except the Poles. Only a few Colonial laws were disallowed or vetoed by the Privy Council. Some customs were collected, but smuggling, often with the connivance of officials, was commonplace. After the Seven Years' War, the North American customs service actually cost more to operate than it collected.

Resulting from the experience of that war, the British policy of "salutary neglect" gave way to a "new imperial policy." Britain had failed to secure close coordination and cooperation among the Colonies, whose legislatures had met requisitions for supplies and money sporadically or not at all. And Colonial traders had persisted in trading with the enemy. At the end of the war, taxes in indebted Britain were high enough to stir internal unrest. Parliament balked at providing further outlays for America and demanded that the Colonists share the expenses of the Empire. These expenses were immediately increased by Pontiac's Indian uprising of 1763, which captured all but one of the ceded French forts north of the Ohio River. The British government sought to pacify the Indians by regulating and restricting westward expansion by negotiated treaties, a measure which gave rise to great dissatisfaction among various elements of Colonial society, especially settlers and land speculators. They also sought to station in the Colonies troops financed by the Colonists themselves. To raise customs duties for this purpose, Parliament first lowered duties on molasses imported from the foreign West Indies, the Colonists' principal source of hard money, but then, in contrast to its earlier relaxed attitude, ordered strict enforcement of customs collection. Specie was already critically short because the balance of payments ran heavily against the Colonies, depriving them of circulating coinage. Further acts of Parliament made the sterling shortage worse. Parliament forbade the Colonies to mint their own money or to pay their debts with (depreciated) currency. Although Colonists paid scant taxes to their provincial governments, compliance with these acts was exceedingly difficult. Britain's new policies were challenged before the bars of law and public opinion, but resistance to assuming a share of imperial burdens did not become general before the Stamp Act of 1765.

This attempt to raise taxes for Colonial

*WILLIAM JACKSON,*

an *IMPORTER*; at the

*BRAZEN HEAD,*

*North Side of the* TOWN-HOUSE,

and *Opposite the Town-Pump, in*

*Corn-hill,* B O S T O N.

*Rioting against the Stamp Act in New York.*

**It is desired that the SONS and DAUGHTERS of *LIBERTY*, would not buy any one thing of him, for in so doing they will bring Disgrace upon *themselves,* and their *Posterity,* for *ever* and *ever,* AMEN.**

*Poster urging boycott of Loyalist merchant during the Stamp Act crisis.*

administrative and military expenses did not really threaten the local currency supply, but it did set off a decade of constitutional debate. Providing for an excise on newspapers, business records, and legal documents (much lower, incidentally, than a current stamp duty in Britain itself), the Stamp Act stepped on the toes of the most articulate, educated, and influential segments of the population. Riots prohibited its enforcement, while a Stamp Act Congress representing nine of the Colonies met in New York to protest formally. The Congress denounced "taxation without representation," but rejected representation in Parliament as impracticable. It affirmed American loyalty to Britain but offered no substitute, as Britain had requested, for requisition as a means of raising revenues. Parliament repealed the tax, but both the issue of the right

to tax and the means of supporting the Colonial army and administration were left unsettled.

Quartering acts and subsequent customs measures met a similar rebuff. Against the Townshend tariffs of 1767, a boycott enforced by local "Sons of Liberty" threatened sales by British merchants. Again Britain yielded by repealing most of the acts, but it reaffirmed the principle of parliamentary taxation by leaving a tax on imports of tea. A period of relative quiet followed until 1773, when the Home Government sought to relieve the financial distress of the foundering East India Company by selling taxed tea at reduced prices, which even smugglers could not meet. Colonial port authorities quietly refused to unload the British tea, but in Boston radicals started a chain of events that led to violence and open pronouncement of revolutionary aims.

Following a minor collision between British troops and local citizens in 1770 (the "Boston Massacre"), Revolutionary leaders had gained increased power over public opinion and government in Massachusetts. Now they disguised themselves as Indians and dumped cargoes of tea into Boston harbor. This destruction of property by the "Boston Tea Party" alienated many moderate and conservative Colonists, but more significantly it drew from Britain, whose government had vacillated between strict enforcement and concessions, a series of coercive acts. They closed Boston's harbor until the tea might be paid for; altered the government of Massachusetts Bay to make the council appointive rather than elective; and suspended the town meetings where such radicals as Samuel Adams held sway. Adams and John Hancock began to organize the collection of arms. In 1775 when British troops tried to seize them and their supplies, an armed clash occurred at Lexington and Concord. Coercion of the Massachusetts Bay government and bloodshed gave the radicals their most convincing demonstration that Britain was bent on tyranny. This they had seen as the intent of every act of the British government, including its belated fulfillment of its 1763 treaty obligations to recognize French law and Catholicism in conquered Quebec. Neither side had planned a war, but the outbreak of armed hostilities brought the constitutional debate to a climax in an atmosphere favoring American advocates of total independence.

After the Stamp Act, the constitutional positions of Colonial leaders fell into three general categories. Some held parliamentary sovereignty to be indivisible and therefore competent to tax and regulate commerce. Although they opposed specific measures as bad policy, they were Loyalists from the start. Others invoked English constitutional precedents to deny tax and tariff powers to Parliament, but they advocated an American legislature that would be equal to Parliament under the British crown. Prominent Colonists, some of whom later became Loyalists as well as some Revolutionaries, were in this camp: Franklin, Jefferson, James Wilson, and Joseph Galloway. A third group, the radicals, best represented by Patrick Henry in Virginia and Samuel Adams in Massachusetts, described any authority outside the local legislatures and courts as tyranny and slavery. They organized "committees of correspondence" to coordinate their efforts and wielded effective propaganda through the press. They set the tasks for the local "Sons of Liberty." In the

*A Colonial antidote for Loyalists.*

absence of local police, these groups enforced boycotts and intimidated their opposition by threats and violence. Their aim was not just local autonomy but the breaking of British ties that supported entrenched oligarchies.

In 1775 the radicals gained control of the Second Continental Congress, which met to organize Colonial resistance. Within individual Colonies they carried out revolutions that produced state constitutions curtailing executive authority, curbing existing oligarchies, and providing bills of rights. Their campaign for independence was reinforced by the writings of Thomas Paine, a recent radical immigrant from England who there had agitated unsuccessfully for reform of the British constitution. The success of the radicals became clear when the Second Continental Congress opened American ports and adopted the Declaration of Independence. The Declaration, drafted by Jefferson, invoked a natural universal right of revolution whenever existing governments persistently trampled on the natural rights of the governed to life, liberty, and the pursuit of happiness. To demonstrate the Revolution's legitimacy, the Declaration attributed to George III, heretofore praised as the one accepted link between Britain and America, a long list of tyrannical acts. In reality, Parliament was primarily responsible for them.

Powers accorded to the Revolutionary Congress reflected the radicals' opposition to any central government, British or American, possessing power to tax or regulate commerce. The same was true of the Articles of Confederation, which operated as the first American constitution between 1781 and 1789. The radicals devoted their attention largely to the state governments whose failure to cooperate fully had made the Continental Congress' task of prosecuting the war reminiscent of Britain's experience during the French and Indian War.

## The Achievement of American Independence

From the point of view of materials, industry, wealth, and manpower, the Colonists' revolt against the world's strongest maritime power was inauspicious. But the Colonies had the advantages of geographical remoteness and British reluctance to proceed vigorously. And, as we have seen, the revolt also caught Britain isolated diplomatically, giving the Colonists the opportunity to harness imperial rivalries for their own purposes.

Independence left the radicals in control under the new Articles of Confederation. The unicameral Congress representing the confederated states had some successes. The Northwest Ordinance of 1787, for example, provided a new method of territorial government that repudiated slavery and provided for the admission of new states on equal terms with the old. Problems of the postwar years, however, undermined the new government. As the Loyalists had predicted, the new country was excluded from world markets. The expenses of the war, largely financed by depreciated paper money and loans, went unpaid. And the newborn nation

was caught in a depression aggravated by the uncoordinated commercial policies of the different states. After the revolutionary fervor abated, state constitutions were rewritten more in accordance with the British past. They incorporated stronger executive power and devices to insulate part of the government from direct popular control. The states' failure to restore confiscated Loyalist estates in accordance with treaty commitments seemed a dangerous precedent for property relationships. In several states, sharp conflicts between factions of debtor-farmers and creditor-merchants broke out. By 1787 conservative and national forces joined hands to replace the Articles of Confederation with a new constitution, which provided for a federal government wielding the power of taxation, controlled commerce, and protected property from expropriation in the future without due process of law.

Although the drafters of the Constitution of 1787 were obliged to compromise with advocates of a bill of rights defining individual and states' rights against the central government, the new instrument represented a mild resurgence of conservatism. Nevertheless, American conservatism had been weakened by the permanent exclusion of the Loyalists, who found new homes in Canada, England, or elsewhere. Finally, the Constitution's espousal of popular sovereignty made it a distinctly radical document. It was, after all, the product of a democratic revolution, a precedent that soon inspired other revolutions.

## The Failure of French Absolutism, 1743 to 1786

The difficulties of the British government at home and abroad were matched by a more gradual, but in the long run even more serious, disorganization of royal government in France. After the competent but superannuated Fleury died in 1743, Louis XV took personal charge of the government but without giving it direction. Affairs of state drifted dangerously for over a decade. Frederick II

*Louis XV's influential mistress, the Marquise de Pompadour, by Boucher.*

*Nature-art of the French Court: Boucher's "Spring."*

quipped astutely that France in this period really had four kings—the Secretaries of State—whose policies contradicted one another. Their disagreements were to some extent a direct result of the policy of Louis, who deliberately chose rival personalities as ministers in order to prevent the possibility of ministerial conspiracy. For the king, these were years of growing unpopularity. His personal lassitude and disinterest in governmental and administrative affairs introduced a creeping paralysis into the central government, and he was particularly vulnerable to the charge that his mistress, the Marquise de Pompadour, an upstart commoner, was manipulating decisions and appointments behind the scenes. Worse still, France lost heavily as a result of the Seven Years' War. Some very able and progressive administrators, especially among the *intendants* of the provinces, were able to check some of the chaotic tendencies of the center but not the

slow disintegration of absolute royal command.

Louis' unpopularity, however, was not entirely his own doing. His administration was obstructed by the *parlements* while their members, armed with Montesquieu's aristocratic arguments, raked him for tyranny. In such attacks they appealed to the nation over and above the king and presented themselves as its true representatives. In actuality, they represented the old hierarchical and corporate structure of the privileged orders of French society, which commercialization was steadily undermining and whose legal safeguards Louis' ministers were beginning to dismantle. The *parlements* cooperated to interfere with royal administration in numerous ways. In 1770 they were implicated in a successful court intrigue to dismiss de Choiseul, the able royal minister who had been responsible for breaking the guilds' legal hold over domestic industry and for opening trade to the Indies by private traders. The king then took the momentous step of abolishing the troublesome *parlements* and replacing them with panels of nonhereditary jurists appointed on the basis of merit. This reform of the courts, primarily a political measure, was also intended as a prelude to the establishment of uniform codes of civil and criminal law. But the monarchy did not justify its action in secular, utilitarian terms; instead, it merely made a blunt declaration of the monarchy's divine right. Far from settling the conflict, this judicial reorganization initiated a period of heightened discontent that lasted until the accession of Louis XVI in 1774.

Louis XVI, a good-hearted but none too intelligent man, immediately terminated the crisis by an appeasing act of weakness; he restored the *parlements* with all of their traditional rights, including the power to register new laws and taxes and to remonstrate with the king on decrees they regarded as detrimental to the country (or their own interests). Ultimately, taxes became the nub of their renewed conflict with the royal government. Although commercial wealth was accumulating in private hands, monarchical finances were rapidly approaching bankruptcy; even the expediency of heavy borrowing was becoming difficult except at ruinous interest rates, which reflected the government's failing reputation among the financial community. Louis' controller-general of finance, the one-time *intendant* Turgot, might have saved the situation when he was called to office in 1774. He abolished costly sinecures, tried to curb the waste and corruption that allowed half the revenues collected to find their way into private hands, and sought to abolish clerical and noble exemptions from a new single tax on land. Turgot abolished the guilds and instituted free trade in grain. However, famine, speculation, and skyrocketing grain prices undid this last act, and the other acts were opposed by the offended privileged orders, which denounced and conspired against him. In 1776 Louis dismissed Turgot and recalled almost all of his reforms. Thereafter France entered the American Revolution, an action that Turgot rightly predicted would bankrupt the royal treasury.

His successor, Jacques Necker (who held office from 1776 to 1781), a Protestant Genevan banker, faced a hopeless task. First, trading on his reputation as a banker, he floated vast new loans to finance the new war and to gain time for more thorough reform. Subject to increasing attacks (not all of them unjustified) from the privileged classes as well as from some financial circles, Necker sought to protect his position by publishing in 1781 the famous *Account Rendered to the King*. This document purported to make public the details of royal financial administration. By juggling figures, Necker contrived to show a surplus in the treasury; in reality, the government's indebtedness was greater than ever. Nor did this publication have the effect Necker intended; by revealing to the public the tremendous sums spent by the monarchy on gifts and pensions to the parasitic court nobility, it not only deepened popular distrust of the government but also called down on Necker's head a fury of opposition from the court, which forced his dismissal in 1781. His successors, including the able Calonne, resorted to one expedient after another but were unable to make any dent in the budgetary deficits of the government. Failing to secure consent to increased but also more equitable taxation from the *parlements,* clergy, and nobility, their efforts were doomed. The rapidly deepening financial crisis proved to be the undoing of the Bourbons' nominal absolutism, for it enabled the ascendant privileged orders to make a revolutionary assault on royal authority in the years after 1786.

For the years ahead, both the American Revolution and the phenomenon of enlightened despotism presented alternative solutions to the problems of eighteenth-century political and social life. In their different ways, both had the same objective: the strengthening of the secular power of the state to overcome the power of traditional corporate "intermediate bodies" between the state and the individual. In this sense, new revolutionary governments would effect the centralization of authority that absolute monarchs had heralded ideologically and implemented imperfectly with limited bureaucracies. But neither divine-right monarchy nor even its modern cousin, enlightened despotism, were really evolutionary stepping-stones toward the establishment of a parliamentary government responsible to the governed. The aristocratic resurgence after 1715 again gave evidence that under normal circumstances the successors to the great absolute monarchs were special interest groups whose privileges the throne had created or maintained. In theory, enlightened despotism marked a departure from this pattern by its assaults on social and economic as well as political privileges. But its practical results in this direction were scanty. Joseph II's failures testified to the weakness of monarchical fiat in overcoming vested interests. As matters of practical power politics, both Frederick II and Catherine II yielded still greater political powers to the privileged. And in France even the emergence of enlightened despotism was largely blocked by the coincidence of royal timidity and the obstructive power of the higher orders of society. Here and there, to be sure, enlightened despots scored some successes that tended toward the benefit of society as a whole, but they did not lead in the direction of popular government.

Eighteenth-century experience indicated that without fundamental alterations in the nature of society itself, something which enlightened despots were unwilling to consider, governments had little ability to legislate basic changes in the distribution of power and prestige. Even where external conditions were seriously undermining the basis of the traditional social structure, as in France, there was no guarantee that the monarchy could adapt to or appropriate such conditions for its own purposes. The same uncertainty hung over entrenched oligarchies like the English Parliament, which claimed powers scarcely less sovereign than those of the enlightened despots.

But in contrast to enlightened despotism, the parliamentary reform movement in England and the American Revolution were on courses that would reconcile greater individual liberty and initiative with stronger government based on legal equality and the active consent of the governed. Both Britain and her mainland colonies already had some degree of popular participation in their constitutional fabric. But the task of expanding that participation proved to be much easier in America than in Britain. Indeed, the ease with which the American revolutionaries succeeded in establishing their "new order of the ages" gave birth to illusions. They had no powerful neighbors except Britain, to threaten counterrevolutionary intervention, and the balance of power worked in their favor to offset any threat from that quarter. They had no entrenched feudal order to contend with, and the violence-laden miseries produced by population growth in Europe were outside their ken. In Britain, economic growth and the existence of popular elements in the constitution made an accommodation to change possible so that Britons would not follow America's revolutionary example. But the succeeding age of revolutions demonstrated that conditions on the Continent were quite different.

## SELECTED READINGS

*Anderson, M. S., *Europe in the Eighteenth Century 1713–1783,* Holt, Rinehart, and Winston, New York, 1961; Oxford Paperback.

Up-to-date textbook written as comparative history.

Barber, Elinor G., *The Bourgeoisie in Eighteenth-Century France,* Princeton University Press, Princeton, 1955.

An analysis of social stratification of prerevolutionary France. Good for indicating bourgeois imitation of the nobility but becomes prisoner of its preconceived social theories.

Blum, Jerome, *Lord and Peasant in Russia from the Ninth to the Nineteenth Century,* Princeton University Press, Princeton, 1961.

An authoritative history of the Russian

* Asterisk (*) denotes paperback.

peasant in the bondage that reached its apogee in the eighteenth century.

*Brunn, Geoffrey, *The Enlightened Despots,* Holt, New York, 1929.
Brief, comprehensive summary well suited for the beginning student.

*Dorn, Walter L., *Competition for Empire, 1740–1763,* Harper and Brothers, New York and London, 1940, and a Harper Torchbook.
Comprehensive account of the renewed power struggle, well-balanced between colonial and continental rivalries; also excellent on the thought of the Enlightenment.

Ford, Franklin L., *Robe and Sword, the Regrouping of the French Aristocracy after Louis XIV,* Harvard University Press, Cambridge, 1953.
Demonstrates the growing community of interest between the two major branches of the French nobility during the eighteenth century.

*Gershoy, Leo, *From Despotism to Revolution, 1763–1789,* Harper and Brothers, New York, 1944, and a Harper Torchbook.
One of the best accounts in English; part of the Rise of Modern Europe series.

*Gipson, Lawrence H., *The Coming of the Revolution 1763–1775,* Harper and Brothers, New York, 1954.
Presents the origins of the American revolution from the point of view of the British Empire.

Gooch, George P., *Maria Theresa and Other Studies,* Longmans, Green, London and New York, 1951.
One of the author's several biographical studies of the period, which tend to be rather old-fashioned.

Goodwin, Albert, ed., *The European Nobility in the Eighteenth Century,* A. and C. Black, London, 1953.
Studies of the nobility in each of the major states showing that "enlightened despots" in Eastern Europe actually favored the nobility.

Kluchevsky, V. O., *A History of Russia,* translated by C. J. Hogarth, 5 volumes, Russell and Russell, New York, 1960.

Volume V relates to the reign of Catherine II; particularly clear in establishing serfdom as the basic social institution of Russia.

Lindsay, J., ed., *The Old Regime, 1713–1763,* Vol. VII, *The New Cambridge Modern History,* Cambridge University Press, Cambridge, 1957.
Thorough reference work particularly good for diplomatic and general military developments.

Link, Edith M., *The Emancipation of the Austrian Peasant 1740–1798,* Columbia University Press, New York, 1949.
Critical for an understanding of peasant conditions in Central Europe and for the aims of Joseph II.

Namier, Lewis B., *England in the Age of the American Revolution,* 2nd ed., St. Martin's Press, New York, 1961, and
———, *The Structure of Politics at the Accession of George III,* 2nd ed., Macmillan, London; St. Martin's Press, New York, 1957.
Detailed analyses of British political life that focus on the personal connections of its factions.

*Ogg, David, *Europe of the Ancien Régime 1715–1783,* Harper and Row, New York, 1965.
A new conventional history distinguished by its recognition of geographic factors in political and economic developments.

Palmer, Robert R., *The Age of the Democratic Revolution, A Political History of Europe and America 1760–1800,* Vol. I, *The Challenge,* Princeton University Press, Princeton, 1959.
Sets forth lucidly the consolidation of aristocratic power against which both democrats and enlightened despots contended.

Pares, Richard, *War and Trade in the West Indies, 1739–1763,* F. Cass, London, 1963.
The standard account of the subject.

Petrie, C. A., *Diplomatic History, 1713–1933,* Hollis and Carter, London, 1946.
A manual of diplomatic events that sketches the balance of power in the eighteenth century.

*Plumb, J. H., *England in the Eighteenth Century,* Penguin Books, Baltimore, Md., 1950.
A social, cultural, and technological sum-

mary by the leading biographer of Robert Walpole and the elder Pitt.

Priestley, Herbert I., *France Overseas through the Old Regime: A Study of European Expansion,* Appleton-Century-Crofts, New York and London, 1939.
A survey from the beginning of the French empire through Napoleon.

Reddaway, W. H. *et al.,* eds., *The Cambridge History of Poland,* Vol. II, The University Press, Cambridge, 1941.
The major large-scale study of Poland in the English language edited by a major contributor to the history of the eighteenth century.

*Roberts, Penfield, *The Quest for Security, 1715–1740,* Harper and Brothers, New York, 1947, and a Harper Torchbook.
A basic study of the oligarchical politics of stability in the Rise of Modern Europe series.

Thomson, Gladys Scott, *Catherine the Great and the Expansion of Russia,* The Universities Press, London, 1959.
Short readable and scholarly treatment of Russia under an "enlightened despot" in the Teach Yourself History Series.

Williams, Basil, *The Whig Supremacy, 1714–1760,* Clarendon Press, Oxford, 1936.
A competent survey in the Oxford History of England series.

Wilson, A. M., *French Foreign Policy during the Administration of Cardinal Fleury, 1726–1743,* Harvard University Press, Cambridge, 1936.
A monographic study, one of the few modern scholarly histories of the reign of Louis XV.

See also the works by Boxer, Holborn, and Rosenberg listed at the end of Chapter I and the great work on mercantilism by Elie Heckscher cited at the end of Volume, I, Chapter XV.

# IV

# A Generation of Revolution, 1787 to 1815

On the heels of the American Revolution a wave of political and social upheavals swept through Western societies. In France, the most populous and powerful state on the Continent,* the balance between the social classes was disrupted, the old political order shattered, and the King himself executed in a rapid and often violent series of events between 1787 and 1792. In Sweden and in the Dutch Republic, rulers who had withstood the threats of reforming minorities in the 1780s lost their places in the next decade when the revolutionary leadership of France exerted its influence. Gustavus III of Sweden fell, murdered by his own nobility in 1792, and the House of Orange was driven into exile from Holland in 1795. In Poland and in Ireland, unstable neighbors of two staunchly antirevolutionary powers, Russia and England, large minorities welcomed the course of revolution and openly sought French mili-

tary aid to achieve it. In German-speaking and Italian-speaking lands, lawyers, teachers, and other intellectuals banded together to discuss and plan the revolutionary pattern. Not even England, where the monarchy was more secure and political institutions more venerated than in most countries, escaped a wave of radical protests against the old order, although the causes of parliamentary democracy and justice for the workingman were set back by many years in the ensuing prosecutions.

No single pattern of events, no short list of causes, no simple division into forces of revolution and forces of counterrevolution encompasses these European upheavals in the generation after the achievement of American independence. The influence of the American victory itself is difficult to assess. Polish patriots and liberal French noblemen alike returned from the New World to seek written constitutions and the guarantee of certain inalienable rights in the Old, but other Europeans expressed their

* About one of every seven Europeans was French in 1787.

135

discontent in phrases that were native to the Continent. By the time the American Constitution, ratified by conventions that represented popular sovereignty, went into effect in 1789, counterrevolutionaries aided by major foreign powers had snuffed out revolts in Geneva, Liège, and the Dutch Republic. In the long run, the American experience could not simply be transferred to Europe, because the social composition and the political power of the factions differed greatly on the opposite sides of the Atlantic.

We saw in Chapter III that the second half of the eighteenth century was characterized by a three-way division of contending forces. Kings and ministers, in the best tradition of enlightened despotism, sought to preserve their deteriorating positions and even to deprive the opposition of its grievances by reform programs. Broader in base, often more conservative, and relying on historic claims to an exalted place in the constitution were the aristocratic groups. These "constituted bodies" sought not only to dominate reform movements, but also to protect their privileges against despot and democrat alike. They included the two houses of the British Parliament (which were essentially alike in representing the great landowners' interests), the leading members of the French sovereign law courts or *parlements,* and the patrician "Estates" party of Belgium, which drove out the Austrians and declared a United States of Belgium in 1789. The third party was composed of democrats in the political sense only—men usually of relatively high social standing (lawyers, bureaucrats, journalists, teachers, businessmen) who sought to broaden existing political institutions. Although these "democrats" were not all middle-class, they usually came from the elite of the Third Estate, which was below the ranks of clergy and nobility. In France and elsewhere, they suffered from inexperience in politics, but enjoyed high expectations of participation. Dutch Patriots, Belgian Vonckists, and Genevan "representatives" all aimed to popularize their constitutions; in the city-state of Geneva, the struggle from 1768 to 1782 was waged between aristocrats and democrats, with no monarchical element present.

From the vantage point of 1815, it is difficult to assess the exact roles of these three great factions. The subjugation of the most expansionist and revolutionary power (France) by a congress of states dedicated to Christian, legitimate monarchy (Austria, Prussia, Russia, and England) would seem to indicate that counterrevolution had triumphed. Yet within each nation the revolutionary virus had left an infection. Below the level of courts and ministers, institutions had changed, especially the bureaucracies and the military establishments. The map of Europe, particularly of Germany, had been redrawn. A new spirit of national self-determination and pride in lingual and cultural achievement had arisen to shatter the easy cosmopolitanism of the eighteenth century.

## THE FRENCH REVOLUTION, 1787 TO 1792

Historians have argued about the general causes of the upheaval in France ever since it took place in the 1790s. Churchmen in exile were among the first to blame the subversive ideas of political philosophers such as Rousseau and critics of the Church such as Voltaire for the seduction of an entire population. The evil genius of the Enlightenment still lurks in the writings of many conservative Frenchmen today. The concept of a fanatic minority seizing power while right-thinking men acted too slowly has been entertained by modern enemies of the Revolution, not only those of the "Right" but of the "Left" as well. Since 1917, socialist critics have championed a few leaders of the decade as precursors of Lenin in their attempts to seize power on behalf of the masses.

The current generation of less doctrinaire scholars, primarily university professors on both sides of the Atlantic, have held the deteriorating economic and social conditions in France from about 1770 responsible for the popular unrest that characterized the revolutionary situation. In the 1930s, beginning with the work of such influential professors as Ernest Labrousse and Georges Lefebvre in Paris, historians came to recognize the picture of a nation that was overpopulated for its food supply, in an era of erratic harvests and poor communications, and subject to inflated prices, and in which the relations between landlord and tenant, producer and consumer were strained. After 1786, a full-scale depression set in. By the winter of 1788 to 1789, the landless peasantry was fleeing unemployment in the countryside to join the relief projects of the city, while working-class families in Paris were spending almost nine tenths of their budget on bread. The wealthier classes also suffered after 1786. Businessmen in such cities as Bordeaux and Marseilles, lacking a central bank and other institutions of credit and yielding control of government funds to court speculators, found their customers at home impoverished and their markets overseas, especially in the West Indies, overcrowded with competition. Textile manufacturers in Rouen and Lille watched their sales dwindle and laid off many workers. Producers of wine and cereal grains faced a long-term decline in prices after about 1770, yet the poor-harvest years of the late 1780s so reduced their crops that few buyers could afford them. There were very few Frenchmen without serious economic grievance by 1787. If the country bailiff or the city notary was doing a good business, many more rural and urban people had begun to live an existence bordering on starvation.

Poverty does not, however, account for the actual succession of events after 1787. Spain, East Prussia, or Russia might have laid claim to the great revolution of the century, if economic conditions alone had given rise to action. In France, the overt break with the past occurred when Louis XVI and his Finance Minister Calonne tried to fore-stall the impending crisis with a thorough set of reform measures. Within three years, factions of the nobility and of the common estate were to force their own versions of reform on the nation. The threefold revolutionary pattern, partially realized in the Thirteen Colonies, in Geneva, and in the Low Countries, appeared in full dress in France.

## The Revolt of the Nobility

As 1786 came to a close, Louis XVI and his ministers realized that they could no longer ignore the growing state deficit. Calonne, the Controller General (in charge of finances), announced that the total deficit was well over 100 million livres, almost one fourth of the yearly revenue. The old tax structure, which put the burden so heavily on peasant income and on consumer goods, would stand no further increase in a time of depression. The interest on short-term loans already accounted for almost one half of the royal treasury's payments. Calonne proposed large reductions in the operation of the royal household, abolition of many internal taxes, free trade in grain, the extension of a stamp tax, and a single income tax based on the yield of the land in each harvest. Provincial assemblies were to administer the new tax. Such a program would have reduced the royal debts, provided steady income, and alleviated the discontent of the rural masses. The program was in the best tradition of enlightened despotism, recalling the brief career of Turgot as reforming minister (1774–1776).*

A serious question of tactics now presented itself. Would the privileged bodies of the land, especially the bishops of the Catholic Church and the nobility of the thirteen *parlements,* acquiesce to such sweeping changes? The clergy, rich in land and in income from feudal dues, paid no individual taxes, but granted a "free gift" to the crown every fifth year. Noblemen were exempt from the *taille,* a tax on individual wealth, and paid

* See p. 130, *supra.*

relatively little income and poll taxes. To summon the Estates General of delegates from clergy, nobility, and commoners seemed risky, even though the last Estates had met in 1614. The nobility still insisted on a quasi-constitutional right to approve taxation when meeting in such an assembly. Similarly, the Parlement of Paris claimed the right to register royal edicts before they took the force of law. Louis XVI decided to summon a special advisory group, the Assembly of Notables. A few were liberal noblemen, such as the young Marquis de Lafayette who had recently returned home from the American wars. But one quarter of the 144 members were magistrates of the *parlements,* and the majority of the others, including the King's two brothers, were suspicious of reform. Calonne himself became the first victim of these suspicions when he announced that Necker, the supposed financial genius of the late 1770s, had lied in his published accounts of 1781.* Calonne foolishly lost the support even of Lafayette and his "Patriots" when he addressed the Parisian populace on the evils of privilege. For his rashness he was replaced, in May 1787, by the Archbishop of Toulouse, Brienne, who was an advocate of clerical reform but was more trusted at Court than Calonne.

The Notables nonetheless proved willing to discuss many serious reform measures before they dispersed in late May, after their work as advisers had been completed. Almost all of Calonne's proposals were approved. The King, for his part, showed his goodwill by cutting the army pension list and reducing the Queen's expenses. Both King and ministers accepted the principle that taxes should be raised only to satisfy actual needs, which led one critic to remark that the king of France had become the king of England, who was obliged to assemble his people yearly to approve taxes. The granting of civil status to Protestants (legalizing marriage and inheritance, legitimizing birth),

which became law in November 1787, was another edict that originated in this period. Less popular and more a product of zealous ministers was reform of the *parlements,* which restricted their jurisdiction in civil and criminal cases, enforced a minimum age for members, and ended the use of torture after conviction.

It was, in fact, the magistrates of the sovereign courts, not the nobility of Versailles or the country squires, who revolted against the royal reforms. No better example of an aristocratic body may be found than the members of the *parlements.* Although a few of them followed Lafayette in hopes of a constitutional change along English lines, the large majority were more determined to protect their fiscal and political privilege than to accept a ministerial reform program, even a good one. Eloquent in their own defense, they were violently opposed to enlightenment and enlightened advisers. Many of the *parlement* members were young, under 35. Nominally, their offices were for sale, but after mid-century they had increasingly excluded commoners from their ranks. Finally, they had already taken the lead in opposing royal absolutism.

In the summer of 1787, the Parisian magistrates refused to register the new tax edicts. They began to call for an Estates General as the only acceptable vehicle for reform. When the taxes were proclaimed despite their protests, they told the King that his program was against the national interest. By mid-August, Louis XVI felt that he had no choice but to banish the Parlement from Paris. Yet the monarch and his ministers had no real party of their own to support this measure for badly needed revenue. Late in September, the government agreed to give up the idea of new taxes. The Parlement of Paris, enjoying the enthusiastic support of most Parisians, was allowed to return. An Estates General was promised some time in the next five years, but the ministers clung to the hope that an Estates would only solemnize the .royal will.

---

* See p. 130, *supra.*

This first victory of the Parlement only increased its intransigence. By January of 1788, the Parlement of Paris freely discussed aspects of royal power that were not included in the reforms. The magistrates tried to subvert the new provincial assemblies instituted by Calonne. Most dangerous of all for the monarchy was the fact that provincial *parlements* sympathized with their Parisian colleagues. In a minor *coup d'état,* early in May 1788, the King and his chancellor struck at the offending bodies. The Parisian court system was replaced with a plenary court that was well-laced with notables, and the provincial *parlements* were suspended. The Parisian magistrates, however, successfully defied the King in refusing to hand over their leaders. Their popular supporters in Paris and Rennes (Brittany) threatened royal officials, while in Grenoble (Provence) four men died in street fighting. The disgrace of the ministerial solution was complete when Brienne was forced to admit, early in August, that the treasury was almost empty. The plenary court was abandoned and the *parlements* reinstated. The Estates General, which was feared by the ministers but hailed as a panacea by most factions of the nobility, was promised for May of 1789. Jacques Necker, the bourgeois Protestant financier, was recalled to replace Brienne. The noble revolt seemed to have taken command.

Yet the *parlements* saw their prize slip from their hands in the next six months. Although they offended liberals by proclaiming that the Estates General would be assembled and composed as in 1614, the judicial nobility really bowed before the aspirations of the third Estate.

## The Emergence of the Third Estate

The Estates General as the historic form of a national representative body was only a fiction in terms of the French population in 1789. Nobility and clergy totaled about 750,-000 members. In previous Estates, each of these orders had enjoyed one of the three votes. Their delegates combined had out-

*The first page of* What is the Third Estate?

numbered those of the Third Estate. By 1789, the single vote accorded to the commoners was to represent 25,000,000 men and women. Although the ranks of the nobility and clergy included rich and poor alike, the variation of social classes within the Third was staggering. It may be argued that the sharecropper accepted the judgment of his clerical or noble landlord, and that the wholesale merchant often sought to imitate the titled nobility. Yet bourgeois lawyers, journalists, and other professionals were highly critical of noble privilege and of the venality of the 130 bishops, all of whom were noblemen in 1789. Many businessmen and independent farmers were ambitious for a role in the reform movements in their own localities and within their own Estate. Criticism of privilege was at heart a moral position, however. The most outspoken detractor of the Versailles nobility was the Comte de Mirabeau. The pamphleteer who made his mark arguing that the Third Estate demanded a place in politics commensurate with its talents was the Abbé Sieyès.

In the autumn of 1788, Parisian and provincial lawyers attacked the pretensions of the *parlements* and urged the "doubling of the Third," so that the number of commoners' delegates would equal those of the first two orders together. Press censorship was suspended to allow the nation to advise the King, and a flood of petitions from the cities convinced Louis XVI to accept the principle of double representation. In so doing, the King followed the advice of his subjects at large, not that of his aristocratic notables. He and Necker refused to answer the more difficult question of whether the Estates should vote by order or by head, with one vote for each delegate.

Elections to the Estates took place in the spring of 1789. Although a nearly universal male suffrage existed, a complicated series of electoral assemblies within the old administrative districts unbalanced the representation in favor of urban interests. Each electoral assembly, even at the lowest levels of guild and country parish, drafted a "notebook of grievances." There was broad agreement among the orders on the need to guarantee civil rights and impose fiscal equality. However, the nobility, which elected only a small minority of liberals among its 270 delegates, demanded a return to archaic social practices and the protection of seigneurial (manor lords') rights. The clergy was more clearly divided, because the parish priests outnumbered the bishops five to one. The notebooks of grievances produced by the Third Estate's assemblies, in which the humbler citizens had little influence, displayed great variety in discussing local economic conditions. The commoners occasionally used phrases borrowed from the *phi-*

*losophes,* went further in their demands for civil liberties and constitutional government, and demanded the surrender of ancient privileges conveyed by birth. Two thirds of the 648 deputies to the order were lawyers or former royal bureaucrats. Only one in seven was a businessman, and one in ten was a country dweller.

When the Estates General met at Versailles on May 5, 1789, the deputies were given little indication that they were to participate in decisions. No reform program was offered to them. The commons found themselves treated as inferiors, left to deliberate as a separate assembly without assurance that they might later vote by head. For five weeks the commoners urged members of the nobility and clergy to join them in one great assembly. Although only the delegates from Dauphiny had had any experience in the fusion of the three orders, the commoners' determination soon split the clergy, some of whom crossed over to join the Third on June 15. Two days later this already mixed group assumed the title of National Assembly, representing the nation as a whole. If the King were to dissolve their new Assembly, the deputies declared, no taxes would be valid. With this step the constitutional history of France took a new and profound turn. On June 20 the Assembly, finding itself locked out of its hall, retired to the royal tennis court where they took a solemn oath not to disperse until the constitution of the realm should be on a firm foundation. The first great symbolic act of the Revolution was thus consummated; it is immortalized on David's canvas.*

Faced with the commoners' revolt, Louis XVI listened to his courtiers' advice. Three days after the Tennis Court Oath, he assembled the orders and informed the National Assembly that its resolutions were void. He offered penal and fiscal reform, and he offered to raise no loans or taxes without

---

* Jacques Louis David (1748–1826) was the most famous artist of the Revolution.

The Oath of the Tennis Court, *by Jacques Louis David.*

consent. He made it clear, however, that the first two orders alone would discuss their special privileges and immunities. The King did not realize that it was too late to settle the crisis on his own terms. The Third Estate claimed parliamentary immunity and refused to leave the hall. On the next day the majority of the clergy defected, and on the following day almost fifty noblemen walked out on their order. On June 27, Louis reluctantly ordered the remnants of the other orders to merge with the National Assembly. An English traveler who knew France well was moved to write in his diary that "the whole business now seems over, and the revolution complete."[1]

1. Arthur Young, *Travels in France,* London, 1909, p. 182.

## Completion of the Bourgeois Revolt

But the third phase of revolution, that of the politically aware Third Estate, was far from complete. The court party began at once to move troops (including Swiss and German regiments) into the vicinity of Paris, probably not so much to occupy the city as to prepare to dissolve the Assembly. Meanwhile, within the city itself, the electors of the Third Estate remained sitting as an informal new government for Paris, while more daring journalists sought to win over the French Guards from the court. Finally, the city lay in readiness for a typical eighteenth-century urban riot; food prices soared, and the lives of grain merchants and bakers were endangered.

*The creation of a revolutionary symbol: the fall of the Bastille, July 14, 1789.*

The crisis broke on July 11. At Versailles, Necker was dismissed. In Paris, customs posts were systematically demolished and documents burned. On July 12, the insurrection became more general when groups of marchers forced the royal garrison to withdraw from Paris. The electors quietly took over the city hall in an attempt to curb the popular agitation, but by the night of July 12 to 13 crowds were looting homes in a search for weapons. The electors tried unsuccess-fully to control the ferment by announcing the formation of a National Guard, a militia for the respectable bourgeoisie. On the morning of July 14, the shortage of arms and gunpowder led the crowds first to an arsenal, where they removed 30,000 muskets, and then across the city to the Bastille. The old fortress for state prisoners was said to be another arms depot. There in the east end of Paris the first bloody act of the Revolution was played out when the governor refused to open the gates. Ninety-eight of the civilian attackers—laborers and master craftsmen for the most part—died at the Bastille. Seven of the defenders were murdered after the governor capitulated; his head and the mayor's were paraded through the city on pikes.

The Bastille became "the shot heard 'round the world" of 1789. The National Assembly was saved. Louis XVI even journeyed to Paris to recognize the electors as a municipal council, Lafayette as Commander of the National Guard, and the tricolor as the symbol of the new regime in Paris. Necker was recalled, and many ultras of the court, including the two royal brothers, fled the country. If the National Assembly had not been involved in the fighting, it nonetheless shared power with the lower elements of the Third Estate.

In much of France political power in the cities changed hands in the summer of 1789. The provincial bourgeoisie responded first to Necker's dismissal and then to the Bastille. Although the timing of these urban revolts varied, in most cases a civilian National Guard effectively held the military balance, while a political elite of merchants and lawyers took control. In a few cities the old corporation merely expanded its ranks. Other cities, including Bordeaux, replaced their old governments with the electors of the Third, as Paris had done. Many cities (Dijon, Rouen) installed men new to politics. The primary effect of these changes was to drive out royal officials and weaken the King's authority.

In the countryside, agitation was far less organized. Rural riot was endemic to France after 1775. Starting in the fall of 1788, there had been sporadic violence and protest against game laws, royal taxes, and feudal dues. After the Bastille fell, waves of rumor affected much of the country. The peasantry envisaged imaginary oppressors—brigands, Poles and Spaniards, aristocrats. The exact relationship between this "Great Fear" and the economic condition of the peasantry is

*Cartoon showing a French peasant holding up the privileged orders.*

unclear. There is little doubt that the smaller leaseholders, sharecroppers, and wage earners in the countryside were most affected by obsolete methods of agriculture, overpopulation, and taxes. But manorial records and houses were the principal targets of peasant action in 1789. Perhaps the peasants believed that they were carrying out the King's reform program in attacking the seigneurial privileges of the nobility. At any rate, the Great Fear was the signal for a magnanimous gesture by the liberal aristocracy and clergy.

Lacking the power to suppress the peasant uprising, the Assembly was obliged to consider peasant grievances. In an emotional session on the night of August 4, 1789, the liberals led the Assembly in renouncing personal services, hunting rights, seigneurial justice, venality of office, and plural benefices. The National Assembly declared that it had destroyed the entire "feudal system." Its resolutions put an end to the principle of aristocratic privilege in France. What the nobility and clergy would not give up in May,

*The night of August 4: the Assembly abolishing "feudalism."*

they surrendered in August in response to the peasant uprising.*

Later in August, the Assembly turned to more positive principles in a virtual preamble to the forthcoming constitution. On August 26, 1789, the Assembly proclaimed the Declaration of the Rights of Man and Citizen. Basically a document of the Third Estate, the Declaration made private property "a sacred and inviolable right" along with freedom of conscience, freedom of press, and freedom of the citizen from arbitrary arrest. Equality in the Declaration meant equality before the law and in eligibility for office. Economic equality and state obligation to the poor were not mentioned. Citizens were invited to take part in lawmaking, but no specific rights of suffrage were granted. The Declaration was expressed in good eighteenth-century universals. Law was held to be "the expression of the general will," and there were marked similarities to the American Declaration of 1776. For those who idealize history, the French Decla-

---

* In the committee that framed the laws to implement these resolutions, however, it was decided that peasants would have to pay for release from obligations on property. But most peasants resisted paying this compensation until the revolutionary government of 1793 abandoned the attempt to salvage manorial rights as indemnifiable property of their owners. Thus, by resisting the National Assembly, the peasantry increased its vested interest in the preservation of its own autonomous revolution.

ration reads as strong philosophy. For its authors, it prepared a nation for the constitutional changes to come.

No discussion of a constitution could be fruitful until the King's powers were more carefully defined. He refused his assent to the August decrees and to the Declaration of Rights. Moreover, a faction within the Assembly which embraced both commoners and nobility wanted an "English" constitution, with an upper chamber and a royal absolute veto. This first clear division into political attitudes had its effect on Paris, where there was talk of marching on Versailles. The more radical group in the Assembly won its point in mid-September when a suspensive veto was passed. The King, still convinced that he was the first defender of privilege, showed his disapproval by allowing Versailles to become a hotbed of emotional demonstration for the monarchy.

Paris had soon had enough of insults to the tricolor. On October 5, 1789, a group of women from the central markets set off in the rain to Versailles to demand bread from "the baker." Lafayette's National Guard took to the road in their van. Historians will probably never know just how spontaneous was the expedition. It had been preached in the radical press for weeks, but it is difficult to identify its leaders or its connections to the Assembly. The King made haste to sign the decrees and the Declaration, but the crowd was not satisfied. Early in the morning of October 6, the royal quarters were invaded and some of the bodyguard murdered. Louis XVI had no choice but to accompany the marchers back to Paris. Ten days later the National Assembly joined the royal family there.

The last of the great days of 1789 ended all hope of a compromise between the royal party and the more determined reformers. The King and Queen henceforth felt themselves imprisoned, as they secretly wrote their friends abroad. The "English" faction was driven from the Assembly. As it set forth to give France a constitution worthy of a revolution, the middle class found itself indebted to the popular classes for victory over aristocracy and court. This uneasy alliance was to characterize the next six years of the Revolution.

## THE CONSTITUTIONAL MONARCHY, 1789 TO 1792

### The National Assembly

The National Assembly took two years to produce a constitution, as well as a series of laws that were among the most constructive of the decade. Although the Assembly was in fact a permanent constitutional convention, the planning of the new regime was not confined to the narrow hall near the royal palace where the "Constituent" sat. Editors and polemicists came into their own as political journals flourished. The range of opinion covered the aristocratic (the Swiss Mallet du Pan's *Mercure de France*), the patriotic (Brissot's *Patriote Français*), and the democratic (Marat's *L'Ami du Peuple*). Political clubs, which had sprung up in the cafés of Versailles, now dotted the neighborhood of the Assembly.

Often taking their names from the vacated monasteries and convents in which they met, the clubs reviewed the agenda of the Assembly and sought favorable legislation through petitions. Relatively high dues and a concern for a constitution that would be balanced between King and Assembly marked the Feuillants, whose members included Lafayette. The Club des Cordeliers, frequented by radical journalists and politicians such as Jacques Hébert and Georges Danton, had low dues and even accepted a few artisans as members. The Cordeliers challenged the Parisian government and adopted as the club's symbol the single eye of vigilance. Politically midway between these two was the most famous organization of its kind—the Society of the Friends of the Constitution, or Jacobin Club. At Versailles, the group had paid high dues and had included Sieyès and Mirabeau. By 1791, the Jacobins of Paris

had more nominal dues, an upper-middle-class membership, and about 400 provincial affiliates. The deputies from Paris dominated debates, although few were as outspoken in support of civil liberties as a young provincial lawyer turned Parisian journalist, Maximilien Robespierre.

More than 200 clergy and 50 nobles sat in the National Assembly. Nevertheless, the electoral arrangements were, at least on first glance, quite liberal. Citizens were divided into "actives" and "passives." The vote in primary assemblies was reserved for active citizens—males of age 25 or over who were domiciled for a year and paid a direct tax equivalent to three-days' wages. This primary electorate of about 4¼ million, or two thirds of the adult males, was by far the largest in Europe. The actual election of deputies, however, was reserved for electors, one to be selected for every one hundred active citizens. Lack of local polling places and the absence of party candidates greatly reduced actual political participation.

In economic policy, the Assembly's bourgeois character was more evident. The landlord's dues were upheld, unless the peasant could disprove their validity with documents. The redemption price of dues was high, at least twenty times the annual cash payment. Most sharecroppers and landless laborers remained unaffected, and probably a majority of peasant leaseholders simply refused to pay any compensation. The establishment of unitary metric weights and measures and the abolition of internal customs and monopolistic trading companies suited private commerce. The prohibition of all forms of association by employers and employees in June 1791 (the Chapelier Law) was designed to prevent political agitation, but such zealous liberalism pleased manufacturers more than workingmen. The end of the corporate regime was most clearly signaled by the abolition of titles and hereditary nobility.

The National Assembly revealed its concern for rationality more than its class interests in redrawing the map of France.

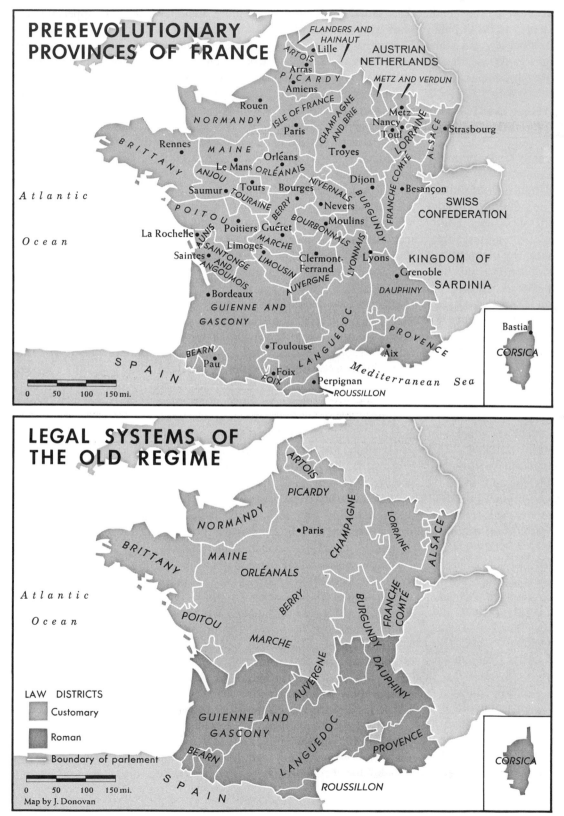

# PREREVOLUTIONARY PROVINCES OF FRANCE

FLANDERS AND HAINAUT

ARTOIS
Lille
AUSTRIAN NETHERLANDS

Arras
PICARDY
Amiens
METZ AND VERDUN

Rouen
NORMANDY
ISLE OF FRANCE
CHAMPAGNE AND BRIE
Metz
Nancy
Toul
LORRAINE
ALSACE
Strasbourg

Rennes
MAINE
Paris
Troyes

BRITTANY
Le Mans
Orléans
ORLÉANAIS

ANJOU
Saumur
Tours
TOURAINE
Bourges
BERRY
Dijon
BURGUNDY
FRANCHE COMTÉ
Besançon
SWISS CONFEDERATION

Atlantic
Ocean
POITOU
AUNIS
Poitiers
Guéret
NIVERNAIS
Nevers
Moulins
BOURBONNAIS
LYONNAIS

La Rochelle
SAINTONGE AND ANGOUMOIS
MARCHE
Limoges
LIMOUSIN
Clermont-Ferrand
AUVERGNE
Lyons
Grenoble
DAUPHINY
KINGDOM OF SARDINIA

Saintes
Bordeaux
GUIENNE AND GASCONY

BEARN
Pau
Toulouse
LANGUEDOC
PROVENCE
Aix
Mediterranean Sea

SPAIN
Foix
FOIX
Perpignan
ROUSSILLON

Bastia
CORSICA

0   50   100   150 mi.

# LEGAL SYSTEMS OF THE OLD REGIME

ARTOIS
PICARDY
NORMANDY
Paris
CHAMPAGNE
LORRAINE
ALSACE

BRITTANY
MAINE
ORLÉANALS
BERRY
BURGUNDY
FRANCHE COMTÉ

Atlantic
Ocean
POITOU
MARCHE
AUVERGNE
DAUPHINY

GUIENNE AND GASCONY
LANGUEDOC
PROVENCE

BEARN
SPAIN
ROUSSILLON

CORSICA

**LAW DISTRICTS**

Customary

Roman

Boundary of parlement

0   50   100   150 mi.

Map by J. Donovan

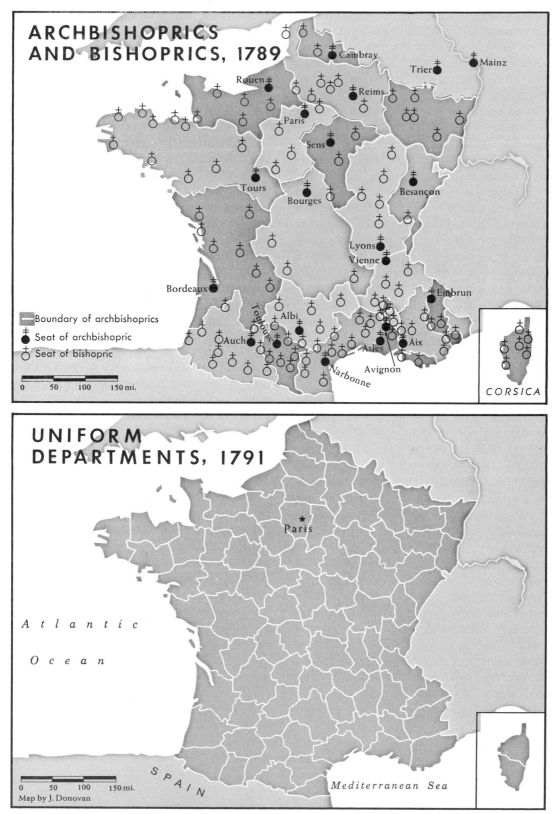

ARCHBISHOPRICS AND BISHOPRICS, 1789

Cambray
Trier
Mainz
Rouen
Reims
Paris
Sens
Besançon
Tours
Bourges
Lyons
Vienne
Bordeaux
Embrun
Toulouse
Albi
Auch
Arles
Aix
Avignon
Narbonne

Boundary of archbishoprics
Seat of archbishopric
Seat of bishopric

0    50    100    150 mi.

CORSICA

UNIFORM DEPARTMENTS, 1791

Paris

Atlantic

Ocean

SPAIN

Mediterranean Sea

0    50    100    150 mi.
Map by J. Donovan

Eighty-three departments, which were approximately equal in size and were named after natural phenomena, replaced the unequal historic provinces. Each department was subdivided into districts, but the real foundation of local government lay in the communes, in which active citizens voted directly for councils. France became a federation, in which village and town politics played an especially important part in training men for national life.

Following the suggestions of Montesquieu and the precedent of America, the Assembly separated the judiciary from the executive. *Parlements* and seigneurial courts disappeared and were replaced by tribunals at municipal and departmental levels. Magistrates were compensated for the loss of their offices.* Justice was free and equal, and judges and criminal juries were elected.

In two other areas the problems facing the Assembly were more profound and the solutions more ephemeral. The replacement of the old fiscal system with a new land tax and income taxes had failed to produce the revenue to meet old debts and current expenditures. The left wing of the Third Estate and many reforming clergymen had singled out the lands of the Catholic Church, estimated now at about 10 per cent of the country's surface, as a potential national resource as early as August 1789. With clerical members leading the way, it was decided in December to sell crown lands and Church property to obtain 400,000,000 livres. These assets would secure an issue of interest-bearing bonds or assignats, with which the state could pay off the holders of the long-term debt. The solution proved so attractive that by June of 1790 all Church holdings of rural and urban property were readied for the auction block, while the assignat became legal tender. Historians are still tracing the sales of Church property, but it seems evi-

dent that the bourgeoisie bought more lands and houses than the peasantry or former nobility. As for the assignat, it relieved a currency shortage in 1790, but by the end of 1791 had lost one third of its nominal value. Afterward it depreciated more rapidly.

## The Assembly and The Church

The most divisive issue facing the National Assembly proved to be the reorganization of the Catholic Church. That the contemplative orders had lost their spiritual justification, that plural benefices were wrong, and that the parish clergy's income was far too low were evils that were recognized by many prelates as well as laymen. The majority of the clergy even accepted the inevitable conclusion that they had to become salaried state servants, once their land was gone. The Assembly granted freedom of worship to Protestants and Jews. But lay and clerical members of the Assembly fell into fundamental conflict over the ratification of the new Civil Constitution of the Clergy, which was approved by the King in August 1790.

Most laymen were free to accept the fact that the National Assembly was empowered to remake all institutions. The clergy, however, could not accept the redistribution of parishes and dioceses, the reduction of bishops from 130 to 83 to correspond with the departments, and popular election of bishops and curés without the approval of the Pope or of a national Church synod. When, by November 1790, no such approval seemed possible, the National Assembly declared the Civil Constitution of the Clergy to be in force and required a loyalty oath to the nation from bishops and priests. The confrontation of spiritual and temporal authority was all the more tragic in a nation that was not noted for its religiosity. Only seven bishops took the loyalty oath, and in some parts of the country, especially in Brittany and in Alsace, up to 90 per cent of the priests would not join the new state Church. Pope Pius VI condemned the arrangement in

---

* As many of them worked for restoration of the Old Regime, however, as accepted the compensation.

the spring of 1791. The newly elected constitutional clergy was regarded by the devout as blasphemous, and the "nonjurors" or refractory priests were considered by the patriotic to be potential counterrevolutionaries. The refractory priests often led their congregations into deep hostility toward the new regime.

## Seeds of Counterrevolution

Other signs of danger had appeared by 1791. Across the border on the east there lived small groups of noblemen including many army officers, who had emigrated from France and were bitterly hostile to the Revolution. The *émigrés* at Turin (Savoy) and Coblentz and Worms (west of the Rhine) were seeking foreign support and even beginning to form a counterrevolutionary army. Unemployment was returning to Paris in the spring of 1791. The Cordeliers Club and its affiliates were moving into open opposition against the restrictions on suffrage.

It was treason of Louis XVI that broke the precarious balance. The King chose the night of June 20–21, 1791, to flee Paris and to attempt to join up with the *émigré* garrisons over the northeastern frontier. Marie Antoinette and her Swedish lover had planned the escape badly, however, and the royal family was detected at Varennes, close to the frontier, and brought ignominiously back to Paris. The King could no longer be seen as a weak monarch with good intentions. His repudiation of the regime very nearly produced his suspension, and the Cordeliers Club called for a republic. Agitation turned into tragedy in mid-July when the National Guard broke up a meeting of would-be republicans on the Champs de Mars, killing about fifty petitioners. Varennes had an international effect, too, because the rulers of Austria and Prussia joined in the Declaration of Pillnitz on August 27, 1791, threatening the restoration of the old order in France.

By this time, the image of the Revolution abroad was already ambiguous. German poets and philosophers, such as Wieland,

*Lafayette as Commander of the National Guard.*

Kant, and Herder,* had hailed the fall of the Bastille. In England, the young poet Wordsworth and the scientist Priestley thought that the first several months after the Estates General had been as glorious as 1688. In 1789, the liberal Polish nobility formed a sympathetic philosophical club, while many of the towns banded together to ask for burgher rights. The potential conflict between entrenched aristocracy and ambitious bourgeoisie was clear, for the Polish gentry dominated the Diet. Yet the constitutional revolution in Poland in May 1791 was based on cooperation between burghers and noblemen. The free veto enjoyed by the great magnates in the Diet disappeared. Burghers were given access to nobility and were granted self-government in the towns. The Poles more than other Europeans needed the French example of sharing privileges in the name of individual liberties, in order to survive their expansionist neighbors.

Another strand of European thought,

---

* For discussions of Kant and Herder, see pp. 84–85 and 183.

*Proclamation of the Constitution of 1791.*

classes. Burke's *Reflections* opened a great debate on the French Revolution, for he was challenged in 1791 by the Anglo-American pamphleteer, Thomas Paine. There were soon self-styled counterrevolutionaries and revolutionaries in Europe. Although the latter were often of the urban middle classes, dissenters from religious orthodoxy, and democrats in political affairs, the debate was at heart ideological rather than social.

## The Legislative Assembly and the Constitution of 1791

In September 1791, the constitution was presented to the King for his assent, and elections to the new government took place. The unicameral Legislative Assembly, like its predecessor, overrepresented urban areas. Its social composition was almost the same; about two thirds of the 745 deputies had some experience in local government or in the courts. But they were all new men on the national scene, because a self-denying ordinance had prevented reelection of members of the Constituent. Men such as Robespierre and Danton had to confine their political ambitions to the clubs, which took on new importance.

The political elite that was most in evidence was a loose coalition of provincial deputies, known to posterity as the Girondins from the river of their native Bordeaux, although contemporaries often called them after their principal spokesman, the impulsive journalist Brissot. Their inspiration was the imaginative Madame Roland, who yearned to make of revolutionary France another, more virtuous Rome. Brissot and the other Girondins rapidly moved to secure strong measures against refractory clergy and *émigrés,* including death sentences for nobility who assembled against the nation. But it was as war hawks that the Girondins left their mark on revolutionary politics.

however, was skeptical of the changes in France. By 1790, when the confiscation of Church property and the emigration were under way, these critics turned into enemies. The most famous of these unfriendly observers was the British statesman Edmund Burke. Formerly a champion of American independence and of Irish rights, Burke was unable to sanction events in France. He was genuinely afraid for the fate of the court and of the clergy by the time he published his *Reflections on the Revolution in France,* in November 1790. Burke's opposition to change in France rested on grounds that have made him one of the pillars of European conservatism. The French experiment was dangerous, irreligious, and bound to fail because it proceeded from abstract principles, he argued. Politics is not a manipulation of contracts, but the indissoluble partnership of succeeding generations in eternal society. The "Rights of Man" were a blind substitution for the experience of the landed, ruling

## The Girondins and the Outbreak of War

Brissot and his friends viewed the idea of a war against France's eastern neighbors, Prussia and Austria, as a crusade to spread revolution against wicked kings. They also sought to use the war issue to gain important posts in the ministry. Austrian and Prussian support for the *émigrés* abroad and the French queen at home, the sister of the Emperor, added both moral fervor and a diplomatic *casus belli* to the cause of the Girondins. Robespierre, at the Jacobin Club, feared that Marie Antoinette would turn an Austrian war into a trap. Brissot's followers carried the day, however, and on April 20, 1792, France declared war on Austria. The Emperor's Prussian ally joined him, and Catherine the Great of Russia promised to send troops.

Foreshadowing events to come, the war went badly for France from the start and led to political upheaval at home. The Prussian forces began a steady advance against a French army that had been weakened by the emigration of more than one half of its officers. Parisians rioted over the high cost of provisions. Rumor grew that the Queen had formed an "Austrian Committee" to deliver the nation. The King tried to stem the rush of events by using his veto against the plan to bring 20,000 National Guards to Paris to celebrate the "Federation Day" on July 14. When Louis XVI dismissed his Girondin ministers in June, an armed band of shopkeepers and artisans invaded the royal apartments and danced about the King as he donned a red liberty cap. Ignoring the royal veto, the Assembly summoned the provincial National Guards to Paris in July. The Marseilles battalion arrived singing a battle hymn that had been written for a northern regiment, but was soon to become a stirring national anthem.

In Paris, the National Guards found a militant atmosphere. The assignat had declined

*Meeting of the Jacobin Club.*

further. The circulation of grain was badly slowed, and shortages were compounded by requisitions for war. There was talk in Paris and elsewhere of price controls and the appropriation of large farms. Jacques Roux, a Parisian vicar, demanded the death penalty for hoarders. Poverty began to be equated with virtue, and vice became the inevitable trait of the wealthy. A ringing phrase that summed it up for many Parisians by the summer of 1792 was the famous negative appellation sans-culotte, that is, he who went without the knee breeches of the upper class. The term was first applied to intransigents after Varennes. It implied contrast with the high bourgeoisie as well as with the nobility. A type of the sans-culotte was the artisan who had no classical education and who saw issues in blacks and whites. He was not represented politically because of the distinction between active and passive citizens, although he was often in attendance at the meetings of the Paris sections, or wards.

In the summer of 1792, the Girondins had a fatal weakening of nerve, for they feared that cooperation between the citizens of the sections and the guardsmen might overpower their opportune leadership. By the end of July, these fears were realized; 47 of the 48 sections had come out for the abdication of the King. The Prussian commander only strengthened the Parisians' will when he pub-

*A Parisian sans-culotte.*

*Revolutionary crowd intimidating Louis XVI at the Tuileries.*

### The Revolution Revolutionized

The August insurrection turned the Parisian government into a revolutionary Commune, which proceeded to imprison many liberal noblemen and clergy as suspects and to assume direction of the war. The Legislative Assembly was shattered when more than half of its members fled Paris. Louis XVI, in reality a condemned man, was suspended by the Assembly's rump and turned over to the Commune for imprisonment. Following Robespierre's aims, the rump announced a National Convention, the deputies to be elected by universal male suffrage. As Lenin was to say many years later after the second upheaval of 1917, the events of August 10, 1792, revolutionized the Revolution.

In the six weeks before the Convention assembled, the implications of August 10 became clear. The deportation of refractory priests was declared. Emigré property was to be sold off by the state. Landlords lost all their dues without compensation unless they could prove title. The egalitarian form of address, "Citizen," was adopted. A distinguished group of foreign intellectuals, including Tom Paine, was given honorary citizenship. But the remnants of the Legislative failed to cooperate with the Commune.

Cooperation was needed, for the Prussian advance quickened after August 10. By the end of the month, the enemy had taken Ver-

lished a manifesto that labeled the National Guards as irregulars and threatened summary treatment after he took the city. On the night of August 9-10, 1792, deputies from the sections took over the city government while the Legislative Assembly stood by, paralyzed. Early the next morning, the insurgents marched on the Tuileries (Royal Palace), while the royal family fled to the Assembly. In the ensuing battle of hand-to-hand and artillery combat, the defenders, mostly Swiss guards, lost more than 600 killed and wounded. The band of shopkeepers, master craftsmen, and provincial guards who had taken up arms suffered 376 casualties.

dun, only 150 miles away. Thousands of Parisians marched off to the front, as the Commune combed the city for arms and for suspects. On September 2, the mood of patriotic frenzy turned to paranoia against the supposed enemy within. Popular bands invaded the prisons, took the unfortunate inmates before hastily erected tribunals, and carried out summary executions. The September massacres went on for several days; between 1100 and 1400 prisoners were slaughtered, including thieves and prostitutes as well as priests and former nobles. The American ambassador reported seeing blood running in the streets. No party would accept responsibility for the massacres, and in reality almost all of the national delegates feared the violence of the city. After August 10, a fourth force thrust itself into the arena where "democrat" had already triumphed over aristocrat and monarch.

## THE REPUBLIC OF THE CONVENTION, 1792 TO 1795

### The Republic and the War

The Convention celebrated its first session on September 21, 1792, by replacing the monarchy with a republic. The occasion was a triumphant one, for news had arrived of the first clear French victory in the field, which had halted the Prussian advance at Valmy, in the Argonne Valley to the north. The battle at Valmy was little more than an artillery duel in the fog, but, as the German poet Goethe remarked, it was to have infinite repercussions. The approach of winter sealed the Prussian defeat. In the next six weeks, the French armies "liberated" Savoy, crossed the Rhine to take Frankfurt, and overran Belgium, after a true victory at Jemappes, where 40,000 sans-culottes overwhelmed the enemy while chanting the "Marseillaise."

By mid-November 1792, the Convention was in a position to promise "aid and fraternity to all peoples wishing to recover their liberty." The simple formula was tested in occupied Belgium, where oligarchical Statists and Democrats disputed the right to organize the new regime. The Convention announced the confiscation of noble and princely property to pay for the occupation. However, the Estates party—victors over the Austrians in 1789 and now considered aristocrats—won the first elections. Alarmed by the results of self-determination, the Convention followed the requests of Democrats and annexed Belgium in February 1793. Whether the universal pattern of democratic revolution could be achieved without French soldiers was to remain a vital question throughout the 1790s.

The Convention had far less success in pacifying the sans-culottes at home than the democrats abroad. Elections to the Paris Commune returned many radicals. The Commune sent its own commissioners to neighboring provinces to requisition men and supplies. Most of the sections demanded price controls for grain. The deputies were alarmed by a virtual rural insurrection south of Paris.

Politics, however, became the great divisive issue in the new Republic. The Girondins had aroused the opposition of a small group of deputies from Paris even before the war. Now the Girondins, who were basically men of the provinces, found their opponents from Paris clustered high on the benches of the Assembly and taking for themselves the name of the Mountain. Both groups were approximately of the same social class, and there was rough agreement on anticlericalism and economic liberalism. The Mountain, however, could accuse the ministers of federalist tendencies, and they were less afraid of an alliance with the sans-culottes. The rapid train of events exaggerated ill feeling between the two groups. The harmony of the first days of the Republic soon faded before the question of the King.

The fate of Louis XVI marked a clear break between the two factions. The Girondins squandered their initiative in trying to blame Danton and the Mountain for the

*Drawing the bluest blood: the execution of Louis XVI.*

September massacres. It was Robespierre who had to remind the Convention early in December that either Louis XVI was guilty of treason or they were. Few could doubt the duplicity of the King after a chest with his secret correspondence was found, but the Girondins could question the competency of the Convention to sit as a jury. They lost their point and also failed to prevent the imposition of the death sentence. Louis XVI was guillotined on January 21, 1793. The real victors were the Mountain and their friends in the Jacobin clubs.

Military and diplomatic events took on a new significance. Despite strong libel laws and press censorship, English democratic societies alarmed their government by sympathizing with France. Both governments regarded war as inevitable after the French intervention in the Low Countries. France declared war on both England and Holland in February. A month later, Spain was in the war along with the Italian states. England was the cornerstone of a coalition of unequal allies, which was negotiated throughout 1793. Englishmen such as Burke believed that the First Coalition would save

European civilization and the aristocracy. Young William Pitt, a great wartime leader like his father, had a more traditional aim—to restore the political equilibrium and contain France. The continental powers were not as strongly convinced that France represented a real threat, for France and England had fought colonial and naval wars for more than a century.

Coalitions against France never held together for very long in the revolutionary years. Eastern members were bent on expanding their own borders. A Russian army had moved into Poland in May 1792, putting down the year-old regime as a criminal plot inspired by France. Prussia similarly crossed the Polish frontier in January 1793. The two invaders formed a holy alliance against "French democratism," but they also sought to annex more Polish territory. By midsummer of 1793, a conservative restored Polish Diet, under Russian pressure, had ceded large areas of Great Poland (with Danzig) to Prussia and of the Ukraine to Russia. The end of Poland as a nation effectively dates from the Second Partition of 1793, which was the greatest victory of the counterrevolution.*

## Internal Crises

The coming together of social unrest, political agitation, and unfavorable foreign entanglements had marked the crises of May-June 1789 and July-August 1792. Now, late in February of 1793, another rapid series of events left the legislative body torn asunder.

High commodity prices and intense suspicion of hoarding and speculation touched off enforced sales at prices that were set by the crowds, often women. Sectional leaders and journalists such as Marat were not ashamed to accept responsibility. Radicals such as Roux and his *enragés* threatened private property with the "agrarian law"— the subdivision of large estates in favor of

* See map, page 111, *supra.*

small agricultural producers. On the front, the spring campaign against Holland opened badly. When the Convention, early in March, turned to recruiting soldiers over all of the Republic, a major civil war broke out in the Vendée, west of Paris and south of Brittany. Rebel bands of peasantry under noble and clerical leadership fought savagely and soon offered a real military threat to the Revolution at home. As the Vendée turned into a siege of western cities, the French General Dumouriez entered into treasonable negotiations in Holland with the enemy. Early in April, French forces were driven from the Rhineland, and the first regiments of English soldiers moved across the Channel.

The response of the Convention necessarily had to be in the direction of increased central authority. Deputies from the Convention, dressed in scarlet cloaks and sporting the tricolor, were made "representatives on mission." By early April, they were acting as political commissars to the armies. A revolutionary tribunal was created on March 10, especially to judge political cases and the refractory priests. The public prosecutor could arrest suspects on the denunciation of a single person. News of the Vendée led to the death penalty for rebels caught in arms. A similar sentence for all *émigrés,* and revocation of their sales and inheritances since 1789, followed. The citizenry at large was enlisted in discovering the enemy within by the establishment of committees of surveillance in the communes. The emergency legislation was capped off on April 10, 1793, by the creation of a Committee of Public Safety to supervise the executive functions of the state.

The Convention was also the scene of a desperate struggle for power between the Girondins and the Mountain. The struggle was mirrored in many provincial cities, especially in the south, where in Lyons, Marseilles, and Bordeaux Jacobins were driven out. While the two factions screamed of plot and counterplot, the *enragés* and the Parisian sections successfully urged price controls on grain. A rough coalition of sectional leaders, Jacobin Club members, and sans-culotte National Guards put an end to the crisis, purging the Convention of 29 Girondin leaders from May 31 to June 2, 1793. Paris had experienced its third great revolutionary day, but the pattern of conflict between aristocrat and democrat had been left behind. The summer of 1793 was to be the summer of the sans-culottes.

Historians who believe that men do exactly what they want to do write of bitterly opposed groups in that summer. The Girondins retained power in Lyons, and in August the Convention opened siege on this city that had executed its Jacobins. In Paris, the sans-culottes wanted their own militia. Instead, the Convention relied on general mobilization, the *levée en masse* of August. The *enragés* wanted to enforce economic controls by violence. The Convention tried to forestall thorough measures by creating public granaries. The sans-culottes wanted social needs to precede the rights of property, but the new constitution stopped short at state responsibility for employment and education. The constitution went on to combine absolute property rights with universal male suffrage. The Parisian world of sectional leaders and journalists sought everywhere to challenge the moderates, but in that summer Marat was assassinated and Roux arrested.

Historians who emphasize the impersonal forces of history are less prone to judge the various republicans as entirely responsible for their actions. The assignat fell from 36 per cent of value in June to 22 per cent of value in late August. Bread shortages were constant. The war went very badly on both northern and southern fronts; the handing over of Toulon and half the navy to the British was the cruelest loss of all. Not until September did the Convention turn back rebel power in the Vendée, and then only with seasoned troops. The argument between historians of plot and of circumstances may never end, but the atmosphere of treason, defeat, and assassination in the summer of

1793 prepared for the period of the Terror that followed.

The Convention triumphed over the sans-culottes with great difficulty in the autumn of 1793. The crisis—still another dramatic turning point—came on September 4 and 5, when crowds of workingmen surrounded the city hall and penetrated to the floor of the national legislature, demanding more bread and a revolutionary army. The day was narrowly saved by a promise to pay indigent sans-culottes for attendance at the sections. Before the end of September, the Convention moved to set up a wide system of price controls on more than forty necessities. Wages as well as foodstuffs, fuel, and clothing were affected. With large-scale requisitions of raw materials and labor, city control of the grain trade, and prices set by the districts, government intervention in economic life was complete.

## The Terror and the Republic of Virtue

An even more profound legacy of the struggle for control of the Revolution was the routinization of Terror in the fall of 1793. A law regarding suspects listed many vague categories of enemies who were to be imprisoned for the duration of the war. The Committee of Public Safety, which Robespierre joined in July, now received two extremist Parisian deputies. On October 10, the new mood of the Committee was expressed by its youngest member, Saint-Just. In a speech justly famous, he defined the principles of the Terror. Not only treachery but indifference would be punished. The Republic has but two parties—the people and their enemies. Justice is reserved for the former and iron for the latter. The Constitution of 1793 was to be suspended (to which the Convention assented) and the "provisional government of France" was to be "revolutionary until the peace."

Saint-Just justified the startling transition in dangerously abstract terms, citing the sovereign will of the people. Neither he nor

*Marie Antoinette led to execution, by Jacques Louis David.*

Rousseau thirty years earlier meant a majority rule when they used the term. The sovereign will expresses the fundamental truth of a community; it must always be just and reasonable. To the men who governed France in the winter of 1793 to 1794, the regime had to be absolutely virtuous. To those who so believed, the seeds of totalitarianism remained hidden.

The principle of a single will was soon institutionalized. A decree of December 4, 1793, became the virtual constitution of the new regime. The Convention was to publish its laws within twenty-four hours. Departmental administrations, suspect of federalism, were shorn of most of their powers. Local surveillance committees, which were busy at purifying popular societies and at screening suspects for the revolutionary tribunals, had to report to the Convention every ten days. The Committee of Public Safety was made officially responsible for war and diplomacy. Its members and representatives on mission visited the armies, checked on the communes, and presided over military tribunals to try the prisoners of civil war. Police power lay with the Committee of General Security, which also presided over the political trials. In mid-October, Marie Antoinette went to the guillotine; the scene, with her proud figure seated in the tumbrel, was caught on canvas at the right moment by the artist David. Two other well-known women followed her—a mistress of the old regime (Madame Du Barry) and one of the new (Madame Roland). Twenty-one Girondin leaders were executed in November.

An old view of the period after the passage of the December laws once held that the Committee of Public Safety emerged with a despotic hold on France. The Committee allegedly condoned the savage reprisals at Lyons, where one of its members oversaw the massacre by cannonade of 350 moderates, and at Nantes, where Carrier, the representative on mission, was present while 3000 Vendéens were shot and 2000 deliberately drowned in the Loire. The Twelve, the members of the Committee, were a remarkable group—young (averaging 37 years) and variously experienced (they included a Protestant pastor, an actor, two army officers, and six lawyers). Until the 1920s, Robespierre, the member without portfolio, was described as a deluded and bloodthirsty fanatic, so secure in his own virtue that he could still wear the powdered hair, frock coat, and frilled shirt of the aristocracy.

It is now evident that the less dramatic members of the Committee, such as Lazare Carnot, an army engineer who was labeled by Napoleon as "the organizer of victory," were more important in the business of governing than were the doctrinaires. Several Committee members and the majority of the representatives on mission were genuinely interested in bringing justice and equality to the provinces that they inspected. The

*Robespierre, spokesman for the Republic of Virtue.*

Committee itself, although temporarily immune from review by the Convention, was opposed on the "Right" by a group that gathered around Danton and on the "Left" by the revolutionary militia and by more radical clubs that were inspired by Hébert, one of history's great yellow journalists. The Committee of Twelve owed their power in 1793 to 1794 far more to circumstances than to cohesion and genius. Their reign after December rested on victory in the civil war in the west and the southeast and on the expulsion of the enemy from French territory. The assignat regained some of its purchasing power by 1794. Through the representatives on mission, the Committee was associated with the widespread anticlericalism that became a veritable campaign for the dechristianization of France. A Republican calendar in which months were named after the seasons had already replaced the Christian year. History began with the year I, on the day of the declaration of the Republic. Sunday be-

*Procession headed by the Goddess of Reason.*

came a workday and every tenth day became a lay holiday. Churches were stripped of their ornaments and vessels. By the end of 1793, Parisian churches were closed and a Festival of Reason had taken place in Notre Dame. Priests were urged to marry, and Jesus became a sans-culotte. If the Committee was in touch with the national mood in matters of religion in the first months of its rule, nevertheless the ultimate effect of dechristianization was to alienate further small communities and the Church from the Revolution.

The apparent rule of the Committee lasted only a few months. By April 1794, it had brought about the trial and execution of Hébert on the Left and Danton on the Right. Robespierre and Saint-Just were crying of a "foreign plot," but were prosecuting domestic enemies. Price controls were altered to allow higher retail profits. The Committee announced the redistribution of traitors' property to the poor, but failed to convince the sans-culottes of a true desire for social equality. Some measures of social justice were passed—free medical care for the aged, free compulsory primary education, the end of slavery—but Robespierre and Saint-Just were increasingly preoccupied with moral absolutes. A series of national festivals of re-

publicanism was arranged by David, who was now the "pageant-master." A Supreme Being was invoked to halt the tide of sacrilegious practice, and it was apparent that Robespierre was at heart still a warm Deist. More ominously, the procedure of the revolutionary tribunals was accelerated with the law of 22nd *Prairial* II (June 10, 1794). The accused was to have no counsel. Moral proof was considered adequate. Only two verdicts were possible—acquittal or death. More than half of the 2639 executions performed in Paris occurred after the *Prairial* law.

Ironically, the final period of the Terror saw the French armies again on the move into Belgium. But the revolutionary government depended on crisis. Now fatigue and personal animosities could take their toll. In the last weeks of their lives, Robespierre and Saint-Just were becoming estranged from their colleagues. The General Security Committee suspected its rival of seeking to take over the police power. The Commune was largely on the side of Robespierre, but the all-important committees of the sections were divided. On July 27, 1794—the 9th *Thermidor,* the hot month—the Convention was persuaded to arrest Robespierre and his immediate followers. He perished on the guillotine on the following day, together with Saint-Just and many of the Commune leaders.

The period of the Terror will forever be weighted by the chilling number of executions. Probably more Frenchmen died in prisons and in summary executions in the year before *Thermidor* than were guillotined following trial (16,594). Three quarters of the death penalties were pronounced in the west and in the Rhône Valley, seats of civil war. Four fifths of the charges specified rebellion or treason. Only one victim in twelve was a nobleman and one in sixteen a priest. Almost 60 per cent were workers and peasants. Some historians have argued that more Frenchmen died in 1871 than in the Terror, but the power of a revolution as his-

*Terrorists executing terrorists: Robespierrists at the guillotine.*

torical myth does not depend on statistics. "Paris in the Terror" still symbolizes a people caught up in moral oppression. Death on the guillotine weighed heavily on men's minds, but equally dominating was the realization that the state demanded complete devotion. Until the enemy without and the enemy within should be vanquished—and only the state could say when that might be —every citizen had to show his dedication. For a few brief months in the Year Two of the Revolution, men and women suspended their ordinary interests and changed their civic symbols, their dress, and even their names. Robespierre, in his most important speech, declared that a popular revolutionary government must have both virtue and terror. What he could not realize in the spring of 1794 is that very few ordinary men shared his profound belief that the Revolution could substitute morality for egotism, principle for habit, and right reason for tyrannical custom.

## The Reaction of Thermidor

The Republic of the Convention hung on for more than a year after Robespierre's death. Some of the divisive issues of the Terror spent themselves. The cult of the Supreme Being passed quickly. In the autumn of 1794, the constitutional Church came to an end, with the state being officially neutral in matters of religion. There is some evidence of a religious revival among the less educated, and in many towns refrac-

tory priests returned to hold Mass. The Committee of Public Safety lost its extensive powers and was purged of the remaining original members. The infamous *Prairial* law survived Robespierre by only three weeks. The Convention negotiated a peace with the rebels of the Vendée and returned their firearms and their clergy. The puritanism of the Republic of Virtue gave way to a cynical press and theater, to the revival of the salon, and to revealing dress.

But Terror itself, especially political assassination, did not end on 9th *Thermidor*. Former Hébertists and Dantonists stirred up gangs of "gilded youths" against supporters of the Mountain and closed the Jacobin Club. The Parisian sections were purged of passive citizens and many of the sans-culottes. The reaction from the Right reached its climax in the spring of 1795 in the southeast. The massacre of prisoners at Marseilles and at Lyons became known as the White Terror.

The most serious unsettled business after *Thermidor* was the reappearance of inflation, after the end of most economic controls in the winter of 1794 to 1795. Price controls ended in December, yet requisition for war continued. By March 1795, the assignat had fallen to 8 per cent of value. Extreme cold added to the misery of the sans-culottes, and the suicide rate rose in Paris. The desperation of the sans-culottes erupted in the spring of 1795. Following a popular threat to the Convention in April, Jacobin survivors were deported. The repression was more severe after an abortive attack on May 20 to 24, in which artillerymen of the working quarters almost fired on the Convention. A military commission condemned the leaders, and the legislature was further purged. Sans-culottes were virtually excluded from the National Guard. The popular phase of the Revolution came to an end, leaving bourgeois democrats solely in command.

Great success on the military front characterized the year after *Thermidor*. The army of occupation in Belgium swept into the

Ruhr. The Palatinate fell, and Prussia withdrew from the war in April 1795, leaving the left bank of the Rhine to France. Spain withdrew from the coalition in the summer of 1795, and French troops gained the Italian Riviera. The most striking success came in the Low Countries, where the Army of the North had crossed the frozen Rhine delta in January 1795. A Batavian Republic was declared; the first of the "sister republics," it was built on the support of the native Dutch Jacobins. The stadtholder of the House of Orange fled to England. Under the Treaty of the Hague (May 1795), the Dutch paid a high price for their independence, joining France as an ally and giving up an indemnity and the mouth of the Scheldt. The Batavian Republic was not to have its constitution for three years, but the French invasion had revealed another genuine group of democrats in Europe, the first to combine in a motto the three keys words, "Liberty, Equality, Fraternity." Of the First Coalition, only Britain at sea and Austria on land still challenged France.

Late in the summer of 1795 the Thermidoreans produced a new, more bourgeois constitution, which specified the duties as well as the rights of man and reinstated the system of a qualified electorate. Fear of centralized power led to a bicameral legislature and a five-man executive, the Directors. When the Convention tried to ensure that two thirds of the new legislature would come from its ranks, however, a royalist revolt in Paris nearly succeeded. The pretender to the throne, the late King's younger brother, was hopelessly anachronistic as Louis XVIII. The royalists bungled an attempt to link up with a British invasion of Brittany in July 1795. The Parisian sections were more dangerous, and the uprising of *Vendémiaire* (October 1795) had to be put down with concentrated artillery fire, not a mere "whiff of grapeshot" as the young General Bonaparte was later to claim. In the confused politics of the Directory (1795-1799), the army was to play an increasing role.

## THE REPUBLIC OF THE DIRECTORY, 1795 TO 1799

### The Bourgeois Republic and Its Enemies

The sans-culottes and their cry for "bread and the Constitution of 1793" had been defeated in 1795. Under the new constitution, the vote was restricted as it had been in 1791. Property qualifications for members of the two houses (Council of Five Hundred and Council of Ancients) were higher than before. There were 158 regicides among the Council members, but an equal number of royalists were returned. Many of the new men not taken from the Convention were businessmen and speculators. Of the five original Directors, only one remained a Jacobin. The Directory was truly the bourgeois republic.

The institutions that the Directory gave to the nation also favored the upper-middle class. The Convention in its last days had decreed elite secondary schools, the forerunners of the present *lycées*. Now the Directory installed central schools in each department. A National Institute dedicated to the sciences symbolized government aid to research. Strict accounting procedures were introduced in the administration of relief to the poor and in the preparation of the national budget. The assignat, worthless by the spring of 1796, was replaced by another paper currency, the conversion rates favoring those who still held gold. Bankers and businessmen in the Councils prepared legislation for a Bank of France, to be created in 1800.

The Directory weathered an attack from the Left in its first days. A radical newspaper editor who had seen rural and urban poverty, François Babeuf, became convinced of the impossibility of a just regime so long as the protection of private property continued to dominate politics. In the autumn of 1795, as prices in Paris rose 75 per cent higher than in 1789, Babeuf prepared an armed "Conspiracy of the Equals" to take over the Republic. With the aid of former Jacobins and terrorists, Babeuf created a secret and highly disciplined organization. The conspiracy's "Manifesto of the Plebeians" ordered the end of private property. The movement has been called "the first attempt in history to establish a communist society by political means."[2] Babeuf was betrayed by a police spy, and the movement was broken up in May 1796; he and his associates were guillotined a year later.

Royalism was as dangerous to the Directory as Jacobinism, however. Purges followed the yearly elections to the legislatures from 1795 to 1799, recalling the years between the English monarchy of the 1640s and Cromwell's Protectorate. In the course of these purges, the Directors relied increasingly on the generals and on the loyalty of the troops to their officers. Generals from two major armies made possible the most sweeping change of regime on the 18th *Fructidor* (September 4, 1797), when more than 200 deputies and even one of the Directors were driven out of office, with 65 persons deported to the "dry guillotine" of Guiana.

## The "Grande Nation"

The latent power of the military rested on the great accomplishment of the Directory —the expansion of France and her revolutionary institutions. This expansion was prepared by the many young generals who had been promoted so rapidly after 1792, by the Jacobin sympathizers who acted as commissars to the armies, and by the hundreds of thousands who served in the ranks. Almost one million men had been mobilized by 1796, and about 450,000 were in service when the Directory began. The Directors themselves were content with having broken the First Coalition.* They made little attempt to encourage revolutions abroad, and it was not until the *coup* of Fructidor allowed more explicit aid to foreign Jacobins that the

* See *supra,* page 154.

2. George Rudé, *Revolutionary Europe 1783–1815,* Harper and Row, New York, p. 172.

Dutch democrats of the Batavian Republic gained their written constitution.

It was in northern Italy that the French army proved that its aims went far beyond simple conquest. The brilliant campaign of the spring of 1796, in which the French army took Milan in five weeks and neutralized the entire peninsula within three months, was planned and led by the most daring of the young generals—Napoleon Bonaparte. Born in 1769 of a landed Italian family on Corsica, and French by reason of the island's annexation the year before, Bonaparte had been educated in France and commissioned in the artillery. He had distinguished himself in action against the British at Toulon in 1793 and against the Parisians on *Vendémiaire.* He also knew how to mix politics with his military career. A good Jacobin in 1791, he was a moderate in 1795 and by 1796 saw that he should seek his fortune at the front, away from the corruption of Paris (where, nevertheless, he had just married Josephine de Beauharnais, the former mistress of a Director). In Italy, Bonaparte settled down at Milan to cultivate his army's loyalty and to send home bullion and art treasures to placate the Directors. But Bonaparte believed in liberty for the Italians as well as in requisitions. Giving material aid to middle-class revolutionaries in Milan, he announced the Cisalpine Republic, in June 1797, the first deliberate copy of the French regime abroad. Bonaparte also ignored instructions in negotiating his own terms with Austria. In October 1797, in the Treaty of Campo Formio, he confirmed French possession of Belgium and sacrificed the ancient Republic of Venice to the Austrians, who withdrew from the war.

The year 1798 has been called "the high tide of revolutionary democracy." Sister republics in Holland, Switzerland, northern Italy, Genoa, Rome, and Naples, had constitutions similar to that of the Directory in France. Each contained a declaration of the rights of man, and most specified citizens' duties as well. Each republic was divided into departments and had two legislatures and a five-man Directory. The republics had been founded with the aid of local patriots, and the citizenry voted in primary and electoral assemblies.* In 1798, Frenchmen were speaking of the *"Grande Nation"* and the "natural frontiers" of the French people, which included the left bank of the Rhine. On the fourth anniversary of Robespierre's fall, a procession wound through Paris honoring Liberty and proudly showing the imperial scope of the Republic. A bear from Berne, lions from Africa, and camels from Egypt were followed by the famous Corinthian bronze horses from Venice.

*Sieyès, the old revolutionary who organized Napoleon's coup d'état.*

## Defeat and Coup d'état

Many contemporaries and modern historians have seen democratic revolution at its height in 1798. The American government reacted with the Alien and Sedition Laws. In England, sailors had mutinied, and the United Irish rose in Ulster—an abortive rebellion to be followed by union with Great Britain. Other historians will admit that revolutionary movements were liberal and bourgeois in character everywhere, but not democratic; only in France did a "Fourth Estate" force its will temporarily on the revolution.

All historians are agreed that French military power was at its height in 1798, the year of the Jourdan law that established universal military service. But military success indirectly brought down the Republic. The actual plot to unseat the Directors and expel the legislators came from within and was carried out by two old clerics who were wise in diplomacy, Sieyès and Talleyrand, and a former Jacobin terrorist, Fouché. The French expansion, however, had driven into a Second Coalition some of the old allies (England, Austria, Russia, Turkey, Sweden). In 1799, Austrian forces drove the French from Switzerland and Germany, while the

Russian general Suvorov liberated northern Italy. A conservative peasant uprising crushed the young Parthenopean Republic in Naples. The Directors took the blame for the reversals, but nevertheless lost the loyalty of their republican generals after 1798 because they remained hostile to the revival of Jacobinism. Bonaparte had again gone his own way and avoided the project of invading England, which he considered too risky. He had instead led an expeditionary force to Egypt, capitalizing on the growing scientific and imperialistic interest in the Near East. That the invasion force lost most of its fleet and that Bonaparte failed to conquer Syria was overlooked by the French public. And although the Coalition had been driven back in Holland, Switzerland, and Italy before Napoleon landed in southern France on October 9, 1799, his dramatic escape through Nelson's fleet enhanced the popular feeling that only he could honorably protect French interests.

Sieyès and his conspirators also needed Bonaparte, as their "man on horseback" to put down the Republican Councils. The General presided over the events of the 19th *Brumaire* (November 10, 1799) when the two Councils were summoned in special ses-

---

* Feudal rights and hereditary nobility were abolished.

sions and then dissolved at sword's point, although he needed the help of his younger brother, Lucien, to regain his nerve in front of the lower house. Within three weeks, the bourgeois Republic had come to an end and Napoleon was First Consul under a Caesarean constitution. Ten years of history had come to a close when the Consuls proclaimed the Revolution to be ended.

## THE REVOLUTION STABILIZED, 1799 TO 1804

### Early Napoleonic Government

The civilian instigators of the *coup* of 1799 sought a more powerful executive who shared their fears of popular government. In Napoleon, a second choice, they thought they had found a man of order without a compromising political past who would be content to name generals and ambassadors and who would be responsible to the Senate, a kind of constitutional jury. Sieyès' proposed constitution called for a tripartite executive with an equal voice in decisions for each of the three consuls.

From the outset Napoleon intended to exercise full command in France, as he had done in Italy and Egypt. He argued successfully that the First Consul was to have final decisions in all matters, although he took care at first to give the appearance of deferring to his legislature and his advisors. The Constitution of the Year VIII set up four bodies to help the First Consul govern, although the wording of the document allowed the executive much room for individual action. Popular sovereignty was an undeniable heritage of the revolutionary decade, but the direct vote of the six million adult male citizens elected only a communal list of candidates. The eventual slate of about 6000 national candidates was co-opted from communal and departmental lists. Members of the Tribunate and the Legislative Corps, the two houses, were named by the Senate from the national lists. Neither of the houses could do more than discuss proposed legislation.

The Senate was a smaller body (60, later 80, members) of more elderly men. In addition to choosing the legislators, the Senate was to elect appeal judges and the Consuls for ten-year terms. Sieyès and his friends had packed the Senate with men of the Directory, but Napoleon bought its complacent cooperation with grants of estates and with military triumphs. The Council of State revived the idea of a royal council. Members were experts in such areas as the Army, Navy, Finance, Legislation, and Internal Affairs. The ministers were subordinate to the Council, which also drafted proposals for laws and rules of administration. The Council was by far the most efficient part of the constitution, and it is to Napoleon's credit that he worked as hard as his advisors and received long periods of service from most of them.

In local administration, Napoleon built upon Jacobin centralization. He appointed prefects in charge of each department, subprefects for the *arrondissements,* and mayors in the communes. The First Consul even had a crude semaphore telegraph system; he was determined to know the mood of his nation as well as he prided himself on knowing his troops. Napoleon financed his state through rational assessment of taxes and more stringent collection, rather than through loans. Physically, the First Consul was worthy of the system. He was tireless in Council meetings, unstinting in his tours of the country, and indefatigable in correspondence; there are more than 40,000 of his letters in print, and perhaps as many are lost.

In the first years after his accession, Napoleon combined his phenomenal energy and the flexibility of the constitution to move the administration of the state into constructive channels. He had asked for and received a mandate for action at the start, submitting the constitution to a national plebiscite. Between 1800 and 1802, Napoleon set up committees to codify civil, criminal, and commercial law. The lawyers combined revolutionary legislation with the ordinances of

Louis XIV and produced succinct and well-defined documents. Napoleon attended the meetings often enough to affix his name to the codes collectively in 1807, but the Civil Code of 1804 especially drew its strength from the Revolution. Napoleon leaned on Roman law to tighten procedures on marriage and divorce, but the granting of absolute property rights, the freedom to bequeath a portion of one's property at will, and the abolition of all servitude were legacies of the 1790s. Although the codes enforced social conformity, especially the rights of husband over wife and father over children, they were sufficiently adaptable to have influenced the law of Italy, Egypt, Canada, Louisiana, and Japan.

Both old-regime authority and revolutionary equality pervaded Napoleon's social and economic policy. He required workers to carry a passbook, thus hardening the law of 1791 against trade unions. In place of the Directory's secondary schools, with their permissive curricula, he established 45 *lycées* with state scholarships to train boys for civil service, the professions, engineering, and the army. With the characteristic statement that girls should believe, not think, Napoleon left their education to religious orders. Napoleon conceived of the national economy more in Colbert's terms than those of Adam Smith. He sought a favorable balance of trade with protective tariffs and excluded English goods. The most obvious attempt to strike a balance between old and new was the Legion of Honor, founded in 1802. The First Consul genuinely sought to bestow distinction, without regard to social rank, on individuals for civic achievement. Yet Napoleon also sought a captive institution named by himself, a kind of republican service nobility.

For reasons of state Napoleon effected a reconciliation with the Church. Although state and Church had been separate since 1795, the Directory's attitude toward the nonjuring clergy had wavered. A great variety of religious practices had appeared;

Notre Dame of Paris had seen worship by Catholics, Protestants, and Theophilanthropists, an intellectualist cult. Bonaparte's own religious attitudes were tolerant and skeptical, and it was for political and social gains that he negotiated with the Pope in 1800. As he so often did, Napoleon had the better of the bargain. The Catholic clergy would be named by the bishops, who in turn were nominated by the First Consul and instituted by the Pope. The distinction between refractory and constitutional clergy came to an end, and the clergy became once again salaried servants of the state. The Pope was persuaded to accept the dispossession and sale of Church lands. Roman Catholicism was declared to be "the religion of the great majority of the citizens." Papal intervention in France and episcopal control of the diocese were limited by the First Consul and the Council of State. The Concordat was published in April 1801. In the long run, the bishops rather than the Pope or the Consul came to control the French Church, but in 1802 Napoleon won his gamble that the legislatures and men of liberal opinion everywhere would accept this charter.

## The Pacification of Europe

Napoleon fulfilled the popular trust that he had come to power to make an honorable peace. To the former general, now forbidden command of troops, this meant rolling back the enemy to the lines of 1798. The campaign to recover Italy proceeded with a hard-fought victory in June 1800, at Marengo, in Lombardy. Napoleon's legendary reputation was enhanced by his crossing the Saint Bernard Pass, albeit in the van of his troops. Even more decisive French victories north of the Alps—over the Russians at Zurich and the Austrians at Hohenlinden—left the Austrian Emperor with little choice but to sign a peace treaty. The Treaty of Lunéville (February 1801) more than restored the terms of 1797, notably in granting France the left bank of the Rhine from Switzerland to Holland. England was ready to sign a peace thirteen

Coronation of Napoleon *by David, artist of the revolution.*

months later, at Amiens, but her final conquest of Egypt was clearly overshadowed by her diplomatic isolation.

Lunéville and Amiens proved to be only a temporary respite for France and Europe. English wealth and maritime power were unimpaired, and a wave of Gallophobia developed in 1802 and 1803 when Napoleon failed to honor the peace treaty and gave every indication of preparing an invasion fleet. When hostilities resumed in May 1803, his military mind argued that self-sufficient France could outlast mercantile and debt-ridden England. The French blockade closed continental ports to English and uncertified neutral ships. Napoleon was also willing to bleed off English wealth by selling smuggling licenses and by allowing English captains to purchase French luxuries in return for needed raw materials. Bonaparte's grandiose scheme—to conquer the sea from the land, as he put it—led to the extension of warfare all over Western Europe.

## Termination of the Revolution

Napoleon's restless energy similarly destroyed the balance between Revolution and Order which he had been creating at home. The First Consul had always been hypersensitive to criticism from his citizens and to opposition from his legislators. At the beginning of his rule, most of the Parisian newspapers were shut down and the rest subjected to strong censorship. Madame de Staël and other writers were particularly harassed by Fouché's secret police. After Lunéville (1801), Napoleon purged the Tribunate. Following a royalist attempt on his life, he deported or executed a number of Jacobin opponents. Napoleon's contempt for parliamentary government emerged in 1802. Counting on the gratitude of the nation for the Peace of Amiens, the First Consul again used a plebiscite to force his plan on the government. He became Life Consul, able to nominate most senators, to declare war and make treaties, and to designate his successor. The legislative and electoral machinery of the constitution was stripped of almost all meaning. Napoleon's power to make law within a new private council and the large number of appointments that he controlled cast a suspicion of dictatorship over the Republic. Ominously, his profile appeared on coinage for the first time.

By 1804, Napoleon had broken openly with the revolutionary past. His arbitrary arrest and murder of the Bourbon Duc d'Enghien, who was kidnapped from the neutral territory of Baden, shocked European opinion and discredited Napoleon more than any other act. The same conspiracy that had doomed the Duc d'Enghien and had removed two of the generals who had won the peace, Moreau and Pichegru, was now used as an excuse to provide for the succession. In May 1804, by proclamation of the private council, Napoleon Bonaparte became "Emperor of the French." The populace was given its third (and most meaningless) plebiscite to approve the proposition that "the Imperial dignity is hereditary." Bonaparte planned to assume the title in a manner calculated to remove any question of Bourbon legitimacy and to humiliate the Habsburgs.

He summoned Pope Pius VII north of the Alps for a coronation rite intended to recall that of Charlemagne. The ceremony of December 2, 1804, was less religious than imperial, with Napoleon unwilling to communicate at Mass or to take an oath of dependence to the Pope, as the title historically demanded. The Emperor crowned himself, bringing to a close the period in which the Revolution in France might have continued.

*Trafalgar, 1805: the eclipse of Napoleon's bid for naval power.*

## THE GRAND EMPIRE, 1804 TO 1815

Napoleon's admirers see the turning point of his career in the military disasters of the three years beginning with the invasion of Russia in 1812. The new Emperor's treatment of France and the republics abroad, however, indicated from the start that he cared little for the pattern of change from the 1790s. A desire to legitimize his family's claim, while he himself had no children to inherit the throne, prompted Napoleon to install his relatives in new monarchies that had once been sister republics. His eldest brother, Louis, became King of Holland in 1804, when the Batavian Republic was abolished. Josephine's son by an earlier marriage went to Venice as King, while Lombardy became part of the Empire. Another brother, Joseph, went to rule Naples in 1806. Before the Empire was complete, the youngest brother, Jerome, was established in Rhenish Prussia.* By 1810 Napoleon realized that Josephine, at 46, would not bear him an heir. The marriage, which had been hastily solemnized in the Church on the eve of the coronation, was now put aside by a French ecclesiastical court. Austria supplied the new Empress, Marie Louise, who bore Napoleon a son within a year. An Imperial court of about 3500 dukes, counts, barons, and chevaliers formed the backdrop for the Empire. Old revolutionary officials and generals

as well as relatives received Italian, Spanish, and Portugese estates as Imperial fiefs. Using the discipline of the Jesuit order as an analogy, Napoleon placed an Imperial University over the entire structure of education. Modern scholars have seen in all of these public actions a private anxiety over the succession. Contemporaries merely saw a man who was insensitive not only to the true meaning of 1789, but even to the aristocratic amenities of the old regime.

### French Expansion

The first three years of the Empire produced stunning victories on the Continent and a stalemate on the seas. The invasion fleet assembled at Boulogne in the summer of 1805 never sailed, having failed to secure the Channel. While Napoleon turned eastward with his Grand Army in the autumn of 1805, the British Admiral, Nelson, crippled the Spanish and French fleets at Trafalgar (October 21, 1805), off the southern coast of Spain.

What Napoleon gave up at sea in 1805, he gained on land, in the Habsburg Empire. The campaign proved Napoleon's faith in himself, for he carried no baggage trains. Nevertheless, the French captured more than 20,000 Austrian troops at Ulm in Bavaria on the day before Trafalgar, and went on to occupy Vienna. The Austrians and Russians still believed that they could defeat Napoleon in a pitched battle, and foolishly engaged him at Austerlitz in Moravia. On the first anniversary of his coronation, the Emperor

---

* Only Lucien broke with his brother, refusing the kingdom of Naples to keep a wife who had been his mistress.

cut the allied force in half, thus gaining his greatest victory.

In the Peace of Pressburg that followed, Francis II gave up Venetia and the Tyrol and recognized Bavaria, Württemburg, and Baden as independent kingdoms. In 1806, the Holy Roman Empire came to an end, and Napoleon reorganized further German territory in the Confederation of the Rhine, taken from Prussia's western provinces. Frederick William II of Prussia, convinced that Napoleon would soon break the truce and expecting Russian aid, mobilized his army. In three weeks and two swift battles (Jena and Auerstadt), Napoleon humiliated the Prussians and went on to Berlin, where he decreed that all continental ports under his protection were closed to British ships. In the spring of 1807, Napoleon's army advanced toward the Baltic and defeated Alexander I of Russia at Friedland. The Emperor and the Tsar met at Tilsit in July 1807 to divide Europe into two spheres of influence, Alexander being particularly eager to set his own course against Sweden and Turkey. Prussia lost her Polish districts to a new French satellite, the Grand Duchy of Warsaw. The campaigns of 1805 and 1807 sealed Napoleon's reputation as a field commander, but it was the failure of the allies to place military cooperation ahead of individual interest that opened the Continent to France.

## The "Continental System"

After Tilsit, the Emperor was convinced that his conquests would reinforce the blockade against the British Isles—a blockade that was changing from one of protection to that of economic warfare. By 1810 the Atlantic, the Baltic, and even the Adriatic had become untenable for neutral ships caught between French Decrees and British Orders in Council. The Continental System, as some perhaps too-rational historians have called it, hurt British exports to Europe, but new markets in Latin America appeared. Although Britain suffered from inflation, bad harvests,

*The result of Spanish resistance to the French:* The Third of May, 1808, *by Goya.*

and mass unemployment in 1811, the blockade probably did less damage than monetary instability, and Britain never lost her continental grain supply. France, too, suffered from a commercial and industrial depression in 1811. Above all, her neighbors' trading interests were damaged, and the Empire began to mean heavy taxes and customs duties.

Napoleon's military reversals also began as a result of the blockade system. He needed the Iberian Peninsula to seal off trade with the enemy, and set out to occupy Portugal in 1807. Napoleon conspired with Godoy, the royal favorite at the Spanish Court, to share the partition of Portugal, but the Emperor's ambitions were drawn to Spain itself. In 1808 he secured the abdication of the Bourbon Spanish king, replacing him with his brother, Joseph, who was transferred from Naples. The Spanish peasantry, which was little affected by the Enlightenment, reacted to French rule as a threat to Church and society as well as a violation of nationality. Guerrilla forces drove Joseph from Madrid and defeated two French divisions in the field at Baylen, in July 1808. Supplied by the Duke of Wellington's British base in Portugal, local militia and juntas fought the savage occupation in scenes that were immortalized by Goya. Until Wellington cleared the Peninsula in 1813, the French

**NAPOLEONIC EMPIRE** AT ITS HEIGHT

Map by J. Donovan

were forced to commit many thousands of troops to the occupation. "The Spanish ulcer," Napoleon later wrote, "destroyed me."

## The Empire at Its Height

Spanish resistance encouraged other continental powers either to resist or to question their obligations to France. Austerlitz had led to patriotic cries for a war of revenge in Austria. By 1808, with troops being pulled back from Germany for the Spanish Front and with Fouché and Talleyrand in dissent at home, Napoleon needed a reconquest of Vienna. The resumption of war between Austria and France was not so one-sided this time, and a peasant uprising in the Tyrol lasted for months. Napoleon went on to cross the Danube and to overturn the Austrians at Wagram in July 1809, but the defeat was not a disaster. The armistice deprived

Francis I* of Salzburg and Cracow, but it also led to Napoleon's marriage to Marie Louise of Habsburg. Napoleon's expansion after Tilsit produced its most unfortunate result in Italy, where the Papal States were annexed to the blockade system in 1808. Pius VII, remembering the many issues that Napoleon had already forced against papal authority, moved toward excommunication of the Emperor. Napoleon's reaction was to kidnap the Pope in July 1808. The captivity lasted five years.

Between 1810 and 1812, the Grand Empire reached its height. A total of 131 departments and about 44 million inhabitants fell under French rule. Napoleon's son, the infant King of Rome, ruled directly over a

---

* The Austrian ruler's title was now Francis I because the Holy Roman Empire, of which he had been Francis II, was dissolved in 1806.

long stretch of the Mediterranean coast and over the Illyrian provinces. The Low Countries and the coastal plain of Germany, including Hamburg, were French territory. Napoleon's relatives in Italy ruled principalities that conformed to older boundaries. Political lines had been redrawn, however, in Germany and in Poland. His youngest brother, Jerome, ruled over a Kingdom of Westphalia which was pieced together from Hanover, Brunswick, Hesse-Cassel, and the Prussian Rhenish provinces. Prussia was in fact the great victim of the Empire's growth, in both West and East, and she was demilitarized between 1806 and 1813.

The Grand Empire never achieved complete unity, but all its parts shared the authoritarian order that was seen in France after 1804. The Emperor allowed religious toleration and internal free trade, but he restricted electoral rights everywhere. He tried to use the Civil Code to destroy the old social order in the Empire by secularizing marriage and education and abolishing feudal dues and corporate bodies. His attack on monasteries and his search for administrative unity recalled the enlightened despotism of Joseph II. Wherever the Directory and Consulate had already touched an educated middle class with these proposals, the Napoleonic regime evoked no great opposition. The assimilation was incomplete in the areas across the Rhine and south of Rome. The price of the French mission—taxes, tariffs, recruitment, loss of political liberty—was not fully apparent until after the fateful invasion of Russia in 1812.

## Collapse of Napoleonic Europe

By 1810 the accord that had been reached between Napoleon and Alexander at Tilsit, the cornerstone of French expansion, had worn thin. French and Russian ambitions collided in the Balkans. Napoleon's reconstitution of Poland as the Grand Duchy of Warsaw was intolerable to Alexander. On the last day of 1810, he renounced the Continental System and began preparations for

war. In 1811, the Emperor retaliated by assembling in Poland a polyglot "grand army" of almost 600,000 men. He recognized the campaign as his greatest gamble, but, as usual, he counted on a short war, that would be won in a great single encounter.

In June of 1812, the grand army crossed the Niemen to start the invasion. By necessity, the Tsar's army retreated, destroying provisions as it went. In August, Napoleon arrived in Smolensk, with almost two thirds of his force dissipated. The expected great encounter took place at Borodino, but Kutusov withdrew the Russian army deeper into the great plain. Napoleon entered Moscow in mid-September, but he found the city deserted and soon in flames. Alexander still refused to negotiate or to engage in a decisive battle. On October 1812, Napoleon gave the order to retreat.

Both armies had wasted away tremendously, but the French retreat through the bitter northern winter finished the destruction of the grand army. About 100,000 were killed, another 100,000 imprisoned, and perhaps 200,000 perished of disease, cold, and famine. In December 1812, Napoleon left the remnants of the army and hastened in disguise to Paris, where the "lawyers" whom he despised awaited him. There was no real threat to the Emperor in the winter of 1812 to 1813, but close observers remarked on his utter lack of concern for the army's suffering and on the decline in his physical capabilities.

In the months after the retreat from Moscow, Napoleon might have extricated himself from the war on the terms of Lunéville, offered by Metternich, the Austrian Foreign Minister. But the Emperor always preferred to negotiate after a victory and not before a campaign. Although forced to restrict his recruiting of men and material to France, Napoleon put together a force of 150,000 for the invasion of Germany. But 1813 was in no way like 1806. German nationalism had been awakened from the Rhine to the Oder by the message of the Civil Code, by

*Napoleon at the Battle of Borodino.*

the example of what an authoritarian administration could do, and especially, as Jerome Bonaparte put it in Westphalia, by "the crushing burden of taxation."*

The reaction to Jena in 1806 had been further cultural nationalism, led by professors and liberal bourgeoisie, but the building of an army to face the French was the work of Prussian ministers. In 1807, Barons Stein and Hardenburg, abolished serfdom and feudal obligations, ended the restrictive allocation of professions and vocations by social rank, and tried to build up a bureaucracy that would be free of privilege. Hardenberg summed up his program as "democratic rules of conduct in a monarchical administration."[3] The most effective reforms took

* The genesis of German nationalism is discussed more fully in Chapter V.

3. Quoted in Geoffrey Brunn, *Europe and the French Imperium, 1799–1814,* Harper and Bothers, New York, 1938, p. 174.

place in the Prussian army, where Scharnhorst and Gneisenau relaxed barbarous punishments, retired incompetent officers, and made universal military service a patriotic duty. Using a rotating reserve to avoid Napoleon's limit on the size of the army, Prussia trained 150,000 men by 1812.

In February 1813, Prussia allied with Russia and declared war on France. Napoleon gained enough time to field 450,000 men by August, but the Prussian *Landwehr,* or civilian militia, had also become available by that time. Austria broke off negotiations and declared war, and the Swedes sent British-subsidized troops. On October 16-19, 1813, in the "Battle of the Nations" at Leipzig, Napoleon was decisively beaten and driven across the Rhine into France.

Napoleon's opponents at first failed to agree on war aims, Metternich being particularly distrustful of Russia. The promise of British subsidy, however, brought the four major powers together at Chaumont in March 1814, binding them to a twenty-year alliance against Napoleon and establishing a cordon of independent states around France. Meanwhile, Wellington's armies had crossed the Pyrenees into France, and the Dutch had recalled their stadtholder. Napoleon had already precluded any repetition of the nationalist crusade of 1793 with his recruitment (a million men were drafted in 1812-1813), requisitions, taxes, and repression of popular movements. The civilian population took the defeat at Leipzig passively and offered little resistance to the allied troops. In Paris, the Senate and legislature prepared to restore Louis XVIII, who promised a liberal charter. Napoleon abdicated on April 6, 1814, retiring with his dignity intact to the island of Elba, while the allies granted pensions to the entire Bonaparte family.

The Treaty of Paris of May 1814 was generous to France. She kept her frontiers of 1792, losing Belgium, Italy, and the left bank of the Rhine, but there was no occupation, no disarmament, and no indemnity. Talleyrand, the versatile Foreign Minister, was to join the discussion of Europe's fate at the Congress of Vienna. Meanwhile, Louis XVIII's Charter had guaranteed the election of two houses by the new nobility and the wealthy bourgeoisie, and had assured the rights of land purchasers, bondholders, army officers, and religious dissenters. The Charter threatened the return of *émigré* nobility, while the King's brother, the Count d'Artois, pressed for full restoration of noble privilege and properties. Army officers went on half pay.

The discontented had good reason to rejoice when Napoleon left his island empire, landed on the southern coast of France, and reached Paris on March 20, 1815, causing the flight of the King. After he had failed to arouse national enthusiasm with a new constitutional "appendix," and after he had been labeled an outlaw by the Congress powers at Vienna, Napoleon mobilized and headed for the Belgian frontier. He had been able to

*Counterrevolution triumphant: The Congress of Vienna.*

raise about 125,000 troops, but the combined forces of Wellington's British and Blücher's Prussians numbered almost twice as many. On June 16, 1815, at Waterloo, the allied generals joined forces in time to break Napoleon's attack. The Chamber in Paris refused him a further chance and submitted to Louis XVIII when he was returned by a Prussian escort. The second Treaty of Paris (November 1815) deprived France of Savoy and the Saar, declared an occupation of three to five years, and set an indemnity of 700 million francs. Napoleon became a British prisoner on the South Atlantic island of Saint Helena where he died six years later, not of cruel treatment by his captors as legend once had it, but of a chronic ulcer.

## THE CONGRESS OF VIENNA

Before Waterloo, the diplomats at Vienna had already agreed on the territorial settlement in Europe. The Congress had nearly disbanded over the question of Poland in January 1815. Talleyrand, Metternich, and Lord Castlereagh, the British delegate, had drawn up a secret alliance against Russia

EUROPE, 1815
AFTER THE CONGRESS OF VIENNA

Map by J. Donovan

and Prussia, which were suspected of designs on Poland and Saxony. The issue was settled by one of the great principles of the Treaty of Vienna (June 1815)—mutual compensation. Prussia received the Rhineland, part of Saxony, and Swedish Pomerania; Alexander I was entrusted to oversee a constitutional monarchy in "Congress Poland" and was guaranteed his conquests in Bessarabia and in Finland. Sweden was compensated for the loss of Finland by Norway, which was taken from Denmark, Napoleon's ally. Austria received Lombardy, Venetia, and Dalmatia, as well as the presidency of a German Confederation of thirty-nine lay states. Holland gained Luxembourg and the Austrian Netherlands. Great Britain's colonial territories were increased by Mauritius, Tobago, Saint Lucia (taken from France), Malta (from the Knights of St. John), and Ceylon and the Cape Colony (from Holland).

Restoration of prerevolutionary dynasties also helped to destroy the Grand Empire. Bourbons were returned in France, Spain, and the Kingdom of the Two Sicilies. The Pope was guaranteed his estates in central Italy and a safe residence in Rome. The Braganzas, who had fled to Brazil, were reinstated in Portugal. The Congress powers respected national self-determination no more than Napoleon had. Eventually the Norwegians, Poles, and Belgians were to gain their independence, and Venetians were to become Italian citizens. Other provisions of the Treaty have remained more acceptable to modern sensibilities: suppression of the international slave trade and piracy and establishment of freer international waterways.

The Hundred Days of Napoleon's reign after his return changed the orientation of the Congress. The four conquering powers entered a Quadruple Alliance, pledging themselves to prevent a Napoleonic restoration, to enforce the second Treaty of Paris, and to provide contingents to occupy France. Castlereagh then bound all five participants at Vienna to a "Concert of Europe," which was not only to protect the settlement, but also to provide machinery to settle disputes without recourse to war. Yet Britain steadfastly refused to support armed intervention in the internal affairs of other states, and it was unclear from the start whether the Congress System would act against nationalist and democratic uprisings after 1815. For Alexander I, maintaining the political divisions after Vienna was not enough. He proposed a "Holy Alliance" or a kind of Christian commonwealth against the rationalism and anticlericalism of the Revolution. The Tsar was probably the only serious believer in the scheme, and his recent interest in religious mysticism was known. All European rulers except the Sultan, the Pope, and the British Regent signed the Holy Alliance, however, and liberals began to identify the Congress System with the counterrevolution.

The Revolution of the 1790s had apparently been overturned at Vienna. Expansionist France was contained, self-determination was denied, and secular ways of thought were refuted—such was the message of the dynastic restoration. Yet the revolutionary generation left a legacy of profound change in European history. The nature of that change was visible to Napoleon in exile, when he cultivated the legend that the Empire had been founded on principles of liberalism, nationalism, and religious toleration.

Liberalism, in its classic sense of the right to make free choices, especially in politics, broadly characterized the hopes of the Constituent Assembly in 1789. The Constitution of 1795 and the Civil Code were perhaps the two most widely imitated documents of the period. Although they promised no great downward redistribution of power in society, each of them was concerned with the protection of inalienable rights. The idea of a

career open to talent entered European thinking about administration. Ecclesiastical and seigneurial justice yielded to national courts within the Empire. But monarchy was the system of government that was most trusted in Western Europe in 1815.

Only a man as egotistical as Napoleon could believe that the generation had given Europe peace. The commercial and dynastic wars of the Old Regime recur in almost epidemic fashion after 1740. Of far more consequence to the future was the conversion of warfare after 1792 from the use of mercenaries and lower-class conscripts under aristocratic officers to the idea of the nation in arms. The emigration of noble officers and the *levée en masse* of 1793 set a pattern for a classless mass army, although no other nation achieved a base of conscription so broad as that of France in 1805. Even England found herself equipping 300,000 men in the army and half as many in the fleet by 1814. War hardened the conflict of social classes in France after 1792, and helped to destroy the attractions of the Empire after 1804. For scholars who see a humanitarian concern in eighteenth-century ideas, the wars of the Revolution have been called "the frustration of the Enlightenment."

Nationalism cannot be attributed directly to the revolutionary generation, although after 1808 the reaction against the Empire was also a reaction against the French. France under the Convention and Western Europe under the Empire enjoyed more national institutions, however. Uniform weights and measures, the end of internal customs, and a single educational system all worked to speed communication within cultural units. Nationalist German and Italian historians consider the national awakenings in their countries, which had their roots in native soil but were nevertheless influenced by the French example, as part of a European-wide phenomenon of the 1790s.

That Napoleon saw correctly the weakening of the temporal power of the Church may have been due to his personal lack of religious conviction. Few historians looking beyond 1815 can describe the Ultramontanism of the next few years as a lesson of the period since 1787, although a clerical revival in Europe coincided with the Pope's captivity. Civil marriage and divorce, lay education, the civic oath as a test of morality, and the loss of Church estates won out over Burke's special protection of religion in the unwritten constitution.

Napoleon was unable to appreciate the passing away of two aspects of the generation. Guided by his own star, he could not have realized that aristocratic privilege received its deathblow between 1787 and 1815. There has been more recent historical argument over the nature and extent of social change than over any other problem, but it seems clear that the constituted noble bodies lost much of their personal privilege, if not their political power or their lands, by 1815. The peasantry neither profited very greatly from the redistribution of land nor solved many of its economic problems, but the legal and social status of rural people improved in France, northern Italy, and western Germany. Bourgeois society, defined in terms of economic activity, especially trade and manufacturing, was retarded by the wars. When considered in terms of the "democrats" of the Jacobin clubs or the civil servants of Prussia, bourgeois society undoubtedly enjoyed greater prestige in 1815 than in 1787.

The Revolution as a historical myth naturally surpassed the vision of Napoleon. Institutions never received all of the sanctity that Burke had desired after 1789. Written constitutions and declarations of rights became living organisms in France and America by 1791, and most Western societies still venerate these documents more than any other civic artifact except the flag. The use of force by France to achieve legitimate ends became blessed with success too many times to allow Europeans to disregard the history of the period. Terror itself became legitimized in 1793, and every major revolution since

then has seen the rationalization—and even glorification—of violence. Few revolutions in history have left such evocative symbols as the sans-culotte and the guillotine. The enigma of the revolutionary Emperor haunted Europe for more than a generation after his death, and still defies the historical imagination.

## SELECTED READINGS

*Amann, Peter, *The Eighteenth-Century Revolution, French or Western?*, Heath, Boston, 1963.

An introduction to a current debate on the scope and nature of the revolutionary movement(s).

*Brinton, Crane, *A Decade of Revolution, 1789–1799*, Harper & Brothers, New York, 1934; also a Harper Torchbook.

A competent general survey in the Rise of Modern Europe series; the revised paperback edition furnishes differing interpretations of the revolution.

———, *The Jacobins*, Macmillan, New York, 1930.

Describes the organization and activities of the dominant revolutionary republican faction.

———, *The Lives of Talleyrand*, Norton, New York, 1936.

Sympathetic biography of a celebrated opportunist who served many phases of the revolution and the restored Bourbons.

*Bruun, Geoffrey, *Europe and the French Imperium, 1799–1814*, Harper & Brothers, New York, 1938; also a Harper Torchbook.

A volume in the Rise of Modern Europe series which treats Napoleon as an enlightened despot.

Cobban, Alfred, *The Social Interpretation of the French Revolution*, Cambridge University Press, Cambridge, 1964.

Historiographical essays on the social history of the revolution raising fundamental questions about all historical writing.

* Asterisk (*) denotes paperback.

————, *Edmund Burke and the Revolt against the Eighteenth Century,* Barnes & Noble, New York, 1961 (2nd ed.).

Sets forth the reversal of Locke's philosophy by Burke and the early romantic poets.

Gershoy, Leo, *The French Revolution and Napoleon,* Appleton-Century-Crofts, New York, 1964.

A standard textbook with an excellent annotated bibliography.

Geyl, Pieter, *Napoleon, For and Against,* Yale University Press, New Haven, 1949.

A collection of judgments passed on Napoleon.

Godechot, Jacques, *France and the Atlantic Revolution of the Eighteenth Century,* translated by Herbert H. Rowen, The Free Press, New York; Collier-Macmillan, London, 1965.

Develops fully the controversial theme that a general "Atlantic revolution" encompassed the Western World.

Goodwin, Albert, *The French Revolution,* Hutchinson University Library, London and New York, 1953.

A short, factual account, especially useful for beginning students.

Herr, Richard, *The Eighteenth-Century Revolution in Spain,* Princeton University Press, Princeton, 1958.

Discovers a belated Spanish Enlightenment produced by the French Revolution between 1792 and 1801.

Hobsbawm, E. J., *The Age of Revolution, Europe 1789–1848,* Weidenfeld and Nicolson, London, 1962.

With Marxist overtones, presents the thesis that two revolutions, one industrial and one political, remade Europe with global consequences.

Hyslop, B. F., *A Guide to the General Cahiers of 1789,* Columbia University Press, New York, 1936.

Discusses the formulation and content of the "notebooks of grievances" compiled by the upper electoral assemblies at the outset of the French Revolution.

*Lefebvre, Georges, *The Coming of the French Revolution,* translated by R. R. Palmer, Alfred A. Knopf, New York, 1957.

Superlative short analysis of the events and background of the revolutionary movements of the year 1789.

————, *The French Revolution,* Routledge and Kegan Paul, London; Columbia University Press, New York, 1962–1964, 2 vols.

Translation of the author's influential work in *Peuples et Civilisations,* an interpretation friendly to the revolutionaries of 1789.

*Kaplow, Jeffry, ed., *New Perspectives on the French Revolution, Readings in Historical Sociology,* John Wiley & Sons, New York, 1965.

A collection of articles on the social and economic pressures behind the revolution, especially those making the lower classes revolutionary.

Markham, F. M. H., *Napoleon and the Awakening of Europe,* Macmillan, New York, 1954.

An easy-to-read account in the Teach Yourself History series.

*Nicolson, Harold, *The Congress of Vienna, A Study in Allied Unity: 1812–1822,* The Viking Press, New York, 1965.

A short treatment of the wartime treaties and the peace settlement.

Palmer, Robert R., *The Age of the Democratic Revolution, A Political History of Europe and America, 1760–1800,* II, *The Struggle,* Princeton University Press, Princeton, 1964.

Recounts the revolutionary conflicts; especially informative on revolutions outside of France.

————, *Twelve Who Ruled: The Committee of Public Safety during the Terror,* Princeton University Press, Princeton, 1941.

An analysis of the men and policies of the Terror, which emphasizes military considerations and treats Robespierre as one—not the most powerful—of the Twelve.

*Rudé, George, *The Crowd in History, A Study of Popular Disturbances in France and England 1730–1848,* John Wiley & Sons, New York, 1964.

Analyzes the origin, composition, and motives of preindustrial crowds; the central chapters deal with the French Revolution.

————, *Revolutionary Europe 1783–1815,* Harper & Row, New York, 1964.
A new general history, which disputes the Palmer-Godechot thesis of a general Atlantic revolution.

Soboul, Albert, *The Parisian Sans-Culottes and the French Revolution 1793–4,* Clarendon Press, Oxford, 1964.
Shows differences between the urban lower-class movements and the Jacobins in power.

Stewart, John Hall, *A Documentary Survey of the French Revolution,* Macmillan, New York, 1951.
A comprehensive collection of the most significant documents up to 1799.

*Thompson, James M., *The French Revolution,* Oxford University Press (Galaxy Books) New York, 1966.
Solid summary by a biographer of Robespierre and Napoleon.

Van Deusen, Glyndon G., *Sieyes: His Life and His Nationalism,* Columbia University Press, New York, 1932.
Biography of an outstanding French nationalist who urged expansion and engineered Napoleon's *coup d'état.*

Webster, Charles K., *The Congress of Vienna, 1814–1815,* Oxford University Press, London, 1934 (2nd ed.).
A detailed exposition.

# V

# *Reaction and Revolution, 1815 to 1850*

French imperialism collapsed with Napoleon, and war-weary populations (anticipating the millennium) at last experienced repose. But the social tensions that had erupted into violence in France in 1789 and had spread over Europe were still unresolved. The old elite of nobles, clerics, and hereditary monarchs, who shunned as dangerous such things as science, intellectual freedom, and secular reform projects, again held most positions of power.

Challenged by revolution, the old elite had produced a counter-ideology of conservatism or traditionalism. Traditionalists asserted that the rights, privileges, and powers that they had acquired in the past were indispensable in governing depraved men. Human experience proved the necessity of such government and providence sanctioned it. Social and political reorganization, natural rights, progress, popular sovereignty, French dominion—these concepts must be repudiated. They stemmed from the presumptuous aspirations and ideology of the bourgeoisie behind whom lurked rootless urban workingmen and insurrectionary peasants. Fearing that any change would invite renewed revolution, traditionalists refused to share power with leaders drawn from the lower classes. They would not tolerate criticism of the marriage between Throne and Altar. It was sacrilegious as well as subversive for the lower orders to question that union.

Not surprisingly, such repression precipitated a renewed struggle with the bourgeoisie, dissatisfied intellectuals, urban workers and, eventually, the peasantry. In 1820, 1830, and 1848 this struggle erupted in waves of revolution that were mostly liberal-national in nature. First and foremost, liberals demanded constitutional, parliamentary government which would provide civic freedoms to the many and political rights to those who held property. Most liberals were convinced that such a regime was possible only when a single nationality constituted the body politic. Hence they were nationalists, men who advocated the formation of states by people who shared a common body of historical and political myth. Not all nationalists were constitutionalists, but the two groups conjoined after 1815 to try to overthrow the Old Regime which the Concert of Europe had reimposed on Europe. Both groups sought to substitute a new elite and establish new purposes for society. Also engaged in these revolts were a smaller number of socialist intellectuals and urban workingmen. They were not primarily interested in individual liberties or the securing of property rights. Rather they sought the creation of a regime that would guarantee social justice and distribute more widely the fruits of industrial productivity. For these purposes they naturally believed democratic government was best suited. In general, however, economic depression, not political or social ideology, kindled revolution among the urban lower classes during these years. The same was true of the peasantry still under old manorial obligations. The peasantry had their own grievances, which population pressure and depression rendered more unbearable. When liberal-nationalist revolutionaries proved unsympathetic to their economic problems, the peasants—still the great bulk of Europe's people—staged their own autonomous revolutions, especially in 1848.

By mid-century the bourgeoisie had gained power in most of Western Europe. Only in Britain and France were the middle classes seriously challenged by urban labor. In Southern, Central, and Eastern Europe, however, military establishments usually came to the aid of the traditionalists and kept them in power.

Superficially these nineteenth-century struggles appear to be between partisans of traditional society on the one side and heirs of the Enlightenment and the French Revolution on the other. Though this generalization contains a large kernel of truth, it is much too simple, because both sides—and

shades of opinion between them—were deeply imbued with romanticism. Traditionalists certainly fought to maintain the inherited social order. But in elaborating their defense of the Old Regime they mingled perceptive observations of society with a species of romanticism. Liberals fought for constitutional government within whose framework policy would be set by the outcome of rational debate. But they, too, invoked irrational sentiment—romantic nationalism—in their quest for the power to reorganize society. Thus, neither side rested its case solely on the precedents of the previous generation of revolution and counterrevolution.

Before turning to the renewed struggle of the liberals to remake Europe and the actions of the traditionalists to prevent it, we must, therefore, give some detailed attention to the admittedly confusing, indeed often baffling, romantic impulse.

## THE ROMANTIC IMPULSE

### The Many Faces of Romanticism

In its broadest sense romanticism meant reliance upon the emotions or intuitive feelings as a test of truth. It appealed especially to intellectuals who found the "cold rationalism," scientific analysis, and material environmentalism of the Enlightenment unsatisfying. It attracted a generation torn by revolution, a generation that had failed to find simple, precise, rational solutions to pressing problems. Although the *philosophes* of the Enlightenment had emphasized feelings as a motive force for constructive work along lines determined by reason, romantics made the stimulation of intense feelings an end in itself, the way of coming into contact with ultimate reality.

Romanticism as a respectable approach to life had literary origins in the late eighteenth century: popular chivalric tales; the novels of Fielding, Sterne, and Richardson, which adapted lower-class heroes and heroines to romantic themes; the studied natural simplicity of Robert Burns' poetry; and the mystical symbolism of William Blake. As early as 1756, Edmund Burke—later a counter-revolutionary writer—strengthened the revolt against neoclassical forms with his *Philosophical Inquiry into the Origin of Our Ideas on the Sublime and Beautiful*. In conscious opposition to the explicit classical ideals of such eighteenth-century painters as Reynolds and Gainsborough, Burke took the position that man's deepest, most sublime emotions were not aroused by proportion, unity, serenity, and decorum. Rather, they were stimulated by disintegration, dissolution, and distortion, awakening horror and incomprehensibility. Instead of rules and reason, the early romantics turned to genius, intuition, and emotions that stirred the soul intensely.

Romantics self-consciously repudiated the Deists' mechanistic world view that conceived of God as a detached author of mathematical, mechanical laws operating the same everywhere. Instead, they viewed the universe as a gigantic organism infused with and directed by spirit—a "World Spirit." Instead of a finished product of past creation they conceived of the cosmos as a "growing world" in which ever-increasing diversity expressed the essence and divinity of nature. During the Enlightenment, uniformities had revealed nature's God, but for the romantics uniqueness was the source of revelation.

Their "growing world" was confirmed by contemporary scholarship and science. Historical research by medievalists, philologists, anthropologists, theologians, and legal scholars pointed to the *evolution* of languages, societies, states, and concepts of God that gave each social organism its peculiar individuality. As geologists explained the formation of the earth's crust over vast time periods by processes still operative, physical and biological sciences were becoming evolutionary. Paleontologists added the fact that forms of life had changed, for some forms had become extinct. A half-century before Darwin's biology appeared, the idea of evolutionary change through time as a key to

understanding nature was "in the air." Romantics first made the concept of an evolving spirit behind the material universe the heart of a world view.

If nature's essence were spiritual and organic, it could not be perceived by analysis and mathematical laws. Nature could be fully understood only by intuition. The individual's feelings enabled him to grasp the spirit dwelling within nature. Most romantics idealized—but never adopted!—the life of the peasant as being most natural and uncorrupted by human invention and artifice. Man's material creations, instead of being man's glory, appeared somehow degenerate to the romantics whether they were poets or advocates of *laissez-faire* economics.

Nor did the spirit dwell only within the external material world. Self-made worlds were no longer consigned to childhood fantasies; they, too, were part of experience and added to the spirit's diverse manifestations. By dreaming themselves into the utopian future or the idealized past—usually the Middle Ages—romantics could vent the frustration and anguish they felt for their contemporary world. In denouncing materialism they asserted the power of will or character over the material environment. Anything done in individual self-interest, on the other hand, would spoil natural spontaneity. Nominally rebels against all rules, they were inclined toward collectivism in their assumption that the individual was always subordinate to the organic whole of which he was a part. That whole, they said, made him what he was.

More than a specific ideology, romanticism was a method of confronting the universe and of answering questions of all kinds. In politics and social theory, romanticism cut across every ideology and gave particular force to varying kinds of nationalism, the identification of self with the nation, the greater whole. Anarchists who proclaimed the iniquity of every restraint on natural freedom were romantics, it is true, of one particular sort. But so were collectivists who

*Romantic painting: Eugene Delacroix,* The Abduction of Rebecca *(1846).*

started with the premise that the individual possessed no reality apart from—or no higher duty than to—the nation. Between these two poles there were humanitarian liberals who would divide loyalties among state, church, family, inherited rights, and the individual's separate identity.

## The Romantic Break from the Classical Mold: Art and Music

Romantic individualism reigned most freely in the creative arts. Here it took the form of the revolt of genius against restrictive rules of composition and form imposed by neoclassicism, a revolt which culminated —in the nineteenth and twentieth centuries —in impressionism and expressionism. This romantic impulse was strongest in music and literature. Some neo-Gothic architecture appeared—the British Houses of Parliament,

*Classicism in painting: Jacques Louis David,* The Death of Socrates.

for example. "Wild" landscape painting flourished; painters such as Goya and Delacroix depicted the idealized writhing emotion of civil war and atrocities. And a pre-Raphaelite cult of prettiness appeared in painting. But neoclassical standards continued to dominate architecture, sculpture, and painting as they had during the eighteenth century.

Simplicity and formality characterized popular music, while Franz Joseph Haydn (1732–1809) and Wolfgang Mozart (1756–1791) were the favorite guests of major courts. The compositions of Ludwig Beethoven (1770–1827), notably his *Eroica* or Third Symphony of 1804, initiated a break from "classical form" to meet the demands of expressing such psychological qualities as heroic strength and vitality, fear, horror, terror, grief, and endless longing. Other modes of musical feeling were created—the adaptation by Franz Schubert of lyric poetry to art songs, and the tone and symphonic poems of Felix Mendelssohn (1809–1847), Robert Schumann, and Frederic Chopin. This generation used a wide variety of new devices to explore tone and color. Their experiments, coupled with the adoption of folk sagas as operatic themes in Germany, opened an era of romanticism for the following generation.

*The attraction of Gothic and unspoiled nature: John Constable,* Salisbury Cathedral.

## Literature

Romantic literature consisted preeminently of lyric poetry, novels—especially historical novels of the Middle Ages— and confessions of personal experiences. Early English novelists had written with sentimentality, but not to the degree that the English romantic poets—William Wordsworth (1770–1850), Samuel Coleridge (1772–1834), and John Keats (1795–1821), for example—were sentimentalists. Choosing natural pastoral or exotic subjects, they evoked emotions ranging from childhood memories to the far-off mistiness of Kublai Khan in Xanadu (Coleridge). Theirs was an attempt to communicate directly and intuitively with nature through inner spirit. At the hands of Sir Walter Scott (1771–1832), history was transformed from the *philosophes'* record of the follies, vices, and manners of mankind to the idealized and legendary local color of King Arthur's court. In America, which lacked the grandeur of a medieval past, James Fenimore Cooper attempted to penetrate the imagined inner soul of the American Indian, presenting him as the truest son of unspoiled nature.

Prerevolutionary France had its romantic prophet, as we have seen,* Rousseau. During the Revolution, Madame de Staël (daughter of Jacques Necker) popularized romanticism by reporting on the land where it had its most extreme and permanent development, Germany.

German literary romantics revolted against the petty, cramped court society of local princes, against French cultural dominance in aristocratic circles, and against the stringent rationalism of pulpit and university. Nowhere else had the classical ideal become such a fetish as in Germany where Johann Winckelmann (1717–1768) maintained a stranglehold on formal culture. When the intellectuals (mostly from the middle and lower middle classes), impotent to change the conditions of real life, shook off Winck-

* See *supra*, pages 83–84.

*Johann Gottfried von Herder, patriarch of cultural nationalism.*

elmann's spell, they veered to the opposite extreme, defying all conventions and restraints during a period of "Storm and Stress" (*Sturm und Drang*), which spent its force between 1770 and 1789. Thereafter Goethe (1749–1832), Friedrich Schiller, and Johann Gottfried Herder strove for a delicate balance in drama and poetry between a rational desire for knowledge and the turbulent spiritualism of romanticism. They welcomed the French Revolution but were disillusioned with it by the end of the century and took flight into an idealism having few contacts with day-to-day reality. Fed by Rousseau, English romanticism, and a revival of baroque literature, the German poets and dramatists Friedrich Schelling (1775–1854), Johann Gottlieb Fichte, and Friedrich von Schlegel (among others) turned to transcendental, creative poetry to express an unrequited yearning for the "Absolute."

From poetry and drama they turned to folk-tales and history, especially the history of the Middle Ages. Eschewing scientific detachment, they made history witness to the manifestations of a World Spirit in successive "spirits of the time" (*Zeitgeiste*) and to the working out of beneficent purpose behind the violence and bloodshed which marked their own time. In rejecting the Enlightenment, they praised all it had condemned: religious fanaticism, the Middle Ages, the baroque, and spirited faith. As former anarchists such as Fichte switched from literature to politics under the impact of the Napoleonic wars, the boundaries between literature, religion, and politics ran together into nationalism closely akin to French Jacobinism.

## Romantic Politics, Law, and Philosophy

Germany was the fountainhead of not only the literature but also the social philosophy of romanticism. The work of Herder (1744–1803) antedated both the French invasion and the circulation of Burke's writings in German. One of the most influential writers for German, if not future Western civilization, Herder developed a cultural nationalism that laid the foundations for subsequent nationalist politics.

Herder conceived of each nationality as a living organism with its own peculiarities and myths. Each had its own divine revelation from the World Spirit in its primitive stages—to its "founding fathers." Germany's national spirit or genius (its *Volksgeist*) had its origins in late medieval folk poetry according to Herder. He was a cosmopolitan who conceived of each genius living side by side with every other in harmony, each with the duty of developing its own peculiar spirit. Accordingly, he popularized early Slavic as well as German literature, laying a basis for Slavic cultural nationalism. But his premises could also be turned into a bigoted creed at the hands of traditionalists and nationalists.

During the Napoleonic invasions the ease with which romantics could switch to collectivist nationalism was demonstrated by Johann Gottlieb Fichte. Fichte, a former anarchist who would accept no law to which he himself did not assent, preached the establishment of a German Jacobin state to repel the invader. Within that state the individual would find freedom by total absorption into the nation-state. It would minutely regulate every aspect of life, including economics. Fichte and his fellow nationalists recognized only two realities, God and country—that is, the nation. And after 1815 some of his disciples considered only Germans capable of holding to either. Friedrich Ludwig Jahn, who organized a patriotic gymnastic society largely for dissatisfied college students, was one of these. In proto-Nazi terms, Jahn vehemently denounced external influences on Germany such as the Jews and the international bourgeoisie. But except for youths who had found no suitable "place" in society, few converts were won to Jahn's strident nationalism.

Political control in the German states rested not with publicists such as Jahn, but with absolute princes and nobles who found their principal spokesman in Friedrich Carl von Savigny (1779–1861). His first work on jurisprudence in 1814 justified cancellation of the Code Napoleon where it had been introduced. He advocated restoring previous legal systems based on the inequality of social estates, thereby founding the "historical school" of legal and political theory that was dominant in Germany for the rest of the century. Repudiating natural rights as a pipe dream, this school of law subjugated the individual's identity to the hierarchic social order and to officials obedient only to the monarchy.

German evolutionary philosophy and social theory—the two became one—was expounded in most classic form by Georg Wilhelm Friedrich Hegel (1770–1831). He depicted an evolving World Spirit, which human reason could "understand" or contemplate but not fathom, directing human affairs. Appearing in a succession of dominant states, eventually it would reach fulfillment in the Absolute, a state of perfection. Meanwhile conflict would rage within existing, imperfect reality. Historical experience was the unfolding of a dialectical clash between opposites, a thesis and an antithesis, which, in collision, would produce a synthesis. This synthesis would, in turn, be a new thesis generating a new opposite or antithesis, and the dialectical process would be repeated. The younger Hegel saw this conflict primarily between economic and social classes which only a reign of absolute law could quell. Later he saw it more as one between states, each bound to assert its peculiar genius against others. Therefore in this spiritual clash it was military leaders who made the real stuff of history. Hegel's contemporary Prussian rulers puzzled over whether to consider him as a revolutionary or an absolutist. In one breath he identified the Prussian autocratic monarchy with perfection. In another, because the present was imperfect, his scheme indicated that change was both necessary and inevitable. His system was sufficiently ambiguous to serve those whose sentiments ranged from radicalism to reactionarism.

In one sense Hegel secularized Protestant theology, and advocated the contemplation of a new providence that was beyond human ability to change. But French social theory was closer to traditional theology. The principal theorists of the restoration—Chateaubriand, Joseph de Maistre, and Louis de Bonald—burned with religious enthusiasm to restore universal papal authority. They built their doctrines around a revitalized union of Throne and Altar. They believed that man, evil by nature, could be made sociable only by inherited, divinely sanctioned institutions wielding force. Therefore they both admired and hated the Jacobin terror, for the executioner, one of them said, was the "savior of society." Romanticism proved too volatile, however, to sustain their authori-

*Hegel lecturing, University of Berlin.*

tarianism. After 1820 several prominent religious romantics, including Chateaubriand, turned to liberalism and social reform, vainly hoping that the Church would follow their leadership.

## THE RELIGIOUS REVIVAL AND THE RESTORATION

In French political thought, close connections between revived Roman Catholicism and the Bourbon restoration were evident. After reaching the nadir of demoralization during the Enlightenment, the Roman Catholic Church revived during the revolutionary wars. Then it regained prestige even in Protestant countries as a bulwark against revolution. From previously fashionable scepticism, most of the aristocracy returned to the fold of the Church. Restored Catholic monarchs, who showered churchmen with favors, proclaimed the union of Throne and Altar as the only legitimate basis for secular authority. For a time the Catholic revival carried overtones of the sixteenth-century Reformation. The Jesuits were re-established, and in Rome and Spain the Inquisition and *Index of Prohibited Books* were resurrected. Moreover romantics who repudiated liberalism and the revolution were attracted by the Church's symbolic rites, art, traditions, and organic social doctrines. Many of them—Chateaubriand, Joseph de Maistre, Louis de Bonald, and the German Novalis, for example—became converts or publicists for a new international order under the papacy.

But papal support of political and social reaction cut short the postwar Catholic revival. Because he feared its blindness and lack of *savoir faire* in dealing with old revolutionaries, even Prince Metternich of Austria shied away from the clerical reaction. In the course of time, however, memories of the revolutionary era dimmed. As they did, one practical reason for the Church's popularity declined. And the spread of science and industry undermined the Catholic resurgence because high churchmen found it difficult to come to terms with modern, urban society.

Even in Protestant countries some romantics and counterrevolutionaries were attracted to Roman Catholicism at the end of the revolutionary wars. But more general in these countries in the eighteenth century were emotional religious revivals.* German Pietism, in particular, merged with romanticism and nationalism. This merger became especially explicit in the writings of Friedrich Schleiermacher (1768–1834), one of the most influential theologians of his era. Schleiermacher separated religion from dogma and from the fear of God—who could be dispensed with in the pure contemplation of the universe. Religion was an intuition, a *feeling* that answered a deep need in man. The Enlightenment's search for a universal religion was all wrong. "If you want to grasp the idea of religion as a factor in the infinite and progressive development of the World Spirit, then you must give up the vain and empty desire for one religion."[1] Cosmopolitanism would disfigure the uniqueness of the individual and his national group. Christianity commands attachment to the nation, and Schleiermacher would make the

*Friedrich Schleiermacher, prophet of religious nationalism.*

nation-state the mediator between God and man.

Some mystical Pietists considered the war against Napoleon a holy crusade against the anti-Christ. Several of these groups called for a new era of peace through the abdication of sovereignty to a supranational government. In Eastern Europe Bible-reading societies propagated such hopes. Some of their converts gained the ear and confidence of Alexander I, who tried to incorporate a supranational state into his Holy Alliance, but it was rejected by the Congress of Vienna. More influential on the peace terms were English Wesleyans. Like the Pietists they identified themselves with English nationalism and repudiated the French Revolution's philosophy of natural rights. But provisions in the peace arrangements to eradicate the slave trade were included largely at their instigation.

---

* See *supra*, pages 86–89.

1. Quoted by Koppel S. Pinson, *Pietism as a Factor in the Rise of German Nationalism,* Columbia University Press, New York, 1934, p. 73.

## POSTWAR POLITICS

Immediately after the Napoleonic wars, the peacemakers' concern was to contain future French aggression. The Concert of Europe, created by the Quadruple Alliance of Britain, Prussia, Austria, and Russia had maintained that purpose. But by 1818 Bourbon France had demonstrated her monarchical respectability. Thereafter the concern of the Concert changed from the containment of France to the repression of liberal and national revolts. French entry into the Alliance—now the Quintuple Alliance—clearly signified that change.

Conforming to the principle of a balance of power, the international settlement at Vienna had been moderate. It laid the basis for a lasting peace. There was no major war before 1854, and no general war until 1914. Headed by Austria, the Concert worked to keep in power restored regimes that were reactionary and often vindictive at home. To maintain themselves, the restored rulers had at their disposal centralized bureaucracies, including secret police and *agents provocateurs.** The Revolution had intensified their fears of the lower classes. Promises of constitutional or social concessions made during the wars were forgotten or emasculated. Piety and fear of all innovations set the tone of the restored governments, which were beset by immense postwar problems. A few aristocrats like Metternich could still appreciate Voltaire, but the wit, frivolity, repartee, and openness of the salons of the Enlightenment were gone. When discontent erupted, the restored elites were determined to stamp it out resolutely and forcibly for fear that a revolutionary movement again would get out of hand. In doing this, they repressed the development of constitutional machinery capable of adapting to social and economic change.

Moreover, reaction had broad acquies-

cence if not popular support. For a generation the prestige of having beaten Napoleon put halos around the triumphant aristocratic leaders. Most people on the Continent were still peasants disinterested in politics. Except in Western Europe, liberal and national revolutionary leaders could count on little popular support. Even in Western Europe they were on the defensive where they were not quiescent in 1815. Their surest aids in producing new revolutionary situations were the policies of the restoration governments themselves.

### *"Austria Over All"*

The pivot of diplomacy on the Continent, and therefore of internal policies enforced by it, was the Habsburg Empire. This multinational conglomeration was held together by its sovereign, the well-intentioned but inflexibly reactionary Francis I. He presided over an uncoordinated central bureaucracy that relied heavily on the army and a secret police network. The Habsburgs had suffered much from the French Revolution, but were little influenced by it. Provincial diets dominated by nobles and clergy were restored but seldom called. From Joseph II's reign and the revolutionary wars, the directors of this "absolutism tempered with inefficiency" concluded that reform did not pay. Francis I sounded the dominant note of the court when he wrote:

I do not want any novelties; all that needs to be done is to apply the laws in a fair way; they are good and satisfactory. The present is no time for reforms. The nations are dangerously wounded. We must avoid provoking them by touching their wounds.[2]

Francis showed signs of benevolence during postwar famine and depression, but his policies at home and abroad were tailored to the *status quo.* He rejected administrative reforms proposed by Metternich, although

---

* Undercover police agents who led illegal activities in order to entrap the participants.

2. Quoted by Hans G. Schenk, *The Aftermath of the Napoleonic Wars,* Kegan Paul, Trench, Trubner and Co., London, 1947, p. 69.

Metternich himself was not committed to any basic social change beyond strengthening the landed aristocracy. Concessions to rapid economic growth, liberalism, and nationalism threatened the structure of the Empire. Hence Metternich's foreign policy (as well as Austrian domestic policy) was intended to squelch their emergence anywhere for fear that they might spread. He understood their implications well and conceived it his duty to preserve a doomed order—to "hold the fort"—as long as possible.

## Unrest in Germany

After the war, Austrian influence predominated in Germany and Italy. The Austrian Chancellor presided over the German Confederation which otherwise lacked real executive, military, or local administrative power. At Vienna the German states had been promised diets, but Austria worked to maintain the princes' powers. Five times between 1807 and 1820 the Prussian King promised a constitution, but Austrian warnings and royal vacillation prevented fulfillment. Four southern princes defied Austria and initiated constitutional assemblies. Although all four constitutions gave ample protection to aristocratic interests and privileges, they seemed to Austria like dangerous concessions to liberalism.

As elsewhere, the war left behind depression and stagnation, disastrous to all social classes in Germany. But Germany's economic problems were aggravated by traditionally anarchical standards for money, weight, measurement, and tolls. Some Germans emigrated, particularly to the United States, but most of the population (the peasantry) remained passive until 1848. Articulate agitation for national unification, constitutional government, and economic reform came primarily from the urban middle classes. Some university professors and students, and a few nobles and government officials also worked for these reforms.

Student societies (the *Burschenschaften*) and patriotic societies such as the *Tugend-*

*Prince Metternich, diplomat of stability and reaction.*

*bund* and *Turnverein* led the nationalist agitation. Despite their meager following, they aroused the fears of the existing authorities. In 1817 the Jena student society led a rally at the Wartburg Castle near Eisenach to celebrate Luther's break from Rome as a great national act. The celebration—the first public protest against the settlement of 1815— ended with the burning of the Napoleonic Code and the symbols of restoration society. In 1819 student radicals caused still greater fears when one of them assassinated a tsarist agent.

Local monarchs reacted sharply and invited the Confederation to intervene. It enacted the Carlsbad decrees of 1819, which banned the student and patriotic societies. It also established rigid newspaper censorship, prevented "objectionable" professors from being employed, and put informers in lecture rooms and some churches. The Confederation set up a central investigating committee in Mainz to snuff out subversive revolutionary ideas, but it uncovered no evidence of an organized revolutionary movement. Finally the Austrian dominated Confederation guaranteed the sovereignty of its princes against limitation. But the more liberal monarchies such as Baden, Württemburg, and Saxe-Weimar were restive under Austrian hegemony, and by 1819 Prussian officials had already started a customs union, the *Zollverein*. By eliminating local tolls between Prussia and her neighbors, the *Zollverein* facilitated commerce and eventually political unification. It gave Prussia a reputation for economic progressivism which contrasted with and highlighted the handicaps which Austrian leadership fostered in the rest of Germany.

## Repression in Italy

In Italy the peace replaced French ascendancy with Austrian ascendancy. Secret police and troops under Austrian control secured political conformity, but economically and administratively the peninsula was as divided as before. In northern Italy enlightened despots and French rule had removed the last remnants of manorial and noble jurisdictions. Ferdinand I (restored Bourbon ruler of the largest state, the southern Kingdom of Two Sicilies) committed himself to respect French reforms. But he also secretly pledged to Austria that he would allow no further constitutional changes. As in the rest of southern Italy, aristocrats and clerics continued to wield great power. Corruption, inefficiency, censorship, and restored clerical power alienated the middle classes and the army. Although one of Europe's largest cities—Naples—was located in the kingdom, it was economically backward and plagued with near-universal illiteracy, poverty, and brigandage. Feudal and theocratic traditions were still more dominant in the restored Papal States. Cardinal Consalvi, papal secretary of state, secured stable finances and refurbished the city of Rome. But here, too, the middle classes were alienated by press censorship, exclusion from government, and

a slack state of public order which fed anti-clerical sentiments throughout Europe.

In the old city-state areas of northern Italy, Habsburg princes ruled Modena, Parma, Lucca, and Tuscany. Lombardy-Venetia—whose geography provided a strategic control over the peninsula—was administered directly from Vienna. These areas were managed efficiently if despotically, and some concern was shown for commerce. Least under Austrian control was the enlarged kingdom of Piedmont-Sardinia, where enlightened despotism, a generation of French rule, and the annexation of Genoa provided institutions and interests which contested the Old Regime's return. Throughout the peninsula political reaction, and clerical and papal resurgence marked the postwar years.

## Bourbon Spain

Conservatives like Metternich, Louis XVIII of France, and the Duke of Wellington feared that flagrant misgovernment by vindictive restored rulers would provoke further revolution. Their worst fears were first realized in Spain. With the possible exception of Russia, no European kingdom had been less influenced by the *philosophes* and revolutionary thought. But Ferdinand VII proceeded against political dissent as though it were a tremendous threat. Clerics and nobles not only tried to erase effects of the revolutionary epoch but also all changes of the eighteenth century. After the counter-revolutionary victory the privileges of the Old Regime were restored. The government identified itself with the Jesuits and the Inquisition. Only two newspapers were authorized, and they were devoted to the weather and religious subjects.

Ferdinand, zealous in pursuing opposition, was incapable of organizing an effective government. During the postwar commercial and agricultural depression (aggravated by revolts in Latin America), state finances collapsed, public services lapsed, and the army and navy went unpaid and underfed. The clergy successfully resisted taxation of their holdings which the papacy was willing to concede in order to save the regime. Despite the narrow social basis of Spanish liberalism, the first open revolution against a government recognized as legitimate at Vienna occurred in Spain.

## Restoration France

Even though Louis XVIII shared the clergy's belief in divine-right kingship and the union of Throne and Altar, he proved to be the most circumspect and practical of the restored monarchs. In 1814 he granted a constitutional charter that created an upper House of Peers and an elected Chamber of Deputies. With this machinery he tried to promote a constitutional royalist movement. Most of the badly divided French population was probably prepared to accept any government that brought peace and guaranteed the Revolution. This Louis was willing to do. He drove the republicans and liberals underground, but his greatest opposition came from recalcitrant nobles and clerics, leaders of the Ultras.

Headed by the King's brother, the Count d'Artois, the Ultras possessed the only open political organization besides the King's. During the first elections, the Ultras inaugurated a bloody white terror against revolutionists, Bonapartists, and Protestants. They thereby secured an irreconcilable assembly "more royalist than the king and more Catholic than the pope." They denounced legal equality as blasphemy against God. They attacked Louis XVIII as "a crowned Jacobin" because of his royal constitutionalism. In their vindictive attack on the Revolution and all its works, they pushed through the Chamber of Deputies laws for administrative arrest and detention, and military courts removed from royal clemency. They also provided for preliminary censorship of the press, and the abolition of divorce. They successfully pressed for the execution of Marshal Ney, a prominent Napoleonic general whom they charged with treason.

Affronted by Ultra opposition in the legislature, Louis dissolved it and, with an electorate broader than England's, secured a moderate royalist assembly in its stead. By 1818, in cooperation with the King, this assembly had put finances in order and paid the war indemnity by raising loans. It also secured the evacuation of occupation troops, and relaxed censorship. The King's attempt to "nationalize the monarchy and royalize France" reconciled the old nobility, some of the Bonapartists, and part of the upper bourgeoisie. But the attempt failed to placate either liberals or urban labor whose organizational efforts during the economic crisis of 1816 to 1817 were sternly repressed. Factions in the new assembly assailed the ministry from both "Right" and "Left," gained at the expense of the middle. The Ultras grew particularly alarmed at liberal gains in the election of 1819. But they were unable to do anything about these gains until the Duke de Berry (son of the Count d'Artois who was in the line of succession) was assassinated in 1820. The shock of Berry's assassination enabled the Ultras to launch another offensive. They doubled the votes of the wealthiest electors. They appointed officers to supervise elections, and secured a renewed crackdown on the press. They were even able to send French troops to suppress a revolution in Spain. When Louis XVIII died in 1824, making way for the Count d'Artois as Charles X, the Ultras' leader held the throne. However, the events after Louis XVIII's reign belong to a new era of revolutions, since he was the last crowned monarch to die on the French throne.

## The Peripheral Victor-States: Russia and Britain

One outcome of the Napoleonic wars was that Britain and Russia—on the periphery of battle—suffered little decline as compared to the war-torn continental states. Neither suffered direct onslaught of revolutionary reorganization—Napoleon's invasion of Russia had been purely military—and both remained little touched in depth by revolutionary ideology. Both emerged from the wars with large territorial acquisitions and, as victors, their traditional institutions acquired the prestige of demonstrated superiority.

The institutions of the Old Regime remained more vitally alive in Russia than in any other state. Catherine the Great's shallow enlightened despotism had yielded to the economic and political power of the serf-owning and landed nobility. At the outbreak of the French Revolution she banned everything French, forbade travel to France, and banished critics of serfdom and internal institutions who used words that the Empress herself had uttered previously. Catherine's unstable son Paul (1796-1801) reverted to reform plans—suspending noble privileges, limiting forced labor, fixing succession to the throne in the male line. But he was strangled in 1801 as the result of a conspiracy to which his son Alexander I (1801–1825) was privy.

Educated by a Swiss Jacobin tutor, Alexander was a late product of the Enlightenment and of religious pietism. Disliking class privilege, he ordered the drafting of a constitution, set about reorganizing the government, and laid plans for serf emancipation and education. He fostered intellectual and religious freedom, and founded three universities and many urban public schools. He also encouraged manufacturing and commerce, and forced serf holders to humanize peasant labor conditions. Theoretically the Tsar wielded unlimited powers but, in practice, Alexander was repeatedly frustrated. Nine tenths of the people were illiterate serfs, turbulently dissatisfied, but not demanding constitutional change. Townsmen, a potential source of discontent, were few in number, for Russia had only two cities of note, Moscow and St. Petersburg. That part of the aristocracy, bureaucracy, and army which had been exposed to European ideas and institutions was reform-minded. But the Tsar was dependent upon irreplaceable administrators who detested reform and were subject to pressure from like-minded landed nobility. Understandably, perhaps, Alexander came to the conclusion that liberty in Russia depended upon unquestioned obedience to royal will.

When the Tsar's domestic reforms had come to nothing by 1804, he turned more exclusively to foreign affairs where entrenched interests were less obstructive. In making proposals for international organization, his cosmopolitan diplomatic corps served the self-interest of the nobles who had lost their foreign grain markets. Alexander, lauding the French Revolution and its principle of national self-determination but deploring its excesses and armed expansion, proposed an international government (the Holy Alliance) that would restrict state sovereignty. Realists everywhere rejected the scheme except to use its moral and religious principles to justify intervention against revolutionary change.

After the Congress of Vienna, the Tsar's hands were tied at home and free abroad. He allowed the Finns to keep their traditional institutions. He emancipated the peasantry in Russian-held Baltic provinces. To "Congress Poland" he granted a constitution ostensibly more liberal than that which existed in France and Britain. In several countries his agents worked with secret societies. In reality his liberalism was partly hollow, for the Baltic peasants failed to receive land and the Polish Diet had no control over the Russian-directed budget or army. "Alexander wants everyone to be free on condition that everyone obey him blindly," a Polish aristocrat lamented.

Repeatedly disillusioned internationally as well as inside Russia, Alexander came around to Metternich's repressive conservatism. After 1818 Russian policy in Poland became reactionary. At home, Count Aleksei Aracheev (1764-1834) and the monk Photius secured sufficient power to undo earlier reforms and apply repression. Already, in 1815, Aracheev began to establish military colonies for soldiers and their families, all subject to military discipline and exorbitant work and drill. These colonies, by their agricultural production, were to make the army self-sufficient. Failing in this, the colonies became nuclei of discontent. Despite a mutiny in 1820, the program of military colonies went on. By 1825, an estimated one third of the army was so deployed. Veterans who imbibed Western ideas began to form secret societies, draw up reform programs, and engage in elementary adult education. Alexander was probably ignorant of the colonies' worst features, but he was aware of the secret societies and their objectives. Presumably he did not suppress them because their leaders had been his friends during his liberal youth. Nevertheless, state policy was directed by circles that upheld the nobility as agents of a divine sovereign and that threatened all dissent with exemplary displays of force, especially after Alexander's death in 1825.

Paradoxically, Britain, whose institutions and liberties inspired revolutionary discontent on the Continent, was as absolute during the revolutionary wars as any monarchy, and the freedoms that had made her liberal reputation were not restored at the wars' close. By the end of the eighteenth century, her entire political-constitutional apparatus was controlled by mercantile families and members of the landed aristocracy. Although assimilating new wealth, the elite in Britain was nearly as closed as the aristocracies on the Continent. Legislation favored the squires and commercial magnates, while population pressure, early industrialization, and the French wars coincided to generate intense social difficulties.* Enclosure acts—private acts of Parliament which consolidated holdings and enclosed common lands—drove yeomen and cottagers off their land, making them (especially between 1794 and 1804) wage laborers heavily dependent

---

* For the Industrial Revolution and the increase of population in Britain, see Chapter VI.

upon relief.† Landlords, producing behind protective agricultural tariffs, increased their profits after 1770—spectacularly after 1793. To finance the war the government relied upon indirect taxes and, to a much greater degree than in France, upon loans. No concessions were made to the reform-minded who were no longer represented inside Parliament. Almost unbroken warfare from 1793 to 1815 enabled the Tories to dominate the government, identifying domestic reformers with external revolutionary foes. To encourage this identification of reform with traitors, the ministry employed *agents provocateurs,* newspaper subsidies, packed juries, and cultivated conservative clergymen to crush the English "Jacobins." Parliamentary reform was thus postponed until 1832, and the English model of Montesquieu and Voltaire became an effective tyranny in ways that war alone did not explain.

## CONSERVATISM IN BRITAIN

The Tory government, basking in the prestige of victory but faced with intense postwar problems, continued repression after Waterloo. Victory proved little more prosperous than defeat. Britain shared Europe's three postwar years of poor harvests. While wages fell and prices and landlord incomes rose, heavy indirect taxes were used to retire the state's debt. Unemployment of artisans (especially in the textile trades) rose because of market fluctuations, technological displacement, and the return of soldiers and sailors. In some parishes, one half of the population is estimated to have been on relief. During the depth of the crisis from 1816 to 1817, there were strikes, bread

---

† By 1795 local justices of the peace met the social crisis by adopting the "Speenhamland system" of relief, which provided aid to underpaid or unemployed workers at rates dependent upon the price of bread and the size of the recipients' families. The government praised the "system" as a deterrent to revolution, but its operation reduced the mobility of labor and detrimentally affected the wage system of remuneration.

*Bread riot, House of Commons, 1815.*

*The charge at "Peterloo."*

riots, machine-breaking demonstrations, and rural incendiarism. Cheap newspapers, reaching the lower middle classes for the first time, occasionally used revolutionary language. But, in Parliament, Whig critics went no further than to complain about using secret agents. Fear, whipped by the ministry's investigation reports, gripped the upper classes.

The government attempted little more than to check agitation and expand the Anglican establishment, but a few key men such as Castlereagh and Wellington sought to relieve the pressure by expanding trade. Probably because of improved harvests, the tensions of 1817 fell short of revolution, but another crisis (a commercial depression) followed in 1819 after a period of rampant financial speculation. All opposition outside Parliament was repressed, and a crowd illegally assembled at the new industrial city of Manchester was charged by cavalry. Following this "battle of Peterloo," the government passed Six Acts, most of which were intended to be permanent. They further curbed public meetings, forbade unauthorized military exercises, provided drastic punishments for offenses against public order and libel laws, and authorized broad powers of search and seizure. Despite all of the tensions within the world's leading commercial, colonial, and industrial nation, popular reformers such as the journalist William Cobbett had few followers prior to 1820.

During the 1820s new men began to form an opposition group in Parliament. They put more emphasis upon commercial and agricultural expansion and relieved part of the population's grievances. They obtained an initial but impotent factory act in 1819 and in 1824 and 1825 lifted some restrictions on trade unions. Later in the decade, political disabilities were removed from religious dissenters, but these changes did not alleviate the grinding submission of Catholic and Protestant Ireland to British rule and exploitation. Both the labor laws and the religious emancipation acts, however, did reflect the growth of humanitarian sentiment and organizations. They attacked slavery, the abusive care of orphans, and conditions in factories, mines, and prisons. These measures and the reform of parliamentary representation were probably the fundamental reason that Britain escaped the wave of revolutions that swept the Continent in 1830.

## A GENERATION OF DISSENT, 1820 TO 1848

Revolutionary élan and liberalism seemed dead after the Napoleonic wars. By censorship, secret police, and surveillance, victorious counterrevolutionary governments drove their remnants into underground conspiracies and secret societies. Active discontent survived mainly among business and professional men, urban labor, displaced or unemployed artisans, intellectuals, and youth. Veterans who remained on active duty but whose prestige and income fell precipitously after Waterloo were also significantly aggrieved. Part of the general discontent resulted from circumstances beyond governments' control: the end of wartime contracts, heavy war debts and taxes, incomplete reassimilation of vast armies into civilian life, poor harvests caused by bad weather, and the flooding of continental markets with British goods. Indeed, the masses became revolutionary only during times of economic depression. Nevertheless, inefficient government and discriminatory economic policies were major causes of the weak, sporadic disturbances that began in 1820.

Once stability was restored, dissent gained a broader base. This was particularly true where expanding economic activity produced a growing middle class, chafing under paternal restraints on its production and profits. Liberalism and nationalism, the two ideologies weakly represented by the revolts of 1820, gained increasing momentum and erupted in a more significant round of revolutions and constitutional changes between 1830 and 1832, especially in France, Belgium, and Britain.

These liberal successes whetted desires for similar changes in the rest of Europe. A climactic series of revolutions and constitutional revisions blanketed the Continent from 1848 to 1850 with varying degrees of success and failure. The failures resulted in part from divisions within the revolutionary movement. Differing objectives between liberal constitutionalists and romantic nationalists came to light in Eastern and Central Europe. In these areas, militant nationalists, whose desires for national unification and self-determination were unsatiated, outstripped liberals who were divided between constitutional monarchists and republicans. In Central Europe the peasantry took a course independent of both. Urban workingmen in the more industrialized areas such as northern England, Paris, and Brussels also challenged the bourgeoisie's brand of liberalism. These divisions crippled the revolutionary movement. But despite them, the generation between 1820 and 1848 secured a more general extension of social and constitutional reorganization than had been won between 1787 and 1815.

## The Resurgence of Liberalism and Nationalism

The liberals' watchword was individual freedom—under law enacted by representative, constitutional government. Nationalism was the belief that ultimate authority should be accorded to the nation-state. The nation —a new word in the century's vocabulary— was defined by language, cultural kinship and, above all, by a subjective feeling of "we-ness." Liberals and nationalists shared some common assumptions such as self-determination of peoples. Historical circumstances joined them in opposition to the Concert of Europe which forcefully represented monarchical legitimacy, the divine right of kings. As a result of the experience after 1815 when nationalism and liberalism were closely associated, these two precepts have been frequently considered inseparable features of a new urban culture. But further experience has amply demonstrated that nationalism has combined with far more ideologies than liberalism. Even in this period, Tsarist Russia, hardly an urban or a liberal state, proclaimed a highly xenophobic nationalist doctrine of Russian uniqueness and mission. By 1848 several European nationalist movements had proved incompatible with liberalism. Nevertheless the revolts between 1820 and 1848 were sufficiently interfused with the two "isms" to be categorized as "liberal-national" affairs.

## The Many Mansions of Liberalism

Liberalism presupposed the individual's rationality. It aimed at a rationally directed social-constitutional structure without legal curbs on individual development or on the

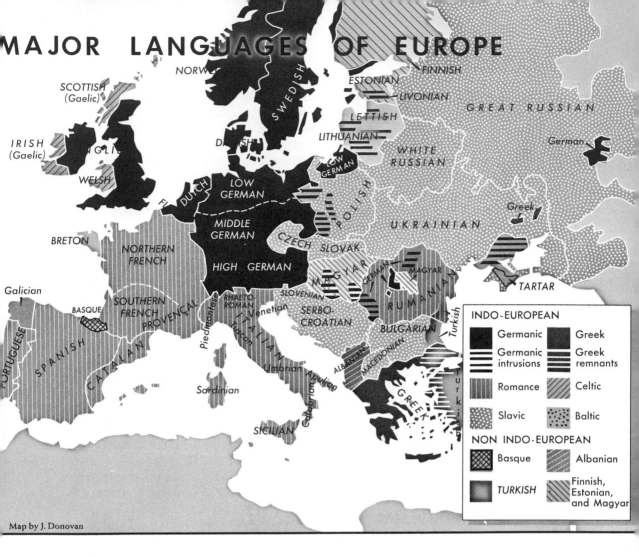

**Map by J. Donovan**

disposition of labor and property. Within the environment of traditional authoritarianism its first tasks were to secure free speech, a free press, religious toleration, and the removal of legal restraints on economic activity. This required changing to a constitutional monarchy or a republic whose legislative authority would be lodged in a representative assembly of those who were capable of independent thought—that is, those who were economically independent of others. Where representative assemblies already existed, liberalism was reformist and evolutionary. Where king, noble, and priest jealously guarded their monopoly of power, it was necessarily revolutionary and anticlerical. Once in power, liberalism's formula was civic rights for all who accepted its constitutional order and political rights for those capable of rational, independent decisions.

Early nineteenth-century liberalism was preeminently the outlook of the bourgeoisie who lived from investments, professional services, large-scale farming, or industrial management. Hence it is usefully called "bourgeois liberalism" to differentiate it from the "democratic liberalism" put in practice during the second half of the century and from the "social liberalism" of the twentieth century. Most bourgeois liberals feared and withheld the franchise from the urban lower classes and the peasantry. The conservatives among them, like François Guizot of France, considered democracy inherently socialist. Radicals like Jeremy Bentham, on the other hand, envisaged a democratic republic based upon an educated electorate. Whatever the hue of their creed, liberals reacted against authoritarianism and its religious sanctions. Instead, they appealed to natural, secular laws. In effect, power in their state would fall to leaders of commerce, industry, and the professions, which they held to be the vivifying elements of society.

At least in the realm of economic production, bourgeois liberals considered all governments necessary evils at best. The state's authority should be limited to justice, defense, and a minimal number of public utilities. Above all, it should protect property, retaining (if necessary) a strong monarch to do so. Theirs was a society based upon contract and wealth rather than inherited legal status. But under their version of *laissez faire* the state should encourage production and distribution by standardizing weights and measures, eliminating internal tariffs, tolls, staple rights, and monopolies, and dissolving guilds and labor organizations. Then each individual, pursuing his own rational self-interest, could serve the common weal, since the natural laws of supply and demand were self-regulating.

Ostensibly by curtailing mercantilism, state police powers—those dealing with health, welfare, and morals—and the harsh legal codes of the Old Regime, liberals would produce a weak government narrowly limited in its functions. But, actually, the liberal state was legally more "absolute," although not more arbitrary, than "absolute" monarchies. It would abolish the legal jurisdictions of the aristocracy and clergy over commoners, outlaw the guilds, and centralize the economy to an unprecedented degree. It would allow no institution except the state to command the ultimate loyalties of the individual. And it could rely on the consent of the governed to a much greater degree. But its reputation as a "watchman state"—Thomas Carlyle dubbed it "anarchy plus the constable"—proved transitory. Wherever liberal economic objectives were achieved, greater and greater centralization of power occurred.

Although liberals opposed them, new comprehensive economic codes followed everywhere on the heels of the industrialization that they advocated. Historically, bourgeois liberals established an economy and representative institutions over which they partially lost control as large, urban lower classes became literate and politically self-conscious.

Major liberal theorists—Jeremy Bentham, Benjamin Constant, and François Guizot—flourished where parliamentary government already existed and the bourgeoisie already had economic and political power. In Southern, Central, and Eastern Europe the liberals' only available channels were secret societies, conspiracies, and the use of force—which contradicted and weakened their own adherence to constitutional procedures. Also in Central and Eastern Europe existing governments were multinational. In this setting romantic nationalism, propagated by literary figures rather than experienced political leaders, came to overshadow liberalism.

## Nationalism

Liberals regarded the self-determination of peoples as the only legitimate basis for government. But, while their outlook was based on this-worldly individual self-interest, romantic nationalism was a religious attitude that looked to the nation-state as the agent of moral regeneration. Nationalism was ethnocentric and demanded self-sacrifice. In Herder's footsteps, most nationalist theorists before 1850 professed a cosmopolitan humanitarianism which would be advanced as each nationality put its own house in order. Some even viewed the achievement of national unity as a stepping-stone to international federation. But others cherished the prospect of exerting their collective military power as the supreme moral good. Either way, the romantic nationalists shared with Giuseppe Mazzini (1805–1872), leader of the Italian unification movement after 1831, the view that the nation was "the God-appointed instrument for the welfare of the human race."

*Giuseppe Mazzini, cosmopolitan Italian nationalist.*

Thereby each particular nationality was the messianic agent for redeeming mankind. Nationalist literary men, journalists, historians, and linguists concentrated on formative periods of national character and eras of past national glory. They instilled in their youth a longing to reclaim lands held in the past. Thus they would not only dissolve supranational empires but also would engage in mortal combat with other "emancipated nationalities" whose territorial claims based on "historic rights" overlapped their own.

## The European Revolts of 1820 and 1821: Spain and Portugal

Before liberalism and nationalism became broad revolutionary movements, discontented soldiers, officials, and townsmen toppled traditionalist regimes in the Iberian and Italian peninsulas. On January 1, 1820, troops embarking from Cadiz to suppress revolts in

Spanish America mutinied against Ferdinand VII. Soon, Madrid and other major cities (which were economically depressed) joined the rebels. A provisional government proclaimed anew the Spanish constitution of 1812. It was a copy of the French constitution of 1791 which Ferdinand had suppressed in 1814.

But most of the population, which was largely illiterate, remained apathetic. Moreover the inexperienced liberal minority in power was split between constitutional monarchists and republican radicals whom the revolutionary military commander supported. The provisional government's actions quickly stirred opposition among nobles, clergy, and peasants. They denounced freedom of the press and legal equality. When the new civilian authorities suppressed the Inquisition, confiscated some Church lands, and abolished some monasteries, they met greater resistance than they could manage. And by granting amnesty to former Bonapartists and changing inheritance laws they only made matters worse. Effective power passed from the *Cortes* or parliament to the army. By 1822, when French invasion was imminent, the army was the sole defender of the revolution. The following year French soldiers, acting in the name of the Concert of Europe, restored Ferdinand. In the name of religion and stability, he suppressed the rebels ruthlessly. But Spain was torn for two generations thereafter by controversies over the succession. This struggle pitted Ferdinand's traditionalist-oriented brother, Don Carlos, against his daughter, Isabella, who was forced to rely on the towns for support.

Meanwhile, in 1820, a revolt in Portugal overturned the Braganza's regency council, which was dominated by a British officer. The rebels persuaded John VI to return from Brazil and proclaimed a constitution and laws similar to those in Spain. John accepted this revolution, but counterrevolutionary forces soon gained the upper hand. They were strengthened when Brazil declared its independence of the revolutionary govern-

UPRISINGS OF THE 1820s

Map by J. Donovan

decried the government's use of lawless, secret counterbrigand bands to check organized thievery—a cure as bad as the malady. On the mainland of the Kingdom of the Two Sicilies, the rebels' victory was ridiculously easy. While it threw the central government into confusion, upper-class leaders demanding self-rule led a revolution in Sicily. Only here did serious fighting occur when Neapolitan forces tried to put down the Sicilian separatists.

The victorious Neapolitan revolutionaries proclaimed the Spanish constitution of 1812, which few if any of them had read and whose provisions had nowhere provided stable government. Moderate inexperienced lawyers, doctors, clerics, officials, and nobles, who were more capable of debating than governing, filled the single-chamber parliament. Their problems were immense. Rifts between radicals and moderates divided them. The masses of the population were illiterate and indifferent. Public order was wracked by brigandage. And the treasury was empty. In early 1821 Austria delivered the *coup de grace* to the revolution by sending an army. Prior to his return to Naples, the king (who requested Austrian intervention) allowed a conservative terror to purge the kingdom of rebel leaders.

Restored Bourbon rule in the Two Sicilies, which now gained the reputation of being the worst rule in Europe, was kept in power and given a measure of stability by the Austrian army. Its garrisons remained (at Neapolitan expense) until 1827. The occupation costs, underwritten by loans that Metternich secured from the Rothschilds, proved ruinous to state finances. Although Metternich feared the repercussions of Ferdinand's mismanagement, his only suggested remedies were to improve administrative efficiency and to apprehend dissident agitators. No fundamental problems of trade, agriculture, customs, industry, or education were tackled and brigandage went unsuppressed. The Neapolitan revolt had been liberal. It was local rather than national, but the mode of

ment and when French troops entered Spain in 1823. Portugal was also torn by factional conflicts over the succession. Spanish and Portuguese absolutists joined forces and received aid from Piedmont-Savoy. Britain and France, however, intervened occasionally on behalf of the liberals.

In both Iberian kingdoms, political instability continued for the remainder of the century. Failing to experience the economic expansion that would have changed the social structure, both kingdoms proved too obdurate for a liberal-national victory. And in both kingdoms, liberal revolutionaries were dependent upon the vacillating support of the army to maintain power.

## In Italy

Repeatedly, the example of one uprising spurred others. News of the Spanish revolt set off a similar one near Naples among discontented military detachments. They were joined by the militia and members of the *Carbonari,* a secret society of clandestine "charcoal burners." Most of the *Carbonari* were well-to-do landholders, professionals, liberal nobles, and judges. Alienated by inept administration and heavy taxes they also its suppression could not have been better calculated to turn reform aspirations into nationalist, anti-Austrian channels.

In crushing the Neapolitan revolution, Austria was making one of her many moves toward dominating the peninsula. In March 1821, liberal aristocrats, intellectuals, army officers, and students in Piedmont revolted. Drawing their inspiration from Naples, Piedmontese insurgents, although intending to unite all of Italy, failed to coordinate their efforts with the Neapolitan rebels. The insurgents were immediately overturned by Austrian arms, which the new king, Charles Felix, had requested.

## In Turkey and Greece

The revolutions of 1820 and 1821 in Latin Europe succumbed to internal divisions and hostile intervention. Except in the minor Portuguese Revolution, no outside power supported the rebels diplomatically or militarily. In both the Balkans and Latin America, however, major powers belonging officially to the Concert of Europe actually supported revolutions against the *status quo* when it was in their interest to do so.

One area where major powers countenanced revolution was the Ottoman Empire in Europe. Its institutional decay and political disintegration invited outside interference. Russia, France, Britain, and Austria were all interested parties except that Austria was temporarily preoccupied elsewhere. During the Napoleonic wars, Russia had taken territory from the sultans and helped the Serbs achieve autonomy. In 1821, while Russia and the Turks were engaged in a dispute over treaty terms, Ypsilanti, a Greco-Russian general, led a body of Greek troops into Walachia and Moldavia expecting Russian aid. Then a more general revolution broke out among the Greek peasants of the Morea and Aegean Islands.

Greek nationalism had been fostered by Greek merchants whose wartime prosperity was reduced by the Viennese peace. The merchants, who had little in common with the illiterate, economically backward, clerically led peasantry, had imbibed revolutionary European ideas. They revived Greek linguistic culture in their schools and founded a secret society, the *Hetaira Philike,* which spread among the Greek mercantile colonies of the Black Sea and Aegean ports. The society's aim was to oust the Ottomans from the Balkans and resurrect the Greek medieval empire. While the peasants' war degenerated into a national-religious struggle of mutual extermination, Greek leaders proclaimed a constitutional government whose separate existence Britain recognized in 1822. Jealousies between leaders vying for political and economic spoils split the revolution into factions. In 1825 it began to collapse before Turco-Egyptian forces.

At this point Greek freedom became the celebrated cause of a liberal romantic (Philhellene) movement in Europe and America. It urged governments whose nationals were economically involved in the area to intervene. In 1827 British and French naval forces destroyed the Turco-Egyptian fleet at Navarino Bay. The following year France interdicted further Egyptian military operations against the Greeks, and Russia launched an invasion that culminated in the conquest of Adrianople in 1829. Foreign intervention thus forced the sultan to concede Greek independence. It was the first triumph of the principle of nationality in Europe since 1815. But the independent state that resulted was confined to the southern tip of the peninsula. By no means did it satiate the thirst of revolutionary leaders for either self-determination or restored empire.

## The Latin American Revolts

Before Greek independence was finally recognized, most of Latin America had successfully broken from Europe. The American revolutions were colored by sharp social cleavages which, as was not the case in Europe, involved racial distinctions. Tensions between the pure-blooded European Creoles born in America and the mixed, ostracized

# LATIN AMERICAN INDEPENDENCE
## c. 1824

*Atlantic Ocean*

*TEXAS*

*Gulf of Mexico*

MEXICO

Mexico City

Havana CUBA (Sp.)

DOMINICAN REPUBLIC

BRITISH HONDURAS

HAITY

PUERTO RICO (Sp.)

GUATEMALA
SALVADOR
HONDURAS
NICARAGUA

*Caribbean Sea*

CENTRAL AMERICA
*Independent, 1821
Divided, 1838*

COSTA RICA

Panama

Caracas

VENEZUELA
*1830*

TRINIDAD
(British)

BRITISH GUIANA
DUTCH GUIANA
FRENCH GUIANA

*Pacific Ocean*

*Equator*

Bogotá

GREAT COLOMBIA
*1819-1830*

Quito

*ECUADOR
1830*

*Amazon R.*

P E R U
*1824*

Lima

EMPIRE OF
B R A Z I L
*1822*

BOLIVIA
*1825*

La Paz

*Chaco dispute*

Rio de Janeiro

C
H
I
L
E
*1818*

PARAGUAY
*1811*

ARGENTINA
*1816*

Buenos Aires

*URUGUAY (Independent, 1828)*

Montevideo

*Patagonia*

---

## c. 1790

VICEROYALTY
OF
NEW SPAIN

CAPTAINCY-GENERAL
OF CUBA

HONDURAS
(Br.)

CAPTAINCY-GENERAL
OF SANTO DOMINGO

JAMAICA
(Br.)

CAPTAINCY-GENERAL
OF
GUATEMALA

DUTCH GUIANA
FRENCH GUIANA

VICEROYALTY
OF
NEW GRANADA

VICEROYALTY
OF PERU

VICEROYALTY
OF
BRAZIL
(Portuguese)

VICEROYALTY
OF
BUENOS AIRES

0   100   200 mi.

Map by J. Donovan

0   50   100   150 mi.

*mestizos* had erupted prior to the French Revolution. So had conflicts between the Creoles and officials sent from the mother countries who were at the top of the social-economic ladder of privilege. A few uprisings had occurred among the Indians but, for the most part, this most grievance-laden class remained inert.

The Creoles were decisive for the Latin American revolutions, but their course was not consistently liberal or national. In the late eighteenth century many of them rallied to the Enlightenment. But when the French Revolution became radical and aggressive, they reverted to orthodox monarchism. Except in Mexico where a social-political revolution was under way, the Spanish Creoles broke with Napoleonic Spain in the name of Ferdinand VII. Royalist Brazil received the Portuguese royal family in exile. Then certain radical Creoles such as the wealthy Simon Bolivar broke from the royalists, demanded total separation from Europe, and involved the colonies in civil wars.

Expulsion of Spanish authority was largely the work of Bolivar in the north and José San Martin in the south. After 1815 Bolivar's fortunes declined sharply, but when the Spanish Revolution broke out in 1820 he drove Spanish garrisons from present-day Venezuela. From there, he pushed southward into Ecuador and Peru, the center of Spanish power. Here he met San Martin leading liberation forces from Argentina and Chile; the southern revolution had begun in Buenos Aires. As early as 1806 Britain unsuccessfully had sought to annex that area by taking advantage of discontent with Spanish trading policies. In 1816 a revolutionary government in Buenos Aires declared its independence. Amid anarchic political conditions, the southern portion of the Spanish empire in South America crumbled into local states. San Martin, military liberator of Argentina, joined with Chilean revolutionaries and proceeded to Peru. By 1824 Spanish America had driven out its European officials, and

Brazil had become an independent empire under a younger son of the Portuguese monarch.

Latin America became independent with the aid of Britain, who reaped commercial rewards for her efforts. British freebooters and veterans gave San Martin provisions, men, and direction. Meanwhile, British trade and investments flowed into the whole Ibero-American area. At first the new states' independence was recognized only by Great Britain and the United States, who engaged in weak competition with one another for the area's trade.

## The Collapse of the Quintuple Alliance

The revolutions of 1820 and 1821 tested the resolve of the Quintuple Alliance of 1818 to keep Europe peaceful and conservative. Metternich's Austria, by its geographical position and interests, was destined to lead the alliance in the crushing of liberal-national uprisings. The Spanish revolt of 1820 presented the first challenge. But Spain was remote, and Metternich hoped that the revolution would burn itself out. Naples, on the other hand, was too close to ignore. At Troppau in 1820 the three Eastern members of the Alliance met with observers from Britain and France to consider these revolts. Here Metternich completed Alexander I's conversion to conservative interventionism. Thereafter, Austria, Russia, and Prussia agreed to the Troppau Protocol justifying intervention against liberal-national revolutions:

States which have undergone a change of government due to revolution, the results of which threaten other states, *ipso facto* cease to be members of the European Alliance, and remain excluded from it until their situation gives guarantees for legal order and stability. If owing to alterations, immediate danger threatens other states, the powers bind themselves, by peaceful means, or if need be by arms, to bring back the guilty state into the bosom of the Great Alliance.[3]

Lord Castlereagh, whose country supported constitutional governments for their stability and openness to British trade, rejected the Troppau Protocol as an illegitimate extension of the postwar treaties. At a subsequent congress at Laibach (in present-day Yugoslavia) the issue of intervention in Italy came to a head. Austria secured authorization (although not from Britain) to destroy both the Neapolitan and Piedmont revolutions. Britain eventually approved this intervention in Italy —as an act of Austrian self-defense, not as a general principle.

To deal with the Spanish, Latin American, and Greek revolts, the powers next assembled in 1822 at Verona in Venetia. Tsar Alexander, who had provided a reserve army to back up the Austrians in Italy, pressed for authorization to send his forces to Spain. His proposal stirred fears of Russia's expansion, just as his proffered—and rejected— naval support against the Barbary pirates and slave traders had done. For Metternich, French intervention in Spain was a palatable substitute. Furthermore, the expedition fit into domestic French politics as a way of reconciling both the Ultras and the army (bored with inactivity) to the government of Louis XVIII. Once more, Britain, fearing further intervention into Latin America under French auspices, stood aloof.

The crushing of the Spanish Revolution in 1823 was the Concert's last victory. Britain's new foreign minister, George Canning, welcomed the return to a situation of "every nation for itself and God for us all." Already he was involved in aiding the Greek and Latin American uprisings. To forestall intervention in Latin America he turned to both the United States and France. He proposed to the United States a mutual declaration guaranteeing Latin American independence and pledging both countries not to acquire territory there themselves. From France he secured a formal disclaimer of intent to intervene. The American President James Monroe, who was advised closely by John Quincy Adams, spurned Canning's proposed joint declaration in favor of a unilateral declaration, later known as the Monroe Doctrine. In it he warned that the Americas were not to be considered subject to further European colonization.* For good measure, he asserted American noninterference into the fundamentally different political system of Europe. The Monroe Doctrine exhilarated America's sense of national pride but, for the time being, the British fleet and Canning's pledge from France were the surest guarantees of Latin American independence.

Reduced to the three Eastern monarchies of Austria, Prussia, and Russia, the Concert continued to function in attenuated form. The formal machinery of cooperation established at Vienna was further weakened, however, by the Greek revolt. Metternich was able to prevent Alexander I from active participation but, after the Tsar's death in 1825, Russia joined with Britain and France to help the Greeks win their independence.

## The Decembrist Epilogue

Alexander I's death in 1825 provided the occasion for Russia's one fleeting revolutionary experience in the nineteenth century. Discontent within the army (among noble officers and men who were inspired by Western liberalism) broke into open revolt in December 1825. A southern group headed by Paul Pestel (1793–1836) agitated for liberation of the serfs, abolition of class privilege, a republic based on manhood suffrage, and the forcible assimilation of non-Russian minorities. Simultaneously a northern secret

---

3. Quoted by W. Allison Phillips, *The Confederation of Europe,* 2nd ed., Longmans, Green & Co., London and New York, 1920, pp. 208–209.

* Monroe was also concerned with Russian territorial expansion on the Pacific coast of North America.

*The end of a line: Louis XVIII (seated) and the Count d'Artois, the future Charles X (left).*

were gaining converts through an expanding press, education, and the popularization of causes such as Greek independence. Although most of Europe remained economically similar to the world of Voltaire, an agricultural revolution was beginning to uproot inherited agrarian relationships. Expanding commerce and industry bred discontent among businessmen and guildsmen. In 1830 only France sustained a revolution without foreign aid, but the revolts of 1830 and the peaceful constitutional changes that occurred in Britain, some Swiss cantons, and a few German states by 1832 indicated a much broader liberal-national base of support than in 1820 and 1821.

### Bourbon Rule Deposed in France

France (or, more specifically, Paris) was the epicenter of the revolutionary quake beginning in 1830. Charles X, whose accession Louis XVIII prophetically feared as the doom of the Bourbon dynasty, could not keep a moderate ministry working under the Charter of 1814. The court, ministries, and legislators were under Ultra influence. At the court, medieval pageantry and the royal touch to cure disease were revived. Ministers openly reckoned on divine assistance for their policies, and laws initiated by the Assembly seemingly were designed toward the restoration of the Old Regime. Legislation tightly restricted an electorate pressured by appointive officials, eliminated jury trials for critics of the government, and advanced clerical education. In 1825 a reduction of the interest rate paid to bondholders compensated *émigrés* for confiscated land. Stern penalties for despoiling Church properties and objects of worship were instituted. Another measure would have restored inheritance by primogeniture among the nobility, but the Chamber of Peers, which contained Bonapartist elements, rejected it. And courts mitigated the censorship laws by acquitting persons accused under them of treason.

Liberal opposition (fanned by journalists) mounted as influential bankers, journalists,

society, which included noble landlords as well as soldiers, took Bourbon France as a model. Neither group had a significantly large following, and both organizations were transient. Their revolt was more a matter of unexpected opportunity than of planning. When Alexander died, the succession was not clear because Constantine, the next in line, had secretly renounced the throne. During the three-week interregnum, military units in St. Petersburg attempted a *coup d'état* under the slogan of "Constantine and Constitution." As Nicholas I took the throne, both insurrections were quickly smashed. Subsequent would-be revolutionaries studied the Decembrists' naïve tactics for knowledge on how *not* to conduct a revolution.

### Tremors of Change, 1830 to 1832

None of the risings of 1820 and 1821 had survived without foreign assistance, and the Italian and Spanish revolutions had collapsed when met with force. But, by 1830, conditions had begun to change perceptibly. The Concert of Europe was in disarray. Ecclesiastics no longer presented a solid counter-revolutionary front. In France a liberal Catholic movement had started. In Poland and the Belgian half of the Kingdom of the Netherlands local churchmen openly opposed the *status quo*. Romantic liberals and nationalists

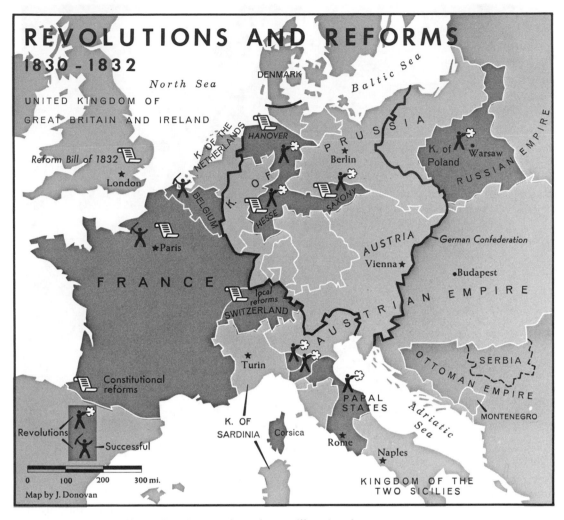

REVOLUTIONS AND REFORMS
1830 - 1832
Map by J. Donovan

and intellectuals joined in denouncing the government. Heretofore, they usually had kept aloof from secret society conspiracies. Hostility to the Bourbons was the major cause of resentment, but there were also economic grievances that made workingmen revolutionary. Lower-class Parisians suffered from a lack of work, low wages, and the high price of bread. Instead of the "dangerous classes," however, it was the more solid artisans who formed the backbone of the revolutionary crowds as they had in 1789. But these crowds were not very interested in the constitutional issues that inspired the liberals. Charles X and his ministers, discovering that mild appeasement failed to satisfy

liberal agitators, turned to vain expedients. As a distraction from domestic tensions and as an appeal to nationalists, Charles X began an invasion of Algeria. When liberal dissent continued to swell, he resorted (in July of 1830) to a series of ordinances that provoked a popular revolution in Paris.

The July ordinances, although promulgated without military precautions, gave popular credence to the charge that Charles X intended to restore royal absolutism. They dismissed an elected assembly before it met, forbade further publications without prior government authorization, reduced the electorate, and placed Ultras in high office. Journalists defied the censorship and de-

*Barricades romanticized: Delacroix's* Liberty Leading the People *(1830).*

nounced the ordinances as violations of the charter, while Talleyrand (among others) negotiated with leading bankers and citizens of the capital to plan a new government. Constitutional monarchists emphasized that no social-economic upheaval was in the making. Paris, however, still nourished a small republican movement that was socially more radical. The revolt began when employers freed their workers to take up arms. The republicans made the first show of force, but they were promptly stranded when Lafayette, their political idol, attached himself to the dominant revolutionary faction: the constitutional monarchists. Their candidate for the throne was Louis Philippe of Orleans, who had participated in the early stages of the French Revolution and who now accepted its symbols.

Louis Philippe, replacing the fleeing Charles X, gave up royal power to issue decrees, recognized Catholicism as the religion of the majority (personally he was a Deist), made civil liberties more firm, and slightly lowered voting qualifications. As in England in 1688, divine-right monarchy was replaced by the rule of an elite defined primarily by wealth. Louis epitomized the ideals of his principal supporters—thrift, investments, and dedication to order. The ideological spokesman for the July or "Bourgeois" Monarchy was a historian—François Guizot—who held office during most of Louis' reign. Guizot's histories and policies identified the interests of the bourgeoisie as the golden mean, the *juste milieu,* between royal absolutism and democracy, which he considered as a stepping-stone to socialism. But his policies alienated the republicans, Bonapartist advocates of power politics, and urban workingmen to whom the government made few concessions.

By means of the revolution of 1830 Paris had overturned a key provision of the counterrevolutionary peace of 1815: the Bourbon restoration. It excited both conservatives and liberals across Europe. Metternich, a constant prophet of doom, judged it as being the end of his life's work. Eager to intervene, Nicholas I of Russia assembled troops in Poland, but he was too far away. Prussia entered into military conversations with him. Louis Philippe reassured the conservative powers that he had no intention of exporting revolution. But, in fact, the French example served to precipitate uprisings in Belgium, Italy, and Poland. It also stirred agitation for constitutional changes in Switzerland, Britain, and several German states. Revolutionary and reform movements spread out in an emotional wave. One revolution encouraged another. Their simultaneous occurrence had the effect of diplomatic coordination. Revolts in Eastern and Central Europe pinned down the military forces of the Eastern empires, precluding their intervention in the West.

## Belgium Achieves Independence

Prior to 1830 there had been no general agitation for Belgian independence. But since the forced Dutch-Belgian union of 1814, latent grievances had been accumulating among the Belgians. More numerous and less-indebted, the Belgians shared equally with the Dutch in representation and combined debts. Although enlightened, the arbitrary administration was Dutch. It laid much of the basis for Belgium's subsequent rapid industrialization in the future, but Belgian critics attributed to it—and particularly to its low, agriculturally oriented tariffs—the problems of the middle and lower classes. The religious rift was more serious. Belgian Cath-

"The Charter or Death," Parisian poster of 1830.

olics opposed the state's monopoly of lower education, and Catholic conservatives resented forced freedom of conscience. The rising in Paris brought to a head the dissatisfaction with the House of Orange. In August the King received demands for reform, but his concessions came too late. A provisional government declared Belgium independent —a clear violation of the peace settlement at Vienna. In 1831 the new state adopted the most liberal constitution in Europe. It provided for popular sovereignty, local self-government for provinces and towns, and basic freedoms (press, assembly, religion, and education—meaning, in practice, clerical education). The constitution contained no restrictions on the suffrage, although later statutory enactments limited voting to the wealthy.

To declare independence, however, was not to achieve it. William of Orange confidently anticipated assistance from the Eastern powers, but Britain and France adhered to the principle of no counterrevolutionary intervention. After the outbreak of a revolt in Poland in November 1830, they secured international recognition of Belgian independence and its perpetual neutrality. When Orangist troops moved to recover the Belgian provinces, both France and Britain intervened to prevent them. Not until 1839 did William, still absolute in the Dutch provinces, acquiesce in Belgian independence.

## Uprisings that Failed, 1830 and 1831

The remainder of the uprisings of 1830 and 1831, whose leaders counted vainly on French assistance, occurred in Eastern and Central Europe. The uprisings ended in failure and renewed reaction. The largest and most significant one was in Poland. In reaction to the repressive policies of Nicholas I, nationalism flared in "Congress Poland" among the aristocracy, army, and intellectuals. A secret society, established in Warsaw at the army-officers' school in 1828, was first in effectively organizing discontent. When rumors spread that Polish troops were to be sent to France and Belgium, soldiers and students rebelled. Then after Russian troops withdrew, the aristocratic Polish Diet declared Nicholas deposed. The aristocrats, fearing radical nationalists who desired social reforms, tried to negotiate with the Tsar. The revolt was weakened by social divisions and by Europe's first cholera epidemic. It took Russian troops only from February to May 1831 to suppress it. Vengeance followed. The universities were closed; lands were confiscated, and the intellectual elite of Poland emigrated *en masse* to Western Europe (especially Paris) and to the United States. In new homelands they helped paint Russia's image as the major suppressor of human liberties.

Revolts in northern Italy—Parma and Modena—and the northeastern Papal States challenged Austria's hold in Italy in 1830. Although literary nationalists revived Dante and Machiavelli and recalled Italy's glory in resisting German rule during the Middle Ages, these revolts were local rather than national. The *Carbonari,* who organized them, seldom aspired to more than provincial independence. Playing upon local rivalries, Austria crushed them one by one in 1831.

The reaction that followed was significant for both Italy and Europe. The papacy, in whose states revolts had occurred, con-

*Polish revolutionary forces, 1831.*

demned liberalism unconditionally in 1832. Liberal Catholics were denounced for supporting freedom of conscience, freedom of the press, separation of church and state, and "other harmful errors of those who possessed by an undue love for liberty, do their utmost to undermine authority." This position sharpened the cleavage between liberalism and the Church, and it encouraged nationalists to uphold their creed as a rival religion. The Italian fiasco of 1831 also discredited the old secret societies. Now Giuseppe Mazzini's Young Italy took the lead. Its tactics were secret and conspiratorial also, but its religious nationalism intended to unite all of Italy by concerted action.

## Nonrevolutionary Changes About 1830

The liberal-national surge of 1830, either because it was weak or because authorities made concessions, did not lead to violence everywhere. Slavic and Magyar nationalists were reviving their literatures and histories. Eventually their cultural nationalism led to political self-consciousness but, for the moment, the Habsburg government, which ruled most of the nationalities involved, kept it in check. In Hesse and a few other German states the revolts of France and Poland served as a goad for constitutional reform. Saxony and Hanover adopted laws that totally emancipated the peasantry from inherited dues and services. But in most of Germany this revolutionary period produced more agitation by professors, students, lawyers, and writers than immediate concrete achievements. Again, as in 1819, the German Confederation thwarted constitutional changes and curbed dissent. Individual Swiss cantons were able to show more liberal results by 1832. Local constitutions now provided for popular sovereignty, a broader suffrage, and secular education. Agitation also occurred in Scandinavia but, except for the establishment of consultative assemblies in Denmark, no institutional changes occurred.

## The Great English Reform Bill

England's Reform Bill of 1832 was the main nonrevolutionary constitutional change in Europe. By 1830, when the first bill to alter Parliament was introduced, industrialization had drastically altered Britain's economic, social, and demographic structure, while the basis for representation to the House of Commons was still that of the seventeenth century. Wealthy landed persons, sometimes a single family in a "rotten borough," elected members to the House of Commons while populous industrial cities like Manchester were totally unrepresented or industrial counties like Yorkshire had only its two old seats. Conservative defenders of the existing constitution claimed that under the old system all Englishmen were "virtually" represented by men of wisdom. Tory repression, however, failed to check pressures for reform. During the 1820s, young humanitarian Tories including Robert Peel, George Canning, and William Huskisson cooperated with moderate Whigs to break the Tories' solid front. But moderate reform did not become a real issue until the Whigs adopted it as a party program. This occurred during the excitement produced by the July revolution in Paris.

Newspapers and popular orators generated public support for the bill that Lord Grey, the new Whig prime minister, submitted to Parliament. But Grey and his titled cabinet ran into a flurry of opposition from

*A Union Jack for the Reform Movement, 1832.*

the older Tories and higher churchmen. When the House of Lords blocked the bill in 1831, mobs patrolled the streets of Bristol and other cities. Armed organizations appeared, and the Bank of England was threatened with a run on its gold reserves. When the Duke of Wellington tried to form a diehard cabinet, Britain came close to civil war. When Wellington failed, the King agreed to threaten the Lords with the mass creation of new peers favorable to the bill. In 1832 the Tory peers decided to let the bill pass rather than risk civil war or dilution with new peers. Thus British conservatives demonstrated greater flexibility than Continental traditionalists. The conservatives, predicting erroneously that reform would cause a revolution, yielded peacefully to popular pressures.

The reform bill cut away some of the worst abuses of the old system without a thorough revision of the electoral machinery. It took seats from smaller boroughs and transferred them to the industrial towns and counties of the north and west. It extended suffrage to the upper middle classes. Landed and commercial wealth still dominated the

House of Commons. But the admission of wealthy industrialists to political power challenged the Tories and established a balance of power that utilitarian radicals and humanitarians exploited to secure reform. Both Whigs and Tories considered the Great Reform Bill "final"—its sharing of power between aristocracy and middle classes provided the axis of politics known as the "Victorian Compromise."* Instead of being final, however, it had broken the principle that only landed property holders could participate in politics. Thereafter, no easily defensible principle separated the one property holder in thirty now entitled to vote from the one in four or five whom universal manhood suffrage would enfranchise.

## THE GENERAL REVOLUTIONARY SWEEP OF 1848 TO 1850

Constitutional changes between 1830 and 1832—by evolution and revolution—drew a boundary between a liberal West and an absolutist East and Center. The major Western states were no longer part of the Concert of Europe. In 1833 the monarchs of Prussia, Russia, and Austria consolidated their triumph at Münchengrätz by reasserting their collective right to intervene against revolts outside their borders. For their severity in repressing revolts, Western liberals disdained the Eastern regimes. Subsequent diplomacy eased this East-West rift, but a crucial question remained to be tested by the next wave of revolutions: How far would the Western states go to aid uprisings against the Eastern empires?

A dispatch from the British foreign minister, Lord Palmerston, to the British ambassador to Russia in April 1848 made clear how transitory the outcome of the revolutions of 1830 had been. Palmerston wrote that, with the exception of Belgium, Britain and Russia "are at present the only two

Powers in Europe . . . that remain standing upright." The fifty-odd revolutions of 1848–1849, whose font was Paris, brought to a climax and exhausted the ideology of the French Revolution in Central Europe.

The social and economic conditions in that part of Europe (except for a few pockets of industrialization, some railroads, and improved communications) were more similar to prerevolutionary France than to industrializing Britain or traditionalist Russia. As in the great revolution of 1789, a combination of factors coincided to make a broad section of the Central European populace revolutionary—at least for a time.

The populace was stirred only in part by the burgeoning liberalism and nationalism of the middle classes and intelligentsia. Rapid population increase, followed by a general crop failure beginning in 1846, heightened the people's unrest. Famine, which was caused primarily by inclement weather and the potato blight that shriveled the peasantry's store of staple foodstuffs from Ireland to Central Europe, created a subsistence crisis and was responsible for commerce and credit collapsing in 1847. Skyrocketing food prices during depression put rural and urban workers and guildsmen in acute distress. In some areas, machines were replacing craftsmen. Discontent among the lower classes (especially the peasantry) paralyzed existing governments. This temporary paralysis left the liberal-national intellectual minority freer to work than they were in 1830. With remarkably little violence, Central Europe seemed won over for liberalism and nationalism at the peak of the revolutions of 1848. Yet, in the causes, gains, and failures, much more than liberalism and nationalism was involved. General economic distress introduced elements into these revolutions that made them no mere repetition of the events of 1830.

The liberals' apparent power was illusory and temporary because they represented only a small segment of the forces working to sustain the revolution. The peasants lost

* For the workings of the Victorian Compromise, its revision, and eventual destruction, see Chapter VIII.

interest in it once they secured release from their old manorial and feudal dues and services. And when self-conscious anticapitalist workingmen became assertive in France and Germany in early summer the bourgeoisie recoiled in horror, leaving further revolutionary activity to a narrow segment of radical republicans. Then, too, nationalist animosities prevented cooperation. When German and Hungarian nationalists first tasted power, for example, they were determined to rule over the Slavs. As the older authorities regained their nerve and the will to use force against their inexperienced foes, the early bubble of success broke before a new wave of reaction. The most durable gains proved to be those of the peasants. Counterrevolution had another unexpected ally in the cholera epidemic. It struck preferentially at the densely populated cities debilitating its surviving victims and terrorizing the spared, since contemporary medicine was helpless against it.

## French Revolution and Counterrevolution, 1848 to 1850

Between 1846 and 1848, Europe's political tranquillity was disturbed by a peasant revolt in Galicia, a civil war between liberal and Catholic cantons in Switzerland, and an uprising in Sicily. Restiveness caused by the economic depression was general. But Paris, a nonindustrialized city of over one million people which had increased by one third since 1830, again set off the revolutionary powder train.

Louis Philippe's government had lost the support of one major segment of the population after another. The French Revolution of 1830, which Victor Hugo described as a "revolution stopped half way," left the republicans totally without influence and hostile to the regime. In opposition to Louis, too, were the Legitimist Bourbons, whose dissent split and weakened French conservatism. The government's Voltairean anticlericalism also alienated Roman Catholics.

Unsatiated by the continuing conquest of Algeria, Bonapartists derided the government for its disregard of national prestige and glory. Frequent attempts were made on the King's life. And François Guizot, his principal minister from 1840 to 1848, found it difficult to maintain the loyalty of the minute electorate which consisted of 3 per cent of the adult males, whose unpaid representatives he manipulated by appointments to remunerative government posts. This narrow bourgeois government not only aroused traditional opposition but also—by a callous policy toward urban labor—contributed to the rise and influence of socialist intellectuals whose plans for economic reorganization will be discussed in Chapter VII. Most of the early socialists, whether advocates of violence such as Auguste Blanqui or humanitarians such as Saint-Simon, Louis Blanc, Victor Hugo, and George Sand, agreed that a democratic republic must succeed Louis Philippe's government. If opposition to the Orleanist monarchy was alarmingly widespread, the divisions rending that opposition were equally ominous for the erection of a stable substitute.

Supporters of opposition deputies, forbidden to hold political meetings, began holding banquets with political toasts and interminable speeches. Eventually they planned a massive banquet and demonstration in Paris on February 22, 1848. When the government ordered the affair canceled, prominent sponsors and members of the assembly withdrew. The banquet was never held, but the government's order stirred resistance, answered by repression. Students and workers clashed with the police, and rioting inspired by martyrs continued for several days. Louis Philippe, reluctant to provoke further bloodshed, successively dismissed Guizot, called off military suppression and, after barricades were thrown up in the working class districts, abdicated.

Republicans and socialists (mostly journalists from two capital newspapers) joined together in proclaiming a provisional gov-

LIBERTÉ

PUT OUT!

*Liberty extinguishes Louis Philippe's candle.*

ernment. Prodded by the Parisian populace, this government proclaimed universal manhood suffrage, absolute freedom of the press, and other radical measures. Slavery, imprisonment for debt, and capital punishment for political offenses were abolished. For urban lower classes it guaranteed a right to work at livable wages, reduced the work day from about fourteen to ten hours, set up an employer-worker council, and authorized the establishment of producer cooperatives as a substitute for private capitalism. The provisional government inherited an empty treasury and an economic crisis which soon became catastrophic. As wealthy Parisians emigrated by the thousands, credit dried up, banks closed, the market slumped, shop closures swelled unemployment, and the cooperatives (Louis Blanc's National Workshops) seldom got beyond unproductive relief work projects. Inexperience and the substitution of zeal for skill plagued the new government.

The provisional government's most severe weakness was its narrow urban basis of support. Election by universal suffrage, even at the height of revolutionary fervor, produced a majority of republicans, monarchists, and clericals determined to wipe out concessions to urban labor which were being financed by rural taxes. The constituent assembly, elected in April, removed Parisian radicals from positions of power. It utilized the National Guard—a bourgeois "honor society," —to thwart pressures from working-class districts. Its decision to abolish workshop relief, giving recipients the choice between draining pestilential swamps in the provinces or joining the army, provoked open warfare between the popularly elected government and the Parisian workers. During the "June Days" (June 23 to 26), about 100,000 workers, whose leaders were in jail for having organized previous risings, took to the barricades. Unlike the liberal cry of "liberty or death," theirs was "bread or lead." The assembly concentrated all authority in the hands of an Algerian veteran general—Cavaignac—who used the new telegraph and railway system to gather troops from the provinces. After bombardment by artillery, the rebels' strongholds fell to Cavaignac's troops. The insurrection's affront to the new government, which represented popular national sovereignty, produced a shock wave of reaction against the "specter of communism." This reaction inspired judicial and military reprisals and the revocation of all social concessions made to the working classes during the revolution.

## Defeat of the Revolutionaries

Cavaignac's victory inspired counter-revolutionary forces throughout Europe. In France, initiative shifted from the republicans to clerical monarchists and frightened bourgeoisie. This occurred as constitutional procedures broke down. In November 1848, the constituent assembly promulgated a constitution that resulted in a stalemate between an elected president and an elected assembly.

*Procession of Napoleon's ashes at the Arc de Triomphe, 1840.*

Whether such a constitution could ever have worked is moot, but the subsequent election of a Bonapartist president and a monarchist assembly in December and January sounded the Republic's death knell.

In electing Louis Napoleon (nephew of the great Emperor) as president, the voters repudiated the socialists, radical republicans, and even the conservative republican, Cavaignac. Louis Napoleon's past smacked of comic opera, but he bore the great general's name and exploited the Napoleonic legend that Napoleon I was the champion of peace and the common man.* To the "Left" he posed as a socialist. To the "Right" he appealed as a disciplinarian of labor, an apostle of authority and order.

The electorate, by returning to the assembly a clerical and monarchist majority pledged to save society from the radicals,

still more explicitly impugned republicanism. Ironically for democratic liberals, universal manhood suffrage in a society that was still basically agrarian had produced a government less liberal than Louis Philippe's government. The clerical monarchists purged urban radicals from the electorate, gave the Church an enlarged role in primary and secondary education, and joined with Napoleon in destroying the short-lived Roman Republic in 1849.† But, by reacting against radicalism more than public opinion warranted, the assembly armed Louis Napoleon with the popular support to destroy it. When it refused to amend the constitution to allow him to succeed himself as president, he staged a *coup d'état* on December 2, 1851—the anniversary of Napoleon I's great victory at Austerlitz. After suppressing republican uprisings, he obtained authority by plebiscite to write his own constitution. Once again a revolutionary French republic had given way to a Napoleon on horseback.

* In addition to the writings of Napoleon himself, Louis Napoleon had contributed to the making of that legend. In 1840 Louis Philippe had the Emperor's remains returned and interred (with much ado) in the Dôme des Invalides in Paris.

† See *infra*, p. 217.

# MAJOR REVOLUTIONS AND REFORMS
## 1848-1849

*Map labels:*

IRELAND — UNITED KINGDOM OF GREAT BRITAIN — K. OF SWEDEN AND NORWAY — DENMARK — K. OF THE NETHERLANDS — RUSSIAN EMPIRE — London — BELGIUM — German Confederation — 1850 — Berlin — K. OF PRUSSIA — POLAND — SAXONY — Prague — FRANCE — PALATINATE — Frankfurt-am-Main — BADEN — Paris — 1847 — SWITZERLAND — PIEDMONT — Milan — Turin — PARMA — MODENA — Custozza — Vienna AUSTRIA — Budapest — HUNGARY — TRANSYLVANIA — MOLDAVIA — WALACHIA — AUSTRIAN EMPIRE — SERBIA — TUSCANY — Florence — PAPAL STATES — K. OF SARDINIA — Rome — MONTENEGRO — OTTOMAN EMPIRE — Naples — SPAIN — KINGDOM OF THE TWO SICILIES — GREECE — *Mediterranean Sea*

Constitutional reforms
Revolutions

0    100    200    300 mi.

Map by J. Donovan

## Habsburg Paralysis:
## The Viennese Revolt

The Parisian uprising of 1848—far more provocative than the July revolution of 1830—not only produced a feared republic, but a republic which, while pledging no aggressive war, disavowed the treaties of 1815 and claimed the right to intervene to protect other revolutions against foreign suppression. But the pace of change in 1848 and 1849 was so rapid that, instead of aiding revolutions abroad, France became conservative and acted only to preserve peace and to put down the Roman Republic in 1849. As for intervention by the Concert of Powers in France, the series of uprisings that followed Paris made any such plans fatuous. Thus, many revolutions followed so quickly that only the more strategic ones can be discussed here. Probably the most significant revolt of the series was the one that toppled the Habsburg bulwark of counterrevolution in Central Europe.

## The Reactionary Elite

Institutionally the Habsburg bureaucracy had become frozen where reaction to the reforms of Joseph II and the French revolution of 1789 had left it. It was a rigid, centralized absolutism, dependent entirely upon the monarch's person for its coordination and unresponsive either to social-economic changes or to burgeoning demands for provincial or national autonomy. Francis I, until his death in 1835, rejected Metternich's proposals to reform the wooden bureaucratic machine. But even Metternich lacked a sense of urgency for domestic reform. Moreover, he (who once quipped that he had sometimes ruled Europe but never Austria) lost influence in domestic affairs under Francis' weak-minded successor, Ferdinand. The upper aristocracy—a self-contained social world oblivious to the pressures for change among its subjects—dominated the bureaucracy. It pursued policies inimical to the provincial German diets, the peasantry, and nationalist movements in the non-German provinces where a majority of the monarchy's population lived. Its repression of the interests of the middle and lower urban classes jeopardized Habsburg economic development, curtailed the monarchy's power, and united the sparse urban classes in opposition. But its failure to cope with the peasant problem was worse, since it alienated both nobles and peasantry.

## The Plight of the Peasants

Before 1848, some landlords adopted changes in agriculture that upset inherited land relationships on the manor. Demand generated by a rapidly increasing population led large landholders, usually organized in agricultural societies, to introduce new crops such as sugar beets and potatoes. They developed more productive strains of cattle, brought old and newly reclaimed lands into more intensive production, and improved transportation to markets. Their greatest needs were twofold: capital or credit, and an efficient supply of hired labor in place of inefficient forced labor. Provincial diets dominated by progressive landlords petitioned the government to establish credit institutions. They also wanted a form of peasant emancipation that would give them a ready labor supply and control over land under communal peasant direction. These landlords were willing to surrender feudal jurisdictions and some peasant obligations *gratis,* but they insisted upon emancipated peasants paying for their land and for release from labor, dues, and fees.

The peasantry constituted about four fifths of the population. Under the existing system, peasant families owed as much as 70 per cent of the product of their labor to Church, state, and landlord. They accepted the idea of emancipation gladly, but balked at paying for it. An uprising in Galicia in 1846, when peasants refused to perform services and pay dues, seemed to forecast general revolt not only in Habsburg areas but in the whole of North-central and Eastern Europe. Fearing that freed peasants would become dangerous bands of idlers and would cease paying taxes, the bureaucracy refused to consider emancipation.

## Revolution in Vienna

A crisis, sparked by economic depression, had been germinating in Vienna and Budapest for several months prior to the revolution in Paris. Then, beginning in early March, popular movements gained progressively greater concessions from the Habsburg government. First, the court dismissed Metternich, symbol of the era just past. He took refuge in Britain. Then the Emperor promised a constitutional convention, agreed to revolutionary Hungarian laws, and promised administrative autonomy to the Bohemians. Croats, Serbs, Slovaks, Czechs, Moravians, Galicians, and Rumanians, who, stirred by nationalism and liberalism, were demanding constitutional rights and local autonomy. Late in April the Emperor promulgated a centralized constitution based on the Belgian constitution of 1830. Slavs distrusted it as being pro-German, and the populace of Vienna rightly suspected that the Emperor was insincere. But further pressure forced him to fulfill his promise of a constituent assembly. Soon thereafter the court left the capital, and a popular government took the place of imperial authorities. This precipitous collapse of Austrian central

*Metternich's flight, a caricature.*

*Popular Viennese revolt against the Habsburgs.*

authority encouraged dissidents in Italy and Germany to revolt, and gave the Habsburg liberals and nationalists an illusory sense of power.

During the summer and fall, the liberal-national tide began to ebb as rapidly as it had risen. Dissipation of pent-up emotional energies, the ruinous impact of political uncertainty upon the economic crisis, and liberal fears of urban lower-class movements partly explained the debacle that began during the summer. However, three interrelated, underlying factors account better for the sudden liberal victories and their equally sudden demise:

1. Conflicting noble and peasant programs for peasant emancipation previously rejected by the government were resolved in July so that both parties assumed victory and stopped opposing the government.

2. Local national movements that had de-

fied the central government became mutually antagonistic after the revolution began.

3. A breakdown in the bureaucracy of military conservatives, who were more politically experienced than the liberals, mended during the summer and fall.

In July of 1848 the revolutionary constituent assembly, composed mainly of urban liberals, proclaimed emancipation of the peasants but postponed a decision on indemnities. The peasantry, the greatest social force behind the whole revolutionary movement, had no interest in constitutions or liberal government. Thinking that the victory was won, they withdrew support from the revolution, leaving the liberals and nationalists to fight their own battles. But the liberals' and nationalists' concept of property closely paralleled that of the nobility. A law passed in September 1848, and retained by the counterrevolution, required the peasants to pay for the release from old obligations in kind, labor, and cash. The outcome was then an unmerited double victory for the Habsburg court. First, the peasantry had withdrawn from the revolution at a critical point. Second, the provincial German aristocracy had lost its principal economic grievance against the bureaucracy. Now the two could work more closely together.

## Slavs and Magyars

In the Habsburg non-German provinces, nationalism as much as the peasants' revolt debilitated the central authorities. Hungarians had long resisted Habsburg encroachments upon the noble Diet's autonomy. In 1825 the Diet vindicated its power to levy troops and taxes. Modern liberalism and nationalism shaped its resistance after 1830, even though Hungary's political, economic, and intellectual life remained almost entirely in the hands of a medieval aristocracy.*

At first the liberal-national Magyar movement was cultural and economic; then it became political. The Magyar language was revived and, in 1844, was made the official language of the kingdom. Count Czecheny (1791–1860), a great noble, worked to imitate Western Europe's economic development and to institute gradual political reform. An agrarian-based liberalism spread rapidly among the gentry and, in 1847, carried the lower house of the Diet. The liberal majority passed on to the upper house of magnates bills to reorganize the Hungarian state and society. They provided for a con-

*Louis Kossuth in the Hungarian Diet.*

stitutional government responsible to parliament, a large list of personal freedoms, the compensated emancipation of the peasantry, and the termination of rigid entails on estates. But they were blocked in 1848 by the magnates and the court.

As revolution swept Europe, Hungarian leadership passed to the radical Louis Kossuth (1802–1894). While the Habsburgs were weakened by the revolt in Vienna, Kossuth secured royal approval of the liberal reforms. Liberalism, however, was the lesser half of the Hungarian reform program. Nationalism—the will of the ruling Magyar minority to impose its language, culture, and rule upon the entire kingdom—immediately alienated the Croatian and Rumanian majority. The Croatians helped the Habsburgs suppress Hungarian independence. The Hungarian gentry, considering itself the whole nation, failed to win the support of its own peasantry. Thus its narrow and aggressively intolerant nationalism played into the hands of the Habsburgs who, with Russian assistance, crushed Kossuth's newly proclaimed Hungarian Republic in 1849.

* The Magyar aristocracy had clung more tenaciously than any other in Europe to semifeudal privileges. Together with the clergy the aristocracy enjoyed the exclusive right to own land; the right to hold peasants and administer justice over them; exemptions from taxes, tolls, and penal laws; and participation in the Diet. The Diet was divided between the magnates and the exceedingly numerous untitled gentry. The magnates held great conglomerations of landed estates, which were universally entailed. They joined with the clergy to form the upper house of the Diet, and they laid exclusive claims to the major offices of state, Church, and army. The gentry's economic and social position varied widely. Its representatives formed the lower house of the Diet: the Table of Deputies.

*Barricade-building on a Prague bridge.*

Nationalist movements among the divided Slavic nationalities were less of a problem for the Habsburgs than for the Magyars. Slavs (particularly the Bohemians) demanded cultural and political autonomy. But because political circumstances dictated otherwise, no major Slavic group attempted to secede from the Habsburg orbit. Divided geographically by Magyars and interpenetrated by German settlements, the Slavs' main concern was to avoid being ruled as subject peoples by either German or Hungarian nationalists. Such a threat came from Vienna, from German unificationists meeting in 1848 in Frankfurt, and (for the Croatians) from the Hungarians. In response to these pressures, the Czechs and Moravians took the initiative in organizing a Pan-Slav Congress in Prague in June 1848, whose objective was a federated empire of equal nationalities. Its leading spirit, Francis Palacky, a historian who glorified Czech independence prior to Habsburg rule, firmly committed himself to the political consolidation of Central Europe. He wrote that if the Austrian Empire did not exist, "in the interest of Europe, nay of humanity, it would be necessary to make haste and create it."

While the Pan-Slavs met in Prague, riots with stronger aspirations for democracy and autonomy broke out among the city's people. The outcome was disastrous to both Czech autonomy and the Pan-Slav Congress. Prince Windischgrätz, a thoroughgoing absolutist whose wife had been an accidental victim of the riot, turned loyal troops on the revolutionary movement—the first time that an 1848 revolt was militarily resisted by Habsburg forces. The Prince, after reducing Prague and Bohemia to a military dictatorship, then prepared to move on Vienna. His action marked the first successful reconstruction of "pre-March" Habsburg authority.

## Italian Revolution and Counterrevolution

Soon thereafter another imperial general, the superannuated but able Joseph Radetzky in Italy, defied the court's orders and began a military rout of the revolutions which had swept the Italian peninsula earlier in the year.*

Austria's grip on Italy had begun to waver prior to 1848. A popular book on political prisons had kept alive resentment to the reprisals of 1831. The Lombard-Venetian population was restive under the arrogance and Germanizing tendencies of their officials appointed from Vienna. Hatred of Austria had become a religion for the angry young men lacking wealth and social position. They heeded Mazzini's call for assassination and guerrilla warfare as a means to unite and regenerate Italy and establish republican freedom. After 1840, moderate constitutional monarchists competed with Mazzini for influence. One group hoped that

* Ironically, the revolutionary government in Vienna ordered him to take the offensive against Italian revolutions.

Charles Albert of Piedmont-Sardinia would lead a crusade for unity. Another group formed around the plan of Abbé Vincenzo Gioberti of Turin, who proposed a federation under the papacy. Gioberti's scheme became popular after 1846 when a new pope, Pius IX, released political prisoners, named a lay advisory council—although without a constitution—adopted plans for gaslights and railroads, and resisted Austrian troop movements in 1847 and 1848.

As in Austria, revolutions were successful only until the army regained control. Before Metternich's fall in 1848, Sicily was in revolt, and rulers in Turin, Florence, and Naples had promised constitutions. Charles Albert of Piedmont-Sardinia, who previously had been hardly liberal, redeemed his promise with the *Statuto*—a royal grant of parliamentary government, individual rights, and a very narrow suffrage—which eventually became the constitution of united Italy. Following Metternich's dismissal, Austrian hegemony quickly collapsed. In a five-day war against Radetzky's garrison, the Milanese drove Austrian troops from their city. Before the end of March, the papacy had granted a constitution, and the Austrian dukes had been evicted from Parma, Modena, and Tuscany. Charles Albert, hoping to extend this dynasty, declared war in late March, helping to drive Austrian garrisons from most of Lombardy and Venetia. They retired to the security of their northern fortifications.

But in June and July, the tide began to turn. Radetzky reorganized his troops while the King of Naples used Swiss mercenaries to break the Neapolitan parliament. After the papacy withdrew its subjects from the north and condemned the revolution, Radetzky began to recover one Venetian town after the other. For a time, however, Venice successfully defended its republican government. On July 25 the Austrians defeated Charles Albert at Custozza. He withdrew from the war, allowing Radetzky to reconquer the Habsburg north. As disillusionment with liberal economic and political ineffectiveness spread, republican movements took over Rome and Florence early in 1849. At the behest of radical nationalists in Piedmont, Charles Albert reentered the war. But Piedmont was quickly defeated again, and by the middle of the year Florence and Rome fell to Austrian and French troops. Apart from the Piedmont Constitution, no positive vestige of the revolution survived the vengeful reaction which again reigned in Italy.

## Habsburg Recovery

Counterrevolution in Italy restored Austrian power. It coincided with the success of counterrevolution in the older Habsburg domains. The ascendant court banished the constituent assembly from Vienna to the Moravian town of Kremsier. In March 1849, the assembly completed a federal, parliamentary constitution with guarantees to individuals and minorities. The Kremsier Constitution was the empire's last chance to avoid nationalist disruption. But it remained a dead letter, for Radetzky's favorite, Prince Schwarzenberg, gained immediate control of Habsburg affairs except in rebellious Hungary. Securing the accession of Francis Joseph I (1848–1916!), who had made no promises to the liberals, Schwarzenberg quashed all concessions and grants except peasant emancipation. He proclaimed his own centralized constitution whose provisions for popular representation were never implemented. It provided for equality of subjects rather than equality of citizens. Successfully crushing the Hungarian revolt with Austro-Slav and Russian assistance, he built a new, modernized bureaucracy, which trampled asunder every local and inherited aristocratic privilege that stood in the way of centralized absolutism. Thus, under military auspices, he remedied the breakdown in the "pre-March" administration. While carrying through the above reforms, which were almost as thorough as the Napoleonic Codes, Schwarzenberg successfully contested Prus-

*Hungarian surrender to the Austrians.*

sian dominance in the German states, where revolutions had also failed.

## The Liberal-National Miscarriage in Germany, 1848 to 1850

Like Italy, Germany lacked an existing central government which liberal-national forces could take over. The Diet of the German Confederation represented Austrian influence and illiberal local German states. Liberal-nationalists were therefore obliged to operate on two competing levels: (1) changing local monarchies and oligarchies while (2) creating a central parliamentary government. The first level divided revolutionary energies and led to conflicts between local and national reformers. The second level was difficult because it would destroy the dynastic rights of the German princes and because German boundaries were ill-defined.

Following revolutions in Paris and Vienna, the populace of nearly every German capital and major city demonstrated to secure greater popular participation and rights. Where parliamentary institutions already existed (as in the Rhineland and some imperial cities), republican movements with proletarian support stirred and spread. Except for a peasant uprising in the Neckar Valley, which troops quickly suppressed, and the revolt in Berlin, almost no violence occurred. No strong conservative power checked liberal gains by force, since Austria was tied down at home, and the Prussian government, which flirted inconstantly with liberal and nationalistic policies, was itself the most significant victim of the German revolutions.

## Prussia in Revolt

Prussia's course was critical for the German liberal-national movement. The Hohenzollerns ruled one third of all Germans. The strength of their army overawed other members of the Confederation including Austria.

And their political-economic policies served as a magnet for popular nationalism, which was only remotely "liberal." A war scare of 1840 advertized Prussian military power as the principal defender of the Germans against their "hereditary foe": France. In 1848 the Prussian foreign minister planned a war to support a Polish revolution against Russia until the Prussian king and French diplomatic aloofness killed the project. Its purpose was to bring about German unification. In 1844 the *Zollverein*—a General Customs Union across northern Germany—was completed, welding together Prussian leadership and a nationalist school of economic reformers founded in 1841 by Friedrich List. List advocated protectionism and state assistance to transportation and industry to initiate economic progress. But also he repudiated individualistic Western liberalism as being materialistic and cosmopolitan, and urged Germans to use their power to civilize the "barbaric" countries of the world.

Catholic liberals from the Rhineland and more orthodox liberals everywhere objected to Prussian bureaucratic and militaristic authoritarianism, but their misgivings were eased by the pronouncements of Frederick William IV (1840–1861). In his romantic quest to restore medieval institutional purity, the Prussian King conceded some liberties to the press and in 1847 called Prussia's first General Diet. He needed it to raise loans for a railroad desired by the eastern Prussian aristocracy (Junkers) to market the grain from their estates. But he retained distinctions of medieval estates as the only natural, Christian order. When he refused to grant a constitution, the Diet refused to underwrite the loan. But the press reported the Diet's proceedings, thus opening public affairs to scrutiny. Press reports prepared the way for a revolt of Berlin's citizenry against the army's administration in March 1848.

Frederick William IV attributed the uprising to the activities of foreign agitators among "my dear Berliners." The ideas of insubordination and civil war repulsed him.

Much to the army's chagrin, he ordered its withdrawal, made repeated liberal promises, and embraced the national cause by declaring that "Prussia will henceforth be merged into Germany." Agitation by workmen and guildsmen,* however, scared the intellectuals and middle classes, who left the capital in droves.

A graver thrust to the revolution emerged from a radical conservative coalition of Junkers, army officers, and Lutheran clergy. These conservatives reckoned on peasant support for suppressing both liberal and urban lower-class agitation. While a Prussian constituent assembly and parliament sat during the summer, the conservative coalition formed a newspaper and a secret ministry which worked to undo every concession made by the official government and to win the King to their policy of military suppression. Otto von Bismarck was among them. The parliament-constituent assembly suffered from inexperience, ministerial instability, peasant passivity toward its constitutional objectives, and failure to control taxation and the army (the two traditional levers of monarchical absolutism). It passed only eight laws. In the end, the King complained that the assembly always gave way to the mob. He returned to his conservative supporters, whose theories of government were his own. Following the army's recapture of Berlin and the proclamation of martial law in December 1848, he proclaimed his own constitution.

His version, gradually amended into final form in 1850, drew from the assembly's work but retained royal initiative. It created

---

* The industrial workers' organizations were national in scope. Besides political democratization they demanded unemployment insurance, consumer cooperatives, free secular schools with free books and elected teachers, housing, income taxes, a ten-hour day, a ministry of labor, and equality for women. Guildsmen, who also began to organize nationally during the summer, wanted a return to a restricted number of guilds and guildmasters—that is, a return to their guaranteed position of the past. Neither organization agitated for the liberal demands of a free press, an armed militia, or commercial reforms.

*Frederick William IV taking oath to the Constitution, 1851.*

*The Frankfurt Assembly in session.*

an upper house of hereditary lords and an assembly elected by universal manhood suffrage. Initially its broad suffrage rallied conservative rural sentiments behind the monarchy. But the Crown retained a veto, prevented the Diet from controlling the ministry and tax collection, and established an indirect electoral college based on tax payments —that is, wealth. The ingenious electoral system was so constructed that the upper two electoral colleges (representing, respectively, 4 and 14 per cent of the electorate) were able to outvote the lower electoral delegates sent by the other 82 per cent of the voters by a vote of two to one. This "sham parliamentary system" lasted in Prussia until 1918. Other German states, the Habsburg Empire, and Russia (1905) borrowed its

features to grant the form of universal suffrage without abandoning political control to the electorate.

## Abortive Unification at Frankfurt

While the local German revolutions ran their course from early success to triumphant reaction, the first all-German parliament in history met at Frankfurt-am-Main. Its purpose was to formulate a constitution and to take direction of German affairs. Dubbed "the professors' parliament" by its detractors because it represented a plethora of scholars to the exclusion of seasoned statesmen, its membership was almost exclusively middle-class lawyers, administrators, judges, and professors. There was a slight sprinkling of landowners and still fewer businessmen. The Assembly lacked more than experience; it lacked a machinery of government and a populace obedient to it. It tried to establish a provisional executive, an army, and a navy, but the dynastic states (whose forces it commissioned for specific tasks) followed its direction at their own discretion. As a government, the Frankfurt Assembly functioned in a vacuum. After the revolutionary movement had receded, a narrow majority tried to enlist Prussian support by making the

Prussian King the constitutional monarch of Germany. But Frederick William refused to accept "a crown of filth and mud"—that is, one based on popular sovereignty. Mortally wounded by this rejection, the Assembly disbanded after an existence of eleven months. A republican remnant, which transferred its seat to Stuttgart, was eventually dissolved by force.

Despite its impotence, the Frankfurt Assembly had significance as a source of constitutional innovations. Parts of its still-born federal constitution were adopted by the North German Confederation of 1867 and by the Weimar Republic of 1919.

The Assembly was more immediately pertinent as a mirror of attitudes within the German liberal-national movement as practical problems arose. Constitutional deliberations were interrupted by circumstances requiring a definition of the German nation-state's frontiers. In June 1848, the Danish sovereign tried to recover the rebellious duchies of Schleswig-Holstein and to incorporate Schleswig into Denmark. Its population was mixed—German and Danish. At that point the Assembly commissioned Prussia to drive the Danes out, unsuccessfully asserting German sovereignty over the duchies. In a more difficult boundary situation between the Germans and the Poles, the Assembly overwhelmingly voted to approve Prussian rule over wholly Polish districts and rule by German minorities in mixed areas. In both the Polish and Danish episodes, nationalism, as the will to dominate or civilize other nationalities, overrode the professed goal of national self-determination of peoples whose practical implementation in East-Central Europe was an ethnographer's nightmare. Even more difficult for the deputies at Frankfurt was the question of the inclusion or exclusion of the Austrian Germans. The Greater German (*grossdeutsch*) radicals would have disrupted the Habsburg Empire by annexing it with its Czech subjects. The Smaller German (*kleindeutsch*)

party favored the exclusion of Austria altogether. For the time being the question was settled by the failure of both the German and Austrian revolutions, but the basic issue remained.

In later eras, the *kleindeutsch* approach dominated Bismarck's unification of Germany around Prussia in 1871, while the *grossdeutsch* solution triumphed with Hitler's annexation of Austria to Germany in 1938 and the incorporation of the *Sudetenland* in 1939.

Factions also formed in the Assembly around constitutional and social issues, but the great majority adhered to constitutional monarchism, considered property inviolate, and rejected the philosophy of natural rights in favor of historically acquired individual rights. Nevertheless, the Frankfurt Constitution would have abolished nobility, patrimonial courts, and entail. Neither the constitutional monarchists nor the republicans favored working-class programs. The Assembly rejected a government-guaranteed right to work and called upon Prussian and Austrian troops to put down a national organization of trade unionists at whose headquarters in Frankfurt disorders designed to influence the Assembly broke out. Still the republicans were alienated on other issues by the constitutional monarchists. By vain new revolutions in Baden, the Palatinate, and Saxony in 1849, they sought to preserve the life of the Assembly against reaction. But they were forcibly dispersed.*

## Failure of German Unification

As Frankfurt's attempted unification of Germany collapsed, princes took the initiative in appealing to nationalist sentiment. In May 1849, Hanover, Saxony, and a number

---

* Following suppression of these revolts, many of their surviving leaders emigrated. In the United States, "Forty-Eighters," such as Carl Schurz, subsequently played leading roles in American liberal politics.

*Execution of a revolutionary in Germany.*

of smaller states signed a Prussian agreement for political union. The larger southern states turned to Austria. Her victory over Hungary had put Schwarzenberg's government in a position to challenge the Prussian union with a reformed Confederation Diet. During a revolt in Hesse-Kassel in 1850, a showdown between Austria and Prussia occurred as battle-ready troops of the Diet and Prussia—both claiming counterrevolutionary jurisdiction—confronted each other. But Russia, trying to maintain the balance of power which a united Germany would overturn, threw its weight behind Austria. At Olmütz, in the same year, Prussia backed down and gave up her union—the "humiliation at Olmütz." The outcome was a standoff between Austria and Prussia. Plans to reform the Austrian-dominated Diet were also scrapped. Thus, Germany remained as before, a loose confederation of thirty-eight states. As a result of these failures in 1848, nationalists

became disillusioned with pacific parliamentary procedures. In the next decade most of them became "realists," ready to follow Bismarck in unifying Germany by "blood and iron."

At both the national and local dynastic levels, the German revolutions of 1848 and 1849 utterly failed to transfer political initiative from kings and their ministers to parliamentary assemblies dominated by the middle classes. No dynasty was unseated. Whatever constitutional changes that followed were granted by sovereigns. They usually allowed the nobility and upper classes a strong voice, although more in an advisory capacity than as directors of affairs. At the same time, programs of workingmen received no recognition whatsoever.

As in Habsburg territories, the peasantry, not the urban populations, gained in legal status. In a few western German states, legal emancipation was far advanced in 1848. In others, it had hardly begun. The revolutions of 1848 forced the aristocracy out of its intermediary role between the peasants and the state. Subject to long-term redemption fees from the peasantry, old feudal-manorial obligations were canceled. At the same time steps were initiated to break up the communal village which had made most peasant agriculture a common undertaking for centuries. The impact of reform was more than to increase the material well-being of the peasants (especially the cottagers and small holders); it was to throw the countryside open to capitalist agriculture which provided foodstuffs for expanding urban populations. Legal emancipation also made the peasantry mobile and more easily drawn into urban industry in subsequent decades. Ultimately, urban industrialization, more than legal freedom, decreased the pressure of population in the countryside which had contributed heavily to the crisis of 1848. In specific instances, reaction after revolution narrowed peasant gains, but nowhere could it thwart the basic change.

## The Lesser Revolutions and Evolutionary Changes, 1848 and 1849

Revolution visited several other European areas in 1848 and 1849 with little success. Poles in the Duchy of Posen became prepared for a Prussian-backed war of unification, which failed to materialize when Prussia changed her policy. Rumanians in Transylvania revolted unsuccessfully against the Magyars. Other Rumanians in Walachia and Moldavia, led by intellectuals returning from Western Europe, also revolted, but were crushed by Turkish and Russian troops.* A revolt in Greece scored no gains. An enfeebled revolution in famine-ridden Ireland was no more successful.

The most successful smaller revolution occurred in Switzerland. In 1847, liberals and Protestants won a twenty-five day war against a conservative league of Catholic cantons before France and Austria could intervene. The victors gave Switzerland economic unity and a federal constitution modeled largely on the Constitution of the United States.

Revolution was a general mood in these years, but in some areas liberal changes were made without an open outbreak of force. Belgium successfully checked riots and radical movements by doubling the electorate to include most of the middle classes. Public works and poor relief sufficed to prevent revolts by workingmen. In 1848, King William II of the Netherlands permitted his wealthier citizens to elect a parliament that could initiate laws and choose the ministry. In 1849 the King of Denmark conceded a national assembly with an elected lower house, but initiative did not clearly pass to popularly elected representatives for the remainder of the century. Unrest under enlightened despotism in Sweden also led to minor popular

*London slums, a source of upper-class fears (by Gustave Doré).*

concessions between 1844 and 1859, but a modern parliamentary system was not established there until 1866. Thus the states that acquired successful democratic governments in the twentieth century were evolving in that direction in 1848. Significantly they escaped the military reactions that plagued liberalism in the revolutionary states.

During the crisis years of 1848 to 1850 the two major peripheral states—Britain and Russia—had neither revolution nor progressive political evolution. Although the middle classes were badly scared by the Chartists, Britain escaped revolution.† In part, she escaped because a functioning parliamentary system made economic concessions to check discontent among the lower and middle classes. Moreover, centuries earlier she had passed through the agrarian crises that rocked Central Europe in the middle of the nineteenth century. Perhaps as important, popu-

---

* Russian troops stayed on in these principalities, becoming one of the causes of the Crimean War (1854–1856).

† For the Chartist Movement see *infra,* Chapter VIII.

lation pressures found release in both Britain (although not in Ireland) and Russia. British industrialization plays a significant role here. Also, British people were going to the colonies in great numbers. Meanwhile the Russian frontier expanded rapidly into Central Asia. Finally, for a variety of reasons, the upper classes, who wielded political power in both countries, remained united and conservative.

## THE STRUGGLE FOR SOCIAL AND POLITICAL POWER: A SUMMING UP

After the French Revolution, the contest between liberalism and nationalism, on the one hand, and traditionalism, on the other hand, became a struggle of the educated middle classes against kings, nobles, and clerics entrenched in power. By mid-century the middle classes were holding or sharing power in Britain, Belgium, the Netherlands, Switzerland, Piedmont-Sardinia, and the Scandinavian kingdoms. Their hold on the political institutions of France slipped temporarily with the rise of Louis Napoleon. And their bid for liberal institutions in Central Europe failed. Although Western liberals sympathized with these ill-fated revolts, their governments failed to intervene. In fact, Britain even sanctioned Russian intervention in Hungary, which was decisive in breaking the Hungarian Republic. Europe continued to be divided between a liberal West, whose orbit was expanding, and a conservative, monarchical East and South.

In theory, Western liberalism held a concept of collective status—the self-determination of nationalities—which it would substitute for the dynastic state. Where national cultural boundaries and the dynastic state approximately coincided, self-determination could be achieved by the evolutionary or revolutionary transformation of existing governments. In Germany and Italy, national unity required the expulsion of Habsburg power and the elimination of existing petty states. Within the Habsburg Empire, self-determination meant either federation of equal, autonomous nationalities (the Pan-Slav approach) or the total disruption of the Empire into separate states (the radical Hungarian position). In this environment, collectivist romantic nationalists gained the upper hand.

During and following the revolutions of 1848, tough-minded nationalists jettisoned all pretense of universal humanitarianism. Reaping a harvest of disillusionment from parliamentary failures of 1848, they became willing allies of radical conservatives and "national liberals," who subordinated the goals of individual liberty and responsible government to the cause of unification by "blood and iron"—power politics abroad, and forced uniformity at home. The liberal catastrophe of 1848 marked the end of an era in which publicists envisaged nationalism as a stepping-stone to international cooperation. Free, unrestrained nationhood had become the highest good.

The year 1848 also became a landmark in social conflict. Politically conscious artisans and workingmen entered the struggle for status and power. The "June Days" in Paris indicated their willingness to use force. With few exceptions, their political and social programs aimed more at "social welfare" than at "socialism" or "communism." Nevertheless, they inspired fear, condemnation, and forcible repression by an alliance of bourgeoisie, peasants, and traditionally privileged classes. The bourgeoisie, frightened by what the obscure Karl Marx called in 1847 "the specter of communism," compromised with conservatives, clerics, and nationalists to preserve the existing distribution of property and its benefits. At mid-century the urban labor movement was a small minority of the population, slow to achieve political self-consciousness. Potentially, however, when industrialization on a par with Britain and Belgium became general, it would constitute the largest segment of society. Urban industrialization meant the transformation of the mobile peasant into an urban wage earner. In 1850, conservatives could count upon the peasants' support, but would this support survive the transition to an industrial society?

## SELECTED READINGS

*Artz, Frederick B., *Reaction and Revolution, 1814–1832,* Harper & Brothers, New York, 1934, and a Harper Torchbook.
A general account in the *Rise of Modern Europe* series, revised in detail by more recent research.

Babbitt, Irving, *Rousseau and Romanticism,* Houghton Mifflin Co., Boston and New York, 1919.
Assaults root and branch the premises and methodology of the romantic thought attributed to Rousseau and his successors.

Barzun, Jacques, *Classic, Romantic and Modern,* Secker and Warburg, London, 1962.
A romantic who believes that twentieth-century critics have vilified his tradition rehabilitates romanticism, narrowly defined.

Blum, Jerome, *Noble Landowners and Agriculture in Austria, 1815–1848: A Study in the Origins of the Peasant Emancipation of 1848,* Johns Hopkins University Press, Baltimore, 1948.
Sets forth the agricultural changes which caused peasant grievances and moved many secular landowners toward a form of emancipation.

Brinton, Crane, *Political Ideas of the English Romanticists,* Oxford University Press, London, 1926.
Demonstrates parallels between German romanticism and the English romantic poets.

*Bruun, Geoffrey, *Revolution and Reaction 1848–1852, A Mid-Century Watershed,* D. Van Nostrand Co., Princeton, N.J., 1958.
A short introduction to the impact and sequel of Europe's most general revolution of the nineteenth century.

Bury, J. P. T., ed., *The Zenith of European Power, 1830–1870,* X, *The New Cambridge Modern History,* Cambridge University Press, 1950.
An exhaustive work useful for reference.

*Butler, Eliza M., *The Tyranny of Greece over Germany,* University Press, Cambridge, 1935, and a Beacon paperback.
Portrays the rigid idealized classicism which dominated German aesthetics and against which an exaggerated romanticism was in revolt.

Englebrecht, H. C., *Johann Gottlieb Fichte, A Study of His Political Writings with Special Reference to His Nationalism,* Columbia University Press, New York; P. S. King and Son, London, 1933.
A monograph which sketches Fichte's drastic change from romantic individualism to collectivist nationalism in response to the French invasion of Germany.

Ergang, R. R., *Herder and the Foundations of German Nationalism,* Columbia University Press, New York, 1931.
A basic work on the fundamental formulator of modern nationalism.

Evans, David Owen, *Social Romanticism in France 1830–1848,* Clarendon Press, Oxford, 1951.
Traces origins of republican socialism in France, especially in literary circles.

Halévy, Elie, *A History of the English People in the Nineteenth Century,* E. Benn, London, 1949–1952, 6 vols. (2nd rev. ed.).
A celebrated study by a perceptive French scholar.

Hayes, Carleton J. H., *The Historical Evolution of Modern Nationalism,* R. R. Smith, New York, 1931.
A study which identifies and describes several different kinds of nationalism.

Herring, Hubert C., *A History of Latin America from the Beginnings to the Present,* Alfred A. Knopf, New York, 1962 (2nd rev. ed.).
A standard textbook excellent for the revolutionary period.

Hovell, Mark, *The Chartist Movement,* Longmans, Green and Co., New York and London, 1918.
Presents an account purely factual and descriptive.

* Asterisk (*) denotes paperback.

Kissinger, Hans A., *A World Restored, Metternich, Castlereagh and the Problems of Peace 1812–1822,* Houghton Mifflin, Boston: The Riverside Press, Cambridge, 1957.

> Both a general theoretical and historical account which finds much to admire in the balance of power established at Vienna.

Marcuse, Herbert, *Reason and Revolution, Hegel and the Rise of Social Theory,* The Humanities Press, New York, 1954 (2nd ed.).

> An attempt to absolve Hegel of fascist implications, interpreting him as a rational critic of the *status quo.*

*May, Arthur, *The Age of Metternich 1814–1848,* Henry Holt, New York, 1933.

> A good short summary in the Berkshire Studies in European History designed for beginning students.

*Namier, Lewis B., *1848: The Revolutions of the Intellectuals,* Doubleday & Co., Garden City, N.Y., 1964.

> Finds evidence that nationalism was overcoming liberalism in Germany.

*Robertson, Priscilla, *Revolutions of 1848: A Social History,* Princeton University Press, Princeton, 1952, and a Harper Torchbook.

> A general study which finds social class lines often more significant than economic and political categories.

*Ruggiero, Guido de, *The History of European Liberalism,* translated by R. G. Collingwood, Beacon Press, Boston, 1959.

> A detailed historical analysis.

*Schapiro, J. Salwyn, *Liberalism: Its Meaning and History,* D. van Nostrand Co., Princeton, N.J., 1958 (an Anvil Book).

> Excellent for differentiating different strains of bourgeois, democratic, and social liberalism.

Schenk, Hans G., *The Aftermath of the Napoleonic Wars, the Concert of Europe—an Experiment,* Kegan Paul, Trench, Trubner and Co., London; Oxford University Press, New York, 1947.

> Deals with postwar difficulties, including economic problems, briefly and well.

Schroeder, Paul W., *Metternich's Diplomacy at its Zenith, 1820–1823,* University of Texas Press, Austin, 1962.

> Uses archival evidence to demonstrate the exploitative nature of Austrian dominance in Italy, thus refuting apologies such as the one which follows.

*Viereck, Peter, *Conservatism Revisited,* Collier Books, New York, 1962 (revised and enlarged ed.).

> A vindication of Metternich whose argument turns upon an undefined and misleading usage of the word "constitution."

Walzel, Oskar, *German Romanticism,* translated by A. L. Lussky, G. P. Putnam's Sons, New York and London, 1932.

> A comprehensive survey covering political views as well as literature.

# VI

# *The Industrialization of Society*

In the preceding chapter we observed the revolts of liberal nationalists against autocratic kings, nobles, and privileged clergymen. The liberals sought to overturn the old social order by removing the legal underpinnings of caste and inherited-status groups. In the place of these underpinnings, the liberals would introduce social mobility and economic relationships based on contract. By this revolution's embodiment of liberalism's economic "laws of nature" in positive legislation, the liberals hoped to stimulate the economy and provide for the amelioration of social problems. But legislation alone was not sufficient to produce economic growth. In the complex interaction of factors that produced it, the climate of governmental policies was but one of many. The product as much as the instigator of economic expansion, liberalism required a broad middle-class social base. When that base was absent —as in the preindustrial economies we have studied—liberal revolt aborted.

Within Europe's conditions, industrialization was necessary for liberalism but did not guarantee it. That the nineteenth century was the century of liberalism par excellence

was due in large measure to the unprecedented economic growth of the Western world. Applied technology gave Western man unheard-of control over the forces of nature and over the remainder of the world. In many parts of the West these changes transformed the very substance of society— its way and place of life, its social stratification, its distribution of power—and necessitated the recasting of its institutions.

England first made the transition from the agrarian, semicommercialized Old Regime to a society dominated by industrial capitalists. With the possible exception of Belgium, only England could properly be called an industrialized nation by 1850, and her industrialization was far from complete. Using steam-powered factories to produce for both foreign and domestic consumers, England literally became—for a limited time —the "workshop of the world." Investments and the export of capital goods followed the paths opened abroad by commerce. Industry, trade, and investment returns supported a dense, rapidly growing population that enjoyed unprecedented security from famine and disease. England pioneered an historic breakthrough in economic growth that Belgium, France, the United States, Germany, Russia, and Japan, among others, would follow during the remainder of the century. These industrial societies achieved standards of living and longevity surpassing those of half of the world's population even today and to which nearly every modern government is committed as a goal.

French observers, comparing England's rapid pace of change with their own revolution of the eighteenth century, coined a phrase that took permanent root in popular usage by the end of the nineteenth century: "the industrial revolution." Noting that food production also expanded rapidly, other observers added the concept of an accompanying "agricultural revolution." Because trade increased more than at any past time, some historians would also apply the term "the commercial revolution" to the industrial epoch. But sober economic historians distrust these "revolutions" as oversimplifications of the complicated process of economic growth. Changes occurred in medicine, population, and public attitudes as well as in industry, agriculture, and commerce. Instead of being iconoclasts, inventors stood on the shoulders of previous generations that had worked toward the solution of generally recognized problems. Requiring capital and organization, their innovations were only gradually adopted. Moreover, the steam-powered factory represented a threshold more than a completed "revolution." With industrialization came organized efforts to develop new technology—the "invention of invention."* Economists are inclined to view "the industrial revolution" as a phase of rapid economic growth made possible by a favorable interaction of people, resources, technology, institutions, and international trade patterns at given times and places. Our appreciation for this complex interaction of factors may be sharpened by studying not

* Today we may gain insight into the continuing impact of this process by debating the effect of "automation" or "modern warfare."

only cases of successful industrialization but also those "underdeveloped areas" whose population growth has outstripped the accumulation of capital and the use of inanimate energy for power—frequently with disastrous political and economic results.

Industrialization has taken place under such divergent ideologies as *laissez faire* and Communism. But regardless of the ideology, certain economic and social elements have always been present in and imperative to the process. The people who industrialize must enjoy enough internal security to permit economic and social innovation. They must accumulate and dispense enough capital to support investment in mechanized means of production and distribution. If this capital is raised domestically, the population must produce more than it consumes. Heavily capitalized machine industry requires markets compatible with technological efficiency, and these markets depend upon domestic or foreign purchasing power. An industrial technology demands inventiveness and depends upon a labor force that is skilled or capable of being trained. The population must be induced to undergo the social dislocations of a mobile labor force and, often, a shift of social, economic, and political power. By the second half of the eighteenth century England met most of these requirements for industrialization.

Geography provided some of these requirements naturally. As an island, Britain was relatively immune from foreign invasion. Deposits of coal and iron were plentiful and close together, and coal—called "sea coal" —was accessible at the water's edge where it could be cheaply transported. Other mineral ores and alum for cloth production were also available. Good ports and central location favored trade with the Continent, the Far East, and the colonial world. A moist, temperate climate favored cotton manufacture—although at the same time it was unsuited to the production of raw cotton.

Old institutions and policies that had adjusted to commerce also provided a relatively favorable environment. English society already had what the French Revolution achieved up to 1791. No tariff barriers separated the counties. Royal justice and the common law courts maintained legal unity and frequently handed down decisions hostile to privilege and responsive to the desires of entrepreneurs. Although Englishmen remained acutely conscious of social rank, they could move from class to class with increasing ease. Production codes, which at first stifled industrial innovations, were enforced less and less strictly during the seventeenth century. The revolutions of that century left the commercial classes with extensive influence in the British government.

English institutions gave considerable latitude to the acquisition of knowledge and the advocacy of novel ideas. Scientists in the Royal Society and from the Scottish University of Glasgow made critical contributions to mechanical invention and industrial chemical processes. Religious dissenters, some of whom had immigrated bringing new industries with them, secured toleration but did not secure places of honor and preferment. Many of the dissenters became prominent in humanitarian reform movements demanding, among other things, a system of production that would better the standard of living for the lower classes. They also called attention to public health and succeeded in turning into public scandals those conditions previously accepted as inevitable. Humanitarianism was related to major economic changes, but its impact—in contrast to that of commercial expansion, agricultural improvements, and industrial inventions—is difficult to assess.

## COMMERCIAL CAPITALISM AS A PRELUDE TO INDUSTRIALIZATION

Since the late Middle Ages new centers of commerce in Europe had been supplanting countries that formerly led in trade. The states along the Atlantic seaboard were the chief beneficiaries of an all-sea route to the Indies, exploitation of the New World, and Europe's carrying trade. The Dutch Republic replaced the Iberian kingdoms and became the trade emporium and financial clearing house of the seventeenth century. But the Dutch were supplanted by France and Britain in the eighteenth century. From a duel with France over commerce and colonies, Britain emerged as the unchallenged mistress of the seas, arbiter of the world's most lucrative trade, and principal center of finance. She thus secured, through war and diplomacy, markets barred formerly by mercantilist regulations.*

### Accumulation and Use of Commercial Capital

By the end of the eighteenth century Britain, the Dutch Republic, and—to a lesser degree—France and a few German cities possessed large accumulations of capital. Successful merchants, investors, and "adventurers" multiplied their assets from shipping, ground rents, the slave trade, and colonial plantations. They also profited from foreign sales and inflation as prices outdistanced wages. They refined and expanded the fund of inherited techniques and institutions for mobilizing capital: stock markets; stock companies for mines, utilities, and colonization; insurance companies; mortgage credit; banks handling state loans, issuing bank notes, and discounting commercial paper. Occasionally these devices resulted in disastrous speculative booms and busts such as the "South Sea Bubble" in England and the "Mississippi Bubble" in France (1720–1721). But capital continued to accumulate, and England and the Dutch Republic prospered from low, stable interest rates which their good credit assured.

* Whatever their stimulus to the economy, the same wars harmed economic growth by destroying capital, raising interest rates, drawing investment money into state loans, dislocating industrial production, causing financial panics, and drawing potential consumption into postwar taxes.

Commercial capital, however, was not necessarily invested in industry. Although "country banking" expanded and the Bank of England gained a stabilizing influence over bank-note issues during the second half of the eighteenth century, English financial institutions were inadequate to meet the demands of agriculture and large-scale industry. English and Dutch bankers did make loans to industrial entrepreneurs, but the bulk of the capital invested in industry during the early stages of mechanization seems to have been raised by individual proprietors and partners. They struggled competitively for survival and those with viable, adequately financed businesses won out.

Nevertheless, industrial production was enlarged and rationalized to meet the demands of large and distant markets. Repeatedly since the Middle Ages merchant capitalists serving large markets had undermined the craft guilds and their industrial production codes. They were the principal organizers of the "domestic" or "entrepreneurial" system of production.* In some areas and trades "merchant manufacturers" extended their control over all phases of production and established large shops where goods were finished under their direction. In this way the manufacturers anticipated the modern factory system of controlling production and directly supervising labor. The entrepreneurial system divided labor into specialized operations and made labor dependent upon wages that varied in accordance with market conditions and the laborers' bargaining power. But this system did not lead inexorably to the modern factory system of production or rapid technological change. Similar developments had taken place in Renaissance Italy and in the Dutch Republic of the seventeenth century. Rather than becoming industrial entrepreneurs, the oligarchic financiers of these areas preferred to invest in further commerce, land, and governmental loans. In England, commercial

capitalists first invested significantly in industrial production during the Napoleonic wars.

Capital investments in transportation also supported industry. Better ships, equipped with chronometers for determining longitude, facilitated overseas trade. Their crews could remain hardy thanks to a method of controlling scurvy discovered in England. Better transportation also served home markets that were economically more significant than colonial trade. Britain, served by coastal shipping and natural waterways, still lagged behind France and the Dutch Republic in building internal transportation systems at the beginning of the eighteenth century. But thereafter, she supplemented river improvements with large-scale canal building and the rapid extension of a network of turnpike roads, some of which were macadamized or hard surfaced. Because of these advances, coal as a fuel could be more easily substituted for wood; grain could be shipped to famine areas; and agriculture entered a market economy.

## Commercialization of Agriculture and Land Redistribution

Centers of grain production, livestock husbandry, and dairying grew up around every major trading city. In northern Italy, England, the Low Countries, Switzerland, and parts of France and Germany, these centers remained free of serfdom and forced labor. But peasant tillage was subsistence agriculture carried out under custom and communal village direction. Where town life ebbed, as in Eastern Europe after the fifteenth century, the peasants were enserfed. Even when the peasants produced for export, their lords relied on intensified discipline rather than economic inducements or improved technology to create a profit.

In both Eastern and Western Europe grain was produced under the three-field system of the Middle Ages. Arable land was distributed in unfenced strips. In planting, sowing, harvesting, and pasturage, every farmer had

* See Volume I, Chapter XIV.

to coordinate his work with every other producer. The technology of this system limited the number of people that the soil could support. Leaving only postharvest stubble and the natural grasses in common meadows, wastes, and forests for cattle, it drastically curbed man's supply of meat, milk, and beasts of burden. A scanty supply of cattle meant a shortage of manure to replenish the soil, a third or more of which had always to lie fallow. And unfertilized soil, even when rested every third crop, became depleted and eventually exhausted. Communal control offered little opportunity for experimentation; it did not even sanction the isolation of herds for selective breeding or quarantine from cattle plagues. As manorial lords increased their control over the land, the peasants lost their initiative to make improvements. Thus traditional agriculture was caught in a closed cycle of diminishing returns. So long as this situation prevailed, famine was endemic.

The "agricultural revolution" broke this cycle. New crops from the New World played a significant role in increasing productivity as their adoption spread. Maize or Indian corn increased cereal production as much as tenfold. Even in poor soils the "Irish" potato had a similar capability of augmenting food supplies. But the heart of this "revolution" was the reorganization of traditional agriculture to use the land more intensively and to maintain or build its fertility. New techniques for this purpose were introduced in Italy and the Low Countries during the sixteenth and seventeenth centuries. England imported and improved upon them in the eighteenth and nineteenth centuries. Since they hinged upon new crop cycles and the enclosure of lands, they required the reorganization of rural institutions and the system of land tenure.

This reorganization of agriculture introduced seed grasses and root crops such as clovers, lucern, alfalfa, and turnips into the crop rotation cycles. The legumes among these served the dual purpose of increasing

*Charles "Turnip" Townshend.*

animal nutrition (and thereby manure) and of rebuilding the chemical composition of the soil. By the judicious rotation of crops—such as turnips to barley to grasses to wheat popularized in England by Lord Townshend—no land lay fallow. By including hayfields in the rotation cycle, the farmers could dispense with their permanent common meadow. They could reclaim many wastes with proper (and expensive) drainage, fertilization, and cultivation. "Turnip" Townshend was not the only experimental producer to support "the agricultural revolution." Robert Bakewell publicized selective breeding of livestock to improve gaunt and bony cattle with results indicated by Table I.

*TABLE I   Average Weight (Pounds) of Cattle Sold at Smithfield*[1]

|        | 1710 | 1795 |
|--------|------|------|
| Oxen   | 370  | 800  |
| Calves | 50   | 150  |
| Sheep  | 38   | 80   |

1. Adapted from J. H. Plumb, *England in the Eighteenth Century,* Penguin Books, Baltimore, Md., 1965, p. 82.

*Robert Bakewell, pioneer of selective breeding.*

In 1731 Jethro Tull published a work urging adoption of horse-drawn "hoes" and drills—the drills to replace inefficient broadcast sowing. These gentlemen farmers created a popular movement for agricultural change. King George III identified himself with their cause, and in 1793 Arthur Young, an unsuccessful farmer but a brilliant publicist and observer, was named secretary of a new Board of Agriculture. Young advocated new techniques and the redistribution of landholding by enclosures, which he described as "sensibly dividing the country among opulent men." Stimulated by the enclosure system and promising to meet the demands of a growing population, commercial agriculture became prosperous. As on the Continent before the revolution of 1848, commercially minded landlords led the campaign against the inherited system of cultivation and tenure.

Enclosure—the consolidation of arable strips and common lands and their redistribution as compact parcels of private, fenced lands—spread progressively in eighteenth-century England. Enclosures were initiated by large holders either by voluntary agreement or in compliance with private acts of Parliament. Parliamentary enclosure acts reached their apogee between 1791 and 1801, the same years in which machine industry was being introduced. By 1851 the process of consolidation and redistribution was nearly complete.

Enclosures had profound but controversial effects. Older historical accounts consider enclosures responsible for destroying small holders and the leasing yeoman class and driving them to industrial cities to work as propertyless laborers. Recent studies of land-tax statistics suggest, however, that in most areas the number of landholders on newly enclosed lands actually increased. But after wartime demands ceased in 1814, only large estates and small, family-worked plots increased in number. Holders of middle-sized farms, backed by insufficient capital, could not sustain themselves. Enclosures brought hardship for unknown numbers of cottagers and small tenants who had no legal title to their plots and pasturage on the commons. Losing access to land they became dependent solely on wages and charity. Critics charged that enclosures were depopulating the countryside and increasing poverty. Advocates such as Arthur Young defended them as indisputably more productive and correctly asserted that the rural population was actually increasing. Although the critics were wrong about depopulation, both sides had their points. Greater productivity sustained a rapidly expanding population even during wars with France. Some of the employed urban workingmen probably enjoyed the new luxury of butcher's meat in winter. At the same time, enclosures unquestionably put economic pressure on the rural poor. After 1795 their inadequate wages were subsidized by relief under the Poor Law (the "Speenhamland system").* Comparison of English enclosures with contemporary agra-

* See *supra*, page 191, note.

rian reform in Denmark suggests that greater productivity could have been obtained with fewer hardships. On the other hand, the example of Ireland demonstrated that a choice worse than enclosures might have been made. Ireland supported exceedingly rapid population growth by intensive potato culture on subdivided plots, but during the 1840s bad weather and potato blight caused famine and massive starvation.

New techniques in agriculture and mechanized innovations in industry were parallel phenomena. It has usually been assumed that enclosures drove people from the country to take urban jobs. But demographic research indicates that industrial labor forces were recruited chiefly from natural population increases in the cities themselves. Large-scale migration from country to city apparently awaited the coming of the railroads and agricultural mechanization. It would be hastened, too, in the second half of the nineteenth century by intensive foreign competition and the agricultural depression following from it. Providing an increasing population with a constant supply of food, "the agricultural revolution" relieved the country of serious famines and stabilized the economy as a whole. In the past, general economic crises were often rooted in food shortages. Harvest failures brought rising food prices, which naturally took a larger portion of the spendable income. Of course, this meant less income was available for industrial goods. By remedying this depression cycle, "the agricultural revolution" undoubtedly assisted industrialization, but new sources of instability in industrial society soon became apparent.

## Population Growth, Subsistence, and Industrialization

Before 1750 famine and disease in Western Europe had checked population growth and held average life expectancy down to thirty years or less. But in the following century these barriers to demographic expansion crumbled, and rates of population growth

and longevity shot upward. Because statistics are sparse and faulty, there is little hope of unraveling the precise relationship between this development and industrialization. But one thing is certain. This demographic "takeoff" is every bit as phenomenal as the increase wrought in industrial productivity by steam-powered factories.

Preindustrial conditions have been obscured by romantic and religious glorifications of the past as well as by a lack of reliable statistics. We know that famines, epidemics, endemic disease, and malnutrition constantly drained the population. Epidemics respected no social rank, but other ravages took their heaviest toll among the poor. Many ills that were later attributed peculiarly to industrialization were commonplace long before 1750: long hours at low pay, occupational diseases, unemployment, dearth during financial panics, and hard labor for women and children. With certain logic, mercantilists had recommended employment of children since it enabled them to survive in impoverished households. Crime and drunkenness were rampant. Except for the Dutch Republic, no country on the Continent had a standard of living as high as England's. Yet late seventeenth-century observers asserted that over one half of the English people was dependent upon charity, relief, or thievery to bridge the gap between income and subsistence costs. One early statistician estimated that half of all incomes went to less than one fifth of the population, while the lower three fifths of the families received one sixth of the national income. Poor Laws gave a measure of social security, but local parishes were adept at avoiding responsibilities by shunting off dependents and children upon their neighbors' charge.

Accumulated capital may have provided the means to alleviate these conditions in certain preindustrial cities, but most of these commercial centers suffered health hazards similar to those in army encampments. Deaths usually exceeded births. Predominantly urban civilization was impossible until

*Industrial slums, an exaggerated view.*

cities became more wholesome places in which to live. City dwellers awaited achievements in sanitation and medicine and a more constant and varied diet provided by improved transportation and agriculture to curb their death rates and establish a net, natural increase in their population.

Cleanliness was the principal development of urban sanitation. As magistrates in England and on the Continent began to heed the advocates of cleanliness, they copied London's vermin-resistant brick and paved streets. Although usually pumping from polluted sources, they enlarged their water supplies.* People began to wash with soap, killing lice, and they replaced woolen clothing—often worn until it rotted—with cheap, washable cottons. Urban leaders had sewer drains installed. They prohibited garbage dumping in the streets and hired street cleaners. Water-closet privies were introduced. Still, water supplies polluted by sewage left the cities vulnerable to cholera and typhoid fever.

Because growth was rapid and unplanned, these advances in hygiene could not combat all the ills of overcrowded industrial centers. Congestion, poverty, crime, ill health, and heavy mortality continued to characterize lower-class districts. A report of 1840 stated

---

* Cleanliness was the main objective since water was little used as a beverage.

that one fifth of the workers in Liverpool and a somewhat smaller proportion in Manchester lived in cellars. Gruesome accounts of the 1830s and the 1840s list three to five persons per bed in Manchester cellars and an utter lack of elementary sanitation in the city's "Little Ireland." Death rates actually increased in some English cities in these decades. Heretofore, these conditions were accepted as providential because the wherewithal to remedy them was unimaginable. Now they were a scandal that provoked the hesitant intervention of the central government.

By twentieth-century standards medicine during England's early industrialization was primitive. It was occasionally harmful and sometimes subject to legitimate satire as quackery; nevertheless, doctors made significant breakthroughs. They identified and largely eliminated nutritional deficiencies as the cause of scurvy and rickets. Probably more than anything else their practice of quarantine checked epidemics of plague by preventing reinfection from abroad. They had malarial swamps drained, checked typhus by fumigation and other means, and controlled smallpox by isolation, inoculation and, after 1805, vaccination. A physician's report of 1813 indicates the significance of controlling just smallpox:

. . . I found that not more than half of the human species died before they were ten years of age and that of this half more than a third part died of Small Pox so that nearly one fifth of all that were born alive perished by this dreadful malady.[2]

Doctors and patrons of charity (frequently the same persons active in other humanitarian causes) established hospitals, dispensaries, and foundling homes—institutions

---

2. Quoted by M. C. Buer, *Health, Wealth and Population in the Early Days of the Industrial Revolution* (George Routledge and Sons, London, 1926), p. 182. It may be added that many who survived smallpox were blinded or otherwise incapacitated.

that rarely received public assistance. Efforts to improve midwifery, a traditional craft which the English government did not regulate until the twentieth century, helped reduce infant mortality, but infant deaths—though fewer than in previous centuries—dropped gradually rather than sharply.

Birth and death rates were both high by present standards, but reductions in mortality rates for specific age groups, especially between the years of one and twenty, enlarged the total population, altered the distribution of age groups, and increased the proportion of Europeans within the world's population. An observer in 1770 estimated that one half of the children in Western Europe died before reaching the age of ten. By 1825 the proportion was probably less than one third; by 1910 two thirds of the population survived their twentieth year. Greater survival of children increased the proportion of young people in the total population during the years of industrialization. During the "Hungry Forties" an extraordinary wave of young adults entered the labor market and contributed to strains upon living standards.* Departing sharply from past trends, England's population increased from an estimated 7.5 million in 1751, to 16.5 million in 1831, to 21 million in 1851, and to more than 37 million in 1901.

Population growth was not peculiar to England. It occurred in all of Europe, in some areas at an even faster rate. But only the industrialized areas utilizing high per capita amounts of energy maintained their security against famine, holding or increasing their standards of living. As Ireland, Eastern Europe, and contemporary parts of the "underdeveloped world" demonstrate, industry cannot be considered a general cause of population growth nor population growth a necessary cause of industrialization. But the introduction of machine industry into England and parts of Western Europe un-

*London's Foundling Hospital.*

doubtedly saved these countries from declining to an "Asian" standard of living during the nineteenth century.

As industrialization occurred or was anticipated, public servants and commentators became acutely conscious of relationships between population size, economic development, and standards of living. For the first time governments took comprehensive censuses of people, manufactures, resources, and commerce, and used this information in making administrative decisions. They supplemented general censuses with special inquiries into conditions of health, poverty, housing, unemployment, and various other facets of economic and social life. England completed her first survey in 1801,† three years after the first appearance of Thomas Malthus' *Essay on Population.* This work injected population and subsistence issues into household conversations.‡ Malthus attacked the optimism of both the *philosophes* and the romantics, for the *philosophes* advocated birth control within marriage and the romantics insisted upon nature's automatic provision for human fecundity. Traditionalists continued to attrib-

* It was also undoubtedly involved in causing the wave of revolutions of 1848.

† Before England, Sweden and the United States instituted regular census taking, and local French *intendants* had carried out local tabulations within their generalities.

‡ Malthus' doctrines and their contributions to the ideologies of the nineteenth century are discussed further in the following chapter.

ute human tragedies of epidemics and early death to the plan of Providence, whereas utilitarian liberals and various categories of humanitarian reformers sought to raise living standards, limit births, or do both. Nineteenth-century Frenchmen chose to limit births. By the end of the nineteenth century the English did the same, since their birth rates eventually adjusted to the ebb and flow of business cycles.

## MACHINES, FACTORIES, AND THE "ENERGY REVOLUTION"

New agriculture and public health were essential to the transition from agrarian to urban industrial society. At the core of this transition was the general adoption of mechanical energy as a source of motive power. Energy-converting machines required entrepreneurs to put up heavy capital. With so much invested they closely supervised the entire production process in their factories. Neither machines nor factories were totally new, but industries adopting coal-fueled steam engines had a more flexible and reliable source of energy than those using older sources of energy. The steam engine made a decisive divide in Western economic history —between "low-energy society" dependent for power upon man, beast, wind, and flowing water and "high-energy society" that gave its population the equivalent of many slaves per capita. High-energy consumption presupposes heavy industry—mining, smelting, metal fabrication, and machine tools of clock-like accuracy. For both heavy industry and the steam engine, iron and coal provided the basic components. Hence, the location of suitable coal and iron deposits and the routes for moving them set the configuration of much early industrial society. The availability of coal and iron deposits continued to be primary until oil partially replaced coal as a source of power and ways were devised to transmit coal-derived electrical energy cheaply.

## Technological Developments in Textiles

Except in a few instances prior to the later eighteenth century, England imitated rather than initiated new technology. But for a time thereafter her chemists, clockworkers, carpenters, locksmiths, iron masters, farmers and others took the lead in inventiveness. Innovations were particularly significant in the cotton textile industry where a long series of inventions culminated in the replacement of spinning wheels and manual looms with power-driven machines.

During the seventeenth century the domestic textile industry generally adopted a pedal-operated knitting machine that was too expensive for individual domestic workers to own. At the same time, silk makers in Italy were beginning to use water-driven spinning and reeling machines. The French and English later duplicated these machines surreptitiously. Silk fibers were relatively easy to handle by machine, but silk was a costly luxury product. Machines did not yet exist that could handle cheaper wool and linen fibers. When Europeans began to import calicos and muslins from India, they saw for the first time a relatively plentiful fiber that was pliable enough for mass machine production: cotton. In England the mechanization of cotton textiles had the additional advantage of being outside the industrial production codes of the established crafts.

The inventions that mechanized English cotton mills were called forth by production problems which many persons had sought to solve. In 1733 John Kay, a clockmaker, patented a "flying shuttle" for throwing the woof across the warp in broadloom weaving, thus eliminating one of the two loom operators. It was not generally used until 1760, but as it spread and as the market demand increased, both wool and cotton yarn became scarce. Experiments to produce mechanical spinners were already underway. Between 1745 and 1760 four separate patents—some incorporating principles that were ultimately practicable—were issued. The cotton yarn shortage was relieved by James Hargreaves' "jenny" of 1767 that spun eight threads at a time by hand. With the addition of mechanical power the capacity of the jenny could be increased many times. Two years later Richard Arkwright (1732–1792), an ambitious barber who secured control over a locksmith's invention and became a large-scale manufacturer of thread, patented a "water frame." This device spun, stretched, and twisted yarn rovings into thread by running them through a series of rollers. Hargreaves' jenny produced fine, weak thread. Arkwright's patent, operated by water or steam power, spun coarse, heavy yarn. In 1770 Samuel Crompton combined features of the two into a "mule" which produced a thread both fine and strong enough to compete successfully with Indian imports. As this machine was adopted in England and Scotland, cotton production soared. The amount of raw cotton imported in this period can be used as an index to this increased production. In 1751 raw cotton imports were less than 3 million pounds. In 1784 they were nearly 11.5 million and by 1800 the figure exceeded 50 million.

Demand for cotton cloth proved highly elastic and was filled as it expanded. Soon the entire process of fabrication—although not the production of raw cotton—was mechanized. Arkwright and others patented machines for preparing cotton fibers for spinning. Chemists produced dyes and bleaches that were plentiful and quickly applied. But no one developed a satisfactory power loom until 1830. At this point the basic features of modern textile machinery were completed in principle, but further refinements between 1840 and 1880 doubled the output per man-hour. By 1830 raw cotton imports rose to over 260 million pounds, and by 1841 to nearly 490 million. For raw cotton, English and Scottish mills depended upon the Near East, India, South America, and the United States. After 1793,

*Hargreave's spinning jenny.*

when Eli Whitney invented the cotton gin to separate seeds from fibers, the American South, relying on slave labor and "soil-mining" agriculture, became the principal supplier of raw cotton. Ironically Great Britain, which had abolished slavery in its Empire in 1833, helped rivet that same institution upon the United States.

By 1860 difficulties in mechanizing the wool industry had been overcome. At the same time, sewing machines—invented in the United States—had further speeded and refined the production of clothing. The power-driven factory system now extended to all manufacturing except that of raw materials and the final operations of clothes-making.

## Spread of the Factory System

The modern factory system—the assembly of workers in centralized locations to carry out specialized operations under the constant supervision of the entrepreneur or his agent —had both economic and technical origins. Factories could and did exist quite apart from power-driven machinery. They had prototypes, with the specialized division of labor, in arsenals, shipyards, mines, ore and metal processing establishments, paper and glass plants, breweries, and finishing sheds for wool and linen cloth. But the factory system did not spread among the textile and other mechanized industries until water- or steam-driven machinery was adopted. Hence,

*Workmen destroying their mechanized competition.*

the early textile mills were concentrated along the rivers in northern and western England and southern Scotland where commercial outlets, coal fields, and proper degrees of humidity were also present.

Factories that were established to make use of mechanized power were no less institutions for the supervision and discipline of labor than their predecessors were. Bells or whistles announced the beginning and end of the work sessions, and machines set the pace of operatives' work. Manufacturers were frequently called "captains of industry" and their organizations were compared to disciplined armies. For labor the most drastic change in the transition from domestic to factory production was the close supervision and regularization of work habits enforced by contract. Owners of highly capitalized interdependent factory operations would not tolerate irregularity or independence in their workers. A doctor disillusioned with the "debilitating consequences of uninterrupted toil" in Manchester described this regularity as follows:

While the engine runs, the people must work —men, women and children are yoked together with iron and steam . . . chained fast to the iron machine, which knows no suffering and no weariness.[3]

By resisting this discipline, the workers retarded the spread of factories. Textile manufacturers recruited labor from the countryside, from Ireland, and particularly from women and children who were least prone to organized resistance.

Factory production completed the destruction of traditional craft organizations which the domestic system had already eroded, and Parliament added the force of law to their dissolution. Craft skills were seldom directly transferable to the factory. Some craftsmen became inventors or practical engineers, but most of them resisted factory employment. Employers considered their independent spirit insufficiently docile for machine work. Because machine industry spread slowly, never more than a small minority of craftsmen was put in competition with machinery at the same time. It was precisely these shifting minorities who suffered the greatest loss of status and security. Their distress sometimes erupted into machine-breaking riots. At the end of the eighteenth century, they petitioned Parliament to enforce old Elizabethan statutes, but Parliament refused. In 1814 it abolished the laws supporting the guild structure. Parliament also had enacted laws preventing combinations of journeymen in various trades against their masters. In 1799 and 1800 it laid a comprehensive ban on collective action by journeymen and factory laborers. Further acts removed surviving wage- and price-fixing authority from local magistrates, and in 1834 a new Poor Law sharply curtailed charity to able-bodied workers. Thus did British laws sanction the discipline of the factory system.

Once it was perfected, mechanized industry served well where the demand for uniform products rose with lower prices. But machines were adopted so slowly as to render

3. Quoted from Dr. James Kay by J. T. Ward, *The Factory Movement 1830–1855,* St. Martin's Press, New York, 1962, p. 65.

*Mule spinning in an English textile mill.*

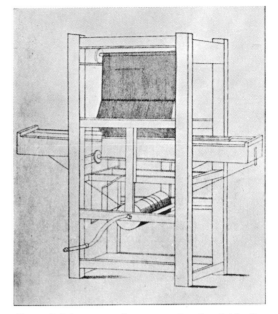

*Cartwright's power loom—a sketch of his first patent.*

inaccurate the phrase "industrial *revolution.*" Even in cotton textiles, factory organization did not spread at a steady, uniform pace. Between the invention of Crompton's spinning "mule" and the general adoption of power looms after 1840, domestic weaving expanded to an unprecedented extent. Throngs of unskilled men entered the weaving trade before the power loom was introduced. Then their wages and work opportunities fell precipitously. In 1831 the "typical Englishman" was still a countryman and the "typical worker" a handicraftsman; only one in eighty was employed in a textile mill. Even in textiles, domestic production continued to coexist with machines, and handicraftsmen prevailed in the metal trades until after the middle of the century. Although the momentum of the factory system spurred the entire economy, as late as 1851 nonmechanized workers outnumbered machine hands three to one and there were twice as many domestic servants as cotton workers.

## Coal and Iron

Without supplies of coal and iron no country could industrialize. Coal not only served as the fuel for steam engines but was essential to the smelting of iron—the basic construction material of the new age. To substitute coal and iron for wood was to replace an increasingly scarce and costly resource with less scarce and cheaper but highly capitalized raw materials. Until coal in the form of coke was adapted to the smelting of iron ore and the processing of bar iron, iron production in England, France, Sweden, and other areas was curbed by dwindling supplies of charcoal. England's early industrial preeminence was due as much to her exceptionally abundant supply of coal and easily smelted iron ore as to her innovations in textile manufacturing.

Iron and coal, hitherto little related to one another, became the keys to the new economic era. Charcoal blast furnaces had been used in Western Europe since the Renaissance, but their operations were more an erratic art than a controlled technical science. After a century of abortive experiments to use coal for smelting, three generations of Darbys—an English Quaker family of ironmasters—finally developed a coke-burning furnace that produced a fairly uniform cast iron. About 1756 the second Abraham Darby used enlarged furnaces, unusually strong bellows, and coke that his father had developed to produce purer cast iron with hotter temperatures. To become malleable

*Boring to locate coal.*

iron or steel, cast iron had to be refined further, but when it was mixed with coke in the same furnace unwanted carbon appeared —a phenomenon chemists would later be able to explain.

Many men experimented with refining processes. Compressed air pumps that raised temperatures and quadrupled furnace productivity were invented and adopted in Scotland. In 1783 or 1784 Henry Cort patented an improved combination of refining techniques that included stirring or "puddling" the molten ore to allow impurities to escape. The simplest product from Cort's rolling mill—itself a new device that replaced hammers for shaping the iron and extruding its impurities—was iron plating that found ready use in boilers, tanks, pipes, and eventually rails. Steel needed for cutting edges and springs remained a costly luxury until the second half of the nineteenth century, but Britain's iron production of 68,000 tons in 1788 had nearly doubled by 1796. While the Continent still relied almost exclusively on charcoal, Britain used mostly coke. By 1806 her annual iron production had risen to 250,000 tons. Thereafter it soared to 750,000 tons in 1830, 3 million tons in 1855, and over 6 million tons in 1870. Except for fine Swedish iron and steel Britain's imports of foreign iron ceased, and her cheaper, plentiful iron products dominated markets wherever inexpensive transportation facilities existed. Although the metal trades were mechanized only slowly,

the heavy metal industries undergirded machine industry itself. Iron parts or whole iron machines replaced wood, leather, and other durable materials in textile and other factories.

Iron production and steam power made coal the basis of nineteenth-century industrialization. Coal deposits were most advantageous when coking-grade coal lay near the surface in the immediate vicinity of low phosphorus iron ore. The unusual proximity of such coal and iron in many places gave Britain an initial advantage over other countries and encouraged the decentralization of her metal industries. While coal production increased tremendously during the nineteenth century, coal and iron mining were only slightly mechanized. Heavy industry in mining was literally heavy labor, and deeper diggings increased hazards. Although the Scots abolished serfdom in their collieries at the end of the eighteenth century, exceedingly onerous labor conditions continued longer in the mines than in the factories. Yet the demand for iron, if it had depended upon charcoal without coal, would have denuded the forests and precipitated an industrial crisis.

## The Harnessing of Steam

Waterwheels were made more efficient during the eighteenth century, but no basic new power source was discovered between the wind and the water mills of the Middle Ages and the steam engine. The development of the steam engine was closely interrelated with the mining and production of coal and iron. Primitive steam engines were first used to force water out of deep coal mines. Air pumps in large rolling mills and new blast furnaces required steam's greater power for their operation. Furthermore, the steam engine was a heavy consumer of both iron and coal.

Generations of technical and scientific progress preceded James Watt's patent of 1769. Scientists had noted the expansive power of steam and the partial vacuum created by its condensation. In 1698 an Englishman patented a steam pump using both the expanding and condensing properties of steam to expel water from mines. It was replaced in 1705 by a "fire engine" patented by the locksmith and blacksmith Thomas Newcomen. For power, Newcomen's pump relied entirely on atmospheric pressure on a piston in a cylinder below which steam was condensed. It wasted fuel and was incapable of producing regular rotary motion, but its largest model generated nearly 75 horsepower. In the development of the steam engine, science influenced technology more than any other invention (with the possible exception of chemical dyes and bleaches). It is romantic fantasy to attribute Watt's ideas to his watching his mother's teapot as a boy. As the son of an architect and shipbuilder, Watt grew up in a scientific environment, became a builder of apparatus for experiments in astronomy and physics at the University of Glasgow, studied chemistry and latent heat under the eminent chemist, Joseph Black, and kept abreast of scientific developments on the Continent. Setting out consciously to improve the university's Newcomen engine, Watt developed ideas for a separate condensing chamber to save heat. He also determined how the expansive power of steam could be used on both sides of the piston, and how regular rotary power could be transferred to machines.

His initial patent was for a concept, not for a completed engine. The building of an actual engine led to further refinements and required heavy financial support. Watt was first financed by John Roebuck, but Matthew Boulton, another entrepreneur, took over when the failure of Roebuck's other businesses forced him to withdraw. Boulton obtained the major share of Watt's patent rights which Parliament extended from 1775 to 1800. Watt's exclusive rights barred the field to men more technologically advanced than he was, and until 1800 all steam-engine designs were marketed by him and Boulton. Technical problems such as the production of

*Newcomen's atmospheric steam-engine pump.*

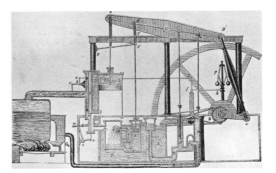

*Watt's double-acting steam engine.*

minutely engineered cylinders, pistons, and automatic valves were more influential than patent rights in retarding early widespread adoption of the engine, however.

## Machine Tools and Engineering

Machine industry destroyed the economic viability of old trades—at least until the tourist trade gave them a flickering revival—but it created new fields for individual talents. Of these, none was more critical than the development of iron, later steel, machine tools engineered to minute tolerance requirements. The lack of these machine tools held Watt back in building and distributing an efficient steam engine. For industry in general the invention of new lathes, borers, and screw-threading machines was a *sine qua non* for the transition from wood to iron. But these tools were not suddenly born out of a void. Although they were not generally known until the nineteenth century, Leonardo da Vinci had made sketches of screw machines and other devices whose principles were later utilized by the iron industry. Seventeenth-century Nuremberg developed stamping machines. Clock- and watchmakers used a variety of instruments to shape springs and moving parts. Stamped, interchangeable, metal parts were used in eighteenth-century Sweden and France.

The key person in England's industrial machine-tool production was James Wilkinson. About 1776 he developed a process for boring cannon applicable also to steam-engine cylinders. He was the first to use the steam engine to operate a forge hammer. He also used improvements in the lathe developed by another innovator, Henry Maudsley. Maudsley developed a slide rest for holding cutting tools that allowed the production of smooth valve facings and true cylinders and pistons. Thus essential operations of making steam-engine parts were mechanized, and Wilkinson became the principal builder of Watt's engines. He experimented with an iron boat and in 1788 sold forty miles of iron pipe to the city of Paris for its water supply—pipe that for the first time prevented seepage between sewers and water lines. Like other successful entrepreneurs, Wilkinson built an autocratic empire whose resources exceeded those of petty states on the Continent. When he died in 1805 he was buried at his own request in an *iron* coffin.

The inventors and designers of industrial tools formed a new engineering profession. Their increasingly versatile and complex creations propelled industrialization along a path of continuing technological advance. Drop forges, die stamps, and pattern turning were used to make interchangeable parts in clock- and watchmaking, rifle manufacture, and (particularly in the United States) the production of sewing machines and reapers. Hydraulic machinery for lifting of all kinds appeared before the middle of the nineteenth century. During the same period, Sir Henry Bessemer, future discoverer of basic steel-making processes, was able to order from several suppliers components of a machine to make gold ink out of bronze shavings without the suppliers having knowledge of his profitable trade secret. Eventually, the machine-tool or capital-goods industry became a critical nerve center of technology whose expansion and contraction economists use to predict economic trends.

## Transportation and Communications

In marketing, production, and finance, industrialization did not reach its maturity until the advent of railroads, the steamship, and instantaneous local and intercontinental communications. Transportation was not mechanized in England until late in the history of her industrialization because a long series of technological inventions had to appear first. Nations industrializing later, however, could transform their transportation systems first. Until the decade of the 1840s Englishmen relied primarily on coastal shipping, canals, roads, and horses. After 1810 horses were used to draw wheeled carts on tramways that had long been used in mining. Despite Watt's diffidence, inventors in both France and England tried to mount early steam engines on wheeled locomotives. Richard Trevithick, who designed a steam engine superior to Watt's but who died penniless, experimented with a steam locomotive in England. It was made practical by a colliery worker, George Stephenson, whose *Rocket* locomotive demonstrated its superiority over stationary pulling engines in 1829. Stephenson was concerned more with a level roadbed than with the engine. His concept opened the railway era in 1830 when a line was laid between Manchester—the leading industrial city—and Liverpool, England's main entrepôt for trade in cotton, iron, and coal products. The first trains were only capable of the (then) sensational and frightening speed of twenty miles per hour, but they progressively reduced the cost of transporting heavy bulk fuel, raw materials, and products over terrain not accessible to the still cheaper waterways.

*Stephenson's* Rocket *locomotive, 1829.*

Railways proved to be profitable investments. During the 1840's Britain's railway construction expanded rapidly. To finance them local stock exchanges mushroomed in provincial towns and cities, mobilizing an excessive amount of capital. Railway construction followed a cyclical pattern of rapid expansion, financial crisis, then further consolidation and expansion. In 1838 Britain had 500 miles of track. By 1843 that figure had been multiplied nearly four times. Almost 5000 miles of rail ran over the island by 1848, and 16,700 miles by 1886. Britain supplied the initial rolling stock, capital, and the rails to start railroads in other parts of the world, whose tracks totalled 4000 miles in 1840. In 1880 the figure had jumped to 200,000. Now, replacing sailing ships and the horse—imperfect instruments of imperialism—with a combination of railroads and iron or steel steamships, Europeans could more thoroughly dominate the world.

Domestically railroads accelerated economic and social changes initiated earlier by roads and canals. Reaching markets previously inaccessible, they enlarged demands and thereby spurred the drive toward mechanized industrial production. Although water transport remained cheaper, it was less flexible, and towns that were dependent solely upon rivers or canals withered or ceased to grow. The construction of railroads resulted in expansion in the coal and iron industries. But it meant contraction in

the business of canal, stagecoach, and freight-wagon companies and in the local trades. Many companies passed to railroad management. Railways broke up local monopolies and for the first time tied provincial economies together. Rapid bulk transport made relief to areas of famine easier and made industrial centers less dependent upon local agriculture. As freight rates fell, imported foodstuffs competed successfully with domestic produce, and England became more and more dependent upon distant continents to sustain her urban population. Within a few years, railroad links between town and country changed rural life more drastically than many successful political revolutions. Because the railroads were private corporations with monopoly powers, their operations also drew the countryside into political controversies over their control.

As the railway displaced stagecoaches, canal boats, and freight wagons on land, the steamboat later pushed other transportation aside at sea. Invented by a Scot—not an American—the steamboat antedated the railroad. Early sidewheelers were more suited for internal waterways than for ocean travel, since fuel supplies needed for long voyages were too large to carry. Commercial sailing ships actually enjoyed their greatest vogue after the invention of both the railroad and the steamboat, but British marine engineering developments during the 1840s and 1850s ultimately sealed their doom. Screw

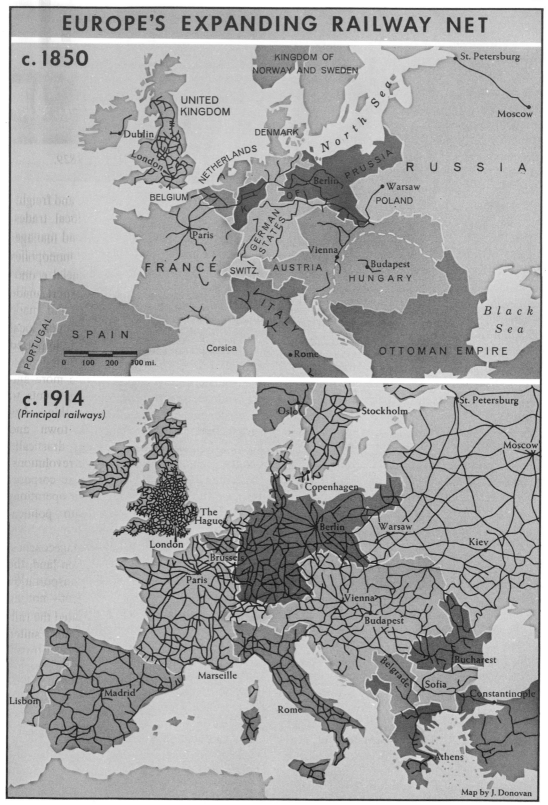

# EUROPE'S EXPANDING RAILWAY NET

**c. 1850**

KINGDOM OF
NORWAY AND SWEDEN

St. Petersburg

UNITED
KINGDOM

North Sea

Moscow

Dublin

DENMARK

London

NETHERLANDS

PRUSSIA

RUSSIA

BELGIUM

Berlin

Warsaw

OF

POLAND

Paris

GERMAN STATES

Vienna

FRANCE

Budapest

SWITZ.

AUSTRIA

HUNGARY

ITALY

Black Sea

PORTUGAL

SPAIN

Corsica

Rome

OTTOMAN EMPIRE

0 100 200 300 mi.

**c. 1914**
*(Principal railways)*

Oslo

Stockholm

St. Petersburg

Moscow

Copenhagen

The Hague

Berlin

Warsaw

London

Kiev

Brussels

Paris

Vienna

Budapest

Bucharest

Belgrade

Marseille

Sofia

Madrid

Constantinople

Lisbon

Rome

Athens

Map by J. Donovan

*Opening of the Suez Canal.*

*Coiling the Atlantic cable aboard the cable-layer, "Agamemnon."*

propellers, better marine engines, and iron hulls—soon replaced by lighter steel ones—gave British liners and merchantmen the lion's share of the world's commerce. But the displacement was slow. The world's total sailing tonnage did not begin to decline until about 1880.

Using mechanized transport, nineteenth-century commerce increased at a rate and scale beside which all previous "commercial revolutions" appear minute—though not insignificant. Advances in communication—which reduced the size of the world even more than trains and steamships—attended the new "commercial revolution." Some of these advances followed from improved machinery and transportation. At the end of the Napoleonic wars, *The London Times* introduced a steam-powered cylindrical printing press that ran 1000 impressions per hour. By 1827 this rate had quadrupled. Railroads and ships carried posts and newspapers, and the Cunard Line of steamships founded in 1840 depended upon subsidized mail contracts as did some railroads. Scientific technology produced a more revolutionary innovation in communications—the electric telegraph. Based upon the discoveries of Michael Faraday and others, the telegraph was first demonstrated in the United States in 1844. Financiers, merchants, governments, and especially railroads pressed for the installation of telegraph lines. In 1851 England was linked to the Continent by

cable. Twenty years later cities on the major continents were connected. Telegraphic contact served to create a world market of capital and commodities, but it also expedited the dispatch of fleets and troops. Technologically and economically the world was becoming a single unit, but political attitudes by no means reflected this wholeness.

## THE ORGANIZATION OF INDUSTRIAL SOCIETY

By 1850 the British began to realize that industrialization had effected drastic changes within their country. Not just their technology, but their basic institutions, their culture, and their very ways of life were taking new form. Less and less could social and economic power be inherited by birth or obtained through the church. More and more did this power belong to those who controlled the means of production, distribution, finance, and communications. But the resilient aristocracy was not entirely displaced, for it adjusted to economic change by investing in mines, factories, urban rents, railroads, and other new forms of wealth. Many nineteenth-century observers claimed that industrialization was dividing society into two antagonistic new classes: capitalists and laborers dependent entirely upon wages. Labor had organized to oppose the expanding power of the capitalists, and their organizations had gained legal recognition. But the British census of 1861 revealed that the notion of two antagonistic classes was oversimplified. Both industrial classes were diverse in composition. Moreover merchants, miners, and especially professionals in law, medicine, teaching, and recreation were increasing more rapidly than other segments of the population. At the same time a declining proportion of the people was absorbed into factory labor.

## Entrepreneurs and Financial Organization

Industrialization was an economic as well as a technological process. To fully exploit machinery and natural resources, capitalists had to invest more heavily than before in plants, mines, and transportation. They then had to reinvest a still higher proportion of profits in capital goods, if the ventures they supported were to become self-sustaining. No new enterprise could survive without long-term credit for capital goods and short-term credit for operations, wages, raw materials, and warehousing. In addition to the entrepreneurs an enlarged, specialized, and increasingly powerful financial community grew up as co-organizers of industrial society.

In England individual proprietorships, entrepreneurial families, and partnerships prevailed as forms of business organization. During the first half of the nineteenth century, corporations required individual grants from Parliament. These grants were limited mainly to transport, insurance, and colonizing enterprises. Large concentrations of economic power resulted as some businesses outstripped and absorbed weaker competitors. But England had only a few monopolistic manufacturing combinations during the nineteenth century. A wide distribution of resources and the government's free-trade policies tended to secure the vitality of competitive, noncorporate concerns.

The characteristics of early entrepreneurs have been the subject of interminable controversies. Nineteenth-century portraits of them ran the gamut of description from

*Machine tools in operation: Stephenson's Locomotive Factory.*

greedy oppressors to honest men of thrift, frugality, and adaptability, whose tragic flaw was that they could not control the market forces upon which their lives depended. Many recent economic historians have focused attention upon the role of the entrepreneurs as creative organizers whose success or failure depended heavily upon their personal attributes or skills. A disproportionate number, though still a minority, were religious dissenters—Quakers, Methodists, and Unitarians. T. S. Ashton, an eminent English economic historian, emphasizes this point as he stresses their integrity, their willingness to run great risks, and their relatively high level of education. Scottish industrialists, who excelled in scientific technology, were particularly well educated. As a total group, entrepreneurs were diverse. Some, especially the Quakers, combined intense competitiveness with equally intense humanitarianism. But while their humanitarianism deserves emphasis, for many "average employers" it may well have stopped short of the factory gate. The entrepreneurs claimed absolute control over production and distribution as the prerogative of ownership. Only mavericks among them welcomed state intervention on behalf of health, safety, and welfare. On the other hand, the entrepreneurs were struggling against unbridled competition, within an imperfect financial framework, subject to the dislocations of war and to adverse fiscal policies of their government. The industrialists who survived accumulated profits and powers greatly exceeding those of earlier capitalists. They were strong enough to keep their principal gains for themselves. They shared these gains with holders of mineral lands and recipients of urban rents and land value appreciation. But as credit facilities expanded and a larger portion of the population became sellers rather than producers, a larger share of total incomes flowed to the financial and commercial sectors of the economy.

At first entrepreneurs and merchants were plagued by a lack of credit and an inelastic money supply consisting largely of coin. They encouraged the founding of country banks that issued bank notes, dealt in mortgages and bonds, and transferred credit where it was most needed. The Bank of England and the major mercantile financial houses catered primarily to the state debt, trading companies, and international exchange. After 1826 the Bank of England established provincial branches and gradually secured a regulatory power over interest rates. In 1844 it was empowered to become the sole issuer of bank notes. But much investment capital flowed through stock exchanges and insurance companies that were relatively independent of the Bank. When joint-stock banks were permitted to form after 1833, consolidation increased more rapidly in banking than among business establishments.

Industrialization expanded the range of adjustments made through the price mechanism of the market, but it failed to eliminate the trade cycles that affected entrepreneurs, merchants, and labor. To remain profitable, heavily capitalized production normally required continuous operation, but sharp commercial crises in 1772, 1792, 1814–1816, 1825, 1839, and 1847 suspended operations sufficiently to remove marginal operators. The causes of these fluctuations are still controversial. England's worst crisis in the nineteenth century occurred after the Napoleonic wars. The crisis can be attributed in part to the aftermath of these wars, in part to Parliament's deflationary taxation and monetary policies. But "boom and bust" cycles recurred in industrial society, and governments were eventually moved to attempt their correction. Although entrepreneurs were affected by these cycles, most efforts to curtail depressions came not from businessmen but from labor organizations, traditional conservatives, and middle-class persons who were sympathetic to lower-class plights or fearful of the political side effects of depressions.

## Labor and Workingmen's Organizations

To generalize about living standards in England prior to 1850 is difficult for several reasons. It is indisputable that manufactured goods sold for lower prices. But the standard of living for wage earners was set by the purchasing power they retained after paying for food and rent. "Labor" was a diversely rewarded class that included pauper children forced to labor, women, agricultural day workers, craftsmen competing with machinery, craftsmen in nonmechanized trades, domestics, and higher-paid builders of new machines. A considerable portion of England's increasing production and consumption went necessarily to support a population that doubled between 1801 and 1851. During the same period excise taxes on items of common consumption placed the main burden of taxation on the most numerous classes. Moreover, wages fluctuated during recurrent periods of unemployment and for the chronically unemployed. Few historians doubt that the *average* standard of living was increasing even during the trying years between 1820 and 1850, but its distribution to the lowest classes is questionable. Poverty has continued in industrialized societies. Only a few "welfare states" of the twentieth century—Sweden is a notable example—have eliminated slums and poverty, and their success has been accompanied in each case

*Carting coal from the mines, 1842.*

by the general adoption of birth control and the avoidance of war.

Whether working conditions worsened during industrialization or whether humanitarian sentiments had made old practices less tolerable is another moot question. Industrialization did bring stringent discipline, new dangers from deeper mines and from power-driven machines, more extensive overcrowding, and the systematization of child labor outside the home. But the conditions of industrial labor were probably no worse than the former environments and, in some respects, were better. At least the factory, mill, or enlarged mine was a unit more open to public exposure and was brought under public regulation more easily than individual homes. Investigations, whether prompted by political, religious, economic, moral, or humanitarian motives, continued to reveal unsavory situations, especially concerning the employment of women and children. They provoked state intervention. Qualified medical observers like Dr. Gaskell noted pallid complexions and spindly frames among miners and industrial workers whose quarters lacked elementary sanitation. Despite efforts towards reform, however, child labor probably expanded. As late as 1841 60 per cent of the employees in cotton mills—where child labor had been regulated—were minors. No action had been taken to curb it in mines and other industries. Hours were long—up to fourteen or more a day—and parents or parish authorities started children to work at ages now considered appropriate for early schooling.

Exposés by commissions and officials may have exaggerated the evils of industrial life. But through them evangelical Tories and Utilitarian reformers could arouse the public conscience and secure laws regulating the hours and working conditions—but not the wages—of women and children. Parliament's Health and Morals of Apprentices Act of 1802 incidentally limited the workday for pauper children to twelve daytime hours, required some education, separated sexes in quarters, and ordered ventilation and white-washing of cotton mills. Another act of 1819 followed further investigations. Applicable only to cotton mills, it banned employment under nine years of age and limited the workweek for youth between nine and eighteen. In 1831 Michael Sadler headed another investigation that resulted in the Factory Act of 1833. It set a milestone along the path to modern factory codes because it provided four paid inspectors to share enforcement powers with local magistrates. High death rates, heavy welfare costs, and cholera epidemics brought further probing of mines and factories in the 1840s. In 1842 an inspector was established for above-the-ground mining operations, and women were banned from the pits. In 1844 women were brought under previous cotton mill laws limiting their day to twelve hours and their week to sixty-nine hours. The same provisions applied to youth between 13 and 18 years of age. The act also introduced the first safety regulations in cotton mills and stripped Justices of the Peace, who had obstructed enforcement of previous acts, of their jurisdiction. In 1847 the workday for women and children was reduced to ten hours, but until the 1860s the scope of these acts was limited to cotton mills and mines. Nevertheless the basis for the systematic factory code of 1901 was being built.

Apart from special laws applicable to dangerous trades, adult males were left to their own devices. To oppose the unprecedented power held by owners and managers, the more independent workingmen took to collective bargaining. Such combinations were illegal until 1824 and 1825, and after 1825 English courts still did not recognize unions as legal personalities. The upper ranks of workingmen formed friendy societies for mutual benefits. Some publicists such as Robert Owen sought to inspire a national labor organization with the goal of substituting cooperative societies for private capitalism. But Owen's union failed to win strikes or deter governmental repression. His early labor movement was engulfed by the wider discontent of Chartism during the 1830s and 1840s, and Chartist agitation to democratize the state also failed.* After the Chartist movement collapsed, highly paid craftsmen led by the engineers succeeded in organizing unions that had sufficient discipline and funds to survive strikes and depressions. But their legal position was insecure until the 1870s. The lower ranks of labor did not organize successfully until prosperity declined in the 1880s. Then they furnished recruiting grounds for socialist unions who sought political redress and a reorganization of the power structure of English industrial society.

* Chartist activities are discussed in Chapter VIII.

## The Impact of Urbanization

If the full complexity of industrial society was obscure to contemporaries, at least one trend was unmistakable—urbanization. Industry, mechanized transport, and increased agricultural productivity had reversed the balance between country and city. Congested cities came to hold the majority of the population. Their skylines displayed brick factory walls, drab apartments, and multiple smokestacks. Until bicycles, electric streetcars, and eventually motor cars partially decentralized cities, workers lived within walking distance of their employment. Up to 1875 England's city authorities lacked legal power to proceed against congestion. City planning was discussed but seldom implemented. Apart from the tavern there were few provisions for recreation. The cultural facilities that existed were usually provided by private philanthropy. A few industrialists like Robert Owen erected model villages, but they were rarely imitated.

As the pioneer of industry, England was also first to face these problems of city life. Before mid-century no other major country exceeded England's proportion of city dwellers in 1801. In 1851 her inhabitants were roughly half urban, half rural. By comparison her degree of urbanization in 1881 was not reached by Germany until 1910 or by the United States until 1960.

Industrial cities brought together a diverse population with labor the most numerous class. Urbanization told heavily against traditionalism and passive acceptance of previous conditions. Customs of dress, diet, and entertainment changed. Children had fewer functions and chores than in a rural environment. After laws and compulsory education curtailed child labor, children became an economic liability rather than an asset. Urban life was more this-worldly and anonymous. Conservatives like the Earl of Shaftesbury feared that *laissez faire* would lead to the degeneration of morals. Ties of kinship—especially the patriarchal family structure—lost their hold, and the rural-oriented, tithe-supported church alienated the working districts. Wealthier citizens lived apart, but the industrial city brought together in close proximity greater differentials of wealth and poverty than before. The towns were dominated by a new aristocracy of wealth, but the lower classes tended to lose their old sense of subordination to their "betters." The traditional social order based on birth, status, and wealth was being eroded further and replaced by a new hierarchy in which wealth predominated.

Urbanization was part of a process that produced sharp political struggles between town and country and between different urban classes. New towns—and hence the centers of population—were located in the industrial Midlands, in the North, and in the West. Landed classes unresponsive to urban problems retained political power during this population shift. Justices of the Peace, for example, obstructed execution of social legislation. Slowly and belatedly local vested interests were overridden by officials of the central government, and between 1832 and 1885 parliamentary districts were redrawn to conform more closely to the distribution of the population. English adaptation to urbanization was slow; still it was rapid enough that the lower classes were not alienated from constitutional procedures. In 1867 the majority of city dwellers obtained the suffrage, and significant laws favoring their interests soon followed.

It was not, however, until the twentieth century that legislation struck at the basic sources of urban insecurity. Propertyless townsmen, divorced from land, were especially vulnerable to economic depressions. Eventually social insurance programs were passed to protect the townsmen against losing their income and purchasing power during involuntary unemployment. Although state-sponsored old age, unemployment, and disability benefits held no place among the ideological traditions of entrepreneurs and Protestant dissenters—they held every indi-

vidual responsible for his own economic conditions—the economic system of the nineteenth century was changing nevertheless. Men of the cities were learning, however slowly, to control their environment.

## The Integration of Industrial Society

English liberals held in 1850 that *laissez faire* caused industrialization. As yet no other economic system had fostered industrial growth to shed doubt on this opinion. Defenders of paternalism and the traditional social hierarchy held that the forces changing their society were forces of anarchy. So did many humanitarian and religious critics of *laissez faire*. Disapprovingly they agreed with its economists that the price mechanism had become the arbiter of religious, moral, and human values. But both sides were ignoring strong indications that industrial society in Britain, although still beset by bitter conflicts of interest, was becoming far more integrated and producing conditions far more uniform than the Old Regime.

Although the control of production, distribution, and finance was divided among private individuals, it was concentrated in larger units than before. In some instances a few men at the top of the economic pyramid possessed immense power. Skilled labor combined to gain a greater share of the benefits of industry. Both capital and labor resisted state interference in their internal affairs. But investors and merchants called upon the state to press their opportunities at home and abroad, and labor sought to secure social security by action of the nation-state or, more rarely, by international organization. Professional groups also organized, but they seldom entered as significantly into the power structure as did capital and labor.

When power became concentrated in the hands of employers, the central government began in an unprecedented fashion to extend its administrative control. This was true not only in England but in every subsequent highly urbanized industrial state. Rapid communications and transportation facilitated the centralized supervision of local affairs, while the increasing complexity of an industrial economy made local control impossible. No longer could families, parishes, counties, towns, or even to some degree national states regulate their own financial affairs. Unable to escape the effects of rapid and far-reaching transportation and communication systems, they were now part of a larger, interrelated community. They either shifted their loyalties accordingly or assumed a hostile stand against contact with different cultures. From now on public opinion would concern itself with international as well as domestic politics. More often than not it would reflect strongly nationalistic sentiments. But the nation-state no longer sufficed as an economic or political institution. Imperialists ignored its borders as they divided the globe among themselves. And an unprecedented number of international institutions were created between 1850 and 1914.* Still none of them created a lasting alternative to the system of competition among sovereign states. International finance transcended national boundaries, but its institutions failed to provide a basis for supranational institutions. Industrial wealth and power went more to domestic manufacturers, traders, and investors than to international financiers. Industrial capitalism organized society into larger and more cohesive functional units, but their effective size continued to be the imperialistic nation-state.

## AN "OPEN-ENDED 'REVOLUTION' "

At the first World's Fair—in London—Britain was hailed as *the* workshop of the world. But industrial technology was still in its infancy. The economic transformation

* In 1914 these included a Universal Postal Union, a Universal Telegraphic Union, copyright conventions, a Parliamentary Union, the socialists' Second International, The Hague Court, the Rotary Club, the Boy Scouts, about thirty scientific societies, many church groups, and about 160 peace organizations with a permanent international headquarters.

*Inside the Crystal Palace, the first World's Fair, 1851.*

which Britain had pioneered proved "open-ended" in a double sense. Changes in technology and economic institutions continued to accelerate and to produce further social changes. Meanwhile other parts of the world adopted power-driven machinery. British exports of capital, men, and machines stimulated industrialization elsewhere. Technical discoveries in making steel between 1859 and 1878 first opened the superior resources of the Continent to exploitation. Continental technicians cut down Britain's geographical advantages in world trade by duplicating the work of her marine engineers. Latecomers were quick to pick up the most advanced technology and to turn it to their best advantage. Britain's industrial leadership declined as rapidly as it had been built up.

The history of industrialization in these other nations was similar to, but not exactly the same as, that in Britain. Nor did it conform to the predictions of Adam Smith and other classical economists. Smith and his immediate successors foretold an interdependent world divided into zones of specialized production that would contribute to peace as well as to the wealth of nations. But nearly every country supported its industrialists with high tariffs that restricted imports and protected domestic monopolies. After 1875 agrarian interests secured tariffs and restrictions against products shipped from America and various colonies by railroad and steamship. Growing trade between industrialized states clearly demonstrated their interdependence, but imperialists and economic nationalists rebelled against it. The most striking sequel to industrialization within the competitive state system was not the creation of new economic mechanisms for international peace or the dominance of economics over political passions, but intensified power differentials, rivalries, and the advent of total war. Industrialization not only changed the tools of war but it also revamped the balance of power and involved entire citizenries in the conduct of hostilities. Since World War II Europeans have looked in many directions—toward the United Nations, the European Economic Community, and in some areas toward Communist parties—for an escape from mutual annihilation.

## The Onward March of Technology

More difficult than an account of the early "revolutionary" inventions is a survey of the often more important technological changes that have occurred since the middle of the nineteenth century. Research laboratories, technical schools, equipment makers, professional journals, and all the new inventions and trades they have fostered, defy compression into a few paragraphs. They also defy control by societies composed of nontechnical persons and specialists whose horizons are bounded by their own particular fields. The most we can hope for here is a general sketch of selected changes that have most conspicuously influenced the course of events.

## Energy Conversion and Power Transmission

Machine industry and heavy industrial metallurgy during the nineteenth century depended directly upon coal. Coal is not just coal; its organic composition varies widely. Only those areas that possessed or had access to good coking coal could establish their own heavy industries. In both metallurgy and

energy conversion new processes reduced coal consumption and increased its flexibility as a source of power. Coal gas, a by-product of coking operations, was easily produced and piped to consumers in densely populated cities. The development of steam turbines between 1840 and 1880, a feat of mathematics and alloy metallurgy, provided much more speed, power, and fuel economy than the reciprocating steam engine. Used to propel newly invented dynamos, the turbines greatly increased coal's potential as a source of power. Electricity permitted industrial centers to branch out and set up regional enterprise. Mines and factories using electricity became further mechanized, and furnaces producing new metals (such as aluminum) could generate greater heat. Cities could relieve their congested streets by building electric tramways. Thus the configuration of towns changed. Electric lights replaced gaslights, and in the twentieth century household tasks have been mechanized.

Although coal remained the key industrial fuel, other sources of energy came to rival it in the twentieth century. Hydroelectricity and natural gas are comparatively insignificant ones. Far more important were petroleum and the internal combustion engine. First used as a lubricant, illuminant, and medicine, petroleum gradually replaced bulky coal as a fuel in situations where transportation costs, cleanliness, and convenience favored it. Early in its history petroleum was employed aboard ship to fire steam boilers. In 1887 Gottlieb Daimler suggested a different use when he adapted Nikolaus Otto's earlier internal-combustion engine to propel both boats and land vehicles using gasoline as a fuel. In the long time span between Daimler's invention and its practical elaboration by engineers on both sides of the Atlantic, Rudolf Diesel invented a heavy oil-burning engine more suited to heavy power needs. Shortly after the turn of the century the Wright brothers in the United States used the light gasoline engine to introduce another dimension into transportation: the airplane. More recently

*The Wright Brothers' airplane, 1903.*

*An early assembly line of the Ford Motor Company.*

oil-fueled jet turbines and engines functioning on rocket principles have added immense speeds to commercial and military transportation. The adoption of petroleum as a fuel in Western Europe was closely tied to the chemistry and physics in which her scientists excelled. However, the supply of petroleum was far more limited than that of coal; Western Europe lacked a domestic source.

The full impact of the internal-combustion engine upon society did not become apparent until after World War I in the United States and after World War II in Europe. Motor transport blurred and eventually effaced the ribbonlike economic patterns established by the railroads. Heavy-duty roadways absorbed heavy capitalization while railway nets ceased to grow or shrank. Motor transport broke down rural isolation far more thoroughly than the railroad did. In agrarian areas where capital and abundant resources were available, motorized mechanization has enabled a trifling percentage of the population to supply food for the urban remainder and to produce unsalable high-cost surpluses. In the cities passenger vehicles opened a trek to the suburbs far greater than that started by electric tramways. Widely owned private cars became new symbols of social status. Cars allowed youth unprecedented separation from adult supervision and weakened family ties—especially among multi-automobile families. Although subject to still undefined limits of space, purchasing power, and atmospheric pollution, cars stimulated the entire economy of more than one nation.

Contemporaries who feel themselves part of the atomic age may protest the omission of atomic energy from this list of power sources, but *at present levels of technology* the input of electrical energy into refined atomic fuel exceeds its economic potential for most uses. So far the "atomic age" terminology relates primarily to military preparations where economic considerations cease to govern human activities.

## Metallurgy and Heavy Industry

Although the greater advantages of steel were known, iron remained the basic structural metal until after 1860 because no means for the mass production of steel were at hand. With a thunderous roar and a shower of sparks from burning silicon and carbon, Henry Bessemer provided such a method in 1859. The Bessemer process oxidizes impurities by injecting an air blast into molten pig iron. While his converter was being improved, the Martin-Siemens open-hearth method was discovered on the Continent. The new processes increased steel production sharply. But the major known iron deposits outside Britain, the United States, and Spain contained ruinous

*Bessemer process of making steel.*

phosphorus. It had to be eliminated by chemical means discovered finally in 1878 by two Londoners, Sidney Gilchrist Thomas and Percy Gilchrist. The Thomas-Gilchrist process was widely adopted on the Continent within a single year. It made the large deposits of iron ore in Lorraine, Luxembourg, and northern Sweden the most valuable in all of Europe. Technology thus helped erase Britain's initial advantage in usable resources, since regions on the Continent were better endowed for the age of steel.

In the quality, variety, and economy of steel production still more significant steps were taken after 1859. Up to 1913 the relative cost of steel was reduced by increasingly economical uses of fuel and by the application of advanced chemistry and physics to production techniques. Tougher-than-steel alloys were produced for machine tools. In this period of technological advance, scattered obsolescent ironworks were closing down and large-scale operations became concentrated in a few favored regions. Within these regions integrated firms combined smelting and refining; some also brought finishing operations under their unified control. Except for producers of specialties, these integrated firms outstripped their competitors by reducing duplicate expenditures on fuel and equipment, by increasing the capital invested in research and mechanization, and by using by-products of one process constructively in another process. In the twentieth century a large array of chemical

processes and the use of electricity and natural gas as sources of heat have encouraged some plants to decentralize and establish sites near larger markets. The depletion of quality ore in such areas as the Mesabi Range in the United States has also affected the location of heavy industry. Culminating after World War II in a "straight-through" converter eliminating almost all hand labor, mechanization ("automation") has preserved the advantages of integration for the largest producers. Also in the twentieth century plastics and new metals such as aluminum have competed successfully with steel for old and new uses.

Besides heavy industry, scientific metallurgy attained general significance during the second half of the nineteenth century in the smelting of gold and silver. New processes were partially responsible for the inflation of the world's gold supply during the 1890s and for the drastic increase of silver supplies during the last third of the century. When this increased supply of silver upset exchange rates between gold and silver—both of which were widely used as monetary metals—silver was demonetized to prevent inflation.

## New Industries

Alongside established trades technology has produced a proliferating series of new industries. Chemicals—notably heavy industrial acids and alkalis, fertilizers, dyes, explosives, photographic materials, pharmaceutical products, plastics, and cosmetics—advanced most rapidly at first in Germany where chemical knowledge and resources were superior. Although more Germans worked in forestry than in chemicals at the end of the nineteenth century, Germany produced three fourths of the world's synthetic dyes and major portions of other lines. In the electrical industries that nation shared leadership with the United States. Starting with the telegraph and telephone, electricity expanded rapidly with the inventions of the turbine-driven dynamo and of procedures for transmitting high-voltage power. Basic re-

*Marconi and his wireless apparatus, 1897.*

*An early steam threshing machine.*

search in electricity continued to yield practical results. At the end of the century Guglielmo Marconi perfected wireless telegraphy. Knowledge of electromagnetism underlay the electronic industries of the twentieth century which have integrated local and regional societies more thoroughly than any previous means of communication and transportation. But with the exception of motion pictures, intercontinental mass communications remain severely limited by cultural, economic, political, and some technical barriers. The military may be the most predominant users of this field of communications.

A host of other new industries and their implications could be cataloged—automobiles, rubber, business and data processing machines, petroleum, synthetic textiles—but our purpose is illustrative rather than exhaustive.

## Scientific and Mechanized Agriculture

During the nineteenth century the peasantry of Western Europe adopted the improvements of "the agricultural revolution." Chemical fertilizers, machinery, and other technological advances increased farm productivity further. Still no industrialized country in Europe could produce enough food on home soil to feed its entire, ever-expanding population. Only one of them, Britain, clearly abandoned a policy of self-sufficiency, but all became dependent upon imports that were paid for in international exchange by indus-

trial exports, shipping, banking, insurance, and investment returns.

Although farming continued to be a major source of wealth in Britain, other countries took the lead in agricultural technology. Germany and to a lesser extent the United States excelled in the application of science —notably chemistry, microbiology, genetics, and veterinary medicine—to agriculture. Temperate parts of the British Empire and the United States, whose agricultural resources far exceeded their own consumption needs, led in the introduction of labor-saving machinery. New milling machines, refrigerated railway cars and steamships, steel cans, and other means of food preservation facilitated the transport of surpluses to Europe. In the twentieth century mechanized scientific farming has extended into Southern and Eastern Europe. Especially since World War II gasoline tractors and nitrogen fertilizers have raised yields in the older industrialized states. France and some other areas have begun to produce high-cost surpluses similar to those in the United States. Although Europe continues to import foodstuffs, its prospects for eventually feeding its own (slowly expanding) population are far stronger than those of other regions of the world. Densely populated areas where the birth rate is extremely high and industrial capability extremely low, and whose purchasing power in international trade is very weak, will not soon satisfy their peoples' hunger by their own production.

## The Evolution of Financial Capitalism

Only heavy capital investment could support the mass production industries and their proliferating technology. Often individual proprietors, partners, and family businesses were incapable of such investment. About the middle of the nineteenth century, Western states enacted general incorporation laws permitting the formation of limited liability stock companies. Shareholders in these corporations were liable only to the extent of their investments—hence, they were "limited." At the end of the century only Russia and the Ottoman Empire still required special grants of incorporation. Limited liability corporations permitted the raising of large amounts of capital and provided the machinery to make ownership easily transferable. The rate at which these corporations were chartered became an index of economic activity. They also provided lines of financial control over economic activity far beyond the capability of small individual entrepreneurs. By the end of the century the bulk of capital investment, production, and employees was under corporate management in every industrial country. In negotiable shares ownership was distributed among many investors. But blocks of stockholders, corporate banks, investment banking firms, or other corporations usually held the real powers of management. In financial institutions that directed the flow of credit (the very lifeblood of capitalist economy), economic power was most centralized. Thus, by corporate organization, an economy dominated by financial institutions supplanted the early capitalism of entrepreneurs.

The dominant financiers made agreements among themselves to curb unrestricted competition and to form combinations through which they could control the markets. To secure the collective monopoly they usually sought and obtained high tariffs. Their first, simplest, and least enduring form of combination was normally an agreement to fix prices or, in the case of the railroads, to establish pools for the prearranged sharing of traffic or profits. Overstocked participants were, of course, tempted to reduce prices and break the agreement. Several devices were used to remedy this defect. German bankers and producers formed cartels or incorporated associations that operated through common sales agencies at high fixed domestic prices and allotted production quotas. This development was in accord with traditional governmental sponsorship of industry and the use of economic power for political ends. Cartels permitted their participants to sell abroad without restrictions, but on occasion they made agreements with similar foreign organizations to allocate markets or set prices. By 1900 practically every German trade had its own cartel organization. So long as newcomers could be excluded or absorbed, the participants obtained security at home and power abroad. At least in the short run they could assure labor of steady employment, but at the cost of higher domestic prices and taxes. The government granted them tariff protection, sales assistance, transportation bounties, and colonies. In return they put their economic power at its disposal to back its foreign policy and to prevent unwanted democratization.

Outside Germany other devices were more common than cartels. Common sales agencies and informal agreements served similar purposes for bankers and producers in France where business dependence upon government was less thoroughly established as a tradition. With some exceptions, free trade and dispersed resources precluded the success of such organizations in Britain. Producers naturally immune from foreign competition did combine, however, and one British combination dominated the world market for cotton thread. High tariffs, major resources concentrated in a few areas, and general dependence upon the railroad fostered the growth of monopolies. In America as in Germany they were held together by major investment banking firms. Their tendency was not toward common sales agencies or cartels but toward the corporate merger or coordination of management in the form of trusts, holding companies, and interlocking directors named by investment bankers who supplied credit. Monopolists improved or—as in the aluminum industry—perfected their control by obtaining exclusive rights to raw materials, by assuming transportation advantages, by absorbing their competitors, or by reaching informal agreements. At the beginning of the twentieth century heavy industry, transportation, fuel, and finance were generally controlled by the apex of a corporate pyramid.

The power of these combinations was soon perceived as a threat to general economic well-being. Different states formulated various remedial policies, but they all attempted government regulation or control. In Europe no substantial party rose urging restoration of competition. Conservatives reluctantly countenanced the government control that socialists welcomed. Liberals tended to be nationalistic and to view monopoly as an indispensable weapon of foreign policy. European governments gave control over credit and a flexible money supply to centralized discount banks. After World War II most of these central banks were nationalized. The United States belatedly adopted a banking system with credit controls in 1913. Alone among the major industrial states, the United States instituted "antitrust" laws aimed at banning certain combinations, divorcing investment banking from corporate management, and restricting interlocking directorates. In practice these laws had little effect. After the Depression of 1929 to 1933, further steps were taken to regulate security and commodity exchanges and to prohibit or tax out of existence those holding companies that controlled chains of firms by owning as little as one fifth of the chain's stock.

As a result of its own growth and the effects upon Europe of two world wars, the United States gained unquestioned dominance in twentieth-century world finance. Meanwhile a "managerial revolution" within American and British corporations took place. It made management substantially autonomous from individual stockholder-owners. Bureaus of technicians took over the management of larger corporations. Devoting their attention to consumer credit, purchasing power, labor relations, and the stimulation of market demand, they raised new capital from undistributed surpluses without recourse to investment houses. In America such corporations came to dominate retailing, many of the service industries, consumer credit, and advertising. Through advertising the mass media became dependent upon these corporations. Soon after World War II some American corporations—in the automotive and electrical industries, for example—replaced investment houses as the largest private financial powers in the world. During the same period new quasi-public institutions such as the International Monetary Fund rose to give greater stability to world exchange.

Differences between Europe and the United States still exist, however. To date Europeans have accepted "trust-busting" nominally if at all. American business circles reject Europe's post-World War II economic planning. And they do not agree (nor in fact do all businessmen in Europe) that supranational organizations such as the European Economic Community are necessary to maintain free trade and the mobility of capital and labor.

## Some Social Implications of Evolving Technology and Finance

Wherever industrialization occurred it produced a period whose social morphology resembled that of Great Britain in the second half of the nineteenth century. This structure was, in turn, modified by subsequent changes in technology, financial organization, and government policies. Except during depressions, the proportion of city dwellers increased. Enlarged spheres of economic activity produced more tightly integrated societies at the national level and have fostered regional "common markets," new international organizations, and foreign conquest. Standards of living clearly rose although they continued to be jeopardized by financial combinations, wars, and depressions.* Scientific medicine, better nutrition, and improved sanitation extended longevity. Private associations and governments then instituted old age and survivor insurance plans. They also sponsored insurance for sickness, disability, and accidents. Since the burdens of accidents fell primarily on employers, investments in safety equipment rose rapidly. Some governments undertook housing projects for the lowest income levels. Labor unions achieved recognition and applied economic and political pressure to reduce hours, increase wages, and improve working conditions for their members. Thus the fruits of science and industry were distributed in part to the lower classes, but wealth and economic power still remained highly concentrated. Revolutionary social-economic doctrines challenging this concentration spread rapidly through late nineteenth-century labor and intellectual circles. But in areas where industry had "matured"—where the proceeds of greater productivity were distributed, and concentrated economic power was policed by democratic political institutions—these movements became constitutional and reformist. Elsewhere revolution born of war, depression, and social dislocations became a reality or a continued threat.

Predictions that industrialization would divide society into only two classes, the bourgeoisie and the industrial proletariat,

---

* Commercial crises, whose scope included the whole industrialized world after 1848, decreased in frequency, but as populations became more urbanized and dependent upon wages and salaries, the individual was left with virtually no protection against them. Major crises occurred in 1857, 1866, 1873, 1896 and, the largest of all, in 1929 to 1933.

were sorely wrong. The bourgeoisie obtained and held great power as owner-managers but, as in England, the proportion of factory workers eventually ceased to grow. More and more, industrial populations entered commerce, finance, managerial staffs, and services. More Americans, for example, were employed during the 1920s in finance than in agriculture. The most rapidly growing segment of the population was the professionals—teachers, doctors, engineers, lawyers, civil servants, recreation directors, and technicians. Professions that required enforced standards for entry were estimated at 1200 for advanced countries in 1929. The number has risen since. In industrial societies increasing attention was paid to education. Systems of both general compulsory education and technical training were widely established. Peoples like the Germans or Swedes could industrialize rapidly and smoothly because they were already highly literate and disciplined intellectually.

If current predictions concerning the impact of "automation" on middle management and routine office positions materialize, continuing technological development may further alter the social structure. So far white-collar workers have tended to identify with the managerial elite or at least to dissociate themselves from labor. Whether they continue to do so under the threat of partial technological displacement remains to be seen.

## Industry in Belgium and France

The first countries to industrialize rapidly after Britain were Belgium and France. Until after 1814 the Napoleonic wars absorbed the Continent's resources and isolated the Continent from Britain's early industrial technology. After the peace, British products undersold their competitors, further delaying economic growth on the Continent. Both Belgium and France had a history of technical skills and commerce, and in both countries the French Revolution had swept traditional institutions away and left behind economic unity. Together with Luxembourg, Belgium and France shared the mineral resources of an international region whose deposits extended eastward into the Prussian Ruhr Valley. Because they lacked credit and cheap overland transportation, their economies developed only slowly at first, but eventually they overcame these scarcities.

Belgium was first to introduce the railways, coke-burning furnaces, machine tools, mechanized textiles, and new banking institutions that made her the gateway of continental industrialization. Immigrants including the English Cockerill family brought advanced technology to Belgium and Luxembourg. After 1813 William Cockerill produced textile machinery. His son, John, went into iron and machine tools near Liège in 1817, where he built the largest industrial empire in Europe during the 1830s. As early as 1822 the Dutch king chartered a promotional investment corporation in the Belgian provinces, the *Société Générale*; most early Belgian industry, however, was financed by French and English investors. The French Rothschilds maintained the new Belgian state of 1830 by loans. The government borrowed heavily between 1834 and 1842 to build a new trunkline railway system that kept transit charges low to encourage commerce and industry. The state later acquired private lines that it added to the network. By mid-century Belgium was keeping pace with England, and its self-sustaining economy was as much admired as its liberal constitution. But toward the end of the nineteenth century, when Belgium's population was the densest in the world, its deep mines failed to produce sufficient coal and iron for domestic use. Belgium then became a net importer of both materials, yielding economic leadership to other areas having superior resources. Capital and engineers flowed out of Belgium into other parts of Europe.

Industrialization in nineteenth-century France was rapid, slow, or hardly existent depending on the area in question. After 1815 Alsatian cotton textiles kept pace with

*A small French canning factory.*

leading British centers. For a brief period before 1870 France—much of whose technology was superior to England's—became a leading producer of iron. But on the whole the country's industrialization was slow before 1895 and not spectacularly fast thereafter. At the beginning of the twentieth century France remained a land of small preindustrial workshops and tiny, inefficient, nonmechanized farms.

Tardy industrialization did not result from a shortage of capital or top-level engineering skills, since France supplied these to other areas of Europe and the world. But the quality, quantity, and geographical location of her mineral resources were major drawbacks. She lacked large deposits of quality coking coal and rich nonsulfurous iron ore. Domestic or imported coal could reach the major iron deposits of Lorraine and the northern departments only by rail. And political disputes and rivalries among promoters delayed completion of a railway network until 1870. It was just completed when Prussia seized the Alsatian textile districts, a sector of the Lorraine iron fields, and part of the railway system. Repeated economic depressions following sprees of wild speculation in securities further retarded French growth. Silkworm and vineyard diseases also affected basic export commodities.

These misfortunes do not entirely account for France's delays in using available resources. Most of the population remained small farmers passionately tied to the soil and to traditional farming methods. Their political spokesmen were provincial town oligarchs or wealthy landlords who preferred to invest in government securities and real estate. Much early industrial investment in France came from Belgium and England. Rampant speculation and political scandals characterized French promotional activities. Productivity increased, but at least until the end of the century most increases in national income went to landlords, financiers, and industrialists. The government encouraged the education of engineers but was slow to promote general secular education and social legislation. Urban labor, remaining semi-agrarian and poorly organized, became the alienated stepchild of a society manipulated by speculators. Largely illiterate, lowly paid, and politically suppressed, the laborers vented their dissatisfaction in revolutionary outbreaks. Until 1874 France had no law comparable to the English Factory Act of 1833 regulating child and female labor. Other social legislation was similarly delayed. After 1884 republican governments made some concessions (not so thorough as the relief measures in England and elsewhere) to the restive "other France." But the conciliation process foundered and is still incomplete.

Although their achievements at home were limited, French capitalists and engineers promoted industrialization on the rest of the Continent. They founded foreign investment firms, constructed railway networks, opened mines, built factories, and established utilities and commercial businesses. By 1914 French foreign loans amounted to about fifty billion francs (ten billion dollars). James de Rothschild and the Pereire brothers, Isaac and Emile, were the principal agents of such investment. In 1852 the Pereires founded the *Crédit Mobilier* in France. With their aid it was imitated in Switzerland, the Netherlands, Spain, Italy, Britain, the United States, and especially Germany and Belgium. Competing to control the railway lines of Europe,

the Pereires and Rothschilds laid lines throughout the Continent, leaving only Germany and Scandinavia uncrossed. French capital and engineers also built the Suez Canal of 1869, over which the British gained control. The French made a scandal-ridden effort to build a similar canal across the Isthmus of Panama. As European areas industrialized, became self-sufficient financially, and paid lower interest rates, French capitalists—like those of England, Belgium, and later Germany and America—began to vie more intensely for investment opportunities in non-European areas of the world.

## German Industrial Preeminence in Europe

Few other early nineteenth-century areas appeared less favored for large-scale industry than Germany. As a battleground divided among thirty-nine mercantilist states, its economy was primitive. Most Germans were peasants bound to the soil or were entering a century-long process of compensated emancipation. Capital was lacking and commercial banking was nonexistent outside a few commercial cities and princely courts. Exchange still occurred primarily at fairs and weekly markets or through peddlers as it had for centuries. Except for a few state enterprises, industrial production was in the hands of local entrepreneurs and privileged guild masters who actually outnumbered their journeymen. In few areas of Europe had traditionalist lords and clerics succeeded so well in preserving a medieval economy.

But several breaches were opened in this economy during the first half of the nineteenth century. French occupation had its most lasting effects in the Rhineland, the areas where most German resources were later discovered. After 1835 individual German states and investors began to construct railroads at a pace more rapid than that of the French. Prussia sponsored a customs union (the *Zollverein*) that in 1844 imposed a tariff on British iron. As the resources of the Ruhr and Rhineland were discovered,

British, French, and Belgian firms sent capital, skills, and labor to exploit them behind German tariff walls. One factor in the revolution of 1848 was the mechanization of the textile industries, which dislocated craftsmen and weakened the traditional social order. The same revolution strained that order further by emancipating the peasantry.

In the quarter century between 1850 and 1875 German political unification created the largest effective single market in Europe. Germans quickly demonstrated their capacity to adopt industrial technology and organization. Literate and rather highly educated, they led in some branches of scientific knowledge. Their technical schools, journals, and equipment manufacturers speeded the spread of technology across their society. During the 1850s they assumed almost exclusive management of foreign-owned plants. Between 1840 and 1870 they increased coal production within the *Zollverein* over 850 per cent, iron about 700 per cent. Newly completed railway lines that opened up both resources and markets largely account for this economic spurt. In 1856 a foreign visitor noted that Germans were devoting as much energy to financial institutions as to railroads. The Darmstadt Bank was founded in 1853 with assistance from the French *Crédit Mobilier*. Thereafter corporate banking was closely tied to industrial management. After 1860 natives began to displace foreign financiers. By 1875 Germany had attained financial self-sufficiency and the German Empire emerged as a competitor for foreign markets and investment opportunities.

By 1875 Germany was producing more iron and coal than Belgium and France. By 1910 it was the greatest industrial producer in Europe and the second trading nation in the world (Britain was the first). Change occurred so rapidly in the German Empire that her rulers had to cope with remnants of peasant emancipation and pressing urban-social problems simultaneously. From the beginning her industrialists adopted the latest technology. That her people were literate and knowledgeable, adaptable, and subject to discipline partially explains her dazzling rate of growth. But nineteenth-century industry was founded on coal and iron, and the German Empire probably possessed as much of these resources as the remainder of Western Europe put together. Furthermore, she had easy access to the rich ores of Sweden after 1890. As John Maynard Keynes observed with little exaggeration, "The German Empire has been built more truly on coal and iron than blood and iron."[4] In addition, the Empire possessed rich chemical resources and deposits of nonferrous metals.

During the six decades ending in 1910 Germany's urban population rose from ten to forty million—from less than 30 to over 60 per cent of the population. An increase in agricultural production effected by enclosures, scientific methods, and partial mechanization coincided with industrial urbanization. Tillage replaced herds of sheep, and Germany became almost totally dependent upon imported raw wool. Potash and electrically produced nitrogen were introduced as chemical fertilizers. Schools and universities added agriculture to the curriculum, and new crops such as sugar beets were promoted. In the quest for self-sufficiency (prompted partly by military considerations) large numbers of pigs were maintained as a source of fats and meat, and agricultural tariffs subsidized large inefficient eastern landlords who produced large quantities of rye with foreign migrant labor. Rural life changed less than life in the cities, but the pull of urban markets caused the countryside to reorganize. Peasants formed cooperatives for banking, purchasing, and marketing. Lest the importance of commercial agriculture in industrial society be excessively de-emphasized, it is worth noting that the cash value of the milk produced in Germany in 1907 exceeded the cash value of the output of all mining industries.

4. *The Economic Consequences of the Peace,* Harcourt, Brace & Howe, New York, 1920, p. 81.

Rapid industrialization quickly brought new social and political problems to the fore. Between 1871 and 1910 Germany's population increased from just over forty-five to nearly sixty-five million. Late in the nineteenth century death rates declined markedly. Birth rates began to decrease shortly after the turn of the century. Despite the swelling population, standards of urban living improved. Meat, sugar, coffee, rice, and cotton were available, especially after 1880, to the dwellers of the cities. Although industrial workingmen suffered fewer hardships than displaced artisans, they organized more thoroughly in Germany than in France or Britain. Unions protested long hours, low pay, and hazardous working conditions. They opposed the government for its tariff policies and for acquiring colonies. Against capitalists they laid the charge of hoarding industry's major benefits and excluding labor from politics. Because electoral districts did not reflect the preponderance of city over rural populations, political power was still held by clerical agrarian aristocrats and the magnates of industry. The dissatisfied labor movement, the most literate of Europe at the time, turned to socialism after the depression of 1873. After failing to destroy the socialist movement with coercion, Bismarck sought after 1880 to undermine it with the most comprehensive social insurance system of the century. The Socialist party, supported by about four fifths of organized labor, had become the largest political party in Germany by 1910. But German labor proved loyal to the regime at the outbreak of World War I.

## The United States' Rise to World Industrial Preeminence

The United States was abundantly endowed for industrialization, and its deficiencies proved remediable. Agricultural and industrial resources were sufficient to sustain the impression for over a century that they were unlimited. Over Europe and contemporary "underdeveloped countries" America had the cardinal advantage of no population pressures. Despite an influx of cheap immigrant labor there was a labor shortage. That shortage helped bolster a per capita purchasing power higher than any other market in the world. It also furnished incentives for mechanizing farm and factory without producing the serious side effects of technological displacement. In Europe industrialization alleviated problems of subsistence, social immobility, and poverty, but in America, industrialization was popularly associated with the first appearance of these problems.

In addition to a shortage of labor, the new republic was also short of capital, international exchange credits, and banking institutions. Banking outside New England was chaotic until after the Civil War, and many of the difficulties of southern and western banks stemmed from a shortage of "hard money." Capital that was accumulated from commerce and land appreciation predated industrialization, but native investment powers were inadequate. Governments—local, state, and federal—used their resources and credit to provide transportation and banking facilities. Heavy foreign investments flowed into the American economy throughout the nineteenth century. Exports of gold, silver, and agricultural products redressed an otherwise unfavorable balance of international accounts, but the United States remained an international debtor until World War I.

American factories originated in cotton mills and gun shops in New England at the end of the eighteenth century. But general industrialization did not occur until the first railway networks were completed during the 1850s. Prior to the Civil War, canals and railways united much of the Ohio River Valley and the eastern seaboard into one economic market. The railroad's massive appetite for iron spurred coke-fueled metallurgy. For the rest of the century the expansion and contraction of railroad building tended to set the pattern of business cycles.

During and after the Civil War the holders of political power were responsive to industry, finance, agricultural expansion, and nationalism. In 1861 the first severe protective tariff was enacted. With few respites it was progressively raised until the 1930s. The Civil War Congress also created a standardized but deflationary banking and monetary system. It established grants for agricultural colleges and for continental railroads with northern terminals. From the Civil War Congress went free land to western settlers, and mineral lands at minimal prices. Northern politicians turned the business climate in their areas into a veritable hothouse.

Between 1865 and 1910 speculation, fraud, flagrant waste, and the emergence of market-controlling monopolies intermingled with solid growth, integration for technical efficiency, and expanding technology. Production in steel, oil, milling, tobacco, meat packing, sugar, agricultural implements, railway equipment, electricals, and scores of other lines soared. At the beginning of the twentieth century the United States led the world in heavy industry, petroleum, and consumer items as well as in agriculture. Except for agriculture, most of this production was consumed domestically.

Urban industrialization produced social phenomena contrary to American traditions. Concentrations of economic power closed off opportunities in many fields of manufacture and commerce. Political developments seemed to follow economic events. Capitalist investors were "in the saddle." Even during depressions investors regularly received their dividends. Courts, police, and military troops stood ready to suppress any challenge to the system from labor. Entrepreneurs and financiers influenced every level of government. Corporation lawyers on the Supreme Court bench reinterpreted the Constitution. Senators were identified by their business interests rather than by their states. The same government that championed capitalism at home strove for imperial expansion abroad. As long as prosperity was widespread and

opportunities open, voices of dissent were scattered and divided. Farmers and local merchants revolted against business and monetary policies. But farm revolts were often anti-urban, anti-Negro, anti-Catholic, and prohibitionist. They rejected the city and often blocked urban attempts at reform. Successful labor organizations, on the other hand, frankly accepted laborer status and pitted their economic power against the collective power of their employers. Professionals and older "patrician" families also rose in protest. They wanted more democracy—at least until the present rulers had been replaced. Socialism appeared but could raise a vote of only 6 per cent in 1912, and part of this was a protest vote.

Combined economic and sectional dissent movements obtained some changes during the first two decades of the twentieth century. But less social legislation was passed and less public control was assumed over the economy in the United States than in most European countries. Still, the American government was more subject to popular control. Antitrust laws and regulatory commissions were established, but their administrators, as well as their opponents, were sympathetic to the interests of those they were expected to regulate. In 1908 federal courts first allowed minimal state legislation to stand concerning the hours and working conditions of women, but a constitutional amendment barring child labor failed. Progressive domestic reformers also tried to substitute arbitration treaties and collective security for imperialism abroad. But the composite coalition behind these reforms proved unstable. After World War I a nationalist reaction set in. Advocates of rural traditionalism, nativism, political isolation, high tariffs, and big business expansion at home and abroad once again held sway. Further expansion and urbanization ended in the crash of 1929, which provoked social legislation comparable to that in Britain and Germany at the turn of the century. Political power, however,

*Stockholm, a city without slums.*

continued to reside disproportionately with the rural minority until after World War II.

## Three Latecomers: Sweden, Russia, and Japan

Technical advances enabled some qualified areas to industrialize more rapidly than all their predecessors. Probably the most sensational and least socially painful case was Sweden. Sweden had immensely rich iron deposits, an active commercial community, and a highly skilled, literate population, but she lacked coal and capital. Imports and electricity made up for the coal. Beginning in the 1860s the government borrowed money—largely from French investors—for railroads, public utilities, and banks. Public officials, whose reputations and resources entitled them to less than private interest rates, carefully administered loans that were huge in proportion to Sweden's revenues and wealth. Foreign firms were at first excluded, and for the most part foreign technicians were not needed. Sweden, which had been 90 per cent rural in 1850, was more than half urban by 1910. Democratization occurred at the outset, and politics passed quickly from a liberal to a welfare stage. The Social Democratic party, practically unknown in 1890, secured one third of the parliamentary seats in 1910 and lasting control during the world depression of the 1930s.

Approximately 92 per cent of Sweden's economy remains privately owned. But welfare-oriented officials working with one of the world's most stable populations have gained a wide reputation for eliminating slums and dire poverty through social legislation, monetary controls, and a pacific foreign policy. Sweden has shared with Switzerland the highest standard of living in twentieth-century Europe.

In sharp contrast stands the Russian Empire whose industrialization was rapid, jerky, and uneven. Russian resources were immense and only partially known, but her institutions were primitive. Commerce was essentially medieval in organization, and domestic industry produced most wares. Illiterate, emancipated, but tradition-bound peasants constituted all but a narrow segment of the population. A landed aristocracy that was only a little more progressive than the peasantry dominated society. As late as 1900 about 80 per cent of the population derived its income from the soil. Still the pressure of a population that nearly doubled during the second half of the century outran the production of foodstuffs. Agriculture remained communal and traditional; it lacked resources, technology, and capital. Industry, science, and mechanization came too late to prevent massive famines that probably carried away between two and three million people between 1892 and World War I. Further famines during the 1920s followed the upheavals of war and revolution.

The Tsarist government, defeated militarily and diplomatically by industrial powers in 1856 and 1878, threw its full weight behind railway construction after 1857 and behind heavy industry after 1880. Railroads stimulated the rise of a modern coal and iron industry in the Donets Basin of the southern Ukraine. Protective tariffs higher than those in the United States and a host of other inducements lured foreign capital and technology. Foreign investors opened the Baku oil fields after 1860 and for a short time at the end of the century, Russia led the world in oil production. Meanwhile, a cotton industry developed on a large scale around Lodz in Poland and around Moscow. Coming late, Russian industry utilized the largest production units in all of Europe. Emphasis fell on heavy industry rather than on consumer goods. At the opening of the twentieth century, Russia was fourth in pig iron production. The period from 1906 to 1914 was one of spectacularly rapid investment and growth. Self-sustained economic growth had not been achieved, however, and technological development was spotty.

More than one third of the total capital invested in prewar Russia came from foreign sources. Domestically the principal source of capital, management, and control was the Tsarist state whose Bank of Russia made industrial loans. The predominance of foreign and state capital precluded the development of a large, native middle class. Heavy tariffs attracted foreign capital but they also protected inefficient state and private enterprise. In the early twentieth century, metal products, machine tools, oils, coal, and sugar were organized into cartels and trusts. The combinations resembled German cartels except that the German state played a lesser role in finance and management.

The Tsarist government pressed industrialization at huge social costs. Power in international affairs was one objective, and considerations of foreign policy prompted loans from France. Like other Eastern autocratic regimes, the bureaucracy mistakenly assumed that industrialization would lessen political and social discontent. Grain was exported even during famine to secure foreign exchange. Instead of supporting the weakened *status quo,* however, the government's revolutionary economic policy produced unwanted social, political, religious, and intellectual effects which the bureaucracy tried to suppress. Stringent factory laws were enacted, but officials were spectators over the worst social situations yet produced by industrialization. Labor organizations were forbidden until 1904, and secret police infiltrated their ranks. Revolutionary socialist parties organized before (revolutionary) liberal parties, and one socialist faction, the Bolsheviks, developed an organization capable of coping with the Tsarist secret police. After a revolution in 1905 the government attempted agrarian reforms, but it lost the race between subsistence and catastrophe. Population pressures and resultant land hunger left the peasantry unappeasable.

Given Western imperialism equipped with industrial technology, the nonindustrialized peoples of the world had either to submit to foreign domination and the disintegration of their institutions or borrow the technology of the Occident to "repel the barbarians." Earlier some countries like China and Japan had successfully maintained a policy of hermetic isolation against mercantilist thrusts from Europe. After the Opium War of 1840, however, China was forced open to European penetration. American, Russian, and British naval forces also forced Japan to abandon isolation. In Japan, a counternationalist reaction set in. During the 1860s a young Japanese warrior class appealed to nationalist sentiments, adopted European military science and economy, united the islands under the emperor, and set out to modernize Japan from above. Eclectically borrowing from advanced nations, the government sponsored industry and commerce. It avoided financial dependence on foreign investors. Despite serious shortages of raw materials, industry—especially electrically powered heavy industry—grew extraordinarily after 1890. Subsidized industry and commerce, combined with low labor costs, enabled Japanese businessmen to expel foreign competitors at home and to undersell them in Asia. By Asian standards the Japanese attained a high standard of living, but the greater portion of their gains in productivity went to maintain a growing military establishment and to support a population that increased from about thirty million in 1850 to seventy million in 1940. A new educational system and the Shinto religion inculcated militant nationalism. Social dissent, which was suppressed by terroristic methods, tended to be extremist and revolutionary.

## Industry and International Rivalry

While Britain, as the single industrial trading nation, dominated commerce and technology, a Pax Britannica prevailed. There was no basis for rivalry between industrialized states. But spreading industry soon deprived Britain of her monopoly. To most Britons free trade was a self-efficient law of nature to which they owed their prosperity and which would remake the world. But to leaders of states that industrialized later in the face of her competition, free trade was an imperialistic British weapon. To initiate local economic development they relied upon tariffs, tax and resource concessions, and subsidized transportation. If the premises of free trade theory had regulated international intercourse, initial protective measures should have lapsed after local concerns became competitive. This was not the case. With a few brief exceptions, the United States, France, and other nominally *laissez-faire* states intensified protectionism the more their "infant" industries became giants of vested interest and political power. From the outset of their industrial growth, the governments of Germany, Russia, and Japan, among others, considered industrialization as a strategic path to power, first defensively then offensively.

In the last decades of the nineteenth century the tools of initial protection were turned into weapons of economic warfare. Temporarily after 1860 France, the leading continental producer at the moment, negotiated low tariffs with Britain and most of the Continent. The experiment was short lived. Uneven distribution of resources between nation-states may have made free trade between them impracticable.* In France the treaties were unpopular. Then the United States (1861) and Germany (1879) adopted severe and moderately high tariffs, respectively. Nationalism spawned by German and Italian wars of unification spread protectionism further. So did the appearance of large quantities of American and Russian grain on European markets after 1880. Tariff wars became conventional diplomacy, often a prelude to military conflict. Russia became the most exclusionist state. Only Britain and the Netherlands held fast to free trade until World War I. Consular services aided merchants and investors abroad. Governments encouraged the export of monopolies and directed investments according to strategic calculations. They seized colonies for purposes of exclusive investment and to extract raw materials.†

Industry was convertible to military power. Hence, uneven economic development increased power differentials between industrialized and nonindustrialized peoples and drastically altered the balance of power among those who were technologically advanced. Germany's superior industry as much as her large population was responsible for her emergence as the strongest military power in Europe. French armies had overrun the Continent at the beginning of the nineteenth century. But now against a united and industrialized Germany the

---

* Late nineteenth- and twentieth-century experience convinced the men behind the contemporary European Economic Community and other economic unions that free trade is a hopeless aspiration unless political institutions that provide for the mobility of labor, capital, and resources and for the judicial reconciliation of economic differences tie trading partners together.

† Popular arguments advanced by the press and industrialists that colonial markets were the principal concern are belied by international trade statistics. Most exchange occurred and still occurs between industrialized countries whose markets possess purchasing power far superior to primitive colonies or states, no matter how numerous their populations are.

French were incapable of standing alone. Recognizing this fact, their leaders not only made foreign alliances but also sank investments in Russia and Eastern Europe hoping to develop a counterbalance. The United States, up to this time preoccupied on the North American continent, began to build a navy during the 1880s and to penetrate distant areas politically and economically. In the Far East, an industrialized Japan defeated China in 1895 and Russia in 1905, annexing territory in each case. While Occidental industrial states were engaged in World War I, Japan established her hegemony in the Far East. In each region dominated by an industrialized power, nominally sovereign but economically backward states lost their self-determination.

As major power rivalries became tense, military expenditures rose and absorbed productive energies that, if directed elsewhere, might have raised stagnating living standards. These developments climaxed in the year of 1914. The disciples of Adam Smith, relying upon *economic* laws to produce a harmonious world, had not foreseen industrialized warfare. Their postulate of interdependence was real enough,* but unless international organization was a utopian dream their rejection of political institutions was naïve. The world wars of the twentieth century produced economic dictatorships that provided the first working models of economies completely controlled and planned by states bent on aggrandizement.

---

* Despite recriminatory tariffs and other weapons of economic warfare, the volume of international trade increased rapidly at the end of the nineteenth century, and no nation possessed self-sufficiency in raw materials. Every highly urbanized industrial country in Europe was running a deficit in trade balances. All of them made up this deficit and gained surpluses from "invisible exports"—shipping, banking services, interests and profits from foreign investments, insurance, salaries of technicians working abroad, and expenditures by travellers.

*Mechanized warfare: tanks on parade, Berlin, 1959.*

## Industrialized Warfare

The second half of the nineteenth century was still a period of relative peace in Europe. Only the United States experienced a long industrialized war of attrition. But in Europe industrial development had become a heavy determinant in localized wars.

Industrial development could unleash superior killing power against enemy forces through inventions such as the magazine-fed breech-loading rifle whose range and accuracy set new standards. An all-weather percussion cap invented in 1856 and smokeless powder adopted in 1886 increased the efficiency of this weapon. With it and its close relative, the discharge gas-operated machine gun, holders of defensive terrain had an advantage over enemy forces whose technical power equalled theirs. In the late nineteenth century projectiles equipped with precision-timed fuses made possible barrages of rapid-fire artillery. Armies equipped with rifles and artillery required rapid communications and fast, heavy transport. The American Civil War served as a laboratory for the large-scale use of railroads, telegraphs, and a host of other devices. Armies were no longer dependent upon horses or mules for their communications, transport, and supplies. The Prussian army learned from American experience and introduced a general staff that

*Mechanized warfare, 1966: jet aircraft on a napalm bombing run.*

both planned and directed the mobilization and deployment of large forces from a central point. Railroads and telegraphs were only the first steps, and were succeeded by telephones, radios, and electronic navigational aids. In military operations as in commerce, the internal combustion engine proved more revolutionary than the railroad. In World War I motorized troop carriers, aircraft, submarines, and tanks were introduced. They could break into enemy lines when artillery could not and were used with poison gas to counter the rifle. Now that the military depended upon gasoline-powered vehicles and oil-driven ships and submarines, petroleum became *the* strategic fuel, and control of oil fields *the* strategic goal. After the beginning of World War I, chemical industries also figured prominently in industrialized warfare, not so much for widely publicized poisonous gases—they proved too volatile to be used as effective killing agents—as for explosives and firebombs.

Perhaps we can best comprehend the welter of military innovations in the twentieth century by studying their results. By World War II military research was no longer ancillary to industry and science; rather it was justified by its contributions to those fields. Contemporaries need no reminder that the end product of industrial-

ized warfare, radioactive thermonuclear energy, threatens the continuation of the very society that produced it.

While high-energy technology multiplied the radius of human killing power, industrialized warfare took on another dimension. Now that societies could produce more, they could expend more—in men and resources —for the battlefield without endangering domestic subsistence standards. In World War I, for example, Britain mobilized 5.7 million men with scant decline in her total production despite shortages and losses. Thus, industrialization quietly reduced material limitations that had restrained past warfare and laid the foundations for "total wars" in the twentieth century. Total war has drawn every able civilian adult into the production of war materials or into essential civilian goods and services. And it has destroyed their immunity from direct military attack. In both World Wars I and II civilian deaths exceeded military deaths. New long-range guns, aircraft, and rockets aimed at industrial complexes were used to create these casualties. Nationalism—fostered by mechanized transport, mass communications, and education—is equally, if not more, responsible for total war than industrialization. With emotional propaganda, national mass media gear the psychology of their populations to war. With their hate-fed civilians behind them, it is not surprising that the governments of industrialized countries have lacked moderation at peace tables or that some defeated powers have turned to totalitarianism to overturn unfavorable peace treaties.

To some observers total war and totalitarianism signal an absolute moral decline. To the historian of crusades, religious wars, and divine-right monarchies, the will to exterminate foes and establish total uniformity appears far from novel. Compared to the warriors of earlier periods, today's military powers justify their deeds by secular rather than religious ideologies. What is decisively new is their access to unprecedented control over technological knowledge including the means of mass communications. From this point of view the industrialized world has been trying to pour new technological oil into old institutional bottles. Whatever interpretation he takes, the student cannot dispute that—no matter how capable industrial society is of recuperating from "conventional warfare"—World Wars I and II drastically reduced Europe's productive capacity and left only one major power yet unscathed.

Long before the implications of this "open-ended 'revolution' " became apparent, industrialization began to affect the popular ideology and politics of Western societies.

## SELECTED READINGS

Ashton, Thomas S., *An Economic History of England: The Eighteenth Century*, Barnes & Noble, New York, 1955.

   Describes the structure of population, agriculture, transportation, manufacturing, shipping, exchange, and labor during the early period of industrialization emphasizing continuity rather than revolutionary developments.

*————, *The Industrial Revolution, 1760–1830,* Home University Library, London, 1949, and a Galaxy Book.

   A lucid short treatment of early English industrialization sympathetic to the plight of entrepreneurs and emphasizing the role of credit and banks.

Bowden, Witt, Michael Karpovich, and A. P. Usher, *An Economic History of Europe Since 1750,* American Book Co., New York, 1937.

   An old account well balanced and still useful.

Buer, M. C., *Health, Wealth and Population in the Early Days of the Industrial Revolution,* Routledge, London, 1926.

   Indispensable for the subjects of subsistence and longevity.

Cameron, Rondo E., *France and the Economic Development of Europe 1800–1914,* Princeton University Press, Princeton, 1961.

* Asterisk (*) denotes paperback.

   Traces the use of French capital on the Continent, especially to build railways, and its impact in spurring industrialization there.

Chambers, Jonathan D., *The Workshop of the World: British Economic History from 1820 to 1880,* Home University Library, London, 1961.

   An analysis of the British economy during its period of world leadership in industrial production.

*Cipolla, Carlo, *Economic History of World Population,* Penguin Books, Baltimore, Md., 1962.

   A very brief history of world population which puts in sharp focus the ability of industrial society to sustain large populations.

Clapham, John, *An Economic History of Modern Britain,* University Press, Cambridge, 1951–1959, 3 vols.

   Detailed running account from the railway age after 1820 to the organization of big business, labor, and government in the twentieth century.

————, *The Economic Development of France and Germany, 1815–1914,* University Press, Cambridge, 1955 (4th ed.).

   A standard descriptive account.

Clough, Shepard B., *The Economic Development of Western Civilization,* McGraw-Hill, New York, 1959.

   An excellent up-to-date economic history.

*Cottrell, William F., *Energy and Society,* McGraw-Hill, New York, 1959.

   Describes the introduction of energy-conversion machines using natural fuels as the basic divide separating "low energy" past and present societies from industrialized societies having "high energy" consumption per capita.

Deane, Phyllis, *The First Industrial Revolution,* University Press, Cambridge, 1965.

   Based on research by others, this study analyzes the factors of economic growth in the British economy between 1750 and 1850.

Deane, Phyllis and W. A. Cole, *British Economic Growth 1688–1959, Trends and Structure,* University Press, Cambridge, 1962.

   Using the oldest industrial economy, the

authors marshal available long-term quantitative data for the testing of theories of economic growth.

Dunham, Arthur L., *The Industrial Revolution in France 1815–1848,* Exposition Press, New York, 1955.
A topic-by-topic survey that provides much detail but it is not easy reading.

Fuller, John F. C., *The Conduct of War 1789–1961, A Study of the Impact of the French, Industrial and Russian Revolutions on War and Its Conduct,* Eyre, Spottiswoode, London, 1961.
A caustic critique of modern total warfare by a British general who finds much of its origins in technological developments beginning with the railroad.

George, M. Dorothy, *England in Transition: Life and Work in the Eighteenth Century,* Penguin Books, London, 1953.
A masterly survey of the social process of early industrialization which destroys romantic myths concerning subsistence and working conditions in preindustrial England.

Griffith, G. T., *Population Problems of the Age of Malthus,* University Press, Cambridge, 1926.
Critical for the early debate on the relationship of population to subsistence.

Habakuk, H. J. and M. Postan, eds., *The Cambridge Economic History of Europe,* Volume VI, *The Industrial Revolution and After: Incomes, Population and Technological Change (I),* University Press, Cambridge, 1965.
Disjointed discussions of income, world population, technological changes in agriculture and industry, and the industrialization of the United States, Russia, and the Far East.

Henderson, William O., *The Industrial Revolution in Europe: Germany, France, Russia, 1900–1914,* Quadrangle Books, Chicago, 1961.
A pioneering and none too successful effort to relate the industrial development of the Continent.

Hobson, J. A., *The Evolution of Modern Capitalism: A Study of Machine Production,* Allen & Unwin, London; Macmillan, New York, 1954 (4th ed.).
A basic study with important observations on trading patterns.

Knowles, Lilian C. A., *Economic Development in the Nineteenth Century, France, Germany, Russia, and the United States,* Routledge, London, 1932.
A general summary that includes information on tariffs and trade policies, domestic and foreign.

*Mantoux, Paul, *The Industrial Revolution in the Eighteenth Century,* Harper & Row, New York, 1962.
A reprint of an old but sound discussion of English industrial mechanization.

Mumford, Lewis, *Technics and Civilization,* Harcourt, Brace & World, New York, 1934.
Insight-filled associations between machines, the culture they arose from, and the problems they present.

Pounds, Norman J. G. and William N. Parker, *Coal and Steel in Western Europe,* Indiana University Press, Bloomington, Indiana, 1957.
Historical geography of the basic industrial resources emphasizing disparities between their distribution and political boundaries.

Rosen, George, *A History of Public Health,* MD Publications, New York, 1958.
Discusses improvements in sanitation and their relationship to population growth.

*Toynbee, A., *The Industrial Revolution,* Beacon Press, Boston, 1956.
The classic that crystallized the term "industrial revolution" in English usage.

*Usher, Abbott P., *A History of Mechanical Inventions,* Beacon Press, Boston, 1959.
Superbly illustrated account of which Chapters XI through XV apply to the era of power machinery.

Ward, J. T., *The Factory Movement 1830–1855,* St. Martin's Press, New York, 1962.
Chronicles the public agitation to secure regulation of factories in England during the first half of the nineteenth century.

# VII

# *Intellectual and Ideological Ferment in the Age of Realism and Science*

Undermined by science and industry, one inherited certainty after another broke down during the nineteenth century. People living in industrial cities were unable to accept the aristocratic paternalism of traditionalists and romantics and therefore joined new political and social movements. Scientists, technologists, and social theorists gained prestige among townspeople at the traditionalists' expense. At least among those who reaped tangible benefits from them, science and industry revived the Enlightenment's faith in progress and social ameliorization. Their visible impact fostered a more pervasive this-worldly realism among their apologists and foes than any previous generation had witnessed. The "realism" so engendered was not that of philosophers; rather, it was a way of looking at human realities apart from supernatural explanations or remedies.

Realism took different and conflicting forms, but they were all consistent in displacing traditional idealistic and theological viewpoints. In the world as a whole, European religions expanded sensationally during the second half of the nineteenth century, but the greatest growth occurred in colonial areas. In industrial Europe itself, the traditional established churches that were hostile to modern thought and society were displaced, at least among urban people, by dogmatic secular rivals. Only churchmen who became involved in new social problems or absorbed secular doctrines as their own were not displaced. They found some doctrines, such as nationalism, congenial because they were "spiritual." They tagged other doctrines, such as socialism, ephemeral "ideologies." Nevertheless, these anticlerical "ideologies" continued to spread.

Secular dogmatists contended among themselves over possession of *the* truth.

271

From a few authoritative premises they deduced conflicting "scientific" world views, which claimed to hold the key to the laws of historical evolution—the new providence—and a solution to the riddles of the universe. Like the clergy, these new metaphysicians described their rivals derogatorily as "ideologists." At higher intellectual levels they wrestled with age-old philosophical problems, such as the origin and validity of human knowledge, the origin of evil, standards of conduct, and providential determinism versus free and conscious will. At the cruder level of propaganda, they sought to harness public passions for ends that, spiritual or material, were secular in orientation.

Above all else, nineteenth-century thinkers attempted to discover natural or scientific laws operating in society. Industrialization persistently and irrepressibly made economic considerations a part of their raw materials. Rapid social change created crises for those who believed in an unchanging, divinely ordained order, and static metaphysics gave way before evolutionary theory and speculative, historical sociology. Social theorists now sought to explain the principles that govern social change itself.

Unlike natural scientists, the new social scientists could not agree on an acceptable method for discovering and demonstrating the laws that govern society. Bona fide empiricists attempted to investigate social data or history without metaphysical, theological, or a priori assumptions, but they were few. Most "social scientists" worked with a set of precepts borrowed from evolutionary philosophy or from physics and biology. Dominant among these various "scientific" ideologists were the various types of Darwinists whose views of nature were taken from evolutionary biology. Significantly, this model had little resemblance to the harmonious Newtonian world of natural laws beneficent to the individual. Rather, it portrayed nature as a sanguinary jungle of natural antagonisms and a struggle to the death for survival in which the species or collective group, not the individual, counted. In espousing the theory of the "survival of the fittest," evolutionists retained the Enlightenment's idea of progress. For them, however, it was an inexorable law of nature, the outgrowth of natural struggles for survival, not the product of human knowledge or humanitarian efforts to mitigate savagery.

Reflecting contemporary social and political antagonisms, evolutionary social doctrines split into several "scientific" ideologies. In industrialized countries conservative "Social Darwinism" provided a rationale for giving all initiative to the industrial and financial elite. Although it was formulated in England, its assumptions more accurately fit conditions in preindustrial societies. Meanwhile, "reform" Social Darwinism provided a new basis for progressive liberalism. Also rising to oppose conservative Social Darwinism was the uncompromising class-conscious socialism of Karl Marx. Marx, who was steeped in Hegel's philosophy of evolutionary progress through conflict, immediately recognized similarities between his advocacy of class warfare and Darwin's natural selection of species. Even though it was intended for industrial workers, Marxism ironically proved more adaptable to retarded but developing areas where traditionalists attempted to repress the social and political effects of industrialization. But the most common form of evolutionary ideology was still a different application of Darwinism—the nationalist and imperialist argument that warfare regenerated human society. Thus realism, an old and recurrent aspect of Western thought, gave cynical, deterministic, and "scientific" connotations to the thirst for bloodshed. By the end of the nineteenth century, "spiritual" Darwinist nationalists were locked in conflict with "materialistic" evolutionary socialists, both of them claiming to have absolute scientific truth.

Their dogmatic clash created a crisis for the whole idea of a social science, because some observers considered this conflict proof that no objective study of society was possible. Romantic realists cast further doubts on the objectivity of any social science by probing the role of instincts and unpredictable, irrational environmental influences in the determination of individual behavior. Mathematicians of "relativity," although they believed in a fixed objective reality, inadvertently gave impetus to the antiscientific revolt by questioning popularly accepted physical "laws of nature." Among the youth of the generation just before World War I, mystical cults of irrationality took root. Nationalist and religious historians everywhere had long been following the subjectivist approach, and now German philosophers and historians were making subjectivism into a formal system. Separating physical science sharply from social studies, they considered social truth to be entirely relative to the investigators' value systems. To these challenges of irrationality and subjectivism, chastened rationalists and empiricists replied with sociological and psychological methods that claimed only tentative and hypothetical validity. Their concessions to irrationality were sufficient, however, to question the basic assumptions of rationality on which classic liberalism rested.*

## RESPONSES TO INDUSTRIALIZATION

Both of the new urban industrial classes—capitalists and workers—faced novel problems to which traditional institutions responded slowly or negatively, and initially both were critical of existing political and religious creeds. Middle-class intellectuals formulated new ideologies for each of them. For entrepreneurs and financiers they elaborated a most congenial tenet from the doctrines of Adam Smith: *laissez faire* or nonintervention by public authority in the management of production and distribution. Outside England, however, *laissez faire* was not generally considered to be a bar to

---

* For the rational premises of nineteenth-century liberalism, see *supra*, pp. 193–195.

tariffs or to public support of business through subsidized commercial facilities. Laborers, left to their own devices, seldom went beyond the organizing of unions for winning immediate economic objectives. Usually only the more highly skilled and paid among them succeeded in holding their organizations together through strikes or depressions. But intellectuals, who were sympathetic to labor's conditions or critical of economic instability, supplied various alternatives to private *laissez-faire* capitalism in the form of state intervention, cooperatives, or state ownership. And by the end of the century, union-based socialist parties headed major movements in most industrialized European nations.

## The Evolution of Liberal Economics

In Britain, the hearth of classical liberal economics, Thomas Malthus dampened Adam Smith's humanitarian optimism with a cold shower of economic realism. In his *Essay on the Principles of Population* (1798), Malthus rejected the idea of progress and predicted gloom. If unchecked, he said, men multiply by a geometric ratio and thus outstrip subsistence, which increases only by an arithmetic ratio. Grossly excess numbers would be removed, luckily, by war, famine, and plague; misery and vice would continue to operate as checks on the multiplication of the poor. Although they blame institutions, the niggardliness of nature, or others for their plight, poor people are responsible for their own want. Government intervention, higher wages, and charity would not relieve it. The only remedy that Malthus sanctioned was moral restraint—late marriages and chastity (he rejected birth-control measures suggested by Condorcet and other advocates of progress). In this and other works, Malthus, a clergyman by training, established himself as the leading early professional economist. To contemporaries who disagreed with him, he was the pessimistic architect of the "dismal science" of economics. Classical economists and Charles Darwin considered that Malthus had contributed an enduring element, foreign to Adam Smith's optimism: an inexorable struggle for survival as the basic law of nature.

Using some of Malthus' premises, David Ricardo (1772–1823) jettisoned Smith's automatic harmony of interests established at the marketplace. He saw the interests of landowners, industrial capitalists, and individual wage earners locked in antagonism. By an iron law of nature, real wages could not rise for long above subsistence levels. If employers increased the fund set aside for wages, the number of competing laborers would increase, which would drive wages back to or below the margin of subsistence. Declining fertility of the soil would cause subsistence costs to rise, thus consuming additional money paid as wages. Industrial entrepreneurs, on the other hand, were threatened, he argued, by the rents of parasitical landlords. As marginal lands were forced into production by a population increase, rents from better lands would rise without any increase in productivity. Industrial profits would then fall as a result of paying unearned rents and higher money wages. Shorn of many qualifications and reservations, Ricardo's pessimistic economics provided a rationale for industrial capitalism's two-front struggle against landlords and labor and gained for its formulator international prominence.

Malthus and Ricardo provided classical economists with their basic assumptions. Economic society operated according to a few natural laws of supply and demand, rent, wages, and population. Intervention by government or charity, public or private, would only upset the operation of these laws. Subsequent economic developments indicated that the classical economists failed to take full account of immense increases in agricultural and industrial productivity. Nevertheless, their doctrines were congenial to captains of industry and finance. For the poor and for those who sympathized with their plight, the conclusions of classical economics had little appeal. Ironically, however, their premises and analyses, especially Ricardo's, served socialists as well as capitalists. Karl Marx, among others, drew heavily upon them.

As economic conditions changed, the economic doctrines of liberalism changed and broke into divergent streams. One was the conservative liberalism of Herbert Spencer (1820–1903), who coined the phrase, the "survival of the fittest." Spencer adjusted the doctrine of *laissez faire* to guard against governmental intervention while corporations and combinations of capital— in some cases monopolies—were replacing individual proprietorships and partnerships in heavy industry. A "synthetic philosopher" who combined deductions both shrewd and erratic with contemporary science and social theory, he wrote prolifically on a vast array of subjects. He described all state intervention—public charity, state banking, sanitation and housing inspection, health and safety codes—as "socialism." His social science demonstrated the impossibility of conscious change, at least for the poor or unfit. Such people should be eliminated to make way for a new human nature in a coming era of peace and industry.

The poverty of the incapable, the distresses that come upon the imprudent, the starvation of the idle, and those shoulderings aside of the weak by the strong, which leave so many "in shallows and in miseries," [he wrote] are the decrees of a large far-seeing benevolence. It seems hard that an unskillfulness, which with all his efforts he cannot overcome, should entail hunger upon the artisan. It seems hard that a laborer incapacitated by sickness from competing with his stronger fellows, should have to bear the resulting privations. It seems hard that widows and orphans should be left to struggle for life and death. Nevertheless, when regarded not separately, but in connection with the interests of universal humanity, these harsh fatalities are seen to be full of the highest beneficence. . . .

There are many very amiable people . . . who have not the nerve to look this matter fairly in the face. Disabled as they are by their sympathies with present suffering, from duly regarding ultimate consequences, they pursue a course which is very injudicious, and in the end even cruel. . . . All defenders of a poor-law must, however, be classed amongst such.[1]

Accompanying Spencer's gospel of resignation for the unfit was his emphasis on the importance of business success for the elite, whose philanthropy should help those who are capable of survival to help themselves. He gathered most of his following from the "self-made men" who built personal industrial and financial empires.

In Britain government intervention was already an accomplished fact when Spencer wrote, but he found a ready response and financial assistance in America from such business leaders as Andrew Carnegie and John D. Rockefeller, and from academics as well. His American followers secured recognition of his laws of nature in court decisions curtailing labor unions, but they were selective in popularizing his work. Few of them, for example, evinced interest in his doctrine of free trade.

"Bourgeois liberalism," which in Europe sought to maintain property restrictions on suffrage and to limit education to those who could afford it, had its culmination in Spencer. Breaking with the bourgeois liberals in Western Europe were "democratic liberals" who, looking to the United States as a model, advocated universal manhood suffrage, primary education at public expense, and some modifications of *laissez faire* to recognize labor organizations and to permit state intervention in matters of health and safety. Motives for this break were probably many. In Britain they were partly political. Liberals were competing with Disraeli's "Tory Democracy" for the political loyalty

*Herbert Spencer, prophet of Social Darwinism.*

of the working classes. Evangelical churchmen were cultivating a social consciousness that held society, not just individual shortcomings, responsible in some measure for the squalor and poverty of the poor. This moral impulse, which impelled many to go beyond liberalism to socialist politics, Christian socialism, and a "social gospel," was reinforced by the Utilitarians whose intellectual leader at mid-century was John Stuart Mill.

The Utilitarians inherited from Jeremy Bentham a tradition of legal reform, empirical methodology, a crude materialistic rational psychology, and the premise that the purpose of government was the greatest good for the greatest number. At first they had been vociferous advocates of *laissez faire*. At the same time, however, they adhered to the use of reason, law, education, eventual manhood suffrage, and the restriction of births as a means of mitigating social conditions. John Stuart Mill (1806–1873) went further in search of a balance between social justice and property rights. Although he remained

1. Herbert Spencer, *Social Statics; or, the Conditions Essential to Human Happiness,* Appleton and Co., New York, 1886, pp. 353–354.

a democratic liberal, he reluctantly became sympathetic to certain socialist points of view. He rejected the Calvinist attitude that poverty was the result of individual moral faults and instead advocated reliance on institutions, leadership, and a secular education that would teach youth a sense of social justice. Thus he contributed to the "social gospel" movement, which at the end of the century brought segments of British liberalism, socialism, and religious reform movements together in a common cause.

In addition to the continuing traditions of bourgeois and democratic liberalism, a new variant—"social liberalism"—became discernible at the turn of the century. Social liberals, such as David Lloyd George in England, advocated the use of social security measures to curb business cycles, the expansion of public educational opportunities, and the introduction of income and inheritance taxes as a means of reducing inequalities in wealth and income. Few social liberals advocated extensive state ownership of the means of distribution and production, but they nevertheless worked more easily with democratic socialist parties, which were committed to partial nationalization, than with Spencerian Darwinists.

## *"Utopian Socialism"*

Although democratic liberals shared some ground with "advanced" or social liberals, they generally stood for a private, competitive economy regulated primarily by the mechanism of the market. They tended, especially at first, to emphasize the economic processes that led to capital formation and increased production. Opposing democratic liberalism, various categories of socialists sought to substitute association and cooperation for competition, to put the ownership of the means of production and distribution in the hands of collective associations or the state, and to bring productive processes and the ups and downs of the business cycle under rational control for a broader distribution of industrial wealth. Socialist objections to the economic and political inequalities of both the Old Regime and industrial society were moral and ideological as well as economic. Ideologically they represented an extension of "liberty, equality, and fraternity" from the legal to the economic realm. Socialists denounced liberal individualistic morality on the grounds that economic freedom of the entrepreneurs amounted to the freedom of the working classes to starve amidst increasing plenty. The labor theory of value held by John Locke, Adam Smith, and David Ricardo led most of the socialists to conclude that the capitalists' economic and political power enabled them to appropriate labor's product for themselves, leaving only subsistence wages for the laborers. Moreover, the propertyless classes bore the brunt of depression and unemployment. They could hardly be expected to acquiesce in Spencer's dictum that their elimination as the "unfit" was a step toward progress and humanitarianism.

Early nineteenth-century socialism arose from the industrial environment of Britain and the revolutionary tradition of France. The men who formulated it ranged from humanitarian intellectuals who abhorred class violence to advocates of violent revolution who were anarchists as well as socialists. Occasionally, industrial managers such as Robert Owen joined in posing alternatives to the *status quo*. Seldom, however, did they build political organizations to achieve their ends. Initially, few socialists had broad support from the working classes in whose cause or name they worked. Because most of them relied on persuasion rather than force or on altruism rather than interest, Karl Marx branded them "Utopians," a label that conservatives have also adopted and made general.

Disillusioned with the course and outcome of the revolution of 1789, French liberals inaugurated criticism of *laissez-faire* capitalism. In 1819, Jean Simonde de Sismondi (1773–1842) questioned Adam Smith's conclusion that an "invisible hand"

*Jean Simonde de Sismondi, "Utopian socialist."*

*Claude Saint-Simon, technocratic "socialist."*

presiding over the marketplace best guaranteed the common weal. His *New Principles of Political Economy* stopped short of socialism or public ownership of the means of production and distribution, but it did advocate credit regulation, division of inheritance, and profit sharing as the means of creating a larger number of intermediate capitalists, checking the business cycles, and preventing the growth of two antagonistic classes of workers and owners. Empirical statistics accumulated by Sismondi's followers to demonstrate the validity of his criticism were subsequently used by French socialists for more drastic purposes.

Another disillusioned French liberal was Henri de Saint-Simon (1760–1825). After having participated in the American Revolution and having renounced his title during the French Revolution, Saint-Simon concluded that revolution had failed to do away with one cardinal privilege—unearned or inherited wealth. His solution was leadership by an elite—bankers, engineers, industrialists—who should rule according to scientific and humanitarian principles. This elite would promote efficiency and assure a more just distribution of wealth. It would also furnish the high priests of a renovated, this-worldly religion, the "New Christianity," which would reinforce humanitarianism. Saint-Simon did not envisage a classless society any more than Sismondi. Rewards were to be distributed on the basis of performance. To achieve that end more equitably, society should provide productive tools from a "social fund," establish a state bank to exercise a monopoly of credit, and abolish inheritance rights. Saint-Simon's technocratic doctrines secured their greatest following among youthful engineers, many of whom became the leading builders and managers of French foreign and domestic enterprise. Bankers and businessmen also welcomed his emphasis on a managerial elite, but they rejected his "New Christianity" and the religious cult of his followers which sent its high priest on the search for a "woman messiah." Literary social critics popularized parts of his conclusions, and

Karl Marx, who considered his reform by persuasion naïve, obtained basic notions from his writings. Saint-Simon's secretary, Auguste Comte, went in still another direction. He developed a scientific concept of an evolutionary society which would rely on military discipline as a means of directing or manipulating the social structure.

Most French Utopians used persuasion in their attempts to replace individualism with some form of organic collective that would emphasize social solidarity and interdependence. Two activist exceptions were Louis Blanc and Auguste Blanqui. Blanc appealed to intellectuals by the written word, but he also secured some labor support and became a member of the short-lived provisional government in Paris in 1848. He attacked *laissez-faire* economics as bestowing the freedom to let men die. As a remedy he proposed a system of "social workshops" to supply machines and tools to workmen and to guarantee employment at a living wage. The government that he served instituted "national workshops," but they were set up more for relief than as a substitute for capitalism as Blanc had intended. The revolutionary government also established a few cooperatives and a labor-employer council under his leadership, but his influence was more ephemeral than the abortive revolution itself. Another consequential but politically impotent socialist was Auguste Blanqui. Jailed for most of his life, he kept the faith in violence alive in revolutionary intellectual circles.

British Utopianism, which was cultivated during the wars of the French Revolution in the anticlerical natural-rights philosophy of Thomas Paine and the anarchism of William Godwin, took a socialist course under the leadership of Robert Owen (1771–1858), manager of a well-known cotton factory in New Lanark, Scotland. His radical contemporaries were turning Ricardo's premises against *laissez faire* when Owen broke with fellow managers, turned New Lanark into a model community, and led agitation for

*Robert Owen's New Lanark.*

labor organization and factory legislation. He accepted mechanized industry and private property, but argued that both should be used to promote general human welfare. He shared with other socialists the Enlightenment's faith in human perfectibility, progress, and the development of a science of society. Convinced that human nature was largely the product of environment, he sought to change that environment to produce greater happiness and morality. His humanitarian environmentalism brought him in direct conflict with the Christian doctrine of the depravity of man, and, as he experimented with communitarian settlements on the American frontier, he became sharply anticlerical. Both his labor organization and communitarian experiments eventually failed. Although only a cooperative store movement that he started has endured, some observers consider him a precursor of twentieth-century "scientific management."

### Marxian Socialism—an Ambiguous Legacy

The transition from "Utopian" to "scientific" socialism, which was introduced by Karl Marx (1818–1883) and Friedrich Engels (1820–1895) in the *Communist Manifesto* of 1848, was part of a general switch of the intellectuals to "realism." Marxian socialism emerged at the same time that romantic nationalists became advocates of national unification by force. Instead of attempting to soften class antagonisms, Marxism sought to spur class consciousness among the workers so that they would come to power and eradicate the roots of class antagonism—private ownership of the means of production and distribution and the irrational economic cycles determined by the market. At first Marxism remained confined to narrow intellectual circles, but during the last quarter of the century it became a major political movement in Central Europe. At this point, however, it began to break into divergent and eventually hostile camps. Marx and Engels recommended different courses of action at different times and places. When some of Marx's predictions failed to occur, revisionists challenged his basic premises. Because local Marxists responded differently to local conditions, some of their parties adopted practically all local reform projects concerned with individual liberty and well-being, whereas others pursued violent revolution and totalitarian objectives. Still others took intermediate positions. Thus Marxism became an ambiguous blueprint for action.

Like Herbert Spencer, whom he resembled in method and utopian expectations, Marx put together a broad synthesis of economics, history, philosophy, politics, prophetic moral judgments, and sociology, which offered a total world view. Hegelian philosophy taught him to derive the key law of nature from historical evolution, but, unlike Hegel, Marx concluded that the purpose of philosophy was not to explain and contemplate evolution, but to change the world within the limits set by the historical context. The extent to which change could be accomplished depended on circumstances, particularly on the prevailing "mode of production" or the ownership, control, and organization of the means of production. He traced the evolution of successive modes of production from primitive communal societies through master-slave, lord-peasant, and capitalist-laborer relationships to a future classless, socialist state. The Hegelian idea of the imperfection

of the present—documented by the downtrodden condition of the proletariat or propertyless citizenry—proved to Marx that evolution toward perfection was still necessary. Thus Marx laid the groundwork, which Engels fully developed into "historical" or "dialectical materialism." But in practice he did not wait passively for its automatic achievement any more than John Calvin had waited idly for divine Providence to produce a Reformation. His career was that of an activist; he ceaselessly researched, wrote, organized, exhorted, and fended off competitors. His dream was to instill class consciousness in the industrial proletariat and to bring forth the promise that he saw in industrial technology.

For Marx, the meat of history was a struggle between classes, but his total interest was devoted to a struggle within industrial society between the owners of the means of production and the proletariat or propertyless workers who, he assumed, would become the overwhelming majority. In the *Communist Manifesto,* he and Engels praised the immense historical role played by the bourgeoisie. But although they expanded production and created a world market, their economic system worked to expropriate the artisan, the peasant, and the weaker capitalists. Marx marshaled the arguments for this conclusion from the classical economists themselves, especially from their labor theory of value. The value added by labor, they had asserted, was divided between wages and profits. Marx saw the withholding of "surplus value" from wages for the accrual of capital as an exploitation that public ownership would terminate. With this simple explanation of poverty and subsistence pressures, with the promise of a golden age in the future under public ownership of the means of production, and with a readily identifiable agent of evil, popularized Marxism eventually secured a favorable reception —in part rational, in part emotional— among *urban industrial* populations. For the countryside and preindustrial society, Marx himself and his orthodox followers prior to Lenin had little interest or sympathy.

Marx proclaimed his basic objectives in 1848, but he and his followers, preoccupied with the means of securing a revolution, offered no detailed blueprint for society after the revolution had occurred. For the most advanced countries, the *Communist Manifesto* called for the abolition of private landed property and the right of inheritance; a graduated income tax; the centralization and control of credit, communications, transportation, and the means of production in the hands of the state; equal obligation of all to work; abolition of distinctions between industry and agriculture; and free public education for children freed from child labor. In highly industrialized countries where democratic channels were open, Marx believed, his program could be obtained peacefully.

After the revolutionary fiasco of 1848 to 1849 in Central Europe and after the suppression of the Paris Commune in 1871, Marx's thoughts returned to the example of the French Revolution. Thereafter he wrote on both sides of the question—evolution and violent revolution. *Das Kapital (Capital),* his last major work, sought to demonstrate that capitalism, beset by inherent, internal contradictions, would fall of its own weight. Centralization and concentration of capital would force small capitalists into the burgeoning ranks of the proletariat, and periodic depressions would bring intolerable pressures to bear on industrial urban classes. With capitalist appropriation of surplus labor value unchecked, the working classes would become increasingly miserable. Moreover, as the rates of domestic profit declined—a thesis that Ricardo had also advanced—capitalism must inevitably expand in imperialism or die. Marx thus left a legacy that called for both violent revolution and inevitable evolution, although preliminary industrialization was necessary in either case.

Before Marx's death in 1883, political parties had begun to organize on the Continent that were composed primarily of non-revolutionary trade-union members but were led by Marxian intellectuals. After 1889, these parties were coordinated by the loosely confederated Second International Workingman's Association,* within which the best-organized and dominant group was the German Social Democratic party. The Social Democrats combined the followers of Ferdinand Lassalle, a nationalist who sought democratization and the establishment of government-financed producers' cooperatives, and Marxian internationalists such as Karl Kautsky (1854–1938) and August Bebel (1840–1913). Party platforms spoke of a coming revolution, but simultaneously demanded comprehensive democratization and social-welfare programs, whose implementation would ultimately diminish revolutionary fervor. Attacked by Bismarck's government, the party became the largest in the German Reichstag, but its members were rigorously excluded from the civil service and from universities. Its leaders refused to share office with the bourgeoisie and the aristocracy, and they used their influence in the Second International in 1904 to force a French socialist minister, Millerand, to resign from the cabinet. The leadership, which rejected cooperation with other social classes, was undermined by the rise of "revisionist" platforms that were formulated, with individual differences, by Eduard Bernstein in Germany, Jean Jaurès in France, and their counterparts elsewhere. Bernstein, who had observed British politics in exile, attacked fundamental Marxist tenets. His *Evolutionary Socialism* (1898) concluded that, in fact, the middle classes were not decreasing under capitalism, that the law of increasing worker

---

* The First International Workingman's Association (1864–1876) dissolved as a result of internal quarrels between Marx and the anarchist Bakunin, and because of controversy surrounding its endorsement of the Paris Commune of 1870 to 1871.

misery was inoperative, and that depressions left behind a higher standard of living than had existed before. Revisionism opened a breach in Marxist orthodoxy through which flowed humanitarian idealism, patriotism, and, as long as the entire population profited from it, imperialism.

Even though most revisionists continued to believe in an inevitable evolution toward socialism, revisionist heresies undercut Marxism as a crusading revolutionary faith. Orthodox Marxist apologists counterattacked, to show that Marx's alleged errors were an illusion. The most common orthodox argument was that monopolistic capitalism, far from uniting the world, was living parasitically from imperialism, and that imperialism would soon turn Europe into a military holocaust. When the predicted cataclysm occurred, revolutionary Marxism reaped the benefit not so much from the fulfillment of prophecy as from the fact that World War I undermined all ideologies of gradual progress, including democratic socialism, and elevated Russia to the center of socialist attention.

The shift of the center of Marxian gravity eastward, where conditions were conducive to violent revolution, involves those who approach history strictly on the basis of professed creeds or ideologies in a logical paradox. Marx related his analysis and predictions to advanced industrial conditions. But, revolutionary Marxism, which was tailored by Lenin and others so as to apply to preindustrial or nascent industrial conditions, has actually appealed more to areas where a life-or-death struggle for existence has existed, whether or not an ideology of the survival of the fittest was professed. Economic crises and war destruction have nurtured revolutionary Marxism in some industrialized Western countries, but since 1917 it has flourished best in climates of economic backwardness under strains of initial industrialization, population pressure, and callous social policies of the Old Regime.

Lenin (Vladimir Ilich Ulyanov), the principal architect of a new program that was later called Marxism-Leninism, was the leader of the minority ("Bolshevik")* faction within the Russian Social Democratic Party after 1903. Because the urban proletarian majority that Marx anticipated did not exist, Lenin relied on a disciplined elitist party to wield a dictatorship of and over the proletariat. That elite would guide a "leap over stages" rather than wait for industrialization under the direction of the bourgeoisie. Opposing reform under existing governments lest it postpone general revolution, Lenin relied on a revolutionary dictatorship, thus sidestepping parliamentary government. For he, like the traditional conservatives, considered representative government a mask for plutocracy. An abortive revolution in 1905 convinced Lenin, who was an attentive student of earlier revolutions, that the Bolsheviks would have to win support of the peasantry in order to disarm the Tsarist armies. He rejected revisionism, attributing the continued vigor of capitalism to its exploitation of colonial peoples. Thus he accepted the claim that imperialism was profitable, and in reply he championed colonial self-determination. Although he anticipated international cooperation among anti-imperialistic forces, he was in fact seeking to align Bolshevism (Communism) with colonial independence movements, thereby cutting off the alleged source of capitalistic strength.

## Christian Socialism, Fabian Socialism, and the Social Gospel

Despite its partial British origins, Marxism was based on a period of crisis which had already passed in Britain. Except in Ireland, British conditions were no longer sufficiently desperate to make extremist programs attractive. Moreover, religious and non-Marxism secular movements had already

* Literally, Bolshevik means "majority," for *at the party congress* in exile, although not in Russia, Lenin obtained a majority.

*Charles Kingsley, advocate of Christian socialism.*

*Fabian election leaflet.*

preempted the field of industrial reform. Unlike the labor movements and the ecclesiastical establishments on the Continent, which were mutually hostile, British labor politics largely grew out of a religious and humanitarian milieu.

"Christian socialism" as a response to industrialization first appeared among Evangelical Anglicans, led by Charles Kingsley (1819–1875), a novelist, historian, priest, and social critic. Kingsley preceded Marx in denouncing merely creedal Christianity as an opiate for the lower classes, and he attacked an economy based exclusively on self-interest as a repudiation of Christian principles. Although he considered socialism a Christian heresy, his practical program was limited to the establishment of cooperatives that were financed at low interest rates by wealthy and pious Christians. His immediate impact was slight, but the "social gospel" continued within Anglicanism, spread to lower-class Non-Conformists, and in the twentieth century espoused more radical proposals with respect to private property.

Evangelical Christian socialism applied such medieval ideals as the "just price" and social solidarity to conditions of farm and urban labor. More secular, usually less romantic, but also imbued with a social-gospel concept were the gradualists who became known as the Fabian socialists. The Fabian Society, whose ultimate goal was the nationalization of the means of production and distribution, included such diverse, independent people as George Bernard Shaw, H. G. Wells, and the husband-wife combination of Sydney and Beatrice Webb, who founded the London School of Economics and Political Science in 1895. Because the Fabians dominated English social thought at the outset of the twentieth century, they wielded influence disproportionate to the numbers, especially within the new Labour party. The Fabian Society and the Labour party contained large contingents of Methodists. Still another departure for the social gospel in welfare work in both Britain and the United States was William Booth's Salvation Army. British socialism, of course, also had purely secular sources and strains. Henry George, American author of *Progress and Poverty* (1879) which advocated a single tax on land to divert unearned increases of land values to public purposes, won more converts from *laissez faire* in Britain (and Scandinavia) than Marx.

Protestant social-reform movements also took root in the United States and Germany after the late nineteenth century. In America, they sympathized with problems of the lower classes, which they viewed as a result not of human depravity but of environment and the economic system. Like the seventeenth-century Quakers, advocates of the American social gospel sought at least partially to build the Kingdom of God on earth, but they usually stopped short of socialism. In Germany, the liberal Christianity of Friedrich Naumann (1860–1919) closely approximated certain aspects of the British and American movements, but whereas the latter had pacifist overtones, Naumann sought to reconcile the working classes to the national quest for power. At the court of William I, Adolph Stöker, the Prussian Lutheran preacher, represented a more radical form of German "Christian Socialism." Stöcker urged income and death taxes, a ten-hour day, and other reforms that would equalize economic opportunities, but he tied his program to authoritarian government and to anti-Semitism that would eliminate Jews from commerce. Bismarck, who also relied upon religious concepts for social legislation and to justify power politics, became alarmed by Stöcker's radicalism and secured his dismissal in 1889.

*Pope Leo XIII.*

After a period of suppressing liberals and modernists, the Roman Catholic hierarchy under Pope Leo XIII (1878–1903) moved to grope with the social problems of industrialization. Following the revolutions of 1848, his predecessor, Pius IX, had repudiated his former concessions to liberalism, cemented the union of Throne and Altar, and extended clerical education in a series of concordats. In 1864, Pius IX turned his back on liberalism, "modern civilization," and progress in the *Syllabus of Errors*. During the 1870s, the Papacy lost its extensive territories in central Italy to the new Kingdom of Italy, anticlerical governments came to power in France and Germany, and secular ideologies were depriving the Church of working-class allegiance. Leo XIII conciliated the modernist Catholics and in 1891 issued a bull, *Rerum Novarum* (*Concerning New Things*), for which he was called in some quarters "the workingman's pope." The bull castigated abuses of economic power and advocated the formation of Catholic trade unions, but it made no concessions to either economic liberalism or socialism. Instead, it advocated under the term "corporatism" medieval ideals of a corporate society of estates, each with mutual moral ties, responsibilities and obligations. Although Leo used stern discipline against dissident clerical reactionaries, his struggle for modernism did not deeply penetrate either traditionalist or labor ranks. Some Catholic unions were formed, but most recruits to the Church's new stance came from the lower and middle classes and from the peasantry. Moreover, the Pope's immediate successor repudiated modernism in every form, and after World War I not a few clerics and parishioners backed the rise to power of totalitarian dictators who tailored their ideology to "corporatist" sentiments.

## Anarchism and Anarcho-Syndicalism

Anarchism, like socialism, originated in Western Europe. Theoretically, the goals of the two movements coincided, but their practical programs diverged sharply, and they took root in different environments. Socialists sought to increase political controls over society, at least until a stateless society would evolve. Anarchists, however, advocated the immediate removal of the social, economic, and political fetters restraining the individual. Their basic premise was that the individual, liberated from repressions, would be virtuous and cooperative. Anarchists shared with socialists an animosity toward existing governments, but they offered no political substitutes. At most, they advocated the building of an ideal society on a system of federations of economic groups. Socialist parties grew in highly industrialized areas, whereas anarchism spread primarily in Latin and Eastern Europe where people lacked confidence in the integrity of state officials.

The ideas of Charles Fourier (1772–1837), a drapery clerk, and Pierre Joseph Proudhon (1809–1865), who are often ranked among the Utopian socialists, reveal a confusing interrelationship between the two ideologies. Fourier rejected urban industrialization and sought to combine agriculture and handicrafts in a series of ideal communes. This combination, he believed, would eliminate business depressions and prevent industrial depersonalization. But the communes' theoretical population, a fanciful cross section of human traits, was unrealizable. Proudhon attacked the existing capitalist society as a contradiction-filled "new feudalism." Adopting the theory that labor alone created value in production, he advocated the establishment of an exchange bank at which labor's products could be exchanged for legal-tender coupons. To Marx's ideas, he contributed the vision of a future stateless, classless society, which would operate under the motto "From each according to his ability, to each according to his need." Despite such opinions and despite his celebrated catch phrase "Property is theft," Proudhon was not a socialist. By "property" in this context he meant unearned income—interest, rents, and promotional profits. Otherwise, he considered private property a bulwark against a strong state and against lower-class socialism. Proudhon, a self-educated printer who was too poor to secure a formal education, formulated a lower-middle-class revolt against both financial capitalism and organized labor. To achieve an ideal society, small property holders and workmen should combine within federations of producers and consumers. Proudhon despised government, including democratic government, but when he thought that Napoleon III would follow his program as a dictator, he welcomed him. Initially venting his wrath on liberal nationalism, Proudhon later glorified warfare as an antidote to socialism. Perhaps exaggerating, some historians have considered Proudhon a precursor of fascism.

Another apostle of anarchism was Mikhail Bakunin (1814–1876), a perennial Russian exile and an agitator for a return to primitive, governmentless nature by violent revo-

*Two anarchists, Proudhon (left) and Bakunin.*

lution. In the late nineteenth century, Bakunin's followers made themselves generally notorious by assassinating heads of state (including a Russian Tsar and presidents of the United States and France) in a futile attempt to do away with the visible badges of political authority. Anarchist terror, which was attributed by public opinion to all radicalism, discredited radical reform in general. In the form of anarcho-syndicalism, Bakunin's ideology penetrated parts of the European and American labor movements. Opposed to political parties, anarcho-syndicalists proposed to rely on syndicates of corporate economic structures, particularly industrial trade unions, which would use direct action such as sabotage or general strikes to weaken and overturn the capitalist order. The principal theorist of anarcho-syndicalism, Georges Sorel (1847–1922), a French engineer, believed that violence was a beneficial, purifying agent which alone could emotionally

unite the revolutionary proletariat. Sorel, a self-trained sociologist who explored irrational social motivations, was a principal popularizer of the general strike, with which Russian revolutionaries experimented in 1905 and which fascinated European socialist unions for a time thereafter.

## MAJOR NINETEENTH-CENTURY SCIENCES

Major syntheses in nineteenth-century physics and biology proved as corrosive of traditional certainties and as productive of ideological changes as the transformation of the social order by industrialization. These syntheses were rational constructs that explained the apparently contradictory phenomena of nature in terms of a single cause, as the operation of inexorable natural laws. These laws not only satisfied curiosity by explaining the world, but also proved valuable in medicine and technology. At the expense of philosophers and theologians, scientists gained more and more prestige as wielders of the only method of acquiring reliable knowledge.

## Physics

Physics, which had produced the world view that the universe operates as a machine, joined with chemistry in probing more significantly and more deeply into the seen and unseen nature of matter and motion. Stimulated by the operation and success of the steam engine to study thermodynamics, physicists formulated a new unifying concept—energy—to relate heat to motion. The Englishman Joule expressed heat in mathematical symbols that indicated its mechanical work potential. The German Ludwig Helmholtz added a general law of the conservation of energy to the already accepted premise that matter was indestructible. The universe's store of force, Helmholtz wrote, "cannot in any way be increased or diminished. . . . The quantity of force in Nature is just as eternal and unalterable as the quantity of matter."[2] In the new field of electricity, from which a whole new technology flowed, energy equivalents were also reduced to mathematical description. Heat produced by chemical reactions was also integrated into the unifying concept of energy. Theories concerning the composition of matter eventually coalesced around John Dalton's atomic theory that all matter was composed of a basic number of elements, and their combining weights were tabulated. Spectrum analysis, assisted by photography, aided the identification of these elements in laboratory and observatory. With the discovery of radium at the end of the century, the number of known elements rose from an initial twenty to more than eighty. Eventually, electrons rather than atoms appeared

to be the smallest units of matter, and many physicists believed, erroneously, that the atom operated as a small replica of the Newtonian solar universe.

Although part of the universe's structure, notably the elusive medium of "ether" through which light and electromagnetic waves passed, could not be empirically described, physics and chemistry until near the end of the century seemed to be filling in details of an absolutely known Newtonian universe. Mathematicians working with three-dimensional space began to conclude, however, that mathematical description yielded only a *symbolic* and incomplete representation of reality. Moreover, minute experimentation convinced Albert Einstein and others that Newtonian concepts were inadequate. In the early twentieth century, Einstein achieved a still broader synthesis in physics, which encompassed mass, energy, light, time, space, and electromagnetism within the same basic formula. But the physics and mathematics of relativity were not a philosophical relativism; they were based, rather, on rigorous experimentation and on the assumption of a fixed objective reality. Man's apprehension of this reality, however, was subject to limits and modifications because of his relative position within cosmic space and time.

## Biology

The premises and achievements of physical science encouraged popularizers to explain the universe, including the body and the mind, solely in terms of matter, but developments in biology were equally significant for nineteenth-century intellectual ferment. Biological research tended to move in two independent directions that seldom converged. One dealt with biochemistry, physiology, and heredity. The other explored the origin of species as a product of environmental influences.

Within the first type of biological science, bacteriology as an adjunct of medicine made the largest popular impact. Foremost among

2. From "The Conservation of Energy," *Classics of Modern Science,* Alfred A. Knopf, New York, 1927, p. 286.

*Louis Pasteur (left) and Robert Koch, "microbe hunters."*

early bacteriologists was Louis Pasteur (1822–1895), who concluded from studying fermentation and putrefaction that living organisms were responsible for certain chemical actions. Pasteur succeeded in controlling wine spoilage, a devastating silkworm disease, rabid hydrophobia, and the transmission of microorganisms in liquids and on surgical instruments. The germ theory of disease, to which Pasteur's work gave credence, was established by Robert Koch (1843–1910), who isolated and identified the bacilli causing tuberculosis and cholera and who identified rat-borne fleas as the transmitters of the bacilli causing bubonic plague. While other microbe hunters sought out and identified disease-causing "germs," surgery was transformed by the combination of chemical anesthesia and aseptic procedures that depended either on Joseph Lister's use of carbolic acid or on Pasteur's more effective heat treatment. Biochemists also added to the security of life by discoveries that were use-

ful in agriculture and nutrition, such as the nitrogen cycle of plant nutrition and the process of photosynthesis.

Other biologists were preoccupied with the mechanism of heredity and the cellular structures common to all living tissue. Developments in genetics were especially significant for later biology. In the 1870s, August Weismann of Freiburg distinguished body (somatic) cells from reproductive cells. During the 1880s, he contested Charles Darwin's thesis of natural selection as the origin of species. During the 1860s, unknown to the general scientific world, an obscure Austrian monk, Gregor Mendel, explored the mathematical distribution of inherited traits by crossing "sport" peas with peas whose ancestors were normal in appearance. Although allowances were made for variations and mutations, the application of mathematics to genetics made the study of heredity an increasingly exact science.

The dominant climate of opinion during

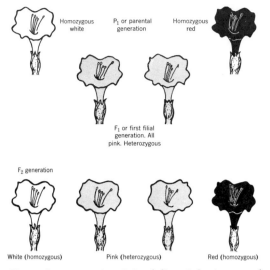

*Chart demonstrating Mendelian inheritance of traits in four-o'clocks.*

the second half of the nineteenth century was less congenial to genetics than to the other major course of biological inquiry which reached a synthesis in the writings of Charles Darwin (1809–1882). Botanists, zoologists, and paleontologists had accumulated large quantities of descriptive data on species and varieties of life extant and extinct, but few had ventured to account for their differentiation into mutually infertile species of plants and animals. Jean Baptiste de Lamarck (1744–1829), stimulated by fossil comparisons and theories of geological evolution, concluded that characteristics acquired by purposeful adaptation to environmental changes were transmitted by inheritance, but his thesis failed to gain general acceptance. In addition to a large store of evidence proving evolutionary changes in the forms of life, Charles Darwin's principal contribution to biology was a theory to account for the origin of new species from common ancestral forms of life. A lengthy voyage on H.M.S. *Beagle* took him to South America and to the islands in the Pacific Ocean, where he observed fossils, geologic formations, and the minute progressive differences in comparable organisms from different locations.

After his return to England, he discussed his evidence with Charles Lyell (1797–1875), a geologist-friend who sought to mediate between gradual evolutionary and cataclysmic theories of the earth's formation and who in *Principles of Geology* (1830–1832) compiled exhaustive evidence on fossils and changes in the earth's structure. It was from the writings of the natural scientist and social theorist Thomas Malthus that Darwin obtained the decisive idea in organizing his data: the origin of species as the result of natural selection.

Spurred by Lyell and by reports that another scientist, Alfred Wallace, was preparing to publicize the same thesis, Darwin published in 1859 a work whose full title reveals its essence: *On the Origin of Species by Means of Natural Selection, or The Preservation of Favored Races in the Struggle for Life*. The *Origin* argued that more creatures were born than could survive, that both within and between species there was a struggle for life, that each creature differed slightly from its parents, and that in the struggle for life those most suited to cope with environment and internecine competition were naturally selected to survive and reproduce their traits. Ultimately, the accumulative preservation of differences produced new species. Thus Darwin's law of nature was not merely a demonstration of biological evolution; it offered a thesis to explain the mechanism that had produced different species and their variations during vast spans of geologic time. Progress and differentiation were rooted in nature where they were exempt from human or divine intervention and where they operated in an amoral "nature red in tooth and claw with ravin," as Tennyson had expressed it poetically before Darwin's *Origin* appeared. Yet on the fundamental point of natural selection, Darwin himself wavered. While it might explain survival of certain traits, it did not explain the origin of the variations preserved. Darwin suggested sexual selection as an auxiliary to natural selection, a theme that he elaborated

Charles Darwin.

Darwinism simplified and satirized.

in the *Origin of Man*. This work made explicit the earlier inference that man stemmed from ancestors common to other life. Sexual selection was at variance with deterministic natural selection, however; it introduced subjective elements or eugenic arguments comparable to the selective breeding that Darwin had noted in animal husbandry.

Because Darwin combined evolution with natural selection, which was a specific explanation of evolution, the scientific reaction to his work was somewhat confused. Lyell, Thomas Huxley, a noted invertebrate zoologist and scientific popularizer, and Herbert Spencer, who shopped among scientific disciplines to find one that would undergird his social doctrines, were immediate converts to Darwin's thesis. Zeal for Darwin's theoretical framework led physical anthropologists to accept as "missing links" some fossil remains that recently have been proved grossly antedated. To geneticists, such as Weismann, and to other biologists natural selection explained the removal of unsuited variations—the stability rather than the change of species—

and they argued that it was a hypothesis that could never be demonstrated empirically. They thought that mutations occurring within the reproductive mechanism were a more likely source of new species.

Darwin's science also drew fire from a variety of moral and religious spokesmen, especially from those who considered his account of human origins irreconcilable with a literal reading of the Book of Genesis. Although the Papacy refused (in *The Syllabus of Errors*) to accommodate religion to science, Roman Catholics, being less committed to Biblical literalism, had less difficulty than Protestants in reconciling evolution with religion. Darwin's works were never placed on the *Index*. Even though some religious apologists insisted that fossils had been planted by God to test the faith of man, Protestant opposition was short-lived, especially in areas where "survival-of-the-fittest" economic doctrines were already prevalent. Protestant fundamentalists had more difficulty with the "death of Adam," but some of them found Social Darwinism quite scientific and acceptable. The clash between evolution and religion was sharp and, in the United States, prolonged; nevertheless, science scored a rapid victory. More critical than the conflict with traditional religions was the collision between proponents of the "survival of the fittest" and humanitarians, religious or secular. The latter eventually included Thomas Huxley, the principal English popularizer of Darwin, who concluded:

As I have already urged, the practice of that which is ethically best—what we call goodness or virtue—involves a course of conduct which, in all respects, is opposed to that which leads to success in the cosmic struggle for existence. In place of ruthless self-assertion it demands self-restraint; in place of thrusting aside, or treading down, all competitors, it requires that the individual shall not merely respect, but shall help his fellows; its influence is directed, not so much to the survival of the fittest, as to the fitting of as many as possible to survive. It repudiates the gladiatorial theory of existence. . . . Let us understand, once for all, that the ethical progress of society depends, not on imitating the cosmic process, still less in running away from it, but in combating it.[3]

Huxley spoke for a losing cause in his generation, however. Most "scientific" ideologies that advocated the use of force—nationalism, racism, class conflict, unrestrained economic competition—seized upon Darwin's biology to prove its agreement with natural law. Once applied, the doctrine that might makes right became a self-fulfilling prophecy, for force could be answered only in kind.

## SOCIAL "SCIENTISM" AND RELATIVISM

Nineteenth-century scientists, respectable social scientists, and ideologists believed that key natural laws of science were absolute parts of the universe's design. By the end of the century physicists, mathematicians, and

sociologists had come to consider their laws useful and pragmatically valid but less than absolute. Nevertheless, the social "scientism" or ideological dogmatism that took deep root during the century continued to assert the absolute validity of natural laws. Those who lost their faith in "scientism" usually went to the opposite pole of total relativism, insisting that all beliefs and knowledge rested on faith alone or on a collectively held myth.

## Positivism

Positivists sought to find the natural laws that govern society. Several nineteenth-century positivists were hailed as the Newtons or Darwins of social science, but their methods and conclusions differed widely. One group believed that when the laws they had discovered were allowed to operate, no further governmental or social controls would be necessary. *Laissez-faire* economists tended to take this view toward the market; anarchists applied it to all facets of government and society; and orthodox Marxists awaited its fulfillment at the end of the evolutionary rainbow. They all borrowed "laws" from physics and biology as fundamental starting points. Another group professed to spurn all metaphysical, religious, and scientific preconceptions for pure empiricism, but they were divided between those who argued that the *status quo,* a product of natural evolution, was the best of all possible worlds and critics of the *status quo* who sought change.

Few positivists stuck more closely over the years to a detached scientific methodology than the British Utilitarians, but the first to fly the positivist banner as such were the disciples of Henri Saint-Simon in post-Napoleonic France. Their claim to scientific standards, however, was more dubious. Saint-Simon insisted simultaneously on both a preconceived law of progress and the conscious change of society by a managerial elite. His successors split between activist reformers and the school of positivism founded by his secretary, Auguste Comte. Comte tried to show that the first condition of progress was

3. *Evolution and Ethics and Other Essays,* Macmillan & Co., London and New York, 1898, pp. 81–82, 83.

the maintenance of order; hence a strong army was indispensable. Like Edmund Burke, he considered social hierarchy inevitable and the existing distribution of wealth the design of providence. Intellectual culture was the instrument of progressive change which ultimately would produce a unified humanity. Like Saint-Simon, Comte reckoned the force of reason and science alone as too weak to enlist popular support. To attract the masses, he founded an abortive scientific religion, which would join with sociology to teach discipline and obedience as mere political action could not.

In France, the United States, and Britain, where Herbert Spencer popularized Comte's positivism, visible signs of intellectual and economic progress validated evolutionary optimism. But in Central, Southern, and Eastern Europe prospects were bleak. Conservatives and clerics forcefully resisted change and justified their privileges as the product of historical evolution. In this environment, critics of the *status quo* tended toward anarchism or, in Russia, Nihilism—a positivism that accepted nothing incapable of scientific proof. Nihilism will be discussed later within its Russian context; more immediately significant for Western civilization was the radicalism in Germany.

"Young Hegelians" such as Ludwig Feuerbach, a philosopher of the revolution of 1848, sought to replace the theology that supported divine-right absolutism with anthropology and love of mankind. Other Hegelians, such as David Friedrich Strauss and Bruno Bauer, employed a "higher criticism" of Biblical texts which eliminated miracles from Scripture and explained their inclusion in the Gospel as pranks or mythological creations of the tension-filled generations following the death of Christ. Another influential revolutionary was Lorenz von Stein, who in 1842 published a German account of the French proletariat's repeated failures to benefit from alliances with the bourgeoisie. In this first "anatomy of revolutions," von Stein announced the discovery of natural laws

that guaranteed the victory of the propertied classes through dictatorships over the proletariat. Although von Stein considered a proletarian revolution impossible and later changed many of his views, he, like the Young Hegelians, influenced Marx and Engels as well as German liberals.

In Britain, the rift between traditionalists and radicals was not so sharp as on the Continent. During the Enlightenment, David Hume had already applied a "higher criticism" to revealed religion, and varying degrees of empiricism were widespread in the sciences, political economy, and public policy. From Utilitarian ranks, John Stuart Mill publicized an inductive logic that bypassed theology and self-evident natural law. The Utilitarian radicals were a distinct and often-attacked minority, but they influenced the government. Churchmen, unlike their counterparts on the Continent, were no longer engaged in authoritarian politics, and some were involved in humanitarian activities. Even leading agnostics considered ecclesiastical institutions socially useful. British positivists were divided, however, between humanitarian advocates of conscious change and conservative Social Darwinists who believed that progress resulted only from a struggle for life and the resulting extinction of the unfit.

## Social Darwinism

When positivists became convinced that they had discovered deterministic laws, their ideologies often became metaphysical, dogmatic, and religious. Social Darwinism—the belief that beneficent change was produced by the survival of the fittest individual, class, nation, or race—became the most dogmatic and widespread form of positivism.

Although Social Darwinists agreed that progress resulted from an unchecked struggle for life, they disagreed on the selective process. According to Herbert Spencer, evolution had carried society beyond a militant era in which warfare had been the selecting agent to an industrial era in which economic success determined survival. Karl Marx cast the conflict as one between classes rather than between individuals or businesses. Both Spencer and Marx combined a belief in the ultimate reality of matter and force with a biological survival of the fittest, but a German biologist, Ernst Haeckel (1834–1919) carried this combination to its logical conclusions. Haeckel's popular *Riddle of the Universe* (1899) was a dogmatic polemic that denied purpose in the universe and taught resignation to the reign of force. Haeckel was a spokesman for the most prevalent form of Social Darwinism—militaristic nationalism. But the crude materialism of Haeckel's nationalism limited its popularity. More widespread was a "spiritualized" or romanticized Darwinism, which regarded national force as the origin of morality and spiritual growth. The moral conflict between nations would, as Hegel had said, produce progress. This "spiritualized" nationalism became the principal foe of "materialistic" socialism and liberalism.

*Heinrich von Treitschke, evangelist of nationalism.*

### Darwinian and Integral Nationalism

Earlier in the century nationalism had been closely linked to liberal constitutionalism. But after 1848, especially during the wars of German and Italian unification, conservatives and radicals fused Darwinian and romantic nationalism into a weapon against the liberals. After 1870 influential publicists, such as Ernest Renan and Heinrich von Treitschke, interpreted the Franco-Prussian War (1870–1871) as a struggle for national survival, stimulating and purifying victors and vanquished alike. Thereafter military men couched their requests for military appropriations in Darwinist terms, and traditional conservatives discovered that they could rally the masses against liberals and minorities by appealing to ethnocentric cultural, religious, and political impulses.

Darwinist nationalists glorified warfare as the agent of human progress. Only the ever-present threat of war could eradicate selfish materialism, comfortable softness, and indo-

lence. But in purely biological terms, Darwinian nationalism could be attacked on the grounds that warfare eliminated the best physical specimens and destroyed the material basis of physical health. Although avowed materialists such as Haeckel continued to be popular, Darwinian nationalism was decked out more and more attractively in romantic, spiritual, and religious clothes. Heinrich von Treitschke wrote:

It is a false conclusion that wars are waged for the sake of material advantage. . . . Here the high moral ideal of national honor is a factor . . . enshrining something positively sacred, and compelling the individual to sacrifice himself to it.[4]

The late nineteenth century may have been a "generation of materialism," but it was dominated by a patriotic religion of force. In Renan's words, which were echoed every-

4. Quoted by Franklin Le Van Baumer, *Main Currents of Western Thought*, Alfred A. Knopf, New York, 1952, p. 547.

where, the nation is a "soul, a spiritual principle." Warfare nurtured that soul and assured progress. "You may hope for a time when the sword shall be turned into the ploughshare," Karl Pearson, an English advocate of imperialism and national eugenics wrote, "but believe me, when that day comes mankind will no longer progress."[5]

This seemingly radical change from biological materialism to cultural idealism is perhaps best explained by the nature of its exponents. Among them, literary romantics were exceedingly significant. To them Darwinism appealed less because it was "scientific" than because of its epic, poetic qualities, harking back to the primitive atavism of the chase, capture, and sudden death of beasts. Fearful that mechanization, urbanization, and science were "uprooting" and killing the human spirit, these romantics sought to keep it alive in an organic universe with struggle, intense feelings, and sudden physical deaths. Moreover, Darwinism supplied a "scientific" rationale for refuting both liberalism and socialism. For freedom under man-made law, Darwinists substituted the superior right of force. For the legal equality of liberalism and the economic equality of socialism, they substituted the natural law of inherent inequality. Socialism, they alleged, would cut off the roots of progress and produce decadence by curbing competition domestically and warfare internationally. Darwinian nationalism, which adopted a "spiritual" terminology, was often clerical and found support within the traditionalist churches. Conservative nationalists, even when atheistic, usually considered otherworldly religion necessary for power politics because it inured people to hardship and self-sacrifice. Churchmen, beset by anticlerical liberalism, socialism, and rational-empirical philosophies, often led in propagating nationalism. Few, however, went as far as the Christian socialist Adolf Stöcker, who compared the majesty of war with the majesty of God. Although conservative nationalism furnished a common meeting ground for all who preferred authoritarianism to liberalism, democracy, or socialism, there were also Darwinists who advocated domestic *laissez faire* or social-welfare legislation to increase national strength in the international arena.

Between 1871 and 1914 there were no major wars to sate the Darwinists' thirst for bloodshed, but domestically "integral nationalists" sought to extirpate internal minorities and to discredit all forms of diversity. After the unification of Germany in 1871, the government placed heavy legal and economic pressures on Polish, Danish, and French minorities, and the imperial government tried to break down the internationalism of Roman Catholics and socialists. After the Hungarians achieved autonomy in 1867, their government attempted to "Magyarize" the Slavic peoples who constituted a majority of the population. Similar policies were applied in the Balkans, but the most extensive attempt to repress all national, religious, and social minorities occurred in Tsarist Russia, where Social Darwinism was less a newfangled ideology than an implicit, traditional policy. Applied most bloodily against the Jews, Russian integralism contributed to the revival of anti-Semitism in Western Europe by driving to it refugees who were less educated, wealthy, and adapted than the older Western Jewish families. Reasons of military security were often advanced to justify persecution of minorities, but in practice the persecutions transformed many of the survivors into dissidents or revolutionaries. International rivalries do not, however, provide a sufficient explanation of integralist pressures for uniformity. Their source more likely was in the domestic ideologies and social pressures that made extremist ideologies attractive.

Whether in Russia, where they were in power, or in France, where they constituted an anti-Republican minority, integral nation-

5. Quoted by Carleton J. H. Hayes, *A Generation of Materialism 1871–1900,* Harper and Row, New York and London, 1941, p. 340.

alists held similar assumptions, objectives, and a burning faith in the uniqueness and God-chosen mission of their own particular nationality. Institutions that antedated the Enlightenment were the natural products of divine evolution, which formed the collective soul of their nation. This soul was most purely represented by the military and the peasantry; it was threatened by "rootless" capitalists, merchants, urban laborers, internationalists, nonconformist minorities, and especially by Jews, whose historical claims as the chosen people of God rankled advocates of other national messianisms. Be it German, French, Russian, Japanese, or American, nativist nationality was God-chosen, and God's chapel was the history classroom. Freedom belonged not to individuals but to collectivities taking arbitrary action. International law or rational restraint in international affairs was, therefore, the antithesis of freedom. And nationalism was divorced from and turned against every "materialist" ideology concerned with the well-being of the individual person. Once more conservatives and traditionalists had at their disposal the means of attack on the values of the Enlightenment and of bourgeois society.

## Racism and Racial Anti-Semitism

Almost invariably, integral nationalists and proponents of imperialism mixed a doctrine of racial superiority with claims to a unique national culture. In the nineteenth century, "race" was a general but imprecise term that was often used interchangeably with "nationality," but racism was a "scientific" ideology that claimed to find *the* key to history within the racial compositions of societies past and present. Modern racism was formulated by aristocratic prophets of doom in France, first in opposition to Louis XIV and more comprehensively later when the French Revolution opened careers to the middle classes. In 1852, the Comte de Gobineau set down in "scientific" form the inherited right of the nobility, as descendants of Germanic conquerors, to rule the Gauls

or French. Understandably, Gobineau societies became more numerous in Germany than in France. Instead of progress in liberal equality, Gobineau predicted doom unless a new "Aryan" elite rose to replace the aristocracy. Gobineau's *Inequality of Human Races* gained little popularity until the late nineteenth century, when the middle classes as well as the traditional privileged classes felt that their positions were being jeopardized by new families rising through educational and economic opportunities. Although ultranationalists preached it, racism generally was an international elitist doctrine. Because it postulated inherent biological inequality, it also became current in the American South and in mixed European colonies around the world. Racial superiority was a constant rationale for imperialism. Domestically its principal manifestation was aggressive anti-Semitism.

Although Darwinism gave anti-Semitism a "scientific" basis, religious and economic sanctions against Jews had long existed in Europe. Sporadic mob murders, riots, inquisitional legal proceedings, segregated housing districts or ghettos, distinctly marked clothing, and exclusion from professions and landholding reach far back into medieval Europe. Protected by rulers who needed their financial knowledge or resources and emancipated by enlightened despots and liberal reformers, the Jews ran afoul of a conservative clerical resurgence that was bidding for popular followings and of some socialist ideologies in the last quarter of the nineteenth century. Romantic nationalists castigated their "rootlessness," their "materialism"—from which both capitalism and socialism were said to flow—and their lack of conformity to the romantics' peasant ideal. In Germany, racial anti-Semitism was best summed up by Houston Stewart Chamberlain (1855–1926) in the *Foundations of the Nineteenth Century* (1899). In addition to elaborating on Gobineau's racial theory of history, Chamberlain, an Englishman who became a naturalized German and married Richard Wagner's daughter, performed the feat of making Christ an Aryan—that is, a Teutonic rather than a Semitic type. Henceforth "scientific" racists relied not on external characteristics but on an intuitively perceived internal soul as the determinant of race. Chamberlain had also built a bridge, ominous for the future, between romantic national religion ("German Christianity") and racial anti-Semitism.

Jews became the scapegoat for all social frustrations and failures. By inventing the fear that wealthy Jews—a minority—were conspiring to rule the world, anti-Semites justified counterconspiracy and violence. British Prime Minister Disraeli warned of such a conspiracy at mid-century, and Rightist critics of the French Republic kept the idea alive after the 1880s. Early in the twentieth century, *The Protocols of the Elders of Zion,* forged in Paris at the instigation of the Tsarist secret police, "proved" the charge. In this widely published proof of Machiavellian chicanery, the modern world had its equivalent to the Spanish Inquisition's charges that Jews habitually conspired with the Archdevil—now the capitalists—to control the world. Generally, Jews responded to persecution and defamation with intensified efforts to assimilate or fled to new homelands. A few turned to the Zionist movement, which aimed to restore a Jewish national state in Palestine.

## Romantic Realism and Naturalism

When romantic protests failed to halt the mechanization of society and the march of "materialistic" science, romantics produced their own competitive brand of "scientific" realism and naturalism. Often the transition from romanticism to realism is treated as a radical departure. In fact, early romantics had had predilections for seeking out minute realistic details of natural diversity. This realistic tradition continued in novels of local color, industrial conditions, and psychological analysis. Besides realism, there was the romantic stream of medieval fantasy, emotional revelation, and triumphs of moral will over

refractory environment. In England, for example, Charles Dickens' exposes of the ills of industrial society were appearing at the same time as Alfred, Lord Tennyson's classic *Idylls of the King.* Both expressed the same social protests, one by criticizing industrial materialism and the other by an exaggerated praise of the chivalric age.

Realists first broke away from romanticism when they became cynically disillusioned with all ideals and enthusiastically advocated instinctual, environmental, or even economic determinism. They championed their new-found absolutes as "scientific," but their conversion was probably inspired more by a thirst for certainty than a commitment to scientific methodology. Romantics ceased to test truth solely by feelings, spirit, and intuition and entered the area of science whose methodology had always been repugnant to them.

Darwinism, because it affirmed fundamental romantic assumptions, proved to be the most attractive path to deterministic naturalism. It furnished proof that nature was organic, that man was an integral part of it, and that life was constantly changing and diversifying. True, the picture of sudden death in a struggle for survival jolted romantic sensitivities, but it also raised the feelings to their highest pitch and showed that the individual's loss was the gain of the species and the universe. Spencerian Darwinism had romantic ingredients that appealed narrowly to a single economic class, as did orthodox Marxism. But nationalism and racism were the two main streams on which the romantic rode into politics.

## Literature of Industrial Criticism

As an escape from environmental restrictions, literary romanticism continued to provide vicarious adventure tales, heroic nationalist histories, love poems, novels, and even detective stories. It also continued to idealize the Middle Ages. At the same time, romantic writers began to produce sociological criticism and "industrial novels." These depicted, in presumably scientific detail, the impact of mechanization and urbanization on humankind. They attacked the demoralization of rural crafts and derided the middle class for its "philistine" conventions and optimistic ideologies.

Within an industrial setting, Thomas Carlyle (1795–1881), a British admirer and imitator of German romanticism, gave early impetus to "realistic" social criticism. Dedicated to the spiritual values of the past which made inequality a divine, moral principle and which denied the dignity and worth of every man, Carlyle produced a doctrine of individualism and personality which would make the masses subservient to an heroic elite—the Noble Few—to whom the responsibility for resolving industrial problems should fall. Carlyle denounced the "cash nexus" of *laissez-faire* capitalism as fervently as any socialist and prescribed moderate paternal reform, work, spirituality, and possible regimentation for labor. He denounced all outlooks, such as Chartism, Utilitarianism, and democracy, which considered human happiness the goal of society. Carlyle advocated a spiritual nationalism that recognized the right of might in foreign affairs. The focus of his hero-oriented biographies was primarily on military men, such as Oliver Cromwell and Frederick II. He failed to gain a personal following in Britain, but his critique of industrialism reappeared in conservative, socialist, and aesthetic indictments of industrial society.

Various other realists strove for greater detail. Some—Jane Austen and Charlotte Brontë in England, for example—wrote sensitive novels of manners and social attitudes without becoming embroiled in social causes. But others employed a new vocabulary generated by industrialization to portray the sufferings and social callousness of mid-century society. In Britain, the industrial novelists included Benjamin Disraeli, later Conservative Prime Minister; Charles Kingsley, a Christian socialist leader;* and two

* See *supra*, p. 282.

*Charles Dickens writing, 1859.*

notable woman, Elizabeth Gaskell and George Eliot, who described lower-class conditions during the "Hungry Forties" and the fate of craftsmen forced to compete with machines. More popular was Charles Dickens, who like Gaskell and Eliot, abhorred revolutions and lower-class activism as well as middle-class acquisitiveness and self-satisfied smugness. Although the industrial novelists stirred up reform sentiments, their proposed remedies were remarkably limited. Principally, they sought "social" as distinct from "political" solutions, a change in the hearts of the possessing classes without the organization of pressure groups by those who were afflicted. They praised workingmen who spurned the Chartists or unions, and they denounced utilitarian reformers who would use "materialistic" data to construct coercive legislation or urge the restriction of births. In the final analysis, their individualism rested on *noblesse oblige.*

The French counterparts of British realists tended to be activist republicans and socialists. Women such as George Sand—who like George Eliot assumed a male name—were among them, but the leading early luminary was Victor Hugo (1802–1885). During the Orleanist monarchy, Hugo took up the cause of the unemployed and the wretched majority whom he contrasted with the selfish and corrupted governing classes.

## Novels of Naturalism and Psychological Analysis

Even though sociological realists dipped deeply into sordid and hitherto unmentionable aspects of life, they were generally more optimistic than the naturalists and psychological novelists. The works of Émile Zola (1840–1902) illustrate the borderline between realism and naturalism. Dwelling upon natural science and heredity and attempting to reduce writing itself to a science, Zola joined with Hugo in defending individual liberties during the Third Republic and in sympathizing with the lower classes in mine, factory, and slum. His naturalistic realism contrasted somberly with the ardent optimism of earlier romantics. Yet he was ultimately optimistic in thinking that the environment itself could be changed.

Other naturalists seldom shared this faith. Zola's older compatriot Honoré de Balzac (1799–1850), for example, devastatingly analyzed the irrational pecuniary and sexual motivations at all levels of society. Mercenary and ambitious for fame and aristocratic connections, Balzac, grandson of a peasant, assumed a noble name and sought out liaisons with titled and wealthy mistresses while he bared the "real" society about him. Politically he was compromised by royalism, and in business his get-rich-quick schemes repeatedly failed. His apology for the sexual infidelity of unhappily married women was carried further by Gustave Flaubert, whose *Madame Bovary* (1857) had to await a naturalistic resurgence among the intelligentsia during the 1880s to be hailed as great art. The English novelist and poet Thomas Hardy (1840–1928) also contributed novels

*Victor Hugo, aged romantic.*

such as *The Return of the Native* which dwelt upon the omnipotence of early environment, instinct, and heredity. As naturalism covered the Western literary world, Jack London, among others in America, experimented with it as a break from earlier realism and local color. Joining the sociological novel, the legitimate theater, partially freed from earlier legal and social restrictions, raised to international fame such playwrights as Henrik Ibsen and George Bernard Shaw, who worked over hypocrisy and respectability in shocking, but avidly attended, drama at the end of the century.

The most somber probing of the murky depths of irrationality was done by Fedor Dostoevsky (1821–1881), the Russian revolutionary turned conservative, conformist, and nationalist. Dostoevsky transformed Russian romantic tradition, established by Gogol and Turgenev, into pessimistic psychological realism. In *Crime and Punishment*

*Nietzsche with his mother.*

(1866) he pilloried reason by making it responsible for the pointless and heinous crimes committed by his central figure, Raskolnikov, whose name literally means "the schismatic." Among the impoverished and none-too-respectable common people he found heroic qualities and virtue. Perhaps greater classical proportions were attained by Dostoevsky's Russian contemporary, Count Leo Tolstoi, who wrote deterministic realism in *War and Peace*. Confronted with the stern realities of Russian social and political life, Tolstoi turned toward radical Christian anarchism, whereas Dostoevsky became an aggressive Pan-Slav nationalist.

## Philosophies of the Will and Neoromanticism

Realism and naturalism deeply influenced German literature, while German philosophy —subjectivism and aesthetics—rivaled and complemented Darwinism in attracting disillusioned idealists. Its theoretical roots ante-

dated the psychological novelists, whose conclusions often pointed in the same direction. Steeped in romanticism and entranced by Oriental asceticism, which he preached but did not practice, Arthur Schopenhauer (1788–1860) published *The World as Will and Idea* shortly after the Congress of Vienna. In this long-obscure treatise Schopenhauer considered the will the fundamental metaphysical reality. Overcome by pessimism, he found an escape in artistic creativity. Although he considered exercise of the will to be evil, his disciple Friedrich Nietzsche (1844–1900) exalted it as the sovereign origin of good. In denouncing equality, utilitarianism, and mechanized culture, Nietzsche had much in common with Carlyle, Sigmund Freud, and Matthew Arnold, the celebrated Victorian literary critic. Both Arnold and Nietzsche assailed the smugness and mediocrity of middle-class society, but Arnold was an emotionally restrained classicist whereas Nietzsche was an exuberant, "Dionysian" enthusiast. Nietzsche's interests were cultural; like Schopenhauer he was no nationalist, racist, or libertine, and he was aloof from politics. When twentieth-century Nazis in their revolt against bourgeois society plagiarized his terms for purposes of political propaganda, they radically perverted his meaning.

As an individualist who demanded that the elite exercise willpower to set standards above the common herd, Nietzsche inspired writers such as George Bernard Shaw. The idea of the primacy of the will also appeared in France in Henri Bergson's evolutionary philosophy of an *élan vital* or life force and in America in William James' pragmatism. Outside formal philosophy, the Nietzschean mantle was re-tailored by continental neoromantics who took advantage of the ambiguity of his loose style, rambling metaphors, polemics against the ethics of the New Testament, and remarks that were probably due to incipient insanity, to make Nietzsche a patron saint of irrationality, nationalism, and racism. Richard Wagner (1813–

*"The Funeral," by Edouard Manet.*

*"Fishermen on the Seine," by Claude Monet.*

1883) grafted Nietzsche's "will to power" and theories of tragic creativity onto romantic German nationalism and racism, thus personally alienating the philosopher. Wagner used his musical drama, a "total work of art," to inculcate the populace with primitivistic, pagan, and chivalric myths and to replace Nietzsche's pessimism with an apocalyptic faith in a future hero-deliverer. Thus transformed, Nietzscheanism became, for the youth of the generation preceding World War I, a nationalist cult that defied all social conventions.

The formation of a band of young Nietzschean romantics on the Continent was only one sign that deterministic naturalism was too confining to harbor the romantic impulse for long. Although some neoromantics defied all social conventions and made vitalistic, irrational urges and willpower the canons for living, numerous liberals and "Marxists of the heart" reasserted humanitarian faith in law and order.

## Romantic Innovations in Art: Impressionism

Another outlet for the romantics' quest for reality was art, especially painting in France. The French Academy, the official arbiter of artistic taste, enforced a neoclassical canon and excelled in encouraging the reproduction of selected items of nature. Until 1857, the Academy barred from its ranks the leading romantic idealist Delacroix, who filled his pathos-laden canvases with political and social themes, often revolutionary uprisings. Courbet, a realist who abandoned Delacroix's idealism to portray the seamier aspects of life, especially squalor in industrial slums, also lacked official favor. Although a new generation of artistic innovators, called Impressionists by a derisive critic, abandoned social and political involvement for the pursuit of "art for art's sake," they were no more acceptable to the Academy. These Impressionists — Monet, Renoir, Pissaro, Cézanne, and Manet, among others—came from varied backgrounds to form an artistic circle in Paris after 1860. For subjects they turned to the open air of coast, forest, and riverbank to catch transitory, fleeting personal or natural moods in unusual combinations of pure, often bright and sharply contrasting or blending colors. Using new knowledge of color perception by the human eye, they left sharp details to be filled in at a distance by the viewer.

Later Impressionists or "Postimpression-

*"D'où Venons Nous . . . Que Sommes Nous . . . Où Allons Nous?" by Paul Gauguin.*

ists" such as Gauguin went further in repudiating photographic reproductions of nature. Gauguin sought to find a primordial unifying link between man and nature antedating the artificiality of complicated modern societies. He found it in the lives of the unspoiled primitives of Tahiti, among whom he lived in conscious revolt against European social conventions. Other Postimpressionists expressed their rejection of bourgeois and industrial society by living as "bohemians" in Europe itself. Preoccupied with planes, geometric forms, and colors, the late Impressionists, especially Cézanne, opened a path to the abstract art of the twentieth century. Continuing in revolt against realistic naturalism, a field preempted by the photographic industry, descendants of the Impressionists have subsequently probed the irrationalities of individuals and society by using a wide range of symbols.

## LATE NINETEENTH-CENTURY SOCIAL THOUGHT

The quest for a science to explain and control the immense political and social changes of the nineteenth century eventually reached a stage of crisis. Ideologies that claimed absolute validity were hopelessly at odds with one another, and their collisions shattered faith in objectivity. Mathematicians

themselves were attacking the absoluteness of physical laws, although not the objective reality of external nature. Darwin's natural selection was under fire from geneticists and those who, like Prince Kropotkin (1842–1912), argued that cooperation rather than internecine rivalry preserved species in nature. Romantics, although rejecting scientific methodology, had amassed evidence that unconscious motivation, myths, and social environment rather than reason dominated social life. German idealist philosophers, notably Wilhelm Dilthey, concluded that the social sciences or "nonphysical disciplines" were subjective and that the writing of history by the historian was an act of faith in his own ideals or traditional values.

These challenges and the rapid spread of liberal constitutionalism and socialism stimulated some continental intellectuals to reconstruct their premises and turn to sociology and psychology for guidance. They reasserted the validity of empiricism and reason as tools of social analysis against relativists and dogmatic ideologists. At the same time, however, they made vast concessions to the role of the irrational in human society. These concessions undermined the basic assumptions of liberal bourgeois society and provided the empirical data that its opponents would use to undermine it in the twentieth century.

## Anthropology, Sociology, and Political Theory

Near the turn of the century, anthropologists and historical sociologists began to revise political thought. James Frazer's *The Golden Bough* in 1890 portrayed divine-right monarchy as a lingering element of primitive society. In countering their opponents, modern conservatives found that invoking nationalism, imperialism, and racism was more effective than appealing for absolutism and a hierarchical class system. At the same time, anthropologists quashed the eighteenth-century myth of the "noble savage." Instead of being an unrestrained natural man, the primitive savage was constrained by innumerable customs and taboos. His actions were guided by myth and rites, rather than reason.

Anthropologists opened new theoretical doors by delving into the role of myth (the personification of collective desires) and its dramatic counterpart, tribal rites—group conduct regulated by magician-rulers. Since the eighteenth century, utilitarian liberals had looked on myth as an irrationality foisted upon society by cunning priests, whereas collectivist romantics had envisaged it as the indispensable soul or personality of society itself. Among others, Edward Tylor (1832–1917), who held the first chair of anthropology at Oxford, saw no essential difference between the myths of primitive and civilized man, except in the materials with which each worked. Scholars disputed the origin and functions of myths, but they regarded them as persistent elements of society. Such theorists as Georges Sorel* joined anthropology with sociology in an effort to inculcate in the irrational masses emotionally satisfying myths. Sorel, who was later claimed by the Fascists and who was personally attracted to Bolshevism, helped to formulate the tactics of those modern political movements which represent a return to

* See *supra*, page 285.

"tribalism"—an instinctive aggregation of the group around an intuitive leader—which in practice nationalism and racism already anticipated.

After having been revamped to exclude physical and biological analogies, sociology no less than anthropology produced revisions in political thought. The impact of the new sociology was exclusively neither liberal nor authoritarian, but it did modify classical liberalism and socialism by casting doubt on their basic premise: the rational self-interest of the individual or class.

On the Continent, Marx's sociology, as distinct from his discredited economic predictions, served as midwife to a new generation of sociological thought. Basically concerned with relating men's ideas and actions to their environment and usually aloof from or hostile to organized Marxism, the new sociologists—like Marx—attempted to get behind facades of ideology and describe only actual practices and behavior shared by all societies. In France, Emile Durkheim, who made sociology an academic discipline, attempted to relate differing ideologies to social stratification and explained Marxism as a moral reaction to a specific set of transitory circumstances. A liberal like Durkheim, the Italian, Gaetano Mosca, concluded that oligarchy or elitism was an inevitable aspect of all states, institutions, and political parties. Like John Stuart Mill, Mosca was perturbed by the authoritarian implications of majority rule, and he insisted that the toleration of dissenting minorities was essential to genuine liberalism.

Mosca's countryman and contemporary, Vilfredo Pareto (1848–1923), made apparent the authoritarian potentialities of anti-intellectual sociology. A *laissez-faire* economist who turned to historical sociology to refute Marx, Pareto was as convinced as Marx that a class struggle underlay historical events. But he denied that revolution would bring a classless society and that economic planning would be effective. Instead, he stressed exclusively the irrational, noneco-

*Vilfredo Pareto, historical sociologist.*

nomic factors in social motivation. Pareto saw social stability as dependent on inherited nonrational behavior patterns (not intellectually acquired creeds) which changed at an almost imperceptibly slow pace. The only certain way to curb irritating minority patterns was to extirpate the groups that follow them. Verbal ideologies only rationalized "illogical" actions and sentiments. Whatever its form, governmental power rested with an elite, which propagated its own myth for the whole society. Governing elites, he concluded, rule either like "foxes" by manipulative resourcefulness or like "lions" by force alone. Any elite that desisted from the use of force entirely would abdicate to a new armed elite in revolution. On the other hand, if the existing oligarchy should become closed and rely wholly on force, it would degenerate and fall. Thus the class struggle was inevitable; a social revolution would only install a new elite. Society might benefit

from a measure of humanitarian ideals, but these could never be fully attained in practice.

As Pareto attacked socialism, he simultaneously laid theoretical grounds for an assault on liberalism. He demonstrated that the rationalism and humanitarianism of the Enlightenment had been a skin-deep affair on most of the Continent and urged existing elites to use force to maintain their power. When Mussolini, a "lion" and former "Leftist", rose to power at the head of the Italian "Right" after World War I, Pareto approved him as a spiritual regenerator of the nation. If Pareto's analysis of elites was correct, however, the terms "Right" and "Left" were no longer meaningful, for after the Bolshevik revolution both extremes were "lions" determined to root out liberal and socialist "foxes."

While Pareto provided continental traditionalists with the conceptual equipment for harnessing mass sentiments and prejudices to authoritarian purposes, the German sociologist Max Weber fought a losing battle to save sociology as an empirical discipline and the rational humanitarian values of the Enlightenment. He supported elitism and imperialism but opposed dogmatism in both its relativist and scientific forms. He popularized "ideal types"—models abstracted from social and political experience which were to be used as analytical tools. Rationally constructed, these models were considered valid only insofar as they rendered empirical data meaningful. Ideal types, often expressed in quantitative or diagrammatic form, have been adopted by the social and behavioral sciences of the twentieth century, especially economics, with considerable success. Weber did not regard his ideal types as absolute pictures of reality any more than contemporary mathematicians considered the "laws" of physics absolute, and even models that were contradictory because of incomplete knowledge could contain partial truths. Although Weber's historical writings traced

*Max Weber, formulator of social science methodology.*

the influence of religious ideas on economic development, he avoided the absolute dichotomy of "materialism" and "idealism" which characterized his German environment, and he found elements of value in Marxism. In comparing Western civilization with other civilizations, he concluded that rationalism in law, thought, science, and industrial organization was its distinguishing feature. Weber was a partisan for the unpopular values of the Enlightenment and feared the rise of a demagogic, charismatic leader who would exploit the mass sentiments that were latent in Germany.

On most of the Continent, Weber's rational-empirical approach *was* in jeopardy, but in Scandinavia, Britain, and the United States political institutions proved responsive to changing conditions, and sociology and political theory became inductive and pragmatic. Individual sociologists varied, but the

methods and conclusions of the American government official and self-educated polymath and sociologist Lester Ward (1841–1913) are representative of their nonsocialist manifestations. Although Ward was an evolutionist, he launched a comprehensive attack on the methods, conclusions, and ethics of the Spencerian Darwinists. Society, he argued in his *Dynamic Sociology* of 1883, is not a branch of biology but a separate field that requires rational-empirical investigation. Speculative deductions drawn from Darwinian biology were not merely an abuse of scientific methodology; they were wrong. Instead of producing competition and individualism, Darwinian *laissez faire* produced monopoly and centralization. Ethically, it justified social oppression, the elimination of the morally best and "fittest," and resignation to a purposeless cosmic law. Historically, *laissez faire* had been instrumental in unseating autocrats, but now representative governments, which used statistics to form their laws, were potential agents of human progress. By modifying natural selection, providing equal educational opportunities, and substituting altruism for indifferent individualism, they would promote man's conquest over nature. Ward's altruistic naturalism was at odds with both religious and Darwinist versions of providence. But his conclusions buttressed the social gospel and were accepted by a new generation of empirical economists and pragmatists who preferred activism to contemplative ideology. They were crucial, too, to the wave of progressive legislation and constitutional changes which swept American government at all levels during the first decades of the twentieth century.

Sociology worked similar changes on political theory in Britain. The rational, autonomous individual who satisfies his own economic self-interest while benefiting society was no longer a tenable object of faith. Studies of mob psychology gave convincing evidence of irrationality, and economists began to incorporate subjective elements in the determination of economic values. Like Ward, British liberal theorists considered the representative state to be an agent of progressive social engineering and to rest not so much on a collection of autonomous individuals as on consensus of the community. Although they were idealists, the British liberal thinkers shared with socialists an extended concern for material well-being. Inspired by their writings, a generation of civil servants used the machinery of state to improve the conditions of British life as World War I approached.

## Psychology

While sociologists made a heavy impact on political theory, findings in the new field of empirical psychology implied a veritable revolution in man's conceptions of his own mental makeup. As early as 1869, Sir Francis Galton, Darwin's cousin, published an analysis of the inheritance of intelligence or abilities, but he was primarily concerned with eugenics—selective breeding and sterilization among humans. Shortly thereafter, William Wundt (1832–1920) inaugurated laboratory methods to explore the physical origins of mental activity. In Russia during the 1890s, Ivan Pavlov experimented with conditioned responses—the memorized reactions of animals to physical stimuli—and suggested that man shared the powers of association and memory with beasts. The most far-reaching speculation about the human mind and its relationship to the social environment emanated from a Viennese circle of psychologists. That circle was dominated by Sigmund Freud.

Freud, who began as a clinical psychologist treating abnormal behavior (neuroses), theorized that emotional disturbances were not purely physical, but rather psychic in their origins. He was principally concerned with the hitherto unrecognized subconscious activities of the mind. Fantasies, dreams, and apparently illogical elements elicited from the patient's "unconscious" became his

raw material for analysis and treatment (psychoanalysis). Eventually, he developed a set of hypotheses about the structure of the mind. Psychic energy, he concluded, originated primarily in the *Id*—a bundle of biologically inherited instincts for food, drink, and especially sex, whose earliest manifestations appeared in infancy. Because unrestrained pursuit of pleasure or the gratification of these instincts would lead to self-destruction, self-preservation required the development of another "layer" of the mind (*Ego*) to mediate between a repressive external reality of scarcity and the desires of the *Id*. Curbed by the *Ego,* the *Id* then found expression in dreams and fantasies. Superimposed on both the *Id* and the *Ego* by parental and social authority was the *Superego* or conscience which imparted a sense of guilt. The function of all three—the *Id,* the *Ego,* and the *Superego*—became unconscious or automatic, but repressions based on early experience could thereafter cause emotional disturbances in adulthood. With this hypothetical construct, which he expected further clinical findings to modify, Freud attempted to reduce the irrational realm thrust forward in thought by the romantics to a rational, scientific, and utilitarian formula.

Although Freud eschewed formal philosophy, he diverted more and more attention away from clinical psychoanalysis to "metapsychology" or the speculative application of his theory to society and culture as a whole, especially after World War I. Because he was concerned with the deep, dark powers of the unconscious and instinctual endowment, Freud interpreted the war not as a fall from a previously attained plateau, but rather as the failure to have reached such a plateau at all. Civilization, he concluded, rests on the repression of instincts, particularly the libido and the aggressive impulse. Society and the individual mind are both arenas of a contest between *Eros*—the power of love and creativity—and *Thanatos,* the wish for death. The will to destroy usually exceeds the strength to create. Tighter social organization, he predicted, would increase repression and the prospects for greater rebelliousness. Religion was no escape, for, although Freud did not teach a break in Puritan ethics, he linked the need for religion and the origin of religious rites to primitive tribal acts of savagery. His social theory was generally pessimistic, but scattered in his works were guarded passages which speculated that the antagonism between repression and instincts would be gradually moderated. His own strivings were toward extending the application of reason. His analysis was mechanistic, but it was not deterministic; he sought a purely secular humanitarianism based on rationalism and realism.

Freud's picture of man and contending forces in the world was similar to the doctrine of human depravity and the cosmic moral struggle which was taught by the traditional churches. Nevertheless, his psychology, particularly his emphasis on sexuality, stirred up popular resentment and helped to divide the adherents of psychoanalysis into antagonistic cults. Psychoanalysts in Zurich, led by Carl Jung, who dealt in ethics, religion, and a racially oriented neoromanticism, rejected Freud's emphasis on sexuality. At the opposite pole, Wilhelm Reich led a school that advocated removing repressions and sanctioning license to remedy individual and social ills. Modern revisionists, such as Erich Fromm and Karen Horney, have objected to the emphasis that Freud placed on biological inheritance. And in the area of Freudian social theory, Herbert Marcuse has suggested that the removal of economic scarcity might release repression and thereby create an improved social environment. In Europe, popular interpretation tended to identify Freud's demand for frankness with free love. Moral indignation that was precipitated by his realism and by faddist perversions of his doctrines conjoined with anti-Semitism, and in 1938 the Nazis, toward whom Jung gravitated, burned Freud's works as a "porno-graphic Jewish specialty." Freudian psychology found its warmest reception in Britain and the United States.

## INTELLECTUAL CURRENTS ON THE EVE OF WORLD WAR I

In the first decades of the twentieth century, Western men had at their disposal a greater number of conflicting and interconnected world views than ever before. Their profusion merely reflected the greater complexity of industrial societies and of social change. A large proportion of the population was literate and engaged in intellectual or professional activities. Freedom of expression had increased with the spread of constitutional government which guaranteed basic civil liberties.

More than in the eighteenth century, science emerged as the criterion for truth. This-worldly outlooks had made deeper inroads than ever before in the history of Western thought. Nevertheless, in most "scientific" ideologies "science" was tantamount to a single-cause explanation deduced from absolute, and often empirically undemonstrable, cosmic laws. When absolutes were questioned or revised by further applications of scientific methodology, most dogmatists chose to look the other way. Others became disillusioned with scientific objectivity as a god that had failed. For them the succeeding years became an "age of anxiety," characterized chiefly by a metaphysical void.

The dogmatic myths of racism and idealistic nationalism were prepared to fill this void. Religiously tinged, these tribalisms became common on the Continent and among imperialist parties everywhere. Polemicists launched frankly irrational and fatalistic assaults on universal concepts of law and justice, proposed governments by special elites, and promised to give the individual "freedom" from responsibility for collective decisions and actions. While empirical sociologists, psychologists, and anthropologists bared the role of irrational behavior in organized society, unbending ideologists threatened to disrupt the institutional framework on which bourgeois society rested. In all of its manifestations, rational individualism was under attack.

To some degree, this disruption of bourgeois values came from within the middle classes. In frantic efforts to combat socialism, part of the bourgeoisie seized upon intellectual weapons that were equally destructive to liberalism, socialism's closest ideological relative. Subsequent experience indicated that well-rooted liberal institutions with lower-class support could survive assault and grave crises. But where they had only a recent and shallow hold, they fell before their combined foes during major crises. Because it precipitated such crises, World War I was the principal catalyst. To understand the political conditions that produced that war, it is necessary to turn to the domestic and international developments of the nineteenth and early twentieth centuries; they are discussed in the next three chapters.

## SELECTED READINGS

*Barzun, Jacques, *Darwin, Marx, Wagner, Critique of a Heritage,* Doubleday Anchor Books, Garden City, New York, 1958.
>Finds a repugnant element of naturalistic determinism in the works of all three men.

*Benda, Julian, *The Betrayal of the Intellectuals,* Beacon Press, Boston, 1955.
>Written after World War I, this essay attacks intellectuals for betraying their mission by becoming propagandists for popular causes, especially national, racial, and class hatreds.

*Bentley, Eric, *A Century of Hero-Worship,* Beacon Press, Boston, 1957 (2nd ed.).
>Studies of Carlyle, Nietzsche, Wagner, and others who preached an antidemocratic doctrine of heroic vitalism, advocating that

\* Asterisk (\*) denotes paperback.

great men should rule and others revere them.

*Berlin, Isiah, *Karl Marx, His Life and Environment,* Oxford University Press, New York, 1959.
>One of the best biographies of the founder of "scientific socialism."

*Brinton, Crane, *The Shaping of Modern Thought,* Prentice-Hall, Englewood Cliffs, New Jersey, 1963.
>An intellectual history especially useful for the development of anti-intellectualism in the early twentieth century.

Cole, G. D. H., *A History of Socialist Thought,* 5 vols., Macmillan, London; St. Martin's Press, New York, 1955–1961.
>Volumes I to III of this extensive work by a British socialist pertain to this period.

Gay, Peter, *The Dilemma of Democratic Socialism, Eduard Bernstein's Challenge to Marx,* Columbia University Press, New York, 1952.
>Sketches the life of the founder of revisionist socialism in Germany, his criticisms of Marxism, and the problems confronting democratic socialists in an increasingly bourgeois society.

*Halévy, Elie, *The Growth of Philosophic Radicalism,* Beacon Press, Boston, 1955.
>Classic analysis of the doctrines and the impact of the English Utilitarians.

*Himmelfarb, Gertrude, *Darwin and the Darwinian Revolution,* Doubleday Anchor Books, Garden City, New York, 1962.
>A critical biography showing the Malthusian origins of Darwin's basic theory which, applied to society and thought, had conservative as well as revolutionary implications.

Homans, George C., and Charles P. Curtis, *An Introduction to Pareto, His Sociology,* A. A. Knopf, New York, 1934.
>A basic summary of Pareto's sociology—his method, categories, and conclusions.

*Hook, Sidney, *Marx and the Marxists, The Ambiguous Legacy,* D. Van Nostrand Co., Princeton, New Jersey, 1955.
>Marx's basic ideas and the divergent strains of thought and politics which evolved from

them set forth, with appended documents, by a philosopher.

*Hughes, H. Stuart, *Consciousness and Society, The Reorientation of European Thought 1890–1930,* A. A. Knopf and Random House, New York, 1958.

A keen intellectual history that portrays a crisis in the search for an objective method to study society at the end of the nineteenth century.

*Irvine, William, *Apes, Angels, and Victorians,* Meridian Books, New York, 1959.

Presents in popular form the careers, contrasting personalities, and writings of the two major evolutionists, Darwin and Huxley, and their relationships with other leading Victorians.

*Kaufmann, Walter, ed., *The Portable Nietzsche,* Viking Press, New York, 1954.

Collection of writings by a leading biographer of Nietzsche and historian of existentialism.

Laidler, H. W., *Social-Economic Movements: An Historical and Comparative Survey of Socialism, Communism, Coöperation, Utopianism,* Crowell, New York, 1949.

Delivers in summary form what the title promises.

*Lichtheim, George, *Marxism, An Historical and Critical Study,* Frederick A. Praeger, New York, 1962.

Shows modifications of Marxist doctrine as it conformed to differing local situations while spreading over Europe.

Manuel, Frank E., *The Prophets of Paris,* Harvard University Press, Cambridge, 1962.

Excellent for Saint-Simon, Fourier, and Comte, set in the environment of their heritage from the Enlightenment.

Mosse, George L., *The Culture of Western Europe, The Nineteenth and Twentieth Centuries,* Rand McNally & Co., Chicago, 1961.

An unusually perceptive intellectual history of modern Europe.

*Puner, Helen Walker, *Freud, His Life and His Mind,* Dell Books, New York, 1959.

A succinct account of Freud's background, his psychoanalytic hypotheses, and the divergent schools of his successors.

Rewald, John, *The History of Impressionism,* Museum of Modern Art, New York, 1955 (2nd ed.).

An illustrated discussion intelligible to non-artists.

Schapiro, Jacob S., *Liberalism and the Challenge of Fascism: Social Forces in England and France, 1815–1870,* McGraw-Hill, New York, 1949.

Makes distinctions between liberalism and certain strains of "utopian socialism" and authoritarianism whose similarities with fascism are overstated.

*Schweitzer, Albert, *The Quest for the Historical Jesus,* The Macmillan Co., New York, 1961.

Sketches a major aspect of nineteenth-century "higher criticism" of Biblical texts, including rational attempts to explain in human terms their recording of miracles and expectations of the end of the world.

Taton, René, ed., *History of Science,* III, *Science in the Nineteenth Century,* Basic Books, New York, 1965.

Translation of a French collaborative manual, including medicine, useful for reference.

*Williams, Raymond, *Culture and Society 1780–1950,* Doubleday & Co., Garden City, New York, 1960.

Exposes romantic novelists who revolted against industrialism as paternalists sharing basic assumptions with traditionalists.

*Wilson, Edmund, *To the Finland Station,* Doubleday & Co., New York, 1953.

A sympathetic account of the socialist tradition before the Bolshevik Revolution.

See also works by Marcuse, Ruggiero, and Schapiro in Selected Readings, Chapter V.

# VIII

# The Politics of Emergent
# Industrial Society—
# About 1850 to 1914

During the decades between 1850 and 1914, the urban industrial type of society that Britain pioneered took root throughout the Western world. Everywhere it raised similar problems. A new industrial and financial elite challenged established elites, usually demanding constitutional changes that would admit them to power. Behind the industrial bourgeoisie came more numerous classes of urban workingmen and intellectuals who sought to democratize political institutions and obtain economic security. Their interests were not those of the elites, whose power they challenged both economically and politically. Governments—autocratic or representative—were called upon to regulate conflicts within this new society, and between it and the old order. The growth of civil services with industrial jurisdictions was nearly as conspicuous a part of this transition as the extension of representative govern-

ment. During these decades, some political leaders attempted to find compromises or accommodations between the preindustrial and industrial segments of society. Usually they appealed to nationalism—often expressed as imperialism—as the common ideology to plaster over cracks in the political structure caused by conflicting interests. But nationalists appealed to traditions that varied widely in different states.

Patterns of adaptation to industrialism varied according to local conditions. The Western democracies, already nation-states with representative governments, were much better equipped to industrialize without revolution. Quite a different set of conditions prevailed in Central and Eastern Europe. For Italy and Germany, nationalism—the ideology of unification and self-determination—took precedence over industry and democracy. Still, unification cleared the path for large-scale industry, especially in Germany. But the new German middle classes were uncertain of themselves and fell under the tutelage of the old military aristocracy and autocratic government. Together they blocked the political "reforms" that were so characteristic of the democratic countries. Thus, they produced a revolutionary situation.

Different rates and degrees of industrialization sharply revised power relationships between states. These differences bore most disadvantageously upon the multinational Eastern empires: Austria-Hungary and Russia. In the absence of wealthy middle classes, their bureaucracies directed modernization to overcome weakness. But at the same time they worked under monarchs and in societies whose traditions and distribution of power were still predominantly from the Old Regime. This contradiction in their policies of maintaining the old order by modernization contributed to instability, but both Austria-Hungary and Russia were beset by other, more serious problems. Nationalism, born of resistance to centralist pressures, threatened to break up both empires, especially Austria-Hungary, while Russia was engaged in a race with catastrophe between population growth and subsistence.

# A. The Western Democracies: Britain, France, and the United States

## THE DEMOCRATIZATION OF GREAT BRITAIN, 1832 TO 1914

Britain was both the industrial leader and the model of constitutional government in nineteenth-century Europe. She alone among Europe's states had a long-established parliamentary government with which to confront industrial problems. Unlike most continental systems which had many parties spread in a continuum from "Left" to "Right" and ruling in coalitions, British politics were based on a two-party structure—one party in power, the other in opposition. In the House of Commons both parties faced each other from opposing benches. Because the executive—the cabinet—depended upon a majority in Parliament, both the voters and the M.P.s had the means of deposing a government. Neither of the two choices at the polls might be entirely satisfactory to the individual voter but, by assuring the victorious party the power to effect its program, Britain's political machinery provided stability. As an alternative or a "shadow" government, the opposition had to keep its program pragmatically in tune with political realities. Splinter parties based on ideology rather than practical politics had little chance of success.

The Reform Bill of 1832 and subsequent reforms ultimately modified the party structure but not the basic constitutional system. Liberals and Conservatives, respectively, replaced the traditional Whigs and Tories, but both upheld the constitutional structure. At the outset, both were firmly committed to maintaining the "Victorian Compromise"— the sharing of power between the gentry and industrial capitalists effected by the first Reform Bill of 1832.* Although it was an informal gentleman's agreement, the Victorian

* See *supra*, pp. 207–208.

Compromise was no less forceful than formal legislation. But the interplay of party politics in a changing social environment led to progressive democratization of the British constitution between 1832 and 1914. The rise of a new political party—the Labour party—prior to World War I indicated that the older parties had not kept abreast of social change, but it did not portend a constitutional revolution. Rather it was a Conservative revolt which threatened to turn the opposition into an insurrection for the first time since 1688.

## Reform Under the Victorian Compromise

Far-reaching reforms began in earnest immediately after the first Reform Bill broke Tory dominance over the House of Commons. Colonial slavery was abolished by compensated emancipation in 1833. The first enforced factory act became law the same year. The Poor Law's administration was centralized and narrowed in scope in 1834 and, in 1835, oligarchies controlling municipal governments were replaced by elected councils. Political concessions to the laboring classes were denied the Chartists, however, in the 1830s and 1840s.

Chartism stemmed from lower-class disillusionment with the Reform Bill, resentment toward the Poor Law's curtailment of alms, religious dissent, and the displacement of domestic weavers by power looms. Representing Britain's first significant labor-in-politics movement, the Chartists aimed to democratize the state. Their petitions to Parliament (called charters) asked for manhood suffrage, vote by secret ballot, annually elected parliaments, equal electoral districts, abolition of property qualifications for voting, and payment to members of Parliament. Some Chartist leaders advocated either violence or a general strike. To Britain's frightened governing classes, these Chartist leaders appeared to be typical of the whole group and, in 1838, they were arrested. But the Chartists recovered from this setback when,

*The House of Commons in session.*

*A Chartist procession, 1848.*

during the economic crises of the 1840s, they sponsored a "Convention" to rival Parliament. A petition of 1848 contained nearly two million signatures—many of them bogus. However, excise tax reductions and repeal of the Corn Laws (agricultural tariffs) in 1846 combined with internal factionalism to eventually undermine their movement. It disappeared as an organized political force during the prosperity of the 1850s.

The Chartist debacle indicated that further reforms required upper-class leadership. This leadership soon appeared and gradually realigned Britain's political parties. In 1834 Sir Robert Peel (son of a manufacturer) committed himself and his Tory followers to further "judicious reforms." Peel had previously sponsored a controversial unarmed model police force in London (the "Bobbies"), and he removed the death pen-

*Lord Palmerston ("Old Pam").*

as Conservative leader in the House of Commons, also followed Peel's tactics of "Tory men and Whig measures." Eventually, under the slogan of "Tory Democracy," he initiated social legislation that went much further than any old Whig or new Liberal was prepared to go.

## Russell and Palmerston's Liberal Nationalism

Liberals took credit for the rising standard of living between 1846 and 1865 under the governments of Lords John Russell and Palmerston. While prosperity sapped the impetus of reform, public attention focused on the personality, pronounced nationalism, and "spirited" foreign policy of Lord Palmerston. His chauvinism electrified the nation when, in 1850, he sent England's fleet to vindicate the claims of a single subject (Don Pacifico) whose property an Athenian mob had destroyed. He began to lose political power, however, as Queen Victoria reasserted royal influence over foreign affairs. When he courted disaster by recognizing Louis Napoleon's overthrow of the French Republic in 1851, he was dropped from the cabinet. But Lord Aberdeen's coalition government mismanaged the Crimean War (discussed later, see pp. 331–332), and thereby created new opportunities for Palmerston. In 1855 he became prime minister. His government successfully repressed the Sepoy Mutiny in India and, in 1857, started a war against China for commercial concessions.* After 1860, his ministry succeeded in negotiating free-trade treaties with other European nations, beginning with France.

Although their special interests differed, no great gulf separated the Conservatives from the Liberals. Entrenched in the House of Lords, the Conservatives—who came increasingly from the ranks of business—were still quick to defend the Anglican Church, agrarian economic interests, and the prerogatives of the nobility. The Liberals were an

alty for more than one hundred offenses. During the great Irish famine he carried his reform efforts too far for the Tory rank and file when he abandoned agricultural protection—the Corn Laws—for free trade. The "Peelites" became the nucleus of the new Liberal party. Meanwhile, Benjamin Disraeli (1804–1881), a social novelist who had started in the Commons as a Radical, used the tariff issue to marshal the opposition of country gentlemen against Peel and to prepare for his own ascent of the "greasy pole" of British political leadership. Too much an opportunist to chain his future to the dying issue of protectionism, Disraeli,

* See *infra,* Chapter IX.

amalgam of Whigs, Dissenters, and former Conservatives who were as respectably upper class as their opponents. Except for some Utilitarian Radicals,* those who agitated for democratic reform were outside of Parliament and were politically impotent. As early as 1852, Lord Russell, architect of the Reform Bill of 1832, proposed an enlargement of the electorate. But as long as Palmerston led the country, his indifference and public apathy toward domestic problems assured the preservation of the Victorian Compromise.

Extensive domestic reforms did not occur in the British Empire during the Liberal era, but a new policy toward Anglo-Saxon colonial settlements evolved. It pointed toward local autonomy for the colonies and looser ties with the mother country. In 1839 Lord Durham reported in favor of such a policy after he had been sent to North America to prevent a Canadian revolt from culminating in another American Revolution. The Canadians were granted a representative assembly where French-Canadian interests were subordinated to those of the English colonists. They secured the abolition of the Navigation Acts in 1849 and, in 1859, were able to introduce local tariffs. The Liberals' colonial policy remained in effect after they had fallen from power and, in 1867, the British North American Act granted Dominion status to Canada.† Later, similar autonomy was extended to Australia, New Zealand, and South Africa. Britain's calculated loosening of ties

*Gladstone, Liberal Reformer.*

---

* The Utilitarian Radicals were followers of Jeremy Bentham who advocated *laissez-faire* economic policies, comprehensive legal reforms, democratization with public education, and an empirical approach to social problems.
† This act, which laid the cornerstone for the later Commonwealth, provided for a popularly elected Commons, an appointive upper house, and an appointive governor-general who remained above party conflicts. Britain retained control over foreign affairs. The Canadian act provided a federal system that was easily expanded and, in 1949, all of British North America, including British Columbia, Prince Edward Island, and the former Dominion of Newfoundland, was brought into a single federation.

with her white settlement colonies contrasted sharply, however, with her aggressive exploitation elsewhere.

## Disraeli and Gladstone Break the Victorian Compromise

After Palmerston's death in 1865, Liberal leadership passed to the Eton-educated son of a wealthy Scottish merchant, William Ewart Gladstone (1809–1898). Gladstone began his long parliamentary career as a Peelite Conservative, dedicated to the preservation of the Anglican Church. Although he was abidingly devoted to a fundamentalist religion that denied Darwinian biology, he became a political reformer and eventually sponsored anticlerical legislation. Competing for leadership with Disraeli, he cast his lot with the Liberals, who accepted him as their "Grand Old Man" long after their younger members had abandoned his faith in *laissez-faire* capitalism. As the pendulum of power swung between Disraeli and Gladstone, reform revived. And often Disraeli's "Tory Democracy"—a system of social reform similar to that which Bismarck later devel-

*Disraeli, advocate of "Tory Democracy."*

oped in Germany—effected more radical change than Gladstone's Liberalism.

Between 1867 and 1885 a series of reforms extended and reorganized the House of Commons' electorate, dismantling the Victorian Compromise. Now the Commons had increased power, and the newly enfranchised classes could pressure the government for more basic reform. In an effort to cement new voters to traditional institutions and to the Conservative party, Disraeli in 1867 sought to outbid the Liberals, "to dish the Whigs," with a greater extension of suffrage. The Liberals countered with amendments even broader in scope. The result was the second Reform Bill of 1867 that doubled the electorate by reducing property qualifications. Now all householders paying poor rates and all renters paying an annual rent of £10 could vote in borough elections. Because most urban workingmen had such means, the bill initiated democracy based on manhood suffrage in urban constituencies, but it failed to enfranchise agricultural laborers. Small boroughs lost their seats, and new or addi-

tional seats were allotted to new and larger towns. In the following year electoral reform was extended to Scotland and Ireland.

Electoral victory in 1868 went to the Liberals. Until 1874, Gladstone presided over a wave of reforms comparable to those following the first Reform Bill. To educate "our masters," as one member put it, the Parliament passed the Forster Education Act of 1870. It instituted the first public primary education system in Britain, although British efforts still lagged far behind those of Germany, Switzerland, and the United States. Parliamentary grants continued to subsidize private religious schools but, where these were lacking, locally-elected school boards were empowered to maintain compulsory, nonsectarian schools financed by local taxes, tuition, and money from Parliament. In the same year, competitive examinations were introduced to open the Civil Service (except the Foreign Office) to all classes, and in 1871 religious qualifications that had barred Dissenters from the universities were removed. Before the reform impetus temporarily flagged, an army reorganization act introduced a reserve system, and stopped the practice of purchasing commissions. Also, secret voting was introduced for the first time, and wide variations in judicial procedures were replaced by a centralized supreme court structure. These measures made British society more competitive but, nonetheless, dominated by the privately schooled sons of the upper classes.

As democracy spread in England, national political parties were formed; leaders began to take issues to the country as a whole; and desires for more democracy were whetted. In 1874 Disraeli campaigned for extended imperialism and state intervention into the relations of capital and labor. He was elected, and before his ministry became engulfed in such foreign adventures as the Balkan crisis of 1875 to 1878, it consolidated and extended public health codes and initiated government housing for the urban poor. It also removed obstacles to labor organization by nullifying common-law doctrines that made contract-breaking a criminal offense and picketing a conspiracy.

Emerging from temporary retirement as leader of the Liberals, Gladstone turned the tide against the aging Disraeli's (now Lord Beaconsfield) imperialism in a national campaign in 1880. Imperialism and relations with Ireland now became the foremost political issues in Britain. But at the same time, the second Gladstone ministry (1880–1885) resumed parliamentary reform on a major scale. Following a Corrupt and Illegal Practices Act of 1883, which set limits on campaign expenses, Gladstone introduced a bill in 1884 that reduced rural property qualifications sufficiently to enfranchise agricultural laborers. To allay Conservative objections that the bill did not abolish electoral inequalities, the Prime Minister secured passage of a second law in 1885 that based representation in the House of Commons on population instead of the traditional boroughs and counties. Within a decade, traditional county government by justices of the peace was replaced by elective councils similar to those introduced in the towns in 1835. Thus democratic procedures reached both the House of Commons and the countryside following the reforms of 1885.

As the next chapter will relate, Disraeli's brand of militant imperialism eventually gained ascendancy in British foreign policy. Gladstone, risking attack as an unpatriotic "Little Englander"—one who would haul down the British flag over parts of the Empire—struggled against the imperialistic foreign policy, but his ultimate failure resulted, in large part, from a split in Liberal ranks caused by his efforts to resolve the irrepressible issue of Ireland.

### The Dilemma of Ireland

In British politics no issue was more intractable to rational resolution than Ireland. By coercive laws and armed force, England had fastened a tithe-supported Anglican Church on Irish Roman Catholics and an

RIVAL STARS.

*The Gladstone-Disraeli rivalry as seen by* Punch, *1868. "Mr. Bendizzy (Hamlet): 'To Be, or Not to Be, that is the question: — Ahem!'*
*"Mr. Gladstone (out of an engagement) (Aside): 'Leading Business, Forsooth! His line is General Utility! Is the manager mad? But no matter — a time will come. . . .' "*

exploitative colonization on the whole population of the island. Resistance to tithes and English rule had repeatedly flared into open rebellion without gaining more than mild concessions. Supported by potato culture rather than industry and commerce, the Irish population almost doubled during the first half of the century only to be caught in massive famines between 1845 and 1847 when poor harvests and potato blight cut into the food supply. Ireland's tragedy contributed to the abandonment of the Corn Laws in 1846, but starvation and emigration combined to drive the population down from 8.2 million in 1841 to 6.5 million in 1851. Yet, landlords were able to raise rents and to deny their Irish tenants security of tenure and compensation for their improvements.

English political leaders ignored the Irish

*Irish tenants resisting eviction.*

"sore" as long as possible, but after 1850 organized resistance made it inescapable. Boycotts were held against English landlords and merchants. A Land League coordinated demands for peasants' freedom to sell their rights, fixity of tenure, and fair rents—the "Three Fs." Irish veterans of the American Civil War organized the Fenian Society that used American funds to instigate violence on the Canadian-American frontier, in English cities, and in the Irish countryside. After the Irish Reform Act of 1868 enlarged the electorate, the staunch Anglophobe, Charles Stewart Parnell, led an Irish Nationalist contingent in the British House of Commons that demanded Home Rule in a separate Irish parliament.

This resistance forced Gladstone and Disraeli—neither of whom had visited Ireland —to consider alternatives to coercion. In 1869 Gladstone secured an act exempting Roman Catholic tenants from paying tithes, but only the Queen's threat to create many new peers secured its passage through the House of Lords where Ireland's submission was a Conservative article of faith. In 1870 Gladstone sponsored a land act to compensate peasants evicted arbitrarily and to provide government loans for those who wished to buy out their landlords. But neither act remedied Irish conditions. After renewed violence, Gladstone offered a second land act in 1881 that granted the "Three Fs." Fearing that the settlement of agrarian issues would jeopardize ultimate Home Rule, Irish Nationalists resisted its enforcement. When terrorists killed the two top civil servants responsible for Irish affairs, both sides again took to violence.

Irish issues became critical in English politics when Irish M.P.s held the balance between evenly divided Conservatives and Liberals. In 1885 both major parties negotiated with the Irish Nationalists in Parliament. But neither party could concede Home Rule without courting unpopularity at the polls and risking a party schism. Nevertheless, Gladstone took the fatal plunge in 1886. When he offered a Home Rule Bill, Liberals, calling themselves "Unionists," defeated him by voting with the Conservatives. Hereafter, Conservatives and Unionists resisted Home Rule. But, in 1892 Gladstone again became dependent on Irish Nationalist votes. Again he offered Ireland Home Rule only to have his bill struck down by the House of Lords. Hereafter, British governments offered generous Land Purchase Acts, but not Home Rule, which was shelved until 1910. Because the House of Lords would not acquiesce in Home Rule voted by the House of Commons, Ireland remained a contentious issue which checked England's evolution toward greater democratization.*

## The Rise of Social Liberalism and the Labour Party

The Liberal split over Ireland delivered power to Conservative governments under Lord Salisbury and Arthur Balfour until 1905. Their governments coincided with the waning of prosperity that had muffled radicalism during the middle of the century. Imports of duty-free agricultural goods after 1880 depressed English agriculture. As other states, such as Germany and the United States became technologically progressive industrial giants, Britain ceased being *the* workshop of the world. Her relative economic and political power in the world de-

* For the resolution of this vexing problem, see Chapter XII.

clined. During that decline, Gladstone's *laissez-faire* Liberalism came under fire from two sides. Conservatives and Unionists advocated imperialist expansion, closer ties with the Empire, industrial tariffs, and the reduction of organized labor's power. On the other side, younger Liberals (such as David Lloyd George) criticized imperialism and campaigned for free trade and greater social welfare. Their social welfare program was enacted after the Liberals were returned to power in 1906, but their advanced social liberalism failed to attract all of labor's votes. During the decline, trade unions picked up marked strength, and Socialists obtained labor followings. When the House of Lords ruled in 1902 that unions could be sued for losses resulting from strikes, the unions' continued existence was threatened. Finding Liberals too little concerned, labor leaders formed their own party and shared in the Liberal victory of 1906. Even though the Taff Vale decision was quickly reversed by legislation, the appearance of laboring men in Parliament as a separate party marked a fundamental divide in British politics. Liberals were losing their ability to hold a solid phalanx against the Conservatives, even with a series of sweeping reforms. As labor grievances accumulated, the unions gained more power and relied less on government support.

The cabinets of Sir Henry Campbell-Bannerman and Herbert Asquith presided over another era of domestic reforms, the implementation of which required drastic reduction in the power of the House of Lords in 1911. These reforms also entailed a large increase in the size of the civil service needed to implement "delegated legislation"—laws, in principle, that were left to the cabinet and civil service to apply to actual conditions. For labor, the reforms made employers responsible for workingmen's accidents—but the Liberals were inactive when a court decision made union political contributions illegal. To the aged and indigent, new laws provided pensions. By 1909 a combination of social welfare costs and naval building appropriations required either large deficits or new sources of revenues. In the "People's Budget" of 1909 the Welsh Chancellor of the Exchequer David Lloyd George spurned the tariff lobby headed by Joseph Chamberlain and proposed heavier income and inheritance taxes. The budget also called for various levies on unearned capital gains. To the House of Lords it appeared to be a social revolution instead of a budget. Breaking precedents, the Lords rejected it overwhelmingly. Thereupon, Prime Minister Asquith took the budget, the issue of the Lords' veto, and—to get Irish support—Irish Home Rule before the electorate. Although weakened, his cabinet kept its majority and promptly challenged the right of the House of Lords to veto money bills and to delay other legislation for more than two years. Again the Liberals held their majority in a new election and, upon the threat that the new king, George V, would create enough peers to break the Lords' opposition, they acquiesced in the Parliament Bill of 1911. By this act the democratically elected House of Commons (whose term was now limited to five years) imposed its will upon the hereditary and appointive constituency of the House of Lords where the power of landed family estates still held sway.

## Prewar Crises

Despite the great Liberal victory of 1911, Asquith's government lost prestige with sectors of the British public, who took to extralegal, extra-Parliamentary tactics to secure redress. One sector was labor, still caught by rising taxes and prices but confident of the growing power of the unions. Another sector was the militant suffragettes who wanted feminine equality, especially at the polls. Both of these groups broke the civil peace, but the third, made up of uncompromising Conservatives and Unionists, who opposed Irish Home Rule, became overtly insurrectionary and threatened Britain with a civil war.

Labor's disillusionment with the Liberal

government and a deteriorating economic position was expressed in a new militant unionism that erupted in a wave of strikes in 1910 and 1911. Some violence occurred, and fears of revolution rippled throughout the press, as miners and transport workers aimed for nationwide settlements. In 1911 Parliament granted a national minimum wage to the miners but displeased both the unions and employers. The government lost prestige, but the number of strikes declined.

Feminist militancy emerged behind the fragile figure of Mrs. Emmeline Pankhurst at the same time the wave of strikes occurred. When Asquith refused to make woman suffrage a party matter or to push it through Parliament, the suffragettes turned to publicity devices involving disorders—window smashing, arson, and chaining themselves to the railings of Buckingham Palace. Imprisoned, they refused to eat, dumbfounding their wardens who tried to force nourishment upon them.

Militant unionists and suffragettes were signs of a declining sense of security in prewar Britain, but neither threatened the security of the established political system as much as the Conservative-Unionist revolt against Home Rule for Ireland. Asquith redeemed his promise of Home Rule to the Irish Nationalists in return for their support in 1910 by introducing a bill in 1912 granting Ireland a bicameral parliament and continued representation in Westminster. The bill became law in 1914 over the opposition of the Lords. Meanwhile, Protestants in Ulster, faced with being subordinated in a parliament in Dublin, became Unionists—to a man. With support from Conservatives, Liberal Unionists, and part of the army, the Protestants set about enlisting a large militia to resist Home Rule by force when World War I broke out. On this issue, opposition to the government had turned to armed resistance. Britain's imminent civil war yielded to a greater war, however, and the problem of Ireland, now rebellious in frustration, awaited settlement after 1918.

## FRANCE: FROM EMPIRE TO REPUBLIC

Compared to England, which had devoted her primary energies to industry, France had been productive of the great political changes affecting all of Europe, especially the revolutions of 1789, 1830, and 1848. But from these revolutions France was yet to find a stable government when Louis Napoleon, whose watchword was order, became Emperor in 1852. The great Emperor's nephew rode to power, as previously mentioned, largely on his uncle's legendary reputation, but he labored constructively to reconcile French traditions with the promotion of industry and finance. When his personal regime foundered, it bequeathed a broader social base for modern legislation and an efficient bureaucracy to the Third Republic. This bureaucracy provided continuity and direction that the unstable ministries of the Third Republic could not. But even with unstable ministries, the Third Republic had the strength to repress traditionalist foes. That strength rested upon a stable French society that was not yet industrial in the sense that England or contemporary Germany were. For in the early twentieth century, French society still consisted mainly of small farmers and small shopkeepers.

### Louis Napoleon and the Authoritarian Empire

As authoritarian president from 1851 to 1852 and as Emperor thereafter, Louis Napoleon managed domestic affairs in the style of his uncle. In late December a plebiscite—a vote "yes" or "no"—authorized him to draft a new constitution. It overwhelmingly approved his *coup d'état* three weeks before when he dissolved the Assembly and called for popular support. His constitution gave him unfettered control over foreign policy, the armed forces, and the administration. Under the constitution, administrative experts drafted laws that the Legislative Assembly could only approve or reject. An appointive Senate worked with the executive to propose constitutional amendments and to prevent violations of the constitution. In November of 1852 a second plebiscite gave approval of Napoleon's conversion of the authoritarian presidency into a hereditary Empire, and ratified the Emperor's title, Napoleon III. By implication this act made all French governments since his uncle's fall usurping, "false" governments.

Lacking an organized political following of his own, Napoleon made concessions to factions that were too strong to destroy. Considering Roman Catholic support indispensable, he wooed churchmen with educational favors and foreign policies calculated to gain their support. At court the Empress Eugenie, the startlingly beautiful daughter of a Spanish nobleman, championed the Church. Catholic leaders responded by calling the Emperor a heaven-sent blessing, and many Bourbon and Orleanist monarchists were impressed by his solicitude for the faith. As long as clerics and monarchists supported him, the Emperor gave them considerable freedom of press and expression. To solidify his authoritarian regime, Louis Napoleon initially repressed liberal constitutionalists, especially the republicans. For a decade summary judicial commissions broke up republican organizations by either imprisoning or exiling their leaders. Public meetings were banned. Newspapers had to be licensed by the government and run by carefully selected editors. Their publishers were required to put up large surety deposits as guarantees against breaches of censorship. Although nonrevolutionary republicans could run for office against officially sponsored candidates, Napoleon III earned their lasting enmity and justified their lasting fears of a strong executive.

Ultimately the Emperor could not reconcile the Napoleonic legend and his alliance with the clerical, traditionalist Right. According to the legend, imposed order was a stepping stone to liberty and material progress—not the permanent condition cherished by traditionalists. In his economic outlook the Emperor differed significantly from them, coming closer to the Saint-Simonians.* His court sponsored banks, credit institutions, railway construction and consolidation, shipping, mining, and urban rebuilding. Remodeled, gaslit Paris, hosting a succession of international expositions, became the showplace of France's industrial progress. Gaiety reigned in the capital, where businessmen served an international clientele and catered to the tastes of the middle class who were displacing landed aristocrats in high society. There was little evidence of the "Moral Order" that the clergy had heralded. Moreover, as the economy expanded, the ranks of urban labor swelled, and workers—dissatisfied with the Empire's paternal welfare services—became a potential force of political opposition. Thus social change came out of Napoleon's economic policies and threatened to end the dominance of his clerical, traditionalist allies on the Right.

## The Liberal Empire and Its Fall

But before such social change had shaken his alliance with the conservatives, the Emperor's foreign policies had already alienated churchmen and had forced him to woo the support of moderates by liberalizing the Empire between 1860 and 1870. Victory in the Crimean War enhanced his prestige, but the result of his intervention in Italy—the creation of an anticlerical kingdom there—cooled clerical and nationalist ardors. Napoleon moved to repair the damage with the clerics by garrisoning Rome and guaranteeing it to the pope. In 1861 he began supporting an ill-fated project to turn Mexico into a conservative, clerical Empire under Emperor Francis Joseph's brother, Maximilian. These actions succeeded more in alienating Italy and the United States than in reenlisting Catholic support. To further attract moderates, Napoleon granted the Legislative As-

* See *supra*, pp. 277–278.

*Emile Ollivier, architect of the French Liberal Empire.*

sembly power to discuss and reply to the address from the throne and to publish its debates in 1860. Pressed by mounting deficits, he made concessions in budgetary matters the following year. The Emperor also appointed a Voltairean historian, Victor Duruy, Minister of Education. Duruy curbed further expansion of clerical schools and—to provide for the educational needs of modern society —sponsored laws calling for compulsory primary education and vocational training. In 1864 the Emperor took the additional step of permitting temporary labor organizations to strike for economic objectives.

These measures fell far short of establishing a liberal government responsible to an elected parliament, but they contributed to pressures for further change to which concessions were made in 1869 and 1870. Opposition in the Legislative Assembly grew. There was a rash of strikes. And radical Republicans—stimulated by the removal of censorship—revived their agitation. Under

the leadership of Emile Ollivier, a former Republican attracted to Napoleon's service by the promise of liberal evolution, the final transition to the "Liberal Empire" began. In 1869 the Legislative Assembly became a parliament empowered to initiate laws, and the following year, just before the outbreak of the Franco-Prussian War, a plebiscite ratified changes making the cabinet responsible to Parliament. The Emperor, however, retained his prerogatives in making constitutional changes and in directing military and diplomatic affairs.

The liberal experiment collapsed when Napoleon III became a Prussian prisoner of war at Sedan in September 1870.* In Paris, Republicans took the initiative by organizing an emergency government to continue the war. An emerging Republican leader, Léon Gambetta, escaped from the encircled capital by a sensational balloon flight and tried to revive the Jacobin spirit of 1792 in order to turn out the German invaders. But it was in vain. Convinced that further resistance was futile, moderates negotiated an armistice that permitted the election of a new government. Regarding the Republicans as war-hawks, the electorate returned a large majority of Orleanists and Legitimist (Bourbon) monarchists who stood for peace. Rather than open the divisive issue of constitutional organization immediately, the new assembly established a provisional government under the aged Adolphe Thiers (1797–1877) to conclude and fulfill the terms of peace.

### Between Monarchy and Republic, 1871 to 1878

Thiers, a seasoned servant of Louis Philippe, a famous historian, and an active moderate who stood on the boundary between republicanism and constitutional monarchism, brought great prestige to the presidency of the provisional government. He led it through three years of reconstruction dur-

* See *infra*, p. 340.

ing which the basic issue of whether France was to be a republic or a monarchy was held in abeyance.

## The Paris Commune and Aftermath

But Parisians—never in close political rapport with their fellow countrymen—had accumulated grievances against the new government. Among them was the defeat of 1870 which Parisian leaders considered a betrayal and an insufferable humiliation, especially since the government had permitted a triumphal German march through the city that had fallen to bombardment and siege. They also resented the government's refusal to extend moratoria on debts and rents, despite the continuing high rate of unemployment. Armed Parisian guardsmen set up a *de facto* government—the Commune—that resisted the central government from March through May 1871. For one week in May of that year, fierce civil war flared as government forces besieged and captured the disorganized city. The casualties and massive revenge in blood exacted by the victors exceeded any single French loss in the Prussian war. In both conservative and Marxian lore, the Commune was portrayed as the first modern Communist experiment, but in fact it was more a resurgence of urban Jacobinism. Except for postponing debts and rents, regulating bakeries, and providing relief, it left private economic interests untouched. Its anticlericalism was no more pronounced than its vengeful anti-Germanism. But lore perhaps reveals better than fact the passions that the Commune rekindled between the "Two Frances"—the urban impoverished one, on the one side, and the traditionalist, rural, and propertied one, on the other.

After making a vindictive example of Paris, the Thiers government, backed by oversubscribed public loans, quickly paid a war indemnity to Germany and secured the evacuation of German troops in 1873. Marshal MacMahon, loser to Prussia but con-

*Parisians buying cat and dog flesh during the German siege, 1871.*

queror of the Commune, replaced Thiers. Then constitutional disputes resumed in earnest. MacMahon's intended role was to preside over a monarchist restoration. This end seemed certain, but the Bourbons and Orleanists could reach no agreement. Symbolized by the Duke of Chambord's stubborn refusal to give up the *fleur de lis* flag (the inviolate symbol of divine right monarchy that was intolerable to the Orleanists), the Bourbons utterly refused to come to terms with modern society. Unable to turn their majority in the Assembly into a restoration, the divided monarchists extended MacMahon's term of office to seven years. Their default gave liberal constitutionalists and Republicans another opportunity.

## Birth of the Third Republic

In 1875 the monarchist assembly passed a series of stopgap constitutional laws which indicated its fear of both a strong executive and the masses. Engrained by the Empire, universal manhood suffrage was retained for the Chamber of Deputies, but most of the upper legislative house was indirectly elected by preponderantly rural voters. Elected by the Senate and the Chamber jointly, the president had no veto but could, with approval by the Senate, dissolve the Chamber. By a majority of only one vote, he received the title "President of the *Republic*." These constitutional laws did not prevent a monarchist restoration. But they became the constitution of the Third Republic—the most enduring constitutional structure that France has had since 1789.

Republicans won control of the Chamber in 1875, but they came into conflict with the monarchist president, MacMahon. Initially he yielded and appointed a Republican, Jules Simon, to head the cabinet. But responding to Rightist fears of Republican anticlericalism, he precipitated a constitutional crisis on May 16, 1877, by dismissing Simon. When the Assembly refused confidence to MacMahon's appointee, he dissolved parliament. After Republicans carried both houses in the ensuing election of 1878, MacMahon resigned. But the reaction against his actions was so strong that, henceforth, no French executive dared dissolve parliament.

This executive weakness—which contrasted sharply to the British Cabinet's ability to command party loyalty by its power to dissolve the House of Commons—was a major factor in France's ministerial instability. Under the Third Republic, parliamentary committees overawed and brought down one cabinet after another. Because of the multiplicity of political parties the cabinets were necessarily coalitions of undisciplined deputies. Mark Twain voiced a common Anglo-Saxon judgment on French politics when he compared the changing of French ministers to the changing of the Royal Guard in Britain. But the Third Republic, steadied by established social patterns and its civil service, proved too stable to warrant this comparison. While ministers changed frequently, their subordinates were permanent employees. Despite—perhaps because of— vacillation at the top, they carried out established routines independently. As long as French society did not change so as to call these routines into question, the subordinates

gave regularity to French public life. Nevertheless, French politics was convulsed by determined contests between the Republic and its enemies.

## The Republic and Its Foes on the "Right"

Up until 1914 the Third Republic succeeded more than preceding regimes in uniting Frenchmen in imperialist expansion, economic development, and fear of the German Empire whose margin of power over France increased. Despite its achievements, it was buffeted by continued attacks from the "Right"—by traditionalists and authoritarians who used its extensive shortcomings and lack of grandeur as weapons against liberal, constitutional government.

No ideological conflict was more fundamental than that between the defenders of Church schools and the Republicans who worked to displace them with compulsory, primary education that would be both secular and free.* Under successive clerical governments, the regular clergy—the monastic orders—had regained most of the ground lost during the great Revolution of 1789, against which churchmen had sworn eternal enmity. Republicans, in turn, viewed the Church's hold on education as a threat to themselves and to France's ability to cope with the modern world. In 1880, Education Minister Jules Ferry (1832–1892) ordered the Jesuits and all unauthorized teaching orders to disband. The government used force when the Jesuits (whose graduates filled the army officer and diplomatic corps and judicial benches) ignored the decrees. But the clergy retained considerable influence as educators, both because Ferry's decrees were laxly enforced and because the government delayed building schools, especially for girls. Animosities lessened when Pope Leo XIII ordered French Catholics to accept the Republic, but substantial parts of

---

* By custom and financial barriers, higher education remained the exclusive preserve of the wealthier classes.

the clergy, especially the regulars, were conspicuous participants in every attack on the Republic from the "Right."

Following sensational conservative gains at the polls in 1885, Republican defenses were weakened by scandals and executive mediocrity. Revelations that his son-in-law was trafficking in Legion of Honor awards forced the resignation of President Jules Grévy in 1887. His successor, Sadi Carnot (chosen because he was a grandson of a revolutionary hero and because he posed no executive threat to Parliament) was faced with the first serious challenge to the Republic since 1877—the Boulanger Affair. General Boulanger was a former commander in Algeria and a stately-appearing figure on horseback. He became Minister of War in 1886 under the aegis of Georges Clemenceau, a Republican who appreciated his lack of aristocratic connections. Stirring public fancy by profuse statements of patriotism and demands for revenge on Germany— themes that Republicans were also wont to play—Boulanger built up a Napoleonic image and following. Clergy, monarchists, revolutionary socialists, and purely adventuresome opponents of the government all looked to him. Stripped of command and military status by apprehensive Republicans, he was elected as a martyrlike hero to the Chamber of Deputies by many constituencies. When the moment for his *coup d'état* arrived, Boulanger proved himself a poor Bonapartist. Threatened with arrest, he fled to Brussels with his mistress where, the following year (1891), he committed suicide.

Fortunate timing spared the Republic. Otherwise, the Panama Scandal, which broke in the courts in 1892, would have coincided with the Boulanger Affair. Investigations revealed to the public that officials, parliamentarians, the press, and high financiers had connived—many for a price—to conceal the bankruptcy of Ferdinand de Lessep's Panama Canal Company. Swamped by losses from yellow fever and technological problems whose solution came too late to stave

*General Boulanger, a would-be Napoleon.*

off ruin, the company collapsed, leaving hundreds of thousands of investors with heavy losses. In the United States, similar scandals had discredited administrations without calling the basic constitutional framework into question. But in France the "Rightist" press used the Panama Scandal as a battering ram against "Republican plutocracy" and its alleged dominance by Jews. Exploiting the prominence of Jews as go-betweens in the affair, "Rightist" journalists such as Eduard Drumont and the nationalist Maurice Barrès —who had financial support from the Mac-Mahon family—sought to stir the populace by using anti-Semitic propaganda in their drive against the Republic.

## Captain Dreyfus and the Eclipse of the "Right"

Anti-Semitism became a central theme of the Dreyfus case, which brought the Republic into conflict with the strongholds of monarchism—the army and the Church. Dreyfus, a Jewish intelligence officer employed in the

*Dreyfus before the court-martial.*

normally Catholic and monarchist General Staff, was arrested for leaking military secrets to Germany. A secret court-martial overrode his plea of innocence, and he was condemned to life imprisonment. But in 1896 a new chief of the Intelligence Section, Georges Picquart, provided his superiors with evidence that the real culprit was Major Esterhazy, a Hungarian adventurer of the Foreign Legion with papal Zouave experience. For his efforts Picquart was transferred to the Tunisian frontier. The case was reopened when a respected senator publicly bared Picquart's findings, but a reluctant court-martial triumphantly acquitted Esterhazy. Emile Zola now joined the efforts of Dreyfus' family to clear his name, by writing the article *J'accuse* in Clemenceau's newspaper. Zola, who escaped to England, was tried and convicted in absentia for his attack on the army's justice. Then Esterhazy, discharged from the army for embezzlement, implicated a Colonel Henry who had become head of the Intelligence Section, but Henry committed suicide rather than testify. The mystery and murkiness of the case deepened when a second court-martial still found Dreyfus guilty but reduced his sentence to ten years. Dreyfus was pardoned in 1899 and fully exonerated in 1906 but, by 1899, his tortuous case had become the basic issue in a realignment of French politics.

From the outset, monarchists, vocal clerics, and all varieties of authoritarian nationalists had defended the army's action as a patriotic duty. Organized in the League of the French Fatherland, they held to a faith in the integrity of the army that made belief in Dreyfus' guilt imperative. They dismissed any other view as subversive and probably foreign-inspired. Mobs, which they urged on, rioted against Jewish shopkeepers and Dreyfusards. For Dreyfus' defenders, a principle vital to the Republic was at stake: impartial justice and a guarantee that the law would always protect individual rights. In opposition to the conservative league, they formed the League of the Rights of Man and, when socialists led by Jean Jaurès threw in their lot with defenders of the Republic, the "Right" lost exclusive control of the streets. In Parliament, a conservative Republican, René Waldeck-Rousseau, formed a ministry for the defense of the Republic. It was dominated by radicals but, for the first time, included a Socialist, Alexandre Millerand. Heretofore the narrow band of French Socialists had been hostile to the Republic and refused to cooperate in any "bourgeois" ministry, but now they rallied to save the Republic. Radical Republicans, however, dominated French politics until the outbreak of World War I.

As a direct sequel to the Dreyfus Affair, the Radicals purged the two citadels of authoritarian opposition, the army and the Church. Henceforth, clerical conservatism, which had been a test for promotion in the past, became a disability for army officers. By building a system of informers and secret personnel files, the government was able to reward friends and punish enemies. Difficulties between the Church and the anticlerical government were inevitable, since the Concordat of 1801 had given the government the right to nominate or appoint prelates. But the Church's involvement in the Dreyfus Affair intensified the conflict. In 1901 a "law of associations" required state approval for the constitution and by-laws of all societies or associations, including religious teaching orders, and required all orders to stop teaching within ten years. Compromise became more difficult with the accession of Pope Pius X, who unilaterally redefined the Concordat and infuriated French public opinion by protesting an official state visit of the French president to the Kingdom of Italy. In 1905 the government legislated almost complete separation of Church and state, and the law required local congregations to take over Church buildings. The papacy objected to both congregational autonomy and separation *per se*. No compromise was reached as long as Pope Pius lived. In the ensuing deadlock, which was marked by corrupt handling of confiscated property and by some violence, the "Right" again benefited from reactions to aggressive Republican anticlerical policies.

## Unresolved Problems

The Republicans had humbled the authoritarian "Right" for the moment, but they also had foes in the anarcho-syndicalist trade unions* and the socialist "Left" which, in part, was unconvinced that bourgeois parties could be trusted in positions of power. And the reputation of the "Left" was derogatorily tinged by lore associating it with the Paris Commune. Prior to 1885 the government pardoned surviving Communards and legalized the formation of permanent trade unions, but further concessions were too few to attract labor loyalties. Politicians, dependent upon the votes of farmers, shopkeepers, and investors, had little sympathy for the urban lower classes. They did legislate a ten-hour day for women and children in 1900 and provide optional social insurance in 1910, but no major industrial state had done so little for its labor force. As in Britain, real wages declined after the turn of the century while investments flowed in heavy streams outside the country. The entry of Socialists into cabinets did little to remedy labor's situation. Socialists themselves were

divided into factions and, when they united in 1905, they were formally committed to noncooperation with middle-class governments. Although "reformism" permeated Socialist ranks before World War I, Socialist ministers were obliged to become independent.

French Socialist weakness reflected the paucity of trade unions and the doctrinaire antipolitical attitudes of those unions that did exist. Organization was difficult for both the Socialists and the unions because French industry was small-scale and dispersed. Textiles still employed the largest number of workers, and half of them still worked at home. Five out of six industrial workers did not belong to any union at all. France—and, for that matter, the rest of Latin Europe—simply lacked the mass labor organizations of large-scale industry in which reformist socialism thrived in England and Germany. Anarcho-syndicalism, which staked its hopes on general strikes and violence rather than a weak minority position in the Assembly, found industrial and political conditions in France especially congenial. The announced intention of the General Confederation of Labor, formed in 1895, was to overturn capitalism and the bourgeois state by sabotage and general strikes. To break strikes, both Socialist and Republican officials used force and threatened to conscript strikers. But labor violence in France probably never equaled that in the United States during the same period, and the vision of a successful general strike began to fade before World War I. The weakness of the "Left" was in large part the natural outcome of France's slow pace of industrialization, the same weakness that caused its power position on the Continent to decline sharply *vis-à-vis* Germany.

Thus despite ministerial instability, the Third Republic achieved a stability that alienated the "other France"—the urban lower classes—at the same time that it broke the "Right's" bastions of power. And that stability faithfully represented the predominant

---

* For the doctrines of anarcho-syndicalism, see *supra*, p. 285.

sectors of French society—the landowning peasants, the professionals, the shopkeepers, the industrialists, and the financiers. Only further industrial urbanization could decisively shift the political center of gravity further from the traditional "Right" and more toward the radical "Left."

## THE EMERGENCE OF THE AMERICAS: THE UNITED STATES

The other major democratic Western state to industrialize during the second half of the nineteenth century was the United States. Like Britain the United States had established representative government. Although her nationhood was put to the test of a great civil war, she was also recognized along with Britain and France as a nation-state, unlike the countries of Central and Eastern Europe in 1850. By the early twentieth century she had become the foremost industrial producer in the world. Yet, like France, only a minority of her population was taken up directly in urban, industrial occupations. In America, as in Britain and France, there were struggles between pre- and postindustrial elites. But especially after the fall of the aristocratic South, the new republic had virtually no institutions comparable to the Old Regime which worked to curb economic opportunity, social mobility, freedom of expression, and the democratization of politics—at least for Americans of European extraction.

A half-century ahead of developments in Great Britain, politics rang with oratorical appeals to the "common man." In the first half of the nineteenth century religious and property qualifications for voting were removed, and state constitutions were repeatedly revised to curb economic and political oligarchies. Compulsory free primary education spread through the northern states, and numerous small denominational colleges —which belonged to no established church— mushroomed. Foreign visitors were impressed and often shocked by the Americans'

egalitarianism, informality, materialism, provincialism, and relative lack of artistic and literary culture. America pulsed with economic activity, but its spread out over an agrarian empire with immense per capita resources also contained the seeds of sectional conflicts which disrupted the national government.

## Territorial Expansion and the Civil War

From the time of its founding the American republic extended its frontiers faster than settlement, land speculation, and the removal of Indian resistance and titles could securely establish them. After the acquisition of the Louisiana Territory in 1803, no powerful neighbors stood in its path. Its imperialism decimated Indians and threatened the inhabitants of bordering states, but it was not applied to new settlement areas within the republic. Under its flexible federal system of government, these territories could be admitted as equal states. Florida was acquired from Spain in 1819. Texas was annexed in 1845. As a result of the ensuing Mexican War, present western and southern borders were nearly rounded out. Agrarian expansion first tipped the balance in the Federal Government away from industrial, tariff-minded New England, but then it became bogged down in the slavery controversy that divided North and South.

The industrial and freehold agricultural economy of the North was not easily reconciled with the plantation-slave system where cotton (produced largely for British textile mills) was "king." The question of admitting new states with or without slaves fired smoldering animosities, especially after 1820. The Missouri Compromise of that year created a temporary balance between slave and free states, but the northwestern United States, attracting immigrants from free states and abroad, outstripped the South in population. When admission of new states acquired by the Mexican War threatened to perpetuate and extend the slave-plantation system, slavery—really the symbol of conflict between two different types of society —became the paramount issue in national politics.

The decade of the 1850s brought the slavery conflict to a head. Southern planters defended their "peculiar institution" aggressively. They drove out antislave groups like the Quakers and suppressed all critical discussion both in their region and Congress. They defended slavery as a Biblically-sanctioned positive moral good on which all civilizations had rested. Southern "poor whites" who did not profit from the plantation system feared the Negro and followed the planters. Only in the North, where an abolition movement became a moral crusade, was antislave agitation tolerated. The abolitionists never converted a majority in the North, but moderates were unable to come up with practicable alternatives. The Compromise of 1850, which gave the free states a majority but provided for the return of fugitive slaves, wore thin and was abridged in 1854, after which violence between pro- and antislave factions broke out in Kansas Territory. The ties of union were finally broken with the formation of a strictly sectional, antislave, free-soil, and industrial tariff party, the Republicans, who won the presidency, although not a majority in Congress, in 1860. Southern secession after Abraham Lincoln's election touched off a four-year dress rehearsal of modern nationalist warfare between the agrarian Southern Confederacy and the North that represented a coalition of freehold farmers and industrialists.

Confronting each other in the Civil War were two nationalist military states fighting for unconditional victory. For Lincoln, the struggle was not to emancipate slaves but to maintain the Union and to secure individual rights. Hopes of quick victory on both sides gave way to a long weary war of attrition. Failing to get expected assistance from Britain, the agrarian South was less able to fight a war successfully. Despite sharp divi-

*An American slave market, 1852.*

*Richmond, Virginia, after the Civil War.*

sions of opinion on the justice of the war, the North remained physically stronger. In 1863 its armies under Ulysses Grant cut the Confederacy in two along the course of the Mississippi River. After Robert E. Lee's counterstroke into Pennsylvania was turned back with unabsorbable losses, General Sherman's army divided the South again by cutting a band of desolation across Georgia. In 1865 the war came to an end in Virginia and the Carolinas—the heart of the Confederacy.

Involving greater bloodshed than any previous modern war, the Civil War evoked a spirit of righteous vengeance with which the victors "reconstructed" the vanquished. The Fourteenth Amendment to the Constitution made citizenship explicitly national, sealing the war's verdict against the right to secede claimed by the southern states. Union victory also doomed the institution of slavery, which a constitutional amendment of 1865 terminated. But the outcome of the war also meant the victory of the Republican party which, relying upon the votes of freedmen to stay in power, made the prosperous North into a veritable hotbed for the development of commercial agriculture and large-scale industry.

## The Postwar Consolidation of Business Dominance

Although interrupted by periodic depressions, the North's postwar boom made the United States the largest industrial and agricultural producer in the world by the end of the century. As railroads crossed the western plains and tied mining centers to the East, grain, meat, and precious metals flowed outward in exchange, and millions of immigrants made their way to burgeoning northern cities and farms. As the continental frontier drew to a close in 1890, American life began to assume an urban, industrial complexion. Although still a majority, the proportionate number of farmers in the population began to shrink, and by 1900 the value of iron and steel production exceeded that of the milling and meat-packing industries.

*Laissez faire* and Social Darwinism, spiced with corruption at every level between government and business, prevailed until the turn of the century. It was not strict *laissez faire,* of course: tariffs were repeatedly raised; banking laws provided for built-in deflation; and western railroads received large subsidies that clever managers diverted partially to their own pockets. Business consolidators strove for monopoly, with more than occasional success, and political power was widely used to secure franchises and special privileges. Neither political party had a corner on corruption. At the national level, the Republicans held fast to power by managing Negro votes and by granting extravagant pensions to organized veterans. Concern

for political reform did not stagnate completely, but efforts to legislate a national civil service merit system consistently failed until after 1881 when President Garfield was assassinated by a disappointed job seeker. Although dissident reform movements rose in both major parties, Democrats controlled the presidency and both houses of Congress for only two years (1893–1895) before 1913, and they were years of serious depression. In the wake of the Civil War the competitive party system broke down, and a new aristocracy of new and rapidly acquired wealth assumed positions of political and economic power.

Union legislation during the Civil War provided western farmers with homesteads, scientific agricultural facilities, and railway transportation. Other laws, however, gave business and financial circles preponderant power. But the farmers, unlike the European peasantry, were literate, enfranchised, and capable of long and organized dissent. They demanded and often received limited amounts of "cheap money." They agitated for government regulation of railroad monopolies and in 1887 secured the Interstate Commerce Commission, a new type of federal regulatory agency. But agrarian discontent reached a peak during the depression of the 1890s. Victimized by falling prices, overproduction, local droughts, and financial-industrial combines protected by tariffs, the farmers organized the People's party. This party demanded a voice in the government, which previously had not been responsive to them. Its platform called for an end to tariffs and grants that subsidized business. It called for an increased supply of money and rural credit. It also urged the adoption of a progressive income tax to relieve property taxation. The Populists failed in their efforts to effect an alliance with organized labor and, in 1896, their organization was broken when Democratic leaders swallowed up the party's principal demand for unrestricted coinage of silver.

Fearing the West's flair for "free silver,"

Easterners threw their support behind the Republicans, giving William McKinley's party undisputed control over the United States. Becoming a citadel of Social Darwinism, the Supreme Court curbed, rather than extended, regulation of the railroads. It restricted enforcement of the Sherman Anti-Trust Act (a law directed against combinations of business but also used against unions) and in 1895 declared the income tax unconstitutional. Ignoring needs for domestic reform, the McKinley administration joined the general quest for an overseas empire.

Industrial growth during the consolidation of business dominance produced a large labor force, but it, like the farmers, had difficulty organizing in a hostile environment. A constant flow of immigrants willing to work for low wages (according to American standards) sapped the ability of unions to negotiate, as did apathy, born of the feeling that labor was a step on "the way up," and that laborers were not part of a permanent working class. Business dominance meant that courts, officials, police, and the armed forces were hostile; the use of force in strikebreaking was commonplace. Although revolutionary ideologies made only slight inroads into the American labor movement, the United States had one of the most violent records of employer-employee relationships. Nevertheless the strongest labor organization (the craft unions assembled in the American Federation of Labor in 1881) did not try to found a separate political party. During the Progressive era, when it obtained some political concessions, its membership grew rapidly (from one-half million to two million, 1900–1914).

## The Progressive Era, 1900 to 1914

By 1900 a new self-conscious urban, industrial society had emerged in America. But it was foreign to inherited agrarian traditions and ideology. It became increasingly popular to speak of America as a unique frontier society breeding individualism and ruggedness. Although Theodore Roosevelt worked for a balance between the new and the old, his *Winning of the West* was an early sample of the romantic literature and entertainment that turned American minds away from urban realities to an idealized, stereotyped frontier. Some, including Roosevelt, tried to keep the frontier spirit going by military expansion overseas. Still others, nativists, attributed all agitation over urban social and economic conditions to immigrants and foreign ideologies. In the name of order and the preservation of American Anglo-Saxonism they advocated the curtailment of immigration. Despite these diversions, however, a general reform movement under the label of "Progressivism" swept the country during the first decades of the twentieth century. It came from many quarters and in many guises. Trade unionists, Socialists, and advocates of the "social gospel" all put forward their own formulas for change. Alone, no one of these programs could succeed. The Progressive Movement, however, effected a combination of urban-rural, northern-southern, and labor-upper class reform elements, joined for the first time since the Civil War in a conscious effort to remold American institutions.

Progressives opposed the concentration of political, economic, and social power that had developed since the Civil War. They made the traditional appeal for fair competition, equal opportunity, and democratic institutions. In doing this, they rejected the Darwinists' definition of liberty as an unrestrained struggle for existence. Like the social Liberals and Labourites of Britain, they appealed to a sense of social justice—a social conscience. Believing that legislation could affect man's environment, they pressed for laws based on statistical social and economic facts.

Congressional investigators, urban journalists (the "Muckrakers"), and elected officials took the lead in exposing foul practices in business and government, the unrepresentative nature of political institutions,

*Theodore Roosevelt cleaning up finance.*

and shocking conditions of public health. While they attracted a wide audience, the youthful President Theodore Roosevelt wielded power after 1901 to dissolve "trusts," protect labor rights, and to strengthen regulatory agents. Although his roar was more radical than his deeds, Roosevelt failed to convince his Republican party that progressivism was necessary to check socialism.

Roosevelt lost the support of his party, but reform swelled at the state and local levels. Expert city officials hired by elective councils supplanted the "bosses." City-owned utilities replaced many former franchises and contracts. At the state level more than 1500 constitutional amendments were adopted. Among other things, the amendments provided for more expert administrators, regulatory commissions, and more direct control by the electorate over legislators and judges. Most cities and states began to hold primary elections, and the states adopted an amendment making the election of United States Senators direct. In the election of 1912, Republicans placed third be-

hind Woodrow Wilson and Roosevelt, who led an independent Progressive campaign. The Socialists polled over 900,000 votes. Clearly, Progressivism had a mandate.

Wilson had campaigned for the "New Freedom," which meant to him the restoration of competition and equal opportunity. He broke precedent by personally asserting his leadership in Congress. First he attacked the tariff, which reformers had long denounced as "the mother of trusts." He won sharp tariff reductions and, to replace revenue losses, an income tax sanctioned by constitutional amendment. He also secured passage of a more stringent antitrust act, outlawing certain types of financial combines. In 1913 the Federal Reserve Act changed the banking system, providing a flexible money supply and vesting fiscal controls in a Federal Reserve Board. As the election of 1916 approached, Wilson pushed for the creation of a Federal Trade Commission (a regulatory agency to police competitive business practices) and for laws regulating working conditions on the railways. In the campaign of 1916 he committed the Democratic party to more social legislation and to membership in a League of Nations after the European war ended. The results of that election seemed to vindicate Roosevelt's judgment that reform would undermine socialism, for the Socialist vote fell off more than one half.

In some instances, American Progressivism paralleled the social legislation of Britain and Germany, but the United States was still overwhelmingly rural. Therefore, urban-based reforms were tenuous, since political power continued to reside in the countryside. Not until the 1930s did the United States secure a social security system, minimum wage legislation, and the prohibition of child labor. With respect to industrial social legislation, her development was closer to France than to the more urbanized, industrial societies.

# B. The Consolidation of Germany and Italy as Nation-States

Of the major countries comprising Europe's state system in 1914, two of them, Italy and Germany, did not exist in 1850, except as geographical and cultural entities. The success of each in achieving unification between 1859 and 1871 meant the realization of the nation-state ideal that the revolutions of 1848 had failed to produce. Nationalism rather than the desire for parliamentary government or industrialization was the leading motivation behind the unifying movements. Yet unification provided a potential stepping-stone toward both representative government and industrialization. Both new states experimented with constitutional government, and one of them, Germany, became Europe's leading industrial state in the early twentieth century.

The unification of each state required breaking the Austrian predominance in Central Europe which had been established by the Congress of Vienna. After revolutions in 1848 failed to overturn that settlement, Count Cavour of Piedmont and Otto von Bismarck of Prussia united their states by means of calculated international war. From their respective capitals of Turin and Berlin they challenged Vienna for control of their own affairs and enlarged their states, which became the nuclei of united Italy and united Germany. Although Cavour and Bismarck maintained and extended parliamentary government, neither of them shrank from manipulating public opinion or illegally suppressing opposition. Because they succeeded in triumphing over both existing domestic and international law, Cavour and Bismarck con-

tributed more than any ideologist to the popular conviction that might—whether national, racial, or economic—was right. Their power politics eclipsed all ideas that national self-determination was a stepping-stone to international organization. The ideal of a federated world would not command lasting attention again until after the history of the twentieth century had two world wars written into it.

Cavour's and Bismarck's methods, however, did not fully account for their success as contrasted to the failure of earlier liberal-nationalists. The path to Italian and German unification was opened to them when Russia broke with Austria as a result of the Crimean War.

## THE DIPLOMATIC PRELUDE: THE CRIMEAN WAR, 1854 TO 1856

Russian encroachment upon Turkey—the "Sick Man of Europe"* whose body lay athwart the straits between the Black and Mediterranean Seas—precipitated Europe's first major war since 1815. Meeting at London in 1840 and 1841 to maintain the balance of power, the major European states guaranteed Ottoman territorial integrity and closed the straits to all foreign warships in time of peace. But Nicholas I of Russia persisted in pursuing bold annexation plans. Backed by France and Britain, the Turks

---

* The phrase came to be used by European diplomats after the reforms of the late eighteenth- and early nineteenth-century sultans failed to check the Empire's steady disintegration.

*The siege of Sevastopol — a break.*

The experience of the war led to domestic reforms in Britain, Turkey, and especially Russia, whose new tsar, Alexander II, instituted an era of comprehensive modernization. For European affairs, the most significant outcome was Russia's diplomatic alienation from Austria. Russia had helped the Habsburgs suppress the Hungarian revolution in 1849, and Russian officials expected favors in return. Instead they were met with hostility between 1853 and 1856. The rift between Russia and Austria broke the conservative Eastern remnant of the Concert of Europe. No longer able to count on Russian support in Central Europe, Austria now faced the Germans and Italians alone.

## ITALY

### Formation of the Kingdom of Italy

Count Cavour had worked at journalism, soldiering, scientific agriculture, banking, and railroad management. Before the Revolution of 1848, he had organized secret political clubs and had agitated through his newspaper, *Il Risorgimento (The Resurrection),* for a constitution and liberal economic reform modeled upon French and British theory. Prior to becoming premier in 1852, he had held a series of cabinet posts and had authored legislation that limited Church property holdings and curbed clerical courts. Relying upon a center coalition hostile to clerical traditionalism on the "Right" and democracy and republicanism on the "Left," he built up a conscript army, negotiated tariff reductions, and fostered the expansion of commerce, industry, and transportation.

resisted. When the Habsburgs also demonstrated their hostility, Russia stood almost alone. Only Prussia was sympathetic.

The Turks declared war in 1853, but Russian annihilation of their wooden Black Sea fleet indicated their inability to resist Russian pressures. After much diplomatic maneuvering, Britain and France came to Turkey's aid in 1854. While Austria kept troops stationed on her frontiers with Russia and while Piedmont-Sardinia sent token forces to the allies, British and French forces destroyed Russian bases along the Black Sea and conquered the fortress of Sevastopol on the Crimean Peninsula.

Notable for the introduction of ironclad warships, for the development of military nursing, and for negligence and inefficiency on both sides, the Crimean War was a shock to the agrarian Russian Empire. With the exception of the Caucasus front, the Russians were defeated on their own soil. These losses were confirmed in the terms of peace.*

Cavour left his greatest mark in foreign affairs. Forced either to indulge the whims of King Victor Immanuel or to resign, he led Italy into the Crimean War as a virtual ally of Austria. But he turned discomfiture into

* In the Peace of Paris of 1856, Europe replaced Russia as the protector of both the Greek Orthodox and Roman Catholic Christians within Turkey. Walachia and Moldavia, which Russian troops had occupied since 1848, were set up as protected, autonomous buffer states against further Russian expansion. And Russian naval

forces were prohibited on the Black Sea, while the Turks could maintain a navy and open the straits to their allies.

*Count Cavour, unifier of Italy.*

*Garibaldi.*

success at the peace conference by publicizing Austrian wrongs in Italy. His pleas enticed Napoleon III, who was eager to regain the influence that France had lost in Italy in 1815. The two met secretly at Plombières in July 1858. In return for Nice and Savoy, Napoleon pledged aid in Piedmont's seizure of Lombardy and Venetia—provided that Cavour could goad Austria into declaring war. Italy was to become a confederation of four kingdoms, two of them under French influence. While Napoleon secretly secured Russian neutrality, Cavour plotted with republican revolutionaries to overthrow the north Italian governments which, instead of going to the projected confederated kingdoms, would be annexed to Piedmont. Cavour baited Austria by conscripting Lombard refugees into the army. As he had anticipated, Austria declared a preventive war, but she found herself confronted unexpectedly by France. No sooner were the Habsburgs driven out of most of Lombardy than Napoleon reconsidered his actions. Under

British diplomatic pressure, and distrustful of Cavour's intentions, he made a separate truce with Austria. Through Napoleon III Piedmont obtained Lombardy, but not until Piedmont was allowed to annex four smaller principalities was Napoleon able to obtain Nice and Savoy. The annexation of Lombardy, Parma, Tuscany, Modena, and Romagna consolidated Piedmont's position in northern Italy and left it with nearly half of the peninsula's population.

In 1860 Cavour's direction of Italian affairs was threatened by Mazzini and his republican followers who instigated an autonomous revolution in Sicily. Cavour had suppressed Mazzini's newspaper and activities in Piedmont, but he had secretly supplied Giuseppe Garibaldi (1807–1882), the principal republican military leader, and had diverted him from attacking Nice to a campaign

UNIFICATION
OF
**ITALY**

Map by J. Donovan

peasants, Catholics, republicans, and particularists with local loyalties. Expenditures of lives and money to suppress internal southern revolts exceeded the costs of all the wars of Italian unification. Moreover, total unification awaited another series of wars in which Italy benefited from Prussian victories. In the Austro-Prussian War of 1866, Italy gained Venetia. Napoleon III, whose plans for Italy had been dashed by Piedmont and whose support of an anticlerical Italian state was unpopular at home, garrisoned Rome and prevented its seizure until the Franco-Prussian War of 1870. Thus, except for scattered "unredeemed Italians" along the Austrian frontier, the Kingdom of Italy realized the dream of national unification.

## Italian Politics, 1871 to 1914

Before World War I, Italian nationalists' visions of greatness remained largely dreams. Italy failed to become a major political and industrial power after attaining national unity. Requisite economic resources such as coal and iron were lacking, and population growth exceeded agricultural and industrial expansion. Moreover, government revenues were insufficient to simultaneously develop commercial facilities, educate a largely illiterate population, and maintain the armed forces necessary to make Italy a great power. Because of internal tensions and marked regional differences, especially between the dominant commercial north and the undeveloped, agrarian, and disorderly south, unity was more an aspiration than a reality. Nationalists were disappointed by Italy's poor showing abroad and the failure of their prediction that unification would bring a "spiritual" or "moral" revival. Nationalism, however, proved more deeply rooted than liberalism. Beset by immense difficulties, corruption, and a lack of consensus on political fundamentals, liberal parliamentarianism was still a delicate flower at the outbreak of World War I.

The Kingdom of Piedmont-Sardinia provided the constitutional apparatus, the

against Sicily. In Sicily the picturesque sea captain, who had learned guerrilla warfare in exile in South America, led his "Thousand Redshirts" to unexpected victory. Escorted by British naval units to the mainland, Garibaldi took advantage of a peasant revolt and the collapse of the existing government to topple the Bourbon Kingdom of Naples before Cavour could stop him. To cut off Garibaldi's projected march on Rome and Venetia, which would have involved war with France and Austria, Cavour's army invaded the Papal States to "save them from revolution" and brought Garibaldi under control in Naples. In the spring of 1861 plebiscites, conducted by the Piedmontese army, joined Sicily, Naples, and the Papal States (except Rome) to the newly declared Kingdom of Italy.

A few months after the Kingdom of Italy was proclaimed by Victor Emmanuel, Cavour died, leaving the tasks of organizing the expanded kingdom to contending cliques. The Turin government's economic, political, and religious policies antagonized southern early leadership, and the initial policies for the kingdom as a whole. The Ministry was responsible to Parliament—an upper house of appointed lifetime peers and a lower house elected by property holders comprising a little more than 2 per cent of the total population. Northern leaders, who were constitutional monarchists rather than republicans in outlook, initially guided the centralization of law, administration, finance, taxation, and the army. Local administration was organized on the French model, which managed affairs uniformly from the capital. Inevitably its policies of free trade and anticlericalism collided with the interests of southern Italians (who tended to look upon the government as an alien power) and with the papacy, most of whose territories had been seized during unification. Following Sardinian precedent, the Parliament enacted a Law of Papal Guarantees in 1871. It guaranteed to His Holiness certain rights and privileges, and an annual subsidy. Although the state retained Roman Catholicism as the established faith and paid its clergy, subsequent measures curbed Church control over education, property, and marriage. The Pope responded by declaring himself a "prisoner" in the Vatican (no pope left the city until 1929), by rejecting the subsidy, and by encouraging—later in 1886 requiring—loyal Catholics to be "neither electors nor elected." This breach with the Church did not heal after the northern conservative liberals fell from power. The northern leaders built roads, railroads, and harbors and asserted Italian greatness by maintaining a large army. But, by making large expenditures and meeting interest payments on an immense debt, they also exacted the heaviest taxes in Europe. They postponed education and democratization. Accumulated grievances, especially among the southern middle classes, augured their downfall. In 1876 a new set of leaders, committed to educational reform and widening of the franchise, replaced them.

If any student of Italian politics relied on election slogans, he would assume that the governments of Agostino Depritis (1876–1887) and Francesco Crispi (1887–1896) moved toward democratic liberalism. But, in fact, opportunism (*transformismo*—the "transformation" of opponents into supporters by favors) characterized the politics of their era. Using patronage and favors to recruit a majority of deputies irrespective of party affiliation, Depritis and Crispi virtually substituted "personal dictatorships" for a functioning party system. Appointed by the Minister of the Interior, local prefects collaborated in corruption and in the election of deputies loyal to the government. Their reliance on patronage, bribery, election manipulation, and occasional gangster terrorism led, it is said, to rule over "thirty millions by three thousand for the benefit of three hundred thousand."[1] Money to alleviate rural and industrial poverty was scarce and often spent instead on the military. Unresolved social discontent erupted in anarchism, anarcho-syndicalism, and Marxian socialism. More forcefully than Bismarck,* Crispi attempted to extirpate socialism, but as a substitute for bread he had little more than imperialism to offer. A humiliating defeat of Italian arms by French-supported Ethiopians at Aduwa in 1896 brought his downfall and another opportunity for liberal experimentation.

Both remarkable material progress and widespread social unrest characterized the period 1896 to 1914, when the dominant political personality was Giovanni Giolitti. Northern Italy industrialized rapidly at this time, even though her high production costs penalized her in foreign trade. Hydroelectricity was harnessed as a native source of power, and the government provided tariff protection. But, drained by costly attempts to become a major military power, Italy continued on the verge of bankruptcy. Her lower classes experienced little if any relief from

1. Quoted by H. Stuart Hughes, *The United States and Italy,* rev. ed.; Harvard University Press, Cambridge, Mass., 1965, p. 53.

* See *infra,* pp. 341–342.

hardship. Her population growth so out-stripped the rate of emigration and economic development that she maintained one of the lowest standards of living in Europe. In industrial centers Marxian socialism spread rapidly. Uncompromising class-conscious Marxists sponsored insurrections that were harshly suppressed, while socialists of various revisionist schools attempted to shore up the weakly-supported liberal institutions of Italy.

Although serious financial scandals shook Giolitti's government, he was able to proceed with much of the socialists' reform program. Progress in education sharply reduced illiteracy. His government encouraged the organization of industrial and agricultural labor organizations and, in 1912, the franchise was extended to almost all adult males. In addition, some social insurance was adopted, a weekly day of rest was guaranteed to labor, and the railroads were nationalized.

Giolitti's "Leftist" politics and an attempted general strike in 1904 provoked a conservative reaction. In 1905 the papacy lifted its ban on political activity and founded Catholic Action groups that advocated a corporatist economy. The Church proclaimed itself defender of the existing social order against both liberalism and socialism. More ominous in the light of future events was the following gathered by Gabriele d'Annunzio. A prominent nationalist poet, d'Annunzio made overtures to the Church and to forces of monarchism as he pressed for a more imperialistic foreign policy.* By attempting to gain colonies in Africa and the eastern Mediterranean—a policy that came to a climax with Italy's entrance into World War I—the government played into the hands of proclerical and imperialistic nationalists who proposed to deal with domestic, social, and foreign problems

---

* For his unauthorized seizure of the neighboring city of Fiume after World War I, see *infra*, Chapter XIII.

by force. Just prior to World War I, the government suppressed a second general strike and republican revolutions in the former Papal States.

## GERMANY

### Otto von Bismarck and Austria's Expulsion from Germany

Italian unification proceeded at Austrian expense by the enlargement of Piedmont. German unification likewise cost Austria her control over German affairs. Supported by Russia, Austria had frustrated a Prussian attempt to assume leadership in northern Germany in 1850. Prussia, on the other hand, prevented Austrian admittance to the *Zollverein,* or Customs Union, which included all the other German states. In subsequent encounters between Austria and Prussia, the principal anti-Austrian spokesman was the same man who had distinguished himself as the most uncompromising foe of liberal constitutionalism, Otto von Bismarck. Although he served in major diplomatic posts, Bismarck's outspoken monarchical absolutism barred his rise to power until the semi-absolutist Prussian monarchy reached a constitutional impasse with the Prussian lower house in 1862.

Reacting against Conservative violations of constitutional rights and inspired by the Italo-Austrian war of 1859, the Prussian electorate returned a Liberal majority to the lower house in 1859. Although pledged to uphold the constitution, the new king, William I, set out to reform and enlarge the Prussian army. He appointed two autocratic Junker generals, Alfred von Roon and Helmuth von Moltke (1800–1891), as Minister of War and Chief of the General Staff, respectively. Roon and Moltke wanted to lengthen the army's conscription period and bring the militia, whose commissions were the treasured possessions of the middle class, directly under the regular army. Since both measures were intended to reduce civilian

*Roon (left) and Moltke.*

influence upon the army, the lower house refused to vote the necessary budget. The government retaliated by collecting and spending tax moneys at its own volition. These actions were repudiated at the polls, but the cabinet did not resign or change its policy, since it depended upon royal confidence, not upon a parliamentary majority. As the constitutional crisis deepened, Roon and Moltke prevailed upon the King to appoint as minister-president their candidate, Otto von Bismarck, who had no scruples against ruling in violation of the constitution.

Bismarck was not an ordinary Prussian Conservative. His aims—the aggrandizement of Prussian power and the maintenance of rule by the Junkers—were orthodox enough, but his methods at home and abroad were radical. In international affairs he respected only state egotism and power, not the principle of monarchical legitimacy. As Prussian emissary to the Diet of the German Confederation at Frankfurt he had treated Austria,

the embodiment of international conservatism, as the paramount enemy. The cornerstone of his diplomacy was Roon's and Moltke's maintenance of the army in a constant state of readiness for the exploitation of international crises. This enabled Bismarck to mobilize last and to appear as the injured, defensive party. Unlike other Conservatives, Bismarck appealed directly to the populace with universal, direct manhood suffrage. The purpose was neither liberal nor democratic, however, for Bismarck would not surrender control of affairs of state to a popularly elected assembly. From the Liberals he appropriated the goal of national unity and secured the support of a majority of them without conceding parliamentary government. Bismarck's unification of Germany amounted to an extension of Prussian dominance over the whole Empire.

At every step he used diplomacy to prepare for crises which Prussian power could exploit. Initially he frustrated Austrian plans to reform the German Confederation. Then he secured the lasting friendship of Russia by cooperating with the Tsar's ruthless suppression of a Polish revolution in 1863. In the same year the death of the Danish sovereign reopened the Schleswig-Holstein question* and provided him his first opportunity to turn a major diplomatic crisis into a Prussian advantage.

Bismarck used a crisis over Schleswig-Holstein to precipitate a war with Austria. When German nationalists had tried to annex the two duchies in 1848, the great powers intervened, proposing in 1852 that the duchies go to the Danish heir to the throne upon his accession, a solution contrary to their laws of succession. The death of the Danish king, therefore, created a crisis into which Bismarck quickly stepped. In 1864 he negotiated an alliance with Austria, and the two jointly conquered the duchies. Refusing to exchange Austria's share for southern territory, Bismarck secured their administrative division in 1865, with Holstein going to Austria. But it gradually became clear that Bismarck intended to annex both duchies. In direct violation of the constitution of the German Confederation, he negotiated a secret alliance with Italy for immediate war with Austria. Already having Russian friendship, he secured French neutrality by dangling prospects before the French ambassador of annexing either the Rhineland or Belgium. In vain, Austria sought to avoid a two-front war. When the Confederation Diet spurned reform plans offered by Prussia, the Prussian armies marched on Austria's northern supporters: Hanover, Saxony, and Hesse. These acts and Prussian occupation of Holstein moved Austria to declare war on Prussia in the summer of 1866.

Instead of a protracted conflict from which Napoleon expected to profit by staying neutral, Prussia humbled Austria in seven weeks. Taking advantage of railroads and telegraphs for mobility and coordination, and using breech-loading rifles to fire from prone positions, Prussian forces defeated the main Austrian army, with heavy losses at Königgrätz (Sadowa), on July 3, 1866. In the peace negotiations that terminated the Seven Weeks' War, Bismarck's strategy dictated leniency to the startled Austrians, whose assistance he might need in the future. Italy gained Venetia, but Austria lost no territory to Prussia. North of the Main River, however, Prussia annexed Austria's allies and in 1867 proclaimed the North German Confederation. Its constitution provided for a Prussian type of executive, an upper house dominated by Prussian votes, and an advisory lower house elected by universal manhood suffrage. The peace terms also authorized the formation of a South German Confederation, but the major southern states, divided by mutual jealousies and fearful of French ambitions in the Rhineland, contracted secret military treaties with Prussia. Although Germany still lacked political unity, the Seven Weeks' War had driven Austria from the German states.

Domestically the war had significant repercussions in both Austria and Prussia. Hungarian nationalists seized the opportunity provided by Habsburg defeat to secure autonomy within a newly proclaimed "Dual Monarchy" in 1867. In Prussia the prestige of victory enabled Bismarck to secure the allegiance of the majority of the Liberal (Progressive) party, which became known as the National Liberal party. The National Liberals gave up demands for further constitutional reform. As Johannes Miquel, one of their leaders explained: "The time for ideals is past, and the duty of politicians is not to ask for what is desirable, but for what is attainable."[2] Moreover, the annexation of

---

* See *supra*, p. 221.

[2] Quoted by Erich Eych, *Bismarck and the German Empire*, W. W. Norton, New York, 1958, p. 141.

**GERMAN EMPIRE 1871**

Kingdom of Prussia to 1866

States annexed in 1866

United with Prussia to form
North German Confederation, 1867

United with North German Confederation
to form German Empire, 1871

Ceded by France, 1871

*(Austrian Dominions excluded from German Confederation, 1866)*

Map by J. Donovan

Hanover put an immense source of secret service funds in Bismarck's personal control.

## The Franco-Prussian War

Prussia's consolidation of northern Germany sharply altered the European balance of power with respect to France and undermined Napoleon III's domestic prestige and influence. Although the civilian government failed to cooperate completely, French military leaders began to modernize their army and to extend conscription. Fearing a future shaped by Germany's rapid industrial, population, and military growth, many editors and generals were calling for a preventive war. The ailing Emperor, who preferred to rely upon international conferences, did not accede to these demands nor did he succeed in gaining allies in the event war should occur. When the war came, it fully revealed the glaring, growing differential between French and German military power.

Bismarck was determined to instigate war with France, but the origins of the Franco-Prussian War of 1870 and 1871 were less the result of his calculations than of French emotional reactions to wounded national honor. The episode that led to war started with efforts of Spanish liberal revolutionaries to secure a new monarch after 1868. One of the few available candidates was Leopold of Hohenzollern, a Roman Catholic. Because it would place a Hohenzollern on France's southern frontier, Bismarck promoted his candidacy. After once rejecting the offer, William I, head of the house, eventually accepted it. But the dynastic secret leaked out prematurely in July 1870. In Paris, journalists, politicians, and military leaders accused Prussia of secretly plotting the destruction of France. When French diplomacy secured Leopold's withdrawal, Bismarck's scheme was defeated—temporarily. But to vindicate French honor, Napoleon's foreign minister demanded a promise from William I that Leopold would never be a candidate again. At the resort city of Ems, the King firmly but courteously rejected this demand. In Berlin, Bismarck, who was dining with Roon and Moltke, received William's report of his interview with the French ambassador and altered it for publication to make it appear that the ambassador and the King had exchanged insults. Bismarck's "editing" of the "Ems dispatch" spurred Napoleon III to declare war.

Lacking allies, France fought alone. She believed that her military forces were superior, but poor generalship and other factors belied her faith. Augmented by southern German forces, Prussian armies broke through Lorraine, encircled major French armies at Metz and Sedan, and besieged Paris. The surrender of the encircled French armies was doubly significant for, at Sedan, Napoleon himself became a prisoner of war. Republican leaders hastily assembled new forces that staved off total defeat for six months, but the terms of peace in February 1871 were costly. In addition to a large indemnity and German occupation at French expense until it was paid, the new French government was obliged to cede Alsace and most of Lorraine to the new German Empire. The cession of Alsace-Lorraine, with its textile and metallurgical industries, was a heavy blow to France. It poisoned international relations for two generations. Bismarck put his most strenuous efforts into keeping France diplomatically isolated to prevent its reconquest. In addition to the territorial settlement, the balance of power was further turned against France by the formation of the German Empire, which was proclaimed in Louis XIV's Hall of Mirrors

*Proclamation of the German Empire at Versailles.*

at Versailles. At the invitation of the German princes but not at the behest of a parliament, the Prussian King became German Emperor.

## Bismarck and the German Empire

German unification and subsequent industrialization made Berlin the capital of continental politics. Bismarck's efforts to retain this ascendancy by a system of defensive alliances will be traced in Chapter X. His striving for international peace, however, was dictated by the delicate balance of social forces that went into the constitutional and political structure of the German Empire. That balance was subject to constant revision due to rapid changes produced by Germany's speedy industrialization and urbanization within a single generation.* Since the internal struggles of Germany occurred within the foremost industrial and military power in late nineteenth-century Europe, the outcome was of general significance.

In creating the German Empire, Bismarck took pains to alleviate fears that preponderant Prussia would dominate the Empire's institutions. Yet those institutions were so designed that Prussia did dominate the Empire and its policies. As emperor the Prussian king had sole initiative in foreign and military affairs. Independent of parliamen-

* See *supra*, Chapter VI.

tary control, he appointed the chancellor (Bismarck until 1890) and federal officials. In the two-house legislature the instructed delegates, sent by the constituent states to the Federal Council (*Bundesrat*), dominated the lower house (*Reichstag*). The *Reichstag* was elected at large by direct, secret ballot. It had to concur with the *Bundesrat* in the passage of laws and budgets. Federal powers were enumerated by the constitution; they were sufficiently broad to secure effective economic, political, and military unity. But in the Federal Council Prussia retained sufficient votes to prevent constitutional change. And that body was more a camouflage for Prussian domination than a policy-originating branch of government. Thus without altering the constitution or policy of Prussia, constitutional reformers could not change the Empire.

At first, Bismarck found support in a coalition of middle-class National Liberals (who admired his success in unifying Germany), and the Prussian Junkers (the military aristocracy that was left in possession of its privileges and power). This combination excluded the "Old German Conservatives" from conspiring against the Prussian-led Empire; never would Bismarck rely upon them as an indispensable prop to his system. Believing that only propertied elements should influence affairs, he feared the proletariat as a revolutionary force bent on the Empire's destruction.

After Austria had been defeated in 1866, Bismarck continued the war against the Catholics by means of the "Falk Laws," the anticlerical National Liberals' legislation in Prussia. These laws launched a "struggle for cultural purity" (*Kulturkampf*) against Roman Catholics, Poles, and Germans alike. Among other things they barred Jesuits, restricted Church offices to Germans, put ecclesiastical education under state control, and made civil marriage compulsory. But instead of destroying Catholic opposition, the laws precipitated the rapid growth of a Roman Catholic opposition party: the Center

party. They also moved Lutheran Conservatives to launch an intolerable attack upon Bismarck. By 1879 the *Kulturkampf* had manifestly failed, and Bismarck, for a variety of reasons, changed his tack. His fears of the Catholics diminished as he drew Austria into an alliance. Moreover, the antimiddle-class Center party would support his plans for a tariff and draw workingmen away from socialist leaders who had attracted labor followings after depression began in 1873.

Bismarck regrouped his political base by a compromise of 1879, which he labeled the "second founding" of the Empire. It reflected rapid socioeconomic changes. Caught in an economic depression, which they blamed on the middle-class liberals whom they had previously supported, peasants turned to the Conservatives for leadership. They sought cheap credit, reduced taxes, higher agricultural prices, and tariffs. The anti-*laissez-faire* Center also advocated tariffs, as did the great industrialists of the National Liberal party who were forming cartels and combines. For Bismarck, agricultural and industrial tariffs would provide military revenues independent of parliamentary obstruction and would reduce his dependence upon levies from individual states. In 1879 the tariff front provided the Chancellor with a new coalition. Despite the *Kulturkampf*, the Center became a supporter, although not entirely trusted, of Bismarck's new system. Domestically, it had a primary purpose in keeping the "red menace" under control.

After the depression of 1873, socialists began to make notable headway among the burgeoning laboring population. They were feared by all conservatives and most of the middle classes. Bismarck saw the growth of labor activism as a threat to his whole structure and resolved to meet it by repression. By falsely attributing attempts to assassinate the Emperor to socialist organizations, he secured laws disbanding their associations and suppressing their press. Although socialists were kept out of the civil service and

*Bismarck and William II.*

DROPPING THE PILOT.

*"Dropping the Pilot,"* Punch *cartoon of Bismarck's dismissal.*

the universities, the laws did not prevent their standing for election to the Reichstag. Scrupulously keeping their activities within legal bounds, the Social Democrats responded with electoral gains. To check their growth Bismarck announced in 1881 his support of state intervention to prevent part of the population—the capitalists—from using their power to oppress the rest. Bismarck's social legislation of the 1880s, which began with insurance for sickness, accidents, and old age, became a model for other industrial states. It alienated the National Liberals, but it failed to curb the Social Democrats' growth. As Germany became more and more urban and industrial, the Social Democrats' threat to Bismarck's system (as feared) grew.

## William II and the Failure of Democratization

Bismarck's entire edifice was predicated on a man of his abilities and judgment holding it together. Although never losing control of the army to him, William I had deferred to his judgment. But in 1888 William II, rash in displaying power in both foreign and domestic affairs, came to the throne. By 1890 he and Bismarck came to a parting of the ways. The Emperor broke with Russia, a course that Bismarck considered dis-

astrous because it exposed Germany to the possibility of defeat in a two-front war, a defeat that would destroy the dominance of the Prussian Junkers. William and Bismarck disagreed when Bismarck wanted still more repression of the Social Democrats. The Emperor removed him as intermediary between himself and other ministers and finally dismissed him in 1890. Without Bismarck at the helm, imperial affairs drifted. Once his Napoleonic personality was gone there was no force capable of wringing concessions from the industrialists and the Prussian Conservatives. The Conservatives held on to their control of the army and civil service and successfully resisted progressive income taxes and death duties. Most significantly, they defeated all attempts to democratize the constitution.

Numerically strong, the parties in opposition to William II's government were so divided that a coalition of the Catholic Center and the Lutheran Conservatives sufficed to preserve the *status quo*. Bismarck, himself, had educated the middle classes too thoroughly to follow the Emperor blindly. The aged former chancellor viciously criticized the government, but a Bismarckian opposition party failed to form. On specific issues both the National Liberal party and the more liberal Progressives opposed the government, but neither was committed to the achievement of government responsible to Parliament. Unless the armed Emperor and Junkers were willing to surrender prerogatives voluntarily—which they were not —this could come about only by revolution. The principal party that demanded democratization was the Social Democrats, who polled one third of the vote on the eve of World War I.

William II, himself, provided the principal opportunity for democratization. With Chancellor von Bülow's approval he issued an irresponsible statement to the *Daily Telegraph* in 1908 on foreign affairs. But von Bülow followed public opinion in criticizing that statement, without making it a constitutional issue. His successor, Bethmann-Hollweg, was even more explicit than he in affirming the adequacy of royal confidence and rejecting responsibility to Parliament. Prior to World War I, elections were going against the government, and Parliament voted no confidence in the government on specific issues. But no party could confront the army officered by the Junkers until the military machine at the heart of the imperial system had been overwhelmed by war. But before the debacle of World War I, only a few Social Democrats (such as Friedrich Engels) had been willing to think in these terms.

# C. The Eastern Empires: Austria-Hungary and Russia

Both socially and economically the Eastern empires lagged far behind the more industrialized West. Primarily agrarian, their most severe internal economic problems were agricultural. Despite their great size, they were unable to compete on even terms with the more advanced states. Russia was defeated in the Crimean War, and Austria lost ignominiously to Prussia in 1866. This decline in power spurred their bureaucracies to foster railroads and factories. But at the same time they were committed to the preservation of old institutions. Leading bureaucrats in both states mistakenly assumed that modernization would preserve the Old Regime. However, this urbanization brought new social conditions irreconcilable with it. The Eastern empires' problems were also

compounded by the ferment of nationalism. Whereas nationalist sentiments favored the unification and consolidation of states such as Italy and Germany, they threatened to break up these empires into their constituent national parts.

## THE HABSBURG EMPIRE, 1850 TO 1914

Since the seventeenth century the Habsburgs had served the useful function of organizing the peoples of Eastern Europe. Although its "subject nationalities" worked for more cultural and political autonomy, their peoples on the whole did not yet desire its total disintegration. An apparent anomaly in the age of nation-states, the Empire sur-

*Francis Joseph, guardian of tradition.*

vived until the cataclysm of World War I. Because of slow industrial development, its basic problem was not restive urban populations but the task of reconciling divergent nationalities under the same tradition-bound dynasty.

The Habsburg Empire included a congeries of peoples differing in national culture. Germans were concentrated in the Old Habsburg duchies along the Danube River and were scattered elsewhere in towns and administrative centers. There were also Slavs (Czechs, Slovaks, Poles, Ruthenians [Ukrainians], Serbs, Croats, Slovenes), Rumanians, Magyars, and some Italians. They were held together by the army, the hierarchy of the Roman Catholic Church, a German-speaking bureaucracy, and the inertia of custom. After the revolutions of 1848 and 1849, Habsburg unity was tightened by legal and economic measures, including the building of railroads. But the principal bond

that kept the domains intact was the Emperor Francis Joseph, who ruled from 1848 to 1916. To him fell the task of adjusting traditions to contemporary conditions. Surrounded at court by noble aristocrats, military officers, and high churchmen, he was insulated from full contact with those conditions. Yet he proved open to various proposals—perhaps too many—for reorganizing the empire, as long as his prerogatives were not sacrificed. His successes, however, were limited.

## Federalism Versus Centralization

To run the state, Francis Joseph depended alternatively upon German administrators advocating absolutist efficiency and great aristocrats who favored provincial autonomy and the class privileges of the landed aristocracy. Each shift from one to the other was accompanied by a new proclamation of "irrevocable fundamental laws." In theory, every such constitution recognized liberal principles of legal equality, personal freedom, and ministerial responsibility to elected parliaments. But, in practice, the Emperor was able to preserve his personal prerogatives by playing one interest group or nationality against another. Landed aristocrats and churchmen controlled local politics and the rural economy.

After the victory of the bureaucracy and army over the revolutions of 1848 and 1849, power in Vienna passed to Alexander Bach, Minister of Internal Affairs. He carried out a policy of centralized German absolutism and extended the power of the Roman Catholic Church. As long as prosperity lasted and Bach was successful in foreign affairs, the Emperor retained confidence in him. But non-Germans were alienated. Bach's policies in Hungary required the garrisoning of 150,000 men there. Heavy administrative and military expenses mounted during the Crimean War and far exceeded revenues. Bach's "system" became ever more dependent upon creditors' willingness to take up state loans. The public confidence collapsed during the depression of 1857. Inefficiency, desertions, and finally military defeat in Italy in 1859 led the Emperor to drop Bach from office.

Following Bach's fall, German bureaucrats advocating centralization and nobles standing for provincial autonomy vied for the Emperor's favor. Francis Joseph first agreed to a new constitution of 1860 that divided power between provincial diets and an imperial council. But, by stimulating local political activity, this arrangement alarmed the Emperor. In 1861 he restored the German bureaucrats with a new patent, or constitution. It provided for a parliament representing the various nationalities proportionately. But by "electoral geometry"—the unequal weighting of votes in electoral colleges—it assured power to the Austrian-Germans. The Magyars boycotted it; Czechs and Poles were refractory; and financiers became wary of further state expenditures. Again, Francis Joseph switched policies and constitutions by making a Polish nobleman, Belcredi, his highest official. But his concessions to Slavic autonomy aroused German and Hungarian fears of losing control to the Slavs.

## The Compromise of 1867

Prussia's lightning victory in 1866 brought Belcredi down and precipitated another major constitutional reorganization of the Empire—this one permanent. After his defeat the Emperor could no longer fend off Hungarian demands for autonomy. By the *Ausgleich* or Compromise of 1867, the Empire became the Dual Monarchy of Austria-Hungary. Francis Joseph retained the Hungarian crown, and common ministries sat for military, foreign, and financial affairs. Nominally these three ministries were responsible to a parliament composed of delegations from the Austrian and Hungarian parliaments. Otherwise the two kingdoms became separate entities whose relationships were regulated either by further compromises or treaties negotiated every ten years.

At the core of the *Ausgleich* were the mutual desires of the Germans and the Magyars to prevent their Slavic majorities from challenging their dominance. Neither considered the Slavs fit to rule themselves or the Empire. Hungarian Count Julius Andrassy stated the Compromise's purpose succinctly: "You look after your Slavs and we will look after ours." Besides the Magyars and the Germans, who became masters of their respective halves of the Empire, the Polish aristocracy in Galicia and the Croats received concessions from the Compromise. The Polish magnates obtained full powers over their Ruthenian (Ukrainian) peasants, while the Croats received limited autonomy from Hungary. Thus, by creating privileged groups, the Compromise made a federative empire based on equal national rights even more impossible.

## Social and Nationality Problems After the Compromise

With political domination went economic and cultural domination. Peasant emancipation in 1848 did not break up the *latifundia* (estates owned by the Church or the nobility and worked by landless or smallholding peasants). Ownership and control of industry and transportation were concentrated in German, Viennese, and often Jewish banking hands. Only sporadically did a native middle class exist, and both agricultural and industrial labor was usually recruited from subject nationalities. Such widespread conditions could only exacerbate national animosities and rivalry.

The Magyar oligarchy went farthest with policies of repression. Under Counts Andrassy and Stephen Tisza the Hungarian government after 1875 pressed a vigorous campaign of Magyarization in the schools and administration. The following estimates for the year 1900 indicate its success in crowding out Slavic competition for positions of power: 96% of the judges, 95% of the state officials, 92% of the county officials, 90% of the college students, 89% of the doctors, and 80% of the newspapers were Magyar. Two or three families controlled each county, and sixty families and forty bishops reputedly controlled national affairs. The gentry, which desired further separation from Vienna, dominated the Diet, which 6.5% of the population elected. The more pressure that the Magyars applied to the Slavs, the more they feared Slav treason or separation. The aggressive Magyars attributed all disaffection among the oppressed Slavs to the nationalist agitation emanating from Serbia. At Magyar insistence, Serbian imports were blocked from the Empire. Year by year after 1906, Magyar officials called for the military destruction of Serbia.

In the Austrian half of the Empire, the *Ausgleich* of 1867 restored power to the German bureaucrats who professed liberal principles. In liberal fashion they curtailed the power of the Roman Catholic Church, but they had no desire to make the Emperor and his ministries responsible to Parliament, since he was their only guarantee against dominance by the Slavic majority. But the German Ministry failed to keep the Emperor's confidence and to control his policy. After it was discredited by financial depression and scandals between 1873 and 1878, he overruled its objections and ordered occupation and administration of Bosnia-Herzogovina. Then he replaced it with a new ministry headed by Count Taafe, a personal friend. When Taafe and subsequent ministries made concessions to the Slavs, the German population turned to the Christian Social movement, the Social Democrats, and especially to the Pan-German movement. The Pan-German movement openly sought the annexation of Austrian-Germans to the German Empire. Like Bismarck, Count Taafe fought lower-class political movements with repression and economic concessions, but he lost favor and power when he promised concessions to the Czechs and when he tried to undermine German middle-class nationalists with universal manhood suffrage. Once again, in 1897, a suc-

cessor, Count Badeni, tried to include the Czechs in a coalition, but violent German protests forced him from office. Thereafter, Germans and Czechs staged boisterous demonstrations and counterdemonstrations in Parliament, making orderly debate impossible. Until the Austrian Parliament was suspended indefinitely in 1914, Austrian ministers ruled by emergency decrees without reference to parliamentary majorities. Thus national divisions made parliamentary government difficult, if not impossible.

Shifting from one faction to another, Francis Joseph failed to discover an alternative to nationalist disintegration. In 1907 he granted universal, equal, and direct manhood suffrage in the Austrian half of the Empire. At this point he was attracted by the Social Democrats who attempted to transcend national rivalries and maintain the integrity of the Empire. Soon, however, the Socialists were also rent by national antagonisms. On the eve of World War I, the heir-apparent, Francis Ferdinand, was considering federation as a new basis for the Habsburg Empire. But federation based upon broad popular participation was never tried. It did not appeal to Francis Joseph and his advisers. The point at which it might have succeeded may have already passed, and the assassination of Archduke Ferdinand in 1914 removed its last potential leader. By this time the higher levels of the Dual Monarchy's government had resolved upon the destruction of Serbia as the only possible means of preserving the Empire. On the eve of the war the Dual Monarchy had some success in mitigating national animosities at the local level, but the South Slav problem overrode all other considerations of policy and led to a war that brought the Empire's disintegration.

## RUSSIAN AUTOCRACY ON TRIAL

Triumphant over Napoleon in 1812, Russia's Old Regime displayed its control over the politically apathetic population by the ridiculous ease with which it dispersed the

Decembrist revolt of 1825. Confronting the Ottoman Empire and tribesmen of Central Asia or Siberia, Russia still gave the appearance of strength. But compared to the commercial and industrial countries of Western Europe, she was in a state of relative decline. Confronted by Western military and economic superiority, alert Russians had to choose between drastic internal changes and a decreasing role in European politics.

In making this choice, Russian intellectuals were torn between the "Westerners" and the "nativists"—proponents, respectively, of adding Western ideas and institutions to the Russian heritage and of preserving that heritage unchanged. Although the autocracy in theory had absolute power, it was not actually a free agent. It could use its meager resources to foster commercial agriculture and industrialization only by risking a thorough overhaul of society. Historically dependent upon the serf-owning nobility, the Old Regime had good reason to fear such an overhaul. Compounding the dilemma was the inert overwhelming majority of the population, the enserfed illiterate peasantry on whose immobility and forced labor the entire social pyramid rested. As long as possible the government temporized and expanded its bureaucratic controls. But basic reforms were not introduced until military defeat jolted the complacency of the power structure.

## Nicholas I and the Crimean War

The reign of Nicholas I (1825–1855) became synonymous with increasingly efficient despotism. Some of the Tsar's measures indicated an awareness of basic problems. His decrees limited the power of nobles over their serfs and instigated investigations of serfdom. He ordered the laws codified for the first time since 1649, and he introduced a gold-backed currency. But he was nevertheless preoccupied with asserting the Crown's absolute power over all dissent. Fearful of the nobility because of its complicity in the Decembrist uprising, Nicholas expanded the bureaucracy and forbade nobles to travel or attend schools abroad. Tight censorship prevailed over the universities and the press. The lower schools, reduced in number, championed the formula of Orthodoxy, Autocracy, and Nationalism. Reporting directly to the sovereign, a new Third Section of the Imperial Chancery constituted both a secret police network and a direct source of information on public opinion. The Tsar, already a reactionary, grew increasingly hostile toward liberalism during the revolutions of 1830 and 1848–1849.

He faced opposition at home largely from Western and Slavophile intellectuals. Westerners such as Alexander Herzen (1812–1870), illegitimate son of a nobleman, and the commoner, Belinsky (1811–1848), were attracted by French Utopian Socialism. Herzen, like most Westerners writing in exile, thought Russia was peculiarly suited to socialism because it lacked Roman law, private property, and rational religion. Belinsky, who remained in Russia, could voice his criticism only indirectly in book reviews. The Slavophiles, whose center was Moscow, worshipped Russian traditions and resented railroads and industry. Russian intellectuals formed an impotent class apart from the power structure. Gaining no influence, they vented their frustration in increasing radicalism. Even when Nicholas' regime ran aground in the Crimean War, they were in no position to influence affairs.

Although Nicholas was a standard-bearer of domestic and international reaction, he pursued an aggressive foreign policy that was ill-fated for the Old Regime. After aiding the Greek revolt in 1828 and 1829, he defended the *status quo* only temporarily. In 1831 he rescinded the constitutional privileges that the major powers guaranteed to the Poles in 1815. His undoing came in the Crimean War. The Franco-British victory over Russian forces on Russian soil and coastal waters dispelled the myth of invulnerability that had made traditional institutions sacrosanct after

*Tsar Alexander II, autocratic reformer.*

1812. The new tsar, Alexander II (1855–1881), who ascended the throne at the end of the war, turned immediately to the peasant question, determined to secure action.

## Alexander II, Tsar Emancipator

Failure in foreign affairs and an increasing number of serf revolts fastened Alexander's attention on serfdom, as did the fact that Russian agricultural yields were incredibly low. Landlords using serf labor were going into debt, often mortgaging a majority of their serfs as security chattels. Necessarily, he turned to committees of noblemen and to the bureaucracy to explore the complicated diversity of servile conditions, a procedure that Nicholas I had already used secretly. In the rich "black soil" of the south, peasants primarily owed labor services, and here many landlords favored emancipation, pro-vided that the peasantry could be converted into landless laborers. In the northern more forested regions where the land was less valuable, nobles drew money payments (*Obrok*) from their serfs, many of whom worked part-time in crafts. Other serfs were either landless domestics or worked in a variety of other relationships.

In one of the most complicated decrees in history, Alexander decreed the serfs' emancipation in 1861. Unlike the American slaves emancipated later, these former serfs were granted land. But only their houses and garden plots were their personal property. The remainder of the land was divided between the lords and peasant communes. And land that was ceded to the peasantry (in the decree nobles were recognized as the rightful former owners of the land) was not free nor did it go to individual proprietors. In each locality the elders of the collective village (*Mir* or, literally, "world") were placed in charge of periodic reallotments to families, indemnity payments to the state for forty-nine years, tax and military draft levies, and discipline. To the nobility went the "psychologically best lands," usually the major portion of the former estates. Bonds from the state compensated them for lands and peasant obligations that were lost. Because it favored the nobility, the decree aroused violent peasant resistance. The peasant had legal freedom but was subject to heavy communal supervision and could not accumulate capital when he had to make indemnity payments, most of which fell eventually into arrears. The nobility was no more successful in coping with the new conditions, since the majority of the bond recipients "lived up" their proceeds in luxury instead of using them to introduce scientific agriculture. Thus Russian emancipation stirred more disaffection among the serfs and undermined the nobility. It failed to meet the subsistence crisis produced by an extraordinary increase in population.

Peasant emancipation was part of a larger

goal of legal equality announced by the Tsar at his accession. Together these two reforms necessitated a thorough revamping of the entire administrative and judicial machinery of the Russian state. To substitute its officials for local nobles the government had to expand its bureaucracy greatly. Beginning in 1864 it organized the *Zemstvos,* local elective councils representing nobles, townsmen, and peasants. Given jurisdiction over roads, bridges, local welfare, some police functions, and primary education, the *Zemstvos* served as schools for training local leaders. But they operated on a very narrowly restricted tax basis, and their indirect election system continued to favor the nobility heavily. Beginning in 1870, similar reforms were introduced in municipalities.

Russia's old legal system was based on paternalism and was closely connected with the administrative departments of government. The Tsar replaced it with a new judiciary modeled on French and British practice. The new system provided for public jury trials (with significant political exceptions), legal equality (although peasants still had separate courts), and the separation of judicial from administrative functions. On paper the legal system was the most enlightened in Europe; in practice its impact was more gradual and tentative than revolutionary. More than the *Zemstvo* reforms, Alexander's legal innovations weakened the nobility. And they opened paths to prominence for lawyers who constituted potential opposition to the aristocracy and bureaucracy.

Alexander's enlightened autocracy also spilled over into a number of other areas. Censorship was relaxed and foreign travel permitted again. Drawing a lesson from the Crimean War, the Tsar reorganized the army under a German-style General Staff. Universal conscription for six years of active service and nine reserve years replaced Peter the Great's twenty-five year enlistments from the lower classes. Since the army stressed literacy, military training also became an ad-

junct to Russia's feeble educational system.* To meet deficits left from the Crimean War, the costs of reform, and the capital required for industry and railway construction, Alexander's finance minister introduced the taxation of all classes for the first time. At the very end of his reign, the "Tsar Liberator" was considering an advisory body to the Council of State—which would also function only in an advisory capacity. The new body would have been chosen by the *Zemstvos* and municipal councils. But, in 1881, a terrorist's bomb terminated the Tsar's life. By that year a potent reactionary movement, to which his successor belonged, was gaining ascendancy over both reform and revolutionary sentiment. After 1863, the moderate pro-Western reform position represented by the Tsar was eroded by a new Polish revolution and by rebuffs in foreign policy.

## Reactionary and Revolutionary Polarization, 1863 to 1881

Conservatives found their anxieties that reform would lead inexorably to revolution confirmed by the Polish uprising of 1863. Beginning in 1856, Alexander relaxed the repression of the Polish language and lifted some restraints from Poland's schools and churches. To improve agricultural techniques, the government sponsored agricultural societies that brought the gentry and nobility together. Discussions turned from agriculture to politics. The aristocracy, although divided between radical "Reds" and moderate "Whites," revived aspirations for Polish independence as it existed prior to 1772. When the Polish nobles led a revolution and received sympathy from Western liberals and governments, conservative Rus-

---

* Early in his reign, Alexander pressed for secondary education with heavy emphasis upon science. After a student's attempt on Alexander's life in 1866, however, his minister of education purged the sciences as conducive to materialism and curbed the study of history and modern languages as dangerous subjects.

sians became suspicious of all reforms, whether in Poland or Russia. Meanwhile, radical reformers turned uncompromisingly against tsarist autocracy, whether enlightened or not.

Stimulated by Alexander's reforms, a new generation of radicals, impatient for immediate, more drastic changes, held Russian institutions up to the light of Utopian Socialism and British Utilitarianism. With such spokesmen as Nikolai Chernyshevsky (1828–1889), they focused their attention on economics, economic history, and the exploitation of the lower classes by the upper classes. Dubbed "Nihilists" for their repudiation of traditional authority and institutions, the radical intelligentsia lacked power to effect changes unless they could secure popular— that is, peasant—support. Student sons and daughters of the "conscience-stricken" nobility and middle classes turned to the "dark people," the peasantry, as the potential regenerators of Russian society. A Populist movement (*Narodniki*) sought to educate the peasants to improve their lot, but the tradition-bound peasantry rebuffed them, often reporting them to the police. Stung by this rejection, the radical intelligentsia formed bands of revolutionary elites, which the authorities hunted down. Curbed from above and at least temporarily spurned from below, the revolutionary movements vented their discontent by anarchistic acts of assassination that, in turn, brought more repression.

While the Western-oriented radicals turned Nihilist, an aggressively nationalist nativist and imperialistic Pan-Slav movement gained momentum. During the Polish Revolution, Michael Katkov (1818–1887), formerly the leading liberal publicist in Russia, began to advocate Russification of minorities. In 1869, N. Y. Danilevsky, a biologist, published *Russia and Europe,* a Social Darwinist work that argued that only through war with the West could peace-loving Russians fulfill their messianic mission of rescuing civilization from alien control. Dostoev-

*Pobiedonostsev, arch-conservative in theory and practice.*

sky used his literary fame to spread the Pan-Slav idea of mission: that it was the duty of Russia to save her Orthodox Slavic brethren from the menace of the West. For militant Pan-Slavs, the road to Constantinople ran through Vienna, whose power interests confronted Russian hegemony over the "little Slav Brothers" in the Balkans. Pan-Slavs were instrumental in securing successful Russian intervention in Balkan revolts against the inept Ottoman Empire between 1875 and 1878. When the major powers met at Berlin and stripped Russia and her Balkan wards of their territorial gains, a new wave of anti-Western sentiment flooded Russian conservative circles. The one most significant convert to authoritarian reaction in these years was the highly educated civil servant, Constantine Pobiedonostsev (1827–1907), chief administrator and confidant of Tsars Alexander III (1881–1894) and (until

1905) Nicholas II (1894–1917), whom he also tutored.

## Reaction After 1881

Liberalism had no more competent, consistent, or powerful foe than Pobiedonostsev, for he was mainly responsible for Russian domestic policy until the Revolution of 1905 unseated him. As lay administrator of the Holy Synod of the Russian Orthodox Church, he held superior cabinet rank. Antirational and anti-Western, Pobiedonostsev viewed political society as an organic, historic, and unconscious growth propelled by inertia. To take over parts of another society (to introduce English juries into Russia, for example), violated the uniqueness of the recipient. To separate church and state was to attempt an impossible dichotomy of body and soul. Pobiedonostsev dismissed parliamentary government as an unstable facade for the personal egotism of demagogues and plutocrats. He felt that popular sovereignty would only breed discontent. Secular education corrupted youth by teaching abstractions, and any babbler might start publishing where the press was free. The only laws justifying obedience derived from divine commandments, not from the inventions of man. Equality, he found only in the Russian Orthodox Church, not at the ballot box. He believed that to preserve precious institutions and customs, the ruling elite should prevail —with confident righteousness—against the positivist and utilitarian deceptions of the Western world.

Thus in terms reminiscent of the Western authoritarian nationalists, Pobiedonostsev provided a religious rationale for a full offensive against the reforms of Alexander II, the revolutionary movements, all minority and dissent groups, and the newer urban classes whose rise threatened the declining nobility. Spurred by him, the Interior Ministry enlarged the secret police and its corps of secret agents. They infiltrated revolutionary organi-

*Russian peasants, about 1900.*

zations and incited mobs against unpopular groups. National minorities such as the Finns, the Baltic peoples, the Poles, Asian tribes, and the Georgians were subject to systematic "Russification." Similar pressures were applied to religious minorities—the Roman Catholics, "Old Believers," Baptists, Mohammedans, Tolstoyites, and especially the Jews, who were victims of bloody pogroms. Secret agents were sct to watch secret agents, and an espionage system was established within the church itself to ensure obedience. Thus did "holy terror" mark the policy of Holy Russia, binding the fate of the Russian Church inextricably to the fate of monarchical absolutism. The reforms of Alexander II were also dismantled insofar as was possible. Noble "land captains" regained considerable control over village affairs, public jury trials were canceled for political offenses, and the election and tax bases of the *Zemstvos* and municipal councils were restricted. To prevent dangerous ideas from appearing and spreading, rigid censorship prevailed, and all but the wealthiest classes were deprived of education.

Many oppressed minorities responded to Pobiedonostsev's repression by joining revolutionary movements. But revolutionary pressures also mounted because of economic developments. In part, the government itself under Count Witte was responsible for these developments.* First as an administrator of state railways, then as Minister of Transport, and finally as finance minister between 1892 and 1903, Witte pressed for the expansion of Russian industry and transportation at an unprecedented pace. Building the trans-Siberian railways was his most sensational but not his most solid achievement. By erecting a prohibitive tariff wall, he attracted foreign capital. Industrialization, with few concessions to urban labor, created a large, discontented proletariat separated for the first time from agriculture. But the middle class, whose growth was stifled by state ownership of industry and by foreign capitalists, had little strength to voice their liberalism. Much more significant were the land-hungry peasants whose numbers almost doubled between emancipation and World War I and whose mutterings forbode revolutions. In these prewar years nearly one million peasants emigrated to Siberia, and land prices nearly trebled. But after 1880, starvation threatened about two thirds of the population. For millions, poor harvests in 1891 and 1892 made that threat a reality. Apart from denying the famine's existence, the government abolished poll taxes and reduced peasant indemnity payments. But prior to the Revolution of 1905, discussed below, it offered no policies to cope with the agrarian-population crisis. Agriculture remained collective and technologically backward.

## The Formation of Revolutionary Parties

The government's intolerable economic policies disaffected the peasantry from the autocracy, but they were not attracted to the programs of the revolutionary parties that organized at the turn of the century. The first

party to form was the Marxian Social Democratic party whose appeal was to industrial labor and intellectuals. Not only did Marx, whose *Das Kapital* the censors allowed to circulate as a procapitalist work, offer an extreme answer to an extreme situation, but he also offered a philosophy of history and a prophetic future congenial to Russian patterns of thought. Recovering from an abortive start in 1883, the Russian Social Democratic party reorganized and persevered after 1898. Most of its leadership agitated for democracy, labor reforms, and industrialization, but at the party congress held in London in 1903, advocates of more extreme measures secured a majority and organized as Bolsheviks. Thereafter, their leader, Lenin, and his followers exchanged polemics with the Menshevik ("minority") faction which advocated evolutionary reforms.† The second and largest party to organize was the Social Revolutionaries. Drawn from *Narodnik* (Populist) sources, it was a rustic socialist party that advocated continued communal land ownership, the cultivation of traditional folk customs, and opposition to industry. Although the party supported democratization, part of its numbers engaged in acts of terrorism and assassinated several tsarist officials between 1902 and 1904.

Following the two major socialist parties, the first formal liberal party organized during the early phases of the Revolution of 1905. Its roots were in the *Zemstvo* councils and in professional unions of lawyers, doctors, and teachers. The *Zemstvo* men had first taken the initiative when they attempted to organize a famine relief in 1892. In 1904 they met in a national congress that was called to assist the flagging war effort and to resolve an economic crisis. In May 1905, they joined with the professionals in the Union of Unions led by Professor Pavel

---

* Unlike Pobiedonostsev, Witte never possessed the complete confidence of the Tsar, despite his orthodox absolutism. He was dismissed in 1903, but recalled temporarily in 1905 to negotiate peace with Japan and a large French loan that, in his phrase, "saved Russia." By this he meant that it saved tsarist rule from parliamentary limitations.

† These names reflected Lenin's propaganda tactics rather than the relative strength of the factions in Russia. The Menshevik ("minority") faction had and maintained a larger following than Lenin right down to March 1917.

(Paul) Milyukov to demand parliamentary government, social reform, and civic rights.

All of the revolutionary parties acting as a "popular front" got their first opportunity to gain power not from large popular followings, which they lacked, but from the military and economic embarrassments of the government during the Russo-Japanese War of 1904 and 1905.

## War and Revolution, 1904 and 1905

Russian defeat in Manchuria and Korea began at the outset of the Russo-Japanese War* and continued until the Japanese sank units of the Baltic fleet sent around Africa to the Orient. Facing ridicule at home for these defeats, Nicholas lost more prestige when his palace guards fired on a procession of petitioning workers led by a secret-agent and priest, Father Gapon, on "Bloody Sunday," January 22, 1905. Following strikes and widespread rural disorders, the Tsar began to make concessions which he extended after every fresh major setback. In October 1905, a general strike tied up the economy and forced the dismissal of Pobiedonostsev. Thereafter, Count Witte was restored to favor to promulgate a manifesto promising an elective Duma or parliament and a broad range of civil liberties. As intended, Witte's October Manifesto split the liberals: conservative monarchical Octobrists against liberal Constitutional Democrats, or Cadets, who favored parliamentary government, state education, drastic land reforms, and autonomy for border regions. The Manifesto did not satisfy labor or the socialist parties, however. A labor council (soviet) in St. Petersburg and the Social Democrats organized further strikes and precipitated a conservative reaction among the liberals. When the government arrested the members of the St. Petersburg soviet, Moscow workers led by the Bolsheviks took to the barricades in a short, bloody, and futile revolt. Thus the

* Discussed in Chapter IX.

*Bloody Sunday, 1905.*

revolutionary coalition quickly broke into contending factions with differing interests.

The October Manifesto, a promise rather than a constitution, marked the high point of the Revolution of 1905. Counterrevolution began as soon as peace was obtained. Royal troops returning from the Far East were screened out and set upon rebellious areas. In the countryside, where constitutional issues made no impact, bands of "Black Hundreds," whose membership included the Tsar, high churchmen, and landlords, loosed private terror on rebellious or suspicious peasants. Most important, the Tsar negotiated with France the largest international loan up to that point in history. The loan enabled the Tsar to brush aside the first Duma, which the Cadets dominated. The Tsar consolidated his victory on May 6, 1906, by announcing fundamental laws that reduced the elective Duma to a minor role. Nicholas II, who had not given up his divine-right claims, reserved for himself an absolute veto, decree powers, budgetary initiative, and full control over foreign affairs, the military establishments, the administration and judiciary, and further constitutional changes. Atop the Duma he established an Imperial Council, half appointed and half elected by privileged corporations. When the Duma criticized the government and introduced unacceptable laws for the compensated expropriation and sale of gentry, state, and church lands, he dissolved it. Although not all of its results were erased, the revolution was over.

## Old Russia's "Golden Age," 1906 to 1914

According to aristocratic exiles from the Bolshevik Revolution of November 1917, Russia now entered a period in which her basic problems were being solved, at least until the outbreak of World War I. Actually, substantial progress was recorded. Labor conditions were mitigated, the number of schools increased by 50 per cent, universities were thrown open to the lower and middle classes, and the Russian industrialization rate was one of the most rapid in the world. Censorship relaxed, and persecution of minorities declined. For the first time, the government headed by Peter Stolypin (1862–1911) worked toward a promising program for the peasantry. He secured laws that allowed individual peasants to withdraw and consolidate their private holdings from the communal villages. During the revolution, redemption payments that had drained away capital were abolished. Now peasant banks began to make effective loans to needy peasants for capital improvements, and population pressures were eased somewhat by settlements in Siberia. Stolypin's reforms not only served to change rural conditions, but they also provided the social mobility indispensable for Russia's industrialization. Although ruthless repression of agrarian discontent accompanied Stolypin's reforms, his radical policies aroused reactionary fears. Left carelessly or intentionally unprotected, he was assassinated in 1911.

The socioeconomic problems that the regime faced were immense. Accommodating population increase alone was almost an impossible task. Still, there had been progress

*Rasputin, confidant of the royal family.*

that might have continued with proper direction. But resentment toward Stolypin in the highest government circles was not the only reason to question the adequacy of the prewar tsarist system. At the top of the bureaucracy that held the vast empire together was the Ministry, which lacked organization, coordination, and concern with social problems. Ultimately it depended upon the Tsar's person, and Nicholas II was a weak administrator, preoccupied with preserving his family's prerogatives. In 1907 he altered the election laws to make landowners predominant in the Duma and to sharply curtail the influence of peasants, industrial laborers, and minorities. While this law secured a cooperative, conservative Duma, its success encouraged Nicholas II to think in terms of further reductions of parliamentary government. Eventually alarming to both revolutionaries and conservatives was the power that the erotic "holy devil" Gregory Rasputin held over the Tsar and Tsarina. Their son, the heir apparent, suffered from hemophilia, and Rasputin alone was able to stop the boy's bleeding, apparently by hypnosis. To the Tsarina, who referred to Rasputin as "our friend," he appeared as a divine miracle. Despite the circulation of ugly rumors concerning his personal influence, Rasputin consolidated his position. The Tsar even forbade discussion of him. Ultimately, irate aristocrats assassinated Rasputin during World War I when military reversals were attributed to his advice. His case demonstrated a critical weakness in the Russian state—its dependence upon the Tsar. During the strains of World War I, that dependence proved to be a fatal disability.

## IN CONCLUSION

Between 1850 and 1914, when all Western societies were under the uneven impact of industrialization, every major state had or acquired some form of representative government. All of them had one or more parties committed to such institutions, and often to their democratization. But their powers and ability to respond to changing conditions varied widely.

Representative government fared best in the Western democracies where its hold on popular loyalties was renewed by periodic reforms and by popular education. In Britain and the United States all political parties accepted it as the basic framework. Still there were tensions of class and nationality. Preponderantly urban and industrial, Britain enacted a welfare system that alienated Conservatives, but failed to satisfy labor. The United States relied more on prosperity than on social welfare to maintain cohesion. More dangerous were conflicts of nationality. Southern secession disrupted the American system in the Civil War and, in 1914, the functioning of the British parliamentary system was threatened by the Irish thorn in its side. France, the nation-state par excellence, had no such problems, but her people lacked social and ideological cohesion. Threatened by authoritarian traditionalists, the Third Republic was based on social classes whose policies alienated the urban lower classes. Remaining in a hopeless minority politically, they were tempted by revolutionary programs. After unification, Italy, like France, lacked national minorities. Although clouded by provincialism, corruption, and extreme poverty, her parliamentary system seemed to be making progress by reforms and secular education, especially in the first decades of the twentieth century. But its many enemies had not yet found a single leader and program with which to launch a counterattack.

If thorough industrialization and general literacy sufficed to produce representative government, Germany should have been at the forefront of the liberal constitutional states. Instead, she had much in common with the Eastern empires. Despite imperial elections by universal manhood suffrage, the military aristocracy retained its initiative and power. National minorities were suppressed. Bismarck's remarkable achievement had been to win German liberals to this arrangement. But social welfare legislation did not suffice to check resistance by the Social Democrats and a narrow band of Progressive Liberals who advocated parliamentary government. It was a shaky structure, however, for socialist ranks were still being enlarged by industrial progress and reactions to executive indiscretions.

Still greater instability and a lesser basis for representative government existed in the Eastern empires. Belated but rapid industrialization was only one of several factors upsetting established patterns of political life. The governments of Russia and Austria-Hungary were engaged in suppressing subject nationalities, making them revolutionary and counternationalist in turn. Initiative in both empires rested not with industrial middle classes but with bureaucracies working under divine-right sovereigns. Their role in directing modernization was ambiguous. In Russia it ranged from the emancipation of the serfs to the introduction of large-scale industry. But the bureaucracies' royal masters were loathe to surrender political power to the new social forces that modernization had released. Inspired either by the desire for power or to ward off revolution, reforms were halfhearted or tentative. Moreover, Russia, still a land of peasants, was undergoing an agrarian subsistence crisis that ultimately made the peasantry revolutionary. In Austria, Francis Joseph came to terms with modernization by experimenting with universal manhood suffrage and parliamentary government, but in Russia the Duma arose as a concession to revolution while the tsarist government was embarrassed by defeat in foreign war. It was a concession that did not satisfy liberals and socialists, and that the inept Nicholas II would gladly withdraw at the first favorable moment.

After 1914 the unresolved problems that produced internal instability were temporarily submerged in World War I. How far the outbreak of that war reflected the desires of political leaders to turn attention from them to foreign war is a moot question. Certainly Austria-Hungary's attempt to crush Serbia in 1914 stemmed from the fear of nationalist disintegration. Both Russia and Germany were in revolutionary situations because entrenched power elites would not yield. And Britain's influence was weakened by the prospects of imminent civil war over Ireland. Polemics against socialists generally hit hardest at their internationalism. It is also certain that nationalism, the principal ideology behind the war, was cultivated to secure a feeling of unity despite conflicting interests. But it was most commonly expressed in the quest to rule over and "civilize" other peoples—imperialism. Schisms within industrial societies hardly account for the outbreak of World War I, but the role of imperialism in bringing that war about awaits assessment in the following chapter.

## SELECTED READINGS

*Binkley, Robert C., *Realism and Nationalism 1852–1871,* Harper, New York, 1935, and Harper Torchbook.

A comprehensive history of politics, thought, and business in the Rise of Modern Europe series; particularly good on the foreign policy of Napoleon III.

Briggs, Asa, *Victorian People,* University of Chicago Press, Chicago, 1955.

Depicts Victorian England between the Great Exposition of 1851 and the Reform Bill of 1867 by a biographical approach to major events and institutional changes.

Bury, J. P. T., *Napoleon III and the Second Empire,* English Universities Press, London, 1964.

A short up-to-date analysis, packed with information, in the Teach Yourself History Library by the author of a longer history of France from 1814 to 1940.

Brogan, Denis, *France Under the Republic, 1870–1939,* Harper, New York, 1940.

A solid attention-keeping account, the first seven books of which are relevant to this chapter.

*Dangerfield, George, *The Strange Death of Liberal England 1910–1914,* Capricorn Books, New York, 1961.

A study in the breakdown of parliamentary methods among the suffragettes, labor groups, and conservative opponents of Irish Home Rule on the eve of World War I.

*Eych, Erich, *Bismarck and the German Empire,* W. W. Norton, New York, 1958.

An incisive political biography in the form of lectures based on the author's three-volume life of Bismarck, in German.

*Hamerow, Theodore S., *Otto von Bismarck, A Historical Assessment,* D. C. Heath & Co., Boston, 1962.

A collection of widely different interpretations of Bismarck's career, with an extremely perceptive introduction.

* Asterisk (*) denotes paperback.

*Hayes, Carleton J. H., *A Generation of Materialism 1871–1900,* Harper, New York and London, and Harper Torchbook.

A volume in the Rise of Modern Europe series that sees the end of the nineteenth century, although witnessing the rise of economic imperialism and totalitarian nationalism, as the climax of the Enlightenment.

Jászi, Oszkár, *The Dissolution of the Habsburg Monarchy,* University of Chicago Press, Chicago, 1929.

Emphasizes illiberal Hungarian policies as the basic disintegrating force in Austria-Hungary.

Kann, Robert A., *The Multinational Empire: Nationalism and National Reform in the Habsburg Monarchy, 1848–1918,* Octagon Books, New York, 1964, 2 vols.

Volume I records the growth of nationalism among the Empire's constituent peoples; Volume II surveys the proposals put forth after 1848 to resolve national conflicts within the Empire.

King, Bolton, *A History of Italian Unity 1814–1871,* Nisbet, London, 1924, 2 vols. (rev. ed.).
An old account that is still useful.

Kitson Clark, George, *The Making of Victorian England,* Harvard University Press, Cambridge, 1962.

A revisionist history emphasizing religion, the perculation of wealth downward, and the growth of rule by experts and officials motivated by humanitarianism behind the Victorian ideology of *laissez faire.*

*Pares, Bernard, *The Fall of the Russian Monarchy,* Alfred A. Knopf, New York, 1939, and Vintage Books.

A history of the reign of Alexander II and the first revolution of 1917 by an historian intimately acquainted with source materials and leading persons involved in the events described.

Pobedonostsev, Konstantin Petrovich, *Reflections of a Russian Statesman,* translated by R. C. Fong, University of Michigan Press, Ann Arbor, 1965.

A frank exposition of counterrevolutionary traditionalism by Alexander III's most powerful adviser.

Robinson, Geroid T., *Rural Russia Under the Old Régime,* The Macmillan Co., New York, 1961.

Investigates the peasants' situation before and after the emancipation of 1861 and analyzes in detail the effects of the early twentieth-century reforms.

*Rosenberg, Arthur, *Imperial Germany, The Birth of the German Republic 1871–1918,* Beacon Press, Boston, 1964.

An excellent study based on a parliamentary investigation of the reasons for Germany's loss of World War I by a liberal dissenter who participated in that investigation.

Schorske, Carl E., *German Social Democracy 1905–1917,* Harvard University Press, Cambridge, 1955.

Traces the origins of the great schism between the union-based democratic Socialists and revolutionary Communists within the German Social Democratic party.

Simmons, Ernest J., ed., *Continuity and Change in Russian and Soviet Thought,* Harvard University Press, Cambridge, 1955.

A collection of papers by more than thirty contributors on various aspects of Russian thought before and after the Bolshevik Revolution, several of which are indispensable to Russian history in the nineteenth century.

Simpson, Frederick A., *Louis Napoleon and the Recovery of France,* Longmans, Green & Co., New York and London, 1930.

A worthy pioneering attempt to rescue the Second Empire from inattention, a labor that the author has failed to conclude beyond 1856.

Somervell, D. C., *Disraeli and Gladstone, A Duo-Biographical Sketch,* Garden City Publishing Co., Garden City, N.Y., 1926.

A joint biography based on the classic exhaustive biographies of both men.

Taylor, A. J. P., *The Course of German History,* Coward-McCann, New York, 1946; and *The Habsburg Monarchy, 1809–1918,* H. Hamilton, London, 1948.

Authoritative studies of the two principal powers of Central Europe, rather heavy reading for the beginner.

Thompson, J. M., *Louis Napoleon and the Second Empire,* Blackwell, Oxford, 1965.
Biography of the emperor, based on up-to-date scholarship, that treats the Second Empire as a natural transition to the Third Republic.

*Thomson, David, *England in the Nineteenth Century, 1815–1914,* Penguin Books, Baltimore, 1950.
Traces social changes, mental habits, and social organization during Britain's transition from an agrarian to an industrial society, finding the Victorians liberal enough to have distributed wealth, without bloodshed, throughout the community to an unprecedented extent.

Whyte, A. J. B., *The Making of Modern Italy,* Blackwell, Oxford, 1944.
One of the best accounts of Italian history in English.

*Williams, Roger L., *Gaslight and Shadow, The World of Napoleon III 1851–1870,* The Macmillan Co., New York, 1957, and a paperback under its subtitle.
Biographical sketches illuminating various aspects—including education, culture, and science—of Louis Napoleon's France.

For the United States, see the volumes emphasizing social history by Arthur Cole, Allan Nevins, Ida Tarbell, Arthur M. Schlesinger, and Harold U. Faulkner in *A History of American Life,* edited by Arthur M. Schlesinger and Dixon Ryan Fox. See also:

Link, Arthur S., *Woodrow Wilson and the Progressive Era, 1910–1917,* Harper, New York, 1954, and

Mowry, George E., *Theodore Roosevelt and the Progressive Movement,* University of Wisconsin, Madison, 1946.
Two recent authoritative works on the quest for social justice in industrial America.

# IX

## The New Imperialism and the Posture of Aggression

Much controversy has developed in recent years over the nature, purposes, and consequences of the so-called new imperialism. The opening section of this chapter presents most of the more common arguments that make up this controversy. Brief attention is then given to the salient features of the state and alliance systems, secret diplomacy, militarism, new personalities, and the aims of the powers. The concluding, and major, portion is devoted to a somewhat detailed examination of the global thrusts of the new imperialist surge.

### THE WEB OF FORCES

#### Imperialism

Imperialism may be defined as the extension of control or influence by one people over another. Throughout history it has assumed different forms and exerted varying degrees of influence upon other events, de-

pending upon circumstances and the spirit of the times. In one form it radiates from a power center to contiguous territories. In another it stretches over land and sea to weave itself into the affairs of distant peoples and places. And often it combines both activities.

Sometimes imperialism has been a dominant force, as the history of ancient Rome attests. Sometimes it has faded, in one form at least, to slight significance; for more than a generation after the Vienna settlement of 1815, its extra-European influence was negligible. Later it entered a new phase, of particular importance for our present study. For almost a half century (*c.* 1870–1914) the imperial thrust penetrated seas and continents remote from the heartland of Europe. Pacific isles and ports, almost the whole of Africa, and a large part of Asia came under some degree of imperial rule before the movement, merging with others (particularly nationalism and the attempt to establish a new balance of power), issued in World War I. Continental imperialism was also at work, as we shall see when we come to consider the activities of Pan-Germans and Pan-Slavs in Central and Eastern Europe.

For the most part the new movement was served by conservative or traditionalist interests—the economic elite, their political representatives, the military establishment, and often the church. We know little of the interest and attitude of the common man. Perhaps he felt a glow of pride when the new maps showed his nation spreading over the globe. Certainly this was our own experience in the election of 1900 when—with imperialism the dominant, almost single issue—Americans chose not to "haul down the flag." But it is hard to believe that if the average person had been left to himself he would have shown much interest either way. On the other hand, social democrats and reflective liberals, whatever their party affiliation, almost invariably condemned what they thought of as exploitive expansion.

## Motivating Forces: the White Man's Burden

It is difficult, too, to determine precisely what motivations lay behind the so-called new imperialism. Those who practiced it professed different, sometimes contradictory, aims. And nothing approaching a consensus has been reached by latter-day scholars. Here we will settle for a summary examination of the chief claims of both groups.

Some imperialists believed that modern man was under obligation to share the benefits of his advanced culture with the "lesser breeds" of backward regions. In a sense they may be thought of as missionaries of materialism. (There are important exceptions. Certain English colonial administrators such as Lord Milner and Lord Cromer were motivated by what they honestly thought of as liberal, humane impulses.) In the last quarter of the nineteenth century millions in Western Europe and America achieved a standard of living unmatched in the record of man. In-

*An early anti-imperialist cartoon labeled simply "The Great White Way."*

creasingly, the machine lifted from man menial burdens that bound and coarsened his spirit. But most of the world, especially the colored masses of Africa and Asia, still lived in material wretchedness. Their need, it was argued, spoke to the white man's conscience. The response was accompanied by difficulties and dangers. To bring the benefits of civilization to his colored brothers, the white man, so proponents of this view argued, necessarily had to remake and manage the new societies. In short, the beneficiaries, "half devil and half child," had first to be tamed and then paternalistically governed by their benefactors. Many of them naturally would not understand the need for white control, still less the justifiable "exploitation" which the white man felt must accompany that control. No one knew how long the period of tutelage would last. For however long, both colored and white would probably be beset by wearisome strains and tribulations. But as Rudyard Kipling, the most celebrated exponent of this view, insisted, for the white man there was no choice; his was the challenge to take up, his the burden to bear.

## Religion, Social Darwinism, Prestige

The new imperialism also had a religious perspective. Progress in effective means of getting places and communicating with one another enabled Christians to envision mass conversion of the "pagan" world. The attempt to establish a Christian imperium is of course as old as Christianity. But the advent of the second phase of the industrial revolution—providing as it did relatively easy access to remote areas, reliable channels of communication, and many physical facilities that ameliorated harsh living conditions—multiplied missions around the world. Besides the Christian message, missionaries took with them the cultural accouterments of their own land. More often than not they were also offered and accepted help and protection from the home government; in effect, the flag tended to follow the Cross.

A third apologia of the new expansion of Europe (and later America) grew out of the findings of Charles Darwin as these came to be applied to social behavior. For many persons, "survival of the fittest" explained and justified man's ancient urge to exploit his fellow man. For them, Darwin had shown that the raw and violent sanctions of nature rewarded the strong and penalized the weak. They argued that human existence was subject to the same sanctions. The industrial revolution had brought to white Western societies techniques and powers unknown to the colored masses of Africa, Asia, and Oceania. Refusal to use them was both unnatural and unreasonable. This did not mean that the Social Darwinists demanded or desired the savage destruction of backward peoples. It meant rather that they believed they had the right, indeed the natural duty, to conquer and control retarded peoples so that all might enjoy, according to their different abilities, the benefits of the good life.

Finally, for governments and citizens of the times, the simple desire to gain control over some area before others did was an

*"Modern Apostle," a German cartoon (1904).*

THE WORLD'S PLUNDERERS.
" It's English, you know."

*A Thomas Nast cartoon (1885) pokes at the European powers for their "grab" of the underdeveloped world.*

operating factor in intensifying the imperialist scramble. Pride and prestige are hard to document as causative factors, but certainly among the ruling elites of that period color on the map was a highly sought status symbol.

## Critiques of the New Imperialism

The impact and significance of the new imperialism upon both Western and Eastern societies early attracted and continues to attract the attention of many scholars. Again, only the more prominent of the various interpretations can be examined. One school of thought emphasizes the psychological underpinnings of the movement. Proponents of this view argue that the industrial revolution created a society characterized by boredom, loss of identity, and a store of random energies. Modern machinery had released man from one kind of slavery only to enmesh him in another. Formerly men had physically toiled long hours, which drained them of energies that otherwise could have nurtured mental and spiritual needs. Modern industry had freed man from this exhausting grind but at a frightful price—monotonous attendance upon soulless machines. Out of this new thralldom man periodically sought escape in excitement and adventure. The world's governing elite depended on this reservoir of unchanneled energy and the yen for new experiences when the diplomacy of acquisition entered its final fighting stage.

## The Socialist Critique

Probably the most influential critique of the new imperialism rested upon an elaborate analysis of economic practices. Worked out originally by John A. Hobson, a British liberal economist, it has since served as the classic anticapitalist exposition of the movement. Lenin called it an "accurate description of the fundamental economic and political traits of imperialism" and based one of his own major works upon it. The following paragraphs sketch its main argument.*

Industrial society's newly amassed capital soon overflowed the areas of its origin. This did not mean that home investments vanished. On the contrary, they increased. Even so, capital resources outran investment opportunities as mass consumption (for reasons noted immediately below) lagged behind production. Therefore, capital came to be increasingly invested in "backward" areas where its owners were also seeking markets. In time, as finance capital came to dominate the resources of industrial capital, financial magnates took over leading roles in imperialist ventures.

Moreover, by 1880 the machine, powered now by the dynamo as well as the steam engine, had begun a fundamental transformation of Western society. For the first time in history man had at his disposal tools, skills, and techniques adequate to provide him with not only the necessities of life but many of its conveniences and luxuries. The affluent society seemed in the making.

But society at large did not become affluent, although living standards rose markedly, especially in England, France, Germany, the United States, and Japan. Two circumstances accounted for this anomaly. One was the control of capital by a relatively small entrepreneurial class. A good example of such control was found in our own country. Steel, the backbone of any industrial society, was produced under the direction of a few magnates such as Andrew Carnegie and Henry Frick. Rockefeller and his associates dominated the oil industry. Similar conditions prevailed in other basic businesses such as banking, railroads, meat-packing, sugar refining, and the manufacture of farm implements. Whether called trusts, as in America,

* Two cautions: the words "sketch" and "main" should be emphasized; *in toto* the thesis is long and complicated. Also, the paragraphs should not be read as a condensation of any of Hobson's statements but purely as a rough paraphrase.

or cartels, as in Europe, these giant corporations exercised almost exclusive power to set prices, wages, hours of work, and the methods and amounts of production. For the most part they used this power primarily for their own aggrandizement. Henry Frick, for example, associating himself with Carnegie at the age of twenty-two, became a millionaire before he was thirty. And his counterpart, here and abroad, sprang up with remarkable regularity wherever the machine appeared.

A second circumstance militating against a general distribution of wealth was the almost universal adoption of high tariff policies. In each of the major industrial states during this period, entrepreneurs dominated the government. To protect price levels that would guarantee substantial profits they sought heavy duties on incoming goods, thus keeping foreign competition out of the domestic market.* In the main they were successful. As a consequence consumers, mostly made up of the working class, paid prices set by corporations for purchased goods or went without.

For a while the masses seemed to be content. They sensed that the machine was, at least potentially, the herald and instrument of abundance. Wages, compared to those of former days, were high. Men believed that prices would fall as the machine produced ever greater quantities of goods. Moreover, labor unions were slowly gaining strength, pointing to a promise of yet higher income levels. Altogether, their tomorrows seemed bright.

Actually, the gap between wages and prices was not closed. Corporate wealth continued to dominate governmental policies. Magnates and managers crushed the budding power of organized labor. Such practices, of course, secured the profits of big business; but they also prevented buying power from reaching levels commensurate with produc-

---

* This was not true in England. Far in advance of other nations in industrial efficiency and know-how, she felt she could outproduce and undersell her competitors without tariff aids.

tion. Factories poured out goods into markets that did not exist. True, producers could and did periodically store their surpluses in warehouses, against the coming of better days. But since better days necessarily depended upon higher wages and lower prices, a kind of permanent glut resulted.

So a search for new markets began, particularly in what were called the backward areas of the world. If the door at home seemed closed, perhaps an open one could be found abroad. Other needs produced by the industrial revolution strengthened the trend. Certain raw resources needed to keep the machines going were found only in foreign lands. Tin and tungsten, for example, are basic requisites in any mechanized society. But they were not available in a single one of the Western industrialized states. Obviously the rugged individualist of Europe and America needed to stake out claims abroad.

## The Capitalist Critique

More recently a counter argument has gained wide acceptance among historians and economists. One of its basic postulates is that capitalism, far from prompting imperialist adventures, is fundamentally opposed to them. Depending as it does upon conditions which encourage economic freedom at home and free trade abroad, capitalism naturally opposes war and aggressive expansion. In support of this contention proponents of this view cite the historic record. The birth of modern capitalism occurred in eighteenth-century England. It was characterized by individual liberty, democracy, free trade—ingredients hardly compatible with the imperialist impulse. The capitalist entrepreneur is mainly interested in expanding his business and his profits. War and conquest, the argument goes, disturb, challenge, and often destroy the conditions requisite to healthy capitalist growth. The natural habitat of the businessman is the counting house, not the battlefield. Indeed, not only is he not a war monger, he is actively and genuinely interested in creating a warless world.*

The thesis holds that the historic record also disproves the claim that exportation of capital precipitated nineteenth-century expansionism. For example, at the peak of the new imperialism, England actually exported less capital than it did a generation before when the country was consciously and deliberately pursuing an anticolonial policy. Moreover, such undeniably expansionist powers as Russia and Italy were consistent borrowers rather than exporters of capital.

With these and other arguments, opponents of the surplus profits theory of imperialism sought to disassociate it quite completely from capitalism. They did not, however, minimize the impact of the movement upon world events. According to Schumpeter a great portion of the whole human drama regrettably has been shaped by it. The ruling elites of all peoples are tempted to prostitute their power and eventually to exercise it "disfunctionally." He looked upon nineteenth-century imperialism as a cultural inheritance from ancient warrior societies. Then, as so often before, its primary aim was conquest for the sake of conquest, devoid of rational object and spurred by a "will for . . . forcible expansion, without definite, utilitarian limits. . . ." Only when men rid themselves of this legacy—when, that is, capitalism perfects its own inherent tendencies—will the imperialist impulse fade from history.

Almost all treatments of the causes and course of the new imperialism reject the claim that colonies made money for the home country. With rare exceptions, colonial possessions proved to be economic liabilities. Abundant statistical evidence makes clear that every pre-World War I imperialist power spent far more in military and administrative upkeep than it received as profit from either trade or capital investment.

Indeed, a recent interpretation of the promptings of the new imperialism in Africa holds that it had little or nothing to do with the desire to bring either peoples or markets there under imperial control. Rather, according to this thesis, the aristocratic makers of Victorian policy believed that Britain's existence as a world power depended upon her control of India, and upon her general strength in the East. This control, in turn, hinged upon her dominance of the sea lanes leading to and from the Suez Canal and partly upon control of the waters around the Cape Colony. For a time this dominance was assured through informal "influence" over the weaker and backward peoples of those areas (except in the Cape, of course, where Britons already directly ruled). But when local African governments, "sapped by the strains of previous Western influences," began to collapse and spawn political voids, Britain was forced to occupy and eventually govern territories she would otherwise have had little interest in. The key event that sparked the change in British policy, as proponents of this thesis see it, was the rapid disintegration of normal governmental processes in Egypt in 1882. As the British moved in—reluctantly, almost perforce— many powers grew envious and apprehensive.† Thus began the race of the powers to divide up the Continent, a race that continued until there was practically nothing left to divide.

To summarize, a number of varying and sometimes contradictory theses have been offered by imperialists and by students of the movement to explain the rather sudden burst of expansionist activity that occurred during the late nineteenth and early twentieth centuries: the human yen to aggrandize self,

---

* Joseph Schumpeter, chief exponent of this view, has expressed this opinion in the plainest of terms: ". . . modern pacifism . . . is unquestionably a phenomenon of the capitalist world; [and] wherever capitalism has penetrated, peace parties of such strength arose that virtually every war meant a political struggle on the domestic scene."

† See pp. 371–376. Compare R. Robinson, J. Gallagher, and A. Denny, *Africa and the Africans: the Climax of Imperialism in the Dark Continent,* St. Martins Press, New York, 1961.

family, clan, nation; the white man's urge to share with the nonwhite world (at a price) his "advanced" culture; the desire to make Christianity truly catholic; the belief in the natural right of the strong to subjugate the weak; the need of bourgeois capitalists to export their surplus wealth; the impulse to escape from boredom created by the industrialization of society; "objectless" conquest rooted in atavistic drives; and the necessity to "stabilize" areas situated close to vital sea lanes. (Others, such as the play of Machiavellian diplomacy and the ambitions of certain political leaders, will be considered in the context of specific events in the sections following.) Which of these forces or what combination of them motivated expansion and which, if any, are mere exercises in political theory may be individually determined in the light of events soon to be considered.

## The State System and the Alliance Systems

Both nationalism and imperialism functioned within the sovereign state system. Given philosophic justification by the writings of Hugo Grotius and a kind of official sanction by the treaty of Westphalia (1648), state sovereignty came to be accepted as the only right form of municipal organization. Each state came to believe itself beyond accountability to any authority other than its own. Of course, mutually agreed upon arrangements and compromises were useful, even necessary, for normal intercourse among peoples. But each state jealously guarded its absolute sovereignty as a possession beyond price. By the end of the nineteenth century this outlook and practice had led to what some observers recognized as international anarchy, with war as the ultimate instrument of national policy. Some social scientists and moral philosophers sensed the time had come to set up a supranational organization to preserve international comity and peace; but they were few and without political power or influence. Thus, although by the beginning of our century an amorphous world

community was emerging, there existed no "parliament of man" to legislate for it, no executive body to administer, or court system to adjudicate world law. Rather than set themselves to the task of creating such institutions and a climate of opinion to support them, statesmen of the period sought to secure and enhance interests in ways that eventually led to the creation of an elaborate and ominous system of counterpoised alliances.

The practice of states aligning themselves with other states has its roots in ancient history, as we have seen in Volume I. Before they destroyed each other, Egypt and Hatti were allies,* as were Corinth and Sparta, early Rome and the Latin tribes; the list is beyond compilation. The historic record also includes many instances of alliance clusters; for example, the combinations in the period from 1688 to 1763. The division of Europe in the late nineteenth and early twentieth centuries into two rival camps was therefore far from unprecedented. What was new was the mushrooming technological advances in the construction of war instruments. As the implications of this development were sensed, diplomats sought the protection of long-time alliances and the perfecting of mobilization plans which, as we shall see, tended to make diplomatic situations assume an increasingly inflexible character.

The doctrine of state sovereignty logically implies unending conflict among discrete political divisions, a condition hardly compatible with the basic requisites of civilization. Therefore, the major states had long ago worked out, although fumblingly and inadequately, a pattern of behavior that honored this principle while at the same time mitigating the more intolerable effects of its practice. This compromise often took the form of a balancing of power, characterized either by the formation of alliance complexes or by an extraordinarily strong power ready to act simultaneously as umpire and

---

* See Vol. I, Chap. I.

"Adieu!"
"No, 'au revoir.'   Visits must be returned."

*This cartoon portrays French feelings after the Franco-Prussian War of 1870–1871.*

potential ally of one of the groups. Since Waterloo, England had played this latter role. Throughout this period she had consistently labored to prevent any nation or combination of nations from gaining a predominant position in Europe. Actually, no nation had seemed particularly possessed of such an ambition. Thus, with the Bourbons gone and the Bonapartes weak, with Austria concerned almost exclusively with the preservation of the *status quo,* and with Prussia barely out of its adolescence, Britain's self-assigned chore proved to be not too burdensome. But in the 1870s a combination of events created a new situation. The introduction of the dynamo as an important source of machine power coincided with the unification of Germany. Possessing a large free trade area, access to abundant supplies of coal and iron, and an alert, educated business elite, the new nation soon became a strong contender not only for world markets but, as one of the kaiser's ministers expressed it, a place

in the sun. Germany's victory over France (1871) gave her increased military and political prestige at the same time it reduced France, at least temporarily, to the status of a second-class power; it also clearly marked the end of Habsburg domination in Central Europe. For England these changes came to add up to an ominous challenge.* In short, Europe's balance of power had rather suddenly and quite significantly shifted. Hereafter the course of world politics and international diplomacy had necessarily to change as nations sought to adjust themselves as advantageously as possible to the new conditions.

## Secret Diplomacy, Militarism, and Emergence of New Personalities

Secret diplomacy was an instrument commonly used by all the nations to reestablish a workable balance of power. Although this kind of diplomacy was no innovation, it deserves inclusion in a survey of the forces that shaped events preceding and leading to World War I. It served as a vehicle for a remarkable, and in its ramifications almost unexampled, exercise in international deceit. It kept hidden plans and strategies that citizens might otherwise have refused to countenance. And it constituted a *modus operandi* without which the grand alignments of the period almost certainly would have been impossible. It is particularly important to stress here not only the play of secret agreements on the international situation but the impact it had on emerging democracy. From earliest times the implementation of foreign polity by covert "deals" between the heads of two or more states was delicate and difficult enough. With the advent of democratic advice and consent

---

* But this was not immediately obvious. Indeed some very articulate Englishmen (Thomas Carlyle for one) originally applauded the German victory. By the late 1890s, however (when a clearer view of the new Germany emerged), the challenge was evident to most observers.

in national life, this instrument of international procedure became impossibly difficult. National governments commonly maneuvered themselves out of this dilemma by keeping their own citizens ignorant of such transactions. In short, the new secret diplomacy edged the common man closer to a general European war at the same time that it weakened his power to prevent it.*

By definition power politics ultimately depends upon military sanctions. If war is the ultimate extension of diplomacy—that is, the final arbiter of international "justice"—then a nation's war machine must always be ready, continually undergoing refinement of its striking power. During the period from 1870 to 1914, Europe's armies and navies exceeded in size and power anything the world had yet seen. For the most part they were based upon universal conscription and managed by professional militarists whose views, especially in times of crisis, came increasingly to influence the decisions of their civilian superiors. In other words, militarism constituted one of the primary forces that shaped events throughout the whole of this period.

Whether decisively or only casually, certain personalities also influenced Europe's larger affairs and concerns, as they have influenced group behavior at all times everywhere. Who would care to argue, for example, that the course of American history would have been substantially unaffected had Mr. Lincoln been assassinated a month after his first rather than his second inauguration? Or if the bullet which killed Mayor Cermak had instead killed Mr. Roosevelt? If it is foolish to believe that the drama of human

existence is wholly determined by a few devils or saints, it is naïve to ignore the influence of strong personalities upon the evolution of that drama. Certainly they played a significant role in shaping the events soon to be considered.

## The Aims of the Powers

Finally we need to note the overall aims of the great and lesser powers which framed the developing web of power politics and secret diplomacy. England wanted not only to keep the great empire she already possessed but also to add to it, especially when new markets, raw resources, investment opportunities, or strategic waterways were the prizes. Since her imperial home base was so small and her need for imported goods so great, she claimed a kind of special right to patrol and police the seas. As a "have" nation she preferred peace to war. But she was prepared to oppose by force any attempt to frustrate what she thought of as justifiable national and imperial aims. Although she considered no nation her natural enemy, she was nevertheless disturbed by the German thrust into world markets, by Germany's attempt to supervise continental affairs, and after 1900 Germany's challenge to her dominance on the seas. But until the turn of the century, Britain scorned alliances as crutches needed only by the weak.

During Bismarck's long rule as Chancellor (1871–1890), Germany's basic aim was to keep the peace. Unification had been achieved and France, according to German thought, had been taught a lesson. Also, although industry was expanding, its rate of growth was slow throughout Bismarck's tenure, a circumstance that naturally made him cautious. Moreover, he needed time and peaceful conditions to consolidate the empire he had created. So far as Bismarck was concerned, war could bring Germany only suffering. But he was conscious of France's yearning for revenge. He was aware, too, of imperialist and nationalist fermentations in

---

* It should be understood that "secret diplomacy" refers essentially to the secret protocols attached to the publishable terms of the alliance contracts and not to the alliances themselves. It is also important to understand that knowledgeable people, especially in government circles, were aware that such protocols existed—without, of course, knowing their terms—and they thus encouraged a kind of irrational catering to the whims of their own allies.

the Balkans. So he sought to beguile France (but still keep her friendless), to forestall an Austro-Russian clash in the Balkans, and to woo England as cokeeper of the peace. After Bismarck was dropped, a new course, which we will examine later, was laid out by the Kaiser and his advisers.

France wanted to erase the humiliation of 1871 from the record and to regain her old status as an undisputed first-class power. She believed neither was possible so long as Alsace-Lorraine remained German. She knew she could not achieve her goals without strong help from friends. She also wanted to expand her republican empire; whatever the economic returns might be, the psychological gains would certainly be gratifying. We should not conclude that the citizenry flamed with feelings for *revanche* or periodically demanded additional color on the map. They may have felt both urges, but the actual record tells us little. Presumably French officials represented the electorate, on whose favor they depended. But it is certain that French "cabinet politics," whether citizen inspired or not, were clear and decisive for the nation.

With the same reservations Russia's basic aims may be noted. She sought hegemony over the Straits, including Constantinople (Istanbul) and its environs. Not only would this port give Russia entry to important trade lanes, it would also allow her easier control of the strategic waterway connecting the Black and Mediterranean seas, control long held by the Ottoman Turk and used by him to bottle up at will the Russian Black Sea fleet. Russia also wanted to supervise affairs in the Balkans both because she considered this essential to sound and permanent control of the Straits and because she believed herself to be the natural leader of the Slavic peoples, who constituted the preponderant part of the Balkan populations. Finally, she wanted to expand in the East, particularly in northern China. For many years she was pulled by these polar attractions, unable to go all out for both and seemingly unwilling to decide upon one or the other for sustained concentration.

Across the centuries Austria had built up an empire of assorted peoples. She wanted to keep it from falling apart. With the strong tides of nationalism flowing around her she was not sure she could, particularly since the emperor and his bureaucratic courtiers seemed weary of imperial burdens. Nonetheless, if the danger was not too great she occasionally assumed a posture of offence to forestall action that threatened the *status quo*. At the turn of the century aggressive new leaders were to carry the role beyond posture, into actions that precipitated World War I.

Italy, poorest and weakest of the great powers, wanted credits, colonies, and any friends who could help her to get them. Plagued by poverty, mass illiteracy, and endemic political corruption, she nevertheless nurtured great expectations. Haunted by memories of ancient grandeur and prompted by the urge to keep up with the growing greatness of other powers, throughout this period Italy spent much of her energy in expansionist schemes and in intricate diplomatic maneuvers designed to win friends and fortune.

The Balkan peoples wanted independence and the unification of their ethnic families into true political bodies. For example, Serbia insisted upon the "return" of Bosnia and Herzegovina, peopled mostly by Serbs but long ruled by alien empires. In a number of border areas, nationals were so mixed with other nationals that accurate boundaries were almost impossible to define, even apart from the constant meddling of imperial overlords. But such conditions had little or no effect upon patriotic agitators for national justice. Most Balkan leaders seemed to believe that the sorting-out problem was either inconsequential or negotiable after imperial shackles had been broken. More unfortunately, they also nursed aggrandizing ambitions of their own; what was altogether wrong for Turks or Austrians often became quite legitimate in their own scheming.

## THE WEB OF EVENTS: IMPERIALISM

### *The Imperialist Thrust in Africa*

Such were the general movements, conditions, postures, and aspirations that characterized Europe's political life from 1870 to 1914. Out of them evolved the concrete events we must now consider.

Scarcely more than a century ago almost all of Africa and most of Asia lay beyond the white man's control and some parts of these continents were even unknown to him. Before 1875 European powers possessed only these portions of Africa: Algeria (France), Cape Colony and Natal (Britain), the coastal regions of Angola and Mozambique (Portugal), and scattered trading areas along the western bend of the continent; in all, less than one tenth of the land. A generation later less than one tenth remained under native control. (See maps, pp. 369 and 407.)

### *Belgian Congo*

Interest in Africa was quickened by the combined efforts of missionaries and explorers. In the 1850s and 1860s David Livingstone, a Scottish medical missionary, published two books that gave many Europeans their first understanding of the vast dimensions and resources of this continent. When, around 1870, the outside world lost contact with him as he searched for the headwaters of the Nile, public excitement reached such a pitch that an enterprising newspaper publisher subsidized a search party, headed by the journalist-explorer Henry Stanley. The dramatic meeting of the searcher and the sought stirred millions. Other explorers probed the continent and reported their findings to a reading and lecture-attending public, who were eager to enjoy vicarious encounters with cannibals, jungle beasts, and natural wonders such as the Zambezi (Victoria) Falls and the Sahara's rolling oceans of desert. Many accounts described the potential markets and riches of the "new" world, others the black man's need of the

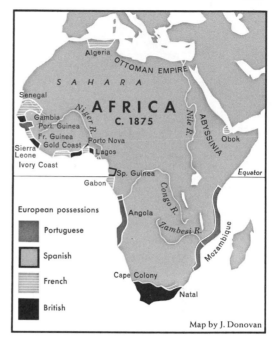

Map by J. Donovan

white man's religion. Sometimes the two themes were interwoven, as in an address Stanley made before the Manchester Chamber of Commerce in which he said:

There are forty millions of people beyond the gateway of the Congo, and the cotton spinners of Manchester are waiting to clothe them. Birmingham foundries are glowing with the red metal that will presently be made into ironwork for them and the trinkets that shall adorn those dusky bosoms, and the ministers of Christ are zealous to bring them, the poor benighted heathens, into the Christian fold.[1]

But it was Belgian royalty rather than British business which made the first significant thrust into Africa. Holding that to "open to civilization the only part of our globe where it has not yet penetrated—is a crusade . . . worthy of this century of progress," King Leopold II organized the International Association of the Congo and sent Stanley back to Africa (1879) to take up the white man's burden. Within a few

1. Quoted in Parker Moon, *Imperialism and World Politics,* The Macmillan Company, New York, 1927, p. 66.

*According to Stanley's own account, this draw-
ing of the famous Stanley-Livingstone meeting
"is as correct as if the scene had been photo-
graphed." Livingstone appears as one of the
few unarmed members of the group.*

*Stanley.*

years the royal crusade had succeeded in
bringing under his control a territory about
eight times larger than Belgium. Ironically,
it came to be called the Congo Free State.
From the beginning the civilizing mission
suffered neglect as concessionary companies
busily set about exploiting the native peoples
and the region's natural resources, particularly rubber and ivory. Later the Free State
was taken over by the Belgian government;
but not before Leopold had accumulated a
personal fortune of about $20 million.

Meanwhile other nations felt apprehension
over Leopold's expansive designs. At their
insistence (and encouraged by Bismarck) an
international conference was held in Berlin
(1885). Behind a facade of humanitarian
concern over the exploitation of primitive
peoples the conference worked out guidelines
intended to regularize the impending partition of Africa. Although Leopold's "free
state" was given official recognition (not in
the diplomatic sense, of course), further acquisitions of the powers were made subject
to certain regulations. A state could not, for
example, claim territory without making a

*Livingstone*

prior public announcement of intention. Moreover, claims had to go beyond paper pronouncements. Only actual exploration, adequate garrisoning, and the institution and maintenance of conventional administrative agencies could legitimatize them. But the agreement, although occasionally appealed to by diplomats overtaken by events, had little effect throughout the next twenty years upon either the scope or methods of expansionist activities. A summary view of those activities follows.

## The British Thrust: Egypt

Britain's ventures in Africa spanned the years from 1882 to 1902. Measured in square miles, her possessions grew to cover an area thirty-five times greater than the homeland. Most of this expansion was concentrated in that part of northern and southern Africa which lay east of the twentieth meridian. The first push was in Egypt. Its ruler had acquired expensive tastes and a habit of borrowing heavily from European financiers. When the American Civil War cut off the South from its world markets, the demand for Egyptian cotton rose sharply. But prosperity only whetted the court's appetite for luxurious living. Increase in bonded debt and the resumption of the export of Southern cotton soon brought Egypt to the brink of bankruptcy. British and French creditors, backed by their governments, demanded measures that would allow them to put the khedive's financial house in order. Another lure compelled English interest. The newly completed Suez Canal (1869) provided easier access to India and the Far East. With her large commitments there, England naturally had a special interest in the new waterway. When the harassed khedive put up a large bloc of canal stock for sale, England (actually Prime Minister Disraeli) snapped up the offer.

In 1882 it became clear that Egypt could not meet her obligations. To impress her ruler with the seriousness of the situation, British and French warships anchored off

*King Leopold II guards the gate of his private African estate.*

Alexandria. Goaded by his nationalist advisers, the khedive prepared to resist. Within three weeks after the landing of British troops (the French having declined this kind of intervention), the contest was over. The British government solemnly announced its troops would withdraw as soon as British economic advisers could unsnarl Egypt's tangled finances. Actually over half a century elapsed before Egypt regained her independence.* Whether British occupation of Egypt (and later the Sudan) sparked the grand scramble for African colonies or not is still a matter of debate among historians. But there is no disagreement over the effect the occupation had on other powers. It endangered French moves to create an east-west axis spanning the continent. It menaced Russian plans to dominate the Straits. And it posed an added problem for Germany whose chancellor favored a vague scheme to divide the Balkans between Austria-Hungary and Russia, a scheme obviously unworkable if British power, at that time hostile to Russian expansion to the southwest, operated from a base so nearby. Put most simply, the eastern Mediterranean was not considered large enough to accommodate two great powers.

Meanwhile explorer-traders were active in

---

* Technically Egypt was not independent when the British occupied it, but Turkish suzerainty was and long had been nominal rather than real.

the Kenya and Uganda regions, some fifteen hundred miles to the south. In 1887 the British East African Association persuaded the sultan of Zanzibar to give it a leasehold over 225,000 square miles of Kenya territory south of Ethiopia.* Several years later the association wrung from the king of Uganda a treaty whose terms invested the company with control over that area which lay adjacent to Kenya and which comprised about 95,000 square miles. But French, English, and Mohammedan religious groups, already settled there, quarreled so violently among themselves that the association appealed to the home government for help. Its London agent also appealed to the Church Missionary Society, the London Chamber of Commerce, and the powerful London *Times*. The respective responses—in the name of peace, Protestantism, profits, and patriotism—were sympathetic but inadequate. In the mid-1890s the Queen's government solved the problem by buying out the association and assuming full responsibility for affairs in both regions.

## From Cairo to the Cape

By this time the imperialist surge had become strong. Spurred by the vision of its dominion extending from Cairo to the Cape of Good Hope, the British government felt deep concern when it learned that France was formulating plans to connect its holdings on the west coast with its Somaliland colony in the east, that is, to conquer and occupy the vast Sudan region south of Egypt. The Sudan (nearly one third as large as the United States) was populated by Negroes (Sudan means black) and ruled by an Arab elite. Following her conquest of Egypt, England had tried to occupy the territory on the flimsy pretext that it was an Egyptian province. But after a massacre of British forces at Khartum (1885) by fierce Arab "dervishes," the attempt was put aside. Now England felt

* For these and subsequent references to African region and territories, see map, p. 407.

A BOUNDARY QUESTION.

*The Fashoda incident as a contemporary* Punch *cartoonist saw it.*

she had no choice; however great the cost, the territory must be secured. Otherwise both her axial plans were worthless and her control of the headwaters of the Nile endangered. When a public warning that a French move into the Sudan would be considered an "unfriendly act" failed to stop her rival, England sent an army under General Kitchener up the Nile. A small French expedition under a Captain Marchand reached Fashoda, a strategic post in southeastern Sudan, ahead of the British and claimed the whole area for France. When Kitchener arrived he ordered the French to leave or fight. Heavily outnumbered, Marchand wired his government for instructions. France might have taken up the challenge had her Russian ally agreed to support her. But Russia demurred, and the French were forced to withdraw (November 1899). British control was thus extended over another million square miles of African territory.

In South Africa the imperialist thrust cut

*Cecil Rhodes (right front) shown several years before his death. He was later buried in southern Rhodesia.*

an equally wide swath. England, as we have seen, had taken over Cape Colony from the Dutch in the early years of the nineteenth century. For almost seventy years the new rulers seemed to feel no urge to expand, although both the climate and the topography of the country to the north were inviting. It is true, many Dutch settlers—in their patois, Boers—had trekked north to escape British rule. Subduing native Bushmen and Hottentots, they had set up two independent republics, the Orange Free State and the Republic of South Africa (Transvaal). For forty or fifty years considerable strife marked relations between Cape Colony and the Dutch republics, but until the advent of the new imperialism a fairly steady, if uneasy, peace prevailed.

## Rhodes—Imperial Colossus

The migration in 1870 of a young Englishman to Cape Colony very much affected the shape of things to come. The young Englishman, John Cecil Rhodes, nursed twin ambitions—to amass a large fortune and to construct an empire. His arrival coincided with the discovery of the Kimberley diamond beds. Within fifteen years Rhodes had created a monopoly that assured abundant realization of his first ambition. The discovery of gold in 1886 in the Orange Free State

gave further scope to his entrepreneurial genius. His methods were contemporary with those of the American monopolists—masterfully astute calculation, ruthless elimination of competition, and unscrupulous manipulation of political controls. His interest in empire building grew out of a sincere if naïve belief that the Anglo-Saxon civilization was God's chosen instrument for the perfection of man. He longed to see a world society established in peace, democracy, and widespread affluence. Although realizing that that day was not imminent, he felt a strong commitment to advance it by the full play of whatever talents he possessed.*

The impact of Rhodes' complex genius upon expansionist activities was, to understate it, considerable. Infecting his fellow nationalists with the heady stimulus of his Cape to Cairo dream, he called for immediate extension of British control over Bechuanaland, an expansive area that lay between German possessions in the west and Portuguese holdings in the east. Delay, he insisted, would invite other powers, especially Germany, to take it over and thus thwart the grand axial scheme. In 1884 the government sent in troops and administrators to claim the whole of Bechuanaland for the crown. Expansionists in both England and Cape Colony were pleased by this success as, of course, was Rhodes. But he sensed a danger too. Smug satisfaction could paralyze the government at just the time when a new effort was called for. Immense stretches still lay to the north. Rivals thwarted in Bechuanaland could recoup there and could still prevent Britain from linking together an unbroken chain of colonies running the length of the continent. At this point the government showed, if not smug satisfaction, at least a certain weariness. So Rhodes took up the burden himself. Out of his own funds

---

* This, however, should not be done in ways that penalized profit taking. He once said that pure philanthropy was good, but philanthropy plus 5 per cent was better.

*A* Punch *cartoon of 1892 shows Cecil Rhodes striding the continent from Cape Town to Cairo.*

*The stubborn Boer resistance that so surprised the British is reflected in the grim expressions of these two Boer warriors standing beside a military train somewhere in South Africa.*

and energy he outfitted expeditions, beguiled missionaries, and sponsored propagandistic publications. Eventually he obtained from a native king an agreement that, according to Rhodes' interpretation, gave him unrestricted rights to mine and control the whole region. Under a charter granted by the London government he then formed an association that ultimately achieved effective dominion over what, fittingly enough, came to be called Rhodesia.

### British versus Dutch: The Boer War

Meanwhile British firms in the Transvaal (of which Rhodes' firm was the largest) were chafing under Boer rule. Although their spokesmen asked only fair enfranchisement laws and a chance to participate in the government, they really wanted to incorporate both republics into Cape Colony. Quarrels between Britons and Boers came to a climax in what is known as Jameson's Raid (1896). For some time Rhodes had openly agitated for the merger of Colony and Republics. In his typical fashion, he had subsidized publicists, paid secret agents, and organized special police forces. His plans miscarried when Doctor Jameson, governor-general of Rhodesia and leader of the military forces that were to oust the Transvaal government, grew impatient and staged an invasion before adequate preparations had been made. Boer troops easily routed the raiders. The fiasco was so complete and the repercussions so strong that Rhodes was forced out of public life. One of the repercussions was an acrimonious exchange between the British and German governments, which almost led to war. On two counts the Germans sided with the Boers: they were ethnic kin; and Germany, or at least the kaiser, hoped some day to see the republics made a part of German southeast Africa. Germans denounced the raid as a typical example of British greed and perfidy. The English became indignant in turn when the kaiser sent an indiscreet telegram to the president of the Transvaal, congratulating him upon frustrating the raiders so promptly and so thoroughly. For a while the public and press of both countries fumed in an orgy of mutual denunciation. Eventually diplomatic salve soothed raw feelings on both sides, but the aftermath of suspicion and fear did nothing to ease growing tensions that eventually found release in World War I.

British residents in the Transvaal continued their agitation for the ballot and for other political privileges. But their real goal still was union with the Cape. Boer leaders, of course, understood this. Behind elaborate negotiations ostensibly aimed at compromise and reconciliation both sides prepared for war. It came in 1899 with British rejection of a Boer ultimatum demanding removal of British frontier troops and the submission of differences to a board of arbitration. It lasted over two years and cost both sides heavy casualties and great material losses. In the end the Boer Republic (Transvaal was joined by the Orange Free State when the fighting began) accepted British dominion but was allowed to retain cultural autonomy. Besides more "color on the map" Britain gained important economic advantages. But the price was higher than she then realized. During the long struggle most of the powers clearly showed their sympathy for the Boers and disgust at what they felt was British rapacity and unjustifiable brutality. What had once been a self-imposed "splendid isolation" took on ominous overtones. Moreover, the war gave tremendous impetus to Anglo-German naval rivalry. During the war several German merchant ships had been captured as prizes. They were later released but not before German wrath had given Germany's big-navy advocates, led by Admiral von Tirpitz, an opportunity to launch their program of building a fleet so large that "war with the mightiest naval power would involve risks threatening

*British scouts on duty in the early part of the Boer War.*

that power's supremacy." For the next two decades the naval race, thus begun, played an important, sometimes decisive, part in weaving the web of events that enmeshed most of the major powers in war in 1914.

## Further British Expansion

On a more modest scale British expansionists were active in west Africa, particularly in the Niger region. The Niger river is one of the largest in the world. It rises in Sierra Leone, curves northeastward for a thousand miles and then drops to the sea about another thousand miles from its source. For explorers, missionaries, traders, and empire builders, it served to lay before them for conquest a vast portion of the continent. It would have been strange indeed had the imperialist thrust neglected it.

Shortly after Stanley set out to trace an empire in the Congo, an enterprising British trader with good financial connections began to talk business with African chieftains along the Niger's lower course. Using trinkets and spirits as lure, he persuaded many tribal rulers to sign treaties with terms that allowed a wide range of interpretations. Soon a half-million-dollar corporation, the United African Company began to show profits marketing cocoa kernels and oil. Its chief worry was the newly formed French Company of

Equatorial Africa, whose agents had also collected a number of "treaties" from native rulers. In the rivalry that followed, the United African Company's larger capital resources enabled it to undersell the French company so effectively that the latter was finally forced to sell out. A later German effort fared no better. In 1886 the British company received from the crown a charter authorizing it not only to trade in the region but also to administer it politically. Renamed the Royal Niger Company, it served as merchant chief and ruler until 1900, when the government took over the colony as a protectorate. From the late 1880s through the 1890s, Britain rounded out its expansion in Africa when British Somaliland, Sierra Leone, and the Gold Coast, much smaller territories, were tucked into the Empire.

It would be tediously repetitive to detail the expansionist activities of the other powers. The same pattern characterized them— explorers were followed by missionaries and traders, native rulers were corrupted or coerced, treaties were signed, troops stationed, and whites assumed political control of the area. It will be enough for us simply to note who took what.

Within the period from 1870 to 1914 France acquired French West Africa, French Equatorial Africa, Senegal, French Somaliland, and Madagascar; Germany took German East Africa, German Southwest Africa, Kamerun, and Togoland; Portugal held Mozambique and Angola; and Italy was in Eritrea, Italian Somaliland, and Libya. By the eve of World War I the entire continent, except for Liberia and Ethiopia,* had been partitioned among a half-dozen or so European powers.

---

* In 1896 Italy invaded Ethiopia and suffered, in the battle of Aduwa, a crushing defeat. This surprising event, the first victory of a "backward" people over the colonial powers, probably saved Ethiopia from attacks from other powers during the "partition period." But it also served, as we shall later see, to invite a new and successful invasion in the next century.

## The Imperialist Thrust: Asia

Most of these powers, and several others which had not participated in the great safari, found in Asia a further field for adventure and expansion. By the outbreak of war in 1914 Japan was the only Asian country retaining full national sovereignty.* In the main, the same methods were used in Asia as in Africa. But there were some differences. Unlike most African states or tribes, Asian societies, such as the Chinese and Indian, were highly civilized. Their culture had been developed over centuries. Also, some had for centuries enjoyed a favorable balance of trade with the outside world. But more often than not their ancient roots eventually bound them to unyielding and stultifying traditions; and their export balance stopped abruptly with the advent of the machine in the West.

## The Conquest of India

Long before the advent of the "new imperialism," English and French interest in the riches of India had led to strong rivalry and a series of clashes, which ultimately forced the French to withdraw (1761). Thereafter for about a hundred years most of India was ruled by the East India Company, a private trading corporation. During this period many Indian states were brought directly under the company's rule; others were left to native princes who kept their thrones by agreeing to take orders from it. The commercial nexus that bound together Britain and India was highly profitable for the British. The factories of Manchester, Birmingham, and other industrial areas hungrily absorbed the flow of raw cotton, wool, flax, leather, and other unprocessed resources that were channeled to the home country. Hundreds of thousands of Indian

---

* Nominally, China and Siam were free from foreign control; and Afghanistan enjoyed a high degree of autonomy. But in each case whatever freedom the state enjoyed rested in one way or another upon the sufferance of Western imperial powers.

"O GOD OF BATTLES! STEEL MY SOLDIERS' HEARTS!"
*Henry V., Act IV.*

*A pious British view of their 1857 clash with the natives of India.*

*British justice: a photograph showing the execution of Indian "mutineers" in the Sepoy Rebellion of 1857.*

artisans and craftsmen were forced out of their jobs by the substitution of foreign machines for native spinning wheels and pit looms. Ultimately, they seem to have merged with the teeming millions of agricultural workers.* With only meager returns from their labor, they were still able to buy England's cheaply priced processed goods, especially cloth and iron manufactured articles. The British also systematically exploited other valuable resources of the great subcontinent—timber, tea, silk, tobacco, precious metals, and gems. For the white man, the burden did not seem intolerable.

## The Sepoy Rebellion and Aftermath

By about the middle of the nineteenth century India's masses had become rebelliously restive. Village communal lands had been divided up among select landholders who were then held responsible for the collection of taxes. The feudal practice of escheat—"lapse," as it was popularly

---

* Some authorities disagree or are unclear on this point. For example, Jawaharlal Nehru tended to the view that many of the displaced craftsmen simply starved to death. In 1770, to cite one instance, over one third the population of Bengal and Bihar was swept away by famine. Others, such as T. Walter Wallbank, simply say there was mass displacement but do not explain what happened to the displaced.

dubbed—was revived to allow the East India Company to claim provinces whose rulers had died without natural heir. The governor-general also took upon himself to decide (or to decide upon the advice of the governing council) which princes were properly administrating their principalities; and if they were not, what changes should be made. For millions of Indians the limit of tolerance was reached when Indian troops were issued new rifles that used cartridges with greased ends that had to be bitten off before they could be fired. The sepoys (as the native soldiers were called) believed the grease came from cows and pigs. Since Hindus held the cow sacred and Moslems considered the pig ceremonially unclean, religious sensibilities were touched off. Insurrections broke out in several provinces and quickly spread over much of north and north-central India (1857). Although called a mutiny by British officials, the widespread uprising was actually a rebellion. Its repression taxed the resources of the British, and before it was crushed they had resorted to atrocities that are hard to match in the record of man's inhumanity to man.

After the Sepoy mutiny, colonial administrative machinery was overhauled. The East India Company surrendered all governing powers to the crown. The "lapse" policy was abandoned, as was the practice of annexing provinces. Local princes were treated so deferentially that they soon became an integral part of the overall ruling elite. Many roads and railroads were built. But the condition of the masses and middle classes remained oppressive. Income from the land remained barely sufficient for subsistence; famines were frequent; wages were low beyond the imagination of Western laborers. Education was deliberately kept from the millions, and for the middle and upper classes it was slanted toward acceptance of Western values and the idea of Western superiority. In short, British rule remained essentially autocratic and exploitative.

Indian intellectuals, business classes, and the more literate portions of the masses continued to agitate for reform, some even for independence. In 1885 the Indian National Congress was reformed to serve as the voice of all dissident Indians, whether Hindus or Moslems. Its original demands were modest enough: participation in making policy at the local level, the right to discuss, if not to decide, legislative measures that would affect all of India; the appointment of some Indians to the highest ranks of the civil service administration. Wherever the British could do it without weakening real control, they granted Congress' requests: the right to elect some members of the Legislative Council (a merely advisory body); discussion in the Council of budgetary items; and the appointment of carefully selected Indians to office in the intermediate echelons of the civil service. Later the Congress increased its demands, at times hinting at complete independence. By the latter part of the nineteenth century virtually all classes, even the most lowly, fully understood the implications of the strict color line Britain had drawn. Increasingly their leaders made racial equality the touchstone of reform agitation. Unfortunately for the Indians their struggle for home rule was made extraordinarily difficult by the existence of a large Moslem minority. As Moslem leaders came to envision an India eventually freed from white control, they saw Hindu domination of the whole land, a spectre little if any more inviting to them. Indeed many Moslems began to collaborate with the British to slow down the Indian nationalist drive. In 1906 their leaders formed the Muslim League as a counterweight to the Congress. Whether English imperialists fostered this fatal split is both debatable and irrelevant, but it is certain that they exploited it. After World War I, in which Indian troops made an impressive record, Britain held out vague promises of self-government, promises that, as we will see later, led to full independence in the 1940s. But India entered the twentieth century still politically dependent, socially segregated, economically exploited, and rent by religious strife. Certainly the imperialist thrust had not created all these unhappy conditions, but there is no doubt it consistently and seriously aggravated them.

## Further British Ventures

Burma, an ancient state lying east of India, attempted an imperialist venture of its own in 1824 when it invaded territory claimed by British India. Two years of fighting ended in a British victory and a remarkably lenient peace treaty. However, from the early 1850s on, new appetites and a new temper spurred the English to add Burma to their Asian empire. By 1885 the whole land (as large as France) was under the control of "white" India. To the south of Burma, in the bulge of the great peninsula into which Siam narrows, a mélange of petty sultanates invited the attention of the British East India Company. The great archipelago stretching from Sumatra to New Guinea had already been conceded to its rival, the Dutch East India Company. But such strategic ports as Singapore, Malacca, and Penang (see map, p. 379) were potentially too valuable to pass over. Early in the nineteenth century they had become the Straits Settlements. Thereafter British merchants and marines worked their way north and east until, by the turn of the twentieth century, the whole bulge was under British control. Local sultans were allowed to keep

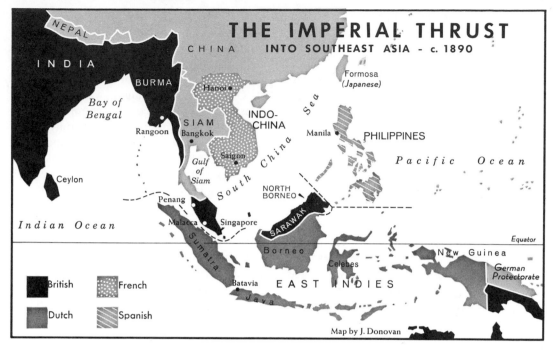

**THE IMPERIAL THRUST**
**INTO SOUTHEAST ASIA - c. 1890**

Map by J. Donovan

their thrones and bureaucratic paraphernalia, but they were closely supervised by the British High Commissioner of the Federated Malay States. Ceylon, just off the tip of India, was occupied by the British in 1833. Until the invention of the automobile its chief resources were tea, coconuts, and pearls; since about 1900 the cultivation of rubber trees has made this island one of the world's foremost producers of latex. Two other states in the Middle East, Afghanistan and Persia, became involved in Anglo-Russian imperialist maneuvers in the early twentieth century. (Consideration of this development will be reserved for a later section.)*

## Dutch Imperialism

Another great empire in southeast Asia was managed by the Netherlands. Like other corporations of its kind, the Dutch East India Company was interested in making profits from whatever lands and peoples

---

* British expansion in China will be taken up
  shortly when we turn to the proposed partition
  of that nation.

lay open for exploitation. The lands and peoples it conquered, lost, and reconquered (in the early 1600s through early 1800s) probably constituted the most profitable colonial empire any European state has created in modern times. Geographically the colonies—Sumatra, Java, Borneo, Celebes, New Guinea, the Moluccas—encompass an area greater than all of Western Europe; and their combined population exceeds that of any Western European power except Germany.

Originally they were coveted for their spices, later for their sugar, rubber, tin, tobacco, coffee, tea, and petroleum. From about 1830 to 1870 their Dutch masters used what was called the "culture system." Natives were forced to set aside and to work, for the exclusive profit of their white rulers, 20 per cent of all land cultivated. The methods to keep native laborers producing were barbarous. Village chiefs, for example, were liable to hanging if quotas set for building roads were not met; and a number of chiefs were hanged. The system was abandoned when journalists published exposés that Dutchmen on the home front found hard to reconcile with even the loosest interpretation of the white man's burden. The new "free labor" system was somewhat, but not much, better. A poll tax was laid on all workers. To save enough from meager earnings to pay it demanded a fatiguing tempo of work. In addition, Dutch planters often tempted natives with long-term loans, which, since they were practically unpayable, bound them in virtual serfdom. Educational facilities were gradually extended throughout the islands. But the offering was especially designed to keep the natives content with their lot. When unrest developed nonetheless, repressive measures were used that made the line between savage and civilized hard to discern. In the 1940s much of this fabulously rich empire was wrested from the Dutch by Japan. Her defeat by the Allies in 1946 returned the archipelago to the Netherlands but only briefly. For by then a new mood was abroad among the so-called backward peoples of the world, a mood that led to the blunting and breaking of the imperialist thrust.

## China's "Time of Troubles"

As the oldest, largest, and at that time the most civilized nation in Asia, China might have been expected to withstand Western expansion. In one sense she did. At no time throughout the period of rampaging imperialism was she wholly subdued or partitioned. But in another sense she fared little better than India or the East Indies. For a century after 1840, a number of foreign states pared down her size and sovereignty so steadily that it seemed, just before World War I, that she must certainly suffer the fate of Africa.

For many centuries China had been a world unto herself as a font of East Asian civilization and later as the "Middle Kingdom," around which other peoples moved and had their cultural origins. Since ancient times she had maintained contacts with the West, but under Manchu rule (established

in the mid-1600s) they diminished in number and kind. By about 1800 the Middle Kingdom had become a hermit nation, living in a past almost wholly, and deliberately, cut off from the forces of life flowing around it. Only one port, Canton, was open to the West; only one activity, commercial exchange, was allowed and that only under severe restrictions.* Not for centuries, if ever, had China's cultural and political life been so static, so moribund, nor her view of the outside world so illusory and distorted.

Since the West was simultaneously experiencing its heady thrust of power, a new and fateful meeting of East and West was hardly surprising. Its first manifestation was the so-called Opium War, 1839 to 1842. For a long time opium, much of it imported from India, had been supplied to an increasing number of Chinese by British and other foreign traders operating out of Canton. In 1839 the Peking government published a decree prohibiting its sale and use. British merchants ignored the decree. When Chinese officials disciplined them they called upon their government for succor. In the war that followed China experienced its first encounter with a military machine served by industrial technology. It was a humiliating experience. In the treaty that ended the uneven struggle, China was forced to legalize the opium traffic, open five ports to foreign trade, pay an indemnity, cede Hong Kong to Britain, reduce tariff duties on British goods to 5 per cent *ad valorem,* and to allow British citizens in the port cities to live under their own rather than Chinese law. Other nations soon forced China to extend the same trade, tariff, and extraterritoriality† provisions to them. A second war in 1857, in which France joined England to enforce ob-

---

* For location of cities and areas cited in this discussion, see map, p. 381.
† This cumbersome term denominates the practice of allowing foreigners to live under the law and in accordance with the customs of their own country.

*This lithograph shows Chinese delegates trying to reach an understanding with British representatives about the opium question. They failed, both at the conference table and, when the British forced the issue, in their first military clash with a Western nation employing modern methods of warfare.*

*This engraving of the British attack in Shapoo during the Opium War shows the suburbs of the city on fire and the disparity of strength between the two navies.*

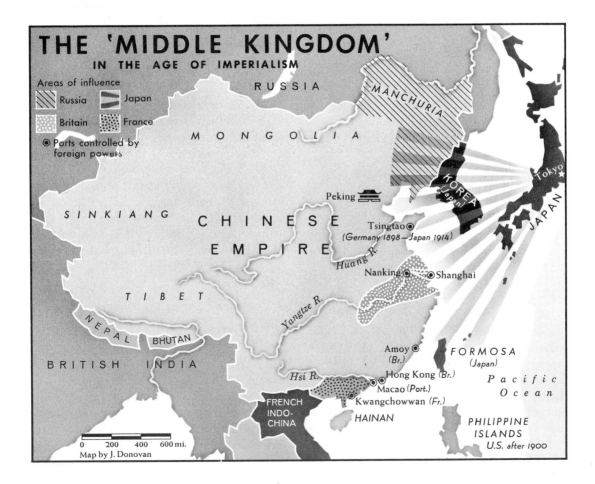

THE 'MIDDLE KINGDOM'
IN THE AGE OF IMPERIALISM

Areas of influence
Russia     Japan
Britain     France
◉ Ports controlled by foreign powers

RUSSIA

MANCHURIA

MONGOLIA

KOREA (Japan)

Tokyo ★

SINKIANG

CHINESE EMPIRE

Peking

Tsingtao ◉
(Germany 1898 – Japan 1914)

Huang R.

Nanking ◉    ◉ Shanghai

JAPAN

TIBET

Yangtze R.

NEPAL
BHUTAN

Amoy ◉
(Br.)

FORMOSA
(Japan)

BRITISH   INDIA

Hsi R.

Hong Kong (Br.)
Macao (Port.)
Kwangchowwan (Fr.)

Pacific
Ocean

FRENCH
INDO-
CHINA

HAINAN

PHILIPPINE
ISLANDS
U.S. after 1900

0   200   400   600 mi.
Map by J. Donovan

*In this satiric slap at European imperialism,* Punch *has the British lion saying, "It's all right, Johnny Chinaman, we've come to a friendly agreement," as the Russian bear responds pleasantly, "We're going to divide you."*

servance of concessionary rights, ended in another victory for the Western powers; and more concessions. Added treaty ports were opened, trading privileges in the Yangtze Valley were granted, and protection for missionaries was promised. At about the same time, by skillful employment of the tricks of diplomacy, Russia was given leave to annex a huge area in Siberia (north of the Amur River).

## Inner Decay: Invitation to Partition

China's troubles with the outside world were compounded by internal troubles. This great kingdom had once exercised authority of one kind or another over an empire twice as large as itself—Mongolia, Sinkiang (Chinese Turkestan), Tibet, Tongking, Korea, Taiwan (Formosa), and—with the coming of the Manchus, of course—Manchuria. By the mid-nineteenth century Outer Mongolia had become more or less autonomous, Sinkiang ruled by warlords, Tibet virtually independent, and Tongking had been absorbed by Annam. Korea and Taiwan were still dependencies of China, but both would be lost to Japan (herself a former Chinese tributary) around the turn of the new century. Moreover, most Chinese, espe-

cially those south of the Yangtze River, had never really reconciled themselves to Manchu rule. In the 1850s a series of uprisings occurred. The most serious and sustained was the T'ai Ping Rebellion, which at one point seemed to promise release from Manchu domination. But the government's importation of outside military leadership and the tendency of patriot generals to turn into self-seeking warlords caused the rebellion to fail, although the deep unrest that had motivated it persisted. In the end, inner decay and dissension paved the way for the new imperialist scramble to partition China.

Soon the principle of extraterritoriality came to be applied in ways which unfairly penalized the economic development of Chinese resources by the Chinese themselves, and also relegated many Chinese to second-class citizenship. Foreign control of tariff duties encouraged Western traders and industrialists, invariably backed by their governments, to block out spheres of influence where they could manage commerce and industry for their own aggrandizement. To tap China's mineral resources, mining concessions were demanded, and these demands too were backed up by force or the show of force. To connect market with market and markets with ports, the right to build and manage railroads was also insisted upon. By the mid-1890s the frantic struggle for East Asia was on, and within a decade large areas of China were parceled out among competing Western nations.

## The Scramble for China

After absorbing Tonkin and Annam into Cochin China-Cambodia, France occupied Laos (1893). As a base to protect and serve French Indochina, France "leased" the mainland port of Kwangchowan (1898). Fearful that France intended to push northward, Britain persuaded China to allow only British power to establish itself in the Yangtze Valley. Fearful too of Russian designs in the north, the British government negotiated a ninety-nine-year lease of Wei-haiwei, in the Shantung peninsula. Although a late comer in the contest, Germany was determined to get her share. The best she could manage was a leasehold on Kiachow, a port strategically located in Shantung some 200 miles down the coast from the British base. Meanwhile Russia was busy consolidating her Siberian gains and devising ways to move into Manchuria. With money borrowed from France (after 1887), she planned to construct a railroad to span Siberia, with a branch line running through Manchuria. Such designs naturally made Japan apprehensive, since she coveted the same prize.

Much of this pattern of imperial aggrandizement was determined by the outcome of the Sino-Japanese War, 1894 to 1895. Although nominally independent, Korea had been a Chinese dependency for many years. Japan desired Korea as a valuable possession in itself but also to use as a springboard for penetration into southern Manchuria and as a strategic defense base. Russia's schemes and China's weakness spurred her to action. A Korean insurrection in 1894 set the stage. Acting under an earlier agreement, both China and Japan sent in troops to restore order. When the insurrection petered out, Japan demanded the removal of Chinese troops and the creation of an independent Korea. Sino-Japanese bickering over the terms of a settlement led to war in 1894. Again China suffered humiliating defeat. In the treaty of Shimonoseki (1895) Korea was recognized as an independent nation. China was forced to pay a large indemnity and to cede Taiwan, the Pescadores, and part of the Liaotung Peninsula to Japan. China also agreed to conclude a new and generous commercial treaty with Japan. Some of the edge was taken from the Japanese victory, however, when Russia, France, and Germany, fearing Japan's appetite would grow embarrassingly large after so much eating, concerted to force her to return the Liaotung cession to China.

In this 1894 Judge cartoon, Japan is shown smashing the Chinese "wall" against the advance of Western civilization.

China's defeat, the third in as many wars during the century, pitilessly laid bare her helplessness. From then on the expansionist powers pondered not whether China might be partitioned but when and how. Moreover, since by that time the imperialist thrust was cutting deeply around the world, the powers felt a sense of urgency. They also had gained some notion of who wanted what. As we have already noted, Germany made haste to secure a foothold on the Shantung Peninsula before Japan, Russia, Britain, or some combination of them should preempt the whole of it. Britain's move into Weihaiwei was similarly motivated. Both Russia and Japan believed no time should be lost staking out their claims in Manchuria and Korea. Their rivalry led to war in 1904 and to the temporary withdrawal of Russian expansionism in the Far East when, for the first time in the modern era, an Asian state defeated a European power (1905). The treaty settlement opened the way for subsequent Japanese expansion in both Korea and southern Manchuria. Japan's surprising victory was due in part to many grave sociopolitical troubles with which Russia was struggling at the time (see p. 502), and the corruption and inefficiency that had long plagued her military establishment. But it was also partly due to the extraordinary, rapid, and multiform metamorphosis Japan had undergone after 1868.

*After the "opening" of Japan, the Japanese set about arming and drilling themselves in Western fashion.*

## The New Japan

Like China, Japan had for centuries nurtured a conservative, almost static, inner and institutional life. Bound by feudal patterns and practices and walled off from the white world to the West, she had not experienced the revolutionary impact of the Enlightenment, the advent of science, industrialism, and political liberalism, which had so profoundly remade that world. Theoretically her divine emperor ruled a united kingdom. Actually he was a figurehead. For centuries the kingdom was almost as much divided by provincial loyalties and institutions as it was bound together by common national sentiments and imperial bureaucratic machinery. At the national level the real ruler was the shogun, a hereditary official somewhat comparable to the early French Merovingian mayor of the Palace. At the provincial level considerable political power was held by the heads of great families.

From the 1600s on, the development of commerce—trade with China, Korea and a few Western outlets—and the flourishing of craft industry created a small but productive middle class that set the stage for the subsequent development of remarkable advances in economic modernization and the establishment of trade connections with Western nations. But Japan's remarkable metamorphosis, signalized by the overthrow of the shogunate and the restoration of imperial power, probably was caused more by political influence than economic developments. Two events were especially portentous. One was the power struggle between two strong feudal forces—on the one hand, barons who supported the shogunate and, on the other, the Satsuma and Chosu barons who sought to capture the shogunate for themselves. The other was the coincidental thrust of the West into the East. In 1853 Commodore Perry anchored an American naval force in Tokyo Bay. The Commodore's purpose was both plain and painful to the Japanese, that is, the opening of the island kingdom to Western trade and Western influence. What the white man had done to China and to other Asian states he now proposed to do to Japan. Pressure was at once put upon the shogun to resist. But the Japanese government was little better prepared to resist the foreigner than were the other Asian governments. Its bowing to the inevitable and the treaties and consuls that followed gave popular support to antishogun forces. Their success in 1868 ushered in the Meiji restoration.* Several years later (in 1877) an attempted reinstatement of the old regime failed. Thereafter imperial forces ruled supreme.†

## The New China

Thus by 1900 great powers, old and new, had in one way or another moved into spheres of control in China: Britain, Russia, Japan, and Germany in the north; France in the south; and Britain in the Yangtze Valley. Few doubted that China could prevent or long postpone its complete partition. Unlike Japan, China seemed unwilling or unable to free herself from stultifying tradition to learn the ways of the West. Perhaps her

* That is, restoring political control to the imperial house.
† Many authorities hold that certain complicated economic developments accounted for the great change in 1868. For a strong presentation of this view see Edwin O. Reischauer, *Japan, Past and Present,* Alfred A. Knopf, 1964, p. 98.

*Some of the Boxers captured during the rebellion of 1900.*

*Aftermath of the Boxer Rebellion: the Chinese are forced to build a memorial arch in Peking in commemoration of the murder of the German minister to China (1900) by the Boxers. At the dedication ceremony in 1903, the Chinese representatives passed through the arch in the presence of German soldiers.*

sprawling vastness induced inertia. Certainly the heavy hand of decadent Manchu rule weakened and wearied her.*

Nonetheless there were restive stirrings in China that gave some hope of a brighter day. Two movements, unrelated to each other, roused enthusiasm. One sought quite simply to solve China's problems by ousting foreigners and all things foreign including, indeed especially, Christianity. It was organized in the northern provinces in the late 1890s. Formally the movement was designated the Society of Harmonious Fists. By Westerners its members were simply called Boxers. In the late spring of 1900 they staged uprisings in Hopei and nearby provinces. For a brief time they were successful. They "captured" Peking and a number of other cities in the north. Many foreigners were killed or captured; many fled before the fury of the Boxers. In Peking foreign officials, missionaries, and their families took refuge in the

*A 1900 cartoon showing Uncle Sam squaring off against a Manchu mandarin. The caption shows the American saying, "I occasionally do a little boxing myself."*

---

\* It probably should be said again that in a general introductory study many details important in specialized works must be passed over. Here, for example, a specialized study of the period would give details of the elaborate reform effort of 1898, which had the sponsorship of no less an authority than the emperor.

foreign legation and appealed to their home countries for help. It was promptly sent. Large and well-equipped contingents of foreign troops—German, Russian, Japanese, British, French, and American—landed in the region of the Taku Forts and soon invested the capital. Within a short time they had established themselves in Peking and had pacified the northern provinces. The position of the dowager empress, who ruled as regent, was ambiguous throughout. It seems fairly clear that at one point she sympathized with and ordered aid to be given to the rebels. When it became clear that the movement would collapse under foreign assault she officially condemned it. In the settlement that followed she was allowed to keep her throne but her government and the country suffered heavy penalties. Among them was an indemnity of $333 million apportioned among the powers; importation of arms and ammunition was prohibited for as long as the powers thought necessary; official decrees were published forbidding the expression of antiforeign sentiments; foreign powers were given the right to occupy certain cities lying between Peking and the sea. Moreover, the great and rich province of Manchuria was brought closer to alienation. The Boxer fiasco had again advertised China's disintegration and the government's inability to control provincial officials. Japan and Russia watched imperial authority fade. They looked at the chaos in Peking and the booty in Manchuria; and they made plans. The Boxer promise of a brighter tomorrow had not only failed, it led to yet darker days.

## The 1912 Revolution

The other movement was broader in scope, more far reaching in consequence. For many years the Manchu regime had given increasingly clear evidence of its inability to cope with the forces of disintegration within and without. Concerned intellectuals and reformers—many of them influenced by study abroad and sensitive to the urgent necessity for drastic social, political, and economic changes based on the Western model—agitated for overthrow of the monarchy and the establishment of a dynamic, democratic, forward-looking regime. In the winter months of 1911 and 1912 revolution-

*Dr. Sun Yat-sen, builder of the "New China," poses with his wife, a member of the famous Soong family.*

ary armies overthrew the Manchus and set up a republic. The most influential leader of the revolt was Dr. Sun Yat-sen, a Cantonese liberal who had been educated in American schools. Dr. Sun's program for rebuilding China was threefold: a government based upon the sovereign will of the people; the unification of all sections and areas into one political body; and an equitable redistribution of the national wealth. Dr. Sun argued that domestic regimes were outmoded, that modern peoples rightly demanded that sovereignty should rest in their own hands. He did not, however, believe in rule *by* the people. Rather he held that the actual construction and administration of law should be undertaken by trained leaders of talent and vision, in short, by an elite. Sectional differences, he insisted, though understandable, and to a point even healthy, should not be allowed to subordinate the whole to its parts. And mass poverty, almost by definition, was incompatible with national strength and humane development. Sun's "three principles" caught the imagination of millions and buoyed their hopes. Thus charted, the new China meant to shake off foreign shackles, create a new identity, and construct a national economy that served all citizens fairly. The implementation of the program was entrusted to the Koumintang, Sun's revolutionary party.

## The Failure of the Revolution

But the demands of China's *risorgimento* were greater than China's capabilities to cope with them. For one thing, hundreds of millions of illiterate peasants could not overnight become sensitive, responsible citizens and voters. The government set up schools and launched a variety of educational campaigns. But chronic ignorance is a tenacious disease. Moreover, sectional strife had become so rooted that when the imperial facade was destroyed, local leaders, the famous warlords, sprang up almost automatically. Civil war became endemic. Also, European and Japanese holdings (of whatever kind) had by then become secure, and they were so protected by a military might which went beyond anything that China could oppose, that real popular sovereignty and national unity were out of the question. Finally, World War I, coming so soon after the revolution, heightened the atmosphere of violence, diverted the attention and energy of Chinese leaders, and sharpened imperialist tensions in China. Dr. Sun's death in 1925 passed leadership of the revolution to Chiang Kai-shek, one of his most trusted disciples. But the trinity of ignorance, sectional strife, and imperialist greed remained to plague the movement. Thirty years after the Sino-Japanese war, which so much influenced the shape of imperialist things to come, China, like most of Asia, was still in bondage. A new day was to come, but it had not yet come.

*Chiang Kai-shek, leader of the Chinese revolution after the death of Dr. Sun.*

## The Imperialist Thrust: The Americas

During this period most of the nations of the western hemisphere also felt constraints imposed from without. Quite in line with the logic of geography, the main thrust came from the United States. Except for a few Caribbean dependencies, by the late 1820s all Latin peoples had set themselves up as independent states.* To shield them from European interference, the United States issued (in 1823) a pronouncement declaring the whole hemisphere henceforth beyond "future colonization by any European powers." Significantly, the declaration did not include a disavowal of future interference by the United States. No European government

* Their number and specific identity remained in flux for a long time. Periodically this or that independent unit became the province of another state or vice versa. Boundary disputes were (and are) seemingly endless.

welcomed the announcement, of course; and Britain explicitly repudiated both its legality and propriety (although in practice her navy gave the "doctrine" probably its chief sanction).*

## The French Fiasco in Mexico

Until the 1860s the new states were left relatively free from imperial harassments. The United States, it is true, carved off a substantial portion of Mexico (1848). But most United States officials and citizens seemed to view this not so much taking land from another people as finally claiming territory that had always been theirs by right of "manifest destiny."

The first new instance of large-scale exploitive imperialism occurred in 1863. Napoleon III, emperor of France, decided the time had come to interpose a Latin block to Anglo-Saxon expansion in the New World (and, some argue, to divert his people's attention from sagging morale at home). Involved in its own profound and protracted domestic strife, the United States could only reply to this violation of the Monroe Doctrine with paper protests. Believing the Union cause was lost, Napoleon landed an army in Mexico and installed a puppet regime. We cannot know what the course of Latin American history might have been had Grant rather than Lee surrendered at Appomattox. Perhaps Napoleon's gamble would have led to the conquest of Latin America by the then dominant powers. Perhaps Mexican revolutionary forces eventually would have expelled the invaders from the land. Actually, Union victory in 1865 released federal troops for whatever action might be needed in Mexico. Unprepared to resist this kind of protest, Napoleon ordered his army home, and the puppet regime collapsed. Since then no European state has attempted to repeat the experiment.

* That is, British insistence on keeping the trade lanes to the South American markets open, in effect, kept Spain from pushing her plans to reconquer her one-time colonies.

*President Theodore Roosevelt's "Big Stick" policy was often cited as a manifestation of America's imperialist designs. Here, a cartoonist of the New York* Herald *(1905) shows "Teddy" policing the Caribbean area.*

## Extension of U. S. Influence in Latin America

But Latin America was not thereby made secure from foreign interference. The emergence of big business (and the passing of the frontier) prompted American entrepreneurs, by then in control of the national government, to give serious thought to the markets and resources of our southern neighbors. By the opening of the new century, hundreds of millions of American dollars were invested in various enterprises in the so-called "banana republics" of the Caribbean area. Some European nations had made large loans to a number of Latin America governments. When these governments defaulted, as they did with disturbing regularity, foreign creditors turned to their own governments for help. Normally, as we have seen, foreign intervention almost invariably followed, but the United States felt bound by the Monroe Doctrine to intervene. It also felt, despite twinges of conscience, that it had the right to interpose its own control when Latin America's chronic political instability flared into unmanageable chaos. Thus in the latter decades of the nineteenth century and the early years of the twentieth, the United States came to exercise an imperial control

JONATHAN'S LATEST.

SHADE OF COLUMBUS (*aside*), "HAD I FORESEEN IT WOULD HAVE COME TO THIS—CARAMBA!—I WOULD NEVER HAVE DISCOVERED AMERICA!"

*This* Punch *cartoon of 1896 shows the United States as an aggressive, militant bully during the period of the Cuban insurrection against Spain.*

*This German cartoon satirizes the claims of the United States and Spain in 1898 to "protect" Cuba. The caption shows the Cubans protesting, "No matter who wins, we lose." The cartoon is prescient of the Cuban dilemma in the 1960s.*

in this hemisphere very similar to the kind it condemned in Europe and Asia. In 1895, for example, the United States Secretary of State publicly announced that "the United States is practically sovereign on this continent, and its fiat is law upon the subjects to which it confines its interposition."

A far reaching act of "interposition" occurred in 1898 when the United States fought a war with Spain over Cuba. For years Cubans had tried to rid themselves of Spanish domination. Widespread uprisings in 1895 and for several years following attracted American attention. Spanish attempts to subdue the revolutionists were so savage that many Americans demanded United States intervention. Some American statesmen, such as the young Theodore Roosevelt and Henry Cabot Lodge, not only sympathized with the mistreated Cubans but saw in the overall situation a chance for America

to expand in the Caribbean area. Other Americans, including many businessmen, although deploring Spanish ruthlessness, did not want to see the United States embark on what they thought of as martial adventures. But by 1898 the prevailing sentiment—shaped by sensational press releases, effective agitation by Roosevelt and his colleagues, the sinking of the battleship *Maine* in Havana harbor, and Spanish blunders—favored war with Spain. The conflict was brief and one-sided. By the Treaty of Paris in 1899, Spain relinquished not only its Caribbean possessions but the Philippine Islands and Guam as well. After a spirited debate, which figured prominently in the election campaign of 1900, the United States somewhat gingerly embarked on its first imperial enterprise. Cuba was granted nominal independence; in actual practice it became a quasi-protectorate. Puerto Rico, Guam,

*The "Maine" as she appeared the day after the explosion.*

and the Philippines became colonial possessions. Hawaii, long desired by American sugar planters on the islands, was annexed in 1900 after the native ruler was overthrown and an interim "planter" republic set up in 1894.

Thereafter, although not consistently or steadily, the United States extended its control over various peoples and areas to the south. At times its motives were innocent enough, even altruistic. For example, in 1902 the United States saved Venezuela from at least temporary occupation by European powers. At that time Germany, Great Britain, and Italy were on the verge of landing troops to compel Venezuela's dictator to pay his government's overdue debts. At the insistence of the United States the matter was referred to an arbitration committee for settlement. But for the most part rather selfish, strategic, economic, and political interests dictated our actions in Latin America. In 1903 the United States asked Colombia to lease to it the isthmus of Panama for the construction of an interocean canal. When Colombia proved difficult to bargain with, Philippe Bunau-Varilla, a "Panamanian" personally interested in the construction of the canal, led a revolt against the Colombian

government. To insure success for the revolution, President Theodore Roosevelt dispatched marines with orders to "interpose" themselves between the Colombian and rebel troops. Almost immediately Panama was given official recognition as an independent nation. Several weeks later it signed a treaty with the United States granting this country the right to build the projected canal.

The next year Santo Domingo was threatened by several European nations seeking to force payment of debts hopelessly in arrears. To forestall its occupation, Roosevelt announced that the United States (alone) would assume the responsibility of supervising the finances of any Latin American country which because of "chronic wrongdoing, or an impotence which results in a general loosening of the ties of civilized society, may . . . ultimately require intervention by some civilized nation."* As it turned out, such intervention led to dominant control over Haiti, Panama, El Salvador, Nicaragua, Honduras, and to a lesser extent Costa Rica. In the last, as well as in several other Latin American states, the United Fruit Company gained a virtual monopoly over their banana plantations. Other American business concerns acquired special rights, and of course special profits, in such diverse fields as sugar, oil, and banking. In Mexico a cooperative dictator, Porfirio Diaz, doled out railroad, land, oil, and mine concessions to a number of foreign nations, including a billion dollars worth to Yankee capitalists.

### The Meaning of Imperialism: A Summation

In summing up the meanings of these various imperial and colonial activities, we naturally note first the variegated abuse of the Afro-Asian and, to a lesser extent, South American peoples by the white-supremacist West. Economically, the nonindustrialized

---

* This is the essence of what has come to be called the Roosevelt Corollary to the Monroe Doctrine.

peoples were subjected to manipulations that kept standards of living low and local economies "subsidiaries to their Western masters. Malaya became a rubber plantation, Rhodesia a copper mine, Ceylon a huge tea plantation, Arabia an oil field."[2] Psychologically, the imperialist thrust cleaved the world into snobbish tutors and sullen pupils. Even when it brought intrinsic good, that good often led to unexpected woe. A significant example is the introduction of Western medical knowledge and skills. Afro-Asians gladly accepted the balm of the healing arts, but by decreasing infant mortality and increasing adult life span, the population soon soared beyond production capacities. As a result, increasing millions suffered the miseries of subsistent, really sub-subsistent, living. Politically, the expansion of European power stimulated rivalries among the European imperialist powers that edged them nearer to crisis and conflict.

On the other hand, benign or potentially benign influences flowed out of the new imperialism. Without it, industrialism would have come even later to Asia and Africa. It also brought with it (although not by conscious design) many of the ideas of the Enlightenment and of the French and American revolutions. Particularly consequential were the concepts of nationalism and democracy and, however amorphously, a sense of movement and progress. Another contribution was the scientific method and attitude toward life. That these influences eventually led, as we shall see in a later chapter, to a sanguine confrontation of sahib and servant does not diminish their significance.

## SELECTED READINGS

Hayes, Carlton J. H., *A Generation of Materialism, 1871–1900,* Harper & Brothers, New York, 1941.

One of the best accounts of the transformation of Western man's outlook and values that were shaped by the impact of the "second" industrial revolution. Emphasis is given to the secularization of society, the rise of the masses, and the genesis of totalitarian nationalism.

Hayes, Carlton J. H., *Essays on Nationalism,* The Macmillan Co., New York, 1926.

A series of essays that deal with nationalism as a religion, its relationship to war, militarism, and intolerence, its basic nature and development. The author is one of the foremost authorities on this hard-to-handle subject. He deserves careful study.

Hayes, Carlton J. H., *Nationalism: a Religion,* The Macmillan Co., New York, 1960.

A strictly historical approach to the study of what nationalism is and how it got to be what it is. The author takes a pessimistic view of the growing power of nationalist sentiment. He believes that it may be "moderated or watered down" only by the imperatives of the Christian faith.

Hobson, J. A., *Imperialism, a Study,* George Allen & Unwin, London, 1905.

Hobson considered imperialism a disease that society had to cure if it was to survive as a culture worthy of the name civilization. In spite of severe attacks, especially in the last 25 years, it remains one of the most illuminating studies the subject has yet received.

Kohn, Hans, *Prophets and Peoples,* The Macmillan Co., New York, 1946.

A study of five brands of nineteenth-century nationalism as it appeared to J. S. Mill, Michelet, Maini, Treitschke, and Dostoevsky in their times.

Kohn, Hans, *The Age of Nationalism,* Harper & Brothers, New York, 1962.

In this work the author argues that in the third decade of our century a metamorphosis developed which is transforming the old state-rooted nationalism into a "garment for the globe." Ethnic bonds, he believes, have not and will not disappear, but over them is being superimposed a pan-nationalism that will make the relation of modern nations to a universal community similar to the old relation of family or clan to state-limited nationalism.

---

2. Robert L. Heilbroner, *The Great Ascent,* Harper and Row, New York, 1963, p. 81.

Langer, William L., *The Diplomacy of Imperialism, 1890–1902,* Alfred A. Knopf, New York, 1935, 2 vols.

Though written more than thirty years ago, this work is still of high value. All of the international clashes of the 12-year period stated in the title are given close examination—the struggle for the Nile, the "Armenian Question," the West's attempt to partition China, and the Boer War. The style is graceful; the temper is judicious; and the evidence is well used.

Lenin, V. I., *Imperialism,* Vol. V of his *Selected Works,* International Publishers, New York, 1943.

The classic Communist exposition of imperialism as the final stage of the capitalist economy.

Moon, Parker Thomas, *Imperialism and World Politics,* The Macmillan Co., New York, 1927.

Defining imperialism has become a kind of academic sport in recent years. There are now so many (and often contradictory) definitions that a student could hardly expect to immerse himself in them and come up with a unified concept. Moon does not concern himself with present-day abstractions. He treats the late nineteenth-century expansion of Europe and America as a strictly historical phenomenon. If only one book on imperialism is read, this could well be the one.

Shafer, Boyd C., *Nationalism, Myth and Reality,* Harcourt, Brace & Co., New York, 1955.

This is a brief examination of the origin, nature, and meaning of an institution that the author believes is the greatest force in the past 150 years. The concluding section is an eloquent diatribe against the evils inherent in the institution.

Thornton, A. P., *Doctrines of Imperialism,* John Wiley & Sons, New York, 1965.

Imperialism is considered as a force used by nations to gain power, wealth, and a position to exert their civilizing influences upon backward peoples. Although some of the examples used to develop his themes are not as clearly related to the themes as others he could have chosen, the author presents a sound account of the wide ranging forces of nineteenth-century European expansion.

Wilson, E. M., *The Pattern of Imperialism—A Study in the Theories of Power,* Columbia University Press, New York, 1947.

The author does not believe that capitalism necessarily issues in imperialism or that economic imperialism caused either of the great world wars. His examination of what has happened in history and what has caused these happenings leads him to conclude that imperialism and war are "political phenomena."

# X

# *Power Politics, 1875 to 1914— The Entangling Web*

## THE WEB OF EVENTS: NATIONALISM, ALLIANCES, AND THE NEW BALANCE OF POWER

In the preceding chapter we noted that other movements and forces besides imperialism helped mold the events of the period: nationalism, the sovereign-state system, militarism, strong personalities. We also noted that certain general conditions significantly bore upon these events: the shift in Europe's balance of power and the consequent development, abetted by secret diplomacy, of two great alliance systems. In this chapter we are concerned with particular European events produced by or made up of these movements and forces as they met and merged with the imperialist thrust. Because the multiple forces and movements are too interrelated for topical treatment, a simple chronological approach is used.

Special attention must be given to the nationalist impulse in the Balkans since, no matter how paradoxically, Balkan affairs

came to form the nexus of events that brought the imperial powers and their imperial schemes into bloody conflict in 1914. Until about 1830 the Balkan peoples were subjects of the sultan of Turkey (as they had been for about five hundred years). With the decline of Ottoman power they increased their agitation for ethnic unity and independence. In 1830 Greece won her independence, and Serbia and parts of Romania (Moldavia and Walachia) were granted autonomy. Both of these semi-independent states grieved publicly and continuously over separation from what they claimed as lands rightfully theirs. Bulgaria gained home rule in the 1870s; but like Greece, Serbia, and Romania, she complained that her true ethnic family had not been joined together. Specifically, Greece wanted a sizable portion of Macedonia, including the Thracian peninsula; Serbia demanded all of Bosnia and Herzegovina (reasonably enough, since these areas were mostly peopled by Serbs), as well as a portion of Macedonia; Romania wanted Transylvania and Bessarabia; Bulgaria quarreled with all three over lands adjacent to her boundaries. Undoubtedly a kind of imperial aggrandizement motivated each of these victims of imperialism. But basically they sought the right to set up ethnic housekeeping for themselves. And they were determined to continue to do all they could to achieve it, whatever the difficulties, however great the sacrifices either to themselves or to others. By itself, the nationalist impulse that roiled throughout the whole Balkan region was likely to stir up trouble from time to time. If this Balkan nationalist impulse were to meet head on with the imperialism of the great powers (both "autocratic, continental," and "new" extracontinental), it was almost certain to create a thunderhead of turbulence that would sweep Europe into cataclysmic violence.

## Balkan Embroglio, 1875 to 1878

In 1875 the oppressed peoples of Bosnia and Herzegovina revolted against their Turkish masters. The event in itself, one of dozens like it before, was hardly worth recording. But at this juncture the revolt touched the imperial interests of three great powers —Russia, Austria-Hungary, and Britain— and set off a chain of reactions that ultimately involved most of the nations of the world. It therefore deserves some detailed attention.

Although the Ottoman Turk—the so-called Sick Man of Europe—was and had long been in decline, he could easily have snuffed out the revolt if it had not led to other Balkan uprisings and, as important, to the intervention of Russia and Austria-Hungary. For several months in the summer of 1875 the Turks busied themselves with savage reprisals against the rebelling provinces and against whatever other Slavic groups supported them. For obvious reasons Serbia gave encouragement to the rebels. Russia, as their big Slav brother, was also sympathetic. Although Austria-Hungary was certainly not sympathetic to this or to any other

A CONSULTATION ABOUT THE STATE OF TURKEY.

*This famous* Punch *cartoon gave vogue to the reference to Turkey as the Sick Man of Europe. France and England are shown mulling over the possibilities that may develop if the Sick Man dies.*

kind of uprising, she was anxious for Turkey to call a halt to brutal repressions before they brought further reprisals against the already ailing power.

Of course, neither Russia nor Austria was motivated by altruism. Russia wanted control of the Straits, with Constantinople as her southern window on the sea. That meant kicking the Sick Man out of Europe. She was also strongly motivated by a complex of vague feelings subsumed under the term Pan-Slavism, "a continental, home-grown imperialist ideology."[1] Basically this movement aimed at uniting all peoples whose languages were Slavic, whose religion was Orthodox, and who claimed allegiance to a common historical heritage. Many of the champions of Pan-Slavism, such as Dosto-

1. H. Stuart Hughes, *Contemporary Europe . . .* , Prentice-Hall, Inc., Englewood Cliffs, N. J., 1961, p. 26.

evsky, sincerely believed that Eastern Europe was threatened with the same debauchery that befell the industrialized West. Others, including more than an occasional diplomat, used the movement simply as a stratagem to promote the interests of their nation or class. But no matter how it was used, Pan-Slavism was a force that shaped events, sometimes decisively.

Austria, in declining health herself, feared not so much Turkey's losing her European holdings as Russia's gaining them. But with the Ottoman Empire seemingly dissolving, and Austria unable to cope single-handedly with Russian designs, she found it expedient to collaborate with her rival.

Pressed by both of these powers, Turkey agreed to effect a series of reforms. The insurgents refused to accept them, however, and from the spring of 1876 on, conditions became worse. Irregular Turkish troops massacred thousands of Bulgarian insurrectionists (the "Bulgarian Horrors"). Serbia, joined by Montenegro, declared war on Turkey. Believing an Ottoman defeat imminent, Austria and Russia came to an understanding (in the secret Reichstadt Agreement) on the projected spoils: Constantinople was to be made a "free city"; Russia was to reincorporate Bessarabia; Austria was given the right to occupy and administer (*but not annex*) Bosnia and Herzegovina; Bulgaria, Rumelia, and Albania were to become autonomous states.

But in September Serbia suffered a crushing defeat, and the whole picture changed. Suddenly the Sick Man seemed fearfully healthy and threatening. This naturally agitated Russia's Pan-Slavists who now demanded direct intervention. After concluding a new agreement with Austria, along the lines of the earlier Reichstadt Agreement, Russia sent her troops marching (April 1877). Her easy victories seemed to promise a quick and uncomplicated conclusion of the war for Russia. But in July, at Plevna, the Turks showed a strength that convinced many European powers that the Ottoman Empire was not so moribund as they had long believed. Indeed, it is thought by some present-day historians that the battle of Plevna not only saved the Ottoman Empire for another forty years but was responsible for Turkey's present control of the Straits.[2] Even so, the battle did not prevent Russian troops, early the next year, from battering their way to the gates of Constantinople. At this point Turkey asked for an armistice and in March 1878 signed the treaty of San Stefano. This treaty created a large Bulgaria under covert Russian control. Since this was clearly contrary to the modified Reichstadt Agreement, Austria objected. So did Britain, who saw Russia now in a position to threaten her own "lifeline" to the East. To implement her objection she sent a naval squadron into the Sea of Marmara where it anchored off the roadsteads of Constantinople.

## The Congress of Berlin and Its Aftermath

Russia, knowing she could not cope with the combined forces of England and Austria, reluctantly agreed to a conference where the settlement might be reviewed. At Austria's suggestion (initiated by Bismarck), the meeting was held in Berlin in June 1878, and was attended by all the major powers. Chaired by Bismarck—who insisted he was acting only as an "honest broker"—the Congress of Berlin thoroughly revised the Russo-Turkish treaty. Bulgaria was divided and the pared-off portions were returned to the direct or indirect control of Turkey. Bosnia-Herzegovina was occupied by Austria; and Russian gains in Asiatic Turkey were cut down.

The reactions of the powers were what might have been expected. Many Russians were furious. Some of the more conventional diplomats, it is true, had all along understood that the inflated terms of the San Ste-

2. Compare A. J. P. Taylor, *The Struggle For Mastery of Europe, 1848–1918,* Clarendon Press, Oxford, 1954, p. 245.

fano treaty were hardly realistic, and that in the revised treaty Russia had not come off too badly. More, however, felt that Russia had won the war and lost the peace. They lamented the loss of both coveted territory and face, for which they chiefly blamed Bismarck who, they insisted, had favored Austria throughout the conference. They felt alarm, too, at Britain's strong insistence that Turkey continue to hold the key to the Straits. England was satisfied—Russia's move toward the Straits had been blocked and an extra and unexpected plum, the island of Cyprus, had been gained. France, invited only because Bismarck hoped it would help her feel like a great power again and perhaps forget the rape of Alsace-Lorraine, was pleased by the Iron Chancellor's coy (and confidential) suggestion that Tunis probably needed her attention. Italy, also invited out of courtesy, felt some alarm at Austria's Balkan gains but did not seem to believe she had really been hurt by them.* Speaking for Germany, Bismarck modestly admitted that a difficult job of brokerage had been concluded and, in his opinion, all parties had been fairly treated. Bulgaria, grieving over her losses, made it plain that sooner or later she would regain her "stolen" territories. Romania resented the loss of Bessarabia to Russia. Serbia protested that her claims for just boundaries, including, of course, Bosnia-Herzegovina, had been shamelessly ignored. Like Bulgaria, Serbia also spoke, though softly, of a coming day of reckoning.

Before considering in detail the events that flowed out of, impinged upon, or became connected with the decisions made at this conference, we may note its overall significance. The occupation of Bosnia-Herze-

"DOCTOR BISMARCK."

*"Doctor Bismarck" prescribed for most of Europe in the 1880s and 1890s. Note the soothing syrup for France, offered in the hope of settling French revanche agitation. It proved to be an ineffective remedy.*

govina by Austria-Hungary was for that state a victory more seeming than real. Instead of consolidating imperial control in the Balkans, the occupation eventually led to crises which, as they culminated in World War I, led to the complete breaking up of the Austro-Hungarian Empire. (See the later section on the Bosnian crisis, 1908 and 1909, and the section on Sarajevo in the next chapter.) The treatment accorded Russia by the Congress of Berlin and the treaty which came out of it contributed to the subsequent formation (1894) of an alliance between that nation and France.† The strength thus gained by each encouraged England, in due time, to associate herself with both—and the Triple Entente was born. Because Russia

---

* There is a difference of opinion among historians on this point. Some hold that Italian fears and chagrin were strong. For a fairly full account of this nation's position at the Congress of Berlin and its reaction to the settlement see Luigi Albertini, *The Origins of the War of 1914*, Vol. 1, Oxford University Press, London, 1952, pp. 26–31.

† But at the time, and for some years thereafter, Russia got along much better with Germany than with England. Really strained relations between Germany and England did not develop until after 1895. The point here is that Russian suspicions of German sympathies, rooted in the unfair treatment she had received at Berlin—unfair as she saw it—predisposed Russia toward a touchiness vis-à-vis Germany which subsequently aborted conciliatory efforts and encouraged her to think of France, the Continent's only other great power, in terms which otherwise would have been quite unlikely.

was so seriously disaffected by the Treaty of Berlin, Bismarck believed that Germany should draw closer to Austria-Hungary; that, indeed, a formal alliance between the two should be effected. Italy's indignation at France's action in Tunis caused her to join France's principal enemy—and the Triple Alliance came into being. Thus, the Congress of Berlin re-created the alliance system of the pre-1815 period, and emphasized afresh the play of power politics. If it prevented a localized European war in 1878, as it almost certainly did, the Congress of Berlin sowed many of the seeds of a far greater conflict to come.

## The Emergence of the Alliance System

After the Congress of Berlin many of the imperio-nationalist elements in Russia became convinced, quite understandably, that in spite of his honest-broker pose Bismarck intended to work more closely with Austria than Russian interests could tolerate. In these circumstances she made overtures to both France and Italy. Bismarck became alarmed when he heard of this. Allied with any power, France might prove dangerous; allied with Russia she would surely one day try to regain Alsace-Lorraine. To counter this possible development Bismarck sought an alliance with Austria. Fearful of what Russia might attempt after her humiliation at Berlin, Austria was willing enough to join forces with the strongest military power in Europe. So in 1879 the two empires joined in a secret, defensive military pact. By its terms each agreed to help the other if Russia attacked either. If a power other than Russia were the aggressor (in other words, France), Austria would observe benevolent neutrality toward Germany. This treaty, later expanded and renewed, became the cornerstone of the grand diplomatic edifice soon to be erected by Bismarck.

The German Chancellor never tired of emphasizing the defensive nature of the pact. He knew Austria would be tempted to use it

to strike out at any power that encouraged disaffection among her restive ethnic groups, particularly against Russia or Italy. To forestall this, Bismarck repeatedly let Austria know that he reserved to himself the right to decide when the treaty should become operative. He thus looked upon the alliance as a safeguard to be used only after conditions had already assumed threatening aspects. But obviously German interests called for the prevention, if possible, of the development of such conditions. In Bismarck's view this came down to the need to establish better relations with Russia; that is, to the re-creation of the Austro-German-Russian league of friendship (the Three Emperors' League) which had dissolved amid the recriminations flowing out of the Berlin settlement.

Favoring this move was Russia's profound reluctance to ally herself with a republican regime. Clearly, her heart was not in the brief flirtation with France of the preceding year. England was out of the question because she considered the eastern Mediterranean to be her own special preserve. Italy was too weak to be of substantial help. But financial exigencies and military weakness precluded Russia's standing alone. Thus the logic of circumstances clearly pointed to Germany. Sensing this, Bismarck sounded out his Austrian colleagues. Austria was reluctant to revive the old partnership with Russia; the Tsar's government, Austria felt, simply could not be trusted. But Bismarck insisted and, rather than risk losing her powerful friend, Austria finally agreed. In 1881 a new (and, again, secret) pact was signed. Its terms protected the interests of Germany by bringing Austria and Russia into peaceful collaboration. The pact protected the interests of Russia by insuring her partners' help if England should move against Russia through the Straits, and by fostering the peaceful union of Bulgaria and Rumelia. Austria's interests were protected by Russia's promise not to attempt to alter conditions in the Balkans without Austria's con-

"THE SISTERS THREE;" OR, THE TRIPLE ALLIANCE.

*This British cartoon likens the members of the newly formed Triple Alliance to the Three Fates who possess complete power to decide when the thread of peace will be snapped. A few years later, German cartoons were picturing France, Russia, and Britain as ominously "encircling" the Fatherland.*

sent, and by Russia's agreement to an eventual absorption of Bosnia-Herzegovina into the Austrian empire.

Thus, only three years after Russia had vowed never to trust Germany again, she became her ally and, even more strangely, the ally of Austria whose influence in the Balkans she most feared. Bismarck, of course, was pleased. He believed the pact would work not only to keep Russia out of France's embrace, but also to render less likely embarrassing friction between Austria and Russia.

In the meantime Italy had been busy readying plans to annex Tunisia. Before she could act, however, France occupied the territory (1881) with the covert support of England and Germany. Italy, thoroughly angered by this *fait accompli* and unaware of Bismarck's role in the affair, turned to him for comfort and aid. Although the terms of the Austro-German alliance were kept secret, the fact that an agreement of some kind existed was well known. Italy now offered to associate herself with the central

powers.* Bismarck received the suggestion with mixed feelings. Poor and often unreliable, Italy was not the most promising candidate for admission into a great-power bloc. On the other hand she was, because of her own west Balkan claims, a potential disturber of the peace. Perhaps she could be kept under control as a colleague. Austria was even less amenable to the suggestion than Germany. But Bismarck's logic, and nudging, persuaded her to agree. So, in 1882, the Triple Alliance was formed. Bismarck again made it plain that the pact was purely defensive. With tongue in cheek, Italy acquiesced. The secret treaty provided that Germany and Austria would give full support to Italy if she were attacked by France *without provocation;* that Italy would join with Germany if Germany were attacked by France without provocation; that all would join together if any one was attacked by two or more powers.

## England's "Splendid Isolation"

Meanwhile England continued to enjoy what she liked to think of as her "splendid isolation." Before sounding Austria in 1879, Bismarck had hinted of an alliance with Britain, but the cool response from across the Channel quickly discouraged him. The position of the island empire did indeed seem secure. Early ventures in industrialism had given England a substantial head start over other powers. Her empire circled the globe. On the high seas she was supreme; not only was her fleet more than double in size and effectiveness that of her nearest rival, France, but she controlled most of the strategic approaches to the sea lanes of the world. Control of Gibraltar and Suez, for example, allowed her to bottle up the Mediterranean whenever she wished (thus tending, incidentally, to make Italy an unofficial and subordi-

* Actually she desired an alliance with Germany alone but Bismarck made it clear that "the road to Berlin ran through Vienna."

nate ally). Squadrons stationed at the tip of South Africa watched over affairs at this juncture of two oceans. Waters washing the great subcontinent of India were policed by English ships. Singapore, Hong Kong, and Shanghai gave her not only entry to east Asian markets but the final word in disputes that might arise in that vast area. Ruling the seas, dominating the major trade areas, rich, secure, and at peace, England disdained entangling alliances. Within the span of a single generation, many of these conditions were to undergo marked change, and the splendor of isolation was to be lost. But at that time, as for so long before, she seemed unchallengeable.

## Balkan Trouble Again; Its Repercussions

For a while European tensions eased, but only for a while. Soon trouble in the Balkans flared again. The presence of Russian troops and advisers in Bulgaria had not been conducive to good relations between these Slav brothers; indeed, just the opposite. Therefore, when the Bulgarian government supported a Rumelian uprising against Turkey (in 1885) which resulted in reunion of the two provinces, Russia was quite put out. This was not the big Bulgaria she wanted. On the other hand, England was pleased at Russia's setback and immediately gave the union her blessing. Thus the situation created earlier by the treaty of San Stefano was quite reversed.

In a rather fantastic attempt to regain control, Russia contrived the kidnapping of Alexander of Battenberg, the Bulgarian ruler, hoping to install a puppet regime. But the Western powers intervened and put a German prince, Ferdinand of Coburg, on the throne in 1887. Thwarted again by Austria and (as she mistakenly thought) Germany, Russia refused to renew the Three Emperors' Alliance, holding that her supposed partners had acted contrary to a provision in

*Here the great powers are pictured as highly disturbed over chronic Balkan crises. What is not shown is their continuing interference in Balkan affairs which contributed greatly to the bubbling fermentation they seem here to find so unholy.*

that treaty which implicitly recognized Russia's special interests in Bulgaria.

The lapse of the treaty once again disturbed Bismarck, especially since the general international situation had deteriorated. In 1885 Russian and British troops clashed in Afghanistan; for a time it appeared that war was inevitable. Eventually a peaceful settlement was reached, but relations between the two powers became even more strained. The next year Italy proved hard to satisfy in negotiations looking to the renewal of the Triple Alliance. If general conditions had been more settled, neither Germany nor Austria would have much cared whether Italy was satisfied or not. But in the existing circumstances rather large and, in Bismarck's eyes, potentially dangerous conces-

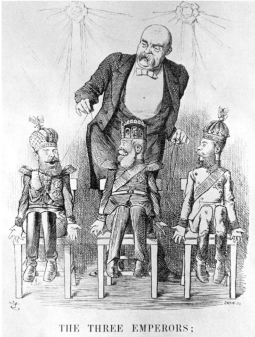

THE THREE EMPERORS;
OR, THE VENTRILOQUIST OF VARZIN!

*By the late 1880s Bismarck was indeed Europe's master diplomat. But at no time did he pull the strings quite so effectively as this drawing would indicate—and certainly not so obviously.*

sions had to be made.* Finally, the situation in France had become threatening. Led by its chauvinistic minister of war, Georges Boulanger, that nation was loudly beating the *revanche* drums which sounded menacingly like drums of war.

In this situation Bismarck again feared a *rapprochement* between Russia and France that might ultimately lead to a two-front war against Germany. He did not doubt that German victory would result (provided England stayed out). But what, save expense and suffering, would be gained? In this mood

---

* In effect, Germany had to promise military support for Italy in circumstances that might be anything but "defensive" for Italy; that is, circumstances involving Italian imperial designs in Africa.

he once more approached England. If Europe understood that Germany, Austria-Hungary, Italy, and England stood together against aggressors, all threat of war would vanish. But England still thought of herself as the uncommitted arbiter of world affairs, and so the second German offer came to nothing.

Now Bismarck executed what many consider his subtlest diplomatic maneuver. In what came to be known as the Mediterranean Pacts (1887), he succeeded, in effect, in drawing England into an informal alliance without that nation quite understanding what had happened. The details are too complicated for our study. Italy and England agreed to work for the maintenance of the *status quo* in the Mediterranean (which eased Bismarck's apprehensions); Italy reaffirmed her approval of English domination of Egypt; England recognized that Italy had special interests in North Africa (particularly in Libya). In short, England, Italy, and Austria (who adhered to the first pact and signed the second) were placed in combination to stave off French aggression in the western half of the Mediterranean and Russian aggression in the eastern half. The agreements were supposedly secret, but enough information was allowed to leak to give Russia pause in her Balkan schemes.

With the Triple Alliance and the Mediterranean agreements in force, Bismarck felt more optimistic about the preservation of peace. Only one link seemed missing—a close and formal tie with Russia. Rather surprisingly, Russia now suggested this herself. Two motives prompted this: rivalry between two factions of the ruling elite, and the menacing implications of the Mediterranean Pacts. For long, a struggle had been carried on between those who wanted to Westernize Russia and those who saw in Westernization the destruction of Russia's Slavic soul. At this time the Westernizers were in sufficient ascendancy to dictate foreign policy. A connection with Germany seemed to them both a good thing in itself,* as well as a setback for Slavophile rivals.

So, in 1887, Russia's minister in Berlin indicated that although Russia could under no conditions consider a renewal of the Three Emperors' Alliance, she was quite willing to discuss a bilateral agreement. Bismarck responded at once. Out of the negotiations that followed there came what is commonly called the Reinsurance Treaty. It stipulated that Germany favored Russia's peaceful penetration of the east Balkans, particularly Bulgaria, and control of the Straits; and that each would observe neutrality toward the other if either became involved in war with a third power. Bismarck made it clear that this provision did not cover a *Russian-provoked* war with Austria and conversely agreed that it would not come into force in the event of a *German-provoked* war with France.

Thus, in the ten years following the Congress of Berlin, Bismarck's diplomacy seemed to have stilled the tempests raised by that conference, and to have laid the groundwork for pacific relations among the powers. The Triple Alliance appeared to insure that neither France nor Russia would quite dare to start big trouble in Europe. The Mediterranean agreements further shored up the forces working against violent modification of the Balkan *status quo*; they also gave ordered recognition to imperial ambitions in Africa. The Reinsurance Treaty brought Russia back within the German orbit without penalizing Russia's peaceful penetration to the south. Quite correctly, then, we may refer to this period as the "Bismarckian Era." Who else could have

constructed a general peace within the framework of the politics of realism?

## Weaknesses of Bismarckian Diplomacy

However, the substance of the Bismarckian achievement was more seeming than real. France, although active in Africa and Asia, had not forgotten the debacle of 1870 and 1871; she still yearned for revenge. For the most part she sought to follow Gambetta's advice—speak of it never, think of it always. She was convinced that her day would come. Russia was willing to *talk* of peaceful penetration. But, granted funds could be found to refurbish her ailing military machine, another kind and instrument of penetration was to be fashioned and held in reserve. As for what came increasingly to be called the Balkan Problem, Bismarck never really understood it. To him the ethnic groups of that region were pawns to be moved in the great game of power politics. He failed utterly to appreciate the dynamic, churning force of Balkan nationalism as a "wave of the future."

He also failed, though perhaps more understandably, to sense the demise of one era—his own—and the birth of another. Essentially he was a transitional figure. True, in the last days of his tenure he supported German industrialists in their efforts to exploit markets and resources in the so-called backward areas of the world. But his support was reluctant and late. At no time did he seem to comprehend the ranging implications of the new industrial age. His own formative period had coincided with the flowering of the Manchester doctrine of free trade and anti-imperialism. Although he came to accept upward industrial tariff revisions and even eventually became somewhat enthusiastic over protection for agricultural produce, he remained basically insensible to the mercantilist, protectionist trend that was already working important changes in world affairs even before he left office. Almost by

---

* Somewhat from a process of elimination. England and Austria seemed irrevocably committed to courses which must necessarily penalize Russia's Balkan plans. France was republican and weak. Although Germany might play fast and loose with her, Bismarck seemed both to understand and to sympathize with Russia's Balkan "needs."

necessity his was, fundamentally, a static Germany and a static world. His boasted policy of "limited liabilities" served well enough the demands of *Europa-politik* (although he denied there existed such a thing as "Europe"). But the ingredients of the new age—industrialism, protectionism, colonies, big navies—called for a *Weltpolitik* beyond his ken. His passing from power in 1890 marked* the transition from the steady-state world to a world of dynamic change.

## NEW PATHS AND NEW COMPACTS

### Beginnings of the "New Course"

Four German chancellors held office in the period from 1890 to 1914. But none was chancellor in the sense that Bismarck had been chancellor. The new emperor, William II (reigned 1888–1918), saw to that. Young, aggressive, and impressionable, he made it clear from the beginning that his royal hand was at the helm. He possessed talent without genius, intelligence without judgment, domineering ways without the capacity actually to dominate. Often he sought advice and almost as often failed to distinguish the sound from the unsound. Unlike Bismarck, he understood the need for a new concert of Europe functioning within the framework of *Weltpolitik*. Unfortunately, and illogically, he wanted a *dominated* concert with Germany in the master role, of course. Moreover, he worked simultaneously to set up a power system of alliances, a system obviously incompatible with his own projected concert. During his reign, therefore, Germany experienced the effects

*A painting of the young Kaiser about two years after he became Emperor.*

of a confused and ineptly directed foreign policy.

The year that Bismarck left office the Reinsurance Treaty came up for renewal. On the advice of Baron von Holstein, head of the political section of the German Foreign Office, William allowed the treaty to lapse.† The excuse given by Chancellor Caprivi was

---

* It should be pointed out that most historians, in contrast to the present writer, would read "made" for "marked." They hold that a kind of capricious abandonment of Bismarck's policies by William II and his advisers pointed international developments toward the war that broke out in 1914. The latest scholarly work which expounds this view is Albertini, *The Origins of the War of 1914* (see, especially, Volume I, p. 64, where it is baldly stated).

† During this period Holstein exerted great influence on German foreign affairs, although probably not as much as was once thought. The older view is best expressed in a statement by Prince Lichnowsky, one-time ambassador to London and a highly knowledgeable person, to whom Holstein was a "master of intrigue (who) knew not only how to impress his superiors but how to intimidate and even completely dominate them . . . in short (Holstein) was a national misfortune and the real begetter of the World War." Quoted by Albertini, *op. cit.*, Vol. I. p. 63, footnote.

that he could not keep five balls in the air at once, a reference to the diplomatic dexterity required to keep all of Germany's friends, some with conflicting aims, from breaking out of the orbits so adroitly set by Bismarck. Actually, the new leaders of Germany, managing what the Kaiser liked to call the "New Course," were afraid of what might happen should news of the treaty's terms leak to Austria and England with whom the Kaiser-Caprivi government hoped to cement relations preparatory to constructing a grand new alliance of states.

*Czar Nicholas II is shown as he is about to embark at Cherbourg. The newspapers of both France and Russia made much of this royal visit.*

## The Franco-Russian Alliance, 1890 to 1894

Naturally Russia became alarmed. To her the severance of the German tie could only mean that Germany was drawing still closer to Austria and Austria's Balkan schemes. Quite naturally she set about seeking a new ally. The *Dreikaiserbund* could probably be reestablished; but to what point? England's Mediterranean interests precluded a meaningful understanding with her. Italy was a frail reed to lean upon. Only France remained. Although still republican, she had money to lend and an abiding hatred of Germany whose western frontier she flanked. Acting together, France and Russia could launch a two-front war in which even the famed Prussian military machine might flounder.

Russian diplomats opened negotiations with their counterparts in Paris. Even before Bismarck left office, Germany had cut off loans to Russia,* loans which Paris banks were happy to make. By 1891 well over one million francs had been put at Russia's disposal; millions more were to follow. Beyond political insecurity, therefore, a cash nexus drew the two empires together. In addition, each nursed a growing animus against England. In 1891 Italy announced renewal of

the Triple Alliance in terms deliberately calculated to make it seem that England had become a member. She had not, of course, but certain current developments lent credence to the sham. Only the year before, England and Germany had effected the Heligoland–Zanzibar exchange. In announcing it the British press, quite groundlessly, had hinted of provisions that went beyond those made public. Finally, a well-advertised visit by the Kaiser to England strengthened the growing suspicions of France and Russia.

In these circumstances the two states worked out a *detente.* More millions were loaned to Russia. As a gesture of friendship, French warships made a courtesy call at Kronstadt where the Tsar stood on the deck of the flagship with bared head as a band played the revolutionary *Marseillaise.* The next year the two governments, in an exchange of letters, promised to confer together when crises threatened. Not satisfied with this, the chiefs of staff in joint meetings framed a convention that stipulated mutual military obligations. But the Tsar felt this was carrying the budding friendship too far, and, for the moment, he put it aside. But new French irritations with Britain and new Russian difficulties with Germany led the diplomats of both countries to press still harder for a pact with teeth in it. That such

---

\* But only, as Bismarck hoped, temporarily—to discipline his ally. The causative factors leading to this decision are complicated beyond the scope of this study.

a pact was indeed approaching the draft stage was symbolized by the appearance, in 1893, of a Russian fleet in the French harbor of Toulon. Not only diplomats but generals and admirals were obviously concerting to transform the entente into a binding military agreement.

The next year the alliance was signed. The political section, made public, repeated the stipulations noted earlier; the military clauses, kept secret, were quite different in aim and definite in detail. They provided that Russia would come to the aid of France if France were attacked by Germany; that France would reciprocate if Russia were attacked by Germany; and that if one or more members of the Triple Alliance should order mobilization each of the contracting parties would do likewise.* France let it be known that she had no desire to see Russia use the pact as an instrument of aggrandizement in the East; Russia, in turn, made it clear that she did not intend France to view the alliance as a weapon in her *revanche* game with Germany.

The significance of the treaty can hardly be overstated. By it Russia acknowledged finally that she was fully cognizant of Germany's practice of saying yes and meaning no; and that Austro-German aims were no longer compatible with her own. Further, the agreement revealed Russia's imperialist ambitions to be so strong that she could even agree to compromise her long-held monarchial principles. It tended, of course, to heighten the confidence of each partner and thus to prepare the ground for more ambi-

---

* It is important to note that all military leaders at this time understood mobilization to mean war. One of the proponents of the Franco-Russian alliance put the matter in these plain terms: "Mobilization is a declaration of war. To mobilize is to require one's neighbor to do the same. Mobilization causes the carrying out of strategic transport and communication plans. Otherwise, to allow a million men to mobilize on one's frontiers without at once doing the same is to forfeit all possibility of following suit. . . ." Quoted by Albertini, *op. cit.,* Vol. I, p. 77.

tious ventures in foreign affairs. And naturally it prompted the central powers, particularly Germany, to become even more suspicious. In short, the treaty made possible a developing pattern of "trial by alliances" which would, within a brief score of years, bring on the first global war.

## Milestones of the "New Course"

In 1890 Germany and England effected an exchange of territory. Heligoland, a British-owned island off the western approaches to the Kiel Canal (soon to be opened), was a natural base for defense of Germany's northern coast. To get it, Germany offered England Zanzibar, a rather sizable African territory. Normally, England did not give up island bases, no matter how remote or difficult to defend. That she now bargained away a European possession for an area to which she already had perhaps a better claim than the state who "offered" it seemed to some observers a hint that her imperial position was becoming more precarious than her vaunted boast of splendid isolation would have the world believe.

Three years later English and French ambitions clashed in Siam. For a while it appeared that war could not be avoided. Officious and full of advice, William II accepted England's hints to mediate the quarrel, hoping by this gambit to draw her into the Triple Alliance. The incident closed peacefully when England agreed to a compromise. Once again the world took note of, if not an English retreat, at least a softening attitude. Germany in particular was impressed by the new British tendency to give ground when pushed. From early 1890s on, as colonial rivalry between England and Germany heightened, Germany increasingly pushed.

In 1896 the Mediterranean Pacts came up for renewal. By then England had a clearer understanding of how strongly the Pacts committed her to support of Austrian interests in the Mediterranean, and she refused to remain a party to them. Frightened, Austria complained to Germany that Germany's conduct had estranged England. To appease her ally, Germany tried again to bring England into the Triple Alliance. Since the projected pact was ever more clearly revealing itself as William's chief instrument to effect German dominance in all matters of large concern, England again rejected the offer.

Two events occurred in 1898 that soon further strained relations between the rival empires. Von Tirpitz, newly appointed minister of marine, pushed a naval bill through the Reichstag which provided for a large high seas fleet. To win nationwide approval he set up a generously subsidized Navy League, with branches scattered throughout the Reich. From each of these units subsequently flowed an endless stream of noisy propaganda. The basis of the race for naval supremacy, soon to be begun in earnest, had been established.

This year also marked a change in Germany's attitude toward Turkey. Up to this time, affairs in the Ottoman Empire had but little interested Berlin officials. But Germany's rapid railroad development and her remarkable commercial expansion now combined with an upward thrust of national confidence to cause her to view Turkey, lying athwart two continents, in a new light. Seemingly limitless markets lay in the East. Could they not be tapped by a land route running from Berlin to Bagdad, thence by sea to India and China? To realize such a grand design, of course, Turkey's cooperation was necessary. Accordingly German diplomats began, as it were, to toast the health of the Sick Man of Europe, while German bankers held amiable discussions with Turkish officials.

Naturally Britain felt concern. For many years she had been Turkey's staunchest ally. While protecting her own lifeline to the East, she had kept the Ottoman Empire from falling apart and had prevented Russia from reaching the Straits. The proposed German railroad across Turkish territory, accompanied by generous loans to the Porte, thus

THE NEW HAROUN AL RASCHID.
A DREAM OF BAGHDAD, MADE IN GERMANY.

*The proposed Berlin to Baghdad railroad gave British merchants and industrialists a lot to fret about. A* Punch *cartoon of the time (1911) shows the Kaiser as a new Haroun Al Raschid dominating the commerce of two continents.*

constituted a triple threat to English interests. To meet it she reversed her position: perhaps it would be better if the Sick Man were allowed to die and his estate duly apportioned among the legitimate heirs.

Policy makers in Russia were also busy. The drive to the south had ground to a halt; meantime the Japanese had inflicted a crushing defeat upon China (1894–1895). Naturally this imperiled Russia's interests in the Far East, and she therefore decided to patch up an understanding with Austria-Hungary which would give her a free hand in the new trouble zone. According to the terms of the rather hastily arranged agreement (1897), the *status quo* in the Balkans was to be respected by each of the powers; if, at a later date, modifications were considered necessary, joint consultations were to precede and pattern any military moves. Thus for the time being the fluid Balkan situation was "put on ice." By this agreement Austria gained a breathing spell and Russia gained a chance to block Japanese expansion. German prodding was behind Austria's rather reluctant cooperation. The dual monarchy had little faith in Russian promises, but the pressure exerted by the Kaiser and his advisers was too strong to resist.

In these ways the New Course revealed its fundamental aims: the creation of a powerful high seas fleet (conveniently based in the North Sea); a stubborn contesting of Britain's commercial supremacy; and a sustained effort to supervise European diplomacy in a manner befitting the Kaiser's coveted role as arbiter of continental affairs. Already William saw himself as a knight in shining armor, a new Siegfried. Thus accoutered he confidently cued the New Course into the world scene. As it turned out, neither confidence nor course was rooted in the realities of the age.

## Emergence of England from Her Isolation

With international rivalries mounting, England found it necessary to reassess her own position. Almost overnight Germany, France, Japan, and the United States had become industrial powers with expanding empires. Sprawled over the globe, the British Empire inevitably invited contests and conflicts. Several examples will illustrate this evolving development of challenge and response.

In March 1894, an agreement with Germany permitted France to join together certain of her Niger-Congo territories. Earlier, this connecting strip had been passed on to Germany by England with the deliberate purpose of preventing France from acquiring it. In May of the same year, an Anglo-Portuguese agreement gave England some territory that added another link to her north-south line. Since, however, the transaction violated provisions of an earlier signed Congo pact, Germany protested and England

was forced to renounce her acquisition. Moreover in 1895, as we have earlier noted, British raiders led by Dr. Jameson invaded the Dutch Republic of Transvaal and were promptly repulsed by the Boers. The Kaiser was moved to dispatch a telegram to the president of the Dutch Republic congratulating him upon this swift and effective action. At this seemingly gratuitous insult, England blazed with fury, sparking a newspaper war between the two countries. Shortly thereafter, as the German high seas fleet began to emerge from its blueprint stage, William publicly declared, "Our future lies on the water." Meanwhile, German overseas trade continued its phenomenal growth.

There seemed, in short, no end to the harassments besetting the British. In 1897 Russia, temporarily disengaged in the Balkans, occupied Port Arthur on the Liaotung Peninsula. Coupled with Japan's infiltration into northern China, this constituted a serious threat to England's commercial interests in the East. In Africa an even graver threat developed. Fashoda, a strategically located fortress in the Sudan region (see p. 372) was occupied in 1898 by a company of French troops under Captain Marchand. To counter the move, General Kitchener marched an English contingent into the area. For a while the Tricolor and the Union Jack flapped in the same breeze, with each commander demanding the other's withdrawal. At this point England took an adamant stand. France could capitulate or fight. Reluctantly the French Foreign Office ordered Marchand to evacuate the fortress, but tension remained high.

## England's Search for Allies

By 1900, then, England was at odds with three of the greatest powers on the Continent. A generation earlier France was beaten and humbled; Germany was in its national infancy; Russia was recovering from the debacle of the Crimean War. Now conditions were changed, and the powers were

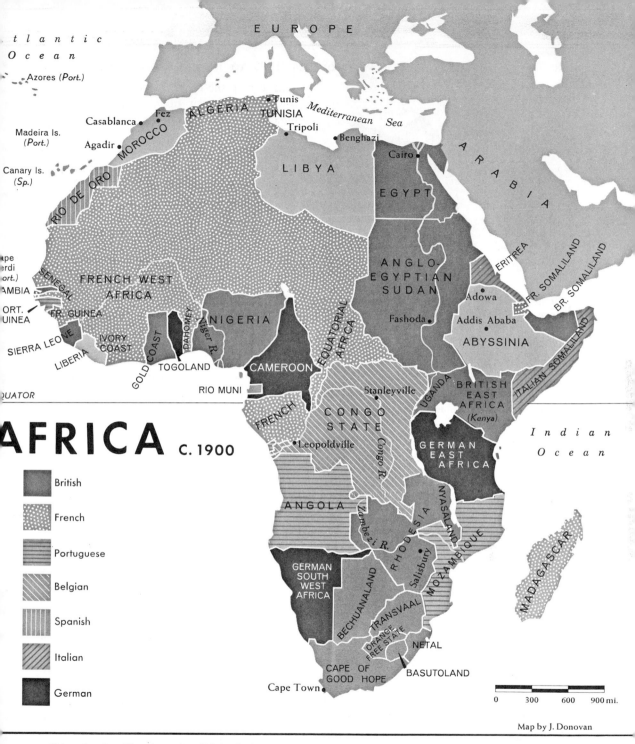

tlantic
Ocean

Azores (Port.)

Madeira Is.
(Port.)

Canary Is.
(Sp.)

ape
erdi
ort.)

AMBIA

ORT.
UINEA

EUROPE

Mediterranean Sea

ALGERIA

TUNISIA

Tunis

Tripoli

Benghazi

Cairo

ARABIA

LIBYA

EGYPT

MOROCCO

Casablanca
Fez

Agadir

RIO DE ORO

SENEGAL

FRENCH WEST
AFRICA

FR. GUINEA

SIERRA LEONE

LIBERIA

IVORY
COAST

GOLD COAST

DAHOMEY

TOGOLAND

Niger R.

NIGERIA

RIO MUNI

CAMEROON

EQUATORIAL AFRICA

ANGLO-
EGYPTIAN
SUDAN

Fashoda

Adowa

Addis Ababa

ABYSSINIA

ERITREA

FR. SOMALILAND

BR. SOMALILAND

QUATOR

# AFRICA C. 1900

British

French

Portuguese

Belgian

Spanish

Italian

German

FRENCH

Leopoldville

CONGO
STATE

Stanleyville

Congo R.

UGANDA

BRITISH
EAST
AFRICA
(Kenya)

ITALIAN SOMALILAND

GERMAN
EAST
AFRICA

Indian
Ocean

ANGOLA

Zambezi R.

NYASALAND

RHODESIA

Salisbury

MOZAMBIQUE

MADAGASCAR

GERMAN
SOUTH
WEST
AFRICA

BECHUANALAND

TRANSVAAL

ORANGE
FREE STATE

NETAL

CAPE OF
GOOD HOPE

BASUTOLAND

Cape Town

0    300    600   900 mi.

Map by J. Donovan

talking back. Clearly splendid isolation was out of date. It was time to make some friends and share the world.

England's first move was to sound out Russia. But Russia insisted upon permanent possession of Port Arthur in the Liaotung Peninsula as a *sine qua non*. Fearing that

this would give Russia an overriding influence in the East, England dropped the venture and turned elsewhere. For a long time Joseph Chamberlain, Britain's Secretary of State for Colonial Affairs, had argued that Germany was England's natural ally. Europe's dominant sea and land powers, he

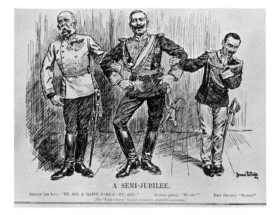

A SEMI-JUBILEE.

*Around 1900 Italy drew so close to Britain and France that her membership in the Triple Alliance was more nominal than real, a situation pointed up by this cartoon (1907).*

believed, should join forces to direct and manage the larger concerns of world politics (particularly since they were of Nordic stock; Chamberlain's general outlook was strongly pervaded by racist and Social Darwinist convictions). But the suspicions of Bulow and the Kaiser blocked Chamberlain's efforts. A third try proved more rewarding. Before considering it we need to note two other related events.

In 1898 Italy was forced to call off the ruinous tariff war it had been waging with France since the Tunisian affair. Both nations had been hurt by it, but it was plain that Italy, poorer than France in both resources and credit, would eventually have to choose between surrender and bankruptcy. Two years earlier she had hinted at her choice when she concluded a pact with her rival recognizing France's Tunisian claims. Now Italy signed a trade agreement which regularized normal commercial relations. A further step toward *rapprochement* was taken in 1900 when the two states blocked out respective spheres of development in North Africa. France was given a free hand in Morocco, Italy in Tripoli. Shortly thereafter a real *entente* materialized when, in an exchange of notes, each prom-

ised to help the other if either was provoked into declaring war upon a third power. In effect, Italy had defined herself out of the Triple Alliance.

In 1902 England offered to join Japan in a formal alliance, hoping thereby to prevent Russia from running amuck—that is, from interfering with English interests in the East. Japan was next door to this source of possible friction; England was thousands of miles away. By itself, this geographic factor loaded the treaty in favor of England; but Japan, flattered by the prospect of joining forces with a great Occidental power, agreed readily enough.* In this year, then, England's famed isolation was formally abandoned. Of itself, the arrangement turned out to be relatively insignificant. But this break with her past made it easier for England to play the alliance game with others, especially in Europe where conditions were rapidly becoming unstable and unpredictable.

Rebuffed by both Russia and Germany, England turned to France. For a long time Holstein had insisted that such a combination was impossible; and his reasoning seemed quite sound. England and France had already fought two wars, each lasting a hundred years. Their overlapping imperial claims provoked mutual suspicion. Temperamentally they were poles apart. Almost any other partnership would seem to make more sense. What Holstein and others failed to realize, however, was England's dawning understanding that, under the conditions of the new era, she could not "stay out of Europe." The exigencies of the new imperialism and the new nationalism clearly foreshadowed the day when she would either fight alone or ally herself in Europe, compromise her world position, and hope to preserve the peace and as much of her empire as she could.

France was willing to talk terms, especially after Fashoda, which had brought home an

---

* Japan also believed an alliance with England would weaken the Franco-Russian alliance.

*Emperor William II as Ruler of the World (pre-World War I cartoon).*

*The center figure is von Tirpitz, creator (with the Kaiser, shown left) of the "risk" navy, designed to keep Britain from interfering with German imperialist expansion.*

old lesson—if you can't lick them, join them. Granted the necessary *quid pro quo,* she was more than passively interested in England's overtures. So in 1904, after the usual diplomatic preliminaries, the two nations reached an understanding in which it was agreed that France would give England a completely free hand in Egypt and the Sudan in return for English support of French interests in Morocco. The significance of the *Entente Cordiale,* as it came to be called, can hardly be exaggerated. It clearly implied that England, forced to choose between sharing naval and industrial supremacy on the one hand and colonial possessions on the other, would choose to share colonial possessions. It showed, too, that France would compromise on colonial issues but not on Alsace-Lorraine or the day of revenge and that her alignments, in short, would always be aimed at Germany.

Strangely, Germany did not show the concern that might have been expected. Already Italy had virtually slipped out of the

Triple Alliance, France and Russia and now England and France had drawn together. All of the dangers warned against by Bismarck were threatening. William, it is true, complained that Germany was becoming the object of encirclement. But the leaders of the New Course were either unaware of the serious turn that events were taking or, if they knew, were uncertain what to do about it. The Kaiser still dreamed his foolish dreams of a Continental System, with Germany virtually directing the foreign affairs of Austria-Hungary, Italy, France, and Russia. Von Tirpitz continued to believe that a big German navy would solve most of Germany's problems. Holstein, although admitting surprise at Anglo-French *rapprochement,* insisted that the real crux of the international situation lay in the unbridgeable gulf separating England and Russia. Of all these master mistake-makers, none erred more grievously than Holstein; for within three years the impossible gulf was bridged, and the Triple Entente stood poised against the Triple Alliance. We may now examine the progression of events that led to this ominous rebalancing of the forces of power.

## Formation of the Triple Entente

We have already noted that Russia, bogged down in her Balkan schemes, had decided to try her fortunes in north China. The same decision was reached by Japan at the same time. For the next several years each staked out its claims until in 1904 the expected collision occurred (see supra, p. 383). In the Treaty of Portsmouth which ended the war Russia ceded to Japan half of the island of Sakhalin, yielded up her foothold on the Liaotung Peninsula, and acknowledged special Japanese interests in Korea. Although Japan had been victorious, her financial and manpower resources had been so severely drained that she was willing to forgo demands regarding Manchuria, except those we have noted in an earlier section.

Russia, balked both in Europe and Asia, battered by war, and finally torn by revolution (see p. 502), looked about for means to recoup. England and France offered their services for a price. Both had been alarmed by the war. Linked to the rising Japanese power by the treaty of 1902, England was fearful that a too ambitious Japan might involve her in a large-scale war. France, quite understandably, wished to see her Russian ally unencumber herself in the East. Thus both worked to effect a *detente* between the late belligerents, a chore successfully concluded in 1907 when Russia and Japan signed an agreement acknowledging each other's spheres of influence in Manchuria. More by accident than design, then, the outlines of a Franco-Russo-English entente be-

gan to take shape. England had been remarkably friendly toward Russia in the Portsmouth negotiations. France was the ally of both. Why should not the friends of a friend themselves become friends? Logic and self-interest gave strong point to the question.

Another wrench tightening the alliance system was the authorization given in 1907 to French and English military and naval officials to meet and work out joint plans of action. From these discussions there ultimately emerged a pattern of reciprocal responsibilities. For example, the French fleet was assigned exclusively to the Mediterranean, leaving British squadrons to guard the Atlantic coasts. In the famous Plan XVII (counterpart to Germany's von Schleiffen plan) the deployment of French troops was shifted away from the Channel ports from which incoming British forces were to fan out. Political authorities in both countries took pains to point out (to each other; the public knew nothing of them) that these arrangements had no binding political force, that both nations remained free to act as their interests dictated. Some may actually have taken the disclaimer seriously.

This tripartite commingling encouraged Russia to turn again to the Balkans. But this time her courtship of her little Slav brother was more carefully planned. Her brusque treatment of Bulgarian officials was gone. Serbian complaints against Austria-Hungary were given sympathetic attention, even encouragement. Russian money and Russian agents filtered into Belgrade to foster the creation of a "blood brotherhood" designed to harass the Teutonic masters out of Bosnia and Herzegovina in preparation for the day of their reunion with the motherland.

But consolidation of Russia's position in the Balkans depended upon some kind of working rapport with Britain. Already, as we have seen, the groundwork for this had been laid. In 1907, as a token of her friendly feelings toward an old rival, Russia sent a squadron of warships into Portsmouth harbor on a courtesy call. Promptly responding to this amiable gesture, British admirals toasted their visitors while officials in Downing Street initiated an exchange of notes with ministers in the Russian embassy. More than the amenities of international intercourse were involved. Indeed, nothing less than the smoothing out of large imperial cross-purposes, under formal guarantees, was about to be undertaken. And if successful, that step would surely lead to others.

For years both nations had sought to establish hegemony over a sizable portion of the Middle and Far East—Persia, Afghanistan, and Tibet. Presumably, some kind of settlement there could prepare the way for the peaceful adjustment of general differences, both current and to come. A settlement of this type, moreover, could not but serve as a caution to Germany and Austria-Hungary. Under these benign promptings an agreement was formally concluded in June 1907. Persia was divided into three parts. The northern area was to be regarded as a Russian sphere of influence; the southern portion was "assigned" to Britain; a central section was to remain under Persian control as a buffer region. (In none of these decisions, incidentally, was the shah of Persia consulted.) Both states gave formal recognition to China's suzerainty over Tibet. Russia agreed to carry on all future negotiations between her government and Afghanistan through the good offices of the British.

## Mutual Distrust; "Alliance over All"

The juxtaposition of two great rival power blocs charged the European atmosphere with tense distrust. Entente diplomats increasingly feared what they thought of as the Machiavellian machinations of the Triple Alliance, particularly the schemes of Germany and Austria-Hungary. Germany's amazing industrial growth seemed to Britain a threat to her own supremacy, perhaps

even to her security. Germany's claim to "a place in the sun," coupled with von Tirpitz's plans to build a formidable "risk" navy, heightened Britain's concern. Austria's refusal to heed her subject peoples' demands for self-rule gave further credence to the charge that the Triple Alliance was an unholy combination based upon medieval principles of autocracy and elitism.

Germany and Austria in turn looked upon the Triple Entente as an international instrument of evil. Again and again the Kaiser protested what he called the malicious encirclement of Germany. France, he complained, rebuffed all his efforts to reach a friendly understanding; England persisted in regarding the high seas, world markets, and a large portion of the globe as hers by a kind of divine right. Similarly, Austria-Hungary considered the Triple Entente a direct threat to her existence as an empire. Austrian officials argued that Russia (aided by France whose commitments to Russia gave her even greater confidence) would never rest until Serbs, Croats, Slovenes, Czechs, Slovakians, and other subject peoples were pried loose from the control of the dual monarchy, and until she had firmly established herself in the Straits.

These attitudes and circumstances naturally fostered mutual suspicion and recrimination. Of course, diplomatic niceties contined to be observed. From time to time the major powers published ringing affirmations of their respect for such commonly held ideals as peace, the territorial integrity and independence of all peoples, and international cooperation. But the bread-and-butter business of diplomacy was something else. Ministers of state could not bring themselves to believe that their counterparts in other lands could be expected to be any more forthright than they were themselves. And "national interests" seemed to require both calculated disingenuousness (if not deception) and when the pacts of "acquisitive diplomacy" failed, big guns and loyal allies.

*For both Germany and France, Morocco was prized more for prestige than for economic purposes. The caption of this cartoon has one Moroccan asking, "Why do the French and Germans quarrel over our deserts? Now if we were only rich!" and the other replying, "If we were rich, my friend, the British would have seized us long ago."*

An increasingly disquieting development was the growing tendency of each of the great powers to regard its individual destiny as intricately bound up with the power and prestige of the group to which it belonged. If the Triple Entente suffered a diplomatic setback, France (or England or Russia) felt it had been weakened. The same was true of members of the Triple Alliance. Eventually an absurd kind of diplomatic algebra was worked out. The triumphs of alliance $T$ in conflicts 1 and 2 penalized alliance $E$ by x number of points. If $E$ in conflict 3 scored heavily enough, the balance might be righted or even tipped in its favor. If, however, either $T$ or $E$ consecutively lost y number of times, no future redress was possible. Admittedly these terms are somewhat fantastic. But they contain a hard core of truth, re-

peatedly revealed as European diplomacy unfolded its disastrous course in the opening years of the new century.*

Thus the imperialist thrust, the nationalist impulse, and the creation of a system of alliances designed to redress the balance of power had divided Europe into two armed camps before 1910. Piling armaments upon armaments each protested its horror of war and begged the other to mend its ways before a holocaust engulfed them all. Both met new, emergent crises with fear and fulmination and with an increasing conviction that compromise would only make matters worse. No one knew how many crises could occur before one of them would spark the conflagration. But each side hoped that the other would gain its senses long before that fatal fusing and call off its pyrotechnic displays of stubborn aggression.

## THE TAUTENED WEB: TESTING THE NEW BALANCE OF POWER

### The First Moroccan Crisis, 1905

Actually about fifteen more or less serious conflicts occurred in the period between 1904 and 1914. Each conflict added to the menace of the next and built up a cumulative tension. Several are worth examining in some detail: the first Moroccan crisis (1905); the so-called Buchlau Bargain and its aftermath (1908–1909); the second Moroccan crisis (1911); and the Balkan Wars (1912–1913).

The coming together of England and France in the "cordial understanding" of 1904 alarmed Germany. The Franco-Russian alliance was bad enough; the new entente, it was felt, would restrict Germany's freedom of action even more. Bulow, to be sure, pretended to regard it as a further

---

* Consider, for example, the British Foreign Secretary's remark when Delcassé was forced to resign as French Foreign Minister at Germany's insistence in 1905: "The fall of Delcassé is disgusting and has sent the *Entente* down any number of points on the market." Albertini, *op. cit.,* Vol. I, p. 158.

guarantee of the peace of Europe. But his public pose belied grave private apprehension. Holstein was even more agitated. Between them they agreed to break up the entente as quickly as possible. The Kaiser gave his full approval to this project, going so far as to warn, in another of his endless public pronunciamentos, that what had happened in 1871 could happen again.

Two developments conjoined to precipitate what has since been called the first Moroccan crisis. By 1904, even as Tirpitz had predicted, the German navy was well on its way to becoming the deterrent "risk" navy planned some years before. From now on English admirals would have to sing more softly. The second development evolved from a scheme of French Minister of Foreign Affairs Delcassé, one of the "new leaders" in European politics. Favoring an aggressive foreign policy Delcassé proposed, in 1905, to bring Morocco under French control. As a first move he asked England, Spain, and Italy to join with him in demanding financial and political "reforms" in that Arab state. With their approval he sent off a note to the sultan which clearly indicated forthcoming French pressure. Holstein, who had been waiting for such an opportunity, urged Bulow to enter a vigorous protest. As it happened, the Germans had international law on their side. In the so-called Madrid Convention of 1880 all the major western European powers had underwritten the neutral status of Morocco. Actually Bulow did not need urging. Delcassé's blunder, he believed, gave Germany its chance to inflict upon France—and thus upon the newly formed *Entente Cordiale*—a humiliating setback.

Accordingly the Kaiser paid a visit to Tangier in 1905 where he bluntly announced Germany's intention to safeguard the independence and territorial integrity of the threatened Moslem state. The next month, in a Reichstag speech, Bulow deplored the French action and demanded an international conference to deal with the crisis. The challenge could scarcely have been put more bluntly: France could pull out or fight.

Believing the Germans were bluffing, and in any case supported by the British government, Delcassé called for a showdown. He got it, but not the kind he had anticipated because his own colleagues, including the premier, demurred. They argued that the Madrid Convention gave the Germans a strong case, that Bulow was not bluffing, and that in the event of war the English navy could hardly help in the defense of Paris. Delcassé, they insisted, must resign. When he did, the German press jubilantly hailed the event as the just desserts of a warmonger. Rouvier, the French premier, had hoped that by thus appeasing Germany the demand for an international conference would be dropped. But Bulow and Holstein were not satisfied; the conference must be held and the French action must be officially condemned.

Now both the French and English governments felt alarm. What were Germany's intentions? Did she wish to protect her commercial interests in Morocco? If so, the dismissal of Delcassé had given clear proof that the French would do nothing to jeopardize them. Did she, perhaps, actually want a war? This was not easy to believe; but who could be sure? Certainly Germany's posture in international affairs had assumed an increasingly aggressive character. France's ally, Russia, was fighting a losing battle with Japan. Perhaps Germany believed the time was ripe to administer England, France, and Russia a crippling blow, and to make herself *the* European power. Diplomatic documents of the period reflect Entente apprehension. In a memorandum dated February 20, 1906, Sir Edward Grey, the newly appointed British Secretary of State for Foreign Affairs, wrote:

If there is a war between France and Germany, it will be very difficult for us to keep out of it. The *Entente,* and still more the constant and emphatic demonstrations of affection (official, naval, political, commercial, municipal and in

*Sir Edward Grey, British Minister for Foreign Affairs, was a strong, though cautious, advocate of Entente solidarity.*

the press) have created in France a belief that we should support her in war. . . . If this expectation is disappointed, the French will never forgive us. There would be, I think, a general feeling in every country that we had behaved meanly and left France in the lurch. The United States would despise us. Russia would not think it worth while to make a friendly arrangement with us about Asia, Japan would prepare to re-insure herself elsewhere, and Germany would take some pleasure, after what has passed, in exploiting the whole situation to our disadvantage. . . . On the other hand, the prospect of a European war and of our being involved in it is horrible.[3]

Germany, convinced that she held the trump cards, made it plain only an international conference would satisfy her. France yielded to this pressure. Meeting in Algeciras in January 1906, the powers debated the

3. Quoted by Albertini, *op. cit.,* Vol. I, pp. 166-167.

question for nearly three months. For a time it appeared that no agreement could be reached. Germany insisted upon genuine international supervision of Moroccan affairs. France argued that her position in Algeria made it necessary for her to exercise some kind of police power in the neighboring state. In the end a compromise was reached. All nations, including of course Germany, were guaranteed the right of free trade in Morocco. A police force under international control, but supervised by France and Spain, was created to maintain internal order. Overall supervision of the execution of the agreement was entrusted to the Diplomatic Corps at Tangier.

In a sense the Entente powers had suffered a serious setback. Clearly France had begun something she could not finish. Virtually at Germany's dictation a French foreign minister had been forced to resign. International, not French, control was established in Morocco. But it was an empty victory for Germany and her allies, since out of it came an even closer drawing together of England and France. Each felt it had been ordered about by Germany for all the world to see. Each believed the Entente could not survive another such public humiliation. Both agreed to work together more closely against the day when Germany should rattle the sword again.

Accordingly, Sir Edward Grey "entered into conversations" with Paul Cambon, the French ambassador (without, it should be added, obtaining the approval of his colleagues in the cabinet or even informing them of his action). They arranged for military persons of both countries to hold meetings periodically and work out joint plans of "defense." In the words of Sidney B. Fay:

The conversations continued right down to the outbreak of the war in 1914, and inevitably came to involve England in increasingly binding obligations of honor to support France in case of a European war arising out of any question whatsoever—not merely one arising out of the Morocco question—provided that

*As this cartoon rightly shows, the* Entente Cordiale *grew all the stronger as a result of the Moroccan affair of 1905–1906.*

*Count von Aehrenthal, Minister for Foreign Affairs for Austria-Hungary (1906–1912), was a strong proponent of Habsburg domination of the western Balkans.*

France did not appear to be the active aggressor. Probably Sir Edward Grey did not at the time see the full implications and danger of these "conversations" . . . . It was not until 1912 that circumstances caused (them) to be revealed to the whole Cabinet, and not until Grey's speech on August 3, 1914, that Parliament and the British public had any inkling of them.[4]

In a word, the Algeciras "settlement," far from reducing diplomatic tensions, increased them. Another crisis of this order might snap the thread that bound together the bristling powers in what passed for the peace of Europe. This test came soon.

## The "Buchlau Bargain": the Bosnian Crisis, 1908 to 1909

Several months after the Algeciras settlement, Count von Aehrenthal was made Austria's minister for foreign affairs. He had

4. *Origins of the World War,* 2 vols., Macmillan, New York, 1928, Vol. I, p. 208.

long felt great dissatisfaction with his country's posture in world affairs. The Empire, he believed, suffered from two chronic deficiencies. One was failure of nerve, a refusal to risk all to save all. The other was a remarkable inability to understand its true interest in the Balkans. He believed that a bold venture, resolutely carried out, would serve a double purpose. A coup of this type would inject *élan* and confidence into the body politic and prepare the Empire for a resumption of its old leadership; and at the same time it would provide a means for regaining world respect. Moreover, if this venture were to have its locus in the Balkans, by that very fact an immense shoring up of the

Empire's general European position would be effected. Many of its subject peoples were Slavs whose constant carping for unity and autonomy had kept the double state in continuous ferment. Especially troublesome were the Bosnians and Herzegovinians, forever clamoring for union with Serbia. If they were allowed to join their motherland, other ethnic groups would be encouraged to intensify their own nationalistic agitation. Surrender to one group would invite surrender to another, and another, until the Empire no longer existed. On the other hand, if Bosnia and Herzegovina were formally annexed and Serbia at the same time were dealt a crippling blow, prospects for the Empire's tomorrows would brighten. Gnawing fear of the Empire's dissolution would itself dissolve. Also, the plans of Austrian capitalists to invest in various Balkan projects would of course be rendered more secure.

A number of circumstances rather fortuitously combined to encourage Aehrenthal. For one thing, a long-overdue revolution in Turkey occurred in 1908, led by "the Young Turks," as they called themselves. Wearying under the corrupt rule of the sultans, they rallied support from all parts of the Ottoman Empire to set up a new and professedly liberal regime. Before long, it is true, the Young Turks succumbed to the same temptations which had corrupted the old rulers, but for a time the promise of a new day seemed bright. Oppressed peoples in the Balkans and throughout the Near East took heart; a kind of judgment day seemed at hand.

The revolution surprised and disturbed Aehrenthal. He cared not at all who managed Turkey's internal affairs. But the Young Turks showed signs of extending their reforms throughout the Ottoman Empire, of which Bosnia and Herzegovina were (at least technically) still parts. This made a difference. Aehrenthal intended his public justification for annexing the provinces to be the "enlightened" rule of Austria-Hungary. If the Young Turks anticipated him and moved

in with their baggage of promises, he could hardly pose as a reformer.*

At this point help came from an unlikely quarter. Rebuffed in the Far East, Russia turned her attention again to the Straits. Izvolsky, minister of foreign affairs, believed he could gain by shrewd maneuvering and compromise what an earlier show of force had failed to win. His overall plan was simple: Russia would wink at Austria's annexation of Bosnia-Herzegovina in return for Austria's sympathetic neutrality toward Russian efforts to open the Straits to Russian warships. To this end he sought an exchange of views with Aehrenthal.

The meeting was held on Aehrenthal's Buchlau estate in the fall of 1908. Since no official record was kept of the discussions, it is hard to say precisely what agreements were reached. Subsequently both parties published full accounts of their conversations, but they differed widely in important details. According to Izvolsky, Aehrenthal approved of Russian expansion in the south in return for a free hand for Austria in Bosnia-Herzegovina. Neither, however, was to act until both were ready and had agreed upon the proper moment or, in other words, until Izvolsky had sounded out Italy, France, and England and had obtained their consent. Aehrenthal later agreed that they had sympathetically discussed reciprocal support for each other's respective aims, but emphatically denied that any kind of timetable was involved.

Meanwhile Izvolsky had set out to make his rounds of the capitals. Rome had shown sympathetic interest, especially since the Russian minister had promised a benevolent attitude toward Italian interests in Tripoli. In Paris, the busy bargainer hoped to find an equally favorable response. But events over-

---

* At this early stage of the Young Turk revolt, neither Aehrenthal nor the beguiled Balkan peoples understood that the Young Turks, as one scholar has phrased it, "were not planning to liberate anyone but Turks."

took him. On the day of his arrival Parisian journals sensationally reported the Austrian *fait accompli.*

The reactions of most of the European states were prompt and vigorous. Serbian officials and their journalistic mouthpieces called upon all patriots to gird themselves for a final showdown with Austria. Bosnia and Herzegovina were their Alsace-Lorraine. If the Habsburgs were allowed to keep these provinces, all hope for a greater Serbia would vanish. Izvolsky, of course, was furious. The Russian half of the Buchlau bargain depended upon Anglo-French cooperation, the groundwork for which had not yet been laid. Moreover, he had plotted the affair without fully informing Tsar Nicholas or Prime Minister Stolypin of its details, particularly of the all-important commitment to Austria's annexation of Bosnia and Herzegovina. Caught in the dilemma, he decided to brazen it out and he thus called upon his Entente colleagues to demand an international conference. But Austria (strongly backed by Germany) stubbornly refused to agree to a conference. When Serbia ordered partial mobilization, Aehrenthal made it clear that Austria was not bluffing. He assured Serbia that if she did not demobilize and behave reasonably Austria would have to meet force with force.

Serbia's adamant stand presented Russia with the choice of backing her up or calling her off. When England and France shied away from all-out support for their ally, Russia was forced to accept a compromise solution offered by Germany. In essence the proposal was this: Germany would send notes to all the interested powers asking whether they would agree to Austria's annexation of the provinces. Affirmative responses would make an international conference unnecessary and at the same time would honor the principle of mutual consultation. Care would be taken, of course, to see that all parties agreed beforehand to the desired response. In addition, Serbia was

forced, at Aehrenthal's insistence, to issue a separate statement acknowledging that the annexation had violated none of her rights, and that henceforth she would conduct her relations with Austria-Hungary in a spirit of friendliness and good will. So the crisis was brought to an end. Troops were demobilized, the newspaper war was called off.

The Bosnian crisis and its aftermath led directly to World War I, then only five years away. As France had done in 1905, so Russia in 1909 bowed to the central powers. Austria, long regarded as a dying empire, had gained strength and initiative. In this new situation, Entente statesmen pondered two dolorous queries. What future was there for the Triple Entente if it gave the way whenever the managers of the Triple Alliance rattled the sword? And how, if the Entente had no future, could the individual nations that composed it hope to remain great powers in an Alliance-dominated world? Diplomats in St. Petersburg, Paris, and London agreed in their answers to both questions. They reasoned that unless the current power trend was reversed, all three states were destined ultimately to become pawns of the central powers. Clearly there must not be another Algeciras or another Bosnia.*

The annexation crisis prompted Serbian leaders, assisted by Russia, to form a secret terrorist organization (the *Narodna Obrana* —"National Defense") to prepare for the day of reckoning. It also prodded the quarreling Balkan states to put aside their ancient rivalries and create a united front. The aims of the Balkan League were to prepare for a favorable moment for a combined attack against Turkey, eject the Sick Man from Europe, and divide the spoils among themselves. Naturally Russia supported the

* The international scene just before World War II presented a remarkably similar pattern. How many more Munichs could England and France (and in effect, Russia) accept before acknowledging that Hitler's Germany was master of Europe? For an account of the Munich crisis, see *infra,* p. 573.

*A cartoon on the Second Moroccan crisis in 1911 which was sparked by Germany sending the gunboat* Panther *to Agadir.*

League (indeed, she helped to set it up). As its protectress and benefactor she could expect to share in the gains of the general settlement. France was also affected by the League's aims and activities because by this time she had come to rely heavily upon Russian support vis-à-vis a future showdown with Germany. France had also increasingly invested in Balkan commercial and industrial ventures. England was less directly interested in the plots and counterplots of Eastern Europe, but her commitments to France bound her much more intimately to Balkan affairs than her statesmen cared to admit.

## The Second Moroccan Crisis

The interdependence of ally upon ally was further shown in the second Moroccan crisis (1911). As signatory to the Act of Algeciras, France had publicly affirmed her recognition of Moroccan independence. But her intention to make that Arab state part of her African empire was as strong as ever. French loans to the sultan had made him a kept sovereign.

By fomenting disturbances in outlying areas, France created an excuse to intervene in the name of peace and order. In 1911 she occupied Fez, the capital city. At this point the German foreign minister held conversations with the French ambassador. The German minister made it plain that Germany was ready to recognize French control of Morocco, but only at a price. No precise demands were made, but the implication was clear that France should make a good offer. When the French showed no signs of discussing "compensation," Germany sent a gunboat to the Moroccan port of Agadir.

Apprising England of this development, France declared that she could not tolerate a repetition of the humiliation of 1905. This time, she made it clear, England must stand by her. In response the British foreign minister, Sir Edward Grey, suggested either a reasonable concession in the French Congo, or a division of Morocco into three spheres of control—French, German, and Spanish—with France receiving the lion's share. But Germany would not accept the first proposal, insisting now upon the whole of the French Congo, and France would not accept the second.

The pieces of the now-familiar pattern of challenge-counterchallenge again fell into place. Each power bloc charged the other with making unreasonable demands and of acting aggressively. Each fed its newspapers chauvinistic propaganda. Each feared that giving in to the other would deal its own prestige a serious, perhaps fatal, blow.

Finding France and Germany unwilling to carry on further conversations, England indirectly invited Germany to reconsider occupation of a part of the Congo. Receiving no reply, the British Cabinet began to wonder if Germany might be intending to remain in Agadir and "convert it into a formidable fortress within easy access of the Canaries, a threat to British interests . . . ." To warn Germany of the danger she was risking, the British Prime Minister authorized Lloyd George (then Chancellor of the Exchequer)

*David Lloyd George, British Prime Minister, 1916 to 1922.*

*In 1897, when this cartoon was drawn, the great powers favored peace in the Balkans because their imperialistic interests were centered elsewhere at the time.*

to make a forthright statement. Speaking at a Mansion House banquet in London, Lloyd George bluntly declared:

I believe it is essential in the highest interests, not only of this country, but of the world, that Britain should *at all hazards* maintain her place and prestige amongst the Great Powers of the world . . . . If a situation were to be forced upon us in which peace could only be served by the surrender of the great and beneficent position Britain has won by centuries of heroism and achievement, by allowing Britain to be treated when her interests were vitally affected as if she were of no account in the Cabinet of Nations, then I say emphatically that peace at *that price would be a humiliation intolerable for a great country such as ours to endure.*[5]

The challenge created a furor in Germany

5. Albertini, *op. cit.*, pp. 330–331 (italics added).

and brought Europe to the brink of war. At one point Grey himself believed hostilities might break out in a matter of hours. In a meeting with Lloyd George and Winston Churchill he said, "The Fleet might be attacked at any moment. I have sent for McKenna [First Lord of the Admiralty] to warn him." But in the end Germany moderated her demands and agreed to accept a large portion rather than the whole of the Congo. On November 4, 1911, a treaty was concluded which assigned certain African territories to Germany and the "protection" of Morocco to France. War was averted, but again at the price of increased international tension and bitterness.

## Balkan Wars, 1912 to 1913

In 1912 and 1913 another crisis occurred which brought Europe to the abyss that, a year later, engulfed it and eventually a large part of the rest of the world. The new crisis was a Balkan war deliberately precipitated by the newly formed League.

The League was made up of Serbia, Bul-

*Raymond Poincaré, French Minister of Foreign Affairs (1912–1913), and President of the Republic during the war, was a strong supporter of aggressive action by the Triple Entente.*

garia, Greece, and Montenegro. After Turkey's defeat by Italy in a brief war, 1910–11, these states believed their hour had come. By 1912 the great powers were so delicately balanced in their alignments that no single member dared to act unilaterally to prevent a Balkan flare-up. Russia and Austria, not yet ready for a showdown between themselves, warned the Balkan states not to attack Turkey. But the warning was ignored.

Thus Russia lost control of the Balkan League, which she had sponsored in order to use for her purposes. Instead of following the lead of their Russian patron, the Balkan statesmen struck out on their own and turned against the weakened Ottoman Empire. The French premier, Raymond Poincaré, described the situation aptly when on October 5, 1912, a week after the outbreak of the war, he remarked that "it is too late to wipe out the movement which she

(Russia) had called forth . . . she is trying to put on the brakes, but it is she who started the motor."[6]

Beaten on all fronts, Turkey capitulated in May 1913. Almost all of her European territory was taken from her by the victorious Balkan states. After more than four hundred years of foreign domination, the peoples of southeastern Europe could call their land their own. For the moment, nationalism had won over imperialism. But this was only for a moment because fresh quarrels broke out almost immediately among the victors. What land belonged to whom? Where did Bulgaria leave off and Greece begin? What were the "true" boundary lines of Serbia, Romania, and Montenegro? A new state, Albania, had been created by the treaty settlement. What were to be its boundaries, fixed at whose expense? Bulgaria, having made larger gains than the others, was the special object of recriminatory charges. In an effort to redress the balance Serbia, Greece, and Montenegro concerted to force a rewriting of the treaty. When Bulgaria refused to negotiate, the three states promptly sent their armies marching against their erstwhile ally. Romania joined them, soon followed by Turkey. In this second Balkan war, Bulgaria was unable to stand against attackers who completely ringed her. In August 1913, she agreed, in the Treaty of Bucharest, to a sharp whittling down of her original demands. Naturally this intra-Slav bitterness dissolved the Balkan League, which, in turn, led to further complications. In the words of Sir Edward Grey, the Treaty of Bucharest

had in it the seeds of inevitable future trouble. It left Bulgaria sore, injured, and despoiled and deprived of what she believed belonged to her . . . Turkey, of course, was also sore and despoiled . . . . The settlement after the second Balkan War was not one of justice but of force. It stored up inevitable trouble for the time to come. To make peace secure for the future, it

6. Stavrianos, *The Balkans Since 1453*, pp. 534-535.

*The powers of both alliance systems were apprehensive over inter-Balkan squabbles in 1912 and 1913, as this German cartoon suggests.*

*Maurice Paléologue was French Ambassador to Russia in the years immediately preceding World War I. He could always be counted on to give vigorous support to Entente aggressiveness.*

would have been necessary for the Great Powers to have intervened to make the settlement of Bucharest a just one. This they did not do, being too afraid of trouble among themselves. They were afraid to move lest they should come into contact with each other, and yet their very care to prevent falling out among themselves in 1913 was, in fact, going to render peace more precarious in the year that followed.[7]

## The Aftermath of the Balkan Wars

Several of the Balkan states emerged from the war against Turkey with sharpened tastes and tempers. Extreme Serbian nationalists, for example, formed the Union of Death (more commonly known as the Black Hand Society), a secret organization dedicated to effecting the early "return" of Bosnia-Herzegovina to the motherland. Their methods were frankly terroristic. Cov-

ertly supported by Russian agents, the Society sought to convince Austria that the retention of the provinces was not worth an endless future of bombings and assassinations. The Serbian government did not support, or even favor, such sanguine activities. Nevertheless, it continued to agitate for satisfaction of its irredentist claims. So both officially and unofficially Serbia stepped up its pressures on Austria-Hungary. Similarly, other Balkan states nurtured territorial ambitions and made preparations for the next round.

Although not a direct outcome of the Balkan wars, a French army bill that was passed in 1913 further heightened the atmosphere of crisis in European chancelleries. This bill lengthened the term of conscript service from two to three years. Alliance powers denounced it as clear evidence of Entente ag-

7. Edward Grey, *Twenty-Five Years,* Frederick A. Stokes Company, New York, 1925, 2 vols., Vol. I, pp. 253–254.

gressive designs. Naturally Russia saw nothing but good in it. Inspired perhaps by the Tsar's minister of war, an article in a Russian newspaper put it bluntly: "Russia is prepared; France too must be so." Maurice Paléologue, an influential French ambassador to Russia when World War I broke out and a close friend of Poincaré, repeatedly stressed the need for an army build-up if the Entente powers hoped to stand up to their rivals. Urging passage of the bill in 1913, Paléologue argued "that the probability of war with Germany, or more exactly, of a great European conflict, increases from day to day . . . . We must make ourselves strong without delay." One year later he told a colleague, "I have the inward conviction that we are moving towards the storm. At what point on the horizon and on what date it will break I am unable to say, but war is now irrevocable."[8]

Derived from whatever sources and shaped by whatever purposes, the ambassador's conviction proved terribly true.

## Assessment of the Effect of the Alliance System

It is arguable whether or not the entangling web of interlacing forces and events had so caught up the powers of Europe in the Alliance system that that system automatically, as it were, prescribed and prefixed the responses and postures of the committed nations. We have seen that as crisis succeeded crisis the range of choice seemed to narrow almost to zero and the direction of movement seemed to point irreversibly toward war. But historians are not agreed that this was quite the situation. What appears to some latter-day historians as the "eve of war" may not, others hold, have appeared so to many statesmen and citizens of that time. It cannot be disputed that alliance confronted alliance. But the "interpenetration of alliances" was also a fact beyond dispute. For example, in late 1912 Austria and Russia worked together in an attempt to prevent a

flare-up in the Balkans. When it occurred in spite of this inter-alliance pressure, Austria opposed letting the Serbs gain access to the Adriatic. Here German support for her ally was both reluctant and qualified. More significantly, on this same issue England supported Austria against her own ally's wishes. In June 1914, the thorny question of the Berlin-to-Baghdad railroad was settled when Britain and Germany initiated a compromise that suggested the possibility of other settlements of interalliance disputes by peaceful negotiation. As a final example of flexibility within the seemingly inflexible alliance system, Germany, in this same month, insisted upon a Balkan policy vis-à-vis Austrian reconciliation with Serbia, Romania, and Greece quite consonant with Russian and French interests but decidedly opposed by the Austrians.

On the other hand, other developments seemed to give point to Palélogue's conviction that "we are moving toward the storm." In November and December of 1913, the Turkish government appointed a German general, Liman von Sanders, to reorganize the Turkish army and to take command of its first corps at Constantinople. To edgy Russian officials this seemed a clear signal that the Triple Alliance powers were moving to thwart, once for all, Russia's designs to open the Straits to their warships. When France strongly supported her ally, it appeared that war was imminent. Although a compromise was finally worked out (January 1914), the episode heightened the atmosphere of suspicion that already made "alliance coexistence" a precarious undertaking. Evidence of its somewhat ghostly quality is found, for example, in documents which reveal discussions in a Russian crown council held February 21, 1914. In this meeting the council ominously concluded that Russian aims in the Straits "could be attained only in case of a European war." Simultaneously, British and Russian representatives were busy working out details of a naval convention whose purpose was to synchronize the functions

8. Albertini, *op. cit.*, pp. 554–555.

and spheres of activity of their squadrons in the event of war.

Thus the Alliance system, marked in its actual workings by elements of both flexibility and inflexibility, should not be thought of as a monolithic structure inescapably driving the world to war. Still, it would be inexcusable casuistry to underestimate the tug toward war that was so manifestly a feature of that system. In the opening section of the next chapter we will note the alliance system's relative position among the causes of World War I.

## SELECTED READINGS

Albertini, L., *The Origins of the War of 1914,* translated by I. M. Massey, Oxford University Press, London, 1952–1957, 3 vols.

> The most recent study of this much written about subject. Except for important new material on Italy's behavior and position in —and outside of—the politics of the Triple Alliance, there is little in these volumes that is not found in Fay, cited below.

Angell, Norman, *The Great Illusion,* G. P. Putnam's Sons, New York, 1913.

> An eloquent argument on the incompatability of war and modern civilization. The author treats the economic, moral, psychological, and biological conditions that argue against war in a way that is so convincing that the book became a classic in a remarkably short time but, as its publication date suggests, it was not convincing enough to prevent or even postpone the 1914 to 1918 reenactment of "the great illusion."

Brandenburg, Erich, *From Bismarck to the World War,* translated by Ann Adams, Oxford University Press, London, 1927.

> Another study, this time from the German point of view, of the coming of World War I. For those who have read Fay or Sontag, this work is chiefly interesting for the opportunity it offers to evaluate the force of national bias in historical narration.

Coolidge, Archibald Cary, *Origins of the Triple Alliance,* Charles Scribner's Sons, New York, 1926.

> This is a good short treatment of the subject. The "Notes" section in which the author makes use of material not available to him when the book first appeared in 1917 is particularly interesting. Students thus have the rather rare opportunity of noting how a competent professional historian revises his material, recognizes and corrects original misinterpretations, and integrates new data into a previously written account.

Dickinson, G. L., *The International Anarchy,* The Century Co., New York, 1926.

> Based on the belief that the absence of world government produced World War I and will continue to produce world wars, this book examines the general condition of the great powers after the Franco-Prussian War, the formation of the Triple Alliance and the Triple Entente, and the long series of crises, beginning with the Moroccan crisis of 1905 and 1906, which culminated in World War I. It is one of the most effective polemics that has been written against the sovereign-state system since that system was established.

Fay, Sidney B., *The Origins of the World War,* The Macmillan Co., New York, 1929, 2 vols.

> Written nearly 40 years ago, this is still the best general account of the diplomatic background of World War I. It divides responsibility among the powers of both alliance systems. Although the author warns against assigning guilt according to any definite formula, he nevertheless ends up giving the reader a fairly clear feeling of which powers are more to blame than other powers for the coming of the war, and why they are blameworthy. All of the crises cited in this and the succeeding chapter are treated in detail. Excellent character sketches of the statesmen of the period (1870–1914) are woven into the narrative. Volume I deals with the background causes of the war; Volume II deals with the immediate causes.

Gooch, G. P., *Recent Revelations of European Diplomacy,* Longmans, Green & Co., London, 1928.

*Asterisk (*) denotes paperback.

This is a book about people and the books they wrote dealing with, justifying, condemning or, too rarely, apologizing for events that led to World War I. Almost all of the foremost statesmen of the time either wrote of their roles themselves or were made the subjects of the accounts of others. In addition to being a significant contribution to an understanding of why the war came, the book is highly readable as a literary work.

Langer, William L., *European Alliances and Alignments, 1871–1890,* Alfred A. Knopf, New York, 1931.

Concerned with "the fundamental forces and broad currents that influenced the relations of states to each other" in the twenty-year period following the Franco-Prussian War. Among these forces are religion, Balkan nationalism, colonial activity, and Bismarck's efforts to keep both the peace and Prussia's new position of power in Germany and Europe. Although it covers much of the same ground as the first volume of Fay's book, its approach is different. Fay writes to explain why the war came; Langer is more interested in examining the developments for their own sake.

Manhart, George B., *Alliance and Entente, 1871–1914,* F. S. Crafts & Co., New York, 1932.

One of the *Landmarks in History Series,* this little work (of less than 100 pages) offers a taste of source material that stimulates the appetite. Pertinent portions of most of the basic diplomatic agreements are presented—the first treaty between Austria, Germany, and Italy; the First Mediterranean Pact; the Dual Alliance; the naval convention between France and Russia; and about thirty other treaties, conventions, or statements by leading diplomats of the period.

Medlicott, W. N., *Bismarck, Gladstone, and the Concert of Europe,* The Athlone Press, London, 1956.

The author develops the thesis that from the late 1870s until the early 1880s the more basic features of European politics were fixed by the contest between Gladstone and Disraeli in which Gladstone tried to revive the old Concert of Europe and Disraeli worked to set up a system of close alliances.

————, *The Congress of Berlin and After,* Methuen and Co., London, 1938.

Useful for those who have not read the author's *Bismarck, Gladstone, and the Concert of Europe,* cited above.

Mowat, R. B., *The Concert of Europe,* Macmillan and Co., London, 1930.

A general account of the main developments in international affairs in the period from 1870 to 1914.

Nicolson, Harold, *Portrait of a Diplomatist,* Harcourt, Brace & Co., New York, 1930.

A study of the "old diplomacy" as portrayed in the assumptions and behavior of a genteel Englishman—the author's father—whose nineteenth-century patriotism is held up as a sad example of what was wrong with the civilization that produced World War I. Good for details of the first Moroccan crisis and the Anglo-Russian entente.

Pribram, Alfred Franzis, *The Secret Treaties of Austria-Hungary, 1879–1914,* Harvard University Press, Cambridge, 1920–1921, 2 vols.

Since the dual empire was significantly involved in most of the political affairs of Central and Eastern Europe as these touched international relations, this carefully researched work is of high importance. Although the author was an Austrian, he has kept his bias well within bounds in both his selection of documents and his comments upon them.

Renouvin, Pierre, *The Immediate Origins of the War,* translated by Theodore Carswell Hume, Yale University Press, New Haven, 1928.

This is an extended treatment of the diplomatic and military activity of the great powers and Serbia during the fateful six weeks that followed the assassination of Archduke Franz Ferdinand. Despite claims of objectivity for the book, the reader must leave it feeling that Germany and Austria-Hungary were culpable beyond any stubborness or shortsightedness shown by

Britain, France, and Russia. As an exercise in comparative historiography, interested students should compare this account with that of Fay or Brandenburg.

*Rosenberg, Arthur, *Imperial Germany, The Birth of the German Republic 1871–1918,* translated by Ian F. D. Morrow, Beacon Press, Boston, 1964.

The first two chapters discuss the social forces at work under Bismarck and the politics of conflict in Kaiser William II's Germany. These chapters are perhaps the best account in brief compass that can be found. The rest of the book (about 200 pages) presents the futile struggle for victory and peace, in a conceptual framework and in an economy of words which deserve careful study.

Schmitt, Bernadotte E., *The Coming of the War, 1914,* Charles Scribners' Sons, New York, 1930, 2 vols.

The chief advantage of this book over Fay's and Sontag's is its great amplitude of detail. For example, almost eighty pages are devoted to the Austro-Hungarian note of 1914, and Serbia's reply to it. The author's readable style is an advantage. It has two other less desirable features. It deals only (except for the first two chapters) with the immediate coming of the war; and it's bias is distinctly pro Entente powers.

Seton-Watson, R. W., *Sarajevo,* Hutchinson & Co., London, 1925.

An intensive and illuminating study of the "Eastern Question," whose ramifications brought on World War I.

Sontag, Raymond James, *European Diplomatic History, 1871–1932,* The Century Co., New York, 1933.

The author's main concern is to present a study of how Europe's diplomats tried, in the period stated in the title, to effect "desirable changes in the international *status quo,*" and how to prevent "undesirable changes . . . without recourse to war." He tries to hold in abeyance postwar judgments as he tells the story of prewar diplomacy, and to view postwar developments in the light in which he believes the diplomats themselves saw them. If Fay's two volumes cannot be read, this one should be.

Taylor, A. J. P., *The Struggle for Mastery in Europe, 1848–1918,* Oxford University Press, Oxford, 1954.

Lively, provocative, highly readable. The author certainly has a thorough command of the facts; his interpretation of some of them makes this one of the most controversial of all of the works dealing with this period. It deserves thorough study, but it should not be the only reference used.

Tyler, Mason Whiting, *The European Powers and the Near East, 1875–1908,* University of Minnesota, Minneapolis, 1925.

A detailed study of the conflicting forces at work in the Balkans in the generation before World War I. If the works of neither Langer, Sontag, nor Fay are read, effort should be made to read this one.

# XI

# *World War I and Its Settlement*

This chapter focuses on four years of violence and the uneasy "settlement" that followed them. But no consideration of this period of war and peace can have much meaning unless we understand why the violence occurred. Most of the requisites for this understanding were presented, either explicitly or by implication, in the preceding chapter. Here they are brought together in a new form in order to deal with the question more directly. Lest false hopes be raised, it must be admitted at once that the "answer" is neither clear-cut nor wholly satisfactory. For one thing, the explanations are both multiple and diverse. For another, it is very difficult to sort them out according to the proportionate weight of their influence. Of the causes discussed here, the first five are treated as contributing agents and the last three as more fundamental causes; however, they were all operative to one degree or another in bringing on the war.

## WHY THE WAR CAME

It was once rather generally believed that the "new" imperialism was the basic cause of the war, and a few scholars still hold this view. For a generation after 1870, as we have seen, most of the great states and some of the lesser ones brought ever-widening portions of Africa, Asia, and America under some kind of control or influence. Whether motivated by the search for new markets or by national pride, these aggressive ventures naturally promoted a spirit of rivalry which seriously strained relations among the powers. For a while in 1898 it seemed that France and England would fight for control of Egypt and the Sudan.* International tensions almost reached the breaking point in Morocco in 1905, and the second Moroccan crisis in 1911 posed another serious threat of war. The list of imperial clashes could easily be multiplied. However, a closer and more critical study of these recurring crises has convinced most historians that overseas expansion was not the main cause of the war. They argue that statesmen seemed to sense that their peoples were not of a mind to go to war over color on the map. They point to the effective dampening of the flame of each crisis, however high it might flicker

* For these and the following references, see map, *supra*, p. 407.

for a time, as proof of their thesis that issues that are consistently the subject of successful compromise can scarcely be considered causes of war. Nevertheless, they all agree that the new imperialism accentuated and conditioned the drift toward war.

The system of counterpoised alliances which formed after the Congress of Berlin (1878) certainly allowed their members to indulge in a more venturesome and even reckless outlook and posture than they would otherwise have done. It is quite impossible, for example, to believe that Austria-Hungary would have annexed Bosnia-Herzegovina in 1908, had she not been convinced that Germany would stand between her. and an outraged Russia.* Or that France would have allowed herself to become so deeply committed to Russian schemes in the Balkans after 1912, had she not felt that she could count heavily on British help in case of serious trouble. We should not, of course, confuse the alliance system with the many threatening conditions that caused its creation. By itself, the alliance system was harmless; as a contributory agent, it had influence that must not be overlooked or underestimated.

The same is true of secret diplomacy. If the peoples of the world had known the details of the bargains and commitments made by their political leaders in the half century before the war, possibly neither leaders nor commitments would have long survived. But diplomacy, secret or open, is a procedure; it is not a goal, a hope, a vision, or any of the other things men fight over and for.

The collective forces labeled Pan-Slavism and Pan-Germanism fed aspirations and excited passions that gave an ominous cast to certain critical decisions. Russia's return to the troubled Balkans after her defeat by Japan in 1905 cannot be explained without acknowledging such aspirations and passions,

although of course they were not the only motivating forces. As we shall see, Serbia decided in 1914 to stand against a great empire which, she knew, was backed by an even mightier empire. That she counted on Russia, her big Slav brother, to come to her aid is beyond dispute. Germany's thrust through the Balkans and into Mesopotamian lands, necessitated by her Berlin-to-Bagdad railroad project (see *supra,* p. 405), would have been highly unlikely in the absence of close ties with the Teutonic ruling elite of Austria, which was interested in developing hegemony over lands to the east. The force of ethnic feelings cannot, of course, be calibrated by any tool at the historian's disposal, but its deep and abiding influence is an evident fact of life. Even so, Pan-Slavism and Pan-Germanism, like the new imperialism and the alliance system, encouraged rather than caused the drift to war.

In recent years there has been a revival of interest in the idea that domestic conditions played a crucial role in the coming of the war. In his *Political Origins of the New Diplomacy, 1917-1918,* Arno Mayer argues that domestic unrest in Germany, France, England, Austria-Hungary, and Russia deserves serious study in a general assessment of the forces that produced the war. He suggests, for example, that Tsar Nicholas II may "have been prepared to repeat the 1904–05 experiment [the war with Japan] of seeking to ward off pressures for internal reform by engaging in an international venture."[1] Another historian has gone much further:

In the last resort the First World War was brought about by the coincidence of two opposite beliefs. The rulers of Austria-Hungary believed that there would be revolution if they did not launch a war; the rulers of Germany were confident that there would not be a revolution if they did.[2]

---

\* It will be recalled that Isvolski had agreed to annexation in the "Buchlau bargain." But Austria knew that her precipitate action in annexing the province before Isvolski had matured his schemes would cause trouble.

1. Yale University Press, New Haven, 1959, p. 11.
2. A. J. P. Taylor, *The Struggle for Mastery of Europe, 1848–1918,* Clarendon Press, Oxford, 1954, p. xxix.

It is true that in each of the great states, including the United States, labor unrest and, in some countries, socialist agitation gave the ruling classes considerable concern in the years before the war. It is reasonable to suppose, at least for the autocratic regimes of Germany, Austria-Hungary, and Russia, that conservative rulers may have wondered whether a grand, patriotic rally might not divert the working man's attention from home conditions. The force of this argument is somewhat weakened, however, by available documentary evidence. In 1914 less than 10 per cent of the French labor force belonged to unions. In England, strikes were substantially fewer than they had been in the four years immediately preceding 1914. The same general situation prevailed in Germany and Russia.* Many industrialists and their political spokesmen, moreover, believed that a war, far from dampening labor unrest and agitation, might turn them into a real revolution. Sir Edward Grey, for example, warned an Austrian diplomat in the last days of peace in the summer of 1914: "Beware, a war would be accompanied or followed by a complete collapse of European credit and industry. In these days, in great industrial states, this would mean a state of things worse than that of 1848."[3] Nevertheless, domestic unrest as a condition fostering international war should be kept in calculation in any serious assessment of the forces that brought on World War I.

Anglo-German economic rivalry played a large part in bringing on the world conflict. From 1898 to 1913, Germany made enormous export gains over England. For example, in this period England barely doubled her exports to the United States;

Germany increased hers five times over. Figures for other areas show the same trend: English exports to India increased a little more than twofold, while Germany's increase was sixfold; England tripled her exports to Argentina, Germany quintupled hers; English exports to China increased about 100 per cent, German exports increased nearly 200 per cent. Germany's rate of increase exceeded England's in the construction of merchant ships by about 400 per cent. Naturally, both British industrialists and merchants and British statesmen were deeply troubled by this situation. On the other hand, as the clouds of war gathered in 1914, British industrial and financial concerns almost frantically implored the government to save the peace. Still, it is hard to believe that this rivalry did not incline England toward some kind of drastic solution to preserve her favorable balance of trade, and that in Germany it did not foster a heightened determination to gain what its merchants and industrialists considered their fair share of the world's wealth.

The strong emphasis in the prewar years on military buildup was a substantial force in the creation of the conditions that caused the war. The formation of large conscript armies and the massive stockpiling of armaments naturally developed in both the leaders and the people an outlook that was conducive to an easy acceptance of war as an instrument of national policy. The influence of chiefs of staff and other military leaders became so decisive in the crucial weeks of 1914 that it dominated all other influences. All the evidence indicates that most of the civilian leaders of the Alliance and Entente powers wanted to find a way to avoid war in the summer of 1914; however, as we shall see, generals, not diplomats and political leaders, had the last word.

There can be no doubt that nationalism was a prime cause of the war, both the "my-country-right-or-wrong" variety and the kind that aimed to free ethnic groups from foreign influence or dominance. The five-thousand-

---

* In Germany, it should be noted, the Socialists became, in the 1912 elections, the largest party in the Reich.

---

3. *British Documents on the Origins of the War,* Vol. XI, p. 70, quoted in Élie Hálevy, *The Era of Tyrannies,* Anchor Books, New York, 1965, p. 222.

year record of civilization makes it clear that all peoples, of whatever race, language, or habitat, have, at least potentially, the same general virtues and vices. In spite of this, ethnic groups—large or small, advanced or backward, rich or poor—tend to fall victim to a universal illusion. Each group thinks of itself as a kind of sacred community, a special God-touched breed whose "national interests," to use the current phrase, must take precedence over all other interests within or without that sacred community. When this emotion is whipped up by either outside circumstances or inside political machinations, its force is incalculable. It is also almost beyond explaining. For years German socialists preached the evil of war as an instrument of national policy when formulated and executed by capitalist rulers. Even as late as one month before the war, German and French socialist leaders urged worker nonparticipation if the two countries should be drawn into a capitalist war. Yet, when the war came, they virtually unanimously voted war credits for their own country and urged patriotic support of the government.

Nevertheless, it was ethnic nationalism that directly precipitated the war. In the next section we shall discuss pertinent details of the surge of nationalism in the Balkans, which directly led to wholesale declarations of war among the great powers of Europe. Here our purpose is best served, perhaps, by noting the judgment of a longtime student of the war crisis:

We should ask not *who,* but *what,* was responsible for the three declarations of war [of the Central Powers against Serbia, Russia, France]; and the answer should be: "The rotten condition of the Austro-Hungarian Empire, the fact that the revolutionary principle of nationality was at work within its limits, and that it was about to break up into a number of independent states."[4]

We do not know enough yet to go much beyond this general assessment of the underlying causes of the war. The record is sadly satisfying, however, as to *why* it began *where* it did.

## THE WAR

### *Sarajevo*

By 1914, Franz Josef, Emperor of Austria, had ruled his sprawling Empire for nearly seventy years. His apparent successor-to-be, Archduke Franz Ferdinand, quite understandably had long been preparing for the

4. Hálevy, *op. cit.,* p. 234.

day when he would become the Empire's royal master. Of special interest to him was the thorny Bosnian question. He believed that the solution lay in a reorganization of the basic political structure of the Empire. Hungarian dissidence had been reduced to manageable proportions by the creation of the Dual Monarchy. Would not Slavic disaffection yield to the same treatment? Convinced that it would, he urged that the Dual Monarchy be changed into a Trial Monarchy in which the Serbian inhabitants of Bosnia-Herzegovina would enjoy autonomy as well as limited participation in Empire affairs. To Serbian nationalists the proposal represented an insidious danger. It blunted the edge of their propaganda and would, if put into effect, destroy all hope of reunion within any future time that they cared to think about. They were determined, therefore, to abort the Trialist program. If this should mean more trouble with Austria, as it surely would, then Austria must expect to experience the humiliation that Serbia had experienced in 1908, because Serbia was sure that this time Russia (backed by France) would stand firmly with her Slav brother.

In the confused and volatile atmosphere generated by these ethnic, military, and diplomatic combustibles, the Austrian Archduke visited Bosnia on an inspection tour in the spring of 1914. Widely publicized in advance, the visit gave the Bosnian conspirators who were based in Serbia a rare opportunity to combine terror with the elimination of the architect of the hated Trialist program. Accordingly, a contingent of assassins converged on Sarajevo, the Bosnian capital, which the Archduke and his party planned to honor with a one-day visit. The particular day for the visit, June 28, could scarcely have been less opportunely chosen. To Serbians it was known as Vidoudan (St. Vitus Day), an annual day of mourning "commemorating the battle of Kosovo, which in 1389 rang the death knell of the medieval Serbian empire." Thus for some Serbian nationalists hallowed memories

*Archduke Franz Ferdinand and his family. The Archduke and his wife were assassinated by Gavrilo Princip, right.*

merged with present miseries to transmute murder into high patriotism.

On the day of the visit the official motorcade had scarcely entered the city's limits when a bomb was thrown at the Archduke's car. It rolled off the hood and wrecked the next car behind it. A second attempt was successful when an assassin stepped from the curb and fired directly into the royal carriage. Both the Archduke and his wife (an accidental victim) were killed. More literally than those celebrated by Emerson in the *Concord Hymn,* these shots were heard round the world. Exactly thirty-eight days after the fateful shooting most of the major nations of Europe were involved in a war which, before its bloody end, encompassed the world.

Austria's immediate reaction belied her real intentions. The government was determined to exploit the crime so effectively that Serbia would be destroyed as an independent power. Such drastic action would put an end, once for all, to the insidious Slavic agitation that for so long had eaten away at the foundations of the Empire. In short, the sword must finish in 1914 what Austrian diplomacy had begun in 1908. But secret preparations had first to be worked out in detail. Consequently, the immediate official reaction was surprisingly mild.

Behind the scenes the diplomats were busy. Without an absolute guarantee of German support, Austria's grand purpose was vain. Would Germany pledge such support? To gain it, a special emissary was sent to Berlin. He argued that "the gulf between the Monarchy and Serbia is beyond bridging over." If Serbia remained unpunished, the Empire's days were numbered. Without the Empire, the Triple Alliance was a scrap of paper. And with the Treaty destroyed, Germany would be left standing alone, encircled by the Entente powers. The emissary relayed the Kaiser's prompt response to the Austrian government.

As regards any action on our [Austria's] part against Serbia, he thought such action should not be delayed. Russia's attitude would doubtless be hostile, but he had been prepared for that for years, and even if it should come to a war between Austria and Russia, we would be convinced that Germany would stand by our side with her accustomed faithfulness as an ally.[5]

Later the Kaiser was to regret having given what came to be called the "blank check"; but by then events made it difficult for Germany to reverse her course.* Hungary's consent, at first withheld, was bought by the promise of compensations.

After these diplomatic roadblocks had been removed, Austrian officials set themselves to composing an ultimatum that was deliberately designed to be unacceptable. On July 23, 1914, it was presented to Serbia, who was given forty-eight hours in which to reply. Anticipating such a note, Serbia had earlier consulted her Russian ally. If Serbia resisted, would Russia support her? Convinced that France by now was too intricately and irrevocably involved in Russia's Balkan

5. Quoted in Sidney B. Fay, *The Origins of the World War,* Vol. II, pp. 203–204.

---

* A good deal of scholarly hassling has gone on concerning the nature and significance of the "blank check." Good detailed accounts are found in the cited works of Fay and Albertini.

commitments to yield again to German pressure, Russia counseled Serbia to stand firm against humiliating demands. The position of England was more obscure. But France believed that her ally across the Channel would not permit the Central Powers to destroy the Entente, particularly because the military and naval conversations from 1912 on had so deeply, albeit unofficially, committed the forces of both to joint action.

Serbia was conciliatory in her reply, but refused the demands that infringed on her sovereignty. Austria rejected the reply immediately and ordered mobilization. Russia announced her intention to stand by Serbia and accordingly mobilized against Austria. Because Russia was certain that Germany would enter the war on Austria's side, mobilization along the German border was also ordered. The great showdown was at hand.

## The Futile Search for Peace

During these moments when, as Sir Edward Grey later put it, the lights were going out all over Europe, a last-minute flurry of fear caused civilian authorities in most chancelleries to try to change the course of the events that their own policies had predestined. Almost frantically the Kaiser sought a formula that would save the peace. In this doomed endeavor Tsar Nicholas joined him in his typically befuddled manner. The aged Austrian Emperor did what he could to localize the conflict. Grey and his colleagues in London proposed a general conference of the powers. But military considerations blocked all such efforts. The Tsar was told by his Chief of Staff that partial mobilization—that is, only against Austria— was senseless.* Everybody knew, he argued,

that if Russia supported Serbia, which meant fighting Austria, Germany would join Austria, which meant fighting Russia. Unless Russia was prepared for this, action against Austria alone was worse than no action at all. Similarly, German military officials assured the Kaiser that support of Austria automatically meant war with Russia, which in turn meant war with France† because France could not be expected to disavow her obligations to Russia. Similar pressures were at work in Austria and France. Thus when World War I came in the opening days of August 1914, the dictates of military strategy were the primary force that triggered it.

The specific events that put the armies in motion may be briefly summarized. On July 28, 1914, Austria-Hungary declared war on Serbia and the next day bombarded its capital, Belgrade. On July 30, Russia ordered general mobilization. On July 31, England asked France and Germany to respect the neutrality of Belgium. Germany declined to commit herself; France readily agreed. At the same time Germany dispatched warning notes to Russia and France. On this day, too, Austria ordered mobilization along the Russian border. On August 1, Germany, receiving an unsatisfactory reply from Russia, declared war against her. The next day the English cabinet authorized Sir Edward Grey to inform the French ambassador that "if the German fleet comes into the Channel or through the North Sea to undertake hostile operations against the French coast or shipping, the British fleet will give all the protection within its power."[6] Belgium received notification from Germany that German troops must be granted right of free passage across her territory. When this was refused, August 3, Belgian fortifications

---

* Technically, it was more than senseless—it was impossible. Neither Russia nor Germany had plans that allowed for partial mobilization. In this sense the fears of the chiefs of staff were well grounded; either they totally mobilized their armies or they saw them stand helpless before the mobilization of foreign armies.

† That is, according to the assumptions and provision of the Schlieffen Plan (discussed later) which in effect made any war in Europe but a phase of a developing general war.

6. Quoted by Fay, *Origins of the World War*, Vol. II, p. 540.

were attacked. The German government also declared war against France when that nation, in reply to the German ultimatum, refused to promise neutrality. On August 4, England sent an ultimatum to Germany demanding the evacuation of Belgium. When Germany ignored it, England declared war against her.

Italy refused to join her partners on the ground that Austria was the aggressor. Her real purpose in staying out was to bargain for territory. Because her irredentist claims were directed against Austria, only one outcome was possible. In May 1915, after concluding a secret treaty with the Entente powers, who promised her nearly all that she wanted, Italy entered the war against her former ally. Other states had become involved even earlier. Turkey and Bulgaria joined the Central Powers in the Fall of 1914 in the hope of participating in the partition of Serbia. Japan declared war against Germany at about the same time. Her aim was simple—to take over German interests in the Far East. All together, before the guns fell silent four years later, over sixty nations were actively or passively involved in the war.

## Western Stalemate

Germany's plans called for a holding action against Russia, which would permit her main forces to execute an overpowering thrust into France. According to the German timetable,* about six weeks would be needed to crush the French and Allied armies, encircle and occupy Paris, and force the Western powers to sue for peace. The holding action against Russia would then be turned into an all-out offensive. Altogether four or five months of serious fighting should bring the war to a victorious close. For their part, the French planned to launch an attack in the Metz-Strasbourg area (south of the

German attack), break through into Germany, and join the Russians in Berlin. To hold and later encircle the German thrust through Belgium, French and Belgian troops were scheduled to link up with the British forces that would filter down from the Channel ports. The Allies also counted on a sharp, short war. Both plans miscarried as the war turned first from one of thrust and movement into one of position and, finally, of attrition. We need now to consider its overall course and significance.

Seven German armies participated in the assault against France. The three southernmost groups, which stretched from Luxembourg's southern border to Strasbourg, had two responsibilities—to turn back French invaders and to serve as anchor weights for the wide-sweeping armies to the north. As the northern armies moved scythe-like through Belgium and France, French armies drove northeastward into Germany (in the manner, as a recent writer has expressed it, of two persons simultaneously entering and leaving a revolving door). The French offensive was based on the belief that Germany had thrown so many men into the great northern movement that her Southern Front could not stand against a strong attack. Actually, German manpower in this sector was equal to that of the invaders. Moreover, the Germans had the advantage of fighting in fortified positions which nestled on wooded and hilly terrain. Communication between and coordination of the various units of the attacking forces proved difficult, so that advance was slow and uneven. The French were further penalized by their foolish and persistent preference for light field guns (the famous French "75's"); these alone, they believed, allowed the mobility essential to success. On the other hand, the Germans were well supplied with heavy "105's" and used them with devastating effect. Within a fortnight after launching their "march to Berlin," the French suffered a severe mauling that sent them staggering back to their own fortifications.

---

* Based on the famous Schlieffen Plan. Von Schlieffen was chief of the German general staff, 1891–1905.

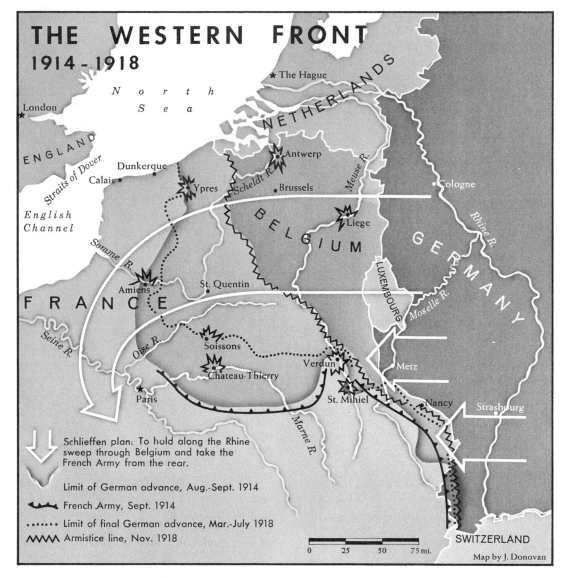

THE WESTERN FRONT
1914-1918

Schlieffen plan: To hold along the Rhine
sweep through Belgium and take the
French Army from the rear.

Limit of German advance, Aug.-Sept. 1914

French Army, Sept. 1914

Limit of final German advance, Mar.-July 1918

Armistice line, Nov. 1918

Map by J. Donovan

Meanwhile, the German scythe had cut a broad swath through Belgium. English troops, it is true, had landed (August 7–17) and had linked up with their allies, but the German thrust could not be stopped. By the end of August, Allied armies had retreated to the Marne (see map, p. 435). The French government abandoned Paris and settled in Bordeaux, far to the south and west. The possible realization of the German vision of a sharp, short war was becoming an emerging specter for the Allies.

At this point the German High Command made two costly miscalculations. Its plans, we have noted, called for a holding action against Russia to allow for the swift destruction of French forces. This was a feasible plan, the Germans believed, because all signs pointed to Russia's inability to mobilize quickly. After France's defeat, Germany could wheel her first-line armies around and repeat her lightning victories in the east.

However, Russia surprised the Central Powers, and perhaps herself, by staging a reasonably swift mobilization. By mid-August large forces had been deployed along the borders of both Germany and Austria-Hungary. Soon her troops had broken into East Prussia, thus posing a problem that the Germans had not anticipated. To meet it, von Moltke detached several divisions from the French Front to reinforce his faltering armies in the east.[7] Although reluctant to modify the Schlieffen Plan, he felt that the move could not seriously affect the course of events in France. Everything there seemed to be going according to plan, with Allied collapse imminent.

Meanwhile the German "anchor" armies in the west clamored for action. The French offensive had been stopped cold. Should not a counterattack be launched, which would allow a double pincers to encircle Paris and bring the war to an even swifter conclusion? Once again the German General Staff hesitated to authorize a modification of its original plans, but the pressures proved too strong to resist.

The Allied situation seemed desperate. The French offensive had failed; the German sweep moved on with ever-increasing momentum. Almost all of Belgium was lost. Paris was threatened. Whatever was to be done, the Allies must do it quickly and on a grand scale. They decided to risk all on a massive counteroffensive. Accordingly, on September 6, Allied armies were ordered to make a general turnabout and drive against their attackers. By September 10 the German High Command was faced with a serious dilemma. The decision to detach several divisions for service in the east still seemed sound; yet the Allied counteroffensive demanded every man whom the Germans could call up. To meet the new situation, the German Command made still another mod-

*Part of the "taxicab army" rushed to the Marne from Paris to meet and stop the German offensive, September 1914.*

ification of its basic plan. It ordered the troops that constituted the point of the sweeping scythe to break off their encircling movement and turn south to avoid widening a gap that had developed under the blows of the counterattack. In effect, the whole line fell back to preserve itself as a line. The Allies made repeated assaults against this line in vain. But from a point near the Marne River (less than twenty miles from Paris) the Germans had retreated about forty miles to a position north of the River Aisne. Here they dug in and settled down to trench warfare. The Battle of the Marne, as it came to be called, thus ended the German offensive and, as it turned out, all hope of a short war.[*]

### Action on the Two Fronts

The stalemate in the west did not have its counterpart in the east. There the soon-to-become famous team of Ludendorff and Hindenburg was sent to stop the Russian advance.[†] While the German offensive was

---

7. Actually, the detached divisions did not reach the Eastern Front in time for the action that Ludendorff had planned. It should also be noted here that some authorities dispute claims that Germany's Western Front was weakened to any serious degree by Moltke's decision.

* For a detailed account of the many and intricate engagements lumped together as "the Battle of the Marne," see Barbara W. Tuchman, *The Guns of August*, the Macmillan Company, New York, 1962.
† Erich Ludendorff, appointed Quartermaster General of the Army in 1916, developed into Germany's most brilliant strategist. Paul von Hindenburg, called from retirement in 1914, efficiently executed Ludendorff's plans and became Germany's foremost field commander.

*Hindenburg (left) and Ludendorff, the military team that shaped Germany's war plans and programs, 1916 to 1918.*

*Gas was used by both sides in World War I. Here, German soldiers wear masks to protect themselves as they move into an attacking position on the Western Front.*

slowly grinding to a bloody halt along the Marne, a series of mauling attacks in East Prussia broke the back of the Russian effort and ended in a decisive German victory. Soon the German Command in the east called on the General Staff for reinforcements with which, they were convinced, they could knock Russia out of the war. However, the strategy makers in Germany believed that the conditions in the west were too unsatisfactory to allow the front there to be weakened. So no reinforcements were sent to Ludendorff, and the knockout blow was postponed. Although entrenchment and stalemate did not develop, the commitment of German armies in the east prevented a grand unification of German might and thus indirectly contributed to the stalemate in France.

Stalemate did not necessarily mean inaction. On the contrary, each side periodically mounted gigantic offensives. Usually these assaults were opened with earthshaking artillery barrages, which were intended to force the enemy to abandon its entrenched forward

positions. They were followed by an attacking infantry, which used bayonets, rifles, machine guns, grenades, and often, after the spring of 1915, poison gas. In most of these offensives the killed, mutilated, and captured numbered in the tens of thousands; in some cases they numbered in the hundreds of thousands. For example, in February 1916, the Germans launched an attack in the Verdun region. For more than four months the two armies grappled in a indescribable embrace of death and destruction. On July 11, the Germans gave up the attack. The ground gained was slight, hardly to be measured in acres. German casualties numbered about 300,000; French losses were even higher. The next month the Allies (mainly the British) opened an offensive of their own in the Somme sector. It ground on for about five months. In November it "gradually ran out in mud and rain." For a net advance of about six miles, the British and French sacrificed about 600,000 lives. The German loss was around 500,000.

## Life in the Trenches

To speak of the "loss of about 500,000 men" is to express a historic fact that is easily recorded and easily understood. Nevertheless, this and similar phrases—such as "position warfare," "entrenched positions,"

*Trench warfare in World War I. Here, a German outpost is going into action against a British advance.*

and "flank attacks"—are abstract and de-personalized. They are like a newspaper account which records the death of thousands from a tidal wave or a hurricane—the statistics are impressive, but the reader has little sense of involvement and less understanding of the unheroic fury of the destructive force. More meaningful, in this instance, although still inadequate, are memoirs by men who lived in the trenches. The following is an extract from an account written by Gustav Regler, a soldier in the German army.

As we detrained in a village near Soissons a party of ten soldiers came along the street. They were caked with mud, having come straight out of the line. Some of us went over to them as they stretched themselves on the floor of a shed, after putting aside their rifles and gas-masks. "It's hell," one of them said, wiping the sweat off his forehead. He rolled over and closed his eyes, as the others had already done. We stood staring at the ten recumbent bodies, and now we knew—it was hell.

The distant mumble of artillery-fire answered the thoughts in our minds.

The German line lay along the northern ridge of the Chemin des Dames, and communication with the valley was maintained by means of a tunnel through which the wounded were carried to the rear. I went along this tunnel on the first day not knowing anything about the recumbent figures I passed and marvelling that they should lie so quietly. But just as I was about to mount the steps a hand gripped my arm. "Shoot me," a voice said out of the darkness, and as though everyone in the tunnel had been awaiting these words a sound of groaning arose, the more appalling since we had to walk bent double and, dazzled by the light breaking in at the entrance, could see very little. I wrenched myself free of the restraining hand, which was like the hand of death itself, and climbed up into the trench, over which shrapnel was exploding at that moment. This was my baptism of fire and it was almost a relief.

It rained for a fortnight. Their company lived in mud, a relentless mud that at every instant reminded us what we were. It sucked at us, clinging tightly to our boots, and it swallowed up the hands of anyone who fell. We strove against it, but even when at nightfall we laid planks on the squelching earth and relapsed into unquiet slumber, the mud was still there; sometimes a hand slipped off the plank, to be gripped round the wrist as though by a handcuff.

Every seventh day we were sent out to an advanced post from our position in a wood. We walked looking neither to right nor left, but once I found a destroyed ammunition-cart in my path. The wheels had tried to get away, but had been brought up against the steep banks of the lane. The horses were stiff already, and in a last heart-rending gesture of tenderness had crossed their necks the one over the other; worms were writhing in their burst bellies. The dead driver of the cart lay in a dark puddle and looked as though he were drinking. "He's drinking his own blood," I thought, and went on hurriedly, as though someone had pushed me from behind.

It was not so much that they were all dead, the wheels, the horses and the man, but that they looked so terribly deserted. Mankind had abandoned them.

On the same day I had a new view of Gabens, a youth of my own age who came from Berlin. We scrambled up a muddy hillock, with Gabens in front of me. Watching him as he plodded on, a shudder ran through me so that I had to pause for a moment and rest. It seemed to me that I had suddenly grasped the truth of what was happening to us.

*Time out for dinner in the trenches. The heavy boots were worn by sentinels who often had to stand for hours in the mud.*

*German troops cutting barbed wire in no-man's-land.*

He looked, in his uniform, like a child in fancy-dress. The whole thing was such an evil joke. The churned-up, ratgrey earth around us, where for years nothing would grow, was slung round his waist which he would detach to fling in the faces of strangers. Back in the wood Gabens had always been full of poetry; he was like an aeolian harp amid the trees, moved to song by every puff of the wind. Now, however, he was like a damned soul, with lice in his shirt, gases in his entrails, sores on his toes, a strayed, eighteen-year old. . . .

We lived in a lunar landscape, quite inhuman, carved up in fear-inspired geography of the trenches, strewn with the rotting fragments of corpses; a neutral territory with which no divine spirit could wish to have any further dealings. But then, did any such spirit wish to have dealings with us? I doubted it; there was too little sense in the things we did. At night we crept out between the lines, scarcely knowing one from the other, and flung grenades at random into the shell-holes. We sat in dug-outs shored up with timber and killed rats. We re-

paired telephone-lines and dug saps between the ground by means of which we hoped to blow up the French dug-outs. When our listening apparatus told us that the French were up to the same game, but digging even deeper, we ran for it. Soon after this the French gave up, and we were just as relieved as we were sure they were.

Neither side wanted to attack. When anything of the kind was ordered, from far behind the lines, we delayed matters for as long as we could. If Battalion Command insisted on an assault we stuck out for an artillery barrage. When this came we had to follow behind it. Quite often we over-ran the enemy trenches opposite. Two days later would come the counter-attack. We would be forced back to our original positions, having lost a few men whom we were unable to bury, and everything would be as before.

The worst trial to the nerves was sitting underground. The earth crumbled softly in the dug-outs and sometimes a timber broke. I often went up above it at the risk of being cut to bits by the flying, jagged lumps of metal. Once a rat came up the steps of the dug-out, sniffed the sulphurous air uneasily with its pink nose and then ran off unconcealed along the lateral trench. I let it run.

We were ordered into the Aisne valley to repair a wrecked bridge. The site had to be inspected by daylight to see where we could lay down a corduroy road. A stray shell came whistling our way and exploded near us. As we moved forward again our captain stumbled over a headless man who must have been one of our advance party. I saw nothing but

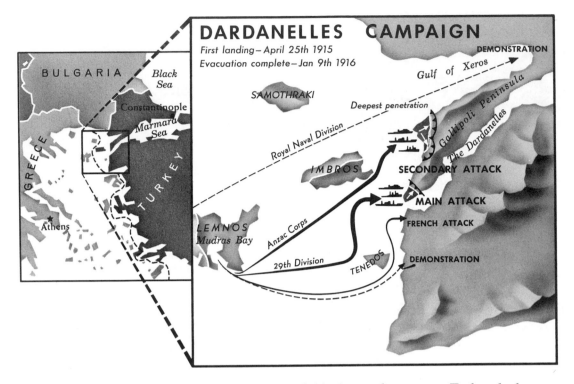

### DARDANELLES CAMPAIGN

First landing – April 25th 1915
Evacuation complete – Jan 9th 1916

the wound, which reminded me of the pictures of martyrs painted by the medieval masters, and the care with which they depicted the anatomical details of a truncated neck.

The captain leaned against a tree and vomited. Then he ordered the man buried, and said that would do for today.

We spent a week laying a corduroy road over the swampy riverbank, and another week repairing the bridge. The next day a French reconnaissance plane spotted the change, and that evening our work was destroyed by an artillery bombardment. The bombardment lasted half an hour.[8]

### English Action in Turkey, and on the Sea

Two developments led England to open a new front: the deadlock in the west (which the entrance of Italy on the side of the Allies hardly affected) and the inability of Russia to do much more than keep her armies in the field. As we have seen, Turkey had come into the war on the side of the Central Powers. In 1915, England decided to attack the "soft underbelly of Europe" and, hopefully, to gain Turkey as a base. From Turkey she might strike a decisive blow against Austria-Hungary as well as threaten Germany from the east. Naval action began in February, followed in April by the landing of about 75,000 troops on the Gallipoli peninsula. The tempo of the offensive was so slow, however, that Turkish battalions were given time to occupy defensive positions from which they could not be driven. Another attempt was made in the fall with the same result. In the end the thrust from the south came to nothing* (see map, p. 440).

8. Gustav Regler, *The Owl of Minerva,* translated by Norman Denny, Farrar, Straus and Cudahy, New York, 1960, pp. 38–41.

* Before the war ended, many other "fronts" were opened—in Mesopotamia, in the Balkans, in Africa, in Asia. These must be passed over in a survey study such as ours. For accounts of the fighting in these areas, see appropriate titles in the bibliography at the end of this chapter.

On the sea another kind of deadlock developed. England's Grand Fleet, although in control of the seas, was vulnerable to mines and torpedoes. Germany's High Seas Fleet, which had been built into an instrument of tremendous power by von Tirpitz, looked forward to the day of battle. But *der Tag* had to be carefully chosen. A well-known analyst has expressed it this way: "The aim of German naval strategy, since August 1914, had been to avoid the risk of a decisive action until the British fleet was so weakened [by mines and torpedoes] that the prospect of success veered from gloomy to fair."[9] Britain's naval strategy was simply to keep the world's sea-lanes open; the destruction of the German fleet, although always something for British Sea Lords to dream about, was a secondary consideration.

Consequently, neither German nor British naval commanders were eager to rush into battle. Indeed, they were so cautious that only one major encounter occurred during the entire war. On May 31, 1916, the two fleets met not far off the Norwegian coast. In the Battle of Jutland, as it is called, each side took care not to expose itself to unnecessary risks. From late afternoon until darkness fell, they "groped towards each other, touched, broke away, touched again." Tonnage loss was greater for the British, but the Germans retreated to home waters, never to offer battle again. Britannia, it seemed, continued to rule the waves.

But not quite. If England was supreme on the seas, Germany was supreme under them. From the beginning, Germany had concentrated on a wide-ranging submarine activity. Cruising beneath the waters of the world's major sea-lanes, her submarines increasingly made Allied shipping a hazardous business. By the fall of 1915, U-boat activity had assumed serious proportions. In the last months of 1916 Germany was sinking an

average of 300,000 tons a month, much more than the Allies could replace. England was especially vulnerable to the submarine menace because she literally lived on imported food, of which she could normally carry only a two-months' supply. For her a tight and continuing submarine blockade spelled certain defeat. In retaliation the British government announced its intention to step up seizure of all "contraband" goods. In practice this meant that England would decide who might send what produce to whom. Neutral nations, she pointed out, were fighting for their right to make profits from international trade; England was fighting for her life.

As Britain's definition of contraband became increasingly arbitrary and all-embracing, her relations with the United States became strained almost to the breaking point. It is pointless to conjecture what the result might have been, because a German action in May 1915 reversed the situation. A large English passenger liner (with a partial cargo of munitions) sailed from New York bound for England. Before its departure, German officials publicly warned American would-be passengers that the liner (the *Lusitania*) would be traveling in what the German government considered a war zone. Several hundred Americans nonetheless booked passage, presumably in the belief that the Germans were bluffing. They were not. On May 7, the *Lusitania* was torpedoed just off the Irish coast. More than 1000 passengers lost their lives, including about 130 Americans. President Wilson, in a series of strong notes (so strong that his secretary of state resigned) demanded not only reparation but an official declaration that such action would not be repeated. When Germany equivocated, the situation became so grave that war seemed imminent. Warned by its ambassador in Washington that the President was preparing to break off relations, the German government finally announced that there would be no more sinkings without warning. It also promised that when vessels

9. B. H. Liddell Hart, *The Real War, 1914–1918,* Little, Brown and Co., Boston, 1930, p. 273.

# NOTICE!

TRAVELLERS intending to embark on the Atlantic voyage are reminded that a state of war exists between Germany and her allies and Great Britain and her allies; that the zone of war includes the waters adjacent to the British Isles; that, in accordance with formal notice given by the Imperial German Government, vessels flying the flag of Great Britain, or of any of her allies, are liable to destruction in those waters and that travellers sailing in the war zone on ships of Great Britain or her allies do so at their own risk.

**IMPERIAL GERMAN EMBASSY**
WASHINGTON, D. C., APRIL 22, 1915.

*This notice appeared in New York newspapers just before the* Lusitania *sailed for England. Few people took the warning seriously.*

*Georges Clemenceau, the "Tiger of France," came to power in late 1917 when French fortunes were at a low ebb. His spirited leadership is credited by many with keeping France on her feet in those dark days.*

## War-Weariness

After two years of trench warfare the belligerents seemed locked in a Laocoön embrace that could be neither broken nor ended. Offensives and counteroffensives on the Western Front killed and wounded hundreds of thousands of men without changing the fundamental position of either side. On the Eastern Front, Germany (but not Austria) consistently defeated but could not destroy Russian forces. On the sea, Allied navies remained unchallenged, but by late 1916 English and French shipping again began to suffer losses that seriously weakened the Entente's home and fighting fronts. More states continued to be drawn into the struggle (for example, Rumania and Greece on the Allied side in the fall of 1916), at the same time that a spreading war-weariness

were sunk care would be taken to rescue noncombatants. In effect this meant that the submarine campaign was reduced to a negligible part of the German war effort. Unless submarines could sink without warning, they could hardly function at all. By necessity their hulls had to be very thin; to surface and warn meant almost certain destruction because most large liners carried deck guns whose firepower could easily pierce thin armor. For the next year and a half Germany complained of this unfair penalty (as she saw it), but in the main she honored her promises to Wilson.

AREAS TO ITALY    SECRET TREATIES OF WORLD WAR I    DIVISION OF TURKEY

made itself felt among all peoples. Political changes reflected the growing discontent. Lloyd George replaced Asquith in December 1916. In France, Briand succeeded Viviani (October 1915) and was himself succeeded by Ribot, Painlevé, and finally (November 1917) Clemenceau. In Italy, Salandra gave way to Boselli, who was replaced by Orlando (October 1917). In other countries the same somewhat frantic search went on for leaders who might bring the bloody impasse to an end. The German Chancellor, Bethmann-Hollweg, was forced to resign (1917) when he objected to the ever-increasing interference in national policy-making by Ludendorff. His successors were Ludendorff's puppets who danced to the General's strident, martial tunes.

## American Involvement

In 1916 President Wilson sent his most trusted adviser, Colonel Edward H. House, to Europe in an attempt to sound out the powers. However, neither Entente nor Alliance leaders showed a willingness to state terms that were clear of ambiguous qualifications or reservations. Unknown at the time to both Wilson and House, secret treaties had been concluded among the Allies, which provided for the virtual partition of the Austro-Hungarian and Ottoman Empires.* In what came to be known (after the war) as the House Memorandum, a quasi commitment was made by this country to Britain which clearly reflected a growing American sympathy—at least among government leaders—for the Allied cause. The memorandum stated that this country was ready to propose peace terms which, if acceptable to the Allies but ignored by the Central Powers, would *probably* lead to America's entering the war on the side of the Entente. Because the proposals fell short of the prizes contained in the secret treaties and because Allied leaders in spite of their fears seemed unable to think in any terms except complete victory, nothing came of the project. Later in the year the President tried again. This time he publicly requested the belligerents to announce negotiable terms. In January 1917, the Allies replied with demands so extreme that Wilson himself could not accept them. The German government entered into confidential conversations with the President which revealed that government's unreason-

---

* Before the war ended, Wilson had learned of the existence of these treaties and some of their provisions.

*After resumption of German submarine warfare (1917), President Wilson addressed Congress to urge the breaking off of diplomatic relations with Germany.*

able claims. Anyway, before practicable reconciliation could be seriously attempted, the German High Command forced a policy on its government that not only ended the negotiations but brought America into the war.

For some time Ludendorff* and his staff had believed that only unrestricted submarine warfare could bring German victory. Civilian authorities opposed resumption of such warfare on the grounds that it would at once make the United States a belligerent. Ludendorff argued that this consideration, even though true, was irrelevant. He believed that unrestricted use of the submarine meant certain English capitulation within six or eight weeks, long before the United States could mobilize or make her influence felt on the Continent. With England out of the war, France could not endure. (This argument was probably stronger than its proponents realized, for disaffection was widespread in the French armies. Within months, tens of thousands of French troops were to mutiny, thus creating a situation that the government was barely able to control.) Russia was

* In 1916, he and Hindenburg were given supreme command of the German armies. Thereafter they decided to concentrate their attention on the Western Front.

already practically eliminated, and Italy was nothing without its allies. A strong blow against England, then, could smash the whole Allied effort.

The Chancellor and his civilian advisers were anything but enthusiastic about the proposal, but they were not in a position to counter it. For one thing, the only available alternative—the opening of peace negotiations—was still considered unpatriotic or subversive. For another, Ludendorff by now had assumed virtually dictatorial powers.

Thus on January 31, 1917, the German government announced resumption of unrestricted submarine warfare. Three days later the United States broke off diplomatic relations with Germany. President Wilson indicated that he would not ask Congress for a declaration of war until the Germans had actually put their policy into practice. When they did—and they did it promptly and energetically—the President, on April 6, 1917, asked a willing Congress to declare that a state of war existed with Germany.

Although the resumption of submarine warfare was the proximate cause of America's entry into the war, it was not the sole cause. Allied propaganda, especially British, had created an American climate of public opinion which, by 1917, had made the United States a kind of informal member of the Entente. By emphasizing the idealistic aims of their struggle—democracy, the primacy of reason over the sword, the right of all peoples to self-determination—while passing quickly over questions of territorial and material aggrandizement, the Allies created an increasingly favorable image of themselves on this side of the ocean. German propaganda was much less effective, partly because transoceanic communication media were less available to the Germans and partly because German officialdom was caste-and-sword-minded, hence clumsy in the arts of verbal persuasion. Germany's treatment of Belgium also alienated many Americans. In addition, the feeling grew in the United States that a German victory would foster the spread of autocracy and militarism. Finally, huge American loans to and profitable trade with the Allies gave the United States a sizable financial stake in an Entente victory.

## Allied Resurgence

The first results of Germany's resumption of unrestricted submarine warfare seemed to prove the soundness of Ludendorff's strategy. In April 1917, U-boats destroyed nearly one million tons of Allied shipping. English food supplies were, by the government's own (later) admission, sufficient to feed the country for only six weeks.

About this time the French, attempting a grand offensive, suffered a crushing defeat in what is called the Third Battle of Champagne. Their repulse was so complete and their losses so heavy that whole regiments of troops mutinied. The incidence of desertion also increased alarmingly. "So general was the dry rot that, according to the Minister of War, only two divisions in the Champagne sector could be relied upon fully, and in places the trenches were scarcely even guarded.[10] For a while British troops constituted the only Allied striking power on the Continent.

On the Eastern Front Russian armies, which suffered from lack of competent leadership, adequate materials and munitions, and crumbling morale at home, steadily gave way to combined Austro-German attacks. In March, the Tsarist government was overthrown. Soldiers and sailors alike believed that the war was lost and that further resistance was useless. In December, the new Bolshevik government signed an armistice with Germany; for Russia, the Great War was over.

Despite these catastrophes, however (indeed partly because of them), the Allies were able to improve substantially their overall situation before the year was ended. Badly shaken by the submarine offensive, the

10. Liddell Hart, *op. cit.*, p. 301.

At Petrograd

Russian Officer: "Why these fortifications, your Majesty? Surely the Germans will not get this far!"
The Czar: "But when our own army returns---?"

*This 1915 cartoon, appearing in a radical publication, correctly predicted the revolution that occurred two years later.*

British admiralty was forced to yield to Lloyd George's demand for immediate adoption of the convoy system, which was simple in concept and, from the beginning, highly effective—the assignment of destroyers, torpedo boats, and other warcraft to guard merchant ships on their Atlantic and Channel crossings. The gravity of the peril also stimulated the search for counterweapons, which eventually produced the submarine chaser and the depth bomb. With these weapons available, the convoy system, strengthened by the added resource of the United States Navy, soon broke the back of the submarine menace. Sinkings continued, of course, but not on the scale required by Germany's great gamble.

On the other hand, the Allied blockade of Germany became so severe that in 1917 food riots broke out in Berlin. The encirclement of Germany, which had formed the subject of so many of the Kaiser's harangues, assumed a new and crippling form. German

*General John J. Pershing landing in France on June 13, 1917, to take command of the American Expeditionary Force.*

armies were still in France and were still winning victories, but the victories brought neither bread nor fuel to the home front. Nor did they seem to promise a decisive change in the overall military situation. The feeling grew that the war was a kind of cosmic curse—ceaseless and, beyond the bloody and monotonous capture and recapture of villages and stretches of no-man's-land, senseless. In the hope of lifting morale, the Kaiser in his Easter message of 1917 announced certain political reforms. Prussia's three-class system of voting—the symbol and substance of Junker autocracy—was abolished. This was followed in July by the introduction of universal suffrage and the secret ballot. In the same month the Reichstag, by an almost 2:1 vote, passed a resolution that called on the government to work for "a peace of understanding and the permanent reconciliation of the people," innocent of "forced acquisitions of territory and political . . . oppressions."

In the meantime, the immense resources of America were steadily being funneled into France and Britain. The first contingent of American troops, under General John J. Pershing, landed in France two months after Congress had declared war. It was a small token force, but by the fall of 1917 "doughboy" battalions were taking their place alongside the French and British in the front

line. Within a year two million American soldiers were in Europe.

## Withdrawal of Russia: Brest Litovsk

In the spring of 1918, Russia and Rumania signed treaties of peace with the Central Powers. In the Treaty of Brest Litovsk, Russia suffered immense territorial losses. She was forced to recognize Poland as an "independent" nation. The Ukraine, Russia's vast breadbasket, was set up as a "sovereign" republic. The independence of Finland and the Baltic States—Estonia, Latvia, and Lithuania—was conceded. In the Caucasus region, generous territories were ceded to Turkey. Russia was also forced to agree to pay an enormous indemnity.\* The harsh treaty clearly foretold what was in store for the Allies if they should lose the war. The Treaty of Bucharest was also definitely punitive. The whole of Dobruja was sliced off and given to Bulgaria. Under terms of a ninety-year lease Germany took over all of Rumania's oil wells. Territory adjacent to Transylvania was given to Austria-Hungary.

On the surface it appeared that the position of the Central Powers had been greatly strengthened. Veteran troops from the Eastern Front were now available for service in France. The shipment of food and supplies from the Ukraine and other German-dominated areas would, it was believed, offset the effect of the British blockade. Altogether, civilian morale was given a much-needed boost. But the gains were more illusory than real. The number of troops required to garrison the eastern areas, as

---

\* Technically, it was not indemnity. Articles 8 and 16 of the treaty stipulated that each side should compensate the other for maintenance of its prisoners of war. Because Germany (and Austria-Hungary) had captured many more prisoners than Russia, the resulting net recompense to the Central Powers was very large. At the time the Russian government estimated the net expense to be over four million gold rubles.

finally determined by the German High Command, turned out to be so large that the Western Front received far fewer divisions than had been hoped for. Food and supplies were indeed siphoned off from the east, but they did not make up the enormous losses inflicted by the blockade. Any uplift in German and Austro-Hungarian morale was more than countered by the stiffening of Allied will provoked by the harsh terms of the treaties and by the substantial change that they effected in Wilson's attitude toward the German and Austro-Hungarian peoples.

Two months before the Brest Litovsk Treaty was signed, President Wilson laid before Congress his proposals for a just peace —the famous Fourteen Points.* His timing was motivated by twin hopes: that Russia could be persuaded to remain in the war, and that the German people could be weaned from allegiance to their power-mad warlords. In Point Six the President said: "The treatment accorded Russia by her sister nations in the months to come will be the acid test of their good will, of their comprehension of her needs as distinguished from their own interests . . . ." Speaking of Germany, in Point Fourteen he said: "We have no jealousy of German greatness . . . . We do not wish to injure her or to block in any way her legitimate influence or power . . . . Neither do we presume to suggest to her any alteration or modification of her institutions." In his message to Congress in the preceding month, Wilson had even more clearly emphasized his belief that the Germans should be left to decide what kind of government they wanted (once they had repudiated their military dictators): "We do not intend to inflict any wrong on the German Empire . . . nor to interfere in any way in its internal affairs."[11]

* For a summary of the "points," see *infra,* p. 452.

11. As quoted in John W. Wheeler-Bennett, *The Forgotten Peace,* William Morrow and Company, New York, 1939, p. 364.

Brest Litovsk changed all that. In a public address delivered shortly after the signing of the Treaty, the President said:

I do not wish, even at this moment of utter disillusionment, to judge harshly or unrighteously. I judge only what the German arms have accomplished with unpitying thoroughness throughout every fair region they have touched . . . . For myself, I am ready . . . to discuss a fair and just and honest peace at any time that it is sincerely proposed—a peace in which the strong and the weak shall fare alike. But the answer, when I proposed such a peace, came from the German commanders in Russia, and I cannot mistake the meaning of the answer. I accept the challenge. Germany has once more said that force, and force alone, shall decide whether Justice and Peace shall reign in the affairs of men. . . . There is therefore but one response possible for us: Force, Force to the utmost, Force without stint or limit, the righteous and triumphant force which shall make Right the law of the world, and cast every selfish dominion down in the dust.[12]

A few months later the President announced what amounted to a fifteenth Point. In a public address delivered at Mount Vernon in July 1918, he declared, in effect, that the Central Powers must substitute democratic institutions for autocratic institutions before peace terms could be discussed. We cannot know whether President Wilson would have been able to bring his colleagues at the peace conference to a moderate reasonableness, if there had not been a Brest Litovsk Treaty. It is certain that because of it, the President's new attitude encouraged a harsher interpretation of his original peace terms.

## Germany's Last Throes

By the end of 1917, the German General Staff had become convinced that submarine warfare could not force a decision. Two alternatives remained: capitulation to the

12. *Ibid.,* p. 366.

RUSSIAN LOSSES

After the Treaty of Brest-Litovsk
and supplemental treaties, 1918

Map by J. Donovan

Allies before the military strength of the Central Powers was shattered, thus (hopefully) assuring good peace terms; or a final all-out assault to force Allied capitulation. Ludendorff, now the real ruler of Germany, chose the second alternative and, during the winter of 1917 to 1918, prepared for a last grand offensive. The offensive opened in March 1918 with a ferocity that sent the Allies reeling. In less than a week the British, who bore the brunt of the initial attack, were forced to retreat about forty miles. A second attack on another sector of the British line was also successful. Made desperate by impending catastrophe, the Allies finally gave the supreme command of their combined forces to Marshal Ferdinand Foch, who immediately coordinated holding operations along the whole of the Western Front. Shortly thereafter, he mounted a massive counteroffensive that broke the back of the German effort.

In September, a multinational army under the command of General Franchet d'Esperey opened a new front in Greece. Overwhelmed by Allied forces, Bulgaria, the smallest of the Central Powers, asked for an armistice (September 29) and dropped out of the war. With Allied armies now pouring in the back door of Austria-Hungary, a negotiated peace was out of the question. On November 3, the Dual Monarchy laid down its arms and accepted Allied terms.

A few days before the capitulation, the crews of the High Seas Fleet, which was ordered by the German command to put to sea in the desperate hope of somewhere gaining a victory, had mutinied. As though awaiting this kind of signal, sporadic revolution broke out in Germany. On November 8, Foch received German representatives to discuss armistice terms. On November 9, the abdication of the Kaiser was announced. Two days later German commissioners were received again by Foch in a railroad coach in Compiegne Forest. With the scraping of pen on armistice papers, on November 11, 1918, the four years of fighting ended.

## Consequences of the War

What had the Great War wrought? For the Austro-Hungarian Empire, it brought not vigor and stability but complete destruction. For Russia, not the key to the Straits but defeat and revolution. For Germany, not a place in the sun but humiliation, a huge indemnity, partition of its empire, and the collapse of its monarchical regime. For Italy, the satisfaction of some (although by no means all) of its irredentist claims, economic chaos, and political disruption. For Turkey,

The Chicago Daily Tribune's *front-page story of the end of World War I.*

imperial demise and political upheaval. For England, continued control of the seas, more color on the map, temporary confirmation of her claim to leadership in the balance-of-power system, a colossal burden of debt, and a new rival (the United States) in the exploitation of the world's markets. For France, Alsace-Lorraine, revenge, ravaged earth, and the haunting knowledge that she had been rescued from defeat and German domination by the combined might of England and America. For the United States, vindication of neutral rights, the overthrow of German military autocracy, assured rank as a world power, emergence as the world's creditor, and a great weariness of everything European. For the Balkan peoples, the war brought nationhood, independence, and new quarrels over boundary lines gained or lost.

A German victory would have fastened the yoke of militarism and autocracy upon Europe. However, Allied victory did not prevent the ultimate spread of both throughout the world. Four years after the war that Wilson had hoped would make the world safe for democracy, Fascism was in power in Italy. Even earlier, in Russia one kind of autocracy had been substituted for another. Although ethnically united and free, most of the new—as well as the old—Balkan and Baltic states were run by military "strong men," as was the new Poland. Moreover, in most states national armaments and reliance on them as instruments of national policy increased rather than decreased.

Perhaps the most significant consequence of World War I was that it brought to a climax the process of the West's changing value patterns.* In the century before the war, two divergent *Weltanschauungen* anomalously cradled the developing events and purposes of Western society. One general outlook was characterized by political and economic liberalism, hopeful striving for universal peace, and general optimism regarding the "human condition." The other stressed the inevitability, even desirability, of heroic violent force in the solution of human problems, chauvinistic nationalism, and the need to keep in sharp focus the refractory nature of the human animal. The war gave strong impetus to the second outlook.

For four years much of the world had lived in a feverish atmosphere of hate. To the Allies, the Germans were inhuman Huns; to the Germans, England was perfidious Albion. Long before the war was over, hate had become the great morale builder, the fundamental and indispensable ingredient of patriotism, and the basic force that would determine who should "win" the war. On November 11, 1918, at the stroke of a pen, the slaughterhouse was abandoned. Guns were stacked, armies were demobilized; humankind was expected to resume the ways of peace. But the inner life of man is not so quickly changed. A year after the armistice was signed and "peace" had returned, Wil-

liam Butler Yeats gave expression to this dilemma:

Now days are dragon-ridden, the nightmare
Rides upon sleep: a drunken soldiery
Can leave the mother, murdered at her door,
To crawl in her own blood, and go scot-free;
The night can sweat with terror as before
We pieced our thoughts into philosophy,
And planned to bring the world under a rule,
Who are but weasels fighting in a hole.[13]

In 1922, Sigmund Freud said of the war: "No event ever destroyed so much of the heritage of mankind . . . or so thoroughly debased what is highest." Thirty years later an American historian, Peter Viereck, put it even more bluntly: "World War I is the worst single catastrophe in human history."

## THE UNSETTLING SETTLEMENT

### Motives of the Peacemakers

It is doubtful whether many of the diplomats who gathered in Paris* in January 1919 to write the German peace treaty were conscious of the monumental changes that the war had effected. For the most part the spirit that motivated them was a blend of ancient rivalries, old and new fears, and vaulting ambitions. France clearly understood the significance of the dynamic development of Germanic power—power that had challenged and ultimately destroyed her domination of Western Europe. She remembered the "rape of Alsace-Lorraine." She remembered the Marne and how close she had come to another German-dictated settle-

13. M. L. Ronsenthal, ed., *Selected Poems of William Butler Yeats,* The Macmillan Company, New York, 1962, p. 109.

---

* Discussed in Chapter XVII.

* Most of the real work of the conference was carried on in Paris. The final treaty was signed at Versailles, a few miles outside Paris.

ment. She looked with bitterness and wrath at her scarred earth, torn and hacked for four years by the iron shards of war. Now her arrogant, goose-stepping tormentors were suing for peace. They would get it. But the price would come high. The chairman of the French delegation (as well as of the Conference) was Georges Clemenceau. Born in 1840, Clemenceau had personally experienced the humiliation of 1871; as much as any man he had longed for the day that had now come. Many years of his long life had been spent in an attempt to rebrighten the luster of a civilization that had·once served as the cultural beacon for all of Western Europe. He had been a champion of the enlightened, open society. But at this time, on this occasion, he did not seem to sense civilization's need of a reasoned peace tempered with mercy.* Neither did the English representatives, led by Prime Minister Lloyd George. In the so-called khaki election, which was held shortly after the armistice, the Prime Minister promised to "squeeze Germany until the pips squeak."† Italian delegates were mainly interested in loot, particularly substantial slices of the Tyrol and Dalmatia. Japanese diplomacy was similarly motivated; the prize was the formerly German-held territories in China.

It is natural to wonder what the masses of Europe were thinking, what they wanted to see as a result of the Conference and the new times. In the absence of reliable data, we can only conjecture. That they were determined to gain more political power one way or another can hardly be doubted. The revolutionary surge that marked the immediate postwar period was sufficient evidence of

this. By 1919 popular governments, or at least what seemed to be popular governments, were in the process of establishment in Germany, Hungary, Poland, some of the Baltic States, and, of course, Russia. The British socialist Labour Party made great gains. In Asia, Dr. Sun's program had found energetic champions. There can be little doubt, too, that the world's masses genuinely wanted peace. When Wilson appeared in European cities, he was hailed as a kind of god. His promise that the Great War would end all wars was not forgotten. His unremitting labors to establish the League of Nations to implement that promise were widely acclaimed.

But the masses were affected by other influences, too. No less than their governments, they were moved by great antipathies rooted in the past. Part of a Frenchman's sacred patriotism was an abiding hatred of Germans. The reference is illustrative only; Europe's many nationalities and religions were, with few exceptions, infected by the same disease. Each nurtured, in one degree or another, suspicion, fear, and distrust of the other. Reinforcing and often inflaming these antipathies was the propaganda poured out by national presses. And always the masses' ignorance and gullibility were exploited by ruling elites in their attempts to gain or keep political power.

This web of the past was strengthened by the concept, held by rulers and ruled alike, of war as an instrument of national policy. It is one thing to hail peace; it is something else to pattern individual and national behavior according to its demanding dictates. There is no evidence in the historic record that any people of either hemisphere was ready to pay this price. English diplomats, for example, earnestly labored at Paris to create conditions which, they hoped, would ensure world peace. Not one of them, however, was willing to sacrifice their country's control of the seas to win that prize. Again the reference is purely illustrative. No nation,

---

* For an informative essay on the France of 1918 and after, see René Albrecht-Carrie, *France, Europe and the Two World Wars,* Harper and Brothers, New York, 1961, Chapter III.

† He later admitted that this was campaign talk. But that he considered such talk necessary is itself significant of the mood of the British man in the street.

including the United States, showed the least interest in subordinating its sovereignty to a universal authority, the *sine qua non* of permanent peace.

Finally, it must be emphasized again that the ineffable experience of the war transformed the men who fought it. For four years millions of men had been killed by millions of killers. The universal maiming was abruptly halted at 11:00 A.M., November 11, 1918. The forces that it had generated within man, however, could not be touched so immediately, nor could humane values suddenly be restored.

Some Americans would like to believe that the United States, alone among the great powers at Paris, was motivated by altruism. It is true that Woodrow Wilson, as its spokesman, gave substance to this belief for a while. Wilson was genuinely interested in the creation of a world community living in justice and peace. His famous Fourteen Points, a blueprint for such a world, bespoke ethnic justice, freedom of the seas, "open" diplomacy, reduction of tariff barriers, and a world organization designed and empowered to keep the peace. It is also true that the people of the United States did not ask for or want territorial gains; they did not even demand indemnities. But before the final treaty was drafted, Wilson had agreed, as we shall see, to certain arrangements quite contrary to his much-publicized aims. Moreover, United States citizens never understood, or even tried to understand, the historic forces that gave hard reality to the jealousies, fears, and suspicions that plagued the old world. They, therefore, tended to assume a holier-than-thou attitude toward both their recent opponents and allies, a posture that hardly prepared them for the role and responsibilities which a changing world demanded.

## Writing the "Peace"

Against this variegated background of old-world hates and new-world ignorance and indifference, of dissolving empires and emerging states, of greedy hopes of the victors and the sullen bitterness of the vanquished, the Peace Conference opened at Paris on January 18, 1919. Twenty-seven Allied and Associated powers were represented by seventy delegates. Ostensibly, they met to translate the Wilsonian program, on the basis of which the Germans had surrendered, into a treaty of peace. The points of this program may be paraphrased as follows:

1. The renunciation by all powers of the practice of secret diplomacy.

2. Freedom of the seas, "alike in peace as in war."

3. Equality of trade conditions among the powers.

4. Reduction of national armaments.

5. The settlement of colonial claims according to the wishes of the colonial peoples, as well as "the equitable claims of the government whose title is to be determined."

6. The evacuation of all Russian territory by Germans and Austrians, and recognition of the right of Russia to determine independently her own political development.

7. Restoration of Belgium.

8. Evacuation of French territory and the return to her of Alsace-Lorraine.

9. Ethnic readjustments of the frontiers of Italy.

10. Self-determination of the peoples who made up the former Austro-Hungarian Empire.

11. Evacuation of the Balkan States, and international guarantees to strengthen their political and economic independence and territorial integrity.

12. Self-determination of the non-Turkish populations of the Ottoman Empire.

13. An independent Polish state, with secure access to the sea.

14. Creation of a League of Nations to protect the political independence and territorial integrity of all states, large and small.

Before agreeing to accept this program as the basis of a general settlement, England stipulated that "freedom of the seas" must not be understood to restrict her naval supremacy—a reservation which, of course, canceled this "point." The Allied powers also reserved the right to demand and secure reparations for war damages caused by Germany. Germany was informed of these reservations and, perforce, accepted them.

The actual treaty that emerged four months later contained many provisions that were contrary to the terms of surrender. Very early in the deliberations, an informal Council of five powers—the United States, England, France, Italy, and Japan—took on complete responsibility for writing the treaty. Long before the task was finished, representatives of what came to be called the Big Three—Wilson for the United States, Lloyd George for England, and Clemenceau for France—assumed dominant control of the Council's work. Of these three, only Woodrow Wilson was seriously interested in honoring the spirit and letter of the Fourteen Points.

Back of the dissension that soon developed in the Council's deliberations lay not only ancient grievances and suspicions, but a number of secret treaties negotiated during the war. The treaties contained, among others, the following provisions:

England consented to Russia's take-over of Constantinople and the Straits.

Russia agreed to England's absorption of the hitherto "neutral" portion of Persia.

England, France, and Russia agreed that Italy should receive from a defeated Austria-Hungary: all of the Trentino; Istria; northern Dalmatia; a number of islands off the Dalmation coast; Valona, and sizable portions, after Turkey's defeat, of the Ottoman Empire (see map, p. 454).

Britain, France, and Russia were also to receive "zones of influence and territorial acquisition" in the Ottoman Empire.

Rumania was "given" Transylvania, part of Bukovina, and Banat.

Russia and Japan agreed to concert to prevent other powers from interfering with their "interests" in China.

France and Russia redrew the boundaries of Germany as follows: Alsace-Lorraine was to return to France; the Saar Valley was to be incorporated into France; a neutral state was to be erected, made up of German territories on the left bank of the Rhine; Russia was to receive French support in redrawing her western frontiers.

It is clear that Allied statesman originally agreed to Wilson's Fourteen Points only because they were hard pressed on all battlefronts and because their peoples sympathized with the spirit and provisions of the Wilsonian program. (By the same token, Germany and her allies welcomed the program when the fortunes of war had turned against them.) For four months, until the treaty was put in final form in early May, Wilson fought with his colleagues over its terms. The provisions stipulating the creation of a League of Nations were given prompt attention. Working closely with Lord Robert Cecil, Wilson and other members of the committee selected to draft the League's Covenant spent weeks devising an instrument which would point the way to a warless world. Some old-world diplomats (including Clemenceau), it is true, gave assent to the venture merely to please Wilson and to expedite what they considered the real business of the Conference. In its final form the Covenant provided for a world organization made up of a General Secretariat, an Assembly, and a Council. All members of the League were admitted to representation in the Assembly. The five major powers—England, France, Italy, Japan, and the United States—were given permanent seats in the Council with instructions to elect four lesser powers to share term representation. The main business of the League was to prevent the outbreak of aggressive war. To this end, it was given the power to investigate quarrels that were likely to lead to war and to recommend settlements. If any League member went to war in violation of the Covenant's provisions and of the Assembly's and Council's procedures, it was considered, *ipso facto,* to have made war on all members

of the League. Only the Council could decide whether and when military sanctions were to be used against an aggressor state, and then only after unanimous agreement (unless the designated aggressor was itself represented on the Council).

In the main, Wilson was pleased with both the Covenant (or constitution) of the League and its general structure. It was, however, the only major achievement of the Conference that did please him. At England's insistence he was forced to concede British control of the seas.* The harsh French

* By agreeing to England's demand that she must have the right to interpret Point Two—the "Freedom of the Seas" clause—as her interests dictated.

demands appalled him—partial dismemberment of Germany, astronomical indemnities, annexation of the Saar basin with its rich coal mines, and long-term occupation of the defeated country. He considered Italian claims equally extravagant, including those that called for cession of large areas of the Austro-Hungarian Empire, which had never been part of Italy and which contained only a minority of her nationals. Japan demanded control of Shantung as well as virtual overlordship of all of China (which, ironically, was one of the "victorious" Allies). At one point during the Conference, Wilson became so disgusted by the rapacity of his allies that he threatened to break off discussions and return home.

In the end a series of compromises saved the Conference from falling apart. Many of them cost the President spiritual agony. He agreed to indemnity provisions that went beyond what he believed to be either just or payable. He accepted Italy's Dalmatian claims and Japan's take-over of Shantung. Other provisions to which he reluctantly agreed were French exploitation of the Saar basin, Allied occupation of Germany, and the cession of certain German territories to Poland (some of which clearly contained a majority German population).* In return he obtained agreement that the League's Covenant should become an integral part of the peace treaty, France's reluctant consent to drop her plans for dismembering Germany, a fifteen-year limitation to French exploitation of the Saar coalfields, and temporary occupation of portions of western Germany. Although Wilson was convinced that Germany deserved to be punished, he felt that the treaty spelled out a Punic peace. Nevertheless, he hoped that a strong League of Nations would ultimately rectify what he considered the treaty's grossest wrongs.

Several other major provisions of the treaty should be noted. Article 231 stated that Germany and her allies were solely responsible for causing the war. All German colonies were ceded to the Allies (as "mandated" territories, ostensibly under the supervision of the League). The German army was limited to 100,000 men; her navy was restricted to six warships, none of them larger than 10,000 tons, and a number of smaller vessels. Construction of military planes, tanks, heavy artillery, and submarines was forbidden. The Rhineland was to be demilitarized in perpetuity. Reparation charges were to include payment for all damages to Allied civilians and to their property (the total bill finally came to about $33,000,000,000). In addition, Germany was charged with all expenses incurred by the occupying troops. A corridor of land ceded to Poland divided Germany into two parts. All merchant ships of 1600 tons or more were surrendered to the Allies. Danzig was detached from Germany and made an international "free" city.

The final draft was presented to the Germans in May. Shocked at the severity of its terms, they refused to sign; Count von Brockdorff-Rantzau, chairman of the delegation, protested that the treaty was a cruel caricature of the Fourteen Points. To insist that Germany alone was responsible for the war would be the vilest lie, he said. Germany was defeated; she was not, however, so weak as to sign away her honor. But the victors would make no substantial concessions. Faced with a resumption of hostilities for which it was in no way prepared, the German government appointed a new commission which, on June 28, 1919, signed the treaty under the most solemn protest. Within the next few months the governments of Germany, France, Britain, Italy, and Japan ratified the pact.

## America Rejects the Treaty

Alone of the Great Powers represented at the Conference, the United States refused ratification.† According to the American Constitution, no treaty is valid unless approved by two thirds of the United States Senate. On two occasions the Versailles Treaty was submitted to this body for ratification. In each instance the treaty was approved, but not by the necessary two-thirds majority. Because the League Covenant was inextricably bound up with other terms of the treaty, the United States rejected the world organization for whose creation its President had done so much.

For this failure, the President and certain Republican senators bear mutual responsibility. When Mr. Wilson went to Paris, he

---

* It should be noted that the cession of *some* German territory to Poland was an absolute necessity if Poland was to have, as Wilson and others insisted, free access to the sea.

† Because of the Shantung provision, China also withheld her signature.

was advised by his own friends to take with him several Republican leaders, or at least one outstanding Republican senator. The President refused. The Republicans, he felt, would try to make political capital out of both what went on at the Conference and what came out of it. His own great objective, he believed, was above partisan machination. In a public address just before the Conference convened, he said:

There is a great voice of Humanity abroad in the world just now which [cries out to all who are not deaf]. There is a great compulsion of the Common Conscience now in existence which, if [resisted by] any statesman, will gain for him an unenviable eminence in history. *We are not obeying the mandate of party or politics, we are obeying the mandate of humanity.**

Thus seemingly disassociating the Republicans from the Common Conscience (and implicitly identifying it with the Democratic conscience!), the President blundered badly. Two outstanding Republicans, Elihu Root and former President William Howard Taft, had actually collaborated with Wilson in his early work on the Covenant. Others, such as Charles Evans Hughes, Mr. Wilson's opponent in the 1916 election, were certainly sympathetic to the idea of a world association of nations. It is true, of course, that Republican senators would not overlook opportunities to reap partisan gains wherever they could. Indeed, many were on the *qui vive* for just such opportunities. Knowing this, Mr. Wilson should have taken care to avoid the very kind of blunder that he committed.

By deciding to head personally the American delegation in Paris, the President opened himself to another, perhaps more

debatable, charge. Had he stayed home, it was argued, he would have preserved the world's picture of him as the great impartial arbiter. By entering the arena as a contestant, he perforce lost this advantage.† Finally, the President's personality undeniably contributed to the Senate's repudiation of the treaty. Often high-handed and even haughty in dealing with his own associates and colleagues, he alienated many who genuinely wished to collaborate with him. Those who opposed him, or whom he suspected (but not always correctly) of opposing him, soon learned how nakedly autocratic the great democrat could be. In private conversations he referred to the "pigmy minded" gentlemen of the Senate. "He tactlessly insisted in a public speech, after his return from Paris, that he owed nothing to the Senate."14

On the other hand, a number of Republican senators must share responsibility for America's rejection of the treaty. This was especially true of Henry Cabot Lodge, whose intense personal dislike of Wilson amounted to a kind of irrational hatred. As chairman of the powerful Senate Committee on Foreign Relations, Lodge was in a particularly strategic position to strike at Wilson. He took full advantage of the opportunity. At his instigation fourteen amendments, some of them needlessly crippling, were tacked onto the treaty as the price of Senate approval. Wilson indignantly refused to pay the price. He had already compromised, he argued,

---

* Stephan Bonsal, *Unfinished Business,* Doubleday, Doran, and Co., Inc., New York, 1944, p. 15. Italics added. It should be noted that Henry White, a onetime Republican leader of some eminence, held a place in the delegation. But although still respected, he was no longer a power in the party and played an insignificant role in the deliberations at Paris.

† Wilson's closest adviser, Edward M. House, felt something of this. He confided to his diary: "It may be that Wilson might have had the power and influence ['to blaze a new and better trail'] if he had remained in Washington and kept clear of that Conference. When he stepped from his lofty pedestal and wrangled with representatives of other states upon equal terms, he became as common clay." Charles Seymour, *The Intimate Papers of Colonel House,* Houghton Mifflin Company, Boston, Vol. IV, p. 488.

---

14. Thomas A. Bailey, *Woodrow Wilson and the Lost Peace,* The Macmillan Company, New York, 1944, p. 103.

almost beyond conscience while the treaty was being hammered out at Versailles. He would not, he said, compromise with a compromise; and Democratic senators were instructed accordingly. This, of course, insured a victory for Lodge who now found in his camp not only those Republicans who looked upon him, rightly, as their party's leader, and "bitter-end" isolationists such as Borah of Idaho and Johnson of California, but also a number of Democratic senators. In these circumstances, defeat of the treaty was certain.

In a last effort to force the Republican-dominated Senate to ratify the work of the Peace Conference, the President "went to the people." In early September 1919, he set out on a whistle-stop campaign designed to let the country know what the treaty was all about and in what danger it was. Before he had completed his tour, he suffered a physical breakdown and was hurriedly brought back to Washington. For the next two months, while the President lay stricken and shut off from public affairs, the remade treaty was haggled over in the Senate. Democratic leaders, knowing that the treaty as Wilson wanted it was doomed, begged the President to accept a half loaf rather than none. Turning his face sternly away from this plea, he demanded all or nothing. When the vote was taken in November of 1919, more than twenty Democratic senators bolted and voted for the treaty as revised. All together there were 55 ayes against 39 noes, seven votes short of the required two-thirds majority.* The Senate had spoken. The treaty was dead. Not until nearly two years later did the United States sign a separate, "covenantless" peace with Germany (July 1921). Ironically, the Versailles Treaty, undergirded by a Covenant that was largely the work of Wilson, was promptly signed by the Allied powers which originally had so critically viewed that Covenant.

* Several months later a second vote was taken, with substantially the same result.

## Other Treaties

Treaties with the remaining belligerent powers, named after the suburbs of Paris in which they were signed, were concluded in the period of September 1919 to August 1920. Austria signed the Treaty of St. Germain (September 10, 1919), which officially dissolved the old Austro-Hungarian Empire. The new so-called succession states of Czechoslovakia and Yugoslavia were granted recognition by Austria, as was a reconstituted Poland. Although Austria desired organic union with Germany, she was expressly forbidden this privilege by the treaty (except by permission of the League Council—an unlikely development). Of all the peace settlements, this one made the least sense. Granted that the old Empire had been an amalgam of discontented peoples, it had at least provided the Austrians, as corulers of it, with a political excuse for being. As a great free-trading area, the Empire had also afforded Austria an economic base for existence. The St. Germain settlement, by forbidding union with Germany while (in effect) ringing the newly shorn state (now about the size of South Carolina) with formidable tariff barriers, doomed Austria to political and economic frustration.

The Hungarians experienced similar treatment. By the Treaty of Trianon (July 4, 1920), Hungary too became a truncated state, retaining only one fourth of her old territories and one third of her prewar population. Cessions to Italy and Jugoslavia completely deprived her of access to the sea. Although the old Empire no longer existed, the new Hungary was forced to assume a portion of the Empire's debts in addition to reparations payments. Her army was reduced to 35,000 men.

By the terms of the Treaty of Neuilly (November 27, 1919), Bulgaria (the only remaining state to remain a monarchy) lost her Mediterranean outlet, assumed a reparations debt of nearly one half billion dollars, and was forced to recognize the independence of Yugoslavia, to which she also ceded some territory. Her army was limited by the treaty to 20,000 men.

The original settlement with Turkey (the Treaty of Sèvres, 1920) completely destroyed the Ottoman Empire. Palestine and Mesopotamia were mandated to Britain, and Syria to France. Other areas of the Empire were either granted independence (Armenia, for example), or occupied until a future decision by plebiscite about its disposition, or given outright to the victors (for example, Rhodes and other Dodecanese islands were given to Italy, and Thrace passed to Greece). The Straits were demilitarized and placed under international control. However, nationalist forces in Turkey, under the leadership of Mustapha Kemal, refused to accept the settlement. In the civil war that followed, Kemal's revolutionary armies overthrew the Sultanate and set up a Republic. Acting in the name of the Allies, Greek forces invaded Anatolia. Two years of fighting ended with the Greeks being driven into the sea.* Allied and Turkish representatives then sat down to rewrite the terms of peace. The biggest problem was the question of what to do with the large Turkish population in Thrace and the substantial Greek settlements in western Turkey. It was finally agreed to resettle each group in its original land—a massive exchange of population unparalleled in modern times. In July 1923, a new settlement was reached in the Lausanne Treaty. The Allies agreed to evacuate all Turkish territories; in return Turkey relinquished its claim to non-Turkish territories occupied by the Allies during the war. It is not without significance that the Lausanne Treaty, the only truly negotiated treaty to come out of the war, proved to be the most durable one.

## Consequences of the Settlements

Some of the changes effected by the peace settlements contributed toward a healthier European community and even toward a potentially healthier world community.

* See *infra*, p. 464.

The new League of Nations was a loose association of sovereign states, which was designed principally to provide a forum for the discussion of world problems and, hopefully, an apparatus to adjudicate international disputes. It was made up of three main bodies: the Assembly, composed of delegates from all member states; the Council, whose membership included representatives from the Great Powers on a permanent basis and (eventually) eleven representatives of smaller powers elected periodically by the permanent members; a Secretariat, made up of a Secretary-General and a host of civil servants to man its many bureaus. Under terms of the Covenant, the League was empowered to deal with any threat to the peace and to take "any action that may be deemed wise and effectual to safeguard the peace of nations." Its supporters hoped that the discussion of controversies in open meetings of the Assembly or Council would lead to their peaceful settlements. If it did not, "sanctions" could be voted against recalcitrant states— economic, political, and, if needed, military. In Chapter XV we shall note how the new "parliament of man" functioned in several specific and significant tests of its strength.

The destruction of the Austro-Hungarian, German, Russian, and Ottoman Empires meant that their subject peoples could set up national housekeeping for themselves. Poland was reborn. Yugoslavia was formed by the union of Serbians, Croatians, and Slovenes. Bohemians and Slovakians (and, less felicitously, Ruthenians) united to create Czechoslovakia. Albania, born of the Balkan wars, was recognized as an independent state. The movement for national self-determination did not come to perfect fruition, of course. Czechoslovakia's three million German Sudetenlanders were none too happy in a non-German state. Other Germans, in the Tyrol, violently objected to their forced transmutation into Italian citizens. Russians in Bessarabia protested their being turned into Rumanians. Such discontent was shared by other ethnic minorities which had been swept into this nation or that by the treaty makers. Other unfortunate features also developed out of the application of the nationality principle. Austria, for example, became a head without a body. Cut off from her economic trunk, she became, within three or four years, practically bankrupt. In the old days of the Empire, she had imported relatively little coal and iron, livestock, and grains. With Czechoslovakia, Yugoslavia, and especially Hungary set up as separate nations, Austria now found herself in the unenviable position of requiring huge imports without a fraction of the funds necessary to pay for them. To a lesser, but still serious degree, the same plight was experienced by Hungary. Even the newly freed nations found that the economic price of freedom came high. If the old Empire had been a kind of ethnic prison, it had at the same time been a great free-trading area, which had brought a prosperity that they now found hard to come by.

The democratic movement also made some progress, at least for a time. Germany, Russia, Austria-Hungary, and Turkey all lost their crowned heads. Almost frantic attention was given to the writing (or rewriting) of constitutions. At least in theory, the doctrine of government by consent of the governed flourished in areas where for centuries autocracy or absolutism had been accepted as the natural order of things. And, of course, the League of Nations gave flesh, grafted and weak as it was, to the once utopian concept of the Parliament of Man. Not even the Roman Empire in its most "democratic" phase gave so much promise of realizing man's universal political brotherhood.

However, the unsettling features of the Great Settlement were ominous.* As we have seen, Germany was forced to admit that she and her allies were solely responsible for

* In the following critique of the settlement, no implication that the Central Powers would have fashioned a better one is intended. The treaties of Brest Litovsk and Bucharest are ample evidence to the contrary.

the war. The injustice and hypocrisy of the charge, freely (although always privately) confessed by Allied statesmen, created mounting resentment among all Germans. Damning documents of Entente diplomatic maneuvering, published by the Bolshevik regime, gave added point to their bitter protests.

Moreover, reparations charges, as finally reckoned by the Allies, came to more than thirty billion dollars. This accounting was so unrealistic that a number of Allied economists entered strenuous objections to it. One third of this amount, they argued, was the most that Germany could be expected to pay and still remain solvent; some believed that even this figure was far too high. To meet annual payments, the Germans were forced to use funds that they otherwise could have used to liquidate their huge internal debt and to develop a normal peacetime economy. The attempt to meet both external and internal demands led the government to an extravagant use of printing-press money. Within a few years, spiraling inflation brought the nation into almost complete bankruptcy, with effects that we shall consider in Chapter XII.

The creation of an independent Poland, with "secure access to the sea," resulted in a geographically divided Germany (see map, p. 468). The thrusting Polish Corridor, which separated East Prussia from the rest of Germany, proved a source of endless friction between the two states. In addition to the transit problem, the division caused serious ethnic dislocations. Throughout various regions of the Corridor there were scattered large pockets of settlers whose "Germanness" was rooted in the soil and in the centuries. Now they had suddenly become Polish citizens. Both they and their compatriots on the other side of the Corridor naturally looked forward to a day of reunion —and of reckoning.

Other grievances aggravated Europe's postwar discontents. The Allies had promised to set up and carry out a general disarmament program, consonant with their professed aim of building a warless world. This, indeed, was their justification for insisting that the military establishments of their former foes should be drastically reduced. But the victors showed little inclination to act upon this promise. Pleading her insular needs, England continued to maintain a powerful navy. France kept a large conscript army poised along the Rhine.* On the other side of Germany, Poland, which was soon to become an ally of France, raised an army more than twice as large as that of Germany. Disarmament, it seemed, was for the defeated. More than ever Germans came to believe that the Wilsonian program, heartily endorsed by the Allies when the going was rough, was a sham, a trick to achieve by the pen what they never could have gained by the sword.

The Russian government also found certain parts of the Great Settlement anything but satisfactory. The Allies, it was true, had forced Germany to disavow the infamous Treaty of Brest Litovsk. But they had also concerted to detach from Russia large territories along her western frontier and to set them up as buffer states—Finland, Estonia, Latvia, and Lithuania. The chief complaint of the Bolsheviks was not that these states should become independent units. Indeed, at that time (say, 1917) the Soviet government was leaning over backwards to honor the principle of self-determination. What disturbed it were Allied motivations and purposes. Clearly, the Allies considered Bolshevism a disease that must be kept from spreading. The new small states in reality served as agents of quarantine, as a *cordon sanitaire.*

Nor did treaty settlements give satisfaction to Italy. Always the poorest of the Great Powers, she came out of the war with colossal new debts piled onto the old ones. Like all other belligerents, she had floated loans to buy implements of war that literally

were made for destruction. All of the warring powers, of course, had suffered economic losses. But Italy, retarded industrially and lacking the resources to meet new burdens, found herself quite unable to redeem her debts or to provide adequate employment for her people. Politically she was little better off. Launched on at least a quasi-liberal course by the statesmen of the *risorgimento,* her poverty and lack of liberal traditions had combined to transmute incipient democracy into a political wasteland of corruption and factional parties. Although she came out of the great conflict on the "winning" side, she did not feel like a winner. And even though her territorial acquisitions were substantial, they did not measure up to what her ambitious politicians had led her to expect. Out of these circumstances came bitterness, festering frustrations—and *Il Duce.*

## WAR AS REVOLUTION

In the opening section of this chapter we noted a strong prewar revolutionary ferment at work in various countries. During the early years of the war, this force was largely dissipated by the charged emotions of nationalism. But it was not destroyed. As the war turned from movement to stalemate, patriotic passions subsided and the discontents of the prewar years revived. In Chapter XIII we shall examine in some detail the Russian revolution of 1917, which was the most dramatic explosion of these discontents. Here we merely note the revolution as both a foretoken and a catalyst of the politico-economic storms that were to buffet Europe at the end of the war and for a long time afterward. In England the so-called "forces of movement"—that is, forces that desired the overthrow of established vested interests in favor of a liberal "establishment" —gained some influence and power. In France the Socialist party "took courage and before long became the nucleus of a united front of all parties and factions of move-

---

* Justified by France by the failure of the United States to join with Britain in a guarantee of France's territorial integrity. See *infra,* p. 463.

ment."[15] In Germany the Social Democratic party became vocal and demanded, for example, a reexamination of the whole question of German war aims.

Radical or liberal leaders were not alone in giving expression to the feeling that much more than military decisions were involved in the great struggle. Men of the old order also sensed that the war had unleashed forces that seemed likely to change much of the fabric of Western civilization. Count Czernin, a leading Hungarian statesman, predicted that "the coming generation [would] not call the drama of the last five years the World War, but the world revolution which it [would] realize began with the world war." The German conservative leader Gustav Stresemann "saw the war as part of a world revolution which would profoundly stir all aspects of life [and] predicted that the revolution was destined to continue long after the formal end of hostilities.[16]

It would be a serious misreading of history to see World War I exclusively as one act in a continuing drama of collectivist revolution; our detailed examination of its background should save us from this elementary misjudgment. Nevertheless, unless we understand that from 1917 on the war assumed strong revolutionary overtones, we cannot hope to make sense out of the cataclysmic events that followed it: Communism in Russia; Fascism in Italy, Spain, and a number of central European states; Nazism in Germany; faltering socialism in Britain and France; Gandhism in India; New Dealism in the United States. Throughout the nineteenth century, the forces of industrialism and nationalism worked changes in the Old Order—in class structures, political systems, and the stability of empires. The war gave impetus to the tides of change. State planning in the production and distribution of industrial goods, foretaste of the affluent society for those on the home front,

growing recognition of the bungling and vincibility of ruling classes—these merged with renascent restiveness in the later years of the war to make the strife that circled the globe both war and revolution.

## SELECTED READINGS

Bailey, Thomas A., *Woodrow Wilson and the Lost Peace,* The Macmillan Co., New York, 1944.

A critical interpretation of the Paris Peace Conference, which was written just before the end of World War II to "educate American public opinion to its responsibilities in future peacemaking." Wilson is treated fairly, although, at times, severely. As usual, the author's style makes for easy reading.

Bonsal, Stephen, *Unfinished Business,* Doubleday, Doran & Co., New York, 1944.

The author served as interpreter for Wilson and House at many conferences during the period of peace-writing in Paris after World War I. The book is made up of journal entries that constitute important source material.

Churchill, Winston S., *The World Crisis, 1911–1918,* Odharns Press Ltd., London, 1939, 2 vols.

A close-up view of the coming and the course of the war as seen by a gifted statesman whose rhetoric is compelling, sometimes too much so. But if read with one's guard up, this work is not only one of the most interesting accounts of the great crisis, but one of the most enlightening.

Esposito, Vincent J., ed., *A Concise History of World War I,* Frederick A. Praeger, New York, 1964.

A reprint of various articles on the war published in the 1962 edition of the *Encyclopedia Americana.*

*Halévy, Elie, *The Era of Tyrannies,* translated by R. K. Webb, Anchor Books, Doubleday & Co., New York, 1965.

*Asterisk (*) denotes paperback.

15. Mayer, *op. cit.,* p. 5.
16. *Ibid.*

A reissue of a book originally published in 1938. It is a collection of thought-provoking essays on sociopolitical changes in our century. The section entitled "The World Crisis of 1914–1918" is especially recommended.

Hart, B. H. Liddell, *The Real War, 1914–1918*, Little, Brown, & Co., Boston, 1930.

A short, lucid description of the great battles of World War I. The author uses memoirs, diaries, and autobiographical material to correct, as he sees it, the "essentially superficial" history that comes out of a study of formal, official documents.

Mantoux, Etienne, *The Carthaginian Peace, or the Economic Consequences of Mr. Keynes,* Charles Scribner's Sons, New York, 1952.

A savage attack on the "dogmas" of Keynes' *The Economic Consequences of the Peace.*

May, Ernest R., *The World War and American Isolation, 1914–1918,* Harvard University Press, Cambridge, 1959.

A well-organized study of America's tortuous drift toward war. If longer works on the subject cited elsewhere are not used, this one should be.

Mayer, Arno J., *Political Origins of the New Diplomacy, 1917–1918,* Yale University Press, New Haven, 1959.

A long and effectively constructed argument based on the thesis that any worthwhile study of the basic forces at work among the warring powers must give due cognizance to "domestic political determinants" and must deemphasize the traditional "international" war aims of those powers.

Nicolson, Harold, *Peacemaking, 1919,* Harcourt, Brace & Co., New York, 1939.

There is probably no other work on the Paris Conference that is more interesting and scintillating. Moreover, it offers an amplitude of facts, as well as a broad survey of opinions held by the men who made the peace. Yet it must be read with great caution. The author's opinions—especially his view of Woodrow Wilson—need the corrective of broad reading in other works such as James T. Shotwell, *At the Paris Peace Conference,* Macmillan Company, New York, 1937, and Stephan Bonsal, *Unfinished Business* (cited above).

*Smith, Daniel M., *The Great Departure, The United States and World War I, 1914–1920,* John Wiley & Sons, New York, 1965.

A good brief account of how America became involved in the war despite her long tradition of neutrality, and why Americans repudiated the Wilsonian peace.

Tuchman, Barbara W., *The Guns of August,* The Macmillan Co., New York, 1962.

An extraordinarily well-written account of the plans, performances, and blunders of both Allied and German military leaders in the first month of World War I.

Wheeler-Bennett, John, *The Forgotten Peace,* William Morrow Co., New York, 1939.

The only extended study in English of the "Tilsit Peace" made between Germany and Soviet Russia in 1918. It is probably more revealing and more meaningful today than when it was first published.

# XII

# In the Wake of War: 1919 to 1930s

## INTERNATIONAL RELATIONS, 1919 TO 1929

### The Troubled Years, 1919 to 1924

Despite the grand stacking of arms and the signing of peace treaties, conflict and anguish harassed the peoples of Europe throughout the early 1920s. For France the taste of victory soon turned sour. Twice within half a century she had been overrun by German legions. Only with the timely help of allies had she escaped a repetition of the humiliation of 1871. Only with the continued help of allies, she believed, could she hope to prevent a future day of German reckoning. In June 1919 she had signed a defensive treaty with England and the United States which aimed to secure her against such a reckoning. Less than six months later the United States Senate, reflecting America's isolationist mood, refused to ratify the treaty. Because Britain's promise of assistance was contingent upon American participation, France naturally felt new fears

and frustrations. Outstripped by Germany in manpower and wealth potentials and betrayed (as she saw it) by her former allies, she became obsessed with the urge to protect her precarious security. To this end she persistently used the League of Nations as an instrument to preserve the new *status quo* created by the peace treaties. She tried, unsuccessfully, to detach portions of West Germany and to set them up as puppet states.* She concluded pacts with Poland and the states of the Little Entente—Czechoslovakia, Yugoslavia, Rumania—aimed to keep Germany from shaping the potentials of aggression. To the degree that these efforts were effective, German rancor and recalcitrance understandably increased. This reaction, in turn, stimulated new French efforts to keep the defeated nation down, and so the vicious circle went on.

The flaring of a number of little wars increased European tensions. In 1919

* See *infra*, p. 465.

Poland and Russia fought over the possession of Vilna, a strategically located city south of the Gulf of Riga. Polish troops took the city, but were promptly ordered out by members of the Allied Council who decided that the area lay beyond Poland's proper boundaries. Soviet troops then briefly occupied it before surrendering it to a newly created Lithuania. In the fall of 1920, Polish troops again seized the city. This time the League of Nations intervened and arranged for a plebiscite. When Poland opposed this solution, strained relations with Lithuania developed afresh. The result of an irregularly contrived plebiscite finally gave the city to Poland in 1922.

In 1919 and 1920 conflict spread to the Teschen area, now claimed by two states. Czechoslovakia had occupied the territory in early 1919. In May, heavy fighting broke out between Czech and Polish forces. Members of the Allied Council sought to end the struggle by authorizing plebiscitary procedures. But neither side would agree to a ballot decision, and intermittent clashes continued throughout the early months of 1920. A conference of ambassadors finally succeeded in persuading the contestants to divide the territory. Nevertheless, ill will continued to mark relations between the two states up to the outbreak of World War II.

Particularly bitter and prolonged was the off-and-on fighting carried on between Russia and Poland (of which the Vilna affair was but one episode). In the belief that the Soviet regime was tottering and temporary, the Poles attempted to wrest from Russia the whole of the rich Ukraine. In the spring of 1920, they thrust through the heart of the region and captured Kiev. At this point Trotsky's Red Army rallied and launched a counterattack which not only regained Kiev, Vilna, and almost half of the Ukraine, but penetrated deeply into Polish territory. Aided by France, Poland stopped the Russian advance and again pushed to the east. When it finally became apparent that neither side could hold gains

beyond its own borders, a compromise peace was negotiated (see Treaty of Riga, *infra,* p. 510 fn.).

We have already noted that Turkey refused to accept Allied terms offered in the Treaty of Sèvres (1920). Greece and Turkey had long quarreled over their minorities in Anatolia and Thrace. With Turkey weakened by revolution, Greek armies, supported by the Allies, opened an offensive in Anatolia. For about a year the fighting was confused and indecisive. Turkish forces under the Sultan surrendered and for a while actually joined the Greeks against Turkish nationalist armies. But the latter hung on, encouraged and strengthened by treaties of friendship with Russia and Italy, and by the neutrality of France. In March 1921, a new Greek offensive threatened Ankara, the nationalist capital. When it was finally halted by the determined Turks (aided by Soviet Russia) the Allies sought to bring the fighting to an end and to rewrite the Treaty of Sèvres. But a counterthrust by the Turks defeated the Greeks and forced a conference that ultimately satisfied most of their demands (1923; see the Lausanne Treaty, *supra,* p. 458).

In the same year Greece ran afoul of Italy and its prestige-minded Duce. During boundary negotiations between Greece and Albania, several Italian commissioners were killed by Greek terrorists. Mussolini immediately ordered the occupation of the Greek-controlled island of Corfu. For a time it seemed that a new war would break out. But again the League intervened and successfully mediated a settlement.

A number of plebiscites were held to settle other postwar disputes. Austria and Hungary, for example, accepted Italian mediation in their quarrel over a strip of territory (Burgenland) that lay close to Vienna. Occupied in 1921 by Hungarian forces but populated mostly by Germans, the area was finally divided by plebiscitary action. The question of what to do with Upper Silesia proved harder to settle. Substantial in size and rich in mining and other industrial resources, this territory was coveted by both Poland and Germany. A plebiscite held in 1921 gave the whole district to Germany, but Polish troops (with French support) refused to honor the verdict of the voters. In 1922 the Council of the League of Nations recommended a partition scheme, which both sides grudgingly accepted: the bulk of the land and population was added to the German Republic; the chief industrial centers were given to Poland. In 1920 a dispute between Denmark and Germany over a portion of Schleswig was settled when inhabitants of the area were asked to indicate their wishes. In this election divided loyalties were expressed and reciprocally acknowledged: the northern section was awarded to Denmark, the rest to Germany.

For a number of years after the armistice, European conditions remained troubled by quarrels between victor and vanquished over the payment of war costs. As we have seen, Allied commissioners finally fixed (1921) the reparations sum at about 33 billion dollars. When Germany protested, she was told to accept the obligation or suffer extensive occupation of her Rhineland cities. But the Allied triumph was a Pyrrhic one; Germany simply did not have the resources to meet such demands. War, defeat, and revolution had dislocated her economy; the rich industrial Saar was under French control; most of her merchant marine had been confiscated; and her internal debts were crushing. France nevertheless insisted that full, regular payments be made according to a strict schedule. She also insisted that Britain join her in forcing German payments. By this time, however, British leaders were having second thoughts on the wisdom of mulcting the defeated nation. Actually, British recovery depended on the reopening of German markets, and obviously such markets were beyond recovery so long as Germany was crippled by impossible reparations payments. As Britain veered toward a soft policy, France, feeling herself betrayed

*This German bank note for 10,000 marks, issued in 1922, would not cover the price of a pair of shoes.*

once again, increasingly turned to even more desperate measures.

Arguing that Germany was deliberately wrecking her economy to escape her obligations, France (supported by Belgium) occupied the rich Ruhr valley in 1923. All German officials and many industrial leaders were removed from their positions and were replaced by Frenchmen and Belgians. To make certain that disturbances did not arise, the whole area was placed under strict military control. The elaborate effort proved quite futile. Some German laborers slowed down to an unproductive tempo; most of them simply left their jobs. "The French tightened the screw; they imprisoned all the directors they could lay their hands on, shot seventy-six Germans in street brawls, encouraged their Zouave and Senegalese troops in breaches of discipline, at the expense of the inhabitants, [and] instigated and financed a separatist movement all over the Rhineland."[1] To support their idle citizens, the German government printed money which was hardly off the presses before it lost most of its buying power. With the mark thus inflated beyond practical use (see *infra,* p. 489), the whole

1. J. Hampden Jackson, *The Post War World,* Little, Brown, and Company, Boston, 1935, p. 27.

German economy teetered on the brink of bankruptcy. Meanwhile, British protests, coupled with mounting discontent in France and the appearance of a German statesman, Gustav Stresemann, who promised honest cooperation to the limit of Germany's ability, led to the abandonment (in 1924) of the fateful experiment.

In late 1923, the League of Nations set up two committees to assess the economic facts of the fantastic situation. The mark was clearly beyond rescue (even the franc had depreciated to one fourth of its former value). In these circumstances France reluctantly admitted that she could not "mine coal with bayonets" and agreed to give the new German government a chance to prove its good faith. The United States indicated a desire to contribute what it could to effect a general stabilization. Thus encouraged, England suggested the formation of a new committee to devise a workable plan, under the chairmanship of an American businessman.* With all parties agreeing, the committee, which was headed by former Vice-President Charles Dawes, met in January 1924. In April it was ready with its report. A realistic assessment of Germany's ability to pay was recommended. The German government was to set up a workable budget and a sound unit of currency. Beginning in late 1924, Germany was to make progressively larger reparations payments (from one billion gold marks in 1924 to five billions in 1929). To stabilize international exchange and to "prime the pump" for Germany, the United States and certain European nations agreed to grant her substantial loans (800 million gold marks). This reasonable

---

* Historians themselves may occasionally directly enter and affect the stream of history. The idea that actuated the British move came from a paper read at the 1922 Winter Meetings of the American Historical Association. (See G. M. Gathorne-Hardy, *A Short History of International Affairs,* Oxford University Press, London, 1960, 4th edition, p. 58.)

program—commonly referred to as the Dawes Plan—was promptly accepted by all parties and ushered in "the era of fulfillment."

## The Years of Hope, 1924 to 1929

Although the League of Nations had been set up in 1920 and a Permanent Court of International Justice had convened (at The Hague) in 1922, the nations of the world, as we have seen, had shown little ability and less interest in using either one of these institutions in the true spirit of conciliation. However, flaring "little wars," inter-Allied quarrels, and the reparations debacle had given warnings that were too large to be ignored. Clearly, a new temper and a new approach were imperative if world collapse was to be averted.

Under the aegis of the League, a comprehensive plan of compulsory arbitration was drawn up to permit the peaceful settlement of future disputes or, alternatively, to allow the mobilization of power against a would-be aggressor so as to deter or quickly overcome him. A fundamental feature of the Protocol for the Pacific Settlement of International disputes (1924; popularly called the Geneva Protocol) was its definition of an aggressor. Throughout the ages, nations and their leaders had been plagued by their inability to agree on criteria which would clearly demarcate aggressors from the victims of aggression. The Protocol provided a simple solution—an aggressor was any nation which refused to submit its claims to arbitration. The Protocol also provided detailed machinery of arbitration and, in the event of recalcitrance, a set of sanctions designed to coerce the refractory state. If the nations of the world had accepted the Protocol and had implemented it in the spirit of its designers, war necessarily would have disappeared as an instrument of national policy. But certain components of the British Commonwealth of Nations, particularly Canada, India, Australia, and New

*"Little Miss Peace: 'Isn't it splendid? I've got fifteen—and I hope to get the rest.'"* This 1928 Punch *cartoon reflects the cynicism with which some political observers greeted the Briand-Kellogg proposal to outlaw war.*

Zealand, were unsympathetic to the treaty. They believed that it demanded more of them than it offered; as the Canadian representative in the League expressed it, "In this association of mutual insurance against fire, the risks assumed by the different States are not equal. We live in a fireproof house, far from inflammable materials." The fall of the British Labour government at this time, which had been one of the sponsors of the treaty, also militated against its general acceptance. But its defeat stimulated further efforts.

Even before the formal rejection of the Protocol by Great Britain in March 1925, Germany had persuaded her to support a Rhineland Mutual Guarantee Pact. Seemingly reconciled to the Versailles Rhineland settlement, Germany offered voluntary assent to the Rhineland provisions in return for mutual assurances by France, Belgium, and

Germany that international disputes involving this region would be settled by arbitration.* Out of this suggestion came the Locarno Pacts, which seemed to herald a new era in international relations (for the provisions and significance of the Pacts, see *infra,* p. 483). In the fall of 1925, French troops were withdrawn from several Rhineland cities, further promoting amicable relations between the two long-time enemies.

Other events of hopeful augury followed. Germany had long complained that the victor states could not hope for the realization of world peace until they, as well as the vanquished, disarmed. In the spring of 1926, a preparatory commission for world disarmament was set up and began lengthy deliberations. The next year the Inter-Allied Commission of Military Control in Germany was disbanded in favor of League supervision. In 1929 a new reparations commission was established under the chairmanship of Owen D. Young, an American banker. The new plan liberalized Germany's payments and returned to her domestic economic controls that had long been held by the Allies. In short, vexing political and economic problems seemed finally to be yielding to a new spirit of good will and understanding.†

## THE DEMOCRACIES AFTER THE WAR

### Britain: Domestic Affairs

Germany's surrender in December of 1918 touched off more than wild victory celebrations in the British Isles. For about twenty years Britain had felt Germany's ever-increasing pressures to ease her out of the command of world markets and the sea-lanes that served them. Now the great Teutonic power lay prostrate, her Grand

---

* For details of this agreement, see *infra,* p. 483.
† Other events of the "years of hope" are discussed in another context; see *infra,* p. 490.

# EUROPE, 1929

Map by J. Donovan

High Seas Fleet completely destroyed, and her merchant fleet a potential prize of war. Both trident and trade seemed secure again, and the "nation of shopkeepers" made ready to return to business as usual.

There were also political overtones to the victory celebrations. Four years of war had inflamed passions, rendering them tractable to ambitious manipulation by party leaders. Lloyd George had presided over a coalition government for two years; understandably he wished a renewed mandate.

What better time than now, with the full flush of victory exciting the electorate and favorably inclining it toward the statesmen who had designed that victory? To make very certain of the canvass, the Prime Minister and his colleagues piled promises on passions. Germany must pay to the last farthing; the Kaiser must be brought to the gallows; England must be made a land fit for heroes. In short, if the government were returned to office, the nation could rest secure in the knowledge that the peace, like the war, would be won. In the "Khaki elections" of December 1918, the electorate registered its confidence and its hopes in the coalition government, which at once set about translating promises into policy. For a brief time everything went well. The war had created a backlog of orders, the filling of which now gave the country an economic boost. Moreover, the emergence of Bolshevism had cooled British ardor for bloody justice at Versailles and somewhat relieved Lloyd George of the task of carrying out his extreme and impractical promises.

## Economic Troubles

By 1920, however, the troubles that were to harass Britain for the next twenty years had begun to appear. The postwar boom had inflated prices nearly 100 per cent (between early 1919 and 1920). This unsustainable price level led to a sudden collapse which brought on, in 1921, the worst depression that Great Britain had ever encountered.

Moreover, much of the nation's overall economy depended on the production and exportation of coal. The exploitation of large coal beds that France had taken from Germany naturally depressed that industry and thereby the whole economy. To make matters worse, oil was increasingly coming to be used in place of coal. Even nationalization of the mines would hardly change the situation. Already in 1919 two rather widespread strikes by miners had occurred. In March 1921 the government had passed an emergency unemployment measure which provided jobless men with an income of $2.80 a week. The same month, however, the nation's mines, run by the government during the war, were returned to their private owners. Miners had long advocated government ownership. Now, knowing what they had to expect from the private owners, they again went on strike. Several months later the government offered subsidies to underwrite increased wages, and the strikes ended. Few believed that the stopgap settlement

GOING BACK

*This Low cartoon, drawn some years after the first postwar coal strikes, depicts the spirit of workers and enterprisers as Britain drifts deeper into depressed conditions.*

would lead to a further amelioration of the miners' lot, nor did it. Meanwhile, unemployment became more widespread, and feelings of despair settled over the land. Although national bankruptcy and revolutionary disorders of the kind that occurred in other parts of Europe were avoided, Britain's economy, throughout the interwar period, never recovered its former stability and strength.

The roots of the trouble lay in conditions that we already noted in Chapter X: serious maldistribution of wealth and the adamant refusal of the entrepreneurial class to allow the worker to develop effective bargaining strength. Already before the war these conditions had given shape to a revolutionary spirit which in autocratic countries, such as Russia and Turkey, had led to the overthrow of reactionary governments and the institution of radically new regimes. In Britain the democratic tradition blunted the edge of this thrust and offered alternative courses of action. Nevertheless, the war had given workers on the home front an added taste of power and a new determination to gain a greater share of the nation's resources. It would take another war, as it turned out, for the workers to gain full control of the government and initiate socialistic reforms, but the basic forces of that peaceful revolution were already being marshaled and tested.

Besides the sickness in the coal industry, several other serious economic ailments plagued the country. Britain had been forced to liquidate many of its overseas holdings to help finance the war; its capital investments in America, for example, were practically wiped· out. The old, established patterns of trade, moreover, had necessarily been neglected during the war. It was expected that with the return of peace they would be reestablished. They were, but only in part. The United States had quietly taken over many former British markets, especially in South America; Japan had happily busied herself in the same manner in the East. Less than a decade after the war, British exports were down 40 per cent of the prewar level; on the other hand, imports had increased by more than 15 per cent above the prewar level. For any nation, an unfavorable balance of trade is an embarrassment. For Britain, it spelled near-disaster, because she depended (and still does) on trade surpluses to feed her population and to buy the raw resources needed for her factories.

To finance the war Britain had borrowed heavily at home and abroad. By 1918 she had borrowed from the United States alone well over two billion dollars. Bonded indebtedness to her own citizens reached unprecedented levels. Without an ample supply of investment capital and without a healthy trade balance, it was difficult to meet the huge obligations. Compounding this difficulty was the "unrationalized" state of British industry. In the United States, Germany, and even Japan new machines and new methods of production were devised (for

example, Ford's assembly-line process). These countries thus could and did produce the goods that people wanted more cheaply and in greater quantity. No one doubts that the British were as innately capable of creating new instruments and designing efficient production methods as any other nation in the world. The fact is that they did not. This, of course, further restricted domestic buying power, which inevitably led to curtailed production and layoffs of more workers.

## Political Problems

In the postwar years, the overall political situation was marked by fluidity, change, and not a little confusion. Traditionally, Conservatives and Liberals alike had favored free trade. Almost all Liberals still favored it, but most Conservatives were now ready for protection, although some clung to the old faith. Even though the new Labour party opposed tariffs, its members found little comfort in standing with the Liberals on this or any other issue.

Of the three, the Liberal party was in the most precarious position. It had long been the champion of economic and social reform. In the decade before the war it effected, as we have seen, a substantial change in the sociopolitical structure of British life. Paradoxically, its successes were also its undoing. The feeding of the workingman by the Liberal party had increased the worker's appetite beyond what the party believed it could reasonably tolerate. Thereafter the working class increasingly gave its support to Labour, although neither overwhelmingly nor irreversibly.

The Labour party was not without problems of its own. The tendency of many Englishmen to see the party simply as a cadre of dangerous revolutionaries quite insensible to the English way of life had to be overcome. There was also a lack of political and administrative experience among its leaders. Perhaps the most serious problem was the tendency of party members to split off into doctrinaire groups and to waste strength in intramural fighting. Many of its members were old-line unionists who took a dim view of the nationalization of industry; on this point they were at one with the Conservatives. On the other hand, a group of the younger party members vigorously denounced union reformism and demanded the construction of a socialist democracy. When the political chips were down in an election year, the factions usually voted together; divisional weakness showed when the party was given the responsibility of rule.

Before turning to particular events of the period, we need to note one other aspect of the general political situation—the divided state of mind. Repeated reference has been made to the progressive political fermentation—in plain words, class struggle—which marked British life in the years before the war. The little man had not forgotten the taste of victory, as the growth of the Labour party plainly proved. Clearly, battles on the home front loomed. But all Britons, of whatever class, were wearied and worn by four years of war. They yearned for peace and quiet, for reasonable order, for moderation, and for a return to the normal patterns of life. Although these feelings were hardly compatible with one another, they persisted and eventually led to decisions and developments that were characterized by curious political combinations and strange reversals of position and policy. (For a graphic expression of these combinations and reversals see the chart on p. 475.)

## Strikes, Strife, and "Baldwin Security"

As a wartime leader Lloyd George was bold, imaginative, and effective. His overwhelming electoral victory in 1918 seemed to guarantee an energetic attack on the many problems that faced Britain with the return of peace. But the problems proved too many and too serious for the Prime Minister to handle. When the postwar boom ended in 1920, strikes and unemployment increased. Lloyd George's response was government

*Stanley Baldwin, Conservative leader in the interwar years, often gave the impression of being a folksy country squire without keen political perception. Actually, he possessed a profound understanding of the mood of the country and of what was politically achievable.*

economies, which impaired the nation's education and health programs more than they encouraged new investments in industry. His active participation in arranging for home rule in south Ireland (see p. 476) alienated his Conservative colleagues in the Cabinet. On the other hand, his Liberal followers were anything but enthusiastic about his collaboration with the Conservatives. In 1922 the Conservatives, taking advantage of a minor foreign affair fiasco chargeable to the Prime Minister, withdrew their support from the Coalition government and demanded new elections from which they emerged with a clear majority. The Liberals, indeed, suffered such a thumping defeat that the Labour party became the "loyal opposition." The new Prime Minister, Bonar Law, was an able man, but in failing health. Within a few months he withdrew from politics in favor of Stanley Baldwin. More than any other statesman in the interwar period, Baldwin came to sense the troubled spirit and serve the deeper yearnings of the

British electorate. This is not to imply that either spirit or yearnings were marked by vigor or vision. A mood had found a man; from time to time each bickered with and wearied of the other, but for nearly two decades the two were, for better or worse, really one. During the period, and indeed for some time afterward, this was not clearly discerned. Baldwin's deceptively simple ways made it easy to underestimate him. His willingness to let another man occupy the chief position while he maneuvered behind the scenes also made his place in the affairs of the times ambiguous.

## The First Labour Government

The first postwar Conservative government failed to bring Britain out of her doldrums. Higher tariffs were levied in an attempt to give home industries a boost. The dole was decreased to keep the budget in balance. This resulted in higher prices and lower buying levels which caused, hardly surprisingly, increased distress among the masses. A year of Conservative management convinced the electorate that a change was needed. In January 1924, Baldwin yielded to a Labour government, the first in Britain's history. Ramsay MacDonald, the new Prime Minister, favored a capital levy and high estate taxes as the means of redistributing wealth; he believed that nationalization of the country's basic industries would place the economy on the only foundations that could guarantee the abundant life; he also favored free trade, recognition of Communist Russia, and strong support of the League of Nations. But Labour's representation in Parliament was too small to give him the strength and scope to maneuver. To win the necessary support from Liberal members, he dropped his demand for a capital levy and the immediate nationalization of basic industries. Tariff duties were reduced, however, and large estates were heavily taxed. Russia was given *de jure* recognition, and soon thereafter the two governments agreed to a resumption of

commercial relations. To stimulate Russian purchases, the Labour government underwrote a large loan to the Soviets. To many Britons this seemed little short of treason, and a campaign was begun to throw out the socialist government before it could, as the Conservatives thought of it, subvert the nation to Communism.* Believing that most citizens were not fooled by such scare tactics, MacDonald called for another general election to strengthen his hand. He was mistaken. Suffering from economic disabilities that the Labour government and its Liberal supporters had been unable to moderate, and frightened by Lenin's repeated call for universal revolution, masses and classes alike took the Red scare seriously and voted against both Labour and Liberal candidates. The Conservative party returned to power with an overwhelming majority (1924), denounced the recognition of Russia, abrogated the trade treaties, and again laid tariff duties on certain imports. Thus England returned to about the same condition that she had found so intolerable only two years before.

## The General Strike of 1926

In the meantime, the United States and Japan had consolidated and expanded the trade gains that had been made earlier at Britain's expense. To meet the new competition, British industry further depressed wages, while the government, hoping to work some kind of financial magic, restored the pound sterling to its high prewar level. Both measures reduced domestic buying power, which in turn created greater unemployment. Particularly hard hit was the coal industry. In the spring of 1926 the miners were given substantial wage cuts. Supported by the General Council of the

* The most dramatic feature of the campaign was the publication of a letter, allegedly from the Russian leader, Zinoviev, which called on the British proletariat to rise in revolution. It is the consensus of scholars now that the letter was faked, but at the time it was considered part of a real plot to bring England under the control of the Kremlin.

Trade Union Congress, they refused to accept reduction of their already low earnings and went on strike. Dock and transport workers joined in sympathy strikes, and were themselves soon joined by workmen from other unions. Within a week, one sixth of all union laborers had left their jobs—printers, iron and steel workers, construction laborers —in all, some three million of them. Prime Minister Baldwin declared that the general strike "threatened the basis of ordered government" and directed the workers to return to their jobs. The main thrust of the government forces came from Winston Churchill, who was at that time Chancellor of the Exchequer. Churchill and a few extremist Conservative leaders wanted to discipline labor and make it amenable to the command of England's financial industrial leaders. At the height of the strike, he "seized one quarter of the newsprint supply of *The London Times* and began issuing an official government daily, *The British Gazette,* which headlined the news of the strike as 'Hold-Up of a Nation.' " In one issue the *Gazette* flatly stated: "An organized attempt is being made to starve the people and to wreck the state, and the legal and Constitutional aspects are entering a new phase."[2] Actually, the workers were anything but revolutionary. For example, at the very time of the *Gazette's* thundering diatribes, a football match was played between a team of striking workers and a team of policemen. Nevertheless, the government, in complete command of the news outlets that remained, played up the "insurrectionary" threat and succeeded in enlisting the wholehearted support of Britain's middle and upper-middle classes. Within a fortnight the strike had collapsed and all workers had returned to their jobs, with the exception of the miners. The miners stayed out for six months, but eventually near-starvation drove them back

2. Quoted in Quincy Howe, *The World Between The Wars,* Simon and Schuster, New York, 1953, Vol. II, p. 321.

THE LEVER BREAKS.

*Like most periodicals and newspapers,* Punch *was strongly anti-Labour during the days of the general strike in England.*

to work, at reduced wages. The next year the government passed a bill outlawing certain strikes and lockouts.

## Coalition Governments

For a time the crackdown on labor created a calm without effecting any improvement in economic conditions. Unemployment increased and trade lagged. In the general elections of 1929, the Labour party regained power and Ramsay MacDonald returned as Prime Minister. During the campaign the Labourites again promised to nationalize and modernize Britain's "unrationalized" basic industries, to effect reforms in the tax laws, and generally to bring the nation out of its depression. The antistrike laws were repealed and greater relief was extended to the unemployed. A new trade treaty was negotiated with Russia which, it was hoped, would stimulate the export of British goods. However, no real improvement in general economic conditions resulted. For one thing, the Labourite majority was too small to prevail against Liberals and Conservatives who joined forces in order to block the nationalization of the coal and steel industries. Also, by the time the Labour government had pushed its abbreviated program through Parliament, the whole world was bogged down in depression. In this impasse the

*Prime Minister MacDonald on his way to the House of Commons, 1932. Passersby did not seem to be particularly impressed by this shoulder-rubbing experience.*

government resigned as a Labour government (1931) and reformed with power resting in a National Coalition made up of Conservatives, Labourites, and Liberals. As Prime Minister, MacDonald called on his party to support the coalition for the duration of the economic crisis. But most of his colleagues indignantly refused to accept this repudiation of Labour's program. Instead, they read their leader and the few who remained loyal to him out of the party and went into opposition.

## Return of the Conservatives

MacDonald remained Prime Minister until 1935, but from 1931 until after World War II the government was dominated by Conservatives. Deteriorating economic conditions forced them to adopt a number of measures hardly compatible with their principles. To support sagging farm prices, the government passed legislation that guaranteed a minimum price for some grains; farm credits were also extended. Other legislation shored up the wages of industrial workers and stabilized price levels of various manufactured goods. Like the contemporary American New Deal, the Conservative program also gave limited power to the govern-

ment to supervise some aspects of industrial management. In 1931 the gold standard was abandoned, thus allowing the devalued pound sterling to compete more effectively in the world market. For a time, unemployment was halted and better times seemed on the way. General elections, held in 1935, increased the Conservative majority. Although a pretense of multiparty management was maintained for a while, the replacement of MacDonald by Baldwin in June 1935 marked the end of the coalition. In the meantime the Labour party, reorganized under the leadership of Arthur Henderson, renewed its bid for national leadership. By this time the Nazi menace had grown so threatening that Britain felt forced to undertake extensive rearmament. Moreover, in the spring of 1935 the government introduced military conscription. The combined effects of removing tens of thousands of young men from the ranks of the unemployed and the stimulus given to industry by the rearmament program brought a degree of prosperity that no previous postwar government had been able to create. Naturally, the Labour party lost voter appeal. The prosperity, of course, was artificial. Britain's basic economic and political problems were salved over rather than solved, as the years of the aftermath of another world war were to make plain. But for the time being the nation seemed content to make do with current solutions, however contrived.

In January 1936, King George V died after a reign of twenty-five years. He was succeeded by Edward VIII, the former Prince of Wales. The new king's tenure was brief and ended dramatically. His desire to marry an American divorcee was opposed by the government, which felt that such a marriage was not in the country's interest. When Edward insisted that he had the right to marry "the woman he loved," the government forced his abdication (December 1936). His brother, succeeding to the throne as George VI, promptly offered Edward a dukedom, and the constitutional crisis faded into sentimental legend. Whether wearied by this novel compounding of governmental and romantic chores or harassed by physical ailment, Baldwin soon retired as Prime Minister and was succeeded by Neville Chamberlain. However, not even these dramatic comings and goings could hold the average Englishman's attention. For by then Germany's Führer was springing international surprises with a regularity and virtuosity that blurred domestic triumphs and troubles; these events will be dealt with in Chapter XIII.

---

*BRITISH GOVERNMENTS AND CHIEF DOMESTIC EVENTS, 1919–1937*

*Coalition Government:*

Lloyd George, Liberal, Prime Minister, 1919–1922.

Coal miners' strikes, March 1919; October 1919.

Emergency Unemployment Act, 1921.

Coal miners' strike, March–July, 1921.

Conservatives withdraw from government, 1922.

Resignation of Lloyd George, 1922.

*Conservative Government:*

Cabinet of Bonar Law, October 1922–May 1923.

General election, 1922; Conservative victory.

Labour party displaces Liberal party as opposition party.

Retirement of Bonar Law, 1923.

Stanley Baldwin replaces Bonar Law, 1923–1924.

General election; protective tariffs chief issue; Baldwin defeated; substantial gains by Labour, 1923.

*Labour Government:*

Ramsay MacDonald heads first Labour government, January 1924–November 1924.

Recognition of Russia; commercial treaty with Russia.

General election, 1924; Conservative victory.

*Conservative Government:*

Second Baldwin Ministry, 1924–1929.

Renunciation of treaties with Russia.

Coal miners' strike, May 1926.

General strike, May 3–12, 1926.

Miners accept operators' terms, November 1926.

Trade Union Law, 1927; some strikes and lockouts declared illegal.

Women gain full franchise, 1928.

General election, 1929; Labour victory.

*Labour Government:*

Second MacDonald Labour cabinet, 1929–1931.

Report of the May Committee indicates Britain headed for bankruptcy, 1931.

Issue of governmental economy and cut in unemployment compensation splits cabinet.

Over 2,000,000 unemployed.

MacDonald resigns, 1931.

*National Coalition Government:*

Conservatives, Liberals, and some Labourites form new government. MacDonald's First National (Coalition) Government, August 1931.

Economy measures passed, causing great unrest, 1931.

Abandonment of gold standard, 1931.

General election, 1931; split in ranks of Labour party; coalition government supported by electorate; MacDonald's Second National (Coalition) Government, October 1931.

Baldwin and Conservatives real power in government.

Deepening of depression.

Protective tariff laws passed, 1932.

Subsidies for some farm products voted.

"Buy British" campaign launched, 1933.

Budget balanced.

Slow economic recovery.

Armaments expenditures increased, 1935.

General election; cabinet reconstructed; resignation of MacDonald; Baldwin's National government, June 1935.

Death of George V; accession of Edward VIII, January 1936.

*(Continued)*

Edward's abdication, December 1936; accession of George VI.

Retirement of Baldwin; Neville Chamberlain becomes Prime Minister, 1937.

*National Government:*

(National in name only; actually Conservative.)
Chamberlain, 1937–1940.

*This proclamation appeared at the outbreak of the Irish Rebellion in April 1916. It speaks eloquently of the nationalist feelings of a people long dominated by a foreign power.*

## Imperial Affairs: Ireland

In addition to domestic problems, imperial issues also plagued Britain during the postwar years. Even before the end of the war a serious crisis had developed in Ireland. In the spring of 1916, bands of Irish nationalists organized a rebellion that opened a period of turbulence and violence which lasted for more than twenty years. Since about 1800 Ireland, by Parliament's fiat, had been an organic part of the United Kingdom. Except for the inhabitants of six Protestant northern counties, the Irish people opposed unification. They were of a different ethnic stock, of a different religion, and, generally, of a different psychological character. Moreover, they had sustained over four hundred years of English oppression. England's war with Germany gave them hope that their day of deliverance had come. However, the German help which had been promised was forestalled by a tight British blockade, and the rebellion was savagely crushed. The English then sought to woo their restive subjects by granting amnesty to the rebel leaders, including Eamon de Valera, leader of the nationalist Sinn Fein ("We Ourselves") party. But the rebels would not be wooed. Throughout the next three years relations between governors and governed remained strained. When the Sinn Feiners finally resorted again to widespread terrorism, the English decided to retaliate in kind. For several months in 1920 both sides perpetrated atrocities that neither one of them likes to remember. The carnage was ended when the British Parliament passed the Government of Ireland Act, which gave southern (as well as northern) Ireland its own governing body. By this time, however, many southern Irish were not of a mind to settle for dominion status, and demanded complete, unqualified independence. But others were willing to accept the Act's settlement. Fighting soon broke out between the two factions and continued for over fifteen years. Tension and troubles also continued between Irishmen and Englishmen. Eventually, the harassments became unendurable and brought all parties to negotiations. In 1938, Britain recognized Eire (as the nationalists insisted on calling their land) as completely independent, and Eire agreed to pay about $30 million that was owed to former English landlords. Complete harmony between the two states and between Irish moderates and extremists was hardly to be hoped for, but a reasonably workable peace was achieved.

## Egypt

Nationalists in Egypt were also busy in the postwar period. As we noted in Chapter X. England had occupied Egypt in 1882. Turkish suzerainty was recognized, but only nominally. With the outbreak of World War I, Britain denounced all Turkish claims to Egypt and, to pacify restive Egyptians, promised to defend the land without calling up native conscripts. Before the end of the war, however, conscription was introduced. Egyptian representatives tried to bring their cause before the Paris Peace Conference, but were prevented by the British. For several years opposition of various kinds, ranging from flaring violence to passive resistance, agitated relations between the two peoples. In 1922 England dramatically—and unilaterally—declared Egypt independent. Egyptian nationalists repudiated the action on the grounds, which soon proved to be sound, that the independence was bogus. England reserved the right to intervene in Egyptian foreign affairs, to control communications, especially as they affected the Suez Canal, and to station troops in strategic areas. The next year a constitution was promulgated and elections were held. The nationalist party, the Wafd, gained a majority of seats in the new legislature and proceeded to work for complete independence. In the main their efforts were blocked by British military might and by lavish bribes that kept the native court at odds with its Egyptian subjects. In 1924, Wafd assassins killed the British Commander of the Egyptian army. In the period 1924 to 1925 repeated elections found the nationalist majority growing larger and more recalcitrant. To keep Egypt in line, Britain forced the Egyptian parliament to dissolve for three years, decreed suspension of certain civil rights, particularly free speech and free assembly, and enlarged its military establishment. When the Labourites returned to power in England, Egyptian nationalists hoped that new negotiations would lead to independence. Discussions were resumed, and eventually a new treaty favorable to Egyptian interests was drafted. Unfortunately, the deepening world depression created in both lands internal problems, which first slowed and finally scuttled negotiations. For several years thereafter the British government bribed native leaders to keep down agitation. But the Wafd continued to attract followers and to sabotage English rule. When the Wafdists swept the 1936 elections, Britain agreed to a treaty that gave Egypt a large measure of true independence. Most of the exploitative economic privileges enjoyed by foreign nations were abolished; Egypt was admitted into the League of Nations; Egyptian control was reinstated in the Sudan. Still, the existence of some English troops in the canal zone, together with the maintenance of mixed courts, kept relations between the two states strained. In Chapter XVI we shall note the drastic revisions of the 1936 treaty and the eventual creation of a fully independent Egyptian Republic.

## India

More than one million Indian troops had fought on the side of the Allies during World War I. Their sizable contribution to the war effort and fair words from their British overlords gave Indians strong hope that self-government would soon be granted. British procrastination, combined with serious crop failures (and a crippling influenza epidemic), stirred Indian nationalists to radical agitation in 1918 to 1919. To teach their wards a lesson, Parliament passed the Rowlatt Acts, which stripped Indians accused of sedition of the right of trial by jury. Hindus, Moslems, and Sikhs promptly abandoned the fighting among themselves and united in opposition under the leadership of Mohandas K. Gandhi (popularly called the Mahatma—the Holy One). Gandhi's tactics were unusual. Believing that truth is God and that love is the strongest force in the world, the sainted leader urged his people to meet all wrongs

*Here India's genial Mahatma, Mohandas Gandhi, discusses Indian affairs with his friend, the famed poet and philosopher Rabindranath Tagore.*

of the imperial provinces were given the franchise, and provincial governments were set up with power to act in local matters, such as education, sanitation, and agriculture. The Act did not please many Indians. Although enlarged, the electorate still excluded over 90 per cent of the citizenry; the provincial governments were wholly dependent on British control of the purse; and in overall national affairs the Indians were little better off than they had been before the war.

In 1920, Gandhi led the Congress party* in a renewed campaign for home rule. He urged Indians to boycott British businesses, to make their own homespun garments, and to refuse participation in any governmental affairs until complete home rule was granted. British officials reacted vigorously against what they considered insufferable insubordination. At the same time, serious friction developed between native Hindu and Moslem populations. To increase the pressure on the British, Gandhi launched a widespread civil disobedience program. In spite of the Mahatma's insistence on peaceful resistance, violence spread throughout the land, culminating in the discontinuance of the civil disobedience campaign and the arrest of Gandhi. For several years general confusion marked Indian affairs. Many Indian moderates followed Gandhi in his fight for dominion status but, with their leader in jail, they could make little progress. Other Indians looked to Jawaharlal Nehru for leadership that promised complete independence, but they constituted a minority of the restive masses. Many Indian states were "ruled" by native princes who almost always sided with their imperial masters and did what they could to discourage the fight for either dominion status or independence. As always, caste was arrayed against the great mass of "untouchables," and friction between Moslems and Hindus continued.

After his release from jail in 1924, Gandhi adopted a policy of watchful waiting. Parlia-

with nonviolent resistance. Millions enrolled under his banner. But his straight way was hard to follow, and sometimes the passions of his devotees burst the bonds imposed by the Mahatma. To effect the repeal of the Rowlatt Acts, Gandhi had ordered a massive campaign of peaceful civil disobedience. At Amritsar, British troops fired into a crowd of demonstrators, killing hundreds. India seethed at this act of arrogant brutality and lashed back with violence of its own. To bring the situation under control, Gandhi called off the disobedience campaign and began an expiatory fast. This was to be the Mahatma's basic approach to the solution of India's problems in the years that followed: exhortation of his followers to the use of the love-force (*satyagraha*), trust in its efficacious effect on the British, occasional demonstrations of civil disobedience, fasting and self-sacrifice when either Indians or Englishmen spurned the way of love.

In 1919 the Government of India Act provided for greater participation of Indians in governmental affairs. Propertied citizens

* See *supra*, p. 378.

ment appointed another commission to re-study the problem (1926), but nothing came of its work except increased Indian restlessness. In 1928 strikes broke out in a number of textile establishments and soon spread to the railroads. Nehru's League for Indian Independence gained strength. A new round of violence seemed imminent. At this point Gandhi appealed to the masses for order and discipline, and to the British government for a speedy working out of arrangements that would lead to dominion status. When the London government, by this time plagued by a deepening depression at home, gave Gandhi nothing to hope for, he inaugurated another campaign of civil disobedience (1930). To dramatize the struggle, he organized a great "march to the sea" where, in violation of a British law forbidding the manufacture of untaxed salt, he and hundreds of his followers crudely refined heaps of salt along the shores. Gandhi was again arrested, and another wave of violence spread across the land. Moderates in both India and England insisted that a final resolution of the protracted conflict somehow be found. Several imperial conferences— "Round Tables"—were held. But clearly the white man was not ready to shed his burden, for the meetings produced no policies that had not already been tried.

In 1935, a new Government of India Act was passed by a still hopeful Parliament. Burma and Aden were separated from India and made crown colonies. An increased number of citizens were given the franchise. Extensive control over provincial affairs was granted. But the Act satisfied neither moderates nor radicals. As always, the British government reserved for itself the final word in foreign affairs and defense matters. And, as always, the imperial ministers could decree even local laws if an emergency required it. From then on Gandhi, despairing of partway measures, demanded complete independence. Strife continued between Hindus and Moslems, castes and untouchables, and princes and the people, so that Britain could and did

*Gandhi at his spinning wheel. For Gandhi the spinning wheel was a symbol of both the "non-machine" way of life and India's capabilities of economic self-sustenance.*

argue that she could not withdraw until factional quarrels were settled. But by the outbreak of World War II it was clear that regardless of internal difficulties, a final reckoning could not be long delayed.

## Palestine

As part of the Peace settlement, Britain had been given mandatory control over Palestine. The assignment turned out to be a thirty-year imperial headache. The land was inhabited by two peoples, Jews and Arabs, each claiming the right to the whole territory. Each had strong arguments to support its claims. For nearly two thousand years, from the time of Moses to the Moslem conquest, Palestine had been the homeland of the Jews, as well as the Holy Land for Hebrews everywhere. But certain Moslem tribes had conquered it in 638 and ruled it for well over one thousand years. They had multiplied in greater numbers than the Jews (by 1900 they outnumbered Jews seven to one), and to them, too, Jerusalem was a holy city. Historic and religious ties thus bound both groups to the land.

In these circumstances any mandatory power would have found governing the territory a frustrating ordeal. British interests in the region added further complications. Because of the advent of Communist Russia, England feared eventual Red control of the eastern Mediterranean, which would naturally threaten her lifeline to the East. In addition, some of the great oil conduits that tapped the resources of Iraq and Arabia had their outlets in the Palestinean area. The possession of these pipelines by an enemy could severely penalize Britain's economic interests.

Added to these vexations were the contradictory promises that England had made to the Jews and Arabs when she needed the support of both during World War I. To the Jews she had promised, in the famous Balfour Declaration, help in founding a national homeland. To the Arabs she had given strong hints that she would help them establish independent states. Both peoples called for redemption of these promises after the war. Both charged bad faith and imperial perfidy when England formally took over control of the whole region (including Transjordan) in 1922.

In the years that followed England found herself hung on the horns of a seemingly unresolvable dilemma. Concessions to one group brought anguished protests from the other. Specific Arab complaints included a Jewish immigration policy that threatened ultimately to destroy Arab numerical dominance, allocation of the best land to the Jews, and improper administration of sacred sites in Jerusalem. On the other hand, the growing Jewish population unceasingly lamented Britain's failure to implement the Balfour Declaration. No program seemed acceptable to both groups. In 1937, Britain tried to divide the territory into Jewish and Arab parts. Neither side would agree to the boundaries, nor even to the idea that there should be a division. In 1939, England asked representatives from both groups to meet in London and work out between themselves a satisfactory arrangement. Each side sent representatives, but neither one would sit down with the other. Carrying proposals and counterproposals, Prime Minister Chamber-

lain shuttled back and forth between the rooms that housed the separate delegations. Neither side could compromise on such basic issues as boundaries, if separate states were set up, or representation, immigration, and land sales, if a unitary state was created. So the conference adjourned with nothing accomplished. Following announcement of the meeting's failure, new riots broke out in Palestine, different from the many that had occurred in the preceding years only in the savagery that the almost continuous conflict had nurtured. As we shall see in Chapter XVI, partition and a precarious peace were eventually effected; for the time being, however, Britain continued to bear a burden that had almost no Kiplingesque compensations.

## France

Before turning to postwar events in France, we should note some general considerations. The war inflicted greater physical damage on France than on any other nation. Here most of the four-year fighting along the Western Front took place. Over twenty thousand factories were demolished, nearly one hundred thousand homes and farms were destroyed, almost one half of France's male population between the ages of 22 and 34 were slain.

The war also inflicted a psychic trauma on the nation. Without outside help France would surely have been overrun, and Frenchmen knew it. Clemenceau also admitted that the grandeur of victory was clouded not only by the indescribable misery that had won it but also by haunting fears that a new day of revenge awaited France, as once they had haunted Germany. Naturally, these fears generated a deep yearning for strong safeguards, for security at almost any price. Undestandably, too, these in turn could hardly fail to stimulate ever greater and more persistent preparations for *der Tag* (the day of German vengeance and resurgence of power) across the Rhine.

France suffered also from chronic political

instability. Part of the nation—most of the workers and some intellectuals—clung to the liberal heritage of the Revolution and looked forward to a society truly grounded in liberty, equality, and fraternity. Another part, made up mostly of peasants, petite bourgeoisie, and the industrial elite, feared radical reforms as the prelude to anarchy. Proportional representation was another divisive force. Under it no single party could expect to seat a majority in the Assembly. Consequently, that body was normally made up of a number of blocs whose leaders were forever jockeying for domination of a coalition which only rarely lasted as long as two years and often broke up after several months or even weeks. Twenty different prime ministers, for example, held office during the twenty-year truce between the wars. Under-secretaries, it is true, gave some continuity to both domestic and foreign affairs, but too much has been made of the influence of these civil servants. When chief ministers move in and out of office with a merry-go-round regularity, general political stability is impossible.

For a while the nation enjoyed economic health. Unlike Britain, France produced a large part of the foodstuffs that she needed. The balance between agriculture and industry (the ratio was about 40 to 60) meant less dependence on the vagaries of world trade and exchange, hence greater internal economic stability. Even so, the margin was too close to guarantee sustained prosperity, should the world economy suffer severe depression. Even before this calamity occurred, huge war debts and the falling value of the franc presented grave problems that harried the ever-changing governments.

With these general considerations in mind, we may briefly turn to certain specific events. Ever since the Revolution, France had been divided regarding the place and the power of the Church. Anticlerical governments had, by the early years of the twentieth century, deprived the Church of much of its political influence and most of its property. In 1921 diplomatic relations with the Vatican were reestablished. Three years later confiscated diocesan property was returned to the Church. Republicans bitterly protested both actions. When Republican leaders came to power in 1924, they tried to reverse this "soft" policy toward the Church. But the masses protested so vehemently that the government was forced to reopen its Vatican embassy. Royalist, and later quasi-fascist, overtones complicated this perdurable and divisive issue which vexed ministries throughout the 1920s and 1930s.

By 1924 it was clear that German reparations could not be depended on to pay for the nation's immense rebuilding projects. Plunging deficits, coupled with the chronic tendency of French citizens to evade taxes, sent the exchange rate of the franc down to about two cents, one tenth of its prewar value. When Republican and Leftist parties showed no sign of being able to handle the burgeoning financial crisis, the nation turned to the strong man of the Rightists, Raymond Poincaré (1926). Forming a National Union ministry (which included six former premiers of all parties to the right of the Socialists), Poincaré pushed through a Spartan program of governmental economies and increased taxes. About four fifths of the national debt was repudiated—in effect a capital levy on the rentier class. The nation groaned but suffered the ordeal, realizing that the melancholy choice was between individual belt-tightening and national bankruptcy. The franc was pegged at four cents, and the budget was brought into balance. For the next six or seven years economic conditions improved, although bitter memories of the cost remained to haunt and hamper future ministries.

## Class Struggle

The working classes came out of the war with a new spirit and lively ambitions. They were conscious of their contribution to the great victory. They were impressed by the

gains made by labor in other countries, as
well as emboldened by the cumulative effect
of the preachments of radical doctrinaries,
from their own to those of the Russian Revolution. Some of them joined the Communist
party to work for the overthrow of the whole
capitalist establishment. Many others became
active members of the Socialist party which,
in 1920, joined the Communist-dominated
Third International. Still others remained
independent, voting for the party or bloc
which bid highest for their favor. For about
a decade such bidding was not very vigorous.
Russia's strident call for world revolution
frightened many in the country, encouraging
their bourgeois rulers to weaken working-
class organizations whenever opportunities
for it arose. In 1921 a court order temporarily dissolved the General Confederation of Labor (roughly comparable to our
A.F.L.–C.I.O. except for its strong syndi-
calist leaning); as a partial sop, the government extended the 1898 Workingmen's Compensation Act to include farm laborers. By
1930, however, labor had recovered much
of the ground lost in the Red-scare years.
In that year a National Workman's Insurance Law was passed, which gave to millions
of Frenchmen some protection against the
crippling economic effects of sickness, old
age, and death. Indeed, as we shall soon see,
within half a dozen years a Socialist government had come to power.

So long as prosperity lasted, the conflict
between labor and capital remained minimal
and sporadic; when the Great Depression
spread to France (1931–1932), dissension
became acute. Serious enough in itself, the
conflict was aggravated by other, and in some
cases quite irrelevant, issues. For example,
in 1933 and 1934 the nation seethed with
confused anger over the exposure of corruption in high places. A certain Serge Staviski,
an imaginative rogue with political connections, had overplayed his hand in the promotion of a fraudulent bond issue. He was
killed, it was alleged, resisting arrest. Lead-

*Paris police trying to disperse rioters protesting
the government's handling of the Stavisky affair.*

ers of royalist and quasi-fascist organizations
charged the government with deliberately
murdering a criminal whose public trial
would have embarrassed a number of highly
placed officials, including a Cabinet member
or two. It finally led to the resignation of the
Cabinet. The full facts of the case never became known, nor are they important in our
context. For us the Staviski affair is significant because of the impetus that it gave to
anti-Republican fulminations against "the
system" and to the growing doubts among
French citizens about the ability of democracy to deal with problems of modern
industrial life. For a while it seemed that the
extreme Right might overthrow the Republic
and set up or try to set up an authoritarian
regime.

Members of the working-class parties

gradually came to realize that they could not continue to fight among themselves and still hope to stand against reactionary pressures. Therefore, in the face of growing unemployment, public confusion, and Rightist agitation, the chief parties of the Left drew together in what came to be called the Popular Front. In the spring of 1936 it gained a majority in the Assembly and, under the leadership of Léon Blum, sponsored a wide-ranging program of social reform. The forty-hour week was introduced; arbitration of labor disputes was made compulsory; workers were granted vacations with pay; the munitions industry, one of the largest in the country, was nationalized; and the Bank of France was brought under strict governmental control. For a while France's "new deal" seemed to work. The laboring masses rejoiced in their new rights and in the crippling blow that had been dealt to the so-called ruling two hundred families. Unemployment, never as high as in other industrialized countries, fell. But the Popular Front's "new deal" lacked resources that its American model possessed—potentially abundant supplies of capital to be tapped for public works, a reasonably stable currency, and a geographic isolation which allowed it to concentrate on domestic problems. Within a year, Blum was forced to devalue the franc still further while calling in vain for popular subscription to large and badly needed bond issues. Developments in the savage civil war in Spain also contributed to his declining popularity. Most of his supporters favored giving assistance to the Spanish Republic, but Blum felt the need to stay in line with his British ally which was then (1937) slowly moving toward its appeasement stance. Thus harassed at home and abroad, Blum resigned, bringing to an end the attempted grand breakthrough of socialist reform. Succeeding ministries were no more successful in dealing with socioeconomic problems, but by that time the Nazi menace overshadowed domestic concerns.

## Fear of Germany

From the end of World War I to the outbreak of World War II, national security constituted France's biggest worry. We noted earlier her attempt to bring England and the United States into an alliance with her in order to keep Germany permanently in check (see *supra*, p. 463). Failing in this, France turned to other devices. In 1920 she signed an alliance with Belgium in which each of them promised to support the other in the event of German aggression. The next year she entered into an agreement with Poland in which mutual aid was promised if either party was attacked without provocation. In the period of 1924 to 1927, she linked herself with the three powers of the Little Entente, thus effecting an almost complete encirclement of the German Republic. In this same period *de jure* recognition was given to Soviet Russia, which was followed, with the advent of Nazism, by a formal military alliance (1935) aimed at discouraging Hitler from attempting power plays in the east.

All of these arrangements were motivated by a frankly acknowledged apprehension of revived German power, with little concern, to understate it, with the cultivation of good relations between herself and her defeated foe. One consequential undertaking, however, had precisely this concern as its objective. In 1925 Stresemann, Germany's foreign minister, asked France to concert with Germany in finally dissipating the abiding fear of another war between the two states. Peace-minded Briand happened to be France's premier at the time. He accepted the offer with the proviso that Britain, Belgium, Italy, Poland, and Czechoslovakia be invited to participate in a broad, general settlement of all outstanding issues. Stresemann agreed, and the conference was held at Locarno in the closing months of 1925. Out of it came agreements between France and Germany promising that their facing frontiers were never to be changed by force; that certain areas of the Rhineland (as provided by the Versailles Treaty) were to remain demilitarized in perpetuity; and that neither of them would ever aggressively attack or invade the other.* The pacts were greeted with general acclaim. At Versailles, Germany had been forced to sign away Alsace-Lorraine and to accept demilitarization of the Rhineland. At Locarno she accepted these settlements voluntarily. One great trouble spot, it seemed, had been erased from the European map forever. Cautious critics pointed out that the question of the Polish Corridor, an eastern Alsace-Lorraine, remained unsettled, for Germany refused to make any pledges concerning the boundaries in the east. But the world seemed too happy over the "Locarno miracle" to feel much concern.

To reinsure herself, France began the construction of an elaborate system of fortifications along the German border (1929). The Maginot Line (so called after the name of its chief engineer) was built in such depth and strength that most military experts considered it impregnable. Some skeptics, it is true, professed to see in the costly, complicated works a symbol of the state of the French psyche—an elaborate admission of the nation's loss of vitality and venturesomeness. For most Frenchmen, however, the Line seemed to guarantee the kind of security that they were seeking.

## The United States

The last sections of this and a later chapter take up in some detail certain conditions and policies which significantly marked life in America after the war—inflation, depression, and the New Deal.† Here

we briefly note the condition of the public mind and certain events which developed out of it.

The attitude is associated with a deceptively simple word—normalcy.‡ World War I had sickened America of things European. Casualty lists, governmental restraints, the hypertension of global conflict (to say nothing of strange geographic place names and foreign ways of life)—all had generated in many Americans, perhaps most Americans, a deep longing for disengagement from a world that they did not understand and for an unencumbered opportunity to resume the acquisition and enjoyment of the good things of life. Thus in the campaign of 1920, Harding's call for a "return to normalcy" struck responsive chords. Actually, the phrase was as little grounded in historic reality as it was in grammatical usage. The war had in part shaped and in part revealed America as a world power. Technology had made that world, if not one, at least so interpenetrated and interdependent that no nation could stand alone or even measurably aloof; try as it might, America could never "go home again." Moreover, the forces of modern times had wrought changes internally as well as externally. The American worker had tasted economic affluence; the American entrepreneur had multiplied millions beyond precedent. Although bewitched by the lure of Harding's call, neither would complacently return to the conditions of an earlier day. Furthermore, both were weaned, at least to some degree, from traditional moral restraints and from what came increasingly to be regarded as the naïve demands of a Victorian conscience. Not all Americans became Main Street Babbitts; but the breed multiplied abundantly. Even though Christian America did not disavow its Sunday trinity, it jubilantly made room for a secu-

---

* These constituted the main provisions of a series of multilateral agreements which included a number of arbitration treaties dealing with problems in Eastern as well as Western Europe.
† See *infra,* pp. 487–496; 551–560.

‡ President Harding, whose rhetoric suffered from chronic suffix trouble, is credited with coining this corruption of "normality."

lar workaday worship of nationalism, isolationism, and materialism.*

One manifestation of overcharged nationalism was the "Red scare" which swept the country in 1919 and 1920. Attorney General A. Mitchell Palmer ordered wholesale arrests of aliens who were connected, however slightly, with socialist or liberal groups in this or their own country. A number of states passed laws so stringent that the display of a red flag, for example, was sufficient cause for imprisonment. A visiting English journalist wrote:

No one who was in the United States, as I chanced to be, in the autumn of 1919 will forget the feverish condition of the public mind at that time. It was hagridden by the spectre of Bolshevism. . . . Property was in an agony of fear, and the horrid name "Radical" covered the most innocent departure from conventional thought with a suspicion of desperate purposes.[3]

In 1922 Congress passed the Fordney-McCumber Tariff Act. Its basic purpose, which was frankly stated in the act itself, was to increase the costs of foreign goods to whatever extent was necessary to equalize them with the costs of American-produced goods. The record that it set in producing the highest schedules in our history stood only eight years. In 1930 the Smoot-Hawley

*Despite police orders to the contrary, Klansmen parade through the streets of Tulsa, Oklahoma (1923) in their campaign to keep Tulsa "white, free and 100% American."*

Act increased the rates on some raw materials by as much as 100 per cent. More than one thousand professional economists petitioned President Hoover to veto the new bill, but the President, although voicing some apprehensions, signed it into law. Naturally, other nations retaliated, thus penalizing world trade at a time when its expansion was urgently needed.

In 1924 Congress turned its attention to protecting American workers from the competition offered by immigrants. A law passed in that year reduced the quotas of all countries to 2 per cent of the number of their nationals admitted in 1890. Later the act was amended (it became effective in 1929) so as to put a ceiling of 150,000 to the number of immigrants admitted in any one year. It also prohibited all Japanese from entering the United States except as students or visitors. While Congress was keeping aliens out by law, millions of Americans were busy denigrating non-American cultures. In the early 1920s, a revived Ku Klux Klan launched a sustained attack on all groups beyond the Wasp (White, Anglo-Saxon, Protestant) pale. Ethnic minorities, such as Italians and peoples from the Slavic countries of Europe, were denounced as parasites sucking Amer-

---

* Some historians would sharply disagree with much of the substance of this paragraph. They consider this an "oversimplified myth." In my view, their revisionist treatments provide stimulating reading but dubious history. One of the most incisive and concentrated attacks on what its author would likely call the cult of American myth-makers and their wearisome interpretations is found in David A. Shannon, *Between the Wars; America, 1919–1941*, Houghton Mifflin Co., Boston, 1965. The whole work is a provocative treatment of these times, but see especially pp. 6–7 and 47–57.

3. A. G. Gardiner, *Portraits and Portents*, New York, 1926, p. 13, quoted in Preston Slosson, *The Great Crusade and After*, Macmillan Co., New York, 1930, p. 79.

*Plainclothes Federal enforcement officers empty bottles of liquor confiscated under the Prohibition Act.*

*A typical speakeasy bar of the 1920s.*

ica of its life blood. Catholics were pilloried as conspiratory agents of a nefarious power.* Orientals were branded as unassimilable coolies, Negroes and Jews, not surprisingly, were especially singled out as objects of harassment and, occasionally, of outright brutality. By the mid-1920s, the Klan had become strong enough to impose its rule on many local communities and on at least one state.

### Corruption and "Speakeasies"

Corruption in the higher echelons of national public service also marked the early postwar years. In the Department of Justice, of all places, plundering rascality took over. Before Attorney General Harry M. Daugherty was removed from office in 1924, he and his cronies had turned its bureaus and sections into agencies of personal profit and aggrandizement. Thomas W. Miller, alien-property custodian, was sentenced to a prison term in 1927 for illegal dealings with the American Metals Company. Colonel Charles Forbes, appointed head of the Veterans Bu-

reau, used this office to enrich himself and his friends until a Senatorial investigation revealed the looting to the public. Secretary of the Interior Albert Fall secretly leased the Teapot Dome Oil Reserve to Harry F. Sinclair for an undisclosed consideration; he similarly leased the Elk Hill Reserve to oilman E. L. Doheney who, as later investigations disclosed, had "loaned" the Secretary $100,000 without either interest or security.

Paradoxically, these were also the years when America attempted an experiment, "noble in purpose," which was designed to rid the land of the evil influences of intoxicating drink. In 1920 Congress passed the National Prohibition Act which forbade the manufacture and sale of all beverages that had an alcoholic content greater than one half of 1 per cent. But from the first the law was flouted. "Speakeasies" replaced saloons, and racketeers briskly stepped into the business of illegally supplying a demand for this commodity which Americans had legally banned. Thus in its drinking habits, as in its

* Many Americans actually believed that the Pope, aided by secretly scheming Catholic congregations, was planning to transfer the papal throne to the United States, as an initial move in a long-range plan to take over the country.

economic and political life, the public gave clear evidence of its desire to "return to normalcy."

Our brief review of America's postwar mood and some of the events shaped by it should not lead us to conclude that the country became a carnival of violence and vice. Many of America's millions seriously sought to understand their country's new role in world affairs. Many favored, if not the League as it was, some kind of workable world association of nations. Most Americans were puzzled and saddened by the hate orgies and extremism of the superpatriots; most of them tended to their jobs, their families, and their public duties much as Americans had always done. Nevertheless, the mood that has been described did pervade the land. The rejection of Europe, the erection of tariff barriers, the persecution of minorities, the corrupt management of public affairs, the Prohibition interlude—these events are segments of the historic record which must be placed in calculation if we wish to understand the nature and meaning of American society after the war.

## INFLATION AND DEPRESSION

### The Emergence of Illusory Affluence: America

In the two decades after World War I, economic conditions were alternately marked by inflation and depression. To one degree or another the whole world was affected. We shall give particular attention to their course and consequences in the United States and Germany where their manifestations and significance are most clearly seen.

At war's end all of the major nations of Europe were burdened with huge debts. Great Britain's public debt, for example, was ten times greater in 1919 than it had been four years earlier. France was even worse off. In addition to her bonded debt, she suffered from the effects of the war's destruction of many of her factories and farms. Moreover, her prewar loans to Russia had been completely repudiated by the new Bolshevik regime. Germany's internal public debt was higher than that of any of the Allied countries. During the war Germany had preferred to finance military operations almost exclusively by loans rather than by taxes. Presumably, this decision was based on the intention to force the Allies to make good the redemption of her bonds after her victory; when Allied victory put the shoe on the other foot, Germany was of course seriously pinched. Among other penalties suffered were the loss of many of her world markets and patent rights. Italy, a perennial pauper among the Great Powers, came out of the war somewhat richer in territorial possessions, but with an economy that was teetering on the brink of bankruptcy.

Even the United States, the world's newest and greatest industrial giant, experienced a sharp, if passing, depression in the early postwar period (1921–1922). Nearly seven thousand businesses and banks failed in 1921. Unemployment increased by about 30 per cent. Farm prices fell sharply; corn, for example, which had sold in December 1919 for $1.35 a bushel, dropped within twelve months to 68 cents. In certain key industries such as railroads, textiles, coal, and steel, rates and prices remained high while wages were kept disproportionately low. The Federal Government abruptly curtailed its military spending which naturally affected the overall economy. Foreign markets, of course, dwindled as economic conditions in Europe worsened.

But, paradoxically, economic conditions in America did not become really bad until the nation recovered from its brief depression. The fateful "seven fat years" which followed this recovery—the period of the famous boom—masked basic flaws in the economy which were to bring on the severest depression in modern history. But at the time these years seemed to promise the dawn of an endless age of plenty both in their productivity and in the amazing rapidity with which the nation effected its economic about-face.

No consensus has yet been reached to explain America's rapid emergence from "hard times," although certain elements are obvious. One is the country's transformation during the war years from a debtor to a creditor nation; it became, indeed, the world's leading lender. Another element is the telescoping of technological progress effected by the war itself. It is true that many advances in technology were initiated by Europeans (for example, German chemical engineers and English makers of precision machine tools). But, as one writer has put it:

Big Technology is an integral part of the daily living of Americans . . . . [It] has been for Americans what the Cross was for the Emperor Constantine: *In hoc signo vincas* . . . . The American has been a machine-intoxicated man. The love affair (it has been nothing less) between the Americans and their Big Technology has been fateful, for it has joined the impersonal power of the machine to the dynamism of the American character.[4]

Once out of the slump, American economy went on to set production records never surpassed or even closely approximated. Several relatively new enterprises gave substantial impetus to the boom. One was the automobile industry. By the early 1920s the Ford Motor Company and General Motors, together with a number of smaller corporations, were turning out low-cost cars at such a rate that by 1928 about 25,000,000 automobiles were clogging America's streets and highways.* The automobile's consumption

---

* Again, it must be emphasized that in an introductory study of civilization it is impossible to present a bill of particulars and implications for many generalizations. In the instance just cited, for example, it must be obvious that these millions of cars would have been quite useless had not counties, cities, and states constructed thousands of miles of hard surface roads.

---

4. Max Lerner, *America as a Civilization,* Simon and Schuster, New York, 1957, p. 227.

of oil, gasoline, and rubber naturally stimulated these industries.

Another mushrooming business was that of motion pictures. "By 1926 there were over 20,000 movie theaters in the United States, with an average attendance of 100,000,000 persons a week, a figure only slightly smaller than the total population." By this time, too, the radio had become sufficiently perfected to create a demand that industry energetically set about to meet. Electrical appliances and machines of all kinds poured in a flood upon the market. Also, the war had stimulated the construction and proved the practicability of heavier-than-air craft, and the aviation industry was born. Buildings of all kinds—homes, factories, stadia, business houses—were put up with such speed and in such numbers that in the seven years of 1922 to 1929 America underwent a kind of national face-lifting.

The tempo and scope of this economic bustle imparted to many Americans a feeling that material utopia was at hand. In a special sense of the word, inflation overspread the land—a heady confidence that the realization of stimulated desires and newly felt needs was not only possible but imminent. But inflation in its ordinary sense also marked these times. Price levels stayed fairly high. Real estate values were given dollar values that did not correspond with reality. Stocks of almost all the large corporations were sold—increasingly "on margin"—at figures that only a kind of self-induced delusion prevented the buying public from recognizing as fantastic. In short, a jerry-built economy precariously undergirded America's Jazz Age.

### German Catastrophe: Inflation

European economies also suffered spiraling inflation. Particularly significant was the German experience. Stripped of a good deal of her working industrial wealth (most of the rolling stock of her railways, for example, was handed over to France and Belgium), burdened by impossible reparations, and in-

*A typical payroll scene during the height of the inflation crisis in Germany.*

*This German baker found his inflated paper-mark weekly wage too bulky to fold into his pocket, hence his use of a cigar box.*

wardly determined to prove the economic provisions of the Versailles Treaty unsound, Germany turned to the printing press for relief. This cure of her economic ills, of course, was worse than the disease itself. A few statistics tell the story. Before the war, 4.2 German marks equaled one American dollar in international exchange; in 1919 the ratio was 8.9 to 1; by late 1921 it took nearly 250 marks to equal the buying power of one dollar. As the Allies prodded Germany into maintaining her reparations payments, her economy began to show signs of collapse. The French government insisted, as we have seen (*supra,* p. 465), that the Germans were deliberately sabotaging arrangements provided for in the treaty settlement and demanded direct Allied intervention. When Great Britain questioned the soundness of this move, French forces occupied the Ruhr.

The occupation at once set off bitter and indignant German reactions. Some Germans, such as the young agitator Adolf Hitler, urged the meeting of violence with violence. Some vented their passions in hysterical denunciations. Most supported the German government's decision to oppose the move by passive resistance. Miners refused to go into the pits; factory workers made only a pretense of tending their machines; railroads deliberately maintained hit-and-miss sched-

ules. As unemployment increased, the German government felt obliged to grant aid to the displaced workers. This aid generally took the form of newly printed money.

Naturally, this flood of unsecured currency gave impetus to the already strong inflationary trend. In July 1923, one dollar was worth 200,000 marks; by September it was worth 100,000,000 marks; by November over four trillion marks. Merchants tried to peg prices to the changing value of the mark, but it was difficult for anyone to know at any given time just what that elusive unit was worth. For buyers, the situation became even more fantastic. A German housewife might leave her home with 400,000,000 marks to purchase a loaf of bread only to discover before she had reached the bakery that the price had jumped to 600,000,000 marks. Sometimes housewives borrowed wheelbarrows or carts, not to bring home groceries but to transport bundles of currency. Great quantities of paper money were doled out to employed and unemployed workers, but never in proportion to the soaring prices. Worst hit of all was the large middle class whose fixed income and investment returns made its ruin inevitable. Suppose, for example, that Hermann Schmidt, a civil service employee, had purchased a 15,000-mark annuity policy in 1903 which was to run for twenty years. Throughout these years he had cut expenses to pay his premium against the day when his policy would mature and he would begin to receive benefits which would enable him to purchase some of the comforts that he and his family had denied themselves so long. In 1923 his policy matures and he receives a bundle of paper that does not, literally, buy a postage stamp.

When the harassed German government abandoned passive resistance, the nation's leading financial expert, Hjalmar Schacht, was directed to reform the currency system. He created a new monetary unit, the *Rentenmark,* which "redeemed" the old mark at the ratio of about one trillion to one. Although ostensibly backed by the real estate and industrial establishment of the entire country, the stability of the Rentenmark actually rested on the confidence of the German people. At the same time, and as part of the rejuvenation program, Germany negotiated a series of loans from abroad (mostly from the United States).* By mid-1924, the runaway inflation was brought under control, and German industry began a rapid recovery. But psychic scars had been cut deeply into the German body politic. In Kafka's words, the ghosts had been dispersed; "only as the night advances do they return, in the morning they have all assembled again, even if one cannot recognize them." Before a decade had passed, Germany's ghosts had assembled in their legions, bedecked with brown uniforms and swastikas. For the present, however, things seemed to be going well. The hum of the factories was heard throughout the land. Science combined with technology to produce a dazzling display of entrepreneurial pyrotechnics. To the hopeful it seemed that the age of peace and plenty had dawned.

* During the period of 1925 to 1928, American capitalists loaned huge sums to many European governments and private investors. The total amount exceeded one billion dollars.

## The Mirage of the "Four Good Years"

From 1925 to 1929 business conditions in a large part of the Western World made such marked gains that many economists began to talk of a permanent plateau of prosperity. In 1928 a well-known Harvard economist declared: "There is absolutely no reason why the widely diffused prosperity which we are now witnessing should not permanently increase." One of his German counterparts proposed the rather remarkable thesis that capitalism was unconsciously changing into socialism, which almost automatically would ensure the abundant life:

We are in the period of capitalism, which in the main has overcome the era of free competition and the sway of blind laws of the market, and we are coming to a capitalist organization of economy [which] in reality signifies the supersession, in principle, of the capitalist principle of free competition by the Socialist principle of planned production.[5]

Actually, neither enduring prosperity nor socialism matured by capitalism was rooted in the real conditions of the times. Nevertheless, for a while a kind of economic well-being did flourish. Because of American loans, Germany paid its pared-down reparations installments on time and in full. More loans enabled German industry to rebuild itself, this time in the image of its American assembly-line model. France and England revitalized their own industries, partly out of reparations payments. Soon trade and production, in Europe as well as in America, exceeded their prewar levels.

Currency stabilization and industrial recovery allayed tensions and encouraged humane ventures. During this period, for example, turbulence in German political affairs abated. Nazis and Communists still made much noise, to be sure, but their influence

5. R. Palmer Dutt, *World Politics, 1918–1936,* London, Victor Gallancz, Ltd., 1936, pp. 65–66.

was on the wane. Although the German Republic had not yet grown up to its democratic constitution, the auspices seemed good. Franco-German relations improved. In 1925, as we have seen (*supra,* p. 483), the two former enemies, together with England, Italy, and a number of other states, joined in a large-scale effort to deal with some of the unsettling attitudes and conditions caused by the war and by the treaties that had ended it. Altogether the complex of agreements went a long way—although certainly not the whole way—toward alleviating French fears of future German aggression. For Germany the agreements symbolized her readmittance into the European family. The next year the symbol was made substance by Germany's admission into the League of Nations. Buoyed up by a general feeling of optimism and good will, most states ratified the Pact of Paris (1928; commonly called the Kellogg-Briand Pact) which outlawed aggressive war as an instrument of national policy. In 1929 the Young Plan further scaled down German reparations payments.

One must be either an intellectual smart aleck or an ignoramus to hold that all the hopes and achievements of these "good years" were vaporous products of naïve idealism and shallow Babbittry. Many of the industrial and technological developments were real, lasting, and good. Most of the peacemakers, such as the French Premier Briand and the English Prime Minister MacDonald, were social statesmen of stature, vision, and courage.* Nonetheless, the underpinnings of the prosperous Golden Twenties were shaky. In Chapter XVII we shall survey the spiritual wasteland of those years. The fundamental forces and features of the economic system, more jungle than wasteland, were employed in ways which not

---

* This assessment does not apply to the later years of MacDonald's tenure as Prime Minister, which witnessed such an appalling deterioration of the statesman's competence and ideals that they tend to overshadow completely his earlier strengths and achievements.

only invited catastrophe but made it inevitable. Together with the United States, the leading industrial powers of Europe of that time—England, France, and Germany —share responsibility for the coming of this catastrophe; but our purpose is best served by concentrating on the developments in America and their European repercussions.

Untouched by invasion and bombings, American farms and factories during the war produced prodigious supplies of goods and foodstuffs, which the Allies bought with cash or with credit of one kind or another. By war's end, Europe owed American investors over ten billion dollars. As the chief debtors, France and England hoped to use reparations funds to meet their own obligations. When these funds failed or were scaled down, both countries asked the United States for commensurate debt adjustments. The United States, however, held that there was no connection between debts and reparations and insisted on complete fulfillment of contractual commitments (as Coolidge phrased it, "They hired the money, didn't they?").

Conceivably, the debtor states could have met their obligations even without the suggested scaling down if the United States had been willing to buy European products freely. Actually, it made a point of buying less. The Fordney-McCumber tariff raised duties to a higher level than ever before in American history. Denied both debt adjustment and ready access to American markets, the debtors faced a serious dilemma. With their own economies in the doldrums, they could scarcely raise the money by increasing domestic taxes; thus only default or repudiation remained. But either of these avenues of escape would seriously impair their credit and financial stability at a time when these could not stand further shock.

For a time the debtors were saved by the Dawes and Young plans. But obviously such loans and payments on other debts paid out of them did not make the best of sense, because mere circularity of exchange creates little new wealth. And, of course, the whole complicated process would collapse at any time that America decided to discontinue loans to Germany.

## The Great Depression

Presumably, such loans could go on forever, provided that the United States' economy remained strong. As we have seen, surface signs did suggest that the United States had made a miraculous breakthrough into permanent prosperity. But the signs were wrong. In 1929, the Great Boom came to an abrupt end, and the long lean years of depression completely dried up the dollar flood to Germany. Deprived of this support, the German economy collapsed. Because Germany was a good customer of England, British economic conditions, which were already suffering recession, seriously worsened. By 1930 and 1931, almost all of Europe was affected by the cataclysmic downturn.*

It is natural—and easy—to ask what caused the Depression, which in this country and in much of Europe lasted in one degree or another for a full decade. It is not easy to provide answers that stand the test of serious and informed analysis. The judgments of professional economists, although numerous and elaborate, tend to originate in certain general economic theories. When the theories differ, as they often do, the judgments contradict one another or at least fail to merge into a consensus. Among lay writers, analysis is almost invariably made to fit the political philosophy held by the particular analyst. The analysis here is summary in nature and subject to the same criticism.

If the Golden Twenties had really been golden, there would have existed, among other conditions , a sound economy that served the needs of all citizens equitably. Actually, the economy was anything but sound and basically served the greed of its managers. Throughout the twenties, the national income amounted to approximately 700 billion dollars. Of this about $170 billion, or 25 per cent, went to 5 or 6 per cent of the population.† Obviously, levels of profits on the one hand and wages and salaries on the other were out of balance. This disproportion was maintained throughout most of the decade. "Output per worker in manufacturing industries," for example, "increased by about 43 per cent,"[6] while wages and salaries increased only 7 or 8 per cent.[7]

Another criterion of a sound economy is a responsible and prudent design and management of the corporate structure. It is true that President Hoover's Conference on Unemployment reported (1929) that our economy was marked by "prudence on the part of management; . . . skill on the part of bankers . . . and [an] organic balance of economic forces." But the structure and activities of holding companies and investment trusts, which by that time dominated our national economy, could better be described as a jungle of exploitative forces. One authority expressed it as follows:

. . . the fact is that American enterprise in the twenties had opened its hospitable arms to an exceptional number of promoters, grafters, swindlers, imposters, and frauds. This, in the long history of such activities, was a kind of flood tide of corporate larceny.[8]

---

† A generation later the ratio was still about the same. In 1955, according to a report of the Department of Commerce, 5 per cent of the population received 20.3 per cent of the national income.

---

* France was not seriously affected until about 1932–1933. The U.S.S.R., though beset by various economic problems, cannot be said to have suffered a depression at all, as the word is generally used.

6. John K. Galbraith, *The Great Crash,* Houghton Mifflin Co., Boston, 1955, p. 180.
7. *The Recovery Program in the United States of America,* the Brookings Institute, Washington, D.C., 1936, p. 632.
8. Galbraith, *op. cit.,* p. 183. For both data and interpretive comment dealing with the causes of the depression, I am particularly indebted to this work. *Cf.,* especially, pp. 173–193.

Moreover, at no time throughout this decade had the farmer enjoyed even a modest prosperity; for him the depression had set in as early as 1920. This was due in part to the high tariffs on manufactured goods, which forced the farmer to buy in a dear market while selling in a cheap (world) market. Although the rural population constituted but a minority of the whole, it was a substantial minority whose restricted buying power seriously affected overall economic conditions.

Much of the national "spending" went into capital investment, the profits of which were channeled into further capital investment. In short, the profits of the rich were used in ways which made the wealthy even more wealthy. Obviously, this could not go on forever unless the masses could be counted on to remain satisfied with bare-subsistence living. But, the industrial revolution, and more recently the war, had long since given the masses tastes and expectations hardly calculated to guarantee their easy acceptance of subsistence living conditions.

In 1929 one third of the nation's income was siphoned off by 5 per cent of the population. With its disproportionately small share of the total income, the general public could not buy the flood of goods which steadily poured from the factories. For a while the illusion of a purchasing power commensurate with productive power was maintained by the popular practice of installment buying. But this kind of debt, when long continued, is necessarily self-defeating.

Moreover, the hectic ventures of investment capital during the middle and late twenties encouraged speculation. In the beginning, Wall Street's professional plungers led the way. As the market continued to rise, more conservative men of wealth began to buy and sell. Gradually the good news spread until eager citizens from almost every income level found their way into the market.

In 1927 the increase began in earnest. Day after day and month after month the price of stocks went up. . . . On May 20, when Lindbergh took off from Roosevelt Field and headed for Paris, a fair number of persons were unaware of the event. The market . . . had by then acquired a faithful band of devotees who spared no attention for any celestial matters. . . . Early in 1928, the nature of the boom changed. The mass escape into make-believe, so much a part of the speculative orgy, started in earnest. . . . On March 24 . . . General Motors gained nearly 5 points and the Monday following it went to 199. . . . [John J. Raskob, William Durant, the Fischer brothers, William A. Cutte, and many other veteran operators] were assumed to have put their strength behind the market that spring . . . . Observing the group as a whole Professor [Charles Amos] Dice [of the Ohio State University] was especially struck by this "vision of the future and boundless hope and optimism . . . ." In noting their effect upon the market Professor Dice obviously found the English language verging on inadequacy. "Led by the mighty knights of the automobile industry, the steel industry, the radio industry . . . and finally joined in despair by many [bearish?] professional traders who, after much sackcloth and ashes, had caught the vision of progress, the Coolidge market had gone forward like the phalanxes of Cyrus, parasang upon parasang and again parasang upon parasang. . . ."9

In the last week of October 1929, the market, unable after all to sustain the pace of the fabled phalanxes, collapsed. The Golden Twenties were over.

The depression which followed the crash (not, it should be noted, essentially *caused* by it) is difficult to describe. Statistics are plentiful enough. Industrial production dropped from a high of 110 in 1929 to 58 in 1932.* The Dow-Jones averages of sixty-five strong, selected stocks plunged from

---

* Index numbers 1935–1939 = 100. The statistics cited in this paragraph are from Broadus Mitchell, *Depression Decade*, Rinehart and Co., Inc., New York, 1947, pp. 438–455 *passim*.

9. Galbraith, *op. cit.*, pp. 13–17 *passim*.

*As the Great Depression deepened, Americans queued up before employment agencies, hoping, often futilely, to find any kind of a job that would pay the rent.*

out of four American workers lacked a job. Factories that had once darkened the skies with smoke stood ghostly and silent, like extinct volcanoes. Families slept in tarpaper shacks and tin-lined caves and scavenged like dogs for food in the city dump. In October the New York City Health Department had reported that over-one-fifth of the pupils in public schools were suffering from malnutrition. Thousands of vagabond children were roaming the land, wild boys of the road. Hunger marchers, pinched and bitter, were parading cold streets in New York and Chicago. On the country-side unrest had already flared into violence. Farmers stopped milk trucks along Iowa roads and poured the milk into the ditch. Mobs halted mortgage sales, ran the men from the banks and insurance companies out of town, intimidated courts and judges, demanded a moratorium on debts. When a sales company in Nebraska invaded a farm and seized two trucks, the farmers in the Newman Grove district organized a posse, called it the "Red Army," and took the two trucks back. In West Virginia, mining families, turned out of their homes, lived in tents along the road on pinto beans and black coffee.[10]

$125.43 to $26.82. Exports declined from over $5 billion to about $1.5 billion. Building construction dropped in the same period from $30 billion to $5 billion. In 1929 approximately 3 per cent of the civilian labor force was unemployed; four years later the unemployed made up about 25 per cent of this force.

But statistics do not really tell the story. One may read that more than 40,000 persons are killed annually by automobiles and yet quite fail to sense the ineffable grief of one father whose child is mangled in a wreck. On the other hand, some feeling for the depression is required if its nature and significance are to be even dimly understood. The following paragraph evokes some feeling for the disjointing of life which the depression had effected by 1933, some sense of the darkness that enveloped the country.

The fog of despair hung over the land. One

The United States, of course, was not alone in the deepening misery and despair; much of Europe was mired in it too. The capitalist system had experienced contractions and depressions before. In fact, depression had for centuries been one of its fixed features, a kind of seed-rotting on which the system's subsequent grand flowerings depended. This depression was different. The intolerable material and spiritual sickness of the great decline caused millions in Europe and America to question seriously whether such a system had not served its day. Indeed, it had already been replaced in Russia where, for all the world to see, economic conditions were anything but depressed.

Out of such questionings came the growing belief that national economies should be

10. Arthur M. Schlesinger, Jr., *The Crisis of the Old Order*, Houghton Mifflin Co., Boston, 1957, p. 3.

*Shacks of unemployed along Seattle's waterfront, 1933. Such villages were called "Hoovervilles."*

*A breadline in New York City during the Depression.*

*Two of New York City's many unemployed who tried to earn their daily bread by selling apples on the streets of the city.*

made subject to public planning and management. Nurtured by concerned intellectuals, the collectivist impulse assumed varied forms. In Western Europe (including England) socialist parties grew in strength and respectability. Communism attracted many. In the United States, after the "money changers had fled from their high seats in the temple of our civilization," the people were less sure of what kind and what degree of planning were desirable. But no one could doubt that the majority was ready for almost any innovation and experimentation that could promise food, jobs, and security. Throughout the world it was felt that somewhere there must be a way out of the wilderness, somewhere there must be men who could lead stricken peoples to find that way. And there were. In the United States, Franklin D. Roosevelt improvised a New Deal. In Germany, Adolf Hitler drummed in National Socialism. In France (if only briefly) the Socialist Léon Blum led a "popular front"

in instituting a program of mild social reform. For a while the Labour party in England, under Ramsay MacDonald's timid leadership, gave that country its first faint taste of socialism. In the Scandinavian countries (most notably in Sweden) mixed economies developed, which were in part capitalism and in part socialism.

The creation of one or another kind of managed economies, whether spurred by the depression or generated by the revolutionary ferment stirred by World War I, naturally involved wide-ranging political and social changes. In Chapters XIII and XIV we shall consider the overall transformations that occurred in Russia, Italy, Germany, and the United States.

## SELECTED READINGS

Albrecht-Carrie, René, *France, Europe and the Two World Wars,* Harper & Brothers, New York, 1961.

A very readable account of the main events of Europe's political life, 1914–1939. An epilogue of some 25 pages surveys the "consequences of France's abdication" (in the 1930s) and the impact and consequences of World War II. Particularly worthwhile are the sections on the "false peace"—from Versailles to Locarno—and on the declining power of France after the coming to power of Adolf Hitler in Germany.

Brogan, D. W., *France Under the Republic,* Harper & Brothers, New York, 1940.

One of the best general histories of the political life of France between the fall of Napoleon III and the outbreak of World War II.

Carr, E. H., *International Relations Since the Peace Treaties,* Macmillan & Co., London, 1937.

A brief description of international events for the twenty years following the Versailles Treaty. The organization emphasizes the "period of enforcement," 1920–1924, the "period of pacification," 1924–1930, the "return of power politics," 1930–1933, and the "end of the treaties" with the re-emergence of Germany.

*Chambers, Clarke A., ed., *The New Deal at Home and Abroad, 1929–1945,* The Free Press, New York, 1965.

A very interesting collection of excerpts from the writings of a number of influential Americans of the period—F. Scott Fitzgerald on the Jazz Age; Franklin D. Roosevelt on the New Deal; Grace L. Coyle on "Rebuilding the American

*Asterisk (*) denotes paperback.

Dream"; Reinhold Niebuhr on the state of religion; Gunnar Myrdal on America's black/white problem; and others.

*Galbraith, John Kenneth, *The Great Crash, 1929,* Houghton Mifflin Co., Boston, 1961.

An informative account of the months that preceded the Wall Street debacle and the weeks that followed it. The reader learns more than who did what with the market; he learns something of the outlook of a people at a moment in history. Written in a very graceful and witty style.

*Havighurst, Alfred F., *Twentieth Century Britain,* Harper & Row, New York, 1966 (2nd ed.).

A detailed examination of British political events.

Jackson, Gabriel, *The Spanish Republic and the Civil War, 1931–1939,* Princeton University Press, Princeton, 1965.

Although his sympathies lie with the Loyalists, the author's careful research and judicious evaluation of issues and events assure the interested reader a more nearly full and well-balanced understanding of the rise and fall of the Spanish Republic than he is likely to obtain from any other single source.

Mitchell, Broadus, *Depression Decade,* Rinehart & Co., New York, 1947.

One of the best attempts to describe in graphic form the events of America's Depression and New Deal years. Its chief fault, from the standpoint of the present-day college student, is that it was written before a generation of research and publication had passed. In other words, sections of it are outdated. But it remains well worth reading.

*Rollins, Alfred B., Jr., ed., *Depression, Recovery, and War, 1929–1945,* McGraw-Hill Book Co., New York, 1966.

Although most of the articles of this symposium fall into what many would call the "snippet" category, they are so varied and so well chosen that they can profitably be used by readers who already have a reasonably sound understanding of the broad movements of these times and want or need such source capsules as this collection offers.

*Shannon, David A., *Between the Wars: America, 1919–1941,* Houghton Mifflin Co., Boston, 1965.

A highly readable, interpretative narration of America's domestic and foreign affairs in the interwar period. Introducing each chapter is a section devoted to what the author believes are misconceptions of the events narrated in that chapter and the author's "corrective" comments. One does not always need to agree with these "corrections" to find them highly stimulating.

Slosson, Preston, *The Great Crusade and After, 1914–1928,* The Macmillan Co., New York, 1930.

Concerned with the impact of the violence of war on the fabric of American society in the years after the war—"the blunted conscience, the overwrought nerves, the growth of intolerance . . .," and the development of an interest in the materialistic ways of life that were stimulated by a galloping "prosperity."

*The Recovery Problem in the United States,* The Brookings Institution, Washington, D.C., 1936.

A collection of articles that attempt to point out what obstacles to the return to prosperity lay ahead of the United States in 1936, and what kind of a program should be mapped to overcome them. The first three chapters deal with the background, course, and world impact of the Great Depression.

Toynbee, Arnold J., *The World After the Peace Conference,* Oxford University Press, London, 1925.

An assessment of the general forces at work in the years 1914–1923, forces that brought on the war, and that seemed to prevent its permanent settlement.

Wecter, Dixon, *The Age of the Great Depression, 1929–1941,* The Macmillan Co., New York, 1948.

A volume on the *History of American Life* series. Very readable account of the impact of the Depression on the whole of American culture. Well illustrated.

Werth, Alexander, *The Twilight of France, 1933–1940,* ed. by D. W. Brogan, Harper & Brothers, New York, 1942.

This abridgement of three books includes Rightist groups, Laval, Blum, and interesting accounts of the Popular Front, its response to the Spanish Civil War, the strikes of 1936, France's dilemma *vis à vis* Munich crisis, and an evaluation of the Vichy regime.

# XIII

# *The Collectivist Trend between the Wars: Russia; Italy*

## A. Communist Russia

### BACKGROUND OF THE RUSSIAN REVOLUTION

The ending of the World War I closed one "season of dismay" and inaugurated another, aptly designated by the novelist Arthur Kaestler as the "Age of Longing." By then, many traditional attitudes and modes of behavior seemed outworn and unserviceable. Faith in the old frames of reference gradually gave way to a congeries of doubts and discontents. Out of this creeping confusion came an almost universal yearning for new outlooks, new political and social systems, and new manners. The most radical resolution of these longings occurred in Russia when, in 1917, a splinter political party captured power and created a new society.

It surprised no one that the tzarist regime should one day fall. That it should ultimately fall to a handful of Bolshevik visionaries surprised almost everyone, including many of

the Bolsheviks themselves. From the perspective of the present, however, the radical resolution does not appear so remarkable. Because the industrial revolution had come to Russia so late, no sizable middle class existed. Without such a class, a middle course had little chance to emerge. When change came, it was almost certain to be marked by extremism of one kind or another.[1]

### *The Misery of the Masses: The Peasants*

Certain long-standing characteristics of Russian society clearly pointed to a climactic

---

1. For a more detailed exposition of this point and those immediately following, see John L. Stipp, *Soviet Russia Today*: *Patterns and Prospects,* Harper and Brothers, New York, 1956, Chapter 1. A fuller and richer treatment can be found in John Maynard, *Russia in Flux,* The Macmillan Company, New York, 1948, pp. 22–38, from which much of the material in the cited chapter is taken.

time of troubles. For example, Russia, alone among the great powers, had missed the Renaissance. She did not, therefore, participate in the general reexamination of the meaning and worth of individualism and the escape from medieval inertia that profoundly affected the subsequent development of Western peoples. Russia also missed the Protestant Revolt and the Catholic Reformation that had brought, in the Protestant Revolt, some curb to the repressive force of ecclesiastical power over the peasant and, in the Catholic Reformation, a reinvigoration of the mind and spirit of the clergy.

Cut off from these progressive influences, Russia easily (perhaps inevitably) succumbed to absolutist rule. For nearly 500 years the masses of Russia lived in circumstances that approached the unbelievable. Serfdom, although officially abolished in 1861, still held the impoverished peasant in its grip until the Bolshevik Revolution. The masses were so lacking the refinement of human qualities that they were often referred to in nineteenth-century Russian literature as "dead souls." When, goaded beyond endurance, some rose against their masters, punishment was swift and unmerciful. For example, in 1834 an uprising occurred in the province of Viatka. The landed gentry at once called for troops. The principal agitators were apprehended and, in the forced presence of peasants herded in from the countryside, each was lashed to death. Peasant families normally lived in squalor inconceivable by their counterparts on American farms. They were always hungry and ill-clad. Their huts, until the twentieth century, commonly consisted of one room. The preponderant masses, both peasant and worker, were illiterate. The resulting (almost animal) nature of their daily life is revealed in the following account:

We are not surprised to find that the peasant was brutalized by the conditions of life. One of our writers, whose Siberian stories had great vogue in the seventies, describes the roasting, by their captors, of horse-thieves over

a slow fire. This was the revenge for losses caused to peasant transport-drivers. Fire-raisers were often beaten to death, and this was in the comparative civilization of the Moscow region. The treatment of women was coarse and cruel. The woman was "unclean," and many of the old men would not enter the bath house after her. Wife-beating was entirely approved by public opinion, and a particular kind of possession or hysteria, supposed to be due to grief and ill-treatment, was common among women. Life, and the land, made such pitiless demands that there was no chance of the growth of finer feelings. Peasants marry [off] their girls in autumn, rather than in the spring, for the same reason they sell a cow in autumn rather than in spring—to save winter keep.[2]

## The Misery of the Masses: The Workers

As late as 1914, Russia's industrial workers made up less than fifteen per cent of the population. Most of them were transplanted peasants who were hardly a generation removed from the soil. They worked from twelve to sixteen hours a day; in 1914 their average pay was only about $150 a year. Although few in number, Russian factories tended to be much larger than industrial plants in Western Europe or America. Often the worker and his family were quartered on the factory grounds. As Russia stepped up its military preparedness, the state increasingly became the largest single entrepreneur. Under these conditions Russia's industrial proletariat both worked and lived in a military atmosphere.

Unions were forbidden by law until the opening years of the twentieth century. Even then, the unions that were allowed—under the fantastic system called "police socialism" —were designed to thwart rather than advance worker solidarity. They were, in fact, government-supervised company unions. To counter these unions, certain labor leaders created a new organization modeled after the

2. Maynard, *Russia in Flux,* p. 33.

ancient *Mir*.* Ostensibly this new instrument —called the soviet—dealt only with such matters as workers' complaints about the malfunctioning of established rules and practices. Actually the soviets held secret meetings to discuss revolutionary ideas and mull over schemes for a general day of reckoning. Since their worker-members were peasants under the skin, and since the soviets came to play a significant part in the revolution to come, the new organization may be regarded as one important element in the (at least partial) successes later achieved by the Bolshevik regime in welding together the interests of worker and peasant.

## Emergence of Radical Thought

But by itself, mass misery, no matter how prolonged, does not lead to successful revolution. History indicates the need for two prerequisites: some notion (no matter how vague) of the features of a new and better life (with an accompanying hope, no matter how faint, in its achievability); and able leadership. From the 1820s such notions and hopes, generated by the French Revolution, had begun to infiltrate this desolate land. In 1820 Pushkin published his "Ode to Liberty"—and lost his job in 1824 when he failed to heed official warnings to change the subject. Another young *littérateur,* Lermontov, was expelled (in 1832) from the University of Moscow for his radical views. This excerpt from his *Prophecy* warned of the time to come:

A year, a black year for Russia will come, when the crown will fall off the Tsar's head. The people will forget their old love for [him], and the masses will feed on blood and murder. The destroyed law will protect neither women nor innocent children. And the fetid corpses will cause pestilence in the desolate villages and call victims from the huts. Famine will

* The Mir was a peasant organization of villagers that decided—subject to the lord's veto—such matters as what crops to plant, land allocations, and local administrative affairs.

*Karl Marx, founder of "scientific socialism."*

torment the unfortunate country and rivers will be red with the reflexes of fires.

Belinsky, also expelled from the University of Moscow, wrote movingly of the degradations and sufferings of the "dark people" (writings that particularly influenced the young Dostoevski). Alexander Herzen, forced to flee the country because of his harsh indictments of the regime, founded a periodical—*The Bell*—that was smuggled into Russia and widely read among forward-looking literati.

In the 1870s George Plekhanov translated *Das Kapital,* and thus brought Marxist thought to Russia. Later, a small but energetic Social Democratic party was formed, based on the Marxist blueprint. By the beginning of the century a number of revolutionary parties had been formed. The two major parties were the Social Revolutionary party, which favored the peasant and was imbued with the philosophy of "going to the

*Lenin and Stalin in the early 1920s.*

in a slower tempo†. Other groups were formed from time to time, ranging from liberal parliamentarians to terroristic anarchists. Lermontov's black year for Russia was in the making.

## Illusory Reforms

Basic reforms or the exercise of even elementary prudence, such as cautious avoidance of any test of the regime's strength, might have postponed the calamity prefigured by the centuries. But the rulers of Russia seemed to be beyond the prods of reality. In 1904 to 1905, as already mentioned (p. 383 above), they sought imperial loot in the East. Humiliating defeat by Japan unmasked the basic weaknesses of the regime for all to see. The pent up fury of the long suppressed masses manifested itself in widespread violence. In the villages manors were burned and, in many localities, land was confiscated. Strikes broke out in the larger cities, especially in St. Petersburg where worker soviets, under the leadership of Leon Trotsky, called for a general strike. The Tsar and his court were so shaken that the Tsar promised (in what is called the October Manifesto) the establishment of a constitutional government and an extension of the franchise.

The reforms turned out to be illusory. A constitution—the Fundamental Orders—was promulgated by the Tsar. A legislative body (the Duma) was formed, and the franchise extended. But the constitution specifically recognized the Tsar as autocrat, with power to issue decrees when the Duma was not in session; and even when in session, the Duma had no power to deal with foreign policy and with the armed forces, and very little control over the budget. Moreover, when the first

people," and the Social Democratic party, oriented in the direction of the city worker. The Social Democrats believed that the coming revolution should be directed and managed by professional revolutionaries. Shortly after 1900 the Social Democratic party split into two parts. One part preached violent revolution spear-headed by a disciplined vanguard. This section was headed by Lenin* and a small band of colleagues; it took the name of Bolshevik. The other faction, called Menshevik, was larger (exactly contrary to the literal meaning of the Russian words originally used to differentiate the two groups). It believed in a stricter interpretation of Marxism and consequently

---

* His real name was Vladimir Ilyich Ulyanov. Originally a lawyer, he early became interested in revolutionary activity, especially after the execution of his brother who was implicated in the assassination of Tsar Alexander III.

† That is, it believed a republican bourgeois regime should be allowed, even encouraged, to take over from tsarist autocracy as a necessary preliminary to the establishment of a dictatorship of the proletariat.

*The storming of the Winter Palace in the March Revolution, 1917.*

two Dumas pressed for further reforms, the Tsar dissolved them and severely cut back the already restricted right to vote. Thus, in the end, the Revolution of 1905 brought little overall change in the Russian body politic.*

## THE COMING OF COMMUNISM

### The March Revolution

But the Revolution left memories and sharpened appetites. Another crisis would find the revolutionaries more determined, and the masses more wary of grand, royal promises. This was the case in 1917. By then, Russian armies had been hopelessly smashed by the Kaiser's efficient war machine. Mass desertions were common. Internally, transportation facilities, none too good to begin with, were in a chaotic condition; starvation stalked the cities. Things had become so bad in the House of the Autocrat that even the nobles and gentry were moved to murmured protests.

In February a general strike was called in Petrograd† (present-day Leningrad). Within a week it had spread and merged with uprisings throughout the country. The

*The Tsar and Tsarina in their court robes (1904).*

Tsar ordered the dissolution of the Duma. The deputies accepted the order but remained in the capital awaiting developments. Thousands of workers—yesterday's peasants—demonstrated in the streets. On February 27‡ a significant scene dramatized the rebellious mood of the people. Ordered to disperse the demonstrators, the Tsar's capital guards (numbering about 150,000) not only refused to fire upon the insurrectionists but finally joined them.

By March the Tsar's authority had simply melted away. The strangest thing about the March Revolution was its unrevolutionary character. There were no long drawn out bloody riots; there was little pillaging, little noise and bombast. Soldiers quit fighting; trains stopped running; policemen vanished —in short, the state quietly collapsed. On March 2, 1917 the Tsar of all the Russias signed a simple statement saying ". . . we

---

* But see *supra* (Chapter VIII), for Stolypin's reforms.

† Formerly St. Petersburg. When the war broke out, the government thought the name of the capital should not bear a German form.

‡ See note, p. 505.

have recognized that it is for the good of the country that we should abdicate the Crown of the Russian State. . . ." The autocracy, established in the fifteenth century, thus surrendered to the "dark people," and a provisional government took its place. The new government, however, turned out to be composed mostly of bourgeois moderates rather than toilers. Except for Alexander Kerensky, a radical champion of the peasant classes, members of the Constitutional Democratic party (Cadets) and forward-looking aristocrats took over all high-ranking posts. One of the founders of the Cadets, Professor P. Miliukov, became Minister for Foreign Affairs; Prince Lvov assumed the premiership.

For a short time the new government seemed to enjoy the confidence of the majority of the people. Even the socialist St. Petersburg Soviet supported it. The hated Autocracy had been humbled and harassed from power. A constitutional convention was promised—to be elected by the general adult, male populace. At this point, American, British, and French observers expected, as the next logical step, the setting up of a model of their own bourgeois democracy. Landed aristocrats had stepped out of power; middle-class "democrats" would fill the void, as they had in England in the late seventeenth century and in France in the late eighteenth century.

The provisional government tried to play the role seemingly assigned to it by history. But for middle-class democracy to succeed there must first be a sizable middle class. There also must be available leaders within its ranks who possess political experience and a workable program. In tumultuous times an added ingredient is needed—an iron will. In 1917 Russia, none of these ingredients existed except the iron will. And that, as it turned out, was found only in the leader of the Bolshevik party.

Moreover, it soon became evident that the new regime was more interested in winning a war (which most Russians believed lost) than in reforming the political and social institutions of the land. The St. Petersburg Soviet became increasingly critical. Workers, peasants, soldiers, and sailors—all impatiently demanded an end to their suffering. In July 1917, Prince Lvov resigned in favor of Kerensky. But the new leader, although eager for socialist reform, felt (no less than his predecessor) the need to honor his country's obligations to her allies. Workers in the cities demanded bread; village peasants demanded land and a fair price for their produce. About all Kerensky and his quarreling colleagues could do was make promises. Thus desertion continued at the front, and chaos spread at home.

## The Bolshevik Revolution

Meanwhile, other figures were cueing themselves into the drama. The provisional government promised peace, but only after victory. It promised land and factory reform, but only after a Constituent Assembly could meet and draw up a constitution. The date for the meeting had already been postponed several times. The provisional government neither supported the soviets nor crushed them. On the other hand, Lenin and his Bolshevik comrades were sharp, sure, and simple in their basic strategy and propaganda—almost the only leaders in all Russia who were. Their slogans said what the people wanted to hear: "Peace," now; "Bread," for the cities; "Land," to be taken from the gentry and given to the peasant; and "All the power to the soviets," as the vehicle to effect these aims. (Lenin repeatedly emphasized—privately—that the implementation of this program meant to the Bolsheviks something different from what it meant to the masses. Bread would be given to the city workers—but by forceful requisition, if need be. Land would be "given" to the peasant—but under the ownership of the state. And peace would probably entail, as we have seen that it did, large sacrifices of Russian territory.)

From March to October of 1917, conditions drifted ever closer to pure anarchy. In September, Kerensky launched the last great offensive that, after a faint flicker of success, faded and failed. The Bolshevik coup followed. It was brief, virtually bloodless and, as it turned out, had significant consequence. Lenin and his colleagues already were in controlling positions within the soviets. In October* the Petrograd Soviet, the largest and most powerful in the country, called a Congress of Soviets into session. On the night of the 27th it passed a resolution that declared that all land belonged to the peasants, and all power belonged to the soviets. Back of the Congress stood the peasant-worker army. The provisional government offered only feeble resistance (although in Moscow, Kiev, and several other large cities some sanguinary fighting took place). Within the week, Lenin and the Bolsheviks were in power. Communism had come to Russia.

*Soldiers patrolling the streets of Petrograd in the March Revolution of 1917.*

## THE IDEOLOGICAL CONTENT OF COMMUNISM

### The Basic Concepts

No matter how far-fetched or difficult Marxism-Leninism may strike us, we must give attention to its fundamental ideas, since the greater part of Soviet ideology and practice derives from them.

One basic tenet of Marxism-Leninism is the belief that matter shapes mind; that is, that thought arises from material conditions. Among the material conditions that influence human behavior, economic forces are paramount. These forces are the creators of all societies. They, and they alone, provide satis-

*Leon Trotsky, leader of the Red Army, exhorts some of his troops during the civil war.*

factions for the wants that they have created. Mismanaged, they fail and frustrate these wants.

Another tenet holds that the forces of life are fluid, forever flowing. Change is eternal. At any given moment that which is, is becoming that which it was not. But change is not effected by chance (except incidentally). There is a pattern of development that man can discern and develop, even though he cannot alter it. Its features are simple. Every life force meets opposition in its development. Out of this encounter comes that which is neither the original nor the countering element, but an amalgam. In its turn this new element meets its opposing force that merges with it, and creates a new amalgam—and so on.

---

* In 1917 the Russian calendar was thirteen days behind the calendar used in other parts of Europe and in America. Thus, what is "Octobrist" to a Communist is "Novembrist" to a non-Russian. On February 14, 1918, the Comunist government brought the old Russian calendar into harmony with the one used in the West.

## Class Struggle

Together these two fundamental ideas form the key, in Marxist thought,* that unlocks the mysteries of human existence—past, present, and (up until the establishment of the classless society, at least) future. Proper use of the key produces understandings which, in turn, provide bases for prediction. One understanding is (as the *Communist Manifesto* has it) that "the history of all hitherto existing society is the history of class struggles." From earliest times to the present, human beings have been divided into two groups—the exploited and the exploiters. In ancient Rome, plebeians struggled against patricians. In medieval times the serf sought escape from the dominant rule of the landed lord. In modern society the worker is closing ranks against the bourgeois capitalist.

In the past, dominant minorities have ruled every society. This has been true even when, on the surface, the opposite has appeared to be the case. In "democratic," bourgeois republics, for example, the ruling clique is made up of industrial magnates. The people (that is, the masses) may exercise the franchise and believe they are deciding who shall represent them. In reality they elect candidates who, except for occasional mavericks (or popular leaders that arise during a passing time of troubles), know where the real power lies and behave accordingly. A Marxist reader of American history might point to the following statement to substantiate such a view. Appearing before a Congressional investigating committee in 1911, Frederick Townsend Martin, "an expert witness, an outspoken member of the 'idle rich' . . . remarked with charming frankness":

The class I represent care nothing for politics. . . . Among my people I seldom hear purely political discussions. When we are discussing pro and con the relative merits of candidates or the relative importance of political policies, the question almost invariably comes down to a question of business efficiency. We care absolutely nothing about statehood bills, pension agitation, waterway appropriations, "pork barrels," state rights, or any other political question; save inasmuch as it threatens or fortifies existing conditions. Touch the question of the tariff, touch the issue of the income tax, touch the problem of railroad regulation, or touch the most vital of all business matters, the question of general federal regulation of industrial corporations, and the people amongst whom I live my life become immediately rabid partisans. . . . It matters not one iota what political party is in power or what President holds the reins of office. We are not politicians or public thinkers; we are the rich; we own America; we got it, God knows how, but we intend to keep it if we can by throwing all the tremendous weight of our support, our influence, our money, our political connections, our purchased senators, our hungry congressmen, our public speaking demagogues into the scale against any legislature, any political platform, any presidential campaign that threatens the integrity of our estate. . . .[3]

In Marxist analysis the elite members of the dominant bourgeois minority dig their own graves. They need immense aggregations of workers to labor in the factories that grow ever larger and more numerous. To garner large profits they keep wages depressed and working conditions unsafe and unhealthy. Working in juxtaposition with one another, the workers exchange grievances, form unions, and test their "bargaining" strength. They lose, try again, and lose again, since the bourgeoisie elite control not only industry but also public office and public opinion. But the economic facts of life are not changed by these capitalist victories. For no national

---

* There are several varieties of Marxists. Here, we refer to the Marxist who claims Lenin and his disciples as the true interpreters of original "scientific socialism."

3. Charles A. and Mary R. Beard, *The Rise of American Civilization,* revised college edition, The Macmillan Co., New York, 1934, Vol. II, p. 303.

economy can ever achieve permanent prosperity or even solvency as long as buying power lags behind productive power. And under capitalism the economy of scarcity is a prerequisite.

## Emergence of Classless Society

Eventually (according to Lenin) nations turn to imperialist adventures. They seek to carve out new markets in undeveloped regions. Inevitably this kind of adventure leads to international conflict. The losing powers suffer not only military defeat, but the workers, oppressed beyond endurance, rise against their weakened governments. Radical regimes are established (as briefly, in France in 1871), or revolutions are staged to bring these regimes into being (as in Russia in 1905). Bourgeois power again asserts itself, but the day of reckoning is only postponed. Experience is gained; memories are cherished. In the end the proletariat, led by strong-willed professional revolutionaries, wrest control from the exploiters, and overthrow the dictatorship of the bourgeoisie. In its place they set up the dictatorship of the proletariat.

According to Marxist thought, the class struggle between the proletariat and the bourgeoisie will be the last of the long series, for the coming victory will represent the overpowering majority of the people. Hitherto, victories were won by small minorities: patricians over plebeians; lords over serfs; bourgeoisie over proletariat. When the workers set up their dictatorship, it will function vigorously but relatively briefly, for when the exploiting minority is tamed or "liquidated," the masses will have no enemy to fight.

The final stage is reached when, with no classes and hence no class struggles, the "interference of a state power in social relations becomes superfluous in one sphere after another . . . . Government over persons is replaced by the administration of things and the direction of the processes of produc-

tion. The state is not 'abolished,' it *withers away*."[4]

Such are the concepts that make up the basic framework of Marxist ideology. However, some of these basic concepts were modified (as we shall see) after the Russian Revolution had ended, when the Bolsheviks turned to the business of managing the political affairs of the nation. But in the main, orthodox Marxist ideology supplied the guidelines for the new rulers.

## THE CRITICAL PERIOD —1917 TO 1920

### "War Communism"

In Lenin's view, World War I was but the prelude to world revolution. Under the leadership of Communist elites, the toiling masses—battered by mounting violence and prodded by a growing understanding of the devouring selfishness of rampant capitalism— would rise up against their bourgeois masters and turn the international imperialist war into a universal class war. Uneven as the pace of proletarian victories might be, the day of the "Big Change" had come. The capitalist *nay* was emerging into the socialist *yea*. Russian Communists might lead the way, but anything short of permanent—that is, global—revolution would miss the goal. And for global revolution, the signs were auspicious. Already in Hungary, Germany, and Austria, Communist leaders were preparing for the takeover. As the revolution gained momentum, national governments (even the bourgeois democracies of the West) would be swept away.

Lenin and his colleagues also believed that they immediately could introduce the full Communist program in Russia.* All land and all industry could (and should) be

* Note *introduce*, not put into full scale operation.

4. Quoted from N. Lenin, *State and Revolution,* in Stipp, *loc. cit.,* p. 60.

nationalized at once. True, administrative bottlenecks, even serious and prolonged blundering, would undoubtedly mark the opening phases of the task. But these were details. Once the expropriators were expropriated, the new society could absorb the jolts and jars that inevitably follow when the turning of a grand pivot of history swings one civilization into oblivion and another into being.*

Confident that they were reading the curve of history correctly, Lenin and his colleagues set to work. Numerous contacts were established with Communist leaders in other parts of Europe—Bela Kun in Hungary and Rosa Luxemburg and Karl Liebknecht in Germany were outstanding examples. War weariness, linked with postwar social restiveness, seemed to give promise that workers and peasants were ready for radical ventures. A short-lived Soviet Republic was established in Bavaria; Bela Kun, supported by Russian advisers, took over the government of Hungary (March-August, 1918); a Socialist became the first chancellor of the Austrian Republic; in 1919 and 1920, worker unrest in England erupted in a series of large-scale strikes; German Communists ("Spartacists") staged uprisings in Berlin (January-February, 1919). Throughout Europe, classical radical rhetoric took on the flesh and blood of political reality. The Third International (the Comintern), founded in Moscow,

served as the organizational center for universal revolutionary activity.

In Russia the new government, calling itself the Council of Peoples' Commissars, nationalized banks, land, and factories. A secret police section (the Cheka) was established to deal with reactionary opposition. When the Constituent Assembly, Russia's first and only freely elected national legislative body, convened with a majority of non-Bolsheviks in control, Red guards dispersed the Assembly's members after only a single day's session. The national debt, including of course all foreign loans, was abolished. In March 1918, Trotsky, acting under urgent orders from Lenin, met with German commissioners and signed the Treaty of Brest-Litovsk that took Russia out of the war. History appeared to the coterie of Communist leaders, who held the reins of power, to be running on schedule. Workers of the world were rising under the leadership of men whose mastery of dialectical materialism allowed them perspective and understandings that were denied to others. The words of the famous workers' song, *The International,* seemed quick with life: "Arise ye slaves; no more in thrall! The earth shall rise on new foundations. We have been naught, we shall be all."[5]

## Counterrevolution

But the Communists misread both the spirit and conditions of the times. Except for isolated cells in various countries, the workers of the world were not only unready for world revolution but were profoundly unsympathetic toward it. The pull of nationalism was strong. In Germany, it was not an international workers' song but "Deutschland, Deutschland über Alles" that still stirred masses and classes alike. French spines tingled to the "Marseillaise." British proletarians proudly stood at attention to the strains of "God Save the King." The average

---

* Historians are in dispute on this point. Some hold that Lenin and his colleagues did not want and would never have attempted to introduce "full Communism" immediately had not the regime been threatened by the White armies. Trotsky was working closely with Lenin during this period (1917–1920). He has declared flatly that "the methods of war communism [were] forced on us by the conditions of civil war." Likewise, Lenin held that "the tactics adopted by the capitalist class forced us into a desperate struggle which compelled us to smash up the old relations to a far greater extent than we at first intended." For a detailed account written from this viewpoint, see Edward H. Carr, *A History of Soviet Russia*, Macmillan Company, New York, 1952, Vol. II, pp. 147–269.

5. *I.W.W. Songs,* 21st edition, published by the Industrial Workers of the World, Chicago, 1925, p. 13.

worker, wherever he lived, wanted more to reform the prevailing economic system than to abolish it. Higher wages, fewer working hours, a chance to move up the social ladder (the Horatio Alger dream in America)— these appealed far more than the vision of proletarian dictatorship in a superstate. In light of these conditions, the "permanent revolution" was doomed from the start.

Meanwhile, the Communist rulers of Russia faced such grave domestic difficulties that the prospect of their survival seemed anything but bright. The war had disrupted the Russian transport system which even in peacetime had never been noted for its efficiency. Confiscation of industrial plants had substituted loyal but untrained Communist managers for experienced bourgeois leadership. On the "nationalized" land, peasants worked fields for their own needs and profit. The combined effects of a seriously disrupted transport system, an amateur, improvised industrial management, and a peasant-centered agricultural economy were almost more than the new regime could cope with. Cities lacked food and fuel—partly because the peasants sabotaged government efforts to confiscate "surplus" supplies, and partly because produce could not be shipped to the towns. The countryside lacked the necessary manufactured and processed goods, because too many factory workers had been conscripted into the army, because inept Communist managers slowed down industrial production, and because loss of confidence in the value of the ruble produced a ruinous inflation that virtually eliminated money as a medium of exchange.

To these staggering problems two others were added. The Allied powers encouraged the creation of a number of buffer states along Russia's western borders to counter the advantages gained by Germany in the Treaty of Brest-Litovsk.* Within two months after

* And, almost certainly, to help rid Europe of a socialist state that might serve as an example and rallying point for other peoples who were disillusioned with capitalist ways.

*Baron Wrangel, commander of the White Army in the south, decorates a fellow general.*

the November revolution, the Allies recognized the independence of four states that had been formerly a part of Russia—Finland, Estonia, Latvia, and Lithuania. Furthermore, to help local anti-Communist groups to oust their new Red rulers, the Allied governments sent troops to invade or to infiltrate certain regions of Russia. British troops were sent to Murmansk, Batum, and the Baku oil fields; British, French and American troops to Archangel; French troops to the Odessa region; and Japanese and American troops to Vladivostok. In addition, the Allies encircled Russia with a tight blockade.

At the same time, a half dozen "White" armies, led by die-hard Tsarist officers, moved against the regime. Cossacks, under General Krasnov; troops in White Russia, to the north, under General Yudenitch; forces under Admiral Kolchak in eastern Russia and in Siberia; and General Wrangel's army in the Caucasus region—all converged on Trotsky's hastily formed Red defenders. For three years (1917–1920) the masses (even as Lermontov had predicted) fed on blood and murder. The advantages of numerical strength, financial resources, and experienced leadership lay with the Whites and their foreign allies. By the early months of 1919, the Communist cause seemed hopeless. All of the Ukraine (the breadbasket of Russia) was lost. The Caucasian states of Georgia, Armenia, and Azerbaijan joined Finland, Estonia, Latvia, and Lithuania in declaring their independence. Most of southern Russia was under White rule.

But these months marked the ebb, rather than the flow, of conservative reaction. No single event caused the tide to turn; there were a number of forces that commingled to produce the crest of Red victory. One force was the weight of centuries of oppression. With the overthrow of autocracy, Russia's "Dead Souls" experienced a feeling of release that made any attempt to restore the old regime foolish and futile. Another factor working against the White army was the hard-to-believe stupidity of their generals, for not only was restoration of the old regime precisely their goal but it was plainly, publicly, and boastfully declared. Many Russians, probably most, opposed Red rule and wished to be rid of it, but not at the price that the Whites demanded. Still another force favoring the Communists was the general war-weariness of the Allies. The four-year encounter with the German war machine had weakened the Allies' will for further battle. They detested the new regime; they hoped that the White armies could sweep it away. But they were tired and, after all, the affair (at least for the time) was an internal one for the Russians themselves to settle. Thus, one by one, they withdrew. The Red forces, freed from outside pressure, and operating along interior lines that allowed them to outmaneuver the numerically superior White armies, rallied (in late 1920) to drive out all opposing them.* The counterrevolution had failed

---

* In 1920, Poland entered the war on the side of the Whites, hoping to slice off a portion of the Ukraine. After a kind of stalemate, the two powers reached a boundary settlement in the Treaty of Riga (March 18, 1921).

to restore even a portion of the sprawling stte to capitalist control.

## THE NEW ECONOMIC POLICY

### The Retreat from "War Communism"

New troubles replaced old ones for the triumphant vanguard of the proletariat. Military victory had not educated Red factory managers in economic know-how. At the end of the war, all the joints of the economy were unhinged. Peasants refused to plant more crops than for their own needs. If surpluses developed, they were either hid from government agents or were destroyed. In 1920 drought spread famine across the land. By 1921 economic paralysis was almost complete.

Lenin had hoped, and apparently believed, that uprisings in other nations, particularly in industrialized nations, would open the way to proletarian control of the entire Western economy including, of course, international exchange. With the failure of socialist revolutions to materialize or, as in Bavaria and Hungary, to win to victory, Russia stood alone. For the present, at least, whatever way out there was for the stricken country would have to be found by its revolutionary leaders —if found at all.

Late in 1920, rioting occurred among factory workers in Petrograd. It was an ominous sign. Peasant uprisings could be expected. Few farmers dream socialist dreams; even fewer feel enthusiasm for governments eager to confiscate farm produce. But if the *workers* (the proletarians in whose name the dictatorship was established) were to fall away, all would be lost. In February and March of 1921, Red sailors mutinied at Kronstadt where, but four years before, they had sparked the Revolution. Now the government took drastic action. Up until this point Lenin had somehow hoped to force the peasantry to fall into (socialist) step with the city proletariat. But when the city proletariat turned recalcitrant, Lenin laid aside the Marxist book of rules. Why were the workers wavering? They lacked food. How could they be assured of prompt and sufficient supplies? By pacification of the peasants. How could the peasants be mollified without violating the dictates of socialist policy? They could not. For the present, then, policy must yield. At the Tenth Party Congress (in 1921) Lenin frankly confessed, "Only an agreement with the peasantry can save the socialist revolution in Russia until the revolution has occurred in other countries . . . . The proletariat is the leader of the peasantry . . . but that class cannot be driven out as we drove out the landowners and capitalists. It must be *transformed* with great labor and privations."[6]

The instrument designed to effect agreement with the peasants and, possibly, to transform them was called the New Economic Policy (NEP). It essentially was the substitution of a limited grain tax (or tax in kind) for confiscation of surpluses, and the right to trade surpluses for money or goods in the open market. Some limited private production was also permitted.* Because of a second and even more severe season of drought, the new policy brought little immediate improvement. Peasants planted beyond their own family needs, and sold the surplus for all that the market would bear. With a fairly steady supply of food, factory workers gradually lost their restiveness. Supplied with funds from a banking system now at least partially capitalistic, small producers and merchants set them-

selves up in business, and made a profit. Collection of taxes increased. The budget was brought into balance. The value of the ruble was stabilized (although at a rather fantastic figure). War Communism was dead.

## The Rise of the Nepmen

For the next five or six years the New Economic Policy performed double service for both Lenin and the Party workers. It lulled to a murmur the haunting question of how socialism could develop in a country as backward as Russia. At the same time, it paradoxically provided the means for transforming the country's economic backwardness into at least a measure of economic strength. Critics of the regime could argue (and did) that NEP proved the impracticability of socialism. But while they argued, Russia grew stronger—under Communist rulers, if not by Communist rule. Lenin made it plain that NEP was a stopgap and that the day would come when two steps forward toward socialism would be possible, because one step backward had been ventured. Few people believed him, including some of his most sympathetic supporters, for how could the house of socialism be built upon a capitalist foundation? Lenin shrugged off the question as bourgeois logic; one day the doubters would see.

In 1921, industrial and agricultural prices had been so far apart that economic collapse had seemed certain. Three years later the two were roughly in the same balance that had existed before the war.[7] In fact, the "step backward" was so successful that new embarrassments developed. The "strong and sober" peasants, once courted by Stolypin, managed their farms so efficiently that they soon outstripped the plodding masses. Month after month the disparity between the rich peasant—the *kulak*—and the poor and middling peasant grew greater. By crafty

---

6. Carr, *loc. cit.,* p. 278. Italics added.

---

* Again, Lenin was frank. "Want and destruction," he said, "have gone so far that we cannot *at once* restore large-scale, factory, state, socialist production. . . . That means that it is indispensable in a certain measure to help the restoration of *small* industry which does not require machines, does not require either state-owned or large stocks of raw material, fuel and food, and can immediately render some aid to the peasant economy and raise its productive powers." But it is important to note Lenin's emphasis on *small* industry. Quoted by Carr, *op. cit.,* p. 298.

7. Carr, *op. cit.,* p. 191. For a detailed account of the ups and downs of NEP's course, see *ibid.,* Chapter 5.

calculation and manipulation of market opportunities, *kulak* surpluses were transmuted into more acres and still more surpluses. By 1926 the *kulak* class possessed almost a monopoly of Russian draught animals and farm machinery. Those of the middling class who could afford to rent horses and implements from the *kulaks* did so in the hope of making enough profits in a few years to join the owning class. In this way the ranks of the *kulaks* increased. But many middling peasants failed to clear such profits, or even to make their payment on rented animals and equipment. When this happened, they ran the risk of sinking permanently into the lowest stratum, the "poor peasant" class. To the extent that these developments occurred—and they occurred on an increasing scale—Lenin's NEP countenanced, even aggravated, the class struggle of tsarist times. Certainly, the poor peasant found little substance in the grand promises of the Revolution.

In 1921, Lenin had declared that "only an agreement with the peasantry can save the socialist revolution." Five years later the "black people"—then, as always, the bulk of the peasantry—were well on their way to becoming permanently alienated from their Communist rulers. Here and there, violent opposition to the regime flared up—a president of a village soviet was murdered, or a Party leader was beaten up. Because the government could hardly discipline *all* of the peasant classes and hope to survive, and because it believed that it needed the surpluses produced by the *kulaks* to feed the city workers, it tended for a while to support, by a kind of double talk, the rich peasant: "The man who looks after his land well is not a *kulak,* but a Soviet worker."

## The End of NEP (1928)

If the new policy sharpened conflict among peasant classes, it also divided Red leadership. After Lenin's death in 1924, two of his co-workers, Stalin and Trotsky, began a struggle for power that lasted for nearly three years. NEP was only one of a number of issues over which they quarreled. Trotsky and his followers believed that the purposes of NEP had been achieved. They argued that it was time to begin large-scale efforts to industrialize the country. They also insisted upon the necessity for "permanent revolution." Good Marxists, they held, could not give up hope for proletarian victories abroad. Given enough encouragement and the right kind of leadership, workers of the world would (and must) shake off their chains. "Russian Communism" was a contradiction of terms. Proletarians were proletarians wherever they lived; world revolution was the *sine qua non* of the dictatorship of the proletariat. Those who professed to believe that an island of socialism could stand in a sea of capitalism were either blind or faint of heart. Stalin and his associates, on the other hand, argued that Trotsky was deviating from Leninism, and hence obstructing the true course of the revolution. Socialism in one country was not only possible, but a necessary prelude to world revolution.

But the immediate issue was NEP. Stalin naturally mistrusted the *kulaks,* but he doubted whether it was yet safe to return to socialist agriculture. Bread for the cities still depended on the temporary coddling that Lenin had decreed. It is difficult to determine how sincere Stalin was in defending this position. Throughout most of the twenties the new policy was unquestionably necessary if the regime were to survive. But unless the transition to socialism was begun soon, the *kulaks* would pass beyond control; the revolution would then surely yield to the long expected Thermidorean reaction. Stalin understood this danger clearly enough. But he also understood that if NEP were abandoned while Trotsky was leading the fight for its abandonment, more than transition to socialism would result—the emergence of Trotsky as supreme leader would be assured.

As General Secretary of the Communist Party, Stalin was in a position to put his men into key party offices. He did this with such thoroughness that, by the mid-1920s, his views had become the Party's views. By 1927, he believed that he could defeat Trotsky in a showdown. Therefore, when Trotsky demanded the end of NEP without further delay, Stalin called for a vote by the Party Congress. The decision to continue NEP clearly demonstrated Stalin's supremacy.* With power now his, Stalin first sent Trotsky to Siberia (in 1927) and then (in 1929) expelled him from the country.

This settled the question of Lenin's successor. But the economic dilemma posed by the Nepmen remained. Stalin met it by adopting Trotsky's program. NEP had allowed the Party to weather the post-revolutionary storm. Now (in 1928) socialist planning could be applied to agriculture and industry. If the Nepmen objected, as they surely would, so much the worse for them. The coddling days had passed; from now on, opponents of the regime could expect not compromise, but exile or death.

## SOCIALIST PLANNING

### Goals and Methods

The essence of socialism is public ownership and control of all *productive* forms of wealth for purposes of use instead of profit.† From 1929 on, this principle was applied to all industrial and agricultural activities. (Not literally all. A very small percentage—perhaps 2 or 3 per cent—of all these activities remained in private hands.

---

\* An understatement. Stalin defeated his opponent by a margin of about 200 to 1.
† But Communist theory and practice do not altogether eliminate "private profit." Indeed, the Party had publicly declared its acknowledgement of the importance of the profit motive. But the non-Communist student can easily misunderstand. Actually, "the operation of the profit motive is hedged under the Soviet system by limitations of the opportunities to bargain for supplies, the centralization of decisions concerning plant expansion, and taxation policies that return most of the profit to the state." Barrington Moore, Jr., *Soviet Politics: the Dilemma of Power,* quoted by John L. Stipp, *op. cit.,* p. 95.

*These wives of field workers are operating a separator on a huge collective farm in the Caucasus region.*

Nor should the statement be understood to suggest that no public ownership of productive wealth existed during the NEP period when, indeed, most industry was under state ownership and control.) Individual farms were merged into either of two kinds of collectivized farms: the *kolkhoze* and the *sovkhoze. Kolkhozes* were based on the co-operative principle—farm lands were cleared by communities and worked by their members. In size, they varied from collectives of seventy-five or eighty "households" to a few of nearly one thousand households. Grains, live stock, and other produce were distributed (in amounts determined by the state), to the *kolkhoze,* to the households, and to the state itself. Each family was given a small individual holding for its own cultivation, in addition to the produce allotted to it from the *kolkhoze.* The *sovkhoze* was given over entirely to state management. Workers lived on these units (usually much larger than their collective counterparts) as day laborers. Of the total land brought under cultivation after 1928, about 95 per cent was made up of *kolkhozes.*

All industry was likewise socialized (except, again, inconsequential fragments). A central planning board was created to fix the kinds, purposes, and amounts of capital investment. It also determined the hours and wages of laborers, prices, and priority of goods to be produced—indeed, all conditions of economic activity of both the individual and the nation. Because Russia lacked power facilities and the machines that produce machines, emphasis was naturally placed on heavy industry. This meant, of course, that consumer goods would be sacrificed for a long time to come. Necessarily, power plants would take precedence over shoe factories, the tool and dye industry over house building, locomotives over automobiles, and so on.

The goals, and the methods to achieve them, were set forth in a series of plans, each originally running for five years (later changed to seven years). The task of drawing up the master blueprint for each period was assigned to the State Planning Commission (Gosplan). The plan for each period stipulated what amount of the nation's total economic energy was to be devoted to agriculture, and what amount was to be devoted to industry. It also provided for the estimated consumer needs of the citizenry, the modes and methods of distribution, the construction needs of heavy and light industry, and the goals and operational procedures of all *kolkhozes* and *sovkhozes*.

Such an undertaking, as unprecedented as it was bewilderingly complex and comprehensive, originally seemed to many beyond what human skill and ingenuity could achieve. How could meeting the needs of tens of millions of persons be planned? More basically, who could determine, or even define, the needs of a nation's population? What criteria of priority should be used? How could gross miscalculations be prevented or remedied? What practicable sanctions could be devised to enforce unpopular decisions? What incentives, consistent with socialist doctrines, would keep the nation at work?

From the days of the first Plan (1928–1935) to the present, Soviet leaders have grappled with these and related questions. It is natural to ask: with what success? Unfortunately the answers are many and are often contradictory; they will probably remain that way for a long time to come. Those who believe in the capitalist way of life deny that any people's needs can be planned by a central body, no matter how brilliant and dedicated its leaders may be. They contend that the Communist system is doomed either to ultimate collapse or to gradual changes of such a basic character that, whatever its name, its nature will become essentially capitalistic. Communists themselves point to the historic record. For nearly a half century they have managed an economy that *is* planned; and, of course, it is growing more, not less socialistic.* Still, the problems persist.†

## Party and Government Agencies

A vast complex of Party and government agencies has grown to meet the needs of life in a planned society. Although *Gosplan* drew up the master plan, the Party decided what the basic elements of the Plan were to be. For example, Lenin and his colleagues in the Politbureau early laid down the dictum that Russia's first need was electrification and industrialization. No official in *Gosplan,* no matter how exalted his position, could have altered this decision. On the other hand, once plans had been approved and put into execution by *Gosplan* and its agencies, no local Party official could hope to exempt his community from the plans. Yet, on the local level, considerable discretion was allowed in other ways. For example, local soviets often decided what kind and what amount of recreational equipment and facilities were to be supplied to their communities. And at all times, officials of whatever level—high, low, or intermediate—could suggest changes, new ideas, and techniques, or could point out troubles to come if a current practice were not stopped.

---

* Stalin and his successors claimed even more—that *socialism* has already been achieved in Russia, and that the transition to Communism (that is, the classless, stateless society) is well under way.
† Of course Communists point out that even more serious problems persist under capitalism.

To prevent or to remedy bureaucratic miscalculations, an elaborate system of "self-criticism" was devised. Citizens from whatever part of Russia, or in whatever kind of work, were urged to register complaints about "socialist services" (but not, of course, about policies decided by the Party). Soviet newspapers and magazines regularly published such complaints. In addition to this popular "control," Party inspectors were sent throughout the land to gather information about what seemed to be going either right or wrong. Perhaps the best barometers of public opinion and reaction were the elected officials of the tens of thousands of local soviets (somewhat comparable to our New England town selectmen, or our city councilmen). From their complaints, information and evaluations found their way through the maze of Party and government organizations into the counsels of the Party leadership. Acting on data gathered from all of these sources, the Party leadership decided where pressures were too great to be maintained, how much slack should be loosened in the endless chain of economic activity, and when and where to push forward again.

Behind these agencies and processes loomed the large and dread state organs of sanction—particularly the secret police, Party-packed courts, and concentration camps. In the period of the first Five Year Plan, many *kulaks* refused to cooperate with the government in its drive to collective agriculture. Repeating their tactics of a decade earlier, they ignored crop-planting directives, hoarded or destroyed produce claimed by the state, harassed Party officials, and generally sought to wreck the new program. This time the government used the full force of its coercive power. Many thousands of the protesting "rich peasants" were sent to Siberia, where they labored in "work camps" under conditions so mercilessly severe that most of them died before their sentences were completed. Other thousands, both *kulaks* and middling peasants who sympathized with them, were expelled from collec-

tive farms and left to starve. Throughout the period the secret police were busy. Thus, arrests, deportations, deliberate starving, and massacres marked the bloody transition from capitalistist ways to socialist planning.

The general effect of the sweeping collectivist program is hard to assess. Most *kolkhozniks,* as we have seen, resented the socialist form and the nature of collectivization. If they could have had their way, they would have become the owners of individual plots, to be worked as they desired. Failing this, they would have preferred a cooperative arrangement, similar to the old *Mir* type. They did not like to labor under terms laid down by the state where goals were fixed, and fixed, moreover, in such a way that the preponderant bulk of the produce of the *kolkhoze* went to the state. For this meant, in effect, that the fruits of their labor were drained off to provide state capital for the industrialization of the country. They resented the constant prodding of Party overseers who held them to a fatiguing tempo of labor. Almost always, the small strips assigned to individual families for their own use yielded too little to satisfy the normal demands of hunger. The portion allotted to them from the collective was also invariably meager. They knew that they were being forced at a fearful price to buy a Communist tomorrow out of their own today's sweat and suffering. The fact that Russia was rapidly becoming a strong industrial nation (as it was) might constitute a hinge of history that later generations could marvel over, but their own days and hours still remained onerous, often miserable. As a result, many peasants took little interest in their work, and devised countless tricks and subterfuges to circumvent the steady pressures of Party planners.

On the other hand, incentives of various kinds were devised to entice both the peasants and the workers to speed up production. On the *kolkhozes,* work was rated according to the skill and effort involved in particular jobs. *Kolkhozniks* were also credited with

*TABLE I*

| Product | Unit | 1913[a] | 1928 | 1938 | 1940 | Target for 1942 under Third Five-Year Plan | Plan-Target for 1950 |
|---|---|---|---|---|---|---|---|
| Pig-iron | Million tons | 4.2 | 3.3 | 14.6 | 15.0 | 22 | 19.5 |
| Steel | Million tons | 4.2 | 4.3 | 18 | 18.3 | 27.5 | 25.4 |
| Rolled steel | Million tons | 3.6 | 3.4 | 13.3 | 13.1 | 21 | 17.8 |
| Coal | Million tons | 29.1 | 35.5 | 133 | 166 | 243 | 250 |
| Oil | Million tons | 9.2 | 11.7 | 32 | 31 | 54 | 35.4 |
| Electricity | Md. kilowatts | 2 | 5 | 39 | 48 | 75 | 82 |
| Copper | Thousand tons | — | 19.1 | 83.7 | 107[b] | — | — |
| Aluminum | Thousand tons | — | — | 43.8 | 55 | — | — |
| Cement | Million tons | 1.5 | 1.8 | 5.7 | 5.8 | 11 | 10.5 |
| Railway locomotives | Conventional units | 418 | 478 | 1626 | — | 2340 | 2720 |
| Goods wagons | Thousands | 14.8 | 10.6 | 49.1 | — | 120 | 146 |
| Tractors | Thousands | — | 1.2 | 80[c] | — | — | 112 |
| Motor vehicles | Thousands | — | .7 | 211 | — | 400 | 500 |
| Grain | Million tons | 80–82 | 73 | 95[d] | 119 | 130 | 127 |
| Sugar | Thousand tons | 1290 | 1283 | 2519 | — | 3500 | 2400 |
| Paper | Thousand tons | 205 | 284 | 832[b] | — | 1500 | 1340 |
| Cotton cloth | Million meters | 2227 | 2742 | 3491 | — | 4900 | 4686 |
| Woollen cloth | Million meters | 95 | 93 | 114 | — | 177 | 159 |
| Leather footwear | Million pairs | — | 29.6 | 213 | — | 258 | 240 |
| Rubber footwear | Million pairs | — | — | — | — | — | 88.6 |

[a] 1913 figures are for Russia within the pre-1939 territory of the U.S.S.R.

[b] Figure for 1939.

[c] Figures for 1937.

[d] The previous year, 1937, had been a good harvest year and had shown a figure of 120.

"labor days" that, at the end of the year, were used as units of exchange to determine how much of the *kolkhoze's* produce was to be allotted to the individual farmer. In the factories, piecework and bonuses encouraged workers to keep at the job. Other incentives were adjustment of prices, issuance of priority ration cards, and the awarding of honor badges and ribbons to workers who produced beyond their quota.

## Gains and Costs

The aims of the first Five Year Plan,* as reported by the government, were achieved in four years. A second Plan, also giving em-

phasis to heavy industry, was set up for the years 1932 to 1937. However, Hitler's schemes of aggression caused it to be modified, sometime after 1935, in favor of military preparedness. But in spite of this economic detour, the second Plan was carried off as successfully as the first (the third Plan, 1938 to 1943, was even more seriously disrupted by the war; even so, its achievements were also substantial). Table I gives some indication of the "planned" gains.[8]

Critics of the Soviet regime have pointed out that figures such as those given in Table I prove how far behind the United States and

* After 1958, Seven Year Plans were substituted.

8. From Maurice Dobb, *Soviet Economic Development Since 1917*, International Publishers, New York, 1948, p. 311.

England the Soviet Union was at the time that the statistics were published. And the figures do prove just that. What is much more significant, however, is comparison not with the leading industrial nations of the world but with Russia's own record in tsarist times. Here the contrast is striking, especially in industrial goods. It may be argued, of course, that advances would have been just as great if the old regime had remained in power; there certainly is no way of disproving the claim. But the argument is hardly convincing in the light (if the word is appropriate) of that regime's consistently dismal record of behind-the-times productivity.

There can be no doubt that, from the mid-1930s, the standard of living for both farmers and workers rose markedly above that which had so long prevailed in tsarist times. It is true that food, clothing, and housing remained in short supply, but not nearly as short as before the Revolution. Moreover, a new spirit infused the masses. For the first time in their history they felt as "live souls"; they experienced what one authority has called a release of energy. The regime under which they lived was dictatorial, more absolute than tsarist autocracy. But it was created and managed for them, not for landed or bourgeois aristocrats. The dread secret police were ubiquitous, but they rarely sought out the peasant farmer or the factory worker. In short, things were looking up. If today was hard, it was only in preparation for a tomorrow that was bright, almost beyond imagining.

On the other hand, the costs of fulfilling the Plans were inhumanely high. Thousands of families were deliberately forced into starvation, or into the hell of concentration camps.[9] Many thousands more were subjected to forced labor at government terms (especially during the period 1929 to 1934).

9. For a realistic view of life in a Soviet concentration camp, see Alexander Solzhenitsyn, *One Day in the Life of Ivan Denisovich*, E. B. Dutton, New York, 1963.

*An aluminum plant in the U. S. S. R.*

Those in supervisory or managerial positions were forever in danger, not of mere demotion but of imprisonment and even death if production in their factories or farms consistently fell behind the quotas set for them. For years, *kolkhozniks* were overworked and underfed so that their leaders might buy machinery and hire technicians from abroad. No matter how bright the Soviet tomorrow should turn out to be, millions would be harried to their death before it dawned.

## The Purges

Peasant resistance to the strictures of the first Five Year Plan had been so profound and so stubborn that many Soviet leaders demanded a return to NEP, or to some modification of it. But Stalin would not compromise. He was convinced that the forward step had to be taken then, or else all hope given up that it could ever be taken. Perhaps experience would prove the *mouzhik* (the "subsistence" farmer) unteachable. If so, the regime and the Revolution were lost, no

*Menshevists on trial in Moscow for "counter-revolutionary" activities (1931).*

matter what was done. But more likely, stern socialist leadership could force the peasant first to tolerate, and then finally to cooperate with that leadership. In any case, all would be lost if the effort was not made soon.

But for a time it appeared that Stalin, after all, would have to yield to the peasants. By 1932, *kulak* destruction of cattle had reached such proportions that the entire agrarian economy was threatened. Moreover, the middling peasant, upon whom the Soviet regime had to depend (or else lose the masses who looked to the middling peasant for leadership and example), showed strong signs of siding with the *kulak*. Stalwart old Bolsheviks such as Bukarin, Kamenev, Rykov, and Zinoviev strongly counseled retreat before it was too late.

But in spite of these pressures, Stalin held his ground—for seven years, during NEP, the *kulak* had been pampered; his strength had come to rival that of the government. What socialist good could come from further pampering? If the old Bolsheviks could not understand a situation as simple as this, their advice was not worth listening to. But it was hard to believe that they had actually misread the signs. More probably, Stalin came to believe, they were conspiring among themselves to rid the regime of his leadership. He remembered Trotsky, of course, and the left "deviationists" of the late 1920s. Then Trotsky's exile and the imprisonment and execution of many of his followers had

brought Stalin to power. Now, it seemed, "right deviationists" were plotting his destruction. And if they were, could another purge be avoided?

Since little documentary evidence on the purges is available, conjecture must serve. It seems likely that many of the old Bolsheviks were weary of Stalin's leadership. Lenin, before his death, had cautioned against giving too much power to Stalin. Lenin believed that Stalin was too crude, too rude, and too stubborn. Presumably, most of the "old ones" were of this mind in the early 1930s. It is doubtful, however, whether a real conspiracy to oust Stalin had taken shape. By this time a younger generation of Communists was emerging; many of them had been appointed to high Party and governmental office by Stalin. Indeed, by 1934 both the Central Committee and the Politbureau were dominated by Stalin's followers. Thus, there was not much base left upon which to mount an offensive against the leader. Moreover, the secret police were forever checking against precisely such possibilities. Also, it is hard to understand and to calculate the influence of Stalin's suspicious nature. Presumably a number of Stalin's colleagues wished for a milder program, without at all intending to offer more than verbal opposition to the program proposed by Stalin. But to the edgy Party boss, any opposition increasingly came to be looked upon as treason to the Revolution; he tended, in short, to equate his leadership with the only possible successful completion of the Revolution. And yet, as one authority has pointed out, it

was not ambition alone which had led Stalin in the 20's to amass his great power over the party. The survival in power of the party was at stake during those years, and few communists ever doubted that, for the party to retain its monopoly of power was the first and foremost aim of all policy. But this survival required centralized discipline inside the party, and Stalin was probably the only man who could ensure it . . . since [the] revolution meant an all out war by the communist party against the majority of the population, the peasants, it was unavoidable that Stalin's personal power over party should have increased in the process. . . . Stalin's revolution in agriculture and industry and his assault on the party which consummated this revolution must be seen as integrated parts of one and the same process.[10]

In any case, in the years 1936 to 1938, Stalin purged the Party so mercilessly and so thoroughly that his will emerged as the one voice and guide of the Soviet Union. In this period the "old Bolsheviks" were done away with, almost to the man. In public trials, some of the accused "confessed" heinous crimes against the state. A number of generals, including the commander-in-chief, were condemned to death in secret sessions. In none of these cases can the interested inquirer learn the true facts. Some of the "evidence" has been proved false; as for the rest, we can only surmise that most of the charges were without foundation. However, we cannot be sure. What is certain is that for several years the flaming torch of terror seared the land. When it flickered out in 1939, Russia stood out starkly as a monolithic party-state, still energetic, but purged of all dissent.

*Premier Josef Stalin.*

## FROM GERMAN MARXISM TO RUSSIAN COMMUNISM

Twenty years after their overthrow of the provisional government, the Communist revolutionaries had good reason to believe that they were here to stay. The House of the Autocrat was utterly destroyed. Most of the landed gentry and their military colleagues, the White Generals, had been killed or exiled. More recently the whole of the *kulak* class had been wiped out. Although the peasants still had to be convinced of the worthwhileness of collectivization, they were

no longer sabotaging the experiment. As for the city workers, they had never given the government real cause for concern. In short, Communism was making its way.

But it had somewhat changed over the years. For example (a rather remarkable example) it had come to power in the absence of either a bourgeois or a proletarian revolution.[11] What Bolsheviks liked to call the proletarian revolution was actually a revolution planned and executed by the "Vanguard," an elite group of professional revolutionaries. Furthermore, Communism, in its original form, maintained that the society that emerged from the revolution would be completely democratic. Russian Communism, on the other hand, had never tried to function under democratic processes, although it always insisted that pure democ-

10. Leonard Shapiro, *The Communist Party of the Soviet Union,* Random House, New York, 1959, pp. 429–430.

11. Cf. John Plamenatz, *German Marxism and Russian Communism,* Longmans Green & Co., New York, 1954, p. 312, and pp. 306–329.

racy would characterize the ultimate, stateless society. Another modification of German Marxism was Stalin's decision to develop "socialism in one country." Marx and Engels envisioned the proletarian revolution sweeping over all of Europe. Any less effort, they believed, signified both proletarian unreadiness, and the certain collapse of the revolution wherever, in isolation, it might occur. By 1937, Stalin's reading of the curve of history

appeared sounder than that of his masters. Clearly, Russia's Communism, although rooted in Marxist theory, was a product of history, mostly Russia's own. The new way of life did not too clearly promise during its first decades that it could transcend the bleak, degrading inhumanity of that history. But neither did it seem to presage another time of troubles. The hopes of both rulers and ruled looked to tomorrow.

# B. Fascist Italy

## THE SPIRIT AND CONDITIONS OF POSTWAR ITALY

### Disillusionment and Delusion

The aftermath of World War I worked unexpected changes in Italy. After bargaining with both sides, she had joined forces in 1915 with the *Entente,* which had promised her substantial territorial gains at the expense of the Austrian and Ottoman Empires (see map, p. 443). As one of the victorious powers she could hope to secure indemnities, much needed for her chronically anemic exchequer. In addition, as a victorious power, her heightened prestige would lend luster to a political establishment that had been singularly lacking in grandeur since the days of the Caesars.

In varying degrees, all of these hopes were frustrated within a few years. Although territorial gains had been made in the north and north-east, they fell short of what had been promised. Particularly irritating was the creation of the "international" city of Fiume. Indemnities from both Austria and Germany amounted to virtually nothing. As for glory and prestige, the defeat at Caporetto had dashed, indeed crushed, Italian spirits so

thoroughly that a sense of national shame pervaded the land.

Moreover, war costs had brought the economy close to bankruptcy. Returning veterans could not find jobs. The lira steadily dropped in value. Much of the land was owned by proprietors who lived in the cities, and left the management of their estates to overseers who paid hired laborers the barest subsistence wage. Millions of sharecroppers fared no better. In order to build up her industrial machine so that it might compete with those of her neighbors, Italy needed to import great quantities of coal and iron, of which her Apennine Mountains were strangely barren. She also lacked oil, cotton, and wool. But in the general conditions of financial stringency that prevailed in most of Europe after the war, Italy found little opportunity to borrow the capital required for such expenditures.

Psychic ills were added to depression and disillusionment. The war had warped the value fabric of men who had lived long with violence and death. In a strange, unreasonable way it had sickened many soldiers of the ways of peace.

[They] had grown accustomed to the war

with its excitements and rewards, its exaltation of the personal feat, its freedom from daily cares and uncertainties. When peace 'broke out,' as suddenly and unexpectedly as the war itself, these men experienced a letdown. They unconsciously looked for ways to continue the wartime existence which had lasted so long that it seemed there had been no previous life. [A man might find] in the war self-glorification, fulfillment of his dreams as superman, and an escape from creditors and financial harassment. To him peacetime [meant] a return to debts and old mistresses, and the sad admission that he was getting on in years. To be free from worries and stay young he had to remain a warrior. . . .[12]

Actually, many did remain soldiers. In the new Baltic states, for example, some German soldiers continued a kind of guerrilla struggle against the authorities—almost any authorities. In Germany a number of bored officers founded the "Free Corps" with which to harrass the new republican regime and keep alive the heroic image of the uniformed man. In Italy the most notorious "permanent soldier" was the romantic poet-politician, Gabriele D'Annunzio, who (in 1920) declared war against his own country and lived to write boastful poems about it.

Certain conditions rooted in Italy's past compounded her postwar problems. One condition was a citizenry untrained in democratic behavior. The liberal impulse, it is true, had contributed much to Italian unification. But more than impulse is needed to sustain and develop representative government. Particularly important is an alert, educated citizenry; Italy simply lacked this. In fact, as late as 1911, the census returns showed that 40 per cent of Italy's adult population were illiterate. The historic record also showed growing corruption in almost all government agencies

12. Laura Fermi, *Mussolini,* The University of Chicago Press, Chicago, 1961, p. 172. The quotation specifically refers to D'Annunzio, referred to *infra,* but the observation is applicable generally.

and activities. Thus, the machinery of the state was ineffectually run by politicians most of whom felt little responsibility toward the millions that they ruled. It is no wonder that serious socioeconomic problems multiplied as the nation undertook the complicated task of converting the weapons and ways of war into the tools and the modes of peace. The postwar years, then, were a compound of unemployment and sluggish industrial activity, of cynicism, disillusionment, and frustration. In the late months of 1920, workers in the industrial cities of the north "occupied" some factories; here and there, peasants, made desperate by unrelieved hunger and privation, took over land from absentee owners. The national government eventually negotiated settlements that, however, satisfied neither workers nor owners. Throughout the country there seemed little faith, little hope, much restlessness, and a growing tendency to favor direct—and often violent—action to resolve mounting differences. Landed aristocrats and the bourgeoisie watched the Red tide rolling over Russia. They feared that it could happen to Italy. City and farm workers, on the other hand, wondered when the property-owning classes would learn that exploitation was not the way to the good life, and whether they would learn the lesson before catastrophe overtook them all.

## EMERGENCE OF MUSSOLINI

### The "Cult of Force and Daring"

This was the spirit and the general conditions of the times that prevailed in postwar Italy. Clearly, they pointed to some kind of sociopolitical climax. But this could hardly occur until a forceful and determined leader appeared to work his will upon the roiling furies that stirred the land. For a time it seemed that the Byronic D'Annunzio was the man. He had stormed and taken Fiume, a city supposedly held by a contingent of international troops. He had ruled it for a year by an awesome combination of violent force,

*Benito Mussolini, dictator of Italy (1922–1943), in full Fascist dress, including dagger.*

founded the *Fasci di combattimento*.* The new organization was at first more a movement than a party, and served as an outlet for multiple discontents. Unemployed veterans, passionate nationalists, exploited peasants, former army officers weary of peace, and underpaid workers—all came to see compelling attractions in the Fascists, the self-proclaimed redeemers of Italy's harassed body and soul.

Mussolini's behavior, which normally bordered on the peripatetic, was rooted in a variegated psyche, stirred by longings for power and action. As a young man he had read and responded to the coldly passionate strophes of Machiavelli. "My father," he said, "used to read Machiavelli to us in the evening, while we warmed ourselves by the last embers of the shop's fire, drinking the wine of our countryside. The impression was *profound.*"[14] The German philosopher Nietzsche made an impression no less profound. Mussolini professed to believe that by force of will and high disdain for conventional morality man could become superman. About the time he founded the *Fasci di combattimento* he made this Zarathustrian (the reference is to Nietzsche's, not history's, Zoroaster) declaration: "We who detest from the depth of our soul all Christianity, from Jesus' to Marx's, look with extraordinary sympathy upon this 'resurgence' of modern life in the pagan cult of force and daring."[15]

### The Road to Power

The rough treatment that Mussolini's *fasci* gave to demonstrating Socialists caught the

poetical pronunciamentos, and thespian talents. But he had departed after one broadside from an attacking naval force, and had retired from politics. His disciple, Benito Mussolini, had many of his hero's strengths and a surer sense of political possibilities. And he was to last longer.[13]

Before the war Mussolini had been a Socialist. He was dropped by the party when he openly espoused Italian intervention. Using financial resources difficult for the historian to trace, he founded a newspaper, *Il Popolo d'Italia,* in which he trumpeted the call to arms. During the war he served as a noncommissioned officer. He returned to his paper before the Armistice. For a brief time he continued to support worker causes, though no longer as a Socialist. In 1919 he

* Loosely translated, "groups of fighters." The Italian word *fascio* means "bundle." Its real significance is historic. In Roman days political authority was symbolized by a bundle of rods grouped around an axe. It connoted then—as later—disciplined unity and authoritarian power.

13. A good recent biography of Mussolini is Ivone Kirkpatrick, *Mussolini, a Study in Power,* Hawthorne Books, Inc., New York, New York, 1964.

14. Fermi, *op. cit.,* p. 220.
15. *Ibid.,* p. 170.

eye and interest of industrial and business elements. Throughout 1920 and 1921, street fighting between Red agitators and Mussolini's Blackshirts became distressingly frequent. Army and police units surreptitiously aided the fascist gangs. By 1922, general disorder had become so widespread that the public began to insist on the formation of a government strong enough to keep the peace. Mussolini enthusiastically proclaimed himself in complete agreement with this demand. Communist bands, he said, were trying to disorganize the life of the nation. When Red-inspired anarchy became general, Moscow's minions would take control. He felt that when that happened, the Italian people were finished. Thereafter they would serve as slaves of a vanguard of Marxist racketeers. He believed that only a strong, alert government could forestall this. Liberal parliamentarianism had petered out in futile rhetoric and shameful corruption. The only force standing between the buffeted Italian people and the Red menace was, according to the Fascist *Duce* (leader), himself and his loyal followers.

Actually, there was no serious Communist strength anywhere in Italy. Most Italian Socialists opposed Leninism when they were not fighting among themselves, which was a common occurrence. More often than not, the street fights were started by the Fascists. If Mussolini had been serious in his repeated demands for domestic order, his first constructive move would have been to disband his *squadristi* (bully-boy street fighters). He was serious about nothing except gaining and keeping power. By 1922, conditions were ripe for his bid for power. Cabinet crises were frequent and pointless. Many local politicians had become fascists; orders from the central government to disarm the Blackshirts received little or no attention. Fascist propaganda stepped up its campaign against the "Red menace." At the same time, Mussolini made it clear that the Royal House had nothing to fear from him. "The monarchy," he said, "represents the historical continuity

*This cartoon appeared in an Italian periodical before the Duce had yet gained complete control over the press. The caption has the leaders of opinion in Italy saying, "It's all right! We are only convincing an opponent of the need for collaboration."*

of the Nation; a splendid function and one of incalculable importance."[16] A gauge of the caliber of that institution was its ready acceptance of this supercilious judgment by an upstart agitator.

On October 28, 1922, Mussolini ordered his followers to march on Rome to "restore legality to the representative institutions of Italy." The Prime Minister, Signor Facta, decided to meet force with force, and declared a state of siege. But the king, fearful of civil war (and reassured of Mussolini's good intentions), refused to countersign the declaration. Instead, he invited the Duce to form a new government. In his first interview with the king, Mussolini wore a black shirt, black trousers, and white ankle gaiters. Unconsciously, he had attired himself as the perfect symbol of fascist ruler—political

16. Michael Florinsky, *Fascism and National Socialism,* The Macmillan Company, New York, 1936, pp. 17–18.

*Scene from Mussolini's march on Rome.*

thug and respectable "gent." Thus, fascism came to Italy not in revolutionary storm but in bourgeois spats.[17]

*Mussolini after the "march" on Rome, 1922.*

## FASCISM IN POWER

### The Fascist Credo

In the beginning, Italian fascism had no ideological content. In 1919 Mussolini had declared, "Fascism is a movement of reality, life, adhering to life. It is pragmatist. It has no *a priori* isms. No remote ends. It does not promise the usual heavens of idealism. It does not presume to live forever or for long.[18] In a very real sense its prime moving power was the same as that of latter-day beatnik cyclists—"you don't go someplace, man, you just go!" In his famous 1932 essay on fascist doctrines, Mussolini declared: "The Fascist disdains the comfortable life."

By then, fascist "wild ones" had been given a creed. In essence it elevated the state over the individual citizen, exalted the life of action and violence—"the dangerous life"— lauded rule by the elite, and glorified war as the great catalyst of life. Some explication of

17. For an interesting account of the political scurrying to and fro that preceded the "march," see Ivone Kirkpatrick, *op. cit.*
18. Fermi, *op. cit.,* p. 185. Later the Duce changed his mind about fascism's tenure.

this creed is given in the following excerpts from Mussolini's *La Dottrina del Fascismo.*

Against individualism, the Fascist conception is for the State; and it is for the individual in so far as he coincides with the state, which is the conscience and universal will of man in his historical existence. . . . Fascism reaffirms the State as the true reality of the individual. . . . Therefore for the Fascist, everything is in the State, and nothing human or spiritual exists . . . outside the State. . . . The State . . . is the creator of right . . . [It] is an absolute before which individuals and groups are relative.

Fascism desires an active man, one engaged in activity with all his energies. . . . It conceives of life as a struggle. . . . It does not consider that "happiness" is possible upon earth . . . and hence it rejects all theological theories according to which mankind would reach a definite stabilized condition at a certain point in history. . . . The proud motto of the *Squadrista,* "Me ne frego" ["I don't give a damn"], written on the bandages of a wound is an act of philosophy . . . it is education for combat, the acceptance of the risks which it brings. . . .

. . . Fascism is opposed to Democracy, which equates the nation to the majority, lowering it to the level of that majority . . . if the nation is conceived, as it should be, qualitatively and not quantitatively [then it may be understood as] the most powerful idea . . . which acts within the nation as the conscience and the will of the few, even of One. . . . [Fascism] affirms the irremediable, fruitful and beneficent inequality of man . . . . If it is admitted that the nineteenth century has been the century of Socialism, Liberalism, and Democracy, it does not follow that the twentieth century must also be [so]. Political doctrines pass; peoples remain. It is expected that this century may be that of authority, a century of the "Right," a Fascist century.

Above all, Fascism . . . believes neither in the possibility nor the utility of perpetual peace. It thus repudiates the doctrine of Pacifism. . . . War alone brings up to their highest tension all human energies and puts the stamp of nobility upon the people who have the courage to meet it.[19]

## Consolidation of the Fascist Dictatorship

For several years after taking power, Mussolini respected, at least nominally, the constitutional forms of government. He

"Mussolini, the Conqueror: 'Only when all my opponents are in prison shall we have an Italy that is really free.'" A German cartoonist pokes fun at the Italian Caesar just a few years before his satire boomeranged with the rise of a German führer.

19. Michael Oakeshott, *The Social and Political Doctrines of Contemporary Europe,* Cambridge University Press, Cambridge, 1939, pp. 164–177, *passim.* It is interesting to compare this 1932 definition of the essence of fascism, as Mussolini then thought of it, with his views after his overthrow in 1943. A few months before his death he made this frank statement to a fascist leader: "Let us not delude ourselves; as a doctrine Fascism contains nothing new, it is a product of the modern crisis, the crisis of man, who can no longer remain within the normal bounds of life with its conventionalism, within the bounds of the existing human laws. I would call it irrationalism. There is such a thing as morality, but we're tired of it; and I'd go further and say that it makes no impression on us. That can be changed by going against the stream. We are tormented people; everyone of us would like to be in the sun, the pole of life for himself and for others. There you have the evil at the heart of the modern man: call it irrationalism, Bolshevism, Fascism." Quoted in Herman Finer, *Mussolini's Italy,* Archon Books, Meriden, Conn., 1964 (this excerpt is taken from the unpaged section following the preface in the new edition).

recognized the right of nonfascist parties to exist and to dispute fascist proposals (provided that they did it reasonably, that is, mildly). He went through the forms of honoring the king. He also refrained from efforts to denigrate the Church. In short, he sang softly while he consolidated his power.

But he did consolidate his power. He quietly purged the bureaucracy and the police. By a decree, his "street squads" were transformed into legal militia units. And in late 1923, he forced through a new election law that provided that any party receiving at least 25 per cent of the popular vote was entitled to two thirds of the seats in the Chamber of Deputies. In the election that followed the next year, the Fascists, for the first time, constituted a majority of the Deputies.

In 1924 an event occurred that threatened his regime and then, paradoxically, secured it. The event was the publication by Giacomo Matteotti, a Socialist deputy, of a detailed exposé of fascist corruption and violence. Mussolini was furious. The revelations frightened him, while Matteotti's audacity insulted his image of himself as the new Caesar. To certain confidants he hinted that, for Italy's good, Matteotti ought to be taught a lesson. A few days later the deputy was snatched from the street, bundled into a car and murdered. A wave of indignation surged over Italy. Italians, of course, knew that fascist bully-boys had often brutally broken up meetings, and had often given the castor oil treatment to their opponents. If the average citizen did not give full approval to such tactics, he might have at least believed that they had become necessary. But government-sponsored murder was something else.

For a while, popular support of the regime wavered. Mussolini felt obliged to denounce the crime and to call for apprehension of the guilty ones. For their part, Socialist deputies walked out of the Chamber and vowed that they would not return until the political sins of fascism had been admitted and expiated. But popular indignation faded with the passing of time, and Mussolini, sensing it, regained his courage. Strict press censorship kept the opposition and the public literally out of touch with those who might have led the nation in an assault on the regime. The seats of the "Aventine dissidents"* were declared vacant; many political opponents were rounded up and sent into exile. Local elections were suspended. Mussolini had given himself the power to rule by decree, if and whenever he thought circumstances called for it. Two years after Matteotti's

murder the fascist dictatorship was, in all essentials, complete.

It is hard to pass judgment on the average citizen's attitude toward the regime. After 1926 there were no public signs of serious discontent with it but, by that time, coercive instruments of control were in common use. In 1945 Italian mobs mutilated the bodies of the deposed Duce and his mistress; but by then Italy had not only lost the war but had been occupied, first by the Nazis and then by the Allies. After the war Italy repudiated not only fascism but monarchial government as well. Yet as late as the 1960s a widely circulated Italian history textbook blamed the Versailles Treaty almost entirely for Europe's postwar troubles:

> . . . the discontent caused by the treaty is described [in the text] as having so disoriented Italian soldiers returning from the war that, "instigated by parties of the Left with a criminal propaganda of hatred against the ruling classes, they abandoned themselves to public demonstrations, and even fell so low as to occupy factories"; and it was in this political debilitation, against which the "healthy part of the nation reacted," that Mussolini took over the task of rescuing the country from "the bolshevism spreading over the Peninsula." According to [this text's author] Mussolini was a man of "extraordinary dynamism . . . [and] an admirer of the history and grandeur of Rome . . . who let himself be seduced by the idea, noble in itself, of conferring similar fortunes on the New Italy.[20]

Certainly, Italian industrialists and capitalists generally supported Mussolini, as did the army and the Church.† As for the worker

---

* The reference is to the withdrawal by the plebeians of ancient Rome to Mount Aventine, where they set up an extralegal government in opposition to patrician rule.

† In 1929 Mussolini, with considerable fanfare, signed a concordat with the Roman Catholic Church that restored normal relations between state and Church. For nearly sixty years the Pope had considered himself a "prisoner" in the Vatican. But in recent years, state-Church relations had improved a great deal. The concordat thus officially recognized a situation that had developed before Mussolini came to power.

20. Roland Steel, *Italy*, The H. W. Wilson Co., New York, 1963, pp. 54–55.

and peasant masses, perhaps they welcomed the order and the resurgence of national "glory" that Mussolini so dramatically brought them. Or perhaps they did not like current conditions under the regime, but believed that it was their best promise for a better tomorrow. Or they may genuinely have been attracted to the dynamic Duce whose tones, gestures, and words were always calculated to bring the masses under his spell.

## The Paper Corporate State

Beginning in 1926, Mussolini set about the creation of what he called the "corporate state." As it finally (and rather futilely)* developed, its basic economic aspects took on these features. At the local level, employees and employers each formed their own organizations. Their activities were supervised by a National Council of Corporations. Strikes and lockouts were declared illegal; differences between labor "syndicates" and employer corporations were submitted to arbitration. In 1934 an elaborate modification of the system was effected. All economic activity was divided into twenty-two corporations. These corporations were divided into three groups: one group of eight corporations was concerned with agriculture and nonmineral materials; another group, also of eight corporations, busied itself with mining, construction, and manufacturing; and the third group, of six corporations, administered transportation, finance, and the service industries. Each of the twenty-two corporations was organized as a trade association at the national level. There were also regional associations to mediate conflicts between local and national bodies. In the government the Ministry of Corporations exercised jurisdiction over all local, provincial, and national units.

For the most part, however, the corporate system was a party device used to impose fascism's political as well as economic policies on industrial institutions, particularly as they were concerned with preparations for war, and attempts to achieve autarchy.[21] But, even as such, the system did not constitute a provocation in the eyes of Italian businessmen. Indeed they supported it, as they generally supported the regime. For, in spite of Mussolini's protestation that "Italy is not a capitalist country," it was, as Italian businessmen very well knew. Moreover, in Italy the entrepreneur had economic advantages not found in most industrial states. For example, employers were given the right, by fascist law, "to fine, suspend, or dismiss workers who proved difficult to discipline or who performed acts disturbing to the normal functioning of a concern." Statistics show that even in Europe's boom period of production, Italian workers suffered a reduction in real wages. Actually, Italy experienced the depression well ahead of the rest of the world. "The acceptance of repeated reductions in wages by the workers was praised by Fascist leaders as patriotic sacrifice and as 'a preparation for tomorrow by the renunciations of today.' And yet in 1934 [Mussolini] asserted: 'We are probably moving toward a period of humanity resting on a lower standard of living. Humanity is capable of asceticism such as perhaps we have no conception of.' "[22]

## THE CULT OF FORCE IN ACTION

### In Africa

These prognostications could hardly have caused jubilation among Italy's masses. Their standard of living was already one of the lowest in Europe. It is reasonable to ask whether the timing of Mussolini's decision to carve out a new African empire was related

---

* Or as one authority has expressed it, "the corporate state *outside of labor* remained largely a paper organization." (Italics added.)

21. See Witt Bowden, Michael Karpovich, Abbott Usher, *An Economic History of Europe Since 1750,* New York, 1936, pp. 792 ff.
22. *Ibid.,* p. 797.

*As the Italians advanced into Ethiopia they burned out many thatched-hut villages.*

*An Ethiopian rifleman attempts to harass Italian bombers during a raid on an Ethiopian town in early 1936.*

THE AWFUL WARNING.

FRANCE AND ENGLAND (together ?).    "WE DON'T WANT YOU TO FIGHT, BUT, BY JINGO, IF YOU DO, WE SHALL PROBABLY ISSUE A JOINT MEMORANDUM SUGGESTING A MILD DISAPPROVAL OF YOU."

*Neither England nor France was eager to cross the Duce in his Ethiopian adventure, as this* Punch *cartoon makes clear.*

to domestic miseries.* It is hard to believe that even Mussolini's magic could mesmerize an entire nation into accepting the prospect of permanent poverty. In any case, in 1935 the Duce led Italy down what he thought of as the "glory road" to war. Until the spring of 1936, the nation's attention and energies were absorbed in the conflict with Ethiopia, an underdeveloped, weak country that Mussolini, with a straight face, charged had attacked Italian interests in Africa.

The conquest of this backward state gave

* The conquest of Ethiopia was decided on in late 1933, at the nadir of the great world depression.

the Duce and his people a surge of confidence. Further contributing to Italy's feeling of power was Europe's meek capitulation to overt aggression. Ethiopia had appealed to the League of Nations, whose two chief supporters were England and France. When Mussolini successfully pushed his war in the face of League disapproval, he concluded that he had underestimated fascism's strength and undercalculated democracy's weaknesses. What adventures were not possible if the will was strong and the spirit tough?

## In Spain

Hardly had the African conquest been concluded when, with the outbreak of war in Spain, Italy became involved in new fighting. Reactionary forces under General Francisco Franco attempted a coup against the liberal republican regime in July 1936, which soon turned into a full-scale civil war. Italian troops and material were sent to Spain to help Franco establish his fascist Falangist state. But the new venture led to consequences with which Mussolini had not reckoned. In October of that same year, Italy and Germany signed an agreement which the Duce, with characteristic bombast, labeled the Axis Pact. During the Ethiopian war, Nazi Germany had been the only major power to support Italy's claims. Naturally, Mussolini felt a kind of affinity with his northern neighbor after this experience. Since Hitler was as eager as the Duce to see liberal government liquidated in Europe, he also sent supplies and troops to Franco. It was quite natural that these friends of a friend should themselves become friends.

To dramatize the significance of the new brotherhood, Mussolini paid an official visit to Germany in 1937. What he saw amazed him. Within four years Germany had become one of the strongest military states in Europe. Even more important to the Duce was the clear evidence that Hitler had made only a beginning. Clearly the Prussian power state had been reborn. In contrast, England and France seemed decadent, timid, beguiled by appeasement delusions. In these circumstances, Mussolini modified his general view of things to come. Up to this point he had seen himself as the world's emerging Caesar. Now the ominous stamp of the goose step was again heard in Germany. Another superman had appeared; some sharing of power was inevitable.

## The Deflation of Fascism

Soon, other events made even clearer to Mussolini the power dimensions of the new Germany and its leader. Nazi planes, artillery, and infantrymen in Spain performed with merciless efficiency. The Italian effort probably was superior quantitatively, but even a casual comparative study revealed a Nazi striking power and an offensive spirit that Italy could not match. Moreover, in 1938 Germany incorporated Austria into the

*Mussolini and Hitler in 1936.*

Reich. This time Mussolini made no protest. The "Greater Germany" towered still higher over its continental neighbors, including Italy. In short, events of the mid-1930s reversed the positions of the fascist leaders and their peoples. For fifteen years the German superman had looked to Rome for inspiration and clues to set up the totalitarian state. But by 1938 the pupil had become the master; hereafter, each passing year was to see the diminution of fascist Italy and the aggrandizement of Nazi Germany. In the end, as we shall see, Mussolini became Hitler's puppet, deprived even of opportunity to hide his sorry state from full view of the world. Ten years after the Italian conquest of Ethiopia, Italy herself was conquered. Fascism longed for action, violence, and war. It got them all. Its leaders had boasted *me ne frego.* With whatever sincerity, the masses of Italy said, in 1945, "but we do." The adventure of the 1920s had faded out in fury and futility.

## SELECTED READINGS

Beloff, Max, *The Foreign Policy of Soviet Russia, 1929–1941,* Oxford University Press, London, 1947 to 1949, 2 vols.
> Probably the best study of this subject up to the time of its publication and still of high worth. The author is not unsympathetic to the problems and position of the Soviet Union.

Carr, E. H., *The Bolshevik Revolution, 1917–1923,* Macmillan & Co., London, 1950–1958, 3 vols., variously numbered according to edition.
> Although sympathetic to the aims of the Russian revolutionists, Carr exercises his ample scholarly talents in a much too disciplined manner to allow his own leanings to seriously affect his work. These volumes offer the best account of the great revolution available to date.

Deakin, F. W., *The Brutal Friendship,* Harper & Row, New York, 1962.
> A long, carefully researched study of the tandem efforts of Mussolini and Hitler to construct a new order in Europe. Mussolini's character and talents appear in a somewhat (but not substantially) different light from that given them by the focus of Kirkpatrick, cited below.

*Deutscher, Isaac, *Stalin, A Political Biography,* Vintage Books, New York, c. 1960.
> One of the best studies of Stalin. The author's mild pro-Soviet sympathies are clearly discernible.

Deutscher, Isaac, *The Prophet Armed—Trotsky, 1879–1921,* Oxford University Press, London, 1954.

————, *The Prophet Unarmed—Trotsky 1921–1929* (1959).

————, *The Prophet Outcast—Trotsky 1929–1940* (1963).
> A carefully researched, highly informative trilogy by one who, in his own words, considers Trotsky "one of the most outstanding revolutionary leaders of all times, outstanding as fighter, thinker, martyr."

* Asterisk (*) denotes paperback.

Finer, Herman, *Mussolini's Italy,* Grosset & Dunlap, New York, 1965.
> Except for a ten-page insert, "From Mussolini's Italy to Italy's Italy," this is the same work that was first published in 1935. Part V, "The Manufacture of Obedience," is especially recommended.

Kennan, George F., *Russia and the West under Lenin and Stalin,* Little, Brown & Co., Boston, 1961.
> In the author's words, this is a "series of discussions of individual episodes or problems," instead of "a chronological account of the happenings of this phase of diplomatic history." Kennan's scholarship, personal experience, and intellectual integrity combine to make each "episode or problem"—Brest-Litovsk, the Allies in Siberia, Rappallo, The Soviet-Nazi Pact of 1939, and about 20 others—meaningful beyond any "chronological account" that deals with this material, except perhaps that of Max Beloff's cited above.

Kirkpatrick, Ivone, *Mussolini, A Study in Power,* Hawthorne Books, New York, 1964.
> The best biography of Mussolini yet published. It is well organized and well documented. The author is not inclined to sympathize with the Duce's dictatorial ways, but his feelings for the dynamic power of the Italian leader show through his fundamentally objective account. This book is particularly worthwhile when read in conjunction with Deakin's work, cited above.

Matthews, Herbert L., *The Fruits of Fascism,* Harcourt, Brace & Co., New York, 1943.
> The author, a journalist, spent many years living in and (for a time) admiring Fascist Italy. The Spanish Civil War gave him, according to his own account, a new and (as he believed) a truer view of the fascist ways of life. This book is a polemic against the evil, inhumane conditions that he believed fascism fastened upon all men who submitted to its authority. It is important for the many illustrative episodes and anecdotes that are not found in the accounts of professional historians.

Maynard, John, *Russia in Flux,* The Macmillan Co., New York, 1948.

This abridged edition of Maynard's *Russia in Flux* and *The Russian Peasant and Other Studies* is perhaps the best single source for the American reader to use. It stresses the life and outlook of the pre-Revolution peasant—an understanding of which is a prerequisite of any attempt to probe the meaning of the first two decades of Soviet Russian history. Unfortunately, it understresses the inhumanity of early Bolshevik rule.

Moore, Barrington, Jr., *Terror and Progress USSR,* Harvard University Press, Cambridge, 1954.

The author's main purpose here is to "weigh, with an eye to the future, the sources of stability and the potentialities for change in the Bolshevik regime." He does somewhat more than this as he examines the role of the peasant in a workers' state, Soviet concepts of science and art, and the "function of terror."

Stipp, John L., ed., *Soviet Russia Today,* Harper & Brothers, New York, 1956–1957.

Selected extracts from various authorities on the theory and practice of Marxism in Russia.

Trotsky, Leon, *The History of the Russian Revolution,* translator, Max Eastman, Simon and Schuster, New York, 1932, 3 vols.

Both because Trotsky was one of the "three who made the revolution," and because he writes—and is translated—so well, this history of the Russian Revolution invites serious study. If Lincoln had lived to write a history of the Civil War, it would undoubtedly have been denounced by Southern Confederates and Northern Copperheads as a biased, unreliable tract. And probably they would have been partly right. But the work would have been well worth the effort and the reading. This is also true with respect to this 1400 page history of Russia's "civil war."

*Wolfe, Bertram D., *Three Who Made a Revolution,* The Dial Press, New York, 1948.

The three men are Lenin, Trotsky, and Stalin. They come to life in these pages.

# XIV

# *The Collectivist Trend between the Wars: Germany; the United States*

## A. Nazi Germany

### INTERLUDE OF THE WEIMAR REPUBLIC

The defeat of the German armies by the Allies inflicted traumatic suffering upon the whole nation. Right up to the signing of the armistice most Germans expected Allied, not German, surrender. The legend of Prusso-German military invincibility had long been a fundamental part of the psychic fabric that distinguished the Germans as a people. Nothing that the general public was allowed to learn during even the grim later phases of the war had given indication of anything but eventual victory. The sudden capitulation in the fall of 1918 stunned the nation. For many Germans, life would never have worthwhile meaning until German arms had cauterized the wound and made the nation whole again.

And, of course, the Versailles Treaty compounded German humiliation and hurt, providing as it did for unilateral disarmament, territorial dismemberment, punitive reparations, and degradation of Germany to the tatus of a second class power.*

By refusing to deal with the Kaiser and the military, the Allies also encouraged German liberals to set up a German republic to replace Bismarck's "Second Reich." The government of the new state, commonly called the Weimar Republic after the city in which its constitution was written, functioned under severe handicaps. For one thing, its representatives had signed the hated treaty, and thus incurred an odium which persisted,

---

* For a review of the terms of settlement, see *supra*, p. 455.

however irrationally, throughout its brief life. For another, its democratic apparatus proved puzzling to a people long accustomed to authoritarian rule. From 1871 to 1918 the Imperial Government of Germany rested upon a constitution personally drawn up by Bismarck. From even earlier, Prussia (by far the largest German state) had clung to a constitution that virtually disfranchised most of its adult, male citizens.

For a few years in the mid-1920s the Weimar Republic showed some promise of gaining stability. But at no time did it enjoy the broad public support and imaginative leadership an enduring regime requires. Its troubles were many and began early. In 1919 a Communist uprising (the Spartacist revolt) occurred in Berlin and its environs. Hundreds were killed in the bloody assault and its repulse, including Rosa Luxemburg and Karl Liebknecht, internationally known leaders of the German Marxist Party. The next year monarchist rebels attacked the government. Led by unemployed militarists, the initial thrusts of the insurrection (often referred to as the Kapp Putsch) proved so threatening that the government temporarily abandoned Berlin. In 1923 Adolf Hitler and his Nazi contingents staged what came to be known as the Munich Beer Hall Putsch. Hitler's announced intention was to march on to Berlin, overthrow the Versailles "traitors," and establish a Nazi regime. All of these attempts proved abortive; but they demonstrated how shaky were the underpinnings of the Republic. Contributing to the general confusion were the restiveness and recalcitrance of the German General Staff. Left untouched by the Versailles Treaty,* the Staff worked secretly and ceaselessly against the day when Junker militarism should regain control of a reborn Reich. Also left virtually untouched were the old

imperial civil service and the judicial systems.

Experience has shown that republican regimes are most stable and function most efficiently under the two party system. In the Weimar Republic there were always about a half dozen "major" parties jostling for position and power. On the left were the Communists and Social Democrats. Throughout most of the life of the Republic, the Social Democrats held more seats in the Reichstag (the main governing body) than any other party, but they were never able to command a majority. Until dissolved when the Nazis took over, the Communist party steadily grew in numbers and influence, although at no time did it represent more than about 15 per cent of the total electorate. The Catholic Center party tended to advertise itself as a middle-of-the-road party, but few liberals agreed that the labeling was accurate. Politically, its position could be compared to that of moderate Republicans in this country. Its main strength came from Bavaria and other south German states. The more genuinely middle-of-the-road party was the Democratic party, almost alone in sincerely working to establish a capitalistic republic. It often received less support than either the Communist or Center parties. On the right were the Peoples' party, the Nationalists, and the Nazis. The Peoples' party balanced off the Democrats, the Nationalists balanced off the Centrists; until the last three years of the Republic, Nazi representation in the Reichstag was negligible. In every election a number of splinter parties further complicated the attempt to find a consensus.

By itself, such a situation was bad enough, even for a democratically grounded people, as any Frenchman would admit. In addition, the Weimar Constitution provided for a system of proportional representation which practically guaranteed a perpetual coalition government. This, combined with multiple parties, democratic inexperience, and sustained suspicion of the system responsible for acceptance of the hated Versailles Treaty,

---

* Technically, the General Staff was abolished by the treaty. In actual practice it reformed under another name.

made it difficult indeed for the new Republic to prove itself.

Despite these troubles, so many and so serious, the Republic might still have made its way if the army had been put in its place and kept there. But from the beginning, it was not. Friedrich Ebert, soon to be chosen Germany's first president, reviewed returning troops in Berlin and publicly acclaimed them as "unvanquished [on] the field of battle." The General Staff could hardly have asked for a more welcome sign from the leader of the political party that was to play a major role in the new Republic's government. Soon an even more ominous development occurred. In 1920, as we have seen, the monarchist Kapp Putsch temporarily ousted the government from Berlin. When Ebert asked the army chiefs to support him in routing the insurgents, they flatly refused. It was only when the Social Democrats threatened a general strike that the Putschists withdrew from Berlin.

The determination of General von Seeckt, new commander of the German army, and of his senior officers to rebuild a strong army led to an anomalous diplomatic coup. For several years after the war, Germany shared with Russia the opprobrium and suspicion of most of the world. As "outcasts," they understandably had things to talk over between themselves. One important item to Russia was the hiring of military experts to help build up the Red army; another item was the engagement of German industrial technicians to advise Russian commissars in the intricacies of industrial construction and management. For Germany, association with a European power—even a Communist power—was a psychological lift. Furthermore, a favorable treaty of commerce gave Germany access to much needed markets. Perhaps most important, the assignment of German officers outside their own country where such activities were forbidden enabled them to work out plans and projects designed to modernize army efficiency. Thus the agree-

*General Hans von Seeckt was the father of the new German army, which the strictures of the Versailles Treaty tried to keep small and weak.*

ment of 1922—the Rapallo Treaty—opened the door to arrangements that (from 1923 on) allowed Germany a kind of military "elbowroom" strictly forbidden by the Treaty of Versailles.

The Weimar Constitution (adopted in July 1919) seemed to guarantee democratic development. Free speech, press, assembly, as well as freedom of religion were all underwritten by the new basic law. Representative legislative bodies and an elected president were provided. The Reichsrat, roughly corresponding to the American Senate, participated in making laws, but could be overruled by the more popularly elected lower house, the Reichstag. Nevertheless, the new constitution's democratic surface glossed over several potentially autocratic features. For example, Article 48 gave the president arbitrary power to issue decreees and laws if he believed public order and safety were threatened. During the fifteen years of the Republic's life, several hundred such decrees and ordinances were enacted.* Indeed, in the two-year period before the advent of Hitler, Germany was governed almost exclusively by decree. Also, Article 53 gave the president power to appoint and remove the chancellor. Normally (as in France and Britain), this power is used under the direction of popular leaders. But Germans construed it to mean that a chancellor was responsible not only to the Reichstag but also to the president. In 1932, for example, President Hindenburg removed Chancellor Brüning despite the latter's possession of the confidence of the Reichstag.

In 1925 President Ebert died. Although hardly an aggressive Socialist he at least was completely devoted to maintaining the republican system. His successor, Field Marshal von Hindenburg, was at best a lukewarm supporter of that regime. In the run-off election of that year (no candidate had received a majority in the first canvass) Hindenburg benefited from the vicious struggle between the Socialists and the Communists. If the Marxist parties had supported a single candidate, he would have been elected since, between them, they cast over one million more votes than did the supporters of Hindenburg. Their refusal to vote together allowed a Junker aristocrat and general to head the Republic.

Fortunately, a year before, Gustav Stresemann, Germany's one great statesman in the Weimar years, had become the real working head of the government (first as Chancellor, then as Minister for Foreign Affairs). During the war Stresemann had been a strident nationalist. By 1923, he seemingly had come to see the need for genuine rapprochement between his country and France, and for ac-

* Technically the Reichstag could rescind such decrees. The party system, however, made this provision difficult to implement.

*Dr. Gustav Stresemann, Germany's strongest leader in the new Weimar Republic.*

ceptance of the Versailles settlement, at least in its broad outlines. Under his leadership, Germany signed the Locarno Treaties (see pp. 483), joined the League of Nations, and accepted the Pact of Paris (the so-called Briand-Kellogg Pact, 1928) that outlawed war as an instrument of national policy. His death in 1929 was a blow that had repercussions reaching far beyond Germany's borders. Of course, it did not of itself prefigure for Germans a future time of troubles. But it diminished the likelihood of avoiding it.

The advent of the Great Depression made that future inevitable and imminent. As unemployment spread, millions of Germans tightened their belts, queued up for public relief, and cursed the Weimar system. Increasingly, they came to hold the government responsible for all the ills that had beset them since that fateful day in November 1918. Their reasoning was simple: never before had Germans suffered so cruelly; never before had Germans allowed themselves to experiment with democratic government. To an extent not amenable to reasonable assessment, the doubts and confusions of their present were fused with memories of the past to point to a coming day of rule by "leaders."

## RISE OF HITLER AND THE NAZI PARTY

Cutting through their misery and the general atmosphere of haunting fears, the confident, raucous voice of a rising politician, Adolf Hitler, trumpeted the coming of a new day. Germany, he insisted, had only to awaken, shake off its numbness, and form ranks behind him. There was in National Socialism and its leaders certain salvation for the Fatherland; indeed, more than salvation—a thousand years of power and glory. Scarcely a decade earlier, neither the Nazi party nor its leaders were known by more than a handful of Germans. Formed in 1920, the party membership consisted of a strangely assorted company of economic radicals, restless, unemployed junior military officers, and embittered nationalists. Two years earlier a Bavarian locksmith, Anton Drexler, had gotten together a Committee of Independent Workmen. His aim was to create a mass movement designed to set up a sociopolitical system favorable to the little man, and to regain the lost glory of the old German Reich. In the same year a similar movement was organized* in Austria under the title National Socialist German Workers Party. In 1919 the limping Committee of Independent Workmen merged with several related splinter groups to form the German Workers Party. It was this party that Hitler joined in September 1919. The next year it took over the name of its Austrian counterpart as well as some of that party's followers. Other recruits were some Free Corps officers, including Captain Ernst Röhm, who yearned for the creation of a German state revitalized by an armed citizenry and a quasi-socialist economy.

* Actually reorganized by a change of name and by merging with several other small groups.

*Hitler swearing in new members of the Nazi party about 10 years after its founding. Josef Göbbels appears in the background.*

At no time during this period did any of these parties attract even a moderately large following, until Hitler edged his way into leadership of the National Socialist German Workers Party. By 1923, as we have noted, Hitler considered "his" movement strong enough to attempt an insurrection. But until then, the name Adolf Hitler meant nothing to the German masses. Even for some years after the putsch, the future führer was regarded by most Germans as a rather comical figure destined soon to return to the oblivion from which he had so recently and so unaccountably emerged. Certainly nothing in his record made such a prognosis unreasonable. Born of poor parents in Braunau, a village near Linz, Austria, he had dropped out of school at an early age. As a young man he tried his hand at painting but received no encouragement from professional artists. After the death of his parents he drifted around Vienna and Munich doing odd jobs. For several years he was so destitute that he was forced to live in flophouses and public charitable institutions. The coming of the Great War gave his life, by his own account, a sense of purpose and direction. He joined a Bavarian regiment and

*Hitler (marked by cross) could tolerate but not really join in relief-station horseplay which his fellow soldiers concocted to work off the stresses of front-line fighting.*

served throughout the war with sufficient distinction to earn the Iron Cross. After the war he worked for the army as a kind of spier-out of subversive activities among dissident civilian groups. In this capacity he attended a meeting of the German Workers party. He so much liked what he heard that within a few months he became a member. Shortly afterwards he resigned his army job and devoted all of his energies to the task of making the organization the nucleus of a movement to "awaken" Germany, break the shackles of Versailles, and create a master Reich.

The general conditions described above and the new leader's persuasive oratory combined to bring a measure of life to the struggling party. Two other forces also worked to swell Nazi* ranks. When men suffer long and deeply they tend to seek a scapegoat upon whom to load their psychic woes. Hitler well understood this. In his writings and speeches he tirelessly argued that the ubiquitous Jew was fundamentally responsible for most of Germany's troubles. The Jew was represented as an evil genius eternally bent on exploiting the economic resources and systems

* The term comes from *N*ationalso*z*ialistische; the full name of the party was *Nationalsozialistische Deutsche Arbeiter Partei* (National Socialist German Workers Party).

of all people everywhere. If millions of Germans suffered economic deprivation, it was because the grasping Jew had siphoned off into his already fat coffers national wealth that should have been distributed equitably among honest German workers and peasants. To millions of Germans this was heady talk, especially as many of them, long before Hitler, had nurtured strong anti-Semitic feelings. They looked around and saw affluent Jews untouched by hard times. The Nazi invitation to smash the Jews thus had a double appeal. It offered a way to express pent up feelings of desperation at the same time that it promised an end of economic conditions which produced such feelings.

Another bogey persistently paraded by the Nazis was the "Communist threat." According to Hitler and his colleagues international communism was actively planning a universal take-over. The precipitating agent, of course, was Red Russia. Unless a mighty force was erected against Russian encroachments, the bolshevization of Germany and the rest of Europe was imminent. National Socialism alone was that force. Actually, at the time the Nazis came to power, Russian Communists were busy following the Stalinist line of "Communism in one country." Moreover, the Communist party in Germany, although stronger than it had ever been, constituted but a small minority of the electorate. Nonetheless, Nazi propaganda made headway among the rank and file members of the bourgeois parties, and especially among the industrial magnates who controlled the economy.

But in spite of powerful forces at work for the new party, most Germans withheld support from it. Nazi violence and extremism probably frightened away sober elements of the population. To many, National Socialism either suggested rule by rowdyism, or seemed a ridiculous essay in political amateurism, or both. Still, as the Depression deepened, Nazi victories at the polls became increasingly impressive. In 1928, for example, the party had but 12 representatives in the Reichstag; two years later the number increased to 107. By 1933 it was the largest party in the country.

Textbook accounts rarely extend to detailed examination of the doctrinal origins of political parties. The searing—and lingering—impact of the Nazi state was too strong not to make such inquiry here.

## NAZI IDEOLOGY

### Darwinism

In general, Nazi ideology was rooted in romantic irrationalism. Instinctive urges, mystical inner feeling were honored above pure intellect. In Freudian terms, the id dominated the ego. Hitler and other shapers of Nazi policy never tired of denouncing reliance upon logic—which they looked upon as a kind of child's game—and respect for conscience, which they thought of as a ghost conjured out of foolish guilt feelings. In place of reason and conscience they stressed intuition and iron will. The real leader, as Nazi ideology pictured him, moved toward his goal with the mystic, unerring certainty of a sleepwalker.

Nazi ideological content was shaped by the thought of a number of scientists and philosophers of the nineteenth century.* Particularly prominent was Darwin's theory of the survival of the fittest. To the Nazis, "fittest" meant not only raw, amoral power; it implied a conscious, planned destruction of the nonfit. Quite literally, for them, life was a ceaseless struggle for existence and commanding strength, a struggle which in itself made up the meaning and glory of life. Going beyond Darwin, they argued further that since power was the goal of life, any

---

* Historians are not in agreement on Nazi "roots." Some hold that Hitler and other high Nazi officials created their doctrines mostly out of their own "inner consciousness." They deny explicitly that Nazi leaders were much aware of the detailed arguments and propositions of the nineteenth-century (or any other century) philosophers, much less significantly influenced by them.

scrupulous discrimination between means and ends was ridiculous. Instead, means and ends were interchangeable, like duplicated parts of mass produced machines. Those who could not or would not accept this fact of life were destined to become the manipulated dupes of those who did. Moreover, the amount of power achievable by man was, like physical living space, limited. To achieve power for oneself automatically meant wresting it from another. At any moment of existence the augmentation of an individual or group A necessarily meant the diminution of B.

### Philosophic Supports: Elitism, Racism

The philosophy of Friedrich Nietzsche attracted many of the Nazi elite. Actually, Nietzsche was neither a nationalist nor a socialist, but Hitler and his colleagues shopped around in philosophy as one might shop in a supermarket. They were especially attracted by the Nietzschean dictum that the aim of life was to live in an "ecstasy of power." They also were interested in Nietzsche's doctrine of the transvaluation of values—the transmutation of values into super values. As they saw it, the society of their day exalted the weak and the expedient—that is, evil—and scorned the real good—that is, the frank acceptance of the way of pure power. For example, they believed the whole Versailles world was compounded of hypocrisy and pointless bourgeois strife; its complete and ruthless destruction was an urgently needed good. Unfortunately, most Westerners, including millions of deluded Germans, accepted the Wilsonian principles which undergirded the Versailles system in the foolish belief that these principles, however much violated in practice, derived from eternal Judeo-Christian virtues. For most Nazis, the Christian ethos, characterized by devotion to meekness, gentleness, the turning of the other cheek, was itself a perversion of the truly good. It was, in short, an abiding madness that led to certain destruction. When the time came, a new race of men—the heroic users of raw power—would know how to deal with this complex of follies and its protagonists.

Another influence bearing upon the Nazi *Weltanschauung* was the pessimistic philosophy of Arthur Schopenhauer (1788–1860), one of the most germinal thinkers of the nineteenth century. According to Schopenhauer, the best that man could hope for was a *realization* of the unachievability of meaning and purpose in life. All thought and will were therefore self-defeating; in the end there is only death. It is true that he allowed for stray moments of aesthetic appreciation of some of life's passing phenomena, but they were basically illusory, and always brief. Most human beings, of course, remained naïvely ignorant of the dark secret of life's basic meaninglessness; therefore, their lives suffered double frustration. Nazi ingestion of Schopenhauer's pessimistic revelation of the "No Will" led to differing and occasionally self-contradictory beliefs. Hitler professed to have carried certain of the philosopher's works around in his knapsack throughout the whole of World War I. It is difficult to assess the precise nature of Schopenhauer's influence upon the Führer-to-be. Perhaps the philosopher's sweeping rejection of meaning in life was interpreted by Hitler to apply to life as it was then institutionalized. Perhaps the opening sentence in one of Schopenhauer's major works—"The world is my idea"—misled Hitler into believing not in the overriding "No Will" but rather in the power of a hero's will to create whatever world he desired. In any case, and no matter how strangely, the Nazi leader seemed to gain from Schopenhauer confirmation of his own conviction that he could remake the world according to long nurtured and deeply felt desires.

A third force that shaped the Nazi mind and inflated the Nazi spirit was the music and rhetoric of Richard Wagner. For Hitler,

Göbbels, Rosenberg,* and other Nazi leaders, the roll of Wagnerian thunder shook loose an earth-bound Germany whose head had been bowed by defeat and whose strength had been shackled by Versailles and by the machinations of the ubiquitous Jew. It can scarcely be denied that Hitler consciously thought of himself as the new Siegfried destined to slay the bourgeois Jewish dragon-world. Until the cares of the war made it impossible, Hitler regularly attended performances of Wagnerian operas. In the panorama of Wagnerian magic, both scored and verbalized, were found all the ingredients of the Nazi creed—reliance upon the mystic dynamism of the *Volk,*† anti-intellectualism, anti-Semitism, and the principle of rule by the elite. Two brief quotations underscore this affinity.

WAGNER: I pour young Life through all your veins; life is a law unto itself. . . . We must be brave enough to deny our intellect. . . . The volk must burst the chains of hindering consciousness.

GÖBBELS: [The Nazi mission is] to cause outbursts of fury, to set masses of men on the march, to organize hate and suspicion with ice-cold calculation, to unchain volcanic passions.[1]

Friedrich Ludwig Jahn, early nineteenth-century nationalist, held a high place in Nazi hagiology. From this superpatriot and his

---

* Josef Göbbels was minister of propaganda in the Nazi state. Arthur Rosenberg liked to think of himself as the official philosopher of National Socialism.
† To non-Germans this can be a puzzling word. Literally, it means folk or people. But, in German thought, it was often associated with a union of "blood and soil." Or, as one scholar has put it, "the nature of the Volk is determined by the native landscape." Hence, the Germans, "living in the dark, mist-shrouded forests, are deep, mysterious, profound." See George L. Mosse, *The Crisis of German Ideology,* Grosset and Dunlap, New York, 1964, pp. 4–5.

---

1. Peter Viereck, *The Roots of the Nazi Mind,* Capricorn Books, New York, 1961. See Chapter VI for these and a number of other interesting comparisons.

writings, National Socialism fed on a heady antiforeignism. Jahn's fervent nationalism was inspired by visions of a strong, united Germany. In his day there were dozens of quarreling German states, more interested, as Jahn saw it, in defending their petty particularism than in nurturing the *patrie* which their ethnic kinship made inevitable. He spent most of his life preaching the doctrine of "Germany over all." To him, German greatness lay not in the development of Austrian or even Prussian leadership, but in the creation of a holy *Deutschland*. Woven into his fierce plea for *Volkstum* ("folkdom") was Jahn's insistence that physical fitness was a prerequisite for national greatness. Through his efforts gymnastic societies sprang up in many German states. Their purpose was to develop in German youth an iron body that alone could serve as the temple for an iron will and an unyielding spirit. In Jahn's day such youth were to prepare for the overthrow of French hegemony, the destruction of "effete" French values and manners. In our own century the Jahn heritage helped shape the spirit and formation of Storm Troop battalions.[2] In the mid-1930s two Nazi historians paid these tributes to their folkish saint:

> In Jahn arose another world, a new human type. . . . "Only the overthrow of the nineteenth century by National Socialism has enabled us to see freely and purely the figure of Jahn."
>
> As inventor of the word "folkdom," Jahn is the natural starting-point for every analysis of the concept of Volk.[3]

No little of National Socialism's anti-Semitism was grounded in and strengthened by the writings of Houston Stewart Chamberlain. Chamberlain, an English-born, natur-

2. Compare Edmond Vermeil, "The Origin, Nature, and Development of German National Socialist Ideology in the 19th and 20th Centuries," in *The Third Reich,* Frederick Praeger, New York, 1955, pp. 38–39.
3. Quoted in Viereck, *op. cit.,* p. 63.

"The Emigration to Palestine," an anti-Semitic cartoon in a Vienna periodical, is typical of the kind of propaganda employed by the Nazis in the early years of the Party.

alized German, elaborated the myth of racism in his *Foundations of the Nineteenth Century,* first published in 1899. Highly praised by Hitler, this work belabored a simple thesis: that blood was the bearer of virtue; that the purest, most virtuous blood was Aryan; that the Germans were Aryan elite; that the worst corruptors of virtuous blood were the Jews. The implication was obvious: as the bearers of the highest culture, Germans were under solemn obligation to harry all Jews out of the coming Aryan dominated world.

The works of Oswald Spengler, German philosopher-historian, were also used by Nazi to buttress their soaring *Weltanschauung*. That Spengler himself rejected Nazism (and finally fled from Germany) merely added a paradox to the Nazi mystique—the belief that the non-Nazi mind often failed to understand its own workings.

National Socialists regarded Western society as a cultural cadaver, fit only to be buried. In his *Decline of the West,* Spengler argued that civilization was the sorry mark of the degradation of the human spirit. A vigorous people lives by *élan,* not by effete convention. When it wearies of the call of the spirit it becomes encrusted with complicated status fabrications and falls prey to the scourging power of a new "barbarian" folk. To the Nazi mind the message was clear: the West was a dead waste that needed to be swept away by any means the new elite saw fit to use.

## THREE NAZI BIASES

### Anti-Christianity

The above influences helped* to shape three great negations which characterized National Socialism, often eloquently declaimed in private, all eloquently denied in public. One negation was the corrupting force of the Christian religion. Publicly, the Nazi regime gave conventional support to Christian institutions. In 1933 Hitler's government recognized, in a concordat with the Vatican, the right of Roman Catholics not only to participate in formal religious services but also to conduct schools and to organize societies (so long as such religious activities were kept free of political involvement). Protestant churches and organizations were given similar formal sanction. But these and other overt practices belied the philosophy and long-term aims of the regime. In private conversation Hitler spoke plainly: "We are not out against the one hundred and one different kinds of Christianity, but against Christianity itself. All people who profess creeds are smugglers in foreign coin and traitors to the people. Even those Christians who want to serve the people

---

* But only helped; the thought and power of the personality of Hitler and of some of his colleagues creatively bore upon the construction of the overall framework of Nazi ideology.

—and there are such—will have to be suppressed." Writing in 1942, a Nazi soldier expressed the same spirit: "The German God is an omnipotent power, a vision without form, whose presence one can anticipate and sense —but not see. . . . We Germans have by fate been chosen to be the first to break with Christianity."

Fantastic as it must seem to the non-Nazi mind, hate was conceived as one of man's truly "good" basic drives. The heroic, violent deed was the *raison d'être* of life. Without hate, the motivation for the violent deed was lacking. Scraps of Hitler's private "table talk" made this clear beyond misunderstanding: ". . . through work and industry a people has never grown free, only through hatred"; and, "Germany will not be saved by men who fall victim to universal world love but to those who turn universal world hatred against themselves." The Nazis' almost compulsive emphasis upon hate (against whom was not too important) as a basic drive is reminiscent of an Orwellian scene in which citizens participate, via television, in a weekly five-minute hate exercise.

But if the Nazi hierarchy rejected a theistic God, many of its members professed faith in a vague, inchoate Providence, or Fate. They believed that when called upon by men of superwill and supersensitivity, this power would respond. But, inconsistently, many at the same time saw blind chance as the determinant force in human life. If a particular effort failed, Providence had willed it for a later good. If the effort was successful, iron will and the caprices of chance were responsible. In a public address in 1935 Chancellor Hitler spoke plainly of his own belief in Providence. "Fate has meant well for us. It did not let the [1923 putsch] succeed which, had it succeeded, must finally have foundered because of the inner immaturity of the movement and its faulty organizational and spiritual foundations. We know this today. Then, we acted with courage and manhood. Providence, however, acted with wisdom."

## Antisociety; Antihumanity

A second fundamental negation in the Nazi creed was directed against the whole corpus of Western institutions, as well as the heritage that had molded it. Except for the instrument of sweeping revolution, nothing was really worth saving. General Werner Blomberg, one-time model of the Nazi military mind, declared:

> The existing order is in process of collapse. Apart from that, we are masters of a technique with which we can break all resistance. That is their [the radical Nazis'] contention, and logic is on their side, for progressive radicalization is the law of all revolutionists . . . . Our patterns today are the young generals of the French Revolution. Our model is Napoleon with his pace and his complete change of tactics. It is logical that one should seek in our armies the revolutionary fanaticism of the sans-culottes. And no more of the *bourgeois* patriotism of 1914.[4]

Erich Koch, the notorious *Gauleiter* of East Prussia (later governor of occupied Ukraine) put it in even plainer terms:

> There is no longer . . . in Europe anything left in which to believe. Not even "prosperity." Do you suppose [Americans] still believe in their political ideals? Perhaps the political-minded and the literary people do. But there is no longer any life in the old ideals. They are just empty phrases, useful for muddling peoples' heads in peacetime. Let any great upheaval come in that continent, and we shall see that they are no better off than we are here. I tell you, I see such explosions coming as have never before been known in the world.[5]

Special contempt was felt for the middling classes, the bourgeois community that from the beginning had managed the Industrial Revolution and had shaped the substance and style of the "new West." But this did not mean that Nazi leaders felt sympathy

*Dr. Robert Ley, head of the Nazi Labor Front, preached a classless society to workers who liked to hear this kind of talk; but neither he nor other Nazi leaders believed their own propaganda, much less practiced it.*

for either the old aristocracy or the new proletariat. They hated all classes impartially. Publicly they fulminated against the privileges of the old aristocracy; privately they despised the masses even more than their onetime masters. And at all times they denounced material Thingism and Babbittry. For propaganda purposes they favored a classless society. For example, Dr. Robert Ley, head of the Nazi Labor Front, declaimed in a public address: "No class rule from below, also none from above, but the true classless society of the eternal people, which no longer recognizes parties or special interests but only duties and rights in relation to the people as a whole."[6] Actually, Nazi plans for the coming New Order called for the division of human beings into two classes: the elite and the nonelite. Providence had touched some men. For them, schools should be built (and some actually were), so that from early youth the principles of leadership could be nurtured in gifted future führers. The rest were cattle to be herded at the pleasure of their masters. The leaders should not be squeamish about the herding process; otherwise they invited occasional,

4. Quoted in Hermann Rauschning, *Men of Chaos*, G. P. Putnam's Sons, New York, 1942, pp. 319–320.
5. *Ibid.*, pp. 81–82.
6. *Ibid.*, p. 111.

senseless stampedes. One Nazi leader phrased the idea simply: "Who cares," he said, "about life, fate or interests of the millions, if only the representatives of the racial soul prosper!"

The third bias hardly needs belaboring. In the Nazi outlook, humanity was meaningless as a concept and unspeakably wretched as a phenomenal condition. Pidder Lung, a pedagogue who tried his hand at organizing Nazi philosophy, once said, "Humanity is an abstraction which cannot be translated into practical life." In actual life, inherent human dignity was an illusion. By nature most men were swine. Women were even more inferior than men; essentially they existed as breeding animals, producers of the warrior class. As for children, they were regarded as malleable organisms to be molded as the elite saw fit.

No matter how bizarre these views may seem, they subsumed a terrible program that was soon to be translated into the hard facts of history.

*Fritz Thyssen, wealthy German industrialist, helped Hitler come to power. Later, finding he could not manage his "puppet," he fled to Switzerland. Here he is shown after the war, during the first day of his trial before a denazification court.*

## THE NAZI STATE

### Alliance with Big Business and the Army

From his first venture in politics, in 1920, Hitler remained confident of ultimate victory, providing only that he could bring into full play his propaganda magic. These things would guarantee revolution: massive rallies throughout the Reich, subsidized Storm Troop units controlling the streets, and sustained newspaper support. But how were they to be paid for? Nazi funds had increased with growing membership lists, but dues would not keep such a program going for even a month. The sums needed could come only from the very rich—from such industrial magnates as Fritz Thyssen (steel) and Gustav Krupp von Bohlen (armaments). But until 1931 the great industrialists had not felt inclined to give much support to Nazi agitation. Partly this was because they took seriously the "socialist" element in the Nazi program; and partly because they distrusted

what they thought of as the wild men of the movement. The coming of the Depression changed both their attitude and their behavior. The economic crisis caused many Germans to turn to the left. Worsening conditions could lead to revolution. If they did, only a strong Rightist government backed by the industrialists could save the capitalist system. At this juncture, Hitler's advisers counseled consultation with business leaders. Without their support the Party could not hope to stage the campaigns needed to gain power. With it, victory was certain; and, after victory, the Führer could put whatever construction he pleased on the terms of the bargain. Consequently, each side, compelled by what it considered necessitous conditions, moved closer to the other side. During the period 1930 to 1931, Nazi and industrial leaders held a number of meetings. Otto Dietrich, Nazi press chief for both party and state, later claimed that Hitler spent most of his time in the summer of 1931 wooing business leaders: ". . . he traversed Germany from end to end, holding private interviews with prominent personalities. Any rendezvous was chosen, either in Berlin or in the provinces, in the Hotel Kaiserhof or in some lonely forest-glade."[7]

Besides big business, Hitler needed the army. He doubted (correctly as it turned out) that he could command a parliamentary majority during his earlier days in power. This would necessitate reliance upon power to govern by decree. Under the terms of the Weimar Constitution, only the president could sanction such rule. As president, Field Marshal von Hindenburg assuredly would grant this power only to one who had the confidence of the military. Thus, in 1931 to 1932, Hitler took care to declare publicly that he considered the army the rock upon which any regime must rest, and he assured highly placed military officers of this in many private conversations. Actually, this was in no sense a mere political trick. His grandiose plans of conquest were empty dreams without an efficient military establishment. His courting of the military served a double purpose.

## Hitler Appointed Chancellor

A series of cabinet crises brought Hitler to power in January 1933. During the years 1923 to 1929 Germany had made substantial gains both at home and abroad. Most of her recovery resulted from the patient labors of Gustav Stresemann. Stresemann's death in 1929 left the nation leaderless at a time when talents such as his were most needed. Chancellor Heinrich Brüning (Catholic Center party leader) tried to meet the problems created by the Depression. But they proved more than he could handle. Growing national restiveness and lack of a workable parliamentary majority led him to rule by decree. This

*Shortly after his coming to power, Hitler attended a Tannenberg Memorial celebration with the President of the Republic, Field Marshal von Hindenberg.*

was of little help, however, for his program for economic recovery was anything but bold and imaginative. As a consequence, parties of both the Left and the Right gained extraordinary support, particularly the Communist and the National Socialist parties. Squeezed into this political vise and harassed by the sharp deterioration of economic conditions, Brüning resigned (1932). He was succeeded by a Junker career diplomat, Franz von Papen, who had neither a program nor the wits to devise one. Seven troubled months later he was replaced by Kurt von Schleicher, a political general whose behind-the-scenes wirepulling had been responsible for both the rise and fall of his two predecessors. He lasted barely a month.* Confused by the enveloping political chaos and badly advised by his Junker comrades (particularly by von Papen who—typically—believed that he could tame the Nazi Führer), Hindenburg reluctantly gave Hitler his long awaited chance. For Germany, and indeed for much of the world, the hour of the rough beast had come around at last.

7. Otto Dietrich, *With Hitler on the Road to Power,* London, 1934, quoted by Allan Bullock, *Hitler, A Study in Tyranny,* Harper and Brothers, New York, 1952, p. 157.

* The story of political intrigue and conspiracy that attended these events is too detailed and complicated for treatment in a general study. The bibliography at the end of this chapter includes works that relate this story for those who are interested.

*"The Old Consul (to Hitler): 'This is a heaven-sent opportunity, my lad. If you can't be a dictator now, you never will be.'"* This Punch *cartoon shows Hindenburg urging Hitler to use alleged Communist violence to build himself into a dictator. Actually, Hindenburg disliked the upstart "little corporal."*

## Consolidation of Nazi Power

The new leader clearly understood the difficulties that he faced. Most of the members of his cabinet were not Nazis. The Nazi Party lacked a majority in the Reichstag. Big business and the army had accepted him strictly on the basis of temporary sufferance. Intraparty problems were numerous; some were serious (for example, the insistence by some upon genuine socialization of heavy industry; by others, the transformation of Storm Troop brigades into regular army units).

Hitler's first major decision was to call for new elections. In the words of Göbbels the outcome was assured: "The struggle is a light one, since we are able to employ all the means of the State. Radio and Press are at our disposal. We shall achieve a masterpiece of propaganda. Even money is not lacking this time."[8] The results, however, were disappointing. Most Germans voted against Hitler and his regime. True, 288 Nazi delegates were elected to the Chamber, a gain of 92 seats. But opposition parties won 373 seats. Only an agreement between Nazi leaders and leaders of the Nationalist party (with 52 Reichstag members) gave the National Socialist government a shaky majority.

His next move paved the way for outright dictatorship. A bill was presented to the Chamber empowering the government to decree laws when the interest of the state should require it. In order to obtain the necessary two-thirds majority for passage, Hitler outlawed the Communist party— ostensibly because of the burning of the Reichstag building—and denied its representatives their seats in the Chamber. Mixing flat public promises that the "emergency" powers would be used discreetly with private injunctions to the Storm Troopers to soften up the opposition, the new Chancellor got his Enabling Act, as it was called, by the handsome vote of 441 to 84* (all votes against the measure being cast by the Social Democrats). Thereafter, Germany was ruled by the fiat of one will.†

Ignoring his promise to use the powers of the Enabling Act sparingly, Hitler proceeded at once to bring the nation's political, economic, and cultural institutions into harmony with the "principle of leadership." Within several months all political parties except the National Socialists were disbanded either by voluntary action of their leaders or by government decree. One of the country's oldest and largest parties, the Social Democratic party, was dissolved on the simple grounds that its philosophy and practice

---

* Curiously, the exact figures are in dispute. But all authorities cite a ratio of at least four to one for the Nazi victory.
† The statement is to be taken quite literally. Although the law gave decree-making power to the Cabinet, Hitler thereafter chose not to call the Cabinet into meeting.

8. Quoted in Bullock, *op. cit.,* p. 234.

were subversive of the nation's well-being. All of Germany's sixteen states—Prussia, Bavaria, Saxony, and others—were stripped of autonomous powers and came under the rule of governors appointed by the Nazi hierarchy. A new judicial system, capped by a complex of Peoples' Courts, was super-imposed upon the old. The chief function of the Courts, put in simplest terms, was to protect and promote National Socialist principles and practices. Thoroughgoing changes were made at all levels of civil service personnel by the Civil Service Law of April 1933. Jews, socialists, and all other possible opponents of the new Reich were dismissed, and faithful party members were put in their places.

Hitler knew that these revolutionary changes could endure only if the German masses approved them, or could be brought around at least to tolerate them. To this end he took care to establish close control over all media of mass communication. In March 1933, he appointed an Old Guard Nazi, Dr. Josef Göbbels, to head the newly formed Ministry of Propaganda and En-lightenment. Göbbels was not only a brilliant word artist but also an extremely able administrator. He quickly and effectively established control over the nation's news-papers and periodicals, radio, the cinema and theater, literature, art, and music organiza-tions and activities. Thereafter, the German people read or listened to Nazi news, at-tended Nazi approved plays, read Nazi literature, listened to music calculated to inspire Nazi feelings and emotions. In short, a cultural curtain enshrouded the nation.*

---

* One example of the actual procedures used to effect this all-embracing control is cited by William L. Shirer: "Every morning the editors of the Berlin daily newspapers and the corre-spondents of those published elsewhere in the Reich gathered at the Propaganda Ministry to be told by Dr. Göbbels or by one of his aides what news to print and suppress, how to write the news and headline it, what campaigns to call off or institute and what editorials were desired for the day. In case of any misunderstanding a daily directive was furnished along with oral instruc-

## Instruments of Terror

Coercive agencies were also used to fashion consent. One was the *Sturm Abteilung* (Storm Section) or SA. Originally (in the early 1920s) its marching columns were employed to display Nazi strength and solidarity, to whip up public enthusiasm, and to "dominate the streets" during election campaigns. Its rank and file came mostly from the middle and lower middle classes, its officers from the old Free Corps. It ap-pealed to the typical German's love for uniforms and marching; it doled out pittances welcomed by the unemployed; it provided some relief from gnawing feelings of frustra-tion. During the hectic latter years of the Nazi climb to power it broke up Communist and Socialist political meetings, smashed Jewish shops, bullied provincial authorities into giving it special favors, and served generally as the spearhead of the Nazi Revo-lution (see illustration, p. 548). When Hitler became Chancellor the brown-shirted Storm Troopers let themselves go in a series of frenzied programs directed against Jews, socialists, landlords, aristocrats, and often personal enemies who could safely be "given theirs" in the general turbulence that pre-vailed.† For a while, Hitler tolerated (even approved) the Brown Terror as a natural expression of exuberant spirits tasting the first fruits of victory. Later he administered a bloody disciplining to some SA leaders who made demands on the army, and had dared to talk about socializing industry.

Another instrument of terror was the SS (*Schutz Staffel*—"protective squads"). Originally it served as Hitler's bodyguard. When the SA swelled to proportions difficult

---

tions. For the small out-of-town papers and the periodicals the directives were dispatched by telegram or mail." *The Rise and Fall of the Third Reich,* Simon and Schuster, New York, 1960, pp. 244–245.

† Bullock has described the event succinctly; "The street gangs had seized control of the resources of a great modern State, the gutter had come to power." *Op cit.* p. 245.

*Nazi bully boys staged this now-famous book-burning (1933) to keep their compatriots from becoming infected with "radical" ideas.*

*After the war these German civilians were forced to visit this scene at the onetime concentration camp at Landsberg.*

to handle (and increasingly came to include apostates from socialist and radical organizations—to say nothing of a hoodlum assortment of pimps and homosexuals), Hitler made the SS a special cadre of Nazi elite. In 1929 he entrusted its training and program to Heinrich Himmler, one of the most brutal, vicious men of modern times. Under Himmler's direction the SS became a kind of secret state within a state. Above the law and the courts, even Nazi law and Nazi courts, the SS worked to create a "purified" racial body, a nation of Aryan fanatics ruled by a corps of supermen accountable only to the Führer's master will.

Before the SS achieved its dread distinction, the most feared agency in Germany was the Gestapo (*Geheime Staats Polizei*). Created in 1933 by Hermann Göring, (Hitler's No. 2 man), it served as the secret investigative agency of opposition to, or disaffection with, the Nazi Reich. The Gestapo, like the later SS with which it was soon affiliated, could (and often did) perform outside the law. If, for example, the unlikely occurred and a political prisoner was found not guilty by a state court, the acquitted might be picked up by the Gestapo as he left the court room and hauled off to a camp for detention or execution.

A number of detention camps, or concen-

tration camps, were set up all over Germany (and just before and during the war, in annexed and occupied territories). Chief among these camps were Dachau, near Munich; Buchenwald, outside of Weimar; Sachsenhausen, close to Berlin; Mauthausen, near Linz (Austria); and Auschwitz, in occupied Poland. Often the main gate to these camps was overarched by the slogan *Arbeit Macht Frei*—"Work Makes Free." But the SS commanders of concentration camps were interested in neither work nor freedom. Their job was to so terrorize the inmates that the very idea of opposition to the regime would die out. In the main they were successful. Many never returned from the camps; their absence was a perpetual reminder to their families and friends of the folly of defiance, or even criticism. Those who did return were often living warnings of what happened to citizens who turned "subversive."*

But it is unlikely that Nazi propaganda and Nazi terror, powerful as they were, could have sustained the new regime apart from economic recovery and a growing

* It would be futile to attempt to describe the horrors of life in the concentration camps in such a general work as this. Those with the stomach for such descriptions will find appropriate titles listed in the bibliography at the end of this chapter.

feeling that Germany was regaining her place among the powers of the world. Within a year unemployment had dropped from around seven million to less than one million. Public works and ambitious rearmament projects mainly accounted for economic rehabilitation. Bold defiance of both world opinion and the remaining restrictions of the Versailles Treaty provided stimuli to create anew the comforting image of national greatness. By mid-1934 the hum of factories was heard throughout the land; by then, too, the world had learned to sit up and listen when the Führer spoke. Germany was becoming herself again.

## The Crushing of the "Second Revolution"

Still, all was not well in the Reich. For millions of the SA the taste of recovery was good, but they had not, they insisted, staged a revolution just to get the wheels of industry turning again. They aimed at nothing less than the capture and control of the nation's economy, to be run by them and for them. Also they wanted wholesale absorption of SA military units into the regular army. Hitler had no intention of allowing either. He knew that he needed the support of big business, at least for several years; otherwise, the economic revival, upon which all of his power plans depended, would die aborning. He likewise needed the professional army, for he realized clearly that any day (until, that is, the regime had become firmly rooted) if the army wanted to rout the SA rabble and unseat the government it could do it. When, therefore, certain SA leaders increased their agitation for "completion" of the revolution, Hitler publicly warned them against persisting in what he thought of as treasonous behavior. "The revolution," he said, "is not a permanent state of affairs, and it must not be allowed to develop into such a state. The stream of revolution released must be guided into the safe channel of evolution . . . ."[9]

*Nazi Party Day at Nuremberg, 1934. A few months before this picture was taken Hitler had ordered the murder of a number of Party leaders whom he suspected of fostering a "second revolution."*

But for large masses in the SA battalions (many of whom had been disappointed at the meager economic and prestige advantages doled out to them in return for their arduous efforts to overturn the "System") the talk about "safe channels of evolution" itself seemed treasonous. Ernst Röhm, leader of the SA, publicly answered his Führer in blunt terms. "Anyone who thinks that the tasks of the SA have been accomplished," he warned, "will have to get used to the idea that we are here and intend to stay here, come what may."[10]

But the combination of Hitler, big business, and the army was more than the little men in brown shirts could handle. In June 1934, Hitler loosed his fury against the

9. Bullock, *op. cit.,* p. 255.

10. *Ibid.,* p. 257.

dissidents. Within 48 hours all the chief leaders of the "second revolution" were murdered, including Röhm. Many lesser *leiter* were thrown into concentration camps. While they were at it the new rulers settled a number of other accounts. Former Chancellor Kurt von Schleicher was shot down in his home. Several Bavarian politicians who had played a part in crushing the 1923 Beer Hall Putsch were murdered. Vice Chancellor von Papen's chief aide was killed. No accurate count has ever been made of the slain and maimed of that bloody night. But such macabre arithmetic is quite irrelevant. Whatever the number, the nation had learned a lesson in followership not soon to be forgotten.

The next month a venture in foreign affairs came off less happily for the Führer. Long an advocate of the Greater Reich, Hitler judged the time ripe for the annexation of Austria. To this end a coup was staged July 25, 1934. Austrian Nazis raided the Austrian Chancellory, assassinated Chancellor Dollfuss, and took over the national radio station in Vienna. They were thwarted by the prompt action of the Austrian authorities, supported by Mussolini who had sent Italian troops to the Brenner Pass with instructions to move in if the Austrian government showed signs of yielding. Realizing he was not yet ready for this kind of a showdown, Hitler disavowed the putsch and patched up difficulties with Kurt von Schuschnigg, Dollfuss' successor. But Austria's reprieve was short-lived.*

In August, President von Hindenburg died. The old Field Marshal had been the only man in the government with sufficient power and prestige to stand against the upstart Chancellor (and in his latter months, growing senility had made of even this revered soldier-hero just another Hitler puppet). Using a decree long prepared for the occasion, Hitler virtually abolished the

* The union of Austria and Germany—*Anschluss* —is taken up in the next chapter.

*In violation of the Versailles Treaty, German troops marched into the Rhineland (1936), thus setting the stage for some of Hitler's later aggressions.*

office of president by combining its powers with those of the chancellor. Moreover, all members of the armed forces, from field marshals to privates, were required to swear an oath of allegiance not to the state but personally to Hitler. Now, indeed, *der Führer* stood alone in power.

## Triumph of the Nazi Way

Across the next several years Hitler sprang surprise after surprise upon fellow Germans and foreign peoples alike. In March 1935, he unilaterally denounced that section of the Versailles Treaty which limited German armed forces to 100,000 men. Thereafter, a formidable conscript army was raised, trained, and equipped. A year later he ripped another page from the Treaty when he ordered German troops to march into the Rhineland. For the first time since the Armistice, French soldiers now looked across their frontier into the muzzles of German guns. Within a remarkably short time (about two years or less) a vast military establishment bristled in the area once designated a perpetually demilitarized zone. Foreign powers, especially France and England, protested these violations of the Treaty, but their protests were muted. Germans, of course, hailed the creation of a new army and the remilitarization of the Rhineland as the kind of miracles they were coming to expect of their dazzling Siegfried.

By this time the Nazi hierarchy felt strong enough to begin to establish control over their business and military collaborators. The appointment in 1936 of Hermann Göring as economic dictator under a Nazi-devised Four Year Plan officially marked the end of Nazi tutelage under the leaders of German industry. In early 1938 the army received similar treatment. Hitler simply dispensed with the Ministry of War and made himself supreme commander of the *Wehrmacht*. Both business and the military now mulled over possibilities of checking the Nazi tide. But they were late in sensing what had happened. By then, all instruments of government and news were in Nazi hands. The Blood Purge of 1934, the omnipresent Gestapo, the disciplined SS, the concentration camps—all reminded Germans who might want to dispute the Nazi way of the price involved. With few exceptions, the industrial magnates and generals adjusted themselves to the new situation.

Besides, it is doubtful whether many Germans wanted to dispute the Nazi way.

Everybody was employed. The Reich was again a power in the world. The Versailles Treaty was but an unpleasant memory. There were no unsettling elections, no swift and senseless changes of governments, and no street battles between partisan factions. Some bitter democrats and socialists, it was true, had gone underground, but their grumbling was rarely heard. Foreign newspapers sometimes criticized the regime, but foreigners could hardly be expected to understand the New Order, or approve of the spectacular rise to greatness of the new Germany. Citizens could not, of course, criticize the government, even mildly. This was occasionally irritating, as were the haunting stories of Gestapo midnight visitations, and the hard life in the "camps." But prosperity and order demanded some sacrifices, some inconveniences. In the long run it was better, it seemed, to look the other way when now and then a disturbance occurred. Until later when its soldiers floundered in the snows of Russia and its cities rocked under a hail of bombs, the Third Reich's Nazi ways seemed to speak to the longings and to still the fears of most German citizens.

---

# B. New Deal America

Thus far, we have considered the collectivist trend as it developed in nondemocratic societies. In the United States the movement was hardly less strong. Between 1929 and 1939 it created a Big Government that made the Hamiltonian dream seem pale and paltry. During the same period, Big Labor grew to proportions no realistic A.F.L. leader would have dared predict a few short years before. Accompanying these changes and making them possible was a new climate of public opinion. Its vital center was the growing conviction that no individual was rugged enough to make his way alone in a complex industrial world. Business, though still big and soon to grow bigger, had failed the test of the Depression. Only the general government, speaking in the name of the people and responsive to their needs, could be trusted to manage the national economy.*

It should not be understood that the new attitude toward the nation's business in general and the business of making a living in particular was adopted by all, nor by many, to the same degree. From about 1934, an

---

* "Manage" is here used in the sense of general supervision, not in the sense of direct, day-to-day control. See pp. 559–560.

increasing number of critics of the New Deal pointed to this changed attitude as a kind of sickness that must be cured, unless American civilization was to collapse. Much of the criticism came from professional politicians who, as "outs," naturally wanted to get back in. But much of it came from those whom we think of as typical Americans. A sociological study of an Indiana community, published in 1937, reported the following as a kind of consensus of the town's business leaders:

All these big plans they're making in Washington look well, read well—but they just won't work. They're Utopian, and we don't live and try to do business in a Utopia! By what God-given right do those fellows in Washington think they can do so big a job? . . . You can't make the world all planned and soft. The strongest and best survive—that's the law of nature after all — always has been and always will be.[11]

Nor should it be thought that New Deal collectivism was based on a detailed, carefully thought out planned economy that blanketed the nation's business affairs. At no time did Roosevelt and his top advisers suggest such a program; at no time did they give evidence that they had the slightest sympathy for such planning. From first to last, the New Deal was a work of improvisation, always seeking, sometimes desperately, to locate the weaknesses of the established system and to apply effective remedies. And when, in 1939, it faded into national efforts that were more concerned with foreign than domestic affairs, it left no blueprint for a centrally managed economy.*

Nevertheless, control of the nation's busi-

---

* Some of Roosevelt's early advisers, such as Rexford Tugwell, did favor large-scale central planning. But this should not be confused with total planning such as Mussolini attempted in the Corporate State or as Stalin inaugurated in Russia in 1929.

11. Quoted in Willard Thorp et al., eds., *American Issues, The Social Record,* J. B. Lippincott Company, Philadelphia, 1955, Vol. I p. 1012.

*New York unemployed seeking jobs line up before the State Temporary Relief Association (1933).*

ness and the people's outlook regarding that control, despite these qualifications, were fundamentally changed in the years 1933 to 1939. The lure of the American Dream had faded. The glory road from "rags to riches" was relegated to myth. Unrestricted *laissez-faire* was no longer considered tenable as a philosophy of political economy. In 1964 the Republican Party, under the leadership of Senator Goldwater, tested the reality of the "Big Change." No responsible party or statesman is likely soon to repeat the test. For all its improvising on an old theme, or perhaps because of it, the New Deal had made a very real new America.

## THE FIRST NEW DEAL

### Relief Legislation and the N.R.A.

Franklin Roosevelt took up the duties of the presidency in one of the bleakest periods of American history. By March 1933, almost forty million of the country's population were living a hand-to-mouth existence, without a steady income or, in many cases, without any income at all. The index of industrial production had fallen to an all-time low. The nation's banks were in such perilous condition that those that had not already closed their doors to prevent runs were shut down by the President two days after he took office. Near-hysteria gripped the country as day-to-day business and, as it seemed to some, the business of living from day to day itself appeared to be grinding to a stop. In these circumstances, no grand plans to overhaul the economy were worth immediate attention, even if any had been at hand. In his inaugural address the President spoke plainly of what had to come first:

Our greatest primary task is to put people to work. This is no unsolvable problem if we face it wisely and courageously. It can be accomplished in part by direct recruiting by the government itself, treating the task as we would treat the emergency of war . . . .

The three months of the special session of Congress that Roosevelt had called were spent first in providing that work, and then in setting up a program designed to promote industrial recovery. Under emergency legislation the nation's banks were opened under strict federal supervision. The same month a Civilian Conservation Corps was established providing jobs for about 250,000 male youths working on a variety of projects—reforestation, flood control, road construction, and prevention of soil erosion. The Federal Emergency Relief Act of May 1933 appropriated millions of dollars for direct relief. Under it, sums were granted outright to states and local communities to finance whatever job programs they could devise. Out of that Act two other agencies later evolved (1934–1935)—the Civil Works Administration and the Works Progress Administration. Both were concerned with direct supervision by the Federal Government of an extensive program of public works. Farmers were not forgotten. With passage of the Farm Credit Act in June 1933, they became eligible for loans at low interest rates, with which they could refinance their mortgages. Similarly, home owners were granted loans to meet pressing mortgage obligations and delinquent tax bills.

More ambitious projects, aimed at getting

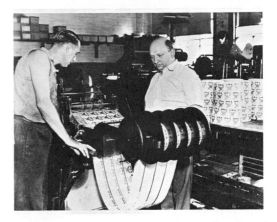

*Millions of N.R.A. labels were distributed throughout the country as the new administration sought to rally the country behind its New Deal program.*

*Civilian Conservation Corps enrollees working on a reforestation project.*

and keeping the wheels of industry turning, were provided by legislation in this same period. The National Industrial Recovery Act (soon shortened to N.R.A.) was the most important. The Act was designed to effect economic recovery by the creation of a set of codes for each industry in the country. Each code, as it was finally developed, spelled out in detail principles and practices which purported to deal fairly with producers, consumers, and laborers. Representatives from each industry were selected to draw up a general plan under which that

*The N.R.A. flag, symbol of Roosevelt's first program to rid the country of the Depression, is hoisted to the mast of the Wisconsin state capitol, August 2, 1933.*

industry would conduct its business. To permit this "benign collusion," the N.R.A. suspended operation of the antitrust laws. By the fall of 1933 almost all businesses in America were operating under such codes. For the most part, industrialists supported the new effort because it allowed them to work together to eliminate the waste and the expensive duplication that are an inevitable part of cut-throat competition. Laborers favored it, both because it promised to provide jobs as industry revived and, particularly, because one section of the new law specifically guaranteed labor's right to organize and bargain collectively. The general public also gave it enthusiastic support since each code, before it became operative, had to be approved by the President who, they believed, genuinely had their interests at heart.

For about a year the N.R.A. seemed to be on the way to meeting many of the stricken country's needs. As unemployment decreased and money began to circulate more freely, the sense of panic subsided. Hopes for a brighter tomorrow sustained millions who still remained unemployed, particularly since the Federal Government, under Section II of the N.R.A., laid extensive plans for the construction of many public buildings and roads. Laborers turned to unionization and the prospects of higher wages through collective bargaining.

## A.A.A.; T.V.A.; and S.E.A.

To guarantee American farmers their fair share of the coming planned prosperity, the government set up an Agricultural Adjustment Administration. Its primary task was to promote the restoration of the buying power of farmers. To accomplish this, the new agency arranged for the elimination of surplus crops through agreements with farmers to reduce plantings, and for a bigger "farmer's dollar" through the determining and underwriting of parity prices for certain basic products such as corn, cotton, wheat, and hogs.

Other important New Deal legislation dealt with such diverse problems as rural electrification and regulation of the stock market. Since 1917 the United States government had owned a huge hydroelectric power plant at Muscle Shoals, Alabama. For years Senator George Norris of Nebraska had urged the Federal Government to use the resources of Muscle Shoals and the power of the Tennessee River to upgrade socioeconomic conditions throughout the whole Tennessee watershed region. Republican presidents had vetoed such schemes on the grounds that government must not compete with business. But in the new atmosphere of the "Roosevelt Revolution," things were seen differently. In May 1933, a Tennessee Valley Authority was established, which went far beyond Norris' dreams. During the next decade the T.V.A. constructed power plants that generated and sold electricity directly and cheaply to many farmers in Tennessee, Alabama, North Carolina, Kentucky, Virginia, and Mississippi. It manufactured and sold fertilizers, planned and executed flood control projects, arrested soil erosion, and encouraged the efficient use of the region's water resources. Naturally, private power companies and industries associated with them protested this "socialist innovation," as they thought of it.

*Lineman at work in the Tennessee Valley, bringing power to the farmers of the region.*

But for most inhabitants of the vast watershed region (and for many outside it who hoped for like benefits in their own areas), the upgrading of living standards and the hum of renewed industrial activity generated by the T.V.A. dulled the edge of such ideological dialectics.

To prevent the recurrence of stock exchange malpractices that preceded and partly caused the crash of 1929, Congress passed (in 1934) a Securities Exchange Act. Through a commission established by the Act, the Federal Government undertook to weed out unfair practices in securities markets. Promoters of new stocks were required to give solid evidence that their issuance was based upon real capital resources. Price manipulation, of new stocks and old, was prohibited with severe penalties for infraction of the rules of trading. Buying stocks "on margin," a practice that inflated the

exchange boom of the late twenties, was discouraged by restrictive regulations. In short, "it was the New Deal answer to the social control of finance."[12]

## The New Deal Moves Left

These and other measures of the first New Deal were based upon curiously conflicting beliefs. From the founding of the Republic until the Roosevelt Administration, presidents and people alike had either never seriously entertained or had consciously rejected the notion that the Federal Government possessed the power or right to directly administer relief to economically distressed citizens. Such an idea constituted, indeed, a kind of affront to the American Dream and to the doctrine of rugged individualism. Three years of the Great Depression had changed much of the popular and political mind about both dream and doctrine. When Roosevelt urged passage of the first federal relief act and the Congress pushed it through almost without debate, both were mirroring the new mood of America.

At the same time, however, both the President and the people seemed to believe that the clearly necessary overhauling of the capitalist system should be entrusted basically to the trained talents of the captains of that system. By 1933, it is true, those captains were no longer regarded with the almost religious awe accorded them in the Golden Twenties. Too many tycoons had publicly stumbled in the wasteland of tickertape for that. Nevertheless, the intricacies of business called for business talents. Moreover, it was reasonable to suppose that the stumbling itself had taught a lesson. Finally, the Federal Government was prepared to act as a surrogate for the people; its laws would serve as guidelines for the reconstruction of the national economy; its leaders would supervise

12. Ralph F. De Bedts, *The New Deal's SEC. . . .* Columbia University Press, New York, 1964, p. 205.

*Huey Long in a typical haranguing posture.*

*The Reverend Gerald L. K. Smith, Father Coughlin, and Dr. Francis Townsend are shown here whipping up interest in "social justice" at an anti-New Deal meeting in 1936.*

the activities of the reconstructionists. At any rate, it was to business leaders that the New Deal turned in its first efforts to set the United States on its feet.

As it turned out, the codes approved by the President had little enduring effect on general conditions beyond stimulating a small upturn in business, which gave industrialists disproportionate profits and renewed confidence in "the old way." Labor leaders soon began to refer to the N.R.A. as the "National Run Around." Low wages and long hours were common in spite of certain provisions of the Act designed to give labor a fairer share of economic returns. Some companies kept two sets of books, one for themselves, and one for N.R.A. inspectors. In fact, many of the codes, even if they had been fairly practiced, were loaded in favor of business, in spite of the President's examination and approval of them. A number of them were verbatim copies of plans drawn up for different purposes when Hoover was president. A year and a half after the N.R.A. had gone into operation, the United States (although slowly climbing up from the Depression's depths, and although buoyed and more hopeful of tomorrow) was ready for a cleaner break with the old system. So were the President and most of his advisers. For some time, various radical dissidents had shown signs of capturing substantial followings. In the southwest, Huey Long, demagogue supreme, preached political homilies on sharing the wealth that set that section ablaze and gave him rising hopes of establishing dictatorial control over the whole country. In the midwest, Father Coughlin, a quasi-fascist Catholic priest, blasted the New Deal as communistic and promised national salvation through his own program of social justice. His weekly radio broadcasts reached millions and influenced many who were beginning to doubt the efficacy of the New Deal. On the West Coast, Dr. Francis Townsend beguiled many senior citizens with his demand for a government grant of $200 a month for every person over 65.

In 1935 a conservative Supreme Court declared the N.R.A. unconstitutional. Roosevelt was troubled by the decision, but he had already given clear indication (in his annual message to Congress) of a new attack upon the country's economic ills. Hereafter, the Federal Government would point more directly toward a managed economy, with the masses of workers and farmers as the prime objects of its concern.

## THE SECOND NEW DEAL

### *Social Security; Growth of Unions*

A sweeping series of reform measures was passed in the period 1935 to 1938. In April 1935, the Government ended its direct relief program and established the Works Progress Administration (W.P.A.). Under the energetic prodding of its director, Harry Hopkins, this agency began a building program that eventually employed more than eight million workers. Before its termination (after the beginning of World War II), it had spent about $11 billion on tens of thousands of projects, ranging from huge public buildings to programs of adult education. Most of the money went directly into wages and salaries, with a consequent jump in mass buying power.

Several months later a comprehensive Social Security Act was passed and put into operation. Among other social services, it provided for unemployment relief, and monthly benefits for those over 65. Under terms of the Act, each state was invited to set up an unemployment insurance plan in cooperation with the Federal Government. Administrative expenses were paid almost completely by the Federal Government, but funds for unemployment benefits came from taxes levied against employer payrolls. Not all workers were covered by the Act—agricultural laborers and domestic workers, for example. But a substantial portion of the American labor force was covered, thus relieving many workers (at least for a period extending to 36 weeks) of the haunting fear of payless Saturdays. Old-age benefits, ranging from $10 to $85 a month, were supplied out of funds provided by taxes paid jointly by employer and employee. Other provisions of the Act set up funds to be spent on relief of homeless, crippled, and delinquent children, for vocational rehabilitation projects, and for maternity and child care.

One of the most important "second" New Deal laws, although not originally sponsored by Roosevelt, was the National Labor Rela-

*Harry Hopkins, one of President Roosevelt's most trusted lieutenants in the New Deal war on the Depression. Evidence indicates that Hopkins was Roosevelt's choice for Democratic candidate for president in 1940. Hopkin's illness caused Roosevelt to run for the office a third time.*

tions Act, commonly called the Wagner Act. Already before its passage, American labor unions had a century-old history behind them. But they had never enjoyed governmental protection; indeed, quite the opposite was true. Since the Civil War, corporate industry had grown to gigantic proportions; individual laborers could not hope to stand up to its multiplying monopolies and trusts. Now with the United States government guaranteeing their right to organize and collectively bargain, workers were given a truly "new deal." They made the most of it. Within five years the majority of the nation's great corporations had recognized bargaining agents of the workers' own choosing. True, for a while the new unions were put to a severe test. The new law guaranteed the right to or-

*Rexford Guy Tugwell, one of Roosevelt's "Brain Trusters," appears before a Senate committee to satisfy his questioners of his fitness for the post of Undersecretary of Agriculture.*

ganize and bargain; it did not, of course, guarantee that companies would sign contracts. Throughout 1936 and 1937 big unions were formed; both the Wagner Act and the advent of industrial unions, such as the Committee of Industrial Organizations (C.I.O.), assured this. But most big industries, such as United States Steel and General Motors, were determined to draw the line at bargaining; that is, *talk*. To force employers to carry through to contracts, many workers struck and threw close-packed picket lines around company plants. Normally, at this point, industrialists and political leaders joined efforts, almost always successfully, to break both picket lines and union strength. This time the Federal Government and most state governments were controlled by political leaders who either sympathized with the workers or were afraid to oppose them. Consequently the

country's business enterprises, large and small, became progressively unionized. For labor the year of decision was 1937. When, in that year, steel companies and the automobile and rubber industries refused union demands for contracts, the workers staged sit-in strikes. Company efforts to dislodge them resulted in bloody fights and considerable property damage. When state and federal government officials showed no signs of coming to their aid, most corporations renewed bargaining negotiations and eventually signed contracts satisfactory to the workers. Big Labor had come to stay.

Other important New Deal legislation was passed in 1935: the Motor Carrier Act, which gave the Federal Government control over conditions of labor, passenger and freight rates, and financial regulations of the country's interstate bus and trucking concerns; the Revenue Act, which sharply increased income, estate, and gift taxes; and the Public Utility Holding Company Act, which forced public utility holding companies to break up their empires of affiliates, empires which had given inordinate financial (and hence political) power to gas and electric monopolies.

In 1938, in what may properly be considered the last year of the New Deal, three other significant bills were enacted into law. The Bituminous Coal Act put most of the soft coal industry under federal regulation. A new Agricultural Adjustment Act replaced the earlier one which had been declared unconstitutional (1935) by the Supreme Court. The new "Triple A" gave the Federal Government the power to establish marketing quotas when farm prices slumped; the right to restrict plantings (contingent upon approval of the farmers involved in producing the enumerated crops); and authority to buy and store surplus produce to keep farm prices at a parity with such levels as the Government should decide were just. The Fair Labor Standards Act put a floor under wages and a ceiling over hours of work for about a million wage earners (subsequently, many more) engaged in work that affected interstate commerce.

## SIGNIFICANCE OF THE NEW DEAL

Many claims and counterclaims have been made regarding the meaning and worth of the New Deal. Some are too extreme for serious attention as, for example, that the "Roosevelt Revolution" ushered in an age of socialism that would inevitably lead to totalitarian communism; or, on the other hand, that the New Deal brought to as much perfection as human talents allow, the Jacksonian vision of an egalitarian America, secure in both political and economic democracy.

Other claims, more limited but still untenable, are that the New Deal not only did not effect economic recovery but actually retarded it. Or, the other side of the coin, that the New Deal brought America out of the Depression. Statistics prove both of these claims wrong. It cannot be argued soundly that the Roosevelt program retarded economic recovery in the face of these demonstrable facts: from 1933 to 1939 national income increased over 65 per cent; in the same period, unemployment decreased nearly 60 per cent. But, on the other hand, nearly seven million workers were still unemployed in 1938 to 1939, and the income level of the average employed worker was still under what such a conservative body as the Brookings Institute described as the minimum for health and decency. In other words, the New Deal substantially ameliorated the hard times of the 1930s, but it did not "cure" the Depression.

Although still unreconcilable, more reasonable views of the worth and meaning of the New Deal were expressed by the chief protagonists of the old and new views. In his *Challenge to Liberty* (one of our century's most closely and cogently reasoned arguments for the private enterprise way of life), Herbert Hoover made the following charge:

We cannot extend the mastery of government over the daily life of a people without somewhere making it master of people's souls and thoughts. That is going on today [1934]. It is part of all regimentation. Even if the government conduct of business could give us the maximum of efficiency instead of least efficiency, it would be purchased at the cost of freedom. It would . . . stifle initiative and invention, undermine the development of leadership, cripple the mental and spiritual energies of our people, extinguish equality of opportunity, and dry up the spirit of liberty and the forces which make progress. It is a false Liberalism that interprets itself into government dictation, or operation of commerce, industry and agriculture. Every move in that direction poisons the very springs of true Liberalism . . . . The nation seeks for solution of its many problems . . . . They cannot be achieved by the destructive forces of Regimentation . . . . the restoration of confidence in the rights of men, the release of the dynamic forces of initiative and enterprise are above all the methods by which these solutions can be found and the purpose of American life assured.[13]

In his second inaugural address, President Roosevelt spoke of the nature of the New Deal in these terms:

When four years ago we met to inaugurate a President, the Republic, single-minded in anxiety, stood in spirit here. We dedicated ourselves to the fulfillment of a vision—to speed the time when there would be for all the people that security and peace essential to the pursuit of happiness. We . . . pledged ourselves to drive from the temple of our ancient faith those who had profaned it . . . .

Our covenant with ourselves did not end there. Instinctively we realized a deeper need —the need to find through government the instrument of our united purpose to solve for the individual the ever-rising problems of a com-

13. Herbert Hoover, *The Challenge of Liberty*, Charles Scribner's Sons, New York, 1934, p. 203.

plex civilization. Repeated attempts at their solution without the aid of government had left us baffled and bewildered . . . . In these last four years, we have made the exercise of power more democratic; for we have begun to bring private autocratic powers into their proper subordination to the public's government. The legend that they were invincible—above and beyond the processes of a democracy—has been shattered. They have been challenged and beaten.

A summary assessment of the New Deal in our own day may stress these developments:

It brought much needed relief to millions of citizens.

It stimulated economic recovery, mainly through governmental spending.

It converted most Americans to a belief in the propriety of governmental regulation of industry and agriculture.

It renovated and strengthened the capitalist system.

The collectivist stamp that the New Deal put upon American life was far stronger than the proportions that its brief tenure might suggest. The strengths or weaknesses that it might have developed after 1939 and the new marks that it might have made upon the course of American history cannot be conjectured. For in that year, World War II flamed across Europe, and soon around the world. In the crucible of this new scourge all systems of society were changed, and some were destroyed. But even global war could not erase the collectivist patterns which had emerged out of the first conflict—indeed, it brought them into sharper focus.

## SELECTED READINGS

*Buchheim, Hans, *The Third Reich,* translated by Allan and Lieselotte Yahraes, Kosel-Verlag, Munich, 1961.
There is nothing new in this ninety-page survey of the origin, development, and end

*Asterisk (*) denotes paperback.

of Hitler's Germany. What is interesting about it is its origin and use. It was written as a handbook of the Western German Federal Defense Ministry for "education in history and current affairs."

Bullock, Alan, *Hitler, A Study in Tyranny,* Harper & Brothers, New York, 1952.
As the author makes clear, this is neither a history of Nazi Germany nor of the Hitler dictatorship. It is a biography of Hitler the man, although naturally the main events of German and European history of the period are intimately involved. The book is soundly researched and interestingly written.

De Bedts, Ralph F., *The New Deal's SEC . . .,* Columbia University Press, New York, 1964.
An exciting account of the formative years of one of the basic reform agencies created by the New Dealers.

Freidel, Frank, *Franklin D. Roosevelt,* Little, Brown & Co., Boston, 1952.
A multivolumed work that deals with almost every question likely to be asked about Roosevelt and his place and behavior in the tumultuous times in which he lived.

Harris, Whitney, *Tyranny on Trial,* Southern Methodist University Press, Dallas, 1954.
The first half is devoted to a study of the coercive processes and practices of Hitler's Nazi state; it includes most of the pertinent —and revolting—material on the Gestapo, SS, concentration camps, and crematoria that one needs in order to understand how inhumane modern man can be. The second half details Hitler's plans for war, 1937 to 1940.

Heiden, Konrad, *Der Fuehrer,* translated by Ralph Manheim, Houghton Mifflin Co., Boston, 1944.
This is by far the best account of Hitler's rise to power. It is also the most enlightening study in English of the Führer's family life, boyhood and schooldays, his early encounter with the party that he would soon make his own, and the Beer Hall Putsch.

Heiden, Konrad, *The History of National Socialism,* Knopf, New York, 1935.
A detailed study of the origins, nature, and

activities (up to the early 1930s) of the Nazi party by one of the earliest fighters against the Hitler movement.

Hitler, Adolf, *Mein Kampf,* Reynal & Hitchcock, New York, 1939.

Hitler's own rambling, revealing story of his "struggle." The book is hard to read, since Hitler had no more sense of organization for written work than he had for speechmaking. This is the edition that should be used.

Kubizek, August, *The Young Hitler I Knew,* Houghton Mifflin Co., Boston, 1955.

Three years of the life of Hitler, dispassionately told by the man who shared them with him in Vienna in the early 1900s. An extraordinarily worthwhile study for those in earnest about learning what were the forces that moved this evil genius.

*Mosse, George L., *The Crisis of German Ideology,* The Universal Library, Grosset & Dunlap, New York, 1964.

An important investigation of the intellectual origin of the Third Reich. The attention given to the Volkish slant of nineteenth-century German youth and their teachers is especially worthwhile because this viewpoint is often neglected.

Neumann, Franz, *Behemoth, the Structure and Practice of National Socialism,* Oxford University Press, London, 1942.

Many other works, some of them cited elsewhere in these Selected Readings, tell the story of the rise and rule of the Nazi state at least as well as this one. But none to date has so thoroughly examined in such short compass the economic workings of the Third Reich (Part Two, about 150 pages).

Pinson, Koppel S., *Modern Germany,* The Macmillan Co., New York, 1954.

A solid, scholarly work that, besides these qualities, contains insights and judgments that make it much more than a fact-on-fact recital of German history.

Schlesinger, Arthur M., *The Crisis of the Old Order,* (1957); *The Coming of the New Deal,* (1959); *The Politics of Upheaval,* (1960); Houghton Mifflin Co., Boston.

An exhaustive and sometimes almost exhausting examination of the causes, nature, and course of the New Deal, 1933 to 1936.

Seligman, Lester G., and Elmer E. Carnwell, Jr., eds., *New Deal Mosaic . . .* University of Oregon Press, Eugene, Oregon, 1965.

The contents of this volume are made up of minutes of the meetings of the National Emergency Council created in 1933. The Council held thirty-one recorded meetings from December 1933 to April 1936. These verbatim minutes probably give a better understanding of the New Deal than any other single volume of the many hundreds published thus far. As Professor Frank Freidel has said, "It is the confidential nature of the Proceedings that gives them their value, since the President could speak so much more freely at the Council meetings than in his press conferences." They also give a close up view of leading New Dealers, from President Roosevelt on down through the higher echelons of the Administration. It is so valuable, indeed, that it may be singled out as the one "New Deal" book to read if students somehow find their time too restricted to read more.

*Shirer, William L., *The Rise and Fall of the Third Reich,* Simon & Schuster, New York, 1960.

Despite a good deal of scholarly scolding over this book it is, in general, well researched and well written. The first four chapters, dealing with pre-Nazi history, fall outside of this evaluation; there are many other works that better portray this part of German history, especially Koppel S. Pinson's volume, cited above. But in the remainder of the book, the account is detailed, enlightening, and absorbingly interesting. Unlike a number of other Americans who have written on the subject, Shirer lived in the Third Reich for a number of years, knew all of the highly placed Nazis, and had access to information that gave him a broad knowledge and keen understanding of the spirit of that ill-fated state.

*The Third Reich,* published by Frederick A. Praeger, New York, under the auspices of UNESCO, 1955.

A collection of 28 essays on various facets of Nazi Germany. Particularly worthwhile are the first and fourth essays on the historical development of German nationalist ideology, the ninth essay on the rise of National Socialism, and the twenty-fourth and twenty-fifth essays on the Catholic and Protestant Churches in Nazi Germany.

*Trevor-Roper, H. R., *The Last Days of Hitler,* Collier Books, New York, 1962 (3rd ed., with a new preface).

This edition should be used in order to profit from the author's updating of events, which are included in the long introduction rather than in the body of the text. The organization is faulty—strict chronology is not an adequate framework for this study. But this is almost the only deficiency of the book. The last three chapters—"The Siege of the Bunker," "Et Tu Brute," and "The Death of Hitler"—are well documented, or they would be quite unbelievable.

*Viereck, Peter, *Metapolitics, The Roots of the Nazi Mind,* Capricorn Books, New York, 1961.

A close—and controversial—examination of historical forces that gave birth to the Nazi "Theology of Terror." This book is especially important when read with Mosse's volume, cited above.

Wheeler-Bennett, John, *The Nemesis of Power,* Macmillan & Co., London, 1953.

The author believes that the outlook and posture of any nation can be gauged by an understanding of the place and power of its armed forces. This book is really an extended warning of what to expect from the new Germanies. It begins with the Kaiser's abdication and ends with the July 20th plot against Hitler. Throughout, the pivotal position and power of the army is emphasized.

# XV

## *The World at War Again, 1939 to 1945*

## A. The Coming of the War

This chapter deals with three subjects: the complex of events that led to World War II; the war's long and tortuous course; and a summary of the ambiguous settlements that followed it.

Listing the major events that preceded and eventually led to war presents no particular problem. Assignment of responsibility for the culmination of these events in global war is another matter. Some historians hold that the question of responsibility is essentially meaningless since "there were no heroes and no villains." Others believe Japanese aggression was the root cause. Still others, perhaps the majority, blame Hitler and the Germans who actively or tacitly supported him.

Part of the problem revolves about the definition of "responsibility." In a previous chapter we noted the indifferent support given to the League of Nations when certain European and Asian problems were brought to it for adjudication. As the Great Depression wore on, many nations became so involved in domestic affairs that even the most flagrant violations of the Covenant produced little more than protests or ineffectual sanctions. Even worse, on occasion some of the powers, particularly Britain and France, connived to permit aggressors to have their way. And, of course, the refusal of the United States to even join the League deprived it of much needed support and involved this country in a kind of international malfeasance through default.

Viewed strictly in this light, the "no heroes, no villains" thesis is sound enough. But this is indeed seeing through a glass darkly because it does not make the necessary distinctions between degrees of accountability. If judgments of this kind were permitted in municipal jurisprudence, those who are guilty of criminal negligence, for example, would be treated no differently from those guilty of premeditated murder. In the following section a clear distinction is made between, on the one hand, conditions that allowed or even encouraged aggressors to wage war and, on the other hand, the *will* to plan for war and actually to bring it about. Even so, each reader must finally weigh the evidence according to his own scale of values and form his own judgment.

## THE ROAD TO WAR

### The "Have-Not" Powers

By the 1930s, Japan's plight was real, serious, and not altogether of her own making. Her people lived on mountaintops that projected from the sea. The total area was small; tillable soil was severely limited. By the third decade of this century many more people lived on the land than it could decently support. A flourishing industrial economy can overcome most living-space problems; England is an obvious example. But such an economy presupposes access to and control of adequate raw resources as well as highly developed technical know-how. By a kind of miracle Japan, within a generation or two, had mastered the necessary technical skills, but she lacked ready access to both supplies of raw materials and markets for finished products. In a world economy characterized by free trade and unrestricted opportunities, a nation needs only patience and application to make its way. But the world economy was not (then, or ever) of this character. Some nations, such as Britain in India and the Netherlands in most of the East Indies, had preempted economic opportunities in various parts of the world. Some others, especially the United States, threw up tariff barriers that slowed down the flow of goods from abroad. Because of these conditions and others related to them, Japan's standard of living remained low.

A warrior mentality that made violence and aggression a prized way of life was more of Japan's own making. Prodded by promptings of the *samurai* spirit,* the Japanese

often formulated both municipal and international policies in terms of raw force. Her attitude toward and resentment of China were an example. China was rich in raw resources of many kinds; she constituted a potential market of almost unlimited demands; she was politically backward and militarily weak. Japan's needs and aggressive spirit naturally tempted her to treat China as an object of exploitation. Inevitably this led to large-scale violence and international turmoil.

Italy, under the leadership of Mussolini, also maintained a posture of belligerence. But Italy was not likely to initiate a general conflict, no matter how pressing her real and imaginary needs were. In spite of his balcony performances and Caesaresque behavior, the Duce well understood where to draw the line in his often dramatic brushes with the other Great Powers.

Weimar Germany, as we have seen, was wracked by political instability, economic adversities, and the psychic strictures of the Versailles Treaty. The "four good years" suggest that the new republic, in spite of all harassments, might have grown in democratic stature and economic health. It needed able, reasonable leadership of the kind provided by Stresemann. It deserved and in 1932 finally was given substantial relief from its intolerable reparations' burden. Enlightened justice from her one-time conquerors—formal admission that Germany and her allies were not solely responsible for the war, reasonable adjustment of the Corridor problem, and general disarmament—conceivably could have cleared the way for genuine democratic development. But it is futile to speculate whether the vision of such enlightened justice might ultimately have been discerned and implemented by peoples and leaders of the time, since the Great Depression (the true "hinge of fate" of these years) turned all nations into desperate

---

* The strong, warrior mentality of the Japanese gentry and lower nobility.

seekers after their own salvation. In the United States, for example, President Roosevelt deliberately scuttled a world economic conference (held in London in 1933) when it seemed to him that it might interfere with his own domestic recovery program. In Germany the Depression gave Hitler his chance to become the voice and vehicle of destruction.

## The Steps to War: the "Manchurian Incident"

The linking episodes that led to war were many and complicated. Not all can be attributed to Hitler's evil planning. Indeed, the first event occurred in Asia when the German Führer was still struggling to gain power. The Japanese called this event the "Manchurian Incident." For some years Japan had sought to carve out an empire in China. Particularly enticing was the expansive, fertile Manchurian "province," loosely controlled by Peiping, actually governed by local war lords.

In 1931 a portion of track of the Japanese-controlled Chinese Eastern Railroad was blown up. Japan blamed Chinese saboteurs and at once moved large bodies of troops into the area.* China appealed to the League of Nations. No one believed the sabotage charge. All informed observers knew the island empire was ready to test its strength in a large-scale imperial adventure.

Legally and morally Japan stood without defense. She was a signatory to the League Covenant that bound her to conduct foreign affairs without the use of unilateral military force apart from League sanction, except in self-defense. In 1922 she had joined seven other powers in formally promising to respect the independence and territorial integrity of China. She had also signed the Pact of Paris (1928), which renounced war as an instrument of national policy.

* After World War II, a Japanese lieutenant colonel admitted that he participated in the destruction of the track.

World opinion was almost solidly against Japan. If unprovoked aggression were to be combated in the name of world order and world peace, it seemed that this was the time and Manchuria was the place to take a

*These two cartoons reflect general American opinion regarding Japan's naked aggression in Manchuria in 1931.*

stand. But the challenge was allowed to pass. The major nations—preoccupied with domestic difficulties, fearful of the costs of a showdown, and seemingly unconvinced of the practicability of world peace under law— in effect looked the other way while Japan overran the whole of Manchuria. Certain half-hearted gestures were made. After prolonged consideration, the League Council set up an investigating committee to "find the facts." Members of the committee trekked halfway around the world to inspect portions of the blown-up Chinese Eastern right-of-way. It called witnesses and solemnly listened to lengthy testimony. It deliberated over its findings, and six months after the "incident" had occurred, the committee issued a voluminous report. The report found Japan guilty of unprovoked aggression, but incongruously recommended the creation of an autonomous Manchuria under Japanese tutelage. Japan replied by withdrawing from the League and ignoring its recommendations. In the meantime the Japanese government had created an "independent" nation out of the conquered province and installed a puppet "regent" to govern it.*

*Italian troops entering Makale, Ethiopia in late 1935. In the lower photograph, natives of the city are shown obediently raising their hands in the required Fascist salute.*

## Subjugation of Ethiopia

Thereafter few took the League of Nations seriously, least of all the autocratic rulers of Italy and Germany. In 1933, one year after the new Manchuria was set up (renamed Manchukuo by the Japanese), Mussolini planned the conquest of Ethiopia. The timing obviously suggests the influence of successful Japanese aggression. Undoubtedly, worsening economic conditions at home also moved the Duce to cast about for some diversionary activity. Historic memory probably served as an added stimulus. In 1896 Italian forces had suffered a humiliating defeat when they had tried to overrun and occupy Ethiopia; vindication of Italian honor had thus been a long time waiting. Finally,

the Fascist yen for action and dangerous excitement made occasional military activity a normal part of the national experience.

In 1935 Mussolini sent his troops marching on the flimsy pretext that Ethiopian soldiers had violated a frontier zone of Italian Somaliland. Haile Selassie, the Emperor of Ethiopia, appeared in person before the League Council in Geneva to plead for protection. Unable to ignore such a blatant violation of its Covenant, the League duly denounced Italy as an aggressor and voted to impose sanctions. If the embargoed items had included oil—essential to Italy's war machine—or if they had even been strictly enforced, as they were not, the Duce's adventure might have been frustrated. But Mussolini threatened war against any state that embargoed oil; and anyway, the major powers were unwilling to attempt much more

_____
* Henry Pu Yi, paradoxically now (1960s) a citizen in good standing of Red China.

THE AWFUL WARNING.

FRANCE AND ENGLAND (together?).

"WE DON'T WANT YOU TO FIGHT,
BUT, BY JINGO, IF YOU DO,
WE SHALL PROBABLY ISSUE A JOINT MEMORANDUM
SUGGESTING A MILD DISAPPROVAL OF YOU."

*Neither England nor France wanted to run the risk of getting deeply involved in the Ethiopian crisis. Their protests were therefore qualified to the point of being quite ineffective, as this satiric Punch cartoon makes clear.*

*Nazi storm troopers march triumphantly into Duesseldorf under Hitler's order to reoccupy the Rhineland.*

than nominal opposition.* Within a year Ethiopia's harassed defenders, matching rifles and spears against airplanes and poison gas, surrendered; later the whole country was annexed by Italy.

## Events in Germany

In the meantime Hitler was mulling over plans of his own. As long as Germany re-

---

* This example is instructive. While the war was going on, the prime minister of France and the foreign secretary of Great Britain secretly met to arrange a settlement of the affair. The terms of the agreement created a popular furore when they were announced: approximately half of Ethiopia was to remain under Haile Selassie's rule; the rest of the country was to be made into an Italian protectorate. Subsequently, the arrangement was denounced by both governments. But the moral was not missed by Mussolini and other potential aggressors.

mained bound by the Versailles Treaty's provision prohibiting land forces to exceed 100,000 men, the Führer's power dreams must necessarily remain dreams only. But already in 1933 orders had secretly been given (and some were given even before 1933) that provided for masked preparations against the day when Germany would openly rearm. Taking advantage of the general confusion caused by Mussolini's preparations to invade Ethiopia, Hitler suddenly announced, in March 1935, the reintroduction of universal conscription. Both France and Great Britain presented the Führer with written protests. But by then a dictator would have to have been a most untypical one to be troubled by such scraps of paper. Throughout the next months and years, Germans heard again the familiar sound of goose-stepping regiments. By 1939 the *Wehrmacht* constituted a formidable fighting machine.

But Hitler knew that even a rearmed

Germany must continue to speak softly so long as its western frontier remained open to easy French invasion. According to the terms of both the Versailles Treaty and the Locarno Pacts, fifty kilometers of German territory on both sides of the Rhine were to remain demilitarized in perpetuity. Plans for aggression were idle games unless the front facing France was fortified. Hitler again chose the ides of March—almost a year to the day after his denunciation of the Versailles rearmament restrictions—to announce Germany's intention to remilitarize the Rhineland. French protests were ignored as he set about constructing a "West Wall" (popularly referred to as the Siegfried Line), sealing off French access to Rhineland industries and farm lands. Three years later the whole frontier bristled with cannon, tank traps, and antiaircraft installations, manned by tough Nazi battalions.

## The Spanish Civil War

The construction of the West Wall in Germany coincided with the destruction of democracy in Spain. Since 1931 various liberal governments in this new republic had tried to redistribute the country's wealth more equitably, to educate the masses to become self-governing, to curtail the power of the Church, to establish a popular educational system, and generally to develop the democratic way of life. The experiment was conducted under anything but favorable auspices. For centuries the monarchy, the Church, and the army had exercised almost total autocratic rule. The common people were uneducated, many were illiterate; wealth was concentrated in the hands of the power elite; provincial separatism was strong; industrial progress slow. By 1936 the forces of reaction felt strong enough to attempt a countercoup which turned into a bloody, three-year civil war. Arrayed against the new regime were the old landlord class, bourgeois wealth, the Church hierarchy and, of course, most of the general officers of the army—one of whom, Francisco Franco, led the revolt.*

*Spanish Loyalists charge Rebels in the Guadarrama mountains (1936).*

Since the conflict so closely partook of the ideological struggle that was rending much of the Western world, it soon took on the character of a miniature world war. Many intellectuals and workers in the free nations sympathized with the Loyalists, as the Spanish republicans came to be called. The Soviet government, always eager to fish in such troubled waters, naturally supported the Loyalists. Fearful that a democratic success might set a bad example for their own peoples, and anxious, anyway, to expand the totalitarian frontier wherever possible, both Mussolini and Hitler sent help to Franco. Early recognizing him as the lawful head of the government, they supplied him first with money and advisers, and then with troops and armaments. Russia also sent armaments and "volunteers" to the Loyalists, although problems of logistics and distance kept them well below the contributions of the fascist states. The attitude of the British government was ambivalent. It continued to give official recognition to the Loyalist regime while witholding tangible aid. France wanted to open her frontier to pass supplies to the Loyalists but was dissuaded by pressure from Britain. The United States officially gave diplomatic support to the republican

---

* General Jose Sanjurjo, leader of a countercoup some years before, had been selected as the new strong man, but he was killed in an airplane accident during the first strike against the republic.

government, and more or less winked at regulations barring United States citizens from joining Loyalist forces.* But at no time did foreign aid for the republicans equal the German and Italian support finally given quite openly to Franco. In the spring of 1939 the rebels routed the dwindling, starved, and ill-equipped Loyalist forces and soon took over complete control of the country. Among thinking people of the free world there was no need to ask, as the novelist Ernest Hemingway had made clear, for whom this bell tolled.†

## Renewed Japanese Aggression in China

In 1937, Japan, encouraged by her easy success in Manchuria, began the conquest of the whole of China. Within two years she had captured Peiping, Shanghai, Nanking, Canton, and other areas along the eastern coast. Again the League of Nations and the United States protested. But Japan's warlords now publicly demanded that Britain and the other powers recognize that Japan's "New Order" in the East was beneficent and inevitable. They insisted they were not waging war against China; rather they were laboring to create an expanded, unified "co-prosperity sphere" in which all East Asian peoples could find happiness and fulfillment. No one believed this nonsense, of course; but no one seemed to know what to do about it. Nagged by internal concerns, conscious of their ambiguous position *vis à vis* their own colonial possessions, and without working faith in the international organizations they themselves controlled, the Western powers fretfully watched world affairs drift into hopeless anarchy.

## Hitler Plans for War

These conditions, and the bemused spirit that enveloped them, well suited Adolf Hitler's Nietzschean promptings. The League of Nations was dead. Serious domestic troubles beset all of the great powers. Italy and Japan had committed outright and large-scale aggression for which they had been mildly slapped on the wrist. In Germany, masses, business, and army were now firmly under Nazi control (in the case of the masses, "spell" is the more accurate word). New military techniques and units had been tested effectively in Spain. Except for Stalin, the leaders of all European states, Hitler believed, were weak and manageable; and Stalin was too preoccupied with his seemingly endless purges to be feared. These and other favorable developments could not be expected to last forever. Germany's great chance had come.‡

Impelled by such prognostications and seemingly goaded by restless inner urges, Hitler called his chief advisers into conference in November 1937. His purpose was not to seek counsel on the plans he was to lay before them. Instead, it was to acquaint his subordinates with the shape destiny was taking and to prepare them for their part in the great events to come.

The detailed minutes of this momentous meeting (taken by Colonel Hossbach, Hitler's adjutant at the time) constitute one of the most significant historical documents of modern times. The minutes baldly set forth calculated plans for military conquest, for large-scale aggression that would by necessity involve some if not all of the great European powers.§ Hitler made it plain that Germany's

---

* The Abraham Lincoln Brigade, made up of some 2000 volunteers, was the most notable American contribution to the Spanish fight for freedom.
† For a sound, well written account of the Spanish Civil War see Gabriel Jackson, *The Spanish Republic and Its Civil War, 1931–1939,* Princeton University Press, Princeton, 1964.

‡ This and the several paragraphs following are based upon material found in captured German documents, particularly the "Hossbach Notes" described below.
§ Some so-called revisionist historians, notably A. J. P. Taylor, dispute the reliability of the Hossbach notes. This is not the place for extended forensics among members of the history

basic need was greater living space, realizable only through military conquest (in *Mein Kampf* and his later work, *Hitler's Secret Book,* he specifically referred to Russia's great breadbasket, the Ukraine). Before successful conquest could be assured, however, several immediately pressing problems demanded attention. One problem was the incorporation—"return" in Hitler's unhistorical view—of Austria into the Reich. Another was domination of Czechoslovakia. Other related problems were the unwanted but probably inevitable conflict with France, and the winning of English support if possible or, if not, her conquest. The Polish problem, of course, had also to be solved. The deadline for this grand program was 1943 to 1945; but, as the Führer pointed out, circumstances might foreshorten the period of watchful waiting. All military preparations were to be completed as swiftly and as thoroughly as possible. He could be trusted, he said, to make the preliminary political arrangements. At the end of the conference Hitler asked if there were any comments. Two of his astounded conferees were bold enough to offer certain objections, emphasizing practical difficulties. Both were soon replaced by more tractable colleagues.

## Anschluss

By 1938 the twenty-years' truce had about run its course. Thereafter, European affairs took their shape and significance from Hitler's grand design for death. In March of that year Austria was absorbed into the Greater German Reich. No one will ever know whether most Austrians of that time wanted *Anschluss*—union with Germany. In

the early thirties, before Hitler, they probably did. Undoubtedly, many Austrians genuinely welcomed the union in 1938; but many did not. Nazi plans for the merger dated (as we have seen) from the abortive coup of 1934. In 1936 an Austro-German pact was signed which nominally brought the two states into friendly relations. In this treaty Hitler promised to treat Austria as an independent nation and to refrain from interfering in her internal political affairs. Austria promised to consider herself as, and to behave as, a "German state," and also to allow Austrian Nazis to develop freely and fully the interests and activities of the party program. Both of the signatory states, as well as Italy which had mediated the agreement, had acted purely from motives of expediency. For his part, Hitler was anxious to set up a fascist bloc to counter the moves and influence of a series of European alliances dominated by France. Mussolini wanted German support for his projected conquest of Ethiopia. Some Austrian leaders, especially Chancellor Kurt von Schuschnigg, dreamed of a reborn Austrian Reich once again under the rule of the Habsburg dynasty. The pact was early and consistently violated by both sides. German Nazi agents infiltrated the little country and kept up a constant barrage of *Anschluss* propaganda. Von Schuschnigg not only kept Austrian Nazis out of official positions but denied them many elementary political rights.

Early in 1938 Hitler arranged a meeting with von Schuschnigg at his Berchtesgaden retreat. The Führer allowed himself in this famous "interview" (von Schuschnigg in effect auditioned a monologue) the luxury of one of his truly Olympian rages. For over two hours he berated his visitor for going back on his promises, for failing to bring a single Nazi into the cabinet, and for generally pursuing policies which dishonored their common German heritage. Unprepared for such a violent assault, von Schuschnigg bowed to the storm and promised better behavior. Once back home, however, he tried to outmaneuver the outraged Führer by

---

fraternity. Let the interested reader go to A. J. P. Taylor, *The Origins of the Second World War,* Atheneum, New York, 1962, and then to a study of the pertinent documents found in the multivolume *Nazi Conspiracy and Aggression* published by the United States Government in 1946 and 1947. A condensed version of these documents is found in John L. Stipp, *Devil's Diary,* Antioch Press, 1955.

*Chancellor Kurt von Schuschnigg as he appeared before a Fatherland Front group in Vienna to ask for a vote of confidence in his government. Less than one month later he was under Nazi arrest.*

arranging for a (somewhat rigged) plebiscite which would give Austrians the opportunity to approve or disapprove of their Chancellor's policies. This was more than Hitler could bear. Immediately, Austrian Nazis were ordered into action to demonstrate in the streets, to rough up the opposition, and to get von Schuschnigg out of office by whatever means were needed. In a public address the Führer indignantly denounced von Schuschnigg's plebiscite trickery, as he thought of it, and promised that German troops would not stand idle while German honor was violated. Unwilling to sanction civil war, von Schuschnigg stepped aside and the Nazi tide rolled in.

Apart from whatever may have been the wishes of the Germans and Austrians, the union itself was of little consequence. But for the broader world, the spirit and tactics displayed in the coup were significant. By both sides, but particularly by Germany, democratic processes were treated with contempt. Beyond this were the cynical chicanery and naked violence of the German manner. For example, at one point in the affair Göring simply rang up Vienna and ordered his henchmen to oust the Austrian government within two hours. He instructed Austrian Nazis to send a telegram, which he himself

dictated, asking for help from German troops. Phoning a short time later he said that the German troops could not be held back much longer, and that even the telegram could be dispensed with; a brief "OK" would suffice. Clearly the Nazis' will to power and their reckless use of violence were passing bounds that the Western powers, for all their internal problems and preoccupations, could tolerate.

## Conquest of Czechoslovakia: Background

But if Hitler sensed this danger he paid little attention to it. Within six months after tucking Austria into the Reich, he demanded a substantial slice of Czechoslovakia. About three million Germans lived in the part of the Bohemian frontier that flanked Germany, called the Sudetenland after the "southern" mountains which dominated the region (see map, p. 577). The inhabitants of this area had never been a part of Germany. Moreover, their status as a minority group in Czechoslovakia had long been the envy of other ethnic minorities spread across Europe. But the Great Depression had created tensions there as elsewhere. Nazi agitators who were sent into the area played upon these discontents and pointed to the glories of the Greater German Reich. Soon a Sudetenland branch of the Party, headed by Konrad Henlein, was holding stormy meetings demanding autonomy and, implicitly, a "return" to the Reich. The Czech government, one of the most enlightened in Europe (and the lone democracy east of the Rhine), made genuine efforts to satisfy the Sudetenlanders. These people were promised more jobs in the Czech civil service and finally, when the agitation had reached hysterical proportions, a substantial degree of home rule. Each concession sent the Führer into new spasms of indignation. In the late summer of 1939 he made it clear that only complete "self-determination" would satisfy the Sudetenlanders, with himself as their protector.

Superficially, German demands for modification of the existing conditions were reasonable. Almost all of the inhabitants of the region were Germans. At Versailles the Allies had argued strongly for the principle of self-determination. There was no doubt that most of the Sudetenlanders wanted to be taken into the Reich. But the problem was not simple. The small nations of Central Europe feared the resurgence of German might. To shield the newly created Czech state from just that danger, the treaty makers of 1919 had deliberately assigned to it (from the old Austrian Empire) the mountainous belt as a defensible frontier. Special care had been taken by the Czech government, as we have noted, to leave local customs and culture untouched. Until the Depression the overall settlement seemed to have worked well enough.

As a further guarantee against possible future aggression, France and Czechoslovakia had signed a treaty of mutual assistance in 1925. Ten years later Russia and Czechoslovakia agreed to a similar pact. The same year, France and Russia concluded an alliance which provided that both, if each acted in concert with the other, would go to Czechoslovakia's defense if she were attacked by Germany.

On paper, then, Czechoslovakia seemed reasonably secure despite Hitler's aggressive posture. But by 1938 France was unwilling to stand against Germany under any conditions unless England stood with her. And England—or at least the Chamberlain government then in power—showed no signs of wanting to risk serious trouble with Germany. Nazi brutalities and gaucheries were, of course, deplored. Hitler's tendency to take unilateral action was condemned. But the evidence—in part to be cited presently—suggests that Chamberlain and some of his conservative colleagues considered the Nazi regime Europe's strongest bulwark against Communism. Without it no part of the Continent, they seemed to believe, would be safe from Soviet imperialism.

As early as 1937 Chamberlain had clearly indicated his intention to appease Hitler. In November of that year he sent Lord Halifax to Berchtesgaden to work out a mutual understanding; it coincided, hardly accidentally, with the first strong push by the Henleinist forces. No formal agreement was reached, but Halifax returned home with words of praise for the Führer. Nine months later, with the Sudeten issue reaching a crisis, Chamberlain dispatched another appeasement-minded statesman, Lord Runciman, to Czechoslovakia to consult with both Czech officials and Henleinists. He returned with the proposal that complete local autonomy be granted to the Sudetenland. Simultaneously, Hitler ordered large-scale military maneuvers, obviously designed to increase pressure on the Czech government.

In the meantime, Henlein and Czech officials carried on a series of conversations that produced little change in the situation. Edward Benes, the president of Czechoslovakia and its chief policy maker, proposed a cantonal organization for the state which he hoped would satisfy Germans both within and without the country. Henlein refused to consider the compromise. Captured German documents now make it clear that the Sudeten leader was acting under direct instructions from Hitler who wanted a settlement exclusively on Nazi terms and in the Nazi manner. The resulting breakdown in negotiations was followed by what can only be called planned disorder. Noisy demonstrations and street fighting occurred throughout the whole region. Against this backdrop of violence, Hitler addressed a Nazi rally at Nuremberg on September 12, 1938. He declared that he could no longer stand by while fellow Germans were being subjected to brutal mistreatment. He was determined to use the full power of the Reich to bring justice and order to the Sudetenland. If foreign nations could not understand this or tried to interfere, so much the worse for them. As at a signal, violence in the Sudetenland increased to almost anarchical proportions. The Czech government declared martial law

*Chamberlain and Hitler at Berchtesgaden as they opened talks on Hitler's Sudetenland demands.*

and indicated that it was prepared, with the help of its allies, to meet German force with force.

## Munich

At this juncture Prime Minister Chamberlain, after consulting with the French premier, asked Hitler for a conference. Hitler agreed and Chamberlain visited him at Berchtesgaden on September 15. Hitler explained that he could wait no longer; the Sudetenlanders, who wanted to return to the Fatherland, had been abused enough. Unless Czechoslovakia agreed to peaceable cession, Germany had no recourse but to use force. Chamberlain agreed that Germans in the Sudeten area should be granted the right of self-determination. If Hitler could assure him that the Czech state would be left in peace after the Sudetenland was ceded to Germany, by an orderly process of progressive occupation, Chamberlain was prepared to urge Czechoslovakia to accept the Führer's demand. Hitler declared that he had no intention of molesting the Czechs; that Germany was for Germans only; and that after this wrong was righted, he would have no more territorial demands to make. Chamberlain expressed satisfaction and returned to London where he again consulted with French officials. Together they agreed to inform Czechoslovakia that unless she agreed to the cession of the Sudetenland both

France and England would have to withdraw from the controversy and let affairs take what course they would. Benes and his colleagues tried to convince their "guarantors" that Czechoslovakia would be at the complete mercy of the Nazis if she were stripped of her defenses. Chamberlain repeated Hitler's pledge and urged prompt acceptance of the proposal. Of the three guarantors, only Russia—if given transit rights for her troops—offered to come to the threatened nation's assistance if she stood firm; but Benes did not believe he could offer resistance without the help of the Western powers. Therefore he reluctantly agreed to the separation. Chamberlain at once arranged another meeting with Hitler—this time at Godesberg—to iron out details of the transfer.

There he found that Hitler had increased his demands. What the Führer really wanted was an immediate and unilateral settlement executed by German troops. Although his "new position" was not described this baldly, he made his point clearly enough. Chamberlain was shocked and affronted. He had given Hitler all he had asked for. Now the German leader was demanding, in addition, British acquiescence in a gratuitous and brutal display of naked Nazi force. Chamberlain could not agree to it. Orderly negotiation, he insisted, was the foundation of civilized international relations. He urged the Führer to reconsider, but Hitler was adamant, and the conference broke down.

For a few days it seemed that war was inevitable. British and French leaders believed that if Hitler were allowed to send his troops marching without regard for any kind of international sanction, much of Europe would eventually fall under his domination. If the alternative were this or war, they felt that they hardly had a choice.

The dilemma was resolved by what seemed to be a concession offered by Hitler. Under pressure from various sources—among them his partner, Mussolini, President Roosevelt, and the highest ranking general officers of

*Mussolini and Chamberlain exchange felicitations after the signing of the Munich Pact. Göring is at the extreme left with Hitler beside him. Count Ciano, Italy's Foreign Minister and Mussolini's son-in-law, stands behind the Duce.*

his own armed forces—Hitler invited Chamberlain, the French premier Daladier, and Mussolini to a conference in Munich (September 29, 1939). A strange scene was enacted there. Hitler offered a program that was in every essential respect the same as the one Chamberlain had earlier refused. Mussolini at once agreed to it (he was the secret author of minor face-saving changes). Chamberlain and Daladier also agreed, satisfied that the principle of multilateral consultation had been honored. Under terms of the agreement, the whole Sudetenland was transferred to German jurisdiction. Occupation by German troops was to begin within forty-eight hours. Certain areas with mixed populations were to vote for or against annexation by Germany. A separate agreement, signed by Hitler and Chamberlain, stipulated that any differences between their two countries in the future would be resolved by negotiation.

Throughout the whole controversy Chamberlain had insisted that his primary purpose was the preservation of peace. It cannot be doubted that this was a fundamental concern. But it may not altogether explain the Prime Minister's actions. Linked to his dedication to peace were his fear of Communism

and his strong belief that Hitler constituted Europe's chief bulwark against its spread. We now know that an elaborate plot to overthrow Hitler was thwarted by the Munich agreement. A number of highly placed civilian and military officials, including the chief of staff of the German army, had concerted to overthrow the regime when conditions seemed right. Hitler's determination to risk war over the Sudeten question set the stage for the planned revolt. The plotters believed that the German people in 1938 were strongly opposed to a war which might involve the major powers. Available evidence indicates they were right. Their plan was to wait until Hitler ordered the army into action, then arrest him and his chief aids, take over the bureaucratic apparatus in Berlin, and set up a provisional government. The plot came within minutes of being put into execution. Among those involved were Halder, Army Chief of Staff, von Witzleben, commanding general of the Berlin Army Corps, von Brauchitsch, Commander in Chief of the Army, and Schacht, former Minister of Economics. Because the course of history might have been changed if the revolt had occurred, the following direct evidence deserves attention. The speaker is Halder, testifying under oath at Nuremberg in 1946:

Adolf Hitler was at the Berghof (in south Germany) at the time when Schacht was with me. Von Witzleben was ready with his preparations. But they could be put into action only after Hitler had come back to Berlin. On the day when Schacht—in the evening—had been to see me, I learned that Hitler had come back to Berlin. I communicated with von Witzleben at once. He came to see me in my office during the noon hours. We discussed the matters. He requested that I give the order of execution. We discussed other details—how much time he needed for the other preparation, etc. During this discussion, the news came that the British Prime Minister and the French Premier had come to Hitler for a discussion. This was in the presence of von Witzleben and therefore I took back the order of execution because, owing to this fact, the entire basis for the action had been taken away.

Now came Mr. Chamberlain, and with one stroke the danger of war was avoided. Hitler returned from Munich as an unbloody victor glorified by Mr. Chamberlain and M. Daladier. Thus, it was a matter of course that the German people greeted and enjoyed his successes. Even in the circles of Hitler's opponents—the senior officers' corps—those successes of Hitler's made an enormous impression. I do not know if a non-military man can understand what it means to have the Czechoslovak army eliminated by the stroke of the pen, and Czechoslovakia, being stripped of all her fortifications, stood as a newly born child, all naked. With the stroke of a pen, an open victory was attained. The critical hour for force was avoided. One could only wait in case any chance should come up again. I want to emphasize once more what extreme importance must be attributed to this Munich Agreement.[1]

Equally significant is the fact that the plotters had kept the British government informed of the planned revolt against the Hitler regime. A natural question is why that government did not act on this information. An antiwar revolution in Germany would seem something to be welcomed by peace-minded Chamberlain. One explanation, of course, is that British officials could not afford to take the risk; plans are one thing, their successful execution another. What if the revolt were quickly put down or, even worse, if the plotters lost courage at the crucial moment and called off or postponed the uprising? On the other hand, it is not unreasonable to suppose that Chamberlain did not want to see Hitler overthrown. Both before and after Munich, the Prime Minister had many good things to say about Hitler. His fear of Communism and his belief that Nazi Germany was the Continent's strongest bulwark against its spread (as we have noted earlier) were well known. Presently we do not have enough evidence to make a firm judgment of Chamberlain's

1. Quoted in Stipp, *op. cit.*, pp. 80–81.

"SHH-HH! HE'LL BE QUIET NOW—MAYBE!"

*An American view of the Munich agreement (1938).*

basic motives at Munich. Until this evidence is available, both views must be kept in calculation in our assessment of the meaning of that fateful conference.

## Occupation of Bohemia and Moravia

Less than a month after signing the Munich Pact, Hitler secretly gave orders to ready Germany's armed forces for the liquidation of the rest of Czecho-Slovakia.* Publicly he had repeatedly asserted that Germany wanted no Czechs in the Reich. Both before and at Munich he had assured Chamberlain that once the Sudeten question was settled he had no further territorial ambitions. It can be argued that his easy victory at Munich created an appetite for fresh adventures. The loss of the heavily fortified Sudetenland left Czecho-Slovakia defenseless. The recent annexation of Austria had made the new Germany a great pincers lying athwart a helpless state. The Little Entente (see *supra,* p.

* After the Munich "settlement" the name of the country was given this hyphenated form to emphasize the autonomy newly granted to Slovakia.

463) was a Munich casualty. Finally, Russia, snubbed by the Western powers and conscious of Czecho-Slovakia's easy vulnerability, could scarcely be counted on to repeat her pre-Munich promises of help.

But the "new appetite" argument is specious. Long before Hitler came to power, he had not only formed but published his program of expansion in the East. He spelled it out clearly in *Mein Kampf*. It was reaffirmed in the early 1930s in conversations with Hermann Rauschning, then Hitler's colleague, and published in a widely read book. As chancellor, Hitler's constant public harangues against "Jewish Bolshevism," as well as at least one public reference to what Germany could do with the Ukraine, could leave no doubt about his intentions. Many persons, it is true, honestly found it impossible to believe him; but this hardly changes the actual circumstances.

As always, Hitler waited for what he considered favorable conditions before he made his move against Czecho-Slovakia. He knew that Hungary coveted certain portions of the truncated state. He also knew that Slovakian extremists could easily be encouraged to agitate for Slovakian independence. To make doubly sure that the necessary crisis conditions would develop, he played each of these states against the other. To Hungary he pointed out the growing restlessness in Slovakia, restlessness which might lead to severance of connections with Czechia. If this happened, he argued, no one could be sure whether the new Slovak state might not insist upon incorporating Ruthenia (the "tail" of Czecho-Slovakia which Hungary felt was rightfully hers) into its own boundaries. Hungary enthusiastically assured the Führer it was ready to take whatever action was necessary to "reclaim" Ruthenia. To Slovakia, Hitler said he would do what he could to help this people find itself but he had to know what it really wanted. Separatist Slovak extremists, for their part, insisted that they knew exactly what they wanted—a complete break from Czechia.

By mid-March 1939, Czecho-Slovakia was threatened by Slovak secession and Hungarian invasion. At this point Hitler summoned the Czecho-Slovakian president—a political nonentity who had taken Benes' place after the Munich settlement—and made a startling announcement. Obviously, he said, the Czech government was unable to keep order in its own house. Violent disturbances in Slovakia and Ruthenia were clear evidence of this. Germany could not tolerate endless discord in Central Europe. Therefore, he had decided to "issue the order for German troops to march in Czecho-Slovakia, and to incorporate this country into the German Reich." In fact, he said that German troops were at that moment on the march (as they were). To save his people needless suffering, he requested that the President at once telegraph Prague to offer no resistance. Before the conference was over the President, surrounded by Nazi generals, not only sent such an order, but signed a statement committing his countrymen to the care of Hitler. Within the week, German troops had occupied all of Bohemia and Moravia. Hungary was allowed to take Ruthenia; Slovakia was recognized as an "independent state."

## The Road from Munich

Now, at last, Chamberlain saw Hitler as many others had long seen him. To stop the Nazi tide, he arranged pacts of mutual assistance with Poland, Rumania, Greece, and Turkey. France joined England in these belated gestures of solidarity against rampant German aggression (March–April 1939). Both nations also stepped up military preparations, already accelerated after the Munich crisis. Both served notice that a German attack upon any of the nations with whom they had signed pacts of defense would be considered an attack upon themselves. Naturally, Poland and the Balkan states welcomed that support, but all understood that they were still far from being out of danger. A German attack upon Poland might, in-

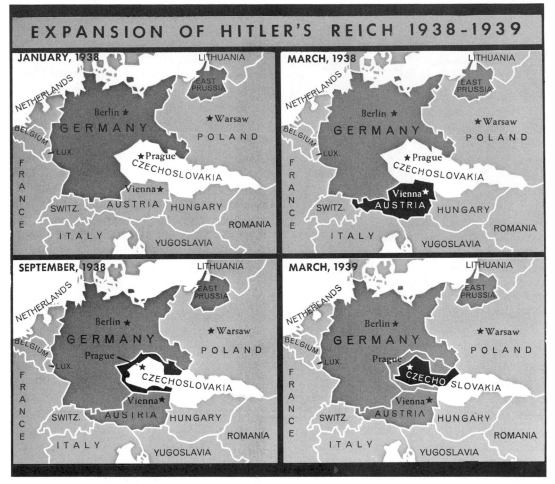

EXPANSION OF HITLER'S REICH 1938-1939

deed, bring England and France into the war. But how could substantial help from either be reasonably expected? England's army and air force were too small to constitute an effective striking force; and, of course, her navy could hardly render assistance to Poland. France was chained, technically and psychologically, to her Maginot Line. This might keep Germans out of France; it could not protect Poland. Still, the guarantees were better than nothing; and they might, some hoped, actually bluff Hitler out of further aggression.

German documents captured by the Allies during and after the war reveal Hitler's decision to push east regardless of pacts and promises. Two months after the occupation of Bohemia and Moravia, Hitler gave secret orders for the attack on Poland to take place "at any time from 1 September 1939 onwards." Hitler never doubted that German forces could easily overrun Poland. What gave him considerable pause was the Russian problem. If, contrary to his hopes, Britain and France supported Poland, he would be compelled to execute a holding action on the Western front until Poland was defeated. This would constitute a considerable nuisance but, he believed, no unsolvable problem. But if Russia entered the war, he would have real trouble on his hands. He must, therefore, neutralize this danger.

## The Nazi-Soviet Pact

To this end Hitler began to prepare for a temporary *detente* with the Communist

*Russian Foreign Minister Molotov signs the Nazi-Soviet Nonaggression Pact as his German counterpart, von Ribbentrop, stands to the left and rear, beside Stalin (August 23, 1939).*

colossus. As so often in the past, he was helped by the very powers now determined to oppose him. In the spring and summer of 1939, Britain and France sounded out the Russians concerning joint action against new German aggression. Clearly, Russia welcomed these advances and wanted a formal treaty to come out of them. But both Britain and France were coy. They wanted Russian help if they needed it. But they were not sure they would need it and, in any case, they were unwilling to put pressure on Poland to allow Russia the freedom to transport troops across Polish territory in the event of war. This made no sense to the Russians who pointed out that their troops could not effectively join battle with attacking Germans if they were forced to stay behind their own boundaries. The half-heartedness of Anglo-French discussions with Russia probably rested on a hope and a fear. The hope was that somehow Germany and Russia would soon become involved in war and thus weaken each other. The fear was that if Russian troops entered Poland, for whatever

reason, they would not leave. In any case, the negotiations remained nebulous, and were allowed to lapse in August 1939.

Meanwhile, Hitler inaugurated discussions of his own. In May the Russian Minister for Foreign Affairs, Litvinov, was dropped in favor of Molotov. Litvinov had established a reputation for being unusually understanding of Western ways, particularly British ways. Molotov had no such leanings. The significance of the change was not missed by Hitler. After a false start, Russian-German discussions moved rapidly from free trade relations, to political accommodations, to the need for a formal alliance. Because of Hitler's long record of violent denunciation of everything Communist, many observers felt that nothing could come of these talks. They failed to understand Hitler's immediate needs, as he saw them, and Russia's deep, abiding resentment at being ignored during the Munich crisis, as well as its own fear of burgeoning Nazi power. By August 20 the diplomatic revolution had been accomplished. Three days later some of the terms of the agreement were published: neither nation would commit aggression against the other; neither would align itself with a third party or any "grouping of Powers whatsoever which is aimed directly or indirectly at the other Party." A secret protocol provided for a division between them of certain territories in Poland should that state become involved in a war with Germany; it also established spheres of influence in Baltic and Balkan regions.

## Plans for the Polish War

Hitler, secure against Russian interference, now completed his plans to attack Poland. Ostensibly his aim was to reincorporate Danzig into the Reich, and to gain a corridor across the corridor in Poland. In reality he sought the complete destruction of Poland and the creation of conditions that would allow him to achieve his ultimate goal—the smashing of Russia and the annexation of "living space" in the Ukraine. Three days before he announced the signing of the Russian pact, he assembled a group of his military commanders at the chancellery for a pep talk (August 20, 1939). The following are some of the notes made by one of the generals who attended this meeting. The notes give us a clear notion of the mood and purposes of the Führer:

Most iron determination on our side. Retreat before nothing. Everybody shall have to make a point of it that we are determined from the beginning to fight the Western powers. Struggle for life or death. Germany has won every war as long as she was united. Iron, unflinching attitude of all superiors, greatest confidence, faith in victory, overcoming of the past by getting used to heaviest strain. A long period of peace will not do us any good. Therefore it is necessary to expect everything. Manly bearing. . . .

Destruction of Poland in the foreground. The aim is elimination of living forces, not the arrival at a certain line: Even if war should break out in the West, the destruction of Poland shall be the primary objective. Quick decision because of the season.

I shall give a propagandistic cause for starting the war—never mind whether it is plausible or not. The victor shall not be asked, later on on, whether we told the truth or not. In starting and making a war, not the Right is what matters but Victory.

Have no pity. Brutal attitude. 80 million people shall get what is their right. Their existence has to be secured. The strongest has the Right. Greatest severity.[2]

On August 25, Britain announced its determination to give full support to Poland if Poland were attacked by Germany. Although Hitler had no intention of staging another Munich—this time he was deter-

*This photograph shows a Polish cavalry column on maneuvers a few days before the Nazi invasion.*

mined to send his troops marching—he was bothered by the British announcement. He did not want to take on England if he could avoid it, particularly since Mussolini had just informed him that Italy was not then in a position to join in a military action. For about a week various conferences were held among British, German, and Polish diplomats. At no time, however, was a truly peaceful settlement possible. Hitler offered England a pact of friendship, to go into effect *after* he had settled accounts with Poland. Chamberlain urged Hitler to enter into normal negotiations with the Polish ambassador in Berlin which, of course, Hitler, refused to consider. On September 1, German troops poured into Poland from three directions. After a delay of two days, Britain and France honored their guarantees to Poland and declared war on Germany. World War II had begun.

2. *Nazi Conspiracy and Aggression,* Office of the United States Chief of Counsel For Prosecution of Axis Criminality, United States Printing Office, Washington, D.C., 1946, 8 Vols., Vol. III, p. 665.

# B. The War

AXIS VICTORIES: 1939 AND 1940

## The Polish Campaign and the "Winter War"

The attack launched by the Germans was so overwhelming that the Poles never had a chance to organize their armies for defensive holding, let alone effectively deploy them for subsequent counterattacks. Two German armies drove into Poland from the north, from Pomerania and East Prussia. Three more poured into central and southern Poland from bases along the Oder River. Simultaneously, swarms of dive-bombers and fighter planes attacked Polish airfields and the Polish planes that managed to get aloft. They also destroyed vital railroad complexes and lines of communication. The air assault was so massive and so devastating that within one day effective concentration of Polish troops became an impossibility; within a week large pockets of these troops were surrounded and soon forced to surrender. Warsaw held out for awhile. Some Polish corps in eastern Poland offered resistance until mid-September. Then Russian troops, advancing from the east, made further struggle altogether hopeless. On September 28, German and Russian diplomats met to settle the final line of demarcation between their spheres of the newly conquered land and to issue a call for a general peace between Germany and her opponents in the West.

Apparently, Hitler believed France and England would seriously consider peace talks. They had given their guarantees to Poland; they had honored them. Now Poland was defeated and occupied. What was there left to fight about? From the first day of the invasion Hitler had ordered his troops on the Western Front neither to attack nor provoke Allied attack. On October 6, Hitler addressed the Reichstag on behalf of peace.

He offered to guarantee the British Empire and French possessions in perpetuity in exchange for cessation of hostilities and for Allied recognition of Germany's new position in Europe. When no word came from London or Paris, he professed first puzzlement and then righteous indignation. Clearly, since both countries were in the grip of warmongers, Germany had no choice but to meet force with force.

No doubt Hitler was sincere in wanting to bring the war to an end. His strategy had always been one conquest at a time. He needed to consolidate his Polish gains and make preparations for the next round. Sooner or later, he believed, he would be under the necessity of fighting France, since he was convinced that France would never acquiesce in the creation of a German-dominated continent. But England was another matter. These tired, conservative people could, he believed, be brought to an understanding. With their empire guaranteed, they could come to view German order not as a menace to Europe but as the bulwark against Bolshevism. With England and Germany in agreement, France would be easy to handle when the time came for that showdown.

As the days passed and no peace sign came from the Allies, Hitler turned to preparations for action in the West. On October 9, 1939, he ordered general plans to be drawn up for an attacking operation, the aim of which was "to defeat as strong contingent of the French operational army as possible as well as allies fighting by its side, and at the same time [to] gain as large an area as possible in Holland, Belgium and Northern France as a base for conducting a promising air and sea war against England. . . ."[3] Hitler hoped to launch this attack in

3. *Nazi Conspiracy and Aggression*, Vol. VI, p. 880.

early November. Actually, about seven months passed before it was put into execution. As a result of this delay a number of persons, both in belligerent and nonbelligerent countries, came to believe that Hitler and the Allies were negotiating a settlement; repeated references were made to the "phony war." They were quite mistaken. The delay was caused by bad weather and a general dragging of heels by certain members of the military High Command who feared an Anglo-French encounter. More than a dozen D-dates were set (the first one, for November 7, 1939). German documents captured after the war show the Führer repeatedly setting the day ahead. On November 7, for example, he issued this order: "A-Day [i.e., D-Day] is postponed . . . by three days. The next decision will be made by 1800 hours [6:00 p.m.] on 9 November 39." On November 9 "the Führer and Supreme Commander of the Armed Forces, after hearing a report on the meteorological situation, has decided: The earliest date designated for A-Day is 19 November"; and so on.

In the meantime another war broke out not only unplanned by Hitler but much against his wishes. According to the terms of the Nazi-Soviet accord of August 23, as modified by the September 28 decisions, Soviet Russia was given a somewhat free hand in dealing with certain of the small states of Eastern Europe. The quick German victory hustled the Russians into rather precipitate demands on Estonia, Latvia, Lithuania, and Finland. Russia's aim was to gain bases and influence in these countries for the double purpose of preparing against the day of a German attack, and eventually to convert them into Communist satellites. Estonia, Latvia, and Lithuania protested but succumbed to Soviet pressure. Finland simply refused Russian demands for certain bases and territorial cessions.

Confident that it could quickly bring Finland to submission the Soviet government, on trumped-up charges, declared war against her November 30, 1939. But Finnish resistance proved stubborn. For a month or two it even appeared that Finland, however incredible it all seemed, might force the Russians to sue for peace. England, France, the United States, and many other nations enthusiastically gave the Finnish people moral or financial support. England and France also made plans to send troops and military supplies across Norway and Sweden, if those nations would give their consent. Evidence indicates that such an arrangement was in its final planning stage when, unable after all to stand against vastly superior forces, Finland capitulated in March 1940. She was forced to cede certain strategic areas to the Soviet Union (the Karelian Isthmus, for example). But she successfully resisted pressures to turn herself into a Soviet puppet state.

## Nazi Occupation of Norway and Denmark

The ending of the "Winter War" proved particularly embarrassing for the British. They had been planning, as we have noted, to send military support to the Finns. But by March 1940, they had completed other plans only incidentally connected with the fighting in Finland. Much of Germany's wartime iron needs were met by extensive importations from Sweden via Narvik, Norway. If these supplies were shut off, the German war effort would seriously suffer. Moreover, Allied occupation of points along Norway's coasts would simultaneously deprive the Germans of their use and give British and French airmen bases from which to bomb Germany and to break up German naval action in the North Sea. In short, the Allies, in the spring of 1940, planned to occupy a number of strategic areas in Norway. It was hoped that the Norwegian government would approve of the action; but evidence indicates that the project might have been carried out without or possibly even against Norwegian approval.

As it turned out, Hitler relieved the British of the necessity to appear as an aggressor by sending his own forces into Norway just ahead of the Allies (April 9, 1940). Originally he had not thought of this action as either needed or desirable. Certain circumstances combined to bring him around to enthusiastic approval. One was Admiral Raeder's insistence that the war against Britain really required German control of Norwegian ports. Another was Raeder's and Rosenberg's request that the Führer have a talk with Vidkun Quisling, a rabid Norwegian Nazi. Quisling told Hitler that the Norwegian government had agreed not to oppose a British invasion of Norway, thus confirming the Führer's fears. But it was the "Winter War" and England's obvious maneuvering in Scandinavia that convinced Hitler that the project required immediate and serious attention. Plans were well along when the Finnish War ended. Its ending destroyed the political basis for the action; but by that time the idea had become so fascinating to Hitler that he decided to go ahead with it anyway, particularly as he had been kept informed of parallel British planning.

Thus on April 9, 1940, air, naval, and army units struck at Denmark (a purely personal decision of the Führer) and Norway. Denmark was occupied in one day. Fighting in Norway went on for about nine weeks. Norwegian troops fought stubbornly and effectively, in the expectation of substantial help from Britain and France. Allied troops were landed in several coastal areas, and made some headway against Nazi land troops. But the German Luftwaffe smashed communication lines, destroyed much of the attacking and supporting strength of British naval units, and heavily bombed Allied strategic centers. Even so, the Germans might eventually have been driven from Norway if Hitler had not launched an invasion of the Lowlands and France on May 10. This gigantic offensive made it impossible for the Allies to supply or even sustain their forces in Norway. By the beginning of June, Allied evacuation was practically complete. Norway and Denmark remained under German domination for the rest of the war.

*This photograph, from a captured German film, shows a paratrooper leaping from a plane over Holland, May 1940.*

## Conquest of the Lowlands and France

Originally, Nazi plans to conquer France were fundamentally based on the Schlieffen Plan used in 1914. Attacking troops were to drive through central Belgium, outflank the Maginot Line defenses, turn southward in wide sweeping movements, and encircle and destroy the trapped Allied armies. This time, however, the Netherlands was not to escape involvement. Hitler believed his forces had to use Dutch and Belgian airfields to strengthen his blitz drive against Anglo-French armies and areas, as well as to prevent Dutch ports and airstrips from falling under enemy control. But during the winter months of 1939 and 1940, von Manstein—one of Hitler's most talented generals—persuaded him to order a significant operational change. The new plan called for the major attack to take place north of Liège and drive through to the Channel ports (for these and later references to places in the war zones, see map, p. 587). If successful, Allied forces would not only be cut in two but would be deprived of the use of Channel ports. Without these, the combined and co-operative functioning of French and British forces was impossible. Simultaneously, a group of armies under Colonel-General (later Field Marshal) von Rundstedt was directed to launch a strong attack south of Liège aimed at both preventing French units from giving support to those under attack in the north, and completing the destruction of Allied means of serious resistance.

Before dawn on May 10, German parachutists were dropped near Rotterdam and The Hague. They had been thoroughly coached for the tasks they performed. For example, they knew exactly which parts of strategic bridges contained demolition charges; they knew where the troops were which guarded each bridge; and they knew the strength of the troops at each bridge. Equipped with this information and carefully drilled for these chores, they wrested several strategic areas from the Dutch defenders within hours after dropping from the sky. Meanwhile, armored forces rolled across the Dutch frontier and raced to establish contact with the paratroop units. The blows were so well planned, so powerful, and so swiftly executed that the Netherlands government asked for an armistice within five days. The same tactics employed against the Belgians gained a complete Nazi victory over them in eighteen days.

The strike against the Lowlands brought the downfall of the tottering Chamberlain government. The glamour of Munich had long since vanished. The conquest of Poland, although hardly chargeable to Chamberlain, had not added to his popularity. The bungling—as many British considered it—in Norway was beyond bearing. When the Lowlands were overrun, Chamberlain did not wait for his parliamentary opponents to rally; he quietly resigned in favor of Winston Churchill, then First Lord of the Admiralty.

With Dutch and Belgian troops knocked out, the German juggernaut pushed relentlessly to the Channel ports. Although French and British forces outnumbered German forces about two to one, neither their troops nor their high commands were prepared for such blitz tactics. By May 20 the German drive had reached the Channel, cutting the defending armies in two. Several attempts were made by both British and French armies to break through the bristling Nazi line; all attempts failed completely. For the British there was nothing to do but try to make it back to their home base. By marshaling a miscellaneous armada of ships ranging from destroyers to fishing smacks (nearly 900 in all), they were able to withdraw from their Dunkerque pocket (May 27–June 4). Over 140,000 French and Belgian troops were evacuated along with about 200,000 British troops. The "miracle of Dunkerque" was rightly made the subject of stirring Churchillian rhetoric; but the fact remained that, except for some forces south of the Somme, the British had been driven off the Continent in less than three weeks of fighting.

On June 10 Mussolini, eager to get in on the kill, joined the war and sent his Fascist forces into southern France. They made little headway, but the end for France was near, since now the full force of German might, converging from both north and south, smashed against crumbling French defenses. Although the Maginot Line was never reduced, this mattered little; with German forces of all kinds flanking it, its massed and massive guns now futilely pointed in the wrong direction. By mid-June most of its defenders surrendered. On June 16, Marshal Henri Pétain, famed for the French stand at Verdun in World War I, took over the premiership from Paul Reynaud (Daladier's recent successor) and the next day asked the Germans for an armistice, which was granted on June 22. Under its terms German troops occupied all of France except the inland southern half. A French totalitarian government, under Pétain and Pierre Laval, estab-

*Nazi troops parade through the Arc de Triomphe, August 1940.*

lished itself at Vichy. It set to work at once to mesh its policies and administrative directives with those of Nazi Germany. For Hitler the war seemed over; France had fallen, Britain was isolated, Russia was his ally. West of Warsaw he dominated most of the Continent. Soon the British would get a taste of the Luftwaffe's power. After that he could expect another request for peace parleys. The New Order seemed about to shape a new epoch.

## The Failure of "Sea Lion"

Because the fall of France had occurred so quickly, Hitler found himself without a detailed plan for the "battle of Britain." Probably he had not anticipated the need for one; his aim had been to destroy the British and French armed forces on French soil. That done, the war would be over, and peace treaties would be made. But thanks to the evacuation at Dunkerque, Britain—although badly battered—was still unbeaten. Or rather, as Hitler insisted, Britain was beaten but did not seem to know it. To

bring home realization of this fact, he ordered an all-out air attack against what he thought of as his stupidly stubborn foe.

In early July the Luftwaffe bombed many English coastal shipping points. Simultaneously, German service troops prepared airstrips and landing fields in various points of northern France and in the Lowlands for the greater assault to follow. It was hoped that, meanwhile, British fighter planes would offer themselves for battle. Experience suggested that they would soon be eliminated as an organized fighting force. Then fleets of German bombers would move inland for the big blow—if that was still needed.

Two weeks of air battle proved somewhat disconcerting for the Führer. British fighter planes were not being knocked out of the sky with the dispatch he had grown accustomed to. Actually, the Luftwaffe itself was taking something of a beating. And, of course, no sounds of surrender were coming from Churchill; quite, indeed, the contrary.

In these circumstances Hitler decided to draw up invasion plans. The code name of the invasion, appropriately enough, was "Sea Lion." In a directive dated July 16, 1940, Hitler laid out the following conditions:

Since England, despite her militarily hopeless situation, still shows no sign of willingness to come to terms, I have decided to prepare a landing operation against England, and, if necessary, to carry it out.

The aim of this operation is to eliminate the English homeland as a basis for carrying on the war against Germany, and if it should become necessary, to occupy it completely.

To this end I order the following:

The *Landing* must be carried out in the form of a surprise crossing on a broad front from Ramsgate to the area west of the Isle of Wight. . . . The preparations for the entire operation must be completed by mid-August. . . . I request the Supreme Commanders to submit to me as soon as possible:

The intentions of the Navy and Air Force for achieving the necessary conditions for the crossing of the channel. . . .

The crossing and operations plans of the army, composition and equipment of the first crossing wave.

Proposals of the army and navy on the overall command *during* the crossing.

Before many weeks, however, it became unmistakably clear that British fighter planes excelled their Luftwaffe counterparts in both armament and maneuverability. Newly devised radar equipment proved highly effective. The morale of British pilots, moreover, was savagely high. In short, air superiority was gained by the British, not the Nazis. This meant that the elaborate plans of Sea Lion had to be postponed or (as it turned out) abandoned. For without air cover, invasion was impossible. By mid-September the Germans were so far from establishing that cover that they had practically given up daytime raids in favor of night bombing of inland cities. These raids were numerous and costly; over 20,000 civilians were killed in London alone; a few cities, such as Coventry, were almost demolished. For a year after the fall of France, Britain stood alone before the Nazi fury. Bombings continued, and British ships fell prey to German submarines in fearful and increasing numbers. For a time it seemed that —invasion or not—England could not hold out. How could a small island stand against a continent?

Perhaps England would not have held out if the United States had not furnished massive aid of many kinds. In the mid-1930s, America had sought to isolate itself from Europe by the passage of a series of neutrality acts. By the terms of these acts, the United States was prohibited from shipping arms to any belligerent (either attacker or attacked); United States citizens might travel in belligerent vessels, but only at their own risk; and loans or credits to warring nations were forbidden. As Nazi aggression grew, a number of citizens, led by President Roosevelt, tried to free the country from its isolationist moorings. Before 1939 they made little headway. After the outbreak of war,

Congress modified neutrality legislation to permit the "cash and carry" supply of arms to belligerent nations, but isolationist sentiment remained strong. The attack on France led President Roosevelt to ask for vastly increased national defense spending, particularly for aircraft and warships. At his direction the War Department released to Britain millions of dollars worth of military supplies. In 1940 Congress authorized compulsory military service. The next year, under the "Lend-Lease" Act, seven billion dollars were allocated for the supply of arms and munitions to any country whose defense, in the opinion of the President, seemed vital to the security of the United States. Under the terms of this Act, Britain received from the United States vast quantities of goods of almost every kind to meet both civilian and military needs. Anomalously, most United States citizens remained isolationist in sentiment at the time that this country became "the great arsenal for democracy." Beleaguered Britain would have preferred America to become her full-time war ally; lacking this, it gratefully accepted aid that very possibly kept it from defeat.

## THE WIDENING OF THE WAR, 1940 TO 1942

### *"Case Barbarossa"*

In the late fall of 1940 Hitler asked the Spanish government to join him in a move to capture Gibraltar and seal off the British from the Western Mediterranean. The Spanish dictator was willing enough to join a *victorious* Hitler in such a venture. But by then he had begun to have some doubt about Nazi invincibility. England had come off the victor in the air war, and talk of invasion had died down. Hitler might, of course, improvise another victory; but until signs of it were a little clearer, Franco preferred to take no chances. Consequently this scheme came to nothing.

Meanwhile, under the code name "Barbarossa," plans for the conquest of Russia were made ready. Historians have long debated Hitler's motives in taking on Russia before Britain was conquered. An opinion commonly held is that the Führer was forced into opening a new front by Russia's aggressive moves in the Balkans. There is no question that Russia was very active there. In June 1940, for example, Stalin forced Rumania to cede Bessarabia and Northern Bukovina, largely inhabited by Russians, to the Soviet Union. Soviet diplomatic relations were resumed with Yugoslavia, clearly indicating a resurgence of traditional Russian interest in Balkan affairs. Naturally, these moves disturbed Hitler who had no intention either of yielding control of vital oil resources in this area or of allowing Russia to create a power block that would render more difficult his ultimate aim of carving out *Lebensraum* in the east. Nevertheless, available and ample evidence proves the unsoundness of this view. Instead it makes clear that he was moved by these considerations: sheer inability to mark time militarily; confidence that an attack on Russia would not create a two-front war— France was beaten and England immobilized; the conquest of Russia would force the capitulation of Britain; and, finally, this conquest would bring to realization the ultimate goal of German foreign policy—living space in the east.

Captured German documents also reveal Hitler's original intention to invade Russia in the early fall of 1940. He was talked out of it by Keitel, one of his chief military advisers, who outlined the impossibly difficult military considerations such an attack would involve —rapid transportation of troops from west to east, lack of "necessary physical preparations for the deployment of the masses of troops once they reached their destination," and the few remaining weeks of operational weather. Thus Hitler ordered full-scale planning for an attack that would open in the spring of 1941.[4] In his directive of December

1940, Hitler led off by insisting that Russia was to be crushed "in a quick campaign before the end of the war against England." Repeatedly he stated to his advisers that the whole action should be completed within five or six weeks. Under "General Purpose," the directive declared: "The mass of the Russian *Army* in Western Russia is to be destroyed in daring operations by driving forward deep wedges with tanks and the retreat of intact battle-ready troops into the wide spaces of Russia is to be prevented."

## Deflection of the War to the South

D-Day was originally scheduled for early or mid-May 1941; by the end of June or early July, Russia would probably be knocked out, and the surrender of England could be expected soon after. Unfortunately for Hitler's planning, one major and one minor hitch unexpectedly developed that threw off his timing. For one thing Mussolini, envious of his colleague's smashing successes, and resentful of the Führer's sometimes peremptory dealings with his now junior partner, decided on an adventure of his own —the conquest of Greece. This was undertaken by a surprise attack in October 1940. Hitler glossed over his irritation and publicly commended the action. He feared, however, that the move might interfere with his own plans. He was right, since the Greek response was nothing like the Duce expected. Indeed, it soon became apparent that the Italians were in serious trouble. By December their situation was so threatening that the commanding general was relieved, and feverish preparations were made to stave off impending defeat. Hitler realized he would probably have to divert some of his "Barbarossa" troops to rescue his Axis partner.

Three months later the regent of Yugoslavia, a Nazi sympathizer, was ousted and young King Peter II assumed the throne (March 27, 1941). This coup, combined with Italian reverses, caused Hitler to postpone "Barbarossa" in order to put his Balkan house in order. Otherwise, he might expect large British landings along Europe's "soft

4. For a detailed examination of this planning, see Stipp, *op. cit.*, pp. 186–221.

# WORLD WAR II

## GERMAN DOMINATED EUROPE, 1942

**Axis Powers**

**Joined Axis in 1941**

**Vichy France**

**Limit of Axis occupation, 1942**

Map by J. Donovan

underbelly" which could wreck his projected one-front war in the east, as well as put in serious danger his oil resources in Rumania. A large contingent of planes, tanks, and infantry troops was therefore detached from the massed forces ready to strike at Russia. In ten days Yugoslavia was overrun and a Nazi government was installed. German troops were then sent against Greek forces and their British allies. By the end of April they had again pushed the British off the Continent and had brought the Greeks to complete surrender. Mussolini, rescued but red-faced, sent occupation troops into Greece. The Allies had suffered another costly and humiliating defeat.

## The Invasion of Russia

Hitler now returned to "Barbarossa." His lightning victories in Poland, Denmark and Norway, the Lowlands and France, and now in the Balkans gave him full confidence that his drive against the Soviet Union would shatter, quickly and decisively, the last great continental state and bring with it, too, the capitulation of beleaguered Britain. On June 22, 1941, he sent three large army groups across Russia's western frontier.*

* Partly from pressure by Germany and partly from desire to regain territory lost in the "Winter War," Finland joined in the attack.

*Soviet guerrillas waiting for stray Nazi units (1941).*

One group headed for Leningrad, another for Moscow, the third for Kiev and, if necessary, points south and east. The main objective was not territory; it was Russian manpower. Otherwise, the Napoleonic debacle might be repeated.

Hitler's expectations of a quick victory were not altogether unreasonable. The "Winter War" had revealed serious weaknesses in the structure and functioning of the Soviet military machine. In part because of the recent purges, members of the Russian high command were seriously deficient in imaginative planning and ability to improvise. Officers of the middle class, from colonels to captains, too often were incompetent. Among the troops, individual initiative was conspicuously lacking—a deficiency mitigated (but not wholly compensated for) by a stubborn determination and stolid endurance of conditions that many soldiers would not have found tolerable. Many Russian planes had been destroyed on the ground in the early days of the war; many others were obsolete. The Russians were superior in artillery and tanks or soon became so; again, however, the tactical use of them (until 1943) was anything but efficient. On the other hand, Russian manpower was vastly superior to that of the Germans. Also, and most important, Soviet propaganda played down the Communist system and emphasized the stark dangers threatening the very life of Mother Russia.

Moreover, it soon became apparent that Stalin's "scorched-earth" policy would deny the Germans and their allies the grain, gasoline, and industrial establishments they were so eager to get their hands on.

By mid-August all three German army groups were deep inside Russia. Army Group North was close to Leningrad; Army Group Center was approaching Moscow; Army Group South had penetrated 350 miles into southern Russia, approaching the Dnieper River. Already the Army Chief of Staff had come to believe that the bulk of the Soviet army west of the Dnieper had been destroyed, giving Hitler the feeling that once again an enemy had been conquered, save for the final *coup de grace*. To accomplish this, he ordered renewed attacks by Group North and Group South. Moscow, he insisted, was only "a geographical expression"; for the time being Army Group Center could send part of its forces to support the drive to the south.

Substantial gains were made in the new offensives. In early November it appeared that Leningrad, now almost completely encircled, must fall. In the south, Rostov was taken (for all cities and areas mentioned in this section, see map, p. 601). Army Group Center, ordered again into action, came to within 25 miles of Moscow. By late November vast Russian spaces were under Nazi control; hundreds of thousands of Russian soldiers had been captured; and Russian casualties were staggeringly high. The end, it seemed, was at hand.

But despite their seizure of vast territories and the inflicting of almost uncountable casualties among Russian troops, the Germans were still not quite victors. They had underestimated the Soviet Union's vast human resources, the stubborn courage of the Russian soldier, and the ability of Russian commanders to learn not only from their own mistakes but also from their enemy's successes. And since Hitler had planned on a scant six weeks war, German troops were not equipped for winter fighting.

*This photograph, showing Nazi troops in Stalingrad, appeared in a Vienna illustrated weekly on September 30, 1941. Part of the caption pointed out that "Each house and factory was converted into a fortress or defended position."*

In early December Russian counteroffensives along the whole line combined with the coming of early subzero weather to halt the Nazi sweep. By mid-December German commanders were calling for the Führer's permission to retreat. Hitler refused to sanction any significant withdrawals. For him, retreat was a kind of non-Aryan concept; victors did not retreat. He also believed that a full-scale withdrawal under existing circumstances would most likely turn into an uncontrollable rout. As a result, all units were ordered to stand where they were and, if necessary, to die there.

By the end of December, Russian thrusts in both the north and the south gave signs of aiming at the encirclement of Army Group Center. Finally sensing the catastrophe that threatened, Hitler ordered a limited withdrawal in mid-January 1942. It did not nearly satisfy the demands of his generals, but it was of sufficient depth to straighten the German line and allow troops that otherwise might have become isolated to guard against strong flanking attacks. Hitler's appeal to the home front for winter clothing for the troops brought enough to give the soldiers some protection against the freezing blasts. Reserve units were also moved up into the line. By early March the Russian offensives had begun to peter out,

due as much perhaps to lack of Russian military expertise as to German countermeasures. Soon spring rains bogged down the whole front in mud, so that operations on both sides came to a virtual standstill.

The effects of the winter fighting were of tremendous significance. Hitler's prestige among the troops was raised even higher. Surprised by an early and indescribably severe winter, and bewildered by the seemingly endless raising of fresh armies by the Russians, the German High Command had clamored for a full-scale retreat. Later the generals themselves admitted that it would have been but the prelude to a disastrous rout. Hitler's iron will had infected the front-line soldiers with a spirit that they came to sense only after the ordeal was over. To symbolize the way of the Nazi will—as well as to rid himself of a "mere professional"— Hitler had practically forced the resignation of the army's Commander in Chief (December 1941) and had taken over the position himself. He had seemingly demonstrated that what Napoleon could not master, he could. On the other hand, the Russian people felt a pride in their leadership that many had not felt before. Since 1939 Hitler had romped from victory to victory. Against the Soviet Union he had stumbled and had been brought to a halt, at least for the time being. Russian morale was raised, even among many behind the German lines who had earlier hoped for a German victory.

In the spring of 1942 Hitler planned a new offensive. Although operative along the entire front, it was to concentrate on the Caucasus oilfields. Hitler believed that Russia could not continue to spend blood as it had done in the first campaign. The "Bolshevik beasts," deprived of their chief oil resources and decimated by even more murderous assaults, would finally have no alternative but complete capitulation.

Before the new campaign opened, the Russians launched an offensive of their own, aimed at driving the Germans out of Kharkov, recapturing the great power plant

*A German anti-aircraft gun crew in the Libyan Desert.*

*Cossacks, new style, charge over a hill and into action somewhere along the Russian front (1942).*

at Dnepropetrovsk, and generally inflicting whatever damage they could on the enemy. Within five days both of the pincers were savagely broken off by newly built-up German units, and the offensive collapsed. The Russians would probably have suffered even greater losses if Hitler's plans for his own offensive had been nearer to completion.

In late June 1942, the Nazi drive opened with gains all along the front but particularly impressive advances in the south. For two months the offensive ground on without, however, either gaining complete control of the oilfields or routing, let alone decimating, Russian ranks which seemed able always to reform after even the most vicious mauling. In mid-October Hitler decided to break off the offensive when his intelligence services informed him that Soviet losses had not been proportionate to their losses in the previous campaign, and that he should anticipate another Russian winter offensive. By this time the new Napoleon doubtless began to understand the magnitude of some of the frustrating problems experienced by the first great conqueror's encounter with the Russians.

## The War in Africa, 1940 to 1942

For a year after the fall of France in June 1940, land fighting between the belligerents was confined to North and East

Africa.* From Libya the Italians sent exploring columns into western Egypt during August and September. The columns reached a point about 60 miles within the border before being stopped by weak British forces. During the next two months each side worked to build up strength for a vigorous offensive. Early in December the British opened a drive that developed unexpected momentum. In January 1941, Bardia fell— a defeat that cost the Italians 25,000 prisoners and a great deal of war material. Several weeks later, Tobruk (an important fortress-port nearly 100 miles inside the Libyan frontier) surrendered, quickly followed by Derna and Benghazi. By the end of the first week of February the British had captured over 120,000 prisoners, hundreds of artillery pieces, and many tanks. Their own losses in men and equipment were very light. The whole operation had been so surprisingly successful that General O'Connor, the British commanding officer, advised renewing the offensive—which then had pushed 500 miles into Libya—with the aim of expelling the Italians from North Africa.

At this point, however, events in Europe intervened. It will be recalled that Mussolini had staged an invasion of Greece the preceding December and by early 1941 had suffered reverses so severe that Hitler had been forced to effect rescuing operations. In

* For places and areas mentioned in the following paragraphs, see map, p. 592.

the meantime British forces had joined the Greeks; so that now the question was whether the African offensive should continue, or whether troops and equipment from there should be diverted to save Greece. The Churchill government finally decided to defend Greece, with the disastrous results (April–May 1941) that we have already noted. Somewhat earlier, German troops, under General (later Field Marshal) Erwin Rommel, were sent to Africa to bolster the faltering Italians.*

These developments drastically changed the North African situation. Rommel had under him not only a number of Italian divisions but also his own *Afrika Korps* that was soon to become famous. His daring, drive, and specially trained units combined to push the British out of their advanced positions and back again to the Egyptian border (mid-April 1941). A hastily contrived British counteroffensive failed to regain any of their lost positions but it deterred Rommel from further action until he had built up his forces. The British used the next several months for the same purpose and, under a new commander, launched a smashing attack against Rommel in December 1941. Hitler's drive into Russia caused him to drain off some of Rommel's forces precisely at this time, so that the British were again able to capture Benghazi, and station outposts at El Agheila. But their stay was brief, for soon Rommel was once again on the offensive. (These somewhat dizzying comings and goings along the rim of North Africa are basically explained by geographic conditions. The coastlines of Egypt and Libya stretch almost 1000 miles. Much of the hinterland is sandy wastes; quite literally, towns are few and far between. A mobile army, if it makes progress at all, can go very far in a relatively short time. However, it

General Rommel (with field glasses) is pictured here in the foremost line of the African Front during the first drive of the Afrika Korps (1941).

also runs into extremely difficult logistical problems, particularly the basic one of water supply. Consequently, unless an army can supply itself on the run *and* keep going until the opposing forces are captured, destroyed, or chased off the continent, the chances are strong that the chaser will soon become the chased. This was the pattern of warfare in North Africa throughout the whole period of 1940 to 1943.)

In late May 1942, Rommel struck again at British and Free French forces, who were themselves preparing for another push. For a while Allied troops held their ground, although at a high price. Soon, however, German-Italian units beat down the defenders and went on to recapture Tobruk and Bardia. They then crossed into Egypt where, at El Alamein, they were stopped—a bare 70 miles from Alexandria. Thereafter, both Allied counterthrusts and Axis attempts to break through British defenses failed; both sides were near exhaustion.

The situation was so serious for the British that Prime Minister Churchill visited Cairo in August to discuss with political and military leaders what was to be done. Out of these meetings came another shakeup in the High Command and a directive by Churchill that the next offensive must be aimed not at gaining ground, but at total destruction of the Axis armies. For the next several months neither side ventured any large-scale action.

---

* Other operations subsequently were carried out in Iraq, Syria, and Ethiopia which cannot, in a general study such as ours, be considered. By late 1941 all of these countries were either occupied or dominated by the Allies.

*The War in the Pacific, 1941 to 1942*

In 1941 Japanese leaders, or at least the military people who increasingly had come to dominate the government and to make Japanese policy, schemed to conquer and rule an empire that would stretch from the mid-Pacific to the western limits of China. It would include the Dutch East Indies, the Philippines, Malaya, Indochina, Burma, and Thailand—in short, areas that contained about one half of the world's population.*

Even before the European war (as we have seen), Japan had begun nibbling away at China. With the coming of the war, the most promising possibilities for the consummation of her plans seemed to offer themselves. France was defeated and unable to defend her possessions in Asia; Britain had her hands full staving off her own defeat; the Dutch could hardly offer serious opposition.

* For details of this planning see Samuel E. Morison, *The Two Ocean War*, Little, Brown and Company, Boston, 1963, Ch. II, especially pp. 38–45.

The most serious obstacle seemed to be the United States, long a champion of the open door in China, and now an unofficial ally of Britain. But America was 6000 miles away. Logistical problems alone would make her striking power weak and uncertain. Moreover, the surprise destruction of her Pacific fleet, stationed in Hawaii, would prevent her from interfering with the construction and consolidation of a sweeping, fortified perimeter that would effectively and permanently shield the new empire from later attacks.

The United States was well aware of Japan's ambitions. Since 1940 she had embargoed iron, steel, oil, and other military or potentially military supplies that would have further strengthened the Japanese war machine. However, her position was complicated and somewhat ambiguous. President Roosevelt believed that involvement in the war, whether in Europe, in Asia, or on both continents, was inevitable. Millions of Americans did not share this belief. Moreover, among those who did share it there were differences over where the main effort should

*This is the group of Japanese statesmen who decided upon the Pearl Harbor attack. Premier Tojo is in the front row, third from the left.*

*This scene from a captured Japanese film shows Japanese airmen heading for their planes aboard a carrier to start the raid on Pearl Harbor.*

be applied, if a two-ocean war were to develop. Some favored concentrating on Japan; others argued that if Hitler completely dominated Europe and the British Isles, nothing that we could do in the East would have much meaning.

Although jingo militarists occupied most governmental ministries in Japan, not all Japanese were eager for war. The Prime Minister, Prince Konoye (1941), was not eager, nor was Emperor Hirohito.* In August 1941, Konoye proposed a conference between himself and President Roosevelt to see if a compromise of some sort could be worked out. From the evidence we now have, it does not appear that such a meeting could have done more than postpone hostilities, if it could have done that. In any case the President, acting upon Secretary of State Hull's advice, rejected the offer. (Hull's reasoning was that Konoye could not be trusted and, even if he could, our demands would not be acceptable to the dominant Japanese militarist clique.) Konoye then resigned and was succeeded by General Tojo,

---

* But it is important to note that Konoye's reluctance to allow Japan to drift into war with the United States did not at all extend to a lessening of Japanese military ventures in China; here he was a thorough-going imperialist.

who busied himself with perfecting the details of the general plan noted earlier. Mostly as a cover for this planning, Tojo resumed negotiations with the United States which continued until late November 1941. By then Japan felt herself ready to strike.

Because American cypher experts, sometime before, had cracked the Japanese diplomatic code, President Roosevelt and his advisers were fully aware that Japan was about to begin offensive operations. They did not, however, know exactly when or where. Admiral Kimmel, in charge of the Pacific fleet stationed in Pearl Harbor, received a warning from Washington, November 27, that "hostile action is possible at any moment." The chief officer of Naval Intelligence requested that another warning be sent December 4, for by that time even more ominous Japanese diplomatic dispatches had been decoded. But the Navy High Command decided to wait for still more specific information. That information came in about five hours before the attack at Pearl Harbor. General George Marshall ordered an alert to be sent at once to the commanding officers at Pearl Harbor. But there "was a foul-up that morning in Army radio, and the officer in charge entrusted the message to commercial channels [Western Union]. A boy on a bicycle delivered it to General

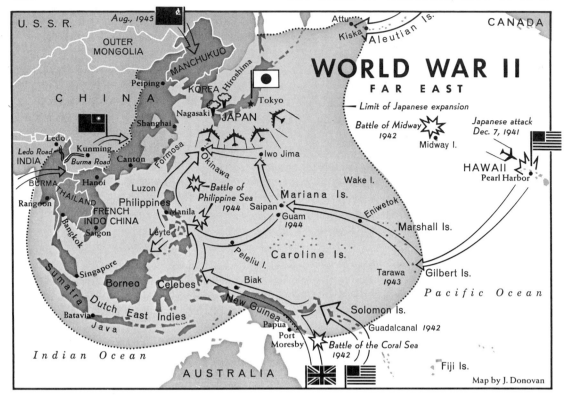

*Hickam airfield, ablaze after the Japanese bombing attack on December 7, 1941.*

The attack on Pearl Harbor on Sunday, December 7, 1941, destroyed half of its large complement of planes, sank or substantially damaged seven battleships, and completely demolished three destroyers. Nearly 2500 lives were lost; hundreds of soldiers, sailors, and civilians were wounded. The nation, though instantly united for war by the savage and unprovoked attacks, suffered a psychic shock. And, as the Japanese had planned, American naval action against Japanese aggression in other parts of the Pacific and in Southeast Asia was seriously hampered for nearly a year. By then most of what the Japanese had blueprinted for their empire—except certain areas of China—was under their control.

On December 13 Guam was surrendered to the Japanese, as was Wake Island on December 20. The same month Thailand agreed to Japanese overlordship, British forces surrendered at Hong Kong, and the Philippines were invaded. Early the next month Manila

Short [in Hawaii] some hours after the attack was over."⁵

5. Morison, *op. cit.,* p. 53. For details of the "Pearl Harbor Question" see Roberta Wohlstetter, *Pearl Harbor: Warning and Decision,* Stanford University Press, Stanford, 1962.

and Cavite were taken by the Japanese, as the Islands' troops, under General Douglas MacArthur, began a slow retreat first to Bataan Peninsula and finally (a remnant under General Jonathan Wainwright) to the island of Corregidor where the final surrender came May 6. In the same period Japanese forces occupied the Netherlands East Indies, Malaya and Singapore, Burma, portions of New Guinea, and all of New Britain. By late spring of 1942 they had made what one writer has called "the most rapid, stupendous conquest in modern times." (For the places and names involved in this conquest see map, p. 594.)

Allowing itself to become infected by what a Japanese admiral later called "Victory Disease," the Imperial General Headquarters decided on action designed to wipe out the United States Pacific fleet and at the same time to extend its "ribbon defense" to include the Western Aleutians and Midway Island. With these objectives gained, the war (it was believed) would be over and Japan would rule most of Asia, as her Axis partners would soon dominate Europe. Even though the designed action against the United States fleet near Midway was bold, its outcome (for the Japanese) was nearly catastrophic. Although outnumbering United States warships nearly three to one, the Japanese striking force, under Admiral Yamamoto, suffered a defeat so severe in the battle of Midway (June 3-4, 1942) that one American naval historian has said it "thrust the war lords back on their heels, caused their ambitious plans for the conquest of Port Moresby, Fiji, New Caledonia, and Samoa to be cancelled, and forced on them an unexpected and unwelcome defensive role."[6]

But, of course, "the most stupendous conquest in modern times" was not undone at once by the battle of Midway, no matter how decisive that battle ultimately turned out to be. For that, three years and much

6. Morison, *op. cit.,* p. 162.

suffering, death, and destruction were to be the price.

## THE YEAR OF DECISION: 1943

### Stalingrad

From September 1939 to late 1942 the Allies had suffered an almost unbroken series of devastating defeats. As we have seen, by the autumn of 1942 German troops had advanced to the Volga; German and Italian forces were within 70 or so miles of Alexandria; the Japanese had conquered and entrenched themselves in most of the Pacific islands west of Hawaii, in the East Indies, Indochina, Burma, and large parts of eastern China. To the cynic it might have seemed that if the Axis powers now went on the defensive it was because they had no place else to go.*

But the situation was not quite so hopeless for the Allies as appearances suggested. For one thing, new Russian armies were being raised, trained, and equipped by Russian officers who were by then much more imaginative and resourceful than they or their predecessors had been a short year before. For another, Axis forces were occupying so many parts of the globe that they were necessarily spread thin. Also, the vast resources and technological skills of the United States were now beginning to be poured into the fearful struggle. Finally, the German submarine, which had played such dread havoc in the "battle of the Atlantic" (1940-1942) that it alone seemed for a while to assure Axis victory, lost its fatal sting when the British perfected "microwave radar and operational research on antisubmarine-warfare methods."

Part of Hitler's directive for the 1942 offense had ordered Army Group B "to develop the Don defences and, by a thrust forward to Stalingrad, to smash the enemy forces concentrated there, to occupy the

* Since Italian efforts were not of a decisive nature, they are not included in this summary statement. But, as we shall see, Italy remained an Axis partner until September 1943.

*German infantry in the process of capturing "Hill 202," a strong point in the industrial suburb of Stalingrad. For a time the hill changed hands daily, sometimes hourly.*

town, and to block the land communications between the Don and the Volga. . . ."[7] In an earlier section we noted that by mid-October 1942, Hitler had halted the new drive after impressive gains, in order to prepare for the expected Russian winter offensive. The aim of the directive just noted, however, was to be carried out that fall. Consequently, the attack in the Stalingrad area continued.

For a while it seemed that the relentless, vicious thrust of German armies would prove too strong for the Russians to withstand. The Sixth Army, under General von Paulus, had penetrated the suburbs of Stalingrad by mid-September. In both armor and aircraft the Germans were, for the time being, superior. The Russian defense, however, was dogged beyond description. When the streets of Stalingrad became the "front" in October and

November, Russian soldiers seemed to occupy every house, every factory, every building of every kind. To gain some notion of the kind of fighting that went on in the burning city from mid-October until the following January, and because Stalingrad came to mark a turning point in the war, the following extended description of that fighting is justified. It is from a letter written by a German lieutenant who took part in it:

We have fought during fifteen days for a single house, with mortars, grenades, machine-guns and bayonets. Already by the third day fifty-four German corpses are strewn in the cellars, on the landings, and the staircases. The front is a corridor between burnt-out rooms; it is the thin ceiling between two floors. Help comes from neighboring houses by fire escapes and chimneys. There is a ceaseless struggle from noon to night. From storey to storey, faces black with sweat, we bombard each other with grenades in the middle of explosions, clouds of dust and smoke, heaps of mortar, floods of blood, fragments of furniture and human beings. Ask any soldier what half-an-hour of hand-to-hand struggle means in such a fight. And imagine Stalingrad; eighty days and eighty nights of hand-to-hand struggles. The street is no longer measured by metres but by corpses. . . .

Stalingrad is no longer a town. By day it is an enormous cloud of burning, blinding smoke; it is a vast furnace lit by the reflection of the flames. And when night arrives, one of those scorching, howling, bleeding nights, the dogs plunge into the Volga and swim desperately to gain the other bank. The nights of Stalingrad are a terror for them. Animals flee this hell; the hardest stones cannot bear it for long; only men endure.[8]

On November 19 the Russians staged a counteroffensive for which they had been long preparing. Within three days the entire German Sixth Army and part of the Fourth Panzer Army were ringed by rampaging Russian forces. Von Paulus requested permission

7. H. R. Trevor-Roper, ed., *Hitler's War Directives, 1939–1945*, Sidgwick and Jackson, London, 1964, p. 130.

8. Alan Clark, *Barbarossa, The Russian–German Conflict, 1941–45*, William Morrow and Company, New York, 1965, p. 238.

GATEWAY TO STALINGRAD

*General Rommel here confers with members of his staff not long before the El Alamein assault.*

*Some Scots Guards press forward behind British tanks in the great thrust from El Alamein.*

to withdraw; Hitler curtly refused, and ordered every man to stand or die. Throughout the next two months the terrible encounter went on. On February 2 von Paulus, unable to carry on the struggle and forbidden to retire (indeed, unable at that point to break out of the Russian encirclement), surrendered what was left of his battered army. The great German drive to occupy the "town" and smash the forces concentrated there had ended in disaster. Never again was the dread Wehrmacht to threaten the Volga; indeed, from this time on, its course was, except for one passing moment, backward to Berlin.

## El Alamein and "Torch"

Meanwhile, in North Africa, a decisive battle was taking place. We have seen that in the spring of 1942 Axis forces under Rommel had pushed to within 70 to 80 miles of Alexandria. Churchill, gravely disturbed by this threat to the Suez Canal and British control of much of the Near East, ordered General Montgomery (newly assigned to Africa) to make whatever preparations were necessary to destroy the *Afrika Korps*. To this end Montgomery reorganized the Eighth Army,

instituted an elaborate program of tactical training for desert warfare, and built up equipment for the coming task.

Before Montgomery was ready for a new offensive, Rommel again attacked (August 31 —September 7, 1942). This time the British lines held. Rommel, unable to break through, and fearing his short fuel supply might leave him stranded in an indefensible position, ordered a general retreat. At this point Churchill urged Montgomery to mount his own attack. But Montgomery insisted that he was not yet ready. He promised that when he did move, in late October, he would not fail. On October 22 and 23 he laid down an artillery barrage designed to destroy Rommel's works on Miteiriya Ridge and then sent his columns

*Guns being brought off the beach by American troops, in the "Torch" operation, North Africa (1943).*

forward. For several days each side inflicted terrible punishment upon the other. Finally on November 5 Rommel began to give way. British and New Zealand troops, encouraged by their initial success, increased the fury of their attack until Rommel was in full retreat. Within three weeks Tobruk and Benghazi were again occupied. In January Tripoli and Mareth fell. In less than three months Allied forces, besides routing the famed *Afrika Korps,* had driven forward over 1000 miles and were within striking distance of Tunis, the gateway to Italy and Europe's "soft underbelly."

By this time a new phase of the North African war had developed. In July 1942, Roosevelt had agreed to Churchill's insistent request for an Anglo-American landing in North Africa. The complicated plans for this operation, whose code name was "Torch" and whose overall commander was General Dwight Eisenhower, were worked out by late October. The first landing occurred November 8, at almost exactly the same time as the beginning of Rommel's 1000 mile retreat. Much of the success of "Torch" hinged upon the responses of the French in Morocco and Algeria, technically under the control of the home government at Vichy. As it turned out, French forces, though ordered by Vichy to resist the landings, offered little opposition;

within three days all French territories in North Africa were ordered by Admiral Darlan, who had defected from his German-dominated homeland, to cooperate with the Allies. To counter this setback, Hitler at once decreed the occupation of all of France and readied plans to dispatch new forces to Tunisia.

The Allies had hoped by their pincer movement—Montgomery from the east, Eisenhower from the west—to close in on Tunis before German reinforcements could be concentrated there. Their hopes ran especially high because of the serious trouble the Germans were experiencing at Stalingrad which, it was believed, would prevent Hitler from feeling easy about diverting forces to Africa which he would need in the east. Despite his setback in the east, however, Hitler did send substantial reinforcements to Africa. During January and February of 1943, powerful attacks were launched against American forces along the Algeria-Tunisia border; for a time it seemed that the Americans might suffer serious defeat. But by early March they had checked the assault and, concerting now with British troops in the south, began a hard, sustained drive that ended in mid-May with the surrender of all Axis forces in Africa. The war was far from over; but Churchill's phrase, applied by him to an earlier development, may be used—for the Allies, it was "the end of the beginning."

## The Invasion of Italy

In early July 1943, British and American troops made landings along the coasts of southern and southeastern Sicily. For over a month they pushed the defending Axis forces, mostly Italians, to the north and east. By this time the Italians were clearly tired of the war. Although some of their troops fought bravely against the invaders, more seemed indifferent or even inclined to court quick defeat. By the end of July most of the island was conquered. No secret was made of what the next move would be. Soon and certainly the peninsula would be under direct attack. In these circumstances grumblings were raised against the Fascist regime. For three years Italy had suffered humiliating defeats—in Greece, in North Africa, in East Africa, and in Sicily. There was no assurance that Mussolini's warriors—what was left of them, for besides tens of thousands killed, hundreds of thousands had been captured—would be able to stop the Allies once they had gained bridgeheads on the peninsula; indeed, quite the contrary.

Faced with this prospect, the Fascist Grand Council called a meeting in Rome on July 25. Although presided over by the Duce, the Council demanded that King Victor Immanuel III form a new government. Mussolini was arrested, and the King appointed Marshal Pietro Badoglio as the new prime minister. To forestall an immediate German take-over of his country, Badoglio assured the Germans that Italy intended to remain in the war as their ally. Actually, secret negotiations were almost immediately opened with the Allies.

Meanwhile the conquest of Sicily was completed (August 17, 1943). Almost at once plans were begun for the invasion of Italy. Lieutenant General Mark Clark was ordered to lead an amphibious attack on Salerno, just north of Naples, a few days after General Montgomery had crossed the Straits of Messina to advance up the toe of the Italian boot. These operations were carried out between September 3 and 9. On September 8 the Italian government announced its withdrawal from the war (in accord with a secret agreement drawn up with the Allies five days before). The "Axis" had bent and broken. *Festung Europa* was now under direct attack.

## Battle of Guadalcanal

Simultaneously with the opening of a new front in southern Europe, American (and later Australian) forces began an offensive in the Pacific. The place chosen was Guadalcanal, one of the southernmost islands of the Solomons (see map, p. 594). Earlier the

*U. S. Marines start ashore from their landing craft on the Guadalcanal beach, August 4, 1942.*

Japanese had established a formidable base at Rabaul on the island of New Britain. From Rabaul Japanese air and naval forces were sent out to defend the southern stretches of the "defensive ribbon." If Rabaul could be eliminated, Allied forces would be in a good position to mount an attack on the Philippines and, ultimately, against the main islands of Japan. A second reason for choosing Guadalcanal was its proximity to the Australian base at Port Moresby, New Guinea, then threatened by the Japanese.

In August 1942, about 17,000 Marines landed on Guadalcanal and set about consolidating their position. The Japanese countered with strong air and naval attacks in an attempt to destroy the landing contingent, or at least to cut off its supply line. The first objective was not achieved, the second only partially. They therefore turned to reinforcing their own garrison. By mid-September the Japanese felt strong enough to launch their first offensive which, however, had to be broken off after only two days of fighting.

For the next four months both sides alternated offensive and defensive actions. Although the island was only about 90 miles long and 20 to 25 miles across, the rugged terrain made advances by either side always hazardous and usually costly. The following account gives some idea of the jungle conditions.

Among and beneath the trees thrives a fantastic tangle of vines, creepers, ferns and bush,

*U. S. Marines move through a tropical jungle of Guadalcanal to attack Japanese forces entrenched along a river a short distance ahead.*

*Japanese prisoners on Guadalcanal. Not many prisoners were taken in the whole operation.*

impenetrable even to the eye for more than a few feet. Exotic birds inhabit its upper regions; the insect world permeate the whole in extraordinary sizes and varieties; ants whose bite feels like a live cigarette against the flesh, improbable spiders, wasps three inches long, scorpions and centipedes. The animal kingdom is less numerous, represented by species of rats, some distant relatives of the possum, lizards ranging in length from three inches to three feet, a few snakes mostly of the constrictor type, and some voracious leeches peculiar in that they live in trees and drop upon the unwary passer-by from above.[9]

But the instruments of modern war, the elaborate, dug-in positions of the Japanese, and the sustained fury of their fighting, made the hazards of jungle or mountain seem almost trivial by comparison. No narrative can really convey the experience of a prolonged, bloody battle. So much has been included here only to indicate something of the nature of the half-year struggle that has been called the turning point in the Pacific War.

By early February 1943, the Japanese were forced to withdraw from Guadalcanal. It was the first land battle in which they had been defeated. No more than the German

9. Frank O. Hough, *The Island War*, J. B. Lippincott Company, Philadelphia and New York, 1947, p. 41.

withdrawal from Africa did it signify the imminent end of the war. But, like that defeat, it did mean that a great aggressor nation had had its seemingly invincible war machine brought to at least a temporary halt. For the Allies it meant new hope and greater confidence in plans they were working out for future offensives.

## THE ROAD BACK, 1943 TO 1945

### Russian Offensives, 1943 to 1944

The Russian offensive that had begun November 19, 1942 did not stop with the surrender of the German Sixth Army and the reoccupation of Stalingrad. The push continued for three months, sending the Germans back to Kharkov and, in the south, to Dnepropetrovsk. In an effort to regain the initiative, Hitler ordered a counteroffensive to begin February 18, 1943. A month's heavy fighting brought the reconquest of Kharkov and Belgorod. Then the Russians stiffened, and the German drive bogged down in March mud.

The fact that Hitler mounted no new offensive in the spring of 1943 was a plain indication that the tide of war had turned. Now he had a number of new and ominous developments to contend with. Axis defeat in Africa clearly heralded an Allied inva-

WORLD WAR II
RUSSIAN COUNTER-THRUST 1943-1945

Map by J. Donovan

sion of Italy. By 1943, too, Russian partisans behind the German line were proving a serious embarrassment.* By this time also,

American aid was pouring into Russia on a colossal scale. It is true that for a week in early July a Nazi rally was attempted, but its slow progress, combined with the Allied invasion of Sicily, caused Hitler to call it off and go on the defensive.

---

* Ironically, this was largely Hitler's own doing. Many Ukrainians had welcomed the early defeat of Stalin's armies. All evidence indicates that if Hitler had treated them as allies, many if not most would have fought for a German victory. But the Führer, caught up in his own racist propaganda, would not listen to this; so

that the Ukrainians soon turned to sabotaging the forces they had originally hailed as saviors.

The next month the Russians opened
a new drive that sent the once-vaunted
Wehrmacht reeling backward. The two-year
siege of Leningrad was finally lifted;
Smolensk, Kiev, and Odessa were retaken.
By June 1944, Soviet troops had not only
cleared large portions of their homeland of
the Nazi invader but were themselves standing on foreign soil (portions of Rumania).

### The Invasion of France

Meanwhile the long-awaited second front,
carpingly demanded by Stalin, had opened
on the Normandy beaches of France. As
early as 1942 it had been broached and debated. But Britain had been too weak and
America too far from massive mobilization
for D-Day to be scheduled that early. By
1943 the changed circumstances we have
noted in the preceding section made realistic
planning for that day feasible. In November
Roosevelt, Churchill, and Stalin had met at
Tehran to work out its broad features and
general timing. For months thereafter about
a half thousand American and British personnel pooled their plans, hopes and, often,
doubts.

D-Day was originally set for June 5, 1944.
All branches and sections of the British,
American, Canadian, and Free French forces
cooperated fully in an effort to make the
landing successful. For several months Allied
planes had systematically bombed terminals
and transport facilities so that German troops
and supplies could not be moved up to the
attack area. They also concentrated on
further clipping the wings of the once-power-
ful Luftwaffe. They were more than moderately successful in both efforts. In addition,
everything was done to convince the Germans (what they already were quite sure of)
that landings would be made in the Calais
area, close to England's Dover Beach. Actually, the chosen site was a 60-mile stretch of
beach along the eastern shores of the Normandy Peninsula, some five times farther
from England than the Calais area.

For their part the Germans had made a

*The Nazis drove many steel pilings along the
coasts facing England to slow down an invasion attempt. Here, some are used by American
troops as cover during their D-Day landing.*

large section of the coast facing England a
vast and vicious obstacle course: under-
water mines and stakes, mined obstacles on
the beaches, and an "Atlantic Wall of case-
mated and mobile guns, so placed as to en-
filade the dry parts of the beaches, with
plenty of land mines planted behind them."[10]
Strong detachments of German troops were
in the area, but the bulk of Hitler's defense
forces remained stationed near Calais.

Because of bad weather General Eisenhower, supreme commander of "Overlord,"
as the whole operation was called, postponed
the invasion one day. Then, on June 6, 1944,
the giant armada moved against the European fortress. The events of the landings,
to be described meaningfully, would take
far more space than a general account
such as ours allows. Here it can only be emphasized that the operation was far more
costly and near to failure than most
Americans still realize. Will, courage, indescribable suffering, and some strange

10. Morison, *op. cit.,* p. 395. For a detailed description of the preparations by both the
Allies and the Germans, and a vivid narration of the first landings, see pp. 384–404.

*Supply ships unloading along the Normandy coast. Barrage balloons were sent up to protect the operation from attacking Nazi planes.*

twists of chance combined to place and maintain parts of seven divisions of Allied troops along that strip of hell. A month later more than a million soldiers had been channeled through the break and had fanned out in three directions.* In mid-August another Allied force invaded southern France. For the next four months the two contend-

* It was at this point that the famous "Generals' Plot" to depose Hitler was carried out. On July 20, 1944, a bomb was planted in Hitler's conference room by Colonel Stauffenburg, one of the leading figures in the German resistance movement. The room was wrecked, and two persons were killed, but Hitler escaped with only minor injuries.

*British troops establishing a beachhead in Normandy, D-Day, June 6, 1944.*

The Third Reich came to an official end on May 8, 1945 when Colonel-General Alfred Jodl, newly appointed Chief of Staff of the German Army, signed the unconditional surrender papers. The ceremony took place in a little red schoolhouse in Reims, France.

ing forces mauled each other in a complicated and often confused series of bloody battles.

## The Collapse of Germany

In the meantime the Russians had launched a new drive (July 1944) that was to evolve, over the next ten months, into a kind of rippling, accordion offensive. At no time were German troops given rest for very long. For a while the Northern Front would ex-

plode into action; as it subsided the southern flank would take fire; then the center, then the Northern or Southern Front again until by January 1945 Soviet troops were poised for the breakthrough into Germany. A month before, Hitler had attempted (in what has come to be called the Battle of the Bulge) to drive the Anglo-American armies back to the coast, establish a new defense line, and turn again to deal with his eastern foes. But by this time he lacked the strength to

## THE ALLIED VICTORY
### D-DAY JUNE 6, 1944 — V-E DAY MAY 8, 1945

SWEDEN

*Baltic Sea*

★Copenhagen

DENMARK

UNITED KINGDOM

*North Sea*

ALLIED AIR ASSAULT

NETHERLANDS
★The Hague

London

Oder R.

★Berlin

Feb.-May, 1945

Russian forces

V-E DAY

D DAY

Calais

★Brussels

*Sept., 1944*

BELGIUM

Battle of the Bulge

Rhine R.

March-May, 1945

GERMANY

Prague

*U.S., United Kingdom and Canadian forces*

LUX.

March-May, 1945

Paris ★

Danube R.

Vienna

FRANCE

SWITZERLAND

Vichy

VICHY FRANCE

Trieste

Milan

*April, 1945*

ITALY

Genoa

Bologna

Free French and U.S. Aug., 1944

SPAIN

Marseilles

0    100    200 mi.

Map by J. Donovan

gain new victories anywhere. German cities and factories were bombed around the clock. Allied forces in Italy had reached the Po Valley. Strong armies were beating in on him from the east and from the west. For nearly six years German armed might had made a terrible and deep mark upon vast stretches of Europe. Now it was opposed by three great industrial powers whose combined populations, armies, navies, air forces, industrial plants, and technological skills were

beyond coping with by any single nation.* During the winter and spring of 1945 German armies steadily retreated on all fronts. On April 30, Hitler, who had entombed himself in an underground compound in Berlin, despaired of effecting a breakthrough and committed suicide. In his last will and testa-

* By this time the Germans stood practically alone; Italy, Rumania, Bulgaria, and Finland had already succumbed to the same driving power that was now crushing Germany.

ment he set up a new government, headed by Grand Admiral Karl Doenitz, to carry on the war. But within the week the new government had agreed to unconditional surrender to the Allies. The 1000 Year Reich had lasted barely twelve years.

## The End of the War in the Pacific

As we have seen, in the late fall of 1942 American amphibious forces had landed on Guadalcanal and, after six months of severe fighting, had forced the Japanese to withdraw. But only a toehold had been gained. All of the great island cluster groups in the Pacific west of Hawaii still remained under Japanese control; all were heavily fortified. The rim of eastern Asia, from Manchuria to Malaya, likewise constituted a formidable redoubt. Japanese land, sea, and air units were at full strength, and were fired with a savage spirit hard for Westerners to understand. If the Allies were to take as long to conquer all the other islands as was taken to capture Guadalcanal, a half-century would be required.

As finally worked out, Allied strategy called for the conquest of two key areas—the Philippines and Burma. If the Philippines could be retaken and held, offensive operations by sea and air could be launched, via Formosa and Okinawa, against Japan itself. Reconquest of Burma would open the way into China and territories to the south. To achieve the conquest of the Philippines, MacArthur decided upon what came to be called the leapfrog approach. Many Japanese bases were stationed along the New Guinea coast. To invest and capture all of them would have taken far more time—and cost far more casualties—than the Americans could afford. So the practice was adopted of attacking certain strategic points, securing them, and then bypassing other Japanese-held bases to attack still others farther on. In this way the bypassed stations were sealed off and allowed to "wither on the vine." The second objective was to be achieved by amphibious

landings among the Solomon Islands until the whole group was under Allied control. Thereafter each giant pincer would close down on the Philippines.

American and Australian troops under MacArthur spent most of 1943 and 1944 inching along the New Guinea coast. All the way the Japanese offered resistance that again must be labeled indescribable and incomprehensible except to the men who encountered it. One example is offered to indicate the impossible proportions of both description and understanding. Off the northeastern coast of New Guinea lies the island of Biak. It is a very small thrust of coral reef jutting out of the sea, some 50 miles long and 25 miles wide. United States forces were landed there May 27, 1944 with orders to take and secure the airfield, and to clear the Japanese from the island. One participant has estimated that walking distance from where the troops landed to the airdrome was hardly a half hour. It took four weeks of heavy fighting for the troops (finally using tanks and flamethrowers) to secure that airstrip "one half hour away."

Two years of this kind of fighting were required to move Americans and Australians along both areas of the pincers. In October 1944 the United States Sixth Army invaded Leyte in the Philippines. By January 1945 its defenders had been cleared out, and American troops occupied the island. For the next eight months the Japanese, under General Tomoyaki Yamashita, fought to keep their hold on Luzon, the largest of the islands. Meanwhile, other Allied forces attacked and occupied Iwo Jima and Okinawa (February to June 1945) in preparation for the grand assault against the home islands of Japan.

On the mainland of Asia the Allies launched a series of offensives (1944 to 1945) to regain Burma and reopen the road to China. By January 1945, the Ledo Road had been cleared and the way opened to join forces with Generalissimo Chiang Kai-shek's

*The battleship* Missouri *was the setting for the end of the Pacific War. In the right foreground, General Douglas MacArthur is being saluted by British General A. E. Percival and American Lieutenant-General Jonathan Wainwright. The Japanese delegation, facing the camera, somberly awaits the signing ceremonies.*

long-isolated armies. This was accomplished in the early spring, breaking Japan's hold on China. By June and July, Chiang's troops controlled nearly 300 miles of the coast north of Hong Kong.

By this time it was clear that Japan's fighting days were numbered. Cut off from the resources of Indonesia by the Philippine-China offensives, open to attack from both the south and the east, her industrial cities under steady bombardment, her carrier force all but annihilated, and her air power seriously crippled, she was unable to mount counteroffensives or even hope to hold on to her severely restricted positions. And, of course, the collapse of Germany in May 1945 meant that even stronger Allied pressures would soon be applied.

On July 16, 1945, the United States completed successful tests of its newly devised nuclear bomb. On August 6 it was dropped on Hiroshima, demolishing almost half of the city and killing some 90,000 persons. Another atomic bomb was dropped on Nagasaki three days later. Simultaneously Russia declared war on Japan and invaded Manchuria. Although the *samurai* spirit of many of Japan's warriors led them to demand a fight to the finish, the Emperor and his advisors opened negotiations with the Allies. On August 14 Japan's virtually unconditional surrender was accepted, bringing to an end nearly six years of global carnage.

## EFFECTS OF THE WAR

Before considering the peace settlements and the events of the postwar years, let us make a summary assessment, leaving the details for later discussion. What had World War II accomplished, and at what price? What changes had it worked in the world? What prefigurations had it effected for the future? What had it done to the spirit of man?

The war had, of course, blocked the expansionist schemes of Germany, Japan, and Italy; it had, indeed, caused the prewar areas under their control to be substantially reduced. It had prevented the establishment of Hitler's New Order in Europe, and the creation of a Japanese "Co-prosperity Sphere" in eastern and southeastern Asia. It had discredited the openly avowed Fascist and Nazi ideologies. It had, at least nominally, given a setback to the notion of "heroic" violence as a way of life. These accomplishments, so easily stated, saved contemporary man from degradations and miseries which, in the turmoil of recent years, he may be tempted to slight. If so, a serious study of the concentration camp culture of Nazi Germany and the savage regimen once imposed over large parts of Asia and the Pacific by the Japanese military—to say nothing of the regimented life concocted by Italy's balcony Caesar—is in order. On the other hand, attention will presently be called to the paradoxical assumption by postwar man, particularly Americans, of some of the totalitarian spirit and habits destroyed at such cost in the years of World War II; neither truth should be allowed to cancel out the other.

The cost in human life and suffering and in material goods is beyond any reasonable calculation. Even if such calculation were possible, the statistical statements would be quite meaningless; the human mind simply cannot personalize abstract figures dealing with such phenomena. Particular statistics may afford a vague hint, hardly more. In Soviet Russia alone military and civilian casualties directly or indirectly resulting from the war have been estimated at twenty million; Chinese battle *deaths* (not casualties, which included the wounded) numbered over two million; probably as many civilians were killed. In Germany, *air raid casualties alone,* military and civilian, approximated one million; over three million German soldiers were killed in battle.

Nor can an accurate, or even very meaningful, assessment be made of the shattering impact upon the overall "human condition" —self-respect, the right of a man to decide for himself what he should or should not do, faith in elemental human dignity and worth —effected by massive dislocations of many nationals during and after the war. Large segments of the populations of Poland, Belgium, the Netherlands, Italy and (to a lesser extent) France were taken into Germany during the war as slave laborers. All were mercilessly overworked, underfed, under-

clothed, and poorly housed. Tens of thousands died from such treatment; many suffered permanent disablement; all were marked by the psychic shock of forced reversion, in the important dimension of decision making, to the dependent status of children. Moreover, millions of Europeans were uprooted from their homelands as a result of the postwar takeover of large areas by Russia and Poland. Naturally, disruption of the normal patterns of living was suffered also by local populations that were forced to make room for and accommodate themselves to the incoming groups.

Out of the war, and partly (although only partly) because of it, emerged two great world powers—the United States and the U.S.S.R. Both had been strong states before the war; in the years that immediately followed it they became, for better or worse, the arbiters of international events. Later— by the mid-1960s—China developed power and influence of such dimensions that it should probably now be counted as the world's third great power.

The war also prefigured certain phases of the developing struggle between capitalism and socialism. Before the twentieth century there was no socialist society (as an organized, sovereign state) anywhere in the world. Between the wars Russia became and remained the sole socialist society.* In the 1960s there were about a dozen socialist states, with combined populations accounting for over one third of the world's total. In a very real sense the contest has taken on aspects closely paralleling the conflict waged in the sixteenth and seventeenth centuries between Protestant and Catholic protagonists. Then, many rulers and peoples alike believed that their opponents were devils, certain to bring destruction to mankind if allowed to

* Several nations, such as Britain and Sweden, have either had socialist governments for a period, or have developed a mixed economy. Here the referent is nationwide nationalization of industry and agriculture under seemingly permanent socialist governments.

preach and practice their doctrines. Then, as now, many on both sides were sincerely convinced that (what today we call) peaceful coexistence was impossible; the only alternatives were conversion or destruction.

This polarization of politico-economic systems naturally led to significant new political alignments. During the war, Britain, France, Russia, China, and the United States were allied against Germany, Italy, and Japan. Spain, under Franco, although not a belligerent, was correctly considered by the Allies as an Axis fellow traveler. Not long after the war an almost complete reversal of commitments developed. As the leader of the so-called free world, the United States came to lean heavily upon the support of West Germany, Japan, Italy and, to a lesser extent, Spain. Conversely, Russia, mainland China, and their allies have become our opponents.

In Africa and Asia, the slogans and energies of the war—as well as the opportunities that were offered at its conclusion—stimulated many of their so-called underdeveloped peoples to shake off colonial bonds. In the next chapter we will consider some of the details of this portentous revolution.

Finally, and no less significantly, the war fastened upon the victors, especially the United States, some of the most reprehensible features of the totalitarian way of life that they had risked so much to destroy. Since the war, and in no small part because of it and the events that flowed out of it, the United States itself has taken on some of the features of a militaristic state. No matter how "normal" peacetime conscription may seem to persons under thirty, it is a drastic postwar innovation that runs counter to a humane tradition dating from Jeffersonian times. The United States military budget annually runs to over fifty billion dollars. The country's industrial complex and its military establishments have become so intimately connected that President Eisenhower, a professional soldier, warned against its ominous implications in his farewell message of 1960. As a further example, our federal secret agencies in recent years have become so numerous and so powerful that neither Congress nor the Chief Executive has always been able to control them, or even, on occasion, to know what they were planning. However anomalously, one of the fateful consequences of World War II was that the victors took on some of the features of the violent Sir Society they had vanquished.

# C. The Road to "Peace"

## MAKING PEACE

### New Conditions of Peacemaking

The normal protocol of peacemaking was only partly followed after World War II. In 1919 representatives of the Allied governments met in Paris, debated, decided what was to be done, composed an elaborate document, and presented it to the German delegates for their signature. With less fanfare and ceremony the same general procedure was followed in dealing with the lesser losing powers. Proceedings after World War II were quite different. It is true that treaties with Bulgaria, Rumania, Italy, Finland, Hungary, Austria, and Japan were written and duly ratified. But, for one thing, the time lapse between the ending of hostilities and the ratification of treaties was much greater—ten years, in the case of Austria. For another, not all of the victorious powers signed all of the treaties that were presented to the vanquished. Russia, for example, refused to ratify the Japanese treaty. Furthermore, many provisions were relatively meaningless because of their *ex post facto* nature. In some treaties the amount of reparations was kept low or even passed over, on the surface a generous gesture. Actually much wealth of various kinds had been taken from the defeated countries (Austria, for example) by the occupying power before the treaties were formulated. Finally, the Allies were unable to agree on a solution to the German problem, leaving that nation divided into Eastern and Western states.

Most of these unsatisfactory and confusing developments grew out of two related circumstances. One was the imposition on the defeated powers of unconditional surrender terms; the second followed naturally —the complete occupation and governance of the defeated nations by the victors or their puppets. At Versailles in 1919 a sovereign German state was, as it were, party of the second part. In 1945 there were no sovereign defeated states.* Their official governments were made up of foreign conquerors who ruled without restrictions, for varying periods of time. Under these conditions formal peace treaties were almost superfluous. The victors arranged what they wanted as completely as the possibilities permitted, including the eventual setting up of local governments preconditioned to accept whatever treaty terms the victors should decide upon. A rough analogue is found in our Reconstruction history; then, the North occupied the South, for a while governed it absolutely, and dictated the new state constitutions.

## The Peace Treaties

In light of these general circumstances let us briefly note the peace arrangements

---

* With the exception of Finland. It should be understood that the Communist Balkan governments—such as Yugoslavia's—were under the control of directives from Moscow. Technically these countries were not subject to unconditional surrender terms and official occupation; actually Russia or its puppets dominated all of them.

that followed the ending of hostilities. In the early years of the war, Finland, together with Bulgaria, Rumania, and Hungary (three Nazi puppets) entered the conflict on the side of Germany, as did Austria, then a German "province." Believing that a general settlement with these nations and with their Axis mentors should not be rushed through as had the Versailles settlement of 1919, Russia, Britain, and the United States decided upon a series of preliminary meetings. At these meetings the foreign ministers of Russia, Britain, the United States, France, and China were to explore the victors' legitimate demands and their relationship to the capacities and reasonable needs of the vanquished. It was hoped that a general blueprint would develop that could be submitted to a plenary conference of Allied representatives.

The scheme did not work out quite as planned. Meetings held during the next nine months in London, Moscow, and Paris revealed serious differences between the Western powers and China on the one hand, and Russia on the other. Reparations, boundary adjustments, and the disposition of Italy's African colonies were major objects of disagreement. Beyond these, and more significant, was the rapidly disintegrating rapport between Russia and the other Allies which the war had created and sustained. Nevertheless, agreements for treaties with Italy, Bulgaria, Rumania, Hungary, and Finland were finally reached at a fourth meeting of the representatives (June to July 1946). All of the treaties required the defeated nations to foreswear enactment of legislation that would discriminate against any of their nationals; all required establishment of democratic procedures; all required the relinquishing of some territories; and most provided for moderate reparations.

Continued efforts were directed toward concluding arrangements with Germany, Austria, and Japan. But by this time (1947) friction between Communist Russia and its wartime allies had increased to alarming proportions; further negotiations seemed only to aggravate it. In brief, a "cold war" was in the making, the features and incidents of which we shall consider later. In these circumstances the United States decided to take the initiative for a settlement with Japan, on the grounds that its occupation was no longer necessary and was also prohibitively expensive. Probably both contentions were true; but America's need to mend its foreign fences against a possible encounter with Russia was undoubtedly another, perhaps stronger, consideration. In 1950 a presidential mission sounded out other nations and recommended a general conference to decide upon acceptable terms. More than fifty nations, including the Soviet Union, met the next year for this purpose. The resulting treaty was ultimately ratified (1952) by most of the states. Russia was conspicuous among the nonsigners.* On the whole the treaty's terms were lenient. No formal reparations were required; the war guilt question was left unmentioned; Japan was invited to join the United Nations; although all of her former colonies and mandated territories were taken from her, her home islands were left intact. Unfortunately for the United States, similar initiative could not be taken to effect a settlement with Germany and Austria, since Russian forces occupied portions of both. Some years later (1955), when relations between Russia and the United States had improved, an Austrian treaty was negotiated not much different from those concluded with the five states mentioned earlier. But the German problem remained unsolved.

## EMERGENT ONE-WORLDISM

### The Pattern of Conferences

Even before the war's end, plans were made for the creation of a world organization that would prevent the coming of another great conflict. The basic motivation, of course, derived from man's growing realization that civilization and modern war are incompatible. Tactically the planning for a new world organization was made considerably easier by the habit formed during the war by the Big Three's leaders of holding face-to-face meetings to discuss mutual concerns. From 1943 to 1945 no less than five of these conferences brought the Allied heads of state together. Because the meetings dramatized the emergence of an incipient one-worldism (as well as produced decisions we need to note), we may give brief notice to them.

The first conference was set up by Roosevelt and Churchill at Casablanca (1943) to decide upon general matters of strategy and policy. Out of it came the decision to land troops in Africa (Operation Torch, see *supra,* p. 592) in preparation for the invasion of Europe, and the policy of unconditional surrender eventually applied to Italy, Germany, and Japan. Later that year Roosevelt, Churchill, and Chiang Kai-shek conferred in Cairo, and Roosevelt and Churchill moved on to Tehran in Persia. This afforded Roosevelt his first opportunity to meet Stalin who, understandably, urged the immediate opening of a Second Front; he also demanded the ultimate breaking up of Germany into a number of small states. In February 1945, as the ring was closing around Germany, the three leaders met again, this time in the Crimea at Yalta. In this meeting certain major decisions were reached: a defeated Germany was to be disarmed, demilitarized, and dismembered, as the Allies "might deem requisite for future peace and security"; Russia promised to declare war against Japan soon after Germany's defeat; certain territories in Asia were to be given to Russia; a new world organization would take the place of the discredited League of Nations. Following Germany's surrender in May 1945, Allied leaders—this time Attlee, who replaced Churchill after a Labour electoral victory, Truman, who became President in April 1945 upon the death of Roosevelt, and

* In 1956 Russia issued a declaration proclaiming that a state of war with Japan no longer existed.

## Creation of the United Nations Organization

*The Potsdam Conference "Big Three" here seem to be in a happy mood: Clement Attlee, British Prime Minister, President Harry Truman, and Premier Joseph Stalin.*

Stalin—met at Potsdam, a suburb of Berlin. To the three d's of the German policy outlined at Yalta, two others were added: denazification and democratization; and dismemberment was toned down to decentralization. It was also decided to divide Germany into four occupation zones until a general peace conference could meet and draw up a definite settlement. Berlin, deep in the Russian assigned area, was also divided into four spheres of occupation, one for each of the Big Three, and one for France.*

---

* For an overall view of America's participation and activities in these conferences, see Gaddis Smith, *American Diplomacy During the Second World War,* John Wiley and Sons, New York, 1965.

Plans for peace as well as war brought representatives to the great powers to the conference table from time to time during the war period. In 1941 Roosevelt and Churchill met in Canada to formulate a statement of war aims. To a later generation harassed by seemingly endless crises, the Atlantic Charter, as it came to be called, may seem highly idealistic. Both America and Britain foreswore any intention to annex foreign territories, promised to honor the wishes of the people concerned in whatever territorial changes were to be effected, unequivocally supported the principle of self-determination for every people, and declared their faith in the possibility of creating a world free from fear and want. In January 1943, representatives of twenty-six countries signed a pact embodying these principles. Later in the year the United Nations Relief and Rehabilitation Administration (U.N.R.R.A.) was created to provide food, clothing, and medical supplies to nations ravaged by the war.

When it became apparent in late 1944 that the war was drawing to an end, representatives of Britain, Russia, China, and the United States held a series of meetings in Dumbarton Oaks (in Washington, D.C.) to lay the groundwork for the creation of the new international organization. Early the next year (April to June 1945) representatives from fifty nations met in San Francisco to draw up a constitution for the new organization, to be called the United Nations. To carry out its purposes—to maintain world peace, to "develop friendly relations among nations," and to "encourage respect for human rights" and freedoms—three main bodies were created. One, the General Assembly, was commissioned to consider world problems of almost any kind and to make recommendations about what should be done. Every member was given one vote; all

The Dumbarton Oaks Conference, 1944, was held to lay the groundwork for an organization to take the place of the League of Nations. Key figures, shown above, beginning second from left, are Lord Halifax, British ambassador to the United States, Cordell Hull, U. S. Secretary of State, Andrei Gromyko, Russian ambassador to the United States, and Edward R. Stettinius, U. S. Undersecretary of State.

Soviet Russia's delegation included these representatives at the opening session of the United Nations General Assembly (October 1946): N. V. Novikov, ambassador to the United States, Andrei Vishinsky, Deputy Foreign Minister, and V. M. Molotov, Foreign Minister. Vishinsky was the ferocious prosecutor of the "Old Bolsheviks" in the 1936 to 1938 purge trials.

resolutions required a majority vote for passage. The size of the second body, the Security Council, was limited to eleven members (now fifteen), including five permanent members: the United States, Britain, France, the Soviet Union, and "Nationalist" China. Both the United States and the U.S.S.R. insisted upon the right of each Council member to exercise an absolute veto whenever its national interests indicated the need for it. Thus, although the Council was given the right to sanction the use of military force to oppose aggression, the negative vote of any one of the Council's members could stop U.N. action. None of the great states would have agreed to become working members of the organization if this provision had not been included. Otherwise, they stood the chance of being outvoted on a sanctions measure by small states that could not assume the power responsibility for making the decision effective. The third branch, the General Secretariat, was set up to exercise

executive functions much in the manner of the American presidency. Finally, like the old League, the U.N. also was given the authority to set up a number of auxiliary organizations dealing, for example, with labor and health conditions, the world's food supply, and the problem of coordinating international civil aviation activities. It should be emphasized that despite the panoply of powers given to the new world body it was intended to be, and remains, a loose confederation of sovereign states.

At war's end most of the peoples of the world seemed genuinely to want an international body strong enough to prevent a recurrence of war. Naturally the construction and use of the A-bomb played a part in shaping this seemingly strong desire. But the six years of violence even without that bomb undoubtedly played a larger part. Many living then had known the horrors of World War I. For them it was not easy to imagine meaningful existence if man were doomed to

*A 1945 United States cartoon, expressing the feeling that probably most Americans then held toward the new world peace organization.*

look forward to World War III, or World War VIII, or World War XXVIII. On the other hand, no people or its leaders stood then—or now—for the abolition of national sovereignty, without which no world organization could substitute its constabulary for national armies. It is beyond the competence of the historian—as historian—to judge the rightness or wrongness of this position; the fact of the position and the implications rising from it, however, cannot be ignored.

In any case, within ten years after the outbreak of World War II, a new world organization, dedicated to peace and human progress, was operating within and occasionally significantly upon the web of world affairs. But in the succeeding decades of mounting crises and tensions its overall influence, hardly surprisingly, rarely prevailed when opposed by the forces of traditional power politics. In the concluding sections of the next chapter we shall point out some of the difficulties with which this organization had to contend.

## SELECTED READINGS

Bailey, Thomas A., *The Diplomatic History of the American People,* Appleton-Century-Crofts, New York, 1958 (6th ed.).

The appropriate chapters of this readable text should be consulted, especially for an understanding of how American public opinion helped to shape the diplomatic decisions of this period.

Churchill, Winston S., *The Second World War,* Houghton Mifflin, Boston, 1948–1953 (6 vols.).

The set, as would be expected, contains very much and very valuable material not found in any other account. But it is not, of course, an unbiased history; and the reader should keep in mind Churchill's admission, made in private conversation before the work was written, that no statesman in writing his memoirs should be so lacking in good sense as to include material which unfavorably reflects upon his own doings and decisions.

Divine, Robert A., *The Reluctant Belligerent: American Entry into World War II,* John Wiley & Sons, New York, 1965.

A brief account of, as the author sees it, America's steady bungling in international affairs from the early 1930s to the Japanese attack at Pearl Harbor.

Hall, Walter Phelps, *Iron Out of Calvary,* Appleton-Century Company, New York, 1946.

An interpretive account of World War II. Where Liddell Hart concentrates on battle plans and actions, Hall tends to subordinate these to narration of why battles turned out as they did, and their political implications.

*Liddell Hart, Basil H., *The German Generals Talk,* Berkeley Publishing Corporation, New York, 1948.

The author held long interviews with many of the leading lights of the *Wehrmacht* and gives here a close, often verbatim account of their views of what went right and wrong with the war.

*Hersey, John, *Hiroshima,* Bantam Books, New York, 1946.

* Asterisk (*) denotes paperback.

There are other, fuller, and more up-to-date books on the bombing of Hiroshima. Probably none can match this first one for total emotional impact.

Langer, William L., and S. Everett Gleason, *The Challenge of Isolation, 1937–1940,* Harper & Brothers, New York, 1952.
Detailed examination of America's response to aggression in Europe and Asia.

Langer, William L., and S. Everett Gleason, *The Undeclared War, 1940–1941,* Harper & Brothers, New York, 1953.
A nearly 1000-page examination of the aggressive ventures of Germany and Japan (1940–1941) and their impact on the policies and practices of Britain and the United States. Other nations—Russia (especially), France, China, Greece, Turkey, and Mexico, for example—are brought into the overall picture of the encounter between Axis powers and "Allied" powers. The authors support, in the main, the view that the United States government genuinely tried to keep out of a shooting war with Japan and Germany.

Morison, S. E., *The Two-Ocean War . . .,* Little, Brown & Company, Boston, 1963.
An abridged edition of the author's multi-volume history of the global operations of the United States Navy. Despite the salty tang and occasional derring-do rhetoric, this work is a rewarding study of some of the great sea battles of World War II.

*Neumann, Robert, with Helga Koppel, *The Pictorial History of the Third Reich,* Bantam Books, New York, 1962.
By strict category this book belongs on the reading list for the chapter on Nazi Germany. But it so much depicts the essence of the war spirit that it can, perhaps, most profitably be read with these books specifically dealing with World War II.

Sherwood, Robert E., *Roosevelt and Hopkins,* Harper & Brothers, New York, 1948.
A sympathetic duo-biography of the two men who administered America's foreign policy from 1941 to 1945.

Stipp, John L., ed., *Devil's Diary,* Antioch Press, Yellow Springs, Ohio, 1955.
A condensation of the more important documents relating to Nazi conspiracy and aggression which were collected by the United States government and published in ten volumes.

Von Wegerer, Alfred, *The Origins of World War II,* Richard R. Smith, New York, 1941.
A brief exposition (125 pages) of the events that led to the outbreak of World War II from the standpoint of a well-known German scholar. Written when the Nazi war machine was running wild in Europe, the book is an interesting study of how documents should not be used.

Wheeler-Bennett, John W., *Munich,* Duell, Sloan & Pearce, New York, 1962.
The best account of this very controversial event. The documentation is full, the interpretation is balanced with and based on the facts. The one area insufficiently covered is the British government's knowledge of and reaction to the plot to overthrow Hitler (an area to which, it should be added, no work has yet done justice).

Wohlstetter, Roberta, *Pearl Harbor, Warning and Decision,* Stanford University Press, Stanford, 1922.
A detailed analysis of the operations of U.S. intelligence agencies as they dealt with Japanese "signals" before the attack on Pearl Harbor. In the author's judgment there were no real villains or even very low level incompetents responsible for the general state of U.S. unreadiness at Pearl Harbor on December 8, 1941. Readers may reach a different conclusion after going through the source material provided.

# XVI

# *The World in Flux, 1940s to 1960s*

---

# A. Domestic Affairs

To bring the complexity and the pace of national and global events that have crowded the postwar years into a manageable unit of study four categories of developments will be considered: major trends within selected nations; the "decolonization" of Asia and Africa; the revival of Europe; and the more outstanding features of the cold war-coexistence syndrome.

## BRITAIN

### *The New and the Old*

An assessment of the meaning of basic developments in Britain since the war is made difficult by our habit of associating, even equating, significant experience with political and economic power. Judged by these two criteria alone, Britain no longer exercises a dominant, at times not even a substantial, influence in affairs that concern the world at large. In a later section we shall see

her war against Egypt abruptly called off by the fiat of other powers, particularly the United States and the U.S.S.R. A generation earlier such an event would have been almost unthinkable. Britain no longer rules the seas. Her once great empire has been transformed into a loose, voluntary association of sovereign states. Where once she was somewhat condescending toward Europe, she is now eager to win the approval of continental nations in her desire to associate with them in common economic and political activity. Her economic stature, like her political position, has changed drastically. At the turn of this century, British merchants controlled about 35 per cent of the world's trade; sixty years later this percentage had been cut in half. Since the end of World War II Britain's standard of living, although higher than any in her history, has failed to keep pace with the rate of rise developed by many other European states. Nevertheless, Britain re-

**At the End of the Rainbow**

*John Bull actually had little reason for showing the surprise that this cartoon depicts. England had never really economically recovered from World War I before World War II overtook her.*

mains one of the most mature societies, possibly the most mature, of the contemporary world. Admittedly the term "mature" is elastic and is susceptible to many categories and shades of meaning. Here it is meant to connote self-discipline, the ability to draw lines, tolerant understanding, respect for both the heritage of the past and the sometimes daring demands of the future—in short, ripe (so far as the limits of any age permit) wisdom. In a later section of this chapter we shall note Britain's (on the whole) graceful disencumbrance of imperial possessions. Although this weakened her command of economic resources that she had once considered vital to her existence and diminished her once strong influence on the flow of world events, in a larger sense it enriched the human basis of her collective life and, among the perceptive, enhanced her prestige. Dean Acheson, a former American secretary of state, publicly asserted in 1962: "Great Britain has lost

an empire and has not yet found a role. The attempt to play a separate power role . . . is about played out." Britain's then prime minister made a polite but pointed reply: "In so far as he appeared to denigrate the resolution and will of Britain and the British people, Mr. Acheson has fallen into an error which had been made by quite a lot of people in the course of the last 40 years."[1]

## Construction of the Welfare State

Probably the dominant theme of British life in the years after the war was the political and economic enlargement of the life of the common man. In feudal and early modern times, as we have seen in the first volume of this book, the landed noble—from knight to king—ruled the country. Later, throughout the eighteenth and nineteenth centuries, first the commercial and then the industrial elite gained dominant political power. In the early years of the twentieth century, particularly after 1910, the "little man," under the aegis of the rising socialist Labour Party, jostled with the privileged middle class for a greater share of both economic affluence and political influence*. Although the early Labour governments were short-lived and seemingly ineffectual, they set the national stage for and conditioned the public mind to the program of nationalization that was inaugurated in 1945.

In the general elections of that year the Conservative party, under the leadership of Winston Churchill, suffered a decisive, and rather surprising, defeat. Labour candidates received an absolute majority of the popular vote, and 61 per cent of the seats in the House of Commons. Although Churchill tended to think of the results of the election as a repudiation of his leadership, they were primarily brought about by other considerations. Britons remembered the doldrums that

* See Chapter XV.

1. Alfred F. Havighurst, *Twentieth Century Britain,* 2nd ed., Harper and Row, New York, 1966, p. 491.

plagued their economic life after World War I when, for most of the period, the Conservatives, either openly or under the cover of the label "coalition," dominated the nation's political life. More important, World War II had worked massive hardships on the home front. The working man was without adequate housing facilities, without prospects of full employment, without reasonable assurance that his subsistence needs would be met, and without a guarantee that his physical and mental health could be ministered to within the limits of his restricted income. On all these counts the Labour party spoke out firmly and in specific detail. The Conservative party, on the other hand, concentrated its efforts on a denunciation of creeping socialism and an acclamation of the merits of free enterprise.

Once in power the new socialist government lost no time in converting its campaign promises into national legislation. By 1947 it had enacted a comprehensive social welfare program that substantially changed the social fabric of the nation. First on its bill of particulars was the national banking system, which was nationalized in March 1946. Later, Conservative critics pointed out that the legislation was of little effect because the close connection between the Bank of England and the Treasury Department that the new Labour law now decreed had essentially existed long before its enactment. This was true, but it was not the whole truth. Although the new law left control of credit in the main to Bank officials, it also transmuted private stock in the Bank to public stock and substituted government-chosen directors for privately selected directors. Perhaps even more important, it effected a psychic gain for Labour leaders who remembered that, under its Conservative governor, the Bank in 1931 had directly participated in bringing down the Labour government.

In July 1946, Parliament passed the Coal Industry Nationalization Act. This law transferred the entire industry from private to public ownership, with compensation given

'I'm afraid we'll have to change your diet, sir'

*An American view of what kept Britain poor. As a Socialist, Prime Minister Clement Attlee was expected to recommend a broad program designed to redistribute the wealth and put the economy on an enduringly sound basis.*

to the private owners. Thereafter all coal mines were operated under the direct responsibility of the Minister of Fuel and Power, who appointed a National Coal Board of nine members to supervise the actual management of operations. The members of this board were drawn from private industry, trade unions, and the ranks of mining engineers. Civil Aviation and cable and wireless corporations were made public institutions during 1946 to 1947. Control of private investment was effected by passage of the Borrowing Act of 1946. The next year the Town and Country Planning Act empowered local authorities to direct the planning of property development. Also in 1947, wartime legislation dealing with the prices and marketing of farm products was extended. In the same year the Inland Transport Act brought railroads and trucking and bus concerns under government ownership and operations.

"It still tastes awful."

© Punch

*This* Punch *cartoon reflects the feelings with which most British physicians greeted the coming of socialized medicine. Twenty years later —in the 1960s—there was still some grumbling, but most practitioners supported the program. The initials on the bonnet stand for Aneurin Bevan, then Britain's Minister for Health.*

During this period a series of social service measures—the National Insurance Act, The Family Allowances Act, and the National Assistance Act (providing weekly food and shelter benefits for those in need of them)—were passed, thus assuring satisfaction of at least minimal subsistence needs for the whole population. In late 1946 one of the most controversial of all the socialist proposals was made into law—The National Health Service Act. The medical profession fiercely attacked the measure as it was originally drawn up. Doctors argued that lay control of medicine through agencies of government, a hospital service dominated by local political officials, and the making of major decisions for the profession by any authority other than licensed practitioners were impossible conditions which they could

not accept. In the end, the legislators contrived a measure that went about as far as any legislation could in providing a national health service in which the patient's needs were met within a framework of a patient-physician relationship that was basically similar to that of private practice.

Finally, housing and educational needs were given close attention. Under two housing acts (1946 and 1949) the government went directly into the business of supplying shelter to a population that was desperately in need of it. Many homes had been destroyed during the war and, because the resources and energies of the people were channeled almost wholly into war activities, few new homes had been built, so that by 1945 Britain was short about two million dwellings. Under the new acts, administered by the Ministry of Health, nearly one million new homes and apartments were built or repaired.

Educational needs were also urgent. Traditionally, what Americans would call "liberal education" beyond grammar school was reserved for children of the "gentlemen" class. In the 1940s, agitation for a more widely educated citizen body became insistent. With its egalitarian outlook, the Labour party naturally gave strong support to this demand. On coming to power, it made education compulsory up to the age of 15, undertook a massive construction of new school buildings, provided much needed facilities for training teachers, and increased instructors' salaries. In higher education, it authorized grants to build new (the famous "red brick") universities and expanded the facilities and programs of technical-training schools.

In short, under five years of Labour government, Britain was transformed into what is now commonly called the welfare state. Although most of the industry remained in private hands, government control was close and alertly watchful. In the main the changes were accepted by most classes in the country. Conservative leaders continued to criticize

the workings of much of the Labour legislation, but they were careful neither to call
for its repeal nor, when they returned to
power, to try to turn back the clock.

## Economic Problems

Because Britain's economy, more than
those of most other powers, fundamentally
rests on a favorable balance of trade—
selling more than buying from abroad—the
short-term value of the many changes that
were made depended on a tolerable prosperity that unfortunately did not develop.
A United States loan of over one and a half
billion dollars in 1945 to 1946 eased the
transition from war production to peacetime
production. But it could not, of course,
reverse the flow of the balance of trade.
As a matter of fact, terms of the loan,
especially the one which forced Britain to
convert pounds to dollars in all currency
areas, aggravated the dollar shortage and
penalized British trade. To redress the
trade balance Clement Attlee, the Labour
Prime Minister, and his colleagues devised
an austerity program that discomfited large
segments of the population. Labor grumbled
at the "Control of Engagements Order"
which, although rarely enforced, was designed to direct labor into jobs deemed most
important by the government. Meat and
gasoline rationing were reintroduced. Temporary monetary laws were passed which
precluded the importation of goods from
dollar areas. These and other restrictions
produced a voter reaction which in the
next general election, held in 1950, cut
into Labour's Parliamentary majority. In an
effort to regain a workable majority, the
Prime Minister dissolved Parliament the
next year (1951) and directed an "educa-
tive" campaign which backfired, resulting in
a Conservative victory.* For the next fifteen

years the Conservative party cautiously combined the more obviously popular achievements of the Attlee government with such
dynamics as remained in the free-enterprise
system. Although the Conservatives won the
elections of 1955 and 1959, the loyalty of
Britain's masses to the general Labour outlook and program was not substantially
weakened; of the seven general elections held
between 1945 and 1966, five produced a
popular majority for the Labour party. It
came as no great surprise, therefore, when
Labour returned to power in 1964 with
promises of "more of the same." Two years
later, in another general election, its Parliamentary majority was substantially increased.

Economic problems, under whatever government, harassed the nation throughout
most of the postwar years. Chief among
them, as already indicated, was the embarrassing gap between what Britain sold and
what she bought from abroad. In a later section we shall note her attempt, after an
initial refusal, to join certain European
powers in what is called the Common
Market. Whether the problems of her trade
imbalance, in or out of the Market, will be
solved, and under what economic system, is
beyond the competence of the historian to
say. Left to the future, too, is her continuing role in the new Commonwealth, her
relationship to the political and cultural life
of Europe, and her influence, or the lack
of it, on world affairs. History has taught us
not to sell Britain short; beyond that it is
not prudent to go.

## FRANCE AND ITALY

### France

Even the briefest survey of the history of
France since World War II presents unusual
difficulties. Encyclopedic details, of course,
could be cited at great length—the rise and
fall of governments, greater and lesser crises
marking intra- and interparty strife, ephemeral "solutions" to colonial problems, the
emergence and disappearance of leading

* Actually, the Labour candidates received, in the
overall count, more votes than the Conservative
candidates. Districting provisions accounted for
the slight Conservative majority in Parliament.

political figures, and the many heated disputes over how France might find herself again. Not all of these events, of course, turned out—or seem to be turning out—to be mere details. But even the strategic events are difficult to treat in a general way, because it is hard to delineate the overall profile of France. Granted that in a world in flux the profile of no one collective society is as clear as the student of history would like, the image of France is nevertheless particularly elusive. The very titles of books dealing with France since the 1930s often reflected this blurred view, such as *The Twilight of France* and *France Against Herself.*

### Economic Recovery; Rise in Birthrate

One development that seems to withstand focal distortion is the country's economic recovery after 1947 to 1948. Whether caused fundamentally by the nationalization of certain industries such as banking, coal, gas and electricity, and the major insurance companies, or by a remarkable venture in economic planning (the Monnet Plan, 1947–1951), the French standard of living in the 1950s and 1960s achieved an unprecedentedly high level. France became, for example, the only agriculturally self-sufficient country in Europe; at the same time the income of her industrial workers allowed mass consumption of such items as automobiles, television sets, and sports and vacation equipment.

Concurrently with the rise in living standards, and undoubtedly partly caused by it, there occurred a substantial increase in the population. Since the Napoleonic Wars, France (alone among the large nations of Europe) had suffered a relative decline in population. The unexpected reversal of this melancholy tradition had dramatic overtones. In many countries, including the United States, the current population explosion has taken on a menacing cast. In France, however, the phenomenon is looked upon

ONE CRISIS AFTER ANOTHER

*Despite an efficient civil service system, Frenchmen found their everchanging governments a constant source of apprehension and insecurity.*

not only as the actual substance of her new life, but also as a promising symbol of future greatness.

### From the Fourth to the Fifth Republic

Probably the most significant postwar event was the establishment of the Fifth Republic in 1958. In Chapter XV we noted the brief, wartime tenure of the Vichy regime. After the war a new constitution set up France's Fourth Republic (1946–1958). Many Frenchmen hoped that under its provisions a way would be found out of the morass of cabinet making-breaking that had marked the tortuous course of the Third Republic (1871–1940). They were disappointed. Premiers rose and fell with the same regularity as before (the average government lasted less than six months). About a half dozen parties sliced up the voting populace so finely and in such a bewildering fashion that no party, with the exception of the highly disciplined Communist party, could ever be sure of its weight from one day to another in the constantly shifting blocs and coalitions. Consequently, consistent policy, for all the vaunted competence of the permanent staff of civil servants, proved teasingly elusive.

Coupled with this embarrassingly carnival aspect of their political life was the tendency of Frenchmen to be plagued by the feeling that their nation had slipped out of the charmed "world-power" circle. Twice within the century they had been rescued from German victory and domination by the intervention of outside powers. As a symbol of their dependent status (as they saw it), the leader of their provisional government, Charles de Gaulle, was not allowed to accompany the first wave of the liberating armies in Normandy. Not until the Americans and British had things well in hand (nine days later) was the General given permission to set foot on his own land. And only by the gracious permission of American and British policy makers was France given a portion of defeated Germany to occupy. Even after her dramatic economic recovery, kaleidoscopic political changes seemed to make her a frail reed to lean upon. If, to many of that time, Europe seemed a diminishing force in world affairs, to sensitive Frenchmen their own country in that shrunken area appeared to count for even less.

De Gaulle's return to politics in 1958 changed this. Sensing the weary despair of his countrymen, he accepted appointment as premier with the express understanding that he would propose drastic constitutional changes pointing toward strong executive leadership.* Although some Frenchmen, and

In 1958 France approved the adoption of a new constitution that brought into being the Fifth Republic. Here, Charles De Gaulle, chief architect of the New Republic, is shown at a Paris campaign rally whipping up enthusiasm for the "New France."

all French Communists, saw this as the first move in the creation of a fascist regime, the majority nevertheless seemed to welcome it as the "sole remaining rampart between the Republic and Fascism." De Gaulle's constitution (he personally supervised the construction of every section of it) was submitted to the electorate in the fall of 1958 and received overwhelming approval. Its terms clearly marked the end of the old ways of the Third and Fourth Republics. The president, elected for seven years and eligible for reelection, was given the power to appoint both the prime minister and members of the cabinet. This meant that the Assembly could no longer overturn ministries at will because the government was not responsible to it. In addition, the Executive exercised the power of suggesting legislation to the Assembly which could approve or disapprove it, as well as initiate legislation itself. Significantly—particularly in view of the current crisis attending the Algerian revolt—the president was also granted the right to issue emergency decrees on his own authority, as well as the power to

---

* The precipitating force that brought France around to the acceptance of drastic change was the Algerian war, described in Section C. For a perceptive study of these "two Frances" and the meaning and methods of the Fifth Republic, see

Dorothy Pickles, *The Fifth French Republic,* Frederick A. Praeger, New York, 1960.

dissolve the Assembly and call for new elections.

Under the new Republic, France experienced a long period of political stability. Throughout de Gaulle's first seven-year term, only one government exercised power —the longest tenure of any government in the history of republican France. Reelected in 1966 for another seven years, the President gave all signs of maintaining this most un-Gallic record. Although welcoming the end of the old "who's in now?" game, opponents of the regime, especially those of the Left, continued to dispute its—as they saw it—essentially undemocratic character. Particularly objectionable to them was the constitutional clause giving the president the right to rule with full powers in a national emergency. In liberals of almost every hue, this clause stirred further fears by giving to the president, and to him alone, the power to decide what conditions constituted an emergency, and what should be done to meet it.

## De Gaulle's France

To the dismay of many Rightists, and particularly the recalcitrant colonialists, de Gaulle insisted on the granting of full independence to Algeria (1962). The next year he caused consternation among the Western European powers making up "The Six" (see *infra,* p. 657) by vetoing Britain's application to join the Common Market. Whatever his official reasons for this action, his real objection lay in his belief that Britain was too closely tied to the United States for Europe's good, especially as he envisioned Europe's good. In his view a most dangerous situation had arisen with the emergence of the United States and the U.S.S.R. as superpowers. Between them they tended to establish a monopoly on the arbitration of world affairs. For de Gaulle, this was a wholly unacceptable development, which relegated not only France but the whole of Europe to a passive role. Throughout his first term as president, he worked hard to reinstate self-confidence among all European peoples. But his program did not find easy acceptance anywhere. His associates in "The Six" favored the admission of Britain. They and the representatives of other states believed also that, superpower or not, the United States was an indispensable ally whose leadership—and financial aid—should not be underestimated as basic props of the democratic world. They objected, too, to the grand de Gaulle "style," which reminded many of the first Bonaparte.

Nevertheless, by the late 1960s, France under de Gaulle seemed to have achieved a condition at home and a position abroad beyond what the most enthusiastic Francophile could have seriously hoped for a decade earlier. At de Gaulle's insistence, France developed a nuclear power that was sufficiently advanced to give her a place in the atom-bomb club. Also at his insistence, France asserted national independence vis-à-vis the strategic demands of the North Atlantic Treaty Organization,* and went so far as to order (1965) the removal of the United States-dominated NATO bases from French soil. Her new posture regarding the claims of her onetime colonies definitely enhanced her international reputation. Furthermore, a substantial measure of economic well-being continued to be enjoyed under Gaullist leadership.

## Italy

In 1943, as we have seen, Italy disposed of Mussolini and switched from being an Axis partner to a "cobelligerent" of the

---

* In a summary history of the contemporary world it is impossible to separate sharply domestic affairs from international affairs. Rather than tediously repeat such directives as "see below" or "discussed in a later section," our account hereafter makes references to related circumstances of this nature on the assumption that the reader will turn to the appropriate parts of Sections B and C on his own initiative.

Allies. But her position was ambiguous. For over twenty years the Fascist way of life had penetrated the interstices of Italy's political and social life. The peremptory dismissal of the Duce, although of course requisite for new policies and a new outlook, could not automatically bring them about. As both an Axis aggressor and an Axis defector, Italy presented, by war's end, a double image that puzzled both herself and the victorious Allies. In the peace treaty of 1947 she was forced to pay an indemnity of $360 million and to agree to a future review of her colonial claims. Eventually she was required to relinquish all foreign possessions —Ethiopia, the coastal colonies of Africa, Somaliland (after a ten-year Italian trusteeship under the United Nations), Eritrea, and the Dodecanese Islands (given to Greece). She also was forced to transfer most of Venezia Giulia and Trieste to Yugoslavia.

In 1946 the monarchy was voted out of existence and a parliamentary republic was set up. The first national elections held under it (1948) gave the Christian Socialist party—much more a Catholic center party than Socialist—an absolute majority. Under its able leader, Alcide de Gasperi, the government vigorously attacked the perennial problems of poverty and illiteracy. In 1950 an elaborate ten-year economic program was announced and, primed by Marshall Plan aid, successfully carried out. The living standard rose to a higher level than Italy had ever enjoyed. But the peasant masses still remained underfed, underhoused, and ill-clothed, especially in the regions south of Rome. Relatively generous sums were allocated for educational projects to create a more than barely literate population; here, too, real advances were made, although compared to other Western nations both the quality and the scope of the educational program left much to be desired.

Because of Italy's economic and social deficiencies, the appeal of Communism proved strong. She has the largest and most

*Italian Premier Alcide De Gasperi, leader of the Christian Democrat party, casts his vote at Rome in the Italian General Elections, April 18, 1948.*

disciplined Communist party in Western Europe, as well as a large congeries of Socialist parties. Generous United States loans and grants were credited with preventing one or the other of these parties, or a coalition of them, from coming to power. The Church also gave strong support to the Christian Socialist regime. The question of whether that regime will not eventually give way to the radical Left remains another one of Italy's uncertainties.

Because of membership in the Common Market and in the North Atlantic Treaty Organization, Italy's general economic and political situation seems for the present to be reasonably secure. But until the yawning gaps between rich and poor, industrial North and agricultural South, and aristocratic elite and uneducated masses can be narrowed, Italy's future, for all her recent socioeconomic gains, remains none too promising.

## THE GERMANIES

### Germany in Defeat

The surrender of Germany in May of 1945 was unconditional. This Allied policy had been fixed, as we have seen in an earlier chapter, before the Allied landings in Africa in 1943. About two years later the closing ring of Russian, British, and American military might left the Germans no alternative to the acceptance of this stipulation. This meant that the victorious powers not only occupied all of Germany but exercised complete political control over it. Until a formal overall Allied administration could be set up to govern the conquered land, the occupying powers divided Germany into four zones. Russia was assigned the northeastern provinces lying between the Elbe and Oder-Neisse rivers, Britain occupied a sector in the northwest, and the United States took over the administration of the south German states, from which two Rhineland areas were reassigned to France.

Even if communist-capitalist stresses had not developed among the occupying powers, the job of managing the country would have remained indescribably difficult. The German population, then as in 1918, was stunned by defeat. The problem was confounded by the unprecedented movement and relocation of millions of people who, during the war years, either had been exploited as foreign laborers in Germany or had lived outside the Reich's borders. Among the foreign laborers were hundreds of thousands of Poles, Russians, Italians, Frenchmen, and Balkan peoples. Masses of refugees poured in from areas overrun by Russian troops. In addition, some fifteen million occupying troops and their families moved in, taking over the best living quarters and in general assuming the traditional prerogatives of conquering powers. To impress on the Germans the inhumanity of the Hitler years, the new rulers distributed films, posters, and books that portrayed concentration-camp life and described other acts of Nazi

criminality. Thus, guilt feelings merged with resentment and despair to produce inner harassments almost beyond bearing.

Besides multilateral occupation, Germany was forced to accept a sharp reduction in territory. In 1939, Russia took over substantial portions of eastern Poland. After the war Poland was compensated by being given certain eastern areas of the old Germany, including half of East Prussia (the other half going to the U.S.S.R.).* Germany was also compelled to accept the dismantling of many of her eastern industrial establishments, which were then shipped to Russia as partial compensation for the massive destruction by German armie. of Russian industry in the Ukraine and in other parts of the Soviet Union.

### Deemphasis of the "De's"

The original Allied aims of deindustrialization, demilitarization, and denazification were only imperfectly carried out. It soon became apparent, at least to Britain and to the United States, that the revival of European economy depended on the revival of German industry, which automatically meant abandonment of any attempt to "pastoralize" Germany. Decentralization plans eventually yielded to the exigencies of the cold war. Total disarmament was quickly achieved; even many Germans—at the time —supported both the policy and its immediate execution. Denazification was a more difficult matter. According to the rules of judgment outlined in the Potsdam and Yalta declarations, not hundreds or thousands of Germans were marked by the swastika brand, but millions. To try them under fair court procedures would take years. Compounding the difficulty was the absence of reasonable criteria that could be used to separate active, convinced Nazis

---

* The annexation of East Prussia by Poland and Russia facilitated the liquidation of the whole of Prussia as an organized province.

from any who had joined the Party or had supported the Hitler regime out of fear of what would happen to them if they did not. In late 1945, twenty-one Nazi leaders were brought to trial at Nuremberg for crimes against the peace, war crimes, and crimes against humanity. All but three were given either sentences of death or terms of imprisonment. Even if we grant the propriety of such trials—which many both in Germany and in the Allied countries did not—the conviction of eighteen leaders hardly denazified Germany. Many trials of lesser Nazi officials were held by Allied and, later, German courts, and a number of those indicted were convicted. Still the basic problem remained —how to root out an ideology that had gripped a large part of the entire nation without immobilizing the economic, political, and social forces that any community requires for even the most elemental kind of organized existence. In the end, the elaborate program of "purification" was allowed to peter out amid the developing agitations of the cold war.*

## Capitalist and Communist Germanies

Rising tensions between the Western Allies and Soviet Russia wrecked the original plan to govern Germany as a "unit." In late 1946 Britain and the United States agreed to an economic fusion of their zones and, the next year, set up a German Economic Council to direct a reconstruction program. Russia soon countered by creating a German Economic Commission in the Soviet sector. Thereafter, both power blocs moved steadily toward the creation of "new Germanies" in their own image. In the spring of 1949 the three Western powers drew up an Occupation Statute which virtually merged their sectors into one, with substantial political control vested in German

* By late 1966, a former Nazi had become Chancellor of West Germany, and the Neo-Nazi National Democratic Party had made substantial election gains.

officials. This was soon followed by the establishment of the Federal Republic of Germany, with Bonn as its capital. Under the leadership of Konrad Adenauer, its first Chancellor and one of Europe's most gifted statesmen, the new Republic quickly gave

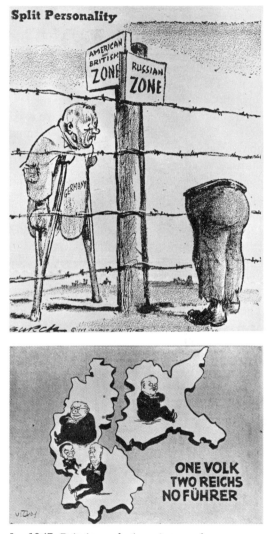

In 1947 Britain and America made one economic unit of their two zones in occupied Germany. Two years later France joined them in drawing up an occupation statute that virtually merged the three zones into one. Meanwhile, Russia had consolidated its control of Eastern Germany. These two cartoons show something of the German predicament that resulted.

signs of spiritual, economic, and political rehabilitation. In reply, the Russians sponsored the creation, in their zone, of the German Democratic Republic. An able statesman, Otto Grotewohl, was named as its Minister President, although real power lay with his Soviet advisers.

Under these circumstances, Western leaders drastically revised the basic provisions of the Potsdam Declaration. They had envisioned the emergence of a new Germany that would be united but weak, sovereign but pliant. Now they worked to make West Germany industrially strong through Marshall Plan aid. Thus stimulated, West Germany's economy soon surpassed prewar levels of production. Indeed, so rapid and so widespread was its recovery that the phrase "economic miracle" came to be used commonly to describe it. Before long, and particularly as the Korean War dramatized the ominous potential of the communist-capitalist conflict, the United States and Britain felt impelled to permit Germany to rearm, with the proviso that the new army would be a part of NATO defense forces rather than an independent organization. The Western Allies also sanctioned a revision of West Germany's political structure which gave greater power to the central government.

With these developments, little hope remained that a general peace conference would ever be assembled. By 1957, West Germany had become thoroughly aligned with the United States, Britain, and France, just as East Germany had become aligned with the Soviet Union. Constant and serious friction marked their relations with one another. Periodically, West German leaders demanded reunion and restoration of the old pre-Hitler frontiers. East German leaders favored reunion—on their own terms—but remained understandably reticent about boundary changes that both Poland and Russia opposed. Divided Berlin remained a continually festering sore. To the West it was a symbol of the containment of Communism. To the East it was a source of unending irritations. As the recipient of Marshall Plan aid money, West Berlin soon became prosperous almost to the point of ostentatious affluence. Its citizens also enjoyed democratic blessings that were denied to their brothers on the other side of the "curtain." Consequently, many East Berliners moved over into the Western sector until the East German government forbade further migration. When, despite this injunction, many smuggled themselves across the line, the Communist government ordered the erection of a wall along the boundary (1961), which was heavily guarded day and night. This stopped wholesale migration of refugees, but at a high price. Tempers were sharpened on both sides, possible avenues of *rapprochement* were shut off, and the cold war took on new and more menacing aspects (although in the long run, it should be added, the presence of the wall eased Russian fears of serious trouble with West Berlin and West Germany, hence reduced European tensions).

In short, the makeshift settlements that followed the defeat of the Nazi state aggravated rather than solved the long troublesome "German problem." Nothing in the whole sweep of German history suggests the acceptance by Germans of a permanently divided country. On the contrary, everything in that history, certainly over the past century and a half, points to an eventual resurgence of the unity movement. By itself, this movement would inevitably create international tensions and would in many ways affect general European conditions. The use of each "Germany" as a pawn in the cold war immeasurably complicates the problem. Even if Germans were amenable to treatment as pawns—which they are not—the human chess game being played by the United States and the U.S.S.R. in the center of Europe cannot, if it is continued, lead to anything but a disastrous "end game." To the world at large this is a deepening cause of concern. To the Germans, it is a prospect too frightening to allow them, however economically affluent they may become, to have the faith and hope that every people must have to construct a humane and stable society.

## RUSSIA

### Economic Losses and Gains

Though mauled by the ravages of the war more than any other nation, Russia emerged from it strong and confident. To Stalin this was clear proof of the superiority of the Soviet way of life. Not yet half a century old, Communist Russia had faced the greatest fighting force in modern times, had absorbed its most vicious thrusts, and had then gone on to overrun and finally destroy its once seemingly invincible legions. As Stalin saw it, the Red Army had won because it was socialist; but behind that army and sustaining it were a socialist economy and a socialist body politic. One does not have to accept Stalin's analysis of victory to acknowledge the stupendous efforts and achievements of the Russian people in that great struggle. Nor is it possible to deny the almost miraculous economic recovery affected after the war. For some three years the Ukraine and parts of other regions of Russia had been laid waste by the violence of war. Over twenty millions of its people had been killed. Great factories and power plants had been destroyed, and much of its agricultural productivity impaired. Losses in livestock, for example, were so great that, in this sector of the economy, Russia was set back a generation. Table I gives a graphic picture of the losses.

*After the war Russia's rulers set the country to work on rebuilding its shattered economic machine. These two pictures show the construction of the gigantic Novo Gorky oil refinery (1958) and cotton pickers at work on the Kyzl Cotton Collective in Uzbekistan (1959).*

Soviet officials have estimated that during the war some 70,000 villages, 98,000 collective farms, 40,000 miles of railroad track, 32,000 factories, and nearly 3,000 tractor stations were destroyed.

By 1948, under the fourth Five Year Plan, recovery was well under way. By then the 1940 level of industrial output had already been exceeded by 14 per cent. By 1953 the production of electrical power had increased by 200 per cent, oil by 70 per cent, and iron, steel, and coal by nearly 100 per cent. New virgin lands in Siberia were brought under cultivation, and many new power and industrial plants were con-

*TABLE I*

| Livestock | 1916 (in Millions) | 1946 (in Millions) |
|---|---|---|
| Horses | 38 | 10.5 |
| Cattle | 58 | 47 |
| Hogs | 23 | 10 |
| Sheep and goats | 96 | 70 |

structed in areas east of the Ural mountains. In the 1960s especial attention was paid to the development of the chemical industry which, in Khrushchev's words, "was a mint from which gold flows." At the Twenty-Second Party Congress (1961), Khrushchev called for more than a 500 per cent increase in industrial production by 1980. It is, of course, easy to call for progress; it is also true that in many instances Soviet goals, announced with much gusto, have subsequently been quietly abandoned or put aside. Nevertheless, the economic achievements of the Soviet Union in the postwar years have been, measured by any reasonable criteria, very real and truly remarkable.

## The Plight of Agriculture— and of Soviet Man

It would be a mistake, however, to conclude that the Soviets had created overnight a material heaven. For one thing, agriculture, which has always been the weakest sector of the Soviet economy, presented serious problems. During the war many farmers had taken over land and equipment for their private use. Party officials were hard put after the war to regain control over the peasants and redirect their efforts along lines required by the fourth Five Year Plan. Even after this had been achieved—at the cost, not surprisingly, of individual productivity —things did not go well. As always, the greater part of the State budget was allocated to the industrial sector, which meant that equipment needs of the kolkhozes, such as tractors and plows, were neglected. Six years after the war, officials publicly admitted that agricultural production did not meet "the demands of the toilers," an admission that can only be characterized as a gross understatement. Nor did the record much improve over the next ten years. In 1961 the government admitted that grain production had missed the planned output by twenty million tons, that the country was suffering from serious shortages of meat

and milk, that, indeed, the agricultural situation in general was in an unhealthy condition.

Moreover, many of the gains were made at the expense of elemental human dignity and freedom. To populate the new farms in the east, for example, the State relied heavily on the Political Police.

The labor involved [in one large project] was convict labor, rounded up by the Political Police and transported by them across the tundra. Technically these prisoners were serving sentences of two to seven years under Article 58 of the criminal code, but if they survived and were given their discharge, they were apt to be retained compulsorily as "free civilian settlers." How many convict laborers have died in [the] Varkurta [project] there is no means of knowing with any accuracy. A Polish engineer . . . who escaped in 1947, estimated that a million had died there by the end of 1946.[2]

Although much of Russia's economic recovery and progress after the war had no such stigma attached to it, much of it did and, as part of the historic record, should be noted.

## Conquest of Space

Even more spectacular than the upgrading of her industrial production were Russia's achievements in science and technology, particularly in the exploration of space. Hard as it may be for Americans—long accustomed to thinking of themselves as the world's most advanced technicians—to accept with any degree of grace, it is nevertheless true that the Soviet Union inaugurated the cosmic age. In 1957 an artificial satellite was successfully put in orbit around the earth; the same year another satellite was sent up, this time carrying a dog. In 1959 a space rocket was fired at the moon and made a direct hit; another rocket, equipped with photographic devices, circled the moon

2. J. Hampden Jackson, The World in the Post-war Decade, Houghton Mifflin Company, Boston, 1956, pp. 208–209.

and took pictures of the side that is turned away from the earth. In 1960 a heavy spaceship carrying two dogs was launched and successfully recovered. The next year a 13,-000-pound spaceship carried aloft an interplanetary station and discharged it in the direction of Venus. In April of 1961, Yuri Gagarin became the first man to orbit the earth; the same year another manned ship orbited the earth seventeen times. In 1962 and 1963, two "companion ships" were sent up—on one occasion with two men, on the other with a man and a woman. In 1964 the three-man *Voskhod* made sixteen trips around the earth. During this period the Russians also launched a number of satellites to gather various kinds of scientific data and to test the possibility of placing "stations" at various levels in preparation for the grand expedition—the landing of a man on the moon. They were also successful in constructing long-range missiles capable of carrying nuclear warheads.

## Expansion in Europe

Not all of Russia's postwar energies were spent in developing her economy and exploring outer space. Equally significant was the extension of Communist control in Eastern Europe. Already before the collapse of the Nazi regime, Russian troops either had occupied or had placed troops and political advisers in Eastern Germany, the Baltic States, Poland, and much of the Balkans. Originally the Soviet Union agreed—on paper—to work with the Western powers toward early free and open elections in the liberated countries. Actually, Stalin and his colleagues did all they could to prevent them. Although the details and timing differed in the various countries, a common pattern of practice was applied to all. Initially a coalition government was established, in which all major parties were usually represented. In almost every government, however, key posts (such as justice, interior, and army) were filled by Communists. With the legal and military apparatus in their hands,

local Communist parties manipulated elections so that Party members soon came either to dominate the legislative bodies or to have the means to prevent them from enacting laws considered inimical to Communist interests. Strong propaganda campaigns, often combined with the nationalization of certain segments of the economy and often backed by the presence of Soviet troops, soon made the Communist faction of the government its dominant force. The next step was the dissolution of the coalition and the assumption by the Communists of dominant control. The final step was the complete acceptance and faithful execution of directives from Moscow. To coordinate its control over the states brought or being brought within its orbit, the Soviet Union set up a Communist Information Center (Cominform, 1947), which was merely the old Comintern under a new name. It also supervised the political activities of the Communist parties of Western Europe, the Americas, and parts of Asia. Throughout the 1950s and 1960s, efforts were made to give a semblance of validity to the Russian claim that the governments of the new "Peoples' Democracies" were operating on a mandate from their own citizens—Russian troops were removed and Russian political advisers were sent home. But no one was fooled. Whoever came and went in the presidencies and premierships of the satellite states, each one of them responded quickly and loyally when the Big Slav Brother in Moscow spoke.

There was one exception. For about a year and a half after the war, Yugoslavia under the exceedingly able leadership of Marshal Tito (whose real name was Josip Broz) maintained close ties with the Soviet Union. Tito also concluded a number of economic and political agreements with Poland, Czechoslovakia, Albania, Hungary, and Bulgaria. As one of the founding members of the Cominform, Yugoslavia could reasonably be expected to follow the Moscow line. It did not. By late 1947, Tito had given unmistakable signs of managing the country as he thought its best interests demanded. When these interests were not compatible with pronouncements from Moscow, he ignored the pronouncements. To bring him to heel, Stalin recalled all technical advisers and military personnel from Yugoslavia and engineered its expulsion from the Cominform, evidently in the belief that Tito would soon see his vulnerability vis-à-vis the capitalist powers that flanked him to the west and south. At great risk, Tito ignored Moscow's threatening gestures and turned to the West for help. The United States and Britain accepted his overtures in the belief that a cracking of the Communist Front might bring about its eventual dissolution; at the very least it would embarrass and somewhat discredit Russia's claim that she spoke for a united Communist world. By 1950, and for several years thereafter, Yugoslavia and the U.S.S.R. went their separate Communist ways. The subsequent "de-Stalinization" of Russia gave the Kremlin's new rulers an opportunity to restudy the situation. Under Khrushchev, cordial relations were reestablished. Yugoslavia rejoined the Cominform, exchanged diplomatic representatives with Russia and her satellites, and, more often than not, stood with them in the recurring confrontations between the East and the West. Still, she did not give up her right to formulate policy independently and according to her own interpretation of Marxist doctrines, even when this implied and sometimes involved a degree of collaboration with the West. In short, after 1947 the Communist world became two worlds (and after China's break with Russia in the early 1960s, three worlds).

The expansion of Soviet control into almost all of Eastern Europe naturally brought heavy criticism from capitalist governments and peoples. What Communists had called imperialist exploitation when capitalist countries overran African and Asian societies, now seemed to Communists a very proper form of good-neighbor relations, an almost sacrificial effort to effect their "liberation." In capitalist eyes this was sheer hypocrisy

which, unless stopped, would lead to the brutal Sovietization of much of the world. There is clearly substantial truth in this charge. Nevertheless, it is not the whole truth. After World War I the Western powers, as we have seen, exerted strong, although short-lived, efforts to overthrow the new regime in Russia. When these failed, the Allies contrived to construct a "cordon sanitaire" around Russia, to isolate it from the community of nations and to weaken its internal position in whatever way they could. Soviet rulers did not forget those years. They were determined that this time the Baltic and Balkan states would not again be used as staging grounds for an eventual assault against their socialist island. Moreover, it should be remembered that some of the Eastern European leaders and regimes, strongly supported by Britain and the United States in the early years after World War II, were reactionary remnants of a past era, which were by no means welcomed by their own people. Our assessment of the nature and meaning of the extension of Russian control in Eastern Europe, therefore, should bring into focus both Western and Soviet images of what Eastern Europe's history was and what its future should be.

### *"de-Stalinization"*

The fourth outstanding event in the life of postwar Russia was its "de-Stalinization." The term can easily be misunderstood. It can be, and unfortunately occasionally has been, construed to mean a consequential deviation from the Marxist-Leninist complex of doctrines that had been administered and developed by Stalin for over a quarter of a century. This is almost completely untrue. Certainly, there has been substitution of one path for another in the post-Stalin era. Soviet leaders have also candidly admitted that the road to socialism may not always be the same for different states. However, the first modification is nothing new in Soviet history. Lenin himself publicly confessed that Bolshevik leaders would have to test out this path and that from time to time to see if it was leading in the direction in which they wanted to go, and this has repeatedly been done. The second "new admission" is truly new, but it is not important from the standpoint of basic Communist goals and basic Communist attitudes. Whether Russian, Yugoslavian, or Chinese, whether dated 1917 or 1967, these goals remain unchanged: the overthrow of capitalist rule; the nationalization of land and industry; the dictatorship of the proletariat (under a "temporary" authoritarian vanguard); the creation of classless society; the final withering away of the state.

More accurately, de-Stalinization signifies the following: the replacement of one-man rule with a more truly collective leadership; a de-emphasis of the power of the police; some relaxation of governmental controls in the creative arts; more reasonable accommodation of the demands of non-Russian Communist regimes; and reforms of one kind or another in education, jurisprudence, and the sciences.

The fact that the Soviet Union had, by the early 1950s, long since passed through its political apprenticeship, and that its leaders were coming increasingly to understand the limitations of terror as a permanent instrument of political administration, undoubtedly played an important part in causing the shift. But two other developments were of perhaps even greater significance. One was the military stalemate created by Russia's construction of the atom and hydrogen bombs (1949, 1953) which forced the two great powers to compete economically and ideologically rather than militarily. At this point Russia's new leadership felt forced to relax some of the more severe Party controls that had long hampered economic and social development. At the same time, of course, Soviet leaders had to keep close watch on the political implications of the new policy lest the Party, the basic instrument of the Soviet system, lose its dominant position. This necessarily meant, as we shall soon note, an ambiguous

Stalin's successor, Georgi Malenkov, is shown here addressing the Supreme Soviet a few months after he took over leadership of the Soviet Union (1953). Within two years he was deposed, for reasons not yet fully known outside of the inner circle of the Communist ruling group.

and confusing periodic alternation of relaxation and tightening of controls.

Procedural changes began almost immediately after the death of Stalin in 1953. For about two years Soviet affairs were administered by three men—Malenkov (Stalin's young protégé); Molotov, an "Old Bolshevik" and an expert in foreign affairs; and Khrushchev, newly made head of the Party Secretariat. One of the first signs of the new approach was the arrest and execution of L. Beria, Minister of Internal Affairs. Whether or not he was, as charged, engaged in a plot to gain control of the government and the Party, his execution marked a turning point in the power of the secret police and of the many agencies of the security apparatus. Such democratic safeguards as those of the American Bill of Rights certainly were not brought into use, but terror as an instrument of government was curtailed.

Another sign of the new times was the nonviolent removal of Malenkov as premier

*Nobel prize winner Boris Pasternak is shown in animated conversation with friends who visited Moscow when the New York Philharmonic made an appearance there in 1959. He is speaking directly to its conductor, Leonard Bernstein, who is sitting at the table with his wife.*

in 1955. It is not possible to accept Malenkov's own publicly announced reasons for his resignation—"nonexperience in Ministerial affairs," his "guilt and responsibility for the unsatisfactory state of affairs which has arisen in agriculture," and his admission that his emphasis on the production of consumer goods had been wrong. The important point is that he was dropped from power but not executed or even arrested; as a matter of fact, he retained high posts for several years, and remains today an unmolested citizen not without some influence.

The most dramatic wrench with the past was Khrushchev's "secret" blast against Stalin at the Twentieth Party Congress in February of 1956. In a detailed indictment that stunned his listeners, Khrushchev charged Stalin with a series of crimes ranging from fostering the "cult of personality" to the murder of hundreds of Bolshevik stalwarts. His leadership during the war was denounced as having been marked by hysteria, incompetence, and, in the early stages, defeatism. "After the first severe disaster and defeats at the front, Stalin thought that this was the end. In one of his speeches in those days he said: 'All that which Lenin created we have lost forever.'" Throughout the speech, Khrushchev took care to underscore Stalin's positive contributions to the building of a socialist state, especially during the trying times of the NEP and the first Five Year Plan. These contributions, he insisted, should never be forgotten. Nor did he bring into question Stalin's complete devotion to the basic aims of the Party. But, the charge ran, sometime after 1934 the temptations of pure power and self-aggrandizement increasingly affected his behavior until, by the time of his death, he had become a demented tyrant. News of this long polemic and some of its more macabre details were allowed to leak out to prepare the people, as Khrushchev thought of it, for Russia's return to true Marxism-Leninism. The term "collective leadership" was made a shibboleth. Censorship, even though by no means abandoned, was sufficiently toned down to permit writers and composers a measure of freedom not enjoyed since Lenin's time (although even then, it should be noted, truly free expression was not permitted). Yugoslavia was wooed and at least partially won back into the fold. Satellite states were treated in a less arbitrary manner. Educational reforms, designed to make higher education for the masses more than a socialist slogan, were introduced.

In short, a politico-cultural "thaw" set in, both making and marking a new style of Soviet life. Many Western critics have made light of the "new departure." They rightly point out that the creative artist is still more a servant of the state than of the muses that move him. When Boris Pasternak was awarded the Nobel Prize in literature, for example, the Party refused to allow him to accept it, arguing that his work, especially his novel *Doctor Zhivago,* was unfairly critical of Soviet life. Uprisings in East Berlin and other East German cities in 1953 were savagely suppressed. Hungarian revolutionists who tried in 1956 to set up a government free from Soviet interference were mercilessly slaughtered. Before Khrushchev had been in power more than a year or two,

*A group of Hungarians gather around coffins in Budapest, seeking to identify the dead, after fighting had swept through the city (1956). One man is lifting the top of a coffin to view the body of a victim.*

*Alexei Kosygin and Leonid Brezhnev, who took over the positions vacated by Nikita Khrushchev, clasp hands during an appearance at Moscow's Sports Palace. This picture was taken about four years before they assumed office, Kosygin as Premier, Brezhnev as Secretary-General of the Communist party (1964).*

highly laudatory articles in the press and other periodicals began to appear, reminiscent of the Byzantine-like worship of Stalin. Nevertheless, the "thaw" is a reality. Poems and novels limn facets of Russian life that are probingly critical despite their subtle phrasing. Most of the satellite states, particularly Poland, have political and cultural elbowroom that they did not have while Stalin lived. Although it often works in collaboration with the Soviet Union, Yugoslavia remains a sovereign power. And, as we have noted earlier, political opponents, although they are still often dealt with harshly, may leave office without necessarily leaving life. Indeed, Khrushchev himself suffered both expulsion from power and rather severe denunciation in 1964 when the Party apparatus installed a new premier, Alexi Kosygin, and a new Party head, Leonid Brezhnev. It is significant that he continued to live in peace and with his family, the same as the leaders whom he himself had from time to time peremptorily dismissed and publicly castigated. It is impossible, of course, to predict what new forms and features Soviet life will assume in the future. It seems highly unlikely, however, that the very marked trends of the "thaw" will be permanently reversed.

## THE UNITED STATES

The main events of American life after the war were industrial expansion accompanied by a general raising of the standard of living, continuing and contentious concern over civil rights, and the emergence of the nation as a consequential arbiter of world affairs.

### Economic Affluence

Elaborate reconversion plans, carefully worked out before the end of the war, saved the country from the economic irregularities that followed World War I. As controls were removed, both wages and prices rose substantially, especially prices. However, the inflationary trend was not so marked as had been feared, except in a few areas of the economy such as rentals and meat produce. Nor did another Great Depression prostrate the country, as it had in the 1930s. Returning veterans found jobs or opportunities to continue their education. In the first five years after the war national production, national income, and consumer income increased by 35 per cent, 30 per cent, and nearly 40 per cent, respectively. After 1950 the indices of all these categories rose even more spectacularly. By the 1960s the trend had continued so markedly that it was commonplace to think of American society as the most affluent of any that the world had ever known.

On the other hand, it should be noted that some critics found both the overall situation and its impact on the national character anything but reassuring. From the end of the Korean War in 1953 to the beginning of large-scale American intervention in Vietnam in 1961 and 1962, the country had suffered three recessions serious enough to give concern to both the government and the general public. Even apart from these periods, the *rate* of America's economic growth did not keep up with, let alone surpass, that of many European and Asian countries. In addition, about 4 or 5 per cent of the population persistently remained unemployed, and nothing that either the government or private industry could do seemed effective. Also, some thought that they saw in the national character a highly developed tendency to measure all meaning of life in materialistic terms. Admittedly man has always craved material comforts and material power. These critics argued, however, that the periods of true human "ascent" have been those when man, however lamentable his failure to put them into practice, held faith in spiritual postulates that subsumed his other activities. They saw contemporary American society headed, therefore, toward the kind of inner crackup which, as they read history, had ultimately destroyed all the great civilizations of the past.

Others pointed to disconcerting conditions beneath the admittedly glittering surface. Most of America's Negroes—over 10 per cent of the country's total population—lived in rural or urban slums. Other segments of the population, such as the white residents of "Appalachia" and of expansive areas in the rural South, lived from birth to death without adequate food, houses, and clothes, to say nothing of educational opportunities.

Even many of the so-called white-collar class, wherever they lived, maintained a seemingly comfortable existence only by the grace of the nation's system of installment buying, supplemented by easy access to the funds of numerous loan companies—in short, by living in continuous, virtually unredeemable debt. Finally, some believed that the economic system itself was living on borrowed time. They pointed out that more than one half of the national budget (well over fifty billion dollars) was devoted to war expenditures of one kind or another. If such expenditures were withdrawn—that is, if the country really lived in the peace that it said it believed in and was working for—the economy would collapse overnight. Whether these judgments of the state of postwar American economic conditions are wholly or partly valid, the historian, of course, cannot say. However, the serious student of history can hardly be excused from including them in his calculations as he assesses the nature of contemporary American society.

## Ordeals Domestic and Foreign: McCarthyism

Another significant development in America's postwar years was the fierce contest between forces that sought to restrict civil rights and the forces that would enlarge them. As used here, the term "civil rights" implies the option of the individual to participate in the general affairs and experiences of the society of which he is a citizen without hindrance, except for the limitations imposed by due process of constitutional law, and without restrictive discrimination because of racial or religious conditions or affinities. American society, as every other society, has never been entirely free from attacks on and infringements of such rights. Some periods of its history have been more marked by them than others; the years following World War II was such a period.

One example of the struggle for dignified "humanhood" was the complex of events that made up the so-called McCarthy era (*c.* 1950–1955). The outbreak of the Korean War in 1950 stimulated patriotic suspicions, already sensitized by earlier cold war events. It is certain that a few Americans allowed themselves to be used as espionage agents by the Soviet Union (as did some Russians by the United States government). It is also certain that their number was minuscule and their effect on the security of the country relatively insignificant. But the tensions of the times allowed ambitious and unscrupulous persons, both in and out of the government, to play on American fears and confusions in such a way that for a time a condition not far from true hysteria gripped the country. Republican Senator Joseph R. McCarthy, of Wisconsin, became almost overnight the anti-Communist voice of America. Before he died seven years later, he had cowed many of the leaders of his own party, captured the rapt attention of millions of Americans, branded certain national leaders (such as Secretary of State George Marshall) as Communist dupes, attacked prominent figures in the Department of the Army, and caused the nation to fret with festering fears and hatreds that were the stronger because they were beyond reasonable analysis. It is doubtful whether Senator McCarthy believed even a small part of his own charges; even if he had, it is doubtful that he would have cared as much as he pretended to care. For his whole political life was characterized by ruthless exploitation of current circumstances and a certain national mood for his own aggrandizement. In the process he mocked and mangled the civil rights of many and, what was worse, conditioned millions of his countrymen to countenance a way of life that denied the basic rubrics of a democratic society. In this atmosphere of hate and suspicion, legislative measures were enacted at both national and state levels which, in effect, made portions of the Bills of Rights of both federal and state constitutions empty phrases, devoid of positive legal life. Many government officials were dismissed from

*For several weeks in the spring of 1954, Americans witnessed the sorry spectacle of the McCarthy Army hearings, conducted almost as much like a carnival as like a serious investigative hearing. Committee members and their counsel, Roy Jenkins, are shown along the table in the rear.*

their posts on the strength of hearsay evidence or because of "guilt by association." Others in private business and in the professions were demoted, dismissed, or viciously harassed. In 1954, McCarthy scathingly denounced an army general for alleged "softness on Communism." The aftermath was a direct confrontation between McCarthy and his aids and the Secretary of the Army and his colleagues. For over a month the televised hearings kept Americans close to their sets. In the end the fantastic and brutal tactics of McCarthy alienated most of the nation and caused the Senate officially to condemn him. Thereafter the country took a more humane, sophisticated attitude toward those accused of subversion by self-serving demagogues, and a more critical attitude toward the accusers. But the price of this "second-look wisdom" had come high.

## The Black-White Problem

No less agonizing was another ordeal whose roots lie deep in American history and whose ramifications still blight the life of almost every section of the country. Its essence is the struggle of American Negroes

McCARTHY'S RULES OF ORDER

*A St. Louis* Post Dispatch *cartoon shows McCarthy running the whole show at the hearings which, before they were over, spelled the end of the Senator's career as America's great Communist witch-hunter.*

to break the bonds of cultural servitude and degradation fastened on them by the white majority of this country after the Civil War. World War I and its aftermath brought a variety of economic opportunities to the colored population. The war, fought in the name of democracy, also stimulated Negro aspirations for political equality and at the same time weakened ideological defenses against it constructed by the white managers of American society. The revival of Klan activities after the war (see Chapter XIII) for a time muted the Negro cry for freedom. So did the cultivated inertia of many white Americans who, although not willing to parade in white sheets and to burn crosses, preferred to look the other way while others did. Nevertheless, white complacency toward and Negro resignation to the Jim Crow way of life were substantially weakened.

The successful revolt of colonial peoples in Asia and in Africa after World War II also spurred Negroes in America to stake out bolder claims. As people after people in Africa achieved independence, became members of the United Nations, and raised their voices both at home and abroad for a world without the color bar, America's "native sons" vicariously participated in the stirring of that continent and in the psychic rewards won by their African cousins. When a black man from a country born only yesterday could stand in the highest council of the nations and command the respectful attention of his white colleagues, American Negroes, who had had cultural advantages for centuries before the advent of the new African states, could not fail to be impressed and to be stimulated to improve their own lot.*

Another landmark in the struggle was the Supreme Court's decision of 1954, which held that the country's public educational facilities must serve colored and white alike. This reversal of an earlier opinion that had supported the "separate but equal" doctrine, enraged the South and opened an era of increasingly violent racial strife. Various artifices were used by Southern lawmakers to circumvent the ruling, such as the nominal transformation of public schools into private schools. In practice almost all Southern schools in one way or another continued to discriminate between the races and to maintain the *status quo*. In one effort to enforce the decision, President Eisenhower sent troops to Little Rock, Arkansas, to protect the handful of colored children who had enrolled in one of the city's "white" schools. Under these circumstances, the colored students were allowed to attend classes, but the tension and harassments to which they were subjected naturally precluded meaningful learning.

In the early 1960s several civil rights or-

---

* However, local developments probably counted for more in the developing civil rights struggles than African events.

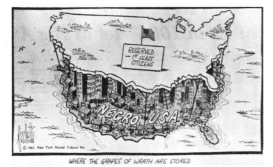

WHERE THE GRAPES OF WRATH ARE STORED

*This cartoon appeared at the time that a new and vigorous race struggle took shape in the early 1960s.*

*When integrationists tried to use this segregated beach (1964), they were attacked by white youths.*

ganizations, such as the Student Nonviolent Coordinating Committee (S.N.C.C.) and the Congress of Racial Equality (CORE), "invaded" the South in a valiant attempt to break the racial barrier and open the way to integration and the building of a more humane social structure. Before these efforts Southern Negroes themselves had already initiated action designed to give them their rightful place in "the land of the free." This action mostly took the form of boycotting enterprises such as city bus lines which drew the color line, and staging "sit-ins" in all-white restaurants. The sustained efforts of both native Negroes and "foreign" whites had the same kind of impact on the social, more general, level as the decision of the Supreme Court had had on education. In 1964 Congress passed a civil rights act which made discrimination by reason of race illegal in all public institutions, such as restaurants, hotels, motels, and theaters. Although sustained by the Supreme Court in a test case and made at least superficially effective in a number of Southern cities, the act did not achieve its main objectives. The same was true of a second civil rights law passed in 1965, which empowered federal officials to supervise the registration of voters in counties where the majority of eligible voters were not registered. It is true that Negro registration picked up noticeably and that more

Negroes exercised their franchise. However, pressures of many kinds were used by the whites to keep down both Negro registration and voting. These were so effective that even after 1965 Negroes still did not influence election results to a degree proportionate to their numbers. Because "white promises" and "white laws" seemed, at least to many reform-minded citizens, to fade out in practice, a new mood took over in some of the foremost civil rights organizations. S.N.C.C., for example, in 1965 repudiated its original non-violent approach and, together with some leaders of CORE, began to speak of "Black Power" as the only path that could lead to the realization of a meaningful life for the Negro. Admittedly an ambiguous term, it nevertheless suggested a turn toward violence in keeping with the views of such very radical Negro organizations as the Black Muslims, which frankly worked for the time when the Negroes could make "Whitey taste a little of his own hell," as one of their leaders put it.

Despite disappointments, setbacks, and sporadic violence, however, the movement for equality between the races is likely to grow in scope and effectiveness. Three hundred years of white domination have ingrained attitudes and practices that cannot be changed in a generation. But a turning point in race relations was reached in the

*More than a year after passage of what seemed to be an effective Civil Rights law (1956), Negroes were still living much the same kind of restricted lives they were before the bill was made law. This picture shows a CORE leader addressing a group of demonstrators who are picketing the main post office in Philadelphia against what they called its discriminatory hiring practices and working conditions.*

postwar years, which promises a more humane way of life for both Black and White America.

## Great-Power Problems

Besides wrestling with the task of reconciling its split economic and racial selves, the United States endeavored to identify and cope with the responsibilities and prerogatives that devolved upon it as an emergent Great Power. Throughout the three and a half centuries of existence, it had played its part in Western world affairs. It had, for example, participated in all of the great "world wars" since 1689. Despite traditional belief to the contrary, it had never really lived an isolated life. In the first half of the twentieth century, as we have seen in earlier chapters, many of its military, political, and economic ventures and activities decisively influenced world affairs. Nevertheless, until the end of the second World War, America had looked upon those affairs as passing phenomena, almost as aberrations, probably to be regretted later. By 1947, however, it was clear to even the

most wistful isolationist that the United States was not only irrevocably of the world but, however reluctantly, one of the arbiters of its problems.

Because it was the possessor of such vast economic and military strength, the United States was naturally regarded as the main support of the Western powers, great and small, as they set about the onerous task of rebuilding their war-ravaged lives. For a year or two after the war, the United States contented itself with generous grants to the United Nations Relief and Rehabilitation Agency (UNRRA). Although this helped to meet Europe's immediate and more pressing needs, it did little or nothing to revive national economies. It soon became apparent that without massive aid they would certainly founder, bringing ruin not only to the peoples of Europe but eventually also to the American economy whose well-being ultimately depended on a reasonably healthy world market. Moreover, languishing economies meant unemployed and restive populations, amenable to the allurements of Communist propaganda.

In these circumstances the United States embarked upon a colossal rescue mission. Billions of dollars, through loans and grants, were poured into those European countries which most needed help. As outlined by Secretary of State George Marshall, such aid was to be used not only to prime Europe's industrial pump, but to create "political and social conditions in which free institutions can exist." Nearly twenty nations, including Britain, France, Italy, and the Scandanavian states, took advantage of American largesse to set their battered economies in order. Russia and her satellites refused all assistance on the grounds that the Plan was an elaborate device designed to bring Europe under American domination. Whether intended or not, the Plan, and later assistance that was offered after the Plan was terminated in 1950, did give the United States a substantial, often decisive, influence in determining both the policies and practices of most West European governments.*

Meanwhile the stockpiling of atomic bombs and the construction of the far more potent hydrogen bomb, together with the lavish production of long- and medium-range ballistic missiles, made the United States a military power surpassed by none and rivaled only by the Soviet Union. Increasingly the country came to base its faith in its own security and that of the Western World on this power, thus initiating a trend away from the nation's long-hallowed Jeffersonian tradition of the complete subservience of military to civilian authority.

By the mid-1960s, America seemed to be less the reluctant world leader that it had appeared to be in the 1940s and more the world's self-appointed policeman. Accompanying this seeming change was a reluctance to accept the goals of disarmament and peace by world law as items of practical and negotiable policy. Leaders in all sectors of society continued, of course, to proclaim the worthwhileness and desirability of such goals. But the heady wine of newly sensed power and the growing feeling that economic prosperity depended on flourishing war industries made it difficult to translate these idealistically desirable goals into acceptable reality.

On the other hand, there were signs in the 1960s that America was troubled by its military might and the international reputation that it was acquiring. Peace organizations multiplied, although none developed a broadly popular base. Growing numbers of United States senators and representatives went on public record against the power and practices of such governmental agencies as the C.I.A. and the House Un-American Activities Committee. Public opinion polls showed

a marked decrease in popular support for the long-term projects of the "Hawks," as the proponents of the "get tougher with Russia" policy were called. It is impossible to predict what the future character of the American mind and spirit will be, or to foretell what use the nation will make of its ample resources and its growing power. But it is hard to believe that the country's long democratic tradition, its established sense of fair play, and its often tested devotion to the imperatives of the good society (whether Great or not) will vanish amid the perplexities and confusions of a world in flux.

## LATIN AMERICA

Postwar conditions in the twenty-one Latin American nations were characterized by contradictions, ambiguities, and uncertainties. In most of these states the standard of living rose over that of the prewar years, particularly in Argentina, Chile, Brazil, and Uruguay. But nowhere was the increase shared equitably. New industries and increased trade brought spectacular affluence to the business elite while heightening the contrast between how they and the illiterate working masses lived. Although most Latin American governments had declared war against the fascist powers, all but a few, such as Chile, Colombia, and Uruguay, were themselves fascist in practice, whatever their democratic professions.

Because they were uneducated and more often than not illiterate, common citizens usually found themselves unable to distinguish between programs that aimed at genuine national welfare and programs that, although decked out in rosy rhetoric, mainly promoted the interests of the already affluent few. Nor could they always, or even reasonably often, be sure that their leaders would not sell them short if, as too often happened, the politics of personal power offered the opportunity. In these circumstances, political parties and political labels underwent rapid

---

* Although the Truman Doctrine was the natural forerunner of the Marshall Plan, it has been thought best to deal with it in a later section. See *infra,* p. 660.

and confusing change. These metamorphoses, in turn, produced abiding uncertainties which increased the "little man's" helplessness, at the same time making him more amenable to demagogic manipulation.

Not surprisingly, the exigencies of the cold war aggravated these conditions. In 1948 all of the American nations joined together in the Organization of the American States (O.A.S.). Although concerned basically with the settlement of inter-American quarrels and problems, the organization lent itself, by reason of the weight of the United States in it, to the checking of Communist moves in world affairs. To effect this, the United States government often favored conservative regimes even when they were corrupt, undemocratic, or both, which more often than not they were. This steadily alienated the Latin American masses from their big "neighbor" to the north and at the same time fomented revolutionary discontent at home. An example of how these forces interacted with one another is the Guatemala crisis of 1954.

In that year the Inter-American Conference of the Organization of the American States met to discuss common problems. The United States was much disturbed by the reform program of the Communist-infiltrated government of Guatemala which had shortly before expropriated lands owned by the American United Fruit Company. To the peasants of Guatemala, and for that matter to the masses in other Latin American countries, this move had been most welcome, signaling the eagerly awaited redistribution of land. To Washington it meant the creation in Latin America of a "beachhead of international Communism." To wipe out this "beachhead," the United States delegation pressured the O.A.S. to approve a resolution holding that "domination or control of the political institutions of any American State by the international Communist movement would constitute a threat to the sovereignty and political independence of the American States, endangering the peace of America." Shortly thereafter an American-financed and trained band of insurrectionists overthrew the Guatemalan government and returned the country to the conditions that had existed before the liberal government had come to power. In the early 1960s a similar coup was executed in Brazil, with strong United States approval, if not direct support. Naturally, such actions by the United States increased the already strong anti-American feelings throughout Latin America and made Communist propaganda even more attractive.

Up to 1967 no substantial progress had been made in dealing with any of Latin America's persistent and pressing problems. Landlords and the merchant elite continued to manipulate economic controls almost exclusively to their own advantage. Little progress had been made in reducing mass poverty and illiteracy. Most of the governments were dominated by militarists, often supported directly or indirectly by the Church. Neither the United States nor the Soviet Union showed any tendency to alter their practice of using these nations as pawns in the cold war. With its two strongest members so inclined, the United Nations naturally could offer little assistance or effective counsel.

# B. The Decolonization of Asia and Africa

## ASIA

### The Revolt Against the West

In Chapter IX we traced the outlines of imperialist ventures in Asia and Africa. By the early 1900s it must have seemed to the empire builders that they were riding the crest of an irreversible tide of world dominion. The great Indian landmass was ruled by Britain. So was Burma, the Malay Peninsula, and a part of Borneo. France managed the affairs of Indochina; the Netherlands controlled almost all of Indonesia; Japan dominated Korea and vied with Russia for control of Manchuria; the United States had taken up the "white man's burden" in the Philippines. In addition, most of the great powers had dreams of partitioning China, or at least of establishing hegemony over large parts of that land. As we have seen, by the early 1900s almost all of Africa was also under white control. Scarcely half a century later the white man, perhaps not quite understanding how it had happened, found himself relieved of his burden as colonial peoples everywhere had either reversed or were in the process of reversing the flow of the once strong imperialist tide. "Between 1945 and 1960 no less than forty countries with a population of eight hundred millions—more than a quarter of the world's inhabitants—revolted against colonialism and won their independence . . . and when the history of the first half of the twentieth century . . . comes to be written in a longer perspective, there is little doubt that no single theme will prove to be of greater importance than the revolt against the west."[3]

Japan's quick and humiliating defeat of Allied forces in the early years of World War II spurred the revolt. For almost three hundred years the power of the white man over his colored brothers had been successfully, often arrogantly, exploited. Here and there in local actions, as in the Russo-Japanese war of 1904 to 1905, Western states had suffered setbacks, but they were on a small scale. The events at Pearl Harbor and Singapore and the vast Japanese conquest in Southeast Asia completely destroyed the image of white invincibility. Thereafter the colored peoples of the world nursed long-deferred hopes—the dissolution of the sahib-servant syndrome and the setting up of independent communities. The achievement of these aims was expedited by the shaken economies and the disturbed social patterns (and in the British experience at least, guilty consciences) produced by six years of world war and long-sustained exploitation. Another dissolving force was a strategem practiced by the Japanese when their own defeat appeared imminent. To consolidate their early conquests they had used local leaders as nominal heads of state wherever possible. The device was transparent and, of course, fooled no one. However, the substitution of eastern masters for western ones, although leaving the ruled far from satisfied, produced a kind of

3. Barraclough, *op. cit.,* pp. 148–149.

racial psychic gain. More important, as the Japanese pulled back before the advancing American and British forces, they gave full independence to the peoples which they could no longer dominate. Thus, when "liberators" arrived, they were more often than not confronted by nationalist governments savoring the turbulent delights of newly gained independence.*

* For this and the following references to emer gent Asian states, see the map on this page.

ASIA, 1967

Countries which gained independence after WW II

Map by J. Donovan

*President Sukarno of Indonesia is shown with two fellow Asians at a conference of African and Asian states. China's Prime Minister, Chou En Lai, is at left; Shojiro Kawashima of Japan at right.*

*Mahatma Gandhi salutes an audience after an address in which he called for Indian independence and unity. This photograph was taken about a year before India gained her independence and about two years before the Mahatma was assassinated by a Hindu fanatic.*

## Indonesia

This was the situation that faced Allied forces entering Indonesia in late 1945. At first the British, who acted as caretakers until Dutch officials could be sent in, gave *de facto* recognition to Sukarno's nationalist republican regime. Their hope was that Dutch and Indonesian leaders could work out a compromise acceptable to both peoples. It was a vain hope. The Dutch failed to understand the new forces at work, and attempted to substitute endless debate for a decisive confrontation of the problem. The Indonesians, supported by world opinion, insisted on self-determination. Lacking the resources to prevent it, the Dutch finally agreed (December 1949) to the establishment of a completely independent Indonesian Republic. For many years thereafter the new nation and its government suffered the buffeting of political strife as militarists fought Communists and both, occasionally (and overtly), fought Sukarno and his bureaucratic apparatus.* Neither economic well-being nor political democracy developed to

* In 1948, Indonesian Communists, probably on orders from Moscow staged an insurrection which Sukarno smashed with a heavy hand. Thereafter the Communists alternately supported and worked against the regime.

the degree or at the pace idealistic reformers had hoped for. But the white master was gone; whatever harassments came from their many fumblings, the Indonesians at long last enjoyed at least the satisfaction of making their own mistakes.

## India

In Chapter IX we noted the formation in India of the Congress party. Long before World War II, it had come to demand dominion status for India. When Britain asked for Indian cooperation in the war and promised home rule after the end of the war, Indian leaders proved stubborn. They pointed out that Britain had made a similar promise during World War I. They argued that they should not be asked to fight for a freedom that they themselves did not enjoy. Gandhi, Nehru, and other leaders were finally jailed. But when the war ended, their pronouncements bespoke the attitude of the Indian masses so clearly and faithfully that Britain could not ignore them unless she was prepared to keep an endless armed watch over all the peoples of the subcontinent. This was out of the question, because Britain needed all of her talents and wealth to restore her own house to some kind of order and comfort. So she began the process of "decolonization."

It was not easy. For years she had used many local princes as willing puppets; they did not welcome the creation of a new state in which they would enjoy neither power nor special privileges. In addition to the problem of the pampered rajahs, there was also the religious rivalry of Hindus and Moslems. Gandhi and most of the leaders of the Congress party wanted a united land with guarantees of religious toleration. Most Moslem leaders insisted on a country of their own. British statesmen* lamented these difficulties and divisions but, by 1948, were determined to leave their solution to the Indians themselves. The independence act of that year recognized a free Hindu India and a free Moslem Pakistan. The problem of how these two states, each of which had a few princes who refused to recognize either state, would get along together, was now their own business. The ceremonial parting, marred neither by petty recriminations nor by officious advice, was quite definite and final. From then on only the bonds of Commonwealth membership bound the three states together, and these of course were voluntary.

## Burma and the Malay States

In 1943 the Japanese had given paper-independence to Burma. When the Japanese

---

* The Labour party was in power. Churchill and other Conservative leaders denounced British withdrawal from India, but it is difficult to believe that a Conservative government could have taken a course other than the one the Labour government took.

withdrew two years later, the returning British found a strongly established Burmese government in operation. The British decision to liquidate its imperial position in India made it easy to open negotiations with Aung San, the determined young leader of Burma's national front party. In late 1947 a popularly elected constituent assembly proclaimed Burma an independent republic; in January of 1948 all British controls were removed. Another new Asian nation was born.

Liquidation of British control in the Malay states did not proceed so smoothly. For one thing, Britain wanted to keep Singapore as a naval and trading base. For another, the peoples of this region were of three distinctly different ethnic strains— Chinese, Indians, and Polynesians. Moreover, Communist guerrillas kept up a steady assault against both foreign and local ruling groups. In 1957 Britain ended her protectorate of Malaysia in return for the right to negotiate a separate agreement with the island colony of Singapore (which was concluded the following year). The struggle against the Communists gave the conglomerate peoples of the Malay states a common purpose, thus serving as a kind of substitute for cultural unity. Even so, serious problems remained. Other territories, such as North Borneo and Sarawak, remained under British control. The peoples of these areas wanted neither British domination nor organic union with Malaysia. In 1963 they rather reluctantly joined the Malay federation after receiving guarantees that they could retain a substantial degree of home rule.

## Indochina, the Philippines, and China

In the following section we shall note the withdrawal of French forces from Vietnam in 1954. The year before, Cambodia and Laos had achieved full independence. France's ultimate withdrawal from Vietnam thus marked both the end of French imperialism in Asia and the heightened development of the struggle of the peoples of Southeast Asia for political, social, and spiritual independence.

Of all the imperialist powers, the United States acted the most promptly in recognizing the new era in Asia. Her dominance of the Philippines, dating from the turn of the century, had never won the wholehearted, enthusiastic support of her people. The new trend, therefore, presented no such problems for them as it had for the French. With obvious reference to its historic significance, Congress chose July 4, 1946 as the day on which to give assent to legislation granting full independence to its former colony. In return, the new Philippine government consented to the establishment of several United States bases in the islands. Intermittent Communist guerrilla attacks gave clear indication that not all Filipinoes were satisfied with the new government, but in the main the transition from colony to independent nation was effected with much less turmoil than that which plagued so many Asian peoples.

Developments in China, more than in any other Asian country, most clearly epitomized the interrelatedness of the forces opposing Western colonialism and the capitalist system which undergirt it. This is not to say that China presented the most typical picture either of Asian colonialism or of the East's revolt against it. In a number of respects it was untypical. Unlike most of the other countries that we have considered, China is huge in geographical dimensions and is the bearer of a culture that is more ancient than any in the West and in some ways more sophisticated. It is untypical, too, in that it has never been conquered and directly ruled by a Western power, even though by the turn of the century it was independent in scarcely more than name.* The point, rather, is that China's successful bid for full national sovereignty was achieved

* For a review of these developments, see Chapter IX.

A 1957 photograph of Chinese Communist leader Mao Tse-tung.

by Communist leaders and Communist troops.

By the early 1940s Japan had occupied substantial portions of northern and eastern China. With the collapse of Japan the foreign war turned into a civil war as Communist forces, under Mao Tse-tung, fought with Nationalist troops under Chiang Kai-shek for control of the country. For a while (1945–1947) it seemed that the Nationalists would emerge as the victors. They could field more divisions, they received generous United States support, and they controlled most of the great urban centers. But Chiang's government was both unpopular with the masses and indescribably corrupt. From 1947 on, the stubborn assaults of Mao's highly disciplined troops, combined with Communist promises of a new day for China's exploited millions, wore down Nationalist strength. In 1949 Chiang took what troops he could to Formosa (renamed Taiwan) to wait for the Communist experiment to fail and then, with American support, to return to the mainland.

Throughout the civil war, Mao had received help from the Soviet Union. After his victory he asked for continued assistance, especially for strategic supplies and trained technicians. For about ten years Chinese agriculture and industry underwent revolutionary development under Russian tutelage, accompanied by astonishing changes in social conditions and general outlook. For many decades regional warlords had prevented the development of national unity, hampered long overdue reforms, and mercilessly mulcted the populace that they controlled. For an even longer period an elitist bureaucracy had kept the face of China turned to the past. And always the landlord class had ground down the peasant masses. Now all of this was changed. For the first time in Chinese history, a grass-roots patriotism developed. Landlords and rich peasants who had more land than they could themselves cultivate were forced to give up the surplus that was not required for their own livelihood. By the mid-1950s industrialization, on which the whole Communist program depended, had made substantial gains under the first Five Year Plan. Warlords became a thing of the past. Except for the Soviet Union, whose help had been requested, no foreign power had a voice in policy making. Dictatorial as Mao's regime was, it afforded more democracy to the awakening masses than they had ever enjoyed. However it appeared to hostile Western eyes, the new regime seemed to the majority of the Chinese people an instrument with which the doors of a more meaningful and abundant life had been opened. In the early 1960s, ideological and political differences dissolved the Chinese-Soviet entente; but by that time the new China was strong enough to stand alone. Its problems were many and serious: periodically food supplies fell below a level to satisfy even minimum requirements; after the break with Russia, capital and technical assistance were hard to come by; "free nations" repeatedly rejected its bid to join the United Nations; prodded by the United States, many nations not only refused to grant recognition to the new regime but insisted on regarding Chiang's Formosa as the "real China." Nevertheless, by the late 1960s the new nation had established itself as the world's third Great Power, and the old days of kowtowing to the West seemed gone forever.

## THE NEAR EAST

The nationalist surge was no less strong in the Near East.* After World War I a species of autonomy or paper-independence was granted to many of the peoples of this region. In 1922, for example, Britain, acting as a "generous" mandatory power, gave Iraq a constitution and eight years later proclaimed it an independent nation. But Iraq was not really independent: a twenty-five-year alliance with Britain gave that country the right to decide foreign-policy matters as well as the right to construct and use certain air bases and transit media. Transjordan had a British general as its strong man for a long time. Indeed, except for Turkey and Saudi Arabia, no people in this region was really the master of its own house. Syria and Lebanon were ruled by the French (supposedly under the general supervision of the League of Nations). Palestine, Iraq, and Jordan were ruled by the English (again, as the mandatory power). Iran was recognized as an independent state, but throughout most of the period between the wars she was closely bound to Britain by economic ties, and for several years during World War II she was occupied by Anglo-Soviet troops.

---

* Some scholars prefer other designations, such as Middle East or Western Asia; some also prefer other boundary limitations than those used here. The peoples and states of this admittedly loosely defined area are here limited to Turkey, Syria, Lebanon, Israel, Jordan, Saudi Arabia, Iraq, Iran, and the small dependencies of the Arabian peninsula.

However, the revolutionary forces of the war transformed the whole area from a checkerboard on which imperial powers moved pieces almost at will to a mosaic of independent states, which were often fierce rivals of one another but were also fiercely alert against renascent colonialism in any of its forms.

## Syria, Lebanon, and Jordan

With the collapse of Germany, France attempted to regain control over Syria and Lebanon. British and French troops had occupied both countries after the surrender of France in 1940 in order to prevent the penetration of the Axis powers. After the war Britain promptly removed her forces. France, however, pointing to the threat of Communist infiltration, argued that her pre-World War II mandate over both countries gave her a legal right to administer their affairs, and claimed that the Catholic population of the region (mostly concentrated in Lebanon) required her protection. Nevertheless, when Syrian and Lebanese nationalists, with the tacit support of Britain and America, staged violent demonstrations, the French government finally withdrew its troops and recognized the independence of both states.

In 1946 Britain proclaimed the independence of Transjordan (which soon renamed itself the Kingdom of Jordan). But there, as in Iraq, British loans, technical assistance, and military aid made practical independence somewhat unreal. In the next two decades, however, the sustained thrust of Jordanese nationalist agitation made the British game there not quite worth the cost; by the 1960s Jordan was substantially free of all external control. In Iraq, Britain attempted to use a sympathetic royal ruling house as the instrument of its control. But, in keeping with the established pattern, patriotic agitators won a sufficiently strong following to overthrow the Western-tainted dynasty and establish (1958) a truly independent state.

## The New Israel and the New Egypt

During and after the war, hundreds of thousands of Jews migrated to Palestine where they and their native coreligionists demanded the immediate creation of the long-promised independent Jewish state. As mandatory of Palestine, Britain tried to work out a compromise that would give some measure of satisfaction to both Jews and Arabs. All her efforts were in vain; whatever plans she suggested irritated either the Jews or the Arabs or both. Prompted by the same forces that caused her to withdraw from Greece, Britain announced in May of 1948 that she was taking her troops and administrators out of Palestine. What happened thereafter would be the responsibility of the Jews and Arabs themselves. The Jews immediately proclaimed the State of Israel under the presidency of Chaim Weizmann. Almost its first act was to call up troops to defend itself against Arab attacks. For over a year bitter fighting, broken by temporary truces, bathed the Holy Land in blood. By the summer of 1949, the superior equipment and resources of the Jews, together with crippling dissension among the Arab states, brought an uneasy peace to the region.

Although Egypt had been granted official recognition as a sovereign nation in 1922 (see Chapter IX), British controls remained strong. As in Iraq, Britain had kept control with the help of a compliant—and fantastically corrupt—royal house. In 1952 the nationalist surge swept the royal debauchee off the throne, and set up a republican government. Three years later Gamal Abdel Nasser, a powerful leader dedicated not only to Egyptian nationalism but to Arab unity, gave the British the choice of withdrawing the last of their troops from Egypt or fighting to keep them there. The British withdrew. The next year, in a bold action that would have been an exercise in fantasy a score of years before, Nasser took over complete control of the Suez Canal.

*Egypt's President Nasser, right, at the Cairo airport where he greeted Russia's Prime Minister, Alexei Kosygin (1966), who is waving to a welcoming crowd.*

The background of this startling move involved more than the stirring of Egyptian nationalism. For some time the new leader had been planning the renovation of the economy of Upper Egypt. A key project in this planning was the construction of a great dam at Aswan which would serve Egypt's power and irrigation needs. For a time the United States and Britain seemed interested in negotiating the necessary loans. But because Nasser continued to maintain cordial relations with the Soviet Union, the loans failed to materialize. Nasser thereupon nationalized the Canal, arguing that Egypt's financial needs made the action necessary. He also arranged for loans from Russia.

Naturally, Egyptian seizure of the Canal infuriated British interests. It also served as a pretext for France to combine with Britain in a retaliatory action. Later we shall consider France's efforts to keep its hold on Algeria; here we merely note it as a factor that generated strong French feelings against Nasser who was supporting the native Algerians in their struggle for freedom. Israel also objected to Egyptian control of the Canal, fearing, with good reason, that shipments to her ports would be jeopardized. Because Russia was at the time heavily in-

volved in subduing an uprising in Hungary and the United States was in the middle of a national election campaign, Britain, France, and Israel decided on armed intervention. Israel's troops invaded the Sinai Peninsula as British and French air forces bombed strategic Egyptian areas and landed troops in the delta region. Russia at once protested to the United Nations, hinting that if it failed to act the Soviet Union would give support to Nasser. When the United States also entered a vigorous protest and insisted on an immediate end to fighting, the three invaders agreed to a cease-fire and soon withdrew their troops. Thereafter Egypt took over full control of the Canal.

Egypt's victory naturally stimulated Pan-Arabism. In 1958 a new United Arab Republic, made up of Egypt, Syria, and (for a while) Yemen, was created. A revolution in Iraq brought to the fore anti-Western leaders who associated themselves with the new republic, as did the successors of Ibn Saud, Saudia Arabia's founding father. When Jordan and Lebanon seemed, under Egyptian pressure, to be moving in the same direction, Britain and the United States landed troops in Lebanon and announced that they would support any Near Eastern nation threatened by "Communist aggression." This rather ambiguous pronouncement and the action which implemented it were not particularly welcomed either by the peoples of the region or by most of the Western nations. Russia, of course, at once charged both Britain and the United States with imperialist aggression.* Amid recriminations between the capitalist and communist blocs and a rising chorus of disapproval from citi-

---

* The American action was planned by the C.I.A., apparently with the interests of American oil companies in mind. If this is true, Soviet Foreign Minister Andrei Gromyko did not altogether miss the mark when he publicly charged that America's greed for oil was the basic force in this operation of the so-called "Eisenhower Doctrine." But the U.S. State Department's fears of Nasser and its desire for military bases were also compelling reasons for the action.

zens of the occupying powers, British and American troops were withdrawn. The fiasco might have led to greater cohesion among the Arab states and a widening of the East-West split, had the nationalist force within the Arab states not proved to be so strong. In the four years following the creation of the United Arab Republic, Syria came increasingly to criticize its domination by Nasser. Yemen's local interests steadily separated that little state from loyalty to the U.A.R. Jordan turned toward Saudi Arabia and away from Egypt. Even so, Pan-Arabism remained a strong force in the Near East. Its official instrument, the Pan-Arab League (founded in 1945), served as both a forum of protest and a rallying center for nearly 300 million Moslems. Whatever differences retarded united action—and they were many and significant—the Arab peoples of the world had made it abundantly clear that Western imperialism was no longer to be borne.

## AFRICA

### Libya, Algeria, and Tanzania

The postwar surge of nationalism in the Far and Near East soon spread to Africa. The pace and scope of its development there have produced results so complex, so novel, and so bewilderingly ramifying as to require study quite beyond the aims of this book. Here we can only sketch its main outlines and, in order to give some body to our understanding, sample a few specific developments.

At the end of World War II there were only four independent nations in Africa: South Africa, Ethiopia, Liberia, and Egypt. Within the short span of twenty years, over thirty other independent states emerged (see the map on p. 652). Many specialists in African affairs predict that the few remaining colonies, such as Angola, Mozambique, and South West Africa, will achieve independence within another score of years or less.

The rapid process of decolonization in Africa was carried out in various ways. For example, Libya, which became an independent state in 1951, had its freedom practically thrust upon it. Before the war, as we have already seen, it was an Italian colony. After the war the new Italian Republic showed signs of wanting to regain complete control. Because Italy had been an Axis belligerent, this claim was given little sympathetic attention. More as a move in the cold war, which by then had assumed serious proportions, than as an act of humane justice, the country was made an independent monarchy, with air bases and other accommodations granted to the Western powers, particularly the United States.

Quite different was the course of Algerian independence. For almost a century Algeria had been a French dependency. By the turn of the century French colonists had staked out the choicest lands and resources for themselves; they had, indeed, come to think of the country as a part of France—their part. Although restive under French rule, most of the native population saw little hope for change. From time to time small-scale demonstrations and riots, generated by the eloquent pleading and daring of liberation-minded leaders, bespoke nationalistic potentials that lay under the surface of regimented French rule. The collapse of France in World War II gave stimulus to these potentials. By the early 1950s many Frenchmen, including influential members of the government, were ready for negotiations that would ease rising tensions. By this time Algerian leaders, and a majority of their countrymen as well, were insisting on complete independence. Even this might have been considered by the French Cabinet had it felt reasonable assurance that their compatriots in the colony would have accepted such a decision. Tentative proposals made it plain that the settlers would not only refuse the granting of independence but also would not accept any substantial change in the *status quo*. At this point large-scale rebellion

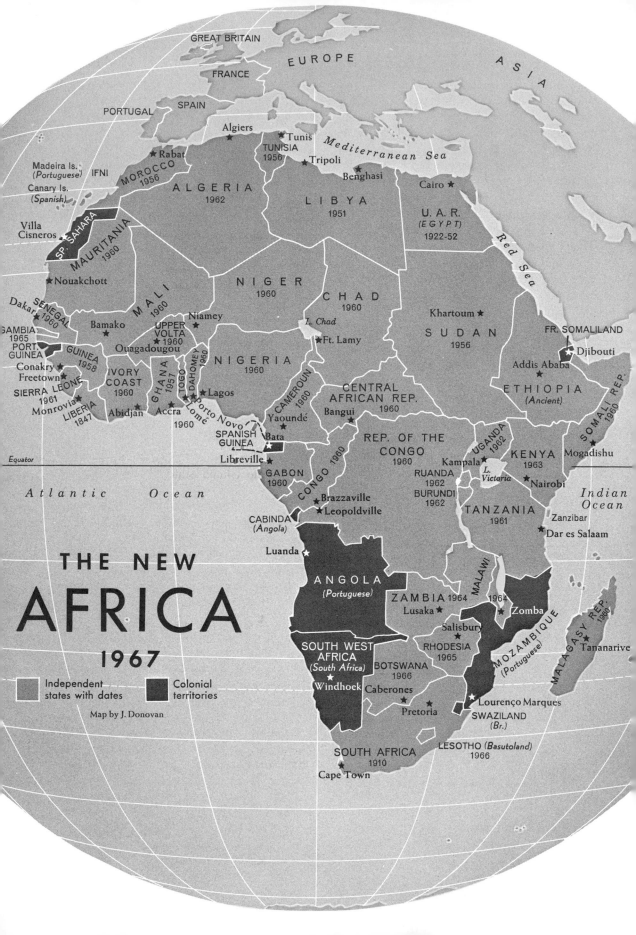

broke out. Under the vigorous leadership of the National Liberation Front, Algerians fought with all the resources at their command for the creation of a free, independent Algerian nation. For seven years (1955–1962) terror roamed the land; each side perpetrated atrocities that both would like to forget today. With de Gaulle's return to power in 1958, new efforts were made by the French government to persuade French colonists to either return home or accept Algerian rule. For a time it appeared that civil war would rend France itself. Only when de Gaulle made ready to use the armed forces on a massive scale against the settlers, did they grudgingly yield. Later a high official of the new Algerian government spoke appreciatively of French understanding "of the dynamics of the postwar colonial change —*European decolonization.*" But bitter memories of the long, bloody struggle could not fail to affect efforts by both sides to achieve a lasting *rapprochement*.

Still another road to independence was taken by Tanzania (formerly called Tanganyika). Long a ward of first the League of Nations and then the United Nations, Tanzania achieved full freedom as an independent state in 1962. Orderly negotiations, reasonable demands, and a mutual recognition of political realities marked the change from colony to nation. Much of the credit for this sophisticated approach to decolonization must go to Julius Nyerere, leader of Tanzania's nationalist party and head of the government. Unlike some African leaders, Nyerere refused to allow excited emotions to affect his judgment of what could be done as against what a long-repressed people would like to see done. For example, he retained large numbers of British civil servants despite the agitation of many of his countrymen to send the white man packing. Without them, he well understood, administrative chaos would follow, intensifying the growing pains that every new nation must suffer. He even went so far as to severely punish Tanzanian soldiers who mutinied in

*In 1964 a Tanzanian army mutiny led to rioting and looting. President Julius Nyerere, left, speaks at a press conference in his residence at Dar-Es-Salaam. The President, although lamenting the strife, felt that the soldiers had real grievances.*

January 1964, in protest against the retention of British officers in the small Tanzanian army. In return, Britain took care not to allow its citizens who remained in the former colony to subvert the plans and processes of the new government.

## The Failure of Nationalism in South Africa

In these three instances of surgent African nationalism, full freedom and independence were achieved. In South Africa, on the contrary, native Africans suffered humiliating defeat. More than two thirds of the population of the Republic of South Africa are Negroes. But all instruments of authority and control are held or dominated by whites. Negroes are denied the right to vote. Their major political parties, such as the African National Congress and the Pan-Africanish Congress, were banned and many of their leaders imprisoned. A detailed and severely enforced program of *apartheid*—segregation —operates at every level of society.

Since 1948, successive Nationalist (that is, white) governments have worked systematically toward the objective of creating a closed, compartmentalized society in which each racial group will have prescribed living areas, kinds of work, levels of wages, and distinctive educational systems. Since the Africans are, in the folklore of apartheid, only "visitors" from their tribal homelands and . . . "do not constitute a homogeneous people," they are not allowed to participate in the government of white-governed South Africa.[4]

Repeatedly the United Nations has tried, always unsuccessfully, to persuade the Nationalist government to grant basic freedoms to the majority black population. Thus, while in almost all other parts of Africa the native peoples have freed themselves from the yoke of colonialism, in South Africa the nationalist surge has been blunted and almost broken.

## The Trend Toward Socialism

In many parts of Africa the movement for independence has been accompanied by the supersession of the capitalist system by one or another form of socialism. Fairly typical of the anticapitalist views of many African leaders is that expressed by Tanzania's president, Julius Nyerere:

In an acquisitive society wealth tends to corrupt those who possess it. It tends to breed in them a desire to live more comfortably than their fellows, to dress better, and in every way to out do them. They begin to feel they must climb as far above their neighbours as they can. . . . Apart from the anti-social effects of the accumulation of personal wealth, the very desire to accumulate it must be interpreted as a vote of "no confidence" in the social system. For when a society is so organized that it cares about its individuals, then, provided he is willing to work, no individual within that society should worry about what will happen to him tomorrow if he does not hoard wealth today. Society itself should look after him, or his widow, or orphans. That is exactly what traditional African society succeeded in doing. Both the "rich" and the "poor" individual were completely secure in African society. Natural catastrophe brought famine, but it brought famine to everybody—"poor" and "rich." Nobody starved, either of food or human dignity, because he lacked personal wealth; he could depend on the wealth possessed by the community of which he was a member. That was socialism. That *is* socialism.[5]

Naturally, this trend away from capitalism has disturbed many leaders in the Western world, as it has encouraged Communist leaders in Europe and Asia. Thus the emergence of African nationalism has solved old problems and created new ones. White imperialism, at least in its old form, is gone. Millions of black people have won the long-lost right to order their lives according to their own genius and their own traditions. In all the new states, however, undeveloped economies and understandably unstable political regimes have invited attention from the two great superpowers which may both prejudice new freedoms and aggravate old tensions.

4. Helen Kitchen, ed., *A Handbook of African Affairs,* Praeger, New York, 1964, p. 139.

5. "Ujamaa: the Basis of African Socialism," by Julius K. Nyerere, from John Albert Luthuli, *Africa's Freedom,* George Allen and Unwin Ltd., London, 1964, pp. 138–139.

# C. The Metamorphosis of Europe

## REGIONAL GROUPINGS

In the interwar years, Western Europe's influence in world affairs declined as the potentials of leadership passed to the United States and, to a lesser degree, to Russia. At the time this was not clearly perceived. For one thing, Europe, sparked by Weimar Germany under the Dawes and Young plans, appeared to be on the road to economic recovery and political stability. For another, Communist Russia seemed to have lost its revolutionary *élan* as it retreated into a New Economic Policy. Moreover, the United States had made it abundantly clear that it was not interested in the responsibilities of world leadership. But these conditions masked rather than revealed the true situation. Europe's postwar "good years," as we have seen, fundamentally rested on American, not European credit. On the other hand, Communist Russia was on the threshold of an amazing industrial upswing under its Five Year Plans. And despite the serious setback soon to be effected by the Great Depression, the United States had created an economic establishment unprecedented in productivity.*

World War II revealed the true situation. By 1947 Great Britain had come to acknowledge openly that she could no longer support Greece in its fight against Soviet aggression, an acknowledgment that heralded the end of Britain's preeminence as arbiter of world affairs. France was nearly prostrate from four years of Nazi occupation and internal dissension. Germany was sundered into two parts. Italy was all but bankrupt both economically and politically. In contrast, the Soviet regime was not only master of its own house but also of most of Eastern Europe. The United States, its homeland unravaged by war, had amassed wealth and power of quite immeasurable dimensions. Europe had not only ceased to "expand" but had shrunk to almost its pre-Columbian condition.

Nevertheless, the early prophets of Europe's doom were more wrong than right. Within twenty years after World War II, Western Europe was again enjoying economic prosperity and, in the main, political stability. Most important, it had taken giant steps towards regional integration. It is certain that this partial break with national compartmentalism contributed to both prosperity and stability. Why the moves toward integration were made is less clear. Some observers believe that they were prompted by a long-overdue realization of the fatal limitations of parochial nationalism. Others hold that "European founders and American godparents designed the new North Atlantic Community as an instrument of the cold war." It is difficult to believe that the cold war was not a compelling force; it is also unlikely that the national advantages of cooperation in a shrinking world were not sensed. In any case, in the years following Germany's surrender, a half dozen or so comprehensive supranational institutions were created.*

## *The Council of Europe and the European Coal and Steel Community*

The first such venture was modest enough. In 1948 Belgium, the Netherlands, and Luxembourg agreed to abolish all tariffs

---

* Compare Geoffrey Barraclough, *An Introduction to Contemporary History,* Basic Books, Inc., New York, 1964, pp. 19–22.

* The emphasis here is upon "comprehensive." In all, large and small, these organizations ran into many dozens.

*Jean Monnet, left, and Robert Schuman attend a reception following the signing of the famous Schuman Plan (1951). Foreign Minister Schuman conceived the plan; Monnet served as its chief "architect."*

it served, and continues to serve, as an important clearing house of debate.

In 1951 the six nations constituting "Little Europe"—France, Italy, Belgium, the Netherlands, Luxembourg, and West Germany—set up the European Coal and Steel Community. In essence this organization, which developed out of what is popularly called the Schuman Plan after its founder Robert Schuman, then French Minister of Foreign Affairs, allowed the member states to pool their basic industrial resources under complicated arrangements designed to do away with restrictive competition and encourage mutually profitable trade. Together with the Marshall Plan it brought Western Europe out of its postwar economic doldrums in a remarkably short time. Because its economic activities were so complex and of such a fundamental character, political decisions were often involved in the Community's undertakings. This practice, in turn, promoted the development of an informal but increasingly effective unity of interests and outlooks that suggests the possible future creation of a true political union.

## The "Western Union"

The outbreak of the Korean War in 1950 prompted the United States to urge the rearmament of West Germany against the possibility of renewed Communist expansion in Europe. Fearful of resurgent German militarism, the Schuman Plan countries debated a French suggestion for the formation of a Western European army—the European Defence Community (E.D.C.). Ironically, the idea caught on with all members of the Plan except France itself. After two years of fretful debate the French Chamber of Deputies, with visions of goose-stepping conquerors still fresh, voted against it. Thus Europe's first serious move to create a truly international army came to nothing. But its approval by the other five nations showed how far along the road to integration many Europeans had traveled.

Failure of the E.D.C. project led, in 1955,

against incoming goods originating within the borders of any of them, and to charge common rates on incoming foreign goods. The resulting enlargement of their free-trade areas stimulated economic activity while it lessened political tensions among them. In 1949 Belgium, Denmark, France, Britain, Ireland, Italy, Luxembourg, the Netherlands, Norway, and Sweden formed a loose political association called the Council of Europe. Meeting in Strasbourg, delegates from each of the countries debated common concerns in a forum called the Consultive Assembly. A Committee of Ministers was set up to act as the Council's executive agent. Each nation retained its full sovereignty, and no measure "passed" by the Consultive Assembly was automatically binding on any member state which chose not to accept it. Although later joined by a number of other states, clearly the Council was no Federated Europe. But

One Big Family

*This Chicago* Sun-Times *cartoon shows Europe's "First Family" happily—and surprisingly—united six years after the holocaust of World War II.*

to the creation of a seven-power Western European Union composed of Belgium, France, West Germany, Italy, Luxembourg, the Netherlands, and Britain. Its purpose was to coordinate the arms production and defense plans of the member states and to promote common political and cultural interests. Its Assembly was made up of the delegates selected to represent the member states of the Consultive Assembly of the Council of Europe. For a time it was hoped that this "Western Union" would mark a real advance toward a Federated Western Europe, but it eventually became little more than another forum of debate. In 1960 its chief cultural and social committees were made adjuncts of the Council of Europe.

## "The Six" and Other Regional Groupings

One of the most momentous steps toward integration was taken in 1958 when the busy "Six"—Belgium, the Netherlands, Luxem-

bourg, France, Italy, and West Germany—formed the European Economic Community (E.E.C.), popularly called the Common Market or "The Six." Fundamentally an extension of the Coal and Steel Community, the new organization set up a program to eliminate import and export duties among themselves, to establish a common tariff policy for trade with the rest of the world, to develop common agricultural and transport policies, and otherwise to "promote throughout the Community a harmonious development of economic activities." At the same time a European Atomic Energy Community (Euratom) was set up to create "the conditions necessary for the speedy establishment and growth of nuclear industries in the Community" through the coordination of public and private research in atomic energy. Like the Coal and Steel Community, the Common Market played a tremendous role in revitalizing the economic life of Western Europe. For a while Britain, originally invited to join the enterprise, felt that her Commonwealth commitments and advantages overbalanced the attractions of the new organization. To strengthen her position, she invited Norway, Sweden, Denmark, Switzerland, Austria, and Portugal to join with her in a similar enterprise which would still permit her to keep her preferential tariff arrangements with the Commonwealth states. When trade gains of "The Seven," as they came to be called, did not keep pace with those of "The Six," she reversed her position and applied for admission (1961). But President Charles de Gaulle of France, fearing that Britain had become too dependent on America for Europe's good, refused to give his consent. Nevertheless, Britain continued her efforts to merge "The Six" and "The Seven."

Meanwhile, other constellations in other parts of Europe and the world were formed, such as the Council for Mutual Economic Aid (1949) made up of the U.S.S.R. and six satellite Communist countries, the Central American Common Market (1960), the

EUROPE, 1967

NORTH AMERICA
Arctic Ocean
ASIA
Atlantic Ocean
Ural Mts.
Caspian Sea
AFRICA
Indian Ocean

Barents Sea

*Atlantic*

*Ocean*

NORWAY
SWEDEN
FINLAND
Helsinki ★
• Leningrad

★ Oslo
Stockholm ★

*North*

*Sea*

*Baltic Sea*

DENMARK
Copenhagen ★

UNION OF SOVIET
SOCIALIST REPUBLI

• Mosc

IRELAND
Dublin ★

UNITED
KINGDOM

London ★
The Hague ★
NETHERLANDS
West Berlin   East Berlin
EAST
GERMANY
Warsaw ★
POLAND
• Kiev

*English Channel*

Brussels ★
BELGIUM
Bonn ★
WEST
GERMANY
Prague ★
CZECHOSLOVAKIA
LUXEMBOURG

Paris ★
FRANCE
LIECHTENSTEIN
Vienna ★
Budapest ★
ROMANIA

*Bay of Biscay*

★ Bern
SWITZERLAND
AUSTRIA
HUNGARY
Bucharest ★

*Black Sea*

ITALY
SAN MARINO
YUGOSLAVIA
Belgrade ★
Sofia ★
BULGARIA
Istanbul

PORTUGAL
ANDORRA
MONACO
Corsica
(France)
Adriatic Sea
ALBANIA
TURKEY
Ank

Lisbon ★
★ Madrid
SPAIN
Rome ★
Tirana ★
GREECE

Sardinia
(Italy)
Aegean Sea

• Gibraltar
(Br.)
Balearic Is.
(Spain)
Athens ★

*Mediterranean*

Sicily

Malta
(Br.)

Crete

*Sea*

Communist countries

"THE SIX"

"THE SEVEN"

0      200      40

Map by J. Donovan

Organization of American States (O.A.S.) which included all nations of the Western hemisphere, and the R.C.D.—Regional Cooperation for Development (1964)—composed of Iran, Pakistan, and Turkey. In short, although national sovereignty was not surrendered or even seriously discussed, in the score of years following World War II

regional communities were established and developed strength and by that fact diminished traditional national prejudices. If Europe, the world's onetime master, loosed its grip on peoples and places beyond it, it also created the model of the "cluster community" that gave some promise of an eventual Great Global Society.

# D. The Capitalist-Communist Conflict

## THE COLD WAR

### *Causes*

Parallel with this promise, an ominous peril appeared—the growing conflict between the capitalist and communist worlds. Were he alive, Hitler could point with some gloating to a statement that he made just before his suicide in 1945: "With the defeat of the Reich . . . there will remain in the world only two powers capable of confronting each other—the United States and Soviet Russia. The laws of both history and geography will compel these two Powers to a trial of strength. . . ."[6] Although we may seek comfort from the fact that one of the age's greatest liars spoke these lines, we cannot deny that the first of the two theses proved itself, at least until the advent of Communist China partially invalidated the Führer's arithmetic.

After the war collaboration between the capitalist and communist worlds came to an abrupt end. It is idle to deny, although some have attempted to, that ideology was a basic cause of the cold war. In 1848 the bourgeois world was horrified at the pronouncements

of the Communist Manifesto. A hundred years later it had much more reason to be apprehensive. Even though, as we have seen, Soviet Russia had lost over twenty million of its people in the war and had suffered a scarring of its earth beyond the comprehension of any who did not live there, it emerged from the long "Years of the Gun" with a greater strength than this ancient land had ever known. Its leaders believed that its Marxist way of life had saved it from destruction. Available evidence plainly indicates that its masses, although weary of Stalin, were not of a mind to turn the clock back to pre-Soviet capitalism.* For millions in Russia and in other lands, Communism had come to stay. But Communists believed that staying meant encountering, battling, and eventually overcoming the non-Communist world. For their part, many among the capitalist ruling elites believed that the world would never know either peace or prosperity so long as the "Communist menace" existed.

But more than ideology was involved in the renewed struggle. Soviet leaders remembered that after World War I the Western powers had ringed Russia with a tight

6. Francois Genoud, *ed., The Testament of Adolf Hitler,* translated by R. H. Stevens, Cassell, London, 1961, p. 107.

* See George Fischer, *Soviet Opposition to Stalin,* Harvard University Press, Cambridge, 1952.

*An anti-Communist view of the American "rescue" of Europe after World War II.*

"cordon sanitaire."* This time they were determined to forestall a repetition of this by doing some ringing of their own. Before the war had ended they had annexed Estonia, Latvia, Lithuania, and a portion of Poland. By 1948 they had set up Communist regimes in Czechoslovakia, Albania, Bulgaria, Rumania, and Hungary. The eastern provinces of Germany, occupied by Russian troops since early 1945, were also consolidated into the German Democratic Republic (1949), under Russian domination. Thus the Russian push westward was motivated by a mixture of ideological concerns, determination to revenge the sealing-off strategy of the Western powers after World War I, and plain, old-fashioned imperial aggrandizement.

### Crises: Greece and the Marshall Plan

The first serious crisis in the renewed capitalist-communist struggle occurred in the Balkans in early 1947. For several years

* See *supra,* p. 460.

Communist insurrectionists had tried to overthrow the reactionary monarchial regime in Greece, but had been thwarted by military and economic aid supplied by Britain. In 1947 the British Labour government, as we have seen, frankly admitted that Britain's own pressing needs necessitated the abandonment of this policy. To prevent an otherwise certain Communist take-over, President Truman ordered American intervention. Thereafter American money, arms, and military advisers were sent to Greece in an ever-increasing volume. With this aid the Greek government was finally able to put down the insurrection and consolidate its position (1949). Because Soviet Russia had put similar pressure on Turkey, aid under the "Truman Doctrine" was extended to that nation.

Simultaneously, United States Secretary of State George Marshall urged Congress to legislate a gigantic economic-recovery program for Europe. Originally the program was designed to stimulate the economic recovery of all of Europe by extending unusually generous loans to countries applying for them. However, between Marshall's formulation of the plan in 1947 and Congressional enactment of it into law in 1948 the occurrence of two events substantially changed its original purpose. One was the American intervention just noted; the other was Soviet Russia's adamant stand against any Communist country accepting American aid. Both events gave the President and his advisers the opportunity they wanted to use the Marshall Plan to forestall the advance of Communism in Western Europe. In short, the European Economic Program became a weapon in the cold war.

### Soviet Response: The Cominform and New Conflicts

To counteract Western pressures the Soviet Union, in late 1947, revived the Third International (see *supra,* p. 508) under a new name—Cominform. Ostensibly an agency to facilitate the exchange of information among Communist states, it actually functioned as a political propaganda instrument supporting anticapitalist solidarity around the world. Its influence was soon felt in important developments in France, Czechoslovakia, Italy, and Germany. In November of 1947, French Communist leaders called for a general strike. Because both economic and political conditions in the Fourth Republic were in anything but a healthy condition, the call posed a real threat to the government. For several weeks it appeared that spreading violence and sabotage might actually destroy the democratic system. Strong government action gradually wore down the insurrectionists, however, so that by mid-December the strike was given up. In February of 1948, events took a different turn in Czechoslovakia. For several years democratic leaders there had been able to keep Soviet influence within moderate bounds. Now Moscow gave the signal for a showdown with which the little country, surrounded by Communist satellite states, was unable to cope. Thereafter it followed a strict Stalinist line. The Communist take-over deeply shocked the Western world and, of course, intensified the cold war.

Soon Italian Communists began a gigantic rally to win mass support for their candidates in the general elections of 1948. Because a majority of Italy's Socialists, under Pietro Nenni, joined with the Communists in what was called the People's Bloc, and because Italy's politico-economic situation was even more unstable than France's, it appeared possible, even likely, that another capitalist regime would fall. But the recent example of Czechoslovakia, combined with American pressure and the Pope's strong support of anti-Bloc efforts, gave the Christian Democrats and their allies a substantial victory.

Much more threatening to the precarious peace of the world was the Berlin crisis of June 1948 to May 1949. To deter the Western powers from creating a West German state, Russia cut off land access to their sectors of divided Berlin, deep within the Soviet zone. Because the city had become a symbol of Western power vis-à-vis Soviet designs in Europe, Western statesmen felt that their sectors of the city had to be supplied at all costs. They therefore organized a gigantic airlift to bring in food, fuel, and other necessities. For a while during the winter months of 1948 and 1949, the city's demands for coal alone almost caused the project to collapse. Somehow enough planes and skilled airmen to fly them were found to carry it off, and in May the Russians admitted defeat by lifting the blockade. The residue of resentment and heightened tensions on both sides, however, further widened the gap between them.

## The Creation of NATO

One rather logical result of this crisis was the creation of the North Atlantic Treaty Organization (1949). It was essentially a military alliance, and its basic purpose was to secure the non-Communist states of Europe against Soviet aggression. The signatories agreed that "an armed attack against one or more of them in Europe or North America shall be considered an attack against them all." Although made up of some fifteen states, the United States, Britain, and France in practice bore the chief responsibility for making the organization strong enough to discharge its principal obligations. Headquarters were established outside of Paris where weekly meetings of the NATO Council were held. General Dwight Eisenhower was appointed supreme commander of NATO's military forces, which were made up of contingents contributed by member states. Eventually, Russia and the Communist states of Eastern Europe formed a similar organization under the terms of the Warsaw Pact (1954). Thus, within ten years after the destruction of Nazi Germany, the major powers, and many of the minor ones, were grouped into two opposing camps, each armed and bitter in its denunciations of the machinations of the other.

## The Korean War and Its Aftermath

In 1950 the capitalist-communist conflict developed into a shooting war in Korea. After the surrender of Germany but before the defeat of Japan the United States and Russia agreed, with Britain concurring, to work for an independent Korea to be set up after the war. As a temporary measure the country was to be divided at the 38th parallel, with the United States occupying the southern half and Russia the northern half. Quite naturally, this eventually resulted in the establishment of a communist regime in the Russian sector and a capitalist regime in the American sector. In 1948 and 1949 both Russia and the United States withdrew their troops from Korea. Shortly thereafter a North Korean army crossed over the dividing line in an attempt to unite the country under Communist rule. President Truman at once ordered United States forces to join those of South Korea in repelling the attack, and called on the United Nations to declare North Korea guilty of flagrant aggression. Owing to the temporary absence of Russia from the United Nations Council, the Council unanimously agreed and directed all members of the United Nations to supply military and other aid. Token forces from some United Nations member states were sent, but the main force opposing North Korean troops was made up of American and South Korean units. General Douglas MacArthur was appointed supreme commander of all forces.

Throughout the period of 1950 to 1952, the war followed a seesaw course. At one point the North Koreans came very close to driving MacArthur's troops into the sea. Not long afterward, a United Nations offensive pushed the North Koreans back to the 38th parallel. MacArthur insisted on continuing the advance until the whole of North Korea was conquered. Sustained by President Truman, MacArthur pushed his forces almost to the Chinese border. At this point Communist China sent massive support to the North

Koreans, and the war thereafter settled into a deadlock. To break it, MacArthur insisted on bombing mainland Chinese bases. Because this would have probably moved Russia to intervene and thus might have led to the total war that President Truman was determined to avoid, the President removed MacArthur from command. Under his successor, General Matthew Ridgeway, United Nations troops, although unable to move much beyond the 38th parallel, stubbornly withstood further North Korean and Chinese offensives. After many months of tedious negotiations a truce was signed, which left the general situation much as it was before the invasion began. Even though repeated attempts to frame a definitive peace settlement failed, a general war was avoided.

The ominous strength displayed by Communist China in the Korean War was the partial cause of the creation of still another regional grouping—the South-East Asia Treaty Organization (SEATO), which was made up of Australia, France, New Zealand, Pakistan, the Philippines, Thailand, Britain, and the United States (1954). Thus in Asia, as in Europe, the capitalist-communist conflict spawned rival alliance systems.

As long as the United States could claim exclusive possession of nuclear weapons, the Communist world naturally operated in world affairs under a severe handicap. From 1950 on, this situation underwent rapid change. From the successful detonation of an atomic bomb the Russians went on to build up a massive arsenal of medium- and long-range missiles. Moreover, in 1957 it announced the successful orbiting of an object in space (the first Sputnik), an event that ushered in the still bewilderingly strange space age. The next year the United States launched its Explorer I, and the cold war took on some of the aspects of fantasy in a kind of Edgar Allen Poe progression—which "side" had the more expert mathematicians and astrophysicists? Which could first send up a man to walk in space? Which would first hit the moon? By the mid-1960s the cold-war equations became even more complicated as China and France joined the lethal "Atomic Club" with political propensities that leaned clearly neither toward the Soviet Union nor the United States.

## COEXISTENCE AND THE "THAW"

In spite, or more probably because, of the rapidly mounting and increasingly fearful developments in destructive power, the tensions of the capitalist-communist conflict showed intermittent easement after 1954. With the emergence of Khrushchev as Russia's chief policy maker in 1956, a new Soviet note was struck—a note that is perhaps best described as cautious leniency at home and measured tolerance abroad.[7] We have already noted the nature and significance of the de-Stalinization of Party and State. Its influence was also felt in varying degrees in international affairs. In April of 1956, for example, the dissolution of the Cominform was announced. Also, the new Soviet leader made a special point of laboring the thesis that socialism was a many-mansioned system, and that the roads leading to it were not limited to the one traveled by Russia. The *detente* with Yugoslavia was further cultivated. Under a native Communist leader, Wladislaw Gomulka, Poland undertook the execution of certain nationalist policies—for example, the restoration of limited liberty to the Catholic Church—without retributive action from Moscow. In 1955, President Eisenhower and the foreign ministers of Britain and France met with Khrushchev in Geneva. No specific program for more peaceful East-West relations came from this "summit" conference, but the cordial atmosphere of the informal discussions suggested a welcome lessening of world tensions. Even new Russian threats—such as Khrushchev's "We will bury you"—took on new tone and meaning. Now the emphasis

was on *outproducing* rather than outshooting the capitalist world, on winning the so-called backward nations to communism by example rather than by Russian-initiated revolution. The "thaw" was far from complete; as we shall soon note, it was not even reasonably progressive. But it was real and marked a possible turning away from "bomb diplomacy" to grudgingly tolerant exploration and adjustment of world problems.

A recurrence in 1961 of the Berlin crisis emphasized the ambiguity of East-West interchanges. By then migrations from East Berlin to West Berlin, for reasons beyond our detailing here, had reached proportions both embarrassing to and economically crippling for the life and leadership of East Berlin. As its mentor, Khrushchev demanded an end of Western occupation. His blunt words and threatening gestures seemed to make an all-out violent showdown inescapable. A meeting between him and President Kennedy in Vienna (June 1961) did not resolve the issue, but it probably helped to forestall Soviet action leading to that showdown.

## THE "REFREEZE"

### The Cuban Crisis

Nevertheless, the "thaw" periodically yielded to distressing periods of "refreeze." After Fidel Castro's establishment of a Communist regime in Cuba, many anti-Communist refugees fled to Florida and other areas not too far from their homeland to prepare for the day of their return. Officials of the United States government, particularly those holding important positions in the Central Intelligence Agency (C.I.A.), actively collaborated with a refugee junta to plan the overthrow of the Castro government. The attempt was made in April of 1961—the "Bay of Pigs" invasion. It was promptly and completely repelled when, to the surprise of many Americans, the Cuban masses not only refused to join the invasion forces but supported the government in dispersing them.

7. See H. Stuart Hughes, *Contemporary Europe; A History,* Prentice-Hall, Inc., Englewood Cliffs, N.J., 1961, pp. 488–489.

IT IS A LONG FUSE, BUT IT IS LIGHTED

*A popular American conception of the Cuban crisis of 1962. Khrushchev is the happy "Cuba Meddler."*

Some American officials urged the President to use United States marines and other military forces to smash the Castro regime. Had the President yielded to this pressure, it is possible, although somewhat improbable, that Russia would have become involved, with consequences quite beyond conjecture. The President's refusal to heed the advice of the war party prevented this; capitalist-communist relations, however, suffered a serious setback. A year and a half later another Cuban crisis occurred when Soviet military technicians began to install and equip missile-launching sites on the island. President Kennedy demanded their immediate removal under threat of military sanctions. This time it was Khrushchev who heeded the voice of caution. The sites were dismantled and their materiel and Soviet personnel were returned to Russia. The resolution of this crisis was of extraordinary significance. Put negatively, it precluded complicating developments that might—some would say almost certainly would—have plunged the nations into nuclear war. Put positively, it resulted

in a *détente* which made it possible for the United States and the U.S.S.R. to collaborate in arranging multilateral talks that resulted in a partial nuclear test-ban treaty. It also led to more East-West contacts, although at the cost of heightening Chinese recalcitrance.

## The War in Vietnam

In 1965 and 1966, another serious East-West confrontation developed, the background of which must be examined in some detail. For many years (since about 1875) the people of Annam, Tonkin, and Cochin China had been ruled by the French. After an interlude of Japanese overlordship (during World War II), some of them won a kind of independence from the restored French rule in 1946. These included most of the people of Annam, but none of Tonkin to the north or Cochin China to the south. Negotiations between leaders of newly established Vietnam ("southern country") and the French soon ran into difficulties. The Vietnamese insisted on both complete independence and unity, by which they meant unity with their ethnic kin in Tonkin and Cochin China. France refused to grant either and, in December of 1946, the leaders resorted to guerrilla war to gain their ends. The fighting went on for eight years, with France (generously supported by United States dollars and other aid) winning many battles but steadily alienating the peasant population. After the Communist victory in China in 1949, Vietnam was supplied by them with arms and aid of many kinds. By 1954 the Communist-dominated Vietminh ("independence party") ruled most of the countryside, with fairly strong peasant support. In that year the French forces suffered a complete defeat at Dien Bien Phu, and France was forced to negotiate a settlement. Although North Vietnam gained its complete independence, France, aided by Western powers at Geneva where the meetings were held, was able to insist on a temporary continuation of the division of the whole land—

*South Vietnamese soldiers disembark from a United States Marine "chopper" to attack Vietcong guerrillas (1962).*

*Ho-Chi-Minh, the North Vietnam leader, is shown chatting with a group of young people after viewing with them an exhibition in Hanoi that featured examples of Chinese support of the North Vietnamese struggle against the United States.*

at the 17th parallel—until general elections could be held in 1956. The anti-Communist government in South Vietnam, however, refused to honor the elections agreement. Its strong man, Ngo Dihn Diem, whose armies were now organized and trained by agents of the United States government, consolidated his power in a dictatorship as tight as North Vietnam's, without the latter's social program. Indeed, Diem's regime became so corrupt and autocratic that, in spite of increased assignment of United States advisers and aid, it was overthrown in 1963 and Diem was executed. His successors, however—all militarists and by 1966 all except one former officers in the French army who had fought from 1946 to 1954 against their own people—were as little inclined toward reform as he.

When the Geneva agreement was abrogated by the Diem government, the North Vietnamese, under Ho Chi Min (a veteran Communist leader who, because of France's long struggle to keep her Asian colonies, was able to blend Communism with nationalism) again agitated for unity. Soon Ho sent Vietminh fighters south of the dividing line to rally the countryside against Diem. In 1964 the United States government, fearful that Ho would succeed in establishing Communist rule throughout the whole land, increased

*This Associated Press photograph shows a United States soldier waiting for Vietcong guerrillas to emerge from a hideout into which a smoke bomb had been thrown (1966).*

its support of the southern regime.* Within two years it had sent a third of a million soldiers to South Vietnam and had bombed various sections of North Vietnam. Thus in Southeast Asia the cold war had turned into a shooting war, which threatened to develop into a conflict the dimensions and end of which were difficult to foresee.

# E. Summary of the Flux and Flow of Contemporary Events

## THE NEW EUROPE

The events that we have considered in this chapter clearly indicate the development of far-reaching changes in the terms and conditions of human existence. During the eighteenth and nineteenth centuries, Europe made itself the world's mentor and, often, master. Since 1914 it has been contracting. But, as we have seen, the historic record plainly gives the lie to the pessimistic claims of those who argued that Europe was finished. Developments of the last ten years, indeed, point rather to its revitalization as a "high culture-carrier." Moreover, the emergent peoples of Africa and Asia have been so deeply marked by Europe's brand of civilization that, whatever their political status and their "awareness of a cultural heritage which did not derive from the west and which it was important to retain and integrate into modern life,"[8] they are and will long remain cultural cousins of their ousted masters. Nevertheless, the "Atlantic Community" is now but one of a cluster of communities, part of a global constellation which is both sign and substance of a new age in human history.

## THE NEW MASSES

Another aspect of the new age is the changed conditions, place, and power of the masses. At no time in the 5000-year record of civilization had mass man counted so much either in his own notion of his worth or in that of the elites who ruled over him. Even in Periclean Athens, we will recall, the free citizens of the city constituted a dominant minority. At the other chronological extreme of "democratic life"—nineteenth-century America—the situation was not very different. Except for most Negroes and Indians, adult males possessed the franchise and often used it with telling effect. Still, the American mass man was rarely the chief architect of the conditions of his own life, nor is he yet. However, over most of the world today the "little man" is on the move —either under his own power, as in the American labor movement; or under the "vanguard of the proletariat," as in communist countries; or working through socialist parties, as in Britain and Scandinavia; or, anomalously, under autocratic "chiefs," such as Jomo Kenyata in Kenya. Everywhere in the world the gap between commoner and "gentleman" is still wide. But mass society is in the making, and the trend hardly seems reversible.†

---

* It should be noted, however, that this was the officially stated aim. Many knowledgeable persons believed that the real purpose of the United States government was consolidation of a base in Asia which could be used in a future struggle against China.

8. Barraclough, *op. cit.*, p. 192.

† A number of scholars, especially among political scientists, sociologists, and psychologists, hold an opposite view. Representative works, easily accessible, are those of Hans Morgenthau, Ortega y Gassett, and Charles E. Skinner.

## BEGINNINGS OF THE "BREAKTHROUGH TO PEACE"

Paradoxically, this century of violence has been marked by a peace move surging far beyond anything of its kind in all human history. It is true that the doctrine of state sovereignty is still strong, thus weakening the will and ability of peoples to use an international constabulary in place of national armies. It is also true that the might of those armies is stronger than ever. Even so, signs of a revolutionary "breakthrough to peace" are clear. "Peace marches" and "peace sit-ins," for example, indicate a kind of grass-roots drive to abolish war as an instrument of national policy. Many academic communities have seen the creation of permanent "peace-research" groups, which seek to educate both themselves and a wider public. Some large foundation grants subsidize this and other kinds of peace activity. An unprecedented number of young men in the United States, at least, are registering as conscientious objectors to war. And, the destructive power of the nuclear bomb has caused even the man in the street to pause and ponder the destruction of civilization, unless large-scale wars are somehow relegated to the limb of outworn human habits. This is not, of course, meant to suggest that contemporary civilization is on the verge of universal disarmament and the creation of a world state under a common law. It is meant rather—and only—to emphasize an unprecedented turn toward peace.

## A NEW AGE

Also undergoing fundamental change is the complex value system of the long-dominant ruling class. In the 1960s, the bearded dissenters from conventional society's "rut and rule of living" were striking symbols of this change. Almost every convention and almost every concept with roots has invited challenge, from the propriety of neckties to the existence of God. We shall consider some of the more significant of these challenges and changes in Chapter XVII.

In short, the overall cumulative force of the often bewildering developments of the postwar years constitutes a huge pivot in human history, swinging one age, which we have long since labeled "modern," to the periphery of our life, while swinging another age, not yet named, into its vital center.

## SELECTED READINGS

Beloff, Max, *Soviet Policy in the Far East, 1944–1951,* Oxford University Press, London, 1953.

> Particularly useful as background for understanding present-day Soviet-Chinese encounters.

*Gatzke, H. W., *The Present in Perspective: A Look at the World Since 1945,* Rand McNally & Co., Chicago, 1965 (3rd ed.).

> A brief (200 pages) factual account of the cold war, the "restoration" of Western Europe, the major trends of events in the United States, Stalin and Stalin's Russia, the rise of new states in Asia and Africa, and "competitive coexistence."

Jackson, J. Hampden, *The World in the Postwar Decade, 1945–1955,* Houghton Mifflin Co., Boston, 1956.

> The events of this decade are grouped under three themes—the power conflict between Russia and the United States; the emergence of nationalism in Latin America, Africa, and Asia; and the more important "home" developments in Russia, the United Kingdom, and the United States.

Kitchen, Helen, ed., *A Handbook of African Affairs,* Praeger, New York, 1964.

> Good brief accounts of developments in the struggle that the peoples of Africa are waging to achieve independence, and a measure of the dignity that their membership in the human race affords them.

Luthuli, John Albert, *Africa's Freedom,* George Allen & Unwin Ltd., London, 1964.

* Asterisk (*) denotes paperback.

A collection of source materials that give the Western student a closer understanding of the aspirations—and agonies—of the emerging peoples of Africa.

*May, Ernest R., ed., *Anxiety and Affluence, 1945–1965,* McGraw-Hill Book Co., New York, 1966.
America's promises and perils, at home and abroad, as shown in "source" excerpts. Examples are the Taft-Hartley Act, Kennedy's "New Frontier" address, the Marshall Plan, a State Department report on the "fate of China," Truman's "Point Four," Kennedy on the Cuban missile crisis, McCarthy on Communists in the State Department, the problem of automation, and the Civil Rights Act of 1965.

Pikles, Dorothy, *The Fifth French Republic,* Frederick A. Praeger, New York, 1960.
A perceptive study of the meaning and methods of de Gaulle's France.

Roberston, Charles L., *International Politics since World War II,* John Wiley & Sons, New York, 1966.
A summary review of the more significant events and policy decisions of the twenty-year period since the war. The author tries to explain these happenings as they developed out of varying assumptions—not necessarily truths, as he points out—of the policy makers, and the changes worked on the old balance-of-power system by mass ideology, technology, and mass communications.

Saunders, John J., *The Age of Revolution,* Roy Publishers, A.N., New York, 1949.
A pessimistic survey of liberal romanticism and nationalist democracy, which ends with the suggestion that Western civilization may be heading for a new Middle Ages.

Toynbee, Arnold, and Veronica M. Toynbee, eds., *Hitler's Europe,* Oxford University Press, London, 1954.
A volume in the *Survey of International Affairs* series. It covers the years 1939 to 1946. The articles by various authors do not deal with battles or strategy, but with the political and economic structures of Germany, Italy from 1940 to 1943, Vichy France and the Free French Movement, the occupied countries of Western and Eastern Europe, and the satellite states. An excellent reference work.

Ward, Barbara, *Five Ideas that Change the World,* W. W. Norton & Co., New York, 1959.
The ideas are nationalism, industrialism, colonialism, communism, and internationalism. Miss Ward treats them with a strong bias for freedom and human dignity as against the approach of those who pin their hope on cold logic and political expediency as the proper criteria for national behavior in the modern world.

*Wright, Gordon, and Arthur Mejia, Jr., *An Age of Controversy,* Dodd, Mead & Co., New York, 1963.
These "Discussion Problems in Twentieth Century Europe" are concerned with the subjects that you would expect to find in a work with this title—the origins of World War I the rise and decline of colonialism, Russian totalitarianism, the Depression, etc. Particularly recommended are the sections entitled "Transition to the Twentieth Century," "The Impact of Freudian Thought," and "A Half-Century in Perspective."

Zagoria, Donald S., *The Sino-Soviet Conflict, 1956–1961,* Princeton University Press, 1962.
A detailed study of the origin and course of the parting of the ways of these two communist giants. The author does not think the conflict, of itself, is necessarily beneficial to the noncommunist world, which, he believes, should not relax in developing its military strength and its ability to respond firmly and rapidly to political challenges.

# XVII

# *The Travail of Contemporary Man*

Not surprisingly, the discontinuities of a world in flux which we considered in the preceding chapter gave contemporary man a sense of insecurity and apprehension. Further disturbing aspects of our unsettled condition were certain changes that took place within the corpus of our institutional life and the frames of reference which encompassed them; and, equally disturbing, at least to the masses of society, the "revolt of the intellectuals" which accompanied and, though not always intentionally, accelerated these changes. The purpose of this brief, concluding chapter is to sketch these two developments. It should be understood that the examples cited can do little more than illustrate them.

# A. The Disintegration of Traditional Institutions and Beliefs

## THE HERITAGE OF HOPE

It is a truism that life is a continuum. No age or epoch of human existence is completely divorced from the experiences that precede and follow it. Indeed, in many aspects the desires and dreams, the fears and foibles of twentieth-century man are basically the same as those of the citizens of ancient Babylon. But though the threads of human existence eternally bind the past with the present and bind both with the future, attitudes and patterns of behavior shift and change. Periclean Athens, for example, subscribed to an overall attitude toward life which shaped and gave substance to distinctive institutions and modes of behavior. A hundred years later Athenian life, though organically descended from its Periclean past, was characterized by quite another temper and a very different societal structure. Another random example of evolutionary change is the contrast between the America of Cotton Mather and that of Andrew Jackson.

A similar contrast also characterized the society of the West before the Great War and the society that emerged and developed from it. The war itself both contributed to and dramatized this change. Many came to believe that the established order and the system of values which sustained it were, if not wholly illusory, shockingly flimsy, fancy facades hiding a dangerous and perhaps fatal complacency that was itself at least partly responsible for the outbreak of the war.

> What was the value of the long looked
>     forward to,
> Long hoped for calm, the autumnal seren-
>     ity
> And the wisdom of age? Had they de-
>     ceived us
> Or deceived themselves, the quiet-voiced
>     elders,
> Bequeathing us merely a receipt for deceit?[1]

Before this transvaluation of values, most men and women of Western society believed in and labored for the realization of a world for which they thought they had a reasonably clearly drawn blueprint. It was often assumed that in this imagined future the individual would be free from arbitrary control by others whether they were princes, plutocrats, or priests—an ideal partly fostered by the egalitarian sentiments of the American and French revolutions. These and related impulses substantially motivated the revolutionaries of 1848 and 1849, the creators of the French Third Republic, English

1. From T. S. Eliot's *Four Quartets*.

commoners, Russian revolutionists and, to a lesser extent, Jacksonian Democrats and, later, Progressives in the United States. In this imagined world, too, man would live a life of moderate affluence based on the machine. Men hoped that technology would one day free humanity from menial drudgery, and the prison house of ignorance and dulled sensibilities which that drudgery had so cruelly built. Conditions and developments of the nineteenth century also led some seers to perceive, however dimly, the lineaments of a world ordered by law. The phrase "peaceful coexistence" had not yet been coined; but the idea it connotes was taking shape in the minds of many, if lesser, latter-day Kants.

Subsuming these projected enlargements of life, and sustaining their proponents with hope and strength, was a complex of institutions and beliefs inherited from the past. Among them was a social structure built around the family. In this microcosm of the larger community, children learned the elements of both self-fulfillment and communal behavior—from the techniques of language to group patterns of morals and manners. In it, too, were found psychic resources which nurtured a sense of security and, at least potentially, encouraged each member to "find himself" as a distinct and worthy individual.

Another basic resource was the inherited concept of man as a creature of reason, purpose, and dignity, flawed by the prostitution of his own powers, but still only a "little lower than the angels." Encompassing these and all of the other common postulates and practices of the Western way of life was the Judeo-Christian ethos. This religious matrix, rent though it was by skeptics, hypocrites, ignorant zealots, and sometimes intelligent atheists, nevertheless bound the Western world in a developing humane and purposeful fellowship. Assuredly the golden age of peace and plenty, of learning and law and love, had not yet flowered; nor would it soon flower. But men believed they had at least a taste of it, and would settle for nothing less.

## THE IMPACT OF SCIENCE AND INDUSTRY

All of these assumptions and ideas, although not completely destroyed in the postwar world, underwent changes so profound that much of their original nature and significance vanished or became suspect. The assault on tradition came from many directions, from the Great War itself, as well as from science, technology, and industry. To gain some sense of the magnitude of the changes that produced the present "time of troubles" we need to sketch the basic outlines of prewar traditionalism, and note to what extent technology, with science as its basis and industry as its beneficiary, repudiated the past and shaped the present.

### *On Religious Institutions and Beliefs*

The Judeo-Christian faith which cradled Western life was formed about 2000 years ago. Its main postulates are these: that "in the beginning God created the heavens and the earth"; that God is good, compassionate, and caring; that He is personal—that is, to His creature, Man, He bears the relationship of father to son and, like an earthly father, when appealed to properly, will provide the help man needs to achieve the good life; that all creation is purposed by Him and ordered in ways that develop that purpose— the ultimate experiencing of pure love; and that He and His way are not limited in time or space, but are "from everlasting to everlasting." Formed out of the still older faith of the Hebrews, it naturally took over many of that religion's beliefs and practices, such as the primacy of revelation as the way to truth, the anthropomorphic nature of God, the concept of the Savior, and the Ten Commandments as the moral requisites of the life of God's chosen. Naturally, too, it accepted the understandings of that time regarding the physical universe: the central and stationary position of the earth; the daily revolution of the sun around the earth, and

*Famed defense lawyer Clarence Darrow, right, is pictured here in a store in Dayton, Tennessee during the Scopes evolution trial.*

the stars as heavenly "extras" studding the skies for man's delight.

With the advent of science in the sixteenth century the cosmological underpinnings of the Christian faith were severely shaken. Although inspired scripture depicts Joshua commanding the sun to stand still, the findings of Copernicus and Galileo clearly demonstrated that, in relation to the earth, the sun was always "standing still." Even more disturbing to orthodox Christians were the principles set forth by Isaac Newton about 150 years later because Newton described a complex body of natural laws that set aside the Judeo-Christian concept of direct and interruptive divine intervention in terrestrial affairs, such as the parting of the Red Sea to provide for the exodus of the Jews from Egypt. In the nineteenth century, faith was even more profoundly shaken by Darwin's discovery of the origin of species which brought the sons of God into direct biological relationship to the lower animal kingdom and, at least implicitly, invalidated the accepted Christian concept of immortality.

Moreover, all phenomena took on new aspects and meaning from the hypotheses advanced by Albert Einstein in the early years of our own century. According to these theories, all phenomenal "objects" take on particular dimensions, characteristics, and

*Albert Einstein in 1931. Flanking him are his wife and the then governor of California.*

were discrediting. Only the barest reference to these revolutionary concepts can be made. Around 1900, Max Planck (1858–1947), the German physicist, presented theoretical evidence controverting the hitherto accepted notion that a continuous "flow" marked the emission and absorption of energy by atomic and subatomic particles. Planck held that rather than transmission through waves, energy was transferred in discrete packets, which he called quanta. A few years later Niels Bohr (1885–1962) developed the principle which successfully resolved a number of problems that physicists had long found baffling. But the quantum theory ran into difficulty when its more thorough application posed serious inconsistencies. In the 1920s, through the work of Louis de Broglie (1892– ), Erwin Schrödinger (1887–1961), and Werner Heisenberg (1901–     )— among others—these inconsistencies were, for the most part, eliminated by a hypothesis which asserted the *wave* character of particles. Thus the "flow" and "packet" explanations of the nature and movement of energy were merged into complementary hypotheses. In addition, Heisenberg advanced the thesis that since the position and speed of an electron can never be simultaneously fixed, scientists must give up all hope of ever determining absolute causality in nature. The dual character of the mode of the transmission of energy, as well as the Heisenberg "principle of uncertainty," continued to be held by most physicists into the second half of this century.

In the life sciences, particularly biology, revolutionary discoveries have been made in recent years. Whereas, for example, geneticists once labored long (and profitably) on the mechanics of heredity alone, their attention now centers on the nature and functioning of gene action. Their application of biochemistry and biophysics to this phenomenon have led them to believe that the "primary carrier of genetic information" is a nucleic acid (deoxyribonucleic acid— DNA). From this they conclude that study

"meaning" strictly in relation to the particular motion and position of their observer, with the exception of the speed of light which is constant. This dissolution of the traditional notion of absolutes applied even to mass and energy which, in Einstein's famous equation ($E = mc^2$, energy equals mass multiplied by the square of the velocity of light), were capable of transformation from one to the other. Time, as a coordinate of the dimensions of length, width, and breadth, took on a dimension of its own which was also subject, like space, to its relatedness, from the standpoint of the particular observer, to all other phenomena.

Probings into the nature of matter by other physicists revealed further intricacies and complications so removed from the workaday world of sense impressions as to rival the mysteries of the religious faith they of the basis of that acid's strand may lead to a complete understanding of the processes that determine the transmission of characteristics, and thus may bring man close to mastery of the production of those forms of living things that he decides are "good."

These complicated findings of science revealed a new and fascinating world to modern man. But they also made it increasingly difficult for educated persons to hold both to these findings and to the orthodox doctrines of the Christian faith. Although churches continued to be built and their services attended—in increasing numbers, as a matter of fact—the certainties and sanctions of the faith weakened. In short, the 2000-year-old God frame of reference, once sharp and compelling, increasingly tended to take on a disconcerting vagueness that left many Christians groping and confused.

## On the Man Frame of Reference

Another troubled frame of reference was man's long-held image of himself. If he had difficulty "picturing" God, he perforce found it unrealistic to view himself as God's son, or as a creature with godly attributes or potentialities. Nor could he rely, as many men of the Enlightenment had assumed he could, upon innate powers of reason and discernment. For here too the impact of science was strong and, to many, disturbing. One such study, of particular significance, was developed by Sigmund Freud, a Viennese psychologist (1856–1939). Fundamental to Freudianism was the hypothesis that men are basically irrational. What man commonly believed to be purposive cognition Freud insisted was a basic response to the sexual frustrations and inhibitions formed in early childhood. By the early decades of the twentieth century this view of man's motives and behavior became quite widely accepted. Its popularization gave many a sense of release from binding and, as they saw them, hypocritical Puritan restrictions and views of the nature and destiny of man. But it also gave to many a growing feeling of alienation from

Sigmund Freud (1936) whose views of the motivations and workings of the human mind revolutionized, for many, the meaning of human existence.

a world which had traditionally been considered to have meaning and humane purpose.

Another twentieth-century view of man was proposed by John B. Watson (1878–1958) and later, in a variant form, by Charles L. Skinner. Watson argued that man had to rid himself of the notion of "mind" if he was ever to understand and control his behavior. All activity is, in this view, grounded in response to stimuli. Like other animals, man has certain needs to meet— such as hunger, sex, and affection. How he responds to these needs ultimately forms his "character." Since responses to stimuli may be conditioned and reconditioned * this

---

* Terms first used, in this context, by the Russian psychologist, Ivan Pavlov (1849–1936). In his famous experiment, Pavlov offered meat to a hungry dog, to cause it to salivate. Later a bell was rung as the meat was offered. Subsequently, merely ringing the bell produced salivation— a "conditioned" response.

character becomes so highly complicated and intricate that it is easy for man to forget— or refuse to believe—that his total personality really rests upon an originally very simple and wholly physical "stimulus-response arc." But, the behaviorists insisted, temptations to accept religious or other non-behavioristic explanations of man's actions must be resisted, if scientific truth was to be a guide to action.

The double thrust of Freudianism and Behaviorism went far to dim and, for many, to destroy the traditional Man frame of reference. The various images of the "new man," constructed by psychologists and others in the behavioral sciences, like the new universe of the physical scientists, gave to a growing number of men a sense of openness and adventurous growth; most people, however, were left puzzled and bewildered.

## On Social Institutions

Industrial and technological developments of the late nineteenth and twentieth centuries significantly altered the old framework of Western man's communal life. The introduction of the dynamo vastly accelerated the industrialization and urbanization of society. Powered by electricity now, as well as by steam, giant machines and machines to make machines helped to provide a material abundance that man had never before experienced, and at the same time the machines spawned sprawling megalopolises. Food, clothing, shelter, gadgets, games, places to go and rapid means of going there—all increased in supply, variety, and novelty. But the distribution of the new abundance was uneven, resulting in social tensions and spreading slums. As it put man on wheels, the mechanized life also frayed his nerves and dulled his sense of the worth of the nonmarketable goods of life. And with the advent, around midcentury, of automation and huge computers, it became increasingly possible to view life as a "program," coldly directed by mysterious engineering elites more interested in models and "games" than in

*A George Grosz watercolor entitled* Republican Automatons *(1920).*

understanding the needs and, as they were once thought of, noble capabilities of human beings.

## Corporate Man

Even apart from the "program" aspects of modern industrial society, its corporate structure had become such as to cause, rightly or wrongly, many of its members to feel they had been "depersonalized." The telescoping of new and intricate communication devices had, for example, grafted onto the typical large corporation a giant, composite ear and a giant, composite mouth. Little opportunity was left for the individual to reflect on the processes that engaged him or even the meaning of his individual contribution. Nor was this true of only the lower-echelon workers. Although there were still individual "stars" in industry, the day of the tycoon seemed past. Policy making was usually the function of a team, its end product the result of group discussions which often involved a complicated hierarchy of committees and subcommittees.

Moreover, the ramifications of the trend toward mergers, and the ever accelerating growth of the "business mind" were no longer separable from society at large, especially in the United States. Also, although government "interference" in business had steadily increased in the postwar years, industry nevertheless probably had more to say about what the individual—at every social level—thought, said, wore, and valued than any other institution in society, including government. For most workers "the code of practice of the firm—[a kind of] body of common law—seems to them to condition their lives and functions more urgently than the ordinances of the city or the laws of the state or nation."[2] Or again, suppose the executives of a supergiant industry decided to lay out several hundred million dollars for plant expansion. This decision,

may well determine the quality of life for a substantial segment of society. Men and materials will move across continents; old communities will decay and new ones will prosper; tastes and habits will alter; new skills will be demanded, and the education of a nation will adjust itself accordingly; even government will fall into line, providing public services that corporate developments make necessary.[3]

Whether "depersonalized," anonymous, or conformist, many men and women of modern industrial society live their lives on the basis of the frame of reference of the corporation, not that of God or man.

## Family

The combination of industrialization and the exigencies of World Wars I and II helped to produce a "new woman" by providing a new place for her in society. As late as the beginning of the twentieth century, the interests of most women centered in home and children. By the second half of the cen-

tury woman's range of activities and her degree of mobility had increased astonishingly. Almost every occupation, business and profession was opened to her or, more accurately, by her. Besides psychic rewards, she achieved a measure of financial independence which, among other things, changed the nature of marital relationships and responsibilities; more specifically, it made divorce of incompatible partners more practicable and eventually more respectable. With more time, money, and freedom of action at her command, the new woman naturally felt greater concern for her formal education. The effects of these changes meant new family relationships—less time spent with children and husband, and more sexual freedom, as examples—greater activity in political affairs, more direct influence in the economy, all resulting in greater responsibility for the general ordering of society. Concurrently, the wide acceptance of the idea that children as well as adults had inalienable rights of expression and creativity gave children, too, a new freedom and mobility. These developments, coupled with industry's growing propensity to move men from place to place as its expanding needs and facilities might indicate, created a new rhythm of life, sometimes exhilarating, sometimes bewildering. In short, the old home, unit of the old society, as well as the hierarchy of relationships within society, underwent changes which increased the scope of human movement and endeavor as it decreased man's sense of community, security, and rootedness.

## THE "ETHICAL REVOLUTION"

The impact of universal war, science, and technology caused Western man to question the old norms of accepted behavior. After the war, much of what had long been considered the "good life" seemed at best to be irrelevant convention, at worst, unbearable hypocrisy. It was an age of retreating answers and probing questions. Had not the

2. Frederick Lewis Allen, *The Big Change,* Harper and Row, New York, 1952, p. 253.
3. Quoted in John Brooks, *The Great Leap . . . ,* Harper and Row, New York, 1966.

face of Western civilization been revealed as a mask? Was its life a husk which hid or distorted dynamic internal forces? If so, how could Western man trust the traditional value system? For if it had not induced, certainly it had not prevented the catastrophic dimension of his experience. On the other hand, if traditional values were illusory, what values were more sound? Was it realistic to believe in any general code of ethics? Was not, perhaps, each individual answerable to whatever powers might lie within himself, and to these powers alone?

These questions were initially—and insistently—pressed by many of the spokesmen of the famous "Lost Generation." *Their answers, often confused and contradictory, were rooted in rebellion against what they regarded as a phony world and its managers. The new spirit of the times both reflected and shaped the whole range of this generation's thought and behavior. Its chief (and mutually contradictory) characteristics were emphasis upon pure subjectivism, hedonistic abandon, and frank acknowledgment of life's anarchic, often cruel, purposelessness. Although the following example of the new subjectivism deals with art, it is typical of the subjectivist approach to all human experience:

> It is true that human imagination can give to the most ordinary object an unexpected distinction; but the magic power of the imagination is put to very feeble use if it serves merely to preserve or reinforce that which already exists. That is an inexcusable abdication. It is impossible in the present state of modern thought, when the exterior world appears more and more suspect, to agree any longer to such a sacrifice. The work of art, if it is to assist in that absolute revision of values upon which we all agree, must base itself upon a purely subjective inspiration or it will cease to exist.[4]

* Which became most active and vocal in the 1920s.

4. Andre Breton, quoted in Quincy Howe, *The World Between the Wars,* Simon and Schuster, 1953, p. 300.

An "ethical revolution"—based in part on the new empasis on the private, personal, and subjective—led many youths (and no few of their elders) into experiments in hedonism. Possessed of (as well as by) a restless energy created in part by the agitations of the Great War and intolerably dammed up by the frustrations of the aborted peace, these youths sought release in a new warfare against inhibitions. One meaning of the notorious Jazz Age was privatization as exemplified in an endless round of parties, sexual adventuring, shocking stunts, as well as the partly impulsive, partly calculated defiance of convention on any level of life they might happen to find themselves.

Mingled with this desperate search for private experience in the external world was a perhaps numbing recognition of life's basic purposelessness. This nihilism affirmed neither existentialist nor hedonistic fulfillment. Instead, its practitioners perceived life as an ongoing, incomprehensible, often hideous nightmare that the individual had somehow to endure, as in E. E. Cummings' *The Enormous Room.* Sensations were felt, events occurred, ideas were conceived; but all were unpurposed, unplanned, unreal, but nonetheless genuinely threatening to both authenticity and even survival. At best, man's elaborate social structures, complex legal systems, and conventional behavior were alluring chimera; at worst, they could destroy first manhood and, eventually, mankind. A clear (and chilling) expression of this view of life is found in Franz Kafka's *The Trial.* Its hero, fittingly nameless, was an assistant bank director who was arrested by authorities of the state Apparatus on an unnamed charge. The case dragged on for months with no intimation to the victim of the nature of his crime. His guilt was assumed; periodically he was interrogated in a vague, ghostly manner. At no time did he face his official accusers; nor was he ever brought to trial. In the end two "warders" led him out to a stone quarry at the edge of town, courteously disrobed him (taking care to fold his clothes neatly), and ran a butcher knife through his heart. Two of many of such entries in Kafka's diaries reflect the hopeless torment that plagued him throughout his brief life:

There are conflicting thoughts always in my head, something like this: My situation in this world would seem to be a dreadful one . . . on a forsaken road . . . where one keeps slipping in the snow in the dark, a sunless road . . . without an earthly goal . . . incapable of striking up a friendship with anyone, incapable of tolerating a friendship . . . . A man is purer [at night] than in the morning; the period before falling asleep is really the time when no ghosts haunt one; they are all dispersed; only as the night advances do they return, in the morning they have all assembled again, even if one cannot recognize them.[5]

In general, these were the attitudes of the postwar generation. With the past discredited and the future frameless, the condition of modern man, on the one hand, paralleled "the position of those few illuminati who, when initiated into the seventh circle of Syria's medieval Order of Assassins, were told the Order's secret of secrets: 'There is no truth; everything is permitted.' Or, to cite an unconscious Broadway jazz echo of the Assassins, 'Anything goes.'"[6] On the other hand, the condition for many of a later period was so characterized by fretful futility that, if they had invented a slogan to describe

their condition (which they seemed to beat to bother about), it might have been "nothing counts."

The characteristic anguish of the 1920s was interrupted by the crises of depression and war. But, beginning in the late 1950s, both hedonistic abandon and nightmarish nothingness tended to yield to an almost frantic concern for "identity" as not only the supreme value but almost the only value. Some individuals, such as Salinger's symptomatic Holden Caulfield, probed their inner self for feelings, insights, and powers which, once encountered and recognized, would give some measure of meaning, perhaps even satisfaction, to existence. This effort was doubly paradoxical: it came to affirm the unique properties of the self at the same time it insisted that the lone individual was brother to all men, also lone individuals, and that all were comrades in a corporate existence that one could pretend to ignore with impunity. It also simultaneously attacked bourgeois materialism while urging the need for contemporary man to face realistically the fact that the new world was an industrial world that simply refused to be buried under an avalanche of protest literature.

Thus by the middle of the twentieth century almost the whole fabric of Western man's culture had undergone or was undergoing cataclysmic change, with little indication that the pace would slacken.

---

# B. The Revolt of the Intellectuals

Concomitant with these changes, and in part causing them, was the complex of cries of defiance or despair, protest movements,

and startling innovations that characterized the revolt of the intellectuals. As in all ages, these probing venturers constituted a very small portion of the population. But their influence can hardly be measured by their

5. Max Brod, ed., *The Diaries of Franz Kafka, 1914–1923,* Schocken Books, Inc., New York, 1949, pp. 214, 217.
6. Peter Viereck, "The Revolution in Values: Roots of the European Catastrophe, 1870–

1952," *The Political Science Quarterly,* Vol. LXVII, No. 3, September 1952, p. 349.

*Chagall's* I and the Village *(1911).*

Woman Combing Her Hair, *a bronze statue by Alexander Archipenko (1915).*

numbers. Long before the average person sensed the superannuation of tradition, the "illuminati" had come to see the need for change even if that change meant sheer destruction as it did for some. Although initially their work was known only to a few, eventually it filtered down, in part, and in one form or another, into the consciousness, outlook, and behavior of the many. We need, therefore, to note the efforts of at least a few of the intellectual innovators, some of whom were rebels while others acquiesced, who manifested this travail and attempted to sketch the outlines of a new way of life. The examples of revolt that we shall note are representative of the century's *Zeitgeist* although a different cast would yield somewhat different results.

## ART AND MUSIC

In art the revolt against the old ranged from expressionism, "metaphysical art," dadaism, surrealism, cubism, and abstractionism, to the styles called "pop" and "op."

It is enough to illustrate only some of the motivating forces at work.

Metaphysical painting flourished in the first two decades of this century. Its founder, Giorgio de Chirico, sought to "transcend human limitations" by creating on canvas

Le Grand Déjeuner, *an oil painting by Fernand Léger (1921).*

poetic fantasies that bore no resemblance to the experiences of this world. His work was permeated by a nightmare mood that transformed objects, which seemed at first examination to resemble (though distortedly) normal features of life, into desolate otherworldly—or nonworldly—apparitions. Dadaism grew out of revolution against the senseless horrors of World War I. "A whole generation had come to the conclusion that nothing was of any importance . . . . [Dadaism's] aim was to make a clean sweep; its methods were confusion and destruction. It proclaimed that everything, especially art, was nonsense.[7] Both its chaotic daubings and its strangely disciplined nihilism—the latter strikingly seen in the works of Max Ernst—

therefore were not meant to be made sense of. It was a culturally significant and symptomatic temper tantrum. Cubism, on the other hand, although rejecting the traditional concepts of representational art, sought to put mind and order back into art by emphasizing geometric form, and to put the emotions in their place by deemphasizing vivid colors. Some of the early works of Pablo Picasso (who did not long remain in any particular school) effectively portray this approach to reality. The Cubists, however, in their effort to reduce their work to visual symbolic representations of parts, often made the object that embraced these parts so unrecognizable as to destroy it. Contrarily, abstract art had this as one of its primary aims. It tried to break through the "superficial" world of sensory impression to reach the essence of harmony and order. In all of modern art, however—

7. Emile Langui, ed., *Fifty Years of Modern Art,* Frederick A. Praeger, New York, 1959, p. 41.

*Picasso's* Seated Woman *(1927).*

*An oil painting by Miro* — Dutch Interior *(1928).*

whether coldly rational, deliberately "insane," or resting somewhere in between—there was clearly discernible the artist's deep concern for coming to terms with a world whose landscape of reality, whatever it might be, was certainly not the one that was once thought to have been so clearly brought into focus.

The same tendency to break from tradition is found in the works of many (though by no means all) modern composers. Charles Ives, for example, created rhythms and harmonies that any music lover a century ago would have found unrecognizable as music and, perhaps, unbearable as naked sound. Ives also felt that the format of traditional composition and performance was often stuffy and cramping. To free composer, performer, and listener alike from "thralldom" to form, Ives wrote some long works without time signature, and in various other ways allowed the performer to establish whatever rhythm patterns appealed to him. He "was a poetic realist in his music . . . . If, for example, he heard several brass bands on the 4th of July marching through the center of his small town of Danbury, Connecticut, he attempted in his music to create what might be called the poetic confusion of these sounds from different points of the compass meeting simultaneously."[8]

Even when the genius of the artist sought to reduce all feeling and thought to cold logical order, the result often was something quite different from the disciplined harmonies and tonal effects of the great masters of the eighteenth and nineteenth centuries. The works of Igor Stravinsky (1882–    ) are perhaps the best examples of this "backing into the future." For Stravinsky, who denied both "inspiration" as a motivating force in the writing of music, and "expression" as an inherent property of it, every valid work was characterized by objectivity and structural order—"Apollonian" (in contrast to the romantic "Dionysian" style). Yet

8. Peter Garvie, ed., *Music and Western Man,* Dent, London, 1958, p. 285.

*Igor Stravinsky (1920s).*

*T. S. Eliot in 1948.*

some of his compositions were frankly based on the works of Tchaikovsky and other romanticists. And his repeated use of irregular rhythms, strong dissonances, and the twelve-tone scale led many to think of him as the "leader of the futurist group in music." In short, although Stravinsky praised constraint and order and in his own way practiced both, that way was itself of the times—bohemian in its protest against bohemianism.

## LITERATURE AND PHILOSOPHY

Much of the serious literature of the twentieth century may be considered as one great polemic against the emptiness and futility of the times. Almost nothing, from general outlook or "spirit" to the most humbly workaday institutions, is spared castigation. In Theodore Dreiser's *An American Tragedy,* for example, man's life is portrayed as a pointless journey through a labyrinth of experiences conditioned by chance beyond man's meaningful control of them. The sociological novels of Sinclair Lewis strip away the conventional masks of "main street" America to reveal it as small and mean in spirit and childishly simple of mind (which Lewis, despite himself, continued to admire). European society is portrayed as equally distraught, as in Arthur Koestler's

*Age of Longing.* Examples could be multiplied almost without end. In this summary survey, we are perhaps best served by T. S. Eliot's *The Waste Land* and *Four Quartets.*

In several ways Eliot was not typical of the literary rebels of the twentieth century. In poetics and religion he was conservative; in contrast to many of his colleagues he revered tradition, and sought to preserve, not destroy, form and order. But he was like them in holding up the profound emptiness of modern life.

In *The Waste Land,* which has been called "in many ways the pivotal poem of the twentieth century,"[9] man is portrayed as bereft of faith, wandering through a maze of disconnected experiences without zest or meaningful awareness. In one section a woman sits in her richly appointed bedroom, bored with herself, her surroundings, and the expected visit of her lover who, when

9. By Wright Thomas and Stuart Brown in *Reading Poetry,* Oxford University Press, New York, 1941, p. 716.

he comes, is also bored with what he sees, what he does, and what he is.

> Footsteps shuffled on the stair.
> Under the firelight, under the brush, her hair
> Spread out in fiery points
> Glowed into words, then would be savagely still.

> "My nerves are bad tonight, Yes, bad. Stay with me.
> Speak to me. Why do you never speak. Speak.
> What are you thinking of? What thinking? What?
> I never know what you are thinking. Think."

> I think we are in a rats' alley
> Where the dead men lost their bones.

.  .  .  .  .  .  .  .  .  .  .  .  .

> "What shall I do now? What shall I do?"
> "I shall rush out as I am, and walk the street
> With my hair down, so. What shall we do tomorrow?
> What shall we ever do?"
>                              The hot water at ten.
> And if it rains, a closed car at four.
> And we shall play a game of chess,
> Pressing lidless eyes and waiting for a knock upon the door.[10]

.  .  .  .  .  .  .  .  .  .  .  .  .

In another poem, "East Coker," from *The Four Quartets,* Eliot weighs the burden of modernity:

> The whole earth is our hospital
> Endowed by the ruined millionaire,
> Wherein, if we do well, we shall
> Die of the absolute paternal care
> That will not leave us, but prevents everywhere.

And the seeming (but not, probably, in Eliot's own view) finale of man:

> O dark dark dark. They all go into the dark,
> The vacant interstellar spaces, the vacant into the vacant,
> The captains, merchant bankers, eminent men of letters,
> The generous patrons of art, the statesmen and the rulers,
> Distinguished civil servants, chairmen of many committees,
> Industrial lords and petty contractors, all go into the dark . . . .
> And we all go with them, into the silent funeral,
> Nobody's funeral, for there is none to bury.[11]

## Philosophy

No more than in any other century did philosophy have but one voice in the twentieth century. For example, in the thought of Henri Bergson (1858–1941), for a time France's foremost philosopher, human existence is powered by a vital force beyond (though not excluding) reason which creatively shapes meaningful existence. On the other hand, logical positivists such as Bertrand Russell (1872–    ) devote almost the whole of their professional study to the determination, by logical analysis, of meaning. And in between these "heart" and "head" schools are a variety of other schools principally concerned with reconciling the new findings of science with a social behavior that does not too radically depart from that which is part of the Western tradition.

Here, however, it will suffice to indicate the main lines of only one philosophy, existentialism; or rather the existentialism of Jean-Paul Sartre (1905–    ). Although Sartre's arguments and outlook are not widely—that is, popularly—known, and even less understood, they may be noted here

10. T. S. Eliot, *The Waste Land,* Boni and Liveright, New York, 1922, pp. 19–22, *passim.*

11. David Cecil and Allen Tate, eds., *Modern Verse in English, 1900–1950,* Macmillan Co., New York, N.Y., 1958, p. 337.

because they appeal to many intellectuals, and because they are so consonant with the modern temper.

The essence of this philosophy is the denial of absolute essence. Things, including man, exist. But "behind" existing things there is no meaning, no pattern, no order—there is, instead, complete *nothingness*. Man is not a creature of goodness, for there is no being or essence of goodness; and if there were he could not know of it. Man is forever confronted with the present and the passing—and meaningless—things of the present. True, he is free; but he is free in a world where all is uncertain, indefinite, and equivocal. His sole satisfaction comes from his ability to exercise choice in ways to engage his freedom, though whatever actions he decides upon are and must always remain wholly unconditioned. Man is therefore radically free to choose; every act is a result of free choice; and every choice carries personal responsibility for consequences. Viewed from any traditional perspective existentialism may afford only small satisfaction. This philosophy denies all historical moral codes, all religious or philosophical purpose, or even—apart from the choosing to act—meaning itself. The best understanding of the everyday meaning of this deeply pessimistic and monstrously demanding philosophy can be obtained from the following excerpt from one of Sartre's dramas (*The Condemned of Altona,* 1956). In it the "hero," Franz, appeals to History, out of his sense of guilt:

Centuries of the future, here is my century, solitary and deformed—the accused . . . . The century might have been a good one had not man been watched from time immemorial by the cruel enemy who had sworn to destroy him, that hairless, evil, flesh-eating beast—man himself. . . . Where does it come from, this rancid, insipid taste in my mouth? From man? From the beast? From myself? It is the taste of the century. [It] knows it is naked. Beautiful children, you who are born of us, our pain has brought you forth. This century is a woman in labor.

*French philosopher and novelist Jean-Paul Sartre (1964).*

To a substantial degree, then, the life of twentieth-century man has been marked by the dissolution of old certitudes and the search for new meaning. Is there God, or No God? Is there purpose in life, and if there is, what is it? Is man a rational creature or a bundle of conditioned reflexes? Where can we hide from purposeless violence, and the shadow of the Great Mushroom? Where can we flee to escape unbearable reality? Mass man did not, of course, fill his days chanting these litanies of despair. He did not voice his uncertainties in the poignant strophes of the poet:

. . . Alas, who is there
we can make use of? Not angels, not men:
and already the knowing brutes are aware
that we don't feel very securely at home
within our interpreted world . . . .[12]

12. The theme of Rainer Maria Rilke's first *Duine Elegy,* quoted in Erich Heller, *The Disinherited Mind,* Farrar, Straus, and Cudahy, New York, 1957, p. 277.

The evidence of everyday observation, however, makes clear that mass man's life was marked by abiding tensions and insecurity.

Still, it would be wrong to conclude, however distraught the temper of the times, that man is drifting to inevitable doom. The reflective student of history knows that the 5000-year record of Western civilization is darkened by recurring "seasons of dismay": the two centuries of confusion that followed the collapse of Egypt's Middle Kingdom; the melancholy straying from the golden mean of Periclean Athens; the long night of the dark ages that blacked out the grandeur that was Rome—the list is long. It is not likely that contemporary man, amid his vanishing frames of reference, will turn away from the genius that has served him so long. Rather, all of history points in the other direction—to his ability to confront the future with that genius, to make new worlds out of old.

## SELECTED READINGS

Barraclough, Geoffrey, *An Introduction to Contemporary History,* Basic Books, New York, 1964.

In this provocative work the author holds that the new age—in transition from about 1890 to the late 1950s—is as different from the "modern" age as the Renaissance is from medieval times. Its chief characteristics, he believes, are global life, mass man, and technological society.

Berger, Peter L., ed., *The Human Shape of Work,* The Macmillan Co., New York, 1964.

A study in the sociology of occupations, from the menial tasks of janitoring to the power positions of business executives. It sharply outlines the values system of modern American society as that system and the role of economic man in our times interact upon each other.

Boulding, Kenneth, *The Meaning of the Twentieth Century,* Harper Colophon Books, New York, 1965.

A large-minded, humane economist goes beyond the bounds of his professional dis-

cipline to probe, in a very provocative way, such questions as: are we living in an age which is so "new" that it can be compared only to the cultural shift that occurred when man passed from precivilization to civilization; what are the signs that may indicate the need for the creative reforming of the prime categories of human living—family, political organization, religion, for example; what are the responses needed to actually formulate these new attitudes and patterns of life?

Clark, Kenneth B., *Dark Ghetto,* Harper & Row, New York, 1965.

A Negro social-psychologist reveals the facts, fantasies, and frustrations of the Harlem "ghetto," and relates them to the white man's posture of mixed pride and fear. Almost every aspect of the Black-White problem in America is dealt with in one or another way in this frank, preceptive study of the American dilemma.

*Contemporary Civilization,* Scott, Foresman & Company, 1959–1964, 3 vols.

Various scholars summarize the more significant happenings of contemporary civilization, relate them to their historic roots, and attempt projection into the future. Sample articles in Volume I are on the crisis in the Communist world, science and technology, the beat generation, and the overall patterns of life today. Volumes II and III update the examination of these and related subjects.

Frankel, Charles, *The Case For Modern Man,* Harper & Brothers, New York, 1956.

The main thesis of this book is a reaffirmation of the liberal interpretation of history and of the potentialities for good in modern man. The author's main method is to detail the arguments of some who oppose that view, such as Jacques Maritain, Reinhold Niehuhr, and Arnold Toynbee, to show how these arguments are invalid.

Goodman, Paul, *Growing Up Absurd,* Random House, New York, 1960.

A strong, sustained attack upon modern society's hypocrisies and futile posturings. He

* Asterisk (*) denotes paperback.

believes the "Organized System," as the author calls the complex of adult social behavior, poses for youth the alternatives of adjusting to a phony way of life and thus growing up absurd, or rebelling against it which, when adults grow wiser and more honest, will seem to these adults the epitomy of absurdity.

*Heilbroner, Robert L., *The Great Ascent*, Harper Torchbooks, Harper & Row, New York, 1963.

In the brief span of 160 pages the author effectively poses the new problem of "development" in the emerging nations of Asia and Africa. He concludes that more, not less, turmoil will mark this development in the years ahead, that the major Western powers should accept this as part of the growing pains of a new age, that Western democracy must not be made a condition for aid, and that how far and how steadily the new nations develop will depend upon "reforms at home" among the older, if not always wiser, societies.

Regler, Gustav, translated by Norman Denny, *The Owl of Minerva,* Farrar, Strauss & Cudahy, New York, 1959.

An autobiographical account of the life of a German who fought in World War I, fled the Nazis, fought in Spain with the Loyalists, joined and finally left the Communist party, and eventually found himself homeless, disillusioned but still hopeful that new understandings will come out of his harassed grappling with half truths and untruths. This sensitively written work gives the reader a close and poignant feeling for the glory and shame of modern man's confrontations of, and usually retreat from or distortion of, the new world's new issues.

Seldes, Gilbert, *The Great Audience,* The Viking Press, New York, 1950.

An examination of the impact on America's general outlook on life, its morals, manners, and intellectual formulations made by the mass media of communication and entertainment, particularly movies, radio, and television. The author concludes that present use of the popular arts is undermining the forces that make for free men, and for the enlarging development of a free society.

*Sinnott, Edmund, *The Biology of the Spirit,* Compass Books, The Viking Press, New York, 1957.

The author, a world-renowned geneticist, presents the thesis that matter and spirit are one, with protoplasm the fundamental stuff of all life. He suggests that life is teleological and God-designed, though his concept of God is certainly not that included in any orthodox religion.

Smith, Lillian, *Killers of the Dream,* W. W. Norton & Co., New York, 1961 (rev. ed.).

The author, who lived all of her life in the South, tries to probe the mysteries of racial prejudice out of the context of her own experiences and reflections. There is no other work on the White-Black problem like it. The book should be read as a whole; but to whet his appetite, the reader might first turn to a section in Part Two entitled, "The Women."

# Illustration Credits

CHAPTER ONE. Page 4: Historical Pictures Service — Chicago. Page 5: Upper left, Historical Pictures Service — Chicago (from a painting by the Le Nain brothers in the Louvre); upper right, Historical Pictures Service — Chicago. Page 6: Historical Pictures Service — Chicago. Page 7: Upper right, The Bettmann Archive; middle right, The Bettmann Archive (from the Bagford Collection, The British Museum); lower right, Historical Pictures Service — Chicago (engraved after a painting by Jan Steen in the Braunschweig Gallery). Page 8: Historical Pictures Service — Chicago. Page 9: Cliché des Musées Nationaux, Louvre. Page 12: The Bettmann Archive (painting by P. Mignard in the Château de Versailles). Page 13: Historical Pictures Service — Chicago (painting by C. Lefevre in the Versailles Museum). Page 15: Historical Pictures Service — Chicago. Page 17: The Bettmann Archive. Page 19: The Bettmann Archive (painting by Claudio Coello). Page 25: The Bettmann Archive (from the Bridge of the Elector, Berlin). Page 27: Historical Pictures Service — Chicago. Page 30: The Bettmann Archive (painting by Jean Marc Nattier). Page 31: Upper left, Historical Pictures Service — Chicago; upper right, The Bettmann Archive. Page 34: Historical Pictures Service — Chicago. Page 39: Historical Pictures Service — Chicago. Page 40: Historical Pictures Service — Chicago. Page 41: Historical Pictures Service — Chicago. Page 43: The Bettmann Archive.

CHAPTER TWO. Page 52: Courtesy of The American Museum of Natural History. Page 53: Upper left, courtesy of The American Museum of Natural History; upper right, Historical Pictures Service — Chicago. Page 54: Historical Pictures Service — Chicago. Page 55: Historical Pictures Service — Chicago. Page 57: Historical Pictures Service — Chicago. Page 58: Historical Pictures Service — Chicago. Page 59: The Bettmann Archive. Page 60: The Bettmann Archive. Page 62: The Bettmann Archive. Page 63: Upper left, Historical Pictures Service — Chicago; upper right, Historical Pictures Service — Chicago. Page 64: The Bettmann Archive. Page 70: Historical Pictures Service — Chicago. Page 71: The Bettmann Archive. Page 73: Historical Pictures Service — Chicago. Page 77: Historical Pictures Service — Chicago. Page 78: The Pennsylvania Academy of the Fine Arts. Page 79: Historical Pictures Service — Chicago. Page 80: Historical Pictures Service — Chicago. Page 83: Historical Pictures Service — Chicago (courtesy of Lloyd's). Page 88: Upper left, Historical Pictures Service — Chicago; upper right, The Bettmann Archive (Essex Institute, Salem). Page 89: The Bettmann Archive.

CHAPTER THREE. Page 96: Historical Pictures Service — Chicago. Page 97: Historical Pictures Service — Chicago. Page 98: Historical Pictures Service — Chicago. Page 99: The Bettmann Archive (painting by Rigaud in the Wallace Collection, London). Page 102: Upper left, The Bettmann Archive (The British Museum); lower left, Historical Pictures Service — Chicago. Page 103: Upper left, Historical Pictures Service — Chicago; upper right, Historical Pictures Service — Chicago. Page 108: Historical Pictures Service — Chicago. Page 109: Historical Pictures Service — Chicago. Page 110: The Bettmann Archive. Page 112: Historical Pictures Service — Chicago. Page 114: Historical Pictures Service — Chicago. Page 115: The Bettmann Archive. Page 117: Historical Pictures Service — Chicago. Page 119: Historical Pictures Service — Chicago. Page 120: Historical Pictures Service — Chicago. Page 122: Historical Pictures Service — Chicago. Page 123: The Metropolitan Museum of Art, Bequest of William K. Vanderbilt, 1920. Page 124: Historical Pictures Service — Chicago. Page 126: Upper left, Historical Pictures Service — Chicago; upper right, Historical Pictures Service — Chicago. Page 127: The Bettmann Archive. Page 129: Upper left, Historical Pictures Service — Chicago; upper right, copyright, The Frick Collection, New York.

CHAPTER FOUR. Page 139: Historical Pictures Service — Chicago. Page 141: The Bettmann Archive (Versailles Museum). Page 142: Historical Pictures Service — Chicago. Page 143: The Bettmann Archive. Page 144: Historical Pictures Service — Chicago. Page 149: The Bettmann Archive. Page 150: Historical Pictures Service — Chicago (Carnavalet Museum). Page 151: Historical Pictures Service — Chicago (Bibliothèque Nationale, Cabinet des Estampes). Page 152: Upper left, Historical Pictures Service — Chicago; upper right, Historical Pictures Service — Chicago (collection Liesville, Ville de Paris). Page 154: The Bettmann Archive (after Manet). Page 156: The Bettmann Archive. Page 157: Bulloz — Art Reference Bureau (Carnavalet Museum). Page 158: Historical Pictures Service — Chicago. Page 159: Historical Pictures Service — Chicago. Page 162: Historical Pictures Service — Chicago. Page 165: Historical Pictures Service — Chicago (Louvre). Page 166: The Bettmann Archive (painting by Clarkson Stanfield in the Royal United Service Institution, London). Page 167: Courtesy of The Prado Museum. Page 170: Historical Pictures Service — Chicago. Page 171: The Bettmann Archive.

CHAPTER FIVE. Page 180: Upper left, The Metropolitan Museum of Art, Wolfe Fund, 1903; bottom, The Metropolitan Museum of Art, Wolfe Fund, 1931. Page 181: Copyright, The Frick Collection, New York. Page 182: The Bettmann Archive. Page 184: Historical Pictures Service — Chicago. Page 185: The Bettmann Archive. Page 187: The Bettmann Archive (painting by Sir Thomas Lawrence). Page 192: Upper left, Historical Pictures Service — Chicago; upper right, Historical Pictures Service — Chicago (drawing by George Cruikshank). Page 196: Historical Pictures Service — Chicago. Page 202: Historical Pictures Service — Chicago. Page 204: Cliché des Musées Nationaux, Louvre. Page 205: Historical Pictures Service — Chicago. Page 206: Historical Pictures Service — Chicago. Page 207: Historical Pictures Service — Chicago. Page 210: Historical Pictures Service — Chicago. Page 211: Marburg — Art Reference Bureau. Page 214: Upper left, Historical Pictures Service — Chicago; upper right, Historical Pictures Service — Chicago. Page 215: The Bettmann Archive. Page 216: Historical Pictures Service — Chicago. Page 218: Historical Pictures Service — Chicago. Page 220: Upper left, Historical Pictures Service — Chicago; upper right, Historical Pictures Service — Chicago. Page 222: Historical Pictures Service — Chicago. Page 223: Bibliothèque Nationale, Paris, Cabinet des Estampes.

CHAPTER SIX. Page 231: Historical Pictures Service — Chicago. Page 232: Historical Pictures Service — Chicago. Page 234: Historical Pictures Service — Chicago. Page 235: Historical Pictures Service — Chicago. Page 237: The Bettmann Archive. Page 238: The Bettmann Archive. Page 239: Upper left, The Bettmann Archive; upper right, Historical Pictures Service — Chicago (British Patent Office). Page 240: The Bettmann Archive. Page 241: Upper right, Historical Pictures Service — Chicago; lower right, Historical Pictures Service — Chicago. Page 243: The Bettmann Archive. Page 245: Upper left, Historical Pictures Service — Chicago; upper right, Historical Pictures Service — Chicago. Page 246: Historical Pictures Service — Chicago. Page 248: Historical Pictures Service — Chicago (from the Report of the Royal Commission, 1842). Page 251: Historical Pictures Service — Chicago. Page 253: Upper left, Historical Pictures Service —

Chicago; upper right, The Bettmann Archive. Page 254: The Bettmann Archive. Page 255: Upper left, The Bettmann Archive; upper left, Historical Pictures Service — Chicago. Page 259: The Bettmann Archive. Page 264: Courtesy of the Swedish Information Service. Page 267: Wide World Photos. Page 268: Wide World Photos.

CHAPTER SEVEN. Page 275; The Bettmann Archive. Page 277: Upper left, The Bettmann Archive; upper right, The Bettmann Archive. Page 278: Historical Pictures Service — Chicago. Page 282: Upper left, The Bettmann Archive; upper right, Historical Pictures Service — Chicago. Page 283: Historical Pictures Service — Chicago. Page 285: Upper left, Historical Pictures Service — Chicago; upper right, Historical Pictures Service — Chicago. Page 287: Upper left, The Bettmann Archive; upper right, The Bettmann Archive. Page 288: From Earl L. Core, Perry D. Strausbaugh, and Bernal R. Weimer, *General Biology,* Fourth Edition, New York: John Wiley & Sons, Inc., p. 245. Page 289: Upper left, Historical Pictures Service — Chicago; upper right, Historical Pictures Service — Chicago. Page 292: Historical Pictures Service — Chicago. Page 296: The Bettmann Archive. Page 297: The Bettmann Archive. Page 298: Historical Pictures Service — Chicago. Page 299: Upper left, The Metropolitan Museum of Art, Wolfe Fund, 1909; upper right, Kunsthistorische Museum, Vienna. Page 300: Courtesy of the Museum of Fine Arts, Boston, Tompkins Collection. Page 302: Historical Pictures Service — Chicago. Page 303: The Bettmann Archive (painting by Otto Neumann).

CHAPTER EIGHT. Page 311: Top right, Historical Pictures Service — Chicago; lower right, Historical Pictures Service — Chicago. Page 312: The Bettmann Archive. Page 313: Historical Pictures Service — Chicago. Page 314: Historical Pictures Service — Chicago. Page 315: Historical Pictures Service — Chicago. Page 316: Historical Pictures Service — Chicago. Page 320: Historical Pictures Service — Chicago. Page 321: Historical Pictures Service — Chicago. Page 323: The Bettmann Archive. Page 324: Historical Pictures Service — Chicago. Page 327: Top right, The Bett-

mann Archive (Taylor painting, 1852, from the Yale University Gallery of Fine Arts); lower right, The Bettmann Archive (photo by Alexander Gardner). Page 330: Historical Pictures Service — Chicago (from *Puck,* September 7, 1907). Page 332: Historical Pictures Service — Chicago (photo by Roger Fenton). Page 333: Upper left, Historical Pictures Service — Chicago; upper right, The Bettmann Archive. Page 337: Left, Historical Pictures Service — Chicago; right, The Bettmann Archive. Page 340: Historical Pictures Service — Chicago. Page 342: Upper left, photo courtesy of W. W. Binns, Portsmouth, Ohio; upper right, Historical Pictures Service — Chicago. Page 344: The Bettmann Archive. Page 348: The Bettmann Archive. Page 350: Historical Pictures Service — Chicago. Page 351: The Bettmann Archive. Page 353: Historical Pictures Service — Chicago. Page 354: Historical Pictures Service — Chicago.

CHAPTER NINE. Page 360: Historical Pictures Service — Chicago (from *Life*). Page 361: Upper right, Historical Pictures Service — Chicago (from *Simplicissimus*); lower right, Historical Pictures Service — Chicago (from *Harper's Weekly*). Page 366: Historical Pictures Service — Chicago (from *Revanche*). Page 370: Upper left, The Bettmann Archive; upper right, The Bettmann Archive; lower right, The Bettmann Archive. Page 371: Historical Pictures Service — Chicago. Page 372: Historical Pictures Service — Chicago. Page 373: The Bettmann Archive. Page 374: Upper left, Historical Pictures Service — Chicago; upper right, Historical Pictures Service — Chicago. Page 375: The Bettmann Archive. Page 377: Upper left, Historical Pictures Service — Chicago (from *Punch*); upper right, Historical Pictures Service — Chicago. Page 381: Upper left, Historical Pictures Service — Chicago; upper right, Historical Pictures Service — Chicago. Page 382: Historical Pictures Service — Chicago. Page 383: Historical Pictures Service — Chicago. Page 384: Historical Pictures Service — Chicago (from the *Illustrated London News*). Page 385: Upper left, Historical Pictures Service — Chicago; upper right, Historical Pictures Service — Chicago; lower right, The Bettmann Archive. Page 386: The Bettmann Archive. Page 387: The Bettmann

Wide World Photos; lower left, Wide World Photos. Page 557: Wide World Photos. Page 558: Wide World Photos.

CHAPTER FIFTEEN. Page 565: upper right, Historical Pictures Service — Chicago (Talburt in the Washington *Daily News,* 1932); lower right, Historical Pictures Service — Chicago (Darling in the New York *Tribune,* 1931). Page 566: Wide World Photos. Page 567: Upper left, Historical Pictures Service — Chicago (Shepard in *Punch,* 1935); upper right, Wide World Photos. Page 568: Wide World Photos. Page 571: Wide World Photos. Page 573: Wide World Photos. Page 574: Wide World Photos. Page 575: Historical Pictures Service — Chicago (Henderson in the Providence, Rhode Island, *Journal,* 1938). Page 578: Wide World Photos. Page 579: Wide World Photos. Page 582: Wide World Photos. Page 584: Wide World Photos. Page 588: Wide World Photos. Page 589: Wide World Photos. Page 590: Upper left, Wide World Photos; upper right, Wide World Photos. Page 591: Wide World Photos. Page 593: Upper left, Wide World Photos; upper right, Wide World Photos. Page 594: Wide World Photos. Page 596: Wide World Photos. Page 597: Upper left, Historical Pictures Service — Chicago; Upper right, Wide World Photos; lower right, Wide World Photos. Page 598: Wide World Photos. Page 599: Wide World Photos. Page 600: Upper left, Wide World Photos; upper right, Wide World Photos. Page 602: Wide World Photos (photo by Robert Capa). Page 603: Top, Wide World Photos; bottom right, Wide World Photos. Page 604: Upper left, Wide World Photos (New York *Times*); lower left, Wide World Photos. Page 607: Upper left, Wide World Photos (New York *Times*); upper right, Wide World Photos. Page 612: Wide World Photos. Page 613: Upper left, Wide World Photos; upper right, Wide World Photos. Page 614: Historical Pictures Service — Chicago.

CHAPTER SIXTEEN. Page 618: Historical Pictures Service — Chicago (Shoemaker in the Chicago *Daily News,* August 9, 1947; reprinted with the permission of the Chicago *Daily News*). Page 619: Historical Pictures Service — Chicago (Burck in the Chicago *Sun-Times,*

July 29, 1945; reprinted from The Chicago *Sun-Times*). Page 520: Historical Pictures Service — Chicago (*Punch,* 1948), Page 622: Historical Pictures Service — Chicago (Fitzpatrick in the St. Louis *Post-Dispatch,* October 6, 1955; reprinted by permission of the St. Louis *Post-Dispatch*). Page 623: Wide World Photos. Page 625: Wide World Photos. Page 627: Upper right, Historical Pictures Service — Chicago (Burck in the Chicago *Sun-Times,* February 23, 1949; reprinted from The Chicago *Sun-Times*); lower right, Historical Pictures Service — Chicago (Vicky in the London *Daily News Chronicle,* 1948). Page 629: Upper right, Wide World Photos; lower right, Wide World Photos. Page 633: Wide World Photos. Page 634: Wide World Photos. Page 635: Upper left, Wide World Photos; upper right, Wide World Photos. Page 637: Wide World Photos. Page 638: Historical Pictures Service — Chicago (Fitzpatrick in the St. Louis *Post-Dispatch,* March 23, 1954; reprinted by permission of the St. Louis *Post-Dispatch*). Page 639: Upper left, Historical Pictures Service — Chicago (Fischetti in the New York *Herald Tribune,* May 30, 1963; permission granted by the Publishers Newspaper Syndicate); upper right, Wide World Photos. Page 640: Wide World Photos. Page 645: Upper left, Wide World Photos; upper left, Wide World Photos. Page 647: Wide World Photos. Page 650: Wide World Photos. Page 653: Wide World Photos. Page 656: Wide World Photos. Page 657: Historical Pictures Service — Chicago (Burck in the Chicago *Sun-Times,* August 13, 1952; reprinted from the Chicago *Sun-Times*). Page 660: Historical Pictures Service — Chicago (Fitzpatrick in the St. Louis *Post-Dispatch,* July 20, 1947; reprinted by permission of the St. Louis *Post-Dispatch*). Page 664: Historical Pictures Service — Chicago (Orr in the Chicago *Tribune,* 1962; copyright by the Chicago *Tribune*). Page 655: Upper left, Wide World Photos; upper right, Wide World Photos; lower right, Wide World Photos.

CHAPTER SEVENTEEN. Page 671: Wide World Photos. Page 672: Wide World Photos. Page 673: Wide World Photos. Page 674: Collection, The Museum of Modern Art, New York, Advisory Committee Fund. Page 678: Upper left, Collection, The Museum of Modern

Art, New York, Mrs. Simon Guggenheim Fund; upper right, Collection, The Museum of Modern Art, New York, acquired through the Lillie P. Bliss Bequest. Page 679: Collection, The Museum of Modern Art, New York, Mrs. Simon Guggenheim Fund. Page 680: Upper left, Collection, The Museum of Modern Art, New York, gift of James Thrall Soby (permission by courtesy of James Thrall Soby); upper right, Collection, The Museum of Modern Art, New York, Mrs. Simon Guggenheim Fund. Page 681: Upper left, Wide World Photos; upper right, Wide World Photos. Page 683: Wide World Photos.

# Index

* The identifying phrases under each entry are listed in order of progressive pagination.